AN HISTORIAN'S WORLD

Selections from the Correspondence
of
JOHN FRANKLIN JAMESON

Edited by
ELIZABETH DONNAN AND LEO F. STOCK

THE AMERICAN PHILOSOPHICAL SOCIETY
INDEPENDENCE SQUARE
PHILADELPHIA
1956

Unless otherwise indicated the letters hereprinted and those cited in the footnotes are among the Jameson Papers. While the work on this collection was going on these papers were in the files of the Carnegie Institution of Washington; they are ultimately to be deposited in the Division of Manuscripts of the Library of Congress.

Though Dr. Jameson was from his student days a voluminous letter writer, often recording in his diary that he had written twelve or fifteen letters that day, these letters were written by hand and for the early years the collection contains only the letters written to his family; a few to his friend Francis A. Christie, contributed by Professor Christie's niece, Elizabeth Tiffany; a few to his classmate E. C. Norton, which came from Professor Norton's daughter; and photostats of early letters to Albert Shaw and Woodrow Wilson, obtained from the Manuscript Division of the New York Public Library and from the Wilson Collection in the Division of Manuscripts of the Library of Congress. No systematic attempt to collect other letters of early years has been made; but in a few instances, where they promised to be of special value, it was learned that they had been destroyed. After 1905, when Dr. Jameson came to the Carnegie Institution, carbon copies of his correspondence remained in the files of the Department of Historical Research; and it is for the most part these copies which have been used for this volume. It is of course true that a letter is not always sent out as it is first written, but since it was Dr. Jameson's practice to correct the carbon as he corrected the letter it is believed that there are few inaccuracies in the copies here used.

In this selection of a comparatively few letters from the great mass of correspondence which has been preserved, the aim has been twofold: to choose those which illustrate the relation of the writer to the many historical projects which he originated or fostered, and those which give some idea of the manner of man who was writing. Quite deliberately, some letters have been included which have small bearing on historical scholarship but tell something of the historical scholar. The editors recognize that no two readers will agree with their choice. Some will question inclusions; others will lament exclusions. That is inevitable. The editors themselves did not always agree. Final judgments did not always approve of the original selections. Some subjects receive less attention than one might like. Others may seem over-emphasized. Where the entire letter has not been printed the excision is either to avoid repetition or to omit news of family and friends that would have little interest for the reader. To save space for more valuable material the customary polite closing of the letters and the signatures are omitted with no indication of omission. If more than the conventional words are missing the omission is indicated in the usual manner. Omissions from the beginning and the end of quotations from the Diary are not shown, since it is not to be assumed that the entire entry for the day is quoted. Any omission within the quotation is indicated.

With the exception of a few letters which have appeared in newspapers, the letters in this selection have not heretofore been printed, though the Jameson Papers supplied the material for Some Bryce-Jameson Correspondence, *American Historical Review* **50**; Senator Beveridge, J. Franklin Jameson, and John Marshall, *Mississippi Valley Historical Review* **35**; and Senator Beveridge, J. Franklin Jameson, and Abraham Lincoln, *ibid.*; Charles McCarthy to J. Franklin Jameson, *Wisconsin Magazine of History* **33**. This collection also provided the material for A Nineteenth-Century Academic Cause Célèbre, *New England Quarterly* **25**, which dealt with the case of President Andrews at Brown University.

Among the many whose aid made the volume possible must first be mentioned a group of alumnae of Wellesley College whose imaginative generosity provided means for the beginning of the work, and the American Philosophical Society, a grant from which helped in its completion. The Carnegie Institution of Washington has given permission for the printing of those letters which come from its files and has hospitably provided working quarters and many conveniences for the editors. The libraries of the University of Rochester and of Wellesley College have also, at times, provided space for the same purpose.

Amherst, Brown, Columbia, Cornell, the Johns Hopkins University, the universities of Chicago and Michigan, the American Antiquarian Society, The Massachusetts Historical Society have patiently answered inquiries, as have many individuals. Four whose help has been unfailing and invaluable are Miss Josephine Cole of the Alumni Office of the Johns Hopkins University, Miss Rena Durkan, curator of the Edward Hitchcock Memorial Room, Amherst, Miss Antoinette Metcalf, reference librarian, retired, of Wellesley College, and Miss Margaret Boyce, present reference librarian of Wellesley. Their patience has known no limit.

It is a matter of sorrow that Mr. Leo F. Stock, executor and trustee of Dr. Jameson's estate, who first conceived the idea of such a selection of letters, did not live to see the completion of the work.

Elizabeth Donnan

Washington, D. C.
November 1, 1954.

As the senior and now the only surviving member of John Franklin Jameson's professional staff of the Department of Historical Research in the Carnegie Institution of Washington it falls to me to precede this collection, with its Preface and Introduction, by an expression of sorrowful regret that the editors, my former colleagues, have not lived to see the publication, or even the first proofs, of their work. Leo Francis Stock died on March 8, 1954, and Elizabeth Donnan on March 16, 1955. Both devoted the last years of their lives, in spite of failing health, to this labor of devotion. Before Miss Donnan's death she had been able to write the Preface which she alone could sign, and to revise the long Introduction, which is in itself a notable contribution to the history of American historical scholarship during half a century, and to transmit the manuscript, ready for the printer, to the American Philosophical Society.

Inasmuch as Miss Donnan's illness during the last months of her life, made it impossible for her to draw from the files of the Division of Manuscripts of the Library of Congress a representative group of letters covering Dr. Jameson's service from 1928 to 1937, such letters have been selected by Mr. John Beverley Riggs, in consultation with Dr. St. George L. Sioussat who succeeded Jameson as chief of the Division, and with the assistance of the present chief, Mr. David C. Mearns, and have been incorporated in the collection as it was in press. Mr. Riggs, who is exceptionally well acquainted with the Jameson Papers, and who followed closely the work of Miss Donnan and Dr. Stock, has performed the labor of reading the proof sheets and of compiling the index. It is also Mr. Riggs who has completed the arrangement of the Jameson Papers, upon which Miss Donnan was engaged for the Carnegie Institution of Washington, preparatory to their presentation to the Library of Congress.

Waldo Gifford Leland

September, 1955

CONTENTS

CONTENTS

PAGE

INTRODUCTION

"He has done more than any living man to promote sound historical research in America and every historian in this country is under personal or professional obligation to him," wrote Charles Ramsdell to Senator Connally not many years before Dr. Jameson's death. Many of his contemporaries warmly endorsed this dictum though today historians may be less conscious of the contribution which he made to the foundations on which they build. His life remains to be written but something of the nature of the man and of the range and value of his work can be gathered from the selection of his letters here presented.

John Franklin Jameson was born in Somerville, Massachusetts, on September 19, 1859. He was prepared for college in the Roxbury Latin School and was ready for Harvard at the age of fifteen. Thinking him too young and not sufficiently robust for the rigors of academic life, the family decreed the delay of a year, much of which he spent on a farm in western Massachusetts. Meanwhile his father, John Jameson, after some legal work and a period of teaching had moved to Amherst, Massachusetts, where some years later he became the village postmaster. By this move John Franklin was diverted from Harvard to Amherst, and spent his four college years living with his parents, an older and a younger sister, and a younger brother, at that time his despair, though later his great pride. During these years he listened to lectures by Alcott and Emerson; he delighted in performances of Pinafore; he played the flute; he read Seneca and Lucan, and Dickens and Howells and Tennyson; he joined the Phi Upsilon fraternity; he made friends, many of whom he retained as long as they lived. And he studied. His great interest was history and he read Green and Hallam, Macaulay and Gibbon. He gained permission, with two of his classmates, to read Stubbs and once a week to discuss that author with Professor Morse, one of his two most loved and respected instructors. So great was his zest for reading that when the library was closed to students he once climbed through a window. On one occasion he begged permission (which was not granted), to carry a lamp with him in order to work there in unsanctioned hours. Often his reading seems unsystematic, as though the mere sight of a book aroused a desire to know what was in it. But this did not prevent his reading with great concentration on subjects assigned to him or selected by him. His academic course, judged by the record of awards for excellence, was highly successful. In his freshman year, the year in which he determined to devote his life to the study of history, he gained the Latin prize for prose composition, the Hutchins prize for the highest standing in Greek, and the Walker prize for excellence in mathematics. All these amounted to $80, no mean sum for a college boy in 1876. His second year he led in Latin and mathematics, winning two prizes, which again amounted to $80. In his junior year excellence in translating German at sight brought him his only prize of the year. This year he was one of the editors of the college paper, the *Amherst Student*. As a senior he was the winner of the Porter prize of $30, for the highest standing in natural philosophy; and the Bertram prize of $100 for "the best examination by seniors upon specified authors not read in the college course." He was one of the six allowed to compete for the Hyde prize, for the best oration by a senior, his being on the Battle of Tours. Here he lost to Henry Folger, founder of the Folger Shakespeare Library, who spoke on Tennyson.

To an ambitious student of those days the next step after college was foreign study, probably in Germany. Such men as John W. Burgess and John Bates Clark, Herbert Baxter Adams, Herbert L. Osgood, and Anson D. Morse had gone from Amherst to Heidelberg or Leipzig, Berlin or Zurich. A number of Jameson's friends were planning similar pilgrimages, and with a naïve faith that a way would be provided for so eminently natural and desirable a course, Jameson not only discussed his plans with his instructors but wrote to several older men of his acquaintance about obtaining the $3,000 or $3,500 which he believed would adequately support him in Europe for the five years he thought of spending in foreign universities. Among his Amherst instructors, Professor Elihu Root agreed with him that he ought to go abroad immediately on graduation but suggested that he procure a position in advance, to be claimed on his return to this country. Professor William S. Tyler went so far as to inquire whether a place could not be thus reserved for him at Smith College. More realistic advice came from Burgess and Morse, Burgess urging a year of graduate study in Harvard, with the hope of a travelling fellowship later; Morse, probably with greater wisdom, telling Jameson that he ought to teach before he plunged into foreign study, and that five years was much too long to remain in Europe.

His roseate day dreams were shattered by the uncompromising replies of the family acquaintances to whom he had turned for financial assistance and April of his senior year found him searching for a teaching position. Having listed those high schools of Massachusetts in which he was willing to teach, he wrote to a few each day until he had sent out some thirty applications. Chance, rather than this systematic industry,

1

brought to him word of a vacancy in the Worcester high school. He applied in person and despite the feeling of the principal that he looked "very young," he was engaged to teach history and Latin.

On September 1, 1879, he wrote in his diary: "This morning the real work of life begins." Not yet twenty, he found the real work of interesting high school youth in the achievements of Caesar or charming them with accounts of Egyptian civilization beyond his powers. As the year passed, disorder in his classes increased and the disapproval of his superiors was apparent. Summer brought (possibly to his relief) notification that his services would no longer be required. Early in his second search for a position he wrote to Herbert Baxter Adams (Amherst 1872, and a resident of Amherst), asking advice. Adams, then teaching in the Johns Hopkins University, advised him to borrow money and begin graduate work at the university, saying that he felt sure there would soon be many college openings for teachers of history. This advice Jameson accepted, perhaps because he recognized its wisdom, perhaps because he obtained no teaching position.

The Johns Hopkins to which J. Franklin Jameson went in 1880 had already acquired a reputation for unusual graduate work and was drawing together a body of young men, many of them destined to be the outstanding scholars of the next decades. The work in history, political science, and political economy was carried by Herbert Baxter Adams, Henry Carter Adams, and Austin Scott. The offering of courses was small, the direction of work slight. Nevertheless, a group of able students derived from the university atmosphere a mental stimulus which they later carried into their own teaching in many parts of the country.

The young Jameson who entered the university in September, 1880, just past his twenty-first birthday, was a compound of youthful insecurity and high ambition, of humility and conceit, of social naïvete and intellectual maturity, of a liking for people yet a dread of formal gatherings lest he do something socially unacceptable. Proud of his New England birth and scornful of anything "westernish," he was yet able to recognize the unusual powers of Thorstein Veblen, a fellow student, and Albert Shaw from Iowa became one of his closest friends. Though he was highly critical, as are most graduate students, and annoyed or disgusted by pretentions of any sort, simple goodness, such as he found in his classmate, Stanton Coit, in George W. Cable, and in Professor C. T. Morris of the Johns Hopkins made a strong appeal to him.

The immediate impact of the new environment upon him is not recorded in his Diary or in the surviving letters to his family, but we know that of those with whom he worked H. C. Adams most impressed him. When Adams left for Cornell University in February, 1881, Jameson's regret was keen. He thought ill of most of the classroom lectures of his first year and at Herbert Baxter Adams's own suggestion he dropped

those in modern European history. For these he substituted work with Professor G. S. Morris in philosophy but within a few weeks that, too, was abandoned, not because of the character of the course, but because of the character of the student, who maintained then and ever after that he was incapable of understanding philosophy. Most of his efforts were expended on topics of special interest to himself, such as the recent troubles in the Barbados and the early history of New York. For these he searched widely for material, early developing that uncanny knowledge of just where to look for what he wanted which was a lifelong characteristic. The first paper which he presented in the Friday evening seminary of the department—that on the Barbados —received little attention, and he returned to his room greatly cast down and admitting to himself that he was too dependent on the opinion of others. Later, seminary discussions in which Woodrow Wilson joined likewise depressed him because of what he believed to be the inferiority of his own powers to those of Wilson.

But life was far from being all work. He played the flute and read poetry; he boxed with his friends and joined in fiery discussions at the dinner table, over theology and politics, immortality and second marriages. He listened to many of the visiting lecturers, who supplied some of the stimulus lacking in the classroom: Bryce, Freeman, Matthew Arnold, G. W. Cable, and many others less well known today, offered a varied intellectual diet. At Thanksgiving time Jameson explored Washington, learned his way to the materials and the officials of the city, both to prove useful to him in future years. In January he received a graduate scholarship, and for his second year one of the history fellowships. These enabled him to finish his graduate work without being deeply in debt.

The thesis presented in the spring of 1882 as part of the work for the degree of doctor of philosophy was Montauk and the common lands of Easthampton, a subject related to his study of early New York history in the preceding year. Like that study it was published in the *Magazine of American History*. The chief importance of this work on early New York was that it interested Jameson in Willem Usselinx and led to his first substantial piece of historical research. His degree was awarded in the spring of 1882, the first Ph.D. degree in history given by the university. On receiving his degree he was appointed assistant in the department for the following year.

Neither to Jameson nor to President Gilman and Herbert B. Adams did it occur that Jameson might well become a permanent member of the department. Adams was not yet a professor and he and Gilman would have agreed that there was no place in the history department of the Johns Hopkins University for an able and ambitious young man. What was wanted was a scholar of renown. Yet Jameson stayed on year after year for six years. During his years in the university, first as student, then as teacher, he frequently expressed dissatisfaction both with the work offered and with his own performance. After a long conference with Herbert Baxter Adams in his first year he wrote:[1]

it made me very blue to think I should have to work with such methods and such objects and perhaps waste my year. . . . It often came into my mind, what would Root think of such doings? Oh dear, what a mistake I made in coming here! And now, once here, I must spoil this year to get a fellowship, and work here next year, if I stay, though I might do the same work better elsewhere, alone, because the over-valued name of the university, and perhaps its degree, will give me a boost in getting a place. . . . It's a hard thing to have to care so much about $500.

In later years it was more often of himself than of the university of which he complained:[2]

I question, when I'm blue, whether I'm not already proved a failure; and I don't know that even when I'm cheerful I feel warranted in denying it very strongly in the face of the obvious facts. . . . I started out this year with the intention to brace up a great deal, and the feeling that I had new and fresher tendencies in my work; but I reckon it has been all in my own mind and not outwardly discernible to others, and now the very impulse seems to have gone and I am ready to sink back where I was and recognize that I'm not so constructed as to succeed here. . . . [Adams] sees in me the same old Jameson, scholarly but ineffective.

During the six years he was a receptive candidate for work elsewhere, yet when he left, he left with reluctance. Possible positions in Western Reserve, in California, in the University of Michigan, in Wesleyan came in sight, only to disappear over the horizon, and not till the spring of 1888 did he find opportunity to leave the Johns Hopkins for Brown University.

During the years in Baltimore something of Jameson's intellectual progress can be measured in his letters, with their indication of his interests and activities. He corresponded with European scholars and reviewed historical publications for the *Historische Zeitschrift*. His work on Usselinx has been mentioned. At one point he grew interested in state history, and gave to the seminary papers on the subject, intended to show to others what needed to be done. He published the town records of Amherst. In 1887 he delivered four public lectures on Historical Writing in America, which, with some revision, a few years later became a small volume. The idea of a collection of essays on the constitutional history of the United States, to be written by members of the seminary, he conceived here but completed the work after he left the university. Not all his labor showed tangible results. When he came to the Johns Hopkins his attitude toward the South had been not unlike that toward the West but life in Baltimore with its agreeable associations gradually dissipated this bias. Slowly he came to the con-

viction that what he really wished to do was to write a history of the South. For this he began building up the material on southern history in the university library and enlarging his knowledge of the location of the sources. Probably this interest was one of the motives which led him to expend great effort to obtain permission from the Congress to publish the records of the Virginia Company. This, his first dealing with a Congressional committee proved, in the end, not only exasperating but futile.

Nor was all his production of serious historical character. It was the custom of the university to hold its alumni reunions on Washington's Birthday and on February 22, 1887, the last reunion during Jameson's service in the university—though he did not then know that he was soon to leave—he was asked for two contributions to the reunion program. The first, sung to the tune of Maryland, My Maryland, became the Alma Mater of the university.[3]

> To thee we come from far and near,
>   Alma Mater, bearing
> Each his gifts to lay them here,
>   Each thine honors sharing.
> At thy feet once more we sit,
>   Find each year returning,
> The torch at which our lamps we lit
>   Still serenely burning.
>
> Afar we see that beacon light,
>   Hear abroad thy praises;
> Oh, feed that holy flame aright,
>   Till none more brightly blazes.
> We, enkindling here anew
>   Light of thy bestowing,
> Bear us as thy servants true,
>   On thine errands going.
>
> Fill us with the highest things
>   O benignant mother,
> All that lifts man, all that brings
>   Brother near to brother,
> Spread the truth that maketh free,
>   Night to daylight turning;
> Let the world receive from thee
>   Noblest fruits of learning.

His second contribution to this reunion represented a gift well known to his friends and occasionally exercised by him in later years. He was asked to read humorous verses of his own composing, the character of which may be judged from a few stanzas.

> It was a stalwart Hopkins man,
>   And he stept up jauntily,

---

[1] Diary, Mar. 22, 1881.

[2] *Ibid.*, Jan. 22, 23, 1886.

[3] An undated newspaper clipping among the Jameson Papers records that this was composed while the author walked up and down in Druid Hill Park. Just as the final stanza was completed a policeman approached and asked: "Is there anything the matter with you sir?" Called thus to earth, Professor Jameson replied that there was not. "Why do you ask?" Whereupon the officer intimated that to him the professor's antics appeared to look toward suicide and ordered him to "move on," as he "didn't want no such thing as that on his hands."

Now up and write, thou gifted wight
 A versicle for me.
    * * * * *
Then in the academic hall
 When speaking doth begin,
Between two speeches, as custom teaches,
 Thy verse we'll sandwich in.

How doth the little Hopkins man
 Improve the shining hour?
He toils to please the twelve trustees,
 Olympians, clothed with power.

He counteth adverbs, to advance
 The love of classic lore.
And on the sly evaluates π
 And sheds the rabbit's gore.
    * * * * *
The storied page of history
 He turneth o'er and o'er,
And conneth well the marks that tell
 Chaldaean brick-bat-lore.

For some years after Jameson left the Johns Hopkins for Brown University he continued to cherish the idea of writing on the South, and a trip to Virginia in 1891, fully described in his letters, was undertaken with this in mind. Eventually, however, he recognized the difficulty of carrying out his ambition in Providence, which in 1890 seemed so remote as to make access to his material difficult and expensive. The circumstances of his family probably contributed to this decision. Indeed, these circumstances determined many of Jameson's activities between 1885 and 1895. They may have been in part responsible for the fact that he never wrote the sustained historical work which, when he left Amherst College he was confident that he would one day produce. In 1885, with the election of Cleveland, his father lost his position as postmaster and from that time it was necessary for the son to provide a considerable part of the family income. To do this he augmented his meager Hopkins stipend by every possible means. Hack work for the Alden *Encyclopaedia* and for the *Century Dictionary* offered opportunities to earn but devoured the time which might have gone into occupations more intellectually rewarding. When he undertook the drudgery of writing a *Dictionary of United States history* it was undoubtedly for the additional income which is provided, not for the pleasure of the work.

By 1895 the pressure to increase his income was somewhat reduced but at this time he became chairman of the newly created Historical Manuscripts Commission of the American Historical Association and accepted the position of managing editor of the *American Historical Review*. Whether he realized it or not, this meant the renunciation of any considerable historical production outside the *Review*. No one with Jameson's meticulous care for detail could edit a journal, act as head of a department and also find time or intellectual vigor for any further substantial production.

To write of his achievement as editor of the *Review* is unnecessary for the successive volumes of that journal are both a tribute to American scholarship and to his success in bringing forth the best of that scholarship each quarter. From 1895 until he left Brown University he was the managing editor and though he had an able and willing board of editors it was inevitable that the heaviest of the work and of the responsibility fell to him. In the early days he wrote the Notes and News unaided; most of the documents he edited himself or supplemented the inadequate editing of their contributors. Articles which satisfied his critical judgment were not always forthcoming. Many of those invited to contribute declined and there was sometimes an alarming dearth of desirable material but there was always a steady flow of unsuitable offerings. The early numbers of the *Review* might have contained an account of the school house where John Brown went to school, or an epic poem on Abraham Lincoln. The "only living man" who knew the facts about certain Southern campaigns offered a series of articles in order that "posterity might know the truth." Many of the would-be contributors were eager to supply illustrations with their manuscripts.

But the time-consuming and patience-demanding section was that of book reviews. The first problem was to obtain books to review. Publishers, even when importuned, often failed to supply their books. One house when asked for an historical work replied: "We do not see the advantage of sending one to your magazine." Frequently publishers demanded that the *Review* pay half the price of the books, a sad drain on the scanty funds of the journal. After the book was promised, the perfect reviewer must be sought. The aims of the editors were high and few were the reviewers who proved ideal. Months after the review had been requested, the sorely tried editor might learn that the book had never been sent, or had never been received by the reviewer, or had been received too late for him to prepare a review for the date promised. From the reviewers, once they received the volumes, the plea for "more space" was almost universal. Yet, in spite of difficulties of timing, of planning, and of procuring scholarly contributions, the *Review* continued, quarter after quarter, to maintain a standard which elicited praise from foreign scholars as well as from those of America.

In 1901 it passed into the hands of Professor Andrew C. McLaughlin, who, in the long list of questions and comments which he sent to Jameson before agreeing to accept the work, especially remarked on the great range from which Jameson drew reviewers and the wide knowledge he displayed in editing the document section. The retiring editor was shortly placed on the board of editors, where he remained until 1905 when he left the University of Chicago to become head of the Bureau (later the Department) of Historical Research of the Carnegie Institution of Washington, and again took up the work of editing the journal as a responsibility of the bureau. This task he continued to perform until 1928, when he left the Institution for the Library of Congress. During these years, though there was at hand more clerical assistance than in the early days, he never relaxed his vigilance, and to the end of his service the journal bore the hall mark of his scholarship. If to it must be attributed the loss of the historical work which he might have written and in early life hoped to write, he gave to the historical profession a periodical of which they had good reason to be proud.

The first occasion of his surrender of the editorship was his move from Brown to the larger responsibilities of the University of Chicago. The years in Brown had been pleasant ones, once the readjustment to the New England atmosphere after eight years in Baltimore was accomplished. The students at first seemed to him unresponsive, even unmannerly, but by his second year they were coming to his "evenings" with pleasure. Among the faculty he found congenial friends. The Rhode Island Historical Society and the Greek Club profited from his presence. With the aid of Henry B. Gardner, who came from the Johns Hopkins to teach economics in Brown the year of Jameson's appointment, and William E. Foster, the librarian of Providence, an excellent lecture course was inaugurated. In a modest way Jameson published a number of the historical studies produced in his seminar. In his first year at Brown he edited the volume of *Essays in the Constitutional History of the United States in the Formative Period, 1775-1789*, which he had planned in Baltimore. This year he also spent many hours in revising a translation of, writing the introduction for, and bringing to date, Victor Duruy's *History of France*. Though this translation was a cherished idea of his, before the work was finished he regarded it as an "incubus" which was interfering sadly with other projects. Once this was out of the way he prepared for print the small volume *History of Historical Writing in America*. A number of his papers read at meetings of the American Historical Association belong to this period, as does his edition of Calhoun's letters edited for the Historical Manuscripts Commission. Twice he gave a series of lectures in Baltimore, and at Barnard College he delivered the lectures which eventually became the volume entitled *The American Revolution considered as a social movement*. In Brown he led the faculty in the fight for academic freedom precipitated by the attempt of the Brown corporation to silence the president, E. Benjamin Andrews, an advocate of free silver.

When President Harper of the University of Chicago tempted him to leave Brown for the new institution in the Middle West, with characteristic caution he hesitated long and sought much advice. His roots were in New England; the South he had come to love through long sojourn in Baltimore; but the West was unknown territory. Even those of his advisers who urged him to accept the offer painted drab pictures. John H. Finley, one of his former students wrote: [4]

Dr. Harper is an organizer and has introduced the system and order of a factory. Everything is *imposed*. Nothing or little has been *evolved*. The institution seems to be rather the expression of President Harper and the rich Trustees than of the Faculty and the students. There are no traditions. The place seems to have no more character than a new school house.

After this dreary characterization he added, "I should like to think of you out here for I think your influence is needed here." Frederick Warren, a Johns Hopkins friend, suggested that the financial situation of the university was bad, and that Rockefeller was growing "restive under the annual deficit." He also warned Jameson that the work put on the head of a department was endless. His comments, however, were not wholly discouraging, for he suggested that in ten years Jameson should have there "the largest body of graduate students in the country—or in Chicagoese 'in the world.' " [5] Much greater enthusiasm was expressed by E. Benjamin Andrews: [6]

If you wish a great chance to do historical work after your own heart in your own way, with ample resources, a great company of earnest students and a minimum amount of drudgery you will never have a better opening than Chicago offers.

The judgment of Professor McLaughlin, who taught in Chicago one quarter in 1900, was that Jameson was invited to take charge of "a somewhat incoherent department," to which he must give "new energy and meaning. . . . I cannot pretend that you have a bed of roses ahead of you as I consider some of the difficulties of the task." [7] He later added that though there was great disorganization he did not think that there was any dissension in the Department.

The subject was opened by President Harper in the summer of 1900; Jameson's acceptance was not final until December of that year. Two stumbling blocks delayed the conclusion of negotiations: Jameson's salary, which was to be $5,000 eventually, but which President Harper wished to hold to $4,000 for the first two years; and Jameson's insistence that he be assured $25,000 at once and $2,500 annually thereafter, to spend on the library. Harper at length yielded, agreeing that the salary should go to $5,000 the second year and that the money for the library should be supplied. The decision once made, Jameson had a long conference with McLaughlin at the meeting of the Historical Association, after which he made a brief visit to the university, where he met his future colleagues in history and discussed plans with each of them. His first teaching was in the spring quarter of 1901; he was back in

---

[4] An undated letter, probably belonging to the autumn of 1900.
[5] Warren to Jameson, Sept. 10, Oct. 15, 1900.
[6] Andrews to Jameson, Sept. 18, 1900.
[7] McLaughlin to Jameson, Oct. 15, 1900.

Providence for commencement, and moved to the West that autumn.

His feeling during his first years in Chicago, as expressed to his closest friend, Francis A. Christie, was not one of complete contentment. The daily routine left small sense of satisfaction in accomplishment. He felt himself too overwhelmed by his duties to make friends. His administrative tasks were heavy. The quarter system under which the university was working involved many complications; the extension courses, though nominally taught by a personnel outside the history department proper, frequently entailed difficult decisions within the department. With an eye to the future needs of the university, Jameson carried on wide-ranging inquiries about the younger historians of the country and searched for European scholars who could, after the manner of the Johns Hopkins University, be brought to Chicago for brief periods. Much consideration had to be given to building up the library. To spend wisely the sum which he had stipulated when he came took time and thought. In the graduate work, where his greatest interest lay, details concerning qualification for admission, amount of credit, programs of work, and plans for theses all passed under his eye. The number of graduate students increased, and the quality of their work improved. It is highly questionable whether they would have accepted his own characterization of his university work as only "partially successful." One disappointment of his service was his failure to see established a series of historical monographs. For such a series he presented a cogent case to President Harper but to no avail.

Despite his preoccupation with details of administration which, partly because of the character of the position and partly because of his own nature, he was unable to shift to others, he still found time to know the younger members of his faculty, and to become familiar not only with the intellectual capacity of his graduate students but with their personal problems. Both the personal and the professional regrets expressed when it was known that he was to leave the University of Chicago suggest that he greatly underestimated the number of enduring friendships which he had made as well as his educational contribution to the institution. The youthful members of the historical club emphasized the personal friendship he had given to each of them as well as the ideal of historical study which he had established. [8] A young instructor wrote: [9]

It means much to a man to feel that his official superior is absolutely fair and just, and that whatever he says may be laid down as a base line, without any correction whatever. It also means much to have such confidence as I have come to have in your standards of what is right and what is of value. Serving under you, I have felt perfectly certain that, if I tried to do honest work, I should win out without any need of advertising.

Another member of his department, E. E. Sparks, later to become president of Pennsylvania State College, after expressing his sense of the loss to the university and his deep personal regret over Jameson's departure, passed beyond the confines of the university to add: [10]

You cannot so easily appreciate the influence you have exerted on the course of historical education in the Middle West during this time.

The first winter in Chicago it fell to Jameson to deliver the Convocation address, which he made a review of modes of historical writing in the past and a consideration of the present fashion, when history "is sent to school, to learn how to sift and to weigh evidence, how to avoid the blunders of amateurs and the vagaries of rhetoricians." It was after reading this address that Albert Bushnell Hart wrote to Jameson: "What I write seems flat and uneventful, just plain rolling prairie, while your style is like Southern New Hampshire."[11] But it is not for style alone that this address is memorable. It was an early and a vivid presentation of the change wrought in historical method and historical writing under the influence of university discipline. Appreciation of the superiority of new methods must not cause students to overlook their dangers. Histories were now written by college professors where once they had been the work of gifted amateurs with wealth and leisure. The professional writer was trained to seek for evidence and to evaluate it but too often he was not trained in literary presentation. It was not enough that history should be based on a study of its sources. To serve its purpose it needed also to be readable. That fact might be forgotten in the new zeal for documentary evidence. This was the doctrine Jameson was preaching.

A knowledge of the complex of duties belonging to his position makes it easy to understand why this four-year period, in which he was relieved of the exacting demands of the *Review*, was not one of prolific writing. Only one considerable piece of research belongs to the Chicago years. This resulted in his History of the Federal Convention of 1787. [12] Interest in this subject he shared with McLaughlin and somewhat later with Max Farrand, to whom he suggested the investigation which resulted in Farrand's *Records of the Federal Convention*. In 1902 he consented to become the general editor of a series of *Original Narratives of Early American History,* projected by the American Historical Association. Of this he wrote in the first volume of the series:

The general editor would not have undertaken the serious labors of preparation and supervision if he had

[8] Their letter was signed by Arthur E. Bestor, Julian P. Bretz, Marcus W. Jernegan, Frederick D. Bramhall, Committee.

[9] Joseph P. Warren to Jameson, May 1, 1905.

[10] E. E. Sparks to Jameson, April 17, 1905.

[11] Hart to Jameson, Jan. 22, 1902.

[12] *Ann. Rept., Am. Hist. Assn.* 1: 87-167, 1902.

not felt sure that it was a genuine benefit to American historical knowledge and American patriotism to make accessible in one collection so large a body of pioneer narrative.

Serious the labor proved to be. Before the final *Narrative* appeared in 1913, Jameson, in addition to editing two volumes, Johnson's *Wonder-Working Providence*, and *Narratives of New Netherland*, and sharing in the editing of a third, *Journal of Jaspar Danckaerts*, had revised and supplemented the editing of many of the other volumes.

Though he found little time in Chicago for research and writing, he could always find time for meditation on the larger needs of historical scholarship. Before he left Brown he had presented to the American Antiquarian Society plans for the exploration of British archives and in Chicago he continued to develop his ideas for this work, later to be carried out by the Carnegie Institution of Washington. A second subject on which he reflected was that of an historical center. He had not been long in Chicago before he presented to the council of the American Historical Association a program for an historical school to be established in Washington. On learning of Andrew Carnegie's gift he at once began to consider methods for advancing historical study by means of this new foundation. All this finds illustration in the letters of the period.

Once the Bureau of Historical Research of the Carnegie Institution was an actuality, with Professor McLaughlin at its head he and Jameson entered into constant correspondence over its work. Few problems arose which were not submitted for Jameson's consideration; few decisions were made in which he did not share. McLaughlin would have been the first to maintain that Jameson's share in organizing the bureau was as large as his own. When he decided to return to teaching he was delighted to learn that Jameson was to step into his place. On the part of the latter there was no hesitation. He did not feel at home in Chicago. He was far from satisfied with himself as a teacher. He no longer believed that he would write the great historical work of his youthful dreams, or, indeed, any historical work. During the years that he had edited the *Review* and served on the Historical Manuscripts Commission he had come to feel that the function he could most successfully perform was, as he frequently said, to make bricks for others to use. To him this was a vastly more humble occupation than building the edifice but it was a necessary one if historical scholarship was to move forward. His choice at this time clearly indicated that he had consciously surrendered early ambitions. Perhaps the surrender was made in 1895 when he became editor of the *Review,* though it is doubtful whether it was consciously and deliberately done then, as it certainly was in 1905 when he abandoned teaching to become head of the Bureau of Historical Research.

The young Jameson, just to begin his teaching, had sententiously recorded in his diary that September 1, 1879, was the beginning of the real work of life. To the mature scholar the real work of his life would probably have seemed that accomplished between 1905 and 1928. Year by year the annual reports of his department set forth its achievements and his hopes and plans for future years. When he left the Carnegie Institution, much had been accomplished, much remained to be accomplished. On library shelves stand rows of *Guides* directing students to the treasures in foreign archives. An impressive array of documentary publications testifies to the zeal of the small staff gathered together by Jameson. *Letters of Members of the Continental Congress, European Treaties, Proceedings and Debates, the Correspondence of Andrew Jackson,* volumes illustrating the slave trade and judicial cases concerned with slavery, an *Atlas of historical geography,* historical documents relating to the Southwest are but a part of the copious legacy he left to future historians of America. All these, no matter what editor's name they bear were planned and supervised by Jameson. To him went all the knotty problems; his was the diplomacy which smoothed the way in foreign archives or with private owners. A second part of his legacy are the volumes of the *Review,* which he again edited as one of the duties of the director of the department as it was set up in 1902. Four times a year it provided an invaluable record of what the historical world was doing as well as of what it was writing.

The public, at least the historical public, was aware of the appearance of a new *Guide* or a volume of *Treaties* or *Judicial Cases,* or of the current number of the *Review,* but one aspect of the work of the department, impossible of measurement, receiving little publicity and easily forgotten, came to absorb perhaps more time than any of those activities which resulted in printed tomes. In the report of the advisory committee of historians presented to the trustees of the Carnegie Institution in 1902,[13] it was recommended that the institute of historical research to be established in Washington "serve as a clearing house for the historical scholars of the country. It should facilitate their personal researches in Washington, and, so far as possible, aid those who are at a distance to avail themselves of its treasures." Under the term "clearing house" can be grouped the innumerable miscellaneous services, large and small, important and trivial, which filled an ever-increasing portion of Dr. Jameson's day. As he expressed it, he was "a sort of *proxenos* of the historical fraternity." Among his papers are a half-dozen swollen folders of "queries" in addition to those scattered throughout the correspondence. The character of some of these questions can be seen in the letters from Albert J. Beveridge to

---

[13] *Year Book,* Carnegie Institution of Washington, 227, 1902.

Jameson.[14] From one historian of the Middle West came questions which illustrate admirably the sort of service Jameson's department was rendering, to the great benefit of the historians but with little permanent record. Where would one find the original grant of land on which Kaskaskia stands? Were there papers in Washington about John Dodge, Canadian refugee? Was a royal proclamation issued encouraging settlers to go to Jamaica? How many papers in the period in which he was interested existed in the State Department and what would it cost to have them copied? Were the territorial laws of Illinois printed? Where did Roosevelt get his references in the *Winning of the West*? Who were the following?—a list of eight or nine names. This is but a small sampling of the questions coming from one worker in one year. All such questions Jameson answered carefully and often in much detail. Even a man who aspired to write a history of the United States and sent sixty-six topics on which he wished suggestions was given good advice though not exactly what he asked for.

A second group of requests came from graduate students who wanted suggestions as to subjects on which to write, or aid in writing on subjects already chosen. From the number who stated that their directors told them to write, one concludes that it was common practice for the professor to say, "Write to Jameson. He'll know." Often he did know. If he did not, he found out, or he referred the questioner to the expert who would know. He declined to answer only those who, he thought, ought to be looking up the matter for themselves.

In addition to these two groups of serious students, there were those members of the public who wished to learn something of history and wrote for guidance. Simple and practical suggestions for reading along many lines were frequently and willingly given.

Unfortunately the public, even the historical public, never learned that the department was in no sense a publishing house and much time was spent explaining to those who offered manuscripts why they could not be published by the Carnegie Institution, or why the Institution could not finance their further work. A much larger group used the department in place of a local library. The variety of requests resulting from curiosity or passing interest can scarcely be indicated here. Most of these, also, were answered though occasionally Jameson rebelled. The correspondent who wanted the full name, the term of office, and the name of his wife, of all our Presidents did not receive her list, nor did the one who asked for a list of all the Carnegie libraries in the United States; but the writer interested in the history of making maple sugar was given help and the teacher who wanted pictures to use in teaching history to children was told where to find them. Possessors of old letters, or old newspapers or rare coins were directed to those who could evaluate them. The kindness, the courtesy, and the sense of the obligation of his position which dictated this policy were essential characteristics of Jameson. Yet it is undoubtedly true that letters, frequently trivial, were answered with an expenditure of time which might well have been applied to more valuable services or even to relaxation and refreshment of spirit.

The exploration of foreign repositories for materials for American history, the publication of documentary material, the editing of the *Review,* and the maintenance of a clearing house for historians were the four main branches of work recommended by the advisory committee of 1902. But there soon proved to be many activities not specifically included in the duties of the director which attached themselves, so to speak, to them, partly because of the location of the department in Washington, partly because it was the one historical center in the country, and partly because Jameson's name carried prestige, but most of all because he was known to be unselfishly ready to serve the cause of history at all times. Many of these accessory duties were connected with the American Historical Association. As an interested and active member of the Association from its organization, as president and member of the executive council, and as a conscientious worker on many committees, Jameson, no matter what his position, would have given much time to the Association, as indeed he had done since its early days. As a resident of Washington it was inevitable that he should be made chairman of many committees whose work must be done in that city. When a lobbyist was needed he was at hand, willing, informed, and persuasive.[15] The location of the offices of the Association in rooms adjacent to those of the department was useful to both, but it undoubtedly brought added burdens to Jameson. Occasionally he rebelled. When in 1908 it was suggested that he act as treasurer of the Association while that officer was out of the country, he listed the responsibilities which he was already carrying for that body. They included chairmanship of the Historical Manuscripts Commission; of the committee on the program for the annual meeting; membership in the committee on local arrangements for that meeting, the secretaryship of the Committee on Documentary Historical Publications of the United States, and membership in the committee dealing with cooperation among historical societies. During long absences of the secretary

[14] Donnan, Elizabeth, and Leo F. Stock, eds., Senator Beveridge, J. Franklin Jameson, and John Marshall, and, Senator Beveridge, J. Franklin Jameson, and Abraham Lincoln, *Miss. Valley Hist. Rev.* **35**: 466-492, December, 1948; 641-673, March, 1949.

[15] Of lobbying Professor McLaughlin wrote to Jameson on Jan. 12, 1907: "How distasteful this must be to you. I swallowed several tons of mortification and reserve hauteur and family pride and aristocratic aloofness and scholarly sensitiveness and academic independence of spirit and what nots two years ago and possibly in your wiser way you have some of the same hesitations."

of the Association, Mr. W. G. Leland, it was customary for Jameson to take over many of his responsibilities. It fell to Jameson to deal with the Smithsonian in skirmishes over the exclusion of material from the *Annual Reports;* his duty it was to present the cause of the Association to a committee of the Congress when its budget was cut. So cogent was his presentation of his case that he invariably obtained the restoration of the larger amount.

A study of the correspondence makes clear what a large part he, involuntarily, had in building the programs of the annual meetings. "Have you any suggestions?" was the question which early in February was likely to come from the chairman of the program committee. From that time until the final copy of the program was printed he was "on call." Such features as the dinner groups, sessions on legal history, conferences of historical societies, an hour of historical music, resulted from his suggestions. From his vantage point in Washington he knew who was working on what and was able to see possibilities for unified and stimulating programs. When a harassed chairman wrote that *A* and *B* and *C* had declined to speak, Dr. Jameson could point to *M, N,* and *O,* as able to supply equally well what was wanted. One letter, typical of many, began: "Program making I discover to be difficult, requiring the patience of Job and 'then some.'" The writer went on to name three of his chosen speakers who had declined, seven who had not answered his letters. This called forth from Jameson eight useful suggestions, and encouragement about certain of the delinquent correspondents. The next letter from the same unhappy chairman reported that for another session four speakers had declined. Here Jameson suggested five or six possible substitutes and a helpful rearrangement. By December as the proofs passed through the Washington office a spate of telegrams might be expected: "*A* cannot preside; telegraph *Y*" or "*J* wishes to change the title of his paper." In January would come: "Accept my deep appreciation of your constant assistance and suggestions. Most of whatever merit is to be found in the results is due to your help and encouragement." That chairman sighed with relief that his task was completed, and Dr. Jameson began the round again with a new chairman who must learn for himself that program-making was difficult business. This work behind the scenes on the annual programs, both lessened the perplexities of the committees and helped to give the sessions unity and vitality. Such services as these can be set down, evaluated, and appreciated, but the intangible results of his wise and disinterested counsel on Association problems must be largely unrecorded.

As president of the Association in 1907, he delivered as his address "The American Acta Sanctorum," [16] which with erudition, felicity of language, and enlivening

---

[16] *Amer. Hist. Rev.* **13**: 286-402, Jan. 1908.

humor, called to the attention of the historians gathered at the annual meeting the rich stores of information to be found in the lives of the American clergy. By a wealth of illustration he demonstrated the contribution which they could make to many aspects of our social history. This was no new doctrine for Jameson. In his class room he had frequently called the attention of his students to the value of the history of religion in America, a subject largely unexplored at that time.

Many of these services Jameson would have performed had he remained in Chicago but it is doubtful whether he would have taken on his shoulders responsibility for the *Writings on American History* had he not become chief of the Bureau of Historical Research. During Professor McLaughlin's two-year service for the Bureau he, with the assistance of William Adams Slade and Ernest Dorman Lewis, had prepared a bibliographical volume, with the idea that a similar work should be issued each year by the department. On this subject, however, the president and the trustees of the Institution were adamant: bibliographies were not to be financed by the Institution. Keenly aware of the need for such a tool for the use of students of American history, Jameson undertook to obtain financial support for the work and during the rest of his life raised by personal solicitation the funds which paid for the preparation of the annual volumes. Various means of publication were found through the years but at no time were there other means of recompensing Miss Grace G. Griffin for her labor in preparing volume after volume than the small gifts obtained by Jameson. At long last the responsibility which he carried has been accepted by the National Archives and the continuance of the work which he for many years maintained, seems now assured.

Among the small tasks begun by Jameson before he joined the Institution but thereafter carried forward as part of the work of the department was the compilation each year of a list of doctoral dissertations in progress in the graduate schools of history in the United States, together with the titles of those which had been printed. These annual lists not only served to warn students off ground already pre-empted and to enable students to confer with those who were writing on related subjects, but also indicated what the interests of future teachers of history might be. The service seemed a small one, yet it was one of increasing value to the historical profession. From the series one can follow the shifting emphasis in the study of history, for example, the increasing interest in Latin American studies and the growth of attention to Far Eastern affairs are clearly indicated in the successive lists.

Another call upon Jameson's time resulted from his wide knowledge of the work of the younger students of history. All teachers, especially teachers in graduate schools, accept as one of the duties of the position the writing of recommendations for their students. Jameson may have thought, if he thought of it at all, that when he left teaching he would no longer be called upon to suggest candidates for college posts. But, removed from connection with any one graduate school, as head of the historical department of the Carnegie Institution, it was rightly assumed by heads of college and university departments of history that he kept in touch with the universities and knew the achievements and potentialities of the younger historians of the country. Many a young man would have been surprised had he seen the careful evaluation of his work which went from Jameson to some enquirer looking for the best possible man to fill a vacancy. Knowledge, discernment, and thoughtful appraisal were combined, in these recommendations, with Jameson's rare gift of expressing exactly what he wished to say, without overstatement.

Another subject on which his advice was at times invoked, obviously because of his long and unique experience, was that of proposals to establish new historical journals. *The American Historical Review* in 1895 stood alone, but as the number of readers and writers of history increased, and specialization became more marked, new projects were conceived, Jameson's opinion as to their feasibility and usefulness was usually solicited before active steps were taken. The originators of the *New England Quarterly*, the *Mississippi Valley Historical Review*, the *Catholic Historical Review*, the *Hispanic-American Historical Review*, and *Modern History* all requested his judgment on the proposed ventures and his advice concerning the problems of editing.

Thus far this account has dwelt on Dr. Jameson's services to the study of history in this country but any review of his work which omits his relations with foreign scholars would be most inadequate. It should be borne in mind that he was one of the few historians of his day who had not studied in Germany. Thus he began his career without the initial acquaintances that most of his contemporaries possessed. Reference has already been made to his early correspondence with European historians while a young instructor in the Johns Hopkins University. As head of the department of history of the University of Chicago he brought to that university foreign lecturers and at one time attempted to find in England a permanent member of his faculty. But his close connection with many European historians began with his work in Washington. Until the close of the First World War his chief concern was probably the exploration of foreign archives but with the war came a sharp realization of the part America should play in international scholarly activities, and his letters of the twenties display the measure of his historical statesmanship. He was by no means satisfied to suggest desirable cooperative projects but was ready to lend aid in carrying them out. Not only letters here published but many more among the Jameson Papers shed light on the international postwar relations in which Jameson took a leading part.

He was well described by the New York *Times* as an ambassador to scholars.

With some department undertakings nearing completion, others midway, and one or two not yet begun, Jameson learned in the autumn of 1927 that it was the intention of the executive committee of the Carnegie Institution to make no new appointments to the department to replace Miss Davenport, who had died, and Mr. Leland, who had resigned. Those projects under way in the hands of Dr. Stock, Dr. Burnett, and Dr. Paullin were to be finished, and with their completion the work of historical research would no longer be carried on by the Institution. For it would be substituted the exploration of Mayan civilization. Dr. Jameson, himself, was asked to retire in two years, when he would have reached seventy. Just at this time Dr. Putnam of the Library of Congress was looking for someone to assume the duties of chief of the Division of Manuscripts of the Library of Congress and to fill the chair of American history recently established by William Evarts Benjamin. The duties of the chair were as yet nebulous and would be largely determined by the new incumbent. On learning that Jameson's work for the Institution was drawing to a close, Dr. Putnam promptly sought his services for the new position and on July 1, 1928, having severed his connection with the Institution, Jameson became chief of the Division of Manuscripts of the Library of Congress. The summer of 1928 he spent in Europe, as had been planned before his resignation, completing some tasks for the Department of Historical Research, and at the same time serving his new position in various ways. His actual presence in the Library began in September, 1928, and for nine years, in Dr. Putnam's phrase, he gave "luster to the entire library."

Of his new position Jameson wrote in the winter before he entered upon his duties:[17]

I hope that my office upon the Hill will continue to be, as Mr. Henry Adams used to declare that this one was, a sort of central telephone exchange by which he (and others like minded) could get into communication with other historical scholars or sources of information.

Such an exchange it certainly became. The questions which once were directed to the Department of Historical Research now came to the Division of Manuscripts and called for much of Jameson's time. In the Division he inherited certain work already begun which it fell to him to carry to completion. The final volumes of the *Journals of the Continental Congress* were edited under supervision, as were the two concluding volumes of the *Records of the Virginia Company*. He also had the satisfaction of aiding Mr. Bernard Mayo in editing the *Instructions to the British Ministers to the United States, 1791-1812*, though this was done, not for the Library of Congress but for the American Historical Association.[18]

---

[17] Jameson to R. D. W. Connor, Jan. 4, 1928.
[18] *Ann. Rept., Amer. Hist. Assn.*, 1936.

A second group of inherited projects, were those known in library parlance as projects A and C. Project A, the most ambitious undertaking of the Library, was the photocopying of material from European archives respecting American history, financed by a generous gift from Mr. John D. Rockefeller, Jr. It was a happy turn of fate that Jameson, who at the end of the nineteenth century, had planned the exploration of those repositories, and during a score of years had been instrumental in preparing guides to their contents should now be in a position to aid in bringing to this country and in making available to scholars coming to Washington a great body of this material. Project C, over which Jameson had general supervision, included a *Census of Mediaeval and Renaissance Manuscripts in the United States,* edited by Seymour de Ricci; and a *Catalogue of Latin and Vernacular Alchemical Manuscripts in the United States and Canada,* edited by William Jerome Wilson; both of these being supported by funds advanced by the American Council of Learned Societies. Carrying forward Project A and building up the collections of domestic papers were Jameson's major achievements as head of the Division. Though foreign sources for the history of America were accumulated rapidly, domestic material was gathered in with equal assiduity. Jameson's first care was to locate and to procure additional papers of our Presidents, cabinet officers, and lesser political figures. His past experience gave him many clues and the results can be read in his successive annual reports to the Librarian, models of English as well as valuable indications of the growing wealth of the Division.

Outside the work of the Division, Jameson still maintained many historical interests, the chief of them being the compilation of the *Dictionary of American Biography,* and the organization of the National Archives, both to be described later. The editors of the volumes still in progress in the former Department of Historical Research turned to him for advice and assistance much as they had in earlier years. He was still available when the American Historical Association wished counsel or needed a committee member in Washington. The pressure of the routine work of the Division, along with such additional demands as these, was heavy and at one point in the decade of his service to the Library he was warned by serious illness that the duties he carried must be reduced. A second interruption to his work came in the spring of 1937, when he was struck by an automobile as he was boarding a street car near the Library of Congress. His attempt to return to his work in September, after a painful summer, proved too difficult. He died on September 28, 1937.

In this review of Jameson's contributions to the development of historical scholarship four projects of his have been omitted altogether or referred to but briefly. Of these, two were never achieved in the form in which he conceived them, two were magnificently successful.

Early in his student days he came to appreciate the richness of the historical materials in Washington and the need to make them widely available. Reference has already been made to his dream, long cherished and reluctantly surrendered, that of editing and publishing the records of the Virginia Company. Though he gained the promise of a publisher he never received the consent of the Library Committee of the Congress to carry out this ambition. His final abandonment of the project by no means indicated that he had lost interest in the scholarly presentation of the historical material of the government. In 1891 he made a one-man survey of the expenditures of other governments for historical publications. From this he drew the conclusion that the United States fell short not in quantity but in quality of production. Expert planning and expert editing were the needs, not larger appropriations. After this report, absorbed in other work, he dropped the subject for a time, but once in Washington, as chief of the Department of Historical Research of the Carnegie Institution it became one of his major interests. He was now prepared to advocate, not the publication of a single series of volumes, but an extensive plan for governmental publication, directed toward need and guided by historical experts.

In 1905, in one of its periodical attempts to oil the machinery of government, the Congress appointed Charles Hallam Keep chairman of a commission which was to report to the President on departmental methods, including such miscellaneous and diverse subjects as intra-department telephone service, methods of accounting, purchase of supplies, and the publication of historical documents. To Gifford Pinchot a member of this commission, Jameson presented his ideas for improving government publications. Later he carried them to President Theodore Roosevelt, who gave them a sympathetic hearing but regretted that he had no funds with which to pay the expenses of the committee for which Jameson asked. From the President, Jameson turned to Secretary Root. When he went to the meeting of the American Historical Association at Madison in December, 1907, he had had no reply from Root. Despairing of a governmental committee to plan historical publications, Jameson asked that the Association appoint a committee to canvas the possibilities of government publications. Such a committee was authorized and the in-coming president, George B. Adams, promptly named as its members Charles Francis Adams, Charles M. Andrews, William A. Dunning, Worthington C. Ford, Albert Bushnell Hart, Alfred T. Mahan, Andrew C. McLaughlin, and Frederick J. Turner, with Jameson as chairman.

On Jameson's return to Washington he learned that, at Secretary Root's suggestion, the Keep Commission was willing to make the committee of the Association a subcommittee of its own, paying its expenses and incorporating its report in the report of the Commission. The committee began its work in March, 1908, and in November its report was ready for the President, who transmitted it to the Congress in February, 1909, where it became Senate Document 714. The report reviewed the course hitherto pursued by the government, indicating costs, criticizing the lack of system, and demonstrating that the present time was opportune for reform. It pointed out the gaps in our history which needed to be filled by government publication. It recommended the policy to be followed in planning historical publications, described the methods of other governments, and indicated the functions of a permanent historical commission. It recommended the publication of a series of State Papers, supplementing the old *American State Papers*. Finally, it included the draft of a bill to create a permanent commission.

In December, 1909, the McCall bill, similar to the bill contained in the report, was introduced in the House. Now began for Dr. Jameson one of the most energetic and in the end one of the most bitterly disappointing lobbying experiences of his professional life, surpassed only by his persistence and his disappointments in the campaign for a national archive building. For a time life to him seemed comprised of letters and visits to legislators, of interviews with heads of executive departments fearful lest the proposed commission deprive them of power or prestige, and of the drafting of amendments to meet this or that objection to the bill. After long delay a favorable report came from the Library Committee and the bill was given a place on the calendar (H. 15428) but the House adjourned before reaching it. In 1911 the weary process of arousing interest in the subject was repeated but with less success. The bill remained in committee in spite of all Jameson's efforts to dislodge it. When President Wilson came to the White House Jameson's request for an interview with him on the subject was met by the statement that it would be hopeless to press for his project at that time. This ended six years of endeavor. The question of an historical commission such as the McCall bill would have created was dropped for twenty years.

But if a commission could not be obtained there were other means by which something might be achieved. Even before all hope of bringing a commission into existence had faded Jameson was advocating a project which would, he believed, create interest in diplomatic material and also educate the members of the Congress. The anniversary of the signing of the Treaty of Ghent was approaching and offered opportunity to bring out a well-edited collection of relevant papers which might serve as a model for future publications. For this idea there is no evidence that he elicited any enthusiasm. About the same time his help was enlisted in forwarding a more ambitious enterprise. On March 3, 1913, the Congress authorized the publication of the records of the Revolutionary War and the War and Navy departments turned to Jameson for advice. For the first time it seemed possible that historians were to have the opportunity to guide an important government project, but the Congress refused to appropriate the necessary money to continue the gathering of material and the only result was the collection of fragmentary papers in Massachusetts, Virginia, and North Carolina.

Gradually Jameson reached the conclusion that the only hope was to induce an individual department to undertake a specific task. The task he had in mind was the publication of the Instructions which went from our Secretaries of State to our foreign embassies. On November 20, 1922, he wrote to Charles Moore:

I have always kept it [a national commission on government publication] in mind, and I do not wish to die without seeing it done, but I expect to. Much as I am discouraged with respect to the National Archive building . . . I am far more discouraged in respect to any scheme of publication. Every other nation has a good professional historical commission, but it has proved impossible to get one instituted by our Congress, and it would not now receive five minutes' consideration. I believe that you and I constitute a committee of the "A.H.A." on the "Documentary Historical Publications of the United States Government," but I regard the whole thing as perfectly hopeless, except possibly by one method: there is a chance that one might stir up the present Secretary of State to initiate in that one Department a scheme of publication of historical materials, relative to our diplomatic history. I outlined such a project to Hunt when he first took his present office, and I have intended, with his approval and yours, when I could get around to it, to draw it up in form and present it to the Secretary; but as, under present financial circumstances, it would almost certainly be instantly killed by Congress, I have spent my time on things more hopeful.

The Secretary of State, Charles E. Hughes, proved interested and agreed that the work should be done. When all seemed propitious for the beginning of a task first advocated by Professor McLaughlin in 1904, an unexpected difficulty arose. In planning the work Jameson had suggested that the first volume be Instructions to our ministers in Great Britain, and had said that a qualified student stood ready to edit the volume with no cost to the government. At this point the Department of State concluded that it could brook no outside aid. That, as Jameson well knew, rang the knell to any hope of results, as the Division of Publications of the Department was far behind in its regular publications and without such additional aid as he had offered could do nothing to push a new enterprise. Once again, in 1925, Jameson raised the question of printing the Instructions, and also urged that the annual volume *Foreign Affairs,* then ten years in arrears, be brought up to date, that an *Historical Register*—a list of ambassadors and ministers—be prepared, and that the Territorial Papers be printed. The Instructions and the desired Register have never appeared; the series *Foreign Affairs* is still far in arrears; the Territorial Papers are appearing. These Jameson had caused to be calendared not long after he moved to Washington. Many years later he lent his aid to Senator Samuel M. Ralston in obtaining a law which provided for the copying, the editing, and the publication of these papers.[19]

Lest the historians themselves forget the need for improvement in the historical work of the government, Dr. Jameson in 1927 presented at the annual meeting of the Association a survey of the expenditures of the government for history. These he found to be not much more than a thousandth part of what is spent for scientific research. Here once again he emphasized the need for a permanent committee of historical experts who could set up a program of publication and guide its execution.

A second project long cherished by Jameson also concerned the historical material in the nation's capital. His efforts to make these materials widely known and easily accessible took many forms. Among these was a recurring attempt to establish in Washington a school or center to which graduate students from universities the country over might come, to work under guidance and without losing their own university connection. The first suggestion for such a school, Jameson attributed to Professor Frederick J. Turner, but it was Jameson who, in 1901, first cast about for means to bring it into existence. He turned, naturally, to the council of the American Historical Association, which in response to his suggestion appointed a committee to consider the project. Consideration had not yet begun when the news that Andrew Carnegie had presented to the nation $10,000,000, to be employed for research was made public. Just how this sum was to be used was for many months in doubt, and while the newly appointed trustees debated possible plans, Jameson and his committee—McLaughlin and Charles Francis Adams—considered what this gift could do for history. When they were asked to advise the trustees of the Carnegie Institution, their suggestions, drawn up by Jameson, were soon ready. Among these they proposed that the Institution should make provision for the "guidance and instruction for such advanced and highly competent graduate students as should resort to it for the purpose." This, in the minds of the committee, was to be a substitute for the historical school which Jameson had proposed. When Professor McLaughlin became head of the Bureau of Historical Research, the first department of the Institution to be established, he discovered among the trustees considerable opposition to the establishment of any such study center as the committee had conceived. The most that he could do was to use a small fund to bring to Washington students who needed to work in that city for short periods. Even this practice was discontinued in 1907.

Nevertheless, the idea of an historical school in Washington was not given up. In New York in May, 1916, Jameson met with a group of historians to examine the possibilities for such a project. A committee appointed here drew up a constitution and sent out a request for a consideration of it at the December meeting of the Historical Association. Consultation was not limited to the historians. The Political Science and the Economic associations, the Librarian of Congress, the secretaries of State and of the Interior and of the Smithsonian, and the director of the Pan American Union were all asked to endorse the constitution and support the effort. But here the First World War intervened.

After the war the idea was revived, though by this time it was so modified as to be a scarcely recognizable portion of the plan of 1901. Hope for a home and a director was, at least for the time, surrendered. Resident Washington advisers were chosen for the various subjects to be covered, and announcement was made that students would be gladly welcomed. But students failed to appear. Jameson, through the *Review* and by notices sent to universities, endeavored to make the machinery set up of some use, but eventually he was forced to believe that, whatever the need had been in 1901, in the middle of the 1920's there were no students eager for aid in pursuing studies in the capital. Even yet there is in Washington no means of rendering the service which he outlined in 1901.

These two concerns of Jameson—a commission of historical experts to plan the publication of the government's documentary material and the establishment of an historical school in Washington—he failed to achieve, though he gave to them both much effort. With two other projects he was completely successful.

Among suggestions made by Jameson to President Gilman in a letter of February 2, 1902, just after the news of the gift of Andrew Carnegie reached Chicago, was that of a dictionary of American biography, comparable to the English *Dictionary of National Biography*.[20] In this letter he gave his reasons for believing that such a work, if it was to meet the scholarly standards of the English publication, could not find a publisher who would bear the risk involved. Therefore, it must be subsidized. Later, when Jameson submitted his ideas to McLaughlin and Charles Francis

---

[19] Parker, David, *Calendar of papers in Washington archives relating to the territories of the United States (to 1873),* Papers of the Department of Historical Research, 1911. The work of editing was placed in the hands of Dr. Clarence E. Carter, whose first volume appeared in 1934. In 1950 the work was transferred from the Department of State to the National Archives. By the summer of 1953, nineteen volumes had appeared.

[20] In December, 1901, Jameson had received a letter from Professor F. M. Anderson suggesting that the American Historical Association undertake a biographical dictionary and that George Howard, who had recently lost his position in Stanford University because of his defense of academic freedom, be made editor.

Adams, the other members of the committee who were to present a program to the new Institution, this was the project which at once appealed to Adams, who wrote: [21]

The thing in your report which commends itself most to my mind, is the idea of an American Biographical Dictionary on the basis of the English work, of which Leslie Stephen was the original editor. A portion of the fund alone devoted to that purpose for a single year would suffice to insure the completion of the work; for at the outside, $50,000 would, I presume, be all that would be necessary to insure that result. The sale of the work would be large; and, though we might find no publisher as bold and public-spirited as Smith [the English publisher], yet, with such an assured support as I have mentioned, many publishers would be eager to take hold of it.

That would be a monument to the new endowment; and one which, I am very confident, would be gratifying to Mr. Carnegie.

In spite of his enthusiasm the idea received but brief reference in the report of the advisory committee to the Carnegie Institution, being classed with those projects which could wait.

With an eye to what he clearly thought was a long-distant future, Jameson, in his second year with the Institution, sent to the director of the *Allegemeine Deutsche Biographie* a series of questions about the method of preparing the German work.[22] With his questions he explained that, though he had in mind a dictionary as something "which this young institution might sometime attempt," the prospect was remote. He feared that the existence of two or three mediocre works might cause the trustees to hesitate over bringing forth another, even though a much better one. It is not clear whether this skepticism echoed expressions from President Woodward or one of the trustees or whether it was his own surmise as to how they might feel. A few years later he offered a different reason for delay, this time to Worthington C. Ford, who had written of the eagerness of Charles Francis Adams to have the Institution undertake a biographical dictionary, and had added his own arguments for such an enterprise. In his reply of May 28, 1909, Jameson explained that he felt that the time was not ripe. The lives of nineteenth-century subjects were not yet fully recorded, possibly not yet fully evaluated. In addition to these two reasons for postponement there may have been a third, that is, that he realized that he had neither time nor strength to undertake so tremendous a project. The production of the *Guides* had proved to be more prolonged and more vexatious than was foreseen. In fact, this could be said for everything undertaken by the Department. He well realized that to carry through the dictionary would be just such a task as had killed Leslie Stephen. To add it to what he had in

process was impossible. This is indicated in a letter to Professor Hart written two years after he wrote to Ford. At that time Hart had two schemes afoot: an *American Year Book* and a biographical dictionary, both to be published by D. Appleton and Company. The *Year Book* was assured; the dictionary promised to succeed though as yet no subsidy had been obtained. He urged Jameson to become one of a board of six or seven to carry out the editorial work. Jameson's reply was revealing.[23]

At the beginning of my work here I held it in mind as a possibility for this Department, though that thought has long since passed. I am, however, still so interested that it gave me quite a pang to decline to take part in the work of the Board. But I had to tell him [Willoughby] that I could not think of undertaking this, or anything else that would require any serious expenditure of time, though of course as much unpaid assistance as I could give would always be at the service of any such enterprise. The truth is that, by reason of various untoward circumstances, or want of sufficient ability on my part to avoid such a situation, I am burdened pretty nearly to the breaking point by what I have to do now. . . . The association with other members of the Board would be agreeable and stimulating; but I must avoid all stimulants until I get over the present indigestion of materials at 500 Bond Building.

Hart's project was not carried out and the question of a scholarly biographical compilation rested until the first meeting of the American Council of Learned Societies in 1920. Here Turner proposed that it be undertaken by that organization. He repeated the suggestion in 1921, and in January, 1922, a committee was appointed to consider it, with Jameson as chairman. It was Jameson who carried the need to Adolph Ochs of the New York *Times* and obtained the gift of $500,-000 which made the dream a certainty. Professor Allen Johnson of Yale was chosen as editor and on his death the work was completed under the editorship of Professor Dumas Malone. Throughout the years of work which followed Jameson was chairman of the committee of management, where his advice was invoked on all questions of policy. Nor did he limit his aid and advice to matters of policy only. Scrupulous accuracy was so much a habit with him that as he read the successive volumes he could not refrain from noting the errors which he found, with the hope that they might be corrected in a second printing. Many of these were errors of dates, of the spelling of proper names, or were typographical slips; occasionally they were questions of interpretation or of fact. His comments were often amusing, as when he found someone described as a direct descendant of Sir Francis Drake: "Sir Francis Drake had no descendants, and we are just helping to put a man in jail for a long term for swindling a million dollars out of credulous persons who think they are descendants." Or when he wrote:

---

[21] Adams to Jameson, Mar. 11, 1902.

[22] Jameson to Rochus Freiherr von Liliencron, Prälat des St. Johannisklosters, Schleswig, Germany, Nov. 15, 1906.

[23] Hart to Jameson, Feb. 21, 1911; Jameson to Hart, Feb. 25, 1911.

I cannot think he [George Logan] can be truly said to have been the only strict Quaker who ever sat in the U. S. Senate; for I remember Jonathan Chace, Senator from Rhode Island, used to walk out of the Senate whenever the appropriations for the War Department were being considered. From what his nephew told me, he was no doubt a strict Quaker.

Jameson lived to see, with satisfaction, the appearance of the last volume of the twenty planned. That volume contains a history of the enterprise, unsigned, but possibly in part his work. He also wrote for the *Dictionary* the biography of Allen Johnson, the first editor. Here his description of the qualities which Johnson brought to the work might with equal truth be used to characterize his own ideals for it: breadth of view, absence of bias and ancestor worship, a desire for accuracy and for literary excellence.

The second successful project, considered by many to be Jameson's greatest achievement, again related to the historical material in the possession of the national government. During a considerable part of Jameson's years in Washington no single subject occupied a larger place in his correspondence (judged by sheer bulk), consumed a greater portion of his time, and more frequently dominated his thoughts than that of a national archive building. To serve the cause of history, a research center in Washington was desirable; an expert commission to advise on the publication by the government of historical sources was sorely needed; but provision for the safe housing and the professional care of the materials themselves was imperative. The agitation for such a building did not originate with the historians but with the executive departments of the government, which as early as 1878 called attention to the need of care for the accumulating mass of government papers. Formal recognition by the historians of this need came at a meeting of the American Historical Association in Washington, in 1901, when they endorsed the request of the departments for a "hall of records." In March, 1903, the Congress provided for the purchase of a site and authorized a building. To those unfamiliar with the ways of legislative bodies, this would have seemed to indicate that before many years the United States would possess an archive building. Not so. It was thirty years before this authorization finally took form in a structure.

When Jameson came to Washington in 1905 nothing had been done to implement the statute of 1903 and it seemed likely to be forgotten. An early interview with President Roosevelt convinced him that the time had not come for the erection of a building but he saw no good reason why he should not keep the need for it alive in the minds of the members of the Congress. This he did. From 1907 until 1934, there were few periods, with the exception of the war years, when legislators were allowed to forget the subject. Confronted by the horrifying evidence of the neglect of irreplaceable material, gathered under Jameson's direction, they were driven to admit the necessity and at

long last to act. The story of the wearisome campaign to bring a building into existence is illustrated by many of the letters here published and has been told in some detail by Fred Shelley in "The Interest of J. Franklin Jameson in the National Archives, 1908-1934."[24] Here it is intended only to review briefly Jameson's efforts in this cause. To appreciate fully the tireless persistence of those efforts, the frustrations and disappointments, one needs to read the entire mass of correspondence which relates to the subject.

In 1908 the council of the American Historical Association created a committee to promote the erection of an archive building. Of this committee Jameson was made chairman. The chief importance of this action was to give him a certain official standing when he appealed to members of the Congress. During 1909 and 1910 he carried on correspondence with the Treasury Department, which was eager for a building, and with senators, who felt no interest whatever. From President Taft he gained an expression of approval in his annual message of 1910. By the summer of 1911 Sheppard of the House and Poindexter of the Senate, both friends of the cause, believed that the time for action had come. They asked Jameson to draft bills, which they introduced. His correspondence with interested members of the Congress, with the office of the supervising architect, and with all those that he thought might abet the movement was extensive and forceful. Pressure was exerted on the Congress from many directions. Jameson proved to be not only a tireless but also an ingenious lobbyist. His circular sent out to historical societies brought quick response from many of them; addresses by Jameson to the Daughters of the American Revolution and to the American Library Association induced them to use their influence with their representatives. The *Review of Reviews,* the *Nation,* the New York *Evening Post,* the Washington *Star* all presented graphic accounts of existing conditions, most of them using material supplied by Jameson and his aids. For a brief season there seemed reason to hope for success but the hope was short-lived. On January 14, 1913, Jameson wrote to W. G. Leland:

Respecting those [archives] of the United States I am still in a condition of black despair, so far as the present session is concerned. We shall have to see whether an Executive Order "Let there be Archives, W. Wilson," will be potent with the 63rd Congress. I am afraid when it should get through them it would emerge in the shape "Let them Archives be."

The public buildings act of March, 1913, which created a commission that was "to straighten out the tangle and reduce the congestion of affairs respecting public buildings" had by the end of October held but one meeting. After it, Jameson wrote to Leland:[25]

The one step they have taken is to ask the Supervising Architect to devise a system for standardizing the

[24] *The American Archivist* 12: 99-130, April, 1949.

plans for federal public buildings in localities. If they are going to build eighty-two thousand buildings for eighty-two thousand post offices, this measure will tend toward great economy and efficiency. . . . I have, however, addressed an eloquent and touching letter to each of the members of this commission, calling attention to the existence of the city of Washington, and to the possible utility of a building or so right here. I have added to my will a request to my executors to continue to push the matter of the National Archive Building. It gives me pleasure to add that all public authorities who admit having read your article are willing to admit that something ought to be done (by somebody else).

The next year the only forward step was the appropriation of $5,000 for work on the plans for a building. Throughout 1915 Jameson's efforts to convince members of the Congress that this building was a pressing necessity continued. In December the American Historical Association, the Economic and Political Science associations, and other national societies held a joint session intended to promote interest in the building. Here Mr. Leo F. Stock displayed slides showing the present condition of valuable records and appropriate resolutions were passed, urging upon the Congress the speedy construction of an archive building. There were now few who did not admit the need even when they were unwilling to take immediate action. Plans were ready for consideration in 1916 but nothing could be done with them because of a troublesome technicality. The act of 1913 had provided that foreign archive buildings must be inspected before plans were adopted. Such inspection was now impossible because of the war; thus, the next move was to obtain the repeal of this clause. The conflict over a desirable site was a further obstacle. The one designated in 1903 had already been devoted to another use. Jameson prepared a comprehensive survey of the possibilities, setting forth the advantages and disadvantages of each but he obtained no response from the Public Buildings Commission. Thus, when America entered the war, all that had been achieved were some excellent plans, a wide-spread knowledge of conditions, and the favorable opinion of a group of legislators; no site had been chosen and there was little prospect of an appropriation for one. By 1919 the only progress Jameson could see was that a site had been selected (not the one finally used). There was still no appropriation for its purchase. A fire in the census records in 1921 gave him new ammunition. He wrote to half a dozen senators, reminding them that between 1833 and 1915 there had been 254 fires in buildings in use by the United States government. That year the American Legion joined forces with Jameson, the interest of the Legion being in the proper care of the war records. In November, 1921, Jameson was sufficiently heartened to write to John S. Bassett that he would like to send one more memorial to the Congress: "There seems to be strong reason to hope that in this next session an

appropriation may be secured if somebody can make a noise like public opinion." A year later, however, it was his melancholy duty to report to the Association that the appropriation bill which went from the House to the Senate carried no appropriation for the purchase of a site or for a building; the Senate inserted an item (drawn by Jameson) appropriating a half million dollars for a building to be placed on land already owned by the government. This was lost in conference.

Early in 1923 a reporter brought to Jameson news, passed along to Leland, that the Hearst papers had come to his support. Strange bedfellows the campaign had made: the American Legion, the Hearst papers, J. F. Jameson, and the American Historical Association! To a friend, Dr. Jameson wrote on January 22, 1923: "I am spending all my time at the capitol. The prospect now of getting the measure through is very discouraging." His discouragement continued. In May he expressed it to Worthington C. Ford:

I presume it is just as well to confine my attention to the business of the Department of Historical Research in the Carnegie Institution of Washington but whenever I say that to myself, I think of the National Archive Building and am aware that my conscience will never allow me to drop that affair, at which I have been hammering for fifteen years and must probably hammer for fifteen more, or until the undertaker hammers the lid over me.

Ford replied:

Of course you will not abate your efforts for the archives building. If it ever comes that will be your monument in stone in Washington, for no man has contributed so much time and valuable service as you have in furthering its coming. . . . If success is to attend the effort it will be intelligence pitted against local narrowness.

When President Coolidge came to office, Jameson enlightened him, as he had previous presidents since Theodore Roosevelt, on the need for a building and the history of the efforts to obtain it. The President, in recommending a public buildings program the next year, specifically mentioned an archive building, and an act embodying his recommendations was passed on May 25, 1926. It was now taken for granted that an archive building was a certainty, as indeed it was, but few people realized how much effort still lay ahead. One correspondent wrote:[26]

You have accomplished much in your life, but this is perhaps the greatest thing you have done. . . . In working for this you've never faltered in the steadiness of your sustained effort—you've had the patience of a myriad of coral insects. And I say, *Well Done.*

In fact, the work was far from *done.* Eight years of effort still lay ahead. A satisfactory site remained to be selected; plans were yet to be drawn, those of 1916 being thought obsolete; and an organization must be established. In all this Jameson took some part, his

25 Jameson to Leland, Oct. 30, 1913.

26 Jeannette Thurber Connor to Jameson, June 4, 1926.

greatest effort being directed toward obtaining a workable organization. Two desirable sites were lost to other projects before one was finally settled upon. There still remained the long process of condemnation and it was more than three years before title to the land was secured. In the office of the architects progress was slow because of a glut of work, and also because it was impossible to prepare plans without knowing on what spot the building was to stand. In these two tasks Jameson's function was vigilantly to prod others into action. In the third he took a more active role. The act of 1926 authorizing a national archive building had scarcely passed before Jameson sent to Tyler Dennett of the State Department notes on proper organization of the work. He was also in prompt communication with Senator Fess, who asked him to draft a bill, the first of many dealing with the subject. This first bill, introduced by Senator Fess, was referred to the Library Committee, where it remained. In 1929 the Public Buildings Commission set up a committee of six, of which Jameson was one, to deliberate on organization. Its work resulted in a bill which Senator Smoot introduced. From this time numerous measures were introduced both in House and Senate, most of them described by Jameson as "good bills," though often made better by his suggested amendments. The one finally passed was a combination of a House bill introduced by Representative Sol Bloom in 1934, and a Senate bill introduced by Senator McKellar. In addition to enumerating the powers and duties of the archivist, to be appointed by the President with the advice and consent of the Senate, it set up what Jameson had long hoped to see, an advisory committee on historical publications. It is true that this was not entirely composed of historians as was Jameson's suggested committee of 1909, but the five government officials who were to serve on it—the archivist, a representative of the Library of Congress, the Chief of the Division of Publications of the Department of State, and representatives of the historical branches of the War and Navy Departments—were those necessarily interested in history. In addition, there were to be two members of the American Historical Association, chosen from the council. The reorganization of 1949 and 1950 have somewhat enlarged the original functions of this advisory body.

Throughout the closing years of this long-sustained effort, Jameson had carefully refrained from any consideration of possible candidates for the position of archivist. His only desire was that the position be held by a trained archivist, chosen for fitness not because of political pressure, but those who realized how large a part Jameson had played in achieving a building and in outlining the functions of the future archivist, insisted that he serve on the committee which selected the first incumbent, R. D. W. Connor, who in 1939, two years after Jameson's death, when describing the history of the struggle to obtain adequate care of government records, said of him:

It was he who guided those efforts during most of that long period; it was he who kept them alive when others despaired, and it was he who finally brought them to fruition. Working through others, he never thought of claiming credit for himself, but we know that if any one person can rightfully be called the Founder of the National Archives, John Franklin Jameson was the person.

At the beginning of this account the statement was made that Dr. Jameson's work was widely and warmly appreciated by his contemporaries. That appreciation was vigorously expressed by Professor A. B. Hart in 1930:

I often think how much the country and the future country owes to your skilled and indefatigably patient historical labors. You have been a sort of crankshaft for (I will not say the cranks) the historical forces of the country. Leave out what James [sic] Franklin Jameson has done in the development of the study and teaching and writing of History, and there would be a bottomless chasm.

Of these historical labors the letters tell much but they scarcely do full justice to the personal qualities of the man. The youth who entered the graduate school of the Johns Hopkins in 1880 was in many ways far removed from the man who came to the Bureau of Historical Research in 1905. Modesty as to his own powers had replaced the boyish conceit with which he left Amherst; personal ambition had given place to ambition to forward historical scholarship. His intellectual integrity, his tolerance, his patience, his perseverance were obvious to all who came in contact with him. The charm of his conversation; the flash of his humor, which enlivened the dullest subject; the apposite quotation which never failed; above all, the kindness which infused his every act, were completely appreciated only by his closer friends but those friends were many. Wrote one of them:[27]

Dr. Jameson stands to me for the finest spirit of New England scholarship—a passion for truth, a wonderful simplicity of character, a contempt for the things of the world that might stand in the way of his fulfilling his utmost ideal, and a sense of humor of which I have rarely seen the equal.

It was well said of him that he had no predecessor and would have no successor.[28]

Elizabeth Donnan

---

[27] Baxter, James Phinney, III., address delivered at Amherst College, Nov. 12, 1938, *Amherst Alumni Council News* 12: 98, December, 1938.

[28] Leland, W. G., *Amer. Hist. Rev.* 43: 252, 1938.

THE JOHNS HOPKINS UNIVERSITY, 1880-1888

To Mrs. John Jameson

Washington, Nov. 29 [1880].
Mon. morn.

Dear Mother:

. . . But you will like to know about my call at the White House. Will and I, having found that Friday evening was a good time, met at a little after eight, and went there.[1] The introduction and cards were sent up, and after waiting some time in a room, we were conducted to the foot of the big stairs by one attendant; at the top of them another met us, and conducted us into a sort of study where the President was. We were fortunate enough to find him alone. He isn't quite as goodlooking as his picture, his face being somewhat pitted. But he was very pleasant indeed, and I liked him ever so much.[2] To tell the truth, I hadn't much liked the idea of calling there, for I thought it must be an awful bore to the President. Very likely it was, but as he didn't in the least show it, but appeared very kind and cordial, I didn't feel uncomfortable at all. He talked about the things to be seen in Washington, and about the odd characters who drifted to the city, and a little about the Johns Hopkins. We didn't "make too long a call," as you will no doubt be delighted to learn, but skipped down stairs. Will was much, and I somewhat, disappointed, on returning to the ante-room, that we hadn't seen Mrs. Hayes, but we hadn't much more than got there, when the President, who had come down, whether specially for that I do not know, appeared at the door and said, "Gentlemen, perhaps you would like to see Mrs. Hayes." We 'lowed we would, so he took us across a big hall, and into a parlor called the Red Room, where we found Mrs. Hayes, Albert the second son,[3] and the great Massa-

chusetts gas-bag, Dr. Geo. B. Loring.[4] No one else was there. I had the chair next Mrs. Hayes. Will sat next the son, and the President sat down and talked with Dr. Loring, which I hope he enjoyed it [sic]. I thought Mrs. Hayes very pleasant, as I suppose every one does. She talked about the college at Kendall Green[5] and about the deaf-and-dumb asylum which was next door to them in Columbus when Mr. Hayes was Governor of Ohio. Here again we were so extraordinarily bright as not to stay more than two or three hours, which announcement I know you will hail with transports of joy. The son took us out into the hall, and said maybe we'd like to see some of the state rooms. N. B. These are not like the state-rooms in a steamer, but larger. He showed us the green room, and the blue room, and the big East room, at one end of the hall, and the state dining-room and conservatory at the other. They were not lighted, and we didn't go in, but the light from the hall was sufficient to enable us to see something what they were like. The son seemed a pleasant, off-hand sort of fellow (a Cornell man, D.K.E.), and the whole concern didn't sling nearly as much style as I expected. On the whole, as you will have seen, we had a very pleasant time, and I am glad I went.

Tell Father I happened to mention to the President that my father was P.M. in Amherst,[6] but I am sure it couldn't have made any impression on him, especially as he sees so many daily. The evening we went was a little unpleasant, so we were fortunate enough to have our calls about to ourselves. . . .

---

[1] During Jameson's first year of graduate work at the Johns Hopkins University, William Seelye, son of President Julius Seelye of Amherst and an Amherst classmate, was a fellow student. *"Wed. Nov. 24 [1880].* Seelye had, as a letter from Father this morning said he would have, a letter from his father to Pres. Hayes, for Will and me. Don't much like the notion." (Diary, July 24, 1880—May 3, 1881).

[2] Rutherford B. Hayes (1822-1893) was to leave the White House in March. The pleasant impression made upon this college youth, just turned twenty-one, was to remain with him. After a White House reception at which he met President Arthur, he wrote: *"Thurs. May 4 [1882].* My personal impresssions of him will always be very different from those of Pres. and Mrs. Hayes. I think we shall some time look back with pride to Hayes as one of the best presidents" (Diary, Apr. 30, 1882-Dec. 31, 1882).

[3] The second son, just graduated from Cornell University when his father entered the White House and then serving as his father's private secretary, was christened Webb Cook. No one of the four sons was named Albert.

[4] George Bailey Loring (1817-1891), a man of many interests, had abandoned a medical practice in 1850 to develop a stock farm. He next turned his attention to politics, first as a Democrat, then as a Republican. At the time of this call he had just failed of election to the Massachusetts senate for a second term, but he was not long without a place as Garfield appointed him Commissioner of Agriculture in 1881. His oratory, described in the *Dictionary of American Biography* as, "as over-decorated as a Victorian interior," was hardly of the sort to please the young Jameson.

[5] Gallaudet College. Edward Miner Gallaudet (1837-1917), son of Thomas Hopkins Gallaudet, a pioneer in the education of the deaf in this country, at the instance of Amos Kendall, had, in 1857, organized at Kendall Green, Washington, the Columbian Institution, similar to his father's school for the deaf in Hartford. Jameson, on his visits to Washington, stayed with his cousins, the Chickerings, who lived at Kendall Green. This accounts for the choice of the topic of conversation.

[6] John Jameson became the Amherst postmaster in 1877.

To JOHN JAMESON

Baltimore, Jan. 16, 1881.

Dear Father:

. . . Dr. Adams[7] has excused me of his own accord from his four-hours-a-week course, (and indeed he might as well, as I was getting next to nothing from it) and has advised me to go into Prof. Morris' class in German philosophy.[8] It seems likely to be of use to me in my work, and to be interesting. It is a course of lectures, and one need do no reading outside, if he doesn't choose. . . . I had a long talk with our political economy lecturer, Dr. Henry Adams, a splendid young man, yesterday morning, in regard to my dissatisfaction with a good many things here;[9] but I got little present encouragement, though he gave me many useful hints for the future. The School of Political Science[10] increased my discontent, and I stay here for the loaves and fishes chiefly. But the worst ground of

blueness is that Norton,[11] who is very bright and cheering, is going to leave for New Haven, and I shall be quite alone, and am pretty nearly now. I have been very lonesome and unhappy since Wheeler died,[12] more and longer than ever before in my life. . . .

To JOHN JAMESON

Baltimore, Jan. 30 [1881].

Dear Father:

. . . In sober truth I don't find much to admire in his [H. B. Adams'] scholarship, and have got from him almost nothing that I couldn't have got from books in less time, and don't think his method a correct one in historical work.[13] But at the same time it is manifestly unwise for me to let him know of any dissatisfaction, when my getting a fellowship next year, and a place later, depend somewhat on him.[14] . . .

I have had an experience this week that is rather novel. I have passed two examinations, finance Monday, and pol. econ. yesterday. Got about as dead a rush as a man could, in both. The first half-year is ended. Dr. Henry C. Adams goes away, for which I am very sorry, as he is a fine man, and an interesting teacher. My courses are, the last half;—4 hr. a week, International Law and History of Diplomacy, with undergraduates; a few of us take Anglo-Saxon, for laws and history; the class in Early Eng. Const. History continues; and once a week a class to study Bluntschli's

---

[7] Herbert Baxter Adams (1850-1901), A.B., Amherst, 1872, aptly described by J. S. Bassett in the *Dictionary of American Biography* as "promoter of historical studies," after receiving the Ph.D. degree from Heidelberg, had come to Baltimore to create at the Johns Hopkins University a graduate school of history modelled on German practices.

[8] George Sylvester Morris (1840-1889), after two years of study in Berlin, had been appointed to the chair of modern languages and literature in the University of Michigan. In 1877 he was made lecturer on the history of philosophy and ethics in the Johns Hopkins University, coming from Michigan for a short time each year. Jameson's association with him was short-lived. *"Mon. Jan. 17 [1881].* The lecture was one on Descartes. I enjoyed it a great deal, and understood it pretty well, but don't think I do entirely."
"Tu. Jan. 25. As to Prof. Morris' lectures, I don't know whether I understand them well enough to make it profitable to attend, but think I shall continue to. This was on Leibnitz."
"Thur. Jan. 27. At noon Prof. Morris' lecture. After it I told him I was going to leave the class, because I couldn't understand it" (Diary, July 24, 1880-May 3, 1881).

[9] Henry Carter Adams (1851-1921), holder of a fellowship in political economy from the Johns Hopkins University, from 1876 to 1879, studied two years in Germany, where he was interviewed by Andrew D. White, who at first mistook him for Herbert B. Adams. As a result of this interview, on his return to America he was asked to lecture on political economy in the Johns Hopkins, Cornell, and Michigan universities. Babst, E. D., and L. G. Van der Velde, *Michigan and the Cleveland era*, 27, Ann Arbor, University of Michigan Press, 1948. For this reference we are indebted to Mr. Frank E. Robbins of the University of Michigan.
In 1879-1880 and 1880-1881 he divided his time between the Johns Hopkins and Cornell. His final Baltimore lecture on this appointment was given on Feb. 1, 1881. He thereafter alternated lecture courses between Cornell and the University of Michigan until 1886, when he left Cornell and shortly afterwards was appointed to a professorship in Michigan. Jameson, during the brief period of his intercourse with Dr. Henry, as he was known to distinguish him from Dr. Herbert, regarded him as the best man with whom he worked, and in later years whenever Adams visited the university he managed to talk with him.

[10] This probably refers to plans for a graduate school in the University of Michigan, though Jameson may have been hearing of the school recently established in Columbia University.

[11] Edwin C. Norton (1856-1943), "Doc" to his Amherst classmates, a life-long friend of Jameson. After his study in Yale he taught in Yankton, N. D., then in Pomona College, Calif., where he eventually became dean.

[12] Arthur W. Wheeler, an Amherst classmate of whom Jameson had seen much during his first months in Baltimore, died suddenly on Jan. 6, 1881. He had come to the university in the spring of 1880, and in 1880-1881 held a fellowship in physics. Many of the responsibilities connected with his sudden death had fallen upon Jameson as his closest friend.

[13] Before Jameson left the university, he grew to appreciate certain qualities and accomplishments of Adams but he never approved of his methods of instruction nor esteemed his scholarship. On Dec. 20, 1884, in an especially bitter humor, he wrote: "He has so little scholarship, his whole tone is so far from intellectual, his motives and purposes so little exalted, his performance of his duties as a teacher so inadequate! And yet he is a success" (Diary, May 14, 1884-Mar. 26, 1885).

[14] *Mon. Jan. 17 [1881].* But at 10 Dr. Herbert [Adams] came in and said I'd been elected to a graduate scholarship. It was very pleasant news, and puts a different aspect on affairs. I shall get through the year with out more debt than Grandfather's $100 and the same from Father, at the end. It also gives me a good show at a fellowship and I didn't lead trumps either, as Adams said, but shall have my best work, and a new essay, for May" (Diary, July 24, 1880-May 3, 1881). The fellowships for 1881-1882 were awarded to others before Jameson left Baltimore in June and he decided to go to Harvard the next year and so told President Gilman. On June 9, while in Worcester, he received word that he was to receive a Hopkins fellowship. This brought him back to Baltimore in the autumn, and here he spent the next seven years.

Staatslehre (Theory of the State, or Politics),[15] a graduate class, thank goodness. But at the same time, my work will be, as before, mostly on N. Y. government, on which I have been working some the last week.[16]

Tu. and Th. eve. John Fiske gave the 3rd and the 4th and last of his lectures on American History, which have been quite good, though popular lectures.[17]

Today I have been dining with Prof. C. D. Morris (not the philosophy one).[18] He is a jolly, hearty old Briton, and has kept up ever since the Univ. began, the pleasant custom of having half a dozen fellows, profs, and students at dinner each Sunday. We had quite a nice dinner,—five courses,—and lots of pleasant talk. . . .

To George Ward

54 McCulloh St.,
Baltimore, Oct. 30 [1881].

Dear Friend Ward:[19]

Well, I didn't get out to see you, did I? Please don't think it was for lack of desire to; but the last time I was in Worcester, in convention week, the evening concerts filled up the whole evening, and the afternoon concerts the whole afternoon. But I mean to succeed some time; I haven't given up hope of seeing you and that wonderful brother. (I *suppose* he is wonderful; they all *are*.)

So you are a junior now, and a very exalted being, I suppose. It makes me feel a little aged, to have my scholars growing older so fast,—and two of them soon to be married, I hear. Dear me, it is a long time since I was teaching in the Worcester High School, and life has quite a different shape.

I rather think, if you were here with me, you would say that my surroundings at least are quite different. Baltimore is a queer city. I don't like the place over well, but many things one sees and hears in it are very curious. Pronunciation, for instance, and to a certain extent phraseology, are quite different, at least among the uneducated. The first sounds I heard as I left the station the night I got here were, as nearly as I can represent them, "Hyer, boss, whur' ye goin' at?" A Boston hackman would have said, "Here, mister, whǎ yer goin' ter?" He was shouting to some other man. Again, if a Baltimorean were describing this morning's weather, he would say "Deed, ther's right smart of a shaowah this mornun." And everybody says "Chewsday," and even pronounces "to," "two" or "too," all alike "tyew," as if it were "tu" in "tutor," (where indeed New Englanders go in the opposite direction, and say "tootor.") I don't know whether I wrote you about any of these things last year; they strike a man a little queerly at first, but by and by one gets used to them, and by the end of last year I found myself using sometimes the Baltimore pronunciation of "u."

As to sights, the great numbers of negroes and mules are the principal points of difference; one often sees six-mule teams with the driver in a saddle on the nigh wheeler instead of in the wagon, and "cŭl'd gemmen 'n' ladies" abound.

Well, I haven't told you much about myself. I have been here long enough to have got to work briskly long before this. The other day I was over in Washington and saw where Garfield was shot.[20]

I don't believe I've written to you since I saw Mr. Mackintosh. I went down to Amesbury in Sept., and had a pleasant visit with him and his wife and a very nice baby, Roger M. I saw Mr. Whittier there. Please write.

---

[15] In Heidelberg Adams had worked under the Swiss jurist, Johann Kaspar Bluntschli, and was much influenced by his emphasis on the community as the foundation of the state. The German citizens of Baltimore had presented to the university Bluntschli's library, which was arranged by Jameson, who described it to the Friday seminary: An account of the contents of the Bluntschli library as received in Baltimore, *Johns Hopkins University circular*, 61-62, February, 1883.

[16] The result of this work was an essay, submitted in the spring with an application for a fellowship, and the publication of two articles: The origin and development of the municipal government of New York City, 1. The Dutch period, 11. The English and American period, *Magazine of American History* 8: 315-330, 598-611, May, September, 1882.

[17] John Fiske (1842-1901, born Edmund Fisk Green) was at this time at the height of his career as a lecturer on historical subjects, though his published work had been chiefly in the fields of science and philosophy. His historical writing was still to come. "*Tu. Jan. 18* [*1881*]. Went to John Fiske's first lecture. . . . It was on the discovery. I was rather disappointed, for there was almost nothing new in it. But thinking it over, it seems to me that it was skilful, complete and well-digested and showed an excellent sense of proportion between different causes and motives." Of the fourth lecture Jameson wrote: "*Thurs. Jan. 27.* On America's Place in History. Good though hopeful. Also took up only one thing, prospects of universal peace" (Diary, July 24, 1880-May 3, 1881).

[18] Charles D. Morris (1827-1889) was appointed not long after Professor Gildersleeve, to teach Latin and Greek to the undergraduates, in order to relieve the latter from all responsibility for them. His dinners, frequently mentioned in the Diary, were always a pleasure to Jameson. There is evidence that Jameson's liking was returned. H. N. Gardiner (Amherst, 1878), teaching in Smith College, wrote on Nov. 7, 1881: "Riding down with him [Morris] from the Park Hotel previous to the meeting, I asked him about some of the Amherst men at the Johns Hopkins, and in reply he specially singled out you for praise; from which I inferred either that you must be a special favorite with Dr. Morris or else that the faculty generally had rated you at your true worth and that you were thus in general esteem."

[19] In 1879-1880 Jameson, fresh from Amherst College and not yet twenty when the year opened, taught history and Latin in the Worcester high school. George Ward was one of his pupils; Mackintosh, mentioned later in the letter, a fellow teacher with whom he roomed.

[20] This was at the old Pennsylvania Railroad station, off Pennsylvania Ave., at 6th street, N.W. On the day that the President was shot Jameson, at home in Amherst, wrote in his diary: "It is a terrible thing; not because he had shown himself a conspicuously strong president, but because Arthur is likely to give us the worst administration we have ever had" (Diary, May 4, 1881-Nov. 11, 1881).

To John Jameson

Baltimore, Jan. 22, 1881 [1882].[21]

Dear Father:

... This last week has been one of hard, solid work. I had lost a week on Hallam,[22] partly from not reading enough in vacation, partly from miscalculation; but made up my mind that, May not being so hard reading,[23] I could catch up. So pitched in, and have read the two volumes of May, which I had thought would take two weeks, in one. So now a few pages more will finish my work in English Constitutional History, and I begin American ditto. tomorrow, reading Curtis, Schouler and Von Holst and some things beside[s].[24] My work on Swedish is progressing fairly, but the language is more complicated and difficult than I had supposed, and I do not expect to become master of it before April, at the present rate of half an hour an evening. But it is quite interesting.

You will see that I can't have been out very much. We had our meeting of the "Historical and Political Association" on Friday evening;[25] but in spite of its long name, there were only nineteen there, and the papers were about as dull as usual. Then Tu. eve. I heard Towle lecture on Gladstone, but Th. eve. on Beac. I cut him.[26] So it has been a very uneventful week; rainy most of the time. ...

[21] Though this letter is clearly dated 1881 the Diary makes it certain that it belongs to 1882.

[22] Doubtless Hallam, Henry, *Constitutional history of England,* 1827.

[23] May, Sir Thomas Erskine, *The constitutional history of England since the accession of George the Third, 1760-1860,* 1861-1863; the 7th edition of this work appeared in 1882.

[24] Curtis, George Ticknor, *History of the origin, formation, and adoption of the Constitution of the United States,* 1, 1854, 2, 1858; Schouler, James, *History of the United States of America under the Constitution,* 1, 1880; 2, 1882; Von Holst, Hermann Eduard, *Constitutional and political history of the United States,* 1, in English, 1876; 2, 1878.

[25] In the early days of the Johns Hopkins University President Gilman conceived the idea of counterbalancing the extreme specialization which it promised, by creating associations of departments which should occasionally meet for discussion of common problems or the presentation of papers. Gilman himself was president of the Historical and Political Science Association. Unlike the other associations of the university it involved but one department, and actually differed from the department seminary only in that it had as members a few citizens of Baltimore who were not connected with the university. Eventually the association and the seminary became indistinguishable.

[26] George Makepeace Towle (1841-1893), a newspaper editor and writer of history. He had published a book on Beaconsfield in 1879. *"Fri. Jan. 10* [*1882*]. Conversation fell upon Bismarck and Cromwell at dinner. As I came away, remembered Towle's lecture at Peabody tonight on Bismarck, so went to it soon. Rainy. Lecture quite popular but showing up a better side of his character than I, from his late course, had been thinking of recently."

"Tu. Jan. 17. Went with Henry [Goodnow] to Towle's lecture; good one, on Gladstone" (Diary, Nov. 12, 1881-Apr. 29, 1882).

To John Jameson

Baltimore, Feb. 13, 1882.

Dear Father:

... I had to spend Wednesday afternoon presiding over one of the said examinations [for the undergraduates]. It was rather a bore, but as it is about the only thing that fellows have to do for their five hundred dollars, one needn't grumble. ...

Tu. and Thurs. evenings I went to Moses Coit Tyler's lectures, on the Pamphleteers, Song-Writers and Satirists of the Revolution.[27] They have been very interesting. You see he has rather a "monotony" of the subject and much that he brings forward is wholly new to me. He seems a very pleasant gentleman. I shall call on him tonight, though of course it is scarcely likely to be of any use as to a place.[28] ... And Friday was spent at our tiresome history meeting, where a fellow read a paper on the origin of the military system of England, which he traced back *nearly* to when our ancestors chattered in the tree-tops.[29] He couldn't *quite,* because, as I suggested to him, standing armies were impossible among those who held on to branches by their tails.

The article in the *Nation* [Feb. 9, 1882] on the Libraries of Baltimore is by Adams, and so is the review of Freeman's Subject and Neighbor Lands of Venice. ...

To John Jameson

Baltimore, June 4, '82.

Dear Father:

... In the first place to answer recent letters. I was half amused and half vexed at Mother's feeling

[27] Moses Coit Tyler (1835-1900), after an unusually varied career, had become professor of English language and literature in the University of Michigan, then professor of American history in Cornell University, the first such appointment in the country. As the author of *History of American literature during the colonial times, 1607-1765,* 1878, and of *The literary history of the American Revolution,* 1897, he broke new ground. At the time of his Baltimore lectures he was doubtless at work on the second study.

[28] *"Wed. Feb. 8* [*1882*]. Got a note from Dr. Henry Adams [Henry Carter Adams, then in Cornell] who advises me to see M. C. Tyler by all means, though there seems to be no present vacancy at Cornell" (Diary, Nov. 12, 1881-Apr. 29, 1882).

"Dear Father . . . . I went to see Prof. Tyler Tuesday evening, one of the pleasantest gentlemen I ever met. There is, however, nothing at Cornell; but he very kindly offered of his own accord, to write to his friend Pres. Cutler, of Western Reserve for me" (Jameson to John Jameson, Feb. 16, 1882). During this month Jameson looked through a large number of college catalogues and as a result wrote, enquiring about a possible teaching position, to President Strong of Carlton College, Pickard of the University of Iowa, Warren of Boston University, Bartlett of Dartmouth, and Robinson of Brown. Dr. Robinson was the only one who held out any hopes of an opening and this came to nothing.

[29] E. R. Gould (1860-1915), the reader of the paper, studied at the Johns Hopkins between 1881 and 1886, his work being interrupted by frequent illness. See *post,* Apr. 13, 1916.

sorry about my mark of 95.[30]   That is a new view to take of it.   Doesn't she know that (to rise to a somewhat personal explanation) that is just a splendid mark to get, that a man gets a Ph.D. if he gets 75, that that was the poorest of my four exam's, and that a *perfect* knowledge of every point in the vast range of constitutional history is impossible?   Why everybody else opens his eyes at my getting *95* on the poorest, so that I don't tell it to many.   It is like my respected Father's telling his Freshman son, when he was delighted at 92, his first term-mark, that if the latter was satisfied with it, *he* was.   So cheer up, old lady, it isn't so *very* disgraceful, after all. . . . My paper is out (pt. I); it is bungled horribly in one place (of course); I've sent for copies and shall send or bring one.[31] . . .

To ALBERT SHAW

54 McCulloh St.,
Baltimore, Nov. 5, 1882.[32]

Dear Friend Shaw:

I have wanted to get time to write to you to congratulate you on the appearance of your article in the Fortnightly,[33] but time is a scarce commodity with me. It is a high honor that Mr. Morley has done your article, and one very well deserved, as everyone thinks. I have also been much pleased to see your article about us in the college paper, and the notice of your lecture. Took the least bit of *personal* interest in the latter, supposing it to be the one in which some of the facts I had noticed in the stupid German articles were to be used.

"We're gettin' on nicely down here to our village," with a good deal that is new, of which I suppose the principal item is the seminary library.   I don't doubt Adams has kept you informed of that.   I don't myself think much of the policy of colonizing sections of the library, one result of which is that a man not in the Greek department, for instance, can't get a sight of a translation of Horace or even a good edition of him (or it, or them) without tramping over to "Bentley Hall" and making personal application to some one there, if he should chance to find anyone in.   All the books under one roof, with special collections in separate rooms, as now, only much larger rooms, and seminary rooms opening from each of these, would be better, I should think.   But vive la specialisation!   Go to, let us centrifugate.

Our men are working much as usual; we have several more, and among them some [very*] bright fellows; the seminary meetings are kept up to their usual level, though I think there is too much mutual admiration and not enough savage criticism.   But then, I always was an Adullamite at the J.H.U.   My own time is mainly taken up with my teaching and with helping Gilman on his James Monroe;[34] very valuable practice in sources for me.   Do almost no writing for sem.; haven't that consuming zeal in the study of the Anglo-Saxon Origin of Policemen's Billies, the Historical Development of Pedlers' Licenses and other points of the hist. of Institutions (with a large I) that I ought to have.

Do you expect to be back here at all this year?   I sincerely hope so.   Shall be glad to have you write to me.[35]   Hoping you are as well in body and mind, and as happy, as the undersigned.

* Crossed out for "chastened" style, not for disparagement.

---

[30] "Wed. A.M. 11.20 [May 24, 1882]. Dear Father: et als: Last exam (the oral) this morning. Got through them all right. Scott [Austin] marked me 95 on his; Ely's [Richard T.] and Adams' I must have done better in than on Scott's, though they mayn't mark so high. The next time you see me I shall be Doctor of Philosophy." This was the first Ph.D. degree awarded in history by the Johns Hopkins University.

His mother's comment had been: "I suppose you hardly felt satisfied with your examination and it would have been a pleasant, nice thing if you could have been 100 as you doubtless would, if you had had a little more time but perhaps it would have been too hard work and you were spared a week's worry and work" (Mrs. John Jameson to Jameson, May 28, 1882). The mother's final remark refers to that fact that her son had taken his examinations a week earlier than he had planned to.

[31] A reference to the first installment of, The origin and development of the municipal government of New York City.

[32] Manuscript Division, New York Public Library. Albert Shaw (1857-1947), at the time of this letter editor of the Grinnell *Herald*, Grinnell, Iowa, had spent part of the previous year in the Johns Hopkins University and Jameson's Diary indicates that they had seen much of each other.

[33] Local government in America, *The Fortnightly Review*, n.s. 190: 485-495, October, 1882. *The Fortnightly* at this time seems to have been giving special attention to America. During 1882 it published an article by James Bryce, Some aspects of American public life, and two articles by Edward A. Freeman on Impressions of America, 190: 634-655, 133-155, 323-346, November, August, September. In Freeman's first article he wrote: "I cannot help mentioning the school which is now devoting itself to the special study of local institutions, a school which is spread over various parts of the Union, but which seems to have its special home in the Johns Hopkins University at Baltimore, as one from which great things may be looked for. And I cannot help adding the name of my friend Mr. Herbert B. Adams as that of one who has done much for the work, and who, to me at least, specially represents it. To trace out the local institutions, and generally the local history of

their own land, to compare them with the history and institutions of elder lands, to show that it is only on the surface that their own land lacks the charm of antiquity, is the work which seems chalked out for the enquirers of this school, and a noble and patriotic work it is."

[34] Daniel Coit Gilman (1831-1908), the first president of the Johns Hopkins University, was writing the volume on James Monroe for the American Statesmen series, published by Houghton Mifflin. Jameson was correcting errors, adding an extensive bibliography on Monroe and the Monroe Doctrine, and reading the proof for Gilman. The 278 hours he spent on this work brought him $100, a sum which he considered adequate return. While dealing with the manuscript he frequently commented to his father that the biography was not the equal of the volumes which had already appeared in the series and the reviews when the biography came out supported his judgment.

[35] Shaw's reply described his present activities and indicated a strong desire to return to Baltimore: "I have no good report to give of myself—except that my career since I came home

To JOHN JAMESON

Baltimore, Feb. 25, 1883.

Dear Father:

. . . I said in Helen's[36] letter that I was going to Gildersleeve's in the evening, and did so.[37] Had a rather stupid time, of course; met Pres. White, of Cornell, but was much disappointed in him, as all were.[38] . . .

To ALBERT SHAW

54 McCulloh St.,
Baltimore, Feb. 27 [1883] [39]

Dear Friend Shaw:

I meant to answer your letter last night,[40] at once upon its receipt, but found myself at evening too sleepy and stupid to answer it properly. Perhaps I shall not succeed in doing so tonight either, partly because the stupidity continues almost unabated, and

partly because what you ask is difficult, though I am glad to serve you as far as I can. No person can understand another's case quite well enough to decide for him, and that is not, probably, what you want; but I can hardly even furnish you with useful materials for forming a decision, because, like most Johns Hopkins men, I have little real knowledge of what others are doing, and less of what they are going to do. Further, I cannot help paying a good deal of regard to Adams' opinion.

But to begin, with the courses. I have absolutely no knowledge of what Ely[41] is doing (except that one of his courses is in finance) and have conflicting accounts of how well he is doing it. Adams has the graduates only one hour a week, at the Peabody, where I believe he lectures to them on the basis of Bluntschli's Staatslehre, and they also work up various topics more or less independently. This course has only recently started, and I cannot say how valuable it is. That depends on how it is practically worked out; the general scheme, however, seems to me a little crude.

The seminary on Friday evening has two sides. In political economy it is a meeting for the reading of papers, somewhat as the historical seminary of last year was, and some excellent papers are read there. From the historical point of view the seminary is without character or unity. It is in a transition stage, in which it is in my opinion allowed to remain too long,—a transition from a state of things where the men were largely devoted to the preparation of institutional studies which were read at the seminary, forming its staple, to a state of things wherein the seminary work consists, as in a German seminary, in practical exercises, giving practice in the use of sources by devoting attention to the most minute and thorough study of a very limited field each meeting. This is what I hope the seminary will become, but this will not be before the opening of the next year. Meanwhile, the men are not writing historical papers, even reviews of current historical literature are not systematically presented, and the staple of the meetings consists of outside "attractions," now a Confederate general to talk on a campaign, now an elderly party exhumed to "reminisce" to us. I wish the seminary could pass more rapidly through this chrysalis state, passing (I hope) in reverse process from what seemed to me the butterfly period of last year to the period of *grub* which I desire to see next year. The public lecture season is about over, and I believe that nothing of especial value is to follow. Dr.

---

from Baltimore last June has been characterized by industry. I have been doing all the politics and editorial writing as well as all the 'local' work on a small semi-weekly sheet [Grinnell *Herald*], besides looking after the advertising, and attending more or less to the miscellaneous business of a thriving steam job office. It is pretty safe to say that I have averaged fourteen solid columns of writing every week this past fall and winter, nearly half of it political . . . . I have succeeded in becoming recognized as a Civil Service Reformer and a Tariff Reformer" (Shaw to Jameson, Jan. 18, 1883).

[36] Helen was Jameson's older sister, who lived at home.

[37] Basil Lanneau Gildersleeve (1831-1924), the first professor appointed to the Johns Hopkins faculty, whose brilliant teaching did much to build its reputation.,

[38] This letter ignores the early part of the evening, when Jameson first saw President White: "*Fri. Feb. 23.* Read a bit in new no. of Historische Zeitschrift, which Adams wanted me to review this evening, when Pres. White of Cornell is expected to be present. . . . At sem, White was present, but I didn't kno it till I had made my report. He made a speech, but it was weak and rambling. I am disappointed in him; he doesn't seem to be any longer a man of much force, and I don't think he will do as a figurehead to my projected Amer. Hist. Assocn" (Diary, Jan. 1, 1883-Sept. 3, 1883). Andrew D. White (1832-1918) had been intimately associated with Gilman since their college days in Yale, after which they had gone abroad together. From this trip White had returned fired with zeal to found a university which should resemble European institutions and, with Ezra Cornell, had created Cornell University. At the time of this visit he had returned to its presidency after serving as minister to Germany. For a number of years his health had been precarious and he had been obliged from time to time to give up his work. Two years after this letter was written he surrendered it permanently. To the highly critical young graduate students his gentle and amiable talk would have carried no suggestion of the force which had created a university regarded at the time of its inception as a radical educational experiment, had built up a faculty, and had carried the institution through a period of great financial stress.

[39] Manuscript Division, New York Public Library.

[40] Shaw had asked Jameson's advice about an immediate return to the university, saying that Adams had suggested that it might be better to wait until the following autumn and use the interval for the study of German and the mastering of Stubbs' *Charters,* one of the sacred books of the history department (Shaw to Jameson, Feb. 23, 1883).

[41] Richard T. Ely (1854-1943), professor of political economy in the Johns Hopkins University from 1881 to 1892, when he began a long career of teaching in the University of Wisconsin. He had been a student in Germany from 1877 to 1880, spending part of his time in Heidelberg, three years after H. B. Adams studied there.

Scott is not to be here at all this year, being settled, with his wife and son, at Rutgers College.[42]

I believe that these are the facts in the matter,—or rather I believe that these are facts. There are others of another sort which I think should be taken into account. The programme I mentioned in the line of history (I am sorry I know so little about the political economy) is not entirely satisfactory, but is just about what it was last year. Next year there will be more in quantity, and a larger number of students in our graduate classes. But I doubt whether our new plans will get to working sufficiently well the first year to make it a striking contrast to this as to instruction given. But after all, it is not the instruction given that is most valuable in the department. One gets here two things principally,—stimulus and method. Now I of course hope that we shall do better next year than this, in both these respects; but it is a question whether one had better do without what he can here get of them, even these three months. At all events, I believe that your programme would be equally feasible here, except the month in Chicago, which might come in the summer, and I suspect that you would find that the work done in accordance with it would be better in quality than the same if done "on the prairie." To sum up, the university does not offer you much in the way of instruction, yet is perhaps a good place to work in.

As to honors at the end of this year, I do not believe you have much chance at them. Adams some time ago arranged that they should be given in great part upon the basis afforded by an examination to be given before many weeks now, and for which a number of the men have been working very hard in the special field set. The competition is going to be sharp, and I fear there will be, with our three prizes, n-3 "soreheads." There is a lad here, (Adams), which hath five barley loaves and two small fishes, but what are they among so many! Indeed I fear that if you *were* to come thus at the eleventh hour and take away a part of the spoil, the hearts of some of the brethren would be turned away. Perhaps you will think this unreasonable, and to be neglected. But aren't you overrating the value, other than the pecuniary, of a scholarship? I should say that, except in so far as it may lead to a fellowship, that is to say, so far as persons outside the university are concerned, it would profit you little. Indeed I doubt whether the pursuit of fellowships and so forth is not exercising a harmful influence upon some of our young men here, in causing them to be guided during these years of preparation by other considerations

than the desire to train themselves, with single-minded devotion, to absolutely the highest sort of historical scholarship.

Now I have written to you at some length, but I am afraid you will think not very definitely. But I really could not do otherwise, for I wished to give you the most correct statements, and, so far as I hinted at advice at all, the wisest advice. I feel a good deal of responsibility in making such suggestions, as you seem likely to pay more attention to them than you should. I ought to conclude with a prayer to Pallas Athênê that no ill-advised word may have escaped the ἕρκος ὀδόντυν [the barrier of the mouth].

All the time, you know that personally I shall be very glad to have you among us as soon as possible, and I hope you will let me know your decision when it is made. All the boys will be glad to see you; (especially, I dare say, if you are "not a candidate for office.") James Monroe is out. Now, hoping that whichever way you decide, you will be happy in the decision.

To ALBERT SHAW

54 McCulloh St.,
Baltimore, Mar. 9, '83.[43]

Dear Shaw:

I have something to ask you about. Mr. George W. Cable,[44] the New Orleans novelist, some of whose novels, such as "The Grandissimes," "Old Creole Days," etc., you may have read, is now lecturing at the university, and boards at the same place where I do. Today, after lunch, he spoke to me in confidence about some historical work which is wanted in New York, and asked me if I knew of any one who could well undertake it. I told him that I happened to know of only one man that I thought could do it well, and that I would write to you at once. You will please say nothing about it to any one else.

It seems that the Produce Exchange of New York wish to engage some one, at very good pay, to write a history, as I understand it, of the produce business of New York from the earliest times, grouping it, I suppose, around the Produce Exchange, whose present site is that of the first produce market in New Amsterdam, it is said. Much of the growth of the business of the city, the canals and railroads of modern times, would come within their scheme, as well as much antiquarian work, which I know from experience would be interesting, in the Dutch and English colonial period. Their intention is to produce a very

---

[42] Austin Scott (1842-1922), associate in history in the Johns Hopkins, 1875-1881, professor, 1882-1883. In 1883 he left the university for Rutgers College, where he remained until his death. Before coming to the university he had been the private secretary of George Bancroft and during his years in the university he still assisted Bancroft in arranging his papers.

[43] Manuscript Division, New York Public Library.

[44] George Washington Cable (1844-1825) was at this time gaining fame by his tales of Creole life but he was in addition to being a novelist a zealous reformer. This was an aspect of his character which made a strong appeal to Jameson. In 1885 Cable left the South to live in Northampton, Mass., and Jameson's Amherst family came to know and enjoy him.

elaborate work, and I do not suppose expense will be spared. Ordinarily, work of this sort has been done in the most superficial and unsatisfactory way, but I believe, from what Mr. Cable tells me, that the gentlemen in charge would appreciate scholarly and good work, of substantial historical value.

I understand that the writer would be provided with an office and whatever assistance he required. How long a time it would take I do not know, but suppose that, while it does last, it will occupy the writer exclusively. The salary would be high, but I do not know how high.

If you choose to think favorably of this, I should imagine that you can get the chance. I should be much obliged if you would answer, if possible, at once, as Mr. Cable leaves town before long.[45]

To JOHN JAMESON

Baltimore, Mar. 11, '83.

My dear Father:

. . . Speaking of pleasant people, there never was a more delightful little man than Mr. Cable. He says the neatest little things, in his quiet, pleasant voice. Miss Young,[46] the other day, on his speaking of his love of music, asked him if Mrs. Cable was musical. "No, ma'am," said he, (he is very polite, as well as so gentle and quiet and unassuming), "but I have never seen any female musician since for whom I wished to swap Mrs. Cable."

Adams wants him to write a paper for the great and glorious series,[47] but he doesn't think he can afford to, (though he would like to) for he has to earn his living by his pen. He said "It is about the same with me in living that it has been in swimming; I could learn to swim, but I have never been able to float."

But I must say I don't care much about his lectures, because new thoughts on the subjects are almost impossible, though his expressions are beautiful.[48] I am going to try to see more of him next week, if I can, than I have this last.

Since my letter to Helen I have done only one kind of work, that on my future essay on the village-communities in Greece, my usual sole occupation of Friday and Saturday.[49] It is going to be lots of work, but I believe I am going to make a good thing of it, my best paper yet.

The proof of my Easthampton-Montauk article lies on my table, but as the Rev. B. F. DeCosta, D.D.,[50] didn't send the copy with it, I await its arrival before examining the proof. It is to appear in the April number of the Magazine (written about last April) and I suppose will cause a profound sensation in European circles. Glad to hear that your paper succeeded so well.[51] You ought to write more, anyway.

I said I had been working on my essay solely, but of course we had our seminary meeting on Friday night, at which time it was, indeed, that young Tiffany invited

[45] Shaw replied with becoming modesty about his equipment for the suggested work, but asked a number of pertinent questions and expressed a desire to hear more. Jameson had little to add and nothing came of the proposal.

[46] Miss Young presided at the dinner table where Jameson boarded, a table round which many animated discussions took place.

[47] *The Johns Hopkins University Studies in Historical and Political Science,* the first number of which appeared in 1883.

[48] As the lectures continued Jameson's opinion grew more favorable and on Mar. 16 he wrote: "Went to Mr. Cable's last lecture, which was much the best of the course and very fine." During Cable's fortnight in Baltimore Jameson had many walks and talks with him and on his departure wrote: "On my part it seems like having a dear friend go away; he is the kindest, pleasantest man, but, *more* than that, he is a warm-hearted Christian . . . . I must see him again in the morning, and tell him how much good he has done me" (Diary, Jan. 1, 1883-Sept. 3, 1883).

[49] "*Thurs. Sept. 7* [*1882*]. In eve. went down to see Adams [Jameson and Adams were both in Amherst at this time]. He is very busy with plenty of projects. He wants me to undertake getting up an essay on village communities in Ancient Greece. I don't take an undying interest in this communal business, and didn't want to have anything more to do in that, or Adams' line; I've no notion of becoming prominent only as a disciple of one whom I can't regard as my equal, at least as equal to what I mean to be at his age. When I come to choose a speciality, it shall not be that. Still it is a good subject and may help me with Adams and especially with Gildersleeve. But to do it well will require much time, and I don't like to defer the "Usselincx work for it" (Diary, Apr. 30, 1882-Dec. 31, 1882). The first half of the year 1882-1883 was devoted to work on Gilman's *Monroe* but once that was completed, Jameson plunged with his usual thoroughness into gathering material for this paper, his interest growing as he worked. Before he began to write, however, other occupations pushed the Greek villages to the background. The "Usselincx work" had been in Jameson' mind as a possible project ever since his work on early New York history during his first winter in the university. His study of Swedish, mentioned in a letter of Jan. 22, 1882, was in preparation for this. See *post,* July 13, 1884, n. 113, for an account of his search for material on Usselincx.

[50] Montauk and the common lands of Easthampton, *Magazine of American History* 9; 225-239, April, 1883. This article contained the substance of the essay submitted by Jameson as part of his work for the degree of doctor of philosophy.

Benjamin Franklin DeCosta (1831-1904), at this time editor of the *Magazine of American History,* was in his day a colorful character. For an account of his career see the *Dictionary of American Biography.*

[51] John Jameson had written to his son some time before, asking for bibliographical aid on a paper comparing the British and American forms of government, to be presented to the Roundabout Club of Amherst. After his reading of the paper, the father wrote, Mar. 9, 1883, much as his son might have: "Last Tuesday night the Club met for the first time since Jan. 31. I shot off my essay. I interpolated remarks explanatory and had to answer quite a number of interpellations. It took about an hour and in view of the attention paid to it and the interest it excited as evinced by the questions it called out it was quite satisfactory, certainly to that portion of the Club whom I expected to interest and also to some of whom I was somewhat doubtful. To myself it was less so and less than I could have made it had my health given me more ability and that of my clerks more time to work."

me to Sunday dinner.[52] The seminary is a regular
farce, and has been all the year. Adams knows that
the time has passed when we could run it on the old
plan, yet he won't spend the time to manage it on a
new scheme. Shinn, the long-winded California ex-
journalist, a veritable child of nature from the far west,
read the principal paper, but received no criticism and
so no benefit.[53] Adams is just a hopeless case so far
as attention to details is concerned.

. . . I read the Nation review of Morison's Macaulay, of course, also a good one in the London Athenaeum.[54] I must get Morison's Macaulay some time,
and his Gibbon too; they must be first-class things,
especially for a young historical student. Grandfather[55] has promised me his Life and Letters of
George Ticknor unasked. I shall be very glad of
it. . . .

To JOHN JAMESON

Mon. P.M. later
[April 2, 1883.]

Dear Father:

Some time ago I prepared a careful review in German of Bancroft's last two volumes, "The Formation

---

[52] Herbert T. Tiffany (d. 1944), A.B., Johns Hopkins, 1882,
was a graduate student in history, 1882-1883. He later re-
ceived an LL.B. and practiced law in Baltimore. During
Jameson's years in Baltimore he was a frequent guest in the
Tiffany home where he enjoyed his association with "young
Tiffany" and his sister.

[53] This was not Charles Shinn's first appearance at the
seminary nor in the family correspondence. For Jan. 19, 1883,
the Diary reads: "Then Shinn, the new member from California, already famous as the worst bore in the university, read
a paper on Oxford and the Oxford Reformers of 1498. It was
a sophomoric compilation from Ullmann, Seebohm, and a few
other books. It was fairly well written though with a great
deal of glow and many mannerisms copied after Carlyle; but
it was just full of errors and of ignorance, and given in a most
bumptious Western manner, as if giving boundless information.
He read and read, and we 'sot and sot,' till after he had read
an hour, Adams felt obliged to choke him off, which he did
with some difficulty. Then what should Adams do but praise
it as very interesting and comprehensive" (Diary, Jan. 1, 1883-
Sept. 3, 1883). To his sister, Jameson wrote: "Oh, such a
time as we had at the sem. A man read a paper, the last one
that eve., more than an hour long;—and he wasn't through
then, by a good deal, when Adams choked him off. Add to
that, that he was or has been hitherto a journalist, add to this
that he was a Californian, add to this that his style was
modelled on Carlyle, his article full of inaccuracies, his reading
declamatory, and his hair red, and you have a faint notion of
our misery" (Jameson to Helen Jameson, Jan. 21, 1883).
On Mar. 9 Shinn presented a second paper to the seminary,
which drew an equally scathing entry in Jameson's diary. The
subject of these remarks, Charles Howard Shinn (1852-1924),
produced before he left the university, Mining camps: a study
in American frontier government, 1883, which was deemed
worthy of later reissue, N. Y., Knopf, 1948.

[54] Morison, J. Cotton, Macaulay, English Men of Letters ser.,
London. Macmillan; N. Y., Harper, reviewed in the Nation
36: 195-196, Mar. 1, 1883; in the Athenaeum, Jan. 13, 1883,
48-50.

[55] George Thompson, who lived in Woburn, Mass.

---

of the Constitution," and sent it to Prof. Von Sybel's
"Historische Zeitschrift," [56] (Historical Journal) the
principal hist. review in Germany, making at the same
time a proposal to contribute to them brief reviews of
American hist. works as they came out, mentioning
3 or 4 recent ones. I have just got word that this
proposal is accepted; they request me to contribute
such regularly. No money in it (tho' p'r'aps can get
some books that way). But a bang-up advertisement;
couldn't become known to hist. men more widely any
other way. And splendid practice.

Gleefully, F.[57]

To JOHN JAMESON

Baltimore, Apr. 15, 1883.

Dear Father:

These three last days, Friday, Saturday and Sunday,
furnish very scant materials for a letter. Of course
the great event was the party at President Gilman's
on Friday evening.[58] It was a very swell affair, and
I did much dread the same; but, on the whole, I had
a pleasant time. I generally feel pretty well on returning from a party if I have not consciously made a
fool of myself in any very bad way. Actual and positive delight is out of the question. It was quite comfortable; no jam, for the Johns Hopkins mansion, which
Gilman occupies, is very spacious, and there were not
more than thirty or forty guests. . . .

In recent days, my special work has been confined to

---

[56] Heinrich von Sybel (1817-1895), a distinguished student
of Ranke, who, while a professor in Munich, established the
Historische Zeitschrift, which served as a model for later
historical journals.

[57] "Wed. Apr. 4 [1883]. I told him [Adams] of my arrangement with the 'Historische Zeitschrift'; but discovered that I
was like children in the market-place; for he didn't dance. Was
evidently vexed. Said that it had been his plan to have that
matter worked out on a cooperative basis, i.e. to have things
reviewed for it by various members of the seminary; and
seemed to think I had been stealing a march on the crowd.
I'm sure I had no such intention. My recollection of what he
had said upon the subject, was that it was a thing some one
here ought to do. I got the impression that he had no intention of doing it himself; nor have I the slightest remembrance
of any such cooperative plan. This P. M. he tried to assure
me that I had no such exclusive engagement as W. F. Allen's
with the Revue Historique, which is to some extent true; also
that I couldn't do it all well myself, and had better parcel it
out among the members of the seminary." Diary, Jan. 1, 1883-
May 18, 1883. See post, Nov. 4, 1883, n. 76.

[58] "Fri. Apr. 13 [1883]. My head ached a little bit and I was
for a time in hopes that it would prevent me from going out
this evening; but the evening air removed it, and I had to go.
The fellows think or seem to think that my unwillingness to
go out is very remarkable and very funny, but I don't see
anything strange in it. I know I am green and ill at ease;
I cannot possible go out enough to make me feel perfectly at
home everywhere and so I would rather not go at all into a
sphere for which I am not fitted. It isn't that I am unsocial;
I like to call, and I like the company of men, but parties I
don't enjoy . . . . In spite of my reluctance to go (some of
which certainly arose from not having a dress suit; I think I

reading Doyle's "Colonies," [59] for a review in the Historische Zeitschrift. It is a mighty good book, written by a young Fellow of Oxford. I shall probably send them two or three more before the term closes. I don't like to have it prevent my finishing my Greek-villages essay, as I am afraid it is going to, but after all the former is more important work, and needs to be done earlier, if a choice must be made. I was asked by Pres. Gilman to come in to his office tomorrow; he is going, evidently, to talk about next year, but I dare say Adams has already given me all the points about it.

I was much amused to see in the Advertiser that Jas. Freeman Clarke took, as his Fast-Day text, Jotham's parable of the trees in Judges IX (ix). [60]

To JOHN JAMESON

[May, 1883?]

Dear Father:

I'll take another sheet and answer your recent inquiries of one sort and another.

As I wrote *via* Helen, I do not agree with Dr. DeCosta's estimate of Doyle. [61] Dr. DeCosta knows nothing but voyages, and the man who has incidentally to say a word about any voyages, is lost if DeCosta is to review him. Every one differs from him in estimate of the other parts of Doyle's book. But even on this point, his remark about the Zeno brothers is a blunder, for in the same footnote (p.18) in which Doyle gives a reference to Bryant and Gay, he replies in full to Mr. Major's book. [62] DeC. loves to be severe.

I see the Mag. Am. Hist. has been sold out by Messrs. Barnes, wise in their generation, and is now published by "The Historical Publication Co." When a publication gets to being published by such nonde-

scripts as this newly-formed company is, from its name, its days are numbered.

I shall be very glad to be of help in the preparation of a historical discourse. I don't think I could very well prepare one myself, tho' I should rather like to. Maybe the town records would afford much illustrative material. . . .

"Arcades ambo" is from one of Virgil's Eclogues, in which two "swains" contend in verse. "Both are Arcadians" to indicate they are equally matched. Whence the expression is sometimes used to denote "they are equally matched in rascality," degenerating; somewhat like our phrase, "there's a pair of 'em."

I shall be an "associate." Salary, first year, $1000; 2d $1500; 3d 1750-2000; 4th 2000-2500; 5th 2250; 6th 2500. (I'm not sure of the successive steps). . . .

These are, I believe, all the things touching the which ye asked me.

To ALBERT SHAW

Baltimore, June 3, 1883. [63]

Dear Shaw:

The other evening, when some of the Amherst men here were gathered together, talking over affairs concerning and not concerning Amherst, a project for increasing the influence of the younger alumni was proposed by a bright young Philadelphia journalist, [64] which was generally approved and will probably be carried into effect, and which may perhaps prove a useful suggestion in your Iowa movement. [65] It is to inaugurate this year the practice of having an annual "Student" breakfast. [66] I.e., some time during Commencement week to have a swell breakfast (chosen as being a little more imposing than a dinner, and because nearly every chance for a dinner is probably occupied in Commencement week, already), at which the editors of the "Amherst Student" shall assemble, with any friends whom each man chooses to invite and pay for. The "Student" was started about 1869, and has had five to eight editors in each class. So we should form quite a little party, each year, and composed of the younger element. At the Alumni Meeting only older men are ever heard, missionaries, D.D.'s, etc., who make pretty stupid speeches; at the Student Breakfast the younger men would have a chance, and their speeches would of course be printed, or reported,

shall have to get one next summer; an assoc. has to go out more) I had a fairly pleasant time, though I had to spend the evening with rather too few persons, which is inevitable when one doesn't go out enough to know everybody. Mrs. Gilman is a charming hostess" (Diary, Jan. 1, 1883-Sept. 3, 1883).

[59] Doyle, John A., *English colonies in America: Virginia, Maryland and the Carolinas*, N. Y., Henry Holt, 1882.

[60] All good New Englanders, such as Jameson and his family, would have been well acquainted with the activities of this famous Unitarian, who established his own church in Boston and preached there many years. His Fast Day text, with the verse which precedes it, was: "The trees went forth on a time to anoint a king over them; and they said unto the olive-tree, Reign thou over us. (9) But the olive-tree said unto them, Should I leave my fatness, wherewith by me they honor God and man and go to wave to and fro over the trees?"

[61] A brief review of Doyle which appeared in the *Magazine of American History* 9: 302, April, 1883, was unsigned but Jameson apparently had no hesitation in ascribing it to DeCosta, perhaps from the severity of its judgments.

[62] Bryant, William Cullen, and Sydney H. Gay, *History of the United States*, 3v., London, Low, 1876-1880. R. H. Major's book was probably his edition of *The voyages of the Venetian brothers to the northern seas in the fourteenth century*, Hakluyt Society, 1873.

[63] Manuscript Division, New York Public Library.

[64] Talcott Williams (1849-1928), A. B., Amherst, 1873, was at this time on the Philadelphia *Press*.

[65] Shaw had written on May 9: "I am a Committee to make a report to our Ia. Coll. Alumni Assoc'n a few weeks hence on the general subject of Alumni Representation in the Board of Trustees." Jameson replied that, knowing nothing of the matter himself, he had turned to a Boston journalist and was sending to Shaw all the material which his Boston friend had sent to him (Jameson to Shaw, May 12, 14, 1883, Manuscript Division, New York Public Library).

[66] Jameson had served as literary editor of the college paper, the *Amherst Student*, during 1877-1878.

at least, in the "Student" and it is hoped w'd have what influence they were worth upon college opinion. I think such an institution would also have a good effect upon the composition of the undergraduate board of editors, making the position more desirable, and thus improving the paper.

I don't know whether such a plan is applicable among you; indeed I don't know that it will be put in practice at Amherst, as yet it is only a scheme. However, it is excuse enough for writing a letter.

My work is just over, and I shall leave as soon as "the boss" will let me. Closing exercises occur on Thursday; who the fellows (2 of 'em) in our dep't are to be, I don't know;[67] nor, in any respect, what the news is.

I hope your studies are going on well, and that when you come back you will take a room in our house; but, long before that, I hope, you will write to me at Amherst, where I shall do most of my summer's work.

To ALBERT SHAW

Amherst, Mass.,
Sept. 5, 1883.[68]

My dear Shaw:

As it is getting toward the time when the Johns Hopkins begins its year, you will perhaps like more definite information about rooms and board than I gave you before. I am sure you will like very much to board at 209 N. Howard, where I have always boarded. I think there is scarcely a better place in the city, and the price is only $5 a week. At the same place are one or two rooms to rent. They are excellent rooms, and would be perfectly taken care of; and the house is only a block from the University. The prices I do not know; but the cheapest would cost, with board ab't $35 a month of four weeks. The house where I room, 54 McCulloh St., is about seven minutes' walk from my boarding-place as well as from the university. Here there will probably be two rooms, one opposite mine, in the third story, at $9 per calendar month, the other under me, a nice room, second story front, at $12 per ditto.

I write these details because you may like to know something of the sort before you leave; but I shall probably be on the ground when you arrive and shall gladly help you further in regard to these or other places. I am very glad that you are coming; and sorry that you are to be with us only one year. But I judge that you have an attractive prospect for the year or years succeeding, and sincerely congratulate you upon it.[69] I hope you have spent your summer in the pleas-

ant way you expected, and that your health will be perfect again by the time we meet again for work. I wish I could report more work accomplished this summer, but some things I have done,[70] and at all events this last month have been having a most pleasant time. . . .[71]

To MRS. GEORGE THOMPSON

54 McCulloh St.,
Baltimore, Oct. 11, 1883.

Dear Grandma:[72]

. . . The other night I was invited by Pres. Gilman to meet Mr. Grey, an English member of Parliament, grandson of Earl Grey the old prime minister, and soon to be Earl Grey himself. An ordinary pleasant young man.

I am enjoying my classes and my teaching very much, more than ever I think. Last year I had only one class and they all had to be in it; I was very much pleased that most of them, including the best scholars, chose to be in my second-year class this year, which is an elective one. So I fancy I am giving satisfaction. . . .

---

[67] The history fellows for 1883-1884 were E. R. L. Gould and Lewis W. Wilhelm.

[68] Manuscript Division, New York Public Library.

[69] On July 18, 1883, Shaw wrote: "I have 'done gone' and hired out for an indefinite length of time dating from the expiration of the university year. It will be my occupation to

write leaders, etc. for the Minnesota *Tribune,* the leading paper of Minneapolis . . . . After all, I guess newspaper work is my true vocation and I shall try to be virtuous and content therein . . . . I wish I might take my degree at the end of the year —i.e. next summer—but I suppose that will be impossible" (Shaw to Jameson, July 18, 1883). Shaw actually took his degree in June, 1884.

[70] One accomplishment of the summer is not here mentioned. Jameson first speaks of it in a letter to his father: "I have an idea of a thing it would be well to do in the vacation, in the interests of historical science. Namely, to publish in the Record the town records of Amherst from the beginning; don't you think John would be willing to have a column or so furnished him for each issue? Such publication is no new idea; but part 2 is; namely, to get him to print said column off on four pages of a sheet of paper, a hundred or so copies, before he distributes the types, sew the sheets, and bind in pamphlets. I believe I'll do it. He can sell the pamphlets to pay him for his trouble. $ d no object to *me!* (Jameson to John Jameson, Apr. 29, 1883).

No sooner was Jameson in Amherst for his summer vacation than he set to work to carry out his plan. *"Mon. June 11.* Got the earliest town records to examine; from such examination I am quite sure they ought to be published. Went down and unfolded my scheme to John Williams, who was kindly disposed toward printing them in the Record . . . . In the afternoon I saw Mr. Carter, the old town clerk, who knows all the history of the town, and he approved . . . . Began the transcription of the records of Hadley Third Precinct, but made only a start . . . . It *is* really going to involve a considerable amount of drudgery; but on the one hand I have not and cannot have in Amherst enough special work to fill all my time, and on the other hand it is a sort of thing that every town ought to have done for it; if all did, it would make an invaluable body of materials for historical work of several kinds" (Diary, Jan. 1, 1883-Sept. 3, 1883). From this time until June 29, he copied steadily, with the exception of the days devoted to Commencement activities. On July 2 he completed his introduction, "and passed back the old book." The copying had been carried to April 30, 1789.

[71] With the opening of the university year Shaw failed to appear and Jameson wrote: "You don't mean to say you aren't

To John Jameson

Baltimore, Nov. 4, 1883.

Dear Father:

...I got a rather flattering invitation from Putnams to edit a volume of Twelve Great American Orations, supplying introductory historical paragraphs on the circumstances and results of each.[73] But Gilman advised me not to take it, though he thought I would get $250, perhaps, for it. But he thinks that, being after all only hack-work it would affect my standing not very favorably to have my name connected with it. I think he is right; that a *young* man should do work of a more scientific character.

I fancy from what Prof. Fredericq of Liège [74] writes me, that I shall have an opportunity to contribute annually to the Revue de Belgique, the principal review in that country, a general account of the progress in American historical work during the year. This will be an excellent thing to have to do. Most of the books will have been already read and reviewed for the *Zeitschrift,* so that this other won't take much time. It will give me practice in ways which that doesn't,

first, because it will be done in French and not in German, and second, because it will be a broad and general account instead of a series of individual reviews. I have written to Count Goblet d'Alviella, one of the directors, to whom Fredericq directed me; but it will be some time before I hear. Also, it will give me a little money, and perhaps if I choose, when it is done, I can very easily make an American rehash of it which some paper in America, like the Advertiser, might like to publish at the end of the year.[75] Practice of the best kind, anyway. Meantime, I have been reviewing the Statesman Lives for the Zeitschrift in what little spare time I can command.[76]...

Warren [77] said a rather good thing the other day, which I was mean enough to think might well be applied to my respected chief. Speaking of some man he said, "Well, no, he's not so much a pillar of the institution as an advertising column.".…

To John Jameson

Baltimore, Dec. 2, 1883.

Dear Father:

I suppose you are now a widower, and need to be consoled; perhaps you are sick or in prison, to be visited. I was glad to get your letter and Helen's note, at Kendall Green. I got it on my arrival Th. 10.10 A. M. and read it as we walked toward church. I thought I had quite a scheme, to get there when they had just gone to church, but was "too previous," and had to go in with them, a grievous calamity, for I am

---

coming, do you? We shall be much disappointed if you let anything change your mind from the purpose of spending this next year among us." Before this message could have reached him, Shaw reported from Grinnell that he had left Minneapolis but a few days before and had matters of business to attend to in Grinnell so that he could not reach Baltimore before Oct. 15. If the room opposite Jameson was still free at that time he hoped to take it. "It will be a real object to me to room in the same house with you, for I have designs upon you. I propose to make you serve as my professional patron and adviser, my mentor and my intellectual father confessor. You will find me an unpromising subject—old and hardened, and cumbered with sordid aims and cares" (Jameson to Shaw, Oct. 1, 1883, Manuscript Division, New York Public Library; Shaw to Jameson, Oct. 4, 1883).

[72] Mrs. Thompson, of Woburn, Mass., was Mrs. John Jameson's mother.

[73] Apparently the publishing company never carried forward this plan.

[74] Jameson's first acquaintance with M. Paul Fredericq (1850-1921), professor of history first in Liège, then Ghent, came about through a brief note on a pamphlet of his which discussed the German teaching of history. The closing sentence of the note (*Nation* **35**: 303, Sept. 7, 1882) read: "Two or three American colleges are in a condition to do this work; and the training at the Johns Hopkins, for example, will, we think, compare fairly with the German model; for most of our colleges the work must be of a lower grade." Jameson wrote to the editor of the *Nation,* asking the name of the author of the note and his inquiry was sent to the author, Professor W. F. Allen of the University of Wisconsin, who courteously sent Jameson the pamphlet which had been the subject of the item. Any student of history in the Johns Hopkins in the eighties was certain to be interested in a discussion of method and especially of German method, and Jameson at once wrote to Professor Fredericq, thus beginning a friendship which lasted until the death of the latter. After 1883 he received from the Belgian scholar whatever he wrote on the teaching of history in Europe and reported on it to the seminary.

In the Diary: "*Sat. Sept. 22* [*1883*]. Writing to Fredericq today to thank him for his pamphlet, consulted him about my preparing an account of American historical literature in 1883 or '82-3 for the *Athenaeum Belge*" (Diary, Sept. 5, 1883-May

18, 1884). Fredericq's monographs, *The study of history in Germany and France* and *The study of history in Belgium and Holland,* appeared in the *Johns Hopkins University Studies,* ser. **8.** Jameson's efforts in behalf of Fredericq during the first World War are described in letters of that period.

[75] In spite of Fredericq's cordial response to the suggestion, the plan was never carried out. *"Mon. Dec. 17* [*1883*]. Got a letter from Count Goblet d'Alviella, in which he explains that my project of an annual account of American historical literature won't suit the nature of the Revue de Belgique, as I see to be the case from the number of it which he sends. Also the pay [is] next to nothing. But he says that if I will sometime prepare a general article on the progress of historical work in this country, he will translate it into French for me. As for that, I should rather have the advantage of writing it in French myself, but of course I am wholly incompetent to prepare such an article, and if I could do it, should send it to some better review" (Diary, Sept. 5, 1883-May 18, 1884).

[76] Between 1883 and 1888 Jameson published in the *Historische Zeitschrift* reviews of Bancroft's *Formation of the Constitution,* Scott's *Development of constitutional liberty,* Doyle's *English colonies,* Lowells' *Hessians,* Schouler's *United States,* **1** and **2,** Curtis's *Buchanan,* McMaster's *People of the United States,* **1,** Parkman's *Montcalm and Wolfe,* the first nine volumes of the American Statesmen series, and Doehn's *Beiträge zur geschichte der Nordamerikanischen union.*

[77] Frederick M. Warren (1859-1931) was an Amherst graduate of 1880. After a year of study in the Johns Hopkins University, he studied at the Sorbonne, then returned to the Hopkins where he received his Ph. D. degree in 1887, and remained as instructor and later associate until 1891. He was for many years professor of modern languages in Yale University.

not, like the Scotchman, "unco' fond o' preachin'," when it is the Rev. Dr. Bartlett.[78] This particular time he preached a "historical" sermon, which was enough to drive a man *wild* (imagine me wild!) with its pretentious ignorance, and that too for a solid hour and a quarter. There was one man in that assembly that, when he came out, felt that he had something to be thankful for.

. . . Friday afternoon, on which I came back to B., I made use of an introduction kindly furnished me, on request, by Pres. Gilman, and called on Mr. Henry Adams, the historian, second son of Charles Francis. I didn't have much time with him, however, as he was going out to ride; but I shall see more of him some other time, I hope. As it was, I got some hints, and was much pleased with him. I entertained the highest opinion of his historical talents, but was afraid he might be freezing, like his pa, but he wasn't. He lives in an old mansion that I fancy might have been J. Q.'s.[79]

I had a pleasant and profitable talk with Mr. Bryce last Monday morning.[80] He advises me not to wait

five or six years before going abroad; and to make a great point of spending some months in Paris and London, during the sessions, and studying politics there at first hand. Said, in illustration, that Mr. Gladstone told him he supposed the progress of the U. S. must be the greatest political fact of the century, but from books he could get no good idea of it.

---

[78] This may have been the Rev. William A. Bartlett, who was in 1883 pastor of the New York Avenue Presbyterian church.

[79] Henry Adams (1838-1918) had abandoned Boston and Harvard for Washington in 1877 and in the years immediately following had published his work on *New England Federalism,* on *Gallatin,* and on *John Randolph.* While Jameson was in Baltimore he several times called on Adams when business took him to Washington and the relation thus established, though never close, continued until the death of Adams. *"Fri. Nov. 30 [1883].* I found Mr. Henry Adams in, but soon going out to ride. He is a grave but pleasant man, looking, in his forehead, like his grandfather, but with a nose like old John's. I fancy the house in which he lives must have been his grandfather's. Our talk was of a general sort; I felt afterward that I might perhaps have got more by speaking and asking of things more specific, suggested for instance by his Gallatin or his Randolph. However, I got some useful thoughts from him. As to state history, he thought it too closely bound up with the history of the general government, and that it was better to widen the scope of one's work and shorten the period. Invited me to come and see him again when over there. I left him with great regret that I couldn't have training from such a man, for I think he is really profound" (Diary, Sept. 5, 1883-May 18, 1884). The reference to state history is explained in a letter to his father, *post,* April 20, 1884. Adams was at this time living in a house known as the old John Slidell house, which was owned by William W. Corcoran, the eminent banker and philanthropist of Washington, D. C.

[80] James Bryce (1838-1922), to become Lord Bryce in 1913, had lectured at the Johns Hopkins University in 1881 but Jameson does not seem to have met him then, though he listened to his lectures with appreciation. *"Mon. Nov. 21 [1881].* At five came the first of Bryce's lectures . . . . This one was on the Crown and the House of Lords, and was one of the very best lectures I ever heard. He speaks readily and fluently, is very interesting and at the same time very fair, moderate, and candid. He gave much that one wouldn't find in any book, even in Bagehot." *"Tu. Nov. 22.* returned to Bryce's lecture at noon . . . . The lecture was on the Church and the Universities and was very good. Adams waylaid me before it and had me take notes to combine with his and make a report of the lecture . . . . Dr.

Bryce lectured [after dinner] on the Suffrage and the Distribution of Seats, and I enjoyed it very much." *"Wed. Nov. 23.* Bryce's lecture on the relations of law and history was good and suggestive. I took notes on it for Adams . . . . Bryce's [lecture], on the Land and the Poor, very fine."

Two years later (1883) Bryce's course on Roman legal history began with much the same lecture on the relations of law to history that he had given in 1881. At a reception given by President Gilman for Bryce, Jameson failed to get a word with him but the next day acquaintance really began. *"Fri. Nov. 23 [1883].* The chief exercise of the evening [the seminary] was a talk by Mr. Bryce upon Tocqueville's Démocratie en Amérique, especially a review of points wherein Mr. B. thought things had now changed. We young men took some part in it, in reply to some of his questions, and after adjournment had a pleasant talk with him upon some of the points, he sitting in an off-hand fashion on the end of the table and we standing around him. Shaw and I came up together, talking of the evening's proceedings" (Diaries, Nov. 12, 1881-Apr. 29, 1882; Sept. 5, 1883-May 18, 1884).

"Mon. Nov. 26 [1883]. As Pres. Gilman had suggested, went down to his house at 9½, and found Mr. Bryce there. Didn't get quite as much from him as the *most* I had hoped; but on the other hand I had fortified myself with the reflection that I might possibly accomplish nothing, because what I really desire is a chance to consult frequently some great historian, while in a few minutes' talk it is hard to ask general questions without being indefinite. There was *this* trouble at this time. But I got some useful points from him; and in particular he advised me, for the best interests of my 'magnum opus' not to delay visiting Europe for several years; that I should learn a great deal for my purposes by going over now, and spending a good deal of time at London and Paris studying the actual operation of politics. I hardly think it will be possible for me to do this, however. He thought of course that I shouldn't get much from lectures. I should get much from Dicey, little from Stubbs; as to Seeley, it would be doubtful how much, though he would gladly make me acquainted with him. At Paris, he said, I should find the French politicians to whom I might have introductions always very willing to talk of the politics of their country. It seems to me however that I should run a much better chance of being well introduced, by waiting a little. He said Mr. Gladstone told him he thought the progress of the U. S. must be the most wonderful thing in modern times but confessed he didn't understand it at all, in spite of having read several books upon it; Mr. Bryce said he was sure he shouldn't have understood us at all if he hadn't been over here. As to my choice of a subject, Massachusetts was, he should think, the best state to take; the states were diminishing quantities in our politics, still that didn't prevent their history from being important, as having formed the present. Certainly I was doing wisely in having my plans in mind so long beforehand; even if it had to be changed, the results of the thought spent on it would remain. As to difficulty in forming strong and definite views and making up my mind upon disputed points, he thought that would settle itself, by increasing maturity and acquaintance with affairs. Imagined my greatest difficulty would be in the social department of my work, (just so, and that is where I expect to make the most novel contributions)" (Diary, Sept. 5, 1883-May 18, 1884).

To wind up this discourse of celebrities, did I tell you that Mr. Schouler invites me to come to see him this winter in Washington? Which I am going to do it, you bet.[81]

As for McMaster, he is a bright man (the *only* one I saw at Princeton)[82] but his book, though readable, is shockingly inaccurate from cover to cover. I think, that the critics are right in thinking his style modelled on that of Macaulay. But, like most imitators of Thomas, he is particularly successful in imitating his defects.[83]

I read Mr. Genung's article in the Christian Union, and liked its spirit.[84] I was very glad to see such appreciative notice of Mr. Cable as that in the Advertiser.[85] The Advertiser does those things up in mighty good shape; and I can endorse every word of praise it gave the dear little man. I wish he were coming here again this winter, but I fear not. As to the critical Matthew, I know not.[86] (I was thinking the other day, that if we only pronounced our Greek as Mr. Freeman does, we might fitly call Matthew by the name F. is so fond of giving the emperor Basil, viz., Βυλγαρόκτονος, "the slayer of the Vulgarians."...)

To John Jameson

Baltimore Jan. 6, 1884.

My dear Father:

...Oh, those fearful, fearful lectures! [on the Relations of Physical Geography to History] They haunt me day and night, especially this first one. After that one, perhaps it won't be so bad. Adams seemed to think I had got to take them, if I wanted the boss to run me in as associate, and very likely he was right. But I'd give $100 to be rid of the necessity of teaching something I can't teach well.[87]

[81] James Schouler (1839-1920) by increasing deafness had been diverted from the practice of law to the writing of legal articles and from that he turned to the writing of history. The first volume of his *History of the United States* appeared in 1880. Jameson had tea with the family on February 24, 1884, the day after his first call.

[82] The purpose of the trip to Princeton is explained, *post*, Jan. 6, 1884, n.l. In committing its events to his Diary Jameson wrote: "*Tu. May 22 [1883].* Had a very pleasant hour with Mr. McMaster, the newly-famous historian, who seemed very much alive, far more so than anybody else here; he's going to get away from here. Was very pleasantly impressed by him. He told me he had done great part of his work in the Antiq. at Worcester" (Diary, Jan. 1, 1883-Sept. 3, 1883).

[83] A reply to his father's remark that he had read McMaster's *History of the people of the United States* and enjoyed it very much but had been surprised to notice a good many inaccuracies (John Jameson to Jameson, Nov. 26, 1883). Two volumes of McMaster's *History* were later sent to Jameson for review and were the occasion of a number of items in his Diary: "*Sun. Aug. 2 [1885].* Then I began to write on my review of McMaster, or rather attempted to do so, for it was three before I got anything written down; shouldn't have then if the men [Dewey and Alden] hadn't been gone. Always have just such a row about beginning to write anything. However, after I got once started, it went fairly well."

"*Tu. Aug. 11.* In eve, finished review, which the fellows praised. Glad it is done." The review, a long one, appeared in *The Independent* 37: 1229-1230 and 1262-1263, Sept. 24, Oct. 1, 1885. and for it Jameson received $36, no small item to the impecunious scholar.

[84] Genung, G. F., The mission of the new theology, *Christian Union* 28: 441-442, Nov. 22, 1883.

Two Genungs, twin brothers, were in Amherst at this time, George Frederick, a clergyman, serving one of the Amherst churches, and John Franklin, instructor in English in the college. Not long after this Jameson wrote: "I am sorry to hear that Mr. Genung is going; but I must confess that it will be a relief to me henceforth to know which one of them I am talking to, a comfort I have seldom hitherto enjoyed" (Jameson to John Jameson, Jan. 27, 1884).

[85] The issues of the *Daily Advertiser* for Nov. 27, 29, and

Dec. 5, contained long and enthusiastic accounts of Cable's readings.

[86] Nor do we know the question which called forth this remark. Arnold lectured in Amherst on Dec. 7 and in Baltimore on Dec. 20 and 22. The account of the Amherst lecture comes from Helen Jameson: "At last we have seen and heard Matthew Arnold, and I hope you will enjoy him as much as we did. His manner is abominable, his enunciation imperfect, he drops his voice at the end of his sentences and his way of swooping down with one eye onto his notes, placed on a music stand at his side and nearly on a level with his head, is very funny. You must just forget all that at once, get near so you can hear, and then enjoy yourself, as we did. There is no use in my attempting to tell you anything of it for I should only make myself ridiculous, but father will write to you about it . . . . The subject was Literature and Science and it wasn't too deep for me at all" (Helen Jameson to Jameson, Dec. 9, 1883). If the father wrote an account of the lecture it has not been preserved. Of the first of those in Baltimore, the only one Jameson heard, he wrote: "*Thurs, Dec. 20.* I enjoyed it greatly, though it was not a specimen of his best products. Couldn't see him well on account of the lights, but his expression was pleasanter than I had expected . . . . At the reception in farewell to Sylvester, Mr. Arnold came in, close by where I stood; he is a tall and noble-looking man, without being handsome. He said only a few words" (Diary, Sept. 3, 1883-May 18, 1884).

[87] For a short time in 1853, while Daniel Gilman studied in Harvard College, he lived in the home of Professor Arnold Guyot, Swiss scientist, who had come to the United States on the advice of Agassiz. To this period can be traced Gilman's strong interest in geography, which led him to call together the members of the historical seminary in February, 1883, to discuss with them the important relation of physical geography to history. Shortly after this conference first Adams, then Gilman, suggested to Jameson that his program for 1884 would include a series of lectures on this subject and also that he would be given the task of arranging a bureau of maps and charts. In May he went to Princeton to interview Professor Guyot, who had been professor of physical geography and geology in Princeton University since 1854. Unfortunately the geographer was ill (he died the following February) but Jameson interviewed his assistants, inspected the museum, learned much of the literature of the subject, met a charming young lady, and returned to Baltimore disappointed but not completely dissatisfied with his expedition. During the rest of the spring he spent considerable time making lists of books to be purchased, examining maps, and planning a room for the new bureau. The lectures he intended to write during the summer but he allowed them to be pushed aside by work in which he was more interested and returned to Baltimore in September with no lectures and very little reading on the subject. His lamentations over them are frequent and though he grew somewhat more interested before the term was over, he was not reconciled to teaching in a field in which he felt inadequately prepared. When Gilman asked him to deliver a

I find the dissatisfaction with Adams, of which I spoke, increasing among his graduate students. One of the best of them came to consult me yesterday afternoon about some advice Adams had given him, and I was surprised at the way in which he spoke of the chief.[88] It is pleasant and rather flattering to be consulted by the graduate students, but a little embarrassing in this form. But I don't think I said anything that could fairly be objected to, though I felt obliged to give the man the truest advice I could. It is really rather hard to steer sometimes. Scaife[89] has been having a beastly row with Adams during vacation; I guess through his own fault, for he is a jealous little 'cuss, although he feels perfectly sure he isn't.

I've received vol. I of McMaster to review, which I shall do carefully, but goodness knows when. . . .

___

public lecture on the subject he unhesitatingly refused. He also refused a tentative suggestion from Gilman that he contribute to the second edition of G. Stanley Hall's *Methods of teaching and studying history,* an article which Gilman himself had promised but now felt unable to write. The few pages on physical geography and history which appeared in this volume are unsigned and were probably the work of Dr. Hall himself, then teaching at the Johns Hopkins.

To his father he wrote again on Jan. 27: "You know I had Lodge's Webster at home with me, and my next work for myself was to read it and write a review of it for the Zeitschrift. Well, I haven't had time to read one word in it since the day I left home. And when I think that it is all on account of this geog.-hist lecture, which is of no earthly use to me or to the class, I grind my teeth audibly. I've given three now, and shall give the fourth tomorrow noon; it interests me a little, but how on earth I am going to string out the meagre materials into seventeen or eighteen lectures, I don't see."

[88] The consulter was Davis R. Dewey (1858-1942), for many years professor of economics in the Massachusetts Institute of Technology, and editor of the *American Economic Review.* "*Sat. Jan. 5* [*1884*]. Dewey asked to talk with me; so we had a long consultation in the geog. room. Adams had been advising him and several others to make a principal study of 'institutional history,' instead of English and Greek constitutional history, as men going in for a degree have been doing. Dewey said outright that he believed all Adams advised it for, was to give an appearance of greater variety to the work of the department; and I know he is right. He wanted advice as to the course to be pursued. I am much pleased to be thought worth consulting by the graduate students, but it is really hard to advise, especially to advise against a course proposed by Adams. Still I was only reinforcing Dewey's own opinion, that other things had much better be worked at first, than 'institutions,' much as Adams includes under that term" (Diary, Sept. 5, 1883-May 18, 1884).

[89] Walter B. Scaife, who had come to the university in the autumn of 1882, a graduate of the Michigan Law School, remained a friend of Jameson until his death. "We have as pleasant times as ever at the table. There is a new member,— a young fellow named Scaife from Pittsburgh. He is in our history crowd, and is a pleasant fellow, though Westernish. He rather amused me by saying he doesn't thoroughly like the Western people, they are a little too free and brusque, so that he was glad to get back to Pittsburg; for I hadn't been accustomed to regard Pittsburg as an Eastern city, and he has, to my mind, exactly those same defects" (Jameson to John Jameson, Oct. 15, 1882).

"*Fri. Dec. 7* [*1882*]. Scaife came up to my room to see a pamphlet. I showed him my new books, and we fell to talking

___

To THE EDITOR OF THE *Nation*

[Baltimore, January 27, 1884.]

SIR:[90] During the reading of the acute and interesting observations of Mr. Dicey[91] in the *Nation* of January 10 and 17, upon the present tendency in England to make more and more use of the agency of the Government in effecting social reform, as contrasted with the strong laissez-faire notions of thirty years ago, it has occurred to me that a strong and interesting evidence of this alteration is presented by the change wrought since that time in English public opinion upon the history of England of the seventeenth century. This is shown not only in the case of the royalist party in general, but especially in the case of Wentworth.[92] A revulsion [reversal?] of feeling has occurred in favor of the party, and especially of the statesman, who wished to gather power into the hands of the Government, to be used for the accomplishment of great internal reforms. It cannot be supposed that this is owing chiefly to Mr. Gardiner's researches, but rather that the change in the current of public opinion as to governmental action of the present time has, to borrow a metaphor from electricity, induced a current in public opinion upon the action of Government in the past.

___

the Columbia Schools of Political Science and at Cambridge. He stayed till five; but I cannot well regret time so spent, as he is going, I foresee, to make a good historical scholar, if he goes on rightly, and it is worth some time and effort to do all of things here and of what he could do at the Michigan and I can to set him going rightly and put proper ideas of work into his head" (Diary, Apr. 30, 1882-Dec. 31, 1882). During Scaife's time in the university, Jameson continued to see much of him, sometimes with pleasure, sometimes with annoyance. He was frequently at odds with Adams, and eventually gave up a Hopkins degree and went abroad. On the "fourth of July [1887 he] got his Ph. D. at Vienna, the first American to get that degree there" (Jameson to John Jameson, July 24, 1887).

[90] *Nation* 38: 122, Feb. 7, 1884. "I hope you read Dicey's articles in the last two Nations on the Social Movement in England; they seemed to me mighty true and good, and interested me a good deal. I have just been 'dashing off' to the Nation some thoughts which they suggested to me. I dno [don't know] as the Nation will print them, but you can look for them and see what you think of them" (Jameson to John Jameson, Jan. 27, 1884).

"*Sat. Feb. 9* [*1884*]. read Nation, in which is my belated communication with a bad misprint" (Diary, Sept. 5, 1883-May 18, 1884). The "bad misprint" is probably the word "revulsion" instead of "reversal." In Dicey's third article (Nation 38: 272-273, Mar 27, 1884) he referred to Jameson as "your ingenious correspondent."

This was not Jameson's first appearance in the *Nation.* A letter dealing with the exaction of party contributions from government employees, signed "A Pampered Placeman" (*ibid.* 35: 285, Oct. 5, 1882), was from his pen. A second letter, dealing with honor among university students, appeared, *ibid.* 36: 360, Apr. 26, 1883.

[91] Albert Venn Dicey (1835-1922), professor of English law in Oxford, fellow of All Souls, 1882-1909.

[92] Thomas Wentworth, first Earl of Strafford (1593-1641), executed for treason in the course of the struggle between Charles I and Parliament.

It seems to me, too, that the increase which Mr. Dicey notices, between 1850 and 1880, in the prominence given to sympathy in English society and political thought, is similarly reflected in the contrast between the characteristic nineteenth century historians of the two periods—between Macaulay's narrowness of sympathy and the broad and impartial appreciativeness which, aside from its scholarship, is the distinctive merit of Mr. Gardiner's great work.[93]

To JOHN JAMESON

Baltimore, Feb. 17, 1884.

Dear Father:

. . . Your statement as to the Greeks and Romans is correct. I.e., I believe no Greeks mention Romans before 238 B.C. But Roman legends in regard to the decemvirs assert that they, as code commissioners, visited Greece in 451 B.C.[94] . . .

Among the many things I haven't gone to, there was given on Thurs. eve. the first concert of the new J. H. U. glee-club. I didn't know'z I cared much to go and see some young men who were old enough to know better, stand up in line and sing "I've lost my doggie" and "Who will hist my old umbrel," and I judge that many were of my opinion, for the attendance from the Univ. was not large. [95] . . .

To GEORGE THOMPSON

54 McCulloh St.,
Baltimore, Mar. 2, 1884.

Dear Grandpa:

. . . A week ago I got a little outing, going over to Washington Saturday and staying until Tuesday morning. The day before, being Washington's birthday, our university had its 8th anniversary. A very fine address was given at noon by President Eliot of Harvard,[96] and in the evening there was a swell reception given by the university, to which I went, although I don't care much about those affairs. . . . I also saw two historians over there [in Washington] whom I wanted to meet, had considerable talk with one of them, Mr. Henry Adams, Charles Francis' 2d son, and took tea with the other, Mr. Schouler, son, I think, of the adjutant general of Massachusetts during the war; I got several valuable suggestions from them.[97] . . .

---

[96] "*Fri. Feb. 22* [*1884*]. At noon came the exercises in the gym, including an admirable address by Pres. Eliot, on revision of our American collegiate system by elevating other studies to a level with Greek, Latin and mathematics. Pres. Gilman's remarks seemed trivial in comparison, and he himself, though so wonderfully able, seems much less fine, dignified and noble than Pres. Eliot" (Diary, Sept. 5, 1883-May 18, 1884).

An interesting contrast to this comparison is furnished a few years later in letters of Charles H. Haskins, who wrote from the University of Wisconsin: "President Eliot is 'doing' the West in the interest of Harvard and is very much agitated by the ascendency of Hopkins in this region. He spent a part of Thursday here, maligning Hopkins all the time. He asked Turner and me why we ever went there. Didn't we know that Harvard was the place to study history, that they alone had the libraries and the instructors? It passed his power of comprehension that students in the West were so ignorant of the proper place to pursue graduate studies. He was quite discourteous in his manner and apparently created a reaction. Even in the West one is expected to be a gentleman."

"We were delighted to have President Gilman with us. The contrast with Harvard's agent was significant and helped the cause of Hopkins in the Northwest" (Haskins to Jameson, Feb. 15, July 11, 1891). Madison was not the only place where President Eliot's words were resented. See F. W. Blackmar (also a former Hopkins student, teaching in the University of Kansas) to H. B. Adams, Apr. 6, 1891, Holt, W. Stull, *Historical scholarship in the United States, 1876-1901: as revealed in the correspondence of Herbert B. Adams*, 150 and n., *Johns Hopkins Univ. Stud.*, ser. **56**, no. 4, 1938.

[97] "*Sat. Feb. 23* [*1884*]. Went first to Mr. Schouler's, and as he was not in, to Mr. Adams', and he also was not, so I went and got some lunch. At one to Mr. Schouler's again by appointment. He soon came, but it was not long before his lunch bell rang, and I withdrew, but any way we hadn't progressed very far, for he is very deaf, and also talked mostly of his law-books . . . . So to Mr. Adams at two and found him in. Had a long and interesting talk with him, and got quite waked up on some points. He showed one of the privately printed advanced copies of his great book on Jefferson's and Madison's administrations, vol. 1, and talked much about an American Historical Society. His abilities impress me greatly; I would give a great deal to be under him, as some of those Harvard fellows were. He strongly advised that the best work for a beginner was editing, and I learned of some chances, though to a man not of distinguished family they are scarcely chances. I don't think my estimate of the probability of success in historical work with my poverty was much raised by my talk with him, still I was in some respects stimulated. Perhaps he will find a chance to use me in some such matter, or to suggest some opening for zealous unremunerated work (no chance on the Monroe MSS. I fancy). I should be glad to put my services at his command, so far as possible, for the benefit of sitting at his feet, for it seems to me he must be Bancroft's successor."

Twice later in 1884 Jameson called on Adams. "*June 3* [*1884*]. Went down to see Mr. Adams, partly on general accounts, partly about the Bayard MSS., of which project he

---

[93] The impressive volumes of Samuel Rawson Gardiner (1829-1902) had been appearing since 1863. The fourth and fifth installments, dealing with Charles I, appeared in 1877 and 1882, and were reissued in ten volumes as the *History of England, 1603-1640* in 1883-1884. The final volume of Gardiner's life work, the history of the Protectorate, was not published until 1901.

[94] "I was much surprised to read last Sunday in Josephus against Apion that that [*sic*] Heroditus and Thucydides knew nothing of Rome—that its existence was unknown to the Greeks till it was 400 yrs old" (John Jameson to Jameson, Feb. 8, 1884).

[95] This was the glee club of which Woodrow Wilson was a charter member. Its first public appearance was on Feb. 14, 1884. Jameson's scorn was not shared by his friends, for F. M. Warren, Arthur Yager, Albert Shaw, R. H. Bayard, Burr J. Ramage, E. R. L. Gould, and C. H. Levermore, all associates of Jameson, sang in it. Only four of its members were undergraduates and of its graduate members five were at one time fellows of the university.

"*Mon. Feb. 11* [*1884*]. Of all kinds of foolishness, I hate college songs the worst, and think the whole business is childish and undignified for the univ. to have in Hopkins Hall; but college songs, like other nonsense, are amusing for once" (Diary, Sept. 5, 1883-May 18, 1884).

To John Jameson
Baltimore, Mar. 23, 1884.

Dear Father:

. . . My week has been a pleasant one, and full, though our cousins didn't come over. Tuesday evening we celebrated the birthday of Francis Lieber at the seminary.[98] Mrs. Lieber had just given us a burst [sic] of him and his copies of his works, full of his annotations for fresh editions and the MSS. of some of them. His son was present,[99] and Gilman, Adams and others talked.

I had the honor of acting by invitation as critic at the meeting of the undergraduates' literary society the other evening.[100] I gave them much fatherly advice, and criticized with distinguished impartiality the debate on the question of the value of secret societies. Sato talked to them that evening on Student-life in Japan, and was intelligible and interesting.[101] . . .

---

thought well. He suggested an 'American Statesman' but I am hardly ripe for that. Saw Mrs. Adams" (Diary, May 19, 1884-Mar. 26, 1885).

Richard H. Bayard (1865-1923) was at this time a student of Jameson and they had had some conversation about the possibility of publishing the family papers in the possession of his grandmother. Nothing came of the project at the time as the family refused to allow the papers to be examined. Many years later *The Papers of James A. Bayard* were published under Jameson's direction as volume 2 of the *Annual Report of the American Historical Association for 1913*.

In the autumn Jameson again called on the historian: "*Nov. 29 [1884]*. I got a good deal of thought from him, and some ideas of value to the seminary papers I am soon to prepare; it humbled me to see how much thought the man has, and I was more than ever impressed with the necessity of abundant leisure to a man who is going to write history. But in some ways it was a little unsatisfactory, for I had a feeling that I did myself less than justice in my talk with him, which I regretted because I should like to have him think it worth while to give me points" (Diary, May 19, 1884-Mar. 26, 1885).

Jameson also saw Mr. Schouler again after his unsatisfactory call on Feb. 23: "*Sun. Feb 24 [1884]*. Went to tea at Mr. Schouler's . . . . A little after tea Mr. Schouler took me upstairs and we talked of more professional matters, with less profit than with Mr. Adams, for Mr. S. is a less interesting man than I had thought, still with interest, and I got a point or two—*e.g.* Blair-Jackson corr.—which may be of value" (Diary, Sept. 5, 1883-May 18, 1884).

[98] Francis Lieber (1800-1872), after a turbulent youth, had come to this country in 1827, and here spent the remainder of his life, teaching in South Carolina College and in Columbia University. He is often credited with having written the first systematic work on political science.

[99] This son was probably Guido Norman Lieber, who became judge advocate of the United States. Lieber's oldest son, Oscar, was killed during the Civil War, fighting on the Southern side; his two younger sons were in the Northern army.

[100] The name of this society, soon to be reorganized by Woodrow Wilson as the Hopkins House of Commons, was the Matriculate Society. One of the debaters of the evening was R. H. Bayard, already mentioned as a student of Jameson (Diary, Sept. 5, 1883-May 18, 1884, entry for Mar. 20).

[101] Sato, a Japanese student who lived across the hall from Jameson, frequently came to him for aid in preparing his work. Jameson's first acquaintance with Sato had come on Sept. 28, 1883, when he had invited the newly-arrived young Japanese

To John Jameson
Baltimore, April 20, 1884.

Dear Father:

. . . Vacation is poor business, and this one was especially so. Accomplished exactly half the work I hoped to, and yet did nothing but grind, sav'g my ride with Williams.[102] My days went about thus; Curtis' Buchanan for three hours and a half in the morning; in the afternoon three hours and a half of Curtis' Buchanan; three and one half hours of Curtis' Buchanan in the evening. And it is a dull book too, mostly consisting of James' heavy speeches and letters. . . .

I've a scheme for next year that you'll be interested in. I think I shall try, during the summer, if my other work will allow, to work up a course of six or eight lectures on the formation and adoption and character of the Massachusetts Constitution of 1780, to read here next year to graduates in order to start a boom in my little hobby of state history.[103] In that

---

student into his room and had "found him a pleasant and intelligent fellow, and likely to prove a good student for our department. Honestly mean to be of great help to him in his studies." Following on this are several references to brief calls from Sato.

A year later a second name is coupled with his: "*Mon. Oct. 30 [1884]*. called dutifully . . . on Sato and Ota."

"*Fri. Jan. 30 [1886]*. Ota came up with some questions about his report of my paper last Friday night. Got some talk with him. He and Sato oughtn't to have been so shy of wasting my time this year; but I haven't been generous in respect to urging them to come up and see me."

These two students both came to the Johns Hopkins University from the Sapporo Agricultural College. Shosuke Sato (1856-1939), Ph.D., Johns Hopkins, 1887, was professor of history and political economy in Sapporo College from 1886 to 1894, and president from 1904 to 1907; from 1907 to 1918 he was dean of Hokkaido Imperial University and its president from 1918 to 1931. In 1913-1914 he was Japanese exchange lecturer in the Johns Hopkins University. He became Baron Sato in 1928.

His companion, Ota, had an even more distinguished career. Inazo Ota Nitobé (1863-1933), after leaving the Johns Hopkins, studied in Germany, then taught in Sapporo College and in the Imperial universities of Tokyo and Kyoto. From 1919 until 1926 he served as a representative of his country in Geneva. Married to a Philadelphia Quaker, he became a Quaker, whose great ambition was to aid in creating a peaceful world. In 1911-1912 he visited this country as Japanese exchange professor, lecturing at several universities among them Brown and the Johns Hopkins. In the Jameson Papers there is no correspondence between Professor Nitobé and Dr. Jameson though occasional references indicate a recollection of Johns Hopkins days: "While in Toyko [sic] I had the felicity of spending the greater portion of a day with Mr. Nitobé. He sent his warmest greetings to you" (J. A. Robertson to Jameson, Mar. 4, 1910).

[102] George H. Williams (1856-1894), A. B. Amherst, 1878, who came to the Johns Hopkins University in 1882 after receiving a Ph. D. from Heidelberg, was a frequent companion of Jameson. Between 1882 and his death in 1894 he built up in the university one of the outstanding departments of geology and mineralogy in the country.

[103] *Thurs. Apr. 10 [1884]*. [Adams] was heartily in favor of my giving a few lectures to them [the graduate students] in the constitutional history of Massachusetts, or perhaps merely

part of the work in which Messrs. Pickering, Metcalf et als.[104] will need to be worked over, I shall lay you under frequent contribution. Good scheme, isn't it? Mr. Goodell will be able to help me on the 'formation' part, and on the 'adoption' I've a scheme of making a raid on the records of various towns. . . .

To JOHN JAMESON

Baltimore, May 11, 1884.

Dear Father:

. . . I am reminded, on re-examining Mother's last letter, that I forgot to look up

"The base foul stone made precious by the foil
Of England's chair."[105]

It refers to the old Stone of Scone, on which the Kings of Scots were crowned, and which has been removed to London and built into the coronation throne of the monarchs of perfidious Albion. But I have to pass on the adjective "base, foul."

I have seen some notice somers of Giffen's paper (M. Paul Leroy-Beaulieu is the boss French economist, and by no means to be put off with a "Mr. Whats'-his-name," as if he were some one of your two-cent Littell galoots).[106] If you possibly can get hold of J. E. Thorold Rogers' "Work and Wages during Six Centuries in England" (not the exact title) now just out, read it by all means.[107] He is the first of living authorities, and if the College Library hasn't it, they ought to get it. It is intensely interesting. . . .

I am much obliged to you for sending me divers papers lately, as well as the maple-sugar. For, to borrow the language of the humorous Alden,[108] (descend-

ant of John Alden and Priscilla Mullins; who, by the way, has just left us, Alden, i.e., not Psil) "the newspapers of this city are not good; in fact, Sheol is full of better newspapers than those of this city." In the realm of past politics, I have been reading Curtis' "James Buchanan," principally consisting of James' letters and speeches. James was a good man, but he didn't know how to keep a hotel; and, like Dr. Todd, he didn't get in the right kind of deacons. . . .

To JOHN JAMESON

Baltimore, May 20, 1884.

Dear Father:

. . . The books came all right; I haven't had a chance to mail them all yet, but the reason I wanted them so soon was, that I might at the last seminary meeting show them to the men and explain my ingenious and cheap plan of record publication, as a move in propagandism. It has already borne fruit in a project of one of our number to publish the records of St. James' Parish, in the county of Ann Arundel and kingdom of Feverandague. I think it is just as well that John put only my name on the title-page, considering how plain and simple an affair the thing was; to do otherwise would be making a pretty large funeral for a very small corpse, I think.

My friend Miss Seaton has again sent me a lot of interesting autographs to examine, this time all of Webster, some quite amusing, and gave me at the same time two of Webster, one of General Scott, one of Richard Rush, one of Robert C. Winthrop, and one of N. P. Willis, that great poet.[109] Miss Seaton is a mighty nice old lady, and I think a great deal of her.[110]

---

on the formation and adoption of the constitution of 1780. I should like to make this the beginning of a boom in state history" (Diary, Sept. 5, 1883-May 18, 1884).

[104] John Pickering (1777-1846), ed., *Revised statutes of Massachusetts,* lv., 1836. Pickering was one of three commissioners appointed by the governor of the state to prepare a revision of the general statutes of the state.

Theron Metcalf (1784-1875) was the compiler of *Reports of cases argued and determined in the Supreme Judicial Court of Massachusetts,* 13v., 1841-1851.

Abner C. Goodell (1831-1914), ed., *Acts and resolves of the province of Massachusetts Bay,* 21v., 1869-1922.

[105] "A base foul stone made precious by the foil
    of England's chair where he is falsely set;
    One that hath ever been God's enemy."
        Richard III, act 5, scene 3.

[106] Pierre Paul Leroy Beaulieu (1845-1916) at this time held the chair of political economy in the Collège de France. *Littell's Living Age,* founded by Eliakim Little in 1844, much read by the father, was not highly regarded by the son.

[107] Rogers, James Edwin Thorold (1823-1890), *Six centuries of work and wages.* N. Y., Putnam's, 1884.

[108] Edmund K. Alden (1858-1938), A. B. Amherst, 1880, a Baltimore companion of Jameson, who added much to the gaiety of table conversation. He and Jameson spent the summer of 1885 in New York together, working on the *Century Dictionary,* and for some time after that Alden worked for the Century Company. From 1891 to 1924 he taught history in the Packer Collegiate Institute.

[109] Nathaniel Parker Willis (1806-1867), a popular writer of verse and of short stories. The reader is not to take Jameson's adjective seriously. Many years later he wrote: "I am very much obliged to you for sending me the copy of the Phillips *Bulletin* containing your article on N. P. Willis. I am old enough to remember days when he was taken more seriously than it is possible to take him now, and when some of his 'pieces' were in every reading book, and when my classmates declaimed 'Pharrhasius and the Captive' and other gems of poesy" (Jameson to Claude M. Fuess, Feb. 14, 1925).

[110] This was undoubtedly Josephine Seaton, daughter of William W. Seaton, until his death in 1866 editor with Joseph Gales of the *National Intelligencer.* This relationship explains Jameson's comments about her and also her possession of the autographs. "*Tu. Nov. 7* [*1882*]. The Youngs tell me that Miss Seaton is soon coming to stay with them. I do hope I can get well acquainted with her and that she will take a fancy to me. If she will I should judge that it might become of the greatest advantage to me, in some ways in American political history work."

"*Sat. Dec. 30* [*1882*]. After lunch went over the univ, with Mrs. Richardson, Miss Young and Miss Seaton, whom I have thus at last met. She is rather entertaining but terribly deaf."

"*Mon. Mar. 24* [*1884*]. At dinner Miss Young handed me a dozen or so of very interesting autograph letters which Miss Seaton had asked her to show me. Two of great interest were from Gov. Wise to Mr. Seaton, about Amos Lawrence's intercession for John Brown."

"*Mon. May 12.* To room to write out a translation of a few Latin verses for Miss Seaton."

My awful dissipation of Wednesday and Thursday evening was in the course of a struggle to work up a lecture on the last ten or a dozen years of English and ditto French history (Have felt badly ever since); no slight job to accomplish within 24 hrs. in a city where the libraries are so archaic as here. Would you believe it, there isn't in this whole city, in any public library, one single volume of the Annual Cyclopedia, supplementary to Appleton's of 1875. . . .

To Albert Shaw

Amherst, July 13, 1884.[111]

My dear Shaw:

You'll think I've been very dilatory in sending on that "recommend," which is now enclosed, but it had to wait till Commencement was over and our houseful of visitors gone. It has struck me, while I was writing it, as a most ludicrous thing that I should be giving you a "character," but if it is of any use to you, you are welcome to it. Scaife says you are going to boom Blaine; if I had known that you were going to do that, I couldn't have conscientiously engaged to recommend you as an instructor of youth; however, the best of us are prone to wander.[112]

I had a very "intense" week from the time I left Baltimore, June 18, till I arrived here, and an especially precious season at Albany, where I did, over the Usselinx papers, as big a half-week's work as I ever did in my life, working day and night, and finding much of value and some things that quite set me wild.[113] I

fancy that this, with going off to Norton's wedding at New Haven (most charming wife; if you go to Yankton take 'em in) and the business I had during Commencement week, were a little more than was good for me at the end of the year; for I felt rather lazy ensuing; but I believe I'm now ready for work.

Our "Student" Editors' Breakfast, (which is really a Trojan horse for the young alumni) was a great success, and I felt much pleased, for as secretary I had the making of the arrangements.[114] It is already, in this its second year, influential; and for myself, it is an excellent thing to have a little business of that sort to manage. Adams made a good speech for young Amherst at the alumni dinner next day. I was glad to learn from Will Seelye that your young alumni at Grinnell had succeeded. But really I don't think you'll make much if you substitute Mears, who has always seemed to me a mere gas-bag.[115]

Adams is in town, less than a mile from my paternal acre, but I see him very seldom. I believe he is somewhat occupied just now with the projected American Historical Association, to meet at Saratoga in September, which I hope to attend.[116] Scaife was here twenty-

[111] Manuscript Division, New York Public Library.

[112] Shaw, at this time on the Minneapolis *Tribune,* replied: "Yes: I am 'booming' Blaine and writing sarcastic things about you Massachusetts and New York fellows. Some of my friends are afraid I am not quite sincere, and am simply scribbling in pursuance of the policy of the paper. But on the whole I think I am sincere and I think I am right. I do not greatly admire Blaine; but I do admire things that are practical and expedient, and I fear that the wisdom of the 'Society for Political Education,' for example, is not of a practical or expedient character. However, I shall not forget my indebtedness to Eastern men and book-writers and political philosophers. I am of such disposition that it is easiest for me to mediate as it were between Matt. Arnold's 'remnant' and Blaine's vulgar majority" (Shaw to Jameson, July 20, 1884).

[113] Jameson had now turned in earnest to the subject about which he had been thinking since 1881. *"Fri. Jan. 21 [1881].* It seems to me that Willem Usselincx would be a good subject for a magazine article some time. The Lenox library would probably have plenty of materials."

"Tu. Mar 8. I can find a good deal here [Library of Congress] for an article on Usselincx, if I choose to write one in June and July" (Diary, July 24, 1880-May 3, 1881).

The project was pushed aside for various other pieces of work but he never lost sight of it and continued to examine material in this country and to collect copies of manuscripts from the archives of Sweden and Holland. The summer of 1884 saw continuous work upon the subject but the monograph was not completed until 1887. It appeared in the *Papers, Amer. Hist. Assn.* 2: 149-383.

The sequel to his Albany research was less happy. *"Tu. Aug. 5 [1884].* Then I returned to Van Rees, and was much vexed to discover that he has in appendix printed, actually

printed, some of the very papers I saw at Albany. In fact, nearly half my work there, and that the more important half, was useless. Tough. Well, I have new things, I think, on the Swedish part, and shall for the first time put all together in a connected biography. Not so satisfactory, however, as bringing out wholly new materials; I hoped this at first, but we live to learn, and I have gradually, during the progress of this work, learned a great deal as to the difficulties involved in doing any really new work. Merely to bring out things unknown in America is worth while, though, I suppose." (Diary, May 19, 1884-Mar. 26, 1885).

[114] *"Tu. July 1 [1884].* Our programme was as follows; Adams on travelling scholars, Plimpton on the catalogue, Fletcher, the librarian, on the new library, Genung on study abroad, Jameson on new blood" (Diary, May 19, 1884-Mar. 29, 1885).

[115] The conjecture of the editors is that Grinnell College (Iowa College) was considering as a possible president the Rev. David O. Mears of Worcester, a prominent clergyman and reformer of Massachusetts. The first wife of Dr. Mears was a young woman from Amherst; his second, whom he had married in 1882, was Mary C. Grinnell, daughter of Josiah B. Grinnell, who for thirty years was a trustee of Grinnell College. Mears would thus probably have been known to both Shaw and Jameson.

[116] The idea of an historical society had been in Jameson's mind even before Henry Adams discussed it with him in 1884. *"Fri. Dec. 8 [1882].* Thought considerably of the desirability of establishing an American Historical Assoc. or Congress, at whose annual meetings professors and others might meet, compare notes, get hints and stir up popular interest. It ought to be done, and I think even a young and unknown man could set the others at it. One can see the good it might do by observing how much interest its greater prototypes, the Scientific, Philological and Social Science excite every summer" (Diary, Apr. 30, 1882-Dec. 31, 1882; see *ante,* Feb. 25, 1883, n. 38). On May 19, 1883, he wrote: "Adams is proposing to work around to the Am. Hist. Ass. I planned." Despite his early interest he seems to have taken little or no part in the plans for the Saratoga meeting. Though he attended it and became a charter member of the Association he did not remain to the end of this first gathering.

four hours Monday and Tuesday, and seemed blessed in respect to life, liberty and the pursuit of happiness. F. M. Warren was here at Commencement. Macy's number in the series has come; I have read part of it again with renewed pleasure.[117]   Our professor of history, Prof. Morse,[118] has gone West for a few weeks; as he will visit Minneapolis before returning, I gave him a letter to you; he's a good man. . . .

July 12, 1884.

[Enclosure]

Dr Albert Shaw was a student of the Johns Hopkins University during the academic years 1881-1882 and 1883-1884.   With an unimportant exception, he was at no time a member of the classes conducted by me; but I saw much of him during those two years, and am well acquainted with the nature of his work while with us, and with the character of his abilities.   His reading in history and political science was extensive and well-planned.   He gave particular attention to the study of the constitutional history of England and of this country.   His opinions upon our political history were noticeably mature and sound.   The papers which he wrote gave evidence of remarkable thoughtfulness and activity of mind, considerable talent for research, great fairness and sobriety of judgment and a high degree of literary skill.   When speaking without notes he was forcible and clear.

I believe that, as a college teacher of history or political science, Dr. Shaw would be decidedly successful; that by his characteristic activity of mind and skill in presentation he would awaken great enthusiasm in his pupils; that he would teach them carefully, conscientiously, and with the best results to their political education; that he would direct their reading wisely and encourage them to further study; and that, winning and deserving their esteem, he would continually exert over them an influence toward good scholarship and high character.

To John Jameson

Baltimore, Nov. 2, 1884.

Dear Father:
   . . . We are to have a "ratification-meeting" at dinner Wednesday evening at the Youngs', Sumner setting up if Cleveland is elected and Worthington[119] if Blaine.   I

have been invited to respond to the toast in honor of the candidate from my state.[120]   We have had much animated and amusing discussion of politics at the table; there are one Bourbon, two Blaine men, eleven mugwumps, and one doodlebug.[121] . . .

———————————

a graduate of Haverford College and for several years a student in the Johns Hopkins University, was greatly beloved by Jameson.   He was a cousin of Logan Pearsall Smith and once took Jameson to visit the Smiths.   "Sat. Jan. 3 [1885].   Tom took me and Hussey to call on his cousins, the Smiths, two bright and attractive girls, of whom the elder, a Smith graduate, is now studying philosophy at the Harvard Annex.   She discussed the utility of metaphysical study with us; I was moderately interested.   Certainly she is extraordinarily clever.   Invited me to come with Tom and spend A.M. over Walt Whitman; they're all Whitmanites; I'd rather go to Quaker meeting."
"Sun. Jan. 4.   Wasn't converted entirely, but was interested, and led to [greater] appreciation of Whitman than hitherto" (Diary, May 9, 1884-Mar. 26, 1885).   For some account of these sisters, later Mrs. Bernard Berenson and Mrs. Bertrand Russell, and of the family interest in Whitman, see Smith, Logan Pearsall, Unforgotten Years, London, Constable, 1938.
Many years later, in a review of one of the volumes of the Cambridge Modern History, Jameson expressed his mature opinion of this poet: "Walt Whitman is not the Messiah of the new dispensation, but rather a clamorous John Baptist, minus the humility, wearing with ostentation his raiment of camel's hair, and eating his locusts and wild honey with theatrical gusto" (Amer. Hist. Rev. 9: 369, January, 1904).
[120] Benjamin Butler (1818-1893), a storm center in politics before, during, and after the Civil War.   In 1882, on his fifth attempt to become governor of Massachusetts, he succeeded but was defeated in 1883.   The next year he was nominated for the Presidency by the Anti-Monopoly and the National (Greenback) parties.   Jameson's response to the toast took the form of a long poem, a small part of which will give an idea of its nature:

"Abou Ben Butler, (may his tribe decrease!)
Went, in his dreams, where fireworks never cease,
   And being known as an arch evil-doer,
Was given a personally-conducted tour
   Either because Nick thought it was his right,
Or that he wouldn't trust him out of sight.
With anxious mind but with a smiling face,
   The Devil shows him all about the place.
. . . .
Lastly they reach, close by the River Styx,
   The realm of history and politics,
Where Ben's delighted eye in troops surveys
   Political dead-beats of former days.
With these congenial friends he fain w'd stay,
   But Laban, nudging, points another way,
To where two thrones are placed, o'erlooking all
   The politicians sent below each fall.
'For whom are these' says Ben.   'One,' said his guide.
   'For him who most outrageously has lied;
And one for him the people of his state
   Agree with most sincerity to hate.'
'I nominate myself for both,' said Ben,
   'I'm sure I've earned them, can't I have them, then?'"
[121] Election day was Nov. 4.   Jameson, who voted for Cleveland and Hendricks, would have called himself a mugwump. The doodlebug was probably one who failed to know his own mind and flopped from side to side.

———————————

[117] Jesse Macy (1842-1919), A. B. Grinnell College, 1870, taught at Grinnell from 1885 to 1912.   The paper was Institutional beginnings of the western state, Johns Hopkins Univ. Stud., ser. 2, no. 7.
[118] Anson D. Morse (1846-1916), A.B., Amherst, 1871, taught history in Amherst from 1876 to 1908.   He was one of the teachers for whom Jameson had great respect and much affection.   His power to interest students is attested by the number of Amherst alumni of his years who retained a keen interest in history throughout their lives.
[119] Thomas Worthington from a Germantown Quaker family,

To Albert Shaw

54 McCulloh St.,
Baltimore, Dec. 14, '84.[122]

My dear Shaw:

The heavy rain outside reminds me of the evening last June, the evening before your examination, when, having parted from the cynical Warren, you and I sat up here by this same window and listened to the heavy rain, and talked. I wish very much that you were here this year, with a chance to see a little more of you this year than I did last year. I really see very little of the graduates; some of them I don't even know by name. You see, I have no work with them, except to read three papers on state constitutional and political history in January, and am really overburdened with my increased undergraduate work. I don't think the new men are a very valuable lot, if one can judge by their looks and such of their performances as I have heard; I've little to judge by, but I think that if any of them were of the stamp of Wilson, Levermore and Dewey I should have seen it. Those three are doing splendid work. Wilson's book has been accepted by Houghton.[123] The versatile and buoyant Shinn was down here a month or so ago;[124] but I suppose he has written you. Wilhelm[125] doesn't come near the university; I see him occasionally at the P. [Peabody Institute], where he reads some pol. econ. in a dull, bovine spirit.

---

[122] Manuscript Division, New York Public Library.

[123] Charles H. Levermore, Davis R. Dewey, and Woodrow Wilson entered the university in the autumn of 1883. The first comment of Jameson on Wilson which has been found, is a diary entry concerning a seminary discussion of states' rights: "*Fri. Jan. 18* [*1884*]. Wilson showed the greatest logical skill and ability in the discussion of it, and I greatly envied him; when I went to my room, had a very discouraged feeling, to see how far I am from being capable of treating constitutional questions with ability, necessary though it is for one who hopes to teach American history." As the year went on, Wilson read to the seminary parts of his *Congressional government, a study in American politics,* which appeared in 1885 before he received his doctor's degree. "*Fri. May 9* [*1884*]. At sem. we had about the ablest and maturest paper ever read there, the introduction to Wilson's series of papers on the national government."

"*Fri. May 16.* Wilson read more of his work at sem" (Diary Sept. 5, 1883-May 18, 1884). For an account of Wilson's progress on this work see Baker, Ray Stannard, *Woodrow Wilson: life and letters* 1: 210-227, 8v., Garden City, Doubleday, Page, 1927-1939.

Levermore (1856-1927), Ph.D., Johns Hopkins, 1886, was one of the fellows in history in 1884-1885; Woodrow Wilson, the other one.

[124] Shinn, after a year of study, had returned to newspaper work. "*Fri. Oct. 31* [*1884*]. one [talk at seminary] by Shinn on his book [*Mining camps: a study in American frontier government*]. Had some talk with Shinn, now here on a visit, in the afternoon; his buoyancy and fertility are astounding; he is still a little of a bore; but a man who can earn from four to five thousand dollars a year by 'outside writing' for papers in N. Y. obviously has some valuable qualities" (Diary, May 19, 1884-Mar. 26, 1885).

[125] Lewis W. Wilhelm, history fellow, 1883-1884, author of Local institutions of Maryland, *Johns Hopkins Univ. Stud.* ser. 3, no. 5, 1885.

The vivacious Ingle[126] also deserted us at the beginning of the year; but his blithe spirit seems now inclined to hover around us occasionally. Worthington is still here, as unselfish and enthusiastic as ever; runs a female industrial school and is treasurer of the beer-club.[127] I got a letter t'other day from Yager; it pained me to see that some sister planet is, if not drawing him from his orbit, at least causing rotations. Ely and Levermore married, Dewey and Wilson engaged, Yager threatened![128] How account for it? The law seems to be that pure history, (or, as in your case, mixed with int. law) is prophylactic; political econ. is the medium whereby the fatal bacteria are propagated! I never thought of this before. But don't you suppose it is Nature's revenge for the invention of the Malthusian doctrine? I must write some fatherly counsel to Yager, so goodnight. Write to me in some of your Sunday leisure.

To Albert Shaw

54 McCulloh St.,
Baltimore, Mar. 30, 1885.[129]

Dear Shaw:

You have long owed me a letter, but I forgive you, and, having a little axe to grind, will even go so far as to write to you myself. To speak it briefly, my father's term as postmaster having expired, he has been superseded, and I must use my leisure, especially my long vacation perhaps, in getting some money.[130] I there-

---

[126] Edward Ingle, whose home was in Baltimore, spent thirty years in newspaper work in that city. He never received a degree.

[127] The beer club had ceased to be the informal Saturday night gathering of graduate students of its early years, without organization or dues, and had become the Johns Hopkins University Club with dues of five dollars a year. In 1887 it became the still more formal and expensive University Club and was no longer frequented by impecunious graduate students.

[128] Arthur Yager (1857-1941), who had taken his Ph. D. degree the spring before and was at this time teaching history in Georgetown College, Kentucky, apparently did not succumb to temptation until 1892, when he married Estill Lewis. In 1913 he left the Kentucky university to become Governor of Porto Rico, an office which he held until 1921.

Richard T. Ely had married, during the preceding summer, Anna Morris Anderson. Levermore's marriage to Mettie Norton Tuttle had taken place on Sept. 4, 1884. Dewey married Mary C. Hopkins in the summer of 1886 and Wilson, Ellen Louise Axson in the summer of 1885.

[129] Manuscript Division, New York Public Library.

[130] The election of 1884 proved a disastrous one for the Jameson family in Amherst, where efforts to replace John Jameson, postmaster, with a "deserving Democrat" were initiated as soon as the election was over. During March the son wrote many letters on the subject, hoping to enlist the interest of the civil service reformers. On March 10, 14, and 16, he was in Washington, trying by personal interviews to save his father's position. Here he saw Secretary Bayard, Judge Endicott, Senator Hoar, General Hancock, and the chief clerk and the first assistant in the Post Office Department, and had a short interview with Cleveland, of whom he wrote: "*Tu. Mar. 10*

fore propose to see if the portion of me above the neck has any commercial value other than for purposes of dissection; in other words, I am going to try to let my upper story furnished. As the colored brethren we once heard in the open air would say, "My inquiry is, have we the intelligence, have we the capacity, to rise to the point of exhibiting the capacity, the intelligence, which we have, in wider fields of intelligence and capacity?" If your paper has use for any such things as I could write, I wish you'd let me know; it would be a great favor.[131] . . .

To ALBERT SHAW

54 McCulloh St.,
Baltimore, Apr. 17, 1885.[132]

My dear Shaw:

Your letter was very kind; and, more than that, it offered really helpful suggestions. I had already, before its arrival, secured what seems likely to be a good job with the Century Co.,[133] and shall accordingly be

---

[1885]. Cleveland is a much worse looking man than his pictures, looks coarse, gross, vulgar, almost repulsive to me; but I have much respect for him as a public man, and certainly no one could have treated me more pleasantly (he was pleasant to everyone, rather after the 'jolly style'). I must have had from three to five minutes talk with him, and got in just about the things I meant to say, in fact quite satisfied myself with my presentation, considering the short time. He said he should remember the case and this interview when the matter came up; but intimated that when a man had had an office eight years there would be much pressure if a man equally fit wanted it" (Diary, May 19, 1884-1885).

From Amherst there had been petitions and counter petitions, the influence of the president and most of the faculty of the college being exerted for Mr. Jameson. One of the arguments used against him was that he had not voted for Cleveland; and he confessed to his son with much chagrin that he had failed to vote, having arrived at the polls after they were closed. The blow fell on March 26, when the Baltimore *Sun* announced the appointment of O. G. Couch to the Amherst post office. Four years later when the *Nation* condemned Harrison's action in supplanting Couch by a Republican, as a violation of civil-service principles, Jameson wrote, pointing out that the paper had failed to condemn Cleveland for a similar action under identical conditions in 1885, The Amherst postmastership, *Nation* **48**: 335, 383-384, Apr. 25, May 9, 1889.

[131] Shaw replied: "As our paper is organized and administered I don't think it would be possible to make the arrangement you suggest . . . . The N. Y. and Boston papers are run differently, (So also are some of the Chicago and St. Louis papers, *to a limited extent.*) They buy good contributed articles. You know Shinn has done well in that way. I imagine that you might do something worth while by contributing to Eastern papers. It would be diverting and good for you to *learn to scribble.* You ought to do some slashing writing, in which you could give free vent to your humor, cynicism, wealth of literary knowledge, etc. I think you would make a tremendous success as a newspaper writer if you would divorce yourself for the time being from your methods of work as a scholar and employ the entirely different methods of the journalist. You can do it if you will. Each method is legitimate in its own sphere" (Shaw to Jameson, Apr. 5, 1885).

[132] Manuscript Division, New York Public Library.

[133] Two years before this, an offer of the assistant editorship

---

in New York all the summer, doing work on their dictionary. I shall have work of another sort to do here at my room in spare time, also upon the dictionary. In New York I shall have my time to myself after 5 o'clock and on Sundays, and I'm going to see whether I can make any money in journalistic work while there, if I don't find that my other work or the heat tire me too much. I am really very much obliged for your suggestions, and shall hope to put them in practice, though I don't quite share your optimistic forecastings; and even supposing glory awaited me in some other path, I've little faith in my ability to switch off from that I've been following. But perhaps the air of the metropolis will act as a tonic on me. I hope so; that of Baltimore is a sedative, and eventually *petrifies* the subject. How can a city be otherwise than invertebrate, when the cause of its existence is the oyster and the acme of its civilization the terrapin?

We have Ross at the seminary tonight,—not Charlie, but Dr. Denman W., of Harvard, who is going to tell us all about it.[134] Subject: methods of instruction in history in the college and the university. I pray that we may have grace to profit by the privilege. Wish you could be with us; we could kill the fatted calf, and have the little pot of red paint all ready.

By the way, if you hear of any nice little college that wants a well-informed, bright and sound professor of English, I wish you would remember Alden and inform me. I go to N. Y. about May 23, if the boss will let me off. Write when you can.

To JOHN JAMESON

New York, June 14, 1885.

My dear Father:

What do you and the family say of the fact that my room, where I am writing this, is the third-story of the tallest brown-stone front on Stuyvesant Park? Yes, sir, here we are, with everything nickel-plated and a library thrown in, a considerable and interesting library chiefly in German, which Mr. Rittig has left here during his rest in Europe. Do you remember a German

---

of the *Century Dictionary* had been made to Jameson and had been the occasion of many letters and telegrams between Baltimore and Amherst. Jameson had promptly declined the offer, then had learned that it commanded a larger salary than he had supposed and had asked to be allowed to reconsider his decision, but in the meantime Benjamin E. Smith, Amherst, 1877, had been engaged. What Jameson did on the *Dictionary* thereafter was done under Smith, who became managing editor in 1889 and editor in 1894.

[134] Denman Waldo Ross (1853-1935), whose work ranged from the *Early history of land-holding among the Germans,* Boston, Soule and Bugbee, 1883, to *A theory of pure design, harmony, balance, rhythm,* Boston, Houghton Mifflin, 1907. In 1890 he became a lecturer on the theory of design in Harvard but at the time of his visit to the Johns Hopkins he seems to have had no official connection with the university.

"Charlie Ross" was the victim of a well-known kidnapping case in the seventies, which was never solved.

weekly paper I used to take? He is the editor,[135] and in his absence Frau Rittig consents to the subinfeudation of a large room, "his" room, to Dewey and me, and a smaller one to Alden, out of the part of this mansion which she rents.[136] Our room has a cabinet bedstead, with excellent bed, for one of us, and an ordinary bedstead put in for the other. It has desks and such appliances for would-be Bohemias, a large closet, an alcove with washing arrangements and bureau-drawers, bath-room opposite, everything excellently cared for, a really cultivated and most agreeable lady to run things, and great comfort. Our room is south, but not top, and even on so hot a day as this it is comfortable enough. Last night was too hot to sleep, people say, but we never knew it. Also, we are out daily till 5 or 6. Also, Mrs. Rittig of her own accord opened everything through her parlor to give us a breeze. Also, we can take to Alden's room in front when warm. We have in front of the house a really beautiful little park, (we're at 318 East 15, at S.E. corner of it,—but address Cent. Co.), we are only four blocks or so from their office, and have found an excellent place to board at, between here and there, (at $5 a week). And all these advantages and helps toward a cheerful and prosperous life we obtain for $26 a month, or $3 a week each. We think the lines have fallen unto us in pleasant places. Search took so much of our time, that I did only a little work at the office yesterday, but was there long enough to see that they were pleasant people, disposed to treat a man well, that their rooms were not only very elegant, but comfortable and likely to be cool, being on the north side of the 5th story of a building on N. of Union Square, and that the work will be much to my taste and not at all wearing, indeed can't be done save with deliberation. . . .

To JOHN JAMESON

Baltimore, Feb. 25, 1886.

Dear Father:

I've only a very few minutes, but I thought you'd perhaps like to know of a little windfall to me. Prof. Morris, the Greek professor who lately died,[137] had one class which was virtually historical, a class engaged in reading with him the Greek historians in translation, at present Thucydides. Gilman proposes I should take this for the remainder of the year for $100. It meets only once a week, so that will be $100 for twelve hours' teaching. Very good pay, especially as it is a very easy class, and will take as little work as any I have.

But just this isn't of so much consequence as that I shall no doubt have it next year and hereafter and it will probably add $200 to my salary. Indeed I see a pretty good prospect hereby, thro' a little rearrangement of my work, of at once securing the desired $1500 for next year, and getting rid of a certain class I don't like in exchange for one I do; that is, if I can get time next summer to write a certain set of lectures I always meant to do, and can the more easily do, as I shall have all May and to June 15 here for it. So, like Deacon Montague, I feel encouraged. Of course I should have liked to get $1500 for no more, and especially for fewer hours' work; but an hour a week is nothing, and I couldn't imagine any *new* course easier than this one will be. But I must stop, and see how I can pick to pieces and pulverize and eviscerate and vilify Dr. G. M. Asher's account of the early years of the late lamented Willem Usselinx.[138] Perhaps I can catch him in a wrong date, or a misprint! Let me whisper in your ear that all previous bibliographical work on Usselinx will be reduced to insignificance by that of an Individual. Positively no other person has correctly understood the relation of the "Argonautica Gustaviana" to the "Octroy ofte Privilegie"![139] . . .

---

[135] *Sonntagsblatt* of the *Staatszeitung*. On June 18 Frau Rittig received word of the sudden death of her husband (Diary, Mar. 27, 1885-Nov. 26, 1885).

[136] "We're going to have quite a gang in New York this summer, apparently. The last I heard from John Gardiner he had some thoughts of being there in the summer, Dewey is to be there all summer, Levermore will drop in once in a while . . . . and now Alden, who gets home by steamer in a week or so, writes that he thinks that he shall spend June in New York. Says that if he fails to get a professorship of English literature, New York is a good place wherein to hear of a primary school vacancy." (Jameson to John Jameson, May 31, 1885).

Henry N. Gardiner (1855-1927), A.B., Amherst, 1878, John to his college friends because of his English birth, taught philosophy in Smith College from 1884 to 1924.

[137] "*Sun.* Feb. 7 [1886]. Much saddened by the news that

Prof. Morris died this afternoon. Dear old fellow, simple-hearted and unselfish and lovely! He was a friend to us all; and as for me, there have been few men for whom I have had so warm an affection, and I shall truly mourn the modest, tender, kindly man. Of all the prominent members of the faculty he was, as Adams intimated tonight, the one conspicuously good man; alas that the unselfish one, the model of unselfishness indeed, should be the first of all the faculty to go" (Diary, Nov. 26, 1885-Apr. 15, 1886).

[138] G. M. Asher, *Bibliographical essay on the Dutch books and pamphlets relating to New Netherland*, Amsterdam, 1854-1867.

[139] Two works by Usselinx. On the appearance of his monograph the next year, Jameson's diary note is: "*Sat. Sept. 10* [*1887*]: the Nation in a few lines, 'sits on' my Usselinx. No fault found with the workmanship, though no praise, for that matter, but the man thinks Usselinx himself wa'n't no gret of a man. Perhaps I did exaggerate his importance, but it seems to me going rather far to deny him the credit of forming the Company." The anonymous reviewer in the *Nation* had written: "Mr. Jameson describes his hero as the Lesseps of the seventeenth century, the founder of the Dutch and Swedish West India Companies, and the originator of two of our colonies—that upon the Hudson and that upon the Delaware. Usselinx was undoubtedly a most enthusiastic projector, but his ideas were of the wildest character, and he must be compared with the Lesseps of the Panama, not of the Suez Canal . . . . Nor do we see that he deserves the credit of founding the Dutch West India Company, whatever that credit may be, for the charter was not such as he desired, and there was no novelty then in the idea of forming companies for foreign trade" (*Nation* 45: 190-191, Sept. 8, 1887).

To John Jameson

Baltimore, Mar. 8, 1886.

My dear Father:

. . . My Va. scheme is, like so many other excellent schemes, lodged in committee for the present.[140] I saw Senator Hoar [141] about it, and think it will be all right, but there'll be some delay; for they want first to settle once for all the general subject of private persons' publishing papers owned by gov't, and that will take a little time. . . .

---

[140] Jameson's interest in the records of the Virginia Company, owned by the Library of Congress, began with a talk to the Hopkins seminary in October, 1883, by Edward D. Neill, who had himself made a futile effort to have them published. Even at that early date Jameson's feeling that the study of American history could not advance without the publication of its sources was strong and his growing attention to southern history, with what he at first believed to be the availability of these records, led to what he called his "Virginia scheme"—a plan to edit the records and publish them by means of subscriptions. Both Dr. Neill and A. R. Spofford, Librarian of Congress, were discouraging, Spofford telling him that the first step was to gain the permission of the Library Committee of the Congress. Undeterred, Jameson presented his project to a number of those attending the American Historical Association at Saratoga in September, 1885, and there talked to Senator Hoar of the Library Committee of the Senate. Then began an effort which occupied a portion of Jameson's leisure for more than three years. A publisher was found without difficulty, Houghton, Mifflin Company agreeing to publish the volumes provided a sufficient number of subscriptions could be obtained, a sufficient number being, in their opinion, two hundred and fifty. On Nov. 24, 1885, they wrote: "Such a work could not be pecuniarily valuable to us, but its character is such that we should be glad to undertake it if we could do it under reasonable security against loss." They at once published a prospectus containing sample pages copied and carefully annotated by Jameson, who also drew up a long list of those to whom the circulars should be sent. Meanwhile, permission from the committee failed to come, it having decided to settle first the general policy concerning the publication of government documents by private individuals. All through 1886 the consideration of general policy postponed any action on Jameson's request. At the end of the year he wrote to his father: "I'm going to make a regular assault on the Library Committee of Congress this week. I have drawn up a manifesto which is undoubtedly one of the ablest state-papers of the nineteenth century. Six type-writen [sic] copies of this are being made and one is to be sent to each of them, with a prospectus enclosed, on Thursday. Then on Friday I shall go over and see them one by one and rub it into them. I don't believe they'll tumble, especially Geo. F. Hoar, Esq., but perhaps they will" (Jameson to John Jameson, Dec. 12, 1886). At last a bill creating a manuscript commission passed and Jameson wrote, in answer to a question from his father: "About Va. Co. Records, the situation is, that I must get Spofford, Bayard and Langley [members of the new commission] to make a separate favorable report for me, to the Committee, then get the thing thro' the Com., then thro' the House. In other words still another stage of work is added by the existence of the Hist. MSS. Commission."

Settled in Providence in 1888, he presently gave up the cherished project though he never lost interest in it. A talk on the records which he gave to the Rhode Island Historical Society received notice in the *Magazine of American History* 21: 32, 1889. In 1902 Professor William MacDonald, who followed Jameson in Brown, suggested that the Public Archives Commission of the American Historical Association sponsor

To John Jameson

1017 McCulloh St.,
Baltimore, Oct. 30, 1886.

My dear Father:

. . . My lectures on the elements of historical criticism are now attended by *twenty* graduates, who seem to approve of them, so far as I can judge. Friday night, at the seminary, I gave an account of the modes by which I had collected materials for Usselinx. In January, when I've got my public lectures done, I shall finish him.[142] . . .

To John Jameson

Baltimore, Dec. 19, 1886.

My dear Father:

. . . I didn't go over to Washington after all. For the Library Committee doesn't meet next Thursday; and I think it better to interview the members only a few days before some meeting.

Dawes was over here Friday night to give a talk on the Indian question before the Hist. and Pol. Sci. As. Seemed quite happy over the passage of his bill the day before. Talked well, though like a country lawyer of no great genius.[143] . . .

To Woodrow Wilson

Amherst, Mass.,
Aug. 7, 1887.[144]

Dear Wilson:

I hoped before this to give you a fuller exposition of

---

the publication of the records, the work to be done by Miss Susan M. Kingsbury, under the guidance of Professor Osgood. This suggestion did not meet with favor as it seemed to encroach on the province of the Historical Manuscripts Commission of the Association but it served to keep alive interest in the records, which were finally published by the Library of Congress: *The records of the Virginia Company of London,* 2v., 1906, edited by Susan Kingsbury under the general supervision of Professor H. L. Osgood. The third and fourth volumes appeared in 1935.

[141] George Frisbie Hoar (1826-1904), Senator from Massachusetts, 1877-1904, during his service in the Senate could be counted upon to interest himself in worthy historical projects. Jameson had presented a letter of introduction to him in the spring of 1881 and continued to turn to him from time to time as long as he was in the Senate.

[142] The public lectures, on the history of historical writing in America, were delivered in Hopkins Hall on Jan. 26, 28, Feb. 2, and 4. They provided the substance of a series of articles which ran under the same title in the *New England Magazine,* January-April, 1891, and later in the same year appeared as a small volume, published by Houghton Mifflin.

[143] Henry Laurens Dawes (1816-1903), Senator from Massachusetts, was chairman of the Committee on Indian affairs and the author of a bill which conferred citizenship upon civilized Indians and granted homesteads to heads of families. It became the Dawes Act of 1887. Before entering politics Dawes had been a country lawyer in North Adams and Pittsfield, Mass. It is doubtless true that he was "no great genius" but his public career was marked by industry, honesty, and competence.

[144] Wilson Papers, Division of Manuscripts, Library of Congress.

the scheme of which I once spoke to you, and in which I sincerely hope you will take a hand.[145]

My plan, (which please keep to yourself for the present), was for the publication, on March 4th or April 30th, 1889, of a commemorative volume of essays by graduates of our department, say you, Shaw, Yager, Dewey, Levermore and I, and certain others,—upon subjects in the constitutional history of the United States during the formation period, 1775-1789. Almost all of us, though getting up a book is hard, can find time to write an essay. But an isolated essay seems to have little weight. If, however, several essays are combined, still more if they are on subjects in the same field of history, still more if they appear at a time which plainly connects them with that field, they have a momentum with the public.

But I think a still better result may be obtained. I think the book can be made to help in establishing a certain tendency in American historical work on the constitutional side. All sorts of labor have been put on the history of the formation and adoption of the documentary Constitution. But meanwhile little has been done to elucidate the origin and development of the elements not comprised therein and of the unwritten elements generally, and to develop the continuity of institutional life between the colonial and the subsequent period. I should hope that such a volume, concerning as it would our constitutional history in this wider sense, would help to emphasize this need in our historical work.

You asked me to send you a list of subjects. I shall rather suggest some that have occurred to me, and leave every man to find, among them or elsewhere, a subject that suits him. I want each man's choice free; it will be better for the book that no one man shall choose subjects. All I care for is that they shall be within the constitutional field in that period, and well done.

Well, I think one man will write on the history of the suffrage during that period, to show how far the Revolution made for democracy. I myself shall probably write on the origin of the Articles of Confederation by imitation of the constitution of the United Provinces. Another man might, e.g., write on the influence of the state constitutions of the revolutionary period on the constitution of 1787; some other, on the use made of history by the founders of the Constitution. There are several subjects connected with the executive departments. The efforts ought to be made to go back of the acts of 1789, not to be content with referring the arrangements then made in the "creative fiat" of some one man, but really to investigate *origins,* e.g., to show how much the colonial and state Treasury Boards and that of the Confederation contributed, how much Hamilton. So of other departments. The relations of the Old Congress to its ministers might be interesting, as bearing on the cabinet; so might the diplomatic functions and organs of the Old Congress. A subject has been suggested to me by Professor Morse which I should think might have special attractions for you, as a man of legal training; that is, the history of the process by which the colonial judiciaries adapted themselves to their new task as independent tribunals, expounders for sovereign states. But you will be able, much better than I, to pick out a subject which will interest you. I can only say that I hope very much that you will be one of our number; and that, if you consent, I shall be very glad to assist you in respect to any thing which you may need.[146]

To ALBERT SHAW

1017 McCulloh St.,
Baltimore, Feb. 14, 1888.[147]

Dear Shaw:

I will not let thee go except thou bless me, by taking a part in the proposed volume. And bless yourself, too, for I think it is already pretty certain of being a creditable thing to have a part in. I understand you are to go to Cornell. Will it not be a good thing to signalize your entrance into the academic field by a good piece of permanent work?[148]

---

[145] "*Thurs. Mar. 4* [*1886*]. An excellent scheme came into my mind, sufficiently in advance, one would say,—of getting up, for the 100th anniversary of Mar. 4, 1789, a combined volume of historical essays bearing on the constitutional history of that period by graduates in hist. of the univ. Subjects are plentiful, and I could perhaps enlist H. C. Adams, Shaw, Yager, Wilson, Levermore, Dewey, Woods and Bayard" (Diary, Nov. 26, 1885-Apr. 15, 1886). The Woods mentioned was probably Allan C. Woods, a member of the seminary, though he did not receive his A.B. degree until June, 1886. He did not live to share in the volume Jameson here contemplated. Occasional entries in later months show that the plan was not forgotten. "*Wed. Dec. 1* [*1886*]. At dinner Adams's saying a thing of W. Wilson led me to think I'd better put in some stakes by speak'g thus in advance of my Am. Hist. 1789-91 scheme, which he approved."
"*Fri. Feb. 11* [*1887*]. Woodrow Wilson was there [the weekly meeting of the seminary]. I spoke to him of my scheme for Mar. 4, 1889, and he may cooperate" (Diary, Apr. 16, 1886-Feb. 16, 1887).

[146] The remainder of this letter is missing. Wilson apparently answered on Aug. 30 but his reply has not been found. From subsequent remarks of Jameson we surmise that he gave tentative consent to write for the volume and suggested as his subject "Chisholm v Georgia." That he did not give Jameson too much encouragement is evident from a diary entry of Feb. 17, 1888: "It is a bad thing for my book that Dewey, Shaw and Wilson are all doubtful, for they are about my best cards."
[147] Manuscript Division, New York Public Library.
[148] "Your remark about my going to Cornell and my 'entrance into the academic field' shows that you are laboring under a misapprehension. I am asked to give a lecture this spring (May 4) before the Cornell political science assoc'n, that's all. I am informed by letters from Drs. Ely and H. C. Adams that my name has been mentioned in connection with a position in that university, but I have had no other intimation of it, and I do not propose to visit Cornell as a candidate for anything, I assure you. If an offer should be made me, I do not know whether I should accept it or not" (Shaw to Jameson, Feb. 18, 1888). In 1890 Shaw was asked to become professor of political institutions and international law in Cornell but he declined

But I suppose you need no conversion as to this aspect of the case, but take refuge supinely in the superficial excuse that the Northwest contains no books. But you shall not escape me thus. I have a good subject to propose to you, for which I believe you will find materials quite accessible. You will remember that our subjects are to be all within the field of the constitutional history of the period, 1775-1789, or till the constitution can be called fully formed. What I have to suggest to you is, the constitutional history of the religious bodies during the same, or nearly the same, period, or, the influence which the formative process in civil constitution had, by attraction, as the grammarians say, on our ecclesiastical constitution. The period of formation in the one is certainly accompanied by a period of formation, or completer organization, (the first general conventions, the first bishops, etc.) in the other. The mutual relations of the two movements seem to me a highly interesting thing to examine. Moreover, the subject does not require recondite materials. City libraries, ecclesiastical societies' libraries, and the libraries of ministers of various sects, will surely furnish you in Minneapolis with nearly all the necessary data. Anything I can send on from here I will. And then the comparison and reflection can be done anywhere. Does not the theme attract you? It seems to me it must. Pray write me that you will undertake it, (and write me soon anyway.) I hate not to have you represented in our book.[149]

To JOHN JAMESON

Baltimore, Apr. 1, 1888.

Dear Father:

... I am much obliged to you also for your data out of Jones,[150] and for your inquiries of Judge Lowell. It will do good to have brought the matter to his mind. His ancestor was indeed a member of this identical court, and some one of the Lowells has his papers, for information as to which I shall apply to the judge or the poet later in my studies.[151] At Washington, in the Clerk's Office of the S.C., I found that they had twenty big tin boxes of the papers of this court,—a wealth of material (mostly chaff, though, in all probability) which I shall probably attack in June, though it is possible I may go down into the mountains of S. Carolina. Mr. Calhoun's son-in-law [152] invites me to come down and see "ole John C's" papers, and I may take some stock in that. Or, again, my application to the Library Committee of Congress for leave to edit the records of the Va. Co. may succeed. There is more chance of this than heretofore, I think, for Phelan, of Tennessee, a history man, (Ph.D. of Leipzig), will push it. Tomorrow he will introduce a joint resolution I drew up, in the House, and Voorhees in the Senate. These being referred to the Committee, I appear before them on Thursday morning, to urge my request.[153] If they are favorable, Phelan will try to run it through. I saw a lot of people, among them Evarts,[154] who is colder than ever any Adams. . . .

---

for that matter, the state admiralty courts under the Confederation. I am doing a little something, when I can get time, toward working up such federal judiciary system as there was under the Old Congress, and of course that Federal Court of Appeals is the main thing. A few of its cases are reported in 2 Dallas, a few are imbedded in subsequent Supreme Court cases, and there are some other sources of information; yet I should be glad to know of more." For the use which Jameson made of this material, see The old federal court of appeals, *Papers, Amer. Hist. Assn.* 3: 383-392, a paper read in Washington, Dec. 27, 1889.

[151] John Lowell (1824-1897) resigned as circuit judge in 1884. His great-grandfather, also John Lowell, was a member of the court of appeals in cases of capture. The poet was, of course, James Russell Lowell.

[152] Col. Thomas G. Clemson of Fort Hill, S. C. Not long after this Colonel Clemson died, leaving the Calhoun papers to the Clemson Agricultural College, which was to be created on his Fort Hill estate.

[153] James Phelan (1856-1891), Ph. D., Leipzig, 1878, member of the House of Representatives from Tennessee, 1887-1891.

Daniel W. Voorhees (1827-1897), senator from Ohio, 1877-1897. "Mr. Voorhees introduced a joint resolution (S.R.67) authorizing and directing the Librarian of Congress to permit Dr. J. F. Jameson to cause to be made a copy of the records of the Virginia Company, and to cause the same to be published; which was read twice by its title, and, with the accompanying papers, referred to the Committee on the Library." The resolution as introduced in the House cautiously inserted the phrase "at his own expense" (*Cong. Rec.* 19, pt. 3, 50 Cong., 1 sess., 2543, 2618).

[154] William M. Evarts (1818-1901) had been elected United States Senator in 1885. At that time Jameson saw him he was already suffering from impaired eyesight and before many years he was totally blind.

---

the request and the next year established the *Review of Reviews*.

[149] Shaw declined to share in the volume on the ground that he was sailing for England in May for an extended foreign sojourn. "It goes without saying that I should like to be represented in the worthy volume you are to issue; and while I am not learned like Dr. Schaff and Dr. Fisher in Church history I should find it interesting to study the subject you outline so suggestively" (Shaw to Jameson, Feb. 18, 1888).

[150] Jones, Leonard A., *An index to legal periodical literature*. On Feb. 26, Jameson had written to his father: "I wish that, some time when you are over there [Boston Bar Library], and have the time, you would note down for me any titles that you may find in it [Soules' *Index to legal periodical literature*] respecting the old Federal Court of Appeals in Admiralty, or,

To WOODROW WILSON

Winchester, Mass.,
Aug. 4, 1888.[1]

My dear Wilson:

I congratulate you sincerely on your translation to a place so much more congenial and advantageous as Wesleyan is likely to prove.[2] I shall be glad to have you so near as Middletown, and, in prospect of that, have a little plan to unfold.

I propose, next winter at Brown, to get up a course of public university lectures in my department. I conceive that it might be a good plan to utilize for that purpose the researches which men have been making for our common volume of essays, and have a course of

lectures by them upon points in the development of the constitution of the United States. This will be timely this winter, and will not be too serious for a Providence audience. Six of the men will be in New England this winter, and one or two others can come up. I think each one will be able to make an edifying and interesting popular lecture upon the subject on which he has been working.

I do not yet know that this scheme can be carried out. I do not know what can be promised the lecturer as a fee; (something like twenty dollars, I expect). But I should like to ask whether you feel disposed to consent to give one of these lectures, on the subject of your essay, or something growing out of it. Also, have you found time to make progress with the essay itself?[3]

To ALBERT SHAW

Winchester, Mass., Aug. 22, 1888.[4]

My dear Shaw:

I have a vague impression that I wrote to you during

[1] Wilson Papers, Division of Manuscripts, Library of Congress. The Jameson family had moved from Amherst to Winchester. The father was now working in a Boston law office.

[2] Wilson was leaving Bryn Mawr for Wesleyan; Jameson was leaving the Johns Hopkins for Brown University. A portion of the earlier history of these changes is recorded in the Diary, Feb. 18, 1887-Oct. 8, 1888. *"Wed. May 23 [1888].* At 11 Adams and Ely sprung on me the question, whether I wanted to go to Wesleyan as professor of history and political economy at $2500. Pres. Van Vleck is coming tonight, and they can apparently give it to whom they will. It struck me with a chill, as the Michigan chance did last year, and I felt as if I couldn't go . . . . I have made up my mind to take it if I can get it, though indeed I think religion will prevent. It would be . . . poor fun teaching scrubby Methodist undergraduates, but the Jamesons need the money and I need the opportunity, whereas there is not much future here; Adams will no doubt stay now."

"Thurs. May 24. Prof. Van Vleck was here and saw me a few minutes. He has other candidates in view, Adams thinks I stand the best chance; Ely thinks Jenks does . . . . Adams thinks religion won't at all stand in the way of my going to Middletown."

"Sat. May 26. At noon, at the univ., Adams told me that he had a better thing on the string for me than Wesleyan. Most likely Wesleyan will go to some one else; but at Brown they will probably divide Andrew's work, giving Gardner the pol. econ., and some one else the history. They would probably pay the history man less than at Wesleyan, most likely $2000, but it would be a much better place to be at. I suppose it will be best to go, if I can get it; yet I hate to change for $500. But probably they would run that up to $2500 before long. . . . Brown and Providence would give me a fine vantage ground for work."

"Fri. June 1. found letters from Gardner, and one from President Robinson. The latter wants me to come up there, and will probably offer me the professorship. From the letters and Gardner's reply to a telegram I sent him I believe it will be best to go. To be sure, they will probably start me at only $2000, but it must be[fore] many years be raised to the $3000 which the professors generally get. Here, there is little opening; and though the work is pleasanter as being with more advanced students, the other is more of a position, quite apart from salary."

Sat. June 2. Went to see Mr. Gilman, who of course advised me to go, though he strongly expressed his regret. Tele-

graphed Dr. Robinson to find out whether I had better wait till the 12th, or leave Monday. He replies for the latter."

Mon. June 4. Gardner met me, and took me at once to see President Robinson, with whom I had some general talk before going to bed. Like him."

Tu. June 5. Dr. Robinson showed me around, and we had much talk. Then met two members of the committee, Mr. Chase [Arnold B. Chace] and Dr. [William] Gammell, the latter of whom walked me around town, and gave me his views. He believes there is a chance to work up a graduate department here. I encouraged him to believe I should do everything possible toward that end. Yet, with all my desire to do these things and to build up a big department here, I doubt whether my love of quiet study may not overcome this acquired taste for booming. . . . After dinner the committee met—Drs. [Samuel L.] Caldwell, Gammell and [Daniel] Leach—and inspected me. Result favorable . . . . the shrewd old man [Dr. Robinson] so fixed it that the rate of $2000 the first year could not be gainsaid. He said it would be $2500 the second year. I left with a feeling that the outlook was very favorable for the new professor."

[3] Not having heard from Wilson, Jameson wrote again on Sept. 21, repeating the substance of this letter. On the twenty-eighth Wilson replied: "Assuredly the fates are against me! I have been delaying my answer to your two last letters, not only because moving and all its legion attendant cares of packing, preparing, unpacking, settling, have robbed me both of all leisure and of all opportunity to write, but also out of sheer reluctance to tell the truth and say 'I can't write the essay, and I can't lecture in Providence—though I would give my head to be able to.' And yet such is the stern truth. Just look at the case: a topic exactly suited to my tastes and my training, to be written up for a volume I should esteem it a genuine honor and privilege to be allowed to contribute to— and the editor a fellow whose friendship I value as highly as I esteem his scholarship; and yet I'm absolutely barred!"

[4] Manuscript Division, New York Public Library.

my last week in Baltimore, and sent it out to the Tribune office. But perhaps I didn't. Perhaps they didn't forward it. Perhaps indeed you are too busy hobnobbing with the mighty ones of the earth and curving your democratic spine before the representatives of the effete despotisms, to find time to notice a humble, untitled individual in crude America. Be it so. Yet if you have no time to write letters, you may have time to read them, and may like to have what little news I can give. If you have not heard of it (I have really no record of having written to you) you will doubtless be interested to know that I have "removed my relations" from Baltimore, and am henceforth to be professor of history at Brown, succeeding Andrews, who goes to Cornell. I do not have political economy, as Diman and Andrews had. That goes to a tutor, a Brown and Hopkins man named Gardner, whom perhaps you know, and whom I greatly like.[5] I have a good salary, few classes, and an excellent outlook altogether, though there will be much for which I shall miss the Hopkins, of course.

Meanwhile, Woodrow Wilson, turning his back upon "the softer Adams of his academe" at Bryn Mawr, becomes professor at Wesleyan (Middletown). Young's place at Harvard is to be filled by Dr. Charles Gross of Troy,[6] who has worked so much on English municipal institutions. Levermore is at present (temporarily) laid on the shelf with granulation of the eyelids. He is at Brookline, where Dewey also is to live the next year. D. is now at Madison. Adams and Ely have both been lecturing at Chautauqua. Adams reports that he has enjoyed it very much, and thinks he may go there next year also. I have been working fairly well, but so variously that the results can't easily be stated in brief. I have enjoyed our new home, but have had an exceed-

ingly quiet summer. My volume of essays scheme is in good train, certain to be carried out now, I think; I propose to have at Brown a course of lectures in which each man shall give one based on these researches he has been making.[7] Are you going to be able to contribute an essay?

If it won't be too much trouble I wish you would lay out a few shillings and sixpences in buying (or get in any honest manner) any pamphlets, papers, prints, etc., which would illustrate the present government of England in any department, for the purposes of a teacher of governments and constitutions, yet are not to be met with in bibliographies. If you will send them to me at Brown, I will ante up. But don't give yourself trouble. Best wishes for your travels.[8]

To WOODROW WILSON

1 College Court,
Providence, Nov. 20, 1888.[9]

My dear Wilson:

I have this morning sent you the desired copy of *Vom Fels zum Meer,* in which you may or may not find something that will interest you. I have enclosed with it my copy of Mr. Cable's pamphlet on the Negro Question, which Mrs. Wilson may like to read.[10] The book

---

[5] E. Benjamin Andrews (1844-1917) remained at Cornell University but one year, then returned to Brown as president. See *post,* June 23, 1897.

Jeremiah L. Diman (1831-1881) left the ministry in 1864 to teach history and political economy in Brown, where until his death he was a stimulating and effective teacher.

Henry B. Gardner (1863-1939), who had been a student in the Johns Hopkins from 1884 to 1888, continued to teach political economy in Brown University until his retirement. He and Jameson remained warm friends so long as they both lived.

[6] Ernest Young had graduated from Harvard in 1873, with highest honors in history: he gained his Ph. D. degree in 1876, one of the earliest degrees in history granted by Harvard. As instructor, assistant professor, and professor he taught in Harvard until his death in 1888.

Charles Gross (1857-1909), A.B., Williams, 1878, had taken his Ph.D. degree at Göttingen in 1883. Returning to this country, he visited the Johns Hopkins University, where he read a paper on guild merchants to the Friday seminary. At this time H. B. Adams had some thought of an appointment for him in the Johns Hopkins department but nothing came of this and he spent the next five years working independently in the archives of England. In 1888 he became instructor in history in Harvard, in 1901, professor, and in 1908 he was made the first incumbent of the Gurney Professorship of History and Political Science in Harvard. Holt, *Historical Scholarship in the United States,* 69; see *post,* Jan. 25, 1916.

[7] Jameson provided a course of lectures for Providence in 1888-1889 (and in many subsequent years) but the speakers were not the contributors to his volume of essays. The series was introduced by Seth Low; Wilson, in spite of his emphatic refusal of Sept. 28, spoke on Jan. 11 and 18; and Albert Bushnell Hart followed. Members of the Brown faculty completed the course. As the lectures had no university subsidy and were free to the students and to the public, Jameson, Gardner, and a few friends organized the Brown University Historical and Economic Association to sponsor them and by the dues of the members to provide the necessary funds. For many years the arrangements for the series occupied much of Jameson's time and thought.

[8] Shaw replied from Edinburgh: "Particularly glad to know of your appointment to Brown and quite surprised at Wilson's acceptance of the Wesleyan place which I had declined with thanks." (Shaw to Jameson, Oct. 22, 1888).

[9] Wilson Papers, Division of Manuscripts, Library of Congress. Jameson had visited the Wilsons on Nov. 15 and 16, and much of this letter relates to subjects discussed during that visit. "*Thurs. Nov. 15* [*1888*] talked till midnight, and had a right good time of it, over Bryn Mawr, and his book [*The State,* soon to appear] and northern colleges. He finds students' manners much as I do, and their plans to be sociable with their students checked" (Diary, Oct. 10, 1888-Dec. 21, 1890). During the first year of Jameson's sojourn in Providence he frequently referred to this subject in his Diary. "*Thurs. Oct. 11* [*1888*]. Much annoyed at rudeness of certain of the students. Unconscious, but they've no manners."

"*Wed. Nov. 14.* Hurried home to be there for students but again none came. Discouraging to try to be social with them." Again and again during the year 1888-1889 the words "none came" are recorded of those evenings set aside for the students, but in the years which followed, the evenings "at home" seem to have become pleasant social occasions.

[10] *Vom Fels zum Meer* was a German illustrated family magazine published in Stuttgart in the eighties.

Cable, George W., *The Negro Question,* N. Y., American Missionary Association, 1888.

for which I referred you to the Academy is entitled "France as it is," and is written by André Lebon and Paul Pelet and translated into English under their supervision. As it is published by Cassell and Co., and they have a house at Philadelphia, you may be able to get a copy in less time than it takes to import one. After I had left you, it occurred to me that your wish for books which might make real and living the political institutions of European countries might to some extent be met, for France, by a little book I saw at Harvard in September, by Jules Simon, entitled Le Livre du petit Citoyen, Hachette, 1880. It was a well-written book, of course. As I remember it, it had a division on the commune, one on the arrondissement, one on the department; or perhaps they were on local, departmental, and central institutions. At all events it was an attempt to describe vividly, from the *petit citoyen's* point of view, the workings of the parts of government with which he might come in contact.

I take it colonial federation comes into your scheme for Great Britain. Have you happened to see about the South African customs union arranged for by a conference last February? It is badly treated of by our consul at Cape Town in pp. 209-219 of Consular Report no. 93, May, 1888; but he gives the essential details.

I don't know when I've had so pleasant a twenty-four hours as that I spent at Middletown. I am greatly obliged to you for making so delightful an addition to the number of my friends as Mrs. Woodrow Wilson, though it was doubtless done more for other reasons than for my benefit, and has already received other rewards than my gratitude. Commend me to her, please; also to the two infants,—the one with the oval face and the one with the spherical body.[11] I wish you were all nearer.

To John Jameson
Providence, January 5, 1889.

Dear Father:

. . . The candid statement of fact is, that the meetings of the American Historical Association were extremely stupid. The meeting, you remember, was to have occurred at Columbus in September, and the result was, that we had much Western history warmed-over from then.[12] Western history is stupid anyway, I think, and

now that the Ohio centennials are over, it all seemed to have a castanean flavor, as it were.[13] Moreover, the other papers were mostly very dull, and all on very dull subjects, mine among the number.[14] Even Senator Hoar's speech at the end of the session was not anything like as good as that of two years and a half ago, when we had a really brilliant session.[15] Our presiding officer this time was W. F. Poole of Chicago, and a very poor president he was.[16] He didn't choke men off at the end of the half-hour, as he ought. Most appalling results ensued on Thursday evening. The evening meetings were held in the hall of Columbian University. Dr. Welling, the president thereof, concluded the evening's session with a most insufferably tedious paper. Well, being in his own hall, the president of the Association didn't want to shut him up, so the old chap, taking advantage of the leniency, kept it a-diggid for nearly an hour, an age it seemed.[17] There was little diversion at the meetings, except such as was furnished one evening by a very athletic kitten, who sprang from lap to lap of the "nobs" on the platform in a most determined manner. There were more nobs than usual in attendance. Indeed, the gathering was all either nobs or advanced students; the men from 27 to 37, the men whom I always find most interesting, were almost entirely absent; and of the New England historical professors, most interesting men, only one was present besides me.[18]

On the whole, I didn't get much out of the meetings,

Columbus at that date by centennial celebrations, army reunions, and political assemblies made it advisable to change the place of meeting to Washington, and the time to this later date. It was understood, however, that the scheme of topics originally proposed, in which, under the circumstances, the Northwest was likely to have a prominent place, would not be changed" (*Papers, Amer. Hist. Assn.* 3: 277, Washington, 1889).

[13] In less elegant terms, the papers were chestnuts.

[14] This was the paper on the old federal court of appeals.

[15] Two years before, Senator Hoar had paid tribute to the retiring president, George Bancroft; this time he dwelt on the advantages of Washington as a great educational center (*Papers, Amer. Hist. Assn.* 3: 262). A. B. Hart, Alexander Brown, F. W. Taussig, and Moses Coit Tyler had read papers at the earlier meeting.

[16] William F. Poole (1821-1894) had gone two years before this from Cincinnati to Chicago as first public librarian of that city. There he organized the Newberry Library and remained its head until his death.

[17] James Clarke Welling (1825-1894), despite the boredom of Jameson, was a man of wide learning and considerable achievement. He had been president of St. John's College, Annapolis, and professor of rhetoric and English literature in the College of New Jersey (Princeton) before becoming president, in 1871, of Columbian College (now George Washington University). During his administration faculties of law and medicine were created and also a school of graduate studies, his dream being to make of Washington a great educational center. His too-long paper on this occasion was a discussion of the States'-rights conflict over the public-lands (*Papers, Amer. Hist. Assn.* 3: 411-432).

[18] The one was Henry Ferguson from Trinity College, Hartford, Conn.

---

[11] Margaret and Jessie Wilson.

[12] At the second annual meeting of the American Historical Association, Saratoga, Sept. 8-10, Jameson read a paper, The Study of the constitutional and political history of the individual states, parts of which he had already read to the Hopkins seminary. At the third meeting, Washington, Apr. 27-29, 1886, he read an abstract of his monograph on Usselinx; the fourth meeting, Boston, May 21-24, he did not attend. The fifth, on which he is here reporting, was held in Washington, Dec. 26-28, 1888. This was the centennial year of the English settlement of the northwestern states and for that reason a September meeting had been planned for Columbus, Ohio. At the beginning of his presidential address, William F. Poole explained the reason for the change: "The preoccupation of

nor out of the gatherings at the Cosmos Club after them. But I had a pleasant time in the afternoons, on which there *was* no meeting. On both days I lunched at the Wards,[19] whose new abode is very pretty and pleasant. Thursday afternoon had to be spent largely in tinkering my "piece," to reduce it in size; then I went to a reception given us by General Horatio C. King,[20] (a tame affair) and out to Kendall Green to a hasty dinner, after which I donned my spike-tail and chest-protector and sallied forth. . . . I was introduced to Mr. Bancroft Davis [21] before the meeting. On the whole, I think I was lucky in having his pamphlet run across my bows. The result was, that he felt obliged to attend, and when my paper was concluded he rose and paid me quite agreeable compliments. He was only too kind, giving the audience an impression that his own had been a much slighter performance that it really was. It will give you an idea of the interest of the papers, that only mine and two others, out of about 14, elicited any remarks, and these from one man each. I am a little inclined to think the thing is getting into the hands of elderly swells who dabble in history, whereas at first it was run by young teachers, which I think made it more interesting.[22]

Friday afternoon I made some necessary calls, and dined with one of my Hopkins students. Those fellows seem to remember me with much interest and kind feeling and even affection; I saw several there and several in Baltimore. I can hardly fancy my students here ever having the same feeling toward me; but I suppose it is like the famous case of Mary and the Little Lamb. One other important item is, however, that there the history-undergraduates were with you three years, here only a year and a half at most.

It is now the Sabbath, for last night I had to stop and go out to tea. Well, the meeting of the Association ended on Friday evening, and it was decided to meet the next time at Washington, but whether at Christmas or Easter is not determined. I'm sorry they are going, apparently, to meet permanently at Washington, it is so remote. It is a good thing for Adams, and in some ways for the Association, but I think it would be better to meet at some more northern town every other time. . . .

Sunday morning I rose betimes, took breakfast with the Youngs, and went to the penitentiary to see my class. They seemed very glad to see me. . . . Then I went and hunted up Tom Warrun, who is now out of the penitentiary and making an honest living shoe-making. He had had made for me, in the prison, and presented to me, a most hideous pin-cushion with a marble base, which I have brought home and value highly, but shall not place upon my mantelpiece. Then, by way of contrast, I called on Gilman, but he was out.[23] . . .

Our course of lectures began that evening, Friday, with ex-mayor Low.[24] It was thoroughly successful, hall almost completely full, and people seemed to think it excellent, which is the main point, though Gardner and I did not think it as good a lecture as we had expected. Wilson's will be much better. Col. Wm. Goddard, president of our association, gave us a stand-up feed after it.[25]

I've been thinking of getting up an association, or a practice of annual meetings of the professors of history in New England. There are 15 or 16, nearly all young, and there is no reason why, being nearly all near, we should have our only meeting-time and place the meeting of the Am. Hist. Assoc. at Washington. The classical teachers and the English teachers in the N. E. colleges have such an organization, and I think I shall try to organize one among *our* men.[26] . . .

---

[19] Mrs. W. N. Ward of Washington and Virginia. Members of this family remained friends of Jameson until his death.

[20] The report of H. B. Adams states that the reception was given by Mr. and Mrs. Horatio King, which seems probable as they lived in Washington, whereas Horatio C. King, a son, lived in New York. King may have been one of the "elderly swells" mentioned below.

[21] J. C. Bancroft Davis (1822-1907), reporter of the Supreme Court of the United States, had been Assistant Secretary of State and had represented the United States in the Geneva Court of Arbitration. He had recently printed a small pamphlet on the subject of Jameson's paper.

[22] Of the eighty-seven who attended the meeting of 1888, about twenty were teachers. Among the others were college presidents, librarians, senators, judges, government officials, and officers of the Army and Navy. An interesting confirmation of Jameson's judgment of the atmosphere of the Association about this time is to be found in a letter from E. D. Adams to Jameson, of Dec. 21, 1914: "I remember so well the impression made upon me by the 1890 meeting in Washington when the bulk of the members present, and a very small attendance it was, seemed to me so utterly dead and the Association so little worth while. Then also I remember the meeting in 1902 in Washington with its live interests and general impression of scholarship and I marveled at the difference. A little inquiry let me know something of how all this had been accomplished, and who the men were that had done it."

[23] Saturday morning Jameson worked on manuscripts in the office of the clerk of the Supreme Court; the evening he devoted to calls in Baltimore. On Monday he worked on newspaper files in Baltimore, returning to Washington on New Year's Day that he might work in the Capitol the next two days. He was back in Providence on Thursday. His Sunday-morning calls remind one that during part of his residence in Baltimore he taught a class at the penitentiary. He also taught a Sunday School class and at one time had plans for a workingmen's club but that scheme was never carried out.

[24] Seth Low (1850-1916) about a year after this lecture became president of Columbia University, where he remained until 1901.

[25] Col. William Goddard (1828-1907), A.B., Brown, 1846, president of the Providence National Bank, and head of the mercantile firm of Brown and Ives, was for many years a member of the corporation of Brown University and a staunch supporter of the lecture association. He was at this time chancellor of the university.

[26] This became a dinner in Providence on Mar. 29, 1889. Of the seventeen New England teachers of history invited, eight accepted. The dinner meetings were not continued, as Jameson had hoped they would be, and the plan as here conceived was not fully carried out until an historical gathering at Branford, Conn., was begun in 1917. See *post*, Aug. 30, 1917, n. 157.

To Woodrow Wilson

Providence, January 22, 1889.[27]

My dear Wilson:

Another set of "Cockrell's Report" on the management of government business, has come to me, though unbound.[28] Would you like it? If so, I will send it. If you have one, I'll give this to Gardner.

It is my fixed habit, when friends are here and there is little time, never to finish a sentence. I remember that I spoke of the Athenian Empire and the Leagues, and did not go on to speak of the other two matters which you will see I have, in the same note, mentioned as omitted. This might create the impression that I regarded that as of much more importance than the other two. So I take this opportunity to say that I regard as equally important the Expansion of Hellas, so to call it, in centt. VIII, VII, and cent. III.[29]

I take it $28 will cover your fares and leave $20; so we send a check to that amount, and remain greatly your debtors for two admirable lectures.

To John Jameson

1 College Court,
Providence, Feb. 14, 1889.

Dear Father:

. . . I had an extremely pleasant visit at Peace Dale last night, and shot off my lecture with great success, especially considering that I began preparation for it at 2.30 and the train left at 4.10. (N.B. didn't run to the station.) Am growing a little more practised in speaking smoothly without notes.[30] Classroom work here is more like public lecturing than with the small classes of the J. H. U.

My juniors really delight me. Reception at Gov. Taft's[31] this P. M., to meet the General Assembly, at Providence Art Club this evening, a tea to go to on Saturday afternoon and another on the ensuing Saturday or Monday, March 4. A giddy, giddy whirl. The lecture association at Peace Dale gave me ten dollars which I did not expect. I am told that when, the other day, Mr. Tom Goddard[32] found himself, by reason of a mistake in bookkeeping discovered, $20,000 richer than he had supposed, he turned it over to the university. I don't expect to follow suit. . . .

To Albert Shaw

1 College Court,
Providence, Feb. 28, 1889.[33]

Why, yes, my dear Shaw, I have written you, and probably you have received my letter before this. When Mr. Goudy's note came, I wrote to him agreeing, and he has replied to that.[34] I supposed I had also replied to your letter preceding his, but find I did not. I thank you very much for your kind offices, and only hope I shall be able to say something not too foolish about so excellent a book.

I don't think the motive that these Edinburgh people would be good to know if I went there weighed much in my conclusion to do the bit of work,[35] for I see no

---

[27] Wilson Papers, Division of Manuscripts, Library of Congress.

[28] Francis M. Cockrell (1834-1915) served from 1875 to 1905 as United States Senator from Missouri. After leaving the Senate he was appointed by Theodore Roosevelt to the Interstate Commerce Commission. At the time of Jameson's letter he was chairman of a Senate committee appointed to "inquire into and examine the methods of business and work in the executive departments, and the cause of delay in transacting public business." The committee presented its first report in 1888 and an additional one in 1889. 50 Cong., 1 sess., Sen. Rept. 507; 51 Cong., spec. sess., 1889, Sen. Rept. 3.

[29] On Wilson's visit to Brown, Jan. 11, he left with Jameson a section of the manuscript of his forthcoming book. In his Diary Jameson wrote: "*Wed. Jan. 16* [*1889*]. went through Wilson's chapter on the governments of Greece and Rome, which he left with me for that purpose. It disappoints me greatly by its insufficiency and want of perspective and entire grasp. Of course it is very clear and well-presented."

"*Thurs. Jan. 17* [*1889*]. Spent the day, outside of classwork, mostly in a quest for Brackett and on Wilson's book, this part of which is better, though still inadequate in respect to many points of detail" (Diary, Oct. 10, 1888-Dec. 21, 1890).

Jeffrey R. Brackett (1860-1949), A.B., Harvard, 1883, Ph.D., Johns Hopkins, 1889, was at work on one of the essays for Jameson's projected volume (see *post*, Aug. 28, 1889, n. 45). From 1900 to 1904 he lectured on social work in the Johns Hopkins University; from 1904 to 1920, he was director of the School for Social Workers in Boston, a department of **Simmons College.**

[30] Peace Dale, R. I., was the home of the Hazard family, members of which were connected with Brown for many years. Rowland G. Hazard was a trustee from 1869 to 1875 and a member of the board of fellows of the Brown corporation from 1875 to 1888. For him a memorial meeting was held by the Rhode Island Historical Society shortly after Jameson began his work in Providence (*Mag. of Amer. Hist.* **20**: 511-512). With another Rowland Hazard, a trustee from 1875 to 1888 and a fellow from 1888 to 1898, Jameson had frequent intercourse.

"*Wed. Feb. 13* [*1889*]. At 2 began preparation for lecture on the Black Death at Peace Dale . . . . Nice time there; good audience; lecture went off extremely well; and most enjoyable talk with Mr. Hazard till after 12" (Diary, Oct. 10, 1888-Dec. 21, 1890).

[31] Royal Chapin Taft (1823-1912), a textile manufacturer, was governor of Rhode Island for one term, 1888, and declined renomination. He was given an A.M. by Brown in 1891.

[32] Thomas Poynton Ives Goddard (1827-1893), A.B., Brown, 1846, a member of the board of fellows of the university from 1889 to 1893, was a Providence manufacturer and president of the Boston and Providence Railroad.

[33] Manuscript Division, New York Public Library.

[34] Henry Goudy, editor of the *Juridical Review of Edinburgh.* Jameson had been asked to review Bryce's *American Commonwealth* for that journal. To his father he wrote on Mar. 6: "Have at last been able to begin the reading of Bryce. Very interesting. The only trouble is, he is so complete and correct that he leaves an ordinary reviewer little to say." The review appeared in the *Juridical Review* **1**: 204-210, April, 1889.

[35] Shaw had written: "I write this time in behalf of the new 'Juridical Review and Quarterly of Political Science' of Edin-

chance of my getting abroad for a long time, yet, if ever. But I am enjoying the thought of all you are seeing and learning. I wish I could know more about it. Do you write letters to any papers at home? I hope to goodness you don't, for you ought to have complete rest, and get rid of that insomniac look. I shall especially want to see what you say on Irish matters.[36] Our American papers all truckle to the Irish so desperately, and my weekly Times is so hopelessly partisan and so hopelessly dull, that I am left in much doubt, between thinking that Balfour is no man to manage them, nor his people, and thinking such children and such ruffians can never manage themselves, any more than those wise fools in whose capital you now sojourn.[37] I enjoy the Temps greatly. A girl in Paris

has sent me several. A sensible girl, by the way, who has been in Paris some time, and whom it might profit and please you to know, so I think I'll enclose a card of introduction which you can use if you like. Her name is Miss Evelyn Ward, and she is a Virginian. She may know things in Paris you don't, and the head of the family with whom she is travelling was once our minister to Denmark and knows people, while his wife is a daughter of your Senator Washburn. Address, 5, Avenue d'Antin.[38]

Buy me any little things that would help my work, in the line of French government, as illustrative, etc. Please remember me to Gould. At last accounts they were pulling the J.H.U. through [39]—Wilson, whom I've seen thrice, is now lecturing at J.H.U.[40] Yes, I'm here, and moderately contented. In a month or so, shall entertain here a gathering of all the history professors of S.N.E., which I am preparing. Dewey and Levermore flourish at Boston. Meeting of A.H.A. at Wash. was dull.

To WOODROW WILSON

Westport, Maine,
August 28, 1889.[41]

My dear Wilson:

You perceive that I am not wholly untrue to my statement that I was going to write to you. I can't profess to have been very prompt about it; but the summer is no time for promptness. And now the summer is nearly over, and in three weeks comes the beginning of a new college year. I shall be interested to see how far things go differently with Andrews as president. Old Perry, you remember, thought such things made little difference. At all events, Andrews may be expected to be a valuable promoter of the interests of the historical department. I expect to like him, for I

---

burgh, the first number of which appears next week. They want a review of Bryce's work, by an American, and have asked me to suggest somebody. I suggested several names, putting yours and that of H. B. Adams first. They want you to do it, if you can give the time. They can't pay for articles, as they are just starting; but the review is in the hands of *excellent* Edinburgh men, and it won't do you a bit of harm to come into relation with them. I met them when in Edinburgh, and have given them a rather random and hasty article on 'Municipal Socialism in Scotland' for the opening number . . . . Mr. Henry Goudy, advocate, is the managing editor, and he will write to you. He is a friend of Professor Kirkpatrick and the Edinb. University people whom you will want to meet when you go to Scotland. So I hope you can comply with his request and give him the article. Mr. Bryce's work has made a great sensation in England; of course I haven't seen the American reviews. Frederic Harrison reviews it in *Nineteenth Century,* and Mr. Bunting of the *Contemporary* had previously engaged Russell Lowell to review it for him; and I suppose his article will appear in the Feb. *Contemporary.* I read 'considerable' proof for Mr. B. while in London, and made a good many suggestions as to minor matters in the last volume. Mr. B. is in India this winter" (Shaw to Jameson, Jan. 10, 1889).

[36] This, it may be remembered, was one of the stormiest periods in Ireland's stormy history. Lord Salisbury, who replaced Gladstone in 1886, had made Arthur Balfour (1848-1930) chief secretary for Ireland, a position which he held until 1892. While filling the Irish jails by a rigorous enforcement of the Crimes Act, he also advocated remedial legislation. The violent anti-Irish and anti-Parnell position of the *Times* eventually brought about the appointment of a Commission of Inquiry, which in 1890 exonerated Parnell from any responsibility for the Phoenix Park murders (of the viceroy and the under-secretary for Ireland) and declared the letter which the *Times* had ascribed to Parnell, which connected him with these murders, to be a forgery. Parnell brought libel suit against the paper and was awarded £5000 damages. For a brief account of these years, see Hayden, Mary, and George A. Moonan, *A short history of the Irish people from the earliest times to 1920,* 527-533, London and N. Y., Longmans, Green, 1921.

[37] "Here in Edinboro', where I have been for about a week, I have been looked after by Mr. J. S. Black, editor of the Encyclopedia Brittanica [*sic*], and Mr. Sheriff (Judge) Mackay, Ex-Professor of Const. Law in Edinb. Univ. I owe my introductions here to Mr. Bryce, of whom I have seen a great deal. Prof. Kirkpatrick (Law and History) and other interesting men I have become acquainted with here, and the bit of a visit is proving very pleasant. Edinburgh dinners are excellent. These good men ask devout Presbyterian blessings over a fine array of wines, whiskies, etc., which I persist

abstemiously and fanatically to decline. Total abstinence seems very absurd over here, but in my feeble way I am a little bit stubborn about some things . . . . Of the Irish in Ireland also I have an experimental knowledge that is thorough. I had some adventures in Ireland that will do to talk about when I get home. At Bath (British Assoc'n) also I met some good men, read a paper on the Am. Rev. [Revenue] System 'by invitation,' and participated in numerous discussions, sitting as a member of the gen'l committee of Section 'F,' (economics and statistics). Really felt quite inflated, and was much amused" (Shaw to Jameson, Oct. 22, 1888).

[38] Charles Payson was appointed chargé d'affaires to Denmark in July, 1881. He served for about a year.

William Drew Washburn (1831-1912), senator from Minnesota, 1889-1895.

[39] The decline in income from Baltimore and Ohio railroad stock had seriously crippled the university and an emergency fund amounting to $108,700 was raised in 1889 to carry it through the crisis.

[40] Wilson, when he accepted the position at Bryn Mawr, had arranged to give a series of lectures at the Johns Hopkins the next winter, largely in order to add to his small income. This he continued to do for ten years.

[41] Wilson Papers, Division of Manuscripts, Library of Congress.

am told he is a genial, whole-souled, and upright man. I fancy he is not perfectly cultivated (I have never met him), and he will not make so imposing a figurehead as old Dr. Robinson.[42] You should have seen the old doctor at Commencement, in his gown, and with the Oxford cap upon his beautiful white hair! But indeed his manners and his sociability lagged much behind his appearance, and Andrews may do as well in impressing people, all things considered. I doubt if he is as good a thinker in philosophy, which chair he is to take in addition to the presidency. In all the other functions than these two, he will be an incomparably better president.

I haven't wholly made up my mind what to do next year with my spare time. It seems a pity to be consuming one's time with pot-boilers or with minor writings, and yet I don't feel quite at the right point for an *opus majus,* at least for any that at the moment attracts me sufficiently to ensure momentum. The history of the South from 1783 to 1827 or so, a topic of which I have spoken with you, seems hard to work in this latitude; yet I may find it possible to do more toward it than now appears. As for a book on modern historians and historiography, I have a good deal of material ready, but I fear I am not ripe enough and, like the candidates whom the mediaeval bishops used to reject, *minus sufficiens in literatura.*[43] In the summer one pauses and reflects and sees that he knows all too little. In term time he finds he can't do much about it.

I see that your book, yea even brace of books, is coming out,[44] and therefore hope you are near a point of rest. You have perhaps seen that Houghton is bringing out the volume edited by me; I wish he were doing it faster. I am not very well satisfied with it; it is but a *frustum* of what I planned, you know. I hope it won't be too awfully sat upon. (The second half of the penultimate sentence seems like an ungracious reference to friends who did not contribute, as if the absence

of their communications were its one failing; Lord! I wish it were).[45]

But meanwhile, where are you spending the summer? Beneath the patulous fage [spreading beech] I hope; but in Georgia or elsewhere? Shall you visit Boston before September 14th? If so, write to me at Winchester, Mass., and tell me when you arrive, that I may meet you and take you home with me, and set meat before you, and bid you discourse, $\Theta \epsilon \alpha$ $\epsilon o \iota \kappa \omega s$ [like a god].[46] And if Mrs. Wilson accompanies you, you will be doubly welcome. Do not come to Boston in those two weeks without letting me know, on pain of our supreme displeasure. And come to Providence whenever you can. I want to hear you talk about your "Epoch." Hart intimated that he was likely to ask you.[47] He is going to entertain us next; whether in fall or spring I do not know. . . .

To WOODROW WILSON

Providence, Oct. 1, 1889.[48]

My dear Wilson:

I have a scheme for getting you over here, which *must* succeed. We propose to begin, on the evening of Monday, November 11th, a course of about six lectures, on social reforms accomplished by legislation, or legislation for social reform, or government's action in social reform; we haven't fixed our title. But whatever the title, there will be such lectures as one on factory legislation, one by Judge Wayland[49] on prison-reform, one

---

[42] Ezekiel G. Robinson (1815-1894) was the president of Brown University from 1872 to 1889. "Old Perry" was probably Amos Perry, once described by Jameson as the despot of the Rhode Island Historical Society since 1871.

[43] Nevertheless it was to this subject that Jameson devoted a part of his leisure during the next academic years. *"Tu. Nov. 26 [1889].* In eve. read paper on Devel. of Mod. Eur. Historiog. to the R.I.H.S. It was praised but it was hardly suited to them. Rogers said there weren't half a dozen men in Providence who could have written it! I wasn't aware there were that number of men in America who had examined the subject" (Diary, Oct. 10, 1888-Dec. 21, 1890). A revision of this paper was published in the *Atlantic Monthly* 66: 322-333, September, 1890. Four articles on the History of historical writing in America appeared in the *New England Magazine,* January, February, March, and April, 1891, and were that same year brought out by Houghton Mifflin as a small volume.

[44] *The State: elements of historical and practical politics: a sketch of institutional history and administration,* Boston, D. C. Heath, 1889.

[45] *Essays in the constitutional history of the United States in the formative period, 1775-1789.* By Graduates and Former Members of the Johns Hopkins University. Edited by J. Franklin Jameson, Late Associate in the John Hopkins University, Professor of History in Brown University, Boston, Houghton Mifflin, 1889. The subjects treated in the completed volume were: the predecessor of the Supreme Court, by Jameson; the movement towards a second Constitutional Convention in 1789, by Edward P. Smith; the development of the executive departments, 1775-1789, by Jay C. Guggenheimer; the period of constitution-making in the American churches, by William P. Trent; the status of the slave, 1775-1789, by Jeffrey R. Brackett.

[46] Wilson replied that he was to be in Boston early in September and on Sept. 8 he visited Winchester, as Jameson here suggested.

[47] Albert Bushnell Hart (1854-1943), teacher of history and government in Harvard from 1883 until 1926, when he became professor emeritus. Jameson gave no hint to Wilson that he had been asked by Hart to write the final volume of the series American Epochs, but had declined and had probably suggested Wilson's name as a possible author. In this series, published by Longmans, Green and Company, Hart himself wrote *Formation of the Union, 1750-1829;* Thwaites, R. G., *The Colonies, 1492-1750* (to be replaced in 1929 by Jernegan's *The American Colonies, 1492-1750);* Wilson supplied *Division and reunion, 1827-1889.* The latest "Epoch" to appear was the work of Bassett, J. S., *Expansion and reform,* 1926.

[48] Wilson Papers, Division of Manuscripts, Library of Congress.

[49] Francis Wayland, son of a former president of Brown bearing the same name, was at this time dean of the Yale Law School.

on state charities, one on the relations of the state to education, etc. For the opening lecture, we want one which shall treat, in a scholarly fashion and with impartiality, the opposing theories respecting the functions of government in such matters; a lecture of this sort, on *laissez faire* and t'other notion, would fitly introduce our course.

I will frankly say that we tried to get Walker [50] to give us this lecture; because I think that there is more of compliment than of the reverse in saying that, since we can't get him, owing to engagements, we want you to come and deliver a lecture on this subject for us. Terms as last year, I am sorry to say. But pray do come. It is vain to say that that isn't just exactly the subject for you, because it evidently is, exactly. So I assume that you will come. Nevertheless, as M. Jourdain would say, make believe that I do not, and write me that you will; [51] write soon, if you can.

Everything starts well with Andrews. Remember me most kindly to Mrs. Wilson and the olive plants.

To ALBERT SHAW

1 College Court,
Providence, Oct. 27, 1889.[52]

My dear Shaw:

Adams gives me your address, and I hasten to write and inquire whether, now you are starring it around the country, you can't come here and lecture some Monday evening after November 11th and before December 16th to the Brown University Historical and Economic

Association, an association of the best of the graduates, which some of us founded last year, to support a lecture course. In November and December we are going to have a course of lectures on social reforms, or more specifically those effected through legislation. Wilson opens, with a lecture on the theories of the function of the state in the matter. Judge Wayland lectures on prison reform. Taussig lectures on workingmen's insurance, compulsory and voluntary. Dr. Edw. Everett Hale winds up, with an informal talk on the state and charities.[53] There'll be one or two more.

Now you will see at once that this is just the course in which you ought to figure. There must be many topics within its scope on which your American experience or European observation would enable you to lecture. There were such in your article on Municipal Socialism in Scotland. Pray consent, if it is a possible thing, to come here and lecture, however informally. We are not able to promise you sudden wealth as the result, but we will pay your expenses and give you a nice ten-dollar bill; and you will also receive a warm welcome from, and a precious opportunity to converse with, Yours very sincerely, J. F. Jameson.[54]
P. S. I hope you're going to Cornell. Adams doubts if they can offer sufficient pecuniary temptations against the Tribune. I'll tell you, though you probably know it, that they gave Andrews $4000, or so I was told.[55]

To JOHN JAMESON

All Saints' Day, 1889.

Dear Father:

. . . No, my book is not out yet.[56] As I was carrying

[50] Francis A. Walker (1840-1897), A.B., Amherst, 1860, president of the Massachusetts Institute of Technology, 1881-1897, had before coming to the Institute been superintendent of the census for 1870 and 1880 and had taught political economy in the Sheffield Scientific School, Yale. The Diary record is: *"Wed. Nov. 28* [1888]. Talked with Gen. Walker, who cannot lecture to us. He invited me to dine with him, and go in the evening to the meeting of the Wed. Eve. Club." Though President Walker was unable to deliver the opening lecture, he spoke in the Brown series on Dec. 9, 1889. To H. B. Adams, Jameson wrote: "Walker's slaughter of Bellamy in the February 'Atlantic' by the way, was his lecture given here in our course" (Holt, *op. cit.,* 129). Of the lecture as it appeared in the *Atlantic,* the *Nation* commented: "The Socialists who go under the name of Nationalists will also find instructive matter in the vigorous exposure of Mr. Bellamy's gospel by Francis Walker, in which sarcastic as the writer is, the most biting passages are his clear statements of the exact meaning of the new doctrines; but President Walker plainly labors at a disadvantage from the flimsiness of the case he demolishes with his root-and-branch logic" (*Nation* **50:** 94, Jan. 20, 1890).
[51] M. Jourdain, the rich tradesman of Moliere's *Le Bourgeois Gentilhomme* (1670), who wishes to be instructed in music, dancing, fencing, and philosophy that he may be accepted as a gentleman of quality. When the professor of philosophy answers a remark of his with a Latin phrase and adds, "You understand that. You know Latin of course," M. Jourdain replies, "Yes; but do as if I did not know it. Explain to me what that means." M. Jourdain's astonishment when he learns that he has been speaking *prose* all his life has passed into a proverb, "Faire de la prose sans le savoir" (Act II, scene 6).
[52] Manuscript Division, New York Public Library.

[53] Frank W. Taussig (1859-1940) for long a distinguished teacher of economics in Harvard University.
Edward Everett Hale (1822-1909), during his forty-five years as a Boston clergyman, had been connected with innumerable charitable organizations, both public and private.
[54] Shaw replied: "I am delighted to hear from you, and flattered by your invitation; but the 'starring' as you call it is so systematized that new dates cannot be made. To drop the theatrical advance tone, let me say that after getting through here I am to spend some days at Baltimore beginning Friday Nov. 8, and some days at Ann Arbor beginning Monday Nov. 18. From Ann Arbor I must go back to Minneapolis" (Shaw to Jameson, Ithaca, Oct. 29, 1889).
[55] Adams had written to Jameson on Oct. 25: "I hope Shaw will prove the coming man at Cornell. He is disposed to return to Academic life, but he now has a $3,000 position as editor of the Minneapolis Tribune, and President Adams [Charles K.] will need to open the chest at Cornell in order to capture so good a professor." Again on Apr. 30, 1890, Adams expressed the hope that Shaw would be elected professor of political science in Cornell. In reply to this letter of Jameson, Shaw wrote from Ithaca, on Oct. 29, 1889: "About the place here of course I don't know as yet. I'm not a candidate, nor am I on the other hand unwilling to entertain proposals. Do you think me equal to a job of this sort? Could you honestly recommend a shilly-shally fellow like me for a dignified professorship? I know I can do newspaper work. Is it safe to trust me in any other line?"
[56] That is, the *Essays in Constitutional history.* The book appeared between the writing of this letter and the next one.

my last letter to you down to the mail, in which I spoke of Dodd, Mead and Co.'s invitation, "the thought come to me" that I could make it further some of my ulterior plans by consenting to write a little book on Richard Henry Lee.[57] I hadn't previously thought of anyone it would profit or help me to do, but *that* seemed a good suggestion, and I may do it. There has been no life of him save a poor one by his grandson sixty-four years ago,[58] and there are documents in existence, to which I could have access through introductions from Mrs. Ward. Having nothing on Fridays and Saturdays this term, I have a vacation that lasts from noon of Dec. 19 to night of Jan. 5, which I can spend at Richmond if necessary. I shall hate to do so, but may have to, in order to do the book properly, so I send word seasonably in advance. A friend here thinks someone is on that job now. I've written to find out. In that case I shall let it alone, though Dodd wants me to do it anyway, regardless of that. . . .

To John Jameson

Providence, Nov. 17, 1889.

My dear Father:

. . . I hear many pleasant expressions from my friends about my book, and only hope the press will be equally complimentary.[59] It is not to be expected that it should be wholly so, however, for the book, though in the main a good one, has some weak points, and never quite satisfied me. I got very pleasant letters about it from

Adams, from Aunt Martha, etc. Judge Bancroft Davis, reporter S.C.U.S., not only wrote a very pleasant letter, but sent me one of the thirty copies, privately and separately issued, of his appendix to the centennial volume (131) of the U. S. Reports. It is very handsomely bound, with portraits of all the chief justices, and contains a historical account of the judiciary under the Confederation, all omitted opinions that he can find, and an interesting list of all the cases in which the Supreme Court has held U. S. or state laws contrary to the Constitution of the U. S. So that "free copy" cast upon the waters did very well by me.

I find old Mr. Lee has a large book on R. H. Lee about done, and don't think he will want a small one published.[60] Shall know conclusively in a few days. Our course of lectures opened excellently. Fine audience. Increasing membership of Association. I did not see as much of Wilson as I could have wished, as he was guest of Andrews. Tomorrow night's lecture conflicts with Salvini, so we may not have so good an audience for Rev. Mr. Brooks.[61] After that I have no fear as to the rest. . . . Just as I was going by letter to tackle Mr. Hazard to start a sub. to fill up the Diman Fund[62] by subscribing $1000, after having tried in vain to see him, he sets off for Europe ten days earlier than he expected, daughter being sick there, and leaves $1000 to the physics dept. as compensation for his absence from the building committee on the new phys. lab. !

---

[57] On October 25, Jameson had written: "There was an emissary of the devil here this afternoon, in the shape of Mead, of Dodd, Mead and Co., trying to tempt me to write a book for a series of 'Makers of America' they are going to get up." The Diary record is: *"Fri. Oct. 25.* I didn't think much of it, —hate to have my work be something laid out for me by a publisher—but afterward it occurred to me that a book on R. H. Lee might be a good introduction to my Southern subjects; and the Wards know all the Lees, and I have so long a vacation this Christmas that I could examine what there is at Richmond, Charlottesville, Stratford and Ravenswood, as well as at Washington. But if I'm going to do it, I'd rather do it for the 'Statesman' Series,—a better series, though in this other Sumner does Hamilton and Schouler does Jefferson" (Diary, Oct. 10, 1888-Dec. 21, 1890).

William Graham Sumner (1840-1910), professor of political and social science, Yale University, wrote for the series the life of Robert Morris as well as that of Hamilton.

Jameson's "'ulterior plans" were for a history of the South, of which he had begun to think while in the Johns Hopkins, where he was building up in the university library a collection of material for the study of Southern history. He still clung to the idea for some time after he settled in Providence and his trip to Virginia in 1891, described in later letters, was with this task in mind. Eventually, however, he concluded that Providence was too far from his material to make the project feasible.

[58] *The memoir of the life of Richard Henry Lee,* by his grandson, R. H. Lee, 2v., 1825.

[59] The review of the *Essays* which appeared in the *Political Science Quarterly* 5: 696-697, December, 1890, was on the whole favorable, giving greatest praise to the essays of Trent and Brackett. Jameson's own essay was dismissed briefly.

[60] *"Fri. Nov. 8* [*1889*]. Mr. Scudder found a letter from Charles H. Lee (to whom a letter from Cassius F. Lee had referred me); he has a book on R. H. Lee, of 1200 pp. MS., about ready. This renders doubtful the Dodd, Mead scheme" (Diary, Oct. 10, 1888-Dec. 21, 1890). Apparently this manuscript was never published. The gap in American history remained in Jameson's mind and twenty years later his advice and aid induced the Colonial Dames to finance the publication of two volumes of Lee's *Letters,* edited by James C. Ballagh, N. Y., Macmillan, 1911-1914.

[61] The Italian actor, Tommaso Salvini, was making what was to be his final tour of the United States. Jameson had seen and greatly admired him in Othello in Baltimore two years before.

John Graham Brooks (1846-1938), though an ordained minister, served no church but wrote and lectured on economic subjects, chiefly in the field of labor.

[62] When Jameson went to Brown he found that after the death of one of his predecessors, Jeremiah L. Diman, an effort had been made to raise $10,000 to be called the Diman Memorial Fund, the income of which was to be used to buy books in mediaeval and modern history for the university library. Only $1500 had been raised and the income from this could not be used until the entire sum was achieved. As an untried source of gifts Jameson turned to the Providence women who had been in private classes offered by Professor Diman and from them nearly $6000 was received. In the spring of 1891 a special appeal was made to all the classes that had been in the university during Professor Diman's terms of service and Jameson had the satisfaction of seeing the $10,000 fully subscribed.

To John Jameson

Providence, Nov. 19, 1889.

My dear Father:

. . . I also am disappointed in Smith's paper,[63] not because he did not say all he could on his subject, for I think he found out all there was to find, but because he weakened the effect of it as a piece of new work by retailing all the old chestnuts about the ratifying conventions, which only partially and indirectly concerned him, for the most part. It would be better without this padding. His and Trent's are to my mind the unsatisfactory ones, though both are interesting.[64]

I don't know when my article in the Atlantic will appear,[65]—not for some months, I suppose,—nor how much they are likely to bestow on the gifted author. You will be glad to know that I'm not going to write up the late R. H. Lee, and I am rather relieved myself. . . .[66]

To Arthur H. Jameson

Providence, February 25 [1890].

My dear Brother: [67]

. . . Except for sympathy with your regret I should not be at all disturbed about your marks, because I know you have done good work; I wish my young men here did me as good. But I am very sorry you don't think you are getting as much good as you ought out of your college work. Perhaps you expect too much from it. Its profitableness will shine more conspicuous if you compare its effects with those of a year not spent in study at all. Perhaps you can't even by that device, fully realize the gain which it is bringing to you; but you may be confident that the gain is there, all the same; our own growth is something we seldom appreciate.

If your courses aren't giving you all you could wish, my idea of a remedy would be, that you should not feel tied down to them too much, but should give yourself some latitude in respect to interesting reading. It makes no difference to you or to me whether you get good marks this remaining half-year, it being your last. So, without at all neglecting your chemistry or your German, I advise you do a good-sized amount of reading these ensuing four months. Do it in any line that interests you, but it might be especially well, after finishing Darwin (or before if you choose), to read things connected with Greek life and literature. I especially recommend you to read, for a combination of Greek and psychology, Frederick W. H. Myers' essay on Greek Oracles, in his Classical Essays, a very ingenious and interesting thing. Have you ever read Mahaffy's Social Life in Greece, or his Rambles and Studies in Greece? They are very bright books. Or, read R. C. Jebb's Modern Greece; or D. J. Snider's A Walk in Hellas; or Eunice W. Felton's art. in Atlantic, Domestic Country Life in Greece; or Lawton's recent Atlantic arts.[68] Then, II. you can read good translations, either (a) those you possess, if you haven't read them through, or (b) others, whether (1) of a literary sort, under which head I would recommend (a) Aristophanes either in (a) the very amusing versions of Hookham Frere, or (b) those of B. B. Rogers, and (b) more Aeschylus (Plumptre) [69] and perhaps (c) a good many of old Herodotus' yarns; or, and here I think I have a good suggestion for *you*, (2) the scientific and practical, such (a) as Aristotle's History of Animals or (b) Xenophon's Oeconomica, which they claim is a good book, or (c) his Cynegetica. (We are now in paragraph 951.)

You will say that you could be reading where you are not paying tuition. That is only partly true. You will never again, for a long time, have so good a chance for general reading, and moreover you will do it to much better purpose while you are occupied in Greek studies. I consider it quite as much a legitimate way of spending your time as on your studies, and when these fail to give you what you want, I should neglect them, and get it elsewhere. I am perfectly willing you should devote your time to pleasure these next four months, provided it is intellectual pleasure; and don't read anything that *doesn't* give pleasure to the mind,

---

[63] "I reread yesterday your paper therein [*Essays*] and then read Smith's which I was much interested but somewhat disappointed in. You see its title deceived me, as from it I had expected to find (unreasonably perhaps) disclosures of some movement secret till now, or at all events of which I knew nothing" (John Jameson to Jameson, Nov. 18, 1889). The paper by Edward P. Smith was, The movement towards a second Constitutional Convention in 1788.

[64] William P. Trent's contribution, The period of constitution-making in the American churches, was the topic originally suggested to Shaw.

[65] Probably, The development of modern European historiography, which appeared in September, 1890. See *ante,* Aug. 28, 1889, n. 43.

[66] Some years later Charles D. Warner asked Jameson to write the life of Motley for the American Men of Letters series. From notes among the Jameson Papers it would seem that he gave the idea some consideration but on May 7, 1893, he wrote to his father: "I concluded to fight shy of the Motley book. It would take too much time." He did write, John Lothrop Motley (1814-1877), as the introduction to selections from Motley's *Rise of the Dutch Republic* included in Warner, Charles Dudley, ed., *Library of the world's best literature* 17: 10373-10380, N. Y., International Society, 1897.

[67] Jameson's younger brother Arthur, at this time in the middle of his second year in Harvard, intended to enter the Massachusetts Institute of Technology the following autumn, to study engineering.

[68] Eunice W. Felton's article appeared in the *Atlantic Monthly* 50: 675-685, November, 1882; William C. Lawton's The closing scenes of the Iliad, and, Delphi: the locality and its legends, in the same periodical, 64: 482-499, 801-813, October, December, 1889.

[69] *The works of John Hookham Frere,* collected by his nephews and published in 1872, contained translations of Aristophanes; the translations of Aeschylus by Edward H. Plumptre (1821-1891), published after his death, are to be found in *Tragedies and fragments,* Boston, Heath, 1901, and *Nine Greek dramas,* N. Y., Collier, 1909.

even though it come highly recommended by the undersigned. It is only a little space now, so cheer up; I am sure you are not wasting time, but will be a more capable engineer than those who have not read Ladd and Zeller.[70]

To WOODROW WILSON

1 College Court,
Providence, March 9, 1890.[71]

My dear Wilson:

I have so long delayed writing to you that now I am uncertain whether you are at Baltimore or whether you have returned to your "respective home." I'll address to the latter at a venture; and hope you have had a prosperous session at the former. I have heard from Mrs. Carey[72] that you were ill during a part of the time, but hope that that is now far back in the past. I hope, too, that Mrs. Wilson has fully recovered from the accident, of which I was extremely sorry to hear.[73] While you were in Baltimore I got some news of you and others in a pleasant letter from Adams. He was, as usual, in a high state of satisfaction with the progress of the Association, but I, for my part, have my doubts about some of its developments,—and made free to tell him so.[74] It seems to me to be giving more

and more weight to those members who are simply "prominent citizens," presidents of local historical societies and that class of person, distinguished for being distinguished, and to be injuring its scientific value by striving to achieve popular distinction and prestige. But I may be wrong; I was unable to be present at this last meeting.

I am using your book, and at present enjoying the use of it, though, if you will not exclaim with Canning, "But of all plagues, kind Heaven, thy wrath can send, Save, save, or save me from the candid friend!"[75] I will say that I think the chapter on Germany, which we have just traversed, includes too many details. I did not think so until I came to use that chapter with a class; but they found it very hard. I am noting misprints, as well as a few things which seem to me to be errors, in order some time to send them to you, and chasten, what must needs be chastened in every man, your pride as a proof reader.

I do not know that there is any valuable historical news to be forwarded hence, save that Weeden's *Economic History of New England* is nearly through the press.[76] I am convinced that it will be thought a highly

[70] A number of Edward Zeller's books had already appeared in English translation; among others, *A history of Greek philosophy,* 1881, and *Plato and the older Academy,* 1888. During Jameson's senior year in Amherst he borrowed from Professor Root one of Zeller's works and after Root's death he asked his father to obtain this volume from Root's library for him.

The best-known Ladd of this period was George Trumbull Ladd (1842-1921), a teacher of psychology and philosophy in Yale University from 1881 to 1921. Before the date of this letter he had published a number of works on psychology and his *Introduction to philosophy,* more in line with Jameson's other recommendations to his young brother, may have just appeared.

[71] Wilson Papers, Division of Manuscripts, Library of Congress.

[72] Mrs. Martha Carey, daughter of Mrs. Ward of Washington, and a resident of Baltimore. In her home many of the graduate students of the Johns Hopkins were entertained. Her daughter later became the wife of Frederick M. Warren, one of Jameson's Baltimore companions and long a professor in Yale.

[73] Mrs. Wilson had recently suffered a distressing burn. Wilson to Jameson, Jan. 6, 1890.

[74] On Oct. 24, 1889, Jameson had written to Adams a letter which brought forth a reply on Oct. 25: "In my recent letter to Dr. Hart, I had no notion of repressing young men, but of properly representing the 'old boys' at the next annual meeting. There was some gentle criticism from men like Dr. G. Brown Goode, to the effect that we had too many youngsters on our programme. I believe in young blood, but we must preserve a proper balance between the boys and the patriarchs. If you can give me any valuable hints regarding the makeup of the next programme, I shall be greatly obliged." No direct answer to this letter has been found.

Jameson's specific reference here is to a letter from Adams of Feb. 5, 1890, in which he wrote: "The American Historical Association is now well established in connection with the Smithsonian Institution and the National Museum. Professor

Langley has granted every request that we have made. I regard this new connection as the best stroke ever made for historical organization in this country. We are now planning to secure the co-operation of the State Historical Societies, and shall soon issue a revised version of the enclosed letter." The connection with the Smithsonian to which Adams refers, was accomplished by the act incorporating the Association, Jan. 4, 1889.

Jameson, on Feb. 21, 1890, protested to Adams against the effort to bring into the Association local historical societies, as likely to lower the quality of scholarship represented. "This year, for the first time in the history of the Association, I think, its executive council is mainly composed of persons who do no teaching of history. Now I consider the hope of good historical writing in the future to rest with the teachers, now that the instruction of graduates has reached such an extension as to make 'schools,' personal followings, and the learning of the trade possible. The historical societies I consider of little account intellectually, except as trustees of material and as possible furtherers of publication . . . . A movement to maintain and strengthen the alliance with the professorial body appears to me, therefore, likely to be of more benefit to the *quality* of the Association's operations than this" (Holt, *op cit.,* 128). The executive council of 1890 consisted of G. Brown Goode, assistant secretary of the Smithsonian Institution; John G. Bourinot, clerk of the Canadian House of Commons; two librarians—Justin Winsor and William F. Poole; George Bancroft; Andrew D. White; and George P. Fisher, professor of ecclesiastical history in Yale.

[75] George Canning (1770-1827), in New morality. Canning, it may be remembered, was the author of the rhymed despatch to a British minister:

"In matters of Commerce the fault of the Dutch
Is offering too little and asking too much"

[76] William B. Weeden (1834-1912), one of Jameson's earliest Providence friends, is frequently referred to in the Diary. "*Sun. Nov. 25* [*1888*]. spent a large part of the evening talking over his book with him."

"*Wed. Apr. 10* [*1889*]. In eve. the 'historical group' of the B.U.H. and E. Assoc. [Brown University Historical and Economic Association] met at Mr. Weeden's. He read a chapter of his book and we talked. An auspicious start."

important and valuable contribution, as well as a very laborious piece of truly original research. Our lecture course was exceedingly successful. During our first course our hall was full every night, crowded sometimes, and even in the second, with less popular topics, we had larger audiences than last year. The Boston Herald had an editorial commending the movement as a new move of the Andrews administration, quite oblivious of the three mighty men who last year fought their way through to the remote wells of Middletown and elsewhere, and brought thence refreshment for our thirsty college and its friends. But we don't mind that, for really we are delighted with the success with which Andrews is urging the college forward and at the favorable turn which public opinion respecting it is taking. To speak a moment of material things, I am, on my own account, carrying on a still-hunt for subscriptions to the Diman Fund, and, though it is new business for me, have so far $4500 of the necessary $8500 from five people (out of six I have so far spoken to). But don't tell anyone of this; for I am not certain of the remainder till I get it. . . . I hear nothing from Hart, and hardly like to poke him up. It is not impossible that Mrs. Hart may be in a state which makes them unwilling to entertain. In that case, would you like to have them (i.e. the men) come to Middletown? If you would, I can use that on Hart, delicately, so as to make him show his hand. Morse is ill, and probably cannot ask us. Write me soon about this.[77]

I suppose one may properly congratulate you, if what I hear is true;[78] you will enjoy your life there, but I shall be sorry to have you and Mrs. Wilson leave New England. I suppose Turner is booked for Allen's place.[79] Is there a better man in the country to take yours than Levermore? I know he would go there, and, with your consent and in support of your efforts if they tend that way, I should be glad to write to Raymond on his behalf, for I have great respect for his abilities and acquirements.[80]

[77] Wilson replied that he was unable to invite the group to Middletown. So far as the editors know, there was no successor to the dinner for New England historians given by Jameson.

[78] After a year of doubt, Wilson's appointment to Princeton was now certain.

[79] Professor W. F. Allen's death had occurred early in January. Frederick J. Turner, who had been in the department of history of Wisconsin for a year, was retained and after another year Charles H. Haskins, an instructor in the Johns Hopkins University, was called to Madison. He and Turner had received their Ph.D. degrees from the Johns Hopkins in 1890; Haskins at the age of twenty.

[80] In a reply written on Mar. 20, Wilson agreed that Levermore, then in the Massachusetts Institute of Technology, would be an excellent choice but doubted whether he could be appointed. The position was, after some time, filled by Max Farrand.

Bradford Paul Raymond (1846-1916) was the president of Wesleyan from 1889 to 1908.

To John Jameson

Nov. 24, 1890.

Dear Father:

Hooray! Also Whoop te Doodle! I have done likewise my dreaded lecture in the B.U.H. and E.A.[81] course in two days,—or at any rate two days and two hours. And for this I had not as for the "Spanish Historians," the aid of any previous lecture.[82] I'm much pleased. I said to myself I'd do it, and I done it,—and am none the worse for it, and can spend the P.M. and eve. and tomorrow A.M. with Morse[83] with a clear conscience. Tomorrow evening the Boys' Club opens.[84] Wednesday I must make some beginning on my second lecture on the Sp. Hists., if other writing doesn't spring up to prevent. . . . I will bring my lecture home. I think you'll be interested in it.

To Albert Shaw

1 College Court,
Providence, April 11, 1891.[85]

My dear Shaw:

I thank you very much for your kindness in sending me the first number of your new "Review."[86] I appreciate the difficulties of which you speak, but am sure that even this first number does not require anything like the indulgence you suggest. It seems to me that you are doing a good and useful work, so useful that I rather think I shall subscribe to it when I get a little time to think. What you are pleased to term

[81] Brown University Historical and Economic Association. In the lecture series which this organization sponsored Jameson was to lecture, Dec. 1, on the Origin of political parties in the United States.

[82] Of the lecture on the Spanish historians, built up from a part of the Baltimore lectures of 1887, Jameson wrote: "Sat. Nov. 1 [1890]. Having resolved last night that I would do that lecture in two days, I worked at the top of my speed, and got, if not half, at any rate 5/12 of it done before I went to bed."

"Sun. Nov. 2. Worked at the top of my speed all day, except that 5.25-6.05 I walked to Red Bridge, and at 10.40 my lecture was done. Quite an achievement for two days, I think. But I am tired." The lecture was delivered to the Rhode Island Women's Club on Nov. 5. On Dec. 3, he gave to this group a second lecture on the same subject, this time completed late in the morning of the day it was delivered.

[83] "Mon. Nov. 24 [1890]. Morse came at 4, and at 8 gave us an exceedingly fine lecture on 'Political Parties,'—wise and thoughtful and fair. Enjoyed talk with him."

The final lecture of the series on political parties in the United States, was delivered by Levermore, who spoke on the rise of the Whig party (Providence Journal, Dec. 16, 1890).

[84] During Jameson's early years in Providence the Boys' Club took the place of his Baltimore visits to the group in the penitentiary.

[85] Manuscript Division, New York Public Library.

[86] With the copy of the Review of Reviews, Shaw wrote: "If you knew how many practical difficulties we have been obliged to encounter in getting out this April number, sympathy would well up to such an extent that your critical judgment would have no chance to get in its deadly work" (Shaw to Jameson, Apr. 6, 1891).

severe scholarly and critical standards are, it seems to me, much better satisfied than you intimate. May I make one suggestion? With all recognition of your better knowledge of what should be done a suggestion from a single individual may sometimes be helpful. An exceedingly valuable part of the publication for my purposes is the monthly record of current events; and I should be very glad to see this summary carried to greater length. I used to value quite as much as anything else in the "Nation" the two pages of summary of the week's news, which that paper formerly contained, and was very sorry it dropped the practice. What I should like to see would be, like that, a record in which each item of news was developed a little more than it is in the brief jottings which your review contains on pages 233 and 234, and fuller obituaries, in some cases. Until I received your letter I had not observed the complimentary remarks which you utter respecting my highly valuable publication. Having my attention thus drawn to the matter, I proceeded to read them, and at once found my confidence in the good judgment with which the Review is to be managed seriously impaired. However, I am very much obliged to you.[87]

I suppose it is impossible for you to get away and it certainly is impossible for me to do so, but I heartily wish I could see you even once in a while. Perhaps I may get the poor consolation of an hour or two with you when I go through New York on the 5th of May on my way to lecture at the J.H.U.[88] I hope you may very much enjoy your new work. I watch everything you do with the greatest interest, and *confidence,* and high respect.

---

[87] The comment on the contents of the *New England Magazine* was: "Prof. J. F. Jameson of Brown University continues his invaluable papers on 'The History of Historical Writing in America.' These papers constitute the most important critical and informational review that has ever been made of the development of American historical literature. Their appearance in book form will be awaited with much interest." (*Review of Reviews* 3: 299, April, 1891).

[88] In May, 1891, Jameson was to deliver at the Johns Hopkins University a series of ten lectures on the history of the South, his return to be $250. When these were completed he was to spend some weeks in Virginia, searching for historical material. About his preparation of these lectures he wrote to his father, Apr. 15, 1891: "Lectures booming too. Monday and Tuesday prepared and dictated the whole of the second one. Today pitch into 3d; rule, one every three days." And to his brother he wrote on Apr. 26: "I am prospering with my lectures; the sixth is nearly done. I have just received an invitation to give four lectures at the Peabody Institute in Baltimore next winter, and receive $400 therefor; not 'wholly unsolicited' but agreeable." After reaching Baltimore he reported: "My lectures have opened up satisfactorily. They come opportunely, for a very large collection of books and pamphlets respecting Southern history has just been presented to the University. So the papers have reported my lectures, which is not usual with class lectures, and a good many older men around town seem to have taken an interest in them." (Jameson to Arthur H. Jameson, Baltimore, May 10, 1891). The gift to which reference is made was from Col. J. Thomas Scharf.

Believe me, with very best wishes for the prosperity of the *Review* and of yourself,
P. S.   I subscribe, and enclose $2.00.

To JOHN JAMESON
                                    Baltimore, May 22, 1891.
Dear Father:
    . . . Adams has lent me (don't say anything about this save at home, because it is perhaps doubtful whether he ought to have done it) two MS. volumes containing the journals which Jared Sparks kept during historical tours in the South in 1826, 1827, etc. He was engaged in just such errands in Virginia as mine will be, the search for historical MSS., and therefore his journals contain much information which may prove of value to me. So I have felt it necessary to go through them and take notes, as I may not have a chance to see them again.[89] . . .

To JOHN JAMESON
                                    Richmond, May 31, 1891.
My dear Dad:
    I wish you were here. You would enjoy this very much. I've no doubt I miss a great deal of the interest which would be felt by one who remembers the war as you do. I don't remember it, and I'm not well read in it, and you'd get much more out of it in that way.

    However, in my own line and for my own purpose I am going, I am sure, to have much profit from the visit. Not much has been accomplished yet, except in the way of getting acquainted. I got here yesterday afternoon. The ride from Washington is uninteresting. You go through the poorest part of the state, gravelly soil, and sparse population. Fredericksburg is interesting, and Ashland is as pretty a village as one would see in New England, not down at the heels like most Southern villages. Randolph-Macon College was removed to A. some years ago. Henry Clay was born near it. The recent constant rains have swollen the "Jeems" River, and made it more than usually muddy.

    I put up at the Davis House, at Lawford's[90] suggestion:—all the Richmond hotels are bad. Today I have begun to board at Col. Colston's, father-in-law of Professor Gildersleeve of J. H. U., and tomorrow I get into a room opposite there. My address for about two weeks will therefore be, In care of H. D. Hoge [pron. Hōg] 716 E. Franklin St., Richmond. Mrs. Hoge and Mrs. Colston will make me very comfortable, I expect. The latter's husband is one of the officials of the record-

---

[89] Adams was probably at work upon his *Life and Writings of Jared Sparks,* which appeared in 1893. This would account for the fact that he had these journals in his possession. The notes made by Jameson are still among the Jameson Papers.

[90] J. W. Lawford, a member of the insurance firm of Lawford and McKim of Baltimore, had been a table companion of Jameson in his Hopkins days. Lawford was a descendant of the Mauduit family and at one time provided Jameson with considerable information about Jasper Mauduit.

office, and an old historical scholar sits next me. By the way, he says they are going to pay the debt.[91] Mrs. Colston's daughters are agreeable women of the Virginian type, and make things pleasant for a stranger. So also do the grandchildren, and the young men who board,—Mr. Randolph Tucker, nephew of J. R. T.,[92] and others. Admirable grub and great sociability of cultivated people, and all for about the price Annie[93] pays for the privilege of feed and social intercourse at Mrs. Knapp's.

Yesterday I called on the secretary of the Va. Hist. Soc.,[94] who promises me aid. After that, I was prevented by heavy rains from walking about the city or even getting a map. In the evening Lawford and Geo. Williams came from Baltimore, and this morning they left for "Lawford," P.O.; G. is going to look at some mineral lands near L.'s farm for him. I had a lot of Brown and other writing in the evening and to-day.

Tomorrow I am to be taken to see the treasures of the Va. Hist. Soc. and the Capitol, and shall make further acquaintances. I have eight or nine introductions to prominent people, historical and other, from Baltimore friends, and shall soon know everybody that is worth my while to know. Today I made two calls, on Mr. Beverly Crump and Mrs. Peyton Wise, and have met the secretary of state.[95] These Virginians certainly are nice sociable people, and treat you exceedingly well. People you have known ten minutes offer to introduce you to anybody they think it will be useful for you to know, or to write you letters of introduction to friends at country-houses. So it takes no time to get acquainted, even if they are pretty slow in other things.[96]

Richmond is a beautiful city. Not so beautiful as Providence, but very pretty. Somewhat like Providence and Worcester. Very hilly. This hotel adjoins the Capitol grounds, which are as beautiful as the campus of Brown. On the top of the hill are the Capitol (like old chapel at Amherst, but bigger and with no tower) and the official residence of the governor. Va. Hist. Soc. (in Westmoreland Club House) and Capitol are near together, and 716 E. Franklin is between the two. June 10 occurs the 150th anniversary of St. John's Church, Henrico Parish. . . .

To John Jameson

Richmond, June 11, 1891.

My dear Father:

. . . You would have enjoyed being with me last night, and I should have enjoyed having you. They celebrated the 150th anniversary of old St. John's Church, Henrico Parish, in which Patrick Henry made his memorable speech to the Convention of 1775 ("Give me liberty," etc.), and Mr. Wm. Wirt Henry, his grandson, president of the Va. Hist. Soc., gave a historical address.[97] He has not his grandfather's eloquence, but the place was eloquent. They showed me the pew in which tradition says Henry stood. Col. Edw. Carrington,[98] as a young man, heard the speech, looking in at a window, and at his request is buried outside just under that window. The yard is full of old flat tombs of Richmond worthies. Gov. John Page and Chancellor Wythe are buried there.[99] I shall have a great deal to tell you when I come home. I mustn't write at great length, because I must get in all the work I can at the Capitol and Va. Hist. Soc. Had some talk with Judge Crump yesterday about Ritchie and the Polk campaign,[100] and about Judge Marshall, whom he knew. . . .

---

[91] The "historical scholar" was probably William P. Palmer, editor of the first volume of the *Virginia Calendar of State Papers.* Years later Jameson quoted to Senator Beveridge tales told him at this table. See Senator Beveridge, J. Franklin Jameson, and John Marshall, *Mississippi Valley Historical Review* 35: 468, December, 1948.

For some account of the tangled problem of the Virginia debt, see Randall, James G., Virginia debt controversy, *Pol. Sci. Quart.* 30: 553-577, December, 1915.

[92] John Randolph Tucker (1823-1897), who had served in the Congress from 1875 to 1887, was at this time professor of constitutional and international law in Washington and Lee University, where two years later he became dean of the law school.

[93] Annie, later known by her second name, Esther, was Jameson's younger sister.

[94] Robert A. Brock (1839-1914) was corresponding secretary of the Virginia Historical Society, 1875-1893.

[95] Beverley Tucker Crump, son of Judge William W. Crump mentioned below. The two practised law together until the death of the father. The Secretary of State at the time was H. W. Flournoy.

[96] To his brother Jameson wrote: "I enjoy the Virginians very much. I believe they are the most pleasant and cordial people in the world, as kind and genial as could be. Everyone seems to want to help me, and anyway it is a pleasure to be surrounded by people so good-natured and agreeable. It is quite a lesson to a Yankee" (Jameson to Arthur H. Jameson, June 5, 1891).

[97] William Wirt Henry (1831-1900) had a brief political career but throughout most of his life was more interested in history than in politics. At the American Historical Association of 1886 he read a paper on the part taken by Virginia under the leadership of Patrick Henry in establishing religious liberty as a foundation of American government. In 1891 he was president of the Association.

[98] Edward Carrington (1749-1794), John Marshall's brother-in-law, was United States marshall of Virginia and supervisor of revenues for that state during Washington's presidency.

[99] John Page (1743-1808) succeeded Monroe as governor of Virginia in 1802.

George Wythe (1726-1806), signer of the Declaration of Independence, member of the Virginia House of Burgesses, of the Continental Congress and of the Virginia high court of chancery, established the first chair of law in an American college, the professorship of law and police in William and Mary.

[100] Thomas Ritchie (1778-1854), for over forty years editor of the Richmond *Enquirer* and a power in Virginia politics, by abruptly throwing his support from Van Buren to Polk, with the slogan, "Polk and Texas," did much to bring about the nomination of Polk in 1844. Following Polk's election, he became editor of the *Union,* the administration organ in Washington. See Ambler, Charles H., *Thomas Ritchie: a study in Virginia politics,* ch. 8, Richmond, Va., Bell Book and Stationery Company, 1913.

To JOHN JAMESON

Richmond, June 16, 1891.

My dear Dad:

. . . I expect to leave Friday morning by the James River steamer for Shirley (Carter's) and Westover (Byrd's), (see June Century).[101] There I hope to stay but a few hours; but Virginian travel is so slow, one can't predict. Friday night or Saturday I go up from City Point to Petersburg, to see a man. Monday I go back to the river and steam down to Brandon,[102] to see what papers the Harrisons have, and then, after a day or two, on to Jamestown and Williamsburg. There I strike a hotel. Up to that point, save at Petersburg, my resource is to be the hospitality of the owners of these old places. A day or two at Williamsburg will suffice, then Norfolk, then Yorktown. At Williamsburg I shall be under the charge of a granddaughter of St. George Tucker and of John Tyler's son, Lyon Gardiner Tyler, President of William and Mary College, now revived.[103] Up to next Monday, inclusive, mail may be sent to his care. After that, I don't know where I shall be for a few days, but I shall bring up in care of Mrs. W. N. Ward, Lyell's P. O., Richmond Co., Va., so that will be the next address. My uncertainty as to those few days arises from a very gratifying thing. Mrs. Carey's cousin Dr. Barney used before the war to be a great collector of autographs and MS., and knows all Va. from that point of view. At my first interview the old gentleman offered to take four or five days off, and go on a journey with me in Essex and Middlesex, where he knew of some things, and scented others, that I ought to see. The dear old boy is slow, but the time it will take will probably be well spent. You will perceive that it takes a good while to make a trip of research in Virginia. . . . I must do things here while I *am* here. I haven't accomplished all I thought of, for the mass of material at the Capitol is much greater than I supposed. But I carry off a great amount of spoil, and have learned and

enjoyed much. This morning I went around to see the plain old brick house of Judge Marshall. This eve. I go to a reception of the Bar Association to C. J. Fuller[104] at the Westmoreland Club. . . .

To JOHN JAMESON

Wm. and Mary College,
Williamsburg, Va.
June 27, 1891.

My dear Father:

I'll just start a letter here. I am writing in the old president's house, built in 1723. Opposite diagonally is the old college, built in 1693, and from the college buildings extends the long street (Duke of Gloucester Street) past the quaint old houses, Bruton Parish Church, the Palace Green, the Court-house Green, the Red Lion Inn and the site of the old Raleigh, to where the old Capitol stood. I came here for a day, and have stayed three and a half, for I found an old lady here, granddaughter of St. George Tucker, possessing a nearly complete set of the Journals of the House of Burgesses, a thing I suppose not to be found elsewhere in the world. I have been kept under the hospitable roof of Lyon Gardiner Tyler, president of Wm. and Mary, and son of Pres. John Tyler. I went to the hotel, but he made me come up here, and I have had a most delightful visit with him and his wife. He is a man of about 37, the ablest historical man I have met in Va., and one of the best fellows in the world. But I must prepare to depart for Norfolk, and leave this delightful village,—a sort of Virginia Hadley.[105] The college has come up from 0 to 200 in three years under his management.

Newport News, June 28, 1891.

I left there, with much regret, yesterday morning, and came down the peninsula to here and over to Norfolk, where I have been until this morning. I got some good points at Norfolk, but was disappointed in my hope of seeing the correspondence of Gov. Littleton W. Tazewell and his father.[106] His daughter, an old lady,

---

[101] Harrison, Constance Cary (Mrs. Burton Harrison), Colonel William Byrd of Westover, Virginia, *Century Magazine* 42: 163-178. Shirley passed into the possession of the Carter family in 1723, when its owner, Elizabeth Hill, married John Carter, the eldest son of "King" Carter of Corotoman. Westover, seat of the Byrds, was built by William Byrd the second, about 1730.

[102] Brandon, on the James River about nine miles from Richmond, seat of the Harrisons, was built about 1765.

[103] This granddaughter, mentioned again in the letter of June 27, was Cynthia Beverley Tucker (1832-1908), who became Mrs. Charles Coleman.

Lyon Gardiner Tyler (1853-1935), president of William and Mary College from 1888 to 1919, editor of the *William and Mary College Quarterly and Genealogical Magazine*, and of numerous books dealing with Virginia history. William and Mary College, founded in 1693 and forced to close during the Civil War, had reopened in 1869 but financial difficulties had caused its suspension from 1881 to 1888. In the latter year the state granted it $10,000 annually (later made $15,000) and in 1893 the Congress gave it $64,000 indemnity for damage suffered during the Civil War.

[104] Melville Weston Fuller (1833-1910), Chief Justice of the United States, 1888 to 1910, was a member of the American Venezuela Boundary Commission, for which Jameson made a study in 1896. Fuller was also a member of the Arbitration Tribunal of 1899 which settled the Venezuelan boundary dispute. In 1897 he became a member of the executive council of the American Historical Association.

[105] If the presence of a college created part of the similarity, Jameson meant not the village of Hadley but that of South Hadley, not far from Amherst, and the seat of Mount Holyoke College.

[106] Gov. Littleton Waller Tazewell (1774-1860), an able lawyer, a member of the United States Senate (and its president *pro tempora*), from which he resigned in the midst of his term; governor of Virginia, 1834-1836, which office he also resigned. His father, Henry Tazewell (1753-1799), "most popular Virginian of his day," served in the Senate, where he too was for a time president pro tempora. He died before the completion of his term.

was ill; but I saw her nephew, and made some arrangements that may lead to seeing them later, or getting them into print through the American Historical Association, through which also I mean to get printed a good many letters Tyler has.

One of my Hopkins pupils, a quite devoted one, came from Norfolk.[107] He was not at home, but his brother showed me much kindness. Norfolk was so much a Federalist stronghold that I hoped to find some Federal correspondence, but the town has been damaged so much that I learned of none. Still, I got word of some other materials, and picked up some books *very* cheap.

I came over here early this morning. Two or three hours to wait for a train to Hampton and Old Point. This is a newly-boomed place, and looks flourishing, and is neater than any other place in Virginia I have seen. I fancy the boom has anticipated a good deal, and doubt whether the 12-story elevator, lettered C and O in letters you can read from Norfolk, 12 or 15 miles away, is yet worked to its full capacity. A few coal steamers are at the wharves, two of them bearing the meteor flag of England,[108] which I have not seen for some years. Tyler drove me all around the country every evening from 6½ to dark. The last time we saw York River; beautiful. Sorry not to see Yorktown, but can't.

Hampton, June 29.

I wish you could have been with me the rest of the day. Hard to imagine things at once more beautiful and more interesting. First, came over here, and went around Gen. Armstrong's school.[109] Beautiful water views all around. Then to Old Point Comfort by electric car; dinner at the Hygeia, with its beautiful sea-view. The white fleet lay off the hotel. In the latter part of the afternoon I went out to the Yorktown, of which a friend, Lieut. Bradbury, is navigating officer, saw it, and dined with the officers. On returning, walked all around the ramparts of Fortress Monroe. I should hate to have to take it. Beautiful village within, and wonderful sea-views without. Lovely day added. Spent night here. Now up to Richmond by C. and A., not being able otherwise to reach Lester Manor, whence to Tappahannock and Mrs. Ward's, address Lyell's Richmond Co.[110] I hope you follow me

---

[107] Walter Herren Taylor, who received his A.B. degree from the Johns Hopkins in 1889.

[108] "The meteor-flag of England
Shall yet terrific burn."
Thomas Campbell, Ye mariners of England.

[109] Gen. Samuel Chapman Armstrong (1839-1893), born in the Hawaiian Islands, educated at Williams College under Mark Hopkins, during the Civil War a commander of negro troops, and after the war an agent of the Freedmen's Bureau, was the creator of the Hampton Normal and Industrial Institute in 1868.

[110] Bladensfield, Lyell's P. O., Va., was the summer home of the Ward family of Washington, and of Mrs. Carey of Baltimore.

with Smith's Invaluable Atlas. Dr. Barney can't go, which saves the 2 or 3 days I lost at Wmsbg. probably. . . .

To John Jameson

Bladensfield, July 7, 1891.

My dear Father:

. . . I spent yesterday at the court-house and clerk's office. They are separate buildings, the former 160 years old, but somewhat changed within. King William C. H., which I visited a week ago, is apparently just as it was. I sat up with the judge a little while. He is a great friend of Mrs. Ward's, an old squire looked up to and trusted by all, but with little knowledge of law. There was little business; the jail is empty. But many farmers, and most of the more worthless part of the population, were out on the green, —three or four hundred of them,—buying and selling and talking of crops, etc. The crowd after all seemed not so different from a crowd up in New Hampshire as I had expected. The clerk was an elderly man from Harvard, Massachusetts, named Warner, who had drifted down there. I sat in the corner of his office, working over an old book of records, and listened with great interest while the local worthies talked horse, or law cases, or lumber, or crops, or land. Then I went over to the church festival, and saw Washingtons and Tayloes and other good country people scooping out ice-cream after much the manner of Amherst lawn parties. But the people are so different!

Today I write letters all day; tomorrow I examine the papers at Sabine Hall,[111] and so on, in Richmond and Westmoreland. . . .

To John Jameson

Bladensfield, Va.,
July 19, 1891.

My dear Father:

I dare say you are surprised that I am still here; but I changed my plan. I have got word from King George C. H. which makes it unnecessary for me to go through that county. Indeed, there is nothing for me to do between Westmoreland and Alexandria. So, instead of going up to Westmoreland and then on, I changed my plan, and have worked Westmoreland from this point as a centre; for this place is on the borders of the two counties. Then I could go up to Alexandria without delay or difficulty by steamer, which I much prefer to Northern Neck roads, of which I have had enough. Tomorrow I was to go, but news of last night delays me a day more. Tomorrow I drive down

---

[111] Sabine Hall, on the north bank of the Rappahannock, built by "King" Carter for his son Landon in 1730. The Carters intermarried with Byrds, Tayloes, and Harrisons, and their correspondents included the great names of Virginia.

to "Edgehill,"[112] where I am told I may find papers enough to reward me for a ride of 45 miles in all. The next day I leave here and, after a day at Blandfield,[113] the old Beverley place, I go to Alexandria and an old place in Loudoun. I shall reach Washington at the end of the week; there I shall stay a week with Jack,[114] working in the Lib. Cong., then home, stopping a day in Princeton with Woodrow Wilson.[115] So you see I shall be late in arriving, and for that I am very sorry, but it has been a paying trip, even though Va. be slower to work than one thinks. The Northern Neck has paid me well; my notes are as numerous as from Richmond. The past week has had some disappointments. Monday I went to Mt. Airy (Mr. Tayloe's)[116] where I found nothing. Tuesday I went over into southern Westmoreland, a fine country. Rode about 20 miles, stopping at various places, almost wholly in vain. The next day we went to Stratford, one of the Lee houses, where Gen. Lee was born.[117] Nothing there but the place, but on the way back we stopped at Westmoreland C. H. long enough for me to get some very good materials. The whole ride was one of 40 miles, much of it over the worst road I ever saw; therefore I rested Thursday, reading, writing, and talking, and made some calls. Friday I set out on an expedition from which I had to come back, but got some materials before returning. Yesterday I went through a rare pph. I had borrowed, which must be returned; and saw some people. Today I was going to Yeocomico Church[118] in Westmoreland, but couldn't. To-morrow the old Carter-Chinn place, where in the haunted garret were things a little while ago, belonging to those families and the Balls. No tenants one can learn from. The road is not bad. . . .

Word from Providence tells me I am to have Munro as assoc. prof. history, and Wilson as assistant in pol. science. My former graduates you know.[119] Result, boom of department. . . .

[112] The first house at Edgehill was built before 1800 by Thomas Mann Randolph of Albemarle County, who married Martha Jefferson. This was inherited by Thomas Jefferson Randolph, who in 1828 built the brick house which Jameson visited. After the builder's death the Randolphs used Edgehill for a boarding school until 1896 when it passed from the possession of the family.

[113] Blandfield, built by Col. William Beverley about 1760, was named for his wife, Elizabeth Bland.

[114] John Jameson Chickering, one of the Kendall Green cousins, also an Amherst classmate of Jameson.

[115] This visit was in response to a letter from Wilson of June 29, 1891: "We are spending the Summer here [Princeton] at home and nothing would cheer and delight us so much as a visit from you, whenever you return this way."

[116] Mount Airy, home of the Tayloes, was built by Col. John Tayloe 2nd.

[117] Stratford Hall, built about 1725, was the birthplace of Richard Henry, Francis Lightfoot, and Robert E. Lee.

[118] Yeocomico Church, in Cople Parish, built in 1706, was not far from Wakefield, the Washington home, and several Lee homes.

[119] Wilford H. Munro (1849-1934), A.B., Brown, 1870, had

To John Jameson

Providence, December 6, 1891.

My dear Father:
. . . Our lecture-course began very successfully on Monday evening, and was continued on Thursday evening.[120] Hamlin, who gives the first, is the son of Dr. Cyrus Hamlin of Constantinople. Was of Amherst '75. Used to be called Turkey Hamlin.

The ball on Wednesday evening was a fine affair, and I quite enjoyed it, even though I did not get to bed until two. The gymnasium looked very pretty, and so did the girls.

"And Jullien's band it tuk its stand
    So swately in the middle there,
And soft bassoons played heavenly chunes,
    And violins did fiddle there."[121]

Thursday night I dined at the Blakes', which is always a great pleasure.[122] Friday afternoon our seminary had its second meeting,[123] and I dined at the Gardners'. Last night I took tea with Mrs. Poland, and then went to the Greek Club,[124] where Andrews read an excellent

done graduate work under Jameson during 1889-1890; the next year he studied in Germany. He remained in Brown until he became professor emeritus in 1911. George Grafton Wilson was Jameson's first graduate student in Brown, receiving his Ph.D. degree in 1889. In 1910 he left Brown to become professor of international law in Harvard University.

[120] "Monday evening came our first lecture; it was numerously attended and much admired. I receive much commendation for the composition of the course,—all which I would swap for five new subscribers. . . . In intervals, have prowled around down street, seeking the fugacious five dollar bill for the association. *Only* 90 more to get. *Sic itur ad astra*" (Jameson to Arthur H. Jameson, Dec. 6, 1891). This was the year in which the association, deciding to broaden the scope of the lectures, changed its name to the Brown University Lecture Association. The course included lectures by Albert Shaw, Josiah Royce, A. D. F. Hamlin, C. T. Winchester, and Walter Damrosch, with others perhaps less well known.

[121] Thackeray's Mr. Moloney's account of the ball.

[122] Possibly the family of Eli Whitney Blake, professor of physics, Brown University.

[123] "I start a seminary of history, political economy, and political science here Friday evening" (Jameson to Arthur H. Jameson, Nov. 15, 1891).

[124] Mrs. William Carey Poland. Her husband, connected with Brown since 1870, was at this time director of the Museum of Classical Archaeology. Two years later he became director of the Museum of Fine Arts of Brown.
The Greek Club, a Providence institution to which Jameson belonged during his years in Brown, finds frequent mention in his Diary. "*Sat. Dec. 8* [*1888*]. to the Greek Club at Poland's. Went in a most unwilling and disgusted frame of mind, but before long was really enjoying it. They read The Persians, and read it very well. They read from one translation mostly . . . and I, with Mrs. Chace, followed them in another. This gave a good chance to see the real force of the poet as never before."
"*Sat. Mar. 15* [*1890*]. Great amount of work on hand and no heart for it. But the Greek Club, and a jolly hour at the Chace's after it, set me all right (pro tem.). . . . We read at the Club 'Antigone.' I read the Chorus, in place of Granger" (Diary, Oct. 10, 1888-Dec. 21, 1890).
The program of the club, planned to cover a span of eleven

paper, of which I did not understand a single sentence.[125] When it comes to metaphysics, I'm not in it. . . .

To Sara Elwell

Woburn,[126] July 4, 1892.
(Monday afternoon).

My dearest Sweetheart :[127]

It is six o'clock on the afternoon of the Ever-Glorious Fourth, and I gladly stop work to write to my dear. It is a horrid grind, this writing of an article, and I have finished only one of the Atlantic's big pages, whereas I must write about four, and am permitted to write six. It is a review of Mr. W. W. Henry's life of Patrick Henry and of Miss Kate Mason Rowland's life of George Mason that I am doing. Mr. Scudder asked me to do them because of my interest in Virginian history in that particular period, and the reading of the books is in itself enjoyable enough.[128] But I always have a fit of depression and groaning and travailing when I get to the beginning of writing anything. I warn you to be very peaceable at them [sic] times in

the future. This morning was remarkably clear and cool, and I thought I was booked for a good long day's work on the article. The morning mail brought so many letters that had to be attended to, that I did not get a whack at the article until after dinner. And I don't venture to work in the evening, lest it prevent my sleeping enough to do fair work the next day. Well, I always do manage to scrape through somehow, and get a thing done just at the last minute, and so I suppose it will be this time. But I can't compose rapidly in hot weather. . . .

To Edwin C. Norton

27 Franklin Street,
Woburn, Mass., August 7, 1892.

My dear Doc :[129]

You know full well that you owe me a letter, and therefore you will argue that something extraordinary has happened, to cause me magnanimously to waive all scruples thence arising, and write to you notwithstanding. You are right. Something extraordinary has happened. To wit, I am engaged. Having experienced this yourself, you will easily imagine all that it involves to me; and will also perhaps recollect how hopeless appeared the attempt to give your correspondents any idea of so interesting a personality. In your case my remedy was, to see for myself how charming a being it was; and I hereby invite you, whenever subsequently to next spring you visit these regions, to take the same mode of supplementing whatever attempts I may make to describe to you my dear friend. But not to wait for that. I remark in the first place that she is named Sara or Sallie Elwell, is of Brooklyn, New York, and spent last winter in Providence; that she is half a dozen years younger than I am; and that she is tall,—nearly five feet nine, to be precise. So far, we are dealing with facts about which there can obviously be no dispute. Not less indisputable, as I conceive, are the following statements. She is of a particularly happy disposition,—sweet-tempered, warm-hearted, generous, and unselfish to the last degree. She is vivacious, cheerful, active, energetic, and amusing. She is social, and much used to society. She never says an ill word of any one, is a good, conscientious, religious girl, and has a bright, quick and fairly well-educated mind. And she is very fond of me, and I of her, and we are very happy. To all the above I hereby make affidavit, as being, not praise, but mere description. These things being so, tell me, beloved, am I not entitled to congratulations? . . .

years, was outlined by Arnold B. Chace. At the end of this period it was disbanded, to reorganize as the Review Club. During the time of Jameson's membership, he presented papers on Greece in the fourth [fifth?] century; Aristotle in the Middle Ages; the Ancients and natural scenery; Greek athletics; St. Augustine; and the times of Dante (*Greek Club, November 5th, 1887-November 5th, 1898*). Of the first paper which he prepared for the club, he wrote: *Sat. Oct. 26* [*1889*]. At noon began the preparation, at Mr. Chace's request, of a paper for the Greek Club, on the political history of Greece in the 5th cent., and its relations to the literary history. Resolved to rush it through in 24 hours, and without looking in a book, (haven't looked in a book of Greek history for two years)."

"*Sun. Oct. 27.* Got it done at 12.07! and it is not so bad. Glad to have it off my mind" (Diary, Oct. 10, 1888-Dec. 21, 1890).

[125] The paper by President Andrews was on the metaphysics of Aristotle. He had the year before presented one on the philosophy of Plato.

[126] George Thompson, Jameson's grandfather, died in 1891 and the Jameson family moved to 27 Franklin Street, Woburn, Mass., the home of the grandparents, to live with the grandmother. This remained the family home until the death of the older sister, Helen, in 1945.

[127] Sara Elwell, the future Mrs. Jameson, was from Brooklyn but had been spending the winter in Providence, teaching in Miss Wheeler's school, and boarding where Jameson boarded. They had become engaged some weeks before this. For some account of Miss Elwell's family, see *post*, June 7, 1924.

[128] In, Two Virginians, *Atlantic* 70: 407-414, July, 1892, Jameson reviewed William Wirt Henry's *Patrick Henry, life, correspondence and speeches,* 3v., N. Y., Scribner's, 1891, and Kate Mason Rowland's *The life of George Mason*, 2v., N. Y., Putnam's, 1892.

Horace E. Scudder (1838-1902), reader and editorial assistant for Hurd and Company, remained with that firm through various changes until Houghton, Mifflin and Company emerged in 1880. From 1890 to 1898 he was editor of the *Atlantic Monthly*. In addition to his demanding editorial duties and his own considerable writing he found time to serve as friend and counsellor to many young authors, among them, Woodrow Wilson and J. Franklin Jameson.

[129] Edwin C. Norton was at this time teacher of Greek and dean in Pomona College, Claremont, Calif. Jameson wrote at the top of this letter: "I have to use caligraph because of writer's cramp. I like it."

To Sara Elwell

Woburn, August 20, 1892.
Saturday, 4:30 P.M

My dear, dear Sweetheart:

. . . Yes, I manage to keep busy. I have nearly finished going through Campbell's book.[130] Then I shall write what I have to say about it, and gladly wash my hands of him. I only agreed to do it on account of the mon'. When he is disposed of, my time will be free for some most fascinating work, on which I shall be occupied nearly all the time until term opens, though I hope to have a little time left for some preliminary labors on my little book on the House of Burgesses.[131] . . . Aren't any of your rich relatives Baptists that could be induced to blow in a few hundred thousands for the benefit of Brown University, on account of your official connection with that highly meritorious institution? I am developing a scheme for a little series of historical papers, after the model of the Johns Hopkins Studies in History, the Harvard Historical Monographs, Columbia College Studies in History, etc. I shall be duly modest about it, and not put forth the immature work of undergraduates with a great flourish of trumpets. But really a few of the papers my young men did in History 9 last term, (that is the course in practical original research), were excellent, and deserving of permanent preservation in print. I have no printing fund, but I think I can manage without it at first, and perhaps eventually get one, as the fellows have at these other places, if Brown gets any money. Such a series will be a new thing at Brown. I believe it is quite practicable. I am now "pulling the leg" of the editor of a certain Rhode Island

publication, to get the first part of the scheme worked off through him.[132]

To Sara Elwell

Woburn, September 18, 1892.
Sunday, 4 P. M.

My dearest Love:

. . . Yesterday was a lovely day, of which we were very glad, because it enabled many of Grandma's old friends,—the good old people to whom I am still "Frankie,"—to come when otherwise they might not have been able to do so.[133] One of the three old Irish washerwomen who came said, "Och, she has a lovely day to go home," and after she had looked at the dear old face, with its peaceful smile, she said, "Ah, then, if she ain't happy it's bad for the rest of us." We heard many things to help make us happy in the thought that, in spite of her humble self-effacement and the quietness of her life, she had been widely appreciated. The old minister said that many times, when he had come from the pulpit feeling discouraged with the thought that he had preached too imperfectly, he had been cheered by some kind and simple word of appreciation from this good woman. People wouldn't say that she had at all an acute mind; and yet the right place in which to drop a kind word was something she never failed to see. Now for instance, a man came to this town some years ago, a cousin of my father's whom she hardly knew at all, who, because of domestic unhappiness, was, though not at all a bad man, always a little in danger of forgetting some of the best that was in him. She knew this and, feeling that the influences of the church were very good for him, she never failed, when she saw him as they came out, to say some kind or cheerful word, in a welcoming sort of manner. Well, it was all she could do, yet one would say it was only a chance if it really did any good in helping to hold him to what was best. But he tells us, in a letter, that Sunday after Sunday he used to try to come out so

[130] This was Douglas Campbell's *The Puritan in Holland, England and America,* 2v., N. Y., Harper, 1892. Before the appearance of this volume Jameson had criticised a paper given by Campbell at the meeting of the American Historical Association of 1890 (*Papers, Amer. Hist. Assn.* 5: 165-186). Campbell, he felt, placed undue emphasis on the Dutch origins of American institutions. On the appearance of the book, Horace Scudder of the *Atlantic* sent it to Jameson with the remark that it needed close scrutiny. Jameson's review was severe. One of his contentions was that the author's inability to read Dutch, in itself rendered him incapable of investigating his subject properly. "We welcome all attempts to set forth duly the influence of Dutch, French, Scotch or Irish in our history. But, in order to be successful, they must be made by writers who possess abundant scholarship, temperate judgment, and the ability to distinguish between assertion and proof." Though the article (*Atlantic* 70: 698-704, November, 1892) was unsigned, Campbell at once attributed it to Jameson, remarking that there were only two people in the United States who could have written it. A considerable correspondence between the author and the reviewer followed.

[131] A book which was never written, though Dr. Jameson gave addresses on the subject to the Virginia and the Rhode Island historical societies. A list of the journals of the House of Burgesses is to be found in the *Ann. Rept., Amer. Hist. Assn.,* 1897: 432-437. What the "most fascinating work" was we are not told.

[132] This was probably the editor for the Rhode Island Historical Society. Ten papers appeared between 1894 and 1899, and were brought together as *Papers from the historical seminary of Brown University.* The first ones were reprints from the *Publications* of the Rhode Island Historical Society, others were reprints from the *Annual Reports* of the American Historical Association, the *Political Science Quarterly,* the *Pennsylvania Magazine of History and Biography,* and those of 1896 and 1897 were printed by Preston and Rounds of Providence. Mary E. Woolley, Harold D. Hazeltine, Marcus W. Jernegan, and Edmund C. Burnett were among the contributors.

[133] This letter was written the day after the funeral of Jameson's maternal grandmother, Esther Ames Thompson. He was devoted to both his grandparents throughout their lives. After the death of his grandfather Jameson presented some of his books to the library of Fisk University with this inscription: "In memory of George Thompson, 1812-1891, of Woburn, Massachusetts, one of the Early Abolitionists and a Friend of Negroes, this set of Harper's Monthly Magazine, which he began taking at its beginning, is presented to the Library of Fisk University by his grandson."

that he would meet her, for the sake of the few kind words he knew he should have. I know it was often a little tedious to me, she would stop and speak to so many, coming out of church,—mostly strangers to me. But I see now that it all had an importance that neither she nor I dreamt of. It has greatly freshened up for me the commonplace moral of the boundless influence of any single good life. I say to myself, if this frail, modest little woman, poor during most of her days, and with only such education as she had been able to get before her marriage at sixteen, could do so much good in the world, just by an endless succession of little good deeds, how shamed I ought to be, with my youth and health and strength and long course of expensive education, to do more than I do. I will try to do more. . . .

To SARA ELWELL

Providence, October 2, 1892.
Sunday, 9 P. M.

My dearest Love:

Hooray, hooray, hooray! Now oughn't I to be a happy man! Friday evening I secured and ensured the success of my pet scheme for this year by an interview with the editor through whom I want to publish the first numbers of my little series of "Papers from the Historical Seminary of Brown University." Saturday morning that admirable student whom I told you of a while ago was going to Harvard as a post-graduate because of the temptations of their loaves and fishes arrived here and gladdens my heart by resolving to spend the year with me.[134] Saturday evening I have Christie with me at tea at Woburn, and feel again that I have for a friend one of the best men in the world.[135] . . .

To SARA ELWELL

Providence, February 3, 1893.
Friday, 5 P. M.

My dearest Sallie:

. . . I have just got the publisher's account for my

last book during the past six months.[136] During that time, no less than nine (9) copies of it have been sold, and I am enriched by the sum of $5.63. With a neat little income of $11.26 per annum, I should soon get rich by authorship; but of course it is hardly to be expected that the sales should always continue so enormous. . . .

To ALBERT SHAW

(Box 810),
Providence, June 15, 1893.[137]

My dear Shaw:

I have just had to pay out a lot of money unexpectedly, and must proceed to recoup myself in various ways.[138] One which occurs to me is to persuade the "Review of Reviews," with which I understand you have some influence, to let me get up an article for them. What do you think of the idea of making an article which shall lay before the public the ultimate total expense of the pension system, based on the figures of the mortality of pensioners of the Revolution and the War of 1812? It seems to me that, from our experiences in those cases, we can predict pretty securely what the future extent of the system will be; that the public ought to know, and will be interested to know, how much the system is going to cost before we are through with it; and that the facts and statistics are not without enough of the humorous element to make possible a treatment not too heavy. The article could be illustrated with a few diagrams showing for the three wars the curves of mortality or longevity of pensioners or widows.[139] I have indicated at the be-

---

[134] It is impossible to identify this student with any certainty. It may have been the one about whom Jameson wrote to his father on June 29, 1893: "My pleasure is great at having been able to place my best graduate student in an instructorship at the University of Michigan at $900, a fine opening for him." This was Marshall S. Brown, who was graduated in 1892 and received his A.M., in 1893. He remained in Michigan but one year, then went to New York University where he served for many years as professor of history and dean. In Michigan his place was taken by William D. Johnston, also a graduate student of Jameson, who remained in Michigan till 1897.

[135] Francis A. Christie (1858-1938), A.B., Amherst, 1881, was probably Jameson's closest friend from Amherst days until his death. After some time spent in German universities, Christie came to the Johns Hopkins for further work and during 1885-1887 he and Jameson were together daily. For many years he was professor of church history in Meadville Theological Seminary.

[136] This was *The history of historical writing in America.* Of the returns from the earlier volume, *Essays in constitutional history,* Jameson recorded: "*Tu. Nov. 11* [*1890*]. Houghton inform that of my book published just a year ago Sunday, only 30 copies remain unsold. Pity not copyrighted" (Diary, Oct. 10, 1888-Dec. 21, 1890). "I have just got my semi-annual accounts respecting my book. Five copies are left. When they are sold, I shall have cleared, from the whole transaction, $2.81, a truly enormous sum. It would about pay postage on the correspondence in the matter. Wealth is not to be obtained by authorship. Well, I am lucky to have come out even." Jameson to Arthur H. Jameson, Feb. 2, 1891.

[137] Manuscript Division, New York Public Library. The answer to this letter has not been found.

[138] Jameson and Sara Elwell were married in Brooklyn on April 13, 1893, and spent a brief honeymoon in Washington. During the spring of 1893 they lived in Wickford, R. I., from which Jameson carried on his work in Brown and also watched the progress of his new house at 108 (later 196) Bowen Street, Providence. The unexpected expenditures may have been in connection with the house or the result of some need of his own family, largely dependent on him. This was the year in which his young brother, Arthur, was graduated from the Massachusetts Institute of Technology.

[139] There is no further reference to the projected article in the correspondence and it was apparently never written. The need for money referred to in the first line was probably what induced Jameson to undertake the preparation of the *Dictionary*

ginning the sordid and rapacious spirit in which I approach the matter, so that I need not remark at the close that this subject can be commuted for any other you prefer and I think I could do.[140]

To ALBERT SHAW

New York, March 12, 1895.[141]

My dear Shaw:

Firstly, thank you very much for your friendliness and counsel. As I have not seen Low or any of the Columbia men today, there apparently remains time for further consideration. I ask you to consider one thing I did not speak. Mr. Low's proposition was that one should come on Barnard's guarantee, and that was, a guarantee for three years.[142] I suppose Columbia's election for a term of three years would be thought equivalent to a permanency by any man who imagined he would not ultimately disappoint their expectations. But should you think it wise to put that (prophetic) interpretation on such a proposal as this? Will Barnard always have the money? If she doesn't, will Columbia at the end of the three years assume the burden of my support?

At my lecture I met the Dean of Barnard College,

Miss Smith,[143] who said she was "sorry Barnard College was not to have the benefit of my services." This I should take as concluding the whole matter, if I had thought Miss Smith a young woman of experience and tact; but on first impression she seemed to me to have not much of either. Still, I transmit the information, for the utterance may have been "inspired," and may mean that l'incident Jameson is closed. If they can find money to offer Clark $5000 and do not care to offer me more than $3500 they can't want me much.[144] Quite without assuming that Clark and I are on the same basis, I am glad to know about their offer to him. Well, I am very happy in Providence, and can stay there with content. Brown is growing, too. But I shall see you Tuesday, somewhere about 11:30.

To ALBERT SHAW

196 Bowen Street, Providence,
March 21, 1895.[145]

My dear Shaw:

After spending the evening writing about other people's candidacies, I am surely entitled to write a few words about my own, if only to say that I thank you, more than I had time to say in your office before Finley[146] came in, for your furtherance of it, so zealous yet so discreet. I saw Burgess a few minutes, but we had no talk of these things.[147] The invitations to the conference respecting an American Historical Journal are out.[148] The time is Saturday, April 6, most awkward for me, but I shall come, and the place the rooms of the New York Reform Club. In spare moments, if you ever have any, think of a good man for editor. Professors are too busy, and few others occur to my mind. Why couldn't they have had it on a Tuesday? Regards to Finley. Please tell Lanier[149] I am sorry to have missed him.

---

of United States History, which he began this year. Earlier in the year, possibly also in an effort to increase an inadequate income, he had written, Greek history and the Constitution of the United States, for The Chautauquan 17: 285-289, June, 1893. He had also published articles in The Chautauquan in 1890 and 1891. In 1893 he tried his hand at something for The Youths' Companion, where he hoped to place accounts of Jamestown, Williamsburg, and William and Mary College. These never appeared (Jameson to Sara Elwell, Feb. 26, Mar. 19, 1893).

[140] Possibly the financial exigencies of the summer following Jameson's marriage prevented him from attending the meeting of the American Historical Association held in Chicago, July 11-13, 1893, in connection with the World's Fair. For this meeting he wrote, The origin of the standing committee system in American legislative bodies (Ann. Rept., Amer. Hist. Assn., 1893: 393-399), a part of which was read by the secretary at the closing session.

The plan to meet in Chicago had been opposed by Justin Winsor, who wrote to Herbert B. Adams on Mar. 22, 1893, that the list of those who had agreed to read papers made a "pitiful show" and that their quality was not such as to warrant "asking any reputable writer to take part in the Congress to the extent of reading a paper" (Holt, op. cit., 198-199). One turns to the list of contributors to the meeting, to find among them, Ainsworth R. Spofford, James Schouler, Ephraim Emerton, Edward G. Bourne, Bernard Moses, Lucy M. Salmon, George P. Fisher, Reuben G. Thwaites, James R. Woodburn, J. F. Jameson, and F. J. Turner, who here presented his epoch-making paper, The significance of the frontier in American history, Ann. Rept., Amer. Hist. Assn., 1893: 199-227.

[141] Manuscript Division, New York Public Library.
[142] Seth Low had been president of Columbia University since 1890. Jameson was in New York to consider a possible position in Barnard College and also to deliver a series of lectures in that college. See post, Apr. 1, 1895, n. 151.

[143] Emily J. Smith, dean of Barnard, 1894-1900. In 1899 she married George Haven Putnam and soon after resigned her college position.
[144] John Bates Clark (1847-1938), A.B., Amherst, 1872, taught political economy in Amherst from 1892 till 1895 when he went to Columbia, where he remained until his retirement in 1923.
[145] Manuscript Division, New York Public Library.
[146] Probably Robert J. Finley (1868-1897), A.B., Knox, 1888. While a graduate student at the Johns Hopkins University he supported himself by lectures and editorial work and acted as assistant to Professor Smith Ely. He left the university for newspaper work in New York in the winter of 1890-1891, without completing the work for the degree. In the early days of the Review of Reviews he worked with Albert Shaw and was for a short time managing editor of that periodical.
[147] John William Burgess (1844-1931), A.B., Amherst, 1867, professor of history and political science in Amherst, 1873-1876; professor of political science and constitutional law, Columbia, 1876-1912.
[148] For an account of the genesis of this meeting, see post, Apr. 1, 1895, n. 152.
[149] This was probably Charles Day Lanier (1868-1945), A.B., Johns Hopkins, 1888. He continued as a graduate student in history in the university for the year 1888-1889.

To Francis A. Christie

196 Bowen Street, Providence,
April 1, 1895.

Beloved:

Imprimis, N. B. the new number, with which an ingenious municipal government has, for unknown reasons, endowed us. You will think me shabby not to have written before concerning the progress of affairs between me and Columbia. I have wanted to write thus, but there was no progress. A month ago Low offered me a salary which, in view of the superior expense of New York, was less advantageous than what I shall have here next year. It was $3500, which would not admit of that magnificence with which, in your glowing visions, you saw me surrounded. I declined, letting it be seen that $4000 would probably fetch me. I rather wanted to be fetched, much as we should suffer in going from here, but I was coy. Not unduly so, I thought, for the Barnard College people, who give Columbia these new chairs, had given J. B. Clark an offer of $5000; also, to go down there and do extra work to make both ends meet was no snap. Today I am informed that the Barnard people can't offer more than $3500, and they are going to call Robinson of the U. of P.[150] They and Columbia can't have wanted me very badly. Of course I shall give out that I have "declined a call to Columbia," but I should have been glad to go, as I think they have the future with them, in respect to graduate work, and I should probably have more time for writing. But so I shall here, for they will raise my salary. No time for more, beloved. I have to go down to New York this evening for my lectures to the Columbia seminary and to the Daughters of the Revolution.[151] I wish I had time to tell you about the two secret-rival projects for an Amer. Hist. Review,—an amusing tale.[152] It will keep till I see you, perhaps. May that be soon. . . .

To John Jameson

May 6, 1895.

My dear Father:

. . . The family will be glad to know that the committee on the new "American Historical Review," who serve for one year, have elected me managing editor for one term. To be its first editor is a great pleasure to me. Such a position has long been one of my chief ambitions, and now here we are.[153] It is a responsible and difficult job, but I shall do my best.

in Cambridge during Easter week. The Cornell project, communicated to Jameson on Feb. 17, 1895, had advanced much further. A call sent out on that date, signed by Moses Coit Tyler, George L. Burr, and H. Morse Stephens, indicated that Cornell University had granted money for a journal, that H. Morse Stephens (1857-1919), who had recently come to Cornell from England, had been chosen as editor-in-chief, and that a body of associate editors from various parts of the country was to be designated. Jameson was invited to act as one of these associates. Probably in an attempt to unite the two plans a group of twenty-six historians met in New York on April 6, and chose a board of editors empowered to choose an editor-in-chief, both board and editor to act for but a year. On May 5, Hart, a member of the board, wrote asking Jameson to accept the position of managing editor. Since Cornell was no longer to be the sponsor of the new journal a group of guarantors was secured, who promised three annual payments. These guarantors in December elected a board of editors for six-year terms: George B. Adams (1851-1925) of Yale, Albert Bushnell Hart (1854-1943) of Harvard, John Bach McMaster (1852-1932) of the University of Pennsylvania, William M. Sloane (1850-1928), of Princeton (to go to Columbia the next year), and H. Morse Stephens (1857-1919) of Cornell. Harry Pratt Judson (1849-1927) of the University of Chicago was added shortly afterward. This board continued unchanged until 1899, when Andrew C. McLaughlin took McMaster's place. A comparison of the first number of the *Review* with the careful plans outlined by the Cornell group indicates that though Cornell University did not publish the journal its department of history, with the able cooperation of Jameson, had much to do with its character. For an account of the merging of the two plans and of a third brewing at the University of Pennsylvania, see Jameson's article on the history of the journal, *Amer. Hist. Rev.* 26: 2-6, October, 1920. In this account Jameson refers to his own interest in the establishment of an historical journal as having been roused by the visit to this country in 1886 of Dr. Mandell Creighton, editor of the *English Historical Review.*

[153] Two items in Jameson's Diary indicate that when he went to Brown he was seriously considering the possibility of establishing an historical journal: "*Mon. June 4* [*1888*]. To N. Y. had the company of Dr. Hall, with whom I had much talk about Brown, the J.H.U., and my various plans, one of which in particular for an Amer. Hist. Rev."
"*Thur. June 28.* told him [Gardner] of my plan of an American Historical Review, the chief scheme I take to Providence." Diary, Feb. 18, 1887-Oct. 9, 1888.
A year in Brown seems to have convinced him that his plan was visionary. He wrote, after a day spent in Boston and Cambridge: "*Fri. Nov. 29* [*1889*]. In the morning I met Pres. Eliot; from things he said, and things Taussig said, I believe those Harvard people are thinking of establishing an Am. Hist. Review. I have sometimes dreamed of doing that, but of course it is mere foolishness to think of it" (Diary, Oct. 10-1888-Dec. 21, 1890). References to a number of abortive plans for an historical journal are to be found in the correspondence of H. B. Adams. See Holt, *op. cit.,* 47-53, 57, 111, 121, 127, 260, 269.

[150] James Harvey Robinson (1863-1936), lecturer in European history in the University of Pennsylvania. He went to Columbia as associate professor in 1895. Some weeks later Jameson wrote to Shaw: "Since I saw you, the Columbia affair has blown over. It seems Barnard had only so much, and having got their men for mathematics and political economy, they had only a fixed sum left for history. . . . I don't care" (May 20, 1895, Manuscript Division, New York Public Library).

[151] The New York chapter of the Daughters of the American Revolution had undertaken to establish a chair of American history in Barnard College and as a temporary occupant of that chair Dr. Jameson delivered six lectures in Hamilton Hall, Columbia, in March and April, 1895, the general subject being the Revolution as a social movement. A revision of these lectures was presented to a Princeton audience in 1926 and subsequently appeared as a small volume, *The American Revolution considered as a social movement*, Princeton, Princeton Univ. Press, 1926. See *post*, Aug. 10, 1926.

[152] The rival projects emanated from Harvard and Cornell. From the former A. B. Hart wrote to Jameson on Jan. 24, 1895, that the department of history of Harvard felt that the professors of history in the country ought to cooperate in maintaining an historical journal, and asked whether Brown would send a representative to a conference on the subject to be held

The pay will be such that I can withdraw, during my period of office, from enough of my work at B. U. to permit me to do the work, about a third of it, I suppose. [154] . . .

To FRANCIS A. CHRISTIE

196 Bowen Street, Providence,
February 4, 1896.

My dear Christie:

We are delighted with the pictures, and thank you very much for sending them. It is a great pleasure to have a glimpse of your surroundings, even though one has the pain of seeing six medicine-bottles on your mantel. The one containing them and yourself is excellent. One knows you are going to write a great book,—bahnbrechend, colossal. I will assume your permission to have it reproduced in half-tone for use on the circulars advertising your sermon here in April. Well, I hope you are as comfortable as you look, materially speaking. As to intellectual comfort, I wish I had a pull on the right sort of institution, say Columbia. But alas, I cannot even make my own calling and election sure, it appears. The January meeting of their trustees passed without my hearing a word from Burgess, and that of February occurred yesterday, I suppose, but no word this morning. I think I told you I had learned that Levermore was gunning for it. I have done nothing. Burgess knows whether he wants me or not. Have you seen that I am made chairman of the Historical Manuscripts Commission.[155] It ought to be a useful thing.

The other men are excellent, unless one may have a doubt as to Talcott Williams. Adams truly urged that he would be full of suggestions, however. If we go to England this summer, I shall pay some attention to the workings of their Commission. I imagine this will also bring me in the way of pleasant and profitable acquaintance there.[156] Where shall you spend the summer? Could you give any lessons or lectures in early church history to my pupil Miss Woolley, now a professor at Wellesley, instructor rather?[157] She specially wants to go into that period, and is an excellent scholar. I wish you would go across the ocean with us. There is talk of organizing an Amherst Alumni Association in Rhode Island. It seems there are 34 alumni in and around Providence. The New England alumni of J. H. U. dine in Boston February 22. Did I tell you Allinson is here now, and lives around the corner from me?[158] He read us a capital paper on Lucian at the "Greek Club" Saturday night. Monday is my parents' fortieth anniversary, and my mother's birthday. We shall spend the Sunday and Monday there. Probably Father will sail for Jamaica the next day, having got a pass through a friend. It will keep [him] away from some of the winter weather. The April number of the Review goes merrily on. I think it will be as good as the

---

[154] The difficulty of preparing the first number of the *Review* was increased by Morse Stephen's well-known disinclination to answer letters. Under the rules set up by the board of editors the managing editor was to submit to Stephens his choice of reviewers in certain fields of history. It was also arranged by the board that the first number was to contain an article by Professor Stephens. Letters to Professor Burr on July 30 and Sept. 6 indicate that Jameson had had no word from Stephens during the summer and did not yet know whether he was to receive the article (Papers of George L. Burr, Cornell University Library). G. B. Adams, to whom Jameson had confided his uneasiness over the article which Stephens was to prepare, wrote on Aug. 8, 1895: "I imagine he is one of the men who give editors, printers and correspondents no end of trouble, and he must be allowed, in the main, to take his own time with his contributions, but he will be in at the death. [P.S.]. No historian, trained in the study of documents, would consider the evidence sufficient to warrant the deduction that 'the death' above refers to the death of the managing editor, brought on by the troubles of the first number!" In this instance Professor Stephens apparently failed to be "in at the death" for no article of his appeared until April, 1896, and even this was of the nature of a combined review of a number of books which had been sent to him: Recent memoirs of the French Directory, *Amer. Hist. Rev.* 1: 473-489. Cornell was represented in the first number by Moses Coit Tyler's The party of the Loyalists in the American Revolution, 24-45.

[155] At the American Historical Association meeting held in Washington in 1890 Dr. Jameson presented a carefully prepared paper on the expenditures of foreign governments in behalf of history, including expenditures for printing, publica-

tion, editing, archives, and subventions. While admitting that the United States spent as much as other countries he maintained that the distribution had been bad, that more should have been spent on archives, and that machinery should be provided whereby the government could make use of expert aid. His concrete suggestion was that original materials competently edited be brought to the annual meeting of the Association and if approved be incorporated in the annual report made to the Congress and printed as a Smithsonian report. No action was taken on this suggestion until 1895 when at the December meeting it was announced that the executive council had created an Historical Manuscripts Commission, "for the preparation or supervision of a calendar of original manuscripts and records of national interest relating to Colonial and later history of the United States." The members of the commission were: Douglas Brymner, Ottawa, Talcott Williams, Philadelphia, William P. Trent, Sewanee, Tenn., F. J. Turner, Madison, with Jameson as chairman. (*Ann. Rept., Amer. Hist. Assn.,* 1890: 9-10; 1895: 10). Jameson remained chairman of the commission until he completed his edition of the correspondence of Calhoun in 1899 and was again made chairman in 1906.

[156] Part of the summer of 1896 was spent in England, where Jameson consulted Hubert Hall, of the Public Record Office, Bishop Stubbs, a member of the Royal Manuscripts Commission, and J. J. Cartwright, secretary of the commission.

[157] Mary E. Woolley (1863-1947), A.B., Brown, 1894, A.M., 1895. After five years of teaching in Wellesley College, Miss Woolley became president of Mount Holyoke, where she remained until 1937.

[158] Francis G. Allinson (1856-1931) received his Ph.D. degree from the Johns Hopkins University in 1880. From 1882 to 1891 he was head master in classics in the university school of Baltimore and during part of that time was at the boarding-house table so much enjoyed by Jameson. In 1895 he came to Brown as associate professor of Greek and classical philology. Ten years later he married Anne Crosby Emery, dean of the Women's College of Brown. The two remained warm friends of Jameson for many years.

January number or better. Last call for luncheon, so I must close. What is your article to be about? Be of good cheer, brother. You won't have to stay there always. Meanwhile you are doing much. Those youths will "catch on" to more or less and will propagate you.

To Sara Jameson

Washington, D. C.,
May 1, 1896.

My dearest Sallie:

. . . I go back now to the club, to lunch with Burr, and begin to be crammed up by him.[159] One or the other of us must go to the Hague in a week or so; he, I suppose.

Evening. Yes, he will without doubt be the one to go. He would be more useful, and he is free to go, while I can't leave the Review just now and don't want to fail of my date on June 13.[160] He and I had

---

[159] George Lincoln Burr (1857-1938), a member of the history faculty of Cornell University, from 1888 to 1938, and a distinguished mediaevalist. The Jameson papers indicate no intercourse between Burr and Jameson until the establishment of the *Review* brought them together. From that time until Jameson's death they were close friends.

The boundary between British Guiana and Venezuela had long been in dispute, the British basing their claims on the early Dutch claims, the government of Venezuela, on those of Spain. Offers by the United States to arbitrate met with rebuffs from England, and on Dec. 17, 1895, Cleveland, acting, he maintained, in accordance with the Monroe Doctrine, asked the Congress for a commission which should determine the correct boundary historically, with the tacit understanding that once the line was determined the United States would maintain it, by force if necessary. The Congress responded at once with an appropriation and a commission was appointed, consisting of Associate Justice David J. Brewer, Richard A. Almy, chief justice of the court of appeals of the District of Columbia, Andrew D. White, Frederic R. Coudert, and D. C. Gilman. In March Burr was engaged as historical investigator. A letter from Gilman asking Jameson to share in the work has not been found, but on Apr. 18, 1896, Burr wrote from Washington a long and persuasive letter to him: "You are the one man in the country for the most essential part of this work. Your noble study on Usselinx has shown, not merely your remarkable powers of research, of which there is abundant other proof, but your acquaintance, exceptional both in intimacy and extent, with the precise channels of knowledge from which most is to be expected for our problem. I am convinced that it is from Dutch records, printed or unprinted, that we must chiefly hope for the exact data which can alone give definiteness and finality to the work of the Commission. . . . I know that you are at this moment—what with the Historical Review and the new commission on American manuscripts—the busiest historian in America. But I am sure that this is a more pressing call; and I cannot think it unworthy even of your powers."

[160] Jameson's part in the study proved to be comparatively small; he examined all available printed materials before 1648 and from these reported on the facts as there presented. His work was finished on June 11, in time for him to sail with his family for England on June 13, the date he had not wished to miss. His report was submitted from Switzerland. Slightly modified in the light of Burr's later discoveries, it was printed

---

a long séance this afternoon over the "British Case" and other books and papers, and go at it in more regular form tomorrow. After getting through with him I did Gertrude's proof[161] and sent it off and then went out to Kendall Green to supper. Lovely there and in Washington generally . . . .

To the Jameson Family

Cosmos Club,
Washington, D. C.
May 4, 1896.

My dear Father (and Mother, and Helen):

. . . Today I dictated Review letters from 9 to 10, as I usually shall do, having a very good typewriter; then worked on the Guiana matters till four. Burr sails for Europe Saturday. Meantime my effort is to get posted by him. It is too soon to say how well I shall succeed in doing the work, or how rapidly. I have not found it very interesting yet, but shall when I have my own hand. . . .

To Albert Shaw

196 Bowen St., Providence,
November 3, 1896.[162]

My dear Shaw:

You have helped me so much and so often that I very much wish to do anything I can for you. I have tried hard to persuade myself this morning that I could rightly undertake to do what you ask in your letter of yesterday; but I have not succeeded, in view of the plain facts of the case.[163] It may be otherwise after Christmas, but from now until Christmas I have on my mind, beside my college work and my work for the Review, both of which are now heavier than heretofore, the necessity of preparing, for the Christmas meeting of the American Historical Association, an elaborate report for the Historical Manuscripts Commission.[164] That Commission is a thing I care a great

---

in the autumn as *Report on Spanish and Dutch settlements prior to 1648.* Before the commission completed its work Great Britain agreed to arbitrate, so that no American conclusion was called for. To represent Venezuela on the arbitration commission that country named two Americans, Chief Justice Fuller and Justice Brewer. Meeting in Paris, the commission rendered a unanimous decision in 1899.

[161] Gertrude Selwyn Kimball (1863-1910), a student of Jameson, and a friend of both Mrs. and Mr. Jameson, was the author of *The East India trade of Providence,* 1896, which appeared as one of the *Papers from the historical seminary of Brown.*

[162] Manuscript Division, New York Public Library.

[163] The letter of Nov. 2, 1896, has not been found.

[164] The first report of the Historical Manuscripts Commission (*Ann. Rept., Amer. Hist. Assn.,* 1896: 1: 467-1107) was an ambitious attempt to illustrate the kind of work which needed to be done and the character of the historical documents available. After a list of printed guides to materials, the letters of Phineas Bond were chosen from British sources

deal about. I believe that, if rightly managed, it can do a great deal for the future of historical work in this country. I believe also that much depends upon the way it starts out. In view of these facts, and of the difficulty of managing its business by correspondence among five persons so remote from each other, I feel already quite nervous as to the possibility of my not getting the report into shape within the time allowed; so I shall have to decline what I should be glad to do for you. The only way in which I can make any amends is by saying this promptly, which I have now done, and by suggesting some one else. Dunning at Columbia would do the thing very well; so would Hart; and so, I think, would C. F. A. Currier, Levermore's successor at the Institute of Technology.[165] With much regret.

To George L. Burr

196 Bowen Street, Providence
December 21, 1896 [166]

My dear Burr:

You have a grievance, and I don't deny it. I can only say that, what with examination-papers, class essays, the quarterly crisis of the Review (now struggling with a new printer), and the first annual crisis of the Historical Manuscripts Commission (which has involved an amount of work greater than I expected) I hardly know where I am or how to get time to do even *IN*justice to any of these things or to Guiana. I must also plead (a very rare thing with me) a little indisposition just after Thanksgiving,—though not caused thereby—which has left me a little less strong than usual.

However, I rather think I can send you tomorrow night the alterations which I suggest in my report to the Commission.[167] . . . I am sorry to see that your paper has dropped out from the programme of the Association. It seemed to me the most interesting item they had, and I should have been glad that the Fachgenossen should all have a chance to see how

exquisitely you have carried on the whole inquiry.[168] But the printed volume will show that.

I have thought of all you have written about form, but I cannot agree to the suggestion that what you have found out regarding the Dutch in Guiana before 1648 should be "run in" as footnotes to my paper. I know what my work has been, in comparison with yours, too well to be willing to fall in with such a plan. I go farther, and declare that, unless under positive instructions from the Commission or the Secretary, I will not consent to what I think would be not only inappropriate but wrong, as giving a false impression respecting the relative importance of our researches. Personal considerations ought not to hold the first place; but when other things are equal I feel justified in bringing such considerations in, to the extent of defending you against yourself. Now it seems to me that, if other things are *not* equal, it is only that on the whole more is to be said for printing the papers separately and at length, than for trying to avoid overlapping by devices which will, to my mind, appear cumbrous and will certainly confuse the reader.

What I shall send on, for you to do what you please with, is framed on the other plan. I shall make few changes in the text of my report, changes mainly confined to the elision of statements which you have found to be erroneous. The text will thus appear to be what it really is: a report submitted in June, based on printed books. It is that, and I can't make anything else of it in the time at my disposal within the period before you go to press. What little overlapping there is in our reports will be best explained to the reader by his seeing my report as such a June document. So it seems to me.

Where it seems not proper to operate simply by "subtraction and silence" I shall suggest footnotes. I placed all my references and quotations in the text, mainly because, going away with only three copies made, I thought to run it all in after that manner would guard against the chance of copyists' misplacing footnotes. This arrangement, otherwise not perhaps the most advisable one, now gives me a chance to use genuine footnotes as the means of conveying later corrections or additions, such as your Raleigh and Harcourt matter, either by full state-

to demonstrate the importance to American history of British material; and from Canadian archives, a selection of the intercepted letters to the Duke de Mirepoix. The letters of Stephen Higginson, prominent Boston merchant and member of the Essex Junto; the diary of Stephen Hooker; and the Clark-Genêt correspondence completed the report. For all this the chairman of the commission did a large part of the editorial work.

[165] William A. Dunning (1857-1922) was, with the exception of a short period of study in Germany, associated with Columbia University, as student and teacher from 1878 until his death.

Charles Francis Adams Currier (1862-1919) came to the Massachusetts Institute of Technology in 1891. Levermore, who began to teach in the Institute the same year that Jameson came to Brown, had gone to Adelphi College, of which he became president in 1896.

[166] George L. Burr Papers, Cornell University Library.

[167] See *ante,* May 1, 1896, n. 160.

[168] Burr's paper, The search for the Venezuela-Guiana boundary, was read at the New Haven meeting of the Association in 1898 and was printed in the *Amer. Hist. Rev.* 4: 470-477, April, 1899; in 1900, the *Review* 6: 49-64, October, 1900, contained a second article by Burr, The Guiana boundary: a postscript. For an account of his work for the Venezuelan Commission, see Bainton, Roland H., and Lois O. Gibbons, *George Lincoln Burr,* 70-83, Ithaca, N. Y., Cornell Univ. Press, 1943. Jameson in his introduction to *Persecution and liberty: essays in honor of George Lincoln Burr,* xvii, N. Y., Century Company, 1931, called Burr's work for the commission "as fine a piece of historical research and criticism as ever was buried in a government report."

ment or by reference to your pages.[169]   But you may think it better that my original reference and citations should appear as footnotes.   I give you discretionary authority to deal with my offspring.

Mrs. Jameson would send kind regards if she were in.   I might say roundly and boldly that she does send such; but I feel that in all this correspondence connected with the great Venezuela question we ought to be very accurate.   I wish you a Merry Christmas.   I sincerely hope we are to see you at New York after all.

To John Jameson

Huntington, June 23, 1897.

Dear Father:

Thank you for your letter and also for the clippings.   If they organize a Vigilance Committee in Woburn, your San Francisco training will make you invaluable.   As to the Transcript's article, I suppose we must expect that many newspapers will side with the trustees.[170]   For my part, I despise their bigotry and ingratitude, and also their pretence of solemn regard for the well-being of the college, for which the whole pack of them has not done as much as Andrews alone.   Goddard and Durfee and Wayland are to show him the muzzle,[171] it seems.   I hope the

good man will not back down.   It will be a bad state of things for us all if a lot of conceited parvenues like Joe Walker,[172] who get put on boards of trustees simply because they are rich, can dictate to us what we shall say both inside and outside the college.   The papers also show that Gates has brought things to such a pass as to get Morse's resignation.[173]   I have perceived for some time that he was after Morse's scalp,—especially when he was at our house this spring.   Gates is not thoroughly honest, and is a man of such remarkable vanity that the popularity of some of the older professors is a source of irritation to him, "the jealous Turk, that brooks no brother near his throne."[174]   I'll bet the alumni will make Rome howl this Commencement.   Pity Morse's health is so poor; the case for him would be much stronger but for that . . . .

To John Jameson

June 30, 1897

My dear Father:

. . . Thank you for all the interesting clippings about Morse and Gates.   I almost wish I could be up there to help in the fight or (less enthusiastically) in the pacification.   But there is enough to fight about here at home, what with Sid Sherman's affair[175] and

---

[169] Jameson had referred to a statement made by James I, in his *Declaration of the demeanor and carriage of Sir Walter Raleigh*, 1618, which implied early Spanish settlement.   Burr suggested that the statement had come to James from the Spanish ambassador and was therefore valueless.   In support of this he cited Robert Harcourt's *Relation of a voyage to Guiana*, 1626.   See Jameson, *Report*, 50, n. 1.

[170] At its meeting of June 16, 1897, the corporation of Brown University, after some discussion of a speech by Joseph Walker of Worcester, in which he attributed the failure of the university to increase its endowment to the views of the president on the silver question, appointed a committee to confer with President Andrews in "regard to the interests of the university."   At this time the president was in Europe, having been on leave during the preceding academic year.   For an account of this episode in the history of Brown, see Donnan, Elizabeth, A nineteenth-century academic cause célèbre, *New England Quart.* 25: 23-46, March, 1952.
The clipping from the Boston *Transcript* was probably an editorial which appeared in the issue of June 19, p. 7, the same issue which carried a news item describing the action of the corporation.   The editorial began: "The action of the trustees of Brown University in appointing a committee headed by Chancellor Goddard to wait upon President Andrews. . . . is tantamount to calling for his resignation."   It continued: "We suppose that the Trustees of Brown will come in for a good deal of hot censure, notably from that element of Populism which has pointed with pride to President Andrews as evidence that its financial views had won the sympathy of learned men in New England.   The Trustees' side is, however, plain to anyone who will see it.   They must be the final authority for the direction of the curriculum, and the difference between them and President Andrews is personal as well as official.   Free coinage is a question of ethics."
[171] The committee to wait upon the president consisted of William Goddard, chancellor of the university, William Durfee, a former chief justice of Rhode Island, and Francis Wayland, dean of the Yale Law School.

[172] Joseph H. Walker (1829-1907), a Worcester manufacturer and a member of the Congress, was chairman of the House Committee on Money and Banking.   He had for some time been a critic of President Andrews.
[173] Merrill Edward Gates (1848-1922) was the president of Amherst College from 1890 till 1899.   It proved to be *his* term which was drawing to a close, not that of Professor Morse, who served Amherst until 1907.   The immediate occasion of Morse's resignation at this time was the appointment to the history department of an assistant whom he had not recommended.   News of his resignation and his reason roused a storm of protest from the alumni and at their June meeting the trustees, who took full responsibility for the appointment, asked Morse to withdraw his resignation, and assured him that at the close of 1897-1898 he should have full charge of his department.   On this assurance he agreed to remain but the opponents of President Gates were by no means satisfied with the retention of Morse.   They wished also to be rid of Gates.   The trustees, anxious to avoid a scandal, refused to make public the case against the president or to take action, hoping vainly that the opposition would subside.   In the desire to avoid publicity the senior class shared, for though they sent to the trustees a statement of their case against Gates they refused to give it to the press (Boston *Transcript*, June 30, 1897, pp. 1, 5, 14, July 1, p. 6).   Opposition to the president did not decrease and two years later his services were brought to an end.
[174] "Should such a man, too fond to rule alone,
        Bear, like the Turk, no brother near the throne,
          View him with scornful, yet with jealous eyes?"
        Pope, Epistle to Dr. Arbuthnot, Prologue to the Satires.
[175] Sidney A. Sherman, an assistant principal in the Providence high school, and secretary of the Union for Practical Progress, had, in the spring of 1895, written four letters to the Providence *Journal* on municipal affairs.   The first two, described by Dr. Jameson as "temperate discussions of public affairs such as every citizen has a right to print," argued that

that of President Andrews. Thank you for the Andrews clippings, too. Andrews arrived this afternoon, and Gardner and I went to see him at once. I don't think he will resign, though he has no personal attachment to the job; indeed I don't think the corporation want him to resign. Also, I am sure he will not put on the muzzle. Whether the faculty will both concur in my manifesto and think it wise to promulgate it I do not know.[176] I shall not be clear of its wisdom myself for a day or two, certainly . . . . [P. S.] Andrews takes the whole thing philosophically and is not inclined to magnify it. Hadn't heard anything about it till today.

To JOHN JAMESON

Providence, July 9, 1897.

My dear Father and Mother:
. . . Here, though I try to keep up with my work most of one's thought is taken up now with this affair between Andrews and the Corporation. The triumviri will meet him soon, perhaps today. My expectation that, after all that has been said, they will roar very gently, has diminished. I fear they will put pressure on him. In that case there will be a fight. The faculty, I am glad to say, are mostly determined to stand by him and to stand up for freedom of speech. This is all private at present. We want to keep the peace if Andrews feels, after the interview, that the Corporation do not mean to put restrictions upon him. So we say nothing about the meeting we had the other day, at which I read a somewhat detailed address to the alumni I had prepared. It was almost universally approved by those in town, and nearly all would sign it in the contingency mentioned.[177] Probably enough it might first be recast slightly, and take the form of an open letter sent during vacation to the members of the Corporation and to all the alumni. Gardner and I have been taking the chief part in the thing, and he is so very prudent and temperate a man that I am confirmed in my feeling that the only course is some such protest. Apart from the question of right, it would be very injurious for the college to have Andrews resign, or to have it supposed that he has been put under bonds. For that matter he never would be, but I think they will try it. I am much obliged for the clippings, and hope you will send me any more you see, though those that come out now are apt to be "inspired" rather than the spontaneous expressions of editorial opinions. For instance, an editorial on p. 13 of the "Independent" of yesterday was written by Dr. Heman Wayland, son of the old president and brother of one of the triumvirs, who is one of the Corporation. He wrote it for the "Examiner." The editor declined to print it, substituting one of his own which I have not yet seen, but which I was told would be irenic in its tendency.[178] I believe that if necessary we can at least work upon the alumni enough to prevent Andrews's being forced to resign, if that is the design. I don't think it is the plan of most of the board, but it is of some, and they will work hard between now and September 2. As to Sidney Sherman, it now looks as if the main school-committee, on being made acquainted with the facts, could be induced at their September meeting, to undo the injustice committed. We think we can count up a majority. Well, enough of war's alarms. I am still editing the American Historical Review, and working

---

the city council was giving a valuable franchise to the Union Railroad Company too cheaply. The secretary of the company and one member of the council were also members of the school committee and through their influence Sherman was notified that his publications must cease. Not content with this, by means of a "reorganization," the school committee reduced his salary by $400, though he continued to do the same work as before. The efforts to rouse the public to an understanding of what had happened, to restore Sherman's salary, and to establish the right of a teacher to express himself on public questions failed, in spite of three forthright letters from Jameson to the *Journal*. To his father Jameson wrote: "Monday morning, November 1, 1897. (Festo Omnium Sanctorum). . . . I shall send from down town two copies of the Journal, in which I presume they have printed a communication I prepared setting forth the affair of Sid Sherman. The Union Railroad Company has such possession of the reporters and city editors of the papers that Saturday's papers gave an account of Friday night's debate so garbled that no mention of the Company was made." Jameson's long letter of Nov. 1 (*Journal*, 8, cols. 3-4) described the situation in detail. A defense of the school committee appeared in the *Journal* of Nov. 7, p. 4.

[176] This document eventually appeared as, *An open letter addressed to the corporation of Brown University by members of the faculty*, 1897.

[177] The committee conferred with President Andrews on July 16 and on July 17 he sent in his resignation, whereupon twenty-five of the thirty-seven members of the faculty of professorial rank signed Jameson's manifesto.

[178] Dr. Heman Wayland's article in the *Independent* of July 8, 1897, said in substance that while free trade was a "subject on which it is felt that wise and honest men may differ. . . . it is a public calamity and menace when Bryan and his followers can quote in favor of their scheme of hardly recognized repudiation the authority of the President of a leading New England college."
The editorial in the *Examiner* of the same date stated that "it would be extremely unfortunate if the unpardonable publicity given to the recent action of the board should result in depriving the university of Dr. Andrew's invaluable services."
In reply to criticisms, Dr. Wayland again wrote to the *Independent* (Aug. 5), agreeing that Baptist doctrine upheld religious liberty, but arguing that that did not prevent a corporation from requesting a president to refrain from advocating unsound or dishonest economic policies. Meanwhile, the protest of the faculty appeared and the *Independent* commented favorably upon it. This brought forth a third letter from Dr. Wayland in which he wrote that the editorial contained many erroneous statements. On this the *Independent* dryly remarked that readers would find it difficult to discover from Dr. Wayland's letter what the erroneous statements were.

at various other things. Burnett[179] hasn't collared a job yet, so tell me of any vacant professorships of history you read of in any paper. John C. Calhoun's heirs seem disposed to accede to my plan of letting the Historical Manuscripts Commission print a collection of his letters.[180] I think this would be an exceedingly important contribution to American history . . . .

To JOHN JAMESON

Seal Harbor, Me., August 8, 1897.

Dear Father:

. . . In the *Transcript* Judge Gaskill[181] modestly serves notice that he has no mind to be represented by Walker and does not hold certain views which Joseph says the Corp. hold unanimously, and further saith not. I hear from Providence that the alumni movement goes on well. I secretly instigated, before I left, a movement of the women graduates, who of course are especially indebted to A.[182] Saw Gilman yesterday, who entirely sides with Andrews, and has written him. We drove over to N. E. Harbor. On the way met a lot of people we knew, among them two Esty boys and Professor Cowles, who are at S. W. [Southwest Harbor].[183] James Bryce is expected by the Gilmans today. I mean to see him and President Eliot tomorrow.[184] . . .

---

[179] Edmund C. Burnett (1864-1948), A.B., 1890, A.M., 1895, Ph.D., 1897, Brown, was instructor in history in Brown from 1895 to 1899. After a brief period of teaching in the South he joined the staff of the Department of Historical Research of the Carnegie Institution of Washington in 1907.

[180] *The correspondence of John C. Calhoun,* edited by Jameson as the fourth annual report of the Historical Manuscripts Commission, appeared in the *Ann. Rept., Amer. Hist. Assn.,* 1899: 2: 11-1218.

[181] Congressman Joseph Walker was reported by the Boston *Transcript* as saying that the corporation of Brown University was unanimous in the belief that the question over which Dr. Andrews and the corporation were at variance was far more vital to the well being of the country than were the questions upon which the Civil War was fought. Judge F. A. Gaskill, one of the members of the corporation, expressed courteous dissent. *Transcript,* Aug. 7, 1897.

[182] It was during the administration of President Andrews that women were admitted as candidates for all degrees and that women graduate students were taught in university classrooms. Just a year before this the Women's College had become an accepted department of the university. Over six hundred alumni and forty-four of the forty-nine women graduates petitioned the corporation in behalf of Andrews.

[183] William Lyman Cowles (1856-1929), A.B., Amherst, 1878, taught Latin in Amherst from 1880 to 1925. The "Esty boys" were probably the sons of William Cole Esty (1838-1916), A.B., Amherst, 1860, who taught mathematics in the college from 1862 till 1905. The older son, William (1868-1928), was graduated from Amherst in the class of 1889; the younger, Edward (1874-1942), in that of 1897. He returned to the college as instructor in mathematics for the year 1897-1898.

[184] For the part in the crusade taken by President Eliot, see *New England Quart.* **25**: 41-42, March, 1952.

To ALBERT SHAW

Seal Harbor, Me., August 8, 1897.[185]

My dear Shaw:

I received your letter late last night, and make prompt reply. I do not see why it would not be a *very* good thing to print in your September issue a character-sketch of President Andrews. If you do it, by the way, I suggest that the copies of the Review which go to Providence arrive there on August 30 or 31 if possible, that they may have their due influence on the Corporation meeting of September 1. Not at all that I suppose they would be polemical in character, but that, (I imagine) they would tend to promote a just appreciation of Andrews and his services. That sentiment will have large influence. (I don't quite think the Corporation will ask him to withdraw his resignation, but the more they are worked on the more they will do in the way of setting and keeping the college right in the eyes of the world).

As to a man, your best man is Professor C. T. Winchester of Middletown, Conn.[186] You know how admirable a writer he is; and he has been a life-long friend, from school-days. He knows all parts of his career about equally well, and certainly knows his characteristics. If he desires any information about his administration at Brown, I can supply most of it, probably. *Between you and me,* I wrote the professors' memorial; of course many statistical facts that were not used are out of mind now, and out of reach up here; but I could most likely give Winchester what he wanted. In case of absolute need, i.e., if W. didn't want to write on these recent years, I could write you a *brief* account of them, with a fair-minded acct. of this controversy; for (apart from the present question of principle, vital to any university) I believe I know the faults of Andrews and the merits of our Corporation, several of whom are my friends. This would have to be anonymous (I mean it would be more decent, and more weighty) "by a member of the faculty," whether a protestor or not would not need to be said; there is little divergence of opinion in the faculty respecting Andrews, and no such split as the papers have inferred, from the fact that some (in most cases because they disliked the method) did not sign.

Winchester may be out of the country. Manatt,[187] who is now at Old Orchard, might do it too warmly. I know no one who could do it so well as Winchester,

---

[185] Manuscript Division, New York Public Library.

[186] Caleb T. Winchester (1847-1920), A.B., Wesleyan, 1869, of whom Woodrow Wilson once wrote to Jameson: "He is one of the most interesting and admirable of lecturers. I can never hear him too much. He is the man who ought to be Donovan professor of English literature in Baltimore" (Wilson to Jameson, Jan. 1, 1892).

[187] James I. Manatt, professor of Greek literature and history in Brown, 1893-1915.

except certain members of the Corporation, who wouldn't and certain of the faculty, who oughtn't. Professor Richard Colwell, of Denison University, at Granville, Ohio, knows well several parts of Andrews' varied career;[188] but is he any sort of a writer? On the whole, perhaps the best after Winchester would be a Brown ('72?) man who is an editor of the *Tribune*. I know his name well, but can't think of it; it begins with B.,[189] but don't think I mean Joe Bishop of the *Post*, who hates Andrews. Another Brown contemporary and friend is W. C. Hamm, of the Phila. *Press*. Next I might put Henry Robinson Palmer, Brown '90, an able writer on the Providence *Journal*, but, *at the last that I knew*, uncorrupted by the *Journal*'s crabbed hatred of Andrews.[190]

I hope all this will help you. Andrews has had few intimates, or I could do better. He is so noble a fellow, and has done so much good at Providence, that I shall be glad to see him "well shown up" in the esteemed contemporary over which you preside.

Hoping you are having a happy summer, and wishing you were here,

To JOHN JAMESON

Thursday evening [Sept. 2, 1897].

Dear Father:

You have heard our good news, but I thought you might like to see fuller accounts, so I send you yesterday's Telegram and today's Journal. You will note that the Journal omits the last part of the list of signatures to the presidents' memorial and ignores that of the economists. . . .The Olney letter appeared in the Journal of Wednesday morning.[191] Collins, with whom I talked till after midnight, thought it would not irritate the trustees at the stage arrived at,

and wanted to print it to help stiffen up some members. I consented, provided it came out as made public by a member of the Corporation who had seen it, which it did. Well, the Corp. have behaved splendidly. I hope Andrews will stay, but anyhow, the fight is won, so far as the essential thing is concerned. I think the effect of the whole struggle on the universities and colleges of the land will be excellent, even if it does hurt this college temporarily. . . .

To ALBERT SHAW

October 15, 1897.[192]

My dear Shaw:

In view of a meeting of the Board of Editors of the American Historical Review which is to take place next Friday, I should like to bother you with a question or two. The guarantee fund of the Review, which was arranged to continue three years, will expire next spring. At Christmas at Cleveland at the time of the meeting of the American Historical Association, a meeting of the association of guarantors will be held, at which the question of the future basis of the Review will be settled. Our meeting of next Friday is the last meeting we shall have before that. We shall, therefore, have to decide then as to what recommendation the Board will make to the association of guarantors. Mr. Brett the manager of the Macmillan Co.,[193] has a project respecting which I should like to have your advice. His idea is that an arrangement might be made with the American Historical Association whereby they raising $5.00 from each member instead of $3.00 could turn over $2.00 to us, in return for which we should supply each member with the Review; and that secondly a greater popular success of the Review should be made by paying generously for say two articles in each number, of such a sort, as would give the Review a larger circulation without lowering its quality, the rest of the contents being kept about the same as now. He thinks the enlargement of the circulation would pay the expenses of such an experiment. At present we rarely pay for an article. The alternative plan would be, so far as I can see, to get the American Historical Association to give us $500 outright, which I understand they would be willing to do, and to get half the guarantee fund continued for another three years. It appears from the accounts that half the guarantee money, plus $500 would enable us to go on as we do at present.

What I most wish to ask you is whether, in your opinion, Mr. Brett's plan can be carried out in exact terms. He speaks of Captain Mahan, Theodore

[188] Andrews was president of Denison University from 1875 to 1879, years in which two future presidents of the University of Chicago were connected with Denison: E. D. Burton as a member of the class of 1876, and William R. Harper as a young instructor.

[189] The editor on the New York *Tribune* was Arthur F. Bowers, A.B., Brown, 1871.

[190] Shaw apparently did not accept the suggestions of this letter, for on Aug. 12 Jameson agreed to write three thousand words on President Andrews for the *Review of Reviews* and on Aug. 14 he stated that he was sending them. Among the Jameson Papers are the proofs of this article, which appeared as an editorial rather than a signed contribution. *Review of Reviews* 16: 259-261, Sept. 1897.

On Aug. 9 Jameson wrote to Shaw of the memorial which was being circulated to be signed by "many college presidents and professors and many men of affairs," and on the fourteenth he asked Shaw to procure signatures to this memorial from "Mr. Mabie, Dr. Abbott, Mr. Gilder, Mr. Howells, etc." (Manuscript Division, New York Public Library).

[191] Also in the Providence *Bulletin*, Sept. 1, 1897. This letter from the ex-Secretary of State rebuked the corporation and championed the right of free speech and independent thought. In its meeting of September 1, the corporation voted to request President Andrews to withdraw his resignation.

[192] Manuscript Division, New York Public Library.

[193] George P. Brett (1858-1936) was for many years president of the Macmillan Company, which published the *American Historical Review* from its beginning.

Roosevelt, Moses Coit Tyler, and such writers, who can write things that are above criticism in point of quality and yet are highly popular. Do you think that there are enough such men to insure us a supply, in return for increased payments, of two articles per quarter of really popular historical matter, which is, nevertheless, first rate from a scientific point of view? Or would the result of the attempt be that the scientific quality of the Review would be impaired?[194] I ask these questions partly because I wish to give well-considered advice at the meeting, and partly because if any plan is adopted which will lower the scientific standing of the Review, I shall want to drop the position of managing editor. It is pretty laborious when managed in connection with my teaching, and prevents me from doing any historical writing, and I don't care to keep it up unless it is to contribute steadily toward maintaining the highest standards of historical scholarship in the country.

Busy as you are, I am asking a good deal of you in requesting you to turn your thoughts away temporarily from your own magazine to consider the affairs of ours. But I know that you are interested in the welfare of historical scholarship and its organs, and shall be very much obliged by any help you may find it possible to render.[195]

---

[194] George B. Adams on Sept. 20, 1897, wrote to Herbert B. Adams, setting forth Mr. Brett's plan and asking whether it would work. Holt, *op. cit.,* 244-245.

[195] Because of illness Shaw did not reply until Oct. 26, when he wrote: "My impression as to the other proposition, namely that you should pay a good price to such men as Captain Mahan, Theodore Roosevelt, and so on, for popular features, was [that it was] a wholly bad plan. If those men are not willing once in a while to give the American Historical Review a piece of good work for the pleasure they ought to feel in being in such company, not to speak of pride and duty as regards the maintenance of such a periodical in this country, there is no use trying to get them to do it by the inducement of an honorarium. The public in one way and another is contributing generously to the maintenance of these gentlemen, and if they have from time to time some good material that they could give the American Historical Review they ought not to have money in mind at all. Of course I may be all wrong, but I am giving you my very firm opinion. If these so-called popular writers are not willing to write for the American Historical Review on precisely the same terms that your more restrictedly scholarly men write, I think it would be a mistake to let them in. My belief, however, is that if the matter were put to them plainly they would be only too glad to say that they would deem it an honor to contribute to the Review, when they found themselves with something worthy of its standards.

"Personally let me say that while I appreciate very highly the excellence of the American Historical Review, and your own skill and judgment in editing it, I should be sorry if in the long run this editorial work should prevent your doing the historical writing that you are so well qualified for."

TO ALBERT SHAW

October 27, 1897.[196]

My dear Shaw:

I readily understand both your willingness to help us and the particular difficulties that stood in the way last week. I am glad to say that when we came to the meeting and had all the accounts respecting the first two volumes laid before us, we found the financial situation of the Review to be considerably more hopeful than we had expected, and the plan of popularizing it was not urged. The American Historical Association can probably be induced at Christmas to make a direct grant, and the publisher will probably make proposals that will make it possible for us to continue with but a small guarantee fund, if any at all is requisite.[197] Nothing is yet settled, but everything looks well at present. I am very much obliged by your letter.

[P. S.] I am very sorry you have been ill.

TO JOHN JAMESON

196 Bowen Street, Providence,
April 2, 1898.

Dear Father:

. . . We left here on Thursday morning and got to Princeton at evening. Woodrow Wilson and his wife were most hospitable and kind. Friday morning I went all over the college with Wilson. Since I was there seven years ago several *very* handsome buildings have been added. In the afternoon we were taken upon a drive. In the evening came the debate, on the question whether national party politics should be disregarded in municipal elections.[198] Mr. Cleveland presided. The other two judges were William L. Wilson, formerly Postmaster-General and now president of Washington and Lee University, and Mr. Everett P. Wheeler of New York.[199] We found it

---

[196] Manuscript Division, New York Public Library.

[197] At its December meeting the Association appropriated $1000 for the support of the *Review* from July 1, 1898, to July 1, 1899. In return each member was to receive the first two numbers of the volume which began with October, 1898. This was the first official relationship between the Association and the *Review.* A year later, at the New Haven meeting, the Association voted an annual subsidy to the editors and the publisher of the *Review,* with the provision that each member was thereafter to receive the *Review* and that vacancies on the board of editors were to be filled by the executive council of the Association. The legal ownership of the journal still rested in the hands of the editors. *Ann. Rept., Amer. Hist. Assn.,* 1897; **6**; 1898: 5-6, 8; *Amer. Hist. Rev.* **4**: 409-410, April, 1899.

[198] See *post,* Dec. 3, 1913.

[199] William L. Wilson (1843-1900) was Postmaster-General in Cleveland's cabinet from 1895 to 1897; from 1898 until 1900 he was president of Washington and Lee; Everett P. Wheeler (1840-1925), a New York lawyer much interested in honest public administration, some time after this married the daughter of President Gilman.

very hard to decide. The debate was excellent on both sides, and although the award was made to Yale, there was really not much to choose. After the debate came a Yale-Princeton banquet at the now famous Princeton Inn, at which everybody made speeches from Grover Cleveland down to J. F. Jameson . . . . Tillman had appointed our interview for Sunday evening, so I went over there.[200] All that he had to say might have been put upon a two-page letter and sent to me. However, he was a very interesting man to see—in many ways much superior to what I had been led to expect, though pretty rough. In these days when nobody quotes Latin in the Senate as Sumner used to, and perhaps when one would think nobody *could* except Hoar and Lodge, it was amusing to get a Latin quotation from Tillman of all men. He had the Calhoun papers, those possessed by Clemson College,[201] and they are now in the library of Brown University. Four or five hundred letters from Mr. Calhoun and twenty-four or twenty-five hundred to him. I shan't do anything with them for a little while, but have no doubt they will prove very interesting when I get at them.[202] The next time you come down I shall be able to show you some of the chief plums, no doubt. I had to go over and see Tillman again the next morning and he took me up to the Capitol and installed me in the private gallery of the Senate, from which I saw the President's message brought in and heard it and the Maine report read.[203] The galleries were of course packed. . . .

I have an impression that Higginson was *not* the first to suggest that the constitution should be ratified by conventions elected especially for the purpose, but I cannot lay my hand on a reference to that effect.[204]

Mr. Cleveland looks very well, much less repulsive looking than in 1895 [1885].[205] Mrs. Cleveland I did not see, though Sallie did.[206] . . .

To John Jameson
Providence, October 20, 1898.
My dear Father:
. . . I have arranged at six a meeting with Patrick Calhoun.[207] It looks as if the Lord had softened his heart. This was apparently largely due to my setting J. F. Rhodes on him. This particular historian, being a brother-in-law of Mark Hanna counted for something with Calhoun, who lives in Cleveland.[208] I had nearly given up hope of the Calhoun MSS. possessed by the present Calhouns, and of course I may not get them yet. But I hope I shall, for I imagine they would make a considerable addition to what I now have,—the Clemson and other MSS. at the library. . . .

To John Jameson
196 Bowen Street, Providence,
November 19, 1898.
Dear Father:
. . . Froude is always interesting, but you never can put full confidence in his statements. If you happen to be especially interested in Erasmus, don't fail to read the article upon him in the Britannica. It is by the late Dr. Mark Pattison, and is unusually interesting.[209]

---

[200] Early the next morning Jameson and his wife left Princeton, he to go to New York for a meeting of the board of editors of the *Review;* to Philadelphia to see his sister, Esther, who taught in a school for the deaf in Mount Airy; and thence to the Chickerings in Kendall Green. While with the Chickerings his interview with Tillman took place.

Benjamin R. Tillman (1847-1918), coming into political prominence in South Carolina as a champion of agrarian interests, had served as governor from 1890 to 1894, when he was elected United States Senator, an office which he held for twelve years.

[201] Possible Tillman's most useful service to South Carolina was his inducing the state to accept the gift of Thomas G. Clemson and helping to create the agricultural college which Clemson intended. See *ante,* Apr. 1, 1888, n. 152.

[202] It was now ten years since Jameson had first considered editing the Calhoun letters. In the second annual report of the Historical Manuscripts Commission, 1897, he made a preliminary statement of the plan to publish them. This was further developed in the report of 1898 (*Ann. Rept., Amer. Hist. Assn.,* 1897: 401-403; 1898: 567-569).

[203] William McKinley (1843-1901) delivered to the Congress on Monday, Mar. 28, 1898, the report of the Naval Board on the explosion of Feb. 15, 1898, which destroyed the *Maine* in the harbor of Havana, with the loss of 266 lives. The gist of the report was that the explosion was caused by an external mine. Steps toward war followed swiftly after the presentation of this report.

[204] Stephen Higginson (1743-1828), in a letter to General Henry Knox of Feb. 8, 1787, suggested the plan for the adoption of the Constitution which was later followed. *Ann. Rept., Amer. Hist. Assn.,* 1896: 1: 748-749.

[205] See *ante,* Mar. 30, 1885, n. 130.

[206] Jameson in this letter also reported that Professor C. E. Norton's lectures on Dante were to be given in Providence, 175 subscribers having been secured, and that the April *Review* was out, containing two articles of his own, one the report of the December Association meeting, the other, Early political uses of the word convention, *Amer. Hist. Rev.* 3: 477-487, 1897.

[207] Patrick Calhoun was a grandson of John C. Calhoun, a son of Col. Andrew Pickens Calhoun. Jameson not only secured his papers but also those of his sister, Margaret Calhoun of Wallace, Ga.

[208] James Ford Rhodes (1848-1927) was not only Hanna's brother-in-law but also his business partner in the firm of Rhodes and Company, until he withdrew from the firm in 1885 to devote his time to the writing of history. Soon after, he moved from Cleveland to Cambridge, Mass. When this letter was written he was first vice-president of the American Historical Association and was shortly to become its president. He had already published the first two volumes of his *History of the United States from the Compromise of 1850,* N. Y., Harper, 1893.

Marcus Alonzo Hanna (1837-1904), then at the height of his political power, was a member of the Senate and a close adviser of McKinley. His wife was Charlotte Augusta Rhodes.

[209] James Anthony Froude (1818-1894), as regius professor of modern history in Oxford after the death of Freeman, was said to have drawn large audiences to his lectures on Erasmus. These were published as *Life and letters of Erasmus,* London, Longmans; N. Y., Scribner's, 1894.

Mark Pattison (1813-1894) was rector of Lincoln College, Oxford. His chief published work was *Isaac Casaubon,* 1875.

Emerton of Harvard is preparing a book on Erasmus in the same series in which Professor Jacobs's Luther and Professor Richard's Melancthon have just come out.[210] Yes; I noticed the article on original work in this week's Nation.[211] I will not refuse all sympathy to the writer. No doubt freehand drawing in history is better than mechanical drawing, but I don't see that we should increase the amount of the former by diminishing the amount of the latter. If a man is not a genius, he will not write historical works of genius; yet I should think it was better that he should do what he can to advance the cause rather than to be forbidden to do anything. If a man cannot be an architect, he can make bricks, and that will be a great cause to the architects. . . .

To Albert Shaw

December 15, 1898.[212]

My dear Shaw:

I wish you would give me your advice as to the proper reviewer for Frederic Bancroft's forthcoming Life of Seward.[213] It is no ordinary political biography, but a labor of many years and of high intelligence and scholarship. It will be a book to rank with Randall's Jefferson or Rives's Madison.[214] It ought to have the most competent reviewer and the most careful reviewing. It seems to call for a man who knows well both the history of the Republican Party in New York and the modern history of American diplomacy. I thought I had fixed upon just the man in President White, and labored strenuously with him, but in vain. He is too busy. I don't know exactly whom to ask next. I should rather apply to a public man who had lived through some of those times (provided he were not too old), than an academic student of them. Few of these public men are competent to write such a review

as a journal of high standing should desire. Edward M. Shepard gave us an admirable review of Bigelow's Tilden, but I should rather have a Republican. Bigelow himself seems to be, without good ground, a little out with us at present. Schurz is not a New Yorker and probably would not do it for us.[215] I am thinking most seriously of Gov. Daniel Chamberlain. He reviews books of that period extremely well, and is very well disposed towards us (which counts for something since our pay is no great temptation to lawyers or public men), but he was not in New York during those days, nor ever much concerned with diplomacy.[216] Can't you, out of your abundant knowledge as to who is who in New York, suggest a better man, or two or three better men? White was just the combination, and I am very much vexed that he will not do it. It is a pity to bother you about a matter which I ought to know enough to settle for myself, but perhaps you will do it if I flatter you by alluding to your well-known good nature.[217]

I hope we shall see you at the meetings of the American Historical Association in New Haven.

To John Jameson

Providence, December 18, 1898.

Dear Father:

. . . I went over to Boston on Friday evening and dined at Mr. J. F. Rhodes's invitation with him at the University Club. Fine dinner,—terrapin and champagne and other "wanities." It was a first session of the Historical Manuscripts Committee of the Massachusetts Historical Society. They have lately established this, with Hart as chairman, and Rhodes, Schouler and John C. Ropes as members (C. F. Adams, too, I guess, though he could not be present, and with power to add from the corresponding members, upon which they added me, and Franklin Dexter of New Haven,

[210] Ephraim Emerton (1851-1935) published *Desiderius Erasmus of Rotterdam* in 1899; Jacobs, Henry Eyster (1844-1932), *Martin Luther, the hero of the Reformation, 1483-1546,* in 1898; *Phillip Melanchton,* by James W. Richard (1848-1909) also appeared in 1898.

[211] *Nation* 67: 366-367, Nov. 17, 1898. The editorial, a discussion of an article by Frederic Harrison in the *Nineteenth Century* which was highly critical of the historical method of Freeman and his followers, said: "it is this sort of research which is killing the art of historical narrative, and rendering history, instead of a synthetic whole, instead of a life-like picture, a mass of dreary facsimiles of Queen's washing-lists and inventories of the number of swine kept on a baronial manor in the twelfth century."

[212] Manuscript Division, New York Public Library.

[213] Frederic Bancroft (1860-1945), A.B., Amherst, 1882, Ph.D., Columbia, 1885, librarian of the Department of State, 1888-1892, lecturer in Amherst, Columbia, the Johns Hopkins, and the University of Chicago; a friend of Jameson until 1915, as will appear in later letters.

[214] H. S. Randall's three-volume life of Thomas Jefferson appeared in 1857; William C. Rives published his three-volume *History of the life and times of James Madison* between 1859 and 1868.

[215] John Bigelow, Jr. (1817-1911) published *Writings and speeches of Samuel J. Tilden* in 1885 and the *Life of Samuel J. Tilden* in 1895. His annoyance may have been due to the frank criticism by the reviewer of the latter volume (*Amer. Hist. Rev.* 1: 174-182, October, 1895). The reviewer, Edward Morse Shepard (1850-1911), a New York lawyer prominent in Democratic politics, was himself the author of *Martin Van Buren* in the American Statesmen series.

Carl Schurz (1829-1906) at this time was president of the National Civil Service Reform League, his active political career being over.

[216] Daniel H. Chamberlain (1835-1907), born in Massachusetts, a graduate of Yale, 1862, and of the Harvard Law School, had, after the war, become a cotton planter, attorney general of South Carolina, and from 1874 to 1877, governor of that state.

[217] Shaw suggested W. M. Jones of Rochester, once Seward's private secretary, John Hay, or Joseph H. Choate (Shaw to Jameson, Dec. 23, 1898). The review, in the end written by Chamberlain, was severely critical, attributing to Bancroft an unattractive style, many partisan judgments, and the neglect of new material (*Amer. Hist. Rev.* 6: 152-157, Oct. 1900).

later).[218] I had a fine time, and enjoyed their talk very much, especially Ropes's. Caught the midnight train home. I think I told you the Calhoun heirs had sent me what they had. . . . I have just acquired, ultimately for the Library of B. U., a collection of seventy contemporary S. C. pamphlets relating to the nullification controversy. President Gilman has sent me his collection of addresses on University Problems. Ours here is, Whom in the world can the Corporation persuade to take the job of reigning over us? [219]

To JOHN JAMESON

Providence, March 7, 1899.

My dear Father:

Anti-expansionism makes strange bed-fellows. To see Senator Hoar and the New York Evening Post joining hands lovingly was like the joining of Herod and Pilate. To see you and Jerry Simpson falling on each other's neck is still more diverting to the unregenerate.[220] I return to you his valuable communication, and also the clippings, which show how great an influence may be exerted at crises of our national history by quiet thinkers meditating in their own studies. I fear their fate will be like that of the wise man in the scriptures that saved the city. . . .

---

[218] John C. Ropes (1836-1899), founder of the Military History Society of Massachusetts, had already published *The first Napoleon,* 1885, and *The campaign of Waterloo,* 1892. His *Story of the Civil War* was not completed when he died, less than a year after this dinner (*Amer. Hist. Rev.* 5: 406, Jan., 1900).
Charles Francis Adams (1835-1915) was president of the Massachusetts Historical Society from 1895 until his death. Franklin B. Dexter (1842-1920) was connected with Yale University in various capacities from 1863 till the end of his life. In 1898 he was secretary of the Yale corporation.

[219] President Andrews had not withdrawn his resignation in September, 1897, but had consented to remain one year longer. His successor was William H. P. Faunce (1859-1930), A.B., Brown, 1880, who resigned as pastor of the Fifth Avenue Baptist Church in New York City to come to Brown. In the autumn Jameson wrote: "Faunce seems to give universal satisfaction, and it was especially plain how strong a hold he had already acquired in only a month, upon the undergraduates" (Jameson to John Jameson, Oct. 23, 1899).

[220] The New York *Evening Post* was, and continued to be, bitterly opposed to the annexation of the Philippines. Some two years after this, the *Post* published a "balance sheet" of the Philippine policy in which the writer pointed to the loss of lives, the ruined health, and the maimed bodies both of Americans and of natives of the islands. In addition, "our stock of false pretences, hypocritical professions, and silly boasting has been enormously increased by our two years in the Philippines" (New York *Evening Post,* Feb. 6, 1901 p. 6, editorial).
Jerry Simpson (1842-1905), disrespectfully known as "sockless Jerry," had served three terms in the Congress between 1890 and 1898, as a Populist representative from Kansas. He was now in retirement, having been defeated in 1898.

To THE EDITOR OF *The Evening Post*

[Brown University, Providence, R. I. Feb. 21, 1901.]

Sir: [221]

As I perceive that the defenders of President Jordan [222] intend to lay much stress on the report of the committee of the Stanford alumni, I think it important that a few facts respecting it should be remarked. First, it ought to be remembered that nearly all the alumni of Stanford are very young men. The oldest member of the committee was of the class of 1895; the Chairman of the meeting, of 1899. Secondly, it appears from the San Francisco paper in which I first saw the report that the meeting in which it was adopted was a small one; it was carried by less than forty affirmative votes. Thirdly, the committee, as was pointed out at the meeting, report in the main, not pertinent facts and evidences, but their own conclusions. The academic public, and that larger public whose interest in the controversy has been so gratifying, would gladly barter these conclusions for one piece of evidence which should answer the plain but pointed question, Why did Mrs. Stanford, four years having peacefully passed since the campaign of 1896, require the dismissal of Professor Ross, shortly after the speeches in question, if it was not *because* of those speeches? That question has never yet been squarely met by President Jordan and his friends. The truth is, it admits of but one answer; and for that answer there are evidences before which the labored defence crumbles and collapses instantly. If I know anything of the historical students of the country, I could guarantee that these evidences would convince nine out of ten among those who have no personal interest whatever in the matter.

It is not worth while to take up much of your space

---

[221] New York *Evening Post,* Feb. 23, 1901. Professor E. A. Ross, who had been a member of the faculty of Stanford University since 1893, was dismissed from the university in November, 1900. He had been reappointed on June 2, 1900, and on June 5 he had resigned, his resignation to take effect at the close of the academic year, 1900-1901. On Nov. 14, Ross published his reasons for resigning—that his views on coolie immigration and municipal ownership of public utilities were not acceptable to Mrs. Stanford. Because of this public statement, President Jordan asked him to leave at once. At its December meeting the American Economic Association appointed Professors Seligman of Columbia, Farnum of Yale, and Gardner of Brown to investigate the case. Their report, signed not only by the committee but by fifteen leading economists, exonerated Ross from charges of incompetence, of failure to discharge his duties, and of the use of confidential material in his published statement. The issue of the *Post* which contained Jameson's letter also contained the report of the alumni about which Jameson wrote, and the report of the economists.

[222] David Starr Jordan (1851-1931), M.S., Cornell, 1872, president of Indiana University, 1885-1891, was president of Stanford University from its opening in 1891 until 1913, when he became chancellor. The economists in their report had not hesitated to point to his failure to answer the questions put to him and to what appeared to be his yielding to pressure from Mrs. Stanford. He presented his defense in a letter to the *Post,* Feb. 25, 1901, p. 7.

with criticisms of the committee's report. It has been very neatly dissected in an editorial article in the Boston *Herald* of February 14. I make only a few comments. It is a natural question, why, if Mrs. Stanford's objections of 1896 were based not on economic, but on general grounds, it happens that in December of that year Dr. Ross's chair was changed from economics to social science. To say that Dr. Ross's willingness to remain at the university despite Mrs. Stanford's criticisms shows that he did not think his freedom of speech abridged is to draw an inference by no means logical. Finally, if "a university rule against the participation in politics by a university professor of economics during the progress of a political campaign" would not "impair the proper right of academic freedom," what would? Might he vote?

The Stanford alumnus also quotes Vice-President Branner's remarks on Professor Howard's manly protest, which, after two months, was found to have been a mortal offence.[223] They sound well. Academic propriety is a precious possession. To arraign the university management in the presence of one's class is a course of action which, in perhaps every sort of case but one, deserves severe punishment. But this case was of that one sort. There are some things more precious than decorum. When a fellow-professor is suddenly dismissed from his chair by a rich trustee,

distinctly because of sober public pronouncements in the field of his science, in the face of so deadly a blow at the life of the university, it is no time to be mindful of etiquette. In such a crisis, surely no one would wish to see Professor Howard tithing the mint and anise and cummin of academic propriety, and ignoring those weightier matters of the law apart from which universities are worthless.

As to Professor Flügel, a second reading of Professor Ashley's admirable letter in your issue of February answers him sufficiently. Professor Ashley in the plainest terms, declines to prejudge the case.[224] He only says, what is perfectly true, that an honorable man, who does not wish to countenance a species of iniquity fatal to the general good of his profession ought to satisfy himself, by appropriate evidence, that Mrs. Stanford did right before he accepts a call to her university. If he is unable so to satisfy himself, he ought to remember Milton's resolve "to prefer a blameless silence before the sacred office of speaking, bought and begun with servitude and forswearing." [225]

[223] John Casper Branner (1850-1922), B.S., Cornell, 1874, Ph.D., Indiana University, 1885, was professor of geology in Stanford, 1892-1915; acting president, 1898-1899; vice-president, 1899-1913; president, 1913-1915.
George Elliott Howard (1849-1928), A.B., University of Nebraska, 1876, Ph.D., 1894, had been a professor of history in the University of Nebraska from 1879 to 1891, when he came to Stanford as one of the fifteen professors chosen by President Jordan to organize the university. His outspoken defence of Professor Ross caused Jordan to demand that he withdraw his words or resign. His resignation was followed by that of several other members of the university faculty. After two years Professor Howard returned to the University of Nebraska, where he organized the department of political science and sociology.

[224] Ewald Flügel (1863-1914), born in Leipzig, where he received the Ph.D. degree in 1885, was professor of English philology in Stanford from 1892 to 1914.
W. J. Ashley (1860-1927), whose service as professor of economic history in Harvard University ended in 1901 when he accepted a post in the University of Birmingham, felt strongly on this subject, as two young Harvard men, G. T. Lapsley and Joseph P. Warren, had accepted positions in the department of history of Stanford, on the ground that there was reasonable doubt as to the facts. At the end of their first year of service they declined permanent appointment, being by that time convinced that the university had imposed restrictions on academic freedom. T. C. Smith, A. C. McLaughlin, and perhaps an unnamed third declined offers from the university. The vacancy left by Howard's resignation was filled by Max Farrand, after considerable correspondence with Jameson and others as to whether Stanford should be boycotted. His letters indicate that Jameson was the only historian consulted who felt that the facts as known justified such a course (Farrand to Jameson, Mar. 22, 27, Apr. 1, 10, 1901).
[225] The reason of church-government urged against prelaty, *Works of John Milton* 2 (2): 242, N. Y., Columbia Univ. Press, 1931-1938.

To John Jameson

The University of Chicago[1]
April 5, 1901.

Dear Father, . . .

The teaching begins very pleasantly. I shall always have a "seminary course" (this term on the Convention of 1787) on Mondays from 4 to 6, and a lecture-course Tuesday, Wednesday, Thursday and Friday forenoon, one hour (at present 9:30 - 10:30, and on Colonial Charters and other Colonial Letters Patent). That is all. The students seem to me excellent, and the number I have shows that graduate instruction in American history meets "a long-felt want." They come, those I have thus far talked with, from Minnesota, North Dakota, Iowa, Missouri, Arkansas, Texas, and Mississippi, and they seem well educated, and certainly mean business. . . .

To Clarence W. Bowen

5516 Woodlawn Ave., Chicago, Oct. 15/01

My dear Bowen:[2]

Can you tell me anything of Adams's bequest of which I saw a mention in the newspapers?[3] Was it in any way conditioned or restricted? If not, I have had some thought of proposing to the Council that it might be used in partial support of an Historical School at Washington, conducted on the same general plans as the American schools at Athens and Rome. The idea of such a thing was suggested to me last year by the fruitful mind of Turner.[4] I think it is a good scheme, and

to connect it with Herbert Adams' benefaction would be peculiarly appropriate in view of his well-known interest in the furtherance of study at Washington. A sufficient house in a good and convenient quarter of Washington could be had for the income of $5000 plus certain room rents. I believe the important universities would be willing to take their turns in providing teachers to conduct the school, and probably some connection with the Washington Memorial Institution could be worked out with President Gilman.[5] What do you think of this? Would it run counter to any existing interest of the Association? Educationally, it might prove an exceedingly useful thing. Would it be worth while to present it to the Council?[6] But the first question is as to the conditions of the bequest, if any. I should be glad to hear from you respecting this.

To Francis A. Christie

5516 Woodlawn Avenue, Chicago,
November 24, 1901.

Dear Christie:

The enclosed may perhaps interest you, merely as a scheme.[7] Nothing may come of it, or it may be merged in some other and larger plan. There are several possibilities. By the way, are you going to the Washington meeting? I hope so, on general grounds of utility, though the Reverend Sam Jackson's programme for the Church History Section does not seem so alluring as to impel you to the journey. Why don't you come over here and spend Christmas with us, and go down to Washington with me the next day? Come as much before Christmas as you can. We join in urging you to come and make our Christmas less lonesome. I would ask you for Thanksgiving, but we are going to have the unattached Brown boys at the University come to dinner here, and that might not interest you. Also, I am going to be fearfully busy these next days, because

---

[1] After long consideration and much correspondence with president William R. Harper, Jameson had resigned his position in Brown University and had accepted that of head of the department of history of the University of Chicago. He began his teaching there in April, 1901, but Mrs. Jameson and the daughter, Katrina, did not go to Chicago until September.

[2] Clarence W. Bowen (1852-1935) was treasurer of the American Historical Association from 1884 to 1917.

[3] Herbert Baxter Adams was secretary of the American Historical Association from its founding until 1900, when ill health forced his resignation. He died in 1901, leaving $5,000 to the Association. Bowen made no direct reply to the question concerning conditions attached to the bequest, but reported that the gift would yield $200 a year and that he saw no harm in Jameson's presenting his idea to the council, which was to meet in New York on Nov. 29 (Bowen to Jameson, Oct. 23, 1901). The decision of the Association was not to keep the bequest in a specific fund, and the Herbert Baxter Adams prize which was established was paid from the general revenue of the Association (Jameson to Matilda Dunning, June 5, 1923).

[4] Frederick J. Turner (1861-1923), Ph.D., Johns Hopkins University, 1890, entered the graduate school of the Johns Hopkins the autumn after Jameson left the university.

[5] The Washington Memorial Institution, of which Gilman was head, was organized in the summer of 1901 for a purpose similar to the one Jameson and Turner had in mind, but mainly for students of the natural sciences, at least so the historians believed. With the establishment of the Carnegie Institution, the Memorial Institution disappeared.

[6] On Nov. 23, 1901, in a detailed statement to the members of the executive council of the American Historical Association, Jameson set forth the advantages of such a school and certain of the practical possibilities. The council in response set up a committee consisting of Jameson, James Ford Rhodes, and Andrew C. McLaughlin, to consider the project. Before the committee met Charles Francis Adams took the place of Rhodes.

[7] The enclosure was without doubt Jameson's plan for a Washington school of history.

I have agreed to give the Convocation Address on December 17. It is to be made a sort of inaugural address. In justice to President Harper, however, I will say that he tried hard to get proper persons to do it, and on failing fell back on "home talent." He means to invite all the historical people from Tidyuscung to Oscaloosa, and I shall talk on "The Effects of the Dominance of Universities upon Historical Work," or some such title. I don't know but it will be better to take some vaguer title like "The Present State and Prospects of Historical Writing in America," and then talk of the same things.[8] If you could come over as early as that, we should be delighted to have you, and I do not expect to be busy then, as instruction will have ceased.

I keep myself or am kept very busy. On the whole I like it, especially the semi-scholarly part which consists in preparing new lectures for graduate students. That is relatively a much larger part of my work than at Brown. I cannot say, privately, that I get all the satisfaction I ought to get out of a position which, when I stop to think, I know is influential. I haven't imagination to have that fact steadily before me, and am too apt to bury myself in the details of the day, which, Heaven knows, are abundant. It would do me good to have you come over and fire my youthful mind with a sense of what I am really about. My students, I hasten to say, are good material, and I find no fault with them.

I met Mr. Pulsford for the first time last Sunday. It was only for a brief time, on a casual introduction; but I fear he is not just the sort of man to take keen interest in the promotion of a theological school. But we shall see later. I do not give up the idea, though what you write is not encouraging.[9] I wonder if you needed to decline the real presidency? Don't you feel pretty sure that, once in the saddle, you could boss your trustees as so many presidents do? Even people who are somewhat blind as to the highest scholarship, and somewhat inert as to getting it, often do not interfere with its course when once set going; they have many

other interests, and attend to Meadville when it importuneth them.[10] But I must stop. Good-night, and good luck to you.

To DANIEL C. GILMAN

February 14, 1902.

My dear Mr. Gilman:

Ever since I saw in the newspaper that you had been elected president of the Carnegie Institution, I have wished to write and express my congratulations, though we had understood that it was a foregone conclusion. It seems to me you are immensely to be envied. I am sure it never happened before in the history of the world that a man should be given the opportunity, twice over, to organize the institutions which, each in its respective day and generation, take the leading part in the promotion of research in a given country.[11]

I have found myself so warmly interested in the project of the Carnegie Institution and in the question of what it might do for history, that I conclude to be emboldened by your letter of some time ago to set before you a lot of suggestions which have occurred to me on that topic, even at the risk of boring you by a

---

[8] The address, The influence of universities upon historical writing, printed in the *University Record* of the University of Chicago (**6**: 294-300, January, 1902), is well worth reading at the present time.

[9] The Reverend William Hanson Pulsford (1859-1934), born and educated in Scotland, after serving churches in Canada and in New England, was pastor of the First Unitarian Church of Chicago from 1901 to 1923. Jameson and Christie had discussed the possibility of a theological seminary in Chicago and were casting about for a suitable head. In a discouraged letter of Oct. 31, 1901, Christie wrote: "I do not regard it as possible that a school could be established at Chicago for a long time to come. Large endowments are already given to Meadville and more are in prospect—not simply the contingent Pratt bequest, but most likely a Presidential salary fund from another source. Even now the whole income is not used—there is always apparent ground for that. Not only will the Unitarians feel that enough has been done for the provision of theological study for the few students who turn up, but they are going to have other projects on hand which will call for large gifts."

[10] In a letter of Sept. 19, 1901, Christie had written: "The state of our school is most disheartening. It could not be worse. . . . I understand that the Trustees will meet at Saratoga—unofficially perhaps—and that it is proposed by some to make me acting President. That would be intolerable." A letter of Oct. 6 is missing, but in that of Oct. 31, already cited, he continued: "So far as the Presidency is concerned, nothing is done. I put a stop to the idea that I would take the thankless job of acting President and on finding that a New York paper published me as a candidate for the Presidency I informed the committee that I could not be considered at all." On Feb. 18, 1902, Meadville was still without a president and Christie wrote: "Would Pulsford be a good man and would he accept? Salary $3000 and a house—though they can afford to pay more." The president finally appointed was Francis Chester Southworth (1863-1944), a choice entirely satisfactory to Christie. President Southworth, who served as president from 1902 to 1929, had been secretary of the Western Unitarian Conference from 1899 to 1902.

[11] A letter from Gilman of Nov. 11, 1901, indicates that he had heard from Jameson early in November, probably in connection with the idea of the school of history in Washington. In reply, Gilman wrote: "The organization of the Washington Memorial Institution awaits the return of Professor Walcott from the far West and the meeting of the executive committee will be held before the close of the present month. I will then consult my colleagues on your plan and endeavor to get them to send you some concrete information. . . . At present the Washington Institution has not so much as a postage stamp of its own." On Dec. 23, he added: "Mr. Carnegie delays any statement of his plans and I see no reason why you should not proceed, as you proposed to do before the reports of his gift were made." On Jan. 14, 1902, he advised Jameson to present to the trustees of the Carnegie Institution, who were to hold their first meeting on Jan. 29, a formal application for approval of his projects. At this meeting Gilman's election as president of the Carnegie Institution of Washington took place, though for some time it had been well understood that he was to hold this office. The "two institutions" were the Johns Hopkins University and the Carnegie Institution. The letter which follows offers one reason for the writing of this letter.

voluminous epistle. My excuse must be the solicitude of a professor for the proper progress of his science, a progress which in this case certainly can be very greatly aided by the spending of money. No doubt our committee, of which I wrote you, will send in some document later, though we concluded not to begin consulting till the meeting of January 29 had taken place;[12] but very likely they may not care to go much into detail, and (black horrid thought!) they may not agree with all my notions.

I perceive that many persons are supposing that the promotion of researches undertaken by individuals will be the leading work of the Institution, or that its money will largely go to irrigate the universities. So far as history is concerned, I think that to pursue such a policy, save to a quite minor extent, would be entirely a mistake. In the first place, what hinders historical research on the part of the men most competent to pursue it is not so much lack of money as lack of time. They are busy professors. While university organization in the United States remains what it is, subsidies cannot give the older men the chance for original work on a large scale. To subsidize the younger men, on the other hand, is to make it easier to write doctoral dissertations, to increase the quantity and improve the quality of the more immature part of the work now done. I have no doubt that this is a good thing to do, even though we are all sometimes discouraged about the ultimate results of fellowships. But I cannot think that to do much of it is to make the most signal contribution which money can make to the progress of historical science in America.

For in the second place I feel that general enterprises ought to take precedence of particular enterprises, that there are undertakings which the common voice of the profession would declare to be, if only we could afford them, the necessary preliminaries to generations of successful individual work, and that so long as these hold out they ought to have the first place as objects of expenditure. The most fruitful use of subsidies, I should think, is in application to general enterprises. Take the American Historical Review as an instance.[13] The American Historical Association is giving it what it can afford, and this enables it to live, and to grow a little. But if it had seven or eight hundred dollars more a year it could pay two dollars a page for body-

articles. In my judgment this would do more than any other one thing to raise its quality as an organ of American historical scholarship, because it would enable the Review to command articles from the best specialists or the leading professors of history. It has in six years got conspicuously little from these. They are often, instead, writing for journals that pay;[14] but would rather write the kind of articles the Review desires, if they could get something for it, though it were less than the popular magazines pay.

Some money might be given to the Historical Manuscripts Commission with profit to the profession at large. Not perhaps a great deal, for its work has definite limitations. On the one hand it ought to confine itself, among manuscripts in private hands, to those which are national in their bearings, leaving to the local historical societies those manuscripts which in the main illustrate only local history. On the other hand there is a definite limit to the amount of editorial work which the chairman of that commission can attend to, if, as must usually be the case, he is a competent and therefore busy professor.

The work of the Public Archives Commission,[15] on the other hand, has mostly to be done by local persons hired to do it. The chairman must usually rely, in each state or in each great city, on some local antiquary who by years of experience has acquired an intimate knowledge of a particular archive, and who can make an inventory of it under direction from the chairman, if paid for his time. In a few years, by the expenditure of a few hundred dollars a year, the task of this commission could be done once for all. But such a series of inventories, or archive-reports, is an indispensable preliminary to most of the tasks of scholarship in American history. It would be easy to bring forward, from every country in Europe, numerous evidences that such work is viewed in precisely this light over there.

But I must say I think the Carnegie Institution (always speaking of history alone) could do much better than to spend most of its money in subsidies. There is something to be said, I am sure, on grounds of éclat, in favor of the Institution's having its own enterprises; but grounds of general utility are the main thing. There are many historical tasks which no one is now attempting, which could not be made to pay, which are suffering to be done, and the doing of which would be of great and constant benefit to all sorts of individual and collective researches. Prominent among these is that projected School of American Historical Studies, of which, as the Autocrat says, "I was speaking when

---

[12] See *ante*, Oct. 15, 1901, n. 6. The executive committee of the Institution, consisting of John S. Billings, D. C. Gilman, Abram S. Hewett, S. Weir Mitchell, Elihu Root, Charles D. Walcott, and Carroll D. Wright, during the year 1902 set up eighteen advisory committees. For history they appointed Jameson, Adams, and McLaughlin, who henceforth acted as a committee for the Institution rather than for the Association. Their report is to be found in the *Year Book* of the Institution, 1902, 226-231. See *post*, Oct. 13, 1902, n. 29.

[13] Jameson, on going to the University of Chicago, had resigned as managing editor of the *Review*, but he was soon made a member of its board of editors. McLaughlin became the managing editor.

[14] A conspicuous example of this was Woodrow Wilson, who from the establishment of the *Review* firmly refused to write for it, on the ground that the popular magazines paid him generously for his work.

[15] This commission was created at the Boston meeting of the American Historical Association in 1899, to report on the "character, contents, and functions of our public repositories of manuscript records" (*Ann. Rept., Amer. Hist. Assn.*, 1900: 2: 5-16).

I was interrupted,"—which was proposed to the Council of the American Historical Association in November, in a printed communication of which you have perhaps preserved a copy, which its committee had begun to consider, but which went naturally into suspense on the announcement of Mr. Carnegie's donation. Such a school, which would give the advantages of Washington study, under an experienced trainer or trainers of graduates, to a select body of graduate students (say men who have already had a year of strictly graduate work in some approved university) would exercise a fine influence upon the preparation of college teachers of American history. The rotation of professors which I proposed in the printed project might be maintained along with the presence of a permanent man, as is done in the case of the Schools of Classical Studies at Athens and Rome.[16]

Then there is the project of an American school of history at Rome. This has been warmly advocated by some members of the American Historical Association, and has much to recommend it. If it is true, as Mr. C. F. Adams has told me, that Mr. Pierpont Morgan's aid has been enlisted in the scheme of an American university or academy at Rome, the project mentioned may find its place in that larger scheme.[17] If not, it might be deemed a legitimate, as it certainly would be a useful, object of expenditure. There is likewise a large field for the prosecution in European archives of researches relating to the history of the United States. I think our new possessions cause us all to feel especially the need of such studies in Spain, with a view to a completer knowledge of the previous development of these islands.

Again, there is a great deal to be done at Washington in the way of scientific editing of historical materials possessed by the government. To this day, the real journals of the Continental Congress have not been printed in their integrity, to say nothing of their papers.[18] A great amount of material illustrating the earlier history of American diplomacy, withheld from publicity in contemporaneous prints and in the American State Papers, could perfectly well be made public

now. These are only two conspicuous examples. The reason why Congress has done so little of this sort of thing is not altogether want of appreciation or fear of expense, but very largely an apprehension that the task would be made a job, or that it would be badly done. There have been examples of both kinds, and I really don't think that government editing is improving. But if the Congressmen knew that the historical department of an institution which they respected as they do the Smithsonian stood ready to do the editing and pay for it, I have no doubt they would be glad to pay any necessary amount for the printing. Certainly this sort of thing, the provision of material, stands in the front rank among tasks which the present state of historical work among us calls for as prerequisite to further progress.

Another enterprise, which might be thought not to belong so distinctly to this class, but which nevertheless would be of great utility to all historical workers and to many others, is the preparation of a Dictionary of National Biography, worthy to rank with the English series and with the Allgemeine Deutsche Biographie. It is true there is a market for such series. But in this country the market has been spoiled by the historically bad but extensive and well-pushed collections which have been brought out in recent years. I do not believe that one marked by high scholarship could be floated, as the English has been. It would have to be done as the German one was, through a semi-governmental organization. No publisher, I fancy, would think that he could afford to pay for the necessary scholarship. But the Carnegie Institution could, and, beside[s] the main result, its doing so would have on many good scholars the effect which I can see that in many cases the D. N. B. has had in England, viz., that they can afford, each within the limits of his own locality and his own fragmentary spare time, to do good research work which because combined counts for something, and which often sets him upon other and larger researches.

For one more instance, I do not see how by any other means we can ever arrive at the completion of a really first-rate atlas of American historical geography. This is a great desideratum. Like the preceding, it is a book which any publisher could afford to manufacture, if that were all, but which none could afford to prepare, because most of the maps would require a large and expensive amount of pioneer research-work. It is also like it in that it could only be done by extensive cooperation.[19]

---

[16] The suggestion made by Jameson to the executive council was that one professor be released each year from one of the twelve or fifteen universities which might be expected to unite in the project. This man, on half-pay from his institution, would act as adviser to the students, at the same time carrying on researches of his own. No permanent director seemed to him necessary.

[17] The American Academy in Rome, chartered by act of Congress in 1905, received from J. Pierpont Morgan $100,000.

[18] The publication of the *Journals of the Continental Congress,* under the editorship of Worthington C. Ford, then chief of the Division of Manuscripts of the Library of Congress, began in 1905. The final volume appeared in 1936. From his early years in the Johns Hopkins, when he began his long and unavailing struggle to edit and publish the Records of the Virginia Company, the proper publication of the historical material owned by the government was much in Jameson's mind and his interest in the subject will appear in many of the letters in this volume.

[19] In 1903 Jameson sent to the Bureau of Historical Research a plan for an atlas and soon after he became chief of that bureau work was begun along the lines he had suggested. Though the atlas was thus conceived as one of the first enterprises of the department, its execution was slow and it was not until 1932 that it finally appeared, as the joint publication of the Carnegie Institution of Washington and the American Geographical Society of New York. Until 1928, when Jameson left the department, he supervised each step, enlisting the aid

In short, I am sure there are enough historical tasks for the Carnegie Institution to do by itself, quite apart from the existing enterprises which it might choose to subsidize; and I sincerely hope that it will undertake, if not those which I have mentioned by way of important example, at any rate tasks of that general type, adapted to the fructifying or improvement of historical work at large.

I don't know whether my colleagues on our committee will choose to enter upon the subject of organization at all; but I feel moved to do so, and hope it will not be thought an impertinence,—at least no greater impertinence than the whole of this letter may seem to be. I feel moved to do so because the one plan which has been prominently advocated in the press is that of having each department of the work in charge of an advisory committee of specialists in that branch of knowledge. That may be the wisest plan in other sciences. I don't pretend to know; and I appreciate that the type of organization must be determined, with some uniformity, by considerations which are general, rather than by those which are special to one subject. But in history, at any rate, I feel impelled to say, as the result of what experience I have had as former editor of the Review and as former chairman of the Historical Manuscripts Commission, and in work for the Rhode Island Historical Society and the American Antiquarian Society, that this is not the best form of organization. There should be an advisory committee or committees, and I have no doubt the Council of the American Historical Association would be glad, if it were desired to do so, to co-operate in forming it or them. But, for execution, the plan of a paid individual head works far better. I have seen many instances of bad results when a highly competent committee selects subordinates of less than full maturity of scholarship, winds them up once in two or three or four months, and then goes away and leaves them to go on by themselves. Too large a part of what is most desirable in historical scholarship depends on perfection of detail to permit this plan to work successfully. The people that one hires for compilations and such work, and supposes to be entirely competent, prove to require constant supervision. I feel clear that an institution that can afford it ought not to content itself without getting, for its historical work, a director of historical studies of a grade with our best university teachers or private scholars. I can see that this would be true by thinking over the details of several of the enterprises which I have mentioned above as possible and typical. And I am confirmed in the opinion by perceiving that precisely this

is the course which is pursued in the land which beyond all others knows how enterprises of historical scholarship ought to be conducted. The Monumenta Germaniae Historica, to take an instance, the chief German historical enterprise, is primarily in the charge of Dr. Ernst Duemmler, whose standing and salary are like those of the best professors, and who gives all his time to this work.[20] There is an advisory committee, having a certain connection with the Berlin Academy. Similar, I believe, is the organization of the Prussian and Austrian historical institutes at Rome.

I have no doubt, by the way, that such a director of historical studies would be made secretary, or recording secretary, of the American Historical Association, if such a connection were approved by the Carnegie Institution. When Howard Clark[21] resigned that post, at Christmas, the Council was greatly embarrassed, and, after much anxious deliberation, was unable to find the right man in Washington. Finally Clark resumed his duties for a year; but any good historical scholar that went to Washington to live would be welcomed to that influential post in the Association.

Pardon me, Mr. Gilman, if I have overdone this business of making suggestions. I have run on to much greater length than I expected; but I hope my interest in all that can promote the general good of my profession is well enough known, to you at least, to furnish some sort of apology.[22] With pleasant anticipation of seeing you at the celebration next week.[23]

To Francis A. Christie

5516 Woodlawn Avenue, Chicago,
February 15, 1902.

Dear Christie:

The enclosed, a copy of a long letter with which I have bored Uncle Daniel (or shall when it reaches him, Monday) will show you what I am chiefly thinking of. There is a bee in my bonnet, and I cannot dislodge it:

---

of many collaborators. The preface to the *Atlas*, by Charles O. Paullin, shows how widely the scholarly world was drawn upon during these years. It finally appeared as *Atlas of the Historical Geography of the United States*, by Charles O. Paullin, edited by John K. Wright, Washington, Carnegie Institution, publication no. 401, and N. Y., Nat. Geog. Society, 1932.

[20] Ernst Ludwig Duemmler (1830-1902), at one time professor in Halle and author of *History of East Franconian Empire*, began work on the *Monumenta Germaniae Historica* in 1873.

[21] A. Howard Clark (1850-1918), curator of the historical section of the National Museum, became assistant secretary of the Association in 1889 and secretary in 1900. He continued to hold this office until 1908. See *Ann. Rept., Amer. Hist. Assn.,* 1918: 1: 36.

[22] In reply President Gilman wrote on Feb. 17: "At present we have determined to postpone the particular consideration of the very interesting suggestions that have been made to us until we begin to receive income, toward the end of the summer, and until we can decide upon a general plan of procedure."

[23] At the twenty-fifth anniversary of the opening of the Johns Hopkins University, Feb. 22, 1902, which was also the occasion of the inauguration of the new president, Ira Remsen (1846-1927), the university conferred on Jameson the degree of LL.D. For an account of this occasion see French, John C., *A history of the university founded by Johns Hopkins,* 143-145, Baltimore, Johns Hopkins Univ. Press, 1946.

the notion, namely, that I should like that post myself. What would you think of that? [24] Not that this job doesn't please me. On the whole, I like my work quite a bit better than that which I was doing in Providence. But it appears to me that I should like such a position as that which I have outlined, still better. Its influence on the work of the profession would be great, or might be made so. I think there is as good a chance that Mr. Gilman would want me as anybody. In part this letter is intended to let him see that I might be willing to take it if he wanted me to. Does it sound too much like that? Uncle Daniel is of course shrewd enough to read that between the lines,—or indeed to infer it from the portentous length of the document. But on the whole I concluded there was no great harm in that.

I think I sent you a copy of the printed communication on a school at Washington which I sent on to the meeting of our Council in November. I also sent one to Gilman, not knowing anything of Carnegie's scheme at that time; (and glad I did). The Council referred the project to a committee—Jameson, Rhodes, McLaughlin—to report at Washington. Then came Carnegie's announcement, which disposed of this scheme in its first form. I concluded, and the committee agreed, that our best course was to ask that we be discharged, and that instead the Council appoint a committee "on the promotion of historical research at Washington," i.e., a committee to wait and see what the Carnegie Institution could be persuaded to do for history. This the Council did, appointing the same committee, with the addition of the retiring president, Charles Francis Adams, because he knows Mr. Carnegie well. This will explain what opening I had for such a communication. I write you of it because I like to have you know of my scheme, and should be glad to know your thoughts on the subject. But I have never mentioned it to anyone else, except Sara, and ask you to keep it very dark, for there is one particular in which it would work harm if known. . . .

I wish you were going down to Baltimore, but I suppose you aren't. . . . We are all well. Chicago seems to agree with us finely. Sara has no sore-throat, which was frequent in Providence; and she is so contented, people are so kind and take to her so manifestly, that she is having as good a time as she ever had in her life, though it be our first year. It seems a pity to think of uprooting her again. But certainly Washington is a delightful city. And after all I have not yet been asked to go there. As for me, I do not find Chicago delight-

ful. My work is so agreeable that I am contented, and to me my work has now become, in Matthew Arnold's minutely accurate phrase, seven-eighths of life. I am not making friends, unless imperceptibly, because I have no time to. Nor do I much enjoy the town, not having much imagination. Imagination occasionally makes one see its great future; but its present is unlovely, save that its sky is usually bright, this winter. But enow of this. I must now go to a delightful institution of function called faculty-meeting. . . .

[P.S.]   Please return the document.

To George L. Burr

Red Gables, New London, N.H.,[25]
September 4, 1902

My dear Burr:

Sill was over here the other day.[26] I wish I had known earlier that he was so near. He told me that you were now in Ithaca again. Although I firmly believe that you ought not to be, judging from what he tells me of the previous extent of your actual vacation in 1902, still the news emboldens me to write, on a subject on which I should have written before if I had known just where to write to. I feel a good deal of remorse about asking any aid of you, but I really don't know anyone else to whom to apply. So forgive me.

Though for the most part I teach American history to my graduates, yet each autumn I mean to run a course on general or special problems of method. Last year it was on the elements of historical criticism and historical bibliography and heuristic. This year, the auxiliary sciences and the methods by which they are used for the benefit of history; next year, the historians, composition, the history of historiography. Now out of about forty lectures on the auxiliary sciences, accompanied as largely as may be with reading and practical exercises on the part of the class, I mean in October to give the first ten to historical geography, or, more broadly, to the use of geography for the benefit of history. I know that you have conducted a formal course in historical geography, and I do not know of any other man in this country who has. Therefore, I ask you to be so kind as to tell me briefly what you did, that you thought worked well, or to make me some suggestions of things I might not otherwise think of, or, best of all, because making you least trouble, to send me a printed or manifolded syllabus if you had one. Anything will help. My great worry in asking is, that you will take too much time and trouble in the matter, I believe my best plan is, to beg you to limit yourself to four pages of your note-paper, and to hint that if the letter weighs over half an ounce my conscience will compel me to

---

[24] In fact, Christie had already expressed his feeling, though at the time he did so he was under a misconception as to the character of the new institution: "Will you not go to Carnegie's new university in Washington? I think that might be ideal for you and I shall work for it as soon as I see who the responsible and responsive heads are. . . . I like to think of you helping to found the right kind of research in this wonderful new school. I suppose this will supersede your project of a school of American History in Washington" (Christie to Jameson, Dec. 10, 1901).

[25] Burr Papers, Cornell University Library.

[26] Henry A. Sill (1878-1917) began to teach Greek and Roman history in Cornell University in the autumn of 1902.

send it back unopened. Give me a chance some time to aid you if you can find one.[27] . . .

To George L. Burr

5551 Lexington Avenue, Chicago [28]
October 13, 1902

My dear Burr: . . .

Why do I never get a chance to do anything for you before the time comes around again when I must trouble you? This time, however, it is not for my own benefit but for that of the profession at large. At Christmas the Council of the American Historical Society [Association] appointed a committee, three of whom acted, to enter into relations with the Carnegie Institution, and see what could be done for History through its means. In the summer (the delay was not my fault) we sent to them the memorial of which I enclose a copy.[29] Now, the Carnegie Institution has requested the same three persons, Mr. C. F. Adams, Pro-

fessor McLaughlin and myself, the last being for the present designated as chairman, to act as their advisory committee in matters of History. They have appointed us late, and we have little time before we must meet and frame a report. In fact, we meet on October 23. They have turned over to us all the papers which they have received. Few of these have any significance. I fancy that practically what we shall send in to them will be a revised version of our own memorial, carried out somewhat more in detail if we find that they are already disposed to accept our main propositions. It is in this revision that I should like your aid. If you could find the time, I wish you would read over the memorial, and send me any suggestions which occur to you that might improve it, or that ought to be incorporated with it as additions. I value your judgment very highly, and am well aware of my own want of experience, especially on the European side. I should be very grateful for your aid.

To Francis A. Christie

5551 Lexington Avenue, Chicago,
October 31, 1902.

My dear Christie:—

. . . The inauguration of Woodrow Wilson was a very pleasing and interesting event. I saw the great Mr.

---

[27] Professor Burr's answer to this was a full description of a course given by a rare teacher: "To tell you of my course in Historical Geography is a short and easy task, so simple—perhaps so crude—is my method. As a brief text for all my work on the auxiliary sciences I use the articles in the Encyclopediae Britannica. For geography, however, I can use this for scarcely more than a warning; and, if I am still prone to send my pupils to Markham's article, it is only that they may the more clearly discern the distinction between the history of geography (whether the history of the science or the history of discovery), which we are not to study (save as an incident) and the geography of history, which we are.

"Nor do I now broaden Historical Geography, as I was long wont to do, to include the whole story of the relations of the earth to man—what Ratzel has christened 'Anthropo-Geography.' He might better call it *Geo-anthropology;* and I pause over the subject long enough not only to point out its importance but to call attention to the yet more important (even to History), though more neglected, influence of man on the earth, which might more justly be called anthropo-geography. To make this clear I love not only to send them to such books as March's *The Earth as modified by Human Action* and Hehn's *Wanderings of Cultivated Plants and Domestic Animals* (usually reading with them those striking opening paragraphs of Hehn, in which he shows how all visible Italy, even its very landscape and climate, is the work of man), but I usually set them as a task the study of some one land, say Egypt, making them find out how, on the one hand, by its configuration, its climate, its soil, its vegetation, its animals, and its landscape it might influence its inhabitants, and how, on the other, by the evolution of shelter, sustenance, commerce, travel, irrigation, landscape-changing, government, they have utilized or baffled its powers. While I honor a Buckle or a Taine for calling our attention at last to sadly neglected factors in human development, whose results must be eliminated from our matter before we can study History at all, there could be no sorrier rot than seems to me what is talked by even such thoughtful historians as Bryce and Goldwin Smith when they fall foul of this topic. Even the cautious and sensible though rambling new book of Hereford George on *The Relations of Geography to [and] History* seems to me to go much too far. That the earth—man's environment—is man's *material* goes without saying; but whether obstacle checks or stimulates, whether opportunity nerves or enervates, depends in each case on the given man—what he already is and what he wills to be. If he is

ever (which I doubt) but the victim of geography, that is not his accident but his fault, and still it is man we must study.

"Heigh-o! Well, that's about all. Now I turn to what I count Historical Geography proper (the geography which was *present* geography to *past* ages), studying it both statically and dynamically—*das Sinn und das Werden*—epoch-wise and in development. I divide the historical world into a manageable number of regions—'potamic' worlds of Nile and Euphrates, the eastern Mediterranean lands, the three great Mediterranean peninsulas (taken one by one), the Danube valley, the great northern plain of Europe, the Rhine-Rhone hollow, and so on. To my students I leave, as the easier task, the following of their political fortunes, and the boundaries of their peoples and states, prescribing points and periods for definite investigation—it is mainly a study of maps, aided by Freeman and Himly—while I not only quiz them on all this but try to trace the deeper changes, whether of natural or of human origin, so far as they intersect History. And that's all" (Burr to Jameson, Sept. 10, 1902).

[28] Burr Papers, Cornell University Library.

[29] In July, 1902, the committee of the council of the American Historical Association—Jameson, McLaughlin, Adams—in a memorial to the president and executive committee of the Carnegie Institution, suggested the establishment of an institute of historical research in Washington, with a permanent director and a select body of students; the exploration of the Washington archives and those of Europe; a subvention for the *American Historical Review* and for the Historical Manuscripts Commission; and the carrying out of such projects as a dictionary of American biography and an atlas of American history.

This drew from Gilman, then in Switzerland, cautious approval, on July 28, 1902: "Your statement is clear and could not be more persuasive; but more than this I cannot say before my return,—as we agreed, (i.e. the executive committee of the Carnegie Institution) that we would not make any plan until we re-assembled in the autumn."

Morgan, Mark Twain, Tom Reed, Stedman—various people, and dined very pleasantly at John Finley's, whom I used to know at Hopkins. Wilson's speech was beautiful, and was most salutory doctrine for all of us—except the Princeton men, who I should suppose undoubtedly needed instigation into some participation in the errors of the rest of us, lest Princeton, surrounded by the plutocracy, become a sleepy Oxford on a much inferior basis of acquirements.

Our Carnegie committee meeting went as well as could be expected. I have great respect and regard for Mr. Charles Francis Adams, but I suppose it is agreed by historical students that it never was easy to get members of the great house of Adams to adopt the views of others.[30] . . .

To Francis A. Christie

> 5551 Lexington Avenue, Chicago,
> March 6, 1903.

Dear Christie:

I am stirred up to start a letter to you by the mere fact of finding upon my desk a circular respecting the Alumni Trustee election at Amherst. If you have any views on the subject, please communicate them promptly. I will vote just as you say. Except that I will not vote for [——], whom I judge on brief inspection to be a donkey.

I have been meaning to write to you for a long while to say that you were perfectly right (as, indeed, might have been foreseen) respecting Moody's poems.[31] I have an almost invincible repugnance to the examination of new poets, not having caught up yet with a great deal of the old, so it was not until lately that I read more than a few lines of what he has written. Those few lines I misunderstood, I find, and so conceived an opinion that the volume was simply some more Spring poetry; but in reality it is great stuff. I do not see that anyone in America has done anything equal to it for a couple of decades, or, let us say, since Lowell died. Also, I meant to write of the very keen pleasure which I had had in reading, while waiting for somebody, the first few pages of William James' "Varieties of Religious Experience." No doubt you have read it, you who have time to read books. I really tore myself

away from it with difficulty, and long to read more of it, but no doubt never shall.

I thank you for sending your catalogue. It conveys a very pleasing impression of new life and of definite intention on the part of the institution to make use of the intellect in the process of education. I do not speak of this as a novelty in the case of all the professors; but I judge that it is so, so far as the executive is concerned. Meanwhile, in my corner of the vineyard, all is depression and disgust. This is usual at the end of a Quarter, but I never was much gladder to get to the end of a Quarter than I shall be in this case.

The main point is (now that I have got rid of the stenographer,—whose intervention I know you will excuse), the way in which the Carnegie affair has turned out. I would not tell any other man how deeply disappointed I am. You perhaps remember that we (I mean our advisory committee) among other things recommended the establishment at Washington of an institute of historical research, a cross between the American School at Athens or Rome and the Prussian or Austrian Institut für Geschichtsforschung; also, an appropriation of $2000 per annum for the American Historical Review. In what I must think a rather parsimonious spirit toward the history of their country, they have resolved on a combination whereby McLaughlin goes to Washington to be Director of Historical Work for them, and also to edit there the Review, getting $5000 and dividing his time about equally between the two functions. It is a fine thing for the Review, setting free for its improvement all the money which went to editorial expense; and I could not fail to approve as a member of the Board, though unable to go on to the meeting.[32] But in its personal aspect it

---

[30] The first comment of Charles Francis Adams on Jameson's original suggestions was that he felt it to be a mistake to scatter the funds of the Institution over so wide a program, and believed it would be better to concentrate on a single project, such as a dictionary of American biography. In the end he signed the report drawn up by Jameson, only commenting that it said in 2300 words what he had said in 750 (Adams to Jameson, Mar. 11, Nov. 8, 1902).

[31] William Vaughn Moody (1869-1910), an assistant professor in the University of Chicago, had published *Poems* in 1901. Christie had written on Feb. 18, 1902: "I recently blossomed in a new role—giving a public reading of Wm. Vaughn Moody's poems. I am now full of Stephen Phillips' Ulysses and I may read that in public."

[32] In Jameson's letter to Gilman of Feb. 14, 1902, he suggested a subsidy of $700 or $800 per annum for the *Review;* in the report to the trustees of the Carnegie Institution made by its advisory committee on Oct. 25, 1902, the recommendation was for a subsidy of $2000 yearly. Early in January, 1903, Professor William M. Sloane, one of the editors of the *Review,* conferred with John S. Billings, director of the New York Public Library and a trustee of the new Institution. This conference, Sloane reported to Jameson on Jan. 19: "he favours immediate action for us, however, and thinks we may get it at the meeting on the 23rd. I am sending a formal petition in the name of our board for the subvention on the plan you outline. But he thinks the Trustees will suggest an alternative, viz., an appropriation from the publication fund. This means that the publication bureau of the Institute would take over the entire work of publication and assign $5000 for editorial salary, articles, and editorial expenses generally, including the travelling expenses of the editorial board. Our board would continue to be appointed as it is, exercise the powers it has, and be under no restraint except that none of its members should receive pay for his editorial work. Only its employee or employees could receive pay. Since there is a possibility of this alternative being offered please think it over and write to Adams. I heartily favour the plan. It evades the question of subvention. Billings says every technical and scientific journal in the country has asked for a subvention, that the present policy is to refuse, and then to take on for the publication fund about four such journals as ours."

is as bitter a disappointment as I have experienced for many years. Foolishly, no doubt, but because I could not help it, I had been counting on this post of Director of Historical Work at Washington for more than a year. I had thought that I was more especially fitted for it than anyone else I could think of. I do not think this is vanity. I know I am not good in many branches of historical work: I could never be an excellent historian,[33] I am not a first-rate teacher, I am not making a distinct success of my present position. My one talent, if I know myself, lies in the direction of Heuristik, and I thought I had shown this to the historical world, and also the necessary ability to get the other men to co-operate in historical tasks, and some, though not the best, qualities in instruction of graduates. So I counted my chickens. I had thought of it every hour, and had made many and minute and to me interesting plans. All the disagreements of my present position (and there are some, though I enjoy my work better than in Providence), and all the discomforts of life in this lonely and hideous town, were pretty easily borne, under the constant thought that I should soon be out of it. I had especially enjoyed the thought that in winters I could have my dear father and mother with me, and be nearer all the year to them and my friends. It sounds foolish, now that I recount it, that I should so have counted on it. But I did, and the readjustment, the facing anew as permanent and inevitable the things I don't like here, the mere thought of living and dying in Chicago, seemed for a while insupportable. At the time I had a violent cold, Sallie had to leave me and go east for a week on account of her brother's death at South Weymouth, and the cold week came, with its eternal shovelling of coal and its vain endeavors to keep comfortable. I am more reconciled to it now, but I cannot be cheerful over it. I often wonder whether I should be a fool to write and tell Remsen I was at his service. A year or more ago he asked me if under any conditions I would go there, and said that would please him best, and a few weeks ago hadn't chosen any other man. I could live the rest of my days more happily

in Baltimore. But I suppose I should now find it hard to live on that pay; and I suppose my work here is more important than that would be, though I do not actually see important results flowing or to flow from it. I suppose I shall not do this. But I hope I may end my days in the East. I have not the imagination which is necessary to enjoy Chicago, which is doubtless destined to be an endurable and perhaps admirable town long after I am dead. . . . One of my assistants has just dropped in, down stairs, for afternoon tea, which we now provide on Sunday afternoons; so I must go down. Here endeth the Lamentation of yours truly, J. F. Jameson.

Meantime I have found solace in finishing some (to me) interesting Studies in the History of the Federal Convention of 1787 for the next A. H. A. volume.[34]

TO IRA REMSEN

Confidential
[University of Chicago]
March 24, [1903].

My dear Mr. Remsen:[35]

My friend Christie has sent me your recent letter to him, with some statement of what he wrote to you. I may as well write to you directly. I will also write fully, partly because your time in this matter must be precious now, and partly because I have always thought you were a man to whom one could write with entire frankness. I will tell you just what I think.

I had no idea that Christie was likely to see you or speak or write to you. At a time of discouragement, when the outlook here seemed less satisfactory than it sometimes does, I wrote to him—he being from old college and Hopkins days my best friend—and among other things said that I sometimes wondered whether I had been foolish to decline your kind invitation to go to the Hopkins (which, by the way, I don't think I have mentioned to any other man). It was evidently because of this that he wrote to you. In justice to him and in due appreciation of his kindness I ought to say that what I said was not merely the expression of a transient feeling. There was a permanent, (though not prevailing), element in it, as may appear.

When you wrote me before, I did not in fact deliberate long, because, to speak now plainly, I am getting a salary of $5000 a year, and I did not suppose the Johns Hopkins could afford to pay anything like so much as that, if it wished; and therefore it seemed in-

---

On Feb. 1, G. B. Adams, chairman of the board of editors of the *Review,* wrote to Jameson: "Dr. Billings has given Sloane the outlines of a plan which it is expected the Carnegie Board will propose to us at their next meeting. . . . It is a modification of the plan which I prepared but a modification much in our favor, I think, and it is certainly an extremely important proposition. It seems necessary to have a meeting of the board and I have called this for Feb. 14 at 10 A.M. at Sloane's house. . . . In the afternoon there will be a meeting with Dr. Billings. You must make an effort to be present if it is in any way possible, the question is so important. [P. S.] The Carnegie Board meets on the 19th."

The arrangement which the trustees made at that meeting, as here described by Jameson, modified the proposal made by Dr. Billings and also avoided the granting of a direct subvention.

[33] Some years later Jameson wrote: "I should give the title of 'historian' to very few of the members of my profession; for instance, I never allow any one to apply it to myself if I can help it" (Jameson to Col. Henry McCain, Mar. 21, 1912).

[34] Published in the *Ann. Rept., Amer. Hist. Assn.,* 1902: 1: 87-167.

[35] Ira Remsen continued as president of the Johns Hopkins until 1912. In a Diary jotting of March 29, 1903, Jameson wrote: "Remsen not thought likely to be permanent president, hardly young enough, takes things too lightly, not a man of as many ideas as Gilman. . . somewhat a disappointed man; yet very agreeable to the Baltimorians, and as likely to get money from them as anybody" (Diary, 1900-1904).

decent to reply to your inquiry, as to conditions on which I might come, by naming impossible stipulations as to money. So I dropped the other considerations, and gave a general reply. But now, perhaps I had better make a fuller statement.

I am not on the whole discontented with my position. I enjoy my work here more than my work in Providence. But Christie is quite right in thinking that I should feel more at home in the East. It often makes me sad to be so far away from my father and mother and among [many?] old friends. I do not like Chicago. I feel somewhat the severity of its climate, and look forward with apprehension to the spending of old age here, or rather to the attempt, for one sees few old people here. I miss the Eastern libraries. I dislike the amount of administrative detail which our ambitious and complicated system forces upon the head of a department. I like the tone and atmosphere of the Johns Hopkins much better, and have a vivid remembrance, fortified by my visit thirteen months ago, of the pleasantness of social life in Baltimore and the kindness of my old friends there.

On the other hand, permanent satisfaction in one's work depends on the sense of its importance and value, and, though I have little present knowledge of your students and of your relations to the South, I should not easily be convinced that the work of a chief professor of history at Baltimore is likely to have the same influence on the future of historical work in this country as, in view of our hold on the West and our prospective wealth and size, might be exercised by the head of the department here. I say "might be" partly from a sense of my own deficiencies, partly because I am told that President Harper has taken an action which would much diminish the influence of the head of the department; whether this is true or not I shall not know till after his return from the East.

Again, when I look over your list,—it may be simply because I miss so many of my old friends, but it does not appear to me that on the philosophical—philological—political—literary side the men of my own age would afford me as stimulating companionship as that which might be derived here, though indeed that is tempered by the fact that we are all too busy to see much of each other.

Another question which would have caused me much hesitation is the question how largely the staff of the department would be subject to renovation.[36] That was a very important cause of hesitation as to coming here. There were nine men in the department already, some excellent, some not so good, and there

would be little opportunity to make the list better.[37] Also, I do not know how removal to Homewood will affect the Johns Hopkins, especially as to the use of libraries in the city.[38] I have $2500 a year to spend for historical books, which I suppose is more than the department at Baltimore enjoys, and which, though the process is slow and laborious, might in time provide me with library opportunities equal to yours. And our trustees are understood to be considering a scheme for pensions.

I think I have told you all that is in my mind that relates in any direct way to the Johns Hopkins. I wish I had done it earlier if to do so would have aided you more. I should expect that it would cause you to pass by my name again, but shall be content if it causes you to do so with a mind better satisfied.

I hope I have not expressed myself so frankly as to seem to depreciate the Hopkins and your offer, which I am far from wishing to do. I thank you sincerely for the patience with which you have reopened the question.[39]

To FRANCIS A. CHRISTIE

5551 Lexington Avenue, Chicago
April 18, [1903].

My dear Christie:

In view of all your friendly kindness in the matter, I certainly ought to have written to you sooner after sending Remsen a final word.[40] My excuse is the old one, pressure of work. I told him without going down there that I had concluded not to come. If I had felt that there was plenty of time I should have taken it, and I was sorry not to make the most thorough sort of investigation. But by a certain day it seemed, in view of what information I had been able to get together, distinctly probable that I should decline after the fullest scrutiny. It seemed to me that, if that was the case, I ought to think more of Remsen's now short time in case I declined, rather than of taking the time to

[36] The department consisted of John M. Vincent, associate professor, and two associates in history—Bernard C. Steiner and James C. Ballagh. Guy C. Lee aided in the teaching of the undergraduates; James Schouler gave a short lecture course each year; Bloomfield taught Oriental history; and a series of lectures in diplomatic history, known as the Albert Shaw lectures, was offered each year by a visiting professor.

[37] These were: Benjamin Terry and George Stephen Goodspeed, professors; Oliver J. Thatcher and Edwin E. Sparks, associate professors; George E. Fellows, Francis W. Shepardson, and Ferdinand Schwill [later Schevill], assistant professors; and R. C. H. Catterall and James W. Thompson, instructors. Professor Hermann Eduard von Holst was still nominally a member of the department but was too infirm to take any part in its activities and was on leave from the time of Jameson's appointment until his death in 1904. By the end of 1903 Professor Goodspeed had died and Fellows and Catterall had resigned.

[38] The gift of the Homewood land, 180 acres once owned by Charles Carroll, had been made not long before the celebration of Feb. 22, 1902. Not until 1910 were funds sufficient to begin building on the new site.

[39] In reply to this letter President Remsen wrote that the salary would be $5000, that the department could be largely renovated if desirable, and that the university would pay Jameson's expenses if he wished to come to Baltimore to talk over the position (Jameson to Christie, Mar. 31, 1903).

[40] The final reply has not been found.

look into everything in the fullest way for the chance that I might conclude to accept. If I went down I should have to go down at once, as a vacation was imminent and I must see the men (students, especially) in term-time. I ran some risk of making Remsen think that I was again not giving his proposals the full consideration they merited, and indeed I believe he is displeased, for he has made no reply. But I can't help it, though I am sorry; I was acting in his interest, as I thought.

As to why I concluded against going, those things are complex to state. The moving and settling last autumn was so disagreeable a process, and so much more expensive than I had expected, (it has kept us unpleasantly poor all the year), that I could not contemplate another uprooting, another removal and settling, and another year of pinching unless it was very clear I was to gain.[41] That seemed doubtful. I should still be far from my family. My father would not probably come down to Baltimore in the winter. While our climate is disagreeable, and may some time kill a body with pneumonia, it meanwhile agrees finely with us all,—never better in our lives, Katrina and Sallie never so well,—and I was advised that the enervating climate of Baltimore might not suit us so well. But also, I was led to believe there was a pretty definite limit to the money the Hopkins could get, so definite that I did not see much chance to build up a department faculty of a conspicuously excellent sort. A large part of the present material is not good, not as good as what I have here. Unless I could surround myself with a distinctly better set than I have here, I did not care to move, so far as my functions as head of a department are concerned. With regard to teaching, the balance was on the J. H. side. I like Southern young men better than Western, and should fit in better there. As to research and writing—well, in the first place I must not give more than a secondary place to that consideration if I am to be head of a department at all; I am certain to have to teach and manage, in order to get my living. That I shall write anything important is nowise so certain, now that 43 years have gone without my doing so. But Baltimore is not a first-rate place for it, in my line. 2d-rate; Chicago 3d-rate or 4th, to be sure. Taking it all together, I concluded there wasn't enough prospect of gain to make me move. I hope I didn't decide wrongly. I don't think I did. The things you brought forward were significant. They were *the* significant things on their side.[42] But

there was the other side. Yet do feel sure that I am immensely grateful to you for all your course in the matter. It was a great encouragement to me, at a time when I greatly needed encouragement.[43] . . .

To the Editor of the *Nation*

University of Chicago,
March 11, [1904].[44]

Sir:

I have received a flamboyant advertisement of a work in twenty volumes which calls itself "A Definitive, Authoritative and Inclusive Narrative History of North America," edited by Guy Carleton Lee and published by George Barrie and Sons of Philadelphia. Some publishers allow themselves such latitude in the praising of their wares that, although the present advertisement is, I think, the most pretentious I have ever seen, carries self-laudation almost beyond the bounds of rhetoric, and commends the editor in most fulsome terms, I do not intend to comment on these things. It is a more serious matter that, in the heading below the extraordinary title or legend I have quoted, occur the words, "Based on a plan suggested by the American Historical Association." Every one who has attended the meetings of the American Historical Association during recent years knows well that it has never suggested or approved any plan for any coöperative history of America. The nearest approach to such action was when, at the Washington meeting of 1901, "the council reported that, at a meeting held in New York, November 29, the proposition of a coöperative history of America was carefully considered, and in view of the difficulties involved, the council had voted that it would not be expedient for the American Historical Association to take part in forming or carrying out a plan for the composition or publication of a coöperative history of the United States. On motion the action of the council was unanimously approved by the Association." (Proceedings, Annual Report for 1901, p. 37.) The project then submitted and rejected was not this of Mr. Lee's. Yet the circular before me, after speaking of the plan of the proposed work, proceeds to say:

"The American Historical Association some time ago considered the question and determined on a plan for a history that should be: (1) coöperative; (2) under the direction of an editor-in-chief; (3) that the publication be made in small volumes, each complete in itself. The plan of the Association has been improved upon in that," etc.

---

[41] Moving was always a trial to Jameson. Years later he wrote of a move from 1757 to 2231 Q Street, Washington, "I'll bet that it cost us more trouble than it caused Abraham to move from Ur to Hebron" (Jameson to J. R. Jewett, June 22, 1910).

[42] Christie had argued: that the financial situation of the Johns Hopkins was greatly improved; that the establishment of the Carnegie Technical School at Pittsburgh would prevent the university from becoming too "practical"; that it had a unique position in the scholarly world; that Jameson would

build up the department of history, would be near Washington, and, though a Yankee, understood the traditions of the South and would be welcomed by Southern students.

[43] The omitted section deals chiefly with plans for a summer in Maine, in which Christie and Professor Burr, both bachelors, were to join the Jameson family.

[44] A protest to the Editor of the Nation, *Nation* **78**: 210, Mar. 17, 1904.

The statement here made is completely and notoriously false. It is likely that the writers of the circular have shrewdly chosen language which exempts them from legal consequences. But the intention to deceive the public into the belief that the American Historical Association is in some manner connected with the enterprise is none the less manifest, and none the less contemptible.[45]

---

[45] The *Nation* of Mar. 31 carried Lee's reply, which contended that the publishers were essentially correct in their statements, since a committee to consider publishing a cooperative history was appointed by the Association in 1899 and reported favorably on the plan in 1900 (*Ann. Rept.,* 1899: 1: 27; 1900: 1: 18). Lee conceded that the circular should have read: "The American Historical Association some time, through a committee, favorably considered." For information on this committee, of which A. B. Hart was chairman, see Holt, *op. cit.,* 276, 281-287; a letter from Haskins to the members of the executive council of the Association set forth the status of the committee on Jan. 25, 1901.

Jameson's communication brought to him a number of approving letters, one of them from President Remsen, Mar. 28, 1904, telling him that the editor-in-chief of the series in question would cease to be connected with the Johns Hopkins University at the close of the current academic year. Two letters from Professor Van Tyne of Michigan, the first undated, the second of May 26, 1904, throw some light on the character of the series which Lee was editing. The first tells of a Michigan student "who spent last summer copying passages from a dozen or so histories for a clergyman in Newark, N. Y. The learned divine proposed to patchwork these pieces together—changing them some—to construct a volume for the G. C. Lee 'definitive, non-sectional, non-partizan, non-entity etc.' history of America. This young lady says that this reverend, moral prop of society was not even taking the work seriously but thought it a good joke that he who knew nothing of Am. Hist. should be providing historical pabulum for the gullible American public. So you see that occasionally you critics, you 'cut-throat bandits in the path of fame' do 'hold up' real rascality instead of innocent stupidity." In Van Tyne's second letter he reported that this student had typed from the dictation of the same clergyman much of G. C. Lee's *True history of the Civil War,* Philadelphia, Lippincott, 1903, which she says was done in a great hurry. The series under discussion was *The history of North America,* 20v., Philadelphia, G. Barrie's Sons, 1903-1907, "for subscribers only." Lee, the general editor, was the author of v. 1 to 8, 10 to 14, and 17.

One more item can be added to this story. Lee, before sending his reply to the *Nation,* telegraphed to Hart, asking whether Jameson was doing a volume in Hart's American Nation series. To this Hart replied: "Professor Jameson has no connection with my series nor I infer with yours" (Hart to Jameson, Mar. 21, 1904).

THE DEPARTMENT OF HISTORICAL RESEARCH OF THE
CARNEGIE INSTITUTION OF WASHINGTON:
THE FIRST DECADE, 1905-1914

To ROBERT S. WOODWARD

January 20, 1905.

Dear Sir:[1]

The Board of Editors of the American Historical Review hope that they will not seem to be taking too much upon themselves in assuming to address you on behalf of the whole historical profession in the United States, with reference to an object not directly connected with the Review. We are deeply gratified by the founding and rapid development of the Carnegie Institution's Bureau of Historical Research, the variety of activities which it has found, the interesting and important results which it has already achieved. We believe, however, that the usefulness of the Bureau would be greatly heightened by the addition of one more function, namely by provision for more systematic assistance to advanced graduate students of history. Such provision was contemplated in the report made by the Advisory Committee on History to the Executive Committee of the Carnegie Institution;[2] it is entirely compatible with, indeed would probably further, the present activities of the Bureau; and we venture to think that it is in harmony with the desire of the founder of the Institution, expressed in his deed of trust, "to afford instruction of an advanced character to students properly qualified to profit thereby."

It is conceded that the Carnegie Institution should not duplicate existing educational agencies, and therefore there should be no effort to provide those ordinary kinds of historical instruction for graduate students which a dozen universities are already supplying. But to the advanced historical student Washington is a unique treasure-house of material. Never have its riches, and the opportunity which they present, been so fully disclosed as by the Carnegie institution's recently published "Guide to the Archives of the Government of the United States."[3] It is capable of affording, to students of the advanced type designated, an element in their historical training which no university can possibly supply. We submit that it is better for the intellectual interests of the country that this unique element in American historical training should be supplied generously to élite students, and that it should be supplied systematically if supplied at all. The Director of the Bureau, and his assistants, beside advising and aiding individual students, could give systematic lectures on the bibliography of American history, on the history and contents of the various collections at Washington, or on similar topics. It is known that he would welcome such an opportunity.

We suggest that the privileges of such instruction should be confined to students who have at least two years of graduate historical work in one or more of the institutions belonging to the Association of American Universities. This rule would exclude, as is proper, the elementary student. It would include each year several excellent men who are preparing dissertations for the doctor's degree, and who would be glad of the chance to work at Washington under proper guidance. This we believe to be wise. Under existing conditions, we must expect that much of the most useful research work, much of the needed exploiting of the national archives, shall be performed by the makers of doctoral theses. Monographs of this type constitute already a large and valued part of the work of historical investigation achieved in the United States. To encourage the best of them we believe to be a proper scientific policy.

We feel sure that any of the universities in the group mentioned would welcome such an adjunct to their scientific apparatus in history, and would cooperate in making it effective, by allowing work done under such supervision to count toward the higher degrees, and perhaps by the occasional loan of professors to assist in supervising it.

Without wishing to press imperfect analogies, we believe that the success and usefulness of the French School at Rome, and of the Austrian, Prussian, Hungarian, Polish and Belgian historical institutes in that city, furnish an argument for such a development as we have in mind. Such monumental series of publications as have been instituted by some of these organizations, and as we hope to see proceeding from our own Bureau of Historical Research, would be made much easier of execution if, year after year, it should

---

[1] On Dec. 13, 1904, President Gilman resigned as head of the Carnegie Institution and Dr. Robert S. Woodward (1849-1924), dean of the School of Pure Sciences of Columbia University was chosen president, an office which he held until 1920.

[2] See *Year Book,* Carnegie Institution, 1902: 227. McLaughlin had by no means forgotten this. In an article, A bureau of historical research, contributed by him to the *Iowa Journal of History and Politics,* April, 1904, he cited this as one of the purposes of the bureau.

[3] By Claude H. Van Tyne and Waldo G. Leland, Carnegie Institution, publication no. 14, Papers of the Bureau of Historical Research. This work was undertaken in accordance with a plan presented to the Institution by Worthington C. Ford in 1902 (*Year Book,* 1903: xxxvi).

draw into close association with itself the best of our graduate students of American history.

But after all the chief argument for such a step is the fructifying effect it would have on historical studies in the country at large, if every year some of the ablest of our future teachers of American history should have an opportunity, under favorable conditions, to derive historical knowledge and inspiration from contact with the national capital and the national archives.[4]

To GIFFORD PINCHOT

November 23, 1905.

My dear Mr. Pinchot:[5]

At your request I write out, somewhat more fully and deliberately, what I said to your friend this morning.

I spoke of two things: first, the process by which European governments bring expert judgment to bear upon the problem of governmental historical publications; secondly, the procedure by which this might be done in the United States. The practice in European countries varies more or less. Yet in general it may be said that the typical procedure is the creation and maintenance of a commission of the persons most expert or of most eminence in dealing with these problems, which serves permanently, and usually without pay. It is the function of this commission to look over the field, to see what needs to be done, to recommend the most important and pressing of these tasks, and if the approval of the ministry of public instruction is won, to engage editors and supervise and approve their work.

These commissions are made up mostly of unofficial persons. Generally the head of the national archives is a member and sometimes other similar officials, but these are usually historical experts or they would not have the places which they now occupy. The getting of qualified members who have by experience proved their fitness is simplified in most countries by the fact that the members of these commissions are chosen from out of the great learned academies, bodies which the government has formed and in which the work done by the members inevitably tests their judgment and their fitness in other respects for the work of the historical commissions.

An exceedingly good example of a rational mode of procedure is the Dutch. Two years ago the Queen of the Netherlands—I presume at the instance of Professor Blok of Leyden,[6] the most prominent of the Dutch historians, who was her instructor in history—constituted a commission of eight or ten men, called Commission of Advice for National Historical Publications. After due deliberation, in labors and sessions extending over nearly two years, they have made a report—an extremely interesting publication of a hundred pages or so, which I have lately been reading. They set themselves or their individual members at a systematic survey of the whole field of Dutch history with reference to the question, what gaps existed in the historical record as at present published. It is to be observed that they decisively rejected any thought that the government should undertake the preparation of narrative histories. recognizing that its proper function lies in the direction of documentary publication—the printing of the original sources which individual investigators might use at their pleasure in the elaboration of the national history. They took up all the various portions of Dutch history, all the various aspects of it, both those which hitherto have been attentively pursued by historians and those which seemed likely in the immediate future to be regarded with an amount of interest that has not yet been bestowed upon them. They considered in each case what documentary materials had been printed, what had not, what portions were relatively over-documented so that it was superfluous at present to bring out more material relating to them, and what were marked by genuine gaps in the historical record. They considered what desiderata there were that could be met only by long series of volumes, what moderate series seemed to be called for, what cases there were where individual volumes would suffice. Having thus surveyed the field they were ready to recommend that, of the various tasks thus systematically outlined, a beginning should be made with certain ones which could be planned for as component parts of the great general scheme.

This is a rational mode of procedure, such as anyone would expect the Dutch to adopt. It is to be observed, too, that this Commission of Advice is not dismissed as soon as it has set forth its scheme. It is realized that it is impossible for anybody to provide all the advice necessary for a generation of historical publication and then go away and leave the scheme to execute itself, as one winds up a clock and leaves it to run. The same commission continues in existence as an advisory board, has framed excellent regulations

---

[4] Between the time of writing this letter and the next one, McLaughlin had resigned as head of the Bureau of Historical Research and Jameson had been appointed to succeed him, to begin work in October, 1905. McLaughlin returned to the University of Michigan for a year, then accepted Jameson's vacant place in Chicago. During the years which he had spent in Washington he and Jameson had been in constant communication and few decisions had been made which had not been submitted to the latter for approval.

[5] Gifford Pinchot (1865-1947), best known for his services to forest conservation in this country, had in June, 1905, been appointed a member of the Keep Commission to consider department methods, including among many miscellaneous problems, the care of department records and the publication of historical materials. Jameson's prolonged effort to obtain the competent editing of the historical documents of the United States government, is further illustrated by numerous later letters. See *post*, Dec. 13, 1907, Jan. 24, 1910.

[6] Petrus Johannes Blok (1855-1929), historian and achivist of Leiden.

safeguarding and regulating the issue of the historical volumes which may be resolved upon, and will supervise these through committees of one or more assigned to each. Something like this, though not in all cases so well worked out, is the plan pursued by other European countries.

As to the historical publications made by the United States government, I feel clear that in general terms some such plan would, if adopted, secure much more satisfactory results for given sums of money than the system or want of system now employed. A good deal of money has been spent for historical publication by Congress and some of it with exceedingly useful results. But the process has been haphazard. Congress has spent more than two million dollars for the official records of the war and declined last winter to appropriate five thousand dollars for five years for the preparation of the diplomatic correspondence of the years from 1789 to 18[61]. Some of its historical publications have been prepared with great care, while in some many of the most ordinary recognized rules of documentary publication have been neglected. It is a matter of chance if a properly qualified person edits one of these volumes; and there has almost never been an endeavor which a properly composed commission would exercise, to secure for it the very best person that existed in the country.

That such a commission could be called into existence, and if called into existence would perform its functions smoothly and efficiently, there can be no doubt. The historical profession in this country is a singularly united and harmonious body of men and has many members who would cheerfully serve on such a board with or without payment (though it would be unreasonable not to pay their travelling expenses). Just how such a commission should be constituted is not an easy question. I should say that it ought to consist of seven or eight members. That there should be more, would not be useful; that there should be fewer, might work awkwardly in a country with so large distances as ours. The tenure should be indefinite. I do not believe that it would be advantageous that there should be any members ex officio. There is no office, so far as I can see, the holder of which is inevitably one of the seven or eight men best qualified for such a service. The official most likely to be so qualified is, perhaps, the chief of the Division of Manuscripts in the Library of Congress. Yet it is quite conceivable that at some future period a man might be in that office, and be very well qualified for most of its work, whose judgment with regard to governmental historical publications would not be one of the seven or eight best judgments in the country. And so of other offices. Nor do I think it is useful to institute a representation of historical societies as such. Most of them are occupied with problems of local rather than of national history; most of them are indifferent to periods since the Revolution, while the historical publications of the United States government

will be almost confined to the period since 1776. I should say therefore, pick out the seven or eight people best qualified, regardless, or almost regardless of their official positions.

I do not know whether these suggestions will be of any use to you; but if they should be, I should be very glad. Certainly if anything could be done to systematize and improve the annual historical product of the United States government it would be a fine thing. I also think, as I said to your friend, that our government now does less in the way of historical publication, proportionally, than is done by most of the European states, and that we might well do more. That, however, is another matter. I will merely take the liberty to mention a paper on the Expenditures of Foreign Governments in Behalf of History which I contributed to the Annual Report of the American Historical Association for 1892 [1891], which may present some suggestions, though of course it is now thirteen [fourteen] years behind the times.

To ROBERT S. WOODWARD

Department of Historical Research,
Carnegie Institution,
February 1, 1906.

Dear Sir:

You have communicated to me two votes passed by the Executive Committee of the Trustees at their meeting of January 9, reading as follows:

Resolved, That the consideration of allotments for researches in foreign archives be postponed until the reports on those archives now in progress are submitted by the Department of Historical Research to the Executive Committee.

Resolved, That the Department of Historical Research be requested to report to the Executive Committee what transcripts from foreign archives of American historical documents are available in the United States.[7]

In attempting to respond to the second of these resolutions, I find it necessary to call attention to an important distinction, which may not have been in the minds of the Committee, but which may have decisive weight if, as I suppose, there is some relation between the two resolutions. If the resolve to delay further work in European archives was in any degree founded on a doubt whether the material to be disclosed was not already available in the United States in the form of transcripts, it becomes essential to remark that the English archives, for whose thorough inspection provision

---

[7] Jameson had received word of the passing of these resolutions on Jan. 20, and on Jan. 22 had written McLaughlin a long letter on the general situation and his own feeling: "These things I learned two days ago from President Woodward. I have been too enraged ever since to digest anything, but have not perceived that that does any good. The next thing is to return to that charge with a view to their meeting on February 12."

has already been made, stand in respect to such transcripts in a class apart from all others in Europe.[8] Three-fourths of all the transcripts of documents in European archives relating to the history of the United States which are now to be found in this country have been derived from the English archives. It is too late to inquire whether these last are so numerous as to make superfluous the archive-searches contemplated by this Department, for the Executive Committee provided in December 1903 for the report on the English archives and the data are now nearly all collected. But I proceed to answer the Committee's inquiry both with respect to English and with respect to other foreign archives.

First as to England. According to the best estimate now obtainable, it is probable that there are between 250,000 and 300,000 documents relating to the history of the United States in the British archives and British Museum. Of these, it may be estimated that about 25,000 are represented in this country by transcripts. The number of transcripts is probably nearer 30,000, but at least 5,000 should be deducted on account of duplication. Moreover, at least 8,000 of the transcripts are only extracts or abstracts, not complete copies of the documents. It is also to be remarked that, of the existing transcripts, more than one-half, perhaps two-thirds, relate to the period of thirty years from 1754 to 1784, the longer period before 1754 being little represented; and that many of the earlier transcripts are highly inaccurate.

Secondly, as to Spain. The best estimate now obtainable is to the effect that the three chief archives in that country contain, roughly speaking, 500,000 documents relating to the history of the United States. It is not known that more than 1500 of these are represented by transcripts in the more accessible parts of the country, though certain unopened boxes in New Orleans and the H. H. Bancroft Library in California, not yet open to the public, doubtless contain others, and more are supposed to exist in Florida. In part the same remark may be made of Spain, as has already been made concerning England. An agent of this Department, under authority conferred upon my predecessor, has completed an examination of the three chief archives in Spain;[9] but much yet remains to be done in other repositories, public and private. From the Cuban archives practically no transcripts have been made.

If, however, the inquiry respecting transcripts is intended to cast light on the problem of future archive-searches, the really important question, as has been remarked, is the question how many transcripts we have from documents relating to the history of the United States found in the archives of other countries than England and Spain. In these cases it is not possible to present for comparison even approximate estimates of the total number of such documents; but the number of transcripts is in all cases small.

From France there are not six thousand such transcripts in the country, though the printed inventories, in which the French archives surpass those of all other countries, show a rich store of material for American history. The proportion of transcripts is no doubt greater than in the case of Spain and much less than in the case of England. From the archives of Mexico there are a few hundred, though undoubtedly these archives contain many thousands of relevant documents. From the Netherlands we have the nine hundred transcripts which Brodhead made sixty years ago, and two collections of about three hundred each, largely duplicating each other, and relating to the period of the American Revolution. These last, it is certain, represent but a small part of what is available in various Dutch archives. From the German archives, the wealth of which for various aspects of American history is not generally suspected, we have little else than the two thousand transcripts which George Bancroft collected to illustrate the diplomatic history of the American Revolution. From Sweden we have only some two or three hundred transcripts; from Russia practically nothing except what may be contained in the H. H. Bancroft Library in California, though there is much American material in St. Petersburg and Moscow. Of Canadian archives much the same story is to be told, while from the various archives in Rome, which doubtless contain United States documents by the thousand, it is not known that two hundred copies exist in the country.

[8] The history of the early exploration of the English archives is a long and involved one. In 1899 Jameson had drawn up for the American Antiquarian Society a scheme for a search, which it was agreed should be carried out by Professor Charles M. Andrews under the sponsorship of the society. Obstacles developed, however, and when it appeared that the venture would be too costly, the Antiquarian Society dropped the project, giving what material it had gathered in this country to the Bureau of Historical Research of the Carnegie Institution, which had from its inception an examination of European archives as part of its program. Professor Andrews was the obvious agent, both because of his own work in London and because of his connection with the earlier plans. See Andrews, Charles M., and Frances G. Davenport, *Guide to the manuscript materials for the history of the United States to 1783, in the British Museum, in minor London archives, and in the libraries of Oxford and Cambridge,* iii-v, Carnegie Institution, publication no. 90, 1908.

Andrews made a preliminary examination in 1904, as a result of which he read at the December meeting of the American Historical Association a paper on Materials in British archives for American colonial history (*Amer. Hist. Rev.* **10**: 325-349, Jan. 1905). In the summer of 1905 he returned to England to continue his work.

It is worth noting here that for a preliminary survey of the resources of European archives, also part of the earliest plans for the bureau, Professor George L. Burr was the choice but that he firmly refused to be lured away from teaching and from the writing which he then hoped to do (Burr to McLaughlin, June 24, 1904).

[9] W. R. Shepherd (1871-1934), of Columbia University, sailed for Spain in June, 1905, and returned to this country in September. His examination included the archives of Simancas, the Archives of the Indies at Seville, and the Archivo Historico Nacional at Madrid. His *Guide to the materials for the history of the United States in Spanish archives,* Carnegie Institution, publication no. 91, appeared in 1907.

The information desired by the Committee may be presented in another way. It is certain that, of all periods of American history, the twenty years from 1763 to 1783 are those most fully covered by transcripts obtained from abroad. The late B. F. Stevens,[10] in his printed statement regarding his Catalogue Index of Manuscripts in European Archives relating to America for these twenty years, computes the number of documents represented in his index as 161,000. But not one-eighth of that number are to be found in transcript form in America. For earlier periods the proportion must be much smaller.

It should perhaps be added that from the beginning, all the European archive-searches instituted by this Department have been conducted with full regard to all the problems raised by the presence in America of transcripts of some of the documents.

I ask permission to add some remarks on the first of the two resolutions of the Executive Committee quoted above. The reports now in progress, alluded to in that vote, are three in number. That of Mr. Perez on the Cuban archives, the smallest of the three, will probably be ready before the end of the present month.[11] That of Professor Shepherd on the three chief Spanish archives will not be finished until October, that of Professor Andrews on the London archives not until some time next autumn, since in both cases these gentlemen will need the summer vacation for the fullest opportunity to work over their notes. Add to these periods some time spent in printing, and it will be seen that the vote of the Executive Committee calls for a delay of a year before further advances can be considered.

A year is a short period in the life of the Carnegie Institution, and a year's delay in one of the chief services which I came here to render to my profession may matter little if at the end of it appropriations can be made with a confidence as to the outcome which is not to be attained in any other way. But I venture to suggest that there are at least four modes by which a close approach to a satisfactory judgment on the final result can be obtained now.

I. All three of these books bear much resemblance, in general plan and even in many of the details of arrangement, to Messrs. Van Tyne and Leland's *Guide to the Archives of the Government at Washington,* a book which is already familiar to the Committee and of which the plan has met with general approval during the two years during which it has been before the historical public. Its utility is well established; I believe it was the first scientific publication of the Carnegie Institution to become out of print.

II. Since nearly all modern European national plans for extensive historical work have opened in a manner similar to ours, there are many, and in some cases celebrated, European volumes which more or less resemble those contemplated by this Department, and by means of which the usefulness of the latter can be judged. Perhaps the closest analogy is presented by Langlois and Stein's *Les Archives de l'Histoire de France,* a copy of which I have left in your room—though that is a much larger book than either one of our three.

III. The nature of the proposed volumes could be securely inferred from the statement I gave in my letter of December 16, 1905, respecting the purposes of such searches.[12] But since the form and the value of the description must depend upon the nature of the things described, a still closer notion may be obtained by examining Professor Andrews's article on "Materials in British Archives for American Colonial History" in the *American Historical Review* for January 1905, and that of Professor Shepherd on "The Spanish Archives and their Importance for the History of the United States" in the *Annual Report of the American Historical Association* for 1903. Copies of both these I have left in your room.

IV. Finally, the work of preparing all three of the books has progressed far enough to make it possible to submit, as I do herewith, a considerable number of specimen pages. These pages have been carefully chosen with a view to exhibiting, in sufficient variety, average specimens of the actual contents of the three volumes now in preparation. I do not think that the finished volumes will enable the members of the Committee to form a closer estimate than can be framed from these specimens as to the form and value of the results to be obtained from future researches in other archives.

If it is possible to secure a reconsideration of the first vote of the Committee, I hope that in the light of these remarks it may be thought unnecessary to wait a year before authorizing further searches in foreign archives. The delay will be especially disadvantageous in the cases of France and Mexico. I wish also to point out a disadvantage connected with the tour of inspection in Europe which the Committee have authorized me to make this spring.[13] One of the most impor-

---

[10] Benjamin F. Stevens (1833-1902), and his older brother, Henry, were pioneers in opening the riches of European archives to students of American history. Benjamin indexed one hundred and eighty manuscript volumes, and prepared transcripts and facsimiles of many documents. His *Catalogue Index of Manuscripts in the Archives of England, France, Holland, and Spain Relating to America, 1763 to 1783,* to which Jameson here refers, was purchased by the Library of Congress in 1906.

[11] Pérez, Luis Marino, *Guide to the materials for American history in Cuban archives,* Carnegie Institution, publication no. 83, July, 1907. Pérez began his work in June, 1905; he returned from Cuba in December, 1905.

[12] With that letter Jameson undoubtedly hoped to win the approval of the executive committee of the Institution and the necessary funds ($4,000) for the projected searches.

[13] Although the vote of the executive committee was not rescinded, Jameson made the tour of inspection to which he here refers, and from March until the middle of July, 1906, was engaged in visiting the chief European archives. For the expenses of this trip the Institution allowed him $350. During his absence Frances G. Davenport was in charge of the Washington office.

tant objects of that mission was to do all that could now be done to pave the way for those future archive-researches which I had supposed to have been, from the foundation of this bureau or department, constantly contemplated. If general approval of such a policy can now be manifested, I can take while in Europe many preparative steps which I should hesitate to take under the present conditions.

It is possible that $4,000 may seem a disproportionately large sum to devote to these European searches when only $3,000 have thus far been allotted *eo nomine* to American researches. It is only right therefore to call attention to the fact that, from the necessity of the case, nearly all of the $9,600 allotted for the salaries of the office staff is an expenditure for historical researches in America.[14]

Understanding that no allotment has yet been made for the continuation of the annual bibliography of American history, *Writings on American History, 1903,* recently published by the Institution, I ask leave to say a few words on that subject.

It may be true of some or of all the physical sciences that their bibliographies have an unimportant relation to research, or that the annual bibliography of their product is already so well presented, in the International Catalogue of Scientific Literature, that an institution of research has no duty or function in the matter. But the situation of history, and particularly of American history, is radically different. On the one hand, while the French, the Germans and the Italians have such handbooks of their annual historical product, composed upon a plan now well agreed upon, we have none such for American history, and the profession needs and actively desires it.

On the other hand, bibliography holds a more vital relation to history than to the physical sciences. The latter rest primarily on the observation of natural processes or tangible objects; the literature, what men have written about these phenomena, has in research-work a secondary position. But in the case of history both the primary material for observation and the secondary elaboration consist almost wholly of the written statements of men. Historical bibliographies are guides to both documents and interpretation, to both the original and the secondary material. They answer both the purposes which in astronomy are served by the catalogue of stars plus the bibliography of astronomical publications, or in physics by the list of recorded observations in a given field plus the list of monographs. An institution of American historical research, which, leaving to others the writing of histories and the making of

monographs, attempts to serve its generation where its aid is most needed, by guiding workers to their materials and laying those materials before them in increasing abundance, can never properly neglect certain forms of bibliographical list.

As to the specific case of an annual list of writings on American history, it is strongly desired by the best workers in the profession. If such a thing met no real demand, it would not have existed for seven years in France and for nearly as long in Germany. Its preparation is an appropriate part of the work of this Department, and can best be carried on in Washington. I see no prospect that any other agency will undertake it. That the Library of Congress will not do so has been stated to me in writing by Mr. Putnam. The American Historical Association has not the money. As a trade venture, it would not succeed.

I may add that, while $700 is asked for this object this year, after we have "caught up" with 1904 and 1905 an annual volume could apparently be prepared for $400. I sincerely hope that the $700 may be appropriated.[15]

To Waldo G. Leland

Munich, May 13, 1906.

My dear Leland:[16]

I think I sent you a card from somewhere, but have been going at such a rate I hardly know what I have done. Here at Munich I find your letter—very welcome and very interesting. I congratulate you on hav-

---

[14] Fearing the worst, Jameson, on Feb. 9, asked for $1,500 to complete the projects already under way, in case he was not to receive the grant of $4,000. On Mar. 9, being informed that his letter of Feb. 1 did not give to the executive committee the information it wanted, he pointed out that McLaughlin's reports for 1904 and 1905 had presented the facts which the committee seemed to desire (*Year Book,* 1904: 66; 1905: 232-233).

[15] The committee also adhered to its determination not to publish the *Writings on American History* and Dr. Jameson at once began a search for ways to finance that indispensable publication, a search which continued as long as he lived. For 1902 the *Writings* had been prepared by Ernest C. Richardson of Princeton and Anson E. Morse, and published at Princeton in 1904. For 1903, McLaughlin, William A. Slade, and Ernest D. Lewis prepared a volume, which was published by the Carnegie Institution in 1905. For the next two years there are no bibliographies but with 1906, Miss Grace G. Griffin began the series which continued until 1939-1940 (thirty-three volumes in all), in the early years single-handed, in the later period with aid.

The problem of publication was not so satisfactorily solved. The *Writings* for 1906, 1907, and 1908 were published by Macmillan; for 1909, 1910, and 1911, they were incorporated in the *Annual Reports* of the Association. From 1912 to 1917 they were brought out by the Yale Press. After that date they appeared as supplementary volumes of the *Annual Reports.* Their compilation has now been taken over by the National Archives; their printing still rests with the American Historical Association. No volumes have been prepared for the years 1941-1947; the bibliography for 1948 (appropriately dedicated to Miss Griffin) appeared in 1952 as volume 2 of the *Annual Report* of the Association.

[16] Waldo G. Leland, already mentioned in connection with the *Guide to the archives of the government of the United States in Washington,* remained a member of the staff of the Bureau (later the Department) of Historical Research of the Carnegie Institution of Washington from 1903 to 1927. He had been an undergraduate student of Jameson's at Brown University, in 1899-1900.

ing accomplished so much.[17] I wish I could tell you at equal length of my adventures; but neither my hand nor my time permits. It must almost suffice to say that I have kept to my schedule. We think the pace is too much for Mrs. Jameson, and I think that she and Katrina will rest at Weimar while I do what I have to do at Leipzig and Berlin. She thanks you for your kind message, and so would my mother, but that she is temporarily separated from us in order to have a trip in Switzerland, which we alas cannot.

However, we have just had a fine trip from Venice here. At a friend's suggestion, and to give ourselves a bit of equivalent for Switzerland, we diverged from the beaten R.R. path at Verona, kept on to Peschiera, sailed up Lake Garda (beautiful) to Riva, then had a magnificent drive of 22 miles through the mountains to Trent. From Trent to Innsbruck, rail, and from I. to Munich, where I am pumping the Bavarian Hist. Commission and trying to get in a little rest before tackling Leipzig and Berlin.

I really feel pretty well satisfied over my Roman expedition. I did not accomplish very much that is tangible, but quite as much as I expected, and I learned a great deal. I was immensely interested in it. Venice too.

We keep well. I hope Mrs. Leland is steadily improving. Please give her my kind regards. I will tell you both a great deal more in Massachusetts, if I am not rendered incapable of coherent oral discourse in any one language. Probably the H. M. C. is not tainted by temporary personal relations with the C. I. After a period of silence, the Pinckney MSS. might thus be got at. Beer and Fortier to Paris nit. I will

see Cape Fear Mercuries [18] and ask Tantet as desired.[19] I hear McL. has decided to go to Chicago. Greatest good fortune for the dept., and I think a right move on his part.

To Nathaniel Paine

October 18, 1906.

Dear Mr. Paine: [20]

I find myself, to my great regret, unable to attend the meeting of the American Antiquarian Society on October 24. Therefore I avail myself of your suggestion, that I communicate to the Council some things which, if I were present, I might like to say. Not to be too formal about it, I will say what I have to say in this letter, and if you think fit to lay it before the Council I shall be obliged to you.

I think that many of us have warmly desired that in the work of publication the Society should branch out a little beyond the simple issue of its semi-annual "Proceedings"—that after so long an interval as that since 1885 it should add a volume to the "Archaelogia Americana." Perhaps the chief difficulty has been that of finding means for anything considerable. But the Lincoln Legacy Fund has an income which must by this time amount to $320.00, and which has, I think, been used only in one year; and I judge from the last report of the Council that some augmentation of this might be derived from the income of the Collection and Research Fund; perhaps more could be obtained from that of Mr. Salisbury's bequest. While the Society might not feel that it had the means to embark on any very extensive series, I should think that provision might be made for one more volume, and I take the occasion of this meeting, when I suppose many matters of future policy may be considered with fresh attention, to make a few suggestions as to a possible single volume, understanding that in each case provision would probably have to be made not only for the expense of printing, but for proper compensation to an editor or compiler.

By name and by aspiration the American Antiquarian Society has always been a national, as distinct from a

---

[17] Mr. Leland's second assignment for the bureau was a search for historical material in the South. In 1905 he spent about six months in Richmond, Raleigh, and Columbia, and the next year he visited a half-dozen other Southern cities. During the first of these trips McLaughlin resigned and Jameson was appointed to his post. In a letter of Apr. 18, 1906, Mr. Leland reported to Jameson visits to Richmond, Raleigh, Columbia, Charleston, Savannah, Montgomery, Mobile, and New Orleans. He gave special attention to locating and listing transcripts of American materials which had been copied from foreign archives, and also letters from delegates to the Continental Congress, both of these activities being preparatory to major undertakings of the Department.

[18] These cryptic remarks refer to items in Mr. Leland's letter. In Charleston he had seen two chests of Pinckney papers, the owner of which, "being a misled idealist, believes that Andrew's money is tainted which lends a bad odor to the Inst." Jameson suggests that the Historical Manuscripts Commission may obtain the papers later. William Beer and Professor Alcée Fortier, with whom Mr. Leland had talked in New Orleans, both wished the Carnegie Institution to send them to Paris to examine French archives. A. S. Salley, Jr., of Columbia, S. C., had asked that Jameson, while in London, look at copies of the *Cape Fear Mercury.* This request calls for explanation. Before Jameson left Washington he had arranged to publish in the April number of the *American Historical Review,* an article by Salley and W. C. Ford on the fraudulent *Cape Fear Mercury* containing the much-discussed Mecklenburg Declaration of July 3, 1776, which had recently been displayed to the

public as a sensational historical find. The article appeared as Dr. S. Millington Miller and the Mecklenburg Declaration (*Amer. Hist. Rev.* 11: 548-558). Ford was allowed by Miller to make a personal examination of the paper, and pronounced it as being a very clever imitation. Much of Leland's correspondence during the summer of 1906 relates to the matter.

[19] "Also, it would be well to ask M. Tantet in Paris if Forstall's list of documents in the French archives relating to Louisiana (published in French's *Collections*) shows the present location of the documents or if it is entirely useless in that respect." M. Victor Tantet was archivist of the Ministry of the Colonies. Not long after this it developed that his services to Canadian and American historians had been the means of lining his own pockets and distributing very bad transcripts to his clients, who could not protect themselves. On the eve of an investigation he committed suicide (Leland to Jameson, Mar. 20, 1908).

[20] Nathaniel Paine (1832-1917), a Worcester banker, for forty-five years treasurer of the American Antiquarian Society.

local, society. In any additional volume of the "Archaelogia Americana" it ought, I think, to justify its name and its aspirations, as it has justified them in the past, by publications which have more than a local scope and which will, if possible, be of large assistance to historical scholars throughout the United States. I am aware that the suggestion has been made that its first duty might be to publish some portions of its own stores of unprinted material. Unless, however, a collection can be pointed out which has unity, high importance, and a general bearing on American history, I think it would be a better course to define the additional volume, not by the casual circumstances of deposit, but by considerations growing out of the subject-matter, and especially to see if there is not a body of material relating to the colonies as a whole or to some large part of American history, which scholars greatly need. Is it not the best recommendation of a documentary publication that it has been so devised as to help the largest possible number of makers of worthy monographs in important fields?

I should be more concerned to advocate these principles of selection than to urge the choice of any one body of material. But I think of three such bodies which I should be glad to have the Council or the Society consider.

1. In an article, which I take the liberty to send to you herewith, I have suggested (pp. 820-821)[21] that, for a proper understanding of our colonial history, we ought to have in print all the American portions of the Acts and Papers of the King in Council, the royal proclamations, and the debates of Parliament. The first and the third would be a long and an expensive series. A movement is on foot in England for the achievement of the first.[22] If the British government does not print them, I think the Carnegie Institution will; if the English do the first, I think the Carnegie Institution will do the third. But a collection of the royal proclamations respecting America, brought down to 1815, would be a thing of manageable size for the American Antiquarian Society to undertake. It would be general in its character, and illustrate all or many different portions of American colonial history. It would open up to researchers an important class of material now almost unknown and unused because of its rarity, for though the proclamations were printed individually, few copies of any can be seen except in London. Probably there are members of the Society who have examined them there, which I have not done, and who would know much more than I do about the usefulness of such a collection. I simply make the suggestion.[23]

2. An enterprise of a different character which occurs to me as appropriate to a time when thoughts are turning to the first Virginian settlement, is the making of a facsimile-edition, in colors, of John White's very remarkable water-color drawings of men and things seen in America at the time of the Raleigh expeditions. It is a truly wonderful thing that there should have been preserved to our time such an exhibit of native America as seen by the eyes of an accomplished draughtsman, at the very beginning of English colonization. Yet only a part of the drawings have been reproduced, and these in the main not accurately or at least not with that complete fidelity which modern processes permit. Until lately the best of the reproductions were in De Bry, and few have seen them. The half dozen which are reproduced in the eighth volume of the new Hakluyt, and in a less degree those which our associate Dr. Eggleston printed in the "Century Magazine" (November 1882 and May 1883), though not colored, show what might be done in a modern reproduction.[24] The drawings have been in the Grenville library of the British Museum since 1865, and I have no doubt the Society could readily secure the necessary permission to photograph. There is a set of seventeenth-century copies of White's drawings among the Sloane manuscripts in the British Museum which could be used in a supplementary way because, if I understand the matter rightly, it contains some drawings which are not in the original series. I think the Society might take special interest in such a publication from the fact that these drawings of White (in the Sloane series) were first described by our asso-

---

Chicago, had been considering the desirability of embarking on these projects. All three were subsequently carried out, though under different auspices. The Antiquarian Society promptly appointed a committee, consisting of Waldo Lincoln, newly appointed vice-president (virtually acting president), William MacDonald, and Jameson, to consider the publication of the Royal Proclamations. Jameson at once began arranging for the work which could be done in this country and establishing the necessary connections in London. The report of the committee on the amount of material and approximate cost was acceptable to the society; Clarence S. Brigham (A.B., Brown, 1899), was chosen editor, and, obtaining a three-months' leave from the Rhode Island Historical Society, he began work in London in May, 1908. A full account of his London work is to be found in the Jameson Papers, along with the preliminary correspondence. British Royal Proclamations relating to America, 1603-1783, appeared as *Transactions and Collections, Amer. Ant. Soc.* 14.

Another of Jameson's suggestions was carried out by the Carnegie Institution of Washington, which between 1924 and 1941 published five volumes of *Proceedings and debates of the British Parliament respecting North America*, ed. by Leo F. Stock.

[24] *Century Magazine* 25: 66-73; 26: 105-111; Hakluyt, Richard, *Voyages, traffiques and discoveries,* 8, contains a catalogue of voyages to Virginia, a letter of John White to Hakluyt, and a few reproductions of White's drawings. An item in the *Magazine of American History* (1): 221, calls attention to the reproductions in the *Century*. More recently Randolph Adams in, An effort to identify John White, *Am. Hist. Rev.* 41: 87-89, referred to Laurence Binyon's The drawings of John White in *Walpole Society* 13: 19-24, 1924-1925.

---

[21] Gaps in the published records of United States history (*Amer. Hist. Rev.* 11: 817-831, July, 1906), a paper read before the Columbia Historical Society, Washington, D. C., Feb. 12, 1906.

[22] See *post,* Nov. 1, 1907, for the details of this plan.

[23] From a note to Jameson written by George W. Prothero on Feb. 23, 1904, it is evident that Jameson, even before he left

ciate Dr. Hale in the fourth volume of the "Archae-logia," pages 21-24. Dr. Deane, in the "Proceedings" for October 1866, page 12, describes the original series, which he saw at the British Museum soon after it was acquired from Henry Stevens.[25] It is likely that some of the present members of the Society may have seen both sets. A facsimile-edition work of this sort is expensive, but I believe that it would meet with a ready and profitable sale.[26]

3. Another sort of volume which might be thought of is a calendar or reference list of all those letters (perhaps, also, other documents) written in New England in the seventeenth century which have been printed. Of the letters and documents written on New England soil before 1701, a vast number have been printed and in a great variety of volumes. It is hard to keep track of them, and yet, unless we have some such index, arranged in convenient chronological or local order, the historian of New England matters can never be sure that he has all his evidences before him. In a future publication of the Carnegie Institution a guide will be furnished to all those documents in British archives relating to America which have been printed in a great variety of volumes.[27] With this, and the proposed list for New England, writers would be well furnished with references to their material. If such a volume were undertaken it could be followed with a similar index to printed New England letters of the period 1701-1775,

or extended to cover the middle and southern colonies.

This letter grows to too great a length. I hope that you will excuse this. My apology must be that I have thought, from conversation with some of the members, that the time was ripe for the consideration of a more active policy with respect to documentary publication. If the Council, having their annual report all finished, prefer that the matter should be discussed from the floor, it can be done by the bringing forward of a resolution which I will send to our friend Foster,[28] and which he can offer if he thinks fit to do so and if you want him to. I inclose a copy of it. If any discussion of the general subject does occur, I hope that it may be possible for the stenographic report of it to be sent to me, when convenient after the meeting. I may get from it suggestions that would be useful to me in my work here at Washington.[29] . . .

To CLARENCE W. ALVORD

October 24, 1906.

My dear Mr. Alvord: [30]

I have thought your letter of October 17 important and interesting, and have wished to take a little time to reflect about it.

First, let me explain our own position. In almost all European archives there are portions which have, because of their character or their circumstances, commended themselves immediately to American investigators or copyists as rich fields for a harvest of materials for American history, while other masses of papers, sometimes almost as valuable, have been neglected because they were less obvious or less accessible, perhaps not known of, perhaps not yet thrown open at the time when the agents made their visits. I think that this department, which should try to plan for as long a future as possible and should try to serve the interests of all present and future investigators, cannot well pur-

---

[25] Edward Everett Hale, a member of the American Antiquarian Society from 1847 until his death, was its president in 1906-1907 and a member of its committee to determine publications from 1849 to 1907.

Charles Deane (1813-1889) became a member of the Massachusetts Historical Society in 1849, of the American Antiquarian Society in 1851. He was the editor of eleven volumes of *Proceedings* of the first society, of Bradford's *History of Plymouth Plantation* (1856) for that society, and of the first series of Prince Society volumes. His especial interest was early Virginia and New England history and he gave much encouragement to Jameson when he was endeavoring to publish the Virginia records. See *Dictionary of American Biography*.

Henry Stevens (1819-1886), older brother of Benjamin, after some years spent in collecting materials in this country for the Lenox Library and the Library of Congress, established himself as collector and bookseller in London. Here he supplied many transcripts of foreign documents for American scholars. His business was carried on after his death by his son and his grandson.

[26] The society seems not to have been interested in this suggestion. For at least six years Jameson dwelt on the idea of publishing the prints as a volume of the department publications and took various preliminary steps toward that end. Whatever the reason, he never achieved his desire, but forty years after this letter to Mr. Paine was written and more than three hundred and fifty years after the drawings were made, reproductions were published which would have brought great satisfaction to him: *The new world: the first pictures of America made by John White and Jacques Le Moyne and engraved by Theodore de Bry,* edited by Stefan Lorant, N. Y., Duell, Sloan and Pearce, 1946. This contains reproductions made from "photographic hand-colored facsimilies" of White's watercolors, now in the possession of the William L. Clements Library in Ann Arbor, Mich., and from the de Bry engravings.

[27] This plan was never carried out.

[28] William E. Foster (1851-1930), librarian of the Providence public library, 1877-1930.

[29] There are numerous evidences at this time of Jameson's far-reaching plans for documentary publications. Early in 1907, encouraged by Judge Simeon E. Baldwin, he wrote a long letter to Mrs. Sage, who was then considering what disposition to make of her wealth. In this he suggested as a possibility a generous endowment for the American Historical Association, the income from which might be used in the preparation of a "monumental series of volumes embracing the important documentary materials for American history which now lie in the archives of western Europe, especially those of England, France, Spain, and Rome." This letter received no reply (Jameson to Mrs. Russell Sage, Feb. 9, 1907).

[30] Clarence W. Alvord (1868-1928) was from 1906 to 1920 editor of the Illinois Historical Collections, as well as teacher of history in the University of Illinois. In 1920 he left Illinois for the University of Minnesota. From 1914 to 1923 he was managing editor of the *Mississippi Valley Historical Review*.

In a postscript to a letter of Sept. 30, Alvord had written: "I am interested in the Louisiana documents in Paris and have obtained a good inventory of them from M. Tantet. I am anxious to get to work on them as soon as possible. . . . But before all I wish to know what Carnegie is doing or is going

sue any other course than to make first in each capital a systematic endeavor to locate and find out what there is and all there is before proceeding to the next stages of exploitation. I can see that in our relations to state historical societies and historical departments this may make some difficulties, because the latter, while they might wish to wait for the completion of this first process on our part, may feel that they will lose valuable momentum by doing so. I should wish to do everything possible to bring our slower processes into co-ordination with their programme, and will do so so far as I can without sacrifice of what I believe to be an important and fundamental principle for us. I am fairly certain, though it would not be wise to give at present any publicity to the statement, that I shall be able next June to send a qualified agent to make in Paris the same sort of comprehensive guide to the materials for American history in the French archives which Professor Andrews has been making for those in London. The appropriation, however, if made, will not be made until December 10. Meantime please regard my prediction as private.

Steps toward mutual co-operation of the western states and historical societies ought, as you say, not to be delayed. If you think, as you appear to think, that my position makes me the best person to take the initiative, I shall be very glad to do so. I believe, however, that a general and public call for a conference on the subject will not be the best mode. Generally there is in each case one man whom we ought to call into consultation, and this I can do by quietly passing word to five or six individuals to meet with us in Providence if they are so disposed. It is better at the beginning that few agencies should be brought into play rather than many. I should say that your organization, the State Historical Society of Wisconsin, the Michigan Pioneer and Historical Society, the Missouri Historical Society, and the Chicago Historical Society need alone be involved at the start. I speak of the Chicago Historical Society because, reasoning from the state of

things when I left Chicago, it is quite ready to undertake any large, good work, can find plenty of money for it, and is very ready to adopt good suggestions. After a period of difficulty it has brought itself up on a sound basis, and is only waiting to have good works urgently brought to its attention. It is, however, not well organized for such purposes. I mean to say that the motive power which would bring about participation in such an endeavor does not lie in its chief officers, president, secretary, and librarian (I am speaking in confidence and with high appreciation of them, personally), but in certain members of its council. You will know better than I whether in Missouri the leading part in such an endeavor should be taken by the Missouri Historical Society or by the State Historical Society. Perhaps you will kindly tell me, if we resolve on immediate action, which of the two has the resources and the energy to take the matter up in concert with the other agencies that I have named?[31] I do not now speak of the Historical Department of Indiana. Mr. Lindlay, formerly a student of mine at Chicago, is an excellent man, but has hardly got to going yet.[32] He and his organization can come in at a later time; upon this I have a suggestion to make later.

Now you will doubtless be able to speak in an informal, representative capacity for Illinois, and it is obvious that we should ask Mr. Burton and Mr. Thwaites to meet with us on behalf of the two northern states.[33] For the Chicago Historical Society I should think it best to ask Dr. Otto Schmidt to meet with [us], if he is able to do so. His is their Maecenas, and though he is not primarily a student of history he is a very intelligent man, having an exceedingly open and liberal mind. As to Missouri, perhaps you can say who had best be invoked; that is to say, who, if himself convinced that a given course of action was the best, could be relied upon to bring the Society into it. I shall write confidentially to a friend in St. Louis for further advice on this point.

But let us be thinking beforehand what can be proposed with good prospect of success. The minimum of co-operation would be the mere avoidance of duplication in copying. Probably this could be effected through M. Tantet so far as his archives are concerned, and until our general survey of all the archives was completed; or by all agreeing to use this department as

---

to do about them, as we must avoid duplicating work. Yet as altruistic as I may be theoretically, the personal element will play a part and I am inclined to make my major field for the next few years French colonization in the Mississippi. It is a field also which appeals to the taxpayer of Illinois on account of its romantic character and therefore one for which the State Historical Library can get money. Therefore unless Carnegie Institution has already begun and there is hope that results, which the public can use, are to be forthcoming, I may lend my influence towards urging the Library in that direction."

Jameson replied, Oct. 8, that he could answer the question only after the meeting of the Carnegie trustees, and went on to explain his plan for surveying foreign archives. He added that when he went to Chicago he had in mind some sort of co-operative publication of the records of the Old Northwest, a statement borne out by a brief memorandum of May 4-5, 1901, referring to a discussion of such a series with F. J. Turner (Diary, 1900-1904).

Alvord answered that he felt that such a survey as Jameson proposed ought to be accompanied by the copying of the documents listed. All this explains the background of this letter.

[31] Alvord suggested the Missouri Historical Society and named Walter B. Douglas of the circuit court as its best representative. Alvord to Jameson, Oct. 29, 1906.

[32] Harlow Lindley was at the time librarian of Earlham College, Richmond, Ind.

[33] Clarence M. Burton (1853-1932), Detroit lawyer and collector of books and manuscripts relating to the Northwest, and a member of the Michigan Historical Commission. In 1914 he presented his library to the Public Library Commission of Detroit.

Reuben Gold Thwaites (1853-1913), secretary of the Wisconsin History Commission and editor of the *Wisconsin Historical Collections*.

a clearing-house. The maximum of co-operation would be that all should unite in the publication of a great series, embracing the whole mass, not already published, of documentary material from European, Washington, and Richmond archives relating to the upper half of the Mississippi valley before 1803. This would on the whole be the best, but I fear that it may not be thought practicable. The possible plan is probably an intermediate course of such a sort as will in the end lead to the total result, yet will be elastic and will leave to each organization its own portion of the field, to be cultivated according to methods which, suited to each, nevertheless are by mutual conference brought into a considerable degree of uniformity. One mode of such division is the geographical; but I do not see how this can be worked out satisfactorily when so very large a proportion of the documents that will be found cannot be assigned wholly to either one or another of the present state divisions.

I venture tentatively to suggest for your consideration, and shall perhaps, if you approve of it, suggest to the conference, if it occurs, another mode of sub-division a good deal like that which the various German and Austrian institutes at Rome agreed upon as a means of settling a somewhat similar problem with respect to the Nuntiaturberichte. Why is it not possible to divide the archive-material chronologically, and to give to each of these five or six agencies its independent portion of the great task? For instance, might we not suggest that the Wisconsin people should undertake to publish all those documents to be found in the French archives which relate to the history of the upper half of the Mississippi valley before 1701, with omission of what they and others have published (save that the latter should, in their chronological place, be mentioned by title, with a reference to the place where printed); to the Michigan people that they should publish all documents from the French archives of date from 1701 to 1753; to Illinois, that it should deal with the French papers from 1754 to 1783. Those from 1783 to 1803 have been so largely worked by Professor Turner that they also might be assigned to Wisconsin. The Chicago Historical Society might take as its part the relevant papers in the English archives from the earliest times down to 1803; Missouri might undertake the Spanish papers from 1762 to that date; and at a later time Indiana might come in and print what is to be found in the archives of Virginia and of the United States from 1763 to 1789, or later.[34]

This is only a preliminary suggestion. I have tried, as you will no doubt see, to assign to each agency the field in which it has done the most work hitherto, or in which it can most conveniently work. It would of course be for the participant to make any final assignment of territory, for it would require more thought than I have deemed necessary toward a mere illustration, so to divide the fields that the amount of archive-material in each, minus what has already been printed in each, should either be equal or should correspond to the available resources of each agency. No doubt such a delimitation would entail on the part of the various societies some sacrifice of portions of pet projects, as it did in the German-Austrian case I have mentioned above. But I believe that in the end all might be as well satisfied as those people are; and I do not just now see a better mode of working out the problem. It is obvious that copying could begin, or if already begun (as in the Michigan case) could be continued without fear of duplication, long before the preparation of our report, and our agent could aid it, in the French case, to any extent desired; while in the English case, a report extending to 1783, and in the Spanish case a report embracing the three most important archives, may be expected to be available before the end of this winter. Before that time also we hope to have completed on cards a list of the documents for United States history found in the French archives which have already been printed. A similar list of the Spanish archives will be finished in about a month; while our lists of transcripts existing in manuscript in this country, derived from the English and Spanish archives, will probably be finished before the winter is over, though the French is much farther from completion because the archive-report, which it will accompany, has not yet been undertaken.[35]

One additional matter, not to be left out of sight, but not to be dealt with for a good while yet; the Roman archives contain doubtless a good deal of material for northwestern history. But the Roman archives present a difficult and complicated problem, upon which I spent a good deal of time in Europe and shall spend a good deal here. By and by we shall, I hope, be able to

---

[34] "It is with some regret that I have to acknowledge that your proposal of a possible cooperation is the better one. I feel that we are going to lose much by not attempting one publication under the direction of a commission but our states are too independent, I fear, and their societies too conscious of the ego to unite in such an undertaking" (Alvord to Jameson, Oct. 29, 1906).

Later in the same letter Alvord wrote: "Would it not be feasible to have a central committee to draw up the scheme of publication as you propose, dividing the field into sub-periods such as the period of discovery, of settlement, of the wars, of American settlement etc. This central committee should decide on certain principles of editing, of format, paper and printing. Then each of the societies should publish all the volumes of the period or subject assigned to it as volume 1, 2, 3, etc. of such a series of the 'Old Northwest Collection.' This is your plan with a little more uniformity and centralization than you had in mind."

[35] The English report was to be the *Guide* on which Professor Andrews was embarked, the first volume of which, the work of Andrews and Frances G. Davenport, did not appear until 1908; the final volumes in 1912 and 1914; Shepherd's *Guide* was out in 1907; J. A. Robertson's *List* of printed manuscripts and transcripts from Spanish archives, in 1910 (see *post*, Apr. 28, 1910, n. 152). The first volume of the Paris *Guide* appeared in 1932. Lists similar to that of Robertson, for the English and French archives, though they were compiled, were never printed.

undertake a thorough exploitation of these archives; but it is needless at present to make any assignment of the material. What I have already proposed will probably sufficiently frighten most state legislatures.

I agree, and have always agreed, with your notion that there should be two of these series, one for the northwest and one for the southwest. I shall be glad if I am ever able to do anything toward promoting co-operation of a similar sort in the southwest. I have had some talk with Mr. Dunbar Rowland about the problem, in general terms. He has in the fullest degree the spirit of co-operation, and so, I dare say, has Mr. Owen of Alabama,[36] but Florida and Louisiana have not yet progressed far enough to make any large scheme of co-operation as practicable in the southwest as I really believe it to be in your region.[37]

One other consideration, and perhaps an additional reason for caution about copying, in case that no such scheme as that which I have propounded is accepted, nor any scheme for expensive print. Suppose, in other words, that each of the five or six organizations concludes to content itself with manuscript copies, regardless of duplication, each would then wish to have at its headquarters a complete set of what related to its state. This would involve the making of from two to six copies. Now it is quite possible that in such case photographic facsimiles will be cheaper. As a result of study of the proceedings of the Congrès pour la Reproduction des Manuscrits, I made up my mind last year that there probably were processes which we could profitably use in respect to the letters of delegates to the Continental Congress, although *we* need but one copy. Mr. Leland is engaged with this photographic problem. It may cost a little more, but that will very likely be balanced by our having in the office an exact text for proof-reading, and indeed, when it is question of the handwriting of 1775, one adequate for printers' copy. In the case of four or five sets of transcripts, it might be *a fortiori* more profitable.

---

[36] Thomas M. Owen (1866-1920), director of the State Department of Archives and History, Alabama.
Dunbar Rowland (1864-1937), director of the Mississippi State Department of Archives and History.

[37] So many of the group invited to join in the discussion of this matter at the meeting of the Association in Providence were unable to be there that for the time the subject was dropped, but the next year at a conference of historical societies held during the annual meeting of the Association a committee was appointed to set going the work, which in spite of many obstacles, at long last contributed to the production of the *Calendar of manuscripts in Paris archives relating to the history of the Mississippi Valley to 1803*, edited by N. M. Miller Surrey, 2v., Carnegie Institution, 1928. The preparatory listing of the documents included in the *Calendar* was done under the direction of Mr. Leland as a by-product of his general exploration of Paris archives and collections for materials relating to American history.

To EDMUND K. ALDEN
October 31, 1906.

My dear Alden:

I have many times thought of a certain form of compilation as likely to be useful to students of American political history; and this morning, in that period of meditation which precedes getting up, it came into my mind that you are exactly the man to execute it. The thought is, Why would it not be a good thing to execute in moderate dimensions a Check-list of brothers-in-law in American political history? That would probably sound fantastic and humorous to everyone at the first glance; but is there not a good deal in it? That is to say, have we not all often felt when we discovered that "A" had married "B's" sister that that explained a lot of things in their mutual relations that we had not thought of before? Suppose a list of two or three hundred items, arranged in alphabetical order, after this manner:

Adams, Charles Francis: Edward Everett, *m. s.*
Burr, Aaron, *s.m.* Tapping Reeve.
Everett, Edward: Charles Francis Adams, *m.s.*
Gallatin, Albert, *m.s.* Joseph Nicholson.
Nicholson, Joseph: *s. m.* Albert Gallatin.
Reeve, Tapping: *m. s.* Aaron Burr.

Meaning that Charles Francis Adams and Edward Everett married sisters, that Aaron Burr's sister married Tapping Reeve, and that Albert Gallatin married a sister of Joseph Nicholson.

What do you think? Would not two or three hundred such items give students new notions respecting certain political relations? If you think well enough of it to get it up, I don't see why eight or ten pages of such matter might not readily be got into the Annual Report of the American Historical Asociation. I am not a member of the publication committee; but if they wouldn't do it, I know of one or two other places where it could be put, though less effectively. Of one point there is no doubt, that you could do it better than anybody else.[38]

To ARTHUR G. DOUGHTY
December 20, 1906.

Dear Doughty:[39]

I wonder if anyone has written to you respecting the letter of Thomas Lynch[40] mentioned on page 379 of your Report for 1904. If no one has done so, I write to say that if it is a genuine A. L. S., you ought to guard it with care as it is probably worth three thou-

---

[38] The choice of Alden for such a work was natural since he had compiled a large part of the *Cyclopedia of Names* of the *Century Dictionary*. He seems never to have acted on Jameson's suggestion.

[39] Arthur G. Doughty (1860-1936), archivist of the Dominion of Canada, Ottawa.

[40] Thomas Lynch, Jr. (1749-1779), member of the Second Continental Congress and one of the signers of the Declaration of Independence.

sand dollars at least. I do not say this on the basis of sales, because there is only one other A. L. S. of Thomas Lynch, jr., known and that has never been sold except in the following sense: the owner sold a full set of autographs of the signers of the Declaration to another man, including this, repented over night, and the next day made an agreement with the buyer whereby it was omitted from the sale and a difference of three thousand dollars made in the total price on account of this omission. It is absurd that any man's letters should be so highly valued on account of mere rarity. I know well that I am constantly diminishing the value of mine by writing so many letters, but I cannot help it.

To Robert S. Woodward

December 22, 1906.

My dear Dr. Woodward:

In the conversation which I said I might continue in writing, we were speaking of the striking fact that the trustees of the Carnegie Institution have come to the point where their income is nearly all employed, without making for the philological sciences any provision based on recommendations elicited from constituted representatives of those sciences. Your main positions, as I understood them, were: (1) that authorities concerned with the sustainment of research, the world over, were manifesting a similar disposition to throw all their emphasis on the side of the physical sciences; (2) that by whatever process our trustees and these other authorities had been led into this course, it responded to a profound sense among intelligent mankind that the physical sciences were of much greater utility to the development of the human mind than any others. These positions I am deeply concerned to combat.

In the first place, I do not believe it to be true that authorities primarily concerned with the sustaining of research and having a free hand to do what they think to be wisest for its well-rounded development exhibit in their expenditures such a disproportionate emphasis on the physical sciences. To test this, I have taken what I believe to be the most apposite examples. I understand that we are not talking of educational expenditures, which should properly be ruled out because those who have charge of them, from university trustees to school committees, regard primarily, and are obliged by their position to regard, other interests than those of the advancement of science. The same is true of governmental expenditures. In this country for instance the amount which the government spends for geology or the amounts which universities spend for chemistry are not dictated by an estimate of the scientific value of these studies to the development of the human mind, but by a popular estimate of the probability that we shall get our money back through the results of industrial development. Many learned organizations are ruled out of our consideration by another reason, that their organization gives them a permanent set in one direc-

tion or another; the Institut de France for example has a peculiar organization which affects its expenditures in such a way that no one could take it as a clear evidence of what those men, if they met in one body and had a perfectly free hand, would do with their money.

Quite regardless of how the inquiry was likely to turn out, for indeed I did not know, I made up my mind after our conversation that the crucial test of your first position might best be made by seeing what the great German academies did. Except for the possession of certain bequests destined to particular ends, and which I therefore ruled out of consideration (they are not numerous), these academies are in the position of institutions devoted to the advancement of the highest researches and spending their money, not in accordance with the notions of politicians or "prominent citizens," but in accordance with the judgment of the chief scholars and scientists of the German lands. I do not think that a direct knowledge of the distribution of these academic expenditures between the mathematical-physical and the philosophical-historical classes can be obtained in Washington. The budgets are not presented in such a manner as to show. I have tried to tabulate them, but find the data wholly insufficient. Indirectly, however, a strong presumption can be obtained by classifying the published volumes of these academies in recent years. The tabulation counts anthropology and ethnology among the physical sciences, art and archaeology in the philosophical-historical class. The tabulated figures before me show that in the years 1890 to 1899 the Berlin Academy published 447 Schriften in the mathematical-physical division and 250 in the philosophical-historical, nearly half of which—105—lay in the field of language and literature. For the Bavarian Academy I have only the figures for, on the average, the years 1898 to 1904. They total 39 Hefte in the mathematical-physical class and 45 in the philosophical-historical. For the Vienna Academy I have only the figures since 1848, not classified by decades. They are, mathematical-physical 218 volumes, philosophical-historical 386.

I do not believe that these figures are without significance and I submit that, if the course of these three academies is to be taken as evidence of what the most intelligent of mankind deem appropriate in the distribution of scientific expenditure—and I do not know why they should not be taken—they at least do not show an overwhelming emphasis on the side of the physical sciences and at any rate make it impossible to defend by analogy a scheme of expenditure on the part of the Carnegie Institution which ignores philological studies so far as enterprises undertaken at the suggestion of advisory committees in that field are concerned.

I come now to the second and more important point, the examination not of analogies, nor of the opinion of the world, but of the rights of the matter. You held, as I understood you, that astronomy alone had been of more service in clarifying the human mind and improving to its texture than any two of the other physical sciences, say nothing of the humanities.[41] I know little of the history of astronomy, but I should think that this statement was based rather on the earlier than on the later achievements of that science, whereas in shaping the course of a learned institution in the twentieth century it is only the more recent portion of the past that can be brought in as evidence to show that this or that science is likely in the immediate future to produce results of great benefit to the human mind. I understand that we are not speaking at all, throughout anything that follows, of questions of practical utility, but only of intellectual results to be produced upon and for mankind. The chief services which astronomy has performed in this direction, I suppose, have lain in those shiftings of the point of view of human thought which resulted from the discovery of the actual character and position of the solar system. All this was done once for all long ago. I do not see that what astronomy has done in the last fifty years is in any sense revolutionary, even in the case of spectral analysis, the development of which I should suppose to have been its most brilliant achievement. But apart from all this it appears to me that, speaking broadly, it is just as essential to clear the human mind of error and set it to thinking correctly upon the relations of man to man and of nation to nation as upon the relations of man to the universe, and that an establishment dispensing money for such purposes in the twentieth century neglects a large part of its duty if it makes no systematic provision for those philological and literary studies out of which in the last fifty years so much has come to enable different races of men to understand each other and so much to improve our knowledge of mental development in the past. I do not hesitate to say, for instance, that no discovery that I have heard of as occurring in the physical sciences during the last fifty years has done so much to improve the quality of European thinking as those advances which have been made by the study of Oriental religions alone; and that is only one aspect of the developments which have come out of comparative religion and comparative jurisprudence, based on comparative philology. Take another example. I do not believe that any scientific books, except one or two of Darwin's, have exerted more salutary influence on English thinking than Maine's "Ancient Law." There are now more than three hundred million non-Europeans ruled over by European administrators; and all that work is done with enormously greater intelligence on account of the work of the students of comparative jurisprudence, which but for comparative philology would in the field of India at any rate have been able to make little headway.

But I should not take the trouble to set down these rather hasty statements if I thought that nothing practical could be proposed. You asked me to bear that in mind, and to suggest what the Carnegie Institution could do for the philological studies. I suggest four things.

1. That it should make up its mind upon the definite sum which it is willing to spend annually for several years in the promotion of such studies, in order that advisors may not work in the dark.

2. That it ask about seven men, representing respectively Indo-Iranian, Semitic, Greek, Latin, English, Germanic, and Romance philology, to act as an advisory committee in philology.

3. That they hold the first meeting here, at which you shall make perfectly clear to them what they are to do and under what limitations.

4. That they shall then be at liberty to divide into sub-committees or otherwise to develop their proposals and present them before the summer.

I suggest one committee with power of subdivision rather than separate committees for Oriental, classical, and modern philology respectively, because I think that the latter plan would result in the exclusion of many projects that lie on the borders of two subdivisions and because general consultations of the seven would result in a broader view of the whole task.

I do not believe that it would be difficult to select seven men, each of whom should be of high standing in his specialty, accustomed to consider large problems of research, farseeing in respect to their bearings, capable of being judicious and conciliatory in such mutual consultations as would be requisite, and free from the desire to push personal ambitions or act for individual rather than for general interests. I can name four men of whom all this is true, and I think a fifth. For the Indo-Iranian representative I feel no question that you would have an ideal man in Professor Maurice Bloomfield of Johns Hopkins,[42] a very sagacious person, who meets all the requirements; so does Professor C. H. Toy of Harvard for the Semitic field, and this I think would be universally conceded, for every Orientalist recognizes the wide range of his scholarship and his unfailing wisdom.[43] I am not equally clear that Paul Shorey of Chicago is ideally representative of Greek philology, I do not think that there is any professor of Greek in the country who has so much depth and so extraordinarily fertile an intelligence; but he has not the gifts of a practical administrator, though I do not think of one who has those gifts in high measure and whose name at the same time would command anything like the same respect in his profession. John M.

---

[41] President Woodward was himself a mathematician and an astronomer.

[42] Maurice Bloomfield (1855-1928), Ph.D., Johns Hopkins, 1879, became professor of Sanskrit and comparative philology in the Johns Hopkins in 1881. For a time he was one of Jameson's table companions and in those early days Jameson sometimes expressed irritation over what he considered Bloomfield's German arrogance.

[43] Crawford H. Toy (1836-1919), Hancock professor of Hebrew and other Oriental languages, Harvard University, 1880-1909.

Manly [44] of Chicago would be, of all that I know, the best representative of English philology for your purposes, which, so far as I can see, he would meet ideally. Almost as much might be said of Frederick M. Warren of Yale for Romance philology; there are some better Romance philologians but they are mostly weak in general and practical views, in which he is very strong. I do not know the ideal man for Latin or for Germanic philology, but have no doubt that some of those who attend the meetings of the American Philological Association would have such persons in mind.

To Henry Adams

January 31, 1907.

Dear Sir:

I have taken the liberty to send you a copy of my first Annual Report, separately reprinted from the Fifth of the Year Book[s] of the Carnegie Institution, with a more definite object than one sometimes has in inflicting such pamphlets upon one's friends and acquaintances. You were very good to me when I was a young student and teacher in the Johns Hopkins University, and have shown yourself friendly several times since then. I am very anxious to make my present office, somewhat novel in American practice, count for as much as possible in the proper development of historical work in America. If I can keep it up for twenty years I ought to be able to improve very much the documentation of American history. But in order to do this rightly I wish to get the advice of those who have more wisdom and experience than I in historic matters. I remember that you have written me respecting the reasons for your own abandonment of historical work, and your doubts as to the extent of its present utility.[45] But I, who have always made my living by history, am estopped from taking that view. I am like that king of France who declared that it was his métier d'être royaliste.

So, while I am reluctant to worry your retirement with matters for which you have perhaps ceased to care greatly, I cannot refrain from asking the privilege of coming to see you, at such time as may be convenient to you, and asking you to give me your ideas and suggestions with regard to my future work. Since in the report, if you are so good as to read it, you will find me referring to an article on "Gaps in the Published Records of United States History" which you may not have seen and which in a sense is a part of the document which I have sent, I take the liberty of sending you a copy herewith.[46]

To Waldo G. Leland

Washington, D. C.
February 8, 1907.

Dear Leland:

. . . Ford told me yesterday that Admiral Chadwick [47] on going over the Pickett papers discovered that the section relating to the commissioners to Washington, referred to under that head against the arabic figures "1 to 8" on page 43 of your immortal work,[48] had not been transferred to the Library but remained at the Treasury Department. On telephoning about it he found that they had not been sent up on the ground that they were not diplomatic. This is a noble constitutional scruple. For any branch of the executive government to admit for a moment that the Confederate Commission to Washington was a diplomatic body would be equivalent to recognizing the Confederacy, and would go far to undo the results of the Civil War. I am glad that they took so lofty a stand upon the subject, and hope that no official of this office had any part in presenting to them this insidious temptation to make the Treasury Department accessory to treason after the fact. I dare say that Ford will endeavor to secure the papers, but think it best to communicate to you the present facts for use in the new edition. . . .

[44] John M. Manley (1865-1940) taught in Brown with Jameson from 1891 to 1898, when he went to the University of Chicago.

[45] This reference is to the reply of Adams to a request from Jameson for an article for the *Review*: "Long absences are one cause which has broken my relations with the world. The other and more serious cause is that, in the chaotic and unintelligible condition in which I found—and left—the field of knowledge which is called History, I became overpoweringly conscious that any further pretence on my part of acting as instructor would be something worse than humbug, unless I could clear my mind in regard to what I wanted to teach. As History stands, it is a sort of Chinese Play, without end and without lesson. With these impressions I write [*sic*] the last line of my History, asking for a round century before going further. Five or six or even more years have passed since then, and I am still a student and a scholar—and a mighty modest one too,—without consciousness of a mission as teacher. In short, I am like most other men who have studied much, and know that they know nothing. I have nothing to say. I would much rather wipe out all I have ever said, than go on with more. I am glad to hear other men, if they think they have something worth saying; but it is as a scholar, and not as a teacher that I have taken my seat" (Adams to Jameson, Nov. 17, 1896). Part of this letter Jameson quoted in his article, The American Historical Review, 1895-1920 (*Amer. Hist. Rev.* 26: 9, October, 1920). For an acute discussion of the attitude of Adams toward history, see Becker, Carl, The education of Henry Adams, *ibid.* 24: 428-429, April, 1919.

[46] Adams replied: "Thanks for your letter and Report. You deal with the subject so well that I have no place to fill for suggestions. I fear you will coddle our future historians too much, and swamp them in material; but luckily our second-period society (1815-1850) wrote little, and wrote that exceedingly ill, so that there will always be a literary gap there, for the imagination to fill." Adams to Jameson, Feb. 3, 1907, used by Cater, H. D., *Henry Adams and his friends*, 588, Boston, Houghton Mifflin, 1947.

[47] Worthington C. Ford (1858-1941) was chief of the Division of Manuscripts of the Library of Congress from 1902 till 1909.

Admiral French Ensor Chadwick (1844-1919) retired Feb. 28, 1906. His *Causes of the Civil War*, American Nation series, N. Y., Harper, appeared the same year.

[48] *Guide to the archives of the government of the United States in Washington.* The new edition, to which reference is made at the end of this letter, appeared in 1908, Carnegie Institution, publication no. 92. It bears the date 1907.

To JAMES BRYCE

April 17, 1907.

My dear Mr. Bryce: [49]

After I got home last night I saw in a newspaper the passage which I inclose. It is evidently possible that some changes may be made in the constitution of Oklahoma, so that the Blue Book already printed may not in the end represent exactly the completed instrument. But in writing to the secretary of the Constitutional Convention for a copy I have asked him to use his judgment, and to send the existing draft if no changes of importance are likely to be made.[50]

I know of an excellent walk on which I should like to take you, if you would permit me; but as it may be some time before you would have freedom for any such excursion, I will ask leave now to lay before you one or two considerations which may not have occurred to you with respect to the Madison invitation.[51]

It is a certain fact that the Middle West is much less conscious of relation to England than the East. It was very perceptible to me when I was in charge of the historical department at the University of Chicago. There was a much less number of students who took a strong interest in English history than there would be in an eastern university of the same size, and among the various portions of mediaeval or modern European history there was no such distinct preference for English topics as among students on the Atlantic coast. Partly by reason of less purely English blood among the educated classes, partly by reason of greater remoteness from Europe and less frequency of journeys across the Atlantic, regard for England is much less strong in that region than in the East.

Though I have no wish to be importunate, and am sure that the programme committees of the various societies concerned would not wish to ask of you heavy sacrifices of personal convenience, still I have thought

---

[49] For other letters to (and from) Mr. Bryce, who had recently come to Washington as the British ambassador, see Stock, L. F., Some Bryce-Jameson correspondence (*Amer. Hist. Rev.* 50: 262-266, Jan., 1945). The letters contained in this volume had not come to light when the first collection was printed.

[50] The situation in Oklahoma at this time was one likely to interest Bryce. The constitutional convention had drafted a state constitution, had adjourned for a month, and had then reconvened to sign the document. Meanwhile, the supreme court of the territory had ruled that the convention had exceeded its powers, and at the moment it looked as though at least part of the work would have to be done over.

Bryce's attention to state constitutions was of long standing. "In the course of preparing a book on the U. S. government and institutions I have been reading with great pleasure and profit your remarks on State Constitutions, a subject which I began to study four years ago, when there were practically no helps to it. It is pleasant to find that so much is being now done in America; and your study was I think the first to point out their importance" (Bryce to Jameson, Mar. 4, 1888). The study to which Bryce referred was, An introduction to the study of the constitutional and political history of the states, *Johns Hopkins Univ. Stud., ser.* 4, 1886.

The ambassador's interest in Oklahoma was evidently considerable, for on May 29, 1907, he wrote: "I have arranged to pass a rapid visit to Oklahoma and the Indian territory between June 14 and 19; if there are any historical or constitutional phenomena there which specially deserve enquiry by questions addressed to persons on the spot, and if you have any acquaintance there fitted to answer such questions will you let me know?" Jameson replied: "I am sorry that I am not able to be of any use with respect to your visit to Oklahoma and Indian Territory. I do not know anyone in either of them, and have not even succeeded in obtaining any reply from the official to whom I wrote for a copy of the constitution, which rather chagrins me as I believe I professed to you that it would not be difficult to obtain it" (Bryce to Jameson, May 29; Jameson to Bryce, May 31, 1907).

For an examination of the constitution adopted by Oklahoma, see Beard, Charles A., Constitution of Oklahoma, *Political Science Quart.* 24: 95-114, March, 1919.

[51] The story of the attempt to induce Bryce, who was at this time the sole honorary member of the American Historical Association, to speak at its annual meeting at Madison, is a long one. On Jan. 17, 1907, A. L. P. Dennis (1874-1930), then teaching in the University of Wisconsin and chairman of the program committee for the December meeting, wrote to

Jameson: "One point in connection with the program which has occurred to me is that if Professor James Bryce is British Ambassador at Washington next year, it would be both suitable and desirable to ask him to address at Madison a joint meeting of all four associations [economics, history, political science, sociology], perhaps giving him an entire evening session for that purpose." On Feb. 28, Jameson reported that he had not yet seen Mr. Bryce. "I wrote him asking for the making of an appointment at which Senator Spooner [from Wisconsin] and Veditz, representing the sociologists, and I could see him about the matter, but have not yet heard from him; nor have I heard anything from the Economic and Political Science associations, though I understood that you had set them in motion. I should be glad if I could represent the invitation as coming from all the societies. It is doubtful if Senator Spooner in these last days of the sessions can take part in the assault."

After an interview with Bryce, Jameson reported on Mar. 5, that the ambassador hesitated for several reasons: the social demands upon him during the holiday season; the difficulty of travel during the winter; and the difficulty he found in writing a speech. No definite negative was given, however, and after a period Jameson sent this letter, to which Bryce replied on Apr. 25: "I have promised to go to Chicago (barring accidents) in June to deliver Commencement addresses at the Univ. and also at the Univ. of Illinois. In one of these I shall adopt your suggestion and talk about history. This however is irrespective of the gathering at Madison in Dec. While keeping the hope of that before me, I must add that it is more and more becoming clear to me that I must husband my strength and undertake fewer and shorter journeys and fewer speeches." Not yet discouraged, Dennis wrote on May 13: "I am hoping something from the message which Professor Vinogradoff will carry to Mr. Bryce when he goes to visit him in June. For in speaking of the matter, Vinogradoff declared emphatically that he would make it a personal matter to urge Mr. Bryce to come, and said that he knew the sort of arguments which might convince Mr. Bryce." The invitation to speak was in the end declined but a subsequent invitation to dine with the executive council of the Association during their November meeting in New York was accepted (Jameson to Bryce, Nov. 5, 1907).

In Madison, Bryce was elected president of the Political Science Association and at a joint meeting of the two societies in Washington in 1908 he delivered his presidential address, The relations of political science to history and to practice. See *Amer. Political Science Rev.* 3: 1-19, Feb, 1909.

that the facts I have mentioned above might help to persuade you that it was worth while of a British ambassador, whom we all look upon as likely to do more than any of his predecessors to fortify good feeling and mutual understanding between the two nations, to take the opportunity to address such a meeting as that which will take place at Madison next Christmas. While a good many members will come from other parts of the country, the audience will in the main consist of persons who lead and form public opinion in the Middle West or Old Northwest, in English Canada, and in those parts of the United States that have most intercourse with English Canada.

I wish to add my words to those of others in appreciation of the very fraternal and kindly remarks which you made to us last evening.[52]

To PATRICK H. MELL

April 22, 1907.

Dear Sir:[53]

It seems so clear from your letter of April 19 that my informant, a western gentleman who had visited Fort Hill, was mistaken that I shall not undertake in June to go down to the college, great as the pleasure of visiting it would undoubtedly be.

In speaking of the permission which your Board of Trustees gave me to make use of the letters in their possession when I was editing the "Correspondence of John C. Calhoun," you say, "Some of these, I have been informed, were of a private nature and the Board did not desire to have them published." I am very much concerned at this statement, and beg you to permit me to state the actual facts. The Board of Trustees agreed that I should have the use of their collection and appointed Senator Tillman a committee to make the necessary arrangements with me. I met him in Washington. He there delivered the manuscripts to me, saying that the Board made but two conditions or restrictions upon their use. The first was that I should print nothing which reflected injuriously upon the memory of Mr. Calhoun. In making this condition Senator Tillman said that neither he nor the Board anticipated that I should find anything of the sort among Mr. Calhoun's letters. This was indeed the case. It was one of the

most striking things about the collection that not only in his own letters but in the whole mass of letters to him, perhaps 2500 in number, from the most various and often intimate correspondents, there was nothing which might not with freedom be published to all the world so far as Mr. Calhoun was concerned. No one of these letters ever proposes that he should do anything inconsistent with the most transparent integrity. I thought this, by the way, to be no slight tribute to a man, that his correspondents—hack politicians in many cases—all knew that there was no use in proposing to him anything that savored of indirection.

The second restriction was that I should print nothing calculated to give pain to any living person. With this condition also it was perfectly easy to comply, for Mr. Calhoun stood above all gossip and had in his character no trace of malice or of personal ill feeling.

With these conditions I complied with perfect candor. Dealing with a time so subject to controversy, and making inevitably a selection from among papers too numerous for total publication, I considered it no small advantage to be able to say, as I did in the preface to the book, that no omissions had "been made for ulterior purposes—patriotism or partiality, hero worship or conventional decorum. . . . No passages have been omitted in order to support or to weaken any particular opinions in politics or history. Nor has a single word been omitted for the supposed benefit of Calhoun's reputation." And in eight years no person has ever hinted that I did otherwise than as above stated; and accordingly I believe that the volume has been used with far more confidence than is common in such cases of selected publication.

When the matter began to come from the press Senator Tillman had proof-sheets regularly sent to him and examined them, without ever making any comment, until the exigencies of the political campaign of 1900 compelled him to abandon the task. He requested one of the members of the Board of Trustees to continue it in his stead. My surprise was great on receiving a certain batch of the page-proofs to perceive that, without the slightest communication with me, this gentleman had cut out three short letters. They were three letters in which Mr. Calhoun, when some of his slaves had escaped, requested friends to look them up, punish them, and send them home. I protested warmly, arguing that I had lived up to all requirements made by the Board and imposed upon me by its committee and that no single member of the Board had any right to intervene and cut out material which in my judgment belonged in the book. To say that they should have been kept out because they were of a private nature, is far beside the mark, since most of the letters of Mr. Calhoun which the Board turned over to me for publication were private letters, written to members of his family, and to have ruled out private letters would have deprived the collection of one of its chief charms, as exhibiting the nobility of Mr. Calhoun's character as a

---

[52] The occasion on which Bryce spoke was a dinner at Rauscher's at which Dr. Simon Newcomb was host and the members of the American Academy and other distinguished guests were gathered to meet the new ambassador. What he said we do not know. Washington *Post,* Apr. 17, 1907, p. 13, c. 3.

[53] Patrick H. Mell (1850-1918), president of Clemson Agricultural College. Jameson had written to him on Apr. 17, 1907, asking permission to inspect additional Calhoun letters which he was informed had been discovered in an old office building at Fort Hill. President Mell replied that so far as he knew, no additions to the Clemson collection had been made. The sentence from his letter quoted below is ambiguous. It may not have been meant to carry the implication which Jameson ascribed to it.

husband and father and in relation to his cousins. Obviously the reason why these letters were cut out was because of their relation to slavery. Frankly, I thought this silly. Did anybody in 1900 suppose or fail to know that Mr. Calhoun had servants of the sort usual in his region, and did anybody suppose that he omitted all efforts to reclaim them if they ran away, or that he failed to punish them under circumstances when a humane master, which he plainly was, from all the correspondence, usually felt that punishment was requisite? It seemed to me an ostrich-like mode of hiding what after all did not need to be hidden. But my reason for protest was that if those three letters were omitted I could not truthfully say what I had said in the preface, the proof-sheets of which had already received the approval of Senator Tillman, and to have been unable to make that profession of perfect candor in the editing of Mr. Calhoun's correspondence would have damaged the whole publication beyond repair, as there would have been no way of successfully meeting the suspicions to which friendly editors are usually exposed when they are known to have selected what they pleased from among letters. As I have said above, everyone now knows with certainty that I have told the whole story, or rather have let the letters do so.

Upon my making this protest to the secretary of the American Historical Association, through whose hands the printing was passing, I appealed to Senator Tillman, who entirely sustained me, restored the excluded letters, and declared that the course which I had taken was entirely justified. I dare say, however, that some dissatisfaction may have remained in the mind of the trustee affected, and possibly in the minds of the others, since I never received any word of appreciation from the trustees, although I think that I may claim, by having performed gratis the large labor of collecting from all over the country and editing and printing Mr. Calhoun's correspondence, to have done more for the memory of Mr. Calhoun than anyone else in my generation. Mistaken impressions of what has actually occurred in such a case are so apt to be circulated, that I have thought it worth while to tell you the whole story. You will find, I am sure, that Senator Tillman will corroborate it in every detail.

Thanking you for the reference to Dr. Hartzog's address.[54]

To Waldo G. Leland

Washington, D. C.
July 31st, 1907.

Dear Leland: [55]

. . . Bowman left Washington a week or two ago.

He is practically appointed to a pretty good position under Doughty. I suppose, however, that we shall see him in Washington for a month or two in the autumn, as his first work for the Canadian Commission will be in the Washington Archives.[56] To have secured this, to have got Manning into an assistant professorship of diplomatic history in George Washington University, and to have landed Stephens at the eleventh hour in an instructorship at the University of Missouri, are three achievements of the year in which I take more satisfaction than in almost any other.[57] Speaking of the others, by the way, President Roosevelt has agreed to my proposal for the establishment of a Commission on National Historical Publication—a temporary commission to make a preliminary survey and lay out a plan— and he is all ready to appoint it but for the need of making provision for paying the travelling expenses of the members.[58] He agrees with me that this is necessary, but he has no money which he could use for the purpose and I thought perhaps I had in one of my appropriations, but President Woodward does not think that that interpretation of my statute would stand, so I shall try to get it out of the Dii Majores [59] in October, or more exactly, December. . . .

To Charles Francis Adams

September 12, 1907.

My dear Mr. Adams:

Since our talk I have kept constantly in mind the problem which you proposed respecting the choice of a director of research and publication for the Massachusetts Historical Society and I now make such suggestions as have occurred to me.[60]

I remain of the same mind about the question regarding Bradford and Winthrop. If the society has not

[54] Dr. Mell had given the name of a former president, Henry S. Hartzog of Fort Smith, Ark., as a possible owner of Calhoun letters.

[55] Mr. Leland had begun a survey of the French archives. After this time most of the letters to him are directed to Paris.

[56] Hervey M. Bowman worked for the department in 1906-1907 and at the same time was investigating Washington archives for the Canadian Boundary Commission. The position here mentioned he never occupied, first, because of postponements in ratifying the appointment, and later because of prolonged illness.

[57] William R. Manning (1871-1942) had been a fellow and assistant under Jameson in the University of Chicago, 1902-1904. From 1904 to 1907 he was assistant professor of American history in Purdue University. The position in George Washington University he held from 1907 to 1910, when he went to the University of Texas. In 1915 he returned to Washington as an editor attached to the Department of State.

Frank F. Stephens, who had received a Ph.B. from the University of Chicago in 1904, and a Ph.D. from the University of Pennsylvania in 1907, was an instructor in American history in the University of Missouri, 1907-1908.

[58] The history of this plan can be followed in other letters; see those of Nov. 23, 1905, Dec. 13, 1907, Jan. 24, 1910.

[59] The trustees of the Carnegie Institution.

[60] Jameson's correspondence with Charles Francis Adams over historical matters of common interest began as early as 1891. The subject of this letter was opened on Aug. 10 by a note from Adams asking for suggestions. Evidently much ground had been covered in a personal interview between that time and the date of the present letter.

been able to think of the ideal editor for those proposed editions I do not think that it would reach any good solution of the present question by adding to the requirements for the position now contemplated, a position undoubtedly difficult to fill, the *sine qua non* that the man should be also an ideal editor of Bradford and Winthrop.[61] I still think that it would be better to select a man with reference to qualifications for a permanent position, without regard to these two specific tasks, and let him find a man to do them if he can. I do believe, however, that beside the desiderata of an ideal editor of the society's publications we ought also to look out for a man who would have the needful gifts to draw out from the members of the society the best contributions they are capable of affording. That is to say that whatever future may be mapped out for the Collections we have also the Proceedings to think of. That series will almost certainly be kept up. It would not be difficult to find a man who could edit its volumes properly. But the actual content of those volumes is in danger of being marked by diminishing importance. As I went over the last volume, recently received, it seemed to me, as it always seems, that too much space is given to biographies of deceased members. I also thought that with the exception of the president, few members seemed to feel that it was incumbent on them to make important contributions; or at all events few did so. I should think, therefore, that a man ought if possible to be procured who by tact, by prevision, by

the sense of what is really worth while in historical composition, should be able to elicit a better and more important product from gentlemen many of whom are capable of it but either do not write such things or send them elsewhere for publication. I emphasize the importance of this because however well an editor does the especial work allotted to him, general participation by others is requisite to a healthy life in the society.

Now as to persons. Unquestionably Ford is the best man.[62] Next after him perhaps the best man is Frederick J. Turner of the University of Wisconsin. I will say deliberately that he presents more perfectly than any other man in the country occupied with American history the combination of accurate scholarship and large views and the power of sound generalization. If he could be persuaded to undertake the task he would give it the utmost meaning and significance it could have, by reason of his remarkable judgment as to what is really important and his insight into the main problems of American history. Of course, however, he has now one of the most desirable positions in the university world, at the head of the historical department in the most rapidly developing of American universities; and he has now a standing arrangement for freedom during half the academic year and wishes to write. Moreover, he might feel that he would not do his best work in the atmosphere of Boston, but rather in that more plastic society of the Middle West, to whose history he has chiefly devoted himself. However, if he can be got it would be the best thing.

Next in adaptedness to such a position I should place Professor Claude H. Van Tyne of the University of Michigan.[63] He has a very good position, has lately refused a Yale professorship, is a clever and interesting writer and probably wishes to continue to write, more or less, though he might think that in such a position as you describe he might fairly obtain as much time for writing as in a professorship. He is a man of most engaging ways, plenty of tact, energy and good sense. His scholarship and judgment are both excellent and he has shown that he is a good editor.

Next I should place Professor Carl R. Fish of the University of Wisconsin,[64] a man of about thirty, who did his undergraduate work at Brown and his graduate

---

[61] Adams had written: "We could set the editor at work at once on monumental editions of Winthrop and Bradford. . . . In such an edition, the cartography, the reproduction of portraits and of utensils, etc.,—in fact, of everything serving to throw light on the content, including specimens of handwriting, etc., should be as perfect as science, industry and art can make it. The price should be high, but I have no question that the public libraries alone would absorb an edition." What Jameson's mind was on this we do not know. His own plans for editions of Bradford and Winthrop among the *Original Narratives* were already made and the volumes appeared in 1908. See Oct. 22, 1907, n. 74.

It will be remembered that the Massachusetts Historical Society had published William Bradford's *History of Plymouth Plantation,* edited by Charles Deane, in 1856, *Collections, Mass. Hist. Soc.,* ser. 4, 3; in 1912 appeared the Bradford volumes envisaged by Adams, edited by Worthington C. Ford, 2v., Boston, Houghton Mifflin. A more recent edition is that of Morison, Samuel E., *Of Plymouth Plantation, 1620-1647,* N. Y., Knopf, 1952. Morison, in his interesting introduction, recounts the history of the manuscript and describes the various editions which have appeared.

Of the Winthrop *Journal,* Adams spoke at the meeting of the Massachusetts Historical Society in June, 1913, expressing his great desire to have it appear while he was still president of the society. In order that there might be no fear of financial loss he guaranteed that no portion of the cost of the edition should fall upon the society. It was agreed that Ford should proceed upon this work but with the death of Mr. Adams the plan was for the time dropped (*Proc. Mass. Hist. Soc.* **46:** 427-431, June, 1913). The society, however, still hopes to carry out the plan of Mr. Adams for a definitive edition of Winthrop's *Journal.* Letter of Stephen T. Riley, Dec. 22, 1952.

[62] Adams on Sept. 19 wrote in reply to this letter: "On the second page of your letter you say. . . 'Unquestionably Ford is the best man.' I take it 'Ford' was an error of dictation. I have no question Bourne is probably the best man." Nevertheless, in January, 1909, W. C. Ford left the Division of Manuscripts of the Library of Congress for the Massachusetts Historical Society.

[63] Claude H. Van Tyne (1869-1930), already mentioned as joint compiler of the *Guide to the archives of the government of the United States in Washington,* was connected with the University of Michigan from 1901 until his death.

[64] Carl Russell Fish (1876-1932), A.B., Brown, 1897, had been teaching history in the University of Wisconsin since 1900. During 1908-1909 he was research associate with the Department of Historical Research for the purpose of exploring the Italian archives for American material. See *post,* Nov. 4, 1907.

work at Harvard. He has just been promoted to associate professor at Wisconsin. His scholarship has a wider range than Mr. Van Tyne's and he has especially interested himself in New England history, in the teaching of which in Wisconsin he has shown a particularly strong grasp of its relations to the history of the rest of the country. He would be a capital editor, and though I do not think that he has quite as perfect tact as Mr. Van Tyne, and could not at his age deal with historical problems with as much authority as Mr. Turner, still I think that he would in the end succeed in organizing the work of the members to good effect.

There is also one of your present members that might well be thought of, Professor Theodore Clarke Smith of Williams College, a man of about thirty-five, a graduate of Harvard, who has taught in several places before settling at Williamstown. He is a man of much force and judgment. The character of his powers can most easily be judged by looking at the chapter which he contributed to the seventh or eleventh volume of the "Cambridge Modern History." [65]   Except that some of the members might think him a little to aggressive in manner, he is well adapted to the work, being learned, sensible, and energetic. He is chiefly devoted to the most modern periods of American history, *e.g.*, the period from 1850 to 1876.

All these men I know intimately and can speak with confidence of their adaptedness to all the requirements of the situation, though I do not at the time go into detail about each such quality. If it should prove that none of these are available I fancy that among younger men the best choice might be Mr. Frederic L. Paxson, whose book on the "Independence of the South American Republics" I think you probably know. He has lately been made assistant professor in the University of Michigan.[66] I do not know him personally, but I have been told that he is a man of excellent address and well liked. Certainly he has plenty of scholarship, and I have observed that wherever he has been placed, sometimes in rather unpromising soil, he has turned to the local materials for history and has extracted from them good matter for the general history of the United States. Therefore, though I do not know that he has given much attention to New England history I see that he could do so with rapid effect and would do it with an eye to what is important rather than with a merely antiquarian predilection.

I shall be glad if any of these suggestions are of the slightest use to you or to the society. I shall be glad also, if you see any occasion for it, to write further respecting these men or others that you may hear of. After Thursday it will be best to address me at Washington, though I shall not reach that city until September 28.[67]

To Waldo G. Leland

October 11, 1907.

Dear Leland:

I am proposing to put you to a little trouble on behalf of the "American Historical Review" by a letter which I am writing to Señor Manuel González de la Rosa, who lives at 157, rue de la Convention, XV., Paris. He is a Peruvian, formerly, I think, a professor at Lima, who has, however, lived many years in Paris and who has done quite a remarkable lot of investigation in respect to Columbus. He was the original or main assailant of the Toscanelli letters. Vignaud is his friend and knows all about him.[68] In 1900 he read before the Congress of Américanistes of Paris a paper having the somewhat bumptious title, "Solution de Tous les Problèmes relatifs á Christophe Colomb," printed in 1902, in which he gave an outline of his various new views respecting Columbus. But poverty and paralysis of the right side have prevented him from bringing his researches before the public, or perhaps from giving to most of them even in manuscript a final form. Last spring he wrote me asking for a subvention from the Carnegie Institution. This seemed impossible; but I think perhaps I gave him some encouragement to submit an article for the "Review." He consulted Biggar,[69] who believed that a chapter entitled "Columbus's Marriage and His Mysterious Wife" would be the most suitable. I do not see why Biggar should think so.

[65] Political reconstruction (1865-1885), ch. XX, *Cambridge Modern History* 7: 622-654, Cambridge, University Press, 1905. On Oct. 13, 1902, George W. Prothero wrote to Jameson: "I have just received your letter of Sept. 30, from which I learn, to my great relief and pleasure, that you have been able to secure an author for the C.M.H., to fill up the one gap that remained.

"I need hardly say that if you advise Professor Clarke Smith's appointment, we are perfectly ready to abide by your choice; and I can only repeat what I have already said as to our gratitude to you for the trouble you have taken."

[66] Frederic L. Paxson (1877-1948) before going to Michigan had taught in the University of Colorado. He remained in Michigan until 1910; from 1910 to 1932 he taught in the University of Wisconsin; from 1932 until his death he was connected with the University of California. He was a member of the committee on management of the *Dictionary of American Biography* from 1924 to 1936, and was president of the American Historical Association in 1938.

[67] In reply Adams wrote: "Among those you mention I incline to think most favorably of Prof. Smith of Williams. He is of the right age. I think decidedly well, too, of Mr. Paxon [*sic*]. I am afraid, however, of these writers of history. What we want is an editor and investigator. If a man goes to writing history he is for our purposes practically lost."

[68] Henry Vignaud (1830-1922), of New Orleans birth, as a member of the American legation in Paris, rendered many services to American historians. In 1900 both he and De la Rosa presented papers to the Congress of Americanists on the subject of the Toscanelli letter to Columbus of 1474, which was supposed to have guided Columbus. Vignaud later published *La lettre et la carte de Toscanelli*, Paris, Leroux, 1901, and *Toscanelli and Columbus*, London, Sands and Company, 1902. See Bourne, E. G., *Amer. Hist. Rev.* 8: 341-346, Jan., 1903.

[69] H. P. Biggar, attached to the Canadian archives, was working in Paris.

But some time ago the article arrived, written with the left hand in a sort of English, marked by much acuteness in investigation and real learning, but after all merely identifying a lady concerning whom American curiosity is not active so far as anything in our daily papers would show.

I feel very sorry for the poor man but have felt obliged to return the article. I have said to him that our public would care more for an article on one of the following subjects: "Columbus and João II." or "Columbus and the House of Braganza"; "Bartholomew Columbus and the Count de Penamacar"; "Bartholomew Columbus and Henry VII" or "Bartholomew Columbus in England"; "The Academy of Sagres." At this distance and with no more than the outline he has given in the "Solution," etc., I cannot say which of them would be the most suitable, and perhaps he will be too discouraged to resume the attempt, though no doubt he would be glad of the honorarium, and I have told him that he can send his article in French or Spanish if he prefers. But if he chooses to make the attempt, I have suggested that he call you into consultation. If he does so, read the pamphlet "Solution," etc., and then either make up your mind what he had better do, if you can do so offhand, or write to me. I should not wish you to be diverted from your present work into any considerable investigation of Columbus.[70] . . . .

When the October number of the "Review" had been out three days I received a letter from R. O. Alexander, cotton merchant in Charlotte, presumably the one we met in Baltimore then serving as a member of that sagacious committee of investigation. He thoughtfully inclosed three dollars to pay his arrears in the American Historical Association, and expressed confidence that I would certainly allow him the privilege of answering Salley's article in our next number. As an ender of controversy, Salley is not a great success.[71] Perhaps you will see why on reading the article. I eliminated as

much of the inflammable matter as he would permit, but even now the article gives an acid reaction. I labored with him to cut out the futile attempt which fills his last pages, to track the original iniquity to its lair and nail its skin upon the doors of the Alexander family, pointing out to him that once it was proved that the original document was a forgery nobody cared a hang who was responsible for it. But no, all that detective work was too precious to be lost. The world must be instructed in morals as well as in history, and the writer sighed for more Alexanders to conquer.

I regretfully pointed to R. O. Alexander that his confidence was misplaced. There are about ten historical writers in the United States to whom I would promise to print any article they might send in and Mr. R. O. Alexander is not one of them. But no doubt something will come along from Charlotte, and I shall have either to print it or to turn it down on the ground that it is too atrocious, and meantime must expect all my letters to be printed in the "Charlotte Observer," with a running accompaniment of eggs. Such is editorial life—and me a peaceable man, who regards the Mecklenburg Declaration as of no account one way or the other.

Professor Scomp has just come in (on another matter) whose name you may remember as being signed to a small contribution in the "Magazine of American History" respecting a family Bible of Morris Brown which proves the Mecklenburg Declaration to be genuine by irrevocable testimony written down by him within a hundred years of the time of its occurrence. Anyhow, he told me one good piece of news for you. Some years ago he had in his house six thousand dollars' worth of English transcripts belonging to the state of Georgia, which the governor had most improperly lent to him, and they were all burned up when his house took fire. So Providence does have a little regard for this department in spite of some appearances. . . .

To Albert Matthews

October 22, 1907.

My dear Sir:[72]

I am pleased that my suggestion respecting Plymouth interests you. I should suppose that even if few additional manuscript letters having any historical value could be discovered it might yet be a service to bring together into one volume the many that have already appeared in print.[73] But I hope you will not think that

---

[70] This was not the last Jameson was to see of the rejected article. "Here comes from the 'Atlantic Monthly' an article which they think to be not quite suitable to their pages but quite so to ours. It is an article by one Gonzalez de la Rosa, 'Columbus's Marriage and his Mysterious Wife.' Where have I heard something about that before? A man in London has kindly fixed it up for him and sent it to the 'Atlantic,' with the suggestion that if they do not want it they should send it to us" (Jameson to Leland, Aug. 27, 1908).

[71] In an article reviewing two recent books (Graham, G. W., *The Mecklenberg Declaration of Independence, May 20, 1775,* N. Y., Neale Publishing Company, 1905; and Hoyt, W. H., *The Mecklenberg Declaration of Independence: a study of evidence showing that the alleged early Declaration of Independence by Mecklenberg Country, North Carolina, on May 20th, 1775, is spurious,* N. Y., Putnam's, 1907). A. S. Salley, Jr., secretary of the South Carolina Historical Commission, had presented the evidence which he had been gathering since the publication of his first article. This second article, The Mecklenberg Declaration: the present status of the question (*Amer. Hist. Rev.* 12: 16-43), brought forth from Graham a communication, The Mecklenberg Declaration: what did the governor see? *Amer. Hist. Rev.* 13: 394-397, Jan., 1908.

[72] Albert Matthews (1860-1946), for many years corresponding secretary of the Prince Society and editor for the Colonial Society of Massachusetts from 1904 to 1924.

[73] Matthews had written to Jameson on Sept. 29, 1907, asking for suggestions for some piece of work which Miss Mary F. Ayer might edit and the Prince Society publish. Jameson answered that all the letters of historical value written in the Plymouth jurisdiction between 1620 and 1686, whether published or unpublished, might well be gathered into a single

this was more than a casual suggestion. I do not pretend to have thought over the proposal very much, and have not any quantitative notion of the extent to which such a publication would run.

I am very much obliged by your two suggestions respecting Johnson's "Wonder-Working Providence." I do expect to edit it for this series sometime this winter or spring and to bring it out a year from now, moved thereto by filial piety as Edward was one of my ancestors, though I hope when I say anything about history I am more accurate than he was. Savage you may remember, remarks in one of his terse foot-notes that Johnson was precise in nothing but his creed.[74] I shall certainly pay the fullest attention to the Gorges question, though I have not yet gone into it.[75] As to the other matter, I judge that you have not anywhere set forth in print the history of the term "Pilgrim fathers" and that I am therefore to take your letter as an authoritative announcement upon the subject. It is therefore very welcome.

I did notice, being in Boston this summer, that some persons fell foul of President Roosevelt because he did not distinguish between the "Pilgrims" of the Plymouth colony and the "Puritans" of the Massachusetts colony.[76] I wonder if I am wrong—and if I am, no

doubt you can correct me—but I have always supposed that it was just as erroneous to deny that the Plymouth people were "Puritans" as to maintain that the Bay people were "Pilgrims." In other words, it seems to me that the distinction has been overdone and that the two terms do not stand at all upon the same plane, Pilgrim being a specific designation of the founders of Plymouth while Puritan, if I understand the word rightly, is a term so general that Pilgrim is subsumed under it. To put it in another way, the Pilgrims and all other separatists were the "extreme left" of the English Puritans. Is not this the real fact? After having beaten it into the heads of sciolists that they must not call the Bay people Pilgrims, must we not turn around and laboriously keep them from narrowing unduly the term Puritan? Aside from Plymouth, I think it would have surprised Roger Williams and Gorton and Mrs. Hutchinson to be told that they were not Puritans. But on all these matters I should defer to any contrary opinion to which your very solid and patient researches may have led you.

I have not yet heard from Nova Scotia but hope to do so soon.[77]

To Charles H. Haskins

November 1, 1907.

Dear Haskins:

I suppose you are looking around for items for the programme of the Council meeting on November 29.[78] Here is one:

Almeric FitzRoy, clerk of the Privy Council, and Egerton, the Oxford professor of colonial history, arranged a scheme for the drawing off from the registers of the Privy Council of all those items relating to British colonies, down to 1775 at least, and proposed to the British government the publication of these in volumes resembling those in the series of "Acts of the Privy Council," which series is not to be continued

---

volume. It does not appear that the society ever acted upon this suggestion. A similar idea, in this instance for a list of the letters written from New England during the seventeenth century, Jameson had proposed to the American Antiquarian Society. See *ante,* Oct. 18, 1906, and Jameson to W. C. Ford, Dec. 2, 1908.

[74] The American Historical Association, at its annual meeting in 1902, approved the publication of a series of original narratives deemed important to American history. Dr. Jameson was chosen general editor. In December, 1905, a publication contract for twenty volumes was completed with Charles Scribner's Sons. The first volume of the series appeared in 1906. At the time of this letter four volumes had been issued. Jameson's edition of Johnson's *Wonder-Working Providence* was not published until March, 1910. The edition of this work published by the Massachusetts Historical Society in 1846 had been edited by James Savage.

[75] The letter from Matthews to which this replies has not been found, but the editors conjecture that the "Gorges question" is that explained by Jameson in the introduction to his edition of *Wonder-Working Providence,* 3-4. Here he states that the London publisher of this manuscript, first issued anonymously and entitled *A history of New-England, from the English planting in the yeere 1628 untill the yeere 1652,* five years after its issue inserted the unsold sheets of the volume as part III of *America painted to the life,* and ascribed them to Sir Fernando Gorges, grandfather of the author of the first and fourth parts of that work.

[76] President Theodore Roosevelt, in an address at the laying of the cornerstone of a monument at Provincetown on Aug. 20, 1907, had made frequent reference to the Puritans, never to the Pilgrims, but in an extemporaneous introduction he had confessed that when he wrote the address he had not known that there was a distinction to be observed. This created some ripples in the New England press and is referred to by Albert Matthews at the beginning of an article in which he treated what was evidently one of the topics of his undiscovered letter to Jameson: The term Pilgrim Fathers and early celebrations of forefathers' day, *Trans. Col. Soc. of Mass.* 17: 293-384, 1913-1914.

[77] This probably refers to a paragraph in an earlier letter: "Meanwhile could not the Prince Society undertake an issue of some body of documents derived from the archives of the maritime provinces? There is a great deal there which is of value to Massachusetts history and little attempt has been made to utilize it. I speak of this because a gentleman residing there has been making a survey of this material for us, and although he has been doing it slowly I think that he probably by this time has the matter in such shape that if you desired it I could before long get his completed report from him" (Jameson to Matthews, Oct. 5, 1907). Matthews replied (in a letter incorrectly dated September for October 13): "Your suggestion in regard to the maritime provinces is a good one, and when the gentleman who has been making a survey of the materials there has made his report, I shall be very glad to hear further about it." The man to whom Jameson here referred was probably James Hannay of Halifax, Nova Scotia.

[78] Charles H. Haskins (1870-1937), A.B., 1887, Ph.D., 1890, Johns Hopkins, teacher of history in the University of Wisconsin, 1891-1902, in Harvard, 1902-1937, became corresponding secretary of the American Historical Association in 1900; in 1908 his title became secretary of the council of the Association.

beyond 1603. They elicited from the Commissioners of the Treasury the following vote:

"Assuming that the gentleman appointed to do this work (i.e. selecting, preparing and transcribing, etc.) would also see the volumes through the press, and make the indices, as part of his duty, so that no charge for editing, indexing or otherwise would fall on the Vote for the Privy Council Office, and that the only charges falling on public funds would be for paper, printing and binding, My Lords are willing to allow these latter charges to be defrayed by the Stationery Office, provided that it is understood beforehand that the number of volumes will be limited, say, to three, and that the style of printing, etc., is not more expensive than that adopted for the volumes of the Privy Council Register already published."

Upon this showing FitzRoy and Egerton had before them the task of finding the necessary money for transcribing and editing, which FitzRoy computes at $1500.00 a year for two or three years. Egerton, Andrews told me, proposed to subscribe, if needed, a hundred pounds per annum from his own salary. I thought that the United States had quite as much interest in the matter as Great Britain, and also imagined that this country was a more easy prey to the pusher of subscription papers than the more conservative country from which we have sprung. President Woodward gave me some encouragement in the spring to think that our trustees might do something. I proposed to them that they make a subvention of $500.00 a year for two years toward this "worthy object." The Executive Committee at a recent meeting have turned the proposal down, along with some others, the Institution having already at the end of six years reached the normal condition of educational institutions (if this is an educational institution) by becoming poor. Dr. Doughty, the Canadian Archivist, who has a free-hand and has but to dip into his own copious appropriations, promised $250 per annum. I have written to FitzRoy and Egerton to learn details as to the status of the subscription in England. I heartily wish that the United States might do something. I do not suppose the American Historical Association has much money to spare; but whether it could make subscription or not, it would, I think, be worth while to have the matter discussed at the meeting of the Council.[79]

I go on Tuesday to Chicago, McLaughlin having

wished me to lecture to his students for a couple of weeks.[80] ...

To Carl R. Fish

November 4, 1907.

My dear Fish:

Thank you very much for your letter. Doubtless several matters in it can be more thoroughly canvassed when I see you at Madison.[81] Meantime I will only say that some ability to speak both French and Italian will be requisite. Many of those with whom you would have to deal speak English, most speak French; but, for instance, Mgr. Wenzel, the archivist of the Vatican, seemed to speak only Italian. You can pick all these things up in a short time. When Senator Elkins proposed to President McKinley the substitution of the present Fish Commissioner for Marshall MacDonald, the objection was made that he knew nothing about fish. Senator Elkins[82] said, "Oh well, he is a smart fellow and will catch on." This anecdote I commend to the author of the valuable work on the Civil Service.[83] ...

P. S. The clearest possible handwriting is a beautiful trait for one who is preparing notes in Rome to be printed in Washington; But I pass rapidly over this delicate subject. Did you ever see Leland's handwriting? Yet he is doing noble work for us in Paris.

To Elihu Root

December 13, 1907.

Sir:[84]

I ask leave to propose an action on your part which at slight expense would accomplish a great deal for the future improvement of government historical publications. I address myself to the Secretary of State because his statutory relations to the archives of the government seem to indicate his department as the most appropriate for such a purpose. The President, who is cordially in favor of the measure which I have proposed, assures me that he is unable to take the action desired for lack of any appropriation out of which the

---

[79] The council of the Association voted to provide £100 a year for two years. Half of this Jameson and the treasurer undertook to raise from interested individuals and from such societies as the Daughters of the American Revolution and the Society of Colonial Wars. Once the work of assembling the material was begun, it was evident that the three volumes planned would not be sufficient. The series was increased to five and further subscriptions were raised by Jameson. See the Jameson Papers for correspondence from 1907 through 1910 with Sir Almeric FitzRoy, W. L. Grant, Hugh Egerton, C. M. Andrews, and interested subscribers.

[80] The general subject of these lectures was slavery in America before 1820.

[81] On the subject of the exploration of the Roman archives, Jameson and Fish had had an interview in September, 1906, but the matter was for a time dropped because of lack of an appropriation for the purpose. The money was not forthcoming until Jan. 13, 1908, and then came as an appropriation of $2,800 for a research associate for fourteen months. The work was begun in July, 1908.

[82] Stephen B. Elkins (1841-1911), Senator from West Virginia, 1895-1911. The Commissioner of the Bureau of Fisheries in 1907 was George M. Bowers.

[83] Fish, Carl R., *The Civil Service and the Patronage*, Cambridge, Harvard Univ. Press, 1904; N. Y., Longmans, 1905.

[84] Elihu Root (1845-1937) was Secretary of State from 1905 till 1909. The letter of Nov. 23, 1905, to Gifford Pinchot (ante) had thus far seemed to produce no results.

slight expense contemplated can be defrayed. It has seemed to me possible that in the case of the Department of State, however, it might be lodged upon the appropriation for contingent expenses, if the object itself seemed to you desirable.

The inquiry which I wish to raise is, whether it is not now possible to adopt a more systematic and therefore more effective mode of dealing with the problem of documentary historical publications by the United States government. I do not speak of those narrative historical works which are sometimes devised and carried out under departmental or congressional authority, but only of those volumes which consist wholly or mainly of material for history. All governments publish more or less of such material. It is an accepted function of governments, and needs no defense. The United States government has, from the beginning of its history, recognized the obligation, and has issued, especially of late, many such volumes. But in order to fulfill its purpose, and help forward American history with the maximum of economy and efficiency, such publication ought to be based on a well-considered plan, to the framing of which we should apply the best historical intelligence the country affords. This we are far from doing at the present time.

The Present Situation.

That the present situation is far from satisfactory, may be seen by a glance at the list of the volumes of this sort published by the government. For the most convenient example, we may take the product of the last ten years fully reported upon, those of the Fifty-fourth to Fifty-eighth Congresses inclusive. During those ten years the government issued 31 volumes of the "Official Records of the War of the Rebellion," 18 volumes of the "Records of the Union and Confederate Navies," 8 volumes of the "Journals of the Congress of the Confederate States," 3 volumes of the second edition of "The Documentary History of the Constitution," 2 volumes of "Documents relating to the Origin and History of the Smithsonian Institution," 2 volumes of "Indian Affairs: Laws and Treaties," a book of "State Papers and Correspondence relative to the Louisiana Purchase," a volume of "Documents respecting Federal Aid in Disturbances," "The Legislative History of the General Staff of the Army," a supplement to the "Calendar of Jefferson Papers," and the first volume of "Journals of the Continental Congress."

Some of these volumes were well done, some quite badly done; some are of high utility to history, some but slightly needed. The amount of historical material comprised in them is ample. But the list as a whole shows no evidence of a general plan. It is not only miscellaneous but in some respects casual. The question is, whether, with the same amount of expenditure, or less if need be, we could not by having a method make our efforts more effective, and have a product more useful to real historians.

Methods followed in Other Countries.

With some variation in detail, the usual mode by which other countries have dealt with the problem has been by the appointment of a small commission of persons skilled in the valuation and use of historical sources. Nearly every country in Europe has something of the sort. Canada has just established a strong commission of this kind. Those have succeeded most fully which have taken the most pains to form at the beginning a comprehensive and thoroughly digested plan. The best procedure has been that of the Dutch. In 1903 the Queen of the Netherlands instituted a Commission of Advice on National Historical Publications, composed of ten of the best Dutch historical scholars. Before resolving on a single documentary publication, they made a deliberate survey of all parts and aspects of Dutch history, with an eye to their relative degrees of documentation, and constructed a careful report on "Gaps in the Knowledge of Dutch History to be filled by Source-Publications." Having laid before the historical public this general survey of the field, they considered that they had a proper basis on which to found recommendations of particular source-works as really needed. The volumes which they recommended to be undertaken are now in progress, under their supervision. It is submitted that theirs was the rational procedure.

Suggestions as to the First Step of Progress.

Since the establishment of a permanent advisory commission, involving some expense, would require Congressional action which it might not be possible to secure at once, it is suggested that a commission might without significant expense be instituted which should review the whole field of documentary publications for the history of the United States and frame a preliminary plan which should serve to guide subsequent governmental work of this sort into the best channels. The Librarian of Congress,[85] who strongly approves the notion, has suggested to me the analogy of the Park Commission, and the effect which its report has had. By setting up a standard plan, known to represent the deliberate judgment of the best historical experts, such a document would make it more difficult than it now is for ill-advised publications to be entered upon, easier than now for the best projects to win acceptance. A capital basis for the work of such a commission exists already in the detailed survey of all the important historical materials possessed by the government, prepared by the Department of Historical Research in the Carnegie Institution of Washington, Van Tyne and Leland's "Guide to the Archives of the Government at Washington," of which a revised and enlarged edition is now in the press.

I will venture to suggest names for such a commission, naming the men whom I should appoint if in the

---

[85] Herbert Putnam (1861-1955), Librarian of Congress, 1899-1939.

course of my duties as President of the American His-torial Association I had to appoint a commission of eight for analogous work with a regard solely to fitness and the probability of their taking the task seriously and doing effective work. All have at one time or another been members of the Executive Council of the American Historical Association, and their joint pro-nouncements would have the greatest weight with the historical workers of the country. I should suggest:

Mr. Charles Francis Adams, President of the Massachusetts Historical Society

Professor Charles M. Andrews of the Johns Hopkins University [86]

Professor William A. Dunning of Columbia University

Mr. Worthington C. Ford of the Library of Congress

Professor Albert Bushnell Hart of Harvard University

Captain Alfred T. Mahan, U. S. N., retired

Professor Andrew C. McLaughlin of the University of Chicago

Professor Frederick J. Turner of the University of Wisconsin.

While I presume that all these would be willing to give their time to such an undertaking without compensation, I should be unwilling to recommend the project without suggesting the desirability that the travelling expenses which they would incur in attending the necessary meetings should somehow be defrayed. If the Secretary of State is so good as to agree with me in this opinion, perhaps he has some appropriation by means of which the difficulty may be met. I estimate that two general meetings would be necessary and that the cost of the travelling expenses of the members named on the list (it may be taken as a typical list so far as geographical distribution is concerned) would be less than $500.00.

Ultimate Plan.

It is to be hoped that after publication of the report or plan above provided for, it may not be difficult to persuade Congress to establish a permanent commission to regulate and supervise in future the government's publications of documentary historical material. It could easily be arranged for as an adjunct to the work of the American Historical Association, which has statutory relations to Congress. When vacancies should occur, the Executive Council of that Association might make nominations to future Presidents. Such a commission, organizing itself into committees of three upon the materials possessed by the various departments of government, might so act in conjunction with the edi-

torial committees of three established in the various departments by the "Keep Commission" [87] as to ensure that no project of documentary historical publication should be adopted which did not have at once the approval of the Commission on National Historical Publications and of the department concerned, while the commission might make regulations concerning the details of editing and execution, of such a sort as to ensure a scholarly product. These regulations should before going into effect be laid before the President for his approval, and the commission might be charged to report annually to him.

But all this is an ideal for the future. I venture to hope that the preliminary action, described in the earlier paragraph, may be deemed wholly practicable and worthy of present execution. If in any particular it would be of service to you, I should be happy to wait upon you with further explanations of the project.[88]

To WALDO G. LELAND

December 16, 1907.

Dear Leland:

. . . You have probably seen that President Roosevelt has mentioned that he meant it when he said that he would not be president again. I am told that he has since stated that he is going to Europe as soon as his term expires, which is exactly what I supposed he would do. I am thinking whether I ought to give him a job in some of our archive searches, for instance, the Dutch, which I am sure would interest him. He would make the Rijksarchief hum. We missed you at the annual dinner of the Geographic Society Saturday evening. (By the way, I uniformly sequester invitations to such dinners when addressed to you, believing that one who is dining daily in Parisian restaurants would be only bored by any efforts to secure him at our more modest entertainments.) The society's medal was given to Captain Roald Amundsen. The presentation was made by Vice-president Fairbanks.[89] Jusserand

---

[86] Charles M. Andrews (1863-1943), already mentioned in connection with the preparation of a guide to the London archives, received the Ph.D. degree from the Johns Hopkins the year after Dr. Jameson left. From that date until 1907 he taught in Bryn Mawr; the next three years he was in the Johns Hopkins. In 1910 he began his long career in Yale. The other names in the list have already been identified.

[87] See ante, Nov. 23, 1905, n. 5.

[88] When Jameson went to the Madison meeting of the Association, having received no reply to this letter, he, having given up hope of a committee appointed by President Roosevelt, suggested that the Association appoint a committee on documentary historical publications of the United States government. This the Association empowered its newly-elected president, George B. Adams, to do, and he selected the men named by Jameson in his letter to Secretary Root, adding Jameson himself. In February, Jameson learned that Root had suggested that the Keep Commission appoint a subcommittee of historians. That commission took over the committee of the Association which now became a committee of the government. After more than a year of work it made a careful report which included the draft of a bill, to become the McCall bill, the fate of which can be followed in later letters.

[89] Captain Roald Amundsen (1872-1928) had recently returned from a three-year expedition through the Northwest Passage, in which he had established the position of the Magnetic North Pole.

Charles Warren Fairbanks (1852-1918), United States Senator, 1897-1905, was Vice-president from 1905 to 1909.

made a most clever and amusing speech about the voyages of the Northmen; Bryce an interesting and suggestive one about geography in general; all the Americans orated violently. Moore orated in presenting each speaker; Fairbanks orated after the manner of Indiana in presenting the medal; Burton, McGee, Goulder and Hampton orated,[90] at least I know that the first two did and I left at that point, but Bryce told me yesterday that the other two orated even longer than anybody else, pushing the event almost to the point of desecrating the Sabbath. Indisposition of Beveridge alone saved us from an even more portentous oration by that glorified sophomore.[91] By the way, the ministers here are getting up a movement against the desecration of the sabbath in Washington. This really irritates me. I don't know what they mean. This is a good town and I never saw a sabbath desecrated here a little bit [92] . . . .

To ROBERT S. WOODWARD

January 8, 1908.

Dear Dr. Woodward:

I beg leave to request that Dr. Carl Russell Fish, associate professor of American history in the University of Wisconsin, be made one of the proposed group of research associates, with a compensation of two hundred dollars per month, running from about July 1, 1908, to about September 1, 1909.

I ask this not on the ground that he is of all men the one best fitted to assist us in our general work, though he is a brillant and capable man, with a good book and a number of good articles to his credit, but on the ground of his special adaptation to one particular task, that of effecting for American historical scholars a preliminary general exploitation of the archives of Rome. I think it necessary to explain with some fulness how unusual a combination of qualifications is necessary for that task, in order to sustain the opinion that no one else in the country could do it so well. Professor Fish,

I may add, can have leave of absence for a year, beginning next July.

The Vatican archives, specifically so called, were thrown open to the general use of historical scholars by the late pope, Leo XIII., in 1881.[93] At that time or in succeeding years the various European nations, in most cases by governmental authority, have established in Rome historical institutes, manned by from two to ten workers, the object of which is to extract from the enormous masses of material in the Vatican archives those which relate to the history of each particular country. The result has been the publication, by the English, French, Germans, Austrians, Hungarians, Spaniards, Dutch, Swedes, Poles and Russians, of a great variety of volumes of important historical materials, numbering several hundred. The material for the history of North America is much less in volume than that of England, France and Germany. Yet it is a large amount, and the mine is almost completely unworked. The composition of the Vatican archives is such that we may expect it to contain, and indeed it is known to contain, not only the formal and official documents respecting matters in ecclesiastical government but also a great variety of interesting correspondence regarding America, for it is to be borne in mind that most of the area of the United States was before the beginning of the nineteenth century under Catholic control, and all of it since that date has had more or less relation with the papacy. Also, that the Vatican archives are among the most extensive in the world, belonging to a much-writing government.

It results, however, from the ecumenical character of the Roman government, that the materials relating to American history are written in a variety of languages. The agent who should undertake their systematic exploitation for the benefit of American Historical students must be an excellent Latin scholar; he must be able to read Italian and Spanish with facility as well as German and French. Very few professors of American history, I am sorry to say, have this linguistic equipment, except as to French and German, which are relatively much less important in this case. Professor Fish has this equipment, along with a singularly wide range of knowledge of all the various fields of American history. He is also a clear-headed man and a methodical worker.

But the task also demands unusual qualities of address, tact, acute perception, diplomatic skill and social experience. If it were a question of simply working in what are specifically called the Vatican archives, these qualities would not be so necessary, since that collection is open to all properly introduced scholars, regardless of nation or creed. But there are several other collections which are of great importance to America, and are not thus accessible. The Vatican archives contain the papal registers of bulls and briefs, the books of pe-

---

[90] Jean Adrien Antoine Jules Jusserand (1855-1932), French ambassador to the United States, 1902-1925, and president of the American Historical Association in 1920. For an account of this dinner see the Washington *Star*, Dec. 15, 1907, where summaries of the speeches of the two ambassadors are given. Other speakers were Theodore Burton, Harvey D. Goulder, J. Hampton Moore, all members of the House of Representatives, and William J. McGee, geologist and ethnologist, who served the government in various capacities. President Roosevelt appointed him to the Inland Waterways Commission and he was later given charge of the water resources of the country.

[91] Acquaintance with Senator Albert J. Beveridge a few years later greatly modified Jameson's opinion of him. See Donnan, Elizabeth, and L. F. Stock, Senator Beveridge, J. Franklin Jameson, and John Marshall, *Miss. Valley Hist. Rev.* 35: 463-465.

[92] Apparently the clergy of the city continued to agitate, to the annoyance of others besides Jameson, for on Feb. 19, 1913, petitions against legislation to compel observance of the Sabbath as a day of rest were received by the Congress. *Cong. Rec.*, 62 Cong., 3 sess., 4258.

[93] The *Amer. Hist. Rev.* 2: 4-58, Oct. 1896, contained an account of the Vatican archives by Charles H. Haskins.

titions on which these were founded, and the correspondence of the papal secretaries with the nuncios and others. There are several thousand volumes of each of these.

But there are several other archives in Rome of high importance; The archives and libraries of the Italian state, into which much ecclesiastical material has been gathered by confiscation, are of course generally accessible. But this is not true of the archives of the Consistory, of those of the Congregation of the Holy Office, and of those of the Congregation of the Propaganda. Of these, the first and third, imperfectly examined by several scholars, are known to contain much material for American history. Access to them is to be obtained only through diplomatic skill and special favor. I went into the matter when in Rome sufficiently to perceive that much skill would be requisite in order to achieve the desired results.

Moreover, the agent must try to get access to many private collections. The correspondence of the nuncios, very voluminous, with many interesting inclosures, often in earlier times remained in the personal archives of the Secretary of State and has been preserved by his family rather than in the Vatican archives. Sometimes, as in the case of certain of the Farnesi, large collections of this sort have found their final resting place in public collections in other cities than Rome—in the case alluded to, in the Archivio di Stato at Naples. Often, however, these papers are in the archives of the great Roman families, and must be sought through their favor.

Professor Fish is thoroughly a gentleman, with good manners and attractive social qualities, accustomed to society and acute in his perceptions. He is both energetic and careful, and will surely make his way in Rome and produce a most valuable report, which I am confident will astonish American scholars with the wealth of material lying unexplored in that city. He is a man of about thirty-one. Having been in his undergraduate days a pupil of mine, I think I can answer for his being amenable to suggestions and working in harmony with our general plans. I may add that while there are a few places (only a few) in Rome where a Catholic might do better than a Protestant, I know of no Catholic who has enough knowledge of American history to do the task anything like as well as Professor Fish; and that he as a High Church Episcopalian will have many of the same advantages in Rome that a Catholic might have.

To WALDO G. LELAND

February 18, 1908.

Dear Leland:

. . . Your friend Dodd was in here the other day.[94] He dropped in at twelve o'clock, in store clothes. Explanations were not demanded but were soon forthcoming. It appeared that the President of these United States had read his book—or said that he had—and with so much satisfaction that he invited the blushing author to come and have luncheon with him at the White House. I did not see Dodd after, but presume that he enjoyed himself. Another interesting visitor, here the last two or three days, was a young Frenchman named Giraudoux, sent here by Hart, whom I took to Mt. Vernon yesterday, having occasion to go there myself on a curious errand. A nice old lady in this town wished me to act as a sort of referee in a dispute which has arisen concerning two rival carriages of General Washington's.[95] The man for whom she acts presented them some years ago a coachee which is said to have belonged to the General. A few years afterward a society purchased and presented a handsome old coach, said to have been his. You may have seen it in the coach house there, bearing the discreet label "Coach exhibited at the Philadelphia Exposition of 1876 as coach of General Washington." Upon their relegating the humbler vehicle to the rear of the coach house and giving the lime-light to the new acquisition, donor number one was very angry and withdrew his carryall to a storage warehouse in Washington. He then began a campaign of investigation and criticism against the other coach. Both parties, one with enthusiasm, the other somewhat faintly, requested my judgment. After mature investigation I shall now be able to gratify both by pronouncing with great conviction that there is no evidence that either of these ancient vehicles ever belonged to General Washington. So far as I can see, the only portion of any of his carriages which can be satisfactorily proved to exist is one copper medalion, formerly affixed to one of the doors of one of his coaches. It is treasured at the National Museum, and bears a group of cupids said to be by Cipriani, but anyhow, very ugly and apparently of the African race. Thus, as you will see, the cause of history in the United States is progressing with great éclat. Hoping that you are enjoying the same blessings.

To WALDO G. LELAND

March 5, 1908.

Dear Leland:

Rowland has just sent me his Sixth Annual Report and I presume that he will send you one; indeed, I have

---

[94] William E. Dodd (1857-1939), who spent much time on his farm at Round Hill, Va., this year went to the University of Chicago as professor of American history. From this position he was appointed ambassador to Germany, where he served from 1933 to 1937. The book referred to was probably his *Jefferson Davis*, Philadelphia, G. W. Jacobs, 1907.

[95] On Oct. 17, 1907, Jameson wrote to Mrs. Mary Stevens Beall, secretary of the Columbia Historical Society, that he could give no time to the matter of George Washington's coaches until after Dec. 10. He later sent a detailed account of his findings, an account which might well be used as a model for processes of historical research.

asked him to be sure to do so. You will be surprised to find how largely you and I contribute to it. You will also be amused at the correspondence with Ainsworth. I do not blame Rowland for being angry with the General, who treated him very shabbily last spring; but I do not imagine that it will do him any good to contend against that celebrated military commander. Military heroes who have bled (other people) for their country, are firmly entrenched in the hearts of the people.[96]

I could wish that Dr. Rowland had shown something of the same bellicose ardor which he now exhibits toward Ainsworth, when Hart was in Mississippi in January. Hart figured as a "head-liner" in the programme of the Mississippi Historical Society, Riley having made the arrangements in view of Hart's spending that month in a Southern tour.[97] When he got to Jackson he found that his appearance was queering the whole thing. The newspapers had passed around word to boycott the malign Yankee. This is Hart's version of it. I sent for a local newspaper to see exactly what had happened, but of course they sent me the wrong numbers. He says that Riley stuck by him like a little man, and concealed from him as long as possible the awkwardness of the situation; but Rowland came out with a card in the newspaper, disclaiming responsibility for Hart's being there.

Speaking of war-like deeds, you may be interested in the inclosed clipping from the newspaper. I presume that the Paris papers may have given you accounts of the international episode alluded to. If not, I will mention that de Servière was dropped from the Berlitz faculty and Flickinger was made assistant superintendent. Servière, like Mary's lamb, persisted in lingering near, and finally irritated Flickinger to such an extent that he F. stabbed him S. nine times. Not content with this, Servière has hired rooms four doors from the Berlitz, and placarded the front of the building opposite us with a big sign, obviously temporary and inexpensive, reading "Academy of Languages, Professor Rene C. de Servière, Principal. French, Spanish, German, Italian, English, Russian, etc. Native and Experienced Teachers. Trial Lessons Free. Translations from and into all Languages." I do not know whether he is out of the hospital yet. Flickinger meanwhile languishes in another public institution, and things look rather bad for him as Servière seems to have had no weapon save his Gallic tongue.

Thus history continues to be made—made really with more energy and rapidity than we can chronicle it, for the bound volumes of your great work have not yet reached us . . . .

To Harlan H. Barrows

May 28, 1908.

My dear Dr. Barrows:[98]

I am very warmly in sympathy with the project which you mention for offering courses in political geography partly intended as a preparation for work in history, and I should be glad if I were able to offer useful suggestions in the matter. Such as I have I send. But perhaps it is needless to say that I regard instruction in physical geography, or more definitely, instruction on the relations of physical geography to history, as even more necessary. Not perhaps that it is more important

---

[96] The *Sixth annual report of the director of the Department of Archives and History of the state of Mississippi*, 9-13, in a discussion of transcripts of material in French archives, printed letters from Jameson and Leland. The report also published (28-32) letters exchanged between General Ainsworth and Rowland during a vain attempt on the part of the latter to obtain information from the records of the War Department. Major General F. C. Ainsworth (1852-1934), as chief of the record and pension office of the War Department, had been highly successful in organizing the records but had firmly refused to historians and even to agents of the states access to these records. As appreciation of the importance of the historical material which he controlled increased, dissatisfaction with his attitude also increased and finally found expression in an editorial, Withholding public records, in the *Nation* 94: 78-79, Jan. 25, 1912. Following its appearance, the editor, Paul E. More, wrote to Jameson, asking for a contribution on the subject, as he believed that something might be accomplished. Jameson's reply was that Ainsworth was right in his contention that the remedy was a national archive building. "General Ainsworth's arrogance, self-sufficiency, and narrowness of mind are often annoying, and I should be happy to see him retired or transferred to the Philippines or to the stars at any time; but on this particular problem I think that more is to be gained by keeping on good terms with him, or leaving him at one side and hammering away at the movement for a National Archive Building, than by antagonizing him. So please count me out." More replied by asking for a general article on an archive building, which Jameson was about to supply when word came that Ainsworth had been removed. Jameson at once wrote to the Secretary of War, Henry L. Stimson, pointing out the richness of the material in the possession of the department and urging that, under proper restrictions, historical students be given access to it.

Other scholars had responded to the request of More and the *Nation* of Feb. 22 contained an excellent group of letters on the subject. Though these were too late to affect Ainsworth's position they gave added force to Jameson's letter to the Secretary, and the result was a more liberal administration of the War Department records. More to Jameson, Feb. 1, 6; Jameson to More, Feb. 2, 19, 1912; Jameson to the Secretary of War, Feb. 21, 1912.

[97] Franklin L. Riley (1866-1914), professor of history in the University of Mississippi, 1897-1914, one of the originators and a trustee of the Mississippi State Department of Archives and History.

The account of this meeting, contained in the first number of the *Bulletin, Miss. Hist. Soc.*, 5, pays tribute to Hart, perhaps in an endeavor to atone somewhat for his treatment by the newspapers: "A noteworthy feature of the afternoon session was the instructive and inspiring address by Prof. Albert Bushnell Hart of Harvard University, on 'The New England History Teachers Association.' His long and intimate connection with that important organization enabled him to suggest many ways in which a similar association might be maintained and made useful to teachers of Mississippi."

[98] Harlan H. Barrows, at this time an instructor in the department of geology and geography of the University of Chicago, later professor, and chairman of the department of geography.

than the political, which would be a difficult matter to determine, but because students of history are less likely to have pursued it, and are more certain to obtain mental enlargement from the study of aspects and relations of geography which are less likely to have come already into their minds.[99]

Assuming a course confined to political geography, I will not attempt to give a systematic outline of such a course but will only make a few scattering suggestions. One is, that students of history know very little of the process by which maps are made, and might be profited by at least one lecture in which that process should be detailed from the actual surveys of the field to the finished product, including expositions of the mode in which cadastral surveys have been used as the foundation for historical atlases in Saxony and elsewhere. Another suggestion is, that students need to know much more than they do of the qualities of various historical atlases which have been produced and are being produced in different countries, and may profitably be shown what can be done with maps in a variety of ways usually unknown to them—for as a rule they know only of maps showing boundaries and territorial jurisdictions. I think that American students ought to know a good deal about the methods by which the history of American cartography illustrates the progress of discovery and exploration, and of methods such as those which Harrisse has so systematically employed in the case of Newfoundland.[100] Of course they ought also to have an introduction, with plenty of illustrations, to the study of the problems relating to boundary treaties—I mean illustrations of the various difficulties which have attended the effort to lay down in maps and surveys the specifications made in words, often vague words, in treaties, statutes and other documents framed by authorities remote from the terrain.

These are not the central features of such a course as you propose, but simply certain things which I have thought might be less certain to be borne in mind than the central features, because the latter are laid down in plenty of books. A book like Himly's,[101] not having specially in mind the needs of such students of history as I have seen at Chicago, very often does not include all the outlying features which I have named above.

To JUSTIN H. SMITH

244 Goldwin Smith Hall, Ithaca, N. Y., August 25, 1908.

By dear Mr. Smith: [102]
...I am obliged to you for calling my attention to Osgood's review of your book in the "Political Science Quarterly." The difference between his and Van Tyne's is mostly a matter of temperament, I think.[103] Osgood is primarily the patient researcher, indifferent to style; [104] Van Tyne, much less exact in research, takes much more interest in questions of style. Yet in reality both commend and discommend the same things, and an "old hand" at reading reviews would draw much the same conclusions respecting the book from the two reviews if he had not seen it. Indeed, I have thought it quite remarkable how close an agreement there was among all the reviews of your book that I have seen. I think that everyone without exception has praised in very warm terms the care, learning, competence and soundness of judgment which have been displayed by the author in the substantials. On the other hand, everyone that I have seen has indicated the writer's belief that you went too far in pursuing the wish to be readable and picturesque. I speak of this with the more freedom because I think that you yourself expressed to me some doubt that this might be the result of the endeavor, and because it seems plain that the Mexican book, which you said did not call for the same sort of endeavor, will be sure to win all the commendations which the other has won without the reserves with which those latter commendations have been accompanied. I feel very sure of this, and am telling everybody that we have a very highly important book to look forward to, in which we shall feel much pride.[105]

To CHARLES M. ANDREWS

244 Goldwin Smith Hall, Ithaca, New York, August 25, 1908.

My dear Andrews:
What you said about Hall in your recent letter re-

---

[99] The reader may remember that these were scarcely Jameson's sentiments when he was asked to give a course in the Johns Hopkins University on the relation of geography to history.

[100] Henry Harrisse (1830-1910), whose volumes on voyages to the New World had been appearing since 1866. His *Découverte et évolution cartographique de Terre-Neuve*, London, Henry Stevens, was published in 1901.

[101] Himly, Auguste, *Histoire de la formation territoriale des etats de l'Europe Centrale*, Paris, Hachette, 1876.

[102] Justin H. Smith (1857-1930), after eight years as a member of the publishing firm of Ginn and Company and a similar period as professor of modern history in Dartmouth College, 1899-1908, abandoned teaching for the writing of history.

[103] The book here referred to was *Our struggle for the fourteenth colony: Canada and the American Revolution* 2v., N. Y., Putnam's, 1907, of which Van Tyne had written (*Amer. Hist. Rev.* 13: 364-366): "It is a cause for real regret that the author's strivings for literary effects of the tinsel variety have severely vitiated his work." This he followed with a half-page of examples.
Osgood in the *Pol. Sci. Quart.* 23: 323-326, gave to the style of the work a single brief sentence: "The exuberance of Professor Smith's humor may at times offend good taste."

[104] Herbert L. Osgood (1855-1918), A.B., Amherst, 1877, Ph.D., Columbia, 1899, taught in Columbia from 1890 until his death.

[105] *The annexation of Texas*, N. Y., Baker and Taylor, 1911.

minds me to mention some correspondence that I have been having with Miss Davenport about him.[106] We talked sometimes in Washington to the effect that it was very desirable that some anniversary of his connection with the Public Record Office should be marked by a testimonial from the numerous Americans who have been indebted to him for unstinted aid of all sorts. Lately we have been corresponding about it. I believe that Hall's connection with the Public Record Office began in 1879, Miss Davenport has the exact date but I haven't it at hand at the moment. She says that Miss Edith Leonard writes: "Some of us are getting up a little testimonial to Mr. Hall.... The subscriptions vary from 2s. 6d to £1 1s. We have at present collected seventeen pounds." Miss Davenport will write to Miss Leonard for further particulars, such as when the time for subscribing will close and whether there is any reason why Hall's American friends should not be generally notified. I have told her that if the matter can be nursed along until into the autumn I think we in America could do a good deal about it. I would take hold of it earnestly and have no doubt that I could easily find twenty men and women, and perhaps thirty or forty, who would subscribe a guinea apiece. I had hoped that when the time came it might be practicable to subscribe enough to get Hall over to America. I wish that he could be present at one of the meetings of the American Historical Association but I suppose that that would be difficult for him, and I do not know that the English subscribers would care for that.[107] There could, however, be no objection if concurrently with any presentation on their part the Americans should present him with a sum subscribed here, and tell him how glad we should be if it were possible for him to arrange to visit us.[108] What do you think of all this? Ephraim Adams [109] welcomed the idea warmly, and added that he should be glad to have something done to show the Englishmen how much better Hall was appreciated among us than among them, having been a little indignant at their turn of mind respecting him.

Miss Davenport thought that Hall might be asked to give an academic lecture or two. Adams thought that his mode of lecturing was really too bad to admit of this. But the number of Americans whom he has obliged and who would be glad to see him and to contribute to any testimonial must be great. I should not be in favor of a subscription of varying amounts. The same end could, I think, much better be secured by making a level subscription of a guinea apiece, which any of the younger element could stand; and then if it were desired to make up a given sum, let the older element quietly chip in to complete it. I believe that we could get a good sum. My general conviction is that we could teach the British nation a thing or two in the art of pushing around the contribution box.

I should be glad to know what you think of all this. All to whom I have spoken of it in general have regarded the notion with favor.

To HUGH E. EGERTON

January 18, [1909].

My dear Professor Egerton:

I am much obliged by your kindness in sending me a copy of the "Journal of the Royal Colonial Institute" containing your remarks and those of others on Oxford and the Empire.[110] I have found the discussion exceedingly interesting.

May I make one remark apropos of that you say near the foot of page 89? You are right in saying that the more advanced students from American universities prefer to go to German universities rather than to Oxford. Perhaps it is known to you, but I take leave to mention it, that the number who go to either is now small in comparison with the total number of those who undertake post graduate studies. I believe that in spite of the enormous increase in the number of our graduate students the number who go

---

[106] Hubert Hall (1857-1944), first appointed to the Public Record Office in 1879, had been inspecting officer of records since 1905.

Frances G. Davenport (1870-1928), a fellow in the department of history of the University of Chicago, 1903-1904, Ph.D., Chicago, 1904, had joined the staff of the Department of Historical Research in 1905. In London she had been working on the *Guide to the manuscript materials for the history of the United States to 1783, in the British Museum, in minor London archives, and in the Libraries of Oxford and Cambridge*, Carnegie Institution, publication no. 90, 1908, of which she and Professor Charles M. Andrews were joint editors.

[107] The English subscribers presented two pieces of furniture. The American gift was £50, to be used in the purchase of books on America. This was presented to Hall at a dinner at the Holborn restaurant, on Aug. 18, 1909, with twelve Americans present. Along with the purse was a testimonial which read: "Dear Mr. Hall: It is now thirty years since, in June 1879, you entered the service of the Public Record Office. Those thirty years have been marked by assiduous devotion to public duty, by distinguished achievement in historical publication, and by constant efforts to advance the interests of historical scholarship in Great Britain. The trait, however, upon which your American friends dwell with the greatest pleasure, is the generous and untiring helpfulness with which you have throughout these years aided the researches undertaken in London by American historical scholars. They have found in you an invaluable friend, whose kindness has seemed to have no limits. In commemoration of your anniversary, we ask leave to express by this testimonial our gratitude for your constant furtherance of our historical interests, our cordial personal regard, and our best wishes for your future." This was engrossed and presented in the form of a bound book with vellum leaves, containing the signatures of forty-eight American historians who had profited from Hall's kindly assistance.

[108] The desire to bring Hall to this country was satisfied in 1924 when he was one of the English guests at the Richmond meeting of the American Historical Association.

[109] Ephraim D. Adams (1865-1930), professor of history, Stanford University, from 1906 until his death, was a brother of Henry Carter Adams, whom Jameson had so warmly admired in his early days in the Johns Hopkins University.

[110] See the *Journal*, 85-107, January, 1909. Hugh E. Egerton (1855-1927) was Beit Professor of Colonial History in Oxford University, 1905-1920.

to Germany is even absolutely a good deal less than it was twenty-five years ago, when I was a graduate student. At that time a student of history, for instance, thought it his normal course to go and study in Germany. Now he seldom does so. The general opinion in America is that he had better go to Paris, and those who profess to have a better basis for comparison than I could pretend to have say frankly that he may as well stay in America for at least the first two years of his graduate work.

I inclose herewith a list of doctoral dissertations in progress, which I annually prepare. Sir William Anson would think that too much of this was being done and I think our wisest agree with him, that we have made too much of doctoral dissertations as a part of the student's preparation for teaching—which is what graduate study generally means in America— but if we are to make such performance obligatory it is gratifying to see so wide a variety of fields cultivated, even by 'prentice hands.[111]

It is pleasant to know that the Rhodes scholars do well. One of the speakers spoke of them as a picked lot. So they are, but picked from a class which constitutes only a minority and elsewhere than in the North Atlantic States a small minority of our best young men. I am not greatly concerned to apologize for the Rhodes scholars now at Oxford. They seem to be good men and doing very well. But the fact remains that over most portions of the country the greater part of the best young men in the leading universities would not think of undertaking to go to Oxford for three years, because, utilitarian as are their young souls, they do not think that it would so much promote their ambitions to get forward in a good career, already selected, as would the education which they could get in the nearest large university. Several of your speakers mentioned how special were the requirements of Oxford; many of the audience might have been surprised, though I dare say you would not, if told that of my graduate students, when I had charge of the department of history at the University of Chicago, hardly any knew any Greek. Nevertheless, though the Rhodes youths come from a special class, we all feel sure that they will in the course of time do us a great deal of good.

Bowen and I (Bowen is the treasurer of the American Historical Association) are diligently gathering together the American contribution toward the preparation of the volumes of Colonial Entries in the Registers of the Privy Council. I should be much obliged if you would send me a memorandum on the status of the enterprise. If you or Mr. Grant could send this to me so that I should get it by the first of March, I could say something about it in the April number of the "American Historical Review." Please mention the title that has been chosen for the series.[112]

To Henry Vignaud

March 8, 1909.

My dear Mr. Vignaud:

In the newspaper notices of your resignation after having served our country so many years with so much distinction, I observed the statement of the fact—not known to me before—that you had orginally gone to Paris as a secretary to Senator Slidell, then commissioner of the Confederate government.[113] A few days afterward my friend Mr. Charles Francis Adams, who now lives in Washington during a part of the year, came into my office and mentioned that he had been struck by the same statement. He is, as you perhaps know, much occupied with studies of the diplomatic history of the Civil War. I think that he is preparing either a book upon the subject or a more extensive life of his father than the brief one which he contributed to the American Statesmen series. At all events, he is greatly interested in whatever can now be learned respecting the activity in Europe of Mr. Slidell, whom he thought to have been altogether the ablest representative of the Confederacy in Europe and the main spring of its activities there. On his behalf I venture to make an inquiry, and possibly a request, concerning the papers of Mr. Slidell. We are informed by our common friend Dr. Frederic Bancroft, also much interested in the history of the Confederacy, that some eight years ago Mr. Slidell's daughter, Mme la Comtesse de St. Roman, whom he had had the pleasure of meeting in Paris, wrote to him that she had found the box of her father's papers, missing at the time

---

[111] Sir William Anson (1843-1914), warden of All Souls College, in the discussion which followed the reading of Professor Egerton's paper, said: "Something too much is made nowadays of a young man doing what is called a piece of original work. We have a great deal of printed matter poured forth upon us daily, almost hourly, and to have a number of somewhat crude monographs, produced by the student who is eager to show he has the spirit of a researcher, would not, I think, be a benefit either to the researcher or to the human race. What we really want is that a man should understand the advantage of going to original authorities, that he should know when he has got to the bed rock of fact in any subject he is studying, and that he should be able to assist those who can make a full use of the knowledge supplied by doing the necessary drudgery which the researcher must do" (*ibid.*, 100).

[112] See *ante*, Nov. 1, 1907. Shortly after writing this letter Jameson received the first volume of *Acts of the Privy Council, Colonial Series, 1613-1680,* and a letter from Professor Egerton with the news that five rather than three volumes would be necessary to complete the work. Egerton to Jameson, Jan. 28, 1908 [1909].

[113] Vignaud had been attached to the American legation in Paris for thirty-four years.

John Slidell (1793-1871), United States Senator, 1853-1861, but best known for the *Trent* affair during the Civil War, made persistent efforts to obtain the recognition of the Confederacy by the French government. He and his family never returned to the United States.

when he was there, and would examine its contents "on her first full day of leisure."

You have been so kind in all relations with this department of the Carnegie Institution, especially in the very generous assistance which you have afforded to Mr. Leland, that I told Mr. Adams I should venture to ask you if you could supply any information respecting the nature of the collection of papers to which I have referred and if you could offer him any encouragement to believe that its present possessor would be willing that Mr. Adams should see such portions of it as might be of historical importance. I believe that his independence of all sectional or partisan predilection is so well known that she might feel confident of a proper, fair and impartial use of any facts which he might thus be able to obtain. He is, as you probably know, the president of the Massachusetts Historical Society, and the author of historical writings of so high a quality that to aid him is distinctly to aid the cause of American historical scholarship. If it is possible for you to assist his researches in the manner which I have indicated I shall be very greatly obliged and I am sure that he will be grateful to you and to Mme. de St. Roman.[114]

I take this occasion to express the very high appreciation which I share with others of your long continued public service, my best wishes for your enjoyment in a more retired life and my very cordial thanks for all the kindness which you have shown to Mr. Leland and to me.

To MORGAN P. ROBINSON

March 10, 1909.

My dear Mr. Robinson:[115]

It is always a great pleasure, whenever I can do so, to answer such questions as those which you propound in your letter of March 8 and to help such endeavors if I can.[116]

For the purpose of following out the subject as you have proposed it to yourself, I do not think that there are many classes of sources outside those which you mention. The chief ones are three: The newspapers, the local histories and such volumes of local records as have been published, and the biographies of obscure individuals which, though they do not compete with those which you have mentioned under "C," yet in a humble way supplement them and sometimes cast light in obscure corners.

I am not clear, however, that the history of sentiment and opinion respecting slavery is anything like so much in need of thorough examination and scientific treatment as the actual history of slavery as an institution. I believe that the former is better known than the latter and that, although Mr. Ballagh's book makes a very good beginning and Mr. Bruce's has covered the ground in another way,[117] there is still room for a history, subsequent to 1700 in the main (because Bruce's covers the preceding period so well), which shall be based upon the local data preserved in county records, etc., or recorded in the newspapers, or in general such as Mr. E. W. James brought out from time to time in the "Lower Norfolk County Antiquary." I should say also that we knew too little of the history of the eighteenth century importations into Virginia and of the nineteenth century domestic exportations. Generally speaking, it is the economic rather than the political history of slavery which is crying aloud to be written. If, however, you are committed to the history of opinion upon the subject, I believe that you have named the main sources and that with the pursuit of these and perhaps also of some of those additional things which I have indicated you will find plenty to do.

Congratulating you that you can keep up historical research along side your professional work (which, parenthetically, is more than I can do, though you might not suppose so).

To FRANCIS A. CHRISTIE

March 16, 1909.

My dear Christie:

I am writing to you from the hospital where I have spent a profitable though not delightful week. I am to go home tomorrow, I suppose, so I write now in order to secure in your eyes whatever prestige there is in the position. The trouble which laid me low at Munich, and from which you so beautifully aided me to recover during those memorable days at Hei-

[114] In reply to this request, Vignaud sent a letter-book of Henry Hotze, a commercial agent of the Confederate States, reporting that all other papers had been destroyed. Not long afterward he sent a second letter-book and some fifty-five letters which he had discovered. All this material was entrusted to Mr. Charles Francis Adams in May, 1909, to be deposited in the Library of Congress when he had finished with it. From correspondence of 1914 it appears that Mr. Adams forgot the episode and knew not what had become of the manuscripts. The first letter-book was at length found in his safe: "Today the dead are living, and the lost are found today" (Adams to Jameson, May 12, 1914). The second letter-book and the letters were found by W. C. Ford after the death of Mr. Adams (Jameson to Ford, July 1, Ford to Jameson, July 2, 11, 1923). The material was later presented to the Division of Manuscripts, Library of Congress. For some account of these papers, see the introduction to Documents: the London expenditures of the Confederate secret service, *Amer. Hist. Rev.* **35**: 811-812, July, 1930.

[115] Morgan P. Robinson (1876-1943) at this time was practicing law in Richmond. He later became state archivist of Virginia.

[116] Robinson had written, on Mar. 8, 1909, that he was attempting to trace the rise and fall of waves of slavery and anti-slavery sentiment in Virginia. After enumerating the sources he was using, he asked for suggestions.

[117] Ballagh, James C., *A history of slavery in Virginia*, Baltimore, Johns Hopkins Univ. Press, 1902; Bruce, Philip A., *Economic history of Virginia in the seventeenth century*, N. Y., Macmillan, 1895.

delburg, had increased since the first of January to such a degree that a surgical operation was judged expedient. While there was a good deal of pain for the next twenty-four hours, all has gone well since; but I do not like being here, never did see any satisfaction in lying in bed, and find that a week in a hospital is a great interruption to one's work. However, I am the less concerned about that because I had perceived in the last few weeks that my work did not amount to anything, anyhow. The world is hollow and our dolls are stuffed with saw dust. Why you persecute yourself so much about the school and general affairs of Meadville is not certain.[118] You would do well to write out on a sheet of paper the declaration of Lieutenant Pardee, military instructor at Brown University, concerning that institution, "Sick and tired of the whole damn crowd," and paste it on your looking-glass or somewhere where you will see it every few minutes, and especially you had better come away to New England in the early half of April. The real reason why I am writing is that I conclude that after I am a little stronger, and have got some deal with Congress and some business at my office out of the way, I ought to take a vacation. Therefore I am going to take steamer from Baltimore on April 2 and go up and visit at Woburn, inspect summer quarters in and near Brunswick, Maine, see a bit of Providence and of Arthur and wind up with Sallie's sister's silver wedding at Brooklyn on April 15. So if you can think of any duties of the acting president that will justify you in going to the till and getting the price of a journey to Boston about that time, we can meet there, and if you can take a little more than the mere railroad fare, which I should advise, we can blow it in Young's.

I am glad to see by the "Nation" that your excellent friend Mrs. Cortazzo has found innocent and healthful employment in gathering money for a fountain in memory of Ouida;[119] but am sorry on the other hand to learn from the same esteemed journal that your friend W. Sunset Maugham's plays are only so-so....

To FRANKLIN H. HOOPER

April 13, 1909.

My dear Mr. Hooper:[120]

It is always gratifying to be remembered at a dis-

tance of a quarter of a century, especially by one of whom I have so pleasant recollections.

I do not know who owns the plates and copyright of my "Dictionary of United States History." I prepared it in 1893, for a man in Boston named James D. Ball, who called himself the Puritan Publishing Company. He paid me a lump sum and I have therefore had little occasion to follow its fortunes since.[121] About 1899 he became insolvent and a revision which was effected in that year was paid for by a receiver named Reid. Then the thing was bought by a couple of fellows in Philadelphia, one of whom was named Graham and perhaps the other was named Stanley. I understood that they were making two volumes of it, packing it along side of some other publications—Ridpath's *History of the United States* I seem to remember as one of them—calling the whole thing a library of American reference, whatever that may mean. Their agents were in 1900 and 1901 selling the whole composite unscrupuously, in Providence and elsewhere, as my work, though even the minor part of it which was due to me had been altered by the publishers in ways that I should not countenance. I published cards of warning in the papers of Providence, where I then lived, and went to see the two young men in Philadelphia. They assured me that they would stop their garbling; but while I should not wish to be credited as saying that they looked to me like shabby rascals, I did not draw from the interview much confidence in their future performances. I have heard nothing about them for eight years. They usually called themselves the Historical Publishing Company, and had some kind of offices at the corner of Cherry and Juniper streets, but I believe the title-page bore the imprint "The American History Society of Washington," by which designation they undoubtedly intended to persuade the public that the American Historical Association was in some way responsible for their strange composite. I do not think that I have ever seen the whole of the six-volume work, and I do not know how or where the one-volume edition can be procured; I doubt if it is issued by anyone. It is to be hoped for the good of mankind that Messrs.

---

[118] Christie was at this time acting president of Meadville Theological Seminary.

[119] A note asking for contributions from the United States for a memorial to be erected in Bury St. Edmunds to Louise de la Ramée ("Ouida") which appeared in the *Nation* 88: 218-219, Mar. 4, 1909, was signed, "(Miss) Katherine Renée Cortazzo, Meadville, Pa."

[120] Franklin H. Hooper (1862-1940) was with the Century Company from 1883 to 1896, and there Jameson probably knew him as one of the editors of the *Century Dictionary*. From 1899 to 1938, with the exception of the war years, he was connected in editorial capacity with the *Encyclopedia Britannica*.

[121] In a letter to his father, of Sept. 27, 1893, Jameson reported the contract which he had made for the *Dictionary*, and during 1893 and 1894 his home letters often referred to the project. On the delivery of the manuscript he received $1500, and on the first five thousand copies sold he was to receive royalties of $500.

Correspondence in the Jameson Papers shows that he did have some small part in the revision of 1899 and was supposed to have given it his approval, though there is no indication that he received any payment. In the summer and autumn of 1900 David T. Matteson was at work upon a revision, about which he frequently consulted Jameson. On May 5, 1901, he wrote of an "acrimonious correspondence" with the publishers, and on June 30, 1902, he stated that he had not been paid and that the publishers had declared his work so unsatisfactory to the South that they had been obliged to destroy the plates made from his revisions. All this tends to confirm Jameson's judgment of their character. Matteson to Jameson, Aug. 26, Sept. 12, 25, Oct. 17, 22, 1900, May 5, 1901, June 30, 1902.

Graham and Stanley are no more. Perhaps I can find out at the Library of Congress today who is on record as owning the copyright in question.[122] In that case I will append it to this letter before it goes out.

To Albert Bushnell Hart

May 13, 1909.

My dear Hart:

I have just received your letter of April 26, from Athens, and have been able to read nearly every word of it, though it was a little trying not to know whether Van Tyne is "visibly impaired" or "visibly improved." I am sorry that you have not received more notifications about the American Historical Association. I am not guilty. Perhaps your colleague Haskins, who is secretary to the Council, is. I wrote you unofficially that we had a meeting at Richmond at which, beside some transactions of much less moment, we elected you president.[123] I also sent you a "separate" of the article in the April number of the "Review" describing the meeting. I sent it by way of Bremen, and I imagined you as receiving it in Venice and sitting down forthwith among the pigeons on the pedestals of the flag-staffs in the Piazza and refusing to accompany Mrs. Hart into San Marco until you had read the article. I now send another copy directly to Venice. It contains as an appendix the list of committees, and I shall imagine you as committing them to memory while the train goes up through the Brenner Pass. I am glad that anyhow you received the warrant.

I have just been up to New England to find a place for the summer. I did not have time to go out to Cambridge. From the latter part of June until the middle of September we shall be living in a cottage at North Edgecomb, Maine, the other side of the bridge from Wiscasset. The "works" will be at the library of Bowdoin College, to which I shall run down from Wiscasset three or four times a week. I expect to be here until June 16. After that it will be safest to address me at "Bowdoin College Library, Brunswick, Maine." The Board of Editors meets on June 11 and 12. We shall be sorry not to have you with us, but it is for your gain. My kindest regards to Mrs. Hart.

[122] The records of the Library of Congress show these copyright registrations: by James D. Ball, June 28, July 17, 1893; Aug. 18, 1898; by the History Publishing Company, Nov. 15, 1899, Apr. 5, 1900; by E. J. Stanley, May 16, 1900. The latest edition was a revision, 1931, under the supervision of Albert E. McKinley.

[123] To W. G. Leland, Jameson wrote, on Sept. 1, 1908: "I love Hart. But I look forward with an amused apprehension as to what the meetings of the Council under his presidency will be like. It would be [no] surprise [to] me to see us all staggering home from the meetings with a heavy portfolio of new work for each of us to do. Such men are a blessing to an association and keep it from stagnation."

To the Brazilian Ambassador

May 19, 1909.

My dear Mr. Ambassador:[124]

. . . When you were speaking on Sunday evening of the general topic of the influence of America on the progress of modern civilization, it occurred to me to suggest what has often been in my mind and which I now venture to mention. It is obvious enough but I have not felt that its force was always appreciated. It is a suggestion respecting English America, and I have not sufficient learning to know whether it is equally true of the Latin-American regions. It is this: We commonly say that North American society is a section of that of Europe transplanted to the New World. But in reality it is not a completely typical section, not one representing all parts of European society equally. Our population has from the first been, with the exception perhaps of the immigration of the last twenty years, a transplanted portion of the west-European middle class. There never was much to bring any considerable portion of the European aristocracy to North America, while at the other extreme of the scale the cost of transportation (save in the case of convicts) operated somewhat as a property qualification to keep from migration to America the lowest strata of the European population. North American society has therefore been mostly European middle class society transplanted to new surroundings. Affected as it has been by the new surroundings and circumstances, especially by the democratizing influence of the system of small freehold estates, our society has nevertheless retained many of the traits of an European middle class. The ideals of average America are bourgeoise ideals. Its religion is for the most part the religion of the English middle class. What Renan called "cet Américanisme vers lequel le monde marche" is essentially a bourgeoisation of modern society. After writing this I feel a doubt whether it is worth saying; but I let it go. . . .

To Paul Shorey

May 19, 1909.

Dear Shorey:

What a fellow you are! Why cannot I have you on tap and turn you on whenever I want intellectual diversion and edification? You will say that I once did have you on tap. But you are not to add that I did not appreciate you when I had you, for though I came away I knew what I was losing.

Well, anyhow, I thank you for sending me your address,[125] and if you omitted previously to send it because you considered that it was esoteric and I was a rank outsider now, you are very much mistaken. I still share the spirit of the University of Chicago and

[124] Joaquin Aurelio Nabuco d'Aranjo, ambassador to the United States from Brazil, May 24, 1905, to Jan. 17, 1910.

[125] Shorey, Paul, The spirit of the University of Chicago, *University of Chicago Magazine* 1: 229-235, April, 1909.

thank Heaven daily that I had for four years the opportunity to breathe its actual atmosphere. I doubt if I ever had four years more profitable, and I feel fully prepared to agree heartily with all you say respecting it as a strategic point. At the end of a convocation address which I had to give very soon after my arrival at the university I spoke of its fortunate position with respect to the upper half of the Mississippi Valley, "destined apparently to be at some time in the future the chief abode of civilized man," or some such phrase. My mind was convinced that this was the fact—else perhaps I should not have come out there. But the four years spent in the atmosphere of the university and under the influence of President Harper's imaginative visions of the future brought it home to my feelings far more completely—so completely indeed that I have to stop and think quite actively to remind myself why I came away. Your discourse with its mixture of Aristophanes at the beginning and Pericles at the end —not to say both all through—revives for me many thoughts and feelings that were inspiring, and I need not say brings to me many others that had not occurred to my mind. So I thank you very much.

To WORTHINGTON C. FORD

May 28, 1909.

My dear Ford:

. . . The matter of a Dictionary of National Biography has been in my mind from the very inception of the Carnegie Institution, as an enterprise which it might undertake.[126] I have, however, refrained from even proposing the matter. This has been partly due to the belief that I could not carry much more work than at present, until by reason of having a special building near the Library of Congress it was possible for me to organize the work of the Department into such a shape as to give me a little more freedom[127]—and to the remembrance that the Dictionary of National Biography killed Leslie Stephen. It has also been partly due to a belief that the Trustees would not at present or out

---

[126] Ford had written on May 27, 1909: "Mr. Adams tells me, that he once tried to interest the Carnegie people in undertaking an American Biographical Dictionary, on the same scale and general manner as that used in the English Dictionary of National Biography." In Dr. Jameson's letter to President Gilman of Feb. 14, 1902, it will be remembered that he included a Dictionary of Biography among the projects which the new foundation might well undertake.

[127] In a letter of Apr. 8, 1908, Jameson laid before President Woodward his reasons for thinking that his department needed better quarters. To this time the administrative activities of the Institution and the work of the Department of Historical Research had been carried on in the Bond Building in downtown Washington. In 1909 the administrative offices were transferred to a new building on P Street, N. W. For the department Jameson felt that a fire-proof structure was desirable and that for greater efficiency it should be close to the Library of Congress, where much of the work of the staff must be done. The site he selected was opposite the southeast corner of the library.

of the existing funds make additional provision in my Department for anything that would cost perhaps half as much per annum as is now voted to this Department. This is probably not a conclusive reason. It is probable that Mr. Carnegie would himself be interested in such an enterprise—at least Mr. Adams thought so when our advisory committee of three was considering the matter. A determined assault might sometime bring the necessary appropriation, though hardly until after they have made that appropriation for land and building for which I am now clamoring. A more solid reason, which has weighed upon me very greatly, is the conviction that it is not yet possible to make a really first-rate Dictionary of American biography. In the case of the men of the seventeenth and eighteenth centuries, no doubt, the materials are about all in. The case is made up. There are writings respecting them from which the brief biographical notices could be constructed. But this is not true in a very large degree of the men of the nineteenth century. Our nation has during that period not cared for biography to anything like the extent that the English have. Yet the success of a biographical dictionary depends upon the presence of a multitude of works of that kind. Stephen and his men had in most cases a sufficient supply of such material to draw upon. If he had had to have most of his biographies made *de novo* for this particular compilation he could never in the world have got the volumes out promptly, indeed he could hardly have done the thing at all. Now in our case, so far as the nineteenth century is concerned, this preliminary work has not been done in the case of most of the men who have really counted in the history of the nation. Especially is this true of that very important body of men who have made the economic and industrial history of the country. I suspect that we should also find, as a consequence of this same national indifference to a good biography, that we have not a sufficient supply of trained biographers to generate such a dictionary at a proper rate and with sufficient excellence of workmanship.

I set forth all these things as explaining why I have been afraid to tackle the job. I may be wrong, but I think that I should give precedence over this enterprise to the preparation of a scientific Atlas of American Historical Geography. This I am thinking of tackling before long.[128] On the other I am open to conviction. . . .

To CARL BARUS

June 3, 1909.

My dear Dr. Barus:[129]

I have to trouble you with an odd matter and yet one in which you may perhaps feel some interest. Mr. Henry Adams the historian, the younger brother of Mr.

---

[128] See *ante,* Feb. 14, 1902, n. 20.

[129] Carl Barus (1856-1935), physicist, connected with Brown University from 1895 to 1926.

Charles Francis Adams, lives in this town, in much retirement, from autumn to spring and in Paris from spring to autumn. After having produced about twenty years ago the best large historical work which has been produced in America—his History of the United States Under Jefferson and Madison—he dropped history entirely so far as active work was concerned. The last twenty years have been spent in travel and meditation, chiefly the latter. Lately, and just before he made his vernal migration to Paris, he sent me a manuscript entitled "The Rule of Phase in History" and asked me to persuade some competent scientific man to examine it from the scientific point of view, find all possible fault with it, and make such observations upon it as would set him right in any matters wherein he was wrong—a service for which he was willing to pay anything that might be desired.[130]

With my limited acquaintance among scientific men I know of only two or three, and you first of all, whose turn of mind is such that I should feel sure that they could do to edification what he desires. The article is an attempt to apply to the processes of human intelligence, to the development of thought and thus to history what in chemical physics is called the Rule of Phase. Of all those discoveries and reasonings which Willard Gibbs[131] and others have been developing in these recent years, I know extremely little, and I am by nature incapable of following with security any philosophical argument; but it appears that Mr. Adams has taken pains to read attentively in fields for which he was not originally trained and that his reasonings are suggestive and acute. He would, I suppose, wish historical people to criticize ultimately his application to history of doctrine obtained elsewhere; but what he first wishes is to subject his curious paper, especially the earlier part of it, to a good scientific mind of the right type.

Would it be possible for you to undertake to examine the paper, which is not very long—about 7000 words— and to report to me upon it at any time before the first of November? I believe that you might find it interesting. As you might feel that you could not afford to divert your time to it from other things that you had planned to do this summer unless there were a reason in the proposed compensation, I will say respecting this

that, though Mr. Adams named no definite sum, he is a man of liberal disposition and of the greatest courtesy, and would certainly make for the educational service which you rendered to him any compensation which the instructor might deem proper.

If you should wish to see the article before deciding as to whether you could undertake a more serious examination of it, it would be easy for me to send it to you. I shall be here until June 17.

Hoping sincerely that you may feel disposed to undertake what Mr. Adams wishes, . . .

To WILLIAM MacDONALD

Bowdoin College Library, Brunswick, Maine.
September 6, 1909.

My dear Mr. MacDonald :[132]

I read with much interest your article on Summer Schools in the last "Nation." But although, so far as my slight knowledge of the matter extended, I found myself quite in agreement with you, it occurred to me to question the statement that summer teaching does not seem "to have interfered disastrously with the professorial study and writing for which a long vacation has come to be thought essential." Sitting at the receipt of custom on behalf of this Review, as I do, I observe painfully that we do not get an increasing number of articles, that probably in American history at any rate we have in the last few months got a decreasing number from those historical professors who are occupying the best positions and may be spoken of as the leaders. That this disquieting state of things, disquieting not only to an editor but to anyone who wishes to see progress in investigation, is due to any one thing, I do not suppose, unless we can say that it is due to the increasing supply of the world's gold. The rise of prices has increased the attraction to professors of various means of increasing their earnings.[133] But I have had the impression that the summer school had had a pretty large part in diminishing their scientific output. I have seen this to be true in several cases at least.

You know how one reads an article in a journal, finds something to dissent from, thinks he will write to the writer, and then sees the folly of spending his time in that way when so many other things press. If nevertheless I have proceeded to write in this case, it is because you are one of those from whom I have long wanted an article for the *Review* and who has been teaching in summer schools. "De te fabula narratur." If this has not prevented you from sending us an article,

[130] See Cater, H. D., *Henry Adams and his friends*, xci, 646-647, 650, 676-678, for the story of Jameson's efforts to find a critic for The rule of phase. When Professor Barus declined, he tried Wilder D. Bancroft of Cornell, A. G. Webster of Clark, Edgar Buckingham of the Bureau of Standards, and at last Henry A. Bumstead of Yale, who criticized the manuscript in a manner which satisfied Adams. The letters which passed between Jameson and Bumstead are among the Jameson Papers.

After its author's death, The rule of phase was published in the volume entitled by Brooks Adams, *The degradation of the democratic dogma*, N. Y., Macmillan, 1919; reviewed by Carl Becker in the *Amer. Hist. Rev.* 25: 480-482, April, 1920.

[131] Josiah Willard Gibbs (1839-1903) of Yale. The theories of physical chemistry which Gibbs developed held great fascination for Adams.

[132] William MacDonald (1863-1938) had followed Jameson in Brown University, where he remained until 1917. The article referred to was, The status of the summer school, *Nation* 89: 202-203, Sept. 2, 1909.

[133] The price level in this country had been gradually moving upward since 1897. By 1909 the "high cost of living" had become a problem of political as well as economic importance.

please do not let anything else prevent it. Do you know, I think that I have not for six months had an article in American history from any academic that I could accept. That never happened before, and I am beginning to be concerned for the fate of the republic.

To WALDO G. LELAND

October 4, 1909.

Dear Leland:

. . . I am glad to hear that you are going to Brussels, Bruges and Ghent. Bruges is a most delightful place. Go and drink some beer at my expense in a tavern which has been in that business since 1492, and try to recall what event in American history occurred in that year. Since you are going to Ghent, I inclose letters to Fredericq, who is a delightful and loveable man, and to Pirenne,[134] who is a wonderful thinking machine, reminding me much of Haskins. I did not stay at any hotel in Bruges, merely going over for the day from Ghent. But the hotel in Ghent was to me an extremely pleasant one. I am pretty sure that it was called Hotel de la Poste, and I know that it was on the square called the Kouter, which will surely identify it. They had an excellent Grave there. It may interest you to see where the Treaty of Ghent was negotiated and signed. I am not very sure about it. A local antiquary gave an account of the matter in one of the newspapers, which I will send to you if I can find it. But when I got home, in examining the Memoirs of John Quincy Adams I did not think that everything harmonized. However, the story was that the Americans lived in the Hotel Schamp and the British at a former convent, the name of which I have forgotten. The meetings were held alternately at these two abodes, and the treaty was signed at the latter.[135] The Hotel Schamp is now a part of a department store, whose floor-walkers were considerably astonished by my exhibiting an interest in one of their second story rooms, which looked to me to be the main salon of the old hotel. Pirenne can tell you the name of the antiquary. He lived over on the Boulevard St. Michel, I think, though I did not find him in. All my notes are up at the house, so please excuse these vague indications. . . .

To FORMER STUDENTS

October 6, 1909.

Dear Friend and "Former Student":

On the evening before my fiftieth birthday I was, not unnaturally, "considering how my life was spent." Without overmuch beating of the breast or tearing of the hair, I was coming rapidly and easily to the conclusion that I had not played my hand nearly so well as I ought, when a letter was brought in which, brief and simple as it was, immediately changed the whole aspect of the matter. I said to myself at once, and have been saying to myself ever since, that if seventy-five such persons, men and women who are doing such work and occupying such positions in the world, could think well enough of me and my twenty-four years of teaching to write such a letter as that, I had no right ever to feel discouraged. I thank you from the bottom of my heart, dear friend, you and your associates, for your kind thought, your affectionate remembrance, your good wishes. You have increased the happiness with which I always think of the best of those whom I taught, and have made my whole life seem to me better worth while.[136]

I should have been more than content with your friendly letter had it stood alone. But when I got back to Washington, a few days ago, I found in my hall a truly magnificent Tiffany clock, one of the handsomest I ever saw—so handsome indeed that I ought immediately to have the hall re-papered, and get a new suit of clothes! But whether I can ever succeed in living up to it or not, it will be a source of pride and pleasure to me all my days. I thank you most heartily for your part in this beautiful gift, and cordially hope that you will come soon to see it. It is so placed that it is the first thing I see as I enter my house, and I never see it without grateful and happy thoughts of those who sent it.

With the best of wishes, and especially, if you are teaching, with the hope that you may have such men and women to teach as I have had, I am, as always,

To J. LEROY WHITE

October 11, 1909.

My dear Mr. White:[137]

Before my return to Washington one of my assistants had gone over with some care the matters regarding which you inquire in your letter of September 10, and since my return I have myself gone over the ground

---

[134] Henri Pirenne, professor of history at Ghent, who, with Professor Fredericq, was imprisoned by the Germans during the First World War, as appears in later letters.

[135] See *Papers of James A. Bayard*, 1796-1815, *Ann. Rept., Amer. Hist. Assn.*, 1913: 1: 332, ns. 3, 4.

[136] The letter read: "September 19, Dear Professor Jameson, We, your former students, hope that you will accept this birthday present as a mark of our gratitude, appreciation, and warmest regards." Among the names signed were those of Woodrow Wilson, F. J. Turner, J. M. Vincent, C. M. Andrews, W. W. and W. F. Willoughby, D. R. Dewey, Clarence S. Brigham, Charles McCarthy, Mary E. Woolley, H. B. Gardner, Clarence A. Dykstra.

Jameson's letter seems to imply that there had been a letter from this group before the appearance of the clock, but if so it has disappeared.

[137] Julian LeRoy White, brother of Henry White, was a student in Jameson's Hopkins class on the development of modern historiography. Though the family was a Baltimore one, much of the early life of the two sons was spent in France and there Julian later made his home.

with some thoroughness.[138] I regret to say that at the end of it all I cannot see how one can be perfectly sure of the answer to your question respecting the Duc de Lauzun. As you have perceived, he does not himself say in his Memoirs anything that answers the question, whether he was personally present on the occasion of the Yorktown surrender. Unfortunately no other writer whom we have consulted—and I think that we must have got hold of nearly every original authority— indicates specifically his presence. On general grounds it would be extremely unlikely that he should have been absent from such a ceremony, save for one thing: You will have noticed that he and his command were posted on the Gloucester side, under the command of M. de Choisy. Now in the arrangements for the surrender General Washington made a separate occasion of the evacuation of the British works at Gloucester and of the surrender of the troops there, appointing a time for it one hour later than the hour he designated for the surrender in Yorktown proper. Lauzun being one of the two chief commanders under Choisy, he would perhaps have had duties that detained him in Gloucester at the great moment; yet in view of his temperament, we may be pretty sure that he would have got away if possible, and crossed over to see the more interesting spectacle. In short, to my regret, I do not see how we can be sure.

Your second question is happily more easy to answer. It is certain that Count Mathieu Dumas was aide-de-camp to Rochambeau.

Regretting very much that I should not have been able to help you more, I am, with the kindest regards,

To WORTHINGTON C. FORD

January 24, 1910.

Dear Ford:

. . . I had a good talk with Senator Root[139] a few days ago. I wish that I could have got the chance last spring. I knew that it would be profitable and lamented

that I was laid up in the hospital at about the only time when he could have been seen with some ease. After I got around again he was so tied up with tariff matters that he politely declined to give any attention to the matter. At my request he lately introduced in the Senate the same bill which has been introduced in the House.[140] I thought that as a move this would have a good effect. When I came to talk with him about it, and he really applied his mind to the bill—which he had not done when introducing it—it was very interesting to see what a group of criticisms his experience and ingenuity suggested. To put briefly his main points, he thought that the bill as it stood would never pass either House. It in reality gave little power, because, as we know, it must be followed up by appropriations to permit anything to be done; but it appeared to give wide powers, wide enough to excite opposition. He said it was always best, if one could, to fall into line with the sentiments temporarily strong in the mind of Congress; that among such sentiments there was at present a widespread impatience with the waste of public money on any printing; that one would do well to join a definite and restricted and not alarming function in this direction, with a provision for constructive work so phrased as to give latitude subsequently. He made some textual suggestions which I have worked up into a draft. I mean to consult him about it as soon as I can and then to talk of it with McCall, whose committee fortunately has not yet succeeded in getting a quorum since the hearing. I will not send you the draft now because when the mental engine of the Senator from New York gets through with it it may look like something very different. The ideas were, to provide that before starting in on any historical publication the head of a department shall, and a committee of Congress may, require the opinion of the Commission (the commission to serve without compensation). That it should annually report, should have power to recommend things of its own, and to execute them if approved by Congress.

If McCall thinks as Root does, that the present bill cannot pass the House, I think it would be better for his committee to put it into somewhat the shape suggested above. If it can get through the House in the present shape, Senator Root being a member of the Library Committee would have plenty of chance to put it into whatever shape would best pass the Senate.

I feel bound to report to the chairman of our committee from time to time, but you understand that one gets various opinions, various bits of news, and that I

---

[138] In 1907 M. Jean Paul Laurens of Paris was commissioned to paint four panels for the Baltimore court house. Of the $13,000 to be paid for them, the Daughters of the American Revolution contributed $2000, the Municipal Art Society, of which White was one of the founders, $1000, and the city, the rest. The picture—the surrender of Cornwallis at Yorktown —was exhibited at the Paris Salon in May, 1910, then unveiled in the orphans' court room of the Baltimore court house on Dec. 8, 1910.

The questions which Jameson was considering were those raised from time to time by White, in his endeavor to aid the artist in achieving historical accuracy. Some time before this he had asked whether O'Hara, deputed by Cornwallis to make the surrender, presented his sword to General Rochambeau or to Washington, whether Washington took the sword or deputed General Lincoln to do so, and whether French ships were sufficiently close to the shore to appear in the picture.

[139] Elihu Root, after serving as Secretary of War and Secretary of State, was between 1909 and 1915 United States senator.

[140] This was House bill no. 15428, the McCall bill, which was, with some modifications, the bill drafted by the subcommittee of historians who served under the Keep Commission. The core of the bill was the creation of a committee of historians who should advise the government on its documentary publications. A hearing on the bill had taken place early in January and this Jameson had reported to the absent members of his committee on Jan. 7 and 8.

am not likely to report them all but shall have to act on the sum total of them as occasion arises. Meanwhile, of course I am very eager for suggestions.

To Edward B. Krehbiel

February 9, 1910.

My dear Krehbiel:[141]

I do not feel any doubt that it would be better for you not to undertake to write a text-book of the sort which is suggested to you, or indeed of any sort. It is a moderately useful service to historical progress, though there are plenty of good text-books now and the need is a publisher's need rather than a real one. That is to say, the same dinner that will persuade a school committee to adopt our readers may also just as well persuade them to adopt our geographies and histories; therefore let us have a complete line of goods. If not justified from the point of view of helping the science, I am clear that it is the reverse of expedient for you personally. Nobody ought to write a text-book at your age. Nearly all one's earlier published work should be research work. Textbooks should come about the last thing in a man's career, and if thereby they get crowded out it is no great harm.

There, you cannot say that you have applied to me for advice and not got it. Rarely indeed would one fail to get my advice about the text-book question. It must needs be that text-books come, but woe to that man by whom the text-book cometh. . . .

To Julian LeRoy White

February 15, 1910.

My dear Mr. White:

It is a pleasure to get your letter of January 28, and to attempt to answer it. One part of it I am confident that I can answer well.[142] Professor Charles H. Haskins of Harvard, whom you may have known at the Johns Hopkins, where he was quite the infant prodigy of his day, getting his A.B. at seventeen and his Ph.D. at twenty, is by all odds our chief expert in all matters of the history of Normandy in the period of Ordericus Vitalis. I should feel quite confident that he would be strongly interested in the proposed memorial. It may be safer for me to write to him, as I will do today, and ask him if he is disposed to take an interest in the

matter to write to you to that effect. If the Executive Council of the American Historical Association were asked to name a representative, they would surely pitch upon him. He has published a number of valuable articles in the history of Anglo-Norman institutions, and has spent many weeks first and last in the archives of the various Norman cities.

I do not think that it will be appropriate that the Carnegie Institution should be represented on such a committee. I believe that the central authorities of the Institution prefer to avoid such relations.

Besides Mr. Haskins, I should think that Professor Melville M. Bigelow of the Boston University Law School, Professor George B. Adams of Yale University, and perhaps Mr. Justice Oliver Wendell Holmes of the Supreme Court, would by reason of personal studies be interested in this project.[143] It is possible also that Mr. Henry Adams might be interested in it because of his work on the Cathedral of Chartres. He is in Washington now but I suppose that in April he goes to 23 Avenue du Bois de Boulogne, Paris, where he spends half the year.

I do not think that I can do equally well with your other question. I do not feel that my own knowledge entitles me to an opinion on the question, how necessary the French aid was to the American cause, or how useful it proved to be. I do not believe that any authoritative pronouncement has been made upon the matter in recent years, especially from the point of view of the military expert. I should think that one would still have to make his own conclusions from Tower, Doniol, Durand, Lecky, and the like. Only two recent books of importance on the general history of the Revolution have been appearing. One is a good but not large book in Professor Hart's series entitled "The American Nation," namely, Professor C. H. Van Tyne's *American Revolution*. It is a good general survey by a man of much capacity on the political side but not particularly qualified to judge in military questions. The bibliographical appendixes to his book, however, would give useful references to all the important recent books. The other book, Sir George Trevelyan's brilliant but doubtless too amiable *History of the American Revolution* has in the three volumes thus far published arrived only at the end of 1777, and therefore would hardly meet your views. If Major John Bigelow, Jr., had ever yet brought out his military history of the American Revolution it would be more illuminating for the purposes which you have in mind. Perhaps sometime you will

---

[141] Edward B. Krehbiel (1878-1950), Ph.D., University of Chicago, 1906, regarded by Jameson as one of the best of his graduate students. He was associate and instructor in history in the university from 1906 to 1909, and in 1910 became associate professor of European history in Stanford University. He later left university work for a career in business.

[142] Mr. White's first question was, what American societies would like to be represented on a committee to create a memorial to the Norman historian Ordericus Vitalis. The plan, originating with an historical society in the Department of the Orne, was to buy and preserve the ruins of the Abbey of St. Evroult.

[143] A second letter from Jameson to White explained that his reason for suggesting Mr. Justice Holmes was "the extent and thoroughness of his earlier researches in Anglo-Norman jurisprudence. . . . If anybody could persuade him to take up with interest the matter which you have at heart, I should think it would be your brother [Henry White]." Justice Holmes firmly declined, on the ground that he accepted no invitations of this kind and could make no exceptions; Mr. Haskins was appointed official representative of the American Historical Association.

get a chance to talk with him about it. He is now a professor at the Massachusetts Institute of Technology.

To Justin H. Smith

April 5, 1910.

My dear Mr. Smith:

I might have written earlier in response to your letter of March 24, but have been, for a wonder, absent from Washington. Last week, from Tuesday to Saturday inclusive, Burr of Cornell, my friend Christie of Meadville, for whom the small boy is named,[144] and I were occupied in a walking tour along the old National Road, starting from Cumberland, Maryland, and walking across the Alleghenies to Uniontown, Pennsylvania. It was a pleasant trip and did us all much good.

I am glad that you came into contact seasonably with Villard. I do not believe for a moment that he would have taken the pains that you have taken, and while he is very clever, I doubt if he is very solid. As to impartiality, he might however have achieved it in spite of starting with some prejudices, for in the matter of John Brown he must have started with a certain set of fixed opinions derived from his grandfather's circle; and yet I understand that the book, when it appears, will be very far from taking the conventional Abolitionists' view of Brown. But this may not be so; I have not seen the book.[145] Anyhow, it is probably better that not too many books on one subject should come out in one generation, and certainly better that A should escape disappointment by learning early that B has already written his book much better than he himself would. A melancholy aspect of the matter is that if you sit still in an office as I do, dictating letters and receiving publisher's notices, you gradually find that all books you ever thought of writing are being done, and in many cases done very brown, by more active or freer spirits. Not that I am very melancholy about it, however, having plenty to do in other lines, and, since my walk, an improved appetite and digestion. . . .

To Evarts B. Greene

April 26, 1910.

My dear Dr. Greene:[146]

I hope that it is not an impertinence for me to write

to you respecting the invitation which you have had from the Johns Hopkins University, for though neither they nor you have asked me to do so, I am so much interested in their success that I cannot help "butting in." Nearly all the elements of your personal problem are as well known to you as to me, and some of them much better. But if, as I suppose, you have not had a great deal to do with the Hopkins, it may be useful and not inappropriate for me to dwell upon one consideration, and that is, the admirable spirit and atmosphere which pervades that institution. It seems to me quite remarkable how well President Remsen and his colleagues have preserved to the present time that high spirit and clear atmosphere of disinterested scholarship with which the institution started, or which it had in the days when I lived there—halcyon days of an institution then new in type, when it was "joy to be alive, and to be young was very heaven." As time has gone on and graduate schools have multiplied, I have been often extremely disturbed to see in various universities so many signs of commercial or numerical standards of competitive struggle, of academic jealousy. I really think that the Hopkins has kept itself singularly free from these ambitions and mundane desires, and that you would find there still an extraordinary measure of the true spirit of scholarship. I think that you would also greatly enjoy the social spirit of Baltimore, which is singularly genial, springing from unusually warm hearts.

Perhaps I do not need to add, but I will do so, that the pleasure of having you so near at hand would be to me personally a very great one, and that you could always count upon me to help the work of your department by any means that lie within the scope of such a department as this.

To Hubert Hall

April 28, 1910.

My dear Hall:

I see in the *Athenaeum* of April 16, an article relating to my last annual report, concerning the author of which I am able to make a confident guess.[147] I will not be so importunate as to attempt to lift the veil of anonymity. But if you should ever see the writer you might say to him that such extremely amiable treatment of our modest establishment and its plans is in the highest degree gratifying to the undersigned. It is not only extremely

[144] Francis Christie Jameson, born in 1908.

[145] Justin H. Smith had been contemplating writing a book on John Brown but had just learned of the appearance of Villard, Oswald Garrison, *John Brown—a biography fifty years after,* N. Y., Houghton Mifflin, 1910. Villard (1872-1949), grandson of William Lloyd Garrison, was at this time president of the New York *Evening Post.* His *John Brown* was described by a reviewer—James A. Hosmer—as "painstaking and judicial" (*Amer. Hist. Rev.* **16**: 648-649, April, 1911).

[146] Evarts B. Greene (1870-1947) had been a member of the department of history of the University of Illinois since 1894 and since 1906 had been dean of the college of liberal arts. He did not accept the call to the Johns Hopkins University but in 1923 left Illinois for Columbia.

[147] The report referred to, covering the period from Nov. 1, 1908, to Oct. 31, 1909, is to be found in the *Year Book* of the Carnegie Institution, 1909: 108-124. The article in the *Athenaeum* began by saying: "The Annual Report of the Department of Historical Research in the Carnegie Institution at Washington has become an event of importance on both sides of the Atlantic." After some discussion of the distinguished character of the work being done, the author went on, "This distinction is partly due to the peculiar genius of American students for the discovery of historical sources, partly also to the administrative ability, wide interests, and scholarly methods of the Director" (*Athenaeum,* Apr. 16, 1910: 460).

amiable, but excessively so. I can hardly recognize in this glowing description the department concerning whose operations I have so often of late been distinctly despondent. Probably a man, without wishing to deceive his trustees or the public, puts his best foot foremost in his annual report. I wish to Heaven that we were, or were likely to be, anything like as successful as the *Athenaeum* writer represents. However this may turn out, it is not in human nature not to be gratified by the throwing upon our modest stage of so large and fragrant a bouquet, even though the donor's card is not instantly to be found among the leaves and petals. So give the kindly, and partially misled, writer my cordial thanks if you find any opportunity.

I may do well to say for your own information a little more regarding my plans for Paxson and Paullin than I have perhaps communicated in former letters.[148] The report proposed the making of a Guide to the materials in American history subsequent to 1783, in London archives. I knew of course that there was an *if*—if the official permissions in London should be secured. I hope that it did not seem presumptuous to assume this; but this report was primarily addressed to our Trustees, whose consent to my programme for 1910 had first to be obtained and I could not ask for the official permissions in London until the Trustees approved the scheme. Earlier in the present year, however, I got our Secretary of State to instruct the American Ambassador in London[149] to make all the necessary applications with respect to papers over which the ministerial departments have control, and I hope that all such permissions will have been secured by the time Paxson and Paullin arrive in London. Sir Almeric FitzRoy has already promised the needful privileges at the Privy Council Office. I shall of course wish to give the two agents letters of introduction to you (though no doubt you already know Paxson), and while I do not wish them to be a bother to you and a further tax upon your already burdened life, yet I do not suppose that I can keep you from being kind to them and helping them to start right. Paullin sails May 2, but will spend a few weeks on the Continent and will not arrive in London until early in June, probably a few days before Paxson, who sails June 11. Paxson will have three months in London, his academic vacation. Paullin, who is "particulier" not attached to any institution, will be able to stay in London at least five months. In the main the former will naturally attend to Foreign Office papers; the latter, who has been chiefly a student of American naval history, will attend to the Admiralty and War Office papers. As to the Colonial Office papers, various less directly important collections, and those of the British Museum, they will concert a plan between them for covering that territory, though perhaps more of it will fall to Paullin's share than to Paxson's. One of my assistants, as a means of saving their time, has been making as good a catalogue of the British Museum manuscripts relating to American history subsequent to 1783 as can be made from the printed catalogues of the Museum. This they will have in many cases to check up with the manuscript volumes themselves. She has also made a list of the documents presumably in the archives, relating to that period of American history, which are accessible in print in the *American State Papers* and the *British and Foreign State Papers*.

I admit that their time will probably seem a little short. But I suppose that the material must be much less miscellaneous than for the period covered by Andrews; secondly, there will be these aids; thirdly, they can probably use more clerical help than Andrews did, their material lying more largely in long uniform series; and it is after all but a preliminary survey, which I should like to get out pretty soon in order to encourage workers.

I do not lose from mind the private collections of which the writer in the *Athenaeum* speaks. But these are a slower task and must take their place later in our operations. As to archives in the British Chancery here, their counsellor told me two or three years ago that they did not preserve papers beyond a small number of years in the past. I do not know that he said definitely twenty, but I imagine that it is something like that. There is rather a puzzle about this matter, by the way. When I came to Washington I assumed that there was a good deal of material in the embassies and legations of the different states here. Such inquiries as I have made have uniformly been answered in the negative. The statement is that after ten or twenty years everything is sent back to the metropolis. Yet Leland tells me that he has not yet come across in Paris any masses apparently sent back from Washington, and I do not think that Fish heard of any such in Rome. How is this in London?

I do not yet know what I shall do about Canada. The fundamental question is, whether the new stuff which Orders in Council of five or six years ago ordered to be turned in to the archive building has yet been reduced to a permanent classification. Although I had no desire to "indulge in caustic remarks" on the reclassification in London, and am sorry if I seemed to give that tone to what I said, nevertheless I have no mind to start the making of a guide to Ottawa until

---

[148] Charles O. Paullin and Frederic L. Paxson, whose *Guide to the materials in London archives for the history of the United States since 1783* appeared in 1914. Paullin became a permanent member of the research staff of the department in 1911; Paxon joined the faculty of the University of Wisconsin in 1910.

[149] Philander C. Knox (1853-1921) was Secretary of State from Mar. 6, 1909, to 1913. The American ambassador, Whitelaw Reid (1837-1912), was appointed by Theodore Roosevelt in 1905.

a relatively permanent arrangement has been effected.[150] I expected to go up to Ottawa last week but have had to defer it for a few weeks more. Doughty is not a man from whom one can get full information on such questions by letter, and anyhow, there is much to be gained by seeing people myself beforehand.

I have lately sent to press Fish's report on Roman and other Italian archives, and Allison's inventory of materials for American religious history.[151] I do not know when they will be out. Carnegie Institution printing always goes slowly. Robertson's list of documents in the Spanish archives might be out by now if he had not had to go to Manila and take the galleys with him.[152] . . .

By the way, I do not know that I have told you that I have much ampler quarters now—seven rooms where I used to have three; but we are so far from the Library of Congress that I am still clamoring for a small special building.

P. S. Just after this was written there comes a letter from the Department of State saying that a dispatch from the American Ambassador in London states that Paxson and Paullin "will be allowed to see the correspondence of the Foreign Office, the Colonial Office, and the Admiralty down to the year 1837, but that as the records between that date and the year 1860 are now in use for official purposes, it will not be possible to allow Professor Paxson and Dr. Paullin to examine them for the present. Mr. Reid adds that the correspondence of the War Office, however, is open to inspection by the public down to the year 1850, but the date to which the archives of that Department are accessible beyond that year depends on the class of documents to which access is desired."

This date 1837 is very disappointing, inasmuch as E. D. Adams[153] and Justin Smith seem to have been allowed to see things down to 1848. I shall hope, however, that when they are upon the ground the two men may find it possible to push their researches down to a later point. Can you give me advice as to how this should be done? In my letter to the Secretary of State I asked to have the ambassador seek permissions running to 1848.

To EDMOND S. MEANY

April 29, 1910.

My dear Professor Meany:[154]

Thank you for your pamphlet on the name of the American war of 1861-1865. I have read the debate with interest.[155] I am willing to give you my opinion as to the proper name for that war and to state briefly my reasons. But I am not willing to be quoted, because I am editor of the *American Historical Review,* and nine persons out of ten who should not like my choice of name or my reasons respecting it would say, especially in the South, that that showed a fixed attitude of the *American Historical Review* toward the questions involved. In reality it shows nothing of the sort, as I do not think it proper that the personal opinions of the editor in any of those many historical matters which he

---

[150] The "caustic" remark was: "Much sympathy must be felt for Professor Andrews, who will in the end have been compelled to reconstruct nearly every section of his manuscript, and who has already devoted to it more time than a scholar of his eminence would ever willingly devote to the details of such a task" (*Year Book,* Carnegie Institution, 1909: 114).

[151] Fish's *Guide to the materials for American history in Roman and other Italian archives* and Allison's *Inventory of unpublished material for American religious history in Protestant church archives and other repositories,* Carnegie Institution, publications nos. 128, 137, bear the dates 1911 and 1910 respectively. The genesis of the last-named publication has some interest. In the session of the Association meeting of 1905 on church history the church historians present asked for a considerable increase in their share in the activities of the Association. Among other things they requested that the scope of the Public Archives Commission be extended to include denominational archives, and that they be given representation on the Historical Manuscripts Commission. The fact that the reports of the two commissions were printed as government documents by the Smithsonian Institution, which avoided anything with a taint of religious implication, placed obstacles in the way of granting these requests but they stirred Jameson to think of another way to provide a survey of church archives. "An idea has occurred to me over night. If I can get a certain man to do it, and I think I can, I will avoid all difficulty about the Public Archives Commission and give a good forward push to the movement that the church history people desire by causing the preparation this year, as a part of the work of this Department, of an extensive systematic report on all the accessible archives of the religious denominations and missionary societies of the United States. I think this would give real satisfaction to the church history movement,

be in itself a very useful thing to do, and, what interests me as much as any aspect of it, would emphasize from the beginning the disposition to regard with a catholic eye the social and cultural history of the United States rather than to confine itself to the merely constitutional and political. Do you approve?" (Jameson to F. A. Christie, Jan. 13, 1906; see also Christie to G. B. Adams, Jan. 8, 1906, and Jameson to Christie, Jan. 11, 1906, Jameson Papers, and the letter of Nov. 8, 1910, in this volume). The "certain man" was William H. Allison (1870-1941), who had received his Ph.D. degree from the University of Chicago in 1905, had taught history in Bryn Mawr, 1908-1910, and was soon to take a position as professor of ecclesiastical history in Colgate University. See *post,* Jameson to Allison, Jan. 17, 1911.

[152] James A. Robertson (1873-1939) was from 1910 till 1916 librarian of the Philippine library in Manila. Both before and after this work he was attached for brief periods to the Department of Historical Research of the Carnegie Institution. His *List of documents in Spanish archives relating to the history of the United States, which have been printed or of transcripts which are preserved in American libraries,* Carnegie Institution, publication no. 124, appeared in 1910.

[153] In 1910 Adams published *British interests and activities in Texas,* Albert Shaw Lectures in Diplomatic History, Baltimore, Johns Hopkins University Press, 1910, and it may have been in connection with this work that he obtained access to British records.

[154] Edmond S. Meany (1862-1935), professor of history in the University of Washington from 1897 until his death.

[155] *Name of the American War of 1861-1865,* Seattle, 1910, Debate in the United States Senate, Jan. 11, 1907.

conceives to be open to two interpretations should influence the conduct of the Review.

This being made clear, I will say that I prefer the term "Civil War." I believe that the term "War of the Rebellion" is historically correct. But there is an odious sound about the word "rebel" and it is objectionable to many persons, though evidently not to several of the Southern representatives appearing in the debate of 1907. And if I should use the term "War of the Rebellion" without saying more, it would not always be plain that I was fully aware of the considerations which made the war to those who engaged in it something quite different from a rebellion in the ordinary sense. That the war could not properly be termed a *civil* war, is new doctrine to me. The phrase "civil war" to my mind is perfectly applicable to every war the contestants in which have previously been living under the same government. I see nothing in the term which can make it inapplicable to every case that is complicated by the existence of federated states. It would surprise me that anyone should be reluctant to apply the term "civil war" to the Swiss conflict of 1847, or to the Thirty Years' War in Germany. The term "civil war" has also the advantage that it is the term most commonly employed in one language or another by European historians referring to our war.

It seems to me preposterous that anyone should expect a citizen of the present United States to call our war of 1861-1865 the "War between the States." Peace, kind feeling, and magnanimity are all excellent traits; but here when a conflict is admitted to have settled for all time a great constitutional question and given it the answer which the Federal Government constantly maintained that it should have—why should those living under that government stultify its course and deny positions steadily maintained by the executive, legislative, and judiciary, by adopting a name which can be justified only by adopting and approving the constitutional doctrines of the secessionists? If we are in 1910 bound to accept their doctrines as then and now the only correct doctrines, we have a basis for using the term "War between the States." If we are not so bound—and I think it needs no argument to show that we are not so bound—it was a war in which we had on one side the government and forces of the federal republic, and on the other side a body of dissentients, most of whom, to be sure, understood themselves to be seceding with their states, but many of whom were from states that had not seceded, and who as a whole had no common basis but that of opposition to the Federal Government.[156]

---

[156] Many years later, as chief of the Division of Manuscripts of the Library of Congress, Dr. Jameson expressed the same opinion even more emphatically: "I . . . regard 'The War between the States' as entirely improper, especially for use by any establishment under the charge of the United States Government. . . . It was not a war between the states in any proper sense, but a war against the United States by an

To Charles W. Needham

May 2, 1910.

My dear President Needham:[157]

Though I am outside the immediate circle of George Washington University affairs, I do not like to let the newspaper announcement of your resignation pass without expressing for my own part my deep regret. I feel this not solely because you have been so uniformly kind and friendly to me from the time of my coming to Washington, but also because I have been so cordially interested in the success of the experiment which you were making. The transformation of the old college into a modern city university, with endowments and operations of a magnitude worthy the national capital, was from the first not certain to succeed. But it was a noble endeavor, it deserved success, and it seemed to have such very good chances of success that the attempt was well warranted. I am sure that it must have been deeply interesting to engage in such a venture. I hope you will feel that it has also been rewarding, for while you have made many sacrifices for it, and I suppose are making one now, it is impossible not to feel that all this devoted work has borne a great fruit in the public mind, and that, although we may not be certain as to the form in which it will work itself out, it will surely take effect in ways highly valuable to the young people of the District. I wish therefore to congratulate you heartily on having done, with so much intelligence and in so admirable a spirit, so much good work for their ultimate benefit.

To Frances G. Davenport

Preces pro Sorore Francisca a Sancta Clara in navem ascensura.[158]

---

aggregation of states and individuals. The contestant on the Southern side was doubtless an aggregation of states. To represent the contestant on the Northern side as consisting simply of an aggregation of states is to deny the doctrine on which the United States fought the war and which it has always since maintained" (Jameson to Clifford Millard, July 2, 1937, Division of Manuscripts, Library of Congress).

[157] Charles W. Needham (1848-1935), who helped to frame the charter of the University of Chicago and served as one of its early trustees, first served as professor of law in the Columbian University of Washington and then as its president (1902-1910). He was responsible for changing the name of the institution to George Washington University; he originated its School of Comparative Jurisprudence and Diplomacy; and applied to the Congress for an amendment to its charter, enlarging its powers and making it non-sectarian. After his resignation from the presidency of the university he remained in Washington, acting as solicitor with the Interstate Commerce Commission and delivering lectures on legal ethics and constitutional law at the Washington College of Law and the American University.

[158] To Frances G. Davenport, who was sailing for England, to work on her edition of *European treaties bearing on the history of the United States and its dependencies to 1648,* the first volume of which appeared in 1917, Carnegie Institution, publication no. 254.

May 25, 1910.

Lord of the sea, revered Neptunus,
    List, oh list to our humble prayer!
Aeolus, Auster, Notus, Eurus,
    Dreaded powers of the upper air,
Gods above and winds below,
    Favor our friend where'er she go!

Wit ye not, ye winds and waters,
    How precious a freight ye now receive?
Learned'st of all of Adam's daughters
    (Doubtless also of those of Eve)
Peril to her, in the tempest's jaws,
    Is peril to History's holy cause.

Wit ye not how anxious nations,
    Wearily looking for wars to cease,
Wait for some of her annotations,
    Gatling guns in the fight for peace?
Wait for the message, "My book is done
    (Washington, 1921)"?

Smooth ye, then, the floor of ocean,
    Smooth as a diplomatic note;
Calm ye, then, the waves' commotion,
    Calm as the fall of Woman's vote.
Hold your blasts within your den,
    Carry her safe across, and then,
When her treatise on treaties
    At last complete is,
Bring her unharmed to us again.

To WILLIAM E. BURGHARDT DuBOIS

June 22, 1910.

My dear Professor DuBois:[159]

On my return from Maine and Indiana I find here your letter of June 13. It astonishes and afflicts me very much, that I, grandson of an old Abolitionist, brought up to know no difference between black and white, and still—so far as I can see—without a trace of that race prejudice which I see to exist but cannot comprehend, should be thought to inflict upon a professional colleague, contributing to this journal, anything which he can regard as a personal insult. The word "negro" is not a proper noun, not an indication of nationality but of physical traits. We have always held in this journal that it should no more be capitalized than white man, brown man, or red man, or than the Spanish *negro*, black. So far as I have been able to look into the matter without going to the Library of Congress (which is impossible because I leave town

tonight), the authority of dictionaries runs in the same way, and apparently their opinion is based on the same argument. It would be making no more of the white man to capitalize that phrase; it is making no less of the negro to leave the word not capitalized. The question is simply one of typography. I cannot admit that the maintenance of uniform practice with regard to such matters is a small thing. To print "the church" in all our articles for fifteen years and then suddenly and in one article alone to capitalize "the Church" would be nothing short of ridiculous and would justly expose us to the charge of having no typographical standards. The typography of this journal stands, I believe rather high in the scale, and we value our reputation for consistency as well as for accuracy. We should never be above making improvements, but we have never agreed to alter our standards for one article alone, at the request of any contributor. I shall hope that it will ultimately appear to you that we have not treated you in any other manner than that in which we have treated every other contributor from the beginning of the journal.

Believe me, with high regard and with many thanks for the article,

To SARA JAMESON

For Sara's——th birthday, July 29, 1910.

A birthday ode how can a bard compose,
Unless the number of the years he knows?
And this, so needful to the poet's strain,
Even the census man could not obtain.
An English bard there was, well known to fame,
Who "lisped in numbers, for the numbers came";
But shall the Yankee bard perforce be dumb
Because the proper number will not come?
Rather by bold conjecture let him fix
Upon a date. Then art thou thirty-six,
Oh Rose of Youth, Immediate Child of Heaven?
Or can it be that thou art thirty-seven?
Or must one seize a still anterior date,
And, hesitating, hold thee thirty-eight?
Or can it be, in spite of every sign,
That thou hast reached the goal of thirty-nine?
Dost thou the sacred number forty touch?
It is incredible; too much, too much!
Conjecturing pen, no more, audacious run,
Stop ere thou name the name of forty-one.
Art getting warm? Avaunt, 't will never do
To hint at such a thing as forty-two.
But why with numbers palter and with years,
While still the smiling bride her circle cheers?
While still the matron plays her youthful part
With charms unnumbered and unaging heart?
Live on, live on, dear subject of my rhyme,
Disdaining numbers and defying time!

[159] William E. Burghardt Du Bois, of the University of Atlanta, had contributed to the *Amer. Hist. Rev.* **15**: 781-799, Reconstruction and its benefits. On receiving proof of his article he protested against the printing of the word "negro" with a small letter.

To Andrew C. McLaughlin

North Edgecomb, Maine,
August 4, 1910.

Dear McLaughlin:

I send you herewith a check of $1.98, from your excellent institution. I think that I wrote you about this a year ago. When Langlois gave this very excellent lecture at the University he expressed a desire that the university should print it, supposing it to be a matter of course.[160] I found, as one who dealt with the financial branch of your revered institution was apt to find, that there was nothing doing, except on a cash basis. A benevolent individual gave me most of the money, and I blew in the rest, with which I could persuade the University of Chicago Press to print the thing at its usual high rates. The bread thus cast upon the waters had all come back to me a year ago. The donor of the main sum would, I am sure, wish that the small dividends annually declared upon the gift enterprise alluded to above should go to the Historical Department of the University. So I endorse the check, and at the same time will say, as I said a year ago, that if you wish to take over this "best seller" in order that the Historical Department may be if possible more rapidly benefitted by it than by this slow process of annual returns, I will cheerfully hand over my rights therein. In the contrary case, this letter requires no reply, though it is always pleasant to hear from you.

To Frederick M. Kerby

North Edgecomb, Maine,
August 23, 1910.

My dear Sir:[161]

Your letter of August 10, after various forwardings and missendings, has reached me here. I thank you for the compliment implied. But I have lived a life at once so virtuous and so inconspicuous that there has never been any need of a photograph of me in any newspaper, and I imagine that this will continue to be the case. So, as I have at hand no photograph at all, I hope that I may be excused from complying with your request.

To Rafael Altamira y Crevea

North Edgecomb, Maine,
August 25, 1910.

My dear Sir:[162]

I beg leave to recall myself to your recollection as one who had the privilege of being introduced to you at the meeting of the American Historical Association in New York, though unhappily your engagements permitted me to have much less of the pleasure of your company than I wished. You have, however, shown yourself in all ways so friendly toward American historical workers that I venture to ask your advice in a matter of importance which puzzles me.

In dealing with the materials for American history in foreign archives my plan for this Department is that we shall for each important country prepare, first, a general and summary guide, then proceed, secondly, to the more explicit calendaring of some section or sections which have the highest importance for our history, and perhaps proceed, in the third place, to full copying and publication of what restricted portion has the highest claim to such treatment. In the case of the Spanish archives, the first of these processes is represented by Professor Shepherd's "Guide to the Materials for the History of the United States in Spanish Archives (Simancas, the Archivo Historico Nacional, and Seville)," which was published three years ago and which you have doubtless seen.

The time has now come when I can advance from this sketch, which no doubt has been of preliminary use to investigators, to the second stage of procedure. For the whole year 1911 I can have the service in Spain of a very well qualified agent, a young American historical scholar who after living four years in Cuba has been trained in Spanish-American history at Columbia University under Professor Shepherd.[163] I cannot have this opportunity except in the year or fifteen months beginning in January 1911.[164] Naturally I desire to get the utmost possible good for American historical students out of his services in this period of time.

Now the section of the Spanish archives which seems from the account of Professor Shepherd and others to be most deserving of explicit calendaring on our part, both on account of the amount of material, its importance, and its perishing condition, is the section in the Archives of the Indies at Seville called Papeles procedentes de la Isla de Cuba. This great mass of papers, when brought from Cuba in 1886, was found to be infested with the polilla to such a degree that it has never been deemed wise by the archivist to bring it upstairs

---

[160] Langlois, Charles Victor, *The historic rôle of France among the nations,* an address delivered at the University of Chicago, October 18, 1904, Chicago, 1905, reprinted from the *University Record* 9 (10).

Much the same information Jameson had given to McLaugh-

lin in a letter of Aug. 3, 1909, at which time the receipts amounted to thirty-six cents. On Aug. 10, 1911, Jameson reported seventy-two cents.

[161] F. M. Kerby was secretary of the Newspaper Enterprise Association located in Washington.

[162] Rafael Altamira y Crevea, professor in the University of Oviedo, Spain.

[163] Roscoe R. Hill, who had been a graduate student in the University of Chicago while Jameson taught there.

[164] The work on these papers was begun by Mr. Hill in January, 1911, and continued to March, 1913. The body of papers proved too great to calendar but a descriptive list of the bundles was published in 1916: *Descriptive catalogue of the documents relating to the history of the United States in the papeles procedentes de Cuba, deposited in the Archivo General de Indias at Seville,* Carnegie Institution, publication no. 234.

into contact with the remainder of the Archives of the Indies. It has accordingly lain in the basement, slowly, perhaps in some cases rapidly, deteriorating. Documents of priceless value have been found in this mass.

Now to the project of calendaring these manuscripts, important as the task is, there exists one obstacle that is fatal, if it cannot be overcome. It would be vain to make a calendar of a body of papers which have no numbers and whose order of arrangement is not yet fixed, because no references could be given that would guide subsequent investigators. It would be easy to overcome this obstacle by having our agent number the *legajos* as he proceeded. Naturally he might in this process be able to give only a provisional numbering, which the regular officials of the archives might wish to alter completely. But even so, with the aid of a published key from preliminary numbers to final numbers it would be possible to make the calendar a permanent basis for the work of investigators. I speak of this procedure because I have been led to understand that the pecuniary resources of the Archives of the Indies hardly permit the *jefe* to think of causing an orderly arrangement and fixed numbering of these *legajos* within the short time which would elapse before our agent would arrive in Seville.

Against such a procedure there lies the obvious objection, which I am sure any of our American archivists would feel, that it is after all not the business of outsiders to number and arrange bundles or papers; that they may do it in a manner not duly according with the official system locally employed; that they do it without official responsibility to the *jefe*, etc. These objections are so serious that I hesitate to make a direct and formal application to Señor Don Pedro Torres Lanzas of the Archives of the Indies for permission to do what might seem an act of meddlesome interference with archival functions, however it might appear to us as a necessary preliminary to a successful calendaring. I have never had the pleasure of meeting this archivist, though his letters to me have been of the most amiable sort. Another ground of hesitation is that the matter is possibly not within his jurisdiction; that ministerial orders or regulations of the Cuerpo Facultative de Archiveros may stand in the way of permitting one who is not an archive official to do any such provisional arrangement and numbering.

I therefore write to you confidentially to ask you to give me your judgment as to how I should proceed. While I might leave it to the agent to be governed by circumstances and, if he found it impracticable to deal with the Papeles procedentes de la Isla de Cuba, to turn to the Audiencias, or some other collection, of the second degree of importance for United States history, I naturally like better to make definite plans beforehand. I doubt whether the agent is enough of a diplomatist to succeed in bringing about arrangements to which at first there might be some objection. If it is needful, or would give a considerably greater chance

of success to my proposals, I should be prepared to come over to Spain myself, early in January, and use my best endeavors to explain and persuade. But I do not wish to do this unless it is requisite. It would be a great pleasure to me if you would tell me what you think (a) as to the probability of my being able to secure the permission which I desire; (b) as to the means which might best be adopted for securing it by correspondence, in case it is not requisite for me to go over; and (c) as to the steps which might best be taken in correspondence, as preliminaries, in case you deem it best for me to go to the full length in personal endeavors in Spain to discover and meet all possible difficulties and objections. I am, as you see, very anxious to carry through this project, and could not be equally satisfied, as it now appears to me, with any alternative. I am especially moved to this condition of mind by what I have been told of the gradual decay of many of these manuscripts, which I should hope to preserve in the most important instances by large use of photography, in which the designated agent is relatively expert.

I beg you to accept my apologies for troubling you with this long communication respecting my own affairs. If it is ever possible for me to be of service to you in America, you may be sure that I shall be glad of the opportunity.[165]

To CHARLES D. NORTON

North Edgecomb, Maine,
September 7, 1910.

My dear Sir:[166]

I ask leave to trouble you with an inquiry respecting the possibility or the advisability of laying before the President a suggestion intended for use in his annual message to Congress.[167] Various officials of the Government and various persons interested in history have for a long time felt strongly that the Government should have a more satisfactory repository for its archives, in which papers accumulated by the departments but not in current use might be stored in a manner admitting of ready access and consultation, and offering security against fire. So far as the efforts of the Government officials to remedy the situation are concerned, the matter has a long history, running from 1879. Cabinet officials and particularly secretaries of the Treasury have interested themselves in the suggestion of a general archive house, a lot has been acquired, and plans and estimates of a general sort prepared and printed. But there the matter has rested.[168]

Naturally it is with the historical aspects of the matter that I am chiefly concerned. My position with re-

---

[165] In connection with this letter the memorandum, *post*, Mar. 28, 1928, is of interest.

[166] Charles D. Norton was secretary to President Taft.

[167] See *post*, Dec. 12, 1910.

[168] An act of Mar. 3, 1903, Public Act no. 156, authorized a building and provided for the purchase of a site.

lation to the historical profession, as director of this Department and as editor of the "American Historical Review," is somewhat that of an informal consulate in Washington for historians, and I am chairman of a committee (Admiral Mahan, Professor McMaster, and myself) appointed by the Executive Council of the American Historical Association two years ago, to see what could be done to ensure better preservation and housing from our point of view, and to memorialize as found expedient.[169] I have interviewed various persons and have collected a large amount of material regarding the history of the movement and regarding the dangers inherent in the present situation—dangers of pecuniary loss far greater than the cost of a proper archive building. My impression, derived from the history of the matter and from such conversations as I have had in Washington, is that, however heartily the project is approved by individual heads of executive departments, it will not be taken up in earnest by Congress until their attention is pointedly directed to the matter by the President. I cordially wish that the President might be persuaded to insert in his next annual message a brief recommendation upon the subject. If you should deem it expedient I could readily supply a brief memorial as to the need of such a building. It may here suffice to mention, as one typical fact, that the Treasury Department is obliged every few years to hire an additional building in which to store the overflow of papers, and necessarily stores them in such a manner that they are often extremely difficult of access and are highly insecure against damage or destruction.

If after reading any such memorial you should think it expedient, I could readily come to Beverly during the last week of this month, when I shall be in Boston, to supply any further information that might be needed. I believe that a public interest of considerable magnitude is involved in the matter, and that the time is fully ripe for the Government to take the initial steps toward that concentration of archive material in proper repositories (instead of leaving it scattered in a hundred bureaus) which most European governments have carried to a greater or less point of advancement.[170]

To CHARLES MARSHALL GRAVES

October 17, 1910.

Dear Sir:[171]

I reply to your letter of October 15.

While I do not suppose the vote cast by any individual elector for the Hall of Fame is any affair of the public, I have no objection to stating that in the election lately held I cast a vote for Edgar Allan Poe.[172] I did not do this because I supposed him to be a great poet, as apparently a considerable section of the public thinks him to have been. The great poets are surely of much higher class, even in our brief catalogue of American poets I should not put him in the first rank, which I should wish to reserve for poetry exhibiting, along with a keen sense of poetic form, a greater amount of thought than I have ever seen in Poe's verses. But in the list of nominations there were not many literary names of high rank, and I thought that, compared with them, Poe was entitled to one's vote, as a skillful versifier and a clever and forcible writer of short stories.

To HENRY ADAMS

October 31, 1910.

My dear Mr. Adams:

I have duly attended to Mr. Rhode's request and sent him a copy of the *Education*.[173] I am sorry to hear that you are not coming back before Christmas. It would be a pleasure, which I shall miss, to bring around to number 1603 H Street some of the perplexities of my occupation, and have them dissolved in the light of the earnest conviction that they, in common with the whole historical business, do not matter. Meanwhile, I struggle on, making bricks without much idea of how the architects will use them, but believing that the best architect that ever was cannot get along without bricks, and therefore trying to make good ones. I understand philosophical reasonings as little as the estimable Wagner comprehended the remarks of Doctor Faust, but fortunately have an occupation which I do not doubt to be in some degree useful. Over my desk here at the office I keep a photograph of Raphael's School of Athens, which serves to remind me how mankind, though not myself personally, may rise from low mechanic arts

[169] *Ann. Rept., Amer. Hist. Assn.,* 1908: 1: 30. The appointment of this committee was not the first evidence of interest the Association had shown in the proper housing of the papers of the government. At the meeting of 1901 a resolution had been adopted supporting a hall of records (*ibid.,* 1901. 1: 36). For a more complete account than can be given here of Jameson's patient and prolonged efforts to obtain a national archive building, see Shelly, Fred, The interest of J. Franklin Jameson in the National Archives Building, *The American Archivist,* April, 1949.

[170] See *post,* To W. G. Leland, Nov. 21, 1910, n. 180.

[171] Charles Marshall Graves was second assistant to the city editor of the New York *Times.*

[172] The *Times,* Oct. 19, 1910, 10, contains the statement that the paper had asked electors their opinions as to Poe's fitness for a place in the Hall of Fame, the aftermath of the elections of 1900 and 1905 having made it clear that there was a strong popular demand for his choice. On Oct. 22, the *Times* announced: "Poe gets a Place in Hall of Fame," he having received sixty-nine votes and tying with Oliver Wendell Holmes for second place among the eleven elected to the Hall.

[173] "Our amiable friend Rhodes, having got an indigestion from the 'Letter' is now asking for the 'Education.' I wrote him that I thought you could find a copy for him; if he wrote in a sufficiently magisterial tone" (Adams to Jameson, Oct. 21, 1910). The "Letter" was *A letter to American teachers of history,* privately printed, but after the death of Adams included in *The degradation of the democratic dogma.* The "Education" was, of course, *The education of Henry Adams,* also privately printed. Adams had provided Jameson with copies of both books, to be distributed as requests for them were received.

to divine philosophy in the persons of Plato and Aristotle, neither of whose writings I presume to comprehend.

The fame of Eucken has dimly reached me, that of Roosevelt not dimly enough. I believe the Nobel prizes awarded to the two are from different funds, the former, the Swedish foundation for literature, the latter the Norwegian for the promotion of peace.[174] This leaves the matter not less ludicrous in the closing days before election, of 1910, for Roosevelt as he rushes about the State of New York is certainly not, like Lord Falkland at Newbury, "Ingeminating Peace, Peace."[175]

Your brother was here the other day, arranging matters, I am glad to say, to come to Washington earlier than usual this year, I believe about the first of December.

Would it be indiscreet—a phrase we should envy the French—for me to ask the privilege of giving a letter of introduction to you to my assistant and friend, Mr. Waldo G. Leland, now Secretary of the American Historical Association, who is in Paris this autumn and winter? He is a fine young fellow, with many engaging traits, and is occupied, as he has been during the two preceding winters, with the making of a Guide to the materials for American History in the French archives, concerning which you might be able to give him some additional and valuable suggestions.

To Lucius H. Thayer

November 8, 1910.

Dear Lucius :[176]

I wish to speak to you as a member of the Prudential Committee of the American Board regarding a suggestion which has arisen in my mind in connection with one of the publications of this Department. The volume I allude to is "An Inventory of Unpublished Material for American Religious History in Protestant Church Archives and other repositories," prepared by a very competent man of wide knowledge and catholic spirit, Professor William H. Allison of Colgate Theological Seminary, formerly a student of mine at the University of Chicago. The volume is now in press. I undertook the preparation of it because the American church history people wanted to know if I could not do something for the religious history of the United States.[177] I told them I would make this Inventory, and sent a man ranging around through all the archives of denominations and missionary societies, and the libraries of theological schools and denominational colleges. This is a proper and indispensable first step and is in the line of the regular functions of this Department. It will, I think reveal a great variety of interesting materials in American history. When it has appeared, two or three months from now, it will be "up to" the various Protestant bodies to take the steps that come next in the logical processes of history making. I think, by the way, that Ernest Richardson is right in saying that both the Catholics and Jews have surpassed them in documentary historical publication for American history in recent years.[178]

However this may be, I have a thought respecting the archives of the American Board which I should rather like to have you consider, and lay it before the Prudential Committee at a later time if on reflection you see fit. In such an Inventory as Dr. Allison's a deposit of historical materials which consists of isolated letters that have come together by chance and have no organic relation to each other can be treated only by explicit listing. Some other body of papers of much greater importance may occupy a much briefer space in the book because the material is all germane to one purpose, has flowed in in a normal course of office business, and has been systematically filed or bound up into volumes. The archives of the American Board are such a case, and in accordance with the plan of our volume, which is an inventory and not a calendar or catalogue, have been disposed of with a rather brief description. Yet I know that while the later years afford materials for the history of little else than foreign missions, the earlier volumes, because of the domestic work of the Board, are rich in correspondence and other materials for the religious and also in a high degree the social history of parts of the country then remote and not literary. I think there is a rich mine here for historical students, though Allison tells me that the letters of the sort I describe are intermixed with a large amount of merely routine correspondence.

Among the archives which he has visited there are several which have published or are preparing full cal-

---

[174] Adams had written: "What bothers me is that Professor Rudolf Eucken of Jena has been given a Nobel medal for elaborately working out the same result in a big volume called 'The Great Currents of Contemporaneous Thought,' which demonstrates the hopeless imbecility of our whole civilization and society. He has done it so thoroughly as to leave no escape, and I am quite convinced by the cogency of his statement; but I can only conclude that the Nobel medal was given him by way of proving his thesis. This was surely not the original purpose of Nobel. At least, this was not the avowed purpose; although it is supported by the fact of its having been given to my dear friend Theodore Roosevelt,—if I am not mistaken,—which would hardly have been done without some such concealed meaning" (Adams to Jameson, Oct. 21, 1910).

[175] Lucius Cary, 2nd Viscount Falkland (1610?-1643). His name appears with those who, at York on June 15, 1642, protested that they abhorred all designs of making war. See *Dictionary of National Biography* 3: 1155, quoting Clarendon's *History* 7: 233.

[176] Lucius H. Thayer (1857-1931), A.B., Amherst, 1882, pastor of North Church, Portsmouth, N. H., 1890-1928. The "board" was the American Board of Commissioners for Foreign Missions, the archives of which, amounting to nearly three hundred letter-books, are in Congregational House, Beacon Street, Boston.

[177] See *ante*, Apr. 28, 1910, n. 151.

[178] Ernest C. Richardson (1860-1939), A.B., Amherst, 1880, librarian of Princeton University, 1890-1920. He prepared, it will be remembered, the first volume of *Writings on American history*. See *ante*, Feb. 1. 1906, n. 15.

endars of such of their materials as are historically interesting. In the case of these I have had him give but a brief and general description because we can refer to the extended volumes. I wish this were possible in the case of the American Board.

Now I do not expect the Board to think it proper to spend much money in the interest of American historical students. But would it not be possible for the Board to advance the very interests for which it exists by some systematic historical publication from its archives? I think of the notable books which the Society for the Propagation of the Gospel in Foreign Parts, the Society for the Promotion of Christian Knowledge, and the Corporation for the Propagation of the Gospel in New England, have brought out, and of the materials from the archives of the Bishop of London at Fulham Palace which Sadler Phillips published under the title of *Early English Colonies*. I believe that especially the first two societies named have done themselves a very good service in calling attention to their work by these two historical summaries of their record material; and should imagine that with the Congregational Publishing House right at hand a modest account of the archives of the American Board, or ultimately a volume or two of early letters—one volume domestic perhaps, one foreign—might be made to be similarly helpful to your organization.

I should be glad to know if you think there is anything in all this.[179] . . .

To WALDO G. LELAND

November 21, 1910.

My dear Leland:

As Henry Adams intimated in one of his letters that he was likely to stay in Paris till after Christmas I thought it a pity that you should not meet him. I thought this mainly because it would be a pleasure to you to know one whom I think we ought, all things considered, to regard as the foremost of our historical writers; but it also seemed to me not impossible that he might be able to give you some minor suggestions respecting American papers to be found in Paris—though probably this is unlikely. He writes that he would be very glad to see you, though the date of his return is uncertain and he may not stay anything like so long as he formerly thought. Accordingly, I enclose a letter of introduction. His apartment in which he generally lives from May to November is at 23, avenue Bois de Boulogne. You will find him a very interesting being—a small bird-like person, whose conversation is always brilliant and entertaining, but full of paradox and of whimsicalities. It seems impossible that he should believe most of the things that he says; he has his dialect.

You ought to have a copy of his *Letter to American Teachers of History,* privately printed, and distributed to a list of historical professors we made out for him. He has left it to me to send out others to any whom I choose. I think the Secretary of the American Historical Association ought surely to have one, so I send one herewith. If you can understand it all you can do much better than I can. I am in the position of Scotch Janet with the parson. "It was a fine sermon ye gave us yesterday." "Did you understand it, Janet?" "Wad I ha' the presoomption!"

I sent you a copy of Secretary Norton's letter of November 9. I think you should have a copy of the reply I am just writing, so I enclose one herewith. I do not know what Putnam has in mind. I should not wish to run counter, needlessly, to anything he desires. But I conclude the best way to reply when a question is asked me is to say what I really think, on public grounds and disinterestedly.[180] . . .

To MAX FARRAND

November 21, 1910.

Dear Farrand:

I am sorry about the poor proof reader, but I don't suppose that anything can be done, at any rate, until Baldwin comes in as governor.[181] He, being a fellow member of the Council, I might try to prevail on him to order out the militia, or order a day of fasting and prayer, whichever, after consultation with the other members of the Council, I might conclude to be the proper constitutional remedy.

By the way, could not we, for one of the features of the Council dinner, organize a joint debate between

---

[179] This letter was referred to William E. Strong, editorial secretary for the board, who wrote on Mar. 23, 1911, that there was in the material referred to much of historical value, especially concerning our relations with the Indians, but that the board could not publish such a series as Dr. Jameson conceived because of lack of money. He added that much useful material from the letters of missionaries had appeared in the *Missionary Herald,* published by the board.

[180] Norton in his reply to the letter of Sept. 7, asked whether the Library of Congress was not the organization which ought to classify, index, and store the records. On this letter Jameson wrote: "'The hand of Joab is in this thing.' I'd like to know how the Lib got wind of my corr. with Taft and talk with Hilles. It doesn't much matter who bosses the job, perhaps, so it is done." In his reply to Norton, he pointed out that the various departments might more easily be induced to cooperate, if they were provided with a building where they could deposit papers but still maintain ownership. He added that the functions of libraries and of archives were distinct functions, but that the Librarian of Congress might be given general supervision of the archives (Charles Norton to Jameson; Jameson to Norton, Nov. 9, 21, 1910).

[181] Simeon E. Baldwin (1840-1927), governor of Connecticut, 1911-1915, had been president of the American Historical Association, 1905-1906, and as an ex-president was a member of its executive council.

Farrand had complained of the work of the printer in setting up the *Records of the Federal Convention.* The proof reader was reported to have replied to this complaint: "Thank the Lord I don't have to read the damn thing or I would long ago have lepped from the roof."

Baldwin and the second vice president,[182] upon the question of the law respecting workingmen's conspiracies, the decision in the Bakers case (or was it the Hatters?)[183] or the law of libel, or the limitations upon the freedom of speech, or some other live topic of that sort?

To FREDERICK C. HICKS

December 2, 1910.

My dear Sir:[184]

I am glad to answer your letter of November 30. In fact, having for nineteen years taught graduate students in history, some of them members of your own faculty, I do not think that anyone would doubt my personal willingness to help them always, even if it were not one of the functions of this Department to be of use in all proposed researches in Washington libraries or archives. Yet I must confess that your young man's requests, which I return to you herewith, seem inordinate.[185] There are many matters in his formidable looking programme to which he ought surely to give his own attention before asking others to help him. If he is a serious candidate for the doctor's degree, and means to pursue the subject of Tammany in an appropriate manner, he should take all the first steps in acquiring the necessary knowledge, and not expect older scholars at a distance to answer for him questions which he could answer himself if he would make exertions for a few hours in any library. While commenting on some of his questions I feel that it is my duty, and that his professors would wish me, to confine myself to answering only those which my position in Washington might give me an opportunity to answer better than could be done by any inquiries in New York. Thus,

I. (b) I have no information respecting the first paragraph. If I wished to know whether the early almanacs of Philadelphia or Maryland mentioned Tammany or referred to him as a saint, I should go and look at them in some library in New York and should, if I expected to come to Washington, note in Mr. Hugh A. Morrison's "Preliminary Check-List of American Almanacs" those which were not to be found in New York and were to be found in the Library of Congress. If I found the writer of a magazine article saying that John Trumbull was the author of the greatest satire since Hudibras (which is a strange estimate, by the way) I should look up Trumbull's

McFingel, of which there are doubtless forty copies of different editions in New York, before I asked a man two hundred miles away whether Tammany is mentioned in it.

I. (c) Information respecting maypoles can be found in any one of several hundred books.

II. I do not know precisely what the young man means by asking, has the Department of the Interior any references, etc. If he means manuscript materials, I do not believe that they have anything that would be at all useful. Their Indian materials, as he would see by reference to the account of the archives of the Department of the Interior in Van Tyne and Leland's *Guide,* are all of later date. If he means printed books, I do not believe that their library, which is small, is anything like so well supplied with what is needful for the answering of his question as the Lenox, or as indeed your own library. I should think that by means of Field's Indian Bibliography, and the like, he could get hold of all the existing literature on the Delaware Indians.

V. It should be supposed that some correspondence of Colonel Morgan as United States agent would be among the papers of the Continental Congress.[186] I will have inquiry made. As to the references desired at the end of that paragraph, surely they can be got out of Winsor.

VI. The young man could not look in the catalogue of any New York library, under "Sons of Liberty," without running across Dawson's book.

VII. If he has found only one reference to Tammany in the Works of William Penn, I cannot undertake to search through them to see whether he has been thorough. He had better write to Mr. Albert Cook Myers of Moylan, Pennsylvania, making that one inquiry, for Mr. Myers, though upon the point of leaving for Europe for work on his great edition of William Penn's writings, may be able instantly to refer to the desired passage in some writings of Penn not embraced in that edition of his Works which your young man consulted.[187]

VIII. The Library of Congress, as he would see by consulting its "Check-List of American Newspapers," has files of several New York newspapers for the period of which he speaks. They are not in all cases complete but in most cases are nearly so.

[182] Theodore Roosevelt.

[183] The Danbury Hatter's case, Loewe *v.* Lawlor (208 U. S. 274) had been decided by the Supreme Court in 1908; the Bakers' case, Lochner *v.* New York (198 U. S. 45) in 1905.

[184] Frederick C. Hicks was at this time superintendent of the reading rooms of the library of Columbia University.

[185] Requests for information or for aid in finding information poured in to Jameson from students of all ages. If they seemed reasonable they were answered with care; if not, he did not hesitate to say so.

[186] George Morgan (1743-1810) was in April, 1776, made agent for Indian affairs in the middle department. Mr. Hicks was asking his questions in connection with the thesis of Edwin P. Kilroe, which was later published as *Saint Tammany and the origin of the Society of Tammany or Columbian Order in the city of New York,* N. Y., privately printed, 1913. It says of Morgan: "Before setting out [for Fort Pitt] the Delawares gathered and solemnly conferred upon him the name Tamenand or Tamene, signifying 'the affable,' he being the first they had found worthy to bear the name" (67-70).

[187] Though Myers published several minor works on Penn, the "great edition" to which Jameson refers never appeared.

Other newspapers have perhaps come in since the issue of that volume, nine years ago. . . .[188]

*   *   *   *   *   *   *

XI.   As the library of Columbia University has a set of the printed catalogue cards of the Library of Congress, it might be well for the young man to take the trouble of seeing which of the things that he wants are indicated upon those cards as possessed by the library.   If he will send a list of specific titles to the Librarian of Congress, I have no doubt that information will be supplied as to whether those particular items are or are not contained in that collection.

To Edward B. Krehbiel

December 5, 1910.

. . . I am much interested in what you say of the project of the Ginn School of Peace,[189] and should be glad to help in any way toward the preparing of such a historical course as is required, for that examination of the actual results of warfare is of course valuable, and, indeed, essential toward the propaganda.   But I suppose the data will usually have to be collected from scattered places in numerous books of history.   At the moment I can think of only one book the whole of which is a contribution to the matter, and that is Father Denifle's Désolation des Eglises, which is better known to you than to me.   Moreover, the public mind will not be much impressed, and will be justified in not being much impressed, by the tale of calamities ensuing from wars conducted in times far less humane than ours, so that the really cogent arguments are to be derived from the history of the wars conducted since the Geneva Conference of 1864, or in America the issue of Francis Lieber's code.[190]   On the side relating to the sufferings of the soldiers themselves, much curious knowledge could, I suppose, be derived from the reports of the surgeons general, and from such books as Major L. L. Seaman's (if I have the name right) on the medical service of the Japanese army in Manchuria.   Semenoff's books on that war are so impressive as to be almost terrible.[191]   And I don't know that the case has ever been better set

forth than by Tolstoy in *War and Peace,* which is outside your line on two counts, fiction and date.   By the way, I am going to have in either the April or the July number the beginning of a long article on the literature of the Russo Japanese war by the same British officer who two or three years ago gave us an article on the literature of the South African war.[192]

The financial reports of the various states that have been engaged in war at any time in the last fifty years ought to afford a great deal of material, and indeed whatever shows economic effects in those nations. . . .

To Waldo G. Leland

December 12, 1910.

My dear Leland:

. . . In the President's annual message, of which I sent you a copy, he did not mention an archive building.   This was because, as I was told beforehand was likely to be the case, he preferred to make some general remarks on the whole problem of expenditures for public buildings.   The message as a whole, as I think, struck people as disappointingly tame.   It sounds like the work of a supremely capable administrative chief, who had no inspiration to convey respecting political conduct.   The morning's paper announces his nomination of Justice White for Chief Justice, instead of Justice Hughes.   I had been supposing, and most persons had, that it was to be Hughes.   I don't think the substitution will be liked.

As to Roosevelt, I think he has lost some ground by reason of the violence of his language in personal attack, and by reason of his want of simplicity of mind, not to say sincerity, in regard to the tariff problem.   In New York the result was mainly a rebuke to Roosevelt, in the country at large, to the Old Guard.[193] . . .

. . . I wonder if the French admiral's account of the fight between the Alabama and the Kearsarge has ever been printed, or would be interesting to the readers of the Review,[194] but you are looking out for the Review in that respect with a broader vision than I have from here.

I enclose a newspaper clipping respecting the Library of Congress.   This evening and tomorrow and the next day are taken up with the annual round-up of the Carnegie Institution.   Tonight we hear a lecture

[188] The omitted sections are meaningless without the questions to which they refer and these have not come to light.

[189] The School of Peace, established by Edward Ginn (1838-1914), had as its head President David Starr Jordan of Stanford University.   Professor Krehbiel was to give a course in that university on the historical and statistical aspects of the effects of war.   Ginn, head of the publishing house of Ginn and Company, was the founder of the World Peace Foundation, which developed from the School of Peace.

[190] Francis Lieber's *Code of war for the government of the armies of the United States in the field,* was prepared at the request of the President during the Civil War.

[191] Seaman, Louis L., *The real triumph of Japan, the conquest of the silent foe,* N. Y., Appleton, 1906; Vladimir Semenoff, *Rasplata,* N. Y., Dutton, 1909; *The battle of Tsushima,* London, John Murray, 1906; *The price of blood,* London, John Murray, 1910.

[192] A British Officer, The literature of the Russo-Japanese War, *Amer. Hist. Rev.* **16:** 508-528, 736-750, April, July, 1911.   The literature of the South African War, 1899-1902, appeared in the *Review* **12:** 299-371, January, 1907.

[193] The November election, it will be remembered, had returned a Democratic House of Representatives and had made John A. Dix, a Democrat, governor of New York, in spite of the energetic campaigning of Theodore Roosevelt for the Republican candidate, Henry L. Stimson (1867-1950).

[194] The account of this naval engagement, fought off Cherbourg, was printed in the section of Documents of the *Review* **23:** 119-123, Oct. 1917, as *Kearsarge* and *Alabama:* French official report, 1864.

from Davenport on Principles of Heredity,[195] which the president has arranged to have repeated tomorrow afternoon for members of the staffs of departments. Tomorrow noon there is a luncheon, and tomorrow evening a valuable dinner to which the Trustees invited us. You perhaps knew that they "took us up" last year, which was at Root's suggestion. Wednesday the president has a conference of heads of departments and luncheon. An incautious old Trustee told me a few days ago to keep my ears open this week and I would hear some important announcement on behalf of Mr. Carnegie.[196] I will send you newspapers covering these three days.

To WALDO G. LELAND

Washington, D. C.
December 15, 1910.

Dear Leland:

I send some clippings which may interest you. The account of the dinner is, however, open to the following criticisms: That Dr. Woodward did not act as toastmaster; that he did not call upon Flexner, Brookings, and H. P. Walcott; that they were not there; that Root and Wickersham did not respond to toasts, for none were given; and that Parsons did not speak at all.[197]

Once more, Merry Christmas!

To HUBERT HALL

December 21, 1910.

My dear Hall:

I was greatly obliged by your confidential letter of November 12, and the information which you gave respecting the Royal Commission.[198] As to the Amer-

icans, I do not know that they have any special needs or desires different from those of English researchers, though I imagine that any of them who might be in London at a convenient time would be willing to testify if you desired to have them do so. Andrews always declares himself to have been exceedingly well treated, and evidently so have Paullin and Paxson been. It is no doubt somewhat regrettable that Paullin and Paxson could not go down beyond 1837; but there must always be a date, and whatever it is there will always be a good many who wish it were later. Any of us would, I am sure, be glad to co-operate, but none of us are at all certain as to how we could possibly be useful.

If it were conceivable that information respecting American conditions should be desired, Leland has a larger general knowledge of the archives in Washington than any other person, and I should be quite willing to have him go over from Paris (33 rue des Acacias) if it were desired. But in reality our system is no model for anybody on earth; on the contrary it is a fearful want of system. We ought to set our own house in order, or indeed to get an archive house at all, before we presume to advise as to archival housekeeping elsewhere. You always talk very pleasantly about us Americans,[199] but I see the other side of it all. I am going out next week to the meeting of the American Historical Association in Indianapolis. On the preliminary day I am to talk to the Ohio Valley Historical Association. Just look at Ohio, Indiana, and Kentucky when you think that English conditions do not rapidly respond to your desires. Ohio has nearly five million people. There is not a community of five million people in the world whose government has done so little for its history as that. Indiana is about as bad, and Kentucky is a great deal worse, since what little it does spend for history is wasted in the support of an imbecile official and the publication of outrageous twaddle. Therefore

---

[195] Charles B. Davenport (1866-1944), director of the Department of Experimental Evolution of the Carnegie Institution.

[196] At a meeting of the board of trustees of the Institution on Feb. 18, 1911, they acknowledged the gift of $10,000,000, confirmed by Mr. Carnegie in a letter of Jan. 19, 1911. Carnegie had added $2,000,000 to the original endowment in 1907. *Year Book,* Carnegie Institution, 1911: 3.

[197] Simon Flexner (1863-1946), director of medical research of the Rockefeller Institute; Robert S. Brookings (1850-1932), later the founder of the Brookings Institution; Henry P. Walcott (1838-1932), chairman of the Massachusetts State Board of Health; Elihu Root, United States senator; George W. Wickersham (1858-1936), attorney general of the United States; and William B. Parsons (1859-1932), chief engineer of the Cape Cod Canal, were all trustees of the Carnegie Institution. Flexner, Brookings, and Walcott had been elected at the meeting of the board held on Dec. 13, 1910. *Year Book,* Carnegie Institution, 1910: 3.

[198] A Royal Commission had been appointed to inquire into the working of all acts concerning public records, the rules in force at the Public Record Office, the arrangements for the care of public records, the publications of records since 1838, the custody of local records, and the training of archivists. Hubert Hall was secretary of the commission; Sir Frederick Pollock chairman. Hall's letter was not news to Jameson for in the summer Andrews had sent to him an extract from a

letter which he had received from Hall, in which Hall advised that Jameson and Andrews give pointers to Paullin and Paxson in order that they might appear as witnesses before the commission if Andrews himself could not come.

In the autumn Andrews wrote: "I am inclined to think that this means a more or less indefinite postponement of publication [of the *Guide*]. If important changes result from the report of the commission it will [be] necessary that we wait till those changes are completed. My hair will be gray and my MS. (if it survives fire and loss) will be worn out with handling before it gets into print."

Jameson's answer was: "Do not let us take a gloomy view about the Royal Commission. At any rate let us act as if we thought it was not going to injure our work until the contrary is proved. Even a Royal Commission is enitled to be held innocent until it is proved guilty, yet we have our suspicions" (Andrews to Jameson, Jameson to Andrews, July 13, Nov. 4, 7, 1910).

[199] Hall had written: "We are sure to be asking for opinions of the continental archivists anyhow, but I attach more weight to your work than to any other organization for our own purpose" (Hall to Jameson, Nov. 12, 1910).

be of good cheer. You may be pretty bad, but the Americans surely are worse.

I should be delighted to see any memoranda or other documents respecting the Royal Commission that it may be possible to show me, and also to make any announcements to our history people that it may be convenient to have laid before them in the *Review*. . . .

To Waldo G. Leland

January 17, 1911.

Dear Leland:

. . . My dear young friend, do not plan to tap me as a fount of wisdom on Henry Adams's book.[200] I am absolutely no good for that sort of thing. I was perfectly conscious of not having understood it when I read it and now, I give you my word, I have not an idea what it is all about, except of the most general sort. In Raphael's School of Athens, which, as you are aware, hangs before me here, you will see Henry Adams up at the apex of the composition, talking with Plato, and me down in the foreground making little scratches with a stilus on a slate. There is some connection between the two occupations, I suppose, but I cannot make out what it is. In fact, I'll be hanged if I can remember what the second law of thermodynamics is, anyhow. . . .

To William H. Allison

January 17, 1911.

My dear Allison:

. . . I have not the slightest thought of ever publishing the lectures which I gave on the organization of religion in America,[201] or anything whatever in that field. I might also say that I have no expectation of ever publishing any book of my own writing. But anyhow those lectures, though they answered their purpose after a fashion, by drawing the minds of certain excellent graduate students to fields of work in American history which they might otherwise have neglected, were the work of a mere amateur in the subject, who tried to keep a day ahead of the class but whose acquirements in the field did not go beyond that and have not been seriously increased since, but will probably decrease as time goes on. So you have free course to run and be glorified. I sincerely hope that you will enter into that field and do important work in it. You are well qualified. . . .[202]

---

[200] *A letter to American teachers of history.*

[201] Lectures delivered by Jameson while Allison was a graduate student in the University of Chicago. On Jan. 14, Allison had written that if Jameson did not intend to publish these lectures he wished to bring out a book on the organization of religion in America.

[202] Though the book never appeared, Professor Allison worked on the subject for a number of years.

To Hubert Hall

March 17, 1911.

My dear Hall:

Judging from what I have heard from you that American suggestions, if there were any, might be welcomed and might have some chance of being useful during the work of the Royal Commission on the Archives, I have, regarding this office as a sort of clearing-house, written to perhaps a dozen Americans who have worked in the Public Record Office and are judicious persons, asking them if they had any suggestions to offer. Everyone, I am glad to say, expresses himself as having been handsomely treated at the P. R. O. and disclaims all wish to criticize. But some of them make certain suggestions which, with suitable deference to the opinions of those who have had longer experience on the spot, they think might work toward improvement, so far at least as American purposes are concerned. These I codify and transmit to you for any use of which they are capable.

1. As to contents, it is suggested that historical papers lying in other depositories in London, such as the Privy Council Office, should be turned over to the P. R. O.; that those at Lambeth and Fulham should be similarly transferred; and even more boldly, by one man, that it would be convenient if the Irish and Scottish records were deposited in London.

2. As to arrangement, the recent changes of classification having hit the Americans rather hard, it is suggested that as little as possible of such reclassification, as few infractions as possible of the *principe de provenance,* should be entered upon in the future; and that in particular bound volumes of documents should not be broken up if it can be helped.

3. As to publications, it is much wished that some general account of the whole mass of materials in the P. R. O., some *Etat sommaire,* in which the volume should be the unit or item, might before long be prepared and published; that the office should make purchasable by scholars all its printed lists that are still valid, and should print all those which are in manuscript. It is very heartily wished that the publication of the *Calendars of State Papers, Colonial,* might proceed at least twice as rapidly. We are now at 1700. If a volume deals with the papers of one year, and one volume is published annually, we shall always remain 211 years "behind the game." The Calendar of State Papers, Colonial, for the eighteenth century is of course the one in which Americans are most interested. Yet some would be glad to have the rate of speed in the calendaring of Treasury papers heightened, and to have a beginning made on the papers of other departments.

4. As to access, some hope that there is no need for more rigorous rules respecting the admission of American students (embassy, etc.) than for English students. Several express the wish that all restric-

tions upon the use of documents anterior to 1837 may be removed, except where there are real, and not merely traditional, reasons for the occlusion. In many cases the reserved documents, having been read in accessible copies elsewhere, are known to be harmless. In some, *e. g.,* Newfoundland papers from 1759, the reasons have lately expired.[203] It is thought that it would be useful if discretion respecting privilege of access to closed files could be lodged in P. R. O. officials, not solely in those of the original department.

5. As to facilities, it is suggested that there might well be a larger workroom, with a greater and more varied supply of reference books; that the rules regarding the use of records and the number of volumes available at a time might well resemble as closely as possible those of the British Museum; that ink might, under proper conditions, be allowed; and that an authorized stenographer or stenographers and typewriters should be available.

None of these suggestions are made to me still less would the writers wish that I should express them to you, in a tone of complaint. On the contrary all these workers are grateful for the privileges and opportunities which they have had. Many of their suggestions are made with a view quite as much to the convenience of British as of American historical students; and all appear to be made deliberately and with conviction.

To JUSTIN H. SMITH

March 20, 1911.

My dear Mr. Smith:

I ought to have answered your letter earlier but have been pressed by a mass of proof sheets which required so much attention that I have fallen behind a few days with respect to correspondence.

I must thank you very much for mentioning me at all in your preface, and especially for mentioning me in such terms. I am glad to be called your friend. I ought to object to being called your distinguished friend, for which there is no warrant, though it is not human to object violently. But you have put the phrase in such a shape that I cannot easily object without cutting off Ford, Hunt, and Garrison [204] from the privileges of so honorific a designation. How would

it do to say, "to his distinguished friends Mr. Worthington C. Ford, Mr. Gaillard Hunt, and the late Professor George P. Garrison, and to Dr. J. Franklin Jameson, by no means distinguished and yet his friend"? Somehow that does not seem to me as good, stylistically speaking, so I return the slip, grateful but in despair of emendation.

I am glad that you were sorry you did not go home by way of Washington.

To WALDO G. LELAND

April 25, 1911.

Dear Leland:

. . . As to Albany, I think that Paltsits will not be re-appointed. He has had too much friction with Draper,[205] and the fire got so on his nerves that he blazed forth a little indiscreetly. I am sorry; he has done excellent work, but perhaps has a little too much of the prophetic temperament.[206]. Draper was of course anxious to exculpate himself. The episode of the South Carolina Navy Records made him look a little silly, as the leading objection he put forward against returning them was that they would not be so safe in Columbia (where Salley says he has everything of steel) as in Albany. That is the proper mode in which an official of a large or Northern state ought always to talk up to an official of a small or Southern state, but in the present case it seems to have subjected the General to some subsequent correction.

Meanwhile Lowry has been very desirous to utilize the episode, partly no doubt to make "copy," but partly also to help forward the benevolent movement toward

[203] Is this, perhaps, a reference to the fact that the Hague tribunal had in 1910 settled the fishery disputes, and in favor of Newfoundland?

[204] Gaillard Hunt (1862-1924), attached to the Department of State, 1900-1909, chief of the Division of Manuscripts, Library of Congress, 1909-1917. In 1918 he returned to the Department of State.

George P. Garrison (1853-1910) taught history in the University of Texas from 1888 till 1909. His death came just as he was completing the editing of the Diplomatic correspondence of the Republic of Texas, *Ann. Rept., Amer. Hist. Assn.,* 1908: 2; 1909, **2**: (1, 2).

[205] Victor Paltsits (1867-1952), after service in the Lenox and the New York Public libraries, had, in 1907, been appointed by Governor Hughes as state historian of New York, to succeed Hugh Hastings. Andrew S. Draper (1848-1913) was at this time commissioner of education for that state.

[206] In spite of the efforts made by historians, Jameson was correct in his prophecy that Paltsits, on the expiration of his term in April, 1911, would not be reappointed. His four years of service had been stormy ones. Soon after his appointment, a bill which he considered to be a "spite bill" and the work of his predecessor, was introduced, intended to abolish his office. His unwillingness to have his office placed under the control of Draper, an adroit politician, which Paltsits was not, added to his troubles. In March, 1911, came the fire in the Albany Capitol which destroyed about ninety per cent of the manuscript collections of the state. This catastrophe Paltsits was not slow to attribute to Draper's opposition to proper legislation. James A. Holden, a newspaper editor, was appointed historian and the office was placed under the jurisdiction of the commissioner of education. For a letter from Jameson in behalf of Paltsits, see New York *Evening Post,* Feb. 3, 1911, or the *Nation* 92: 140, Feb. 9, 1911. The *Post* of Jan. 26 had published an excellent plea for Paltsits by Edgar M. Bacon, on reading which, Jameson had written to the managing editor: "Thank you . . . for the letter respecting Paltsits, which I have half a mind to follow up with another if there is any danger whatever of slipping back from Paltsits to something like Hastings—'Hyperion to a satyr'" (Jameson to Edward G. Lowry, Feb. 1, 1911).

a National Archive Building (never, never say Hall of Records).[207] He came to me for stuff. I gave him some remarks, and handed out a copy of your memorandum on the actual situation. He asked me over the telephone if he could mention your name. I did not feel sure what you would have said, but told him that it was not prepared by you with a view to publication and perhaps I ought not in your absence to speak affirmatively for you. I see, and you will see from the inclosed article, that he has practically printed the whole of your paper.[208] I do not think that we ought to mind at all. It will do good and does not in the least stand in the way of our using it in any other connection and at any other time. The President of the United States has a copy of it, and doubtless reads a chapter of it every night before he goes to bed; but it is not likely that he on Monday morning got it out and made a rigid comparison of its text with that of Lowry's article in the *Post*.[209] "Lives of great men all remind us" that we can repeat ourselves with the utmost freedom whenever we have really said a good thing; and now that I see this in print I am in the highest degree struck with its excellence—impressed by it more than I will say for fear of getting you on the editorial staff of the *Post*, which would be bad for you in the long run.

To WALDO G. LELAND

May 3, 1911.

Dear Leland:

. . . Miles Poindexter, the new senator from Washington, is a neighbor of my nephew's in Spokane, and through the latter I have known him for quite a while.[210] In the list of committees which the Senate has just made up he has been put on the Committee on Public Buildings and Grounds. I have been putting it up to him that he ought to immortalize himself by becoming the father of the National Archives Building, and am feeding him with information on the sub-

ject in chunks as large as he can masticate at a time. He rather takes to the idea. Meanwhile the House Committee on Public Buildings and Grounds has been poking around the public buildings to see about dangers from fire, and I have been trying with indifferent success to sic them on the trail of the archives.

I put in quite a little time among the statesmen last week, without accomplishing anything very visible, yet it may have done some good. Senator Smoot,[211] to my considerable pleasure, is going to put the quota of the annual reports at 3500 (3000 for the Association, we may presume), and I think that the House will agree to this. But when the new code will go through remains to be seen. The National Historical Commission is at present in the hands of Providence and the new House Library Committee, the chairman of which, Mr. Slayden of Texas, is a well educated and rather cultivated man, but with nothing like the force or influence that McCall had.

In the intervals of these communings with the great I continue to insert commas and semi-colons in various manuscripts at room 500 of the Bond Building. . . .

To WALDO G. LELAND

May 12, 1911.

Dear Leland:

. . . Since beginning this letter I have held the House Committee on Public Buildings and Grounds spellbound for an hour with my eloquence on the archive situation. The eloquence consisted mostly in the facts which you had conveyed to me orally or in writing. I gave due credit to the gifted author at these points. The Committee bore the whole with exemplary fortitude, and it is not impossible that before we die an archive building may be erected in Washington. This will encourage us to continue in existence, which otherwise we might be loth to do. I have also just had a talk about it with Senator Wetmore,[212] who of course is favorable. Three other buildings have the right of way, but the Albany matter may possibly enable this one to step in at the fourth place in the bread line. I do not know that I have ever told you that in July 1910 the Committee on Appropriations succeeded in giving away Square 143 to the Geological Survey; but as the architect's plans for their building would cost two or three times as much as was stipulated (queer lot, architects!) the matter is still at a pause, and the square cannot be said to have been definitely removed from the list of archive possibilities. . . .

---

[207] Edward G. Lowry, Washington correspondent of the New York *Evening Post*, 1904-1911, 1913-1914; managing editor, 1911-1913. The *Post* of Jan. 26, 1911, had published a long editorial on the condition of our government archives as contrasted with the excellent provision made by foreign governments. The editorial ended by quoting the resolution passed by the American Historical Association at its recent meeting (*Ann. Rep.*, 1910: 43). The same account later appeared in the *Nation* **92**: 109, Feb. 2, 1911.

[208] This paper, The present condition of the government archives, is printed in *Hearings . . . relating to the preservation of government archives*, May 12, 1911, 15-16.

[209] Federal archives neglected, New York *Evening Post*, Apr. 22, 1911, 2, Saturday Supplement. In the article Jameson is quoted on the priceless value of the records destroyed in the fire in the Albany capitol and on the nature of archive buildings in other countries.

[210] Miles Poindexter (1868-1946), during his two terms in the Senate, 1911-1923, did valiant work for the archive building. The nephew was Frederick C. Elmendorf, a nephew of Mrs. Jameson.

[211] Reed Smoot (1862-1941), United States Senator from Utah for five terms, 1903-1933.

[212] George Peabody Wetmore (1846-1921), United States Senator from Rhode Island, 1895-1913.

To Max Farrand

May 15, 1911.

Dear Farrand:

. . . This morning has arrived the beautiful and luxurious copy of your *Records*.[213] They have given your book a really beautiful setting. I do not see how the thing could be done in better taste. But the substance is worthy of the exterior, which I apprehend is seldom the case with *éditions de luxe*. Really you have done a splendid as well as a prodigious piece of work, such as a man might be proud to have (I certainly should be) as the one result and monument of his scientific career—and you still a mere youth, with many more excellent volumes in the back part of your head.

I shall now take the volumes, one by one, up to the house. There they will be looked upon by Mrs. Jameson with great admiration and pleasure. A new set of furniture will immediately be ordered to go with them; and young Francis will be trained up to regard them as the chief reason why he should learn to read, and the exemplar of his most ambitious hopes.

Thank you again and again, my dear fellow, for your kindness in sending me this beautiful gift, and for the honor you do me in associating my name with it in so public a way.

To Waldo G. Leland

May 17, 1911.

Dear Leland:

. . . I really think that an impression is being made in archive matters, partly because a subcommittee of this new Democratic House Committee on Public Buildings and Grounds has been poking around in the buildings hired by the government to see about the security against fire. They may not have found the security against fire but they have found a lot of other things that have interested them. I have found no difficulty in getting into print, as a part of last Friday's hearing, as annexes to my feeble remarks, the whole text of your paper on the general archive situation, of Paullin's legislative history of the movement since 1879, and of a modified form of Hunt's Indianapolis paper on the foreign archive buildings.[214] I will send you a copy of the conglomerate soon. The chairman of the subcommittee which I have mentioned is a neighbor and close friend in Kentucky of one of my old Johns Hopkins intimates.[215] He is out in Kentucky now; but when he comes back I am going to get at him, taking Stock[216] along, who can tell him of archive peculiarities that will make him sit up and look around for the Babcock extinguisher. Another member of the committee was a graduate student in political science at Chicago when I was there.[217] Of course no public buildings bill will be introduced until next December or January. It will be good to have you at hand then,

"Th'applause of listening senates to command" . . .

To Francis A. Christie

North Edgecomb, Maine,
August 19, 1911.

My dear Christie:

. . . I have read with much pleasure and profit your article in the *Christian Register* and your interesting review of Allison.[218] The criticisms which you so gently express are well deserved. I ought to have seen to it that the Massachusetts Historical Society was covered. A questionary was sent out to, I think, all promising general libraries and historical societies, and I should suppose that one must have gone to the Massachusetts Historical Society and been ignored by old Dr. Green because that is his nature. I have also been chagrined at the omission of the important and valuable materials at the Fairfax Theological Seminary at Alexandria, Virginia, and if you have no objection shall insert in your review a sentence

---

[213] *The records of the Federal Convention of 1787*, 3v., New Haven, Yale Univ. Press, 1911, were dedicated "To John Franklin Jameson," and a sentence in the preface read: "He [the author] feels still more indebted to two others who have been his constant advisers and have rendered him every assistance ungrudgingly—Mr. Andrew C. McLaughlin of Chicago, and Mr. J. Franklin Jameson, Director of the Department of Historical Research of the Carnegie Institution of Washington. To the latter this work has been dedicated in recognition of his great services to the cause of American historical scholarship." It was at a suggestion of Jameson that Farrand undertook this edition of the *Records of the Convention*. "I suggested it to Mr. Farrand seven or eight years ago, having for some time had it in mind as a thing that would be of great utility but not wanting to suggest it to anyone until I had found a man competent to execute it in accordance with the highest requirements of scholarship" (Jameson to Little, Brown and Company, Nov. 25, 1907).
The omitted paragraphs of this letter deal with plans for Farrand's coming to Washington as "research associate" with the department.

[214] *Hearings before Committee on Public Buildings and Grounds, House of Representatives, relating to the preservation of government archives*, May 12, 1911, contained: History of the movement for a national archive building in Washington, by C. O. Paullin, 4-13; Present condition of the government archives, by W. G. Leland, 15-16; Memorial from a committee of the executive council of the American Historical Association on a national archive building, signed by J. Franklin Jameson, Alfred T. Mahan, and John B. McMaster, 24-25; and Extract from paper on European archive buildings read at the meeting of the American Historical Association, Dec. 30, 1910, by Gaillard Hunt, 25-26.
[215] James C. Cantrell (1870-1923), member of the House from Kentucky, 1909-1923. The Johns Hopkins friend was Arthur Yager.
[216] Leo F. Stock (1878-1954), a member of the staff of the department and one of the editors of this volume.
[217] B. L. French of Idaho, who was a fellow in political science in the University of Chicago, 1901-1903.
[218] Probably, Catholic modernism, *Christian Register*, July 27, 1911.

respecting them.[219] Allison's Inventory was by intention confined to Protestant archives. It was intended to make a similar book some time on our Catholic archives. I still intend to do this, but the time is not yet quite ripe. . . .

I can tell you in very brief space all that I know about Colonel Israel Williams of Hatfield. It is derived from traditionary talk in Amherst or the first pages of Tyler's History of Amherst College, and a paper which Franklin B. Dexter read before us at the American Antiquarian Society at Worcester about eighteen years ago on the Grading of Classes at Harvard and Yale in the Colonial Period.[220] In those days, when college boys were ranked according to the social position of their parents, Colonel Israel Williams, who being one of the "river gods" of the Connecticut valley, had been ranked about number 13 in his class at Harvard, found that his son was put about number 25. He was so incensed that he took his son out of college, and tried to get a charter for an additional college in western Massachusetts, presumably at Hatfield. The movement is one of the origins both of Amherst and of Williams. I think that there is more or less about it in the notes to Goodell's edition of the *Acts and Resolves of the Province of Massachusetts Bay,* about 1760. But all this does not show which way he would jump on the question of saving grace; I judge that he would be an insurgent if the Harvard authorities stood pat, and *vice versa.* . . . .

To EDWARD G. LOWRY

September 28, 1911.

Dear Mr. Lowry:

. . . I don't think it would be rational to edit the Evening Post's Saturday page of college news with my desires in view.[221] It must be that the vast majority of its readers have other interests than mine in the matter. This vast majority consists of the younger alumni of the various colleges. My experience has been that the younger alumni of colleges are even more besotted with the athletic craze than the undergraduates themselves. The undergraduate is forced into a temporary compromise with the notion that intellectual interests have some claim upon the attention of the human mind. The young alumnus has promptly emancipated himself from all such antiquated delusions. For him the bleachers, the waving pennant, the raucous megaphone, the staccato chanting of the rooters. I am not expecting that a page which ought to be made up mainly for the young alumni, and to record, if not athletic progress, at any rate the doings of quite local student organizations, shall occupy anything more than a minor part of its space with the things that a man especially looks for whose main interests are in educational concerns that relate to all colleges alike, and especially in the progress of historical research. Therefore while I answer your queries I hardly make any criticism.

a. I am interested in the news of the progress of the libraries, of gifts to the historical and literary departments (the scientific departments will I know in this American world have a constant stream of gold flowing in upon them), of appointments of the faculties in these lines, of proceedings and discussions at inter-university meetings like those of the Association of American Universities, and to a less extent in news about archaelogical gifts and new buildings. I know so many men in the faculties in so many different colleges that the personal news interests me a good deal.

b. I should be glad to see more about these professors and what they are doing in lines of research, though this would be less interesting to the general public. I think it might be profitable to cover a little more fully the results and discussions of intercollegiate conferences whether with respect to a single line of study or with respect to broad general discussions like those of the Association of American Universities.

c. As intimated above, I naturally do not care very much about the doings of the student organizations, but of course a great many readers do, each in the case of his own college.

If any of this is of any use to you I am glad; but I plainly am not representative. Wishing the greatest success to this and every other page.[222]

To WILLIAM H. TAFT

February 5, 1912.

Mr. President:

I wish to express my gratification at the action

---

[219] Christie's criticisms of Allison's *Inventory* relate entirely to omissions of some of the repositories where documents were to be found. *Amer. Hist. Rev.* **17**: 190-191, Oct., 1911.

[220] *Proc. Amer. Ant. Soc.,* n.s., **9**: 34-59, Oct., 1893. Interested readers may pursue this subject in a study by S. E. Morison, *ibid.,* **42-43**: 371-431, Oct., 1932.

[221] Lowry, at this time managing editor of the *Evening Post,* had written on Sept. 20: "You told me once that you were a subscriber to the Saturday edition of the Evening Post for the page that contains the college news. This page will be resumed September 30. You are the one subscriber personally known to me who is interested in that page, and, therefore I am tempted to have it edited with your demands in view. Therefore, these three queries: (a) What do you find on the page that interests you? (b) What do you not find on the page that you would like to find there? (c) What is there on the page (if anything) that does not interest you? Have you read the page with enough interest to suggest any plans by which its value would be increased to the readers?" An excellent specimen of the page in question can be found in the *Post* for Jan. 28, 1911, 8-9.

[222] Lowry replied, Sept. 29: "Your letter tells me comprehensively and clearly what I want to know. . . . The Saturday page of college news is not addressed to undergraduates, and does not attempt to give any account of their sporting or social activities. It is intended for graduates, for teachers, and other persons interested in educational matters."

which you have taken in drawing the **attention of** Congress to the matter of a National Archive Building, and my sense of the honor which you have done me in referring publicly to my letter on the subject.[223]

May I ask leave to lay before you an historical matter of much less importance than this, though not without significance? I refer to the processes by which the government disposes of useless papers which have accumulated in the departments. The present method is, that the head of the department makes up a list of papers deemed to belong in this class and sends it to the President of the Senate and the Speaker of the House of Representatives. A joint committee is supposed to scrutinize the list, to inspect the documents themselves if necessary, and to take the testimony of chiefs of bureaus or of others who may have more special knowledge of them than is possessed by the head of the Department. If the committee derives from this source no reason why papers designated should be preserved, they are ordered to be destroyed.

While it is a matter of course, and indeed a matter of real importance, that government files should be relieved of useless matter, it has come to my knowledge that papers are thus ordered for destruction which, while they have long survived all usefulness for administrative purposes, are valuable for the uses of historical students and should for such purposes be preserved somewhere. Yet they ought not to be kept in departmental repositories to which they are an embarrassment, and at present we have no National Archive Building in which to preserve them.

Upon the principle that papers ought not to be destroyed unless they are declared by competent authority to be *both* useless for administrative purposes *and* useless for purposes of history, I venture to suggest, as a temporary expedient, in the absence of a general archivist, that there is one official, and I think only one in Washington, who from the nature of the case must always be a good historical scholar, competent to declare whether papers have or have not any historical value. That is the Chief of the Division of Manuscripts in the Library of Congress. My suggestion is, that, without change of existing legislation, an executive order might be issued requiring heads of

departments, before sending such lists of **useless** papers to Congress, to send them to the **Librarian of** Congress in order that they might be examined **by** the chief of the Division of Manuscripts. The **latter** would thus have in the interests of history a second veto upon their destruction. If he should think that any papers in any list had value for history, the Librarian might ask, not that they should be preserved in a department where they were not wanted, but that they should be sent to the Library of Congress for preservation in the Division of Manuscripts, where all such material is preserved.

I may add that I have recently in conversation laid this subject before Honorable Arthur L. Bates of the House of Representatives, who for six years was chairman of the House Committee on Disposition of Useless Papers in the Executive Departments, and that the procedure which I am suggesting met with his very cordial approval.[224]

To EDWARD G. LOWRY

February 26, 1912.

Dear Lowry:

Here is a valuable suggestion for you, for which I make no charge. It ought not to be more difficult to cause the people of Mexico to call imperatively for the services of Colonel Roosevelt as president than it has been to persuade the people of the United States to clamor for the same boon. He is just what they need, and would make Mexico hum. This would solve several difficulties in this city and elsewhere in the United States, and would, I am sure, shed balm upon the wounded spirit of the patriotic Diaz.[225] It is certainly worth trying.[226]

To FRANCES G. DAVENPORT

March 4, 1912.

My dear Miss Davenport:

. . . A few days ago we had a hearing before the Senate Committee on Public Buildings and Grounds on a bill (really written by the undersigned) for a

---

[223] "I cannot close this message without inviting the attention of Congress again to the necessity for the erection of a building to contain the public archives. The unsatisfactory distribution of records, the lack of any proper index or guide to their contents, is well known to those familiar with the needs of the Government in this Capitol. The land has been purchased and nothing remains now but the erection of a proper building. I transmit a letter written by Prof. J. Franklin Jameson, director of the department of historical research of the Carnegie Institution of Washington, in which he speaks upon this subject as a member of a committee appointed by the executive council of the American Historical Association to bring the matter to the attention of the President and Congress" (*Compilation of the messages and papers of the Presidents* 10: 8108, N.Y., Bureau of National Literature, 1913).

[224] President Taft, on Mar. 16, 1912, issued the following executive order: "It is hereby ordered that before reporting to Congress useless files of papers to be disposed of under the provisions of the Act of February 16, 1889, as extended and amended by Section 1, Chapter 189, of the Act of March 2, 1895, lists of such papers shall be submitted to the Librarian of Congress in order that the several Executive Departments may have the benefit of his views as to the wisdom of preserving such of the papers as he may deem to be of historic interest" (Executive Order, no. 1499, *Library of Congress Report,* 1912: 35).

[225] Porfirio Diaz (1830-1915), president of Mexico from 1877 to 1880 and from 1884 to 1911. A successful revolution in 1911 had driven him from the country.

[226] "Your suggestion is a good one. We are all perfectly willing that T. R. should be the next President of Mexico. But who will bell the cat?" (Lowry to Jameson, Feb. 27, 1912).

National Archive Building.[227] Nothing will be done about it this session but we are trying to work up Congressional and public opinion upon the matter. It happens to be a good session for education on such topics, and I really think that in the next session some action will ensue. It will gratify you to know that I have enlisted the aid of the Daughters of the American Revolution in the matter, and have received it in gratifying measure. They are, so to speak, laying bricks in the temple of history, which is much better than heaving them through its windows, now isn't it? I will send you a copy of the hearing as soon as it is printed. The Miss Chiles who figures in it is a magazine writer.[228] She took the matter up independently of us or our committee and had inspected archive places a good deal before I came across her. Lothrop Withington[229] was not on the programme, but requested permission to "butt in" and did so with very good effect, infusing into the proceedings a little of that warmth of rhetoric and imagination in which historical students are so deficient. . . .

To JAMES B. SCOTT

March 11, 1912.

My dear Mr. Scott:[230]

There is a matter in connection with the proposed one hundredth anniversary of the Treaty of Ghent, of which I have meant to speak to you the next time I should see you. . . . My suggestion is this: That the United States government, *respektiv* the Department of State, should commemorate the occasion by publishing in a volume or two all the diplomatic correspondence of any importance relating to and leading up to the negotiations, that can be found in our archives or in those of Great Britain or Russia or in private hands.

It is a very usual thing, as you know, for governments to make this sort of commemoration. The Diaz government prepared and partly published a noble series of volumes of historical documents commemorating the hundredth anniversary of Mexican independence. The Russian government is now undertaking something rather magnificent in scale in commemoration of the great events of 1812. The Italian government, besides the great work which it published in

commemoration of 1492, did a pretty substantial thing with respect to the fiftieth anniversary of 1860—and so on. Our government has been backward about such things, yet they have a great educational importance, and do a great deal to prevent the memory of an anniversary from expiring immediately with the extinction of the last rocket. In 1903, when the centenary of the Louisiana Purchase might have called forth the best kind of a public commemoration along these lines, Congress brought forth the most wretched kind of a little "pub. doc." entitled "Documents relating to the Purchase of Louisiana," and containing perhaps a couple of hundred pages of Lord knows what documents, presented in the most shabby and unscholarly style.

This brings me to the real animus of my suggestion. Such a thing is not worth doing at all unless it is done in a manner to exhibit to all nations, what is the fact, that there is quite enough historical scholarship at the service of the United States government to enable it to do a model piece of editing if it chooses. If such a thing were to be brought out in the usual perfunctory manner by some clerk of a committee, or official untrained in history, I do not care to see it done. A committee of five excellent historical scholars specially versed in the diplomatic history of that period, and most of them willing to do actual work upon it, with Admiral Mahan for chairman, let us say, could prepare a volume or two of which we should be proud, and there is time now in which to do it.

The reason why I should like to see this done is that the use of such a method in such an instance would force upon the Congressional mind the value of a permanent Commission on National Historical Publications. I do not know whether you have known about the plan for such a commission. I send you herewith a copy of a Keep Commission Report on the general subject, prepared by a good and hard-working committee, which President Roosevelt appointed at my instance and of which I was secretary. Ever since he transmitted the report to Congress I have been trying to get the measure adopted, and there has been a favorable report regarding it from the House Committee on the Library, and of this I also send a copy; but I have not yet been able to get anything done beyond this. If the celebration of the treaty of Ghent is taken up with any such appropriation as was spoken of at the meeting at the District Building, I should be glad to see the suggestion acted upon which I have made above.[231]

---

[227] *Hearing before the Committee on Public Buildings and Grounds, United States Senate,* on S. 5179, Mar. 1, 1912, 62 Cong., 2 sess. Jameson's remarks were confined to explaining the competence of the speakers who were to follow him and to winding up the discussion (6-7, 38-40).

[228] Chiles, Rosa Pendleton, The national archives: are they in peril? *Review of Reviews* 45: 209-213, Feb., 1912.

[229] Lothrop Withington, a well-known Washington genealogist and a member of the American Historical Association, who was lost on the *Lusitania*. The *Nation* 92: 165-166, Feb. 16, 1911, contains a letter of his on the subject of the care of government archives.

[230] James Brown Scott (1866-1943), secretary of the Carnegie Endowment for International Peace, and director of its division of international law, 1910-1940.

[231] In the autumn Jameson reverted to this subject: "Last winter I wrote to James Brown Scott the inclosed letter. Please return it; but I thought you might be interested in the suggestion. Some talks which I had at Ghent with an old friend of mine, a professor in the University, revived my interest in this suggestion and I have sent a copy of the letter to Woodrow Wilson, and if he is elected shall follow it up with him, chiefly in the hope that it may do something toward bringing a proper general Commission into existence" (Jameson

To Halvdan Koht

April 12, 1912.

My dear Dr. Koht:[232]

I am very greatly obliged by your kindness in sending me a copy of your paper on the labor movement of 1848 in Norway. The episode was to me a wholly novel one and I have had real pleasure in learning something about it.

Work and life in Washington go on much as usual, so far as I am concerned. The political turmoil is however at present somewhat greater than ordinary, Mr. Roosevelt's candidacy for the Republican nomination having led to more excitement within the party than is customary in such campaigns, because there is at bottom a greater theoretical difference between his supporters and those of President Taft than we usually have between followers of this and that personality for whom the nomination is sought. My impression is strong that Mr. Taft will be nominated at Chicago, but defeated in the election.

To Harold W. V. Temperley

May 7, 1912.

My dear Mr. Temperley:[233]

The invitation which you send me to read a paper at the International Historical Congress in London next April is a great honor, and I appreciate it as such.

I send you at once my acceptance of the invitation, and if a paper of the sort which you describe will best meet your needs and wishes, I will endeavor to prepare it. I put the matter thus, because, remembering that the making of programmes always requires some

shifting and recasting, I think it not improper to say that my personal preference might lie elsewhere. I am so much occupied with matters of the sort which you describe—the prospecting for historical building materials and the quarrying and storing of them—and feel myself so likely to grow stale by reason of such engrossment, that when an invitation to read a paper anywhere is sent me, and it makes no difference to anyone else what subject I choose, I am likely to try to freshen up my mind and keep in contact with real history by taking some theme which calls for historical narrative or exposition. For instance, when I was asked to read a paper at the Berlin Congress, from which I was kept away by an important domestic event,[234] I had it in mind to prepare a paper entitled "Typical Steps of American Expansion," in which I should have attempted to offer comparative data and generalizations regarding certain of the processes by which the Americans have gone up against the land to possess it; and I should still be rather glad of a chance to prepare a paper on that subject. Doubtless it would be more difficult than the one which you propose, but there would be more juice in it for me, and possibly more for an audience.

I mention these thoughts only because, in the kaleidoscopic changes which programmes sometimes have to undergo, it may be useful for you to know of such a notion on my part. But when I am myself occupied with the making of a programme of an historical meeting, I do not wish to compose it of unrelated particles, but rather to bring the various pieces into unity and if possible to make them contribute to some useful and practical end. Therefore I appreciate that if I accept your invitation to read a paper, I ought to give it the form and in so far as I can the character that you wish it to have. So please register me as answering "yes" to both your questions.[235]

Perhaps I ought to say that I do not see, in so pleasant a light as you seem to see it, what we in America have been doing with respect to historical records and materials. I have been so prone, influenced perhaps by hortatory purposes, to paint the situation darkly, that I should have some difficulty in compelling myself to appear patriotic in an international gathering. I send you a copy of a paper which I read before the American Antiquarian Society, which my friends thought not to be very sanguine, but which I thought to be properly veracious.[236] But if it is a question of contributing to general encouragement, one can no doubt dwell upon cheerful aspects of a particu-

---

to W. C. Ford, Sept. 25, 1912). The letter to Wilson was written on Sept. 4.

One further attempt was made by Jameson to bring about some historical publication which should suitably recall the signing of the treaty of Ghent. On learning that Nicholas Murray Butler had been appointed chairman of a committee on publications to commemorate this event, he suggested to him, Jan. 30, 1914, the publication of the family papers of R. H. Bayard, one of Jameson's former students. No reply to this letter has been found and it is probable that the outbreak of the European War brought an end to whatever projects the committee may have had in mind. The Bayard Papers were published as a report of the Historical Manuscripts Commission. See *ante,* Oct. 4, 1909, n. 135.

[232] Professor Halvdan Koht, of the University of Christiania, had visited the United States in 1909. At that time he had already written on Lincoln and on American independence, and the history of this country as well as that of his own continued to interest him. From 1926 to 1933 he was president of the International Committee of Historical Sciences. At the time of the Nazi invasion in 1940 he was Norwegian Minister of Foreign Affairs.

[233] Harold W. V. Temperley (1879-1939), fellow of Peterhouse, and later professor of modern history in Cambridge University and master of Peterhouse, lectured in Harvard University in 1911-1912. He was a member of the committee on the International Congress of Historical Sciences of 1913 and president of the International Committee of Historical Sciences from 1933 to 1938.

[234] Francis Christie Jameson was born during the summer of the Berlin Congress of Historical Studies.

[235] Temperley accepted the suggestion of this letter and the paper read by Jameson at the London Congress was *Typical steps of American expansion.* It later appeared in the *History Teacher's Magazine,* Feb., 1914.

[236] The present state of historical writing in America, *Proc. Amer. Ant. Soc.* **20**: 408-419, Oct., 1910.

lar field.   Anyhow, I place myself in your hands; but I let you know what my very distinct preferences are.

To George L. Burr

June 6, 1912.

My dear Burr:

It does not appear clear to me that I have written adequate replies to your very interesting letters and cards.   It was indeed impossible.   There is nothing for me to write about of any similar degree of interest, and if I were fondly to imagine that we had a theme of passing interest in our politics, whatever I should have said about it in March, April, or May, would probably seem untrue to me in June, and whatever I might write now might seem preposterous to you when you receive it.   If I should plot a curve of Roosevelt's advance from the time when you sailed till now and you should project it on till you meet me in Geneva in the early days of July you would think that we were then in the only remaining important republic except France.   It has quite astonished me how he has gone forward toward the nomination.   I am open to the same astonishment respecting his election.   I believe there is to be an election, though I do not remember to have heard the Democratic party mentioned in the last six weeks unless in some obscure place.

But I am so near the point of sailing[237] that I must not write more except to say that we had a pleasant meeting of the Board a week ago, at which all took pleasure in seeing your window in Grenoble and imagining your pleasure and work, and we hope rest. No revolutionary steps were taken.

*   *   *   *   *   *   *

We reach Geneva on the evening of June 30 and shall hope to find in the Pension Coupier some declaration regarding your whereabouts and those of Christie.   I expect to bring along the same shoes with which I have accompanied you along the Via Nationalis and the classic banks of the Delaware. . . .[238]

---

[237] Jameson's journey was for the purpose of locating material relating to American history in Swiss archives.

[238] In the spring of 1911 Burr, Christie, and Jameson had taken a three-day walk in the Delaware River valley, planned by Jameson, who wrote: "It is exceedingly good of you to agree to go so far in order to walk with a humble worm like me; but you will find me grateful and appreciative, though so destroyed by work as to have no conversation.   I shall be able to walk and I trust to eat, automatically, and perhaps also to sleep; but nothing beyond that, except to take a semi-rational enjoyment in your remarks.   So I look forward to the whole thing with great pleasure after all.   I do not have to be intelligent in order to be happy" (Jameson to Christie, Mar. 24, 1911).

To Waldo G. Leland

An Bord des Dampfers
Prinz Adalbert
June 24, [1912].

Dear Leland:

. . . Today I am thinking of you all as being engaged blythely in the noble task of moving, and of transferring the whole operations of the Department to a higher level.[239]

I do not praise the voyage; I do not praise any ocean voyage.   The boat is good; the captain most excellent; the food good—German, but with plenty of things that Christian Americans can eat; the weather was superb for the first five or six days

"The air was calm, and on the level brine
Sleek panope with all her sisters played."[240]
After that there were four days of rather heavy seas, though without rain; now it is calm again.

The boat is a slow sailor.   The agent in Washington mentioned eleven days.   I automatically added [one], but might better have added 2½, and indeed our arrival in Boulogne will not be many hours less than fourteen days from our departure.   Instead of arriving Tuesday, we are likely to arrive in the early hours of Thursday, but not early enough to catch the 6:52 train for Paris, in which case we get one at 12:30 and arrive in Paris at 4:28.   But such is life, and plans can always be changed and we can arrive in Geneva a day later without unsettling the foundations of Mont Blanc. . . .

P. S.   Landing at Boulogne June 26, Wed., 7 P. M. Spent night there.

To Woodrow Wilson

Rutland Hotel,
29 De Vere Gardens,
Kensington.
August 26, 1912.

My dear Wilson:

A friend has just sent me a newspaper containing your speech of acceptance of the presidential nomina-

---

[239] The Department of Historical Research was moving from the fifth floor of the Bond Building to the eleventh floor of the Woodward Building.   On July 4, Jameson wrote to Mr. Stock: "Brethern, you have my sympathy, although I am happy to say you have not had my aid.   In fact, I admit it to have been, or at any rate to have appeared to be, a skilful stroke to leave the country just before the process had to be carried through.   No doubt I could have contentedly taken a part in the process, but I find that I have found it much more agreeable to drive around Paris and see its beauties, to celebrate Francis's fourth birthday by open-air luncheon in a garden restaurant in the Bois de Boulogne, or to journey down here to Geneva to increasingly picturesque scenery, finally coming up that narrow portion of the valley of the Rhone, from Fort de l'Ecluse to Geneva, which we assisted Caesar to fortify when we were toiling through the first part of the interesting volume he wrote for beginners in Latin."

[240] Milton's Lycidas.

tion, and I have read it with the greatest pleasure.[241] It seems to me difficult for any one to read it without wishing that one who entertains such thoughts and can give them such expression should be put in the highest position of responsibility and usefulness which the nation can give him. Certainly I wish this, with all my heart, and am already looking forward with pleasure to the realization of that wish as probable. I wish that I had many votes to give. As a citizen of Washington, I have not even one; but I can add one voice to the applause at the inaugural speech, three or four spectators for the procession, and can always be counted upon as a warm supporter of the administration, albeit only in conversation.

With the most hearty good wishes, and with the kindest regards to Mrs. Wilson as well as to yourself, I am, as always,[242]

To Henry Adams

October 8, 1912.

My dear Adams:

It is always a pleasure to see your copperplate handwriting, which so shames the formless chirography of most of us younger men. It gave me however a peculiar pleasure to see it again the other day, because it gave such clear evidence of your entire restoration to health.[243] I am much obliged to you for writing regarding the alleged picture of the Ghent commissioners. Perhaps I had better ask the local inquirer to quote his authority for his story.[244]

I had a pleasant summer, thank you, and fondly hope that I accomplished something for our sacred science, though I base this hope rather on the fact that I kept very busy than on anything very impressive in

the sum total of the summer's achievements, now that I look at them with a dispassionate eye.

I am glad that you have enjoyed the summer. I remember that the region immediately about your brother's house is very pleasing. Some of the adjoining townships are familiar to me, and venerable on account of certain "embattled farmers" who did me the honor to stand as progenitors for me. It will be a great pleasure to see you in Washington again, and I shall hope that no result of the election will seem to you so calamitous that you cannot continue to enjoy this town.

To Patrick W. Joyce

November 1, 1912.

My dear Sir:

Without the opportunity and the honor of an introduction, may one who is puzzled in a matter of Irish place-names venture to ask the assistance of one who has published so interesting and so authoritative a book upon the subject?[245] I make my inquiry in connection with an investigation which I am making into the career of John White, who had a leading part in Raleigh's expeditions to North America.[246]

Hakluyt, in the portion of his book relating to these voyages, prints a letter addressed to him by this John White, who writes from "my house at Newtowne in Kylmore the 4 of February, 1593." Would it be possible for you to discern which Kilmore is meant by this? In the Topographical Index published in connection with the Irish census there seem to be a score of Kilmores and several score of Newtowns; but of Newtown in Kilmore I found there only three—one in Cavan, one in Mayo, and one in Wexford. I suppose that Mayo is out of the question in 1593-4, as being too far from the Pale, and that probably the same is true of Cavan; so that my conjecture would be that White is writing from the county of Wexford. But it has occurred to me that you may possibly know of means by which White's residence can be securely identified. Very little is known of him; almost nothing of him otherwise than from Hakluyt.[247] . . .

To Lyon G. Tyler

November 1, 1912.

My dear Dr. Tyler:

Do you know of the existence of any pictures of your college, of Bruton's Parish Church, and of the foundations of the building for the General Assembly,

---

[241] For an account of this ceremony, which took place on Aug. 7, 1912, see Baker, *Woodrow Wilson* 3: 373-374. The speech will be found in full in the *Public Papers of Woodrow Wilson* 2: 452-474, N. Y., Harper, 1927, taken from 62 Cong., 2 sess., Senate Doc. 903.

[242] Shortly after the election Jameson wrote: "I hope you are pleased that our old friend Wilson is elected. I am never perfectly pleased with *sweeping* victories in politics as they are sure to have bad effects, and I do not know how well Wilson will get along with Congress, with whom he is sure to have some bad rows if the Democrats have a large majority. But he is a good man, and does not despise high brows, and knows how to appeal effectively to public opinion behind the representatives; so let us hope for good things" (Jameson to H. B. Gardner, Nov. 6, 1912).

[243] In April, 1912, Henry Adams suffered a slight stroke which caused him to spend the summer in South Lincoln, Mass. On Sept. 29, he wrote to Jameson: "It is the first [summer] in near thirty years that I have passed in the country, and I have found the weather delightful, and the woods charming. The doctors have made me walk again, a habit I had abandoned long since, and, as I have since five years, abandoned writing and study, walking is a resource."

[244] The story of Jameson's search for a picture or pictures of the Ghent commissioners is later told to Professor Sloane. See *post,* Apr. 7, 1914.

[245] Patrick Weston Joyce (1827-1914), a resident of Dublin, was the author of *The origin and history of Irish names of places,* 2v., London and N. Y., Longmans, 1898-1913.

[246] See *ante,* Oct. 18, 1906, and n. 24.

[247] Mr. Joyce replied by adding a fourth Newtown, one in Neath, and saying that it was impossible to fix upon the one mentioned by Hakluyt (Joyce to Jameson, Nov. 12, 1912).

made in the period 1701-1704? I ask because in a manuscript volume in Switzerland this summer, mainly consisting of the diary of a traveller in America in that period, I saw some pen and ink drawings labelled "College standing at Williamsburg wherein the Governor has his dwelling," "a merchant's house," "foundation of the Council house," "the church." If any of these things would be of especial interest to Williamsburg people, I think that photographs of them could be obtained.[248]

To James H. Dillard

November 22, 1912.

Dear Sir:[249]

I have seen in a newspaper a mention of an approaching meeting of the University Commission on Southern Race Questions. I have not hitherto known of this organization. May I ask if in your judgment it would fall within its province to consider an historical question? I have for a long time been persuaded that this department of the Carnegie Institution of Washington might well at some time undertake the preparation and publication of a collection of documentary material respecting the history of the negro in the United States. I have hardly spoken of the plan to anyone and am far from having it fully formed. But my general object has a certain relation to what I should suppose would be the purpose of this University Commission. That is to say, I should wish to publish materials upon the past of the American negro in order to promote a better understanding of his present status and of the problems connected with his future. It is obvious that there are certain varieties of present-day studies, economic and social, which would contribute more directly toward this end, but these lie outside my province. And I should expect, partly by reason of some temporary circumstances in the Carnegie Institution, to leave at one side the period since 1861, though it is doubtless the most important period in the history of the negro.

Without at present going into detail respecting what I have in mind, I write to ask whether it would be a perfectly appropriate thing to ask you to lay before this meeting at Athens on December 19 the question, what variety or varieties of documentary historical publication respecting the history of the American negro before the Civil War would be most useful to the minds of those who are interested in the study of southern race questions of the present day. If you think that these gentlemen, so expert in that study, would be willing to advise respecting this matter, I

should be glad if you would put the item upon your docket or programme. It will be some years before I can undertake anything substantial, but preliminary time for thinking is always useful.[250]

To William H. Taft

November 26, 1912.

Mr. President:

In an interview which you were so good as to give me yesterday, you suggested that I might write to you respecting a National Archive Building as a topic for a portion of your Annual Message to Congress. I am glad to avail myself of the opportunity.

Though the approaching session will be short, there seems to be a very good disposition toward the erection of such a building on the part of all the members of the Committees on Public Buildings and Grounds in both House and Senate. I have strong hopes that a decisive step will be taken this session by the passage of one or the other of the bills now before the two houses. Some headway already gained will be lost if the matter goes over until another Congress, with new committees, especially as the chairman of the House committee, Mr. Sheppard,[251] then goes into the Senate. Therefore a strong impulse from the Executive will be peculiarly timely, and may carry the measure through.

In speaking of the matter, it may be thought advisable to dwell upon the shockingly unsuitable and unsafe conditions under which a large part of the archives of the government is now preserved; upon the fact that a fire, in any one of several buildings, especially in those rented, may at any time cause the government losses much above the cost of an archive building, by the destruction of vouchers and the like; that the rental of space occupied by the overflow of archives, in structures outside the departmental buildings, is nearly equal to the interest upon the sum which an adequate National Archive Building would cost; that the present crowded conditions cause such waste of time in the finding of documents as to constitute a serious drag upon the public business; that modern methods of communication by pneumatic tubes and the like, would make papers in a National Archive Building far more accessible to administrative officials in the departments than they now are when nominally

---

[248] President Tyler replied that they had no pictures as early as these and Jameson at once wrote to Berne for photographs of the drawings which accompanied the journal of Franz Ludwig Michel, who traveled in Virginia in 1699 or 1700.

[249] James H. Dillard, president of the Anna T. Jeans Foundation, New Orleans, secretary of the John F. Slater Fund.

[250] Mr. Dillard replied that he had sent this letter to D. W. M. Hunley, Charlottesville, Va., secretary of the University Commission on Southern Race Questions, with the recommendation that the matter be presented at the meeting of the commission on Dec. 19. At that meeting, held in Athens, Ga., Dr. Jameson's letter was read and it was voted that he be told that the commission could not co-operate with him but that individual members would be glad to give what aid they could. *Minutes of the commission*, 6-7.

[251] Morris Sheppard (1875-1941) was a member of the House of Representatives from Texas, 1902-1913; of the Senate from 1913 until his death.

housed in the departmental buildings; and thus that the erection of such a building would be a measure eminently productive of economy and of heightened administrative efficiency and security. The interests of history are also to be considered. Under present conditions great masses of material valuable to American history are dispersed about the city, so badly housed and so insufficiently made known as to make impossible their effective use by scholars and writers; in a proper National Archive Building they could be made the basis of many important and valuable historical works, official and unofficial. It might also be proper to advert to the fact that every other civilized country has a national archive building in which it has concentrated the documents relating to its past; Canada in particular has set us a splendid example. "The care which a nation devotes to the preservation of the monuments of its past may serve as a true measure of the degree of civilization to which it has attained."

May I also suggest that, in anything which is said of the matter, the term "Hall of Records" should be avoided. That term has been in former times much used in this connection here in Washington, but it is an unsuitable one and misleading to many minds. The structure ought to be anything else than a hall—in reality, a honeycomb of stacks. National Archive Building, or National Archives is the usual and most fitting term.

With much appreciation of the opportunity which you have given me, and with the hope that I have not abused it by writing at too great length.

To CHARLES H. HASKINS

November 27, 1912.

Dear Haskins:

My voice will be among the loudest of those protesting against your resignation; but you may not hear it on Saturday, amid the clamor and lamentation, and so, though this letter will probably not reach you before the meeting, I send it to tell you how sorry I am that you should come to any such conclusion.[252] There is a certain chaste severity about the operations of your mind which makes me believe that it is made up on the present occasion, and that protest is vain. If by the time this letter reaches you this has proved to be the case, at least let me tell you that I for one regard the service which you have performed to the Association as invaluable and never to be forgotten. I will improve upon good Dr. Butler's remark about the strawberry, by saying that I do not believe the Lord could have constructed a better secretary to the council.

If it proves that we must make a change, I do not think of anybody who could do the thing so well as Greene. I should not be willing that Leland should

have both functions to perform, and believe that it is otherwise best to have a special secretary to the council.[253]

To EDWARD B. KREHBIEL

January 14, 1913.

My dear Krehbiel:

Understanding that there was no need of haste about answering the questions which accompany your letter of November 21, I have waited till a number of things were out of the way. In what follows I expect to pass over many numbers in the list, because I cannot pretend to any knowledge respecting them, and sometimes because the matters seem to me not susceptible of any solid determination by any one. I may premise that my opportunities for knowledge in the field are slight. I lived in Baltimore from 1880 to 1888, spent two months of 1891 in Virginia, and have lived seven years in Washington, but I have no personal knowledge of the real South.[254] . . .

On the whole it is no doubt true that the upper classes of Southern society suffered losses of disproportionate severity in warfare. It must, however, not be forgotten that the constitution of Southern society, as of other aristocratic organizations in history, was largely artificial. I do not say with certainty, that the Southern aristocracy had an influence beyond its merits. But I think it was true to a considerable extent that it contained elements no longer worthy of their influential position. Slavery was injurious to practical efficiency and as a result of it many sons of well-to-do families were lazy and dissipated, drinking being very prevalent throughout the South. On the other hand there was in the lower strata of Southern society a great amount of native ability suffering to be liberated, and to a large extent this was liberated, not so much by the war as by the social reorganization which ensued upon it. In that respect the war had somewhat the effect which the period of the Revolution and of Napoleon had in France, the "carrière ouverte aux talents." The political control of the South during the past twenty years seems to have been mainly in the hands of persons whose fathers or grand-fathers were of the class that had one slave apiece or no slaves. Often they have been coarse but vigorous persons like Tillman, though not always with his capacity for growth nor with his in general high character. Now in industrial life the leadership of such persons has been much more beneficial, I imagine, than would have been that of the scions of the old aristocracy who often seem

---

[252] Charles H. Haskins had been secretary of the executive council of the American Historical Association since 1900.

[253] Evarts B. Greene. W. G. Leland was secretary of the Association.

[254] The questions here answered have not been found. The omissions are of answers which mean nothing in the absence of the questions. The numbers given to the paragraphs to indicate the number of the question answered, have also been omitted.

rather helpless persons with more refinement than vigor. These things of which I have spoken are not so much results of war as of this particular war and the crumbling of the old aristocracy. . . .

There is of course a good deal of nonsense about this talk of blood, in the South as elsewhere. In the North and in the South alike, with very few exceptions, the American nation in its first two centuries was composed by transplanting to this country a large section of the European middle class, with a little of the dregs and almost none of the aristocracy. The plain people rose to be aristocrats in the South by acquiring property of one sort, just as in more recent years they have risen to be "society people" in the North by acquiring property of another sort; nevertheless it in many ways does people good to suppose that they are of high descent when they are not. I am accustomed to say to the young people around me that the American nation consists of two sorts of people, those who are descended from lower-middle-class English people and are aware of it, and those who are descended from lower-middle-class English people and are not aware of it. The latter feel much better. . . .

It ought to be added that the Southern aristocracy never was a closed circle. It was always possible for young men of talent but of humble origin to make their way up into it. . . .

What damage came from the non-political carpet-baggers was surely over-balanced by the energizing influence of Northern men who pushed in to make their fortunes; and the most observant person among my acquaintances always maintains, after some months of residence in the South, that they still need more emigration. . . .

Alfred H. Stone,[255] a young planter at Dunleith, Mississippi, might be a useful person to consult. He is a high authority on the economic history of the negro in the South since the war, but is also a person who has read and thought much of all Southern history. Another would be Dr. Frederick Bancroft, Metropolitan Club, Washington, D. C., also a historical scholar of eminence in the Southern field. A third might be Professor H. H. MacPherson, professor of history in the University of Georgia, not perhaps a very acute or able man, but judicious. I am also asking my assistant, Dr. Edmund C. Burnett to write to you. He is an east Tennessee man who had relatives on both sides in the Civil War and was for some years professor of history at Mercer University, Macon, Georgia.

[255] Alfred Holt Stone, president of the Mississippi Historical Society, 1912-1913, and a frequent contributor to the *American Historical Review* and other periodicals, on the economic problems of the South. He later became chairman of the State Tax Commission of Mississippi.

To SARA JAMESON

Brown's Hotel
London W.
April 2, 1913.

Dearest Sara:

Does the enclosed look natural? It isn't Brown's and St. George's, but merely Brown's. A thousand things to tell you each day, but shan't. The congress begins this evening with a reception at the Grafton Galleries. Tomorrow morning opening session, with Mr. Bryce's address; then we split up into nine sections for papers. My piece comes tomorrow afternoon, in sec. IV., Modern History. I read it in the hall of the Royal Society in Burlington House. I have spent part of today at the Br. Mus., filling in certain gaps in it, for which I had not the data on shipboard.[256]

Last night's R. H. S. dinner was a good deal of an affair. The best speech was of course the American one, namely that of Ch. Haskins. I sat next to Mrs. Prothero, and opposite Sir John Laughton the naval historian, Sir Harry Johnston the African explorer and administrator, whom I had met in Washington, and Mons. Bémont, editor of the *Revue Historique*. Eduard Meyer inquired cordially for you. Saw a lot of men I knew.[257]

Tomorrow noon visit Apsley House, (Duke of Wellington's) seldom opened; eve., gov't dinner. Fri. noon Lansdowne House, afternoon, tea at House of Commons with Sir Courtenay Ilbert, clerk of House, eve., special performance "Hamlet," Forbes Robertson. Sat., visit to Windsor Castle, "by invitation of His Majesty the King," eve., dine with Sir George Trevelyan, Sun., I mean to go to the old Dutch Church in Austin Friars; P. M., reception Royal Hist. Soc., eve. dine with Prothero.[258] Mon., lunch with Royal Com-

[256] Jameson was attending the Fourth International Congress of Historical Sciences in London. See *Amer. Hist. Rev.* **18**: 679-691, July, 1913.

[257] Sir John Knox Laughton (1830-1915) was the founder of the Navy Records Society. Sir Harry Johnston (1858-1927) had published *British Empire in Africa* in 1910. His extensive travels in Africa and his voluminous writings on that continent were well known to Dr. Jameson. Charles Bémont (1848-1939) began his work for the *Revue Historique* in 1876 and remained with it till his death.

Eduard Meyer (1853-1930), since 1902 professor of ancient history in the University of Berlin, visited this country in 1909 as the guest of the American Historical Association, at its twenty-fifth anniversary meeting in New York. He served as German exchange professor in Harvard in 1909-1910, and was well known to the Jamesons.

[258] Sir George W. Prothero (1840-1922), whose wife sat next to Jameson, was president of the Royal Historical Society from 1901 to 1910. He had been a guest of the American Historical Association at the New York meeting of 1909 and in 1910 had delivered a series of Lowell lectures in Boston and was the Schouler lecturer in the Johns Hopkins University. His work as one of the editors of the *Cambridge Modern History*, about which he and Jameson had had correspondence (see *ante* Sept. 12, 1907, n. 65), had been completed in 1912.

Sir George Otto Trevelyan (1838-1928), nephew of Lord Macaulay and author of *The American Revolution*, to whom

mission on Historical Records, p.m. reception and tea at Public Record Office, dine with Hall at Lyceum Club. Tu. reception Sir Geo. and Lady Trevelyan. Wed., Oxford, where Prof. and Mrs. Firth put me up; and when I go to Dublin the great Prof. Mahaffy puts me up at Trinity College.[259] Quite a whirl. . . .

To Sara Jameson

Brown's Hotel,
London W.
(Dover St. and Albemarle St.)
April 6, 1913.

Dearest Sara:

. . . Yesterday afternoon at Windsor, where we were taken all around the castle, and where the King provided a tea, but was not present, being in mourning for his uncle, the King of Greece.[260] Dined at Sir George Trevelyan's. Mighty interesting evening, especially the old man's own talk, for I sat next to him. The company: an old English lord, another Englishman, four Americans, three Germans, a Dutchman, a Belgian, a Japanese. (Some 1200 in all) Well, when I got home I found a note from Miss Vinall, thanking for inauguration pictures, and saying, "If you see Sir George Trevelyan, tell him you know an old lady who wishes before she dies to read the third volume of his 'American Revolution.' There are a few things I wish to do before I depart, and to finish that book is one of them." It is out, and I am going to get a copy, have him write in it, and send it to her.[261]

Must now breakfast with a man, then go to the old Dutch Church in Austin Friars and two or three other old E.-end churches I've never seen. Dine with Pro-

thero. Tomorrow eve. Mrs. Humphrey Ward invites me "to meet the Lord Chancellor." [262]

To Sara Jameson

April 13, 1913.

Dearest Sara:

. . . For myself, I have had a very happy day.[263] The weather was the finest we have had since we landed, and we have spent the day in a most lovely country, Buckinghamshire,—meaning Leland, Mrs. L. and I. I tried to get Bancroft and Ford, but they had already agreed to go to Canterbury with C. F. A. [Charles Francis Adams.] We took train to Rickmansworth, a "fly" thence to Chalfont St. Giles, Milton's cottage where he wrote part of "Paradise Lost" and all of "P. Regained," and to which Fr. and I went last August by a somewhat different route. Then to Jordans, where is a quaint old Friends' meeting house, one of the oldest, to which Wm. Penn used to go and where he and his family and Thomas Ellwood [264] are buried, then to Beaconsfield. 8 miles thus in the open carriage, lovely ride; then lunch at the Saracens Head. Burke and Waller are buried in Beac. ch. yard. Thence we walked, 10 m., by Burnham Beeches to Stoke Pogis and Slough, then train home. A day of English country such as you read about—lovely fields, cottages, hedges, gorse in bloom, cherry trees in blossom, robins singing.

I wrote you Thursday night from Bath. The next day was a wonderful one. Awful weather, to be sure, but never mind. Eighteen or 20 of us,—Germans, Russians, one Italian, one Pole, one Ceylonese, one American, various English, went in a big touring-car 20 m. out and 20 back, first to Cheddar, with its wonderful limestone cave, on which we had a little lecture by Professor Boyd Dawkins, whose book on "Cave Hunting" I had long since enjoyed,[265] then Glastonbury and the ruins of its abbey, then Wells and its beautiful cathedral. The dean gave us a tea, and showed us all over the deanery, then the bishop, a most lovable old gentleman, showed us over his palace. Then we drove back in the pouring rain to Bath.

Yesterday morning to Oxford, where again the

Jameson had written during the preceding year, to enlist his aid in his search for debates, notes, or journals in private hands, for use in the projected *Proceedings and debates of British Parliaments respecting North America,* to be edited by L. F. Stock. In reply to Jameson's first letter on the subject, Trevelyan wrote: "Never did debates in any assembly produce a deeper effect on the destinies of mankind" (Trevelyan to Jameson, Feb. 15, 1912).

[259] Sir Charles Harding Firth (1857-1936), regius professor of modern history in Oxford University, 1904-1925, widely known for his work on the period of the Commonwealth and the Protectorate. He was knighted in 1922.

John Pentland Mahaffy (1839-1918), professor of ancient history in Trinity College, Dublin, from 1871. He had long been known to Jameson through his writings on Greek history and civilization.

[260] George I had been assassinated Mar. 18, 1913.

[261] Miss Louise Vinall of Woburn, Mass., was a friend of Jameson's mother. One of the editors remembers hearing Dr. Jameson tell that Sir George Otto Trevelyan wrote in the volume something like this: "To Miss Louise Vinall from the author, with the hope that he will live to write and she will live to read the fourth and final volume of this work." The second part of this wish was not granted; Miss Vinall died at the home of Jameson's mother in Woburn on Dec. 3, 1913 (Jameson to Sara Jameson, Dec. 3, 1913).

[262] Mrs. Humphry Ward (1851-1920), the popular novelist, was Mary Augusta Arnold, daughter of Thomas Arnold, second son of Dr. Arnold of Rugby. The Lord Chancellor was Lord Haldane.

[263] This was Jameson's wedding anniversary.

[264] Among the Jameson Papers is a sheet, possibly meant to accompany this letter, quoting Thomas Ellwood's account of his first meeting with Milton, their subsequent intercourse, and the oft-told story of Ellwood's comment after reading *Paradise Lost:* "Thou hast said much of Paradise Lost, but what hast thou to say of Paradise Found?" To answer this, Milton wrote *Paradise Regained.*

[265] Sir William Boyd Dawkins (1837-1929), author not only of *Cave hunting,* 1874, but also of *Early man in Britain,* 1880, was the discoverer of the first example of the art of the cave man to be found in Britain. He was knighted in 1919.

librarian of Exeter College was absent, so I gave up that MS., worked a while at the Bodleian, came up to London, and slept nine hours. I think I can do it again tonight, after our walk. . . .

To Sara Jameson
                                    April 15, 1913.
Dearest Sara:

I have just got my passage from Liverpool, "Cymric," White Star, sailing May 6, should arrive in Boston May 15—but say 16 or 17, Wash. 22 or 23.

Temperley of Cambridge, who has business with me, has to have me come Saturday, which crowds me a little here, but it's all right. I lunch with the Hazeltines,[266] dine and spend the night with T. [Temperley] at "Peterhouse," and Sunday go on to Bawtry, Scrooby, Austerfield (the Pilgrims' places) [267] and York. Monday arrive at Edinburgh, to be two or three days as Seth's guest.[268] . . . Must be brief, for I must now work hard to go away, and may not write again from London. Tomorrow Ford and I lunch with young George Macaulay Trevelyan.[269] Th. eve. I take F., Bancroft and the Lelands to Albert Hall to hear Coleridge Taylor's "A Tale of Old Japan" (his last work) and pts. I. and III. of "Hiawatha," given by a big choral society, conducted by Sir Frederick Bridge.

To Sara Jameson
                        Trinity College, Dublin
                        April 30, 1913.[270]
Dearest Sara:

. . . I am quite in clover. My host, Prof. Mahaffy, a wonderful old man, whose books I have been reading ever since 1879, has a fine old house in another part of the city, but as a senior fellow of Trinity College has this four-story house in the college quadrangle, where he has his study, in which I am writing, and a bedroom or two, in one of which I sleep, and rattle around in the rest of the house, perfectly at home. Goody McCuen

gives me breakfast in the study, the kind old professor takes me to luncheon with the others in the Fellows' Common-room, and last night had a dinner for me at his beautiful old house. Tonight we dine with some friends of his, tomorrow night with the Viceroy and the Countess of Aberdeen at the Castle (met her at Round Table in Jan.),[271] Fri. to Wales.

"And here I be, as happy as a chipmunk on a wall,
    With nothing to feel riled about, much later'n
Adam's fall."

I like the Irish very much; enormously different from the English, though certainly the English have been very hospitable to me too. Don't know how I can ever repay any of it, but shall try.[272] . . .

To Waldo G. Leland
                        Liverpool, May 6. [1913].

Last Adventure in Great Britain, of J. F. J.

Conceiving that I needed a good walk before embarking at Liverpool, I planned that after leaving Ireland I would treat myself to a three days' tramp in North Wales. The first morning was spent in exploring the numberless staircases and halls and chambers of Carnarvon Castle, and in getting by train to Llanberis, so I was not perfectly fresh when, at two o'clock, I set out for the ascent of Snowdon. Snowdon is 3560 ft. high, the village of Llanberis 370. There is a path up from Llanberis, on the north side of the range, and also a cog-wheel railroad, but the ascent from the east side is finer though rougher, and my plan was to walk around to the east side, to a place called Gorphwysfa, go up from there, spend the night at the hotel on the top, getting the sunset and sunrise perhaps; on the second day to walk down the south side to Beddgelert; and on the third day to skirt the range on the southeast and walk on to Bettws-y-Coed, where is some of the best of the North Welsh scenery.

The six miles to Gorphwysfa were done in a hard rain, by four o'clock. The ascent of Snowdon from there is reckoned at three hours, and though it continued to rain more or less, I figured that by seven I should be under cover, drying my feet before a fire, and eating a good dinner. The path was rough, the rock being slate, and at times was faint. I lost it once

<hr/>

[266] Harold D. Hazeltine, A.B., Brown, 1894, after study in Harvard, the University of Berlin, and the University of London, in 1906 became lecturer on Law in Emmanuel College, Cambridge. In 1919 he was made Downing Professor of Laws of England in the University of Cambridge.

[267] Scrooby was the home of William Brewster; Austerfield, the birthplace of William Bradford. Bawtry was a convenient center for this excursion.

[268] James Seth (1860-1924) taught philosophy in Brown University from 1892 to 1896, when he became Sage Professor of Moral Philosophy in Cornell University; from 1898 till his death he was professor of moral philosophy in the University of Edinburgh, where his brother Andrew was professor of logic and metaphysics.

[269] George Macaulay Trevelyan, younger son of Sir George Otto, was soon to become an even better known historian than his father. His wife is a daughter of Mrs. Humphry Ward.

[270] On the 28th, Jameson wrote to his wife from Belfast, of two days spent in Coleraine and Londonderry, in a search for traces of Jameson forebears.

[271] The Viceroy of Ireland (Lord Lieutenant) was John Campbell Gordon, seventh Earl of Aberdeen.

Luncheons at the Round Table of the Library of Congress, where Herbert Putnam gathered together notable visitors to Washington, residents of the city, and members of his own staff, were famous for the excellence of the conversation.

[272] A similar letter to Leland on the same date added: "Having bought a few more things than I intended—such as a sofa at Coleraine, which my grandchildren will swear came over in the *Molly* in 1746 with their grandfather's grandfather's grandfather, but which is simply a fairly good sofa, which we needed—I have but just enough money to get home, so am not sending you any."

or twice, but easily found it again. But finally the rain turned to snow, and the ascent became slippery, and at a few places perilous. So I was glad when I came, near the summit, to the tracks of the cog-wheel railroad. It was a little disconcerting that presently it ran into a snowdrift. Then I reached the hotel, and found it closed as tight as a drum, uninhabited, and with all its winter shutters fastened over the windows— and a snowstorm going on, and the wind blowing a gale, and the time 7.00 p. m.!

I might have premised that on the station platform of the London and N. W. R. R. I had seen fresh placards of the Snowdon R. R. saying that the following would be their time-table for May and June, and that the hotel was "now open for the season." They generally open in April. Also the L N.W. sta. agt. said it was open.

Though I am in general a respecter of property, it seemed to be my obvious duty to get inside of that hotel. I was quite tired out, thought I could travel no more; and needed a fire and a bed. There was one shutter I could manage to tear off. Using it as a battering-ram, I smashed in the window-sash, and crawled in. I found a half of a loaf of bread, and it was pleasant to sit down where it was dry, and eat something, and chew a little tea which I found. That the bread was a trifle old seemed unimportant under the circumstances. But there was no fuel whatever, except the straw-coverings of a few empty bottles, no oil, no candles, and no beds. The beds, I afterward learned, had been taken down to Llanberis in the autumn.

This gave a different turn to the situation. While I appreciated its humorous aspect, I thought there was danger in staying. It was pretty cold, and no one could tell how long the snow might keep up, and I had a date with the White Star Line less than three days distant. Neither did I have any proper supply of reading matter for the Sabbath (this was Saturday evening). At 7:30 I could still read Baedeker, and I crammed up the directions for the path to Llanberis. I knew it was impossible, after a little snow, to find the path by which I had come up. But if one proceeded by the Llanberis way he could at times follow the railroad track. I concluded the risk in starting down was in that latitude less than the risk in staying. So I crawled out of the window and set out, at twenty minutes of eight. At first I did very well. The snow soon stopped, but it changed to a heavy rain. As it grew darker, it became hard to find the path if one lost it, as I sometimes did. On the other hand, to follow it closely meant to wade in a brook from one to three inches deep, as the rain from the mountain side generally poured down that channel, in part. To follow the railroad would not do, in the lower part of its course, because just before it reached Llanberis it crossed a river, and at ten o'clock of a dark night you can't safely go over high narrow-gauge trestles. So I stumbled on, falling only one or twice. As it grew darker the path

broadened, and I followed it pretty well. Then, quite in sight of the lights of the village, at an unexpected turn, I stepped off a curb or parapet and fell into a stream two feet deep. Fell on my feet, however. The last quarter-mile to Llanberis is a very narrow path through a bit of forest, and I should have been there till morning groping around, or fallen into the river, if a countryman had not come along, and gently led me through it by the hand.

So I got to shelter at an inn at Llanberis, at 10:40 p.m., and mighty glad to get there. Sunday I stayed in bed till noon, and have no worse effects from the whole adventure than a blister made by wet shoes, which still makes me somewhat lame. However, I resumed my journey that afternoon, with modifications appropriate to finding myself on the wrong side of the mountain, walked five or six miles in the rain, and nine the next day in beautiful weather and scenery.

The manager of the Snowdon Railway, whom I went to notify of his open window, said they had expected to open May 1, but a snowstorm a few days before producing the drift I had seen, had prevented. Their posters, scattered all about the country, could not be recalled. But that on the L. and N. W. platform, 300 ft. from their own station in Llanberis, could have been.

Anyhow, it was a good adventure.

To Henry E. Legler

June 5, 1913.

Dear Sir: [273]

I was out of the country when your letter of April 19 arrived. I hope this letter may not seem to be too tardy a reply. I have to make it a brief one.

The specific question which you propound "What can the library do to encourage the study of American history?" is one which I suppose must have very different answers for different sorts of libraries. In the case of libraries of moderate size in small cities, it has sometimes appeared to me that the money used in the purchase of books on American history was too exclusively used in buying the less expensive sort of books, those in one or two or three volumes, of which it is perfectly easy to get a considerable number out of each year's appropriations, while on the other hand the purchase of certain books of value in expensive sets, was never made because it could not easily be made in any one given year. If the purchasing policy were given a somewhat longer range, extending over several years, one might plan to redress this inequality. To avoid speaking as if I were recommending any one long set of Americana for purchase, let me adduce as an instance a library of forty or fifty thousand volumes with which I am familiar which has in the past twenty years bought

---

[273] Henry E. Legler (1861-1917) was a member of the Wisconsin Free Library Commission from 1904 until 1909, when he became head of the Chicago public library. See the sketch of his life in the *Dictionary of American Biography*.

a great many books of English history, without ever yet having afforded the purchase of the *Dictionary of National Biography,* obviously because it was too large a morsel for any one year's budget.

If I were to proceed to make one suggestion for the larger libraries, I might select for comment the relative lack of co-operation among such libraries in respect to the pursuit of the more expensive specialties. It is plain that the interests of students are, in respect to restricted specialties of this class, better served on the whole by their being able to find relatively complete collections in one place, rather than scattered fragments of such collections in various places. The ambition of libraries for possession might well be tempered by some closer approach to systematic organization of these things, whereby certain ones should be recognized as belonging plainly in the field of a certain library without competition on the part of the others. I am speaking, of course, of things which only a few students are seeking, and which they must expect to seek by travel, and not of those things for which there is a separate effective demand in every large city.

May I also suggest the question whether it is not a legitimate use of the funds of a public library to pay recognized experts, resident in its city or summoned from elsewhere, to go over the shelves relating to a particular subject and carefully signalize those gaps which are almost certain to occur; to name, in other words, any important books which have been omitted but which are necessary to make the collection a well-rounded one for the needs of the particular locality as the librarian sees them. I think also that university and college libraries are particularly in need of such periodical redress, because professors are so prone to request books needed for the immediate purposes of their classes, and to exhaust their appropriations by such requests, forgetting the need of building up rounded collections for general purposes; and the librarian, on his part, feels a certain delicacy about suggesting books for which the professor has evinced no desire, though often he will agree they were desirable, if their absence were called to his attention.

To Francis A. Christie

[July ? 1913.]

. . . P. S. Since writing the inclosed letter I have received yours of Franconia. All is forgiven. Once a man agrees to teach systematic theology when he knows he is entitled to occupy himself with church history all his days, the rest follows easily. "The first crime may seem a slight thing, yet it may lead to larceny, and drunkenness, and ultimately to Sabbath-breaking and procrastination." The main point however still remains, namely, that when you have got all of your systematic theology out of your system, you should come over here and have some rational conversation and healthful exercise. . . .

To Robert S. Woodward

North Edgecomb, Maine.
July 3, 1913.

My dear President Woodward:

I thank you for your letter of June 27. I have delayed replying until I should receive your circular letter. I think that the matter is now so clear to me that I shall not need to come down to Boston to make any further inquiries.

I do not think that I can secure a steady supply of proper persons for Research Associates in this Department, and I suppose that such continuous application of the system is not requisite to the plan which you have had in mind. I shall however hope to make occasional use of it, and possibly in 1914. Professors of American history, when able to free themselves from their work of teaching for a year or half-year, will only in a minor number of cases be disposed to spend their time in work affiliated to that of my Department rather than in tasks which they themselves have already planned; and of these men, it is only the most eminent, and only certain individuals even in that class, that I should want. Take, for instance, our friend Osgood. If he were to spend a year in Washington at the cost of the Carnegie Institution he would do a splendid year's work, so far as industry, devotion to his work, and the high quality of the product are concerned; but it would do me and my Department almost no good, because he has no conversation. It would be a separate and distinct thing, perhaps well worth subsidizing, but it would no more meet the purposes which you have in view than if he were doing it in New York. I should want a man overflowing with ideas, who would have his own line of work on which to spend most of his day—some task similar to ours or allied to it—but who in daily talks would wake me and the Department up, and make suggestions affecting our plans and our thinking. One man in America would fill this bill perfectly, and that is Frederick J. Turner of Harvard; but it is useless to think of getting him for two or three years yet. Another man who might be available before that, and who would answer the requirements perhaps half as well, is Edward Channing of the same institution. I dare say that his well-spring of ideas would run dry in much less time, but he is a steady and stimulating researcher. But let me ask if you would feel well inclined toward a proposal that Admiral Mahan should be asked to spend six months with us—say the six months which he ordinarily spends in New York, or from next December to May? I do not know whether it would be possible to persuade him, but I should be glad to try. The only terms on which it would be possible—and this I think would be true of almost any fit person—are that he should have, for the occupation of most of his time, the duty of doing a considerable piece of historical investigation, selected by him and congenial to him. He has not been doing a great deal of that sort of thing lately, but has been writing publicistic articles, which no doubt are profitable. He has already written the historical things which he most desired to write. Yet it is possible that, if the pecuniary conditions were equalized he might like to spend a half-year in Washington in solid historical research, not too exacting, for he is nearly seventy-three years old, and not strong, with only the additional obligation, let us say, of seeing me every day and talking to me. His thinking is of a very high quality, and would do me much good. He is a good talker, lucid, penetrating, and interesting.

To bring a man of such distinction into the system of any institution is not possible except with some elasticity in the system; but I should enjoy making the attempt to present the scheme to him, talking it over with him, and seeing under what conditions if any he could agree to what might be proposed. May I ask what you think of all this? I could get plenty of lesser men to come, but the effect would in most cases be, to aid them but not me. I do not wish to intimate that I cannot be taught anything except by a very few supremely excellent persons; I mean rather to say that I wish to be taught by supremely excellent persons rather than by any others. It must also be remembered that in this department the field of choice is more limited than in others, because on the whole one could not make use of any but Americans since our tasks are in the field of American history, in which no European is at present very high authority.[274]

To the Secretary of War

North Edgecomb, Maine,
July 7, 1913.

Sir:[275]

Soon after my return from Europe in the last days of May I was informed by Professor R. M. Johnston[276] of his endeavors to secure the creation of a proper Historical Commission, to which should be entrusted the efforts made under authority of the War Department to comply with the act of March 2,[277] respecting the collecting and editing of the mili-

---

[274] Admiral Mahan accepted the appointment and came to Washington in the autumn of 1914, prepared to study sea power and American expansion. He died after but a few weeks of work.

[275] Lindley M. Garrison, secretary of War from 1913 to 1916. This letter is marked "Personal."

[276] Robert M. Johnston (1867-1920), at this time assistant professor of history in Harvard, was the editor of the *Military Historian and Economist* and a frequent reviewer for the *American Historical Review*, in the field of military history.

[277] The act appropriated $25,000 and $7,000 for the War and Navy departments respectively, to provide for the collection of the military and naval records of the Revolutionary War, with a view to their publication. From Jameson's statement it is not to be assumed that he had known nothing of the legislative history of this act. In fact, while the bill was in committee he had drafted two sections of the measure. Jameson to Henry A. Vale, clerk of the Committee on the Library, Jan. 19, 1912.

tary records of the Revolutionary War. The act itself had been passed so short a time before my sailing for Europe that I was not aware of its passage. From the time of receiving Professor Johnston's note I earnestly desired to secure the opportunity of seeing you about the matter; but my days in Washington were so few that I was not able to do so.

I think it quite certain that Professor Johnston is in principle right in his judgment that the task which the statute imposes would be better performed by a commission or other body containing representatives of both the military and the historical professions. No doubt this might not have been true of the Official Records of the Civil War. The documents involved in that compilation were so closely similar to those which were in current use by War Department and Army at the time when the compilation was made that there was no danger of incompleteness or misunderstanding on the part of those engaged in the work. But I think the matter stands differently in the case of a war so remote as that of 1775-1783.

1. The system of military organization prevailing at that time, and of military records corresponding, was widely different from anything now prevailing. Hardly any of our military men have occupied themselves with any thoroughgoing researches into the military history of that period. It is unquestionable that army officers, with their modern military knowledge, could contribute an indispensable element toward elucidating the system of documentation then followed. But on the other hand, there are many matters which would be more correctly understood by persons versed in history. It stands to reason that the cooperation of both would bring better results than could be attained by the separate work of either. I have seen, in works of the sort, about an equal number of cases in which matters have been misunderstood for want of historical knowledge on the one hand or of military knowledge on the other.

2. But if such considerations hold good in respect to the subject-matter, or the papers already in Washington, they are still more clearly valid in respect to the task of collection, because of the unusual status of the vast mass of outlying material. In case of a country having a centralized military system, e. g., in the case of the wars of Frederick and of Napoleon, this difficulty does not arise. But the military records of the American War of Independence are those of a federation, of a very loose federation, and of a federation whose members attended rather badly to the business of military administration and showed singular want of system in the keeping of their papers. Now historical scholars have for thirty years been coping with the difficulties produced in historical research by this want of system. They have learned the ins and outs of such research in a thousand particulars in respect to which army officers are amateurs. In dealing with the Revolution under

all its varied aspects they have acquired a fund of special knowledge of the material, which no one taking up *de novo* a particular branch of it could acquire without great waste of time, if at all.[278]

3. Much of the material is in state archives, especially those of the original thirteen states. Of some of these archives no inventory has been printed. None has printed an inventory sufficiently minute to serve the researcher as a guide by which he can be sure of getting all that he wants. Researches on the spot are made difficult by the fact that most of these archives are unscientifically arranged, and one may almost say that they are arranged on thirteen different systems. All these things have been learned by some, would have to be learned by others, and have in each instance their peculiar pitfalls.

4. Many of the outlying materials are in the hands of state and local historical societies. In the libraries or cabinets of most of these great want of order prevails. I could name one in which one of the most expert searchers for Revolutionary materials was almost baffled by the apparently hopeless confusion, and after long efforts felt that he subdued it only incompletely. I could name another in which the only guide is the memory of the librarian, who yields up more and more of his treasures as his confidence is won, but whom one has to learn how to use, like any other piece of bibliographical apparatus.

5. There are other materials in the public libraries which present much less difficulty, and many in the hands of private holders, chiefly collectors of autographs—a class of persons whom historical people have to know and military people do not.

6. A considerable portion of the material, even in the class of official military records so called, is, by reason of capture or other accident, hidden and scattered in European, Canadian, Cuban, or Mexican archives. Historical students know how these repositories are to be approached and exhaustively searched; military men have not had occasion to use these processes.

7. The question, what shall be done with material already printed—either that of which the manuscript is still preserved or that of which the original has disappeared—is bound to come up and to be dealt with. In any case such material will have to be searched for. I can testify from a precisely similar experience, in searching for printed Revolutionary material of another sort, that such bibliographical work is, from the nature of our historical publications, a difficult matter, in which none but well trained historical experts of a particular type can succeed.

8. The term "military records" requires definition. The difficulties of which I have spoken are those attending the finding and treatment of military records in the most restricted official sense. It is probable that the interests of those for whose benefit records of the Revolutionary War are printed will be deemed to require a more liberal construction of the term. The more liberal the scope given to the searcher the greater will be the difficulties suggested above, and the greater the need to bring to bear upon the task the judgment of those to whom American history is their most familiar business.

9. Military records no doubt include muster rolls; in fact, little as we may like to think so, the desire to get interminable muster rolls into print, for the benefit of "patriotic hereditary" societies, is the strongest public feeling behind the passage of this act. It is familiar to many of us that a fierce light doth beat upon a Revolutionary muster roll and upon all the genealogical work connected with it. The knowledge which genealogical experts have acquired concerning documents of this class should be invoked; but historical students know which among the multitude of genealogists can be safely resorted to and drawn upon.

10. I may sum up the whole matter of what I have written by a reference to the indisputable doctrine that in such a matter the government ought to have the very best. Here is a mass of expert knowledge of Revolutionary history which a certain class of men have laboriously acquired, and which would surely be of prime importance to the task in hand. Why should the government be without it when it can perfectly well have it? It is not improper to add, without any thought of disparagement to the general intellectual quality of our army, that, relatively to the armies of other great nations, it has during the last thirty years shown a very small supply of finished students of earlier military history.

I have written because Professor Johnston has requested me to do so, but also because of the strong sense I have long entertained, and often expressed, that our government's historical work, abundant, but often not good, was too largely produced by bureau men, and that it would be better done if the government could be persuaded to draw more largely upon the historical profession, now one of the best equipped professions in the country, though thirty years ago hardly existent.

To GEORGE N. FULLER

North Edgecomb, Maine.
July 31, 1913.

My dear Sir:[279]

I should gladly reply fully to your letter of July

---

[278] In Justin Winsor's presidential address to the American Historical Association, Manuscript sources of American history, delivered in May, 1887, he dealt with the dispersal of sources for the history of the American Revolution. See *Magazine of American History* 18: 20-34, July, 1887.

[279] George N. Fuller had recently become secretary and editor for the Michigan Historical Commission.

30, but probably the method which you suggest is better. I do not think that the larger problems of historical editing are treated profitably in any specific publications that now come to my mind, and if I were to discourse regarding them in general terms it would be to emit a series of sounding generalities that would probably impress you as doctrine already familiar and commonplace. So, if most of what I should say would be superfluous, it would be better if I could have an opportunity to try to answer those particular questions on which you really are in doubt. It is quite true that the books on historical method, like Langlois and Seignobos' *Introduction,* or Bernheim's *Lehrbuch,* or Freeman's *Methods of Historical Study* furnish the mind with all the main principles upon which the purveyor of historical sources for studious mankind has to act; but I imagine that these are familiar to you from graduate work in your university. Let me then, if you please, attempt to answer specific questions as they arise.

May I however make one general suggestion at the beginning of your course of labors, and that is, that you should have a large, comprehensive, general plan. Of course there are probably tasks already undertaken for or in the Pioneer Historical Society's Collections that you will have to finish, so that you cannot at once begin the execution of a large design, nor is it necessary that you should have one single plan; and of course you will not have a perfectly free hand to do what would seem to you the ideal thing, but must adapt yourself to others, either persons in authority or classes of persons who are interested in materials which seem to you not of the first importance. But what I mean is that within the first year of your service you should devote a great amount of time to thinking of what needs to be done in order to fill the gaps in the present documentation of Michigan history. That is to say, think of all the different sorts of monographs that ought yet to be written in order to fill the whole circuit of what we now wish to know, or the men of the next twenty-five years will wish to know, respecting Michigan history, and then see how far the materials for such pursuits are in print and what things are lacking. We had a commission at Washington in President Roosevelt's time which went over United States history with such a purpose, and you may get some suggestions from our work, so I send you a copy of the Report. But it will also be very important for you to think carefully as to what parts of an ideal programme are likely to be carried out by other agencies, to steer clear of duplication, and to be always ready for teamwork with other historical societies or commissions, or at any rate disposed to adjust the boundaries of your tasks to the observed boundaries of theirs.

Also, I should think that you would do well to think a good deal as to what the best historical investigators occupied with Michigan history are at present disposed to undertake in the way of monographic writing, and to see what materials they will need that are not now in print. This list of things that are wanted may be somewhat different from the list of things which in your judgment ought to be wanted; but you will wish to meet desires as well as needs, and to forward Michigan history by instruments already in existence rather than to wait for Providence to raise up a group of persons who have no desire but to do the very most important things. It is sometimes better to provide a lot of materials that are going to be used soon than to provide a *better* lot that is not going to be used soon.

But I fear that after all I am slipping into sounding generalities. Please let me be of use in **any** ways more specific, and believe me.

To Sara Jameson

Woburn, Dec. 3, 1913.
Wed. 8:20 a.m

Dearest Sara:

Much railroading since I last wrote, (on "Bummelzug's" mostly), and much work and seeing people, and no chances to write. I have had an interesting time, though a somewhat tiring one; however, am all right now.

At New Haven, I saw Farrand, Warren and his Martha and James, Allen Johnson, George Adams, and W. L. Phelps.[280] Farrand is to be married the 17th.[281] . . . Phelps showed me, framed on the wall of his study, a menu of the dinner at Princeton at the time of the debate,[282] on which he had the pencilled signatures of presiding officers and judges— Grover Cleveland, Woodrow Wilson, W. L. Wilson, Everett Wheeler, J. F. J.—two pressūstates, to say nothing of me. Lunched at the Graduates Club with F. J. [Farrand, Johnson] and Adams, and then to Middletown, where I spent 2¼ hours, first giving a talk to Dutcher's students, then dining hastily with him and Mrs. Dutcher. They are going to Charleston.[283]

I got to Willimantic at 8:20 and went right to bed, because I was to rise at 5:00, breakfast at 5:30, and take a 6:17 train to Providence. Then, I woke at

[280] Allen Johnson (1870-1931), A.B., Amherst, 1892, after teaching history in Iowa College (Grinnell) and Bowdoin, had come to Yale in 1910. William Lyon Phelps (1865-1943) had been teaching literature in Yale since 1902.

[281] Professor Farrand's wife was Beatrix Jones, distinguished landscape gardener, who in later years served as supervising gardener for Princeton University and consulting landscape gardener for Yale, the University of Chicago, Occidental College, and Oberlin.

[282] See *ante,* Apr. 2, 1898.

[283] The December meeting of the American Historical Association was to be held in Charleston. George M. Dutcher, A.B., Cornell, 1897, had been teaching history in Wesleyan University since 1901.

five minutes of six, and set a noble example to my daughter, indeed to myself, by getting dressed, packed, and out of the house in fifteen minutes. Breakfast was somewhat lacking, but I got to Prov. before nine.

Of course I met an old student of mine before I got to the college. He was one of the earliest and one of the best, and is now attorney-general of R. I.[284] I transacted my business, had a good talk with Faunce, another with Gardner, went all over the John Hay Library, saw Fred Guild, Allinson, Bronson, Manatt, Hill, von Klenze, Winship,[285] all of whom inquired for you most pleasantly; also old janitor William. I went out and called on Mrs. Gardner, who looks as well as ever, really in splendid condition, and saw the young Harry, a fine boy, looking much like Francis. Telephone talk with Mrs. Allinson.[286] Faunce lunched me at the Hope Club with Allinson, MacDonald, and Collier [287] (new young history man). Then I worked at the J. C. B. [John Carter Brown] Library till 5, and got here at 7:30. . . .

To FRENCH ENSOR CHADWICK

January 5, 1914.

My dear Admiral Chadwick:

The last Congress, on March 2, 1913, passed an act respecting documents of the Revolutionary War, of which I enclose a copy. The Secretary of War has this autumn appointed Captain Hollis C. Clark, a youngish retired officer of the regular army, to take charge of the work, so far as the War Department is concerned, and he, as soon as the official arrangement can be completed, will begin, through agents, an extensive work of search and copying in state archives and the like repositories.[288] The search will be done by a properly qualified agent in each state, the copying by the photostat process. The work on the naval side will be done concurrently by the same means.

On Friday last an informal conference respecting the matter was held at the office of the Assistant Secretary of War between the Assistant Secretaries of War and of the Navy, Mr. Breckinridge and Mr. Roosevelt, other military and naval representatives, and several representatives of the Executive Council of the American Historical Association then on their return from its annual meeting at Charleston and Columbia.[289] At the meeting of the Executive Council in Charleston it was voted that the President of the Association should be authorized, at his discretion, to appoint five members of the Association as an advisory committee with relation to this matter. The meaning was, that he should do this if at the conference of January 2 it appeared that the Departments desired this. The two Assistant Secretaries warmly expressed this desire and Professor McLaughlin, the new President of the Association, has appointed the following committee: Major John Bigelow,[290] chairman, Frederic Bancroft, Rear-Admiral F. E. Chadwick, J. F. Jameson, Justin H. Smith. Informing me by telegraph, Professor McLaughlin has requested me to save time by notifying the members of the committee and explaining to them the situation of the matter—instead of leaving the appointment, as has been more usual, to be notified in due course by the Secretary of the Council. I sincerely hope that you will accept the appointment. The undertaking is one of obvious importance and interest, and the desire of the Department to take the advice of qualified historical scholars ought to be met half way, for it is doubtful if such a step has

---

[284] Herbert A. Rice, who held this office from 1912 to 1918.

[285] Most of these were friends of Jameson's years in Providence: Frederick T. Guild was registrar of Brown; Allinson, associate professor of Greek and, after 1898, professor of classical philology; Walter C. Bronson taught English literature from 1892 to 1895; James I. Manatt, Greek; and George Parker Winship was librarian of the John Carter Brown Library from 1895 until 1915, when he became custodian of the Widener collection of the Harvard library. Camille Von Klenze, Jameson had known in Chicago, where he taught Germanic language and literature from 1893 till 1906, when he became head of the department of German in Brown. Hill is unidentified.

[286] Mrs. Allinson (Anne Crosby Emery) was joint author with her husband of Greek lands and letters, Boston, Houghton Mifflin, 1909, and Roads from Rome, N. Y., Macmillan, 1913.

[287] Theodore Collier had come to Brown as associate professor of history after a brief teaching experience in Williams college. He was head of the Brown department of history from 1919 to 1939.

[288] At the November meeting of the executive council of the Association, R. M. Johnston, who during the summer had corresponded with Jameson about obtaining the appointment of a commission to oversee the publication of the Revolutionary records, presented the matter to the council. It was discussed at some length, and a committee of three was appointed to report back to the council in December as to the best possible action to be taken by the Association. In the meantime the Secretary of War, oblivious to the arguments of the historians, had placed Capt. Hollis C. Clark, U. S. A. retired, in charge of the work. Clark at once turned to Jameson for advice and a Washington conference for January was planned (Jameson to McLaughlin, Dec. 8, 1913).

[289] Henry Breckinridge, assistant secretary of War, 1913-1916; Franklin D. Roosevelt, assistant secretary of the Navy, 1913-1920. At the Charleston meeting of the Association, Roosevelt "addressed the conference [on military history] on the unsatisfactory provision now existing for the naval archives of the United States, and on the desire of the two military departments of the government, in the editing of the military records of the Revolution, to produce a publication marked by all possible excellences of preparation and editing" (Amer. Hist. Rev. 19: 482, April, 1914). Others present at the Washington conference were "Rear-Admiral Knight, Major McAndrew, Captain Clark, R. M. Johnston, Hunt, Ames, Bancroft, Burnett, Paullin, Jameson" (Jameson to Hart, Jan. 6, 1914). Charles W. Stewart, librarian of the Navy Department, who was to represent the Navy in the work, was also present at this meeting.

[290] Major John Bigelow, Jr., was at this time attached to the historical division of the General Staff.

ever been taken before in respect to any of the government's historical publications. Service upon the committee will not be laborious. After a preliminary conference upon scope and methods (to be spoken of later) it will consist mostly in answering letters of inquiry from Captain Clark and advising him with respect to fit agents for carrying out his work. It is of very great importance to the success of the undertaking that he should be assisted to obtain, as searchers in the different states, well trained young historical scholars who will act intelligently, accurately, and with perfect integrity toward the government in the matter of hours, etc., instead of having improper appointments made at the instance of Congressmen and politicians. Captain Clark, though a good executive officer, is not an historical scholar, but manifests an excellent spirit with respect to taking the advice of those who are.

The Assistant Secretaries are very desirous that no more time should be lost in making a beginning, and a good showing, that the present appropriations may be followed by adequate continuations. Therefore they have requested that a conference of the proposed committee of the American Historical Association with Captain Clark and with other members representing the war colleges of the two services should be held in Washington, in the office of the Secretary of War, beginning at ten a. m. on Friday, January 16, in order to define the scope and limitations of the proposed collection of materials as well as possible before collecting is begun; to decide upon the methods which shall be followed in collecting, and to frame instructions for those who are to act under Captain Clark's orders as searchers. If no unforeseen difficulty arises (I will write as to this in two or three days), the Departments will pay the traveling expenses of the members who come on behalf of the American Historical Association. The conference may very likely last two days.

I certainly hope that you will be able to be present, and should highly appreciate it if you would let me know by telegram, "collect," addressed to me at 1140 Woodward Building, Washington, D. C., whether I may count upon your presence.

To assist in deliberation respecting the questions of exclusion and inclusion of documents of different sorts, I have drawn up a list which I enclose.[291]

I hope that you will be so good as to take a strong interest in this work. It may be the entering wedge for much fuller participation of trained historical minds in government historical publications, a matter in which I have for some time been keenly interested, and upon which a report was prepared in President

Roosevelt's time, of which I ask leave to send a copy herewith under separate cover.[292]

To Lord Bryce

January 7, 1914.

My dear Lord Bryce:

First let me express my congratulations upon the honor which has been conferred upon you at New Year's.[293] I am sure that it gives much pleasure to your friends here, as it does to me, and the more because the title does not change or hide the name by which you are known and loved among us all.

I have just come back from the annual meeting of the American Historical Association, held in the last days of December in South Carolina, two days in Charleston and one in Columbia. I had never seen either place and was very greatly interested, especially in the old-time Charleston architecture and in the South Carolina character, so far as I could discern it in two days—especially its wide difference from the Virginia character, with which I am tolerably familiar. The Carolinian intelligence seemed to me to bear as plainly the marks of urban origin as the Virginia of rural. Seldom indeed has a city that never had thirty thousand white population made so much of a mark in history. An old gentleman told me of a Charleston schoolgirl who said in her lesson that the Ashley and Cooper rivers flowed past the city on the east and on the west, and joined there to form the Atlantic Ocean. I shall presently go a little further south, for three gentlemen of the Georgia Historical Society appeared upon the scene and made themselves so pleasant to me, and so clearly represented it as my duty, that I agreed to go down next month and give an address at the seventy-fifth anniversary of that Society. My sentiments on returning to my overloaded desk and remembering what I had agreed in a less sober hour to do are of a type which I fancy is familiar to you from days at the Embassy.

One matter was mooted at our Council meeting in respect to which I earnestly hope that we may have your aid, or at least the advantage of your name. We have long felt that American historical students who come to London for the first time, to engage in researches at the Public Records Office, at the British Museum, or elsewhere, have regrettable difficulties in orienting themselves, in getting access to collections, especially those less public than the two I have named, and are apt to lead an isolated existence, when in reality there are always a good number of them in London at any given time, if only they had some means of drawing together. We have

---

[291] This list is among the Jameson Papers, along with minutes of the meetings of the committee and the *Hearings* of Feb. 12, 1914, referred to in the letter of May 7, 1914.

[292] A reference to the report made to the Keep Commission. See *ante,* Dec. 13, 1907, n. 88.

[293] Raised to the peerage as Viscount Bryce in the New Year's honors of 1914.

wished that they might have a headquarters or gathering place, and a friendly advisor of the permanent sort.

A prospect now seems to open toward the securing of these benefits, and some others, through the good offices of Mr. A. Percival Newton, who has just been appointed lecturer in Colonial and Imperial History at Kings College and in American History at University College. I have met him several times in London, and he seems an able young man. If he is not in all respects ideally fitted to be the honorary secretary of the simple organization which might be proposed, at all events he is one of the few Englishmen permanently and deeply interested in American history, and is of the most excellent spirit of helpfulness toward younger fellow students. He proposes that we should establish a branch of the American Historical Association in London, consisting of those of our members who may be at work in London at any given time, and that a room in Gray's Inn, near the quarters of the Royal Historical Society and thus convenient both to the Public Record Office and the British Museum, should be hired, furnished, and kept open as much as possible for the convenience of members, as a place where they might write letters, keep their papers safer than in lodging houses, and meet each other.

The Council of the American Historical Association has taken up the proposal with a strong conviction that to carry it out would very greatly help the work of American students of American or English history, or of the history of the English language and literature, and they have appointed a committee, of which I am chairman and of which the remaining members are Professor Charles M. Andrews of Yale, and Charles H. Haskins of Harvard, to make the necessary arrangements. I shall presently be collecting money for furnishings, from those of our members who have worked in London and appreciate the usefulness of such a headquarters as is proposed. Whether it can be instituted in June or later in the year will depend upon the results of this appeal. The Association will pay the rent, after the start has been made.

Only a simple organization is proposed. We wish to have four honorary officers, president, vice-president, secretary, and treasurer, and an executive committee consisting of these and the three senior members registered at and in London at any given time, which can take action in all details, referring matters of any importance to the officers of the Association here in America. Mr. Newton will act as secretary.

For the offices of president and vice-president we wish, in order to give the whole affair its proper standing in the eyes of American students in London and in those of the interested part of the London public, to have men who are in high positions in our historical world and whose friendly attitude toward American students needs no exposition. I wish to ask, as it was the unanimous desire of our Council that I should ask, whether you, the one honorary member of the Association, will not consent to accept the position of honorary president of this little organization. I earnestly hope that you will agree. I hope and believe that only a small amount of trouble is involved—attending some time in the spring a preliminary meeting, perhaps another if at some later time you care to do so, but for the most part merely lending your name. The whole matter is obviously not one of large importance, but distinctly useful within its range. We mean to ask Mr. Hubert Hall, who for thirty-five years has been the friend of all American students at the Public Record Office, to be honorary vice-president. Please give us your aid if you see no strong reason to the contrary.[294] . . .

To WALDO G. LELAND

January 8, 1914.

My dear Leland:

I have now been at home exactly a week this morning, the whole of which time I have devoted absolutely to the American Historical Asso., in order to clear off once for all, just so far as possible, every item of correspondence that proceeded from the Charleston-Columbia meeting. The result is that I have deferred telling you about it longer than I meant to do, but I will tell you of some things now, and then turn to the *Review* and the Carnegie Institution. The programme you have

---

[294] In 1905 there was an abortive movement for an center of historical research in London, to resemble the American School in Rome. A small group of historians sent circulars to others and received many expressions of approval but nothing seems to have come from this beginning. It may be that the group had hoped the Carnegie Institution would support the project but there is no evidence that Jameson took part in the discussions or that the matter was presented to the trustees. The plan for 1914, a much more modest one, originated in London where those who came in contact with American students were acutely conscious of their need for some guidance. Even before the American Historical Association officially sponsored the idea, Frances G. Davenport and A. P. Newton had begun to collect money in England. Temporary quarters at 8 Southampton Street were opened on June 15 with Lord Bryce in the chair, with Ambassador Page the chief speaker, and with a distinguished group of English and American guests. Of this auspicious beginning Newton wrote a glowing account to Jameson. The early weeks seemed most promising and in December the center rented a permanent room from the Royal Historical Society. But the war brought its usefulness to an end. The executive council of the Association, hard pressed, made no appropriation for rent after 1915, and Jameson, feeling that the commitment to the Royal Historical Society ought to be carried out and also that the room would be needed after the war, for four years obtained by private subscription the money with which to pay the rent. By 1919 the American University Union had been established and it did not appear that the room of the Association was serving any useful purpose. Formal notice of its surrender was given to the Royal Historical Society in January, 1920.

received, and it was carried out almost completely, so we will take that for granted.

I was sorry you were not there, for by reason of your Southern trips you would have found yourself surrounded by familiar things and persons.[295] Mrs. Jameson and I enjoyed Charleston very much, though of course things don't anywhere look their best at the end of December. We stayed at the Villa Margherita on the Battery, a most excellent place, though a little far from the places of meeting and a little dilatory about meals, so that, though the latter were excellent, I did not get the whole of any one of them. On the whole it was a very good meeting, though I hope that we may not again divide a meeting between two towns, especially two towns that are connected by a train that starts at 3:25 in the morning, even with permission to enter your berth at ten. I like the Carolinians, and Stephenson, professor at the College is a delectable man, as is also Mr. Barnwell, president of the South Carolina Historical Society.[296] The latter gave us a very pleasant reception and had there a good exhibition of its treasures. My pleasure in remembering this occasion is marred by the remembrance of my folly in succumbing to the urgency of three representatives of the Georgia Historical Society who came up and persuaded me to give the address at their seventy-fifth anniversary on February 12.

Another pleasure was the excursion to Fort Sumter, where we were allowed to land and inspect, and where Burr, McLaughlin and I, in our capacity of Board of Editors, sat on some piles of rope, in an old shed sheltered from the wind, and held a meeting. How many committee meetings I attended during those three days I cannot now recall, but the chief joy was the business meeting, of which anon. Haskins being absent, I was pressed in to take his place as secretary of the Council. The Council debated much on military things,[297] fixed up the slate of committees, and agreed to what was proposed in respect to London by the committee on that subject, consisting of Jameson (chairman), Andrews and Haskins. The committee was continued with power to make arrangements, including renting a room from January 1, 1915, at not more than twenty pounds. Newton thinks of a room in Gray's Inn near those of the Royal Historical Society. I am starting out to collect money for the furnishings and if some additional

money is got, here or by Miss Davenport and Newton in London, the place may be opened in June. The Association itself has no spare money in 1914. A simple organization is proposed—honorary president (I am asking Bryce), honorary vice-president (I am asking Hall), honorary secretary, Newton, and an honorary treasurer, and an executive committee consisting of these and the three seniors in college graduation among those registered at any given time.

The same committee is charged to make arrangements in Paris if this can, as you say, be done without expense. Now I wish you would write me at length just what you think can be done in Paris.[298] You can see that the Association, though glad to get quarters for nothing, by sharing a room with other organizations, would wish to be careful as to whom it was tied up with and our committee would need advice as to whether the same sort of organization is practicable. Probably the three senior workers could be had, for the executive committee, for I suppose there are almost always three members of the Association in Paris at any given time, but for the officers (secretary and treasurer might be combined, and a vice-president is not very necessary) we should need persons who are always in Paris. I don't know much about the Comité France-Amérique, and though probably Haskins does, you might send one or two of its circulars.

Though Newton can, if need be, introduce people to the Embassy who have forgotten to bring letters to it as a means of getting into the P. R. O., still it is better that the Secretary of the American Historical Association should be the regular channel for such introductions. I wrote to Page[299] early in December, asking him if he would agree to take that secretary's introductions at face value, with a view to performing these requisite formalities. He says he will. No doubt it would be well to make the same arrangement with the Embassy in Paris, if the regulations there (about which I do not know) require that foreign searchers should be introduced by their diplomatic representatives. How is this? If such action is needed and the arrangement as to the Secretary of the A. H. A. is desirable, will you take this up with the Embassy or shall I get it

---

[295] See *ante,* May 13, 1906, n. 17, for reference to Mr. Leland's trips to the South.

[296] Nathaniel W. Stephenson (1867-1935) was professor of history in the College of Charleston from 1902 to 1923. He is well known for his work in Yale on the Chronicles of America photoplays, as well as for two volumes on the period of the Civil War, contributed to the series *Chronicles of America,* and for his life of Senator Nelson Aldrich.

Joseph Barnwell (1846-1930) was president of the South Carolina Historical Society from 1904 to 1930.

[297] Probably the discussion chiefly concerned the best method of assisting in the collection and editing of the records of the Revolutionary War.

[298] Mr. Leland had written in December that he believed that a Paris branch of the Association could be established with little or no expense to the Association and Jameson had agreed that if possible he would bring the matter before the executive council. On Feb. 27, 1914, in reply to this letter, Leland wrote that he, James Hazen Hyde, and Professor Van Tyne, then in Paris, had gone to M. Jules Coulet, director of the Office International, who offered them quarters, and that the Harvard Foundation would provide financial aid. He suggested that the American ambassador to France be made honorary president, Henry Vignaud, president, Charles Langlois, vice-president, and J. H. Hyde, secretary-treasurer. See *Amer. Hist. Rev.* 19: 696, April, 1914. The outbreak of the war brought an end to all such plans.

[299] Walter Hines Page (1855-1918), ambassador to Great Britain, 1913 to 1918.

set in motion from here through Bassett Moore [300] or some such means?

The business meeting went on in the usual cut and dried manner—with possibly a touch of the steam roller because Dunning was anxious to go to a dinner his students were preparing for him—until the committee, which for a year had been incubating nominations, made its report. MacDonald was not there. Alvord read it: McLaughlin, Stephens, Burr; Evarts Greene for secretary of the Council; new councilors, Haskins and Fred Bancroft. Everyone was pleased with the results, but *le nommé* Rowland then arose in his might, and in quite a burst of rhetoric declaimed about the harmfulness of the present method of electing. As he spoke, his emotion and his apprehension of disaster increased and he laid before us with some passion the perils of oligarchy. If there were anybody in the world that was capable of self-government it was the American Historical Association. He thought a ballot ought to be sent out to all members, forgetting that this had been done several times during the twelve years in which he, on his own statement, had been a member without ever feeling that he had any voice in the elections. Various members of the ring pointed out the results, or want of results which we got from the ballot. Even Alvord, once a notorious insurgent, but now, to his own amusement, made conservative by a position on the nominating committee, explained the trouble the committee had taken to get expressions of opinion. Of course you can't make people write to the committee. I did; it appeared that Rowland had not. The discussion was perfectly amiable, and no doubt it did good to have people let off steam, or even hot air, and at the end the new nominating committee was charged to consider and report at the next meeting as to better means of eliciting the general opinion. It was a rather interesting tempest in a teapot, and didn't blow off the lid.

It did not appear that anybody failed to approve heartily the nominations actually made. That is the way it always is, I think. Nobody has much objection to any particular thing that the Council does, but many have an uneasy feeling that they are on the outside of things when they would rather be on the inside. I know no perfect cure for this. You can't have 2845 people on the Council. You have to have a small body, and we all know that it tries its very best to act in the interest of the whole Association. But there should be as much publicity as possible, for I have always found members content when things were fully explained; and so I am writing Jimmy Thompson [301] to be sure to let the business meeting have a whole afternoon. This time it was set at 4:30 by reason of the excursion to

Fort Sumter, and the reluctance of the Local Committee to have their reception in the evening.

The meeting December 1914 is to be held in Chicago. The date for California will be fixed later, after a post card inquiry by the Local Committee (R. J. Taussig appointed for that occasion). E. D. Adams was appointed chairman of the Committee on Special Programme for that occasion, which programme will be confined to Pacific and Panama history.[302] Stephens will give his presidential address then, and then wishes to resign and have Burr elected president for the meeting of 1915, which will be held here in Washington.[303] Save up good thoughts for this; I have a few. Cincinnati was recommended for 1916 by the Council, but the Association did not act. I send you a copy of the list of committees.

At Columbia we were well entertained in a good, new hotel; excellent luncheon by the Chamber of Commerce; rides around town in the afternoon by the automobile club; the Conference of Archives passed a resolution intended to strengthen Salley's hands.[304] . . . Burnett's paper was excellent and well delivered and made a good impression and going to the meeting did him real good.[305]

E. D. Adams arrives in two days to assist C. F. Adams on his book.[306] I don't know how many

---

[300] John Bassett Moore (1860-1947) in 1913-1914 was counselor to the Department of State.

[301] James Westfall Thompson (1869-1941), professor of mediaeval history, University of Chicago, 1913-1932; chairman of the program committee of the Association for the meeting in 1914.

[302] Because of the Panama-Pacific International Exposition in San Francisco in 1915, it was thought an auspicious time to hold an Association meeting on the West Coast. R. J. Taussig (1861-1922), president of the Academy of Pacific Coast History, was also secretary of the Exposition. Later, the work for the Association was undertaken by Professor F. L. Thompson of Amherst, who was in Berkeley for the year. For an account of the meeting see *Amer. Hist. Rev.* 21: 1-11, Oct., 1915.

[303] This plan was not carried out. Professor Stephens gave two presidential addresses: The conflict of European nations in the Pacific, delivered in California in July, was printed in *The Pacific Ocean in history: papers and addresses*, presented at the Panama-Pacific Historical Congress, held at San Francisco, Berkeley, and Palo Alto, Cal., July 19-23, 1915, ed. by H. Morse Stephens and Herbert E. Bolton, N. Y., Macmillan, 1917; and Nationality and history, presented in Washington in December, 1915. See *Amer. Hist. Rev.* 21: 225-236, Jan., 1916.

[304] The resolution expressed the hope that South Carolina would push the work of publishing the archival material which concerned the earlier history of the state. *Ibid.* 19: 486, April, 1914.

[305] Burnett's paper, an outgrowth of his work on *Letters of members of the Continental Congress*, discussed the Committee of the States appointed by the Congress to oversee its business during the summer of 1784. It was published in *Ann. Rept., Amer. Hist. Assn.*, 1913: 1: 141-158.

[306] Ephraim D. Adams worked with Charles Francis Adams, Jr., in Washington until May and in South Lincoln, Mass., until the end of August, on the life of the senior Charles Francis Adams. In this time, C. F. Adams completed volume one, which reached 1848, and E. D. Adams, the second volume, which covered the years 1848 to 1860. They were ready to begin collaboration on the third volume at the time of the sudden death of Charles Francis Adams. The life was never completed and published but subsequently E. D. Adams published *Great Britain and the American Civil War*, 2v., N. Y., Longmans, 1925, which dealt with the period which was to have been covered by the unwritten third volume.

months, but I am glad he is coming.

On the evening of January 1 Bancroft gave an extremely enjoyable dinner at the Metropolitan Club in honor of Dunning. The next day, representatives of the Council had an informal conference with Breckinridge and Roosevelt, Assistant Secretaries of War and the Navy (two very live young men) and some military and naval people,[307] . . . The Departments want to do the thing [publication of Revolutionary Records] rightly and keep clear of political appointees; but Hay of Virginia, chairman of the House Military Committee, hastens to propose a chap none of us ever heard of, when Clark could perfectly well have Morgan Robinson. But I think this is the first time when any Department has invoked the aid of the historical profession as such, for any historical publication, and in this we should rejoice.

In fact, we should no doubt rejoice all the time, but I am going to get some luncheon now or I shall not.

Later. I enjoyed my luncheon very much, thank you; had Albert Shaw and Gilbert Grosvenor and Lowry and heard no end of magazine talk.[308] Heard of several ways in which, by greatly debasing the moral standard of the A. H. R., I could push its circulation right up. Must think of this. Meanwhile a happy new year to you and Mrs. Leland. I hope that she is very well. As for you, I haven't the slightest doubt that you are overworking; and if I had the least influence would command you to desist. All I can say at the beginning of 1914, is what I have said at the beginning of various other years, Go out and play, make sure of your vacation now; do not work as if the universe would collapse if you did not get your Guide done by next November. I don't want to bring agents of the D. of H. R. [Department of Historical Research] home in a litter; it doesn't look well.

To John S. Bassett

January 13, 1914.

My dear Professor Bassett:[309]

. . . Various of the elder brethren spoke [at the business meeting of the Association] declaring the wish, which I am sure they entertained, that the nearest possible approach to a really significant plebiscite might be had, but explaining the difficulty, in the present age of

waste baskets, in bringing out the vote. In the end, the new committee on nominations, which incubates during 1914, and of which Hull is chairman, was charged to report at the next meeting as to any better means that might be devised for eliciting a more general opinion as to nominations. I judged that the explosion did good, not that it was done directly by Rowland's hot air, but that this furnished the means for explanations that satisfied most minds as to the difficulty of improving much on the present plan.

I think that Herbert Adams, whom you quote, was right, as he was pretty apt to be in such matters.[310] A small body of persons deeply interested and willing to work are likely to run things, but the historical profession of the United States being what it is, I do not think they are likely to run them in any other interest than that of the whole society. I think that any one who has ever attended the Council meeting emerges from it with the sense that these men have been acting entirely in the common interest, and with an efficiency that depends somewhat on a conservative policy with respect to the make-up of the Council. Yet efficiency is not the only thing. We should wish members to be satisfied and, as we are likely to have a good many ex-presidents permanently on the Council, we ought to take particular pains to renovate the rest of it and the committee. Haskins, who has for years had the main voice in the making of slates, has always been particularly thoughtful about such points as this, and I think the rest of us have, though less skillful than he in making these arrangements. I have never myself heard of any considerable number of members who were dissatisfied with any particular thing that the Council had done, and I doubt if there is much more insurgency in the whole body than a natural though vague feeling of many men that they are on the outside of it when they would like to be on the inside. For this there is, in the nature of the case, no complete remedy; but we ought to apply what partial remedies that can be thought of. . . .

In the discussion at Charleston good feelings and good nature prevailed universally, except so far as Rowland may have put some things rather more strongly than was warranted. . . .

To Isaac N. Seligman

January 29, 1914.

Dear Sir:[311]

A clergyman in Spokane who is occupied with inves-

---

[307] The omitted paragraph repeats the account given in the letter of Jan. 5, 1914.

[308] Shaw of the *Review of Reviews,* Gilbert H. Grosvenor of the *National Geographic Magazine,* Lowry of the New York *Evening Post.*

[309] John Spencer Bassett (1867-1928), Ph.D., Johns Hopkins, 1894, was professor of history in Smith College from 1906 until his death. In 1914 he held no office in the American Historical Association but he later became its secretary. The omitted paragraphs of this letter recount the episode of the business meeting at Charleston much as it was told in the letter of Jan. 8 to Mr. Leland. For Jameson's published account of this session, see *Amer. Hist. Rev.* 19: 488-490, April, 1914.

[310] Bassett had written on Jan. 9, 1914: "I remember hearing our old friend, Professor H. B. Adams, say that it was inevitable that a few men should direct the policy of the association."

[311] Isaac Newton Seligman (1856-1917), A.B., Columbia, 1876, connected with the banking firm of J. and W. Seligman and Company, New York. No reply to this letter has been found.

tigations into the history of the Oregon country,[312] asks me whether any of the original material used by Washington Irving in writing *Astoria,* and referred to in Mr. Pierre M. Irving's *Life and Letters of Washington Irving,* III. 63, is still in existence.

While the pioneer work of collecting data was done by Mr. M. Irving at the resident [*sic*] of Mr. Astor, and the original draft of *Astoria* written at the same place, yet it is not certain that the papers remained in the possession of Mr. Astor. But if this was the case I am led to believe that they are no longer in existence, since the present agent of the Astor estate writes me that all papers of this sort owned by Mr. Astor were destroyed some years ago.[313] But since I am extremely anxious to answer my correspondent's inquiry, and knowing that you are the possessor of a large amount of Irving material, I write to ask if among these papers there are any of the original documents used by Mr. Irving?

The kindness of your reply to this inquiry will be highly appreciated. . . .

To Andrew C. McLaughlin

March 4, 1914.

My dear McLaughlin:

Thank you for your letter of presumably March 2. I will talk on Monday, March 16, at 1:30 on the Origin of Political Parties in the United States, and on Monday, April 6, at the same hour, on Institutions of Historical Research.

As to Latané's communications,[314] I don't think much of it, and I should think that the affairs of the Association had been dragged before the public quite sufficiently, especially when one considers that it adopted at Charleston a measure intended to amend whatever is amiss, and also when its practices are, so far as I can see from inquiries about here, not seriously different from those of other similar societies. If there is a strong difference between our course and that of the Political Science Association, it is due to the fact that we have money and they have none, that is to say, we have the funds with which to do important tasks which require more permanence than is requisite with them. He seems to imply that their *Review* makes a clean sweep of its Board of Editors in a very short time; the effect of that would be to throw all actual influence over

the journal into the hands of the managing editor if he is permanent.

Latané is not a very strong man, and takes his cue from Hart. I have written to him, but of course shall say nothing more in the *Nation,* though his error in thinking that our Board of Editors could be changed wholesale each year needs to be pointed out to members of the Association. I have however discussed the matter somewhat in the *Review,* taking the caution to sign the article on the Association meeting, because the Board of Editors ought not to be made responsible for the opinions which I express, while on the other hand I don't think I could get together a statement that would stand as the opinion of the whole Board, when only three were present. It seemed to be a sufficiently difficult process to get six men to agree on the phrasing of the short circular to reviewers. My remarks are moderate and conciliatory. If they are not such as other members of the Board would be willing to sign and publish, yet I am sure that they are such as they would be willing to have me sign and publish in their journal.[315] . . .

I lately asked Fay,[316] who is one of the most sensible of men, and has never been on the Council nor attended a Council meeting, to tell me all that he thought about existing dissatisfaction. He thinks as I think, that almost no one objects or ever has objected to any particular thing that the Council has done, that nearly all believe it to have managed well, and that there is not much more in the whole thing than a sense on the part of some that they are quite on the outside, when they would be glad to be more on the inside. The remedy for this is more publicity.

To William M. Sloane

April 7, 1914.

My dear Sloane:

I got your letter just before I left Madison, and at Chicago and Urbana had no chance to reply. I had already written to Mr. Edwards [317] in a provisional manner, saying merely what could be said upon the basis of his second letter, for the first has never reached me. Here, I have not his address, and will ask you to transmit to him what little I have to say beyond what was in my letter to him.

In reality, I have no data whatever respecting the negotiations at Ghent, beyond what is in print. The things of which I spoke to you, though I am glad you found them interesting, illustrate merely the social as-

---

[312] The Rev. J. Neilson Barry, of Spokane, Wash., who for a number of years had a parish on the trail of the overland party of Wilson Price Hunt, and who helped to identify the entire route. Barry to Jameson, Apr. 22, 1914.

[313] C. W. Baldwin to Jameson, Jan. 28, 1914.

[314] *Nation* **98**: 207, Feb. 26, 1914. Professor John H. Latané (1869-1939), of the Johns Hopkins University, had emphasized the longer tenure of office in practice in the Historical Association than in the Political Science Association. Communications had already appeared in the *Nation* from Fay, Rowland, MacDonald, and Jameson. See issues of Jan. 22, 29, Feb. 5, 1914.

[315] *Amer. Hist. Rev.* **20**: 522-525, April, 1914.

[316] Sidney B. Fay, professor of history in Dartmouth College at this time. He had written the account of the Charleston meeting which appeared in the *Nation* **98**: 30-31, Jan. 8, 1914.

[317] G. W. Edwards, a student of Professor Sloane, had asked Jameson for suggestions on his thesis. When he failed to receive prompt reply, Sloane wrote, recommending Edwards as worthy of help.

pects of the sojourn of the American commissioners in that city. They came to me from an official at the city hall of Ghent, who seemed to be rather the moving spirit of the committee which is preparing a local celebration of the treaty. He and the American Consul, Mr. Johnson, were preparing for publication, a small book on the local aspects of the negotiations.[318] They have identified securely the house in which the American commissioners lived most of the time, the hotel of the Baron de Lavendeghem, and are expecting to restore to its original shape and condition the *salle* in the residence of the British commissioners (house of the Carthusians) in which the treaty was signed. He said that while the British commissioners kept themselves very much to themselves, the Americans went about and enjoyed themselves, and were distinctly popular in the society of the town, thus, the *livres d'or* of various societies such as the St. Cecilia and the Society of Agriculture have emblazoned pages recording the admission of the five Americans as honorary members.[319] In the room in which the treaty was signed they mean to create a small museum, in which will be exhibited documents or photographs of documents of this sort. All this, provided they can raise the money. The Carthusians, who keep a sort of old men's home in the building, will give up to the purpose these two rooms, to be restored into one, but cannot afford to do more than that.

This Mr. van Werveke said that Van Huffel, the chief painter of Ghent in that time, was understood to have made a portrait or portraits of the American commissioners. He asked me to see if I could come upon their track in America. When I got back, I wrote to Mr. C. F. Adams, to the present Mrs. Clay, to my old pupil, Richard Bayard, and to Brown University as possessor of the papers of Jonathan Russell,[320] but none knew of any such pictures. Mr. Chas. Adams said that his brother, Henry, who was at that time staying with him, said that in view of the mutual relations of the American commissioners, he did not believe any painter could have kept them in the same room long enough to picture them.[321] A month later, Ford wrote that he had found among the Adams papers a letter of

J. Q. A. to his wife, written a month after the treaty, which cast light upon the matter. Adams says that Mr. Van Huffel, president of the Academy of Design at Ghent, had, during the sessions, made pencil portraits of the other members, and that he himself, though he had been too busy to sit to him, during the time of the sessions, had subsequently given him sittings; that Van Huffel had then wished to proceed to make an oil painting of him; that he had agreed; and that if it were good, she should have it. Mr. C. F. A. said he had never heard of it before, but if such an oil portrait existed, it would probably be found in the possession of his cousin, J. Q. A. Johnson of New York. I traced it to him, and through his kindness got a photograph of it for the people at Ghent. It represents Adams in court costume, with the parchment of the treaty of Ghent in his hand. I believe Ford means to reproduce it as a frontispiece to the third volume of Adams' *Writings*.[322]

Failing to find any trace of the pencil portraits other-

---

[318] The Ghent official was undoubtedly A. van Werveke, whom Jameson quotes in other letters; the consul was Henry A. Johnson. No such pamphlet has been discovered.

[319] See *Papers of James A. Bayard*, 304, n. 1.

[320] Jonathan Russell (1771-1832) was born in Providence and was graduated from Brown University (then Rhode Island College) in 1791. When he joined Adams, Bayard, Clay, and Gallatin in Ghent he was under appointment as minister to Sweden and Norway.

[321] Charles Francis Adams to Jameson, Sept. 30, 1912. The statement which Henry Adams himself made to Jameson was slightly less strong: "I never heard of a crayon sketch of the Ghent commissioners. I have no copy of the Diary here [South Lincoln, Mass.] and nothing to consult, but I shall wait till the sketch turns up before believing in its existence. They were a hard herd to corral, and would have given the artist trouble" (Adams to Jameson, Sept. 20, 1912).

[322] Ford evidently thought better of this for the only portrait of J. Q. Adams in his volumes is that painted by Copley, which is the frontispiece of volume one.

The search made by Charles Francis Adams deserves record. On Oct. 8, 1912, he wrote: "In regard to the crayon likeness of the negotiators at Ghent,—I have at last struck the trail. I found no mention of it in the J. Q. Adams *Memoirs*, and could think of only one other source of possible information,—the familiar letters of J. Q. Adams written to his wife while at Ghent.

I accordingly asked Ford to look in the *MSS*, and see what he could find. He returns me the enclosed, from a letter written by John Quincy Adams to Mrs. Adams, apparently from Paris, January 24, 1915." The enclosure reads: "A few days before Messrs. Bayard, Clay and Gallatin left this city Mr. Van Huffel, a Painter and President of the Société des Beaux Arts, took a fancy to have likenesses of the American Ministers, in miniature drawn with a black lead pencil. Those gentlemen all sat to him each an hour or two, and after their departure I went to his house for the same purpose. But after he had begun with his pencil he persuaded himself, and by dint of importunity persuaded me, to let him put the figure upon canvas instead of paper, and in oil-colours instead of black lead. It was also understood that the picture was to be not for him but for me; that is to say, if you think it worth your acceptance for you. The likeness is good, and the picture not a bad one. I have it here to be finished, and then forwarded . . . to England or to America as the circumstances shall require."

Adams continued: "I am following up the trail in this country. When John Quincy Adams returned to America, he had no home here. He immediately established himself in Washington, as Secretary of State to Monroe. All his household effects, therefore, went to Washington, and there remained during his life.

"My father had a brother who married a Miss Johnson [actually Mary Catherine Hellen],—a cousin of his—in Washington. That brother died in 1833, I think, in Washington. He left two children, both daughters, one of whom died in childhood. The other married, and left descendants. To her and to her descendants all the household effects in Washington went. None of them came to our branch of the family. The male representative of that branch is J. Q. A. Johnson, a lawyer, who lives in New York. I have written to him to ascertain if the whereabouts of this crayon are known."

wise, I thought some trace of them might possibly be obtained through the papers of Christopher Hughes, secretary to the commission.[323] I spoke about it to Mrs. Sioussat of Baltimore, St. George Sioussat's mother.[324] Not long afterward, surprising to say, she found the whole set of these pencil portraits, beautifully executed, pretty good likenesses, and perfectly well preserved, bright and fresh, in the possession of Hughes' grandson. The set comprises, Adams, Bayard,[325] Clay, Gallatin, and Hughes, but not Russell. Legends on the backs show that the painter presented them to Hughes in 1817, as he visited Ghent again on his way to his post as minister to Sweden. My conjecture is that he made the sketches for a large painting of the group, but either found he could not get the Britons or concluded he was not going to finish the task, and handed the sketches over to Hughes as a souvenir.

I really think that this is all I have to contribute, and I fear it will seem trivial to Mr. Edwards' purposes. If, however, he or you should care to see these little pictures, or photographs of the two residences used at Ghent, I can send them from my office, to which I shall return next Monday morning.

I shall have been gone a month, during which I have visited with great pleasure and profit, the universities of Michigan, Chicago, Wisconsin, and Illinois, traveling out with our Spring styles and seeing, to some extent, the "ultimate consumer" of our goods. . . .

To George L. Burr

April 13, 1914.

Dear Burr:

. . . In returning I made with great pleasure the anticipated visit of two days to McLaughlin, and then had a night and a half a day at Urbana with Evarts Greene. I had never seen the University of Illinois, and was much impressed. Then I had some business at Pittsburgh, and, starting out from there with Christie, brought him along to Cumberland, whence we had two days and a half of excellent walking down the towpath of the Chesapeake and Ohio Canal, the most picturesque part, that which goes through the Alleghenies; then we came in here by train Saturday afternoon, but

he was able to tarry only a few hours. It seemed too far to ask you to come over for so excessively short a walk; but short as it was it did us both good, and I feel able to wrestle with whatever there is on my desk. Visiting four of the great western universities has also refreshed my mind, and I hope enlarged it a little.

I came upon no insurgents among the western members of the A. H. A., but I found that a considerable number of men between thirty and forty, thought that other men, between thirty and forty, had been a little more uneasy over the conduct of Association affairs than I had thought, but not much more so. Did you see Rowland's letter of March 19 to the *Nation,* and did you check up his quotation from the constitution? I encountered almost nobody who has done so and who is therefore aware of his discreditable garbling.[326] I had almost a mind to write to the *Nation* again to point this out, it is so outrageous; but I shall content myself with making a rag doll representing him—and stuffed with the same kind of saw-dust—and sticking pins into it. . . .

To James Seth

April 24, 1914.

My dear Seth:

A year ago this morning I was with you, and parted from you to go to Dunfermline and so on. The whole visit is so often in my mind and so vividly enjoyed, that I wish to celebrate its anniversary by writing to you, even though I have nothing much to say—merely the short and simple annals of the poor.

The winter has gone at about the usual rate of one day per diem, and I suppose I have accomplished something in my professional work, though on many days I have been beset by doubts upon that question. There have been few absences from Washington, but one of them was unusually long continued. Mrs. Jameson and I, just after Christmas, went down to Charleston to the meeting of the American Historical Association, and saw a very interesting place which neither of us had

---

[323] Christopher Hughes (1786-1849), a Baltimorean, had been a member of the Maryland House of Delegates. J. Q. Adams wrote to his wife of him: "lively and good-humored, smart at a repartee, and a thorough punster, theory and practice" (*Writings* 5: 69, N. Y., Macmillan, 1915).

[324] Letters to Mrs. Annie L. Sioussat, Mar. 14, 1913, Mar. 9, 1914. For many years Mrs. Sioussat was historian general of the National Society of Colonial Dames and was in frequent communication with Jameson, who acted as historical advisor to the society while it sponsored the publication of the correspondence of William Pitt, William Shirley, and Richard Henry Lee, and *Travels in the American colonies.* It was for this society that Jameson edited his volume, *Privateering and piracy,* N. Y., Macmillan, 1923.

[325] The van Huffel sketch of Bayard is reproduced in *Papers of James A. Bayard.*

[326] Jameson first mentions this communication in a letter of Mar. 24, 1914, to W. E. Dodd, in which he inserts by hand: "See art. 5 and how he cuts it" Art. V read: "The executive council shall have charge of the general interests of the association, including the election of members, the calling of meetings, the selection of papers to be read, and the determination of what papers shall be published." Rowland omitted the words, "shall have charge of the general interests of the association." As adopted in 1916 the constitution made more specific the powers of the executive council: "The executive council shall conduct the business, manage the property, and care for the general interests of the association. In the exercise of its proper functions, the council may appoint such committees, commissions and boards, as it may deem necessary. The council shall make a full report of its activities to the annual meeting of the association. The association may by vote at any annual meeting instruct the executive council to discontinue or enter upon any activity, and may take such other action in directing the affairs of the association as it may deem necessary and proper" (*Ann. Rept., Amer. Hist. Assn.,* 1916: 1: 11-12).

ever seen before. Six weeks later I went down to Savannah to give an address at the seventy-fifth anniversary of the Georgia Historical Society.[327] There was something striking in that, wasn't there—a Massachusetts Yankee giving the commemorative address before the Georgia Historical Society on Lincoln's birthday, though it was Lincoln's birthday only incidentally, but is a day celebrated in Georgia as the date on which the English settlers first landed there.

More recently I was absent a month in the old Northwest. Two days at the University of Michigan, four days at the University of Chicago, two or three weeks at the University of Wisconsin and one day at the University of Illinois, which I had never seen before. All are impressive institutions, with from three to five thousand students and great mental activity, and it did me good to mingle once more in university life, though such attempts as I made at lecturing did not lead me into any longing to return to the teaching profession. On my way back, I managed to get a walk of three days with my old friend Christie, of the Meadville Theological Seminary, for whom my young Francis is named. We walked down the valley of the Potomac through the portion where it breaks through the Alleghanies, namely the part from Cumberland to Hancock, Maryland. We had no adventures, such as my Snowdon expedition of last spring, for our pathway was as nearly level as possible, being the towpath of the old Chesapeake and Ohio Canal. It is a beautiful bit of country and the walk did me much good.

The Washington mind is mainly occupied at the present with our doings in Mexico. The general feeling is that your and my friend, the President, has got us into a very bad position, difficult to defend in both the moral and the military sense, and I fear the effect will be to weaken greatly his prestige, which heretofore has been so remarkable. The general feeling is that, with so many outrages committed by both parties in Mexico, we might easily have grounded our intervention on some grievances of greater magnitude and greater appeal to human feeling than a technical "insult to the flag."[328] It looks to me as if this were true, though I am not one of those who constantly perceive with perfect clearness just what ought to be done when two cut-throats are fighting with each other in the darkness in our back yard.

The American Society of International Law is meeting here now (by accident, though their line of goods is greatly needed here at present) and last night I had some talk at the Cosmos Club with our friend, G. G. Wilson, who confessed to me, you will not be surprised to learn, that he was advising the administration.[329] . . .

To Frances G. Davenport

April 25, 1914.

My dear Miss Davenport:

Thank you very much for your letter of April 17, and the report. I will write to Captain Ashe.[330] Thank you also for the review, which sounds like Pollard.[331] He must be a very superior person. At all events, to be able to say at the end of a review that one would not look for appreciation of Elizabeth's finesse to the Republican simplicity of the Quaker State of Pennsylvania must give one, on quite easy terms, a comfortable sense, as he lays down his pen, of his superiority to those persons who have not had one's own advantages. A thoughtful and judicious historical writer must feel pleasure, on the face of it, that among the six million inhabitants of Pennsylvania there can be no one who understands political trickery, because it is well known that some of the founders were Quakers.[332]

That you have had no vacation since January 4 is an alarming statement. Immediately after finishing the reading of this letter, pack your trunk or valise and start for any place you can think of in Western Europe that is forty miles from a library, and there remain, in the wilderness, forty days and forty nights

[327] The subject of the address was the History of historical societies.

[328] In Tampico, following the arrest of some American sailors, Admiral Mayo demanded an apology and a salute, which Huerta refused. A period of negotiation followed, during which President Wilson ordered into Mexican waters fifty-two vessels. On April 20 he delivered a message to the Congress, following which both houses debated a resolution approving the use of force by the President. On the twenty-first, marines and sailors seized the docks at Vera Cruz to prevent the landing of German munitions intended for the forces of Huerta. An offer of mediation from Argentina, Brazil, and Chile provided a way out of an awkward situation which might easily have ended in war.

[329] George Grafton Wilson, as a member of the department of political science of Brown University, 1891-1910, would have been known to Professor Seth, who had gone to Edinburgh from Brown University, where he had been professor of philosophy during the earlier period of Jameson's tenure.

[330] Capt. Samuel A'Court Ashe of Raleigh, N. C., was the author of a *History of North Carolina,* 2v., Greensboro and Raleigh, N. C., Van Noppen, 1908, 1925, and editor-in-chief of the *Biographical history of North Carolina,* 10v., Greensboro, Van Noppen, 1905-1911. In Mr. Leland's trip to North Carolina in 1905, looking for manuscripts important to American history, Captain Ashe had been of assistance to him. It does not appear from the correspondence why Jameson was now writing to him.

[331] Albert F. Pollard (1869-1948), professor of constitutional history in the University of London. He had some acquaintance with America and Americans as he had delivered the first series of Goldwin Smith lectures in Cornell University in 1913.

[332] The review referred to (*Times Literary Supplement,* Apr. 16, 1914: 184), dealt scathingly with the first volume of Edward P. Cheyney's *History of England from the defeat of the Armada to the death of Elizabeth,* N. Y., Longmans, 1914. It characterized the work not as history, but as a series of essays which "reduced the Tudor period to chaos." To answer Professor Cheyney's verdict that the intellectual powers of Elizabeth were but moderate, Pollard devoted a long and contemptuous paragraph, ending with the statement concerning Republican simplicity which so annoyed Jameson.

(the continuance of rain during that period can, I believe, be taken for granted); after which you can return by way of some available Ararat just in season to open the new headquarters. . . .

The various things I have in hand seem to be advancing rather than retrograding, which at least is a comfort.

I hear that Leland is likely to take a vacation in May; a noble example for others in the foreign mission field.

P.S. Take a vacation.

To LORD BRYCE

April 27, 1914.

My dear Lord Bryce:

You asked me to mention the meritorious new books, especially biographical, which might possibly escape your notice. Perhaps this is hardly likely to occur in the case of the books of Houghton Mifflin; but I derived so much pleasure yesterday from the reading of *Confederate Portraits,* by Gamaliel Bradford, Jr., that I thought I would mention the book for you. His previous book, *Lee, the American,* I have not read. Perhaps you may have seen these studies of Confederate character in the *Atlantic,* where I have a notion that they were published.

We have been having times of great political interest during the last week. I am only a spectator, and one neither very acute nor very well informed in such matters, but the impression seems to be nearly universal that the whole affair has been badly managed. So far as I can report public opinion, it is strongly to the effect that the President, if intervention to any extent was ultimately to be undertaken, ought to have managed to ground it on outrages of greater human consequence than the incident at Tampico; and also that the raising of the embargo upon arms and ammunition passing over the frontier into Northern Mexico was a great mistake. The speeches of Lodge and Root are very widely commended, as placing the matter on a broader ground than that chosen by the President.[333] Yet a week from now the President's stock may be higher. I hardly think that Bryan's will, for the impression that that great politician and excellent man is a misfit as Secretary of State, has deepened. . . .

The American Society of International Law has been meeting here. . . . They confined themselves pretty much to the Monroe doctrine, which was threshed over pretty elaborately, though with what results I have not yet learned, and to the matter of instruction in international law in our colleges, universities and law schools, in respect to which the Society is showing a useful activity.

To FRENCH ENSOR CHADWICK

May 7, 1914.

My dear Admiral Chadwick:

I ought to write to you, as a member of the committee on the Revolutionary records, the fate of the appropriation for that purpose, as I found it on my return from the West.[334] I judge that the hearing went rather badly. Breckinridge made a very good speech to Fitzgerald and his committee.[335] But the committee plainly felt that they would be in for a very great and wholly indefinite expense (Roosevelt and Breckinridge intimated that it might be somewhere between half a million and a million dollars), and they confronted the applicants with the absurdly low figures which had been mentioned in the debate on the original appropriation, on February 28, 1913. I send you a copy of the Congressional Record of that day, and if you will look at pages 4397 to 4400, you will see what was meant.[336]

I think there is really no hope of a continuance this year of the appropriation. The present money may suffice for doing Massachusetts, Virginia and North Carolina, where the searchers have for some time been successfully at work. A year from now, we shall be able, with our experience in these three states as a basis, to frame estimates that can be relied upon. Going before Congress with these, the Departments may hope to secure further appropriations, but it is not possible now.

I do not think our committee need regret the time we spent upon the matter. The text of the hearing shows that what we did was well appreciated by the Departments, and I believe the way is paved for more successful action in the future. . . .

[333] In the Senate debate of Apr. 21, 1914, over the resolution approving the action of the President in sending troops into Mexico, a debate prolonged far into the night, both Lodge and Root spoke. Before morning the resolution was approved by a vote of seventy-two to thirteen (*Congressional Record,* 63 Cong., 2 sess., 6964-7015, esp., 6966-6967, 6985-6988).

[334] On Apr. 15, Jameson wrote to Evarts B. Greene that the departments were not likely to receive a continuance of the appropriation to complete the work of collecting Revolutionary materials, partly, he thought, because Captain Clark had not shown more progress. To Leland he wrote on Apr. 20, that the scheme was probably dead, though the work in Massachusetts, Virginia, and North Carolina might be completed.

[335] John J. Fitzgerald, representative from New York, 1899-1917, was in 1914 chairman of the Committee on Appropriations.

[336] In the House debate of Feb. 28, 1914, the sum considered (and finally granted) was $32,000. At this time, Representative Hay stated that he believed that the work could be completed for this amount (*Cong. Rec.,* 62 Cong., 3 sess., 4327-4329).

To Richard Rathburn

October 10, 1914.

My dear Rathburn: [337]

This is in reply to your letter of September 18, which I received on my arrival in Washington.

I can well understand that the policy of the Smithsonian Institution of avoiding the publication of whatever may awaken question in Congress or on the part of the public on religious grounds may readily be held to apply to the papers of Professor Coleman and Professor Bassett; [338] but, though very reluctant to consume your time, I should like to ask you to take under your personal consideration, or if you have already looked at it somewhat, to consider once again, the paper of Professor Justin H. Smith on "Mexican Feeling toward the United States at the beginning of 1846." Professor Smith, who was chairman of the section before which this paper was read at Charleston, is a really profound student of the history of the Mexican War, not one of those who talk glibly on the subject upon the basis of half-knowledge, but one who has labored for nearly ten years now upon the making of what will surely be the authoritative history of that conflict. While previous writers have usually contented themselves with American sources, he has, besides travelling extensively in Mexico and visiting all the battle-fields, made prolonged researches in the archives of the City of Mexico and in those of the northern provinces. The late President Diaz gave him the most exceptional facilities for this purpose, while President Roosevelt, even during the regime of General Ainsworth, gave him the run of the archives of our War Department as well as those of the State Department —the only historian, I think, who ever had the former privilege during General Ainsworth's time. Professor Smith's spirit is recognized as one of perfect fairness toward both Mexican and American action and opinion. While it would be natural to expect that in a paper of such title, there might be something upon which hostile criticism might lay its hand, I cannot see that there is any such portion of the actual text of the paper. To me it appears to be merely a scientific description of the state of public opinion in a certain country sixty-eight years ago. I do not perceive that it contains any inflammable material whatever, and I am sure that the author can give chapter and verse for every statement which he makes, his system of notes being somewhat celebrated among us.

Accordingly I ask leave to send the manuscript back to you, and request that, as a personal though

I fear a somewhat troublesome favor, you would read it yourself, if you have not already done so. I venture to hope that after such consideration you will think it not only unexceptionable, but a distinctly useful contribution to American history in a field in which we have rather too little—the well documented history of public opinion. [339]

To William H. P. Faunce

October 20, 1914.

My dear Dr. Faunce:

Now that the captains and the kings have gone, and you have settled down once more to academic quiet, and I have got back to my usual routine, I wish to tell you how deeply I enjoyed the whole celebration, how greatly I admire the perfection of all the arrangements, and how highly I appreciate the honor which the university was so good as to confer upon me. I don't know how I can ever live up to a degree of Doctor of Letters, I who can never hope to write a book, having to work out here a life sentence which is incompatible with such an achievement, but I am grateful for the implied expression

---

[337] Richard Rathburn (1852-1918) was assistant secretary of the Smithsonian, 1897-1918.

[338] C. B. Coleman's Some salient features of American Christianity, and J. S. Bassett's The development of popular churches after the Revolution, were read at a session of the Charleston meeting of the Association on American Religious History.

[339] The Smithsonian did not relent and Justin Smith's paper was not published in the Annual Report for 1913. This was the second occasion on which Jameson had protested omissions from the *Annual Report*. In 1909 two contributions were dropped: a paper on the policy of the Great Elector with respect to religious toleration and a classified list of materials for English diplomatic history. Jameson wrote in July that he understood the first exclusion to be in accord with the policy of the Smithsonian not to print anything having to do with the Christian religion, although the article seemed to him to be entirely harmless, but that he could find no reason for the omission of the list of documents. The reply, written in October, stated briefly that the list was omitted because it did not deal with American history. This brought forth a long and illuminating letter from Jameson, which argued that under the act of incorporation the Association was set up, not to promote the study of American history alone but also of history in America, and that this was done with intent, to prevent it from becoming an agency devoted solely to American history. He followed with a table showing the proportion of material not American which had appeared in earlier *Annual Reports* and ended: "But I think it much better to argue solely from the point of view of the good of the country and of the promotion of historical science in the most catholic spirit and thereby in the most healthy and enduring manner." Unfortunately Jameson included with this letter a reprint of his article, The American Historical Association, 1884-1909, *Amer. Hist. Rev.* 15: 1-20, Oct. 1909, and Secretary Walcott's long reply ignored the argument against narrowing the *Report* to American material and devoted itself to the article, which he interpreted as an attack on the conduct of the Smithsonian in its relations with the Association. To this Jameson answered that there was no difference of opinion as to the legal relations between the two organizations and that he was fully aware of the benefits which resulted from that relationship. He had not been complaining of it in his article, still less in his recent letter. Here the correspondence rested (Jameson to C. D. Walcott, July 6, Oct. 16, 25, Dec. 4, 1909; Walcott to Jameson, Oct. 16, 23, Nov. 26, 1909).

of confidence that I could write one if I had the time.[340]

I hope that you are not quite destroyed by your laborious part in these memorable doings of last week. Everyone spoke with great warmth of the complete successes [*sic*] of the whole celebration. To me the most gratifying thing about it was the obvious evidences that Providence and Rhode Island were deeply proud of Brown University, and regarded it as their own in a much fuller sense of affection and support than when I was there. President Angell [341] once told me that when he was in college the college had no more relation to the town than if it had been a Buddhist monastery up there on the hill. That the state of things is so utterly and plainly different now is the work of the last two presidents, and, in different ways, equally of the two, and I congratulate you upon this more warmly than upon any one thing in the whole brilliant celebration.

To Lord Bryce

November 12, 1914.

My dear Lord Bryce:

Miss Davenport, of the staff of my office, returning from London, has brought me a copy of your pamphlet on "Neutral Nations and the War." I had not seen it before, but have read it with much pleasure, and with fortification of the mind. I will take leave to use it as an occasion for writing. I have not written to you, I think, since the war began, and have felt that I had nothing important to say, and nothing in the way of information that did not come to you better from many other American sources. At the same time I have had a slightly uneasy feeling that perhaps in spite of this I ought to write, because in this great and solemn crisis of England's history every Englishman in public life was entitled to receive from every one of his American friends without the burdensome obligation of reply, the assurance of his sympathy for the British cause and admiration for British conduct during these three dreadful months.

Undoubtedly you have heard from others that, almost universally the academic opinion in America is with the allies. A few weeks ago I attended the 150th anniversary of Brown University, where I used to teach, and met there a good many academics from various places. Without exception every one of them who was not of German birth desired the allies to be victorious, though of course not without sympathy for German suffering and for the Germans as human beings, nor without losing appreciation of what we owe to German scholarship and science.

The same is true here in Washington. I know only one person not of German birth who holds that the German cause is better and wishes Germany to prevail. This unanimity has rather surprised me, in a town so full of scientific people, and I have been still more surprised by the warmth, violence even, with which some men here, whom I should have expected to cultivate a neutral serenity, have expressed anti-German feelings. At the Cosmos Club, for instance, most of the members are connected with the government in some way, and subject to the President's injunction as to neutrality of behavior and expression. But the other evening, when a doctor here who had served with the Red Cross in Belgium gave a talk to the club on his very interesting experiences in the warfare, the obvious sentiment of the audience was, as one of my assistants expressed it "neutral only to the extent that the Cosmos Club didn't care who beat the Germans so long as they were beaten 'good and hard.'"

I judge that much the same is the situation in the whole country. Even the German-Americans are by no means of one way of thinking, as one might suppose from the numerous letters of pro-German protest which one sees in the open columns of the New York Evening Post. A New York friend of mine who was lately here, a Jewish lawyer of Austrian antecedents, tells me that, as a rule while persons born in Germany side with the Kaiser, German-Americans born in this country are very largely of the other way of thinking, and the descendants of the Forty-eighters are uniformly so, and that the Jews of German origin are divided much the same way, though the Russian Jews of the East Side are apt to side with the Kaiser, or at any rate against the Czar.

The war presses upon us all. I think of it day and night, and with a heavy heart, hoping and believing that the allies will be victorious in the end, yet seeing that the best result that can be expected will still be attended with enormous calamity to all the civilized world. Wherever two or three intelligent men are gathered together, you presently find them talking about the war, and always with sadness.

Meanwhile the sky of Washington is singularly beautiful all through the autumn, and history is certainly looking up here, so far as increase of numbers of the professional guild is concerned. Mr. Adams came back in good condition a few days ago and is established for the winter. Admiral Mahan is here for six months from the first of November, in the guise of a Research Associate of the Carnegie

---

[340] Jameson had returned from the celebration of the 150th anniversary of the founding of Brown University. In conferring the degree of Doctor of Letters upon him, President Faunce's simple citation was: "John Franklin Jameson; leader in historical research, once professor at Brown, now teacher of teachers throughout the land."

[341] James B. Angell (1829-1916), president of the University of Michigan, 1871-1909, had received his A.B. from Brown in 1849, his A.M., in 1853; he was professor of modern language and literature there from 1853 to 1860, and from 1860 to 1866 was the editor of the Providence *Journal*.

Institution, which means that he is to write what history he pleases and by occasional conversation keep me and this Department out of the ruts into which such an Institution may easily gravitate. He has just been giving an informal talk to our staff on blockading operations in naval warfare, with special reference to the North Sea. He has however been ill in September and October, and does not seem quite well yet.[342] Professor Bernard Moses [343] is also here, and will perhaps settle down in Washington, and Major John Bigelow is finding a furnished house for the same purpose, and several other historical people, rather more than usual because Paris and London seem less eligible than usual to men with sabbatical leaves of absence.

I will ask you to present my very kind regards to Lady Bryce. As I pass the Embassy each morning, taking my small boy to his school and proceeding to my office, I have to lament that you are not still there, but my thoughts and sympathies are with you, and with all who under the English, or French or Belgian flag are fighting for our kind of civilization. By the way, special friendship with four Belgian professors, two at Ghent and two at Louvain, makes me especially appreciate the noble generosity with which Oxford and Cambridge have behaved toward the latter university.[344]

With the most cordial regard, and with the hope that you keep good health in these trying times.

To FRANK M. ANDERSON

November 18, 1914.

My dear Mr. Anderson: [345]

Many years ago I observed, and have always kept in mind, the close relation between the Alien and Sedition Acts and three British statutes on which they seemed to me to be closely modelled, the former on the Alien Act of 1793, the latter on the Treasonable Practices Act and Seditious Meetings Act of 1795. My impression had been that I had never seen the similarity alluded to in print, except in a vaguely remembered foot-note in some book of fifty or sixty years ago, perhaps the *Writings* of John

Adams. A friend however tells me that he seems to remember some reference in print to the affair, and therefore I am led to think that it may have been spoken of more often than I know. If so, you must have come across it. If you can give me any reference I shall be much obliged.[346]

To H. MORSE STEPHENS

November 30, 1914.

My dear Morse Stephens: [347]

Let me put in black and white what I said in conversation the other night.

I stand ready, if you continue to desire it, to give at Berkeley a series of lectures (eight, I understand) during the fortnight beginning with Tuesday, July 6. As to the subject, I suggest "The Development and Organization of Historical Studies in America." If this should continue to seem to you a desirable topic, we can let it stand as the title of the series.

It was a great pleasure to see you, and to hear what you said at the Council dinner. I was greatly pleased with what you said about chauvinistic teaching of history as one of the causes of the present war. I have to talk here on Saturday evening to a club called Federal Schoolmen mostly composed of teachers in secondary schools, and, speaking under the general title "On Teaching Young People to be Fair," had it in mind to speak largely on the responsibility which in this present year must be laid upon those who, for a generation past have been teaching history for the sake of national patriotism rather than for the sake of truth and knowledge and culture. You gave me some very good ammunition. When schoolmasters stop to think, they must see that history furnishes about the only chance they have to teach their pupils anything about human nature and human relations—at least so far as high school curricula in the effete east are concerned. . . .

---

[342] Admiral Mahan died on Dec. 1, 1914.

[343] Bernard Moses (1846-1930), professor of history and political science, University of California.

[344] The Ghent professors were Paul Frédericq and Henri Pirenne; those of Louvain were L. Van der Essen and Dr. S. Delannoy.

[345] Frank Maloy Anderson of Dartmouth College.

[346] Professor Anderson replied, Nov. 26, 1914: "At the time of the Alien and Sedition Acts the possible connection with the British statutes you mention was frequently pointed out by Republicans. Most frequently it took the form of asserting that the suggestion had been obtained from the British acts and that the American acts were more severe than the British. An example of the latter assertion may be found in a speech of W. C. Nicholas in the House of Representatives on July 10th, 1798 (Annals of Congress, 5th Congress, pp. 2144-2145)."

[347] H. Morse Stephens, professor of modern European and English history in Cornell University in the days when he and Jameson worked on the early numbers of the *Review*, had gone to the University of California in 1902.

THE DEPARTMENT OF HISTORICAL RESEARCH OF THE
CARNEGIE INSTITUTION OF WASHINGTON:
THE MIDDLE YEARS, 1915-1924

To CATHARINE C. CLEVELAND

January 21, 1915.

My dear Miss Cleveland: [1]

Thank you very much for your letter of January 16, and for the return of the paper. I didn't know it *was* so good! [2]

What I said about the religious element in the cry of "manifest destiny" meant nothing more specific than this: That national feeling, in its more exalted moods, takes on a character which approaches and resembles that of religious belief. What men worship is, the highest unity they see in nature or in human affairs, and, in the latter aspect, there were many Romans to whom the majesty of the Roman Empire represented the highest unity they saw in human affairs. Now, even after monotheism has prevailed for sixteen hundred years, there are in the large nations many persons so constituted that the highest unity they see really *active* in human affairs or that appeals to their minds with a great deal of force is their own nation. I presume that this present war furnishes wide-spread examples of this way of thinking—patriotism exalted until it becomes indistinguishable from religion, though with less reason perhaps than in the case of the Romans insofar as our states are much less ecumenical than theirs. So I venture to think that there are sentiments in our own day that make the worship of *dea Roma,* or of the Emperor intelligible to us, as we read Dill or Glover.[3] I remember reading of a native regiment in India which on dress parade performed ceremonies which were actually acts of worship toward a big silver épergne which had been presented to them by the Empress—Queen Victoria—toward it as a symbol of the greatest unity in human affairs that appealed to their minds, the British Empire; also how the Puritan Nicholson,[4] to his great annoyance, found it difficult to restrain his native troupes [*sic*] from performing similar acts to him, but to him, I suppose, as a symbol of the same great power.

But these are generalizations of a larger sort, that one ought not to advance save in a suggestive spirit.

To JOHN M. VINCENT

February 3, 1915.

My dear Vincent:

I thank you for your note respecting the lectures, and still more for the other note. Bancroft's attitude and opinion respecting Burr are to me very strange.[5] Plainly, he has no idea of what Burr's standing as a scholar really is; and his excessively masculine mind may easily fail also to appreciate Burr's character. A saint is not half as attractive to Bancroft's mind as a brigadier general.

As for yourself you are too good a medievalist not to know all about Burr, and I know how you regard him personally. And if in any meetings touching organization of the Association I hear you advocating measures that I myself should not advocate, there will be no danger of my thinking any differently of you on that account. In the first place, we are friends of too long standing to misunderstand each other; in the second place, none of these divergencies of opinion are vital or so wide as unthinking persons or outsiders might imagine. Bancroft cannot see any of these things otherwise than in the similitude of a party contest. But what I see is, that some people think that the Council

---

[1] Catharine C. Cleveland (1873-1928), Ph.D., University of Chicago, 1914. Miss Cleveland had written asking to see a copy of a paper by Dr. Jameson, probably, Reasons for studying American religious history, which he had read at the Charleston meeting of the Association. In sending her the paper he wrote: "Very little of European aristocracy ever came over—far less than many societies of resounding claims to ancestry would desire; on the other hand, there was a qualification, about thirty dollars passage money, that deterred the lowest classes from coming over in very abundant quantities. The result is that, on the whole, American religion is *bourgeois* religion" (Jameson to Catharine C. Cleveland, Jan. 5, 1915).

[2] This comment was called forth by Miss Cleveland's enthusiasm over the paper. "If we as students could only wake up to the fact that American history is, as you describe it, 'the rightful heritage of millions' what a different emphasis we should place on our studying and teaching! . . . I should like to know more of the religious element in the cry of 'manifest destiny' and the other ideals which you mentioned. We are so inclined to limit the area of religious thought and thus belittle its historical importance in our development."

[3] Sir Samuel Dill (1844-1924), author of *Roman society in the last century of the Western Empire,* N. Y., Macmillan,

1898, and *Roman society from Nero to Marcus Aurelius,* N. Y., Macmillan, 1904. Terrot Reaveley Glover, among other studies, wrote *The conflict of religions in the early Roman Empire,* 3d ed., London, Methuen, 1909.

[4] John Nicholson (1821 or 1822-1857), an administrator who brought order to the Punjab, where the natives were said to regard him as a god. He was mortally wounded during the siege of Delhi.

[5] J. M. Vincent had written that Frederic Bancroft had taken a dislike to Burr, and was inclined to oppose his promotion to the presidency of the Association, but that he, Vincent, though he might advocate a few changes in organization, would have no part in such a movement.

176

has had too much power, that perhaps it has, that while I think the present arrangements work with extraordinary efficiency I am able to see that contentment of the members is one of the most important ends to keep in mind; and so I see various men differing as to the amount and kind of readjustment necessary, but all having the good of the Association in view, all devoid of personal feeling in the matter, and therefore all likely to come to some harmonious conclusion, which will leave the Association in a healthier condition and perhaps not much less efficient. I presume I made it plain to you that I stood ready to agree to whatever changes the deliberate judgment of the Association resolved upon; and indeed I should think it was plain that that was the attitude of all members of the Council. That of course does not mean that I expect to abandon a member's right to say, in proper form and order, what he thinks should be said for or against particular propositions; but there is no good getting "all het up" and I expect to appreciate and respect the arguments and positions of those who differ from me. And though I do not know whether you and I will differ on questions or propositions not yet before us, I appreciate your writing.

To Lord Bryce

March 8, 1915.

My dear Lord Bryce:

I observed the other day in the *Dictionary of National Biography* that your father was born at Killaig, a few miles from Coleraine, and that your grandfather was a minister there. My great-great-grandfather, Thomas Jameson, and his brother Hugh came from Coleraine to Londonderry, New Hampshire, in 1746. In April 1913, after the International Historical Congress, having to go upon business from Glasgow to Dublin, I treated myself to a hasty foray in the Coleraine-Londonderry region. It was to me a very interesting excursion. In the last hour of my being at Coleraine, just too late for me to act upon the information, I learned of a Thomas and Hugh Jameson of the present day, brothers, who were farmers at Kirkiston in the parish of Ballyrasheine. Later I procured from the Ordnance Office a copy of that portion of the Down Survey which shows the districts about Coleraine and among them this supposed-ancestral place of Kirkiston. So when I saw this bit in the *Dictionary of National Biography* about Killaig I was led to wonder just where it is. I have not found it on this Down Survey map or in any gazetteer at the Library of Congress.[6]

But this is a quite trivial matter—not more than an excuse for writing a letter to you. I never feel as if I were in a position to speak with certainty or fullness of knowledge about political conditions here. Congress has adjourned, doubtless with a sense of relief on the part of the members, and certainly with a sense of relief on the part of the country. In the first two-thirds of its immensely long session it seemed to have and to deserve an unusual amount of respect from the country, but I do not think that in the last four or five months it has behaved better, or has been thought by the country to be behaving better than the average of congresses. The President's prestige seems to have been distinctly impaired by his determined but unsuccessful urgency on behalf of the ship-purchase bill,[7] yet he remains the democratic party's best asset. I think his prestige has also been lessened by the course of events in Mexico. In fact, I think his Mexican policy might have almost destroyed him but for the arising of war in Europe. Those who seem to me to have the best understanding of Mexican character and conditions tell me that he has not understood them at all nor taken any proper measures toward understanding them. They say that he ought to have recognized Huerta and that events are all the time proving that that was the least of the various evils from among which a choice might have been made.[8]

On the other hand, his course with respect to the warring European nations seems to have the approval of most wise men. Mr. Lansing,[9] whom I know somewhat, as he is an Amherst man, is a calm, sensible, judicious man, well-informed in matters of international law, and seems to be regarded as a good man for his position, without being a great man. It is not customary to think that the policy of the Department of State is in any great degree shaped by the Secretary, but that the President directs all these matters of relations to the war with sound assistance from Lansing

---

[6] Bryce answered on Mar. 24, 1915: "Killaig is a place something less than a village and something more than a town which lies about 5 Irish miles, that is nearly 6 English ones, W. S. W. of Coleraine in Co. Londonderry. My grandfather came over there in the very end of the 18th century and lived there as Pastor of the Presbyterian Church till he died in 1854 at the age of 90, having preached twice every Sunday until his death."

[7] In the President's annual message of Dec. 7, 1914, he recommended that provision be made for a fleet of government-owned merchant vessels. A bitter struggle followed in the Congress, in the midst of which the President spoke for the measure at the Jackson Day celebration in Indianapolis on Jan. 8, 1915. The bill was abandoned in March on the threat of a renewed filibuster. For an adequate summary of the history of the bill see *American Year Book*, 1915: 69-71, 74.

[8] The final revolution under Madero's government had broken out in Mexico City in February, 1913. Huerta, chief general in the army, joined it, Madero was overthrown, and Huerta set up a government destined to endure only to the summer of 1914. During its life Wilson refused to grant it recognition. Bryce's comment was: "What you say about the President and Mexico is perfectly true. It astonished me from the first that he should have had so little notion of the conditions that prevail in a Spanish-American Republic. To talk, as he did, of having a legitimate expression of the will of the people and observance of constitution is to use language as inapplicable to Mexico as it would be to the negroes of the Congo. How comes it that a man of so much historical capacity could have remained so ignorant of Spanish-American facts?"

[9] Robert Lansing (1864-1928), A.B., Amherst, 1886, secretary of State, 1915-1920.

and the permanent people. To have arranged that Dacia should be taken in by the French rather than by the British is regarded as a good stroke, for our public is, as you know, sensitive in regard to maritime actions by Great Britain which it will not mind in the case of France.[10] In fact nobody seems at any time to have a word to say against the French. Mr. Jusserand has never once given any occasion for cavil, in fact has been almost completely silent. It is long since I have seen him but he then seemed very much overworked. He told me he had but one assistant, all the rest had gone to the war, and that one knew little English. No propaganda attempted in that quarter, obviously, and none needed.

That of the Germans on the other hand is richly supported, extensive, industrious, and clever. Dernburg evidently knows his America much better than Bernstorff,[11] and is able, ardent, confident, and not over-scrupulous. Still, I do not think that in general the balance of opinion inclines much differently from what I thought when I wrote in November. Probably I should not now say that the German-Americans were anywhere near evenly divided. I judge that while this may be true in country places, yet where there is a great mass of Germans to keep each other warm, as in the large cities they are pretty largely for the Kaiser. But Americans not German by birth or by immediate origin are almost invariably sympathizing with the allies. I should think that this was due to the matter of Belgium as much as to any one thing. Our people have never got over that. As you know, whatever their faults in other directions they are rather exceptionally soft-hearted, and every time they hear of a new requisition extracted from a country they are trying to feed, they squirm inwardly and think many ill things concerning the Germans, some of them of course quite unjust.

But I cannot but think that all this is a great excess of political reflection from a non-political source. I should be so glad to inform you that I am evidently tempted to try it when I cannot. At all events, I send my best sympathy for your anxieties. We all appreciate the justness with which you have spoken of the American government's neutrality. Our own best thought seems to be that such a course as the President

has followed in the long run is the best for the total interests involved. Even Fred. Gillett[12] said that frankly the other day, in the House, while denouncing the President's Mexican policy.

Please give my very kindest regards to Lady Bryce and believe me,

P. S. I might add, that I do not hear from any responsible quarter any criticism of your successor's conduct.[13]

To John Patterson

March 22, 1915.

My dear Sir:

I have just received your letter of March 20 enclosing a two-cent stamp and asking me five questions respecting the Philippines which it would take me an hour to answer if I thought I knew all about the subject, and a year if I did not.[14] No doubt you have written to a number of other persons, for I often get such letters, and it is growing to be a custom among debaters to "work" various professors, or writers, or public men in this manner. Then a debater attempts to confute his opponents by saying that he has written to ninety-one professors or seventy-four public men, and that sixty-three or fifty-seven of them answer in the affirmative, or in the negative as the case might be.

Now let me submit to you in all kindness, that this is not debate at all, in any sense that an educational institution should recognize. If education stands for anything, it stands for the founding of one's opinions on reasoning rather than on authority, and for the effort to do one's own reading and thinking. I would add that, having sometimes been myself a judge in debates, I am convinced that sensible judges think very little of efforts which consist in quoting authorities industriously collected, in order to avoid the trouble of thinking and rate much higher the efforts of youths who show that they have tried to read and think for themselves. Also, if a prize of [sic] an honor is given for debating, that is to

---

[10] The *Dacia* had been purchased from the Hamburg-American line and placed under American registry. Great Britain warned that the ship would be seized if she traded with an enemy country and refused a request that she be allowed to deliver one cargo. In spite of this she left Norfolk with a cargo of cotton for Germany on Feb. 12, 1915. She was shortly after seized by a French cruiser and taken into Brest, where the French flag was hoisted. Throughout the controversy there was great discussion as to whether the sale was bona fide and as to the international law in such cases.

[11] Count von Bernstorff, German ambassador to Washington from 1908 to 1917. Bernhard Dernburg, one-time colonial minister of the Imperial German government, had come to this country in the early days of the war, as a special emissary to conduct the presentation of the German cause. He left not long after the sinking of the *Lusitania*.

[12] Frederick H. Gillett (1851-1935), A.B., Amherst, 1874, member of the House of Representatives from Massachusetts, 1893-1925.

[13] Bryce's successor was Sir Cecil Arthur Spring-Rice, British ambassador, 1913-1918. In response, from Bryce: "Thank you for telling me that Spring-Rice and Jusserand have shown up so well through the crisis. Bernstorff seems generally discredited; and 'tis said he would be recalled to Germany, if he could be got back there! The German mind is an interesting subject of study. So much thoroughness, so much exactness in a knowledge of the outsides of facts, so little power of comprehending their inside, and in particular such an incapacity for seeing things from any angle but their own. One had always felt in their writing of history,—during the last forty years—a sort of want of perception of the life and meaning of men and events, a want of subtlety in discernment."

[14] Among the multitude of letters that came to Dr. Jameson were many from students asking aid. This letter, sent to Baldwin City, Kan., is an excellent illustration of those which he wrote in reply when he felt that the student needed to be encouraged to do the work in question for himself.

say, for argument and reasoning, it is not quite honest to try to obtain it by overaweing the opposition with a show of authorities and names. Therefore, as every man you write to has plenty of other things to do, go to work for yourself, and read up on these subjects, and *think*. Take for instance your second question, about the Filipinos having a common language, why should you ask a score or a hundred of other people to answer that question for you, when you can find the answer in any encyclopedia, indeed cannot read one book on the Philippines without finding it.

All this is not written in a harsh or crabbed spirit, but because, having been a university teacher twenty-three years, I have too much respect for education to countenance any procedure that consists in the utter avoidance of its methods. Get to work, and may you have great success.

To LORD BRYCE

March 25, 1915.

My dear Lord Bryce:

No doubt the cable dispatches have informed you of the death of our friend Mr. Charles Francis Adams, but I believe you will wish to know more particulars than may have been found in the English newspapers.[15]

It has seemed to me throughout the winter that Mr. Adams was not quite as well as in preceding years or showed his age a little more, and yet he was still remarkably vigorous for a man approaching eighty. The war had, from its beginning, pressed upon his mind and spirits with great weight. He was deeply interested in it all and could read little else, though he grew weary with thinking of it. He found it quite impossible to do anything with his book since the war opened and I fear that it still stands where it stood when Professor E. D. Adams of Stanford University, who for some months had been working with him upon it, went back to California in August. This means, if I am rightly informed, that it is about finished down to 1860; but whether anything approaching a satisfactory and continuous narrative after 1860 could be made up from his manuscript by others, for instance by E. D. Adams and Worthington Ford, I do not know though of course that is the part which one would most wish to see completed.

About three weeks ago Mr. Adams's son-in-law Abbott died. Two journeys to Boston within this period, one at that time and one a little later, I believe on account of the Lincoln town-meeting, seemed to have told upon him a good deal, though usually he has made that journey with as little concern or wear as a young man might feel. Tuesday of last week he was out rid-

ing as usual, but at the end of the ride had serious difficulty in dismounting, went home and went to bed. The doctor next morning was apparently not alarmed but the illness, which I understand was classified as grippe, ended his life early Saturday morning. Only Mrs. Adams was with him, and I think she was alone all that day, so far as the family were concerned, for Miss Adams[16] happened to be in Boston and I judge did not get here till Saturday night. There was a brief preliminary service, for the nearer sort of friends, on Monday afternoon, before the train was taken for Boston. The funeral took place at Quincy. It was not known at the house this morning whether Mrs. Adams and Miss Adams would come back to Washington or not.

I feel Mr. Adams's loss deeply. He was a very kind friend, hospitable and generous, and of course exceedingly interesting to us younger men in conversation— his remembrance of American public life being so extensive and various, his comments so incisive, his intelligence so wide and keen. No one can take his place as a centre around whom the men working in history here in Washington might rally;[17] and indeed in the country at large, it is hard to think of anyone making good his place as a writer and speaker on public questions. It is surely a pity that such a man should never have had the opportunities of any public office adequate to his powers; and it is pathetic, even tragic, that even in the field of history, where we all felt his powers to be greater than any one thing he had yet written, he should not have lived to have finished his great book. I have not seen Mr. Henry Adams since his brother's death but shall go there in a day or two. It will be a matter of mournful astonishment to him that he should survive. It is really surprising how well on the whole he continues, in spite of the stroke or seizure of two or three years ago.

To JOHN duFAIS

April 22, 1915.

My dear Sir:[18]

This is in reply to your letter of April 16. I could not reply until I had gone to the Library of Congress, and this I was not able to do for some days. I return herewith your photograph. The lower lines of the inscription should be read, "Ick wil den Here singen [om d] at hy soo wel aen my doet," (literally, "I will

---

[15] Charles Francis Adams died on Mar. 20. Lord Bryce had already learned this when he wrote on Mar. 24. Referring to Adams as "my old friend," he said of him: "There seemed to me to be always a great deal of vigour and independent thought in all that he wrote on historical subjects."

[16] Elizabeth Ogden Adams (1873-1945), third daughter of Charles Francis Adams. She returned to Boston with her mother at this time but was a frequent visitor in her uncle Henry's Washington home as long as he lived.

[17] From a letter of Dec. 4, 1914, to Adams, it appears that it was Dr. Jameson's habit to notify Adams of "historical strangers of eminence" arriving in Washington. In that letter he mentioned David Jayne Hill, Justin H. Smith, and the Right Reverend Monsignor Shahan.

[18] John duFais of Newport had written to Jameson for help in identifying a portrait in the Redwood Library of Newport.

sing the Lord because he doth so well to me"). This is exactly the form, except for insignificant differences of spelling which Psalm 13:6 has in one particular Dutch translation of the Bible. I find it in a copy of the Bible at the Library of Congress, which was printed by Lenaert der Kinderen at Emden in 1563. This Bible is a reprint of that which was printed at Emden in 1560 by Nicolaes Biestkens and the version is known as the Mennonite version or Biestkens Bible, because of the popularity of the edition issued by the latter printer. This version in turn is the same as Mierdman and Gheilliaert's (Emden 1558) which was a translation into Dutch (Low Dutch) from the Lower Saxon translation made by Bugenhaagen (Magdeburg 1554) from Luther's High German version (Wittenberg 1545).

This version was in rather general use until the Staatenbybel or authorized version was brought out in 1636, but, being apparently largely of Mennonite origin (though the translator's name is unknown) was long afterward preferred by the Mennonites and indeed was used by some of them until 1837.

It would accordingly appear probable that either the subject or the painter of this portrait, dated in 1659, was a Mennonite or had some relations with them which would cause him in that year to quote the Beistkens Bible rather than the Staatenbybel.

I should be glad if the above is of any use to you. I think it will have to answer for my contribution to your inquiries, for I know practically nothing of the history of portrait painting. I suggest with respect to that matter that you write to Mr. Charles Henry Hart, 4717 Chester Avenue, Philadelphia, Pa., a well-known expert in the history of portrait painting. I should say that the letters which precede "fecit" were "-eville," or possible "-evisse." These letters are not of quite the same type as the inscription below.[19]

To FREDERICK J. TEGGART

June 19, 1915.

My dear Mr. Teggart:[20]

I have just received your very kind letter of June 14. I beg you not to take the trouble to come over to Third Street. With a map in my hand and a tongue in my head I surely can reach the Faculty Club without trouble, though I appreciate in the highest degree your kindness. I shall not expect you, and yet, in case you do come it probably is wise for me to give of myself precisely the description

which an English lecturer coming to Providence once sent to me beforehand concerning himself, "A lanky individual, with a beard and spectacles." I also think that I must look like a professor for an elevator-boy in this building called me that before I had been here five days.

To WALDO G. LELAND

Santa Fe, New Mexico,
June 25, 1915.

Dear Leland:

The main thing has been that the temperature has hardly ever been too high for my taste. The heat is what I most dreaded. So, though somewhat tired, I am all right, and though the journey has been tedious to me, I have enjoyed myself when on shore. At Chicago I had a very good time with McLaughlin and Christie, and dined with them and the girls. Mrs. McL. had not yet returned from Brown U. commencement. At Lawrence, Kansas, a beautiful town—and the U. has a beautiful view, finer than almost any other Univ. has—I spent my afternoon pleasantly with Becker, and Hodder had a nice dinner.[21] Among those present was MacDonald, who is visiting his wife's mother, then teaching in Univ. of Colo.

I have had an interesting day in Santa Fe. Fine day; delectable mountain air, elevation being over 7000 ft. Chief attraction, the palace of the Spanish governors, built in seventeenth century, now fine museum of School of American Archaeology, pueblo things, etc. Have also visited Church of San Miguel, 1629, and Cathedral, (partly of that time), and talked archives with Archbishop Pitaval. Tell Stock the "Caballeros de Colon" seem to be laudably active here.

My kindest regards to Mrs. Leland, and to everybody at the office. Hope the strain of living without me is not too great.

To CORNELIA M. PIERCE

Berkeley, July 6, 1915.

My dear Miss Pierce:

. . . I don't think I told you, in yesterday's letter, anything about the last stage of my journey. I was much delighted with Santa Barbara and with the railroad ride from there to San Francisco, nearly all of it by daylight, part of it on the brink of the ocean and part of it in beautiful wide and fertile valleys. I have not yet gone over to see the Fair, and am in doubt if I do so this week. I gave my first lecture this morning. There were none killed or seriously

---

[19] In the reply to Jameson's letter the writer stated that the artist had been named by Victor Paltsits, as Crulliam de Ville of Amsterdam (c.1614-1672), and that they were working on the supposition that the subject of the portrait had some connection with the Mennonites.

[20] Frederick J. Teggart (1870-1946), at this time associate professor of Pacific Coast history in the University of California. He later became professor of social institutions.

[21] Carl Becker (1873-1945) taught European history in the University of Kansas from 1902 till 1916; Frank H. Hodder (1860-1935), American history. At this time Professor Hodder was head of the department of history.

wounded, but I fancy that a considerable number will be missing tomorrow, as there are many persons upon the fringe of a summer school who come in for once to see what the lecturer looks like, and these I have no doubt went away disappointed and will not come again. But beauty is anyhow a fleeting thing, while history abideth ever. . . .

To WALDO G. LELAND

Berkeley, July 9, 1915.

Dear Leland:

Last night I saw, and read with much interest, a copy of Bancroft's pamphlet which had been received by one of the younger teachers here.[22] I presume you will agree with me that, while the mode of publication makes an answer on anyone's part difficult, the contents make reply unnecessary. I tried to read with the eyes of a member not personally concerned, and it seemed to me that such a person would be led by its violence of tone, its obvious malice, its clumsy and ineffective style, and also by what he knows respecting the persons alluded to, to attach little importance to the whole performance. It also gratified me to see the name of Rowland on the cover; that name contributes a "powerful element of weakness" to the whole thing. It is also weakened by the conspicuous self-vaunting.

> Thus youthful Horner rolled his roving eye,
> Plucked the dark plum from out the Christmas pie,
> And cried in self-applause, How brave a boy am I!

Nor do I think the whole thing to be much fortified by Latané's efforts at constructive statesmanship. All things considered, though of course the whole thing is an odious and contemptible performance, I think that we may congratulate ourselves that it is so little formidable. My constant belief is that the Lord has a slight preference for the righteous.

I wish you would see, however, what light you can get on the question of distribution. I do not see what list the triumvirs can have used except that in the handbook of 1911, but it would be interesting to know whether they have had the use of the list which I sent to Alvord, or of any other; and I should think this could be discovered.[23]

I am just taking to the woods, namely, I am starting to spend the week-end, with Haskins, in visiting Morse Stephens at the grove of the Bohemian Club.

To GAILLARD HUNT

Berkeley, July 13, 1915.

My dear Hunt:

I thank you most cordially for your letter.[24] As I already knew pretty well what the nature of Bancroft's accusations would be, I was not greatly disquieted by their actual receipt; and yet it would not be in human nature not to be consoled, when the heathen rage and the people imagine a vain thing, by such honest warmth as yours. You are, and always have been, a good friend to me, and while I think you are always a good friend to every historical worker, I have myself very deeply enjoyed the friendship, and have none in Washington, outside my two families at 2231 and 1140, in which I take quite so much satisfaction as in my friendship with you.[25] And such things must inevitably be valued more when one is assailed, even though the assault is so marked by obvious malice and ill temper as not to be really formidable.

You say that you write on the impulse of the moment, but I am glad that if you have ever thought that I, and the members of my department, have seemed to put your division of the Library of Congress in a subordinate position, you should say so with frankness, because it gives me an opportunity to say that such has never been my state of mind, nor I believe that of any of the members of my staff, and that, if anything in our behaviour could ever have given that impression, it must have been something quite misunderstood. Nobody in the country has had a better chance than we have had to appreciate the splendid work of collection and management which has marked your tenure of your present office, and the unsparing and highly efficient service you all render with so much generosity to everyone who comes to work among your manuscripts. So far as I know, there is not in the world a place where a scholar has such splendid facilities for the use of manuscript historical materials, and if I have never said this to you, I have said it many times to other people. Your division is doing splendid work for American historical scholarship. Its functions and those of my department are so different that there could never be, I should think, any thought of rivalry on our part; the only inequality that ever presses upon my mind, and this pretty constantly, is that we are almost never able to do anything for you in requital of the many things which you do for us.

To return to the American Historical Association. There has of course never been any ring. If there has been, as perhaps there has been, too great stability of tenure, or too little regard for the interests of certain elements in the membership—the non-aca-

---

[22] By this time the activities of the three insurgents, Frederic Bancroft, Rowland, and Latané, had ceased to be an effort to modify the organization of the Association and had become a bitter attack on the members of the board of editors of the *Review* and on certain members of the executive council. In carrying on this campaign four pamphlets were sent to members of the Association.

[23] Mr. Leland replied that he had supplied Bancroft with a mailing list of the Association on his request for it.

---

[24] Hunt had written: "I regard his [Bancroft's] charges as trivial and stupid, and, especially so far as they concern you, as absolutely inexcusable" (Hunt to Jameson, July 2, 1915).

[25] 2231 Q St., N.W., was Jameson's home; 1140 Woodward Building, his office.

demics, the younger men, the women—it has never been intentional, but there has been a desire to act for the interests of all classes. It is significant that nobody seems to think otherwise than well of the *work done* in the various offices and committees, or of the decisions taken by the Council or, so far as I hear, of anything *general* in the management of the Review. In respect to persons and offices, or those parts of the constitution and system of operations which relate to them, there may be a need of reform which I have never perceived; but the way to bring about such improvements is not the publication of furious and insulting pamphlets, in which many of the most important facts are concealed from view, while false and misleading accusations are pushed into the foreground and elaborated with clumsy ridicule. . . .

To Arthur H. Jameson

July 29, 1915.

Dear Arthur:

While my Oregon expedition is fresh in my mind I will give you an account of what I saw and learned —not much in the sum total, but very interesting to me.[26]

Coming up from California, I spent a forenoon at Eugene with a Professor in the University of Oregon, who was one of my earliest pupils at the Johns Hopkins. Then I had to stop off at Salem to change trains, and improved the spare hour by finding in the real estate records of Marion County, a deed by which Father on December 17, 1861, conveyed to a certain James A. Holston, of that county, a piece of land about one mile west of Chamboeg, amounting to three hundred and twenty acres, bounded on the north by the Willamette River, and on the east, south and west by neighbors whose names were given. This afterward enabled me to identify the piece. Then I went on by the Oregon Electric Railroad to Butteville, arriving there at 6:30 p.m. There I was met by old Mr. Himes, Assistant Secretary of the Oregon Historical Society and Secretary of the Oregon Pioneer Association, to whom my friend in Eugene, who is Secretary of the former body, had written to meet me.[27] He could stay but two hours, but he had

been familiar with the place for forty years, knew everybody, and could put me on the right trails. He had walked out from Illinois in 1853.

Butteville is hardly a larger place now than it was when Father was there. It had a time of much prosperity in the years after his departure, while steamboat transportation prevailed—six steamers a day each way at one time. Now there is but one sternwheeler, which I had the pleasure of seeing come up to the landing in the same manner in which the *Canemah* does in the picture. In fact, just such a boat. But the railroad was carried some miles from the place and while the new electric railroad goes nearer, the village seems to have no prospect, and is really pretty forlorn.

I spent the night at a kind of hotel, talked at evening and morning with various of the older people about the village. No one was able to remember Father, the earliest of them having come there in 1853, but one woman seemed to remember that Geer, who was the chief storekeeper in her youth, had bought out a Mr. Jameson. If I had gone there two years ago I should have found old François Xavier Mathieu, a famous old French Canadian, whose reminiscences in the *Quarterly* of the Oregon Historical Society I showed to Father in 1900. Father remembered him well, and he would have remembered him, but he died in January 1914, age ninety-five, but of perfect memory.

I saw two or three houses in the village that were there when Father was, one of them was built by the Hudson Bay Company in 1843. The house in which Father lived, as well as I could tell from my remembrance of the picture, was also one that was built by the Company and was standing till 1890, when it was replaced by the house in which the man who drove me around (and wouldn't take a cent) the Mayor of the village now lives.

I shall have some photographs taken of that picture, and send them out to some of the men there who gave me information, and who can identify more securely the location in present times, of Father's house. Also a struggling Congregational Church, which has just been reorganized and is about to call a Pastor, and of which Mother read in the Congregationalist, will be glad of the pulpit Bible, which, I understand, she has a mind to present to it in memory of him. They all seem to be proud of pioneers and pioneer days, indeed my status as a pioneer's son, was the reason why I was taken about so hospitably.

The next forenoon we drove to see a man who, however, proved to have come in 1853 and not to remember Father. Then out in the other direction to see the piece of land he took up. It is about four miles from Butteville, a fine piece of wheat growing land on the river bottom. As I remember it, he used to occasionally close his store, take his rifle on his shoulder, and go out along the Champoeg trail to

---

[26] John Jameson (1828-1905) visited Oregon in 1851, by sailing vessel to San Francisco, and by steamer thence to Portland. After a short stay in Portland, he went to Butteville, where he spent a few months in trade. The next year he returned to Massachusetts, studied law, taught for a few years, and practiced law for a time in Boston, before the family moved to Amherst in September, 1875. Jameson had always been much interested in this western venture of his father and in 1909 had sent to the *Quarterly* of the Oregon Historical Society a letter from his father to a younger brother, R. E. Jameson, later a doctor in Boston. See *Quarterly* 10: 391-395, Dec., 1909.

[27] This professor and secretary was F. G. Young; the assistant secretary, George H. Himes.

the log cabin he had built on his land and spend the night. Both these villages are on the edge of the French Prairie, on which Dr. John McLoughlin, chief factor for the Hudson's Bay Company, established his French Canadians about 1838 to grow wheat for the Company's uses and for sale to the Russians at Sitka.

After a very happy time at Butteville, I went on to Portland, where I had two hours and a half. I rushed down in an automobile to Linnton, seven miles away, to see Adolphe Jetté, ninety years old, whom the Butteville people thought to have been there in 1851, but he did not come there till 1859, and neither he nor his wife, who seemed to be a half breed from the French Prairie, remembered Father. The last person to try for, in that regard, was Mrs. Dwight Geer, François Xavier Mathieu's oldest daughter, who was said to be visiting in Portland; but I found that she had gone back to Seattle where she lives, and I shall try to find her today.[28] She was born about 1848 and may remember hearing people speak of Father, though, of course, his stay was short.

Well, that is about all. I greatly enjoyed it and could also go on indefinitely about California, but I must not keep my friends here waiting. . . .

To Sara Jameson

Glacier National Park
Aug. 5, 1915, Th. 8 A.M.

Dearest Sara:

Well, my first day's walk was pulled off as per schedule, and it was the finest day's walk I ever had in my life. But it was also about the hardest. I started from the N. end of Lake McDonald, which I had come up in steamboat. No more beautiful lake in the world, I am sure. Starting at 10:40 I got to Sperry Chalets at 1:50, going up from a level of 3150 ft. to 6500, a seven-mile climb; then, later in the afternoon, a four hour tramp to this place, over a pass 6900 ft. high, with wonderful views, then down around Lake Ellen Wilson, a lake so beautiful I couldn't help writing the President about it—such colors, from sky and surroundings, red rocks, green rocks, gray rocks, snow—it was really like an opal a mile long. Then up over Gunsight Pass, 6900 ft., splendid views both ways, and down to here. The

trails mostly consist of sharp, loose stones, from the size of your hand down; but my old shoes have held out thus far, also my old feet pretty well. But more than 15 miles of such walking in a day I cannot do, and I shall have to modify the third day's route, as the distance was understated in the circular I was using. . . .

To William B. Munro

Grand Isle, Vermont,
August 20, 1915.

My dear Mr. Munro:[29]

The question you ask is a hard one.[30] It is hard because Colonel Roosevelt very properly sets up as a standard the highest possible grade of achievement in historical literature, toward which ideal various degrees of approach can be made, and your friend's question is, virtually, whether by the application of money one can secure a signally closer approach to that ideal than is likely to be achieved in our generation without the application of considerable sums thus concentrated on one publication.

I am doubtful, but on the whole I should think the experiment was worth making if your friend could make up his mind beforehand not to be disappointed if the result falls considerably short of his highest ideal of historical literature. The number of persons occupied with American history who have what Colonel Roosevelt and your friend would consider to be adequate scholarship and at the same time have literary gifts of a high order is small, and such persons sometimes will not do their best work in a joint enterprise wherein editorial supervision must necessarily have some Procrustean effects that are not felt when a man of literary talent is free to carry out his own ideas of form as well as substance. To put it concretely, no editor can produce a work of genius on American history in ten volumes by as many different authors, because there are not ten competent writers on American history who have literary genius or anything nearly approaching it. But if the question is, as I have put it, whether the application of a considerable amount of money in the way you have suggested might bring better results than will be

---

[28] Added in pen at this point: "Can't find her." On Dec. 24, 1915, Jameson wrote to Professor E. S. Meany that he had located the old lady: "She is the oldest daughter of the locally celebrated François Xavier Mathieu, whose recollections are in the first volume of the *Quarterly* of the Oregon Historical Society. She says that she could have remembered more about my father if she could have talked with me and that is very probable. All she can recollect now, she says, is her father's having my father come over to the house and have dinner with them; also hearing her father say, 'I believe Mr. Jameson will come back to Oregon in a year or two'; but he never came." The article referred to was Lyman, H. S., Reminiscences of F. X. Mathieu, *Quarterly* 1: 73-104, March, 1900.

[29] William B. Munro, teacher in the department of government of Harvard University, 1904-1925.

[30] The question: "A gentleman of means, who has been much impressed by Colonel Roosevelt's essay on 'History as Literature' [*Amer. Hist. Rev.* 18: 473-489, April, 1913], has intimated to me his possible willingness to finance a series of books on American history provided the ideal set forth in that essay could be measurably approached. He would like to know, however, whether our present resources in the way of historical scholarship and literary skill are adequate to any such venture on a considerable scale, granting that generous honoraria were available for the payment of all contributors, and whether, after all, the undertaking would be a real public service if found practicable and carried through" (Munro to Jameson, Aug. 12, 1915).

achieved in the ordinary course of things, I think it may. Anyone who was advising your friend might, for an instance, look over the new Riverside History of the United States. That is a good recent attempt to make a history of the United States that should be more readable, more infused with ideas expressed in literary form, than the ordinary work. The only one of the volumes of which I have yet read any considerable portion, Becker's on the Colonial Period, seemed to me to have great literary merit.[31] Now, unquestionably a certain amount of money, provided by the publishers, constituted an incentive to those four men to make that attempt. It is quite possible that large sums might, with an editor of first-rate historical and literary competence, persuade some of the few men who have greater acquirement or gifts for such work than at least some of these four, to undertake a large enterprise of the same sort with even better results.

It is not certain to my mind that better satisfaction might not be obtained by such a donor if he should subsidize one particular man to write a book on some one great period of American History, especially the period since 1865. In the case of these co-operative histories, there is always a chance that for some of the volumes one has to content oneself with writers of a much less satisfactory grade than the best, or the best of the others, and your friend's ideal might be quite well approached in some cases and much less so in some others. But this is to answer a question which you have not asked. In respect to the question actually put, it may make some difference if one could learn what cooperative projects for histories of the United States are already in contemplation by any of the publishing houses.

I have been very glad to respond to your inquiry though I do not know whether the result will be of any use to you.

To H. Morse Stephens

September 30, 1915.

My dear Stephens:

. . . I see every few days some man of pursuits similar to my own, who has spent a part of the summer in visiting California with the same results as in my own case—a most exceptional refreshment, a new appetite for work, a rejuvenation by from one to five years, according to various estimates. Ponce de Leon's mistake was in seeking the *Fons Juventutis* in the wrong part of America.

---

[31] *The beginnings of the American people*, Boston, Houghton Mifflin, 1915. The other volumes were: Johnson, Allen, *Union and democracy;* Dodd, William E., *Expansion and conflict;* and Paxson, Frederic L., *The new nation.*

To H. Morse Stephens

October 11, 1915.

My dear Stephens:

I promised to keep you informed as to the state of mind prevailing in the East respecting the American Historical Association. I presume that I shall write again, nearer to the time of the meeting, and that this may be regarded as only a preliminary survey.

My route Eastward from Berkeley included visits to the Universities of Oregon, Washington, Minnesota, Wisconsin, and Chicago. I found no one at any of these places, and heard of no one in these faculties, who sympathized with the tone and spirit of Bancroft's attacks, or believed his accusations. I judge from more recent visits to Harvard and Yale that there is no such person there. Cox of Cincinnati [32] reports that substantially no one in his region takes any different attitude than this, and Krehbiel in his travels seems to have found no one.

I imagine that we may well believe that the pamphlet will have little effect in any educational institution of importance, or where there are several historical men to inform each other. On the other hand, it is quite likely that damaging effects have been produced in isolated places and among obscurer members.

The more isolated and less informed members of the Association are numerous, but it is the better informed who constitute the annual business meeting. Bancroft and Latané have been working industriously to build up a party, arranging with "A." in this state and with "B." in that, to organize opposition to the "ring," to the Committee of Nine,[33] and to the election of Burr. How successful they have been, I do not know, for naturally I have heard only of those cases in which they have met with rebuffs. Bancroft will leave no stone unturned to achieve his ends. These ends are personal only in the sense that he feels it personally necessary to succeed, now that he has entered upon the campaign. Whatever his motives, however, he is an unscrupulous person, who will hit below the belt, and that is the only thing that makes

---

[32] Isaac J. Cox, teacher of history, University of Cincinnati, 1904-1919; Northwestern University, 1919-1941.

[33] At the business meeting of the Association in Chicago, on Dec. 30, 1914, the executive council recommended, "That a committee of nine be appointed to consider the constitution, organization, and procedure of the association with instructions to report at the annual meeting of 1915," and, "That the committee of nine, in the event of its appointment, be instructed to consider the relationship between the association and the American Historical Review." The appointment of this committee was assigned to those members of the nominating committee who were present at the Chicago meeting, with the addition of Dunbar Rowland and F. J. Turner. At an adjourned business meeting they reported the following nine: E. D. Adams, R. D. W. Connor, I. J. Cox, W. A. Dunning, Max Farrand, A. C. McLaughlin, James F. Rhodes, W. T. Root, James Sullivan. Rhodes declined to serve and his place was taken by Charles H. Hull (1864-1936). *Ann. Rept., Amer. Hist. Assn.*, 1914: 1: 49-50, 54-55.

him dangerous, for he is a very injudicious tactician —as could be seen from his writing such a letter to you as that of January 27.

In his letter to the *Nation* he takes a more decent tone than in the pamphlet, but is bolder in misrepresentation.[34] The former alteration was a necessity, for his pamphlet was intended for the *Nation,* but the *Nation* would not print it, believing, it is understood, that it might be libelous. As to Phillips's letter, you will observe that it is dated August 6, but released for publication by Bancroft on September 16. I can cast a little light on that, for I remember that Guy Ford[35] told me at Minneapolis on August 8, that since the publication of the pamphlet he had had a letter from Bancroft saying something like this, "You are now in much the same position I was in a year ago, a new member of the Council. You have doubtless seen my pamphlet. I should like to get into correspondence with you, with a view to interchange of opinion of the matters discussed therein." If Bancroft wrote thus to Ford, he of course wrote thus also to Phillips and Barker,[36] the other two new members of the Council. Ford, being a very sagacious bird, avoided the entanglement with ease. Phillips, who is young and impulsive, and always somewhat eager to get into print, "fell for it," and very unwisely publishes his want of balance in believing accusations merely because they are made. Worthington Ford, whose niece he married, told me that he was going to attend to him as a matter of family discipline, but I expect, having so far committed himself, Phillips will vote in the Council as Bancroft wishes. I do not think that any other member will.

Meanwhile, it seems certain that the Historical Statement put forth by the Board of Editors,[37] and the letters of Cheyney[38] and Hart in the *Nation* of September 30, both of them admirably conceived from the respective positions of the two writers, are having excellent effect. Greene writes that you advanced tentatively the suggestion of a conference with Bancroft and Latané before the November meeting of the Council. I earnestly hope that you will not conclude upon anything of the sort. Their agitation lies quite apart from the main current of the movement for reorganization. A great many members desire some reorganization, but those whose answer to the question "Why the American Historical Association needs Reorganization" is because it has hitherto been in the hands of a ring of petty grafters and self-seekers, are very few indeed. There is no reason for regarding Bancroft and Latané as the real leaders of the reformers, except that they say they are. To recognize them as such would be not only to dignify them beyond their deserts and to put a premium on demagoguery, but to do an injustice to the real leaders of reform, for whom I have much respect, men who, before Bancroft took the slightest interest in the Association, have been urging a more open formation, a democratization of our arrangements, but urging it in the manner of gentlemen and in a reasonable spirit. It is with such men that a conference should be held, if at all, but I do not think that there will be any need of it, because the Committee of Nine has been meeting in New York yesterday and the day before, and will present the results of just such comparison of opinions as you would seek. They have been, I know, inquiring into opinions in their localities, and doing this more broadly than you could do it by talking with one or two. Moreover that Committee contains an adequate representation of reform sentiment. Though Bancroft and Latané make base efforts in the *Nation* to discredit the Committee beforehand, it is known to me that four of its original members, three of its present members, were named by Rowland and the three have since been amusingly informed by him that such was the case. Another member was known at Chicago to be a "near-insurgent." I believe that this Committee of Nine has the confidence of the Association, that it will propose important changes, believed by it to be improvements, that what it proposes will be in the main adopted by the Associaton. I imagine they will try to send out their report early, say with the programme. For my own part, I do not imagine myself making opposition to anything that they may suggest. As I said at the meet-

---

[34] *Nation* 101: 356-357, Sept. 16, 1915. Bancroft's long communication in this number is described as an answer to a letter from U. B. Phillips published in the same issue (pp. 355-356). Phillips praised the constructive proposals of Latané; Bancroft assured him that these were but the beginning of the projected reforms, which from the letters which he had received he knew would be widely supported. He then attacked the committee of nine as a tool of the "ring," with which the reformers could have nothing to do. However, if the chairman and one other member would resign and allow their places to be filled by reformers, he and his friends would cooperate with the committee. A letter from Latané in the same issue of the *Nation* opposed the nomination of Professor Burr as the next president of the Association.

[35] Guy Stanton Ford, professor of history and dean of the graduate school, University of Minnesota. In 1931-1932 and 1937-1938 he served as acting president of that institution and was its president from 1938 to 1941. On retiring from the presidency he became executive secretary of the American Historical Association and editor of the *American Historical Review.*

[36] Ullrich B. Phillips (1877-1934), after six years in the University of Wisconsin, was now teaching history in the University of Michigan. E. C. Barker was professor of history in the University of Texas.

[37] *An historical statement concerning the American Historical Review* gave a succinct account of the facts concerning its establishment and its relation to the Association.

[38] Edward P. Cheyney (1861-1947), professor of history in the University of Pennsylvania, was at this time chairman of the board of editors of the *American Historical Review.*

ing of last November, and as everybody present in the Council meeting seemed to agree, the only possible course for the Council is to place itself unreservedly at the disposal of the Association. My own position is this: That while the management of the Association's affairs has long been in the hands of a smallish number of persons, this regime was justified by the acquiescence or indifference of the members; that when the acquiescence has ceased, even on the part of a considerable minority, the equities of the situation have changed, and democratization is in order; that probably some things will not be done so well as they have been done when chiefly deliberated upon by men like Adams, Hart, Haskins, Dunning, and Turner, but that after all the Association belongs to the members, and complete efficiency is less important than harmony. So I will do nothing to "hold the fort," unless some things distinctly unwise for the future are proposed, while at the same time I will with all my force repel, when the proper time comes, any reflections upon the uprightness of my course or that of the Council and the Board.

In sum, we have some unpleasant times before us, but shall pull through without disaster, because the Association is composed of sensible men, accustomed to looking at both sides of a question—or historical training is no good.

To ANDREW C. McLAUGHLIN

November 18, 1915.

My dear McLaughlin:

. . . Why should it be thought that the operations of the Committee of Nine fill the universe, or that all events are related to its labors. There are also scraps going on in the Balkans and elsewhere I understand.

Letter in today's *Nation* from Bancroft. "Watch this Space." SPICY REVELATIONS. HIGH BROWS SHOWN UP. This morning's mail brings me a brief letter from Bancroft, the first I have had since March when I told him that I would have no more. This latter statement remains true, and I shall not reply. What do you suppose he inquires? In pursuing his investigation as to the ownership of the *Review*, he finds statements that astonish him in the article on the New Haven meeting in volume IV. of the *Review*. That article is unsigned and he has looked in vain in Poole's *Index* for an indication of the authorship, and wishes me to state whether I wrote it, or if not, who did.[39]

Isn't this great business for an immortal soul in A. D. 1915, when the whole world is on fire and civilization is going to pieces?[40]

---

[39] *Amer. Hist. Rev.* 4: 409-421, April, 1899. The "astonishing" statements were statements of the relationship between the board of editors of the *Review* and the Association, estab-

To ROBERT S. WOODWARD

November 24, 1915.

My dear President Woodward:

In accordance with your letter of November 23, I shall as a matter of course acquiesce cheerfully in the decision that our work respecting the history of slavery shall not be mentioned in the Year-Book.[41] I wish to say however in respect to the second paragraph of your letter, that the case is not one of announcing a project not yet fully matured. The proposal, which has been mentioned in two or three previous reports, is one to which careful consideration has been given; the plans have, in their outline, been matured in my mind for over a year; the contents of the first volume are quite determined; and between one and two months work has been done. I do not understand that you or the Trustees have formed an opinion that this piece of work, which I think so important, ought not to be undertaken. If you or they think so, I should wish to be told of it soon, in order that, though with regret, I should abandon this part of our work. If, however, I am permitted to proceed with it, as I sincerely hope I shall be, I shall suppose that some description of the undertaking, fuller

---

lished at the meeting of the Association in New Haven. See *ante*, Oct. 27, 1897, n.197.

[40] A month later than the date of this letter and after the appearance of Bancroft's second pamphlet, Jameson wrote: "But I am more incensed at Latané's insolent letter to McLaughlin than by anything Bancroft says in the pamphlet. McLaughlin takes all these things to heart, and is really justified in thinking that he has a pretty poor reward for spending a lot of time reluctantly in the unpleasant task of revising the constitution. I imagine that even "Jeems" Madison would have been somewhat ruffled if, while the Constitutional Convention was dragging on through summer days of 1787 in Philadelphia, three ardent patriots of the variety of James Wilkinson, or Daniel Shays had stood on the sidewalk outside the hall pelting him through the windows with rotten eggs" (Jameson to Jesse S. Reeves, Dec. 15, 1915).

The "insolent letter" is to be found in the compilation of the four pamphlets issued by the three "reformers": *Why the American Historical Association needs thorough reorganization*, 33-35. A single sentence will suffice to illustrate its character: "As soon as I heard of the appointment of the committee of nine I suspected that it was all a scheme arranged in the interests of the ring and that no reforms would be adopted except such as might be necessary to save the ring and its allies."

[41] Jameson's annual report for 1915, to the Board of Trustees of the Carnegie Institution, outlined plans for documenting the history of the negro in this country. On Oct. 13, 1915, President Woodward wrote: "Permit me to state that in broaching this subject, important and vital as it is to the United States, you are trenching on dangerous ground, for two reasons: First, because this ground has been projected for occupancy by a division of our Department of Economics and Sociology. . . . In the second place, the negro question is one which gave our Trustees much trouble before you became a member of the Institution, and it is one with which it must be difficult to deal even in a purely historical way. I would therefore suggest that while your statement with regard to this project may appear in the advance edition of the Year Book prepared especially for the Trustees, it should not appear in the final edition." Jameson, on Oct. 22, sent to President Woodward a letter from Professor Farnam which stated that there could be no

than has appeared in previous Year-Books,[42] and some account of what has been done upon it during the present year 1915-1916, may be given to our public in my next Annual Report. It will then still be true that some persons, after the most careful explanations of what we mean to do, will object to our doing it, because there are some persons who would prefer that the negro should not be mentioned in print; but I shall hope that the objections of such minds will not weigh much with the Carnegie Institution when I am able to show, not merely plans but achievement, of a sort which will, I hope, have the respect and approval of the historical profession—which I am sure that the project has now.

At all events, I shall always be duly mindful—think I have been—of the inexpediency of announcing projects not yet fully matured. Of Mr. Barnum's marginal comment, I naturally thought that it was the result of conversation with you before you and I had our talk on the subject.

---

possible conflict between the project of the Department of Historical Research and that of the Department of Economics and Sociology. This failed to end the matter. On Nov. 16, Jameson wrote to the president: "The receipt of the second set of galley-proofs of my *Annual Report* raises the question whether the Executive Committee, at their October or November meeting, seemed to feel any objection, or whether on subsequent reflection you have yourself felt any objection, against the printing of the last paragraph but one in my report. I raise the question because the proof comes to me with the pencilled comment against this paragraph 'To be inserted in Trustees' edition, omitted in revised edition.'

"In the paragraph alluded to, the first two sentences speak in general terms of three further documentary series, while the other three sentences relate specifically to a project for the publication of materials respecting the history of African slavery in America. I shall hope that at any rate there is no objection against printing the first two sentences in the published edition; but I also very strongly desire that the other three may likewise appear." After adducing some of the reasons for this desire, he added: "If any member of the Executive Committee has, at the October or November meeting, made any objection to the undertaking itself, it would be important to me that I should be informed of it, in order that I might defend the project by more elaborate reasonings than I have yet felt it necessary to prepare, and if these reasonings should not prevail, might bring to a stop all preparations, though for a work which the historical profession would warmly approve. But if there is no objection to the work being done I hope there will be no objection to its being announced."

On Nov. 23, President Woodward replied that he had authorized the sentence quoted from Mr. Barnum: "It appeared to me, however, in view of the experience the Institution has had, that we should avoid the possibility of raising an issue from the negro question although the language of your report may give no adequate basis for such a contingency." Additional paragraphs of this letter advised against announcing projects not fully matured.

[42] The correspondence summarized in the preceding note is the more incomprehensible in view of the fact that Jameson had given notice of what he contemplated in his report for 1913. See *Year Book*, 1913: 162: "It may, however, be well to say that the Department has a definite intention of proceeding, as soon as it can do so without detriment to the work now in hand, toward the preparation of a series of documentary volumes illustrating the history of negro slavery in America. This is a task of great importance, relating to the history of

TO CARL SNYDER

December 6, 1915.

My dear Sir:[43]

In reply to your letter of December 3, I regret to have to say that there are, I feel sure, no trustworthy estimates of the number of immigrants who came to each of the colonies up to the time of the revolution. There are not sufficient data on which to base such estimates, except in isolated spots. Thus, for instance, the Pennsylvania law requiring an oath of allegiance from alien immigrants, led to the keeping of lists of a certain sort at Philadelphia from which statistics could be derived, but they did not cover the case of immigrants who were subjects of the king of Great Britain. The estimates deducted by the Census Bureau in the volume entitled "A Century of Population Growth," to which I presume you allude, seem to me nearly worthless, vitiated by an unsound method, particularly in the matter of reasoning on the form in which surnames were found, and thus quite ignoring the constant habit of translating the foreign surname into English. A great many bits of scattered information can be obtained upon the subject, but nothing complete enough to be of value as a general summation. For the Germans, the volumes of the Pennsylvania German Society contain excellent materials, and most of the facts are summed up in Professor Faust's "The German Element,"[44] though his totals are vitiated by his strange action in lumping all the persons of Dutch descent under the "German element." You would also get useful hints from Professor Dexter's article on the "Population of the Colonies" in the proceedings of the American Antiquarian Society for 1887.[45] That is a good solid piece of work, as far as it goes.

As to nationalities, I once worked through the raw material of that matter and came to the conclusion that of the two million whites of 1775, one might probably assume that about sixty per cent were English stock, seventeen or eighteen per cent Irish, (of whatever origin but mostly protestant), eleven or twelve per cent German, seven or eight per cent Dutch, with a still smaller

---

at least a tenth of our population, and bearing ultimately on one of the greatest problems of American life; yet no governmental commission, either federal or state, is, for well-known reasons, likely to undertake the scientific documentation of this portion of our history." The plans for the department for 1916, as outlined in the *Year Book*, 1915: 180-182, contain no reference to work on slavery or the slave trade but the department report for 1916 (*Year Book*, 1916: 167) refers to the work on the history of the slave trade as already in progress.

[43] Carl Snyder, of 64 Fort Washington Ave., New York City.

[44] Albert B. Faust, A.B., 1889, Ph.D., 1892, Johns Hopkins University, a student of Jameson in 1886-1887, was at the time of this letter a professor of German in Cornell University, where he taught from 1904 to 1938. *The German element in the United States, with special reference to its political, moral, social and educational influence*, 2v., N. Y., Houghton Mifflin, appeared in 1909.

[45] Dexter, Franklin B., Estimates of population in the American colonies, *Proc.*, n. s. 5: 22-50, Oct. 21, 1887.

percentage direct from Scotland and hardly one per cent each of Swedes or French.

Regretting that the materials for a good determination of questions so interesting does [*sic*] not exist, . . .

To CARL SNYDER

December 9, 1915.

My dear Sir:

This is in response to your letter of December 8. I have no wish to interfere with your opinions, but to my mind nothing is more certain than that you are absolutely wrong.[46] I took a good deal of pains with my computations and based them on sound methods of reckoning. The methods you indicate seem to me entirely unsound. You speak of a surprising agreement between the estimate of nationalities in a *Century of Population Growth* and that made by Senator Lodge of the fifteen thousand names included in Appleton's *Cyclopedia of Biography*.[47] That agreement is alone sufficient to condemn the estimates made in the Census book. A radical defect of Senator Lodge's calculations, which seems to me perfectly conclusive, was that he took no account of the way in which cyclopedias of biography are actually compiled. It is a wholly false estimate that those fifteen thousand names represent the fifteen thousand persons who have shown greatest ability in American history. It would be much nearer the truth to say that they are the fifteen thousand persons of whom biographical sketches or books have already been made and who thus come within the range of the editor of these compilations, who can never

afford to do otherwise than to build on the existing material. Now, of two men of equal ability in the nineteenth century, the one who was a minister, military officer, lawyer, or politician has five times the chance of having his biography written than the doctor or the engineer has, and twenty times the chance that the man of business has; a man whose biography would interest English-reading persons has fifty times the chance of having it written than the man has whose biography would be read chiefly by German-Americans; a man who springs from our self-conscious New England stock, in a region where books were constantly made and printed has twenty times the chance of having his biography written, and so of getting into a biographical dictionary that the equally-able native of tide-water Virginia or North Carolina has. For example, Peyton Randolph was of sufficient ability to be made the first president of the Continental Congress and I defy anybody to find two pages of biographical matter about him in print.[48] Senator Lodge's computation, in short, is built on a sandy foundation; and even if it were as solid as Gibraltar, I cannot see how the proportions of different nationalities among the conspicuous persons who are put into a biographical dictionary in 1890 can cast any light on the question what these proportions were in the rank and file of the population of 1750.

Secondly, your conclusion that because immigration of non-English in the years from the revolution to 1840 was very small, therefore immigration of such persons between 1700 and 1775 was small is very astonishing. You conclude that immigration did not reach an average of over 4000 a year before the revolution. It is perfectly well-known that more than twice that number immigrated to America in each of the years 1771, 1772, and 1773 from the North of Ireland alone and it is probable that for fifty years the average from Ireland had been 4000 per annum. There was apparently one year in which 6000 landed at Philadelphia, Wilmington, and New Castle. I have by actual count through a long typical list of names proved that the amount of Dutch and Swedish blood in Delaware was six or seven times what the census people computed it to be. I think that if you will look in the volumes of the Pennsylvania German Society to which I referred you, you will find plenty of years in which more than 4000 Germans came to Philadelphia alone.

In short, the inquiry upon which you have entered is a very difficult one, and the results will in my judgment not be useful unless it is conducted with extreme care as to statistical reasoning and a long period of research, in some cases difficult.[49]

---

[46] On Dec. 8, Mr. Snyder wrote that he felt more confidence in the *Century of population growth* than Jameson expressed; that he believed the number of English stock was much greater than Jameson's sixty per cent; and that the foreign-born in 1750 were probably five per cent, not the one-third estimated by Professor Channing.

[47] Lodge, Henry Cabot, The distribution of ability in the United States, appeared in the *Century*, 1891, and was reprinted in his *Historical and political essays*, 38-168, Boston, Houghton Mifflin, 1892. Of his method and results Lodge wrote: "I therefore took Appleton's Encyclopaedia of American Biography in six volumes, one of the largest and most recent works upon the subject, and classified the persons mentioned therein who were citizens of the United States, according to occupation, birthplace, and race-extraction. . . . I am satisfied, and, I think anyone who will examine dispassionately the tables which follow will be equally satisfied, that the results obtained have a great deal of historical value. The number of names classified and tabulated reaches 14,243, not including the immigrant table, and a number so large includes virtually all the men and women who by their ability have raised themselves even slightly above the general level. The method of classification which I have adopted shows what communities have produced the men who have governed the country and fought its battles, who have educated it and influenced its thought, who have produced its literature, art, and science, and who have made the inventions which in some instances have affected the history of the United States and of mankind" (138-139). On pp. 166-168 Lodge added a note to answer those who criticized the article after its appearance in the *Century*.

[48] An excellent account of Peyton Randolph (1721-1775), written about 1935, is to be found in the *Dictionary of American Biography*, where he is given three columns, still not achieving Jameson's "two pages."

[49] Mr. Snyder stated that he was to publish the results of his population studies elsewhere, but the editors have not been able to find them.

To ANDREW C. MCLAUGHLIN

January 4, 1916.

Dear McLaughlin:

Thank you for your words of congratulations.[50] I certainly feel that, along with Burr, and Turner, and yourself, I am to be congratulated on being released from the pillory in so handsome a manner. I am mighty sorry you could not have been at the business meeting, from this point of view, for while the whole episode has been an unpleasant one, and one can heartily wish that there need not have been a business meeting of this sort at all, yet the Association's approval of the conduct of the Board, and in particular their warm feeling toward the four members chiefly incriminated, was so impressively manifested that I am sure it would have done you good. I was particularly pleased to hear, from others, that the applause on the part of the younger element was particularly cordial. They are the ones whose articles suffer rejection most frequently, and who most commonly see other men chosen as reviewers, so that if they are pleased, it is very creditable to them and very gratifying to present and past members of the Board. So far as the three conspirators were concerned, never were men more decisively repudiated and defeated. I should say that Van Tyne's motion of approbation of the *Review* and reprobation of the pamphleteers was carried by about 400 votes to 1,[51] for I think Latané voted nay and Bancroft was absent and funny old Rowland turned around and rose on the crest of the wave, bowing and smiling and deelighted at the harmonious progress of reform under his leadership, and I judge voted for the resolution wherewith his genial countenance was so vigorously slapped.

But the thing most calling for congratulations is the very impressive demonstration of the abiding unity and harmony of the Association. That is one of the traits of our profession in which I have taken most pride and which I have most vaunted to outsiders. I have not done this much in 1915; but I see no reason why I should not resume the practice. I do not say that there may not have been persons present who agreed with Bancroft throughout, though nobody seems to have heard of any except one unbalanced young woman and one former colleague of Latané's; but they said nothing and we can perfectly well say that, with negligible exceptions, the Association is in unity and harmony. And this unity and harmony are stronger, more effective, and more valid than ever before, because the good-will on which they are based extends in an active and positive form over a far greater number of minds than ever before.

But I really think that you are most of all to be congratulated, because you have done more than anyone else to bring this about. I say this with great emphasis. No doubt the result springs largely from confidence in the characters of a dozen men, whom the members, or various sections of them in the case of each, know and trust and do not think likely to turn into malefactors. But I do not think that this broad and general confidence would with any certainty have landed us on the right shore, or at any rate would have brought about in specific shape the contentment which now reigns, if it had not been for the work of the Committee of Nine, in which everybody knows that yours must have been the leading part. In other words, if that report had not been a wholly satisfactory one, there would have been discontent on the part of a large minority, even if not a majority, of those who on the whole think very well of the personal characters of the present Councilmen and editors. Therefore I hate to have you think that all your unhappy labor and toil of the year was, in your phrase, spent in vain, because I know that it was not but was the essential thing in bringing about the present solution. When the report of the Committee of Nine was made known the victory was won, and won in about the same complete shape and extent in which it .was manifested twenty-eight hours later.[52] Moreover, you are quite wrong in thinking of your report as shelved. It is perfectly true that, partly by reason of a little delay in starting the meeting, partly by reason of the unusual length of Greene's report for the Council and some discussion over it, partly by reason of unexpected and injudicious outpourings from Bowen, partly by reason of the length of Cheyney's report for the Board (which was one of the most admirable informal oral reports I ever heard in my life), partly by reason of a little too much going into detail by the undersigned, there was no time for that full consideration of the report of the Committee of Nine which we should have desired. Nevertheless, it may be said to have been instantly accepted in principle, so that what remains is no more than a consideration of details. The amendments to the constitution could not anyhow be considered conclusively, and they and the by-laws needed to have more time for consideration. Take my own instance; I received the report in the midst of a Council meeting from which I had to go to the archive meeting, from which immediately to a meeting of the Board of Editors that lasted (dinner included) till a late hour, and on Wednesday morning there was a meeting which I had to attend, and in short I had not had the time to read that report through when it was taken up at the business meeting. It was inevitable that most of the consideration of it should go over till next year, and I believe that we shall get a sounder and more deliberate consideration of constitutional and legal details by taking up the matter with

---

[50] McLaughlin's letter has not come to light.

[51] Van Tyne's resolution read: "Resolved, That the attacks made during the last year upon the character and motives of certain prominent and honored members of this association meet with our entire disapproval, and that we hereby express our full confidence in the men whose motives and conduct have been thus impugned" (*Ann. Rept., Amer. Hist. Assn.*, 1915: 1: 51).

[52] For the report of the Committee of Nine, see *ibid.*, 69-75; for its discussion and adoption, 51-54 and 1916: 1: 64-67.

cooler heads, less influenced by the feelings of that particular day. As you indicate, some of the enthusiasm of that moment will pass away; all the more reason why structural matters should be decided later. In respect to the two resolves regarding the *Review,* I could see that, once it was made clear that the Board of Editors were ready to accept the first of them without delay, many members were in a state of contentment who up to that moment had not been quite content. With the matter left at that point, the rest will adjust itself deliberately and without difficulty.[53]

On a survey of the whole affair, I should not have cared to have the Association go farther in enactment than it did, though I agree that it was a pity there was not more time for asking questions as to why this or that detail was proposed, because this would have elicited information useful to many members.

My hat, wouldn't I like to have a couple of hours with you to talk the whole thing over? A lot of interesting things, and a lot of funny things. I hope Thompson [54] has told you of Latané's delicious response to a question from Leland. Never did a man give himself away more entirely to the satisfaction of his opponents. Leland rose and said: "After all, I wish somebody would tell me what definite and tangible gain would come to the Association from owning the Review." Latané jumped up and said, with indignant shaking of the head, "Well, I want to be able to write a letter to the *Nation* when I choose, without being privately reproved for it by the Managing Editor of the *Review.*" Leland said "That's the tangible gain, is it" and sat down. There was great hilarity. Could anything be more petty? And by the way, my "private reproof" was very much distorted in his representation of it and in fact related to another matter than what he declares.

Oh well, that's all over. Pamphlet 3 has since come out and pamphlets 4 and 5 and 6 may come forth, but will fall upon an unheeding world. The Association can now go forward, not without some damage, I admit, but on the whole stronger than ever. And you, I repeat, have done more to bring about that state of things than any other one man, and are more entitled than anybody else to congratulate yourself upon the result. I hope it will ultimately seem to you some compensation for all you have had to go through in this *annus mirablis* of 1915.

I hope that you are by this time entirely well and in good shape for wrestling with the young idea. . . .

To GEORGE L. BURR

January 11, 1916.

Dear Burr:

. . . Everybody seems to be rejoicing in the excellent manner in which the American Historical Association has extricated itself from the difficulties in which it was placed by Korah, Dathan, and Abiran, Ltd.; and a very great part of their satisfaction lies in the fact that one George L. Burr was elected President with the same unanimous vote as previous presidents and with a success in the primaries far beyond anything that any man had ever previously received for that office. There was a time when I feared that a certain portion of the members might be misled, by printed descriptions of the candidate, into supposing that it was Aaron Burr that they were invited to vote for, but it seems that all the members were properly aware of the distinction. . . .

To CHARLES H. HASKINS

January 25, 1916.

Dear Haskins:

Thank you very much for the interesting memoir of Gross.[55] A fine type of man he was, whom it was a great satisfaction to have known; and to have him brought back to the mind in this complete manner, with due emphasis on every one of his fine traits, is a great satisfaction. Recent events have led me often to think of myself as belonging more to the older generation of American historical workers than to this present one, and perhaps it is a sign that this is true that I so often find myself thinking of those who range about Gross's age and about mine, as a superior set to the youngsters now actively coming forward. Probably they *have* been, for the steady diminution of the salaries of professors would work that way, quite apart from any *laudatio temporis acti;* but one must hope for the best from the existing situation, and make the best of it, as you so well did in your admirable remarks at the Council dinner. But in any case, it is good to recall in detail such personalities as those of Gross. . . .

To HENRY L. MOSES

January 27, 1916.

My dear Sir: [56]

This is in reply to your letter of January 26. I am sorry that I misunderstood you, but really one can

---

[53] The Committee of Nine reported that "it is the opinion of the association that full ownership and control of the *American Historical Review* should be vested in the association," and named a committee *instructed* to bring this about. In the business meeting an amendment to the second resolution directed the committee to ascertain what arrangements could be made to accomplish this end and to report at the next meeting. *Ann. Rept., Amer. Hist. Assn.,* 1915: 1: 53-54; for final action on the *Review,* see *ibid.,* 1916: 1: 65-66.

[54] James Westfall Thompson (1869-1941), instructor in the department of history while Jameson was in Chicago, later, professor of mediaeval history in that institution.

[55] The memoir referred to is to be found in *Proc. Mass. Hist. Soc.* 49: 161-166, 1916.

[56] This letter was an answer to a request for information from a New York lawyer who wished to buy for his library that history of the United States which Dr. Jameson considered to be "the best" (Moses to Jameson, Jan. 21, 26, 29, 1915).

hardly say that there is such a thing as a "best" history of the United States. One is best for one purpose, and another for another, one in these respects, and another in those. Understanding you to have in mind a book which treated of the whole period of United States history it did not occur to me to speak of Mr. Rhodes's book, because that treats only of the period from 1850 to 1877.[57] It is a spendid work. For another instance, Edward Channing's *History of the United States,* of which only three volumes have yet been published, runs from 1492, or practically from 1607 to 1789. It is a very good book, but covers only a part of the ground which I suppose you wish to have covered.

Of books which purport to cover the whole period, I should think that a choice would lie between the *Riverside History* and that by President Wilson.[58] The latter is probably somewhat fuller, being in five volumes of larger size than those of the *Riverside History;* and yet I doubt, considering the manner of printing, whether it really contains much more text. It has the advantages which attach to a survey of American history that is made by one and the same mind throughout. On the whole, however, I should recommend the other. It is possible that, if the only object were to read one book on American history, and then have done with the subject for good and all, one might prefer Wilson's book, which certainly is a work of high literary art, though certainly not superior even in this respect to at least the first volume of the *Riverside History,* Mr. Becker's. But the *Riverside History* represents more closely the present state of knowledge on a good many matters in which further investigations have been made since the President wrote his book. It gives you the differing points of view of four excellent scholars, and this I really think is more of an advantage than the unity or homogeneity that attends the work of a single mind. What is still more important, if there is likelihood that you will be tempted to read more extensively in those parts, or upon those special aspects, of American history that most attract your interest, the *Riverside History* has an excellent apparatus of references to more special books, by means of which these desires can be carried out.

My own opinion would be, that one does best to read a history of the United States of moderate compass and then to enlarge in one of two ways. Either one can go over the whole field by a succession of large books, each of which treats of a particular period. First, there would be Channing's book for the period ending 1789; next, one could take Mr. James Schouler's *History of the United States Under the Constitution.* It runs from 1783 to 1877, in seven volumes, of which however

the seventh, for the period after 1865 is less complete than the others. At the beginning it overlaps Channing's, but this is not important because its account of the great constitutional movement of 1787 is somewhat better than Channing's. Then one could take Rhodes's for the period from 1850 to 1877, overlapping Schouler, whose best work lies in the period from 1789 to 1850. This of course leaves the last thirty years of American history, which really are not covered by any great standard book; but Mr. Paxson's volume in the Riverside series will at least have given a general survey of those years. And, by the way, here is an advantage over President Wilson's book, that Mr. Paxson comes down later.

The other mode of procedure after going through the *Riverside History,* would be to take up the special topics in which one has felt the most interest and enlarge upon them by means of the special works upon them which the *Riverside History* recommends.

It should also be said that there is a very excellent larger series on the whole of American history, called the *American Nation,* brought forth under the general editorship of Professor Hart of Harvard and published by Harper and Brothers in 27 volumes. Many of these volumes are excellent. I should hesitate to say that the average quality of the series stands higher than that of the *Riverside History,* but of course you can give a good deal more information about American history in 27 volumes than in 4.

If these remarks do not precisely answer your question, it is because I naturally cannot have the most precise knowledge of your needs and purposes; but perhaps what I have said will enable you to judge for yourself. All the books I have named are of high quality and I think that nearly every competent historical scholar would hesitate, as I have done, to rate the quality of one much above that of others. Their differences are differences of plan or of scope or of adaptation to particular purposes.

To FRANK A. GOLDER

February 1, 1916.

My dear Dr. Golder: [59]

I was to write further about your proposals respecting the history of Russia in English.[60] It does appear to me plainly that we ought to have a better work, of fairly large dimensions, on the whole general subject, which will be of increasing importance to us and which I should suppose would interest our people much more in the future than it has in the

---

[57] Rhodes, James Ford, *History of the United States from the Compromise of 1850,* 4v., N. Y., Harper, 1893; 8v., N. Y., Macmillan, 1904-1919.

[58] See *ante,* Aug. 20, 1915, n. 31. Wilson's work was entitled *A history of the American people,* 5v., N. Y., Harper, 1902.

[59] Frank A. Golder (1877-1929), born in Russia, had been brought to this country as a child. He received an A.B. and a Ph.D. degree from Harvard University and while there became interested in the history of Alaska, where he had lived for three years. From 1910 to 1920, with two leaves of absence, he taught in the State College of Washington, at Pullman; from 1920 until his death he was connected with Stanford University, from 1924 as director of the Hoover War Library,

past. I do not know, however, how publishers feel about such a thing. I imagine that they are all in some difficulties on account of the war, and perhaps especially those that have close connections with the publishing business in England. Considering the plan solely on its merits, however, I should think that it was good and deserving of success. Perhaps my only criticism would be that it would be better to confine the fourth volume to history more closely than you seem to plan. A book which confines itself to history till it gets down to contemporary times and then branches out into full discussions of social, agricultural, political, and intellectual problems sacrifices unity and homogeneity on the one hand and on the other hand enters into fields widely open to dispute. These fields of contemporary life in Russia ought to be treated, but they are being treated, and will be treated by special works, of description or discussion, and on the whole I think that is the best place for them. All the fields of social and economic history ought in the case of Russia, for the same reason as in the case of the United States, to be treated much more fully in proportion to the treatment of political and military and diplomatic history than has ordinarily been the practice in the case of the older countries. In these two new countries, these considerations are all-pervasive and of vast importance. So I should take them into the fullest consideration, in every past century, you understand; but my point is whether there is sufficient reason for giving any other than a strictly historical treatment

---

for which he had gathered vast collections of material in Europe, especially in Russia, after the war.

In May, 1905, while still a student, he wrote to McLaughlin, then chief of the Bureau of Historical Research of the Carnegie Institution, about the possibility of exploring the Russian archives, but it was not until 1914 that this project was decided upon and he was chosen for the work. He arrived in Russia in the early spring of 1914, and in spite of the outbreak of the war, was able to complete his notes for a *Guide* though not to accomplish the personal research which he had planned. In 1917 he returned to Russia to work upon an edition of Bering's journals for the American Geographical Society and to obtain further material for the Department of Historical Research, from archives not yet opened at the time of his earlier visit. He arrived in Russia in time to see the Russian Revolution and worked there during the turbulent summer of 1917, returning to the United States in September, 1917, with much valuable material. In addition to his *Guide to materials for American history in Russian archives,* Carnegie Institution, publication no. 239, 1917, he published *Russian expansion on the Pacific, 1641-1851,* Cleveland, Arthur H. Clark, 1914; *Bering's voyages,* Research ser., no. 1-2, American Geographical Society, 1922; and *John Paul Jones in Russia,* N. Y., Doubleday, 1927.

[60] Golder had proposed to Macmillan the publication of a four-volume history of Russia in English, to be the work of Russians and Americans, with editors supplied by both countries. When he returned to this country in the fall of 1917, he wrote to Jameson that arrangements had been made with Macmillan in London for the publication of the history, the editors to be Golder and Professor Lappo-Danilevskii. Future events made the work impossible (Golder to Jameson, Dec. 21, 1915, Dec. 27, 1916, Oct. 5, 1917).

to the last ten or twenty or thirty years.

In respect to organization, if I were advising a publisher, I should perhaps suggest, a managing committee of three Americans such as you and Lord and Harper,[61] who could plan the scheme, with a view to American needs, engage the proper Russians for the different parts, and if need be, fill in the gaps by writing of your own. I don't think you will get much good out of advisory editors. It sounds well but in practice they would be nothing more than contributors of what you ask them to contribute. . . .

To Henry E. Bourne

February 4, 1916.

My dear Bourne: [62]

. . . I do not find my mind to be exceedingly fertile in suggestions for the Cincinnati meeting, but I will tell you one thing that I think strongly: Of all subjects in history, the one that most interests the mind of American mankind at the present day is this present war. At the Chicago meeting, it was thought best to avoid topics in that field. I thought that to be unnecessary timidity, but even if I were wrong, I believe that divergencies of opinion as to causes and the conduct of different nations have now become better settled, and also the war will by December, 1916 be more largely in the past, more a fit matter for discussions really historical. The matters having any relation to the war which were taken up at this recent Washington meeting, were such that the papers read were quite as fit for a political science society as for an historical society, in several instances, more so. I do not believe in leaving at one side the most interesting and "vital" topics because people may differ respecting them. Such a procedure helps to make our proceedings excessively academic, so that persons who attend our meetings and those of the Political Science Association, tell me that ours suffer in comparison, as if we stood as remote from actualities as the gods of Olympus.

All such criticisms may be unjust, but it is my belief that, in spite of nearness to the events, it is quite possible to lay before our association in December, 1916 some good diplomatic history, military history, and naval history relative to this war. I also

---

[61] Robert H. Lord (1885-1954) for many years taught Russian and Far Eastern history in Harvard University. He was a member of the United States delegation to the Paris Peace Conference as a specialist on Polish affairs. He was ordained a priest in the Roman Catholic Church in 1929, and later taught church history in St. Johns Seminary, Brighton, Mass., and became pastor of St. Paul's, Wellesley, Mass.

Samuel N. Harper (1882-1943), A.B., University of Chicago, 1902, was at this time assistant professor of Russian languages and literature in that university.

[62] Henry E. Bourne, professor of history in Western Reserve University, was chairman of the program committee for the meeting of the Association to be held in Cincinnati in December, 1916.

think that it might be well to try the experiment of having, on one particular evening, no programme, but letting that date remain open for dinners privately organized, at which the men interested in the French Revolution and Napoleon, the men interested in English medieval history, or perhaps larger groups, could, by private and informal organization, come together for an evening of discussion that might produce results in the future. Some beginning of that sort of thing was made here. Krehbiel can tell you about it.

Perhaps it is worth while to suggest that some good might be done by waking up Kentucky, which seems to me in historical, as well as in other respects, one of the most backward of our commonwealths, by a strong concerted movement to exhibit important aspects of its history, e. g. by devoting to that topic alone a joint session with the Ohio and Mississippi Valley associations, but probably the latter would think that offered too little variety to their members. Something distinct ought however to be done for Kentucky and Tennessee.

While much attention has been given to problems of teaching in schools, it is long since any attention has been paid to the teaching of history in colleges and universities. I think it quite possible that there could be a profitable discussion of the status, aims, and value of the doctoral dissertation.[63] . . .

To FERRIS GREENSLET

February 17, 1916.

My dear Mr. Greenslet:[64]

When Mr. Henry Adams gave me a copy of the *Education of Henry Adams* he made one condition, namely that I should tell him of any errors I found. This was a little whimsical; I do not know enough to make it likely that I should discover errors. Still, to make a formal compliance with the condition, though I did not think the matter would ever come up again with him, I did note on a piece of paper, as I read, a certain number of typographical errors to which I thought attention might be directed if ever the book should be published, as I hoped it some time would be.

In view of what you told me the other day, I should think I might well send the list to you, to be kept on file against the time of reprinting, though the errors

are mostly such as your proof readers would anyhow observe.[65] The list is enclosed.

To FERRIS GREENSLET

February 29, 1916.

My dear Mr. Greenslet:

This very slight note calls for no reply. When you told me about the many printings of Thayer's *Hay* [66] I should have mentioned to you a possible correction. There is a letter (I can't tell where and have not the book before me), which Hay is represented as signing "Jo el Hay." Perhaps one ought not to be sure without looking at the original manuscript, but I am confident that what Hay wrote was "Yo el Hay," a humorous perversion of the familiar signature of Spanish kings "Yo el Rey," which, from the difference of pronunciation of "J" and "Y" would not be well represented by the form which appears in print.

To WORTHINGTON C. FORD

March 27, 1916.

My dear Ford:

I received on Friday the *Autobiography* of Mr. Adams [67] and fell upon it with such interest, and had such intervals of street-car riding that within twenty-four hours I had read it. Even to one who had never heard of the man it would be an exceedingly interesting narrative; to me, who had had so much of the privilege of knowing him, it was a constant delight, save in one particular, that there is something distinctly pathetic to me in his over-emphasis upon his sense of imperfection and upon the times at which he fell short of his own ideals of achievement and success. But in these posthumous criticisms, as in his conduct with me when he was alive, he does not succeed in concealing from me that he was a noble and very kind spirit.

I am writing to you to express my thoughts because I suppose the book comes to me as a corresponding member of the Massachusetts Historical Society, which in my mind is always now represented by you. I am very grateful to the society for the gift, as I always am for the volumes that come from them. Everyone of them on its arrival renews my sense of dereliction of duty. Nobody seems to know precisely what the duties of a corresponding member of a historical society are, but it seems that he ought to do something. I should be glad if I could do something for the society. You must of course let

---

[63] The meeting of 1916 offered a session on the teaching of the elementary course in history in colleges and universities, one which dealt with problems of the war, and a number of papers on Southern history, among them Sectionalism in Kentucky from 1855 to 1865, and The influence of the religious press of Cincinnati on the Northern Border States. A trial was made at this meeting of the dinner groups suggested by Jameson.

[64] Ferris Greenslet had been since 1907 literary adviser for the Houghton Mifflin Company.

[65] *The education of Henry Adams* was published by Houghton Mifflin in 1918.

[66] Thayer, William Roscoe (1859-1923), *Life and letters of John Hay*, 2v., N. Y., Houghton Mifflin, 1915.

[67] *Charles Francis Adams, 1835-1915: an autobiography*, prepared by the Mass. Hist. Soc., Boston, Houghton Mifflin, 1916.

me know of anything I can do here in Washington. I have for a long time had in the kettle one or two very slight notes that might be contributed to the proceedings, but it will be of doubtful benefit even if I ever get them finished.[68] Meantime, there are other things which seem to come first.

To J. LeRoy White

April 6, 1916.

Dear Mr. White:

. . . I saw your brother [69] yesterday at luncheon at Mr. Putnam's Round Table at the Library of Congress. He was looking very well, and was making preparations for an address, next Monday, before the Navy League, in which I judged his main subject would be the necessity of not allowing domestic politics to interfere with the proper conduct of foreign relations. It is a lesson very much needed upon the Hill at the east end of Pennsylvania Ave., for, whatever our views may be as to the extent to which the United States should go in military preparations, there is no question that the movements in that direction are being harmfully mingled with a great infusion of politics, especially in the form of machinations of the National Guard, whose pressure from their respective states and localities the members of Congress seem unable to resist, in spite of all warnings.[70]

I am deeply interested in what you write of the sad conditions environing your life. Please be assured of my constant and deep sympathy.[71]

To Albert Shaw

April 13, 1916.

My dear Shaw:

In those early days of the Johns Hopkins University, when you and E. R. L. Gould [72] and I were together, we were all very industrious young men, eagerly busy in making the fullest possible use of the time we had for graduate study. Therefore, my memories of Gould are not those which any of us might have regarding the companions of our undergraduate days, in which there was more leisure for sociability, and a common life extending over a much larger area than that of hard work in a specialty merely. Our enjoyment of each other was simply that which we could get without diverting much time from austere devotion to the muse of history—or to the muses of history and political economy and political science, if the latter have muses, a point concerning which I have no information.

Those three studies constituted one department then, in the charge of Dr. Herbert B. Adams. No one of the graduate students responded more actively than Gould did to the mental stimulus given to us by that brilliant and ingenious teacher. Gould came to Baltimore with a sound education, of the thorough, though not excessively broad type, which Canadian colleges have always known how to give.[73] He showed a capable, eager, responsive mind, good reasoning powers, refinement of thought, and of taste, and a degree of adaptability, distinctly remarkable in a Canadian mind. The atmosphere of the Johns Hopkins in those days was one of the most stimulating ever found in America. "Joy was it in that time to be alive, but to be young was very Heaven." [74] Gould eagerly breathed in that atmosphere, and became an American scholar of a very fine type, whose interests even in those early days showed that public spirit and wish to be of service in large matters which afterwards marked his later career. His work was always done cleverly and substantially and, what is much rarer among American graduate students, was presented in an interesting way. He was indeed a very interesting man, a good talker, devoted to argument, as young students of our subjects ought to be, but never overbearing or quarrelsome. He was the soul of good nature, always kind and courteous and friendly, and very good company. I seldom saw him after those early days, but retain always the impression of a singularly bright young mind, of a singularly pleasant companion, with many evidences of those traits that afterward made him so distinguished and useful a feature in the life of New York.

I sympathize cordially with the desire to com-

---

[68] It is doubtful whether these notes were sent to the society. The next contribution of Jameson to appear in the *Proceedings* was, John Clark of the *Mayflower,* with Spanish documents selected from a group sent to Jameson by Irene Wright. *Proc. Mass. Hist. Soc.* **54**: 61-76, November, 1920.

[69] Henry White (1850-1927), the diplomat, at this time living in Washington, had been retired from foreign service at the beginning of Taft's term. In November, 1918, he was appointed a member of the Paris Peace Conference by President Wilson. Theodore Roosevelt once said of him: "The most useful man in the entire diplomatic service during my own Presidency, and for many years before, was Harry White" (Nevins, Allan, *Henry White: thirty years of American diplomacy,* 305, N. Y., Harper, 1930). If for no other reason Jameson would have known him because since 1913 he had been a member of the board of trustees of the Carnegie Institution of Washington, a position which he held until his death.

[70] See *post,* June 9, 1916, and n. 85.

[71] J. LeRoy White, one of the faithful supporters of Miss Griffin's *Writings on American History,* with his check for that work, wrote from Rabodanges, Orne, France: "Everybody seems to fall ill in these dreadful times. Many of the weak or middle-aged have gone to the wall; who might have lived for years quite happily" (White to Jameson, Mar. 23, 1916).

[72] See *ante,* Feb. 13, 1882, n. 29. Shaw had published a brief obituary of Gould in the *Review of Reviews* **52**: 284, February, 1915.

[73] Gould received his A.B. degree from the University of Toronto in 1881.

[74]   "Bliss was it in that dawn to be alive,
    But to be young was very heaven!"
        Wordsworth, The Prelude, book XI.

memorate him in a substantial manner, and wish that I could make a fuller contribution toward that end.[75]

To ANDREW C. McLAUGHLIN

May 19, 1916.

My dear McLaughlin:

. . . It is so perfectly clear that I ought to be hard at work this afternoon that I shall resist the temptation to discource [*sic*] on public affairs. I was mighty glad to listen to your views, though not as much so as if I could have received them orally; but I hardly know what I myself think.[76] Sometimes I suppose that I do, but then a remembrance springs up of some other turn of thought I had, when the newspapers said something different from what they happen to be saying today. How little I actually know of what is going on at Washington! At present I do not suppose that much *is* going on at the Department of State, though Congress is manifesting its usual activity, with about the usual result. Anyhow, I have never known enough about the situations to be willing to criticize the President very sharply. Perhaps he has done all that public opinion would at any given time bear him out in doing. As I remember it, Lincoln was not very truculent between March 4 and April 14, 1861. We statesmen in a democratic country are obliged I suppose to confine ourselves to what our folks will stand for. I have been seeing more than usual of Congress lately, or at least of the more numerous branch thereof, and I fear that it is indeed a House of Representatives. . . .

To PETRUS J. BLOK

June 6, 1916.

My dear Professor Blok:

We in America who are occupied with history have been very deeply stirred by the news of the imprisonment of Professors Fredericq and Pirenne and soon resolved to take some action in the matter. Our Secretary of State [77] being temporarily ill, I got the Department to send a simple message of inquiry to Mr. Whitlock,[78] but no reply has yet been received. Meanwhile, however, from such Belgian and Dutch newspapers as have come to hand (the latter largely through your Mr. van Loon),[79] we seem to know pretty well what has happened, and the appeal of the Dutch professors, following up the representations of their government, have given us a good model for imitation. I am to see our Secretary of State this afternoon, going to him with a memorial to which 70 professors of history in our leading universities have telegraphed me their permission to append their signatures, and in their names shall urge upon him to send to the American ambassador in Berlin [80] an expression of hope that the two professors, for whom we all feel the highest regard and sympathy, and whom a good number of us know personally (M. Fredericq and I have corresponded for thirty years) may be released on condition of spending the remainder of the war in some neutral country. We should be glad to have them come to America. We appreciate the reasons which you have advanced in your memorial for their continuing their scientific work in Holland. On the other hand, one of our universities (Cornell University, which has a very good library in European history) has voted to offer a good lectureship and a home (very good quarters, indeed, and *pension*) to either one of the two, and it is quite possible that within a few days another university may make a similar offer for the other. I am not authorized to announce all this in any formal way and it may be that both MM. Fredericq and Pirenne would have reasons for remaining in Europe for the present; but I should be glad to have them, and you, and our Dutch confrères, know of our eager interest in their fate, and our warm sympathy for them personally. We are giving no publicity to our efforts here, believing that for the present it may be better that the matter should not be in the newspapers, and perhaps you will kindly regard this as addressed only to you and our two friends, and perhaps a few of your colleagues, if you see occasion. If the release takes place, the president of Cornell University will no doubt send a formal invitation.

Not only in this matter, but in countless others, we Americans have seen the generosity and sympathy

---

[75] This probably refers to the preparation of *Elgin Ralston Lovell Gould: a memorial*, published by the League for Political Education in 1916.

[76] A few sentences from a letter written by Professor McLaughlin on May 3, 1916, will illustrate his feeling: "I am sore over the thoughtless cry for preparedness. Literally over the cry. I am not opposed to a reasonable increase in the army and making it effective. . . . Nobody has on a high plane spoken nobly and high mindedly of the real responsibility of America. Think of an English statesman talking the bunk W. [Wilson] did. Why couldn't he plainly present to the people the whole thing in a straightforward way? . . . T. R. is a brazen Ass. I wouldn't vote for him for assistant coroner of Bird Center. Wilson's Mexican policy may not work out; but it will go down in history among people who have consciences (if any remain) as a fine attempt to be patient, helpful and wise in dealing with an incompetent and unhappy people. . . . As for Wilson's German policy. I don't see that he could do other with reason. Certainly, he could not have gone faster and carried the country with him."

[77] Robert Lansing (1864-1928), secretary of State from June 23, 1915, till Feb. 13, 1920. For a complete account of the case of Fredericq and Pirenne see the next letter.

[78] Brand Whitlock (1869-1934), American minister, later ambassador, to Belgium, 1913-1922.

[79] Hendrik Willem van Loon (1882-1944), born in Holland, A.B., Cornell, 1905, press correspondent in various European countries during the first World War. He afterwards taught, lectured, and wrote in this country.

[80] James W. Gerard (1867-1951), ambassador extraordinary and minister plenipotentiary to Germany, 1913-1917. He was recalled on Feb. 3, 1917.

of the Dutch exhibited toward the Belgians in a degree that awakens our very warm admiration. I wish to express also my cordial sympathy for the sufferings and burdens which the Netherlands themselves are passing through. Also, by the way, let me send my congratulations upon the completion of your second edition, of which I have lately seen the final volume. A rather perfunctory notice of it appears in the forthcoming issue of the *American Historical Review*.[81] I send a clipping from the proofsheet.

To WILLIAM PHILLIPS

June 7, 1916.

My dear Mr. Phillips:[82]

In pursuance of our conversation of yesterday, I enclose two copies of a memorial addressed to the Secretary of State on behalf of Professors Fredericq and Pirenne, and now signed by 93 historical professors, 10 additional names having come in this morning. I also venture to enclose a copy of the draft which I showed to you yesterday, as indicating the nature of the action which we should be glad to have the Department take; but it is of course understood that all matters relating to such action are entirely submitted to the discretion of the Department.

It has appeared to me probable that the Department might wish to have on file a statement of the facts on which our memorial is based, and therefore, and for your own information and reference, I subjoin the following statement:

My sources of information have chiefly been the Belgian, Dutch, and French newspapers in the files of the Library of Congress, or of Cornell University library, or such as have come to a Dutch professor there. I have also had some information from a Belgian professor now residing in Cambridge, England, and there was a statement in the *Nation* of May 18, from its Dutch correspondent.

Professor Paul Fredericq is a man of about 67 years of age, who for perhaps thirty years has been professor of history, and I think also of Flemish literature, in the University of Ghent. He is chiefly known by writings, of a high type of scholarship, on the history of the inquisition in the Netherlands. He is one of the eight members of the Belgian Commission Royale d'Histoire and has the honorary doctorate of the University of Göttingen. Professor Pirenne, a man of 54 years, is also a professor in the same university and a member of the same Commission. His *Histoire de Belgique*, which also exists as a German work in the Heeren-Ukert-

Lamprecht series, is well known. No doubt he is the most distinguished historian of Belgium, and Fredericq the next. At the International Congress of Historical Studies in London in 1913 Pirenne certainly made a larger impression than anyone else of his age.

Both men are personally known to me, as well as to many other American historical students. Fredericq in particular has been my friend for nearly thirty years. Both are exceedingly cultivated men, of the highest character, and not in the least likely to behave otherwise than with propriety on any occasion. Pirenne is the more brilliant; Fredericq is a man of especial gentleness and benignity. In respect to the efforts which have been made to encourage the Flemish element in the university and the literary use of the Flemish language, he has always taken a favorable attitude. I remember that, dining with him when I was last in Ghent, three or four years ago, he told me that he conducted one of his seminaries in French, the other in Flemish. He is an unmarried man, who has lived with two sisters, both of whom have died during the course of the war. He is himself not strong physically, and imprisonment may in his case have very serious consequences. Pirenne is a married man. In the last letter I had from him, in September, 1914, he told me that his three sons were all in the Belgian army. At least one of them has since been killed.

Now as to the facts respecting their cases: None of the Belgian universities is now in active operation. The German government in Belgium, in pursuance of its attempt to build up a Teutonic following by fostering the Flemish language and "releasing the Flemings from the oppressive yoke of the Walloons" has undertaken to create at Ghent a "K. K. Flämische Universität." I have not seen the text of Governor-General von Bissing's decree but I have before me that of Duke Albrecht of Württemberg, commander of the fourth army, dated March 17, and apparently intended to carry out or repeat that decree. (*Indépendance Belge*, April 6, page 3). It reads:

"The courses at the University of Ghent shall be given in the Flemish language. The Verwaltungschef attached to the governor-general in Belgium is authorized to tolerate, for certain branches, the use of another language, as an exception. He is charged to take measures necessary for the execution of this decree." I have also, in French text, General von Bissing's reply to a protest of Belgian deputies against this measure (*Indép. Belge*, March 21), which indicates the same as to the nature of the decree and justifies it, ending:

"As I have already caused the governor of Antwerp to tell you, I cannot permit that the hostile attitude of certain persons against the Flamandization of the University of Ghent, shall continue and shall take on the proportions of a political propaganda. I shall officially oppose every effort whose purpose is to turn aside the professors from collaborating and the students from participating in the work of Flamandization."

---

[81] *Geschiedenis van het Nederlandsche Volk*, 2d ed., v. **4**, Leiden, A. W. Sythoff, 1916; reviewed, *Amer. Hist. Rev.* 21: 853, July, 1916.

[82] William Phillips, third assistant and assistant secretary of State, 1909 and 1914 to 1919; undersecretary of State in 1922 and 1933. He served as envoy extraordinary and minister plenipotentiary to the Netherlands, Luxemburg, Canada, and Italy between 1920 and 1936.

The exact date of the arrest of the two professors I do not find. As nearly as I can make out from the papers, Fredericq was imprisoned for some days, early in February, then released, but rearrested again in the latter part of March (*Indép. Belge*, March 29, quoting *Belgisch Dagblad*), after Pirenne, the German government in Belgium choosing to regard them as the centre of resistance to the re-opening of the University.

The issue of April 19 (page 2) states that Professor Fredericq was at that time in a military prison camp at Gütersloh in Westphalia, "where he is subjected to the treatment of prisoners of war, without consideration for his age and dignity." I have a later statement that his confinement is not so rigorous as this would imply. The issue of April 6, page 3, states that Professor Pirenne is imprisoned in the prison camp at Crefeld. What seems to be the fullest account of the incident is the following (*Indép. Belge*, April 29, page 2) :

Voici à la suite de quelles circonstances le professeur Pirenne a été emmené en Allemagne. Von Bissing avait mandé l'éminent historien. Il lui offrit de devenir recteur de l'Université de Gand flamandisée. Pirenne répondit noblement que, seul, le gouvernement belge avait qualité pour lui offrir les fonctions de recteur.

"Donc, vous refusez?" questionna le gouverneur.

"De toutes mes forces," fut la réponse.

"Très bien. Vous me voyez contraint de vous envoyer en Allemagne."

Le brillant professeur, dès ce moment, ne put plus retourner à Gand et sa femme dut venir à Bruxelles l'embrasser pour la dernière fois.

Le professeur Frédéricq ayant refusé dans les mêmes termes la même offre, le même traitement lui fut réservé.

The same story is given in the *Paris Temps* of May 2, (page 2). In the *Indép. Belge* of April 10, and April 28, and in the *Temps* of May 4, (page 2), it is related that the professors and *chargés de cours* of the existing university were given their choice, either to take part in the work of the new university or to lose their positions and salaries, and that of the whole number, 100 in all, only 2, the one a German, the other a Luxemburger, consented. Since the episode of Pirenne and Fredericq five other professors, all Flemings by birth, who had protested against the decree, had been deported into Germany (*Temps*, April 26, page 2).

After the arrest of Pirenne and Fredericq, the other professors addressed a petition of protest to von Bissing, part of which reads as follows (Amsterdam *Telegraef*, May 1, quoting *Indép. Belge*) :

"The undersigned take the liberty to inform you how deeply moved they have been by the action touching two of their most eminent and most esteemed colleagues, MM. Fredericq and Pirenne. Your Excellency knows that these two honored professors were suddenly arrested and carried off to Germany and that their colleagues questioned in vain as to how they had merited so rigorous a treatment. Your Excellency knows that MM. Fredericq and Pirenne are two scholars whose achievements are everywhere recognized and whose fame transcends our frontiers. . . . As regards the duties of the faculty toward the power now in possession and the relation of these duties to those due the fatherland, there is not the slightest difference between the views of the teachers dealt with and those of their colleagues.

"Your Excellency will without doubt appreciate the feelings of solidarity which in these circumstances unite the members of the University family. You will comprehend that they must all feel themselves affected by the action which has so severely struck two of them. It will not escape you that the shock felt by the University of Ghent will be shared in all lands throughout the scholarly world, in which MM. Fredericq and Pirenne held so high a place."

No reply to this appeal seems to have been rendered, except such as is involved in the arrest and deportation of five more professors.

Meanwhile, about May 6, the Dutch government intervened with the German government to obtain the liberation of the two historians, requesting that they may be allowed to continue their scientific work in some neutral country. Supporting the request made by their government, 182 Dutch savants—members of the Royal Academy of Sciences or professors in the Dutch universities—have sent to the Prussian Academy of Sciences at Berlin and other German academies and the senates of the German universities, an address of which a copy is enclosed.

This Dutch action seeming to indicate a line along which efforts might be made on behalf of our two Belgian colleagues with some prospect of success, a full statement of the facts, much like that which is given above, was prepared by me, after conference with a number of historical professors who happened to come to Washington last week, and was sent to some one in each of a dozen or fifteen of the principal universities. With great unanimity and cordiality, 93 such professors have telegraphed me the authorization of their signatures to a memorial like that which is enclosed, and which is placed in your hands for such action as the Department may see fit to take.

With sincere thanks for your kind attention in our interview of yesterday,

[P. S.]

Princeton telegraphs definite offer of lecturship to Pirenne—Several signers are pro-German.

To ANDREW C. MCLAUGHLIN

June 9, 1916.

Dear McLaughlin:

Thank you very much for your efforts and your letter. There will be no expense, under the method which we succeeded in using. Though you had a laborious celebration, I judge that it must have been an interesting one, and I should have been glad to be there.[83] (I sent a telegram). But now that we have gone through Katrina's days of graduation, and I have seen how much it all meant to her, and have shared in her happiness, I see clearly that I was right in staying here. As for preparedness, I may, for all I know, agree more with you than with Turner, with whom I have not talked in the matter.[84] I really think we ought to have a larger and better preparation against dangers which, to me, seem not unreal. I am not however very enthusiastic about the results we shall get from additional expenditures, when I think of the course which Congress has pursued with respect to the National Guard.[85] The ancient pork barrel of rivers and harbors has begun to smell pretty strong. The almost equally ancient pork barrel of postoffices and court-houses has also of late begun to give out odors which are largely remarked upon. Here, however, is a new pork barrel, has not yet begun to affect the public nose, a third means of getting ourselves re-elected by judicious application of the public millions. Therefore let us joyfully rush toward it, meanwhile pretending that we are patriots, eager to defend our country, and especially that we are more eager to defend our country than the other party, or even other peoples' candidates in our own party. . . .

To JAMES SETH

June 9, 1916.

My dear Seth:[86]

. . . We are waiting this afternoon to hear from Chicago, where the Republican convention, in an hour or two, will be beginning to ballot for its presidential nominee. I hope it will be Hughes, an admirable man—and also a very agreeable one, as we Brown men

here in Washington know.[87] I would be equally content with Root, for whom I have high admiration, but there would be no prospect of his election. For my own part, I think Wilson has done very well in the main, but I believe Hughes would hold with more consistency to high standards, without being impracticable. Whether he is nominated or not, it is a very striking thing that a man in a judicial position, who has been out of politics for several years, and who says not a word about such things now, nevertheless leads the candidates in respect to numbers on the first ballot, merely through force of character, previously exhibited, while the vociferous T. R., struggling for the nomination with all his strength and with all the arts of the most consummate political leader of our time, is losing rather than gaining public favor by his ambition. So at least it appears at 4 P. M. on June 9. . . .

To EDMUND C. BURNETT

North Edgecomb, Maine, July 12, 1916.

Dear Burnett:

I was glad to get your letter of July 8 and to know that you are personally well, however low the state of agriculture. Up here there is no such thing. The season has been so late and so cold that, so well as I can gather, no one will feel justified in planting pease or beans until the first of September, and then he will shoot them into the ground with a gun. Fresh vegetables may be expected early in December; but we have plenty of canned.

Disclaiming all intention to match sufferings and calamities with you, after the manner of Job and his three tactless friends, I will mention that the engine on my boat has not yet begun to run; that the wood was not split when I arrived, and for the most part is not yet cut up—except as I myself, with great reluctance, split enough to last from day to day; that Francis perhaps has the measles; that Katrina perhaps has appendicitis; and that Stock reports my house to have been burglarized, though so far as I can gather with slight loss to me or gain to the misguided youth who made the attempt. Job has little on me, except his detestable patience. . . .

To ALEXANDER S. LAPPO-DANILEVSKII

North Edgecomb, Maine, July 19, 1916.

My dear Professor Lappo-Danilevskii:[88]

I ought before this to have acknowledged the re-

---

[83] The "effort" was to see the Chicago historians about the petition in behalf of Fredericq and Pirenne. McLaughlin had offered to share whatever expense was involved in the action taken. The celebration to which reference is made was that of the quarter-centennial of the University of Chicago.

[84] McLaughlin had written: "I had a pleasant visit with Turner, although I got into a good many arguments with him on the subject of 'Preparedness'. . . . Under the leadership of our friend, Theodore, the people have resorted to what they think is a new idea; 'You may, if you don't like anybody, hit him.' It is possible that the idea was new when Cain and Abel first began to gambol on the greensward of Eden, but it hasn't been new since."

[85] Undoubtedly a reference to the increase in federal control of the National Guards, advocated by the National Guards Association, the lobbying of which drew forth a rebuke from Senator Chamberlain, chairman of the Committee on Military Affairs. The change in organization was made by the National Defense Act, signed June 3, 1916, under which the President received the power to determine the units to be maintained, the rules, the pay, the supply, and all other matters pertaining to the upkeep of the Guards.

[86] The omitted sections relate family news and tell what the Americans were attempting to do for Fredericq and Pirenne.

[87] Charles Evans Hughes (1862-1948) received an A.B. from Brown in 1881, an A.M. in 1884, and was awarded an LL.D. by that university in 1906.

[88] Alexander S. Lappo-Danilevskii, eminent Russian historian, was present at the International Historical Congress in London in 1913 and from that time, he and Jameson exchanged occasional letters. For the tragic end of his life, see post, Jan. 19, 1920, n. 283.

ceipt of your volumes concerning Nyen.[89] I am very much obliged by your kindness. You will appreciate that, in a country where few historical scholars read either Russian or Swedish, there will be difficulty in securing an adequate review of such volumes; but I will see what can be done and shall hope that the result will not be too perfunctory.

I am at present reading the first proofs of Mr. Golder's book. He is lecturing during the summer in Boston. I may yet see him. I continue to be grateful for all your kindness to him.

In the midst of all the terrible calamities which the war is inflicting upon the world, the postponement of our International Historical Congress must, I suppose, be regarded as a very minor matter.[90] And yet it is not a small thing (is it?) that a state of mind has been created which for a long time will make it difficult for the students of history in various nations to come together in a spirit of harmony. It is our (the historical profession's) particular aspect of this general estrangement of civilized minds, in an age when we hoped and believed that such minds were, in all countries, drawing more nearly together. I still hope and believe that, as a general process, this is nevertheless going on. I sometimes remind myself that the Englishman or Frenchman of 1470 might have said to himself "we have supposed that this long period of feudal dissension was developing toward its end, and that this West-European world was evolving into a higher form of organization, organization in great nations—and now comes upon us nevertheless this terrible period of feudal warfare!" And yet he would have been wrong if he had despaired. The evolution he had expected was proceeding and the storm he saw about him was the "clearing-up shower," as we call it in English, after which Western Europe came at once into the larger grouping and the more peaceful condition. So, perhaps when this dreadful war is over, we may advance more speedily to the larger synthesis which we have been expecting. I hope so, though the purely national conduct of most of the socialists has seemed a discouraging evidence to the contrary.

At all events, if the time ever comes when you historical scholars in Russia think a helpful move may be made toward drawing together the historians once more, you can, as a matter of course, count upon especially active help from those of America. . . .

To WALDO G. LELAND

North Edgecomb, Maine.
July 21, 1916.

Dear Leland:

Thank you for various letters, and especially for your endeavors in the matters of those ancient bishops. That the Harvard College Library does not possess the third volume of Conrad Eübel *Hierarchia Catholica* is a scandal of the first magnitude.[91] Haskins and the others may have extenuating circumstances to allege, and therefore I shall keep the deficiency out of the Boston newspapers as long as I possibly can. Meantime you have done much to save my life.

Much was done in the same direction by a day's outing yesterday—a day begun somewhat early by leaving my happy home at 6:40 A. M., and sailing with the Jewetts in their yacht down the river from Wiscasset along the shore of Westport Island to Jewett's birthplace and the Jewett country in general, which he was showing for the first time to his wife and son, and so to my mother's and across to Boothbay Harbor, whence we returned in the Jewetts' car.

Still more will be done toward preservation of the same existence, if you will look in the London *Spectator* for some articles by Lord Cromer (by the way, if you want to see a most excellent epigram, look at the article [on] Cromer in the *Britannica,* the last work into which one would look for humorous verse), letters relative to the American Civil War.[92] I should like the title and the date or dates, for the stuff appears to be important enough to mention as a noteworthy article.

Though the contents of bureau drawers and the like were much tumbled about in my house, it does not appear that anything was taken except Wentworth's *Algebra.* Stock cannot find this, and therefore suspects collusion of the burglar with Katrina. I don't know what to think. . . .

I have today received a very interesting letter from Professor S. Muller of Utrecht, who is in communication with Fredericq and Pirenne, and to whom Blok

---

[89] Nyen was a fortress established by the Swedes on the Neva River above the point where Peter the Great later built his capital. Professor Lappo-Danilevskii had sent to Jameson two volumes on Nyen by A. J. Hipping, which were briefly reviewed, *Amer. Hist. Rev.* **22**: 437-438, Jan. 1917.

[90] It was agreed at the London Congress that the fifth International Congress of Historical Sciences should be held in St. Petersburg in 1918.

[91] Volume 3 of the *Hierarchia Catholica Medii Aevi* appeared in 1910. Jameson's interest in this work will be seen in later letters (*post,* Aug. 3, 1917). He was right in thinking that it would progress slowly. Volume 5, covering the years 1667 to 1730, appeared in 1953, the work of Father R. Ritzler and Father P. Sefrin.

[92] As Lieut. Evelyn Baring, Lord Cromer had visited the American battlefields in 1864, and had written articles on trench fighting before Petersburg, Reminiscences of the American Civil War, *Spectator,* June 3, 10, 1916; see *Amer. Hist. Rev.* **22**, 244, Oct. 1916.
As Major Baring, Cromer had been the dominating influence in the commission of inquiry into the financial practices of the Khedive of Egypt in 1878-1879. The verse referred to is:
"The virtues of Patience are known,
But I think that when put to the touch
The people of Egypt will own with a groan,
There's an Evil in Baring too much."

of Leiden had sent my letter of about June 9. Muller, as president of the chief Dutch historical society, has the matter rather in charge. He is delighted with the American action, believes it will have great effect, and meantime advises that we continue to avoid publicity. I shall have the letter printed here and sent out to all the signers of our memorial in a few days, but shall wait to hear first from the Department of State to whom I am sending inquiry as to any progress. Phillips promised to send me word of any reply he might get, but it is now six weeks. I hope that Muller is right and that Pharaoh's heart will be softened. I am sending copies of his (Muller's, not Pharaoh's) letter at once to Burr and Munro.[93]

To ADAM F. ROSS

October 26, 1916.

My dear Ross:[94]

I should have no objection to answering your question, privately, though I should be opposed to having any publicity given to my opinion, first because it does not deserve it, and secondly because in such cases one always thinks that the man desires his opinion to be known, and I do not.[95] But in reality I hardly have a well-formed opinion on this great question. You see, for eleven years I have had no vote, having no other residence than the District of Columbia. It would perhaps surprise you, to see how largely one is kept from framing political judgments by the mere fact of not having to act upon them. Probably the atmosphere of Washington, where one sees administrations and parties come and go, but sees the work of the government going on much the same under either party, conduces to an indifference to party considerations and to the result of elections. However this may be, I have no doubt that, if I were going to vote, I should long before

this have made up my mind. As it is, I honestly do not know which man I should vote for. I know them both, and esteem them both very highly. Hughes I have known only since he came to Washington to live, Wilson since old Johns Hopkins days. Both are men of the highest character and of extraordinary political intelligence. In either case we should have a most excellent president. I should not think it easy to maintain any preference in respect to the ordinary administrative work of the president's office, or in respect to effective and aggressive effort toward the best ends in any matters outside of the largest questions of foreign affairs and in economic legislation.

In respect to economic legislation, I prefer the Democratic party, but that is to say that in such particulars I prefer a democratic Congress, and perhaps does not answer your question as between Hughes and Wilson. The Democrats have less gift for governmental efficiency, somewhat less intelligence and coherence; but the Republican leaders are too closely allied with capitalistic influences, too much inclined to regard the interests of money rather than the interests of human beings, and if they come into power will, so far at least as Congress is concerned, be dominated by their conservative rather than by their progressive ring. This is bad for the republic.

In the major matters of foreign policy, I should have said three months ago that I should prefer the management which Hughes would give to them. I do not so strongly think so now. His speeches and conduct have somewhat disappointed me. It is true that as a candidate he might put forward too little of constructive statement, yet excel in positive policies when president. But in respect to Mexico his party is likely to push him toward a too aggressive course, and in that and other matters the influence of Roosevelt is always an uncertain factor. I consider it certain that, if he is elected, Roosevelt will turn against him within a year. In that case, what would be the effect upon our foreign policy? It is hard to estimate what it would be, and to my mind not certain that it would be better than Wilson's has been. In some particulars, with respect to Germany especially, Wilson's course has been weaker than I should like to see, though it has been skilful, and has brought results in accordance with public will. On the other hand, the public will is far from being what I should like to see it. The panic of Congress at the time of the McLemore Resolution[96] covered them

---

[93] On Aug. 9, Jameson again wrote to Phillips, calling his attention to an article in the New York Times, Aug. 18, p. 3, col. 3, headed, Deported professors as secret plotters. This accused Fredericq and Pirenne of having engaged in "inadmissible secret agitation." Reminding Phillips that Professor Müller had predicted that this would be the line taken by the Germans, he urged that the State Department renew its efforts to obtain a report from Ambassador Gerard. By Nov. 16 word had come that the two scholars had been refused permission to come to America and had been transferred from a Belgium detention camp to Jena. Here Jameson sent them a sympathetic but cautious letter.

[94] Adam Franklin Ross, one of the last graduate students to be guided by Jameson at Brown, received a Ph.B. from that university in 1899, an A.M. in 1900.

[95] Ross had written to ask whether Jameson favored the election of Hughes or Wilson: "I am writing simply as an old pupil who has profited immeasurably from your instruction and I would like just a bit more of instruction." In acknowledging Jameson's reply he wrote: "One of the best assets that I possess is the fact that I have sat under your instruction" (Ross to Jameson, Oct. 23, 30, 1916).

[96] The McLemore Resolution, introduced by Jefferson McLemore of Texas on Feb. 18, 1916, read: "Resolved, That in the opinion of the House of Representatives citizens of the United States under existing conditions and irrespective of their legal rights ought to refrain from taking passage on armed vessels of belligerent nations except in case of imperative necessity." This was debated in the House on Mar. 7, 1916. (Cong. Rec., 64 Cong., 1 sess., 3717). Speeches of McLemore on his resolution may be found, ibid., Appendix, 361, 453.

with contempt, in my estimation; yet they were probably doing what their constituents wished. Have you ever reflected, as a good schoolmaster, upon the enormous difference with respect to a courageous spirit toward outside aggression, between a nation nearly all of whose members have had nearly all of their teaching from young women between 18 and 28 and a nation taught by men and citizens and soldiers? The Prussian schoolmaster instills into his pupils, in their history classes, a monstrous conviction of German superiority, a monstrous eagerness for national supremacy, which has done much to create the state of mind that makes war possible; but the American schoolmistress, while teaching the little boys to be kind, gentle, and even to be proud of being Americans, does not impart to them a masculine determination to resist with all their strength unlawful aggression from without, because it is not in her to impart. So we have to take our people as we find them, soft streak and all, and cannot too much abuse the President because he has failed to carry out a high and strong policy after he had apparently framed one. I really think Hughes would be bolder, but he would be less skilful in dealing with the European belligerents; and we cannot be sure whether he could have in the State Department the presence of Elihu Root, with better brains than either of them.

Well, as I have said, if I had to vote I should make up my mind, and I should make it up along some such lines as these. After thinking it out with you in this way it looks to me as if I should have voted for Hughes by a small majority in July, and should vote for Wilson by a still smaller majority in November. But the majority either way would be so slight that I should rather have you pay more attention to all other parts of this letter than to that sentence.[97]

I very much appreciate your asking for my opinion, and though I fear that it has been given in a form that will do you no good, it has done me some good to try to formulate it. Thank you also for telling me something about the very interesting and influential position which you hold. To be head of the department of history in a high school of five thousand pupils is to be a man of enormous influence on the future of New York and of the country. I never felt that the slight opportunities for influence presented by my single vote were of more than very

small account in comparison with those presented by the position of a teacher of history. I taught it, to be sure, to much fewer persons than you do; but then, one of them was A. F. Ross. . . .

To Woodrow Wilson

November 15, 1916 [98]

My dear Mr. President:

If you can conveniently do so, I should be glad if you would insert in your next message to Congress, a recommendation for the erection of a suitable national archive building. This is a matter which I have been pressing upon the attention of every Congress since 1908, being chairman of a committee of the Council of the American Historical Association to promote this matter.

The present situation with respect to the archives of the Government in Washington is in many ways very deplorable. They are widely dispersed about the city, bureau by bureau, in a hundred different places, many of them unsafe, most of them unsuitable,—and kept in accordance with many different systems, so that not only is the work of historians more difficult than in any other important national capital, but the work of the Government itself, whenever it ranges into papers more than ten years old, is shockingly inconvenienced and obstructed. Beginning in *1878*, when you and I were in college,[99] bureau chiefs and heads of executive departments have made urgent representations to Congress upon the subject. Since 1908, several societies have co-operated with the American Historical Association in urging the matter. President Taft made forcible recommendations concerning it, in his message of February 2, 1912.[100] The matter has now been brought to the stage where every member of Congress that one meets, agrees that such a building ought to be erected. The Public Buildings Act of March 4, 1913, authorized the making of plans and instituted a commission of five officials which should pass upon the plans and upon the selection of a site. Under a small appropriation subsequently made, sketch-plans of great excellence, have been made in the office of the supervising architect of the Treasury, and have received favorable consideration from the Fine Arts Commission, from the historical people, and from the Librarian of Congress, to all of whom the Treasury officials submitted them for comment. These plans will give us the finest national archive building in the world, and are framed to fall within the limit of cost ($1,500,000 for 3,000,000 cubic feet of space) fixed by the Act of Congress referred to. The con-

[97] A month later Jameson wrote in similar vein to Professor George L. Hendrickson of Yale: "He [Wilson] is a good man, and in nearly all internal matters has made a good President, but in his Mexican policy he has made many bad blunders that he need not have made, and has stuck to them with his iron rigidity, and in respect to European matters has taken a far tamer course than he need have taken, and missed a great opportunity of leadership—in both cases, from being excessively unteachable. That is the way it all looks to me. But I should not have expected better success in foreign affairs from Hughes, and in domestic affairs, I do not trust the old Republican crowd. But I am a mere looker-on in Vienna."

[98] Wilson Papers, Division of Manuscripts, Library of Congress.

[99] Jameson was graduated from Amherst, Wilson from Princeton, in 1879.

[100] See *ante*, Feb. 5, 1912, n. 223.

struction of the building has been authorized by statute.

What we need now is an appropriation for the purchase of a site. I hope to secure this in the next session of Congress. It would, however, be a great help if you would make a strong recommendation of the matter in your message to Congress. Such a recommendation, I need not say, would come with additional force, from one who is not only the Head of the Executive Department of the Government, but is known to speak with authority from the point of view of an historian. I hope that we may count upon your aid in both capacities.

I have abundant data on all aspects of the proposal, and on all stages of the legislative progress of the measure relating to it, and shall be happy to place these at the disposal of any of those who assist you, in case you should designate one of them with whom I might confer.

I hope I may be allowed to add a word expressing the pleasure which, both as a citizen and as an associate in earlier years, I have felt on account of your re-election.

To ANDREW C. McLAUGHLIN

November 20, 1916.

My dear McLaughlin:

I write to notify you that I have taken the liberty to give a letter of introduction to my friend Edward G. Lowry, who for several years was Washington correspondent of the New York *Evening Post,* and of whom I saw a good deal during those years. He is a very intelligent man, and a most entertaining companion. For the last two years he has been in London, but has come back to Washington to live. He is just setting out upon a tour of the West, the objects of which he will explain to you. My letter will no doubt cause the consumption of an hour of your time, but Lowry and the London *Times* are both worth helping and I think you will enjoy meeting him.

It seems ages since I heard from you. Indeed, it is a heavy price we pay for democracy in the American Historical Association, when it cuts me off hearing frequently from you by excuse of some bit of business of the *Review.* But let us summon up the necessary energy to write when we don't have to.

I hope that you and all your family have had a good summer and autumn. Give my warmest regards to all of them. I thought of you and Mrs. McLaughlin with especial frequency at election-time, and hope that the enlarged opportunities of voting for President bred no dissension in so harmonious a household.

I do not mean to talk politics. For my own part while a little inclined toward Wilson, if I had had a vote, I could not see a much better prospect of a satisfactory outcome in the one case than in the other, and now that it is settled, I still have to reflect upon the depressing effect on Washington real estate which according to general prediction will result from four more years of democratic administration, and upon the languid interest taken by the democratic officials in the great cause of the National Archive Building. I cannot expect an appropriation in this ensuing session, for the purchase of a site. I shall be well content if I get the Commission of Five to select one. Perhaps the next Congress may do better. I think Republicans are a little more interested in things like good filing systems than the Democrats are, because they come more largely from Urban centres and less largely from Squashville and Podunk. It is the filing systems of S. and P. which one sees exemplified in the old files of the House of Representatives for instance.

Turner has been with me since the first of November. He is here for six months in capacity of a Research Associate of the Carnegie Institution (Woodward's pet plan) and, while free most of the time to pursue the researches of his own choice, gives me on application a great deal of valuable counsel and suggestion, so that I am delighted thus far with the workings of the plan, as of course with his companionship. Every morning at nine I deposit Francis at his school on California Street, then go to the Brighton opposite and get Turner and we walk down to the Woodward Building together, thereby benefiting the physical health of both and my mental condition. The Round Table, now confined to Wednesdays so far as its more solemn sessions are concerned, has not yet begun, and I have not been up at the Library very much this autumn. . . . I don't know just what stage has been reached in the movement for a Christian Home for Historical Orphans in Washington, but have been told by Leland that it marches somewhat.[101] . . .

To WOODROW WILSON

December 5th, 1916.

My dear Mr. President:

Your letter of November 27th had to be forwarded to me from Washington, and I received it only last night, with no opportunity to reply until this morning.

---

[101] In the spring of 1916 a committee of five—D. C. Munro, A. B. Hart, Charles A. Beard, Gaillard Hunt, and W. G. Leland—was requested to make plans for a Washington center for advanced studies in history, political science, and economics. The committee drew up a constitution and presented a report to a conference of those interested at the December meeting of the American Historical Association. Formal approval was expressed by the Political Science Association and the American Economic Association, and endorsements were obtained from the secretaries of the departments of State and the Interior, from the Librarian of Congress, the director of the Pan-American Union, and the secretary of the Smithsonian. The declaration of war in April caused all thought of this project to be put aside for the time. At the close of the war the plans were brought forward again and in 1918 and 1919 efforts were made to raise the money necessary for their execution. *Amer. Hist. Rev.* **22**: 511, April, 1917; *Ann. Rept., Amer. Hist. Assn.,* 1918: **1**: 43.

I did not know that Charles Chapman was intending to write to you, but he is entirely warranted in using my name as he has done.[102] I have great regard for him. He is intelligent, well trained, and capable, is an assistant professor at the University of California, and has just published a very good book on the Spanish beginnings in that state.[103] Moreover, he is a straightforward and disinterested man, and in this present undertaking concerning a Spanish-American historical journal, has no personal or ulterior motives. That it is he who is agitating the matter is due simply to the fact that, among those interested in it, he is the one who at present has the leave of absence, and is free to go about. His plan seems to have the support of all the best men interested in Spanish-American history, and I believe that, at the dinner and conference in Cincinnati of which he speaks, the project will be resolved upon and launched. I also think that they are going to get needful money.

To some of those who support the project, it is simply a matter of scholarship, in a field in which scholarly interest has, as I have had much occasion to observe, grown rapidly in recent years; but to many of them it is also in a high degree a matter of public spirit, as a thing that will help to increase mutual understanding and good feeling between intelligent people in the United States and in the Spanish-American countries. On both grounds, a word from you, which could be read at our dinner, would be welcome and useful; and, since you are so kind as to ask my advice, my hope is that you will send such a message. I can see no chance of its being misused, and I am sure that it will be a powerful encouragement in a deserving quarter.

I am flattered by Dr. Chapman's assumption that you regularly read the American Historical Review; I shall never ask whether you do.[104]

[P.S.] Dr. Chapman's letter enclosed.

To Charles E. Chapman

December 11, 1916.

My dear Dr. Chapman:

Yours of December 9 is just received. I am very glad that President Wilson has responded so well to your request. I send you, for your files, copies of his letter to me and of my letter to him. I think that, on reading the latter, you will perhaps agree with me that you will not be warranted in using his letter earlier than the occasion for which we may assume that it was intended, the dinner in Cincinnati; nor do I think that it would be expedient to use it in circulars sent out between now and then. Indeed, I do not think you had better send out any circular. On the other hand, there can be no objection against use of the President's letter subsequently to the conference, if such were the mind of those who at that time are appointed a committee to deal with the matter—or of the Board of Editors, if one is created.

May I say that, to my mind, you are quite certainly going too fast? What you have to do at present is best defined in this way, not that you are trying to persuade people to support an Ibero-American Historical Review, but that you are trying to persuade them to attend a conference at which it shall be discussed, whether such a journal shall be founded or not. Mr. Merriman [105] might have been willing to attend such a dinner, if he had not thought that by agreeing to do so one was committing himself to the opinion that such a journal should be founded and maintained. He and many other men who could be useful to you, will decline to commit themselves on that point until they have heard the *pros* and *cons* discussed. You are enthusiastic for the project, but you must expect many other useful men to view it with caution and wish to be shown—both as to the reasons and the effects and as to the number and quality of the persons favoring it, or as to the opinions of this or that man. Don't try to hurry the thing along. Above all, don't discuss now who shall be managing-editor or members of the Board of Editors. The best way to seem to have no personal views as to who shall be in charge is never to express any views on that subject. It suffices to say to people that the enterprise ought to have the broadest base possible, that it should never be the organ of any particular institution or section, and that in order that everybody may see that such is the case, it is expedient that persons from every quarter should attend the conference and that, if a Board of Editors is resolved upon, it should be elected by ballot. From now till the conference, your best course is to take a passive position. You have taken the initial steps, and about all the steps that could profitably be taken now. The thing must be given time to ripen. Much as you are interested in it, it cannot come about in any desirable shape, unless a majority of those present at the conference think it should, and they will insist on doing their own thinking. Much activity on your part cannot now help the thing forward in any signal degree, and may in some respects

[102] Charles E. Chapman (1880-1941), assistant professor of history in the University of California, had asked President Wilson to express his approval of a plan for an Ibero-American Historical Review, the statement to be read at a session of the next meeting of the American Historical Association, in which the project was to be discussed. Wilson, knowing nothing of Chapman nor of the project, asked Jameson for information and advice. On receiving this letter, he sent the desired note to Chapman. See, Wilson to Jameson, Nov. 27, 1916.

[103] *The founding of Spanish California, the northward expansion of New Spain, 1687-1783*, N. Y., Macmillan, 1916.

[104] The *Amer. Hist. Rev.* **22**: 217, Oct., 1916, contained an outline of the plan for the new journal with the suggestion that a session of the December meeting be given to considering it. Chapman evidently assumed in his letter that President Wilson had read this item.

[105] Roger B. Merriman (1876-1945), assistant professor of history in Harvard, already well known for his interest in Spanish-America although the first volume of his *Rise of the Spanish Empire*, N. Y., Macmillan, did not appear until 1918.

be harmful. For instance, there are many persons to whom, if you say a word about who shall be managing-editor, it is at once perfectly clear that that man has been slated by the University of California for that position.

The gentleman whom you mention, though an excellent scholar, would seem to me on several grounds ineligible.

It need surprise no one that the project was not at first cordially received at Harvard. That is not the place to which we are accustomed to look for a glowing reception of ideas generated elsewhere. Go to see Dr. Haskins, and from him to Dr. Coolidge,[106] who is somewhat more likely to be favorable than either Haskins or Merriman, but do not press the matter upon them— merely get them, if you can, to agree to attend the conference. The aid of the Harvard contingent is not indispensable, but it is valuable, and if the project is realized, you will probably find them coming around in due time. Certainly it is not worth while to make a special effort to secure the approval of persons of importance outside the Latin-American field, merely in order to bring in Merriman. They are likely to say that, if the students of Latin-American history care enough about it to make the necessary efforts, very well; it's up to them. No harm to write to Professor Burr as president of the Association, and I dare say that you have done so; but from him and from persons like him you are not likely to get more than general expressions of opinion, which will be of some use at the Cincinnati conference but not indispensable. I can myself take no part in any such circularizing, because it would be resented by those who are agitating the creation of a *Journal of European History,* and would therefore react unfavorably upon the *American Historical Review.* I do not favor the creation of that journal, and I do favor the founding of an *Ibero-American Historical Journal, if* sufficient interest is manifested by those who attend the conference (beyond that I have never gone); and I have my reasons in both cases, but I cannot expect other people to know what they are or to appreciate that the distinction is legitimate and consistently made.[107]

To Max Farrand

December 21, 1916.

Dear Farrand:

I have not wished to thank you for your two articles

in the *New Republic* until I had read them, and that has resulted in a regrettable delay. Thank you very much for sending them. I have read them with a great deal of interest. The field is one to which I have been strongly drawn, though I have never had the time to investigate the matter with as much thoroughness as you.[108] I had never thought that the population of 1775 was less than half of English stock. An estimate I had made, on the one occasion when I undertook to give a lecture in this field, was that of the two million whites of 1775, probably about 60 per cent were of English stock, 17 or 18 per cent Irish (of whatever origin, but mostly protestant), 11 or 12 per cent German, 7 or 8 per cent Dutch. But you have more right to pronounce. Anyhow the articles are very interesting and very well worth while.[109]

To Edmund C. Burnett

Jan. 23, 1917.[110]

When in the course of human events
We reach a day that represents
Ten years finished, I really think
We ought to go out and have a drink.
Ladies are present; we can't do that;
Don't reach out for the hasty hat!
Feminine stars now rule our sky,
And I hear that the District is going dry.
Giving that up, what shall we do
To mark the day and honor you?
Ten long years is a big, big stage
On the road we travel from youth to age.
To spend with Congress a single day
Fills the soul with wild dismay;
Ten times three hundred and sixty-five
You've spent among them and still survive.
Ten years of Lovells and Deanes and Jays,
Ten years of questions and yeas and nays,
Ten years of motions, resolves, and votes,
Varied only by News and Notes,[111]

---

[106] Archibald C. Coolidge (1866-1928), a professor of history in Harvard from 1893 to 1928 and the director of the Harvard Library from 1911 until his death.

[107] Some time later Chapman wrote: "Without your help, I would have been unable to get this project under way, and could not have obtained the letter from President Wilson, from which we expect such big results" (Chapman to Jameson, Jan. 21, 1918). Wilson's note appears at the beginning of volume 1 of the *Hispanic-American Historical Review,* the title given to the new journal.

[108] In all, Professor Farrand published four articles in the *New Republic* under the general title, Immigration in the light of history. Probably the first two were those sent to Jameson: The colonial hyphen and A nation of immigrants, *New Republic* 9: 116-118, 147-149, Dec. 2, 9, 1916. These were followed by, A question of quality and assimilation, *ibid,* 179-181, 208-209, Dec. 16, 23, 1916.

[109] Farrand answered: "The figures which you suggest are, to me, very helpful, and I wish that I had the chance to discuss it with you. I don't think I ever bring out or suggest a subject that I don't find you have more and better material than I" (Farrand to Jameson, Dec. 21, 1916).

[110] Dr. Burnett had completed ten years of service in the Department of Historical Research, much of it devoted to work on the *Letters of members of the Continental Congress.*

[111] Burnett was for many years responsible for the American Notes and News which appeared in the *American Historical Review.*

Ten years of writing and punctuation,
Warrant a mighty celebration.
But how shall we celebrate? No brass band,
No troops of soldiers ready at hand,
No bright banners, to decorate,
Nearer to here than the White House gate.[112]
Fireworks forbidden—not safe or sane;
Speeches—in Washington—wholly vain.
Lofty verse that shall never die?
But the Muse, like the District, is running dry.
Ten years' toil for the D. H. R.
Justifies more than a mere cigar.
Take this box, and as you puff
Forget your Continental stuff,
And let your mind a moment stray,
To think of your friends who hail this day.
(Now don't you believe that we could slink
Away from the ladies and get that drink?)

To WILLIAM W. ROCKWELL

January 29, 1917.

My dear Mr. Rockwell: [113]

. . . I cordially approve the endeavor which your society has in contemplation, and shall be glad to further it if in any way I can. For instance, if you think that any mention of the matter in the April number of the *American Historical Review* will be helpful, please send me such statement as is ripe, before the first of March. I do not think the plan is visionary at all. A journal or some such publication would surely be useful, and would stimulate many persons to greater productivity and of a better sort. I have welcomed an addition to the *American Historical Review* of other professional journals covering part of the historical field, whenever I saw a prospect of success, and in the field of church history, where the *Catholic Historical Review* is making very creditable progress, I should be delighted to see a good journal produced by the Protestant scholars; still more so if it were produced by both Protestants and Catholics, inasmuch as the *Catholic Historical Review* seems to intend to confine itself to the history of Catholicism in America. The other journals which are in my mind are the *Mississippi Valley Historical Review,* the *Military Historian and Economist,* and the *Journal of Negro History*—meaning to speak only of those historical journals which have more than a state or local range—but I do not know that there is anything in the experience of either of these that would be helpful to you. The first has rather hard

sledding, financially speaking, I imagine. The second and third have guaranty funds that will enable them to continue for a while, but I should not look to see them become self-supporting, though they are good in quality. At the Cincinnati meeting of the American Historical Association, plans were discussed for a journal of Latin-American history, and I think that it will be started and will meet with similar success, to a moderate extent.

Why should not one of your best methods of finding money be, by resort to the more affluent among the theological seminaries? Some of them seem to me to have a great deal of money, in proportion to the students they have to deal with and the work they have to do, and while they may still feel poor, as institutions often do, certainly their endowments are much greater than they were ten or twenty years ago. It seems as if they ought to have some spare money for purposes of church history, yet both the Catholics and the Jews have done a great deal more for *American* church history in the last thirty years than any, if not all, of the Protestant denominations. It ought to be possible to tap them.

I suggest that a search might be made through the catalogues and treasurers' reports of theological schools, and also of a good many other denominational institutions, with a view to locating specialized bequests or other funds, that were intended by the donors to be used for purposes like yours. The older institutions have had a great variety of miscellaneous bequests made to them—like a fund for supplying warm winter under-clothing to the students of one theological seminary that I know of—and it would be strange if you should not find somewhere a fund that might be said to have been designed for just such purposes as yours, or by a lenient interpretation might have some of its income diverted in that direction. Also some publishing funds have been bequeathed or established on terms which would make such use possible.

If you could run across a card-catalogue of rich widows and maiden aunts, it would also be useful. I do not think that any has ever been published, but every theological seminary ought to have one in manuscript. . . .

To J. E. CONNER

May 2, 1917.

My dear Mr. Conner: [114]

Since I last wrote you, I have finished the reading

---

[112] The advocates of suffrage for women were probably parading with banners at the gate of the White House as this was written.

[113] William W. Rockwell was assistant, later associate, professor of church history and librarian in Union Theological Seminary from 1905 to 1942. For six years he was secretary of the American Society of Church History and was the editor of three volumes of *Papers* for that society. On Jan. 17, he had written asking Jameson's opinion of the establishment of a journal devoted to church history.

[114] Jacob Elon Conner (1862-1940), A.B., 1891, Ph.D., 1903, University of Iowa, after several years of teaching, served as United States consul in Saigon and St. Petersburg. He was probably the American consul in the latter city when Golder arrived there in 1914. That year he prepared for the National City Bank a report on Russia. In a letter to Jameson of Apr. 25, 1917, he wrote of having been in Russia "last winter," and of returning there after the war. Jameson had written to the Staten Island Club, New Brighton, to locate him, in order to ask him to review Isaac F. Marcosson's *The rebirth of Russia,* N. Y., John Lane, 1917.

of the volume of Artzibashov, as well as of the Gogol play, a classic which I am very glad to have had, by your kindness, an opportunity to read. I am glad too, to have read the Artzibashov volume.[115] I had never read anything of his. In many ways he is terrible and repellent, but he is powerful and illuminating. I find myself constantly wondering what the effect of material progress will be upon the Russian mind and character. The conception of German mind and character which western Europe and America entertained a hundred years ago, or even sixty years ago, was, in many particulars, not unlike that which we now entertain of the Russians. We see how the acquisition of money, and the taste for it, have transformed the German nation, so that, though the President and most writers, speak of the military class as the mainspring of the present German endeavors, the mainspring seems to me to be rather a combination of a military class and a parvenu plutocracy. I wonder if Russia will develop in the same direction, whether, as it grows richer, it will develop the same sort of taste for money and the material good things of life. Therefore, though it has been interesting to read this powerful sketch of one type of Russian millionaire, one hopes (and presumes) that there are and will be other types.

With regard to the library of which you speak, if the old books are Russian, I think the Library of Congress would be particularly interested, because it has so large and valuable a mass of Russian books in the Yudin Collection, yet that collection is, I believe, not so strong in the earlier Russian publications.[116] If, however, the collection is a general one, I shall have no particular suggestion to make, except that a curious institution called the Annmary Memorial Library, Brown Street, Providence,[117] specializes in incunabula and doubtless would be glad to hear of any possible accessions to its store. A catalogue of all the incunabula in the libraries of the United States is, I believe, in process of compilation by the American Library Association. The different libraries have been sending the titles of what each possesses to Mr. Aksel G. S. Josephson of the John Crerar Library in Chicago, who is to edit the mass.[118] The list has not yet been published but Mr. Josephson may have it in print, or, if you have not a list of these incunabula, by the time you get one, he may have his manual so far advanced that he can tell you what libraries possess this or that among your items. The Carnegie Institution of Washington makes no effort to collect a library.

Now, with respect to "Belligerent Occupation"; [119] I have thought that the best thing to do was to call the attention of Dr. James Brown Scott to the matter, and this I have taken the liberty to do by sending him your letter. I have done this because, as secretary of the Carnegie Endowment for International Peace, which publishes a good deal, and as Director of its Division of International Law, and as editor of the *American Journal of International Law,* he may be able to give some advice more useful than any that occurs to me. I hope that you may hear something useful from him, and that you will not disapprove my having consulted in this manner. . . .

To FRANK A. GOLDER

May 23, 1917.

My dear Golder:

Your letter of April 5 was of very great interest to me, and to various other people to whom I have read it. The events and movements of which you speak have lately been shown by the newspapers to have taken a course that might have been expected, and they are viewed here with the gravest interest. We all hope that no harm will befall you. If that is the case, you certainly have before you a very interesting field and period of observation.[120]

---

[115] Mikhail Petrovich Artzibashov (1878-1927), great grandson of Kosciusko, of mixed Polish and Russian blood. Jameson may have been reading his *Tales of the Revolution,* or possibly his novel *Sanin* published several years before. Though Jameson read little fiction he found time for many of the great Russian novels. On going on vacation in 1889, he wrote: *"Tu. Aug. 13.* I took up four novels. . . . Turgenef's Smoke, Mrs. Ward's Robert Elsmere, Middlemarch, and Anna Karenina. The last is the greatest of them, perhaps the greatest novel I ever read: a terrible thing."

[116] "I was offered last winter in Petrograd a library of old books, said to be as many as three thousand. The earliest dates are along about 1471, '74, etc., and there are several valuable incunabula" (Conner to Jameson, Apr. 25, 1917).

[117] Rush Christopher Hawkins (1831-1920) was a New York law student when he first became interested in incunabula and set out to create a collection representative of all the presses in existence before 1500. The Annmary Brown Memorial Library, named for his wife and dedicated in 1907, houses the collection. It is now one of the special libraries of Brown University.

[118] The second census of fifteenth-century books owned in the United States, Canada, and Mexico, *Incunabula in American Libraries, a Second Census,* edited by Margaret Bingham Stillwell, was published in 1940 by the Bibliographical Society of America, with the assistance of the American Council of Learned Societies. It recorded 11,123 titles (35,232 copies) owned by 332 public and 390 private collections.

[119] Mr. Conner had written that he was eager to return to the subject of his doctoral dissertation, "belligerent occupation," as soon as he was financially able to do so, and asked advice on the subject.

[120] Mr. Golder, after writing of the revolution, continued: "The really serious problems are on now. Before the present temporary government was organized a number of workingmen and soldiers formed themselves into the 'Deputies of the Workingmen and Soldiers,' and they wield a great deal of power, more than appears in the papers. Some of them are capable and patriotic, a few are scoundrels and demagogues and have been proven to be such, but the great majority are ignorant, except for a few radical theories. There are 2000 of them in all. . . . They hinder the real government, they sit in judgment on it, and veto, in a quiet and effective way, its measures. They work on the theory that this revolution has been won by the proletariat and that the government as now constituted is bourgeoisie and therefore it behooves the workmen to be on their guard and keep its eye on the bourgeoisie administration." The letter went on to describe the complete demoralization of the Russian army.

I have taken the liberty to tell Mr. Root [121] that if he finds any occasion to invoke your aid, he will have in you a valuable helper toward understanding the state of mind of various classes in Russia. He was glad to know of the possibility, and I feel sure that you would be glad to help him in any way, and that it would be useful to him in having at his disposal intelligence so clear and so disinterested.

Thank you very much for the sugar card and the other interesting prints, which will be carefully saved against your return.[122]

Washington has been a very interesting place since the opening of war. The Cosmos Club is crowded with members of the *Intelligentsia,* here for the purpose of serving the government or the public during the war, in their several capacities. Here in my offices, and gathered together by me, we had on April 28 and 29, a very interesting conference of a dozen or so representative history-men, to talk over the question what members of our profession could do for government or the public in these times. A great variety of useful avenues presented themselves. We formed a National Board for Historical Service, consisting of Shotwell, of Columbia, as chairman, Hull, of Cornell, as vice-chairman, Leland, as secretary, Victor S. Clark, R. D. W. Connor, of North Carolina, Fish, of Wisconsin, Hazen, of Columbia, Gaillard Hunt, and Turner, of Harvard.[123] This Board is now camped down in my offices where I give them such accommodations as I can, and they are very busily engaged in the preparation of educational material and of articles which can enlighten and strengthen public opinion, disseminated through the public Bureau of Information and various press and educational agencies. I believe that much good will come from the movement, and that many history-men, eager to serve the country, but not seeing precisely how, will by these means find an opportunity to be useful. Unfortunately I myself cannot be a member of the Board. I had attacks of grippe, prolonged through the spring, which have left too little strength to do anything beyond my Carnegie and *Review* jobs, especially as a portion of my staff will be drawn off into the service of this Board or similar war work. Leland, I fancy, will do nothing else for some months than his duties as secretary of the Board. . . .

To FREDERICK J. TURNER

May 24, 1917.

Dear Turner:

I am glad that you are comfortably established in the centre of enlightenment and am sorry that Mrs. Turner and you cannot expect to keep up perfect physical comfort there.[124] I miss you greatly as I walk down in the morning, and shall continue to do so, though tomorrow will be the last time that I shall go up to California Street with Francis. His Commencement Exercises occur at noon tomorrow; thereafter it will be his mother's duty to keep him from injuring any part of the universe in his excessive activities. You are also missed in the adjoining rooms. It may be that many proceedings there need to be viewed with alarm. I do not know, but I take some satisfaction in seeing that one who in Washington is a viewer-with-alarm may in the atmosphere of Cambridge be regarded as a pointer-with-pride.[125]

As I look over your summary of individual opinions and attitudes in your department, it appears that only Channing would be disposed to treat the procession with conspicuous disrespect; most of the others, as is natural, seem to be well-affected toward the notion of doing something for the country, with some misgivings as to how skilful other people may do it.[126] Bryce told me once that when all the judges of England were gathered together to deliberate upon a jubilee address to Queen Victoria, and a draft had been presented, several of the members objected to a sentence beginning "Conscious as we are of our imperfections," etc., on the ground that after all, the judges need not be abject in protestations of unworthiness. Lord Justice Bowen suggested that it might be amended to read "Conscious as we are of each other's imperfections."

Well, even if the whole historical faculty of any one university should disapprove the whole movement "I should worry." Anything can be misunderstood, and in fact, experience tempts me to believe that pretty nearly everything is. If I were a member

[121] Root had recently been appointed ambassador extraordinary to Russia.

[122] "Enclosed you will please find an item of historic interest, a sugar ticket, which entitles the bearer to three pounds of sugar a month. We now have a bread ticket, but not always bread."

[123] James T. Shotwell; Charles H. Hull; Victor S. Clark (1868-1946), who was at this time in charge of the division of economics of the Carnegie Institution; Robert D. W. Connor (1878-1950), secretary of the North Carolina Historical Commission and later archivist of the United States; Charles D. Hazen (1868-1941), who had recently left Smith College for Columbia. The others have already been identified.

[124] Professor and Mrs. Turner had gone to Cambridge, where Turner was shortly to undergo an operation.

[125] In Washington Turner had not been among those most enthusiastic for the plans of the Board for Historical Service.

[126] "The historical 'brethering' are, as usual, not one body but many members, with regard to what history can do for the present service. In general they are apprehensive of the danger of twisting historical truth in the service of any cause (and rightly, of course). They point with alarm to German historians and with less alarm, but some, to the English historical tracts. Haskins is busy finishing his book, but is giving the enterprise expectant treatment; and Coolidge I haven't been able to talk with at length; but I think he will be friendly,—without any illusions of an undue optimism of course. Ferguson is taking hold of summer school plans in a way that will be satisfactory to the Board I know. Merriman in khaki (how do you spell it?) is busy interpreting for the French officers who drill Harvard's reserve officer students, and is a private in the same ranks. . . . Lord I understand is ready to help though I haven't seen him. Sammy Morison is of the opinion that if there is any writing to do I ought to set the example,

of a Board occupied with work so plainly useful, and with colleagues so plainly judicious, I should simply saw wood. As it is, I am painfully sawing wood of another kind, but with a sympathetic eye and ear for whatever goes on in 1133 and 1135.[127] . . .

To FREDERICK J. TURNER

June 13, 1917.

My dear Turner:

I have no great supply of events to chronicle since I last wrote, but there is one thing of which I am sure you will be glad to know. The National Board for Historical Service addressed to me, by arrangement, a long letter explaining its activities and asking that the question be raised whether the Carnegie Institution could aid in meeting the expenses of the Board. The letter presented itemized estimates amounting to $450 a month. When President Woodward had read this letter, I found no difficulty in getting him to meet that expenditure, for the remaining months of the present year, by [a] special additional grant to the department of Historical Research, out of funds which the Executive Committee of the Trustees had authorized him to draw for purposes connected with "war-work" on the part of the Institution. The sum is handed over without any restrictions other than those which ordinarily attend allotments to the Department, and therefore the Board will be able to pay clerical and printing expenses, travelling expenses of the Board and of persons who are called here to assist it, and whatever may be right on account of enhanced living expenses. All which is very gratifying to me, and I presume will be to you.

Hull went away Sunday, but Shotwell came Saturday afternoon. He went away again last night but will be here at the end of the week. I presume you know that the Board has added Guy Ford, Evarts Greene, and Henry Johnson to its number.[128] An excellent publication, which it has helped the Committee on Public Information to prepare, and of which I have seen one advance copy, is an annotated edition of the President's war message of May [April] 2.[129] The annotations, prepared by W. S. Davis of Minnesota,[130] by other men there, and by the Board, explain and illustrate in detail, out of history and international law, the allusions made by the President, specific instances being given, and chapter and verse for the various statements. Shotwell is going to have 15,000 copies of the pamphlet and send it to all teachers on McKinley's list.[131] The editor of the *Century Magazine* has requested the Board to fill 32 pages, in each of his issues from November on, with suitable historical matter having some relation to the war.[132] Hazen is not going to edit the series of little books. They are trying to get A. L. P. Dennis[133] to do it. He was here the other day; has resigned the position of Secretary to the State Council of Defence, finding action too much hampered, especially by the Governor.

Perhaps I have been telling you things which you have already heard from Leland or others. On the other hand, I am speaking of only two or three things, where I am sure you would be glad to know about many; but I do not know many details of their operations, though I see them doing a good many interesting things.

We had a pleasant meeting of the Board of Editors on June 2, all being present. My desire was that it should be mostly occupied with discussion of possible articles which, while strictly historical in character,

---

and there he spiked my guns! But he will help if he is *shown*. Channing is, of course, settled in his conviction that it is futile and superficial to try to apply past precedents to present predicaments. He explained at some length to me that the submarine had so modified the art of war that the naval and military lessons of the Revolution and the Civil War were inapplicable to the World War, and, in general, that there was confusion of thought in the research circular and that he was not on duty next year anyway. R. M. Johnston finds the way of salvation in the *Military Historian and Economist*, which ought not to be impeded in its work. Gay is friendly and I have asked him to 'get into touch' when he goes down in June. His historical learning in its depth and breadth and good judgment (and especially in economic history lines) impress me the more I see of him. He is sane and forceful and I hope you men will get at him. The attitude of the men as a whole I should say is (what is natural to all scholars) the fear that history and *ex parte* propaganda will be mixed" (Turner to Jameson, May 20, 1917).

[127] On May 31, in the weekly letter which Jameson sent to Turner during his convalescence, he wrote: "one of their [the board's] correspondents thought that the thing most needful was that the country should be presented with 'a concrete slogan to stand on'—I suppose like those emplacements for artillery which industrious Germans are said to have constructed in the neighborhood of London, possible also Washington."

[128] Henry Johnson (1867-1953) of Teachers' College, Columbia.

[129] *The war message and the facts behind it,* War Information ser., no. 1, published by the Committee on Public Information, June, 1917. The preface was signed by Guy Stanton Ford, as "director of the division on civic and educational cooperation." For the address as delivered, see Baker, R. S., and W. E. Dodd, *Public papers of Woodrow Wilson* 3: 6-21, N. Y., Harper, 1927. For comment on the reception of the pamphlet, see *post*, Aug. 30, 1917.

[130] William S. Davis (1877-1930) was perhaps as well known a novelist as he was as an historian.

[131] Albert E. McKinley (1870-1936) as editor of the *History Teacher's Magazine*, might be expected to have a list of the teachers of history in the United States.

[132] While the *Century Magazine* in the months which followed published much material relating to the war it does not appear that any of it came from members of the board or through their agency.

[133] A. L. P. Dennis was associate professor of history in the University of Chicago during Jameson's last year there. After resigning his position with the State Council of Defense of Wisconsin he became a captain in the Military Intelligence Division of the General Staff. The governor of Wisconsin was E. L. Philipp.

should have some value with respect to the war, but (you know how such things go) a discussion arose over the character and operations of the National Board for Historical Service which took up a good deal more time than it should have, though I dare say it did good in one way. Cheyney and Emerton [134] wanted to be shown, and they were, and I was glad to learn from Cheyney when he went away, that he was well content, perceived that the proper safeguards were in operation, and believed it was a good project. Contentment of both was mainly brought about by a joint session with the National Board during a part of the afternoon, into which they invited the editors for the purpose of getting suggestions and points of view, as is their custom with other historical people that come along. . . .

To Lord Bryce

June 18, 1917.

My dear Lord Bryce:

After worrying you a little (I fear) in the matter of Mr. Balfour, I ought to have reported earlier as to results. In point of fact there were none. Mr. White seemed not to find the opportunity which I desired, and I did not think it right to press the matter, knowing that Mr. Balfour had his mind and time full of things much more important.[135] Also, I was still not very well during the time that he was here, and found it difficult to do each day the work that must be done, and felt little ambition to reach out after new objects which after all cannot be attained, nor any very serious progress made relative to them, till a good while in the future. I did, however, very much appreciate your interest in the matter, and was pleased to see how gladly you would help if Mr. Balfour had not already left England.

I ought to add that I am now nearly as well as ever. In four days I go to North Edgecomb, Maine, as usual, but with this difference of plan, that I shall make the first two or three weeks a genuine vacation, after which I have no doubt that I shall be able to work at the usual rate, with such portion of my staff as I gather around me up there at our summer office.

In many ways I hate to go away from Washington at present, and probably should not do so if considerations of health did not seem to require it. Washington is a very interesting place now, and there is a great deal for any one to do who is able and disposed to work for the country. Scores of interesting men are here. The Cosmos Club is full of them —academics and journalists and scientific men, engaged in the extra work which the larger government operations call for on the part of men of specialized intelligence. I have been giving what attention I could to the organization of work which historical scholars, as such, can do for the government in wartime, or more especially for the informing of the public, by various means, as to all the historical matters, European and American, which have so large a place in the issues of the war. . . .

The Carnegie Institution has placed the services of its departments at the disposition of the government for anything they can do, and several of my staff are working for this Board [National Board for Historical Service]. One of my best assistants I have transferred entirely to it, and he is acting as Secretary of the Board, with great efficiency.[136] I remind myself a little of Artemas Ward's saying, that he would sooner sacrifice all his first wife's relations than have the Union perish, for I appear to be immolating this man and others on the altar of my country while I go off to Maine; but it is necessary, and there will be a plenty that I can do in the autumn and thereafter, as long as the war shall continue.

The nation is taking hold of the war with an excellent spirit, much beyond most people's expectations indeed. The registration of young men passed off far more smoothly than I could have supposed, indeed almost perfectly; and the great loan has been much oversubscribed. The young men who have enlisted seem to be a fine lot, with quite the right spirit. We see it especially in the officers' training camp at Fort Myer, near Washington, where two young friends of ours are under instruction. Even the small boys are doing their part, as the Boy Scouts of the country, by a house to house visitation, have obtained nearly $10,000,000 of subscriptions to the loan which in most cases would not have been obtained otherwise.

The government departments, though overwhelmed with work, seem to be functioning with efficiency, so far as I can judge. In the twelve years that I have lived here, I have seen a steady rise in the appreciation of specialized intelligence on the part of the executive departments, and this is certainly telling now. I cannot say quite as much for Congress, which along with a good deal of patriotism, is showing a good deal of small politics. However, though the legislative machinery may creak and groan, it

---

[134] Ephraim Emerton, Winn professor of ecclesiastical history in Harvard, a member of the board of editors of the *Review* during 1916 and 1917. In 1918 his place was taken by Charles H. Haskins. The board of the *Review* at the time of this meeting consisted of Carl Becker, Edward P. Cheyney, James H. Robinson, Claude H. Van Tyne, Emerton, and Jameson. Turner had left it at the end of 1916.

[135] Arthur J. Balfour, secretary of State for Foreign Affairs, was head of the British mission which reached Washington on Apr. 21, 1917. Henry White had been for many years a close friend of Balfour. On Apr. 23, Lord Bryce wrote that Jameson's telegram did not reach him until after Balfour had left England and that no letter had arrived explaining the matter about which Jameson wished to communicate with Balfour. The surmise of the editors is that it had to do with Jameson's project for collecting the papers of British ministers.

[136] W. G. Leland.

does slowly grind out, in a fairly satisfactory form, the measures which the administration thinks to be necessary, and anyhow votes money with much liberality.

But I do not know that I am able to tell you, about any of these things, anything that you do not get from the newspapers. I am only a spectator in Washington, and not an inside spectator at that.

The visits of the British, French and Italian missions have been extremely successful, from all that I can judge, and have left everywhere most pleasant impressions. A Belgian mission came yesterday, and is installed in Mr. Larz Anderson's house on Massachusetts Avenue.[137] A young relative who is on the General Staff of our army told me yesterday about many interesting and highly valuable and helpful things which it had derived from its conferences with the military members of the British mission; and by the way, he told me that Henry Stimson, who was Secretary of War when you were here, was occupying the next desk to him at the Army War College, having entered the military service as a Major, and been put to work either in the Intelligence Division or in the service of the Judge Advocate General, I forget which.[138] Mr. Taft has a boy at Fort Myer.[139] The Red Cross is in special activity this week, endeavoring, the country over, to raise a special fund of $100,000,000.

To SAMUEL E. MORISON

June 18, 1917.

My dear Dr. Morison:

I have found myself very much interested in your paper on the struggle over the adoption of the constitution of Massachusetts, in the last serial of the Massachusetts Historical Society [140] and it has carried me back, *magnis componere parva,* to an old paper of mine, which I imagine you have never seen, called "An introduction to the study of the constitutional and political history of the individual states," and published in the fourth [fifth] volume of the *Johns Hopkins Studies in History*.[141] It is a slight performance, and marked,

no doubt, by much youthful foolishness, for I was only 25 at the time, but I think that if you will look at part 3 of it, you may possibly find something there to interest you. Your own search in the materials has been so much more complete than mine, which, conducted at a distance from Boston, was nearly confined to printed material, that I doubt if I came upon anything which has escaped you, yet it is not impossible.

More might well be done in New England to elucidate the history of the revolutionary period, by the combination of materials derived from town meeting records. I have been impressed with the intelligence which the local historical journals of France have added to our knowledge of the history of the French Revolution by showing what went on in this or that department or locality. Forty years ago, we were still obliged to take, as our history of the French Revolution, the narrative of what went on in Paris. In respect to the political history of our own revolution, we are still in a corresponding condition, or almost so, knowing not much of what went on elsewhere than in Boston, New York, Philadelphia, Baltimore, and Charleston. A diligent reader of town histories, could pick out a good deal that illustrates local sentiment and action, but the process is somewhat difficult, and does not cover all towns. In my last year at Providence, 1900-1901, I was planning that the Rhode Island Historical Society, of whose publication committee I had just become chairman, should prepare a volume of extracts from the records of its towns (in that state not twenty in number in 1775-1783), comprising all the votes and other records significant as to the progress of local revolutionary sentiment and action. I went away to Chicago then, and the thing has never been done, and perhaps in states of more numerous townships it would be impracticable. But I am glad to see so very intelligent a study made of local public opinion, on one highly important question, upon which, as I thought in 1885, and as you more conclusively show, the local Massachusetts mind was exercising itself intelligently.[142]

To WALDO G. LELAND

North Edgecomb, Maine,
July 6, 1917.

Dear Leland:
. . . The morning papers, hastily read by headlines,

---

[137] Larz Anderson (1866-1937), who had held diplomatic posts in England, Italy, and Belgium, had resigned as ambassador extraordinary to Japan in 1913. His home was at 2118 Massachusetts Ave.

[138] Henry L. Stimson was with the Judge Advocate General. From December, 1917, until August, 1918, he served with the American Expeditionary Force in France.

[139] Charles P. Taft, who was twenty at the time.

[140] *Proc. Mass. Hist. Soc.* 50: 353-402, May, 1917. Morison's interest had been roused by a paper by Arthur Lord on, Some objections made to the state constitution, 1780, presented to the society at the meeting of Nov. 9, 1916 (*ibid.*, 54-60).

[141] Jameson failed to mention to Morison his early printing of the town records of Amherst. See *ante,* Sept. 5, 1883, n. 70; Apr. 20, 1884, n. 103. In his Diary, Mar. 15, 1883, Jameson expressed the hope of devoting this latter half of his working life to a "magnum opus," the constitutional and political history of the *states* of the Union."

[142] Morison replied on June 21: "1885 was two years before I was born, yet I doubt whether any contribution to the internal history of Massachusetts during the Revolution (save Cushing's *Transactions* in the Columbia Studies, a dreadful book to use) has been made from that day to this. We certainly do need more light on the subject; and I am already trying to egg my best graduate student onto it. . . . How strange it is that with the good start you gave it, the subject of state history during the Revolution has been so neglected."

seem to indicate a determined assault on Creel's bureau by the newspapers, and the hope on their part of having the aid of Congress in breaking down the censorship.[143] Newspaper men are an unscrupulous lot, and I hope that none of my young friends in the flat at 1140 will be corrupted by association with them. To their minds, it is much less important that military movements should succeed than that newspapers carrying prompt descriptions of them should be extensively sold. Obvious as is the need of a more rigid censorship (judging from the experience of every other nation), I do not expect its advantages and merits to have any sort of hearing in the newspapers, who are all banded together, by a common interest, chiefly pecuniary, to argue vehemently on the other side. Therefore I wish you would tell me whatever you can about the man who had the paper respecting the behavior of newspapers in the Civil War. I cannot remember the name (was it Everett Brown?), but I cannot imagine that he was able to sell the piece to any newspaper. I am wondering whether he is someone capable of covering that theme with sufficient completeness and historical ability to make out of it a satisfactory article for the American Historical Review. My impression is that it was a man of hardly sufficient experience for that. If I could get a first-rate article upon that subject I might perhaps be able to put it into our October number.[144] By that time some of the evils of the present "unchartered freedom" may be evident to the public, though the newspapers will continue to lay the blame elsewhere. . . .

To ALEXANDER S. LAPPO-DANILEVSKII

North Edgecomb, Maine,
July 16, 1917.

My dear Mr. Lappo-Danilevskii:

Your letter of May 7 arrived at my office just after I had left it for a vacation. Assistants there sent such documents as they thought might partially meet your requirements. I fear that they will not be very useful. The national government of the United States has done practically nothing in the way of concentrating its ar-

chives. We stand in the lowest stage of evolution in that respect, governmental papers, in almost all cases, still remaining in the departments, and even in the bureaus, in which they originated. Therefore the American literature of the subject is a literature of agitation for an improvement rather than anything from which the archivists of another country could learn of achievements that would interest them. I have for nearly ten years been chairman of a committee of the executive council of the American Historical Association for urging upon Congress the construction in Washington of a proper National Archive Building. We have got so far with the matter that sketch-plans have been prepared by the government's architects, in consultation with representatives of historical and archival interests; but efforts to bring on the next stage, the purchase of a site and the erection of a building, are for the present checked by the war. Nevertheless, the matter is in progress, and success is sure to arrive ultimately; and I suppose that, the longer it is delayed, the more we shall be able to avail ourselves of European experience. Therefore it will be a pleasure to learn, by and by, what steps toward concentration have been taken in Russia.

The only code of suggestions for the printing of manuscripts which we were able to send you (and it was sent in typewritten form because the printed edition is exhausted) was a tentative code prepared ten years ago, and I dare say we should change some things in it if we were issuing it now. I presume that you know of the excellent Dutch and Belgian regulations, the latter prepared by our friend Pirenne of Ghent, now for so long a time a prisoner in Germany.

I cordially agree with your suggestion that, since a truly ecumenical gathering of historians is not to be expected for a long time, it might perhaps be distinctly useful, after the war is over, to call together a preliminary meeting of your organizing committee, from all nations from which delegates would be willing to come, in order to deliberate on the means of organizing such kind of international congress as can be successfully achieved. I should hope that it might not only embrace representatives of the allied nations and of the neutrals, but that it might even be possible, by tactful dealings with a few men of the right kind, to bring about some small representation from Germany or Austria, perhaps some broad minded Slavonic-Austrian who was on good terms with Teutonic and Magyar historians in the dual Monarchy, or possibly even some German of the type of Kehr,[145] who has lived out of Germany so long as to be able to think in international terms. Perhaps, if it seems to your committee at all useful to make such an attempt, it might be facilitated by holding this preliminary meeting in Copenhagen rather than in Petrograd. But perhaps all this is fantastic. I am conscious

---

[143] George Creel, who had been editor of the Kansas City *Independent,* the Denver *Post,* and the *Rocky Mountain News,* was appointed by President Wilson chairman of a Committee on Public Information, on Apr. 14, 1917. This office he held until March, 1919. The New York *Times,* on July 6, carried attacks on the censorship imposed by Creel's committee and on the story of a submarine attack which had been released by that committee. On the 7th the same paper reported the demand of Senator Penrose for an inquiry into this story. The double line of criticism—on censorship and on alleged misrepresentation of the news—continued throughout July.

[144] In January, 1918, the *Review* 23: 303-323, printed, The newspaper problem in its bearing upon military secrecy during the Civil War, by James G. Randall, later biographer of Lincoln, who was "historian" of the U. S. Shipping Board during the war. Everett Brown was attached to the U. S. Food Administration.

[145] Paul Kehr, for many years director of the Historical Institute in Rome.

that it is easier to imagine first steps of reconciliation in a seaside summer resort in America than to bring them about in war-stricken Europe; and I advance these thoughts only as a suggestion of a bare possibility, laid before you with all deference to your better judgment.

At all events, I shall probably be able, if you desire it, to come to any important general meeting that is called. Soon after the conclusion of the war I ought to go to England and I could probably so arrange as to go eastward from there, to Copenhagen or to Petrograd.

There has been genuine and very cordial rejoicing all over America, at the entrance of Russia into the list of self-governing republics. I think you might be much gratified if you could see the extraordinary heartiness with which this sentiment has been exhibited by all sorts of people in America. I hope that the missions which have gone to and fro between the two countries will have done much to promote mutual understanding and helpfulness, and that this is only the beginning of closer and closer relations between these two great nations. It is plainly to be seen that the future of Europe lies very largely in the hands of Russia, but we Americans look upon this without misgiving, not expecting your nation to attempt to play the rôle among the nations which Germany has aspired to play—empire or control or hegemony—but rather trusting in the warm and generous Russian temperament to make your mighty republic the "big brother" of the lesser countries to the westward.

The Russian mission under Mr. Bakhmetiev arrived in Washington a few days before I went away,[146] and took up its abode in a house just around the corner from mine; I saw the R flag displayed on many buildings in our city (indeed I have it, with those of the United States, France, Great Britain, and Belgium, in front of the summer cottage which serves me as a summer office here). Mr. Bakhmetiev has been received with great warmth on his public appearances, and has made a fine impression, greatly to his country's advantage. I hope that you will have seen Mr. Root—the leading trustee of the Carnegie Institution, by the way—a statesman for whom I have very great admiration.

Please present my warm regards to Mr. Golder if you see him. I have had from him several very interesting letters, post-cards, and illustrated papers, and am sure that he has been deeply enjoying both his life in the new Russia and his researches, which I know you have greatly aided. . . .

To Waldo G. Leland

North Edgecomb, Maine,
July 17, 1917.

Dear Leland:

Herewith I am sending some pamphlets which appar-

ently are part of Sir Gilbert Parker's output, and which may be of use to the Board.[147] If you find that none of these do anything more than duplicate what you have already received, let me know. The article from the Round Table entitled "The New German Empire" is an interesting and I should think a valuable attempt along the same lines of which I wrote in a recent letter.[148]

Here is another suggestion for Shotwell, or for any of the Board who have such things in charge. Some magazine might like an article which should examine the comparison between the Germany of 1817 and the Russia of 1917. It might be entitled "The Germany of 1817" and run off into the other matter. My point is, that a hundred years ago, in 1817, or in 1813 when Madame de Staël published her book,[149] we all thought of Germany as a country poor in material possessions and too unworldly to acquire them, but abounding in ideas, in sentiments of humanity, vague but strongly held, and in cosmopolitanism. Most of its great writers had little national patriotism, except, in some cases, between 1813 and 1815, but they had a great audience and influence outside Germany. Germany was indeed regarded in somewhat the same way as late as my boyhood and youth—a land of dreamy idealists, capable of being influenced by unworldly professors, moderate and genial, and not so thoroughly capable of seizing on the good things of this world as the English or the Americans. There is no need to point out the enormous contrast between all this and the Germany of the present day, its scholars, professors, and populace. But is it not true that we look upon the Russians of 1917 much as our grandfathers looked at the Germans? Of course Russian nationality has long existed and is a tremendous spiritual power, and that is a great difference. But otherwise, we have a nation whose public opinion, so far as it has one, is largely characterized by unworldly idealism, by high sentiments of generosity, by mysticism, by enthusiasm for humanity. The great literary lights, at least those of the last generation—Tolstoi, Turgeniev, perhaps also Dostoievski—have been spirits that made, and intended to make, a universal appeal to mankind at large, and succeeded in doing so, Tolstoi's influence upon our age being quite analogous to that of Rousseau upon his.

Now, what is to be the result? Russia will grow richer and more powerful. Whether with German or

[146] The Russian mission landed on the West Coast on June 13, and Boris Bakhmetiev, its head, presented his credentials as ambassador to the United States on July 5.

[147] The novelist, Sir Gilbert Parker (1862-1932), was for two and a half years during the first World War, in charge of British publicity in the United States.

[148] The gist of the unsigned article in the Round Table 7: 253-284, March, 1917, was that Germany aspired to become a great colonial empire, in which everything was to be subordinated to its military and economic needs. The relations which it desired with the rest of the world were not those of friendship but of ascendency.

[149] De l'Allemagne, of which the entire edition was condemned when Madame de Staël attempted to publish it in Paris. The summer of 1813 she spent in England and there the book appeared.

with English and American capital, the industrial revolution will come to her. A hundred years from now she will be, not as now, the greatest aggregation of peasants in the world, but the greatest aggregation of industrial city dwellers. I should be glad, for my peace of mind when I come to get out of this mundane coil, if somebody could prove to me that such material development will not give the Russians the same taste for money and material power with which the Germans are now so cursed. I can see some reasons to hope that the parallel will not run the same way, but I think it is not without its interest, and not merely a matter of speculation. In part, these are matters of fact—of fact unknown to me, but on which some man's opinions would be valuable, if you could connect the magazine editor with the right man. Surely the subject is not unimportant. If the course turns one way, the Muscovite Peril, about which the Germans talked so loudly in July 1914, is a great reality, far more formidable to the future of the world than even the German military power of these days; if it turns the other way, Russia becomes simply the "big brother" of the rest of Europe, and mankind and civilization have a chance.

I have a notion that I said something along these lines to Shotwell one day, as he sat amiably beside by bedside in 1137; and anyhow, no editor may think it worth pursuing. But I send it along for what it is worth.

To CHARLES A. SELDEN

North Edgecomb, Maine,
July 28, 1917.

My dear Selden : [150]

I do not remember your course in history to have been marked by any such easy-going negligence as you profess. I fancy that you attended to the work closely enough, but it was some time ago, and it was only to be expected that most of the teaching, even if it had been much more impressive than it was, and most of the accompanying reading should have evaporated by this time. In any case, there is plenty of time still. I expect myself to learn a good deal more history before I die, and I have no doubt that you will do so if you wish to, busy though you are. For instance, you are no doubt making a good many railroad journies [sic], what with the Times office and Washington and the peach farm, and I suppose not all of them at night? As you must be by this time familiar with all the billboards between New York and Washington, even where they run continuously, as from New York to Philadelphia, you have little further need to gaze at the scenery. When one is relieved of that necessity, a railroad journey offers fine opportunities for historical reading.

The main trouble with most people who take up a "course of historical reading" for themselves is that, in order to pursue a complete system that covers the whole ground, they begin with Egypt or Babylonia, or perhaps with the Fall of the Roman Empire, and never get anywhere near to 1917 A.D. With the practical objects in view for which you are reading, the most essential thing is to read about the history of the European states since 1815 (Germany especially) and about certain portions of the history of the United States, especially our diplomatic history and the history of the Civil War.

On the European side, I should first read Europe since 1815, by Professor Charles D. Hazen of Columbia University; the History of Europe since 1814, by Professor Seignobos of Paris (translated) ; and the Political and Social History of Modern Europe, by Carlton J. H. Hayes,[151] another Columbia professor, omitting in the case of the last book the periods before 1815, if you choose to do so. Here are three books covering much the same ground, and you may find it to be a needless duplication of effort to read all three; yet I have generally found that such a practice drives the knowledge in better than to go over the ground but once, and leaves a more solid foundation for subsequent additional reading in special portions of nineteenth and twentieth-century history to which you wish to give more particular attention. Another good book along these same lines, and a little more recent, therefore coming more closely down to the present year, is The Economic Development of Modern Europe, by Professor F. A. Ogg of the University of Wisconsin.

On the diplomatic history of the United States, perhaps I should suggest reading American Diplomacy, by Professor Carl Fish of the University of Wisconsin (Brown 1901), a book with some defects but giving a very intelligent view of the whole matter. On the history of the Civil War, we have had ten times as much matter printed about the battles and campaigns as we have had about the half-civil, half-military arrangements about which we should now be so glad to obtain information for use in present-day thinking. But much that is valuable on these questions, and all that one could desire in the way of solid and judicious treatment of the political history of those days, can be found in those volumes of James Ford Rhodes's History of the United States since 1850 that relate to the Civil War period.

I do not know whether this is the sort of suggestion that will be most useful to you. I have thought that such books as these might well stand first; but if, or when, you wish indications of profitable reading in more special lines than these, I shall always be glad to

[150] Charles A. Selden (1871-1949), A.B., Brown, 1893, was at this time traveling correspondent for the New York Times Magazine; the next year he became Paris correspondent of the Times and reported the signing of the Treaty of Versailles. For an account of his work, see New York Times, Feb. 10, 1949, p. 27.

[151] Hazen, C. D., Europe since 1815, N. Y., Holt, 1910; Seignobos, Charles, Political History of Europe since 1814, N. Y., Holt, 1899; The two volumes by Hayes (N. Y., Macmillan) appeared in 1916; Ogg's work, mentioned below, (Macmillan) had just appeared; Fish, Carl Russell, American Diplomacy, N. Y., Holt, was published in 1915.

be drawn upon, and we shall have many opportunities to talk about such things in Washington, to which I hope your visits will continue to be frequent.

To ALEXANDER S. LAPPO-DANILEVSKII

North Edgecomb, Maine,
August 3, 1917.

My dear Professor Lappo-Danilevskii:

I suppose that the mails are fairly regular now, and that you will have received my letter of July 16. I will however say, by way of precaution, that I fully approved your notion that, after the war shall have ended, it would be well to have a preliminary meeting of the international committee to consider what sort of congress may be possible; and I added that I could probably come to any such meeting if it were desired that I should do so, venturing however to suggest that possibly, if it were not too grossly inconvenient to the Russian members of the committee, it might facilitate attendance of other members if this preliminary gathering should be held in some such place as Copenhagen.

May I proceed to lay before you some thoughts as to an additional reason for desiring that such a preliminary meeting should be held? Interesting as these international congresses of historians have been, and valuable as it has been to bring such men into mutual acquaintance, it may well be felt that these congresses might have done more to promote the progress of historical science than merely to provide an opportunity for the reading of various papers and for social intercourse. Might they not, one is inclined to ask, have brought about some concrete steps of progress, some definite achievements of an international character? I think especially of achievements or works which would aid the historical writers of many or several countries, yet because of the attendant expense or the need of varied co-operation are not likely to be undertaken by the historians or the government of any one nation. I mean, such enterprises as in the field of history may occupy some such position as among the classical philologians, would be occupied by the great *Thesaurus Linguae Latinae.*

The difficulty of utilizing international congresses for the undertaking of such international tasks is that, if they are proposed at the beginning of such a congress, the few days of its sessions do not offer enough time for due consideration of the project in committee, or for the bringing of it into such a shape that it can be laid before the congress before its adjournment; and if projects are simply proposed at one congress and then left to be matured and presented in a final shape to the next congress, years of intervening time are wasted. Now if a variety of worthy projects of the class which I have indicated are presented to an international committee meeting in preliminary conference, it may be quite possible for them to receive some consideration at that time, to be then referred to committees for presentation at the large international gathering, and, when that gathering takes place, to be quite ready for presentation to the general body of representatives of the historical profession and of the various governments, academies, and institutions that send delegates.

It is even possible that the sense of having a common work to do, international enterprises under way, might do something more to bring the historians of warring countries once more into friendly relations, than if there were prospects of nothing else than the reading of isolated papers. There are few international historical enterprises of which we should feel that they could be done just as well without German co-operation, for instance; but Europeans are much better able to judge than we Americans as to the possibility of such co-operation or the expediency of efforts to bring it about.

If you think well of the notion that the preliminary conference should exercise such a probouleutic function, it might be advisable that the formal summons to that conference should carry with it an invitation to those who are members of it to send or bring suggestions of all such international tasks or enterprises as they have thought of, that they may be considered in advance, referred to committees if thought desirable, and laid before the large gathering in a matured form.

I will mention, by way of example, three or four undertakings that have occurred to me:

1. There is Father Conrad Eubel's *Hierarchia Catholica Medii Aevi,* of which the three volumes already published run to 1600. We Americans would be very glad, and I should think all students of European history would be glad, to have this speedily carried down from 1600 to 1918. I do not know Father Eubel, and I know nothing of the financial situation of this undertaking, though I could find out from friends in Rome. It is however obviously expensive, and likely to be produced slowly, so that, if tactful inquiries should show that international co-operation, or pecuniary aid from various nations, would advance the work speedily to completion without diminution of its scholarly excellences, this might be one of the things that an international historical congress might seriously consider, and certainly it has, for western Europe, and for America, an ecumenical character, though its interest for Russians might not be great.

2. Another desideratum, perhaps still more important, and certainly of a sort which would appeal to any international historical congress, is that of a similarly executed list of the ambassadors and ministers sent by the various European governments to each other, from the time when the permanent main-

tenance of embassies and legations began down to the present time—provided with references in proof of the various facts and dates, such as Father Eubel gives in his work or such as Professor Sir Charles Firth has given in his pamphlets listing the diplomatic representatives of Great Britain in various countries, and of various countries in Great Britain.[152]

3. I have no recent information respecting the progress or status of Madam Bang's valuable collection of materials for the history of the commerce of the Baltic, derived from the records of the Sound Dues.[153] This enterprise is surely one that deserves to be sustained and to be brought to its completion. I know that it receives aid from the Carlsborg Foundation, but I know that Professor Dietrich Schaefer[154] has also felt obliged to seek contributions elsewhere, and has obtained them from various countries. The total amount was apparently sufficient for immediate purposes at the time when he last sent me any statement respecting the matter (a statement now in Washington, but which I remember fairly). It seems quite possible that the war may have dried up or diminished the sources of contribution to this enterprise. If so, the means for its continuance might well be taken into general consideration.

4. Perhaps, too, a good deal might be said in favor of some large historical publication of documents respecting events in which European nations have co-operated. The work of co-operation upon such a documentary collection might have salutary effects, drawing minds toward the things that unite instead of toward things that divide. If we could have such a collection of documentary materials from all the archives of Europe on the Congress of Berlin, illuminating all aspects of it from the point of view of the different chanceries, it would certainly furnish a better basis than we now have for the history of the whole era which that congress opened. Some foreign archives might be reluctant to publish some of their documents of so late a date as 1878, but the representatives of the different countries might be able to exert sufficient influence after getting home to overcome this. It would be a fine thing if we

could have all the movements and phenomena of that congress as well documented before us as those of the Congress of Vienna now are,[155] or as those of Dutch history from 1795 on have been illuminated by the searches which Dr. Colenbrander has made in so many different diplomatic archives.[156]

These are merely illustrations. They may or may not be recommendable examples of their class. My thought was merely to lay before you the general notion of such a line of activity on the part of a preliminary conference, and the general question whether it were profitable to attempt in some such way to ensure that the next International Historical Congress should have some results of a more permanent character than any of its predecessors.

To ANDREW C. McLAUGHLIN

North Edgecomb, Maine,
August 30, 1917.

Dear McLaughlin:

I am sorry that you cannot be with us at Branford,[157] but have no difficulty in feeling the chain of reasoning which has led you to the contrary conclusion. "Among those present," as indicated up to the present time, will be C. M. Andrews, G. B. Adams, G. L. Burr, A. I. Andrews, J. W. Black, H. D. Foster, Allen Johnson, your friend W. R. Shepherd,[158] and your friend who signs this letter. I think it will be pleasant.

My brother from Branford was with me yesterday and we went down to Christmas Cove, where I thought fondly of you, remembering your visit and

---

[152] Firth's four pamphlets, *Notes on the diplomatic relations of England and France, 1603-1688* and *1689-1763; Notes on the diplomatic relations of England and Germany, 1689-1727;* and *Notes on the diplomatic relations of England with the north of Europe,* appeared between 1906 and 1913, Oxford, Blackwell.

[153] Bang, Nina Ellinger (1866-1928), *Tabeller over skibsfart og varatransport gennem resund, 1497-1660,* Leipzig, Otto Harrassowitz, 1906. A subsequent volume, which carried part of the data to 1783, was prepared by Madam Bang but was not published until 1930.

[154] Dietrich Schäfer (1846?-1929), professor in Jena, Breslau, Heidelberg, and Berlin. His chief interest was the history of the Hanseatic League. At the time of the International Congress of Historical Sciences in Berlin in 1908 he was responsible for much of the planning of the program and was corresponding with Jameson about it.

[155] The reference is to such volumes as: *Acten des Wiener Congresses in den jahren 1814 und 1815,* 8v, 1815-1819; *Congrès de Vienne: recueil de pièces officielles relatives à cette assemblée des déclarations qu'elles a publiées des protocoles de ses délibérations, et des principaux mémoires qui lui ont été présentés; le tout rangé par ordre chronologique,* 6v., 1816-1818; *Acte du Congrès de Vienne du 9 juin 1815 avec ses annexes, 1815; Recueil des traités et conventions entre la France et les Puissances Alliées en 1814 et 1815,* 1815.

[156] Colenbrander, H. T., *Gedenkstukken des algemeene geschiedenis van Nederland van 1795 tot 1840,* 10v., 's Gravenhage, Nijhoff, 1905-1922.

[157] From this year until his death Dr. Jameson sponsored an annual meeting of professors of history living or vacationing in New England. They gathered for an informal week in a quiet hotel at Branford, Conn., on Long Island Sound. This he called the *convivium historicum,* after the analogy of the *convivium theologicum* which Lord Falkland used to hold at Great Tew, "though I do not entertain or sustain the brethren as he did," he wrote to Professor Seth. "I am merely the convener, to use a British word" (Jameson to James Seth, Oct. 13, 1922).

[158] Arthur I. Andrews, A.B., Brown, 1901, professor of history and international law in Tufts College; James W. Black, professor of history in Colby College, a student of Jameson in the Johns Hopkins; Herbert D. Foster, professor of history in Dartmouth College. The others have already appeared in these letters. C. M. Andrews, Adams, and Johnson were in Yale; Shepherd in Columbia.

the generous conduct of Captain Julius Gamage in the matter of the collar button. Cap'n. Julius and Cap'n. Albion and Cap'n. Llewellyn (*sc.* Gamage) are all well. I visited my friend H. N. Gardiner of Smith (Amherst '78), the Griffins,[159] and in the evening, at Boothbay Harbor, had an hour with W. S. Davis of Minnesota. Allen Johnson is the only other history man in this region, and he is 12 miles below here and I have seen him but twice this summer, so that it will doubtless do me good to gather at the *Schützenfest* of historians next month. From September 18 to 25 I shall probably be at 27 Franklin street, Woburn, working in Boston and Cambridge libraries on a book which I am doing on the side for the National Society of the Colonial Dames of America, viz., *Colonial Privateering and Piracy: Illustrative Documents,* drawn from a wide variety of sources and annotated with the gifted editor's usual felicity—felicity in the original sense of personal enjoyment. Before the end of the month I shall be in Washington.

All the family are well. Yes, I am not sorry that Francis is too young to go to war. As to the Germans, I shall try to make him take moderate views of them ultimately, but that is not his present inclination. With his young companions, he pursues them over the tented fields of Davis Island and, so far as I can judge, keeps them on the run more continuously than his elders in Europe are able to do.

Individually I am all right now. I was sorry and ashamed to go away from Washington while so many excellent historical persons were toiling there in the vineyard of the Lord throughout the heat of the Washington summer, but the only thing for me to do was to come up here, do no mental work for two or three weeks, then a little for two more, then try to carry on my own job. I am not succeeding very well in the latter, but at all events, I can do nothing extra at present. After the first of October I think I can be useful, especially as so many of the N. B. for H. S. will necessarily be absent. Leland has carried a heavy burden through the summer; others could come and go, but for a long time the secretary had to be continuously on the job. Of late however he has had a vacation. I judge that the Board has succeeded very well in some things, not so well in others; in short, as I believe we predicted when it was organized, it has had a development considerably different from what was planned, larger in some directions, lesser in others, but always useful.

You probably saw the newspaper reports from Chautauqua of Latané's bitter criticisms of the pamphlet called "The President's War Message and the Facts Behind It."[160] Since some aid from the Board was acknowledged in a preface (no more than that, and indeed there *was* no more than that), and since I spoke well of the Board in the July number of the Review, he chose to send me lately a "Communication" to be printed in the next number—about seven typewritten pages in length, criticising the pamphlet, and assailing the Board with spiteful contempt, every sentence as mean as he could make it, and hitting at as many people as possible. If you do not see it in the next number, you will readily be able to attribute it to my iniquitous wish to conceal the enormities of various persons who have passed five-dollar bills to me to bring this about. Why did nobody have the intelligence to put him on the Board!

But enow of this; turn we to happier themes. It is a beautiful day, and there are forty letters to write. . . .

To HUGH GIBSON

October 8, 1917.

My dear Mr. Gibson:[161]

Professor Frank Golder, of whom we spoke this morning, is a man about 35 years of age and a professor of history in Washington State College at Pullman, Washington. He has the degree of Doctor of Philosophy, in history, from either Harvard or Chicago, at both of which universities he pursued graduate work in history. His special line of interest at that time was the history of exploration in the northern Pacific and of eastern Siberia and Alaska. This led him to acquire an excellent knowledge of Russian. Indeed, I believe he was born in Russia, though his father and grandfather were not Russian subjects. The fruit of these earlier studies was a book of much value and importance, entitled *Russian Expansion on the Pacific, 1641-1851,* published at Cleveland in 1914.

At the beginning of that year he went to Russia on behalf of the Department of Historical Research in the Carnegie Institution of Washington, to prepare a *Guide to Materials for American History in Russian Archives,* which we published in 1917. The materials for American history in Russian archives relate chiefly to the history of our northwest coast and Alaska, on the one hand, and on the other hand, to the history of diplomatic relations between the United States and Russia. The latter topic occupies two-thirds of the book, and led Mr.

---

[159] A. P. C. Griffin, chief assistant librarian, Library of Congress, and his family.

[160] The pamphlet prepared by Creel's bureau, described in the letter of June 13. For Latané's criticism, see New York *Times,* July 4, 1917, p. 2. At a meeting of the National

Security League at Chautauqua he had said: "Here is a book so full of errors in fact and inference that it is an insult to the intelligence of the American people. It is garbled as badly as the German publications which we have condemned." At the same meeting Professor Hart also commented: "It is a poor job."

[161] Hugh Gibson, who had a long and varied diplomatic career, had been recalled from the embassy in London, where he had gone from the Belgian legation in 1916, to the Department of State, in February, 1917. During the summer of 1917 he had been assigned to the Belgian war mission while it was in this country.

Golder into a minute study of those diplomatic relations. His permissions at that time extended to the year 1854, in the archives of the Ministry of Foreign Affairs, but later permissions have permitted him to pursue the same topic down to times much more recent.[162]

Dr. Golder was in Petrograd and Moscow, chiefly the former, from February to November, 1914, coming back to Washington by way of Siberia and bringing with him as I can testify, a rich store of observations on Russian affairs during the first months of the war. Last January he went to Petrograd again, this time not so much for the Carnegie Institution of Washington as for the American Geographical Society, for which he was to prepare a scientific edition of the journals of Vitus Bering, to be published in commemoration of the bi-centennial of Bering's earlier voyages. The result was that he was in Petrograd through the times of revolution, indeed from February until September. Interesting himself very deeply in what went on, he spent quite as much effort upon informing himself as to political events and social movements as upon his archival researches, and his collections, which have lately passed through my hands on their way to him at Pullman, have embraced a large mass of books, pamphlets, newspapers, and clippings, relating to the events of the past eight months. He is now reducing them to order, with a view to writing.

Deeply impressed with the interest and the enormous importance of what is going on in Russia, Dr. Golder writes me that he would be delighted if in any way he could be of service to our government in respect to matters in that country, or in any other way. I think, as I said this morning, that in respect to certain matters he might be exceedingly useful. He speaks and writes Russian with facility, has a very exceptional familiarity with the history of the diplomatic relations between the two countries, and has had excellent opportunities of observation during several of the earlier and several of the most recent months of the war. But what I should emphasize most, is, that he is an observer of extraordinary intelligence, insight, and good judgment, and that, being a man of catholic sympathies, he has put himself in contact with a quite unusual variety of persons in Russia, so that he is exceptionally able to estimate the opinions and tendencies of different classes there. He is a kind, considerate, sympathetic person, who enters into the minds of all sorts of people and to whom they talk with freedom. He is very likeable and made many friends in Russia. I should also wish to put on record that Mr. Golder is a man of the highest integrity, incapable of any but correct conduct, loyal, trustworthy, and entirely unselfish. Not only is he without a trace of self-seeking, but he is exceptionally indifferent to money matters. Yet, in response to your question, I am obliged to say that I do not suppose he

has such means of his own as would enable him to go to Russia again, immediately, at his own expense. If, on the other hand, the Government finds no possibility or need of sending him to Europe, perhaps there are ways in which his knowledge of recent conditions and his store of notes and printed materials might be made useful.

If there are any matters which I have not covered by this memorandum, I shall be happy to reply to questions.

To Kenneth S. Latourette

October 18, 1917.

My dear Sir:[163]

Picking over some papers in an old desk of my great-grandfather's I found the following note, in the handwriting of his daughter, my great-aunt. The verses, she says, were written as her mother repeated them to her, years before the time of her memorandum, which is apparently of about 1860. The verses are headed with the words:

"Composed and sung when the *Grand Turk* sailed from Salem."

'Twas on the eleventh of March, boys,
    And Sunday was the day,
King Derby, he gave orders
    That she should sail away.

To bear off for the India shores,
    Calcutta was our design,
And we had very good fun my boys
    As we crossed over the line.

And when we got to India, boys,
    And we got safe on shore

We will drink unto our officers
    And all our brave crew,
For a set of better fellows
    Before you never knew.

I thought this old relic of past times might possibly interest you, even though the metre halts, by the omission, I fancy, of two or four lines at the point indicated. The memorandum adds that Captain Ben Hodges of Salem was the first captain of the *Grand Turk,* built by Enos Briggs; that the first mate was Captain Mosley, the second mate, Stephen Phillips, both of Salem, while the crew was of Marblehead. One of them was engaged to my great-grandmother. I don't believe, however, that these details really refer to the first voyage of the *Grand*

---

[162] Carnegie Institution, publication no. 239. A brief addition to this, containing the later material, was published as v. 2, in 1937.

[163] Kenneth S. Latourette, who had been a teacher of history in College of Yale in China, 1910-1912, was at this time professor of history in Denison University, Granville, Ohio, and later became professor of church history in Yale University. His *Early relations between the United States and China (1787-1844),* New Haven, Yale Univ. Press, appeared in 1917.

Turk, which apparently began in November, 1784. The 11th of March fell on Sunday in 1786.[164]

To LORD BRYCE

October 31, 1917.

My dear Lord Bryce:

It is long since I have written to you, but I have not been able to feel that I had anything important to tell you, on which you would not have much better information, and have thought that probably your public duties left you little time to read mere letters of friendship from me, warm as my feeling toward you has always been. Perhaps I have been wrong in this. I do not wish to be like our old friend Simon Newcomb, who at a wedding party was asked if he had spoken to the bride. "No," said he, "I have not perceived that I had any facts to communicate to her."

But at all events, your kindness in sending me a copy of your presidential address, about "The Next Thirty Years," and the thoughts that have occurred to you on the work immediately awaiting the students of the human sciences, ought to lead me to write again now, even if only to say how much pleasure and profit I have derived from that address.[165] You have suggested many things about which I shall continue to think. One part of the address, indeed, your remarks about catalogues of manuscripts, immediately suggested to me a piece of work that I think would be distinctly useful to students of American history, and with which I can profitably use up a bit of an appropriation that was in danger of remaining unexhausted; namely, I think I will get a competent man to draw off systematically from all the printed catalogues of manuscripts, in European libraries (excepting those of London, Oxford, Cambridge, Paris, and Rome, already done) all the items they contain respecting manuscripts having bearing on American history.[166] In the case of the five libraries I have named, agents of this department have already made full notes from personal inspection of the manuscripts, and in four of the five cases these notes have been published. But in addition to these five libraries whose manuscript sections are so abundant in American materials, there are many others which contain some manuscripts of the sort. These libraires are too numerous and too widely scattered for us to make personal examination of their contents, and of those of other, uncatalogued libraries, for a long time to come. It has seemed a more rational course to devote our earlier years to the exploiting of national archives, where the large masses of American material are. But meantime the mere compilation of data from the numerous printed catalogues of the manuscript sections of European libraries, can be done in a short time and will be useful in revealing a good many materials that workers, especially in small libraries where catalogues of foreign collections are not largely kept, might highly value.

What you say on page 17 of the sending out of observers to make surveys of existing conditions in undeveloped countries, makes me think that you would be interested in hearing of one such survey of which I have lately heard a good deal. One of our multi-millionaires who is at the head of a great American organization operating in Mexico, has set aside the sum of $100,000 for a scientific survey of that country in its present economic, social, and political aspects, to be carried out within a year or so by a group of capable men, mostly youngish, of good academic training. They are to have all expenses and receive whatever salaries they are receiving in their present positions, and after much interviewing of Americans who know about Mexico, and of Mexicans, and examination of conditions on the spot, to compile a report which it is hoped will be a readable book for American business men and perhaps for the larger public. The donor seems to be disinterested, at all events makes no conditions or restrictions as to findings, and if his group of men are good, as I know some of them are, useful results may be obtained toward the purpose which he has in mind, which is to inform our people as to real conditions and needs in Mexico.[167]

---

[164] This was the first voyage of the second *Grand Turk* owned by Elias Hasket Derby, 1791-1795. The mate on this voyage, Joseph Moseley, was the captain on the next voyage. Peabody, Robert E., *The Log of the Grand Turks,* Boston, Houghton Mifflin, 1926.

[165] Bryce's address as president of the British Academy was delivered on July 19, 1917, and was published in its *Proceedings* **8**: 1-31.

[166] Compiled by David M. Matteson. This appeared as *List of manuscripts concerning American history preserved in European libraries and noted in their published catalogues and similar printed lists,* Carnegie Institution, publication no. 359, 1925.

[167] A reference to the Doheny Foundation, founded by Edward L. Doheny (1856-1933), who had opened some of the rich petroleum fields of Mexico.

In his reply Bryce expressed great interest in the Mexican inquiry and Jameson in his next letter wrote: "As to the Mexican inquiry, I expect good results, but not the very best. The man who has the matter in charge has selected his investigators a little hastily, so that some of them are not first-rate, and does not pursue, I hear, a steady policy with respect to directing them. They have all gone from here now, but one of them will be here again soon, so that I can learn more; but in any case, I am sure that he and his companions will value in the highest degree Mr. Maudslay's answers to questions propounded by you." Bryce had proposed that he send a list of questions which had occurred to him while he was in Mexico and that he ask the archaeologist Maudslay for suggestions, thinking that these might help to guide the investigation (Bryce to Jameson, Nov. 21, 1917; Jameson to Bryce, Dec. 19, 1917; Stock, L. F. ed., Some Bryce-Jameson correspondence, *Amer. Hist. Rev.* **50**: 268, 269, Jan., 1945).

Jameson's informant may have been Walter F. McCaleb, a graduate student in the University of Chicago while Jameson taught there. He was the author of two volumes published under the auspices of the Doheny Foundation: *Present and past banking in Mexico* and *The public finances of Mexico,* N. Y.,

Your foot-note on page 18, about forms of the Norwegian language, brings to mind what I was told thirty years ago, by a young Minnesota Norwegian who was one of my companions at the Johns Hopkins University.[168] He said that nearly all the people of his township in Minnesota had come from one valley in Norway, and that late comers from that valley told him, on visiting the village, that they were preserving old dialectic forms which in the valley itself had become extinct by reason of the constant influence of the Danish newspapers from Copenhagen and Christiana—the same fossilizing of colonial dialect that is so familiar in the case of Canadian French, South African Dutch, and in a way, the English of Ireland and America. Perhaps also Sicilian Doric, though I speak with bated breath about anything Greek in these days, finding that what I remember from forty years ago is mostly deemed wrong by the experts of the present day.

Our friend Miliukov[169] whose extrusion from the Russian administration has been very grievous to me, told me in the days when we were together in Chicago, that the last old man who spoke Old Croatian had died some twenty years before on one of the outlying Dalmatian islands, but not before a German savant had gone out with a phonograph and taken record of his speech. The last old man—generally it is an old woman, like Dolly Trelease; I remember an amusing passage in one of Gildersleeve's lectures, in which, after speaking of the monument to her on the Cornish coast, he made feeling allusion to the memorial that might yet be erected to "the last old woman, trousered or untrousered, who in America should know anything of Greek."[170]

I do not write of public affairs, for I do not perceive that I know anything about them that is not in all the newspapers, and several Britons here are probably telling you about what goes on in Washington, though they will hardly be aware how strange the

place is with the changes which war has made. Numberless men of special talents and acquirements have come here from all parts of the country to give scientific and other expert assistance to the government. Rents have risen, apartments are impossible to obtain, and so, almost, is luncheon at the Cosmos Club, where the regular members have been "doing their bit" by giving some sort of space and hospitality to many outsiders, and hardly trying to get anything there themselves.

I will, however, venture to tell you of the work of the National Board for Historical Service, which some of us organized last spring, and which has such quarters as I can offer it in my offices here. Or rather, as this letter is already too long, I will send with it a few printed pages that will show the purposes for which the Board was founded, and some of the things it has been doing. I think it has well justified its existence. It is possible that you have seen these pages already in the *American Historical Review*,[171] but I cannot think of you, indeed of anyone else, in wartimes, as a "constant reader" of that humble academic periodical. I do endeavor, however, that it shall in each number have some articles that are helpful toward an understanding of the war, from an historical point of view, such as young Carlton Hayes's article in the last issue, on "The History of German Socialism Reconsidered,"[172] which seemed to me rather good. In the January number I shall be printing an interesting contribution just received from M. Serge Goriainov, formerly archivist of the Ministry of Foreign Affairs in Petrograd, entitled (in the French from which I shall translate it) "La Fin [de] l'Alliance des Empereurs,"[173] exhibiting Russo-German relations from 1883, and especially from 1887 to 1890, on the basis of the documents in his archives, which it seems are now open to inspection by scholars to a surprisingly late date, much beyond anything suggested on page 10 of your address. By the way, a clerk of about 21 in our State Department, once advised his superiors against allowing me to print certain documents of 1799, relating to Toussaint l'Ouverture, on the ground that they reflected upon the conduct of a power with which the United States was now in the most friendly relations—to wit, reflected upon the conduct of one Napoleon Bonaparte, concerning whom I was able to represent to the chief clerk that the worst was now known. . . .

Harper, 1920, 1921. Chester Lloyd Jones, in his preface to *Mexico and its reconstruction*, N. Y., Appleton, 1921, expressed thanks to Edward L. Doheny, "whose establishment of the Doheny Foundation made available valuable source materials relating to Mexican-American relations." The disclosures of the corrupt relations between government officials and the Doheny oil interests in the early twenties probably brought the work of the foundation to an end.

[168] Thorstein Veblen, who entered the Johns Hopkins University the same fall that Jameson did but left it for Yale in a few months. The acquaintance which began at that time was never dropped though communication between the two was infrequent.

[169] Paul Miliukov, professor in the University of Moscow, member of the Duma, 1907-1917, and minister of Foreign Affairs in the provisional government of 1917, escaped to London on the fall of that government, and later settled in Paris, where he wrote on Russian affairs. In the autumn of 1904, Jameson had brought him to Chicago to give twenty lectures.

[170] The monument, in the parish church of Paul, is to Dolly Pentreath, who died in 1777, the last person who spoke Cornish as her mother tongue.

[171] An account of the organization of the board appeared in the *Review* 22: 918-919, July, 1917. Subsequent numbers carried brief statements of its work, *ibid.*, 23: 228, 447, 713, Oct., 1917, Jan., July, 1918. A substantial history of the Board, by Leland, was printed in the *Annual Report* of the American Historical Association for 1919, 1.

[172] *Ibid.*, 62-101, Oct., 1917.

[173] *Ibid.*, 324-349, Jan., 1918.

To ANDREW C. MCLAUGHLIN
                                November 24, 1917.
My dear McLaughlin:

Thank you very much for your excellent and most illuminating article.[174] All through the war I have felt that people did not lay enough stress upon the economic aspects of the argument against the German action in commencing the war. "Super-abundant population requiring additional territory"—and yet a higher wealth *per capita* in the home country than ever before. "Necessity for expansion of German trade"—so you go to work and smash to pieces a trade of $600,000,000 per annum with England, in order to increase a trade of $60,000,000 with your colonies. But, more broadly, the German contention rests upon assumptions in political economy as outworn as those which underlay the endeavors of the confederates, namely the assumption that a nation's economic progress is made only at the expense of another nation, whereas I supposed we all knew that one of the chief elements in any nation's economic progress is the successful progress of its neighbor. But I shall presently get out of my depth. I got my degree at the Johns Hopkins in 1882 with political economy as a minor, got it on very easy terms in that particular, a very minor minor, and then closed the book, and read no more therein, like Paolo and Francesca.

Anyhow, your articles are awfully good and I hope they will have a wide circulation and influence. Why couldn't Ford have them for his war information series? May I ask him? . . .

To JACQUES PIRENNE
                                    March 12, 1918.
My dear Sir: [175]

Your letter of February 21 reached me yesterday, and affected me deeply. All the historical world values your father, and I value him especially on the grounds of personal friendship. I sincerely hope that, in spite of photographs, which are often deceptive, and in spite of anything he has said which may cause you disquieting anxieties, it may after all appear that he has kept up his health as little impaired as is possible under such cruel trials, and his wonderful courage quite unaffected. Nevertheless, we historical men in America shall wish to do all that we can in the line of your suggestions. A hundred of us made a strong effort a year-and-a-half ago through our State Department, to secure the release of M. Pirenne and M. Fredericq from the German government, on condition of their coming to

America, where good lectureships for a year were promised them at two of our universities, but we could not produce any effect upon Herr v. Jagow.[176] We are very ready to do anything we can, under the changed circumstances of the present year, and I hope that we shall be able to accomplish something. I went this morning to the Department of Justice to make inquiries respecting the procedure which you suggested. It did not appear that any exchanging of civilians is at present going on between the American and German governments. It does not seem to be certain that there is any German civilian interned in the United States whom the German government would think it very important to obtain and I fear our Department of State, through which action would ultimately have to be taken, would hold that it was its duty to confine any work of exchange upon which it may embark, to the exchanging of American citizens against German. However, the case of Belgium is always regarded with special interest and feeling, and I will see what can be done.

Though I am not personally known to Madame Pirenne, I should be glad if you would be so kind as to express to her my most cordial sympathy and my high regard.

With abundant sympathy for yourself and with every wish to do anything I can for your father.

To JAMES SETH
                                    March 26, 1918.
My dear Seth:

I have just given my friend McLaughlin a letter of introduction to you, and the needful explanations precipitate a letter which I have owed you a shameful length of time. Please forgive me for this last, but I have been desperately busy. I came back to Washington from Maine, in September, perfectly restored in health, never felt better in my life, but have been rather overworking since then, because it has seemed impossible to me, as to so many others in Washington, not to do whatever extra work one could in times of such pressure. I cannot pretend to have done much toward winning the war, but you will perhaps be interested in the line of work I have been mainly attempting. I think I told you in a former letter something about our National Board for Historical Service. My chief piece of work in connection with it has been to organize and get into operation a series of simple historical lectures on the background and origins of the war and what it is about, perhaps especially the recent European history leading up to it, to be given to the boys in as many as possible of the thirty-two great training-camps. On the whole, they seem to be succeeding very well, and I hope they have done something to make these youths fight better and to make them more adequate citizens of the world afterward.

---

[174] Probably, The Great War: from spectator to participant, *History Teacher's Magazine* 7: 183-187. This article, somewhat revised, was printed by the Committee on Public Information as War Information ser. no. 4.

[175] Jacques Pirenne, son of Henri Pirenne, had written from his army station in Somme, France, a moving letter to Dr. Jameson, urging him to appeal to President Wilson to arrange for an exchange of prisoners which should include his father.

[176] Gottlieb von Jagow was German foreign secretary at the outbreak of the war.

Some months ago there came to me a request from a teacher in the University of London, to find some first-rate American historical scholar, who could go over there and lecture to audiences of London teachers on American institutions, Anglo-American relations, and the relations of United States to the war and to the allies. From this beginning, the scheme has broadened out into something larger, so that now my friend McLaughlin, whom we picked out as the best man, has been set free by the University of Chicago, to go to Great Britain and give a course of lectures at the University of London, and individual lectures to various other bodies, including the universities of Oxford, Cambridge, Birmingham, Manchester, Edinburgh, Glasgow, Dublin, and I think, Belfast; and because he is coming to Edinburgh, I have given him a letter of introduction to you and one to Hume Brown.[177]

I feel sure that you will like McLaughlin. He is one of the finest characters I know, simple, honest, faithful to every duty, public-spirited, kind-hearted, and one of the most likeable of men. He is a son-in-law of President Angell and for a good number of years was professor of history in the University of Michigan. Then he was here in Washington two years, starting this department to which I came in 1905; and then, preferring the work of teaching, succeeded me in charge of the historical department at the University of Chicago. He has been president of the American Historical Association, and has published good things, mostly in the earlier portion of American constitutional history. I hope that his lectures will have great success, and will do much to make the American point of view more completely understood in Great Britain. To us he seems well adapted to accomplish this.

As you will easily imagine from the name, Andrew Cunningham McLaughlin, he is of Scottish extraction; his father came from Peebleshire and his mother from Edinburgh. He tells me that when he was in Edinburgh in 1894, he found a cousin named Miss Margaret Stewart, then dwelling in Thirlestane Road. As I suppose that his stay in Edinburgh will have to be brief, maybe you can find an opportunity to locate this cousin, probably now an elderly woman, unless, indeed, the commonness of the name makes identification difficult. At all events, I feel sure that you will be kind to McLaughlin for his own sake and for mine.

How I wish I could come with him, and see you once more. It seems a long time since that last International Historical Congress. When we adjourned, it was to meet again at St. Petersburg, in April, 1918, on invitation from the Czar. How remote such resolutions now seem. Black days these are in which I

write, but there is general confidence that the British line will not ultimately be broken.[178]

To Homer C. Hockett

April 25, 1918.

My dear Mr. Hockett: [179]

You will think I have been very slow to respond respecting your *Study of Western Influences on Political Parties;* but it is very difficult, and has been peculiarly difficult this winter, for me to find the time to read anything else than the many things which I am positively obliged to read in pursuance of my regular duties. Lately I have had the pleasure of reading much, if not most, of your book, and thank you for the opportunity. It is a good subject, worked out with great intelligence and industry and with good sound thought behind it. If I were to make any suggestion, it would be this: Now that you have so well won your spurs as a monograph writer, by this and preceding similar writings, I would aim hereafter somewhat more at the position of a historian, by paying more attention to skill and felicity in writing. I would, so to speak, get out of the sphere of the doctoral dissertation with its peculiar conventions, and into that of the historian. I think our younger generation hardly realizes how conventional a form has been given to American historical monographs by the habit of the doctoral dissertation. It is a convention that there must always be a bibliography, that every statement must be supported by elaborate footnotes, full of quotations—and other forms that really arise from an academic requirement, intended in order that the young men may easily be brought to book, may realize the responsibility of producing something that shall be shot-proof. I see reviewers sometimes finding fault with books for not containing all these things, though in reality threefourths of what is put into these bibliographies are entirely useless, except for the young writer's proving that he has not neglected his job.

Now the world at large thinks nothing of these conventions, and when one has got one's degree and printed one's thesis, he does well to cut loose from a good many of them. That is to say, if he wishes to take rank as an historian, he must take a wider view. Mr. Henry Adams never thought that he ought to print a bibliography in his great *History,* and he introduced no footnote references but what were strictly necessary, knowing that the general reader would assume that he

---

[177] P. Hume Brown (1849-1918), professor of history, University of Edinburgh; author of *History of Scotland,* 3v., Cambridge, Cambridge Univ. Press, 1902-1909.

[178] It may be remembered that on Mar. 21 the Germans had attacked along a fifty-mile front driving back both British and French forces. At this time Marshal Foch was made commander-in-chief and General Pershing placed the American forces at his disposal. The German successes continued until the early days of April.

[179] Homer C. Hockett, professor of American history in Ohio State University. The work here referred to was published as no. 4 in the Ohio State University series, Contributions in History and Political Science.

had performed the ordinary duties of research (though never likely to know how conscientiously he had performed them), and that the expert would thank him only for those references intended to substantiate statements differing from those to be found in the preceding narratives of the period.

I take Mr. Adams for my instance, as being much the best writer among all the American historians of our time. I do not say that his practice about footnotes is the only one to follow. But I do say that if one wishes to take high rank as a historian, he had better give himself a good long course in close and attentive reading of histories that have high qualities of style, till he develops that sense of form which is so greatly lacking among our writers of monographs, and is incapable of making, as most of them do, sentences so lacking in smoothness that to read them aloud is uncomfortable, sentences that, in Milton's phrase, would have made Quintilian stare and gasp.[180]

I did not intend to write so much, and perhaps I owe you an apology for offering advice not asked for. But you, I know, are one of those who "mean business," mean to attain distinction in our profession, so I hope to be excused. Meanwhile I thank you very much for the pleasure and instruction I have had from the book.

To HERBERT C. BELL

May 1, 1918.

My dear Mr. Bell:[181]

I ought long before this to have written, in some sort of response, to your very kind letter, but, aside from many occupations, have felt as if one had very little to write from this office that was interesting, in comparison with the interesting things that are going on around you and before your eyes. If I write now, it is not because the situation has changed in that respect, but because I hope to get another interesting letter from you.

I judge that the situation of public affairs in Washington is improving. Discontent in Congress with the proceedings of the Administration on the part of most of the Republicans, and a certain number of the Democrats, continues, but I believe has diminished. The Administration seems to have made great endeavors at improvement in those particulars in respect to which criticism has been most active, and to which perhaps the President had hitherto given insufficient attention, and many things are being done much better than they were. The Third Liberty Loan is progressing finely. Men who have been travelling through the country, making speeches, report a good spirit everywhere, especially in the Middle West. Slowly, slowly, this immense mass of somewhat inert public opinion is taking solid shape into something that ought to be ultimately irresistible.

I wish I had more news that I am sure would be interesting to you personally, about our historical fraternity. Mr. Henry Adams died on March 27. Colby, of Montreal,[182] was the last history man to drop in here. He looked very well, and is busy with important matters. Wrong of Toronto,[183] has been commissioned by the Canadian government to take general charge of Canadian propaganda of a proper and very desirable sort, in the United States, and will be here within a few days. I shall certainly wish, and so will the other history men here, to help this forward in every way. It has seemed to me lamentable that our people know so little of what is going on in Canada. The newspapers should do much more. Exchange of professors between these two countries would be particularly desirable. Our National Board for Historical Service, on account of which several excellent history men are here all the time, one after another, will do all it can to push the matter forward this present summer by lectures and addresses and the like in summer schools and sessions and institutes. We have more in common with Canada in this present struggle than with any other nation, and our people ought to be made to feel it.

The Board has been doing a lot of interesting things, and I think valuable ones, but you, from last summer's residence in Washington, know in general the type of thing. You will also have heard of the establishment of a historical section of the General Staff, and no doubt will hear more about it shortly from Professor, now Major, R. M. Johnston.

My own job in the work of the Board this last winter was to organize and keep going a set of lectures, from Y. M. C. A. hut to Y. M. C. A. hut, in each of the great training camps, on the historical background and origins of the war. The historical teachers who engaged in it went to the work with avidity, enjoyed it immensely, and report an excellent spirit among the men and a real desire to know more of modern European history. In the colleges too, everyone says that, in spite of the diminution in the number of students, the number of those electing history courses is as great, or greater, than ever, and relatively much larger than hitherto.

Please write to me when you can. I suppose you are likely to be in France throughout the remainder

---

[180] From Milton's On the detraction which followed upon my writing certain treatises.

[181] Herbert C. Bell, professor of history in Bowdoin College, from 1912 to 1926, except for a brief period of military service during the first World War. He was now lieutenant, General Headquarters, Intelligence, A. E. F., France.

[182] Charles W. Colby, professor in McGill University, 1893-1910, twice declined a position in Chicago University during Jameson's service there. Later he left academic life to enter business.

[183] George M. Wrong (1860-1948), professor of modern history in the University of Toronto and a voluminous writer on Canadian history.

of the war. But at any time that you see a prospect of coming back to this country, please let me know as much in advance as you can. I should wish to have a talk with you if possible and I do not lose from sight the undertakings of which we have talked hitherto.[184] After the war it will be more than ever incumbent upon the United States to come forward with means for promoting historical and other research. . . .

To ROBERT S. WOODWARD

May 24, 1918.

My dear President Woodward:

In accordance with your kind permission, I proceed to write out the outline of the plan of which I spoke to you this morning, first thanking you cordially for your sympathetic reception of it.

I start from the premise that after this war is over all European countries will be so impoverished that they cannot possibly spend as much money as heretofore on governmental and other undertakings in the field of science and learning, must retrench in these lines of expenditure, and must endeavor to think carefully as to how to get the utmost possible good out of what money they do spend in such ways. On the other hand, in any probable event of the war the United States will emerge from it less damaged in a pecuniary sense than any other of the belligerent nations, and will of course be far richer than any of the neutrals. I am eager to see our country appreciate and assume the responsibilities which will arise from such a state of things, to see it step forward into the breach, do all it can to repair the ravages which war will have inflicted on scientific and learned work, bear its proper share, which means a far larger share than it has borne hitherto, in preserving and advancing civilization along all those many lines in which civilization depends upon works of research. We have often satisfied our national conscience in these respects with the statement that we are a new country, from which the finest things in science and learning ought not yet to be expected. It is time that we dropped the excuse. Even if, in a good many lines of scientific and learned endeavor, we may even now be far from able, until considerable modifications have taken place in our social system, to supply the workers who shall make good, in quantity and quality, the fearful personal losses which the war has inflicted

upon the world of scholarship in Europe, we are easily able, if we choose, to make good the pecuniary losses the war will have inflicted in that domain, and it is our bounden duty, our duty to the cause of civilization, to go forward with energy and generosity in that field.

In short, when this sorely damaged world faces the problems of reconstruction, closes up the depleted ranks, and sets out, with a pathetic courage which is already evident, to make a new world, I should like to see the United States take the primacy, so far as it can, in all the works of science and learning, but anyhow should like to see it take at once the primacy in financial support of those works, and, first of all in, so to speak, financing their reorganization.

Almost every science will wear a new aspect when the war is over, I, of course, have special occasion to see this in the field of the historical and social sciences. In social and political respects, we shall emerge into a new and strange world, with a new set of problems. It is perfectly plain already that the historical workers in the United States look at their science in new ways, seeing it in a different perspective, and expecting to work at it by different methods, and I judge that the same is true of the workers in political economy and in political and social science, and presumably in all the humanistic studies. In several of the physical sciences, besides the motives to a new orientation which arise from the changed condition of the world at large, there is an additional motive toward reconsideration, in the striking advance which the sciences have made during and because of the years of warfare. To these considerations should be added the strong impulse toward scientific economy which the impoverished governments must feel, and which should force them to think, more carefully than ever before, what works of science and learning it is most profitable and important for them to support with the diminished resources which it will seem possible for them hereafter to devote to tasks of this nature.

In short, there will be a peculiar need, at the close of the war, to take account of stock, to think out a programme, to consider what should be done next in these fields of science and learning, what lines of work will now seem most important and most profitable to mankind, and to consider these things in an ecumenical and international spirit, as scientific citizens of the world. Many persons will be thinking of these things, doubtless many are already thinking about them more or less. But is it not true that, with so large a problem of reconstruction before the world, with so great an extent of new territory to be surveyed, the best results, even for the individual nations, will come from an international consultation, from some organized international effort to map out the tasks and orient the different forces which can assail them?

---

[184] Professor Bell had agreed to examine the records of the British West Indies for the Department of Historical Research. In June, 1919, released from the service, he listed the West Indian portion of the Colonial Office Papers to 1775; in March, 1920, the Bermuda records; and in 1921 he was again at work for the department in London. To his material some additions were made by Luis M. Pérez and David W. Parker, and the volume appeared as *Guide to British West Indian archive materials, in London and in the Islands, for the history of the United States*, Carnegie Institution, publication no. 372, 1926.

Yet it will be hard for the Europeans, with minds and money engrossed in a thousand tasks that must be immediately taken up, to resolve upon and to organize an international congress for such purposes. Such meetings, in the past, have ordinarily required an invitation from a particular government and a large expenditure on its part, for entertainments and the like; and though much of this expenditure would be inappropriate to a consultation held under the post bellum conditions, governments do not like to be shabby, and will feel that they have all that they can do to look after their own. My suggestion is, that no one can so fitly assume the initiative for such a meeting and take upon itself the main expenditures as the Americans. I should like to see them reach out the hand in this way, and I believe that it would be accepted by the Europeans not merely as a generous and fitting act of the richest of nations, but also as appropriate to our character as an enterprising and forward-looking people with a certain gift for organization.

But what I should like best of all to see, is that this initiative toward fruitful consideration of the future of science and learning in the new world should come from the Carnegie Institution of Washington. For my part, I see no other American source from which it could so fitly come. The National Academy of Sciences would not represent the wide range of *human* studies that is in a peculiar degree called upon for new plans of research, and also it has not the money. A moderate expenditure, such as would not seem like ostentatious, offensive "treating" of our European colleagues, but such as would relieve them of any but those personal expenditures which they or their governments would prefer to carry, would be easily within the means of our Institution. I had thought of Paris, but had felt that it might be uncomfortable to ask the French government to permit the Americans to entertain an international congress in the French capital. Then I had thought of the possibility of using, as being American property, some of those large constructions, cities almost, which our War Department has erected on French soil, and which might for a period after the war be available. To invite such a congress to meet in Washington would, under the circumstances, involve offers of travelling expenses that would put the European colleagues in an uncomfortable position, and even so, we could not expect so complete a representation of the best minds as we could get at some European place. Your suggestion of the Hague and of Mr. Carnegie's Palace of Peace solves all the difficulties most admirably, I should think. If three or four representatives of each branch of science and learning, so chosen that all countries would be represented—Germany and Austria included, if Germans and Austrians would come—could meet at the Hague with thirty or so Americans, to consider what lines of re-

search were most deserving of national and international support, what problems called most loudly for immediate attack and solution, what improvements in international co-operation could be devised—and if the congress were confined to these practical deliberations, without any of the usual reading of papers and exposition of results, the profit to the world of science and learning and to the world at large might be enormous. The value of scientific research to contemporary society would be signally emphasized in the public mind. Incidentally, if the thing were brought about by the method of which I have spoken, it would help to put the Carnegie Institution of Washington in the position which it is entitled to hold in the learned world.

The American representatives could be chosen by the Carnegie Institution through the aid of the professional societies of specialists, such as the American Chemical Society or the American Philological Association. The Europeans to be invited would naturally be selected through consultation of the respective governments, or perhaps through the machinery of the Association Internationale des Académies, if that machinery still exists. But these and all similar details could be easily worked out. My only present object is to set forth the general motion, for any use that you may choose to make of it.[185]

---

[185] Again and again Jameson reverted to some aspect of the general theme of this letter. On Nov. 20, 1918, he wrote to President Woodward: "Some time ago Professor Thorstein Veblen told me that he was preparing to publish a book on the higher education in the United States which he had written before the war. I urged him to take account in it of the new situation in which the United States would be put at the end of the war in respect to the sustainment of learned and scientific researches and laid before him much the same thoughts in that regard that I have at times expressed to you. . . . Lately I received from him for criticism, some pages of text which he had resolved to include in his book on account of my representations. He has, with his usual cleverness, expressed the thing much better than I could and therefore I send his pages to you herewith. . . . The remedy or devices which he suggests for meeting the situation is distinctly . . . his own. . . . But whatever method may be best for achieving profitable results I feel no doubt of the main doctrine of Mr. Veblen's memorandum, nor of the cogency and intelligence with which he has stated it."

The work to which Jameson referred was Veblen's *The higher learning in America*, N. Y., B. W. Huebsch, 1918, of which pages 48-58 were those prompted by Jameson's suggestions. The section begins: "The progress and the further promise of the war hold in prospect new and untried responsibilities, as well as an unexampled opportunity. . . . The fortunes of war promise to leave the American men of learning in a strategic position, in the position of a strategic reserve, of a force to be held in readiness, equipped, and organized to meet the emergency that so arises, and to retrieve so much as may be of those assets of scholarly equipment and personnel that make the substantial code of Western civilization" (52). His proposal is for a great central university where teachers and students of all nationalities may meet as guests of the American people.

Later Jameson took advantage of an application being made to the Carnegie Corporation by Professor F. J. Teggart and

To Elizabeth Donnan

Boston, Mass.,
July 12, 1918.

My dear Miss Donnan:

. . . I have heard almost nothing from returned Americans about the feeling in England with respect to us, but such letters as I have had from Englishmen have been exceptionally friendly in 1917 and 1918. I am quite prepared to suppose that that not very unselfish nation likes us much better now that it has great need of us than it did in 1896, when I was first in England, just after Mr. Cleveland, with an impoliteness which shocked many sensibilities in Boston, indicated to them that they might well stop bullying Venezuela. However, as you know, I admire the best of the English very much, and have felt that the government of England by gentlemen in the period now ended, has, with whatever faults of overbearing conduct and the like, reflected great glory on the nation and been of priceless benefit to the world. I must say that, as rulers of other people, they greatly shine in comparison with all others, not excepting the French and perhaps even the Dutch, both of whom I like better. . . .

To Leo F. Stock

27 Franklin Street
Woburn, Massachusetts,
July 21, 1918.

My dear Stock:

. . . Thank you for your card from the Pennsylvania mining region. Miss Pierce, who arrived Friday afternoon, went through Gettysburg in her automobile trip northward, and through much else of Pennsylvania and New York. She is looking very well. Where do you suppose that I am dictating to her? A

highly historic spot. The libraries which I am using in Boston being closed on Sunday, and I indeed under the necessity of using them every hour that I can on week days, we have trolleyed out to Concord and are seated by the "rude bridge that arched the flood," precisely where "the embattled farmer stood and fired the shot heard round the world." A beautiful scene it is, and not so much changed but that my great great grandfather, who heard from Woburn the sound of the guns and came over to take part in the battle, would recognize the place if he should awake from the repose in which he has been engaged for the last eighty years. . . .

To George B. Adams

North Edgecomb, Maine.
August 15, 1918.

My dear Adams:

I was delighted to receive the beautiful post card showing Bell Island, which I remember well, and in the foreground the lord of the manor in the attitude of one who is monarch of all he surveys and possesses sake and soke, and infangthief and outfangthief. Long may his private jurisdiction continue.

There used to be a post card of the summer office of the D. of H. R. in the C. I. of W., but I can not find one now, and thought it depicts with great fidelity the "red cottage" which is our office, it gives no idea of the heavenly beauty of the scene on which I look as I write to you, or chase the fugacious misprint through the proof sheets of the *Review*. The sky is equal to anything you ever saw in Arizona or California, the Sheepscott River equally blue, and across the cove I see on Palatinus the white porch of my home, with indications that it is so nearly dinner time that I must stop and go over there.[186] . . .

To Albert S. Burleson

North Edgecomb, Maine.
August 27, 1918.

My dear Sir: [187]

It happens that a communication addressed "American Historical Association, Washington, D. C.," which association has desk room in the office of this department of the Carnegie Institution of Washington, has been forwarded to me, and, though it really was not intended for me, I must ask leave to call your attention to what it discloses. It consists of two blanks filled out by a member of a national draft board in the West, giving in the form of a question-

the Association of University Professors to reiterate the need for organized planning and intelligent expenditure after the war: "journeyman tasks of a preparatory character, the providing of the instrumentalities of research, the making accessible of materials, bibliographical work and the like. In these things American wealth and American organizing ability may well perform a shining service." To this President Woodward replied May 23, 1919, that he was familiar with Professor Teggart's plans, that the trustees of the Carnegie Corporation were little disposed to take up post-war problems with the war not yet over, and that he thought them quite right. In this letter he remarked that the Corporation would be forced by the requests which came to it to change its policy (as the Carnegie Institution had been) from that of a receptive disbursing agency to that of a directive and constructive agency.

Jameson's reference is to a committee appointed by the American Association of University Professors in the autumn of 1918, on Apparatus for Productive Scholarship. Professor Teggart made for it a preliminary report on Dec. 28, 1918. The "apparatus" included (*a*) current bibliographies for humanistic subjects; (*b*) annual reports on the progress of studies in these subjects; (*c*) manuals on the subjects in the program. The project never passed beyond the planning stage. *Amer. Assn. Univ. Profs. Bulletin* 4: 8; 5: 35-39, Oct., 1918, March, 1919.

[186] The "red cottage" stood on the bank of the Sheepscott River, directly across from the old farm house on Davis Island in which the Jamesons lived during many summers. It was possible by means of signals to communicate between the two buildings.
[187] Albert Sidney Burleson (1863-1937), postmaster general, 1913-1921.

naire a variety of biographical data respecting him. One of these blanks is headed "The National Army Section of '*America Organized for Victory.*' Published under the auspices of the American Historical Association, Washington, D. C." The other is headed "Biographical Blank for Members of the National Draft Boards," and bears at the foot the request, "Blank when filled out to be sent to the American Historical Association, 1417 You Street, N. W., Washington, D. C."

I submit that this is a bare-faced fraud upon a deserving section of the public. It is plain from the text that the promoters of the enterprise are advertising their intention to bring out a "great biographical work" giving these data respecting their victims, accompanied by portraits (a photograph is enclosed in the reply), and that they are trying to give it authority by falsely pretending that their enterprise is fathered by the American Historical Association. That is an organization of between twenty-five hundred and three thousand members, including every important historian in the country, and enjoying high repute, so that the pretense which is made is, from the advertising point of view, well worth making. Yet that society would never think of engaging in the work of preparing biographical compilations of this county-history variety, "made to sell." It is a distinct injury to the society that such proceedings should go on, and, as promoters of this type seldom live up to their promises, the undertaking is sure to entail upon the genuine American Historical Association a great amount of complaint, trouble, correspondence, and discredit.

Moreover, the American Historical Association is a governmental establishment. It was incorporated by act of Congress of January 4, 1888, and the terms of that act provide for its affiliation with the Smithsonian Institution, and for the printing of its reports, submitted through the secretary of that institution, by the Government Printing Office. The purpose of Congress in instituting a society charged with "the interests of American history and of history in America," and intended to act as the government's official organization in historical matters, is defeated if its title can be used by unknown and irresponsible persons to gather in money from unsuspecting citizens who are devoting themselves to the service of the government in the present crisis.

I understand from a member of my staff in Washington who has communicated with these people over the telephone, that they talk plausibly about making some change of title "when the present stock of printed blanks is exhausted." It would, however, be very extraordinary if a fraudulent organization could continue its fraud indefinitely by merely taking the precaution to print beforehand a sufficient number of deceptive blanks. I beg leave to request very urgently that a fraud order be issued which will forbid these persons to use the United States mails for their dishonest enterprise.

My own position is simply that of one who has been a member of the American Historical Association since the day of its foundation, thirty-four years ago, who is an ex-president of the society, and as such a member of the executive council.[188]

To ANDREW C. McLAUGHLIN

October 30, 1918.

Dear McLaughlin:

Thank you very much for the photograph, I am delighted with it. I wanted to have it for the wall of my particular sanctum and there it shall be placed as soon as it can be framed. It will be the ikon or tutelary divinity of the department. It has, for such a position, a very appropriate appearance of looking thoughtfully into the future, as if to say, "I wonder whether this Department which I have begotten is really going to amount to anything?" Thereby, as it will be so placed as to look toward me, it will stir me up to make good, as indeed the example of your laborious two years here has always done.

Well, after all, the way in which I shall most value it is as the picture of a very dear friend. It does show the man; I call it very successful indeed.

Harper and I had a lot of fun over the Bolshevik documents.[189] It was a mighty interesting seminary exercise for us. He has, I understood, told you something about it. Between you and me, the *Evening Post's* treatment of the matter was highly discreditable.[190] Mr. Creel put the thing to us in an admirable spirit. The stuff no doubt ought to have been better edited before it appeared in the newspapers but the pamphlet edition over which Harding[191] is toiling at present, will be greatly improved,

---

[188] Frauds attempted under the name of the American Historical Association or the American Historical Society were by no means uncommon. In November of this same year Richard W. Hale called Jameson's attention to a fraudulent group operating in Rhode Island, and Jameson wrote of one which was attempting to gain subscriptions to illustrated biographies said to be published by the American Historical Association (Hale to Jameson, Nov. 23; Jameson to Hale, Nov. 26, 1918).

[189] The "Sisson papers," so called because they were brought to this country from Russia by Edgar G. Sisson, purported to prove that the Bolsheviki were pro-German and that their leaders were in the pay of the German government.

[190] On the appearance in print of the first group of Sisson documents the *Evening Post,* in a series of editorials, questioned their authenticity (*Post,* Oct. 15, 16, 17, 1918). When the report of the committee was published the criticism of the *Nation* was savage. Harper was declared to be unfit to serve because he had already committed himself. "The report calls for stern rebuke from every American historical scholar who values the good name of his profession" (*Nation,* Nov. 23, 1918).

[191] Samuel B. Harding (1866-1927), teacher of history, Indiana University, 1895-1918; editor with the Committee on Public Information, Washington, 1917-1919; after that, connected with the University of Minnesota.

as nearly all right as can be in view of a need of haste which has unexpectedly arisen. In view of that need of haste, Creel has seen a draft of our report, and Ford reports him as being much pleased with it, which is very good of him, as in certain parts it is a good deal of a Scottish verdict.

I had not thought of serving on such a committee. We made it up, naturally, of Coolidge (a member of the Board) [192] and Harper and Golder or Lord. But we could not get any of them except Harper (though Coolidge gave useful aid), so had to make it up in a hurry of Harper and me—I fulfilling that useful function, which some one on every committee should fulfil of representing vulgar ignorance.

Ford summons me to the next room to give my valuable opinion on one more of the innumerable points the thing raises, so I must close.

Please give my very kind regards to Mrs. Mc-Laughlin. Katrina is near Constance and Esther I believe.[193] During the epidemic she joined with others in assisting the neighboring farmers, and got $2.00 a day. She knows no more of farming than I do about Russian but she makes more by it. . . .

To DAVID W. PARKER

October 31, 1918.

My dear Parker: [194]

Your letter of June 6, received at North Edgecomb was very much enjoyed, and all who were there appreciated your kind thought of us as I did. It is a bloomin shyme that I have been so slow to answer, but in September I was moving about a great deal and when toward the end of the month I arrived in Washington I had a thousand things to do, partially at the office and partially at the house, where my young Francis and I attempted to set up housekeeping and keep things going without Mrs. Jameson's presence. Later she arrived but she is not at all well, and therefore, I have some additional duties,

also the war makes a good many. My own part in the operations of the National Board for Historical Service is not a large one; but with Leland and Stock entirely given over to its work and others partially so, I, as a sort of residuary legatee have to keep the old department going as well as I can.

I cannot rival your pastoral scenes of warfare,[195] and indeed ought to be rather ashamed to mention military operations to one who is engaging in them when I am not; and as to my reflections upon the high politics of the war, concerning which one staying in Washington ought to have great knowledge, what I should say would be of no real value, because I do not see enough politicians from day to day to learn much that is actual, and also it might lead to the confiscation of the whole letter by the censor.

Keeping down on my own low level I will tell you the recent developments in respect to the National Archive Building. We really seem to have a prospect of a progress this winter, due particularly to pressure on the official mind of the great masses of new papers being made by new bureaus and boards connected with the war. Armies of female children of 18, 19 and 20 have been imported by these boards to cover these papers with typewritten matter, supposed to be of value, but the question where they shall be preserved (the papers, not the children) immediately arises with pressing insistence. The official mind can see the importance of check-stubs relating to the war when it can not see the value of similar documents of 1818. I had brought along the legislation to the point where the purchase of a site and the erection of a building were authorized. The Librarian of Congress has now taken hold of the matter and brought it along a further stage. The site has been decided upon, diagonally southwestward from the big building of the Post Office Department, and agents of the Treasury are securing options upon the property, Meanwhile the plans drawn provisionally three years ago are being adapted to the site now chosen. They are very good plans and I should not be surprised if we had the finest National Archive Building in the world. But in the present state of the building trades, and under the present prices, no more than the essentials will be erected, without the stone facings, or what little severe ornament is contemplated, and without the full provision of work rooms.

The process which the Librarian followed will in-

---

[192] Archibald Coolidge had visited Russia as a special agent for the State Department in 1918.

[193] Katrina Jameson and McLaughlin's two daughters here mentioned were in Smith College, Northampton, Mass.

[194] David W. Parker (d. 1948), at this time a gunner in the 3rd Canadian division of the British Expeditionary Forces located in France, has been named in preceding notes as an assistant in several of the projects of the Department. A Canadian, a graduate of McGill University, he was at times an official of the Dominion Archives. For several years he was connected with the Department of Historical Research of the Carnegie Institution and for it he prepared the *Calendar of papers in Washington archives relating to the Territories of the United States (to 1873)*; and the *Guide to the materials for United States history in Canadian archives*; and with Herbert Bell and others, *Guide to British West Indian archive materials*, Carnegie Institution, publications nos. 148, 172, 372, 1911, 1913, 1926. He also did much work upon Leland's *Guide to materials for American history in the libraries and archives of Paris* **1, 2**, Carnegie Institution, publication no. 392, 1932, 1943.

[195] Parker had written on June 6, 1918: "I can survey a landscape of pleasant green, variegated with the warm tones of tiled dwellings. Magpies flit across the fields chattering as they go, and from the surface of a twisting brook swallows skim the water flies. My fingers itch for a camera as I watch the chiaroscuro of trees, hedge, and meadow dotted with blossoms, while above a sky at the same time brilliant and soft in its coloring is dotted with fleecy clouds. It is a very quiet time, not an aeroplane is in sight, and only an occasional boom from the distance or the staccato note of a machine gun is heard from 'up there.'"

terest you. Dr. Gaillard Hunt, Chief of the Division of Manuscripts in the Library of Congress, was borrowed by the Department of State as soon as the war opened, to help the work of the office which he used to occupy, the Bureau of Citizenship (and Passports). Fitzpatrick has been taking his place.[196] Now, Dr. Putnam has appointed Mr. Charles Moore Acting Chief of the Division of Manuscripts. Moore is an able and experienced man of affairs, skillful in dealing with senators and politicians, a Detroit man, now treasurer of the American Historical Association, who 15 or 20 years ago was secretary of the Senate Committee on Public Buildings and Grounds, and particularly of the Park Commission that made the new plans for the city of Washington. He is at present chairman of the Fine Arts Commission. Dr. Putnam appointed him acting Chief of the Division of Manuscripts with a special view to building it up on the side of war materials, in which it was notably deficient, but likewise with an eye to the collecting and preservation of the records of the mushroom boards and thereby to the securing of an archive building. Moore has been advancing all these matters very successfully, I judge.

I was much interested in what you wrote concerning Public Archives at Ottawa. I had a letter from Doughty two or three days ago sending me a copy of a very interesting little book by Graham Botha of Cape Town, "A Brief Guide to the Various Classes of Documents in the Cape Archives for the Period 1652–1806."

I have not seen Professor Colby for a long time but Professor Wrong was here early in June, and in the summer did some very useful propaganda work of a highly laudable sort by lecturing on Canadian federal institutions and ideals in the summer sessions of a number of American universities. . . .

Leland is in Massachusetts but will be here again soon. Most recently he has been preparing a French War Reader, which a publisher desired our National Board for Historical Service to prepare, and which contains interesting prose and poetry in French respecting the war. In his absence Stock is acting as Secretary of the Board. . . .

To RICHARD W. HALE

December 3, 1918.

My dear Mr. Hale:[197]

I have received your letter of November 29. You are in error in assuming that the discovery of the truth in respect to past transactions, which is the object of historical inquiry, and the doing of justice between man and man, which the object of legal inquiry, are identical ends.

Even a brief and superficial analysis would easily show that their purposes are not identical, but considerably different, and therefore there are large differences between the methods of historical and of legal inquiry. Now the testing of genuineness of documents, occasionally required in legal work is much more often required in historical work. The process has a much larger place in the procedure of my profession than of yours; indeed, a very large part of the development of historical criticism has grown out of the effort to settle questions of forgery in documents. At all events the question laid before Professor Harper and myself was very distinctly a question of historical criticism.[198]

I am fifty-nine years old, more than thirty years ago, I gave at the Johns Hopkins University the first course of formal instruction in the principles and processes of historical criticism that was ever given in the United States, and for many years I taught that subject, in three of our leading universities. Also, as the son of a learned lawyer and myself originally intended for the bar, I am not unfamiliar with the rules of legal evidence and the processes of legal investigation, and the differences between them and those of history, to which I have alluded above. Almost every year from 1886 to 1905, I had occasion to expound those indifferences to graduate students of history; they are indeed commonplaces of historical doctrine.

All these things considered, I think there is something not quite appropriate in any lawyer's telling me, *de haut en bas,* that he regrets that I did not see the need of following the methods of his science rather than of my own in attempting to solve an ordinary and somewhat simple problem which is distinctly in the field of the latter.

My science is quite as old as yours and those who have developed it have been equally intelligent men. For more than two thousand years historians have been elaborating their methods of arriving at the truth in respect to past transactions. It is surely probable that they have devised suitable methods. Surely each science has its own, and if the geologist, for instance, whose labors much resemble those of history, while using some of our methods declines to use others, I am content to believe that those which he selects are the ones which the experience of his profession has led him to consider the best.

To ARTHUR I. ANDREWS

January 24, 1919.

Dear Arthur:

I am interested in what you report. I firmly believe

[196] John C. Fitzpatrick (1876–1940), assistant (and sometimes acting) chief of the Division of Manuscripts of the Library of Congress, editor of the later volumes of the *Journals of the Continental Congress* and of the *Writings of George Washington.*

[197] Richard Walden Hale (1871–1943), cited, *ante,* Aug. 27, 1918, n. 188, was a member of the law firm of Hale and Dorr, of Boston, author of *The Dreyfus story,* Boston, Small, Maynard and Company, 1899, and secretary and treasurer for the United States of the Selden Society.

[198] The question concerned the authenticity of the Sisson papers.

the main series of fifty-three Russian documents to be genuine, and nobody ought from the phrases which Harper and I used to draw the inference that we do not so believe. Since however, from the nature of the case, we could not feel that we had the most absolute proof, beyond the possibility of error, and since historical professors have learned to be cautious in their statements, we did not declare in the loudest possible terms that the documents were as genuine as the Declaration of Independence, that we saw the authors writing them, that no forger could possibly impose upon us, or the like. I suppose we must pay the penalty of our caution.

As to the documents having been published abroad before they were published here, and having been discredited over there—a statement which the *New York Evening Post* has also made, with great show of knowledge and wisdom—all that sort of talk refers, and can only refer, to the dozen documents which Sisson printed in his appendix. Those documents came to him in a mimeographed form (typewritten in Russian) and some other copies were in circulation in Petrograd, and from one of them that brief series was printed in the *Petit Parisien* last January. They were loudly declared by the Bolshevik press to be forgeries. You will have seen that we declined to make any positive pronouncement about them, and why. That is quite another question from that of the main series, though no one would judge so from the not very honest articles in the *New York Post* and *The Nation.*

The examination of that main series was very interesting. It was a good seminary exercise, and seemed to us relatively not a difficult one. We saw originals and photographs, and of course subjected them to all the tests that you or other members of the profession would naturally think of. I think they stood them remarkably well. I need not say to you that *The Nation's* disagreeable accusations of superficiality—"sham investigation," etc.—were without foundation. I knew *The Nation* would assail us, and told Harper so, for that journal is to this extent committed to bolshevism, that it feels obliged always to make out the best case for them it can. For my own part I entered into the investigation, and conducted it, as disinterestedly as if I were adding up a column of figures; and though Harper, because he knows so much more of Russian affairs, has more definite opinions about the Bolsheviki than I have, I did not see him manifest any prejudice at any point of the investigation.

Briefly, we meant just what we said and, though unwilling to exaggerate the degree of certainty which we could attain, were well convinced that the fifty-three documents were genuine.

To ALBERT BUSHNELL HART

January 24, 1919.

My dear Hart:

Thank you for your notes on the *Trail of the Ger-* man.[199] I was glad to have the document, very much interested in it, though of course proof of the loyalty and uprightness of A. B. Hart was the last thing on earth of which I should feel any need.

It was an outrage, for which I cannot find any words strong enough, to print your name in the connection and with the implications with which the Department of Justice gave it out; and from merely the intellectual point of view it is difficult to characterize, the printing as of serious evidential value a paper which is found with no other heading than "Important List" and with nothing to show clearly why it was important.

It is fortunate for you that you are quick on the trigger and a good debater; for, by instantly demanding a hearing and putting things so effectively at the hearing, you did I think succeed completely in what is a very difficult endeavor to succeed in, namely to remove in all quarters the effect of slanderous imputations going out through the Associated Press.

But many a man who is not so quick to respond, or cannot come to Washington to do it, or cannot make an effective appearance before a committee, or has not the ear of press agencies, would be deeply injured by such casting of suspicion and would be unable to remove it. For this reason I tried to have a talk yesterday with old Senator Nelson,[200] whom I know and respect, to urge upon him the impolicy and injustice of doing, what the newspapers said the Committee was going to do, print a list of professors of history, political science and sociology who were indicated to them by a certain Stevenson, of the Military Intelligence Division, whom nobody seems ever to have heard of before, as having been of doubtful loyalty—Pro-German or pacifistic or doubting on August 4, 1914, that the United States ought to enter the war on August 5, or possibly favoring the McLemore resolution,[201] which, outside the Capitol, would it seems have been a criminal state of mind. I was glad to find that the old gentleman considered that you had absolutely and completely cleared yourself, except that your book *The War in Europe* ought to have been more Anti-German

---

[199] The trail of the German, dated Dec. 20, 1918, was Professor Hart's account of his appearance before a subcommittee of the Senate Judiciary Committee. The newspapers of Friday, Dec. 6, had mentioned his name as appearing in a list of names found in the hands of a German spy, one Fuehr. Hart at once demanded a hearing, which was held on Dec. 10, before Senators Overman of North Carolina, Nelson of Minnesota, and Sterling of South Dakota. In the hearing it developed that Otto Merkel of New York had made vigorous but unsuccessful efforts to induce Hart to join the German-American University League and had offered him $200 to write something for it. Hart's interpretation was that Fuehr's list was a list of those whom it was thought desirable to engage in the German cause and that Merkel had been used as an agent to achieve this end. He was able to offer in evidence of his loyalty to America some one hundred articles and three books, all written since the outbreak of the war and all condemning German aggression.

[200] Knute Nelson (1843-1923), senator from Minnesota, 1895-1923.

[201] See *ante,* Oct. 26, 1916, n. 96.

already yet; but I don't think I succeeded in making him see the point that to publish names in the way which was said to be contemplated would inflict upon worthy men severe punishment on insufficient grounds and without a hearing. He did say that no name would be thus published that was not a clear case. He seemed to think that a large number of these professors of political science and history had shown themselves to be a bad lot ("Look at Columbia University"—I looked and chiefly saw Nicholas Murray Butler); it seems they ought all to have been on fire for instant action by the United States from the moment Germany entered Belgium. I refrained from asking him how many senators were so.

Well, triumphantly as you have come out of it, it was a disagreeable experience, and I am sorry you had to go through with it.

To EDWARD B. KREHBIEL

February 13, 1919.

My dear Krehbiel:

I am glad to know more about your recent work, as explained in your letter of February 7. I dare say that business men do not attach much importance to the history of these war organizations, but a good many administrators here in Washington do. Surely they are right. When we entered upon the war it certainly would have been helpful, not only to readers of the American Historical Review, but to persons practically occupied with the administration, to know how certain things worked in what I may call the civilian part of the management of the Civil War. One found that, while there was an enormous amount in print respecting the military operations, matter respecting the economic and industrial mobilization which, though on a much smaller scale than now, accompanied warfare, was almost entirely lacking. Almost nobody in our profession except Carl Fish and some of his students had given much attention to it.[202]

More broadly, again and again one finds new administrative establishments taking up work that to some extent is new and to some extent has been done before, without any knowledge of the previous efforts and systems. Surely it is not reasonable not to have the means of being guided by experience, or at least of taking experience into account. For striking instances, what was known of the frightful blunders of management that marked the war of 1898 saved many of the supply and auxiliary services from making the same mess of things as was made at that time; and the accomplished student of history in the White House did his country a most prodigious service, which almost nobody notices, in causing the appointment of generals,

for the first time in our history, to rest purely on professional opinion and military considerations, without the slightest regard to those political motives which usually govern the appointment of generals at the beginning of the wars of republics, and which cost us so much in 1776, 1812, and 1861. But the typical American mind is after all the Champ Clark[203] mind, which "knows it all" without reading; and not everyone perceives how much federal administration is sure to enlarge its field. . . .

To ANDREW C. McLAUGHLIN

February 13, 1919.

My dear McLaughlin:

We are greatly obliged here for the copies of *America and Britain*. I found them here on my return from a nine days' absence in the regions northward, and shall get into the book as soon as possible, and know I shall enjoy it.

I am sorry about the shabby manner in which the publishers treated you, and I hope (indeed I think I shall see to it) that the reviewer says something about that, of course with indication that you are not to blame.[204] . . .

Fish says that he finds himself in the midst of many plans in London for putting into an organized form closer relations now likely to be established in intellectual matters between Britain and America.[205] The various schemes have not yet reached the stage of compromise or fusion. Apparently one of the chief movements is toward a professorship of American history in the University of London. What do you think about that? I should suppose that an established practice of sending each year some American professor of American history to London, a different one each year, would be better. I saw no evidence in 1913 that anyone in Great Britain was at all interested in American history. In the International Historical Congress, out of two hundred papers read, Britons read one hundred, and not one of them related to the history of the United States, and only one to the history of the British dominions overseas. I should not suppose that there was in Great Britain any person really qualified to be a professor of American history, except Egerton who already has his chair; and I should not suppose that what they ought to have—chiefly incitement toward greater interest in American history, would be so well

---

[202] Among the studies of Fish in this field were: Conscription in the Civil War, Social relief in the Northwest during the Civil War, Northern railroads, 1861, and Back to peace, *Amer. Hist. Rev.* **21**: 100-103; **22**: 309-324, 778-793; **24**: 435-443.

[203] Champ Clark (1850-1921), member of the Congress from Missouri, 1893-1895, 1897-1921; speaker of the House, 1911-1919. In the Democratic convention in Baltimore which nominated Wilson, Champ Clark led on twenty-seven ballots.

[204] *America and Britain*, N. Y., Dutton, 1919, contained the lectures which McLaughlin had delivered in Great Britain. The review of the volume gives no suggestion as to what the injury inflicted by the publisher was (*Amer. Hist. Rev.* **24**: 740-741, July, 1919).

[205] Fish had gone to London to organize the American University Union.

supplied by a permanent professor from America steadily teaching there throughout the session (to few adherents) as by a fresh man coming each year to administer his particular kind of fillip to the British university mind by a moderate series of lectures. But really this is no affair of mine. I should worry.

Moore has been pushing forward the project for a National Archive Building to very good effect this last autumn and winter. The site—12th and 13th, B and C, N. W.—has nearly all been purchased now by the Treasury and it has sent in an estimate for the purchase money.[206] It is hoped with some confidence that what is needed for this purpose can be got between now and the 4th of March, and a million or so for the building either in this session or in the next. A strong additional impulse has come in these recent months from the necessity of making some provision for papers made by the war, perhaps especially in the case of the temporary boards soon to expire.

Friday evening, in my capacity as a back-number official of the American Historical Association, I am to preside over the birth of a society for the study of agricultural history, at a meeting to be held in the new assembly room of the Cosmos Club. Considerable interest is manifested in the scheme, and the organization should be somehow kept under the fostering wing of the A. H. A. perhaps as a section.[207]

Now that the war is ended the foreign missionary enterprises of this Department can recommence, and A. J. F. van Laer, archivist at Albany, is going over in April or May to do the Dutch archives for us.[208] Also I suppose Amandus Johnson will go over to do

those of the three Scandinavian countries;[209] and I had hoped that Herbert C. Bell of Bowdoin would resume our project for a special treatment of the West Indian archives, in the islands and among the Colonial Office papers, but have not heard from him, though I understood he was in London.[210] My annual report of November last will go to you in a few days. . . .

To Leon J. Goodell

February 27, 1919.

Dear Sir:[211]

In 1870 Mr. William J. Canby read a paper before the Historical Society of Pennsylvania in which he related the story of Betsy Ross and the flag as it had come down in the family of Mrs. Ross, who was Mr. Canby's maternal grandmother. The story appears to have been reduced to writing first in 1857 from the lips of a daughter of Mrs. Ross. After Mr. Canby had read his paper he obtained a number of affidavits from other members of the family who had heard Mrs. Ross (spoken of generally as Mrs. Elizabeth Claypoole, from a subsequent marriage) relate the story. The account as related by Mr. Canby was incorporated by Admiral George H. Preble in his *History of the American Flag,* first published in 1872, and thereby gained large currency and quickly caught the popular imagination. These affidavits, together with other materials relating to the history of the flag may conveniently be found in a small volume entitled *The Evolution of the American Flag,* from Materials collected by the late George Canby, by Lloyd Balderston, Ph.D. (Philadelphia, 1909). George Canby was a brother of William J. Canby, mentioned above.

The weakness of the story is the fact that it is not supported by any contemporary documentary evidence. Elizabeth Claypoole (Betsy Ross) died in 1836; her daughter, Clarissa Wilson, related the story to her nephew, William J. Canby, who made some notes of the narrative; in 1870 Mr. Canby wrote out the story and read it before the Historical Society of Pennsylvania; afterward Mr. Canby obtained affirmations from others of the Ross household that the story as related by him was in accordance with their recollections of

---

[206] This was not the site on which the building was later erected.

[207] The newly-created Agricultural History Society met with the American Historical Association in Cleveland in December, 1919. At that meeting an agreement was ratified between the two societies which provided that their annual meetings were to be in the same place; that the *American Historical Review* and the *Annual Reports* were to give space to historical material pertaining to agriculture; and that a representative of the new society was to meet with the council of the American Historical Association (*Ann. Rept., Amer. Hist. Assn.,* 1919: 1: 56).

[208] Failing to obtain results from W. I. Hull, who had undertaken to make the Dutch *Guide* in 1913, Dr. Jameson asked A. J. F. van Laer to spend the summer of 1919 working in the Dutch archives. This he did, but no amount of effort induced him to prepare his manuscript for publication. Miss Mary Griffin, Frank L. van Cleef, custodian of the Dutch records of Brooklyn, and Professor E. W. Pahlow, then of Ohio State University, aided in reducing van Laer's notes to publishable form, but the delay had been so great that it was felt that some sections of the manuscript must be checked before going to press. This was the situation when the work on the *Guides* ceased, with the change in policy of the Carnegie Institution. The necessary revision was done by Dr. Jameson on his visit to the Hague in 1928, and the manuscript, instead of being printed, was deposited in the Division of Manuscripts of the Library of Congress. See *Year Book,* Carnegie Institution, 1925-1926: 88; 1926-1927: 83.

[209] The guide to the materials for American history in Scandinavian archives was the work of many hands. Some of the early notes were taken by Mr. Gunnar J. Malmin, who also aided in preparing the manuscript. Professor Waldemar Westergaard gave some aid. Gaps were to have been filled by Dr. Erik Naumann of the Swedish archives, but he died before his work was done, and it was completed by Dr. Tor Berg of the Stockholm archives. Since, by the time it was completed, the Carnegie Institution was no longer publishing *Guides,* the manuscript was deposited in the Library of Congress (*Year Book,* Carnegie Institution, 1925-1926: 89; 1926-1927: 83; 1927-1928: 94).

[210] See *ante,* May 1, 1918, n. 184.

[211] Leon J. Goodell was a school principal in Little Falls, New Jersey.

the story as they had often heard it from the lips of Betsy Ross.

In addition to the absence of documentary support critics of the Betsy Ross claim call attention to two or three features in particular of the narrative that are out of accord with known facts. The story has a committee of Congress (George Ross and Robert Morris) together with General Washington calling on Mrs. Ross shortly before the Declaration of Independence and receiving from her suggestions in regard to the flag, and adds that the flag agreed upon was shortly afterward adopted by Congress. Actually the first record in the Journals of Congress in regard to the flag was June 14, 1777, when it was

"*Resolved,* That the flag of the thirteen United States be thirteen stripes, alternate red and white: that the union be thirteen stars, white in a blue field, representing a new constellation."

When it is suggested that the conference with Mrs. Ross was in 1777 instead of 1776 it is pointed out that Washington was not in Philadelphia at that time. It is further pointed out that the journals make no mention of such a committee of Congress. In the view of the present writer however this last objection is by no means insuperable. It is also known that flags were in use before June, 1776, although probably not with stars in the union.

What is here said gives only the briefest suggestion of the difficulties in accepting the Betsy Ross narrative. The whole history of the development of the flag in the early Revolutionary period is involved in a good deal of obscurity. In the event that you should be interested in looking further into its history I may suggest, besides the volumes already mentioned, two small volumes, the authors of which do not accept the Besty Ross story: *Our Nation's Flag: in History and Incident,* by Colonel Nicholas Smith (Milwaukee, the Young Churchman Company, 1903); *The True Story of the American Flag,* by John H. Fow (Philadelphia, William J. Campbell, 1908). In a review of Balderston's book, in the American Historical Review for April, 1910 (p. 661), mention is made of a pamphlet by Charles E. Dana, *Notes on the American Flag and Some Others,* which particularly points out the untrustworthiness of the Betsy Ross claim; but I have not been able to lay hands on this pamphlet.

It may be added that in a number of brief histories of the flag which have appeared during the Great War the Betsy Ross story is related without qualification; indeed in some of them it is somewhat embellished.

To DWIGHT W. MORROW

March 18, 1919.

My dear Mr. Morrow: [212]

Thank you for the pleasure which you have given me by the opportunity to read your essay on the Society of Free Nations. I read it with care and with enjoyment, and with the sense that history lost a great deal when you concluded not to accept our good old Morse's invitation.[213] I am glad however that she did not lose it all, but that you are still able to borrow some time from Wall Street for such writing.

I sincerely hope that you will publish the papers as a book.[214] This is not a case where one is justified in refraining from publication because there will be some larger and more thoroughgoing treatise upon the subject, prepared with more leisure, by someone who is primarily an expert in international law and in history. The making of a proper public opinion upon the subject requires that all sorts of minds be assailed by all sorts of books, written from the point of view of the international law expert, of the historian, of the clergyman, of the cultivated lawyer-financier who has for years been reading along these lines, of the uncultivated journalist who has not been reading along any lines, of the senator, of the soldier, of the plain, ordinary pamphleteer. A book by you would go to people, and would be read by people, whether because of your position and connections or because of its own qualities, that would happen not to read the other books, or would help with other books to fortify the thoughts of readers.

I do not know that I have any useful suggestions. One, that occurs to me, I think of as a means of influencing the minds of those who think—and of countering upon the arguments of those who do not think but believe it is a good thing to say—that Washington's advice against entangling alliances is a valid reason against taking part in any superior organization of the world. My suggestion is, might it not be useful to insert somewhere a paragraph which shall show vividly how different a world that of 1919 is from that of 1797, when letters or fleets from Europe would take two months to cross the Atlantic, and when it took about as long to communicate between Mt. Vernon and Philadelphia as it now takes to cross the Atlantic, at the best. Such a paragraph could be inserted somewhere without violence, I should think. Perhaps it could be put more broadly, by dwelling not merely upon the superior means of communication—steamboat, railroad, posts, telegraph, telephone, wireless—but also upon the

[212] Dwight W. Morrow (1873-1931), A.B., Amherst, 1895, member of J. P. Morgan and Company, 1914-1927, adviser to the Allied Maritime Transport Council, 1918, awarded the D.S.M., 1919, for "exceptionally meritorious and distinguished services" in connection with shipping matters. He was a trustee of Amherst College and had shown his interest in history by contributing generously to the support of the London branch of the American Historical Association.

[213] While Morrow was a student in the Columbia law school, Professor Morse asked him to lecture in history in Amherst for a term (Harold Nicolson, *Dwight Morrow,* 56, N. Y., Harcourt, Brace, 1935).

[214] The papers, which appeared originally in the New York *Evening Post,* Feb. 21, 22, 24-28, and March 6 and 7, 1919, were published as *The society of free states,* N. Y., Harper, 1919.

extent to which economic development has made the world one, at the expense of nationalism. Standard Oil is as catholic as the pope.

I often feel that our habit of studying modern European history almost entirely in its political and diplomatic aspects has emphasized unduly the national elements in its growth, and obscured the great processes by which the world has coalesced into what in many respects is already one great society. If we had been devoting our attention to economic history or to the history of civilization we should not be so prone to see the world as chiefly a body of separate entities called nations. It is much with the unity of Europe as it is with the unity of the churches. All my life time people have been talking about church union, and making almost no progress in it by the front door, so to speak. Their front doors still face each other with the same immovable separateness; they negotiate faintly, and faintly declare their desire for increase of formal or organic or constitutional union. And during all this time there has been growing up, unnoticed perhaps by these ecclesiastical constitutionalists, a whole group of societies, a whole body of interests transcending denominations and uniting their members—Christian Endeavor societies, Y. M. C. A., Y. W. C. A., joint missionary endeavors, charity organization societies, movements for social service—until, at the back doors, where the church kitchens and kindergartens and gymnasiums are and where the societies meet, and where all those activities go on that fifty years ago were not thought of, there is a constant and free interchange and communion that makes all the churches one, while their facades still frown at each other across the street.

It can easily be said that this comfortable view of progress might have been entertained in 1913 but has been rather blown to pieces in the four or five years since July 1914. I admit that we were all very much surprised that in that month and those succeeding the forces of nationalism seemed so much stronger, in proportion to those of internationalism, than we had supposed. But I often please myself with the analogy to the last similar period of great change in human organization, and imagine the man of 1470, in England or France or Spain, saying to himself, "We really thought we were getting out of this period of feudalism, and coming into some larger arrangement of mankind, and here we are, enduring the worst of feudal wars." But it was not: warfare of two great aggregations of feudal hosts, in England or in France or in Spain, was nothing like as bad as the state of things that went on when every man's hand was against every man, in earlier feudal periods. Two parties at war in a country were better than a hundred, and made an approach to the system of great nations, such as our two great alliances now make to an international organization. The man of 1470 would have been wrong: what he saw was the clearing-up shower and presently Europe emerged into the system of great monarchies which was the in-

evitable development out of feudal *Kleinstaaterei*. Similarly, all through the war I have held to the faith that it would inevitably pave the way to a larger synthesis, a league of nations of some sort. It is sure to come, and the United States is sure to fall in line, and make the required sacrifices of particularism, with considerably better grace than the states were able to in 1788. The details of the covenant need of course to be carefully scrutinized, and I dare say amended. I think that your comments upon the articles will surely be among the most helpful parts of your book, if, as I hope, you issue it.[215]

To CHARLES H. FIRTH

March 19, 1919.

My dear Firth:

A design is in my mind, one part of which overlaps something that you had been doing, not I hope in such a way as to constitute any objection against its being carried out, if practicable, but in such a way at any rate that you will be my best adviser respecting it. I believe that after the war the study of modern diplomatic history will be more largely pursued than hitherto, and that it ought to be especially furthered, as a means toward bringing about that better understanding between nations the promotion of which is so much in the public mind. Secondly, I believe that that study would be very greatly facilitated if there were in existence a handbook for all such workers, containing dated lists of the diplomatic representatives of each power at the various other courts. We now have a variety of books in which some of this information is listed or from which it can be picked out, but why not have a general manual covering the whole field?

You will say that this is a difficult, ambitious and expensive undertaking, and that you have had much trouble in doing only certain parts of the English section of it in your *Notes on the Diplomatic Relations* (of which I have four pamphlets—are there more?),[216] but I should rather relish having an American institution, viz., this one, "do its bit" for the international fraternity of students of diplomatic history by providing for such a compilation; and furthermore, I should not contemplate the inclusion of such notes respecting materials for the history of embassies and missions as those exceedingly useful and valuable data of this sort which you have printed. The mere making of authoritative lists of ambassadors and envoys and commissioners, with dates of commissions and I suppose also of presentations or arrivals and withdrawals, would be trouble enough, and would constitute a manual of a distinct genus, like Father Eubel's *Hierarchia*. The bibliographical

---

[215] Chap. 9, pp. 156-187, presented a lucid account of the contents of the Covenant and the criticisms offered against it.
[216] See *ante*, Aug. 3, 1917, n. 152.

indication of printed and manuscript sources of information respecting the missions can logically be separated from such a task, and I fear that the attempt to include them would make the whole labor so great that it could not be achieved during the remainder of my lifetime—even though that will be *hoffentlich* considerable. I am writing about this only in a tentative spirit, to ask you what you think about it. If you think it practicable, and can as I judge you would, think it useful enough to warrant its fuller consideration, I wish you would give me your thoughts on plans and persons.

For one thing, how far back had one better begin? If the transition from occasional missions to permanent embassies was a definite one, for which a definite date could be fixed even in one country, one might be inclined to begin there; but I imagine that on the contrary the transition was gradual, would be hard to define, and have to be defined differently in different countries, and the fifteenth and sixteenth centuries would present greater difficulties than all the rest of the work put together. I do not like to embark upon an enterprise the first part of which would take so long that those scholars who would like to use the latter part of it, the very men I should most wish to help, would along with myself have passed away before the last section emerges from the press. I think it might be better to begin with 1648; or, as one especially anxious to serve all interests in connection with the history of the United States, I might like to begin with the first year of the seventeenth century as an arbitrary point of departure. The earlier periods might be tackled later. Please tell me what you think of this.

Again, please tell me what you think about the states to be included. It is painful to think of hunting up not only all the agents that Brunswick-Wolfenbuttel or Silbergroschen-Schreckenstein sent to the Court of St. James, or still more so to think of hunting up all the agents they sent to each other, or to Guastalla or Piombino;[217] but is there a principle on which one can draw a line between important and unimportant, that would be at all defensible? It will also be needful to take some careful thought as to classes of diplomatic representatives that shall be included. In other words, how far down from ambassadors shall one go, or, on the papal side, how far down from nuncios?

I foresee a great many perplexities, and suppose that the best way of dealing with the matter, if you think favorably of my attempting to deal with it at all, will be to get together a few representatives of the diplomatic history of different countries and shape the enterprise by discussion in common, when I next go to Europe, which I suppose will be about a year

from now. But meantime I write to you first about the matter, because you have done a portion of it already, in so fine a fashion, and know the possibilities and the pitfalls.

What do you suppose it would cost to do the whole thing for Great Britain, from 1601 down? Could you probably name, when the time arrives, a good young man or young woman to do all that, or would it be necessary, in order to secure good results, to make use of the services of special experts in special fields, as you have done in the case of Mr. Chance?[218] . . .

Another matter[219] about which I wish to consult you is that of possible deliberations, say in the spring of 1920, about another international historical congress. Those meetings ought not to be given up, and yet the paralysis of all powers of organization for such purposes in Russia, and the death of Lappo-Danilevskii, chairman of the committee on organization, makes it quite possible that the series might be permanently or for a long while interrupted, because no country might feel that it was its special function to take the matter up again. I remember that within a year after the acceptance in April 1913 of the invitation from Russia, Lappo-Danilevskii wrote me about the organization of their Russian committee, and asked me to be the representative of the United States in the group they were organizing of adjunct members, comprising, I suppose, one man in each of the

---

[217] Guastalla, a city on the Po, was once the capital of a duchy; Piombino, a Tuscan town, was formerly the seat of a principality.

[218] J. F. Chance contributed the List of diplomatic representatives and agents to the third and fourth of Firth's pamphlets. Professor Firth's answer of Apr. 15, 1919, expressed much interest in the plan and gave advice on all the points raised by Jameson. He selected 1604 as the best starting point and regretted that he knew of no young man able to aid the project. The idea took root slowly. It was presented to the International Congress of Historical Sciences at Brussels in 1923 and the international committee created by that congress at length decided to embark upon the making of such a manual as Jameson had described. A subcommittee consisting of Ludwig Bittner of Vienna, Michel Lhéritier of Paris, Harold Temperley of Cambridge, and Jameson, was appointed to forward the plan. Jameson at once began casting about for the money necessary to carry out his part of the undertaking (Jameson to Frederic A. Ogg, Apr. 7, Ogg to Jameson, Apr. 15, 1927). Through his efforts the Social Science Research Council was induced to provide funds for the work, which was done by Mrs. Lowell J. Ragatz. A useful preliminary step was achieved in 1928—the publication of, A provisional list of printed lists of ambassadors and other diplomatic representatives, compiled by Frances G. Davenport, in the *Bulletin* of the International Committee of Historical Sciences, no. 4, March, 1928. By June, 1932, the completed list of diplomatic agents sent to the United States between 1776 and 1815 was ready for Dr. Bittner. Two volumes, beginning with 1648, have now been published; the third and final volume, to cover the years from 1783 to 1815, is in preparation (1954). In the meantime the Department of State began work on a list of those diplomatic agents sent from the United States, which was to be published as an Historical Register. This has not appeared.

[219] The matter omitted above describes another project which is more fully set forth in a letter to Bryce, see *post*, June 12, 1919.

other large countries. I never knew who the others were, and suppose there is no means of finding out from Russia, or otherwise than piece-meal. Do you know who was asked to represent Great Britain in that committee, or France, or any other country? It occurs to me that if some of these names could be recovered, those men might legitimately serve as a means of calling into existence a larger international committee, that might meet somewhere and make preparations for an international historical congress a year or two afterward. Some invitation to meet in one particular country might develop at such a committee meeting. It would be a great pleasure to the Americans to invite their colleagues to hold a congress in this country, but I fear that this is for the present out of the question. It would seem too far to go, and the steamship rates are much higher than they used to be, and we should not have an adequate attendance.

An additional reason for suggesting a preliminary meeting of an international organizing committee lies, it seems to me, in the fact that the congresses thus far held have had too little of permanent result beyond what has flowed from the listening to papers and the making of acquaintance. Such congresses might be made to lead to the achievement of definite historical enterprises of an international character. One can without much difficulty think of several such that might be planned. Indeed the manual of ambassadors and envoys of which I have spoken might fall within that class, tho' it could also, I hope, be performed by one agency in one country. There are however others, for which international cooperation would be almost requisite. Some such have been proposed at the congresses, but the sessions never afforded time for adequate consideration of them. Now such projects could be discussed at a small international committee meeting, and those which seem to have merit could be examined more deliberately and recommended, a year or so afterward, to a congress, in a form so elaborated that they could be resolved upon, and subsequently executed; and so the congresses would not "expire with the fireworks."

Do you either know the names of persons who might be considered authorized to take up the matter afresh, or have you any thought as to another method by which such a committee could be called into existence? I think that all who attended the congress in London had great pleasure and satisfaction in it, and would wish that such meetings might recur even in the new world which is separated by so much from that of 1913.[220] . . .

---

[220] While Firth agreed that plans for an international congress of historians ought at once to be initiated, he commented: "Most English historians will decline to cooperate with German or Austrian historians either by meeting them in a Congress or by taking part in joint enterprises. Historical Congresses for the next 20 years or so must be composed of representatives

To George B. Adams and Andrew C. McLaughlin

March 31, 1919.

Dear Adams and McLaughlin:

As neither of the other two members of our committee seems to set the ball rolling, in the matter of honorary and corresponding members, I will make my spiel, and that may start discussion.[221]

In the first place I am not much in favor of increasing the list of honorary members, and am quite opposed to increasing it more than a little, and don't believe in electing any corresponding members at all. I don't see what good corresponding members are. I am a corresponding member of a number of historical societies, as you also are, and so far as I am concerned, I do not see that those societies get a blessed thing out of the relation. Every time I get one of their volumes I am ashamed of myself—probably blush, but am too color-blind to notice it—and say to myself that I really must send to that society some sort of a contribution; but I never get around to it. Also I should think that Europeans who should be made corresponding members of the American Historical Association might perfectly well be more vexed at not being put into class I. than pleased at being put into class II.

As to honorary members, I should be quite content to leave things as they are. It cannot be doubted that when we make a man our sole honorary member we do him an honor, and the more of them we make the less the honor; but the vote of the council, if its form is deliberate, seems to imply that we are to suggest some more names. I mention some of my humble thoughts respecting such a list.

Among Englishmen, I have not been able to think of any who would trot in that first class except Firth, Trevelyan and Bury. Firth has never done anything of such brilliant scholarship as some of Bury's things, nor that was as brilliant literature as Trevelyan's books, but is more representative of the historical profession in England, especially since Bury's health has prevented him in recent years from doing much. If I had to choose but one of the three I think it

---

of the allies and neutrals only. Bryce does not take this view, but so large a number of prominent historians do that it must be accepted as a fact" (Firth to Jameson, Apr. 15, 1919. On this subject see *post*, Jan. 30, 1923, and n. 439-441).

[221] It was voted by the council of the Association on Feb. 1, 1919: "To appoint a special committee of three which shall be, and hereby is, instructed to present to the council at its next meeting nominations, not to exceed nine in number, for corresponding and honorary membership in the association. Messrs. G. B. Adams, J. F. Jameson, and A. C. McLaughlin were named as members of this committee" (*Ann. Rept., Amer. Hist. Assn.*, 1918: 1: 38).

This was not the first time Jameson had been called upon to suggest additions to the list of honorary members. In 1902 he, Turner, and Haskins were made a committee for this purpose. At this time Jameson's suggestions were Maitland, Lecky, Bryce, Harnack, and Lamprecht. The custom has now been resumed with the number limited to fifteen.

would be Trevelyan, leaving Firth and Bury for a later occasion, Sir George being so old. I do not think that Ward or Oman or Egerton or Prothero or Fitzmaurice or Fisher "attains unto the first three."

As to Frenchmen, I should distrust my judgment still more, but from what I could gather I should think that Lavisse was regarded in France as having the first claim. I have read little of him, and much more of Seignobos, who seems to have a great talent, and by now to have acquired a high standing. Langlois and Bémont I know very well, and have read a good deal of what they have written, but while they are admirable scholars and men of great learning, and exceedingly useful in their profession, my impression would be that they would not be considered great historians. Aulard and Hanotaux I should suppose to be not quite the type of which we should make honorary members, but I should think a good case might be made out for Gaston Maspero if he is still living, concerning which I am in doubt.

I should be much in favor of making honorary members of Fredericq and Pirenne. It would be a *beau geste,* and I should think entirely appropriate intrinsically. Pirenne seems to me to be a man of prodigious talent, and if Fredericq is not of quite the same caliber, still his writings have been excellent, his influence as a teacher important, and in view of the association of their fates during the war I should feel a little delicacy about making the younger man and the pupil an honorary member to the exclusion of his teacher—though this may not be sound.

I should feel that Blok of Leyden had a claim like Pirenne's. He is not so brilliant but he is similar in being very distinctly the chief historian of his country, and in having given it its standard history.

In the other countries (I leave Germany out of account) I should think a great deal could be said for Altamira, Païs and Rostovtsev. So far as I can see, all three are men of the highest grade. I should not judge that Borgeaud and Dierauer were quite that.

I have thought that, besides talent and scholarship, we ought to consider conspicuousness, the regard with which men are held in their own country, and their having presented it and the general world with substantial achievements including standard works. If I had to keep the number down to six or seven I suppose I might suggest as my selection Trevelyan, Lavisse, Fredericq, Pirenne, Blok, Altamira, Païs, leaving out Rostovtsev as less known to our public, though I judge quite equal to some of these others. If I had to reduce it still further I don't know just what I should do. This letter is only a straw vote any way.[222]

---

[222] McLaughlin's letter in reply to this, endorsed the list which was here suggested, if the Association was committed to increasing the number of honorary members to this extent. G. B. Adams was more emphatic in his disapproval of adding to the honorary members, maintaining that to do so was to lower the

To Frederick C. Elmendorf

April 2, 1919.

My dear Frederick:[223]

. . . As for me, I am perfectly well. Last week I took my vacation, in the form which had been usual each year, but of late had been interrupted, of a spring hike with my friend Francis Christie, for whom Francis is named. He is a theological professor at Meadville, Pennsylvania. We joined at Harrisburg and walked up the Susquehanna to Northumberland, some sixty-two miles, in four days. Cloudless sunshine, good temperature, good roads, no mud, little dust, few automobiles, and very beautiful scenery. It did me much good. When, not having taken a long walk for four or five years, I found myself at the end of the first day to have covered seventeen miles without being more than healthily tired, I felt very well about myself, not believing that every man in his sixtieth year can do so well and keep it up. As to my work, I wish I succeeded as well in that. I keep busy all the time, but never quite catch up with the job.

As to the league of nations, your remarks are rather flattering. How happy I should be if I *could* give you the correct and authoritative dope upon the matter, and what a lot of money I could make out of it, considering that I should be the only man in the world that could do it! However, some things seem to be clear. I have never felt the slightest doubt that a league of nations ought to be formed, and that the United States ought to accede to it on terms not much different from those which were provisionally set forth in the first draft that was printed; and if so, still more so in the case of the doubtless improved draft in which it will probably be published before this letter gets to you. Moreover, I have little doubt that the Senate will feel obliged to agree to it. And though the President treated them with little tact and skill, I said from the first that they would have to come into the reservation, as gradually they learned how much more the people cared about it than they thought. I said that what would happen would be that, when the time came, the opposing senators would explain that they had always been in favor in principle, and now that, in deference to their objections, it has been so very much improved, they felt they could agree to it; and I have been amused to see

---

previous standard for such members. Indeed he went so far as to say: "None of those you have named would measure up with our past honorary members." He suggested that the classification be dropped and that the group under consideration be labelled corresponding members, in order not to lower the standard set when Ranke, Stubbs, Gardiner, Mommsen, and Bryce were made honorary members. This recommendation was made to the council with a marked lack of enthusiasm and the council decided to take no action in the matter (McLaughlin to Jameson, Apr. 4, 1919; Adams to Jameson, Apr. 3, May 31, 1919; *Ann. Rept., Amer. Hist. Assn.,* 1919: 1: 82). Leopold von Ranke was made an honorary member of the Association in 1885, Bishop Stubbs and Samuel R. Gardiner in 1899, Theodore Mommsen in 1900, and James Bryce in 1906.

[223] Frederick Elmendorf was a nephew of Mrs. Jameson.

them, as time goes on, beginning to hedge around in just about that way.[224]

All over the world the people desire some such arrangement. Not every one has seen beforehand that it was impossible to effect it without some sacrifices of nationalism, some sacrifices of perfect freedom of action on the part of each participating state. When they are brought up against those sacrifices, they naturally shrink from them, but after sufficient reflection, those who have any sufficient sense of what the world has suffered from the greatest calamity that ever befell it will conclude that a better machinery for controlling international relations would be worth the price they have to pay.

The price the United States will have to pay does not seem to me a very great one. A man who says he wishes always to keep the peace ought not to make much objection to being bound over to keep it. Many senators, with dishonest partisanship or hostility to the President, have represented the covenant to the public as putting all sorts of restraints upon American sovereignty which are not to be found in its text nor derived from it by fair implication. I wish the newspapers had carried the text of it daily, instead of only once, but I suppose they rightly thought of it as merely a preliminary draft, not quite the secure basis of argument that the final draft might be.

Our uncle William Taft, I have many times observed, says at the beginning, respecting any matter, just about what the sober sense of the rank and file of the Republican party comes around to at the end. That is because he has no selfish or personal desires to think of, and is not figuring for position in front of any partisan wicket of the political croquet-ground. Much the same is true of Root. I sent you yesterday Boston papers containing the full text of the debate between Lodge and President Lowell,[225] but Root's letter, which of course is carried in your newspaper, was much better than what either Lodge or Lowell said.[226] Lodge showed himself a more skillful debater than Lowell, and made better appeals to the galleries, but Lowell after all talked much more about the actual provisions

of the covenant, and less about glittering generalities, such as the dear old Monroe Doctrine. The Monroe Doctrine means to the public mind several different things, some of which I think we are not entitled to, but what are right in it seem to me to be sufficiently covered by the covenant. I see however that Root does not, and that fact is very important, but I imagine that the matter is being safely attended to at Paris. I am glad to see any improvements made there that can be, but one can't be easy that any one power should insist on a lot of amendments at a late stage in the proceedings, because that re-opens so many questions on which other powers are clamorous, and meanwhile the situation in Europe seems to me so dreadful that I find myself about as anxious this week as I was in that last week of March, 1918.[227]

The whole thing is somewhat as it was when the constitution of the United States was made. The representatives of the twelve states wrangled a long while, and each one had to give up much that it was sorry to relinquish, and when the document was made, Virginia and Massachusetts and the rest had lost a large part of their freedom of action, and the more provincial-minded sort of people opposed ratification because they could see what the state lost, and could not see, because it was so largely in the future, what all states gained. Similar are the minds of many of our senators from whom one does not hear a word but about the interests of the United States, as if the United States could go forward well unless the whole world went forward well. . . .

To Morris Jastrow, Jr.

April 10, 1919.

My dear Mr. Jastrow:[228]

May I make a suggestion, pursuant to your recent correspondence with President Woodward? I do not write to criticize your letter, but only with a view to producing useful results. Please regard this letter as confidential.

President Woodward is perhaps more sensitive to criticism than he need be, and has become restive under faultfinding, of which indeed he has received a good deal on the particular lines within which you wrote. But he is in reality very good natured, and though his previous activities and acquirements have lain mainly in the field of political [physical?] science, yet in disposition he is very liberal, and means to do what is right by the humanities, "however otherwise bounded or described." My estimate of the future course of the trustees is to the effect that his successor is likely to be some scientific man of a less liberal disposition. President Woodward is in good health, but will be seventy this summer, so that, if in any matter more favorable

---

[224] Time was to show how greatly Jameson underestimated both the strength of the opposition and the bitterness which the conflict evoked.

[225] On Mar. 6, 1919, President Lowell proposed to Senator Lodge, a debate on the League. Lodge accepted and the debate was held in Symphony Hall, Boston, on Mar. 19. The letters of the two men are to be found in an "extra" of the Boston *Herald,* of Mar. 9, and the full text of the debate appears in the Boston *Transcript,* supplement, Mar. 20, pp. 2-3, and in an "extra" of the *Herald* of the same date.

[226] On Mar. 31, 1919, the New York *Times* published a long and thoughtful letter from Elihu Root, now ex-secretary of State and ex-senator, written to W. H. Hayes, chairman of the Republican National Committee, at his request. The letter, which occupied about a page of the *Times* (1, 4), offered six amendments to the document under discussion in the Senate, all intended to safeguard American interests but none meant to weaken the League in any fundamental way.

[227] See *ante,* Mar. 26, 1918, n. 178.

[228] Morris Jastrow, Jr. (1861-1921), professor of Semitic languages, University of Pennsylvania.

action is to be expected from him than from his successor, the attempt should be made now.

In the second place, in any at all probable adjustment of the present dreadful tangle in the world's affairs, there is likely to be a wide and immediate opening of opportunities for archaeological explorations in Western Asia. I take it that, though you wrote to President Woodward in the interest of humanistic studies generally, effort by the Carnegie Institution in Western Asiatic archaeology would appeal to you most, and moreover, there is far more hope of securing something by effort in a single department like that than by a general movement to compel or persuade the Carnegie Institution to "do what it ought to do for the humanities." Indeed, I think there is practically no chance of success from such general movements, while, among the departments into which humanistic studies might be divided up, I know of none more likely to appeal to our trustees than archaeology. For instance, they have been doing a good deal lately for Central American archaeology.

What I wish most to emphasize in this letter is that, as I see it, criticism of the Carnegie Institution has in the main not proceeded on profitable lines, or along lines in which the critics are likely to persuade President Woodward and his trustees that their criticism is just. In general the criticisms may be summed up as being to the effect that more should be done for the humanities. That brings one, and in practice it has actually led, to two insoluble questions. Just what are the humanities, and just how much ought the Institution to spend upon them? The trustees have spent a good deal in those lines, possibly enough in number of dollars. The real criticism to which I think they might justly be subjected is that they have followed two different methods in the case of the physical sciences and the other studies respectively, one of them a right method for such an institution to follow, the other distinctly a wrong method. The proper question for them to ask themselves, with respect, let us say, to the expenditure of $10,000 is, Of all the ways in which this sum could be spent, what is the one that will be most useful to the science under consideration. If one wishes a first-rate answer to that question, one gathers together a small committee of experts known to be reasonable and sagacious and to have the confidence of their fellows, and invests them with the responsibility of giving advice, of making out a programme, or selecting and shaping one particular project, as with the voice of the whole profession. When that is done, that committee, however divergent the views of the individual members, is as likely to come down to an agreement as twelve jurymen locked up until they can agree. Now this was on the whole the procedure which the Institution pursued in the case of the physical sciences. In most cases it was followed up by the creation of permanent departments, to whose direc-

tors such a responsibility for giving advice, presumably advice founded on knowledge of professional opinion, was transferred. Such a procedure not only gives a higher degree of security that the right things shall be undertaken, but also promotes harmonious relations between the university and the scientific man. And so far as I can see, this state of things equally prevails with respect to the Department of Historical Research. Its operations, confined to American history for reasons which I need not now enter upon, are treated by the trustees and the president with just as much consideration as those of any of the other departments. For seven or eight years past, they have given me everything I asked for (except in a matter of two where the exigencies of war prevented).

Now the wrong method of procedure, with respect to any given expenditure of $10,000, is to wait for the projects to be proposed and then, laying one before the trustees, to ask, Shall this be done or shall it not? If the decision is affirmative, you then have a book published or a thing done that may be quite good, but there is no security that it is the very best thing that could be done with the money. Now in most of the human subjects this latter procedure has been followed, rather than the former; and here in I think is the point on which alone the Institution can be criticized with any security as unfair to the humanities, namely, that in respect to all of them but history and political economy it has followed a radically different procedure to that which has been deemed wise in the case of the physical sciences.

Why not then proceed constructively? Why not ask whether, in view of the immense and brilliant possibilities likely to be now opened up for West-Asiatic archaeology, the Carnegie Institution would not be willing to select a committee of three or five experts on whom it could place the responsibility of giving professional advice as to what might be done with a moderate sum of money—I say moderate because only moderate sums seem to be available now, though large ones may be available in two or three years.

Let us suppose that a committee were formed consisting of two members of the Archaeological Institute of America, one member of the Oriental Society, one member of the Society for Biblical Literature and Exegesis, and one member of the American Historical Association, five in all, and that they should memorialize President Woodward this spring upon the extraordinary opportunities which the turn of things now seems to present in Asiatic Turkey, on the desirability of America's doing her part, and some of the things that need to be done and the reasons therefor. If this were done and I were notified at the time, I could perhaps persuade the president, to persuade his executive Committee, to ask those five gentlemen to serve as an advisory committee and agree upon specific recommendations falling within a given limit of expenditure. As a matter of fact, history has its present position in the organization of the Carnegie Institution largely because just such a committee was promptly formed by the American Historical Association, at my instance, within three weeks after Mr. Carnegie's announcement of his gift—whereupon the trustees requested that same committee to be their advisory committee in history.[229] It may at least be worth trying, but it would be desirable that the committee, though composed of men of high standing and well-known names, should not include persons who had engaged in previous attempts of larger scope, and not succeeding therein, have thereupon expressed in public or to President Woodward their resulting convictions as to the inefficiency or iniquity of the trustees of the Carnegie Institution.

You know better than I whether harmony in respect to such planning can readily be expected. My own belief is, contrary to that of President Woodward, that persons occupied with the humanities are just as prone to agree as scientific men, provided the method taken for enlisting their opinions is the same, namely, one that encourages concert of opinion, rather than one that, by individual inquiry, tends to elicit merely individual opinion. We have all heard of some striking instances of dissension among Oriental Archaeologists in America, but I presume that they can act harmoniously. You will also know better than I whether any such undertaking as I have described on the part of the Carnegie Institution is even desirable, or whether it would merely produce injurious competition with schemes which individual universities or museums already have in mind—though at this point something might be said about the merits of a scheme which, emanating from an institution having no museum, might have no ambition to carry archaeological objects away from lands henceforward belonging to new nations to whom it might be important and valuable to retain them.

Whatever you may think about what I have proposed, please understand I shall always desire to be helpful.[230]

To CHARLES H. HASKINS

April 17, 1919.

My dear Haskins:

Leland has shown me your letter and that of Professor Cagnat respecting the arrangements for promoting cooperation in historical and philological studies between the academies, and similar institutions of the allied (and I should hope as soon as possible the neutral) countries.[231] I am greatly pleased that something of the sort has been set on foot, and the whole of the French memorandum is admirably conceived. I had greatly hoped that something of the sort would be done, and the method they propose seems to be the best. I think that we of the American Historical Association are very fortunate in having you and Shotwell in Paris to represent us in the matter.[232]

In respect to other societies in this country, I have nothing to add to what you say. The situation is just as you describe it, and I do not see a perfect solution of the perplexities. We have nothing corresponding to the British Academy, or the "phil.-hist. Classe" of the German academies, and I do not know that it is worth while, any more than possible, to create one. The American Academy of Arts and Letters has of course no such representative position, and indeed does not represent scholarship, in respect to which alone there is question of international cooperation, but *belles lettres,* and so is not likely to have any international standing except on occasions of ceremony. The A. H. A., the Archaeological Institute of America, the American Oriental Society, the American Philological Association, and the Modern Language Association of America are the only societies that I can think of that need to be represented in the scheme proposed by the Academy of Inscriptions, and I do not know just how a representation of all five had better be managed; but this presents no difficulties to you gentlemen who can accommodate a council of the League of Nations to the composite character of the British Empire by giving each dominion a seat.[233]

So, though I will make some suggestions, inasmuch as your letter to Leland seems to give me the opportunity, they will not be along the line of organization but of *agenda.* Whatever organization is provided will no doubt be excellent, and, speaking for one member of the Committee on Relations in the council of the A. H. A., I will do what I can to bring about proper coordination of effort on this side of the water. The whole matter interests me deeply, and I had had some hope, after a talk I had with President Woodward last spring and a memorandum I prepared for him,[234] that the Carnegie Institution would be moved to do some-

[229] See *ante,* Feb. 14, 1902, n. 12.

[230] Examination of the *Year Books* shows that Jameson was right in thinking that the Institution was spending considerable sums for archaeology. No change in its policy appears to have taken place at this time. When archaeological work was extended, about ten years later, it was done in Yucatan, not in the Far East, and, ironically enough, was done at the expense of the activities of Dr. Jameson's own department.

[231] M. René Cagnat was a professor at the Collège de France and permanent secretary of the Academy of Inscriptions and Belles Lettres. The plan to which reference is here made was for a Union Académique Internationale to aid in restoring international cooperation in scholarly activities.

[232] At the Paris Peace Conference, 1918-1919, Haskins was chief of the Division of Western Europe, of the American Commission, American member of the Commission on Belgian and Danish Affairs, and Special Commissioner on Alsace-Lorraine and the Saar Valley; Shotwell was chief of the Division of History.

[233] The solution eventually arrived at was the creation of the American Council of Learned Societies. See *post,* Jan. 19, 1920, n. 284.

[234] See *ante,* May 24, 1918.

thing substantial to promote such union of forces in the conquests of science. I gather that he did not receive much encouragement from his executive committee respecting the matter; perhaps President Washington's warning against entangling alliances was still too fresh and recent in their minds. Contracting my thoughts therefore to the mere work of history, I wrote some time ago to Prothero [235] about the possibility of creating some sort of international committee out of what is left of the committee on organization formed by the Russians in 1914 with a view to the St. Petersburg congress; and more lately I wrote along similar lines to Firth. [236] I have had a reply from Prothero, and if he is still in Paris, I am sure that you will find him interested and ready to help in this larger project, into which anything of the sort that I spoke of can well be subsumed. [237] . . .

To Lord Bryce
                                                    June 12, 1919.

My dear Lord Bryce:

I have a project in mind upon which I should be glad to receive any advice or suggestions that may occur to you. It is not a matter for immediate execution, but in the ten months or so that will intervene before I shall begin actually to carry it out I wish to ruminate upon the matter and make a mental and other preparations. I believe it is something in which you will be interested, and indeed perhaps I have written of it before, at some less definite stage of my thinking about it. I cannot now say that I have positively resolved upon it, for there are certain quantitative details to be known before one can conclude that it is not too large an enterprise to be practicable, but it now seems to me probable.

Assuming that the consent of the British government can be obtained, I should like to print, in a series of volumes, the correspondence of the British ministers in Washington (or, earlier, Philadelphia) down as far as may be thought expedient. I mean their correspondence with the foreign secretaries, both official and private, and other correspondence with friends or with relatives in Great Britain.

Of the interchanges between our secretary of state and our minister in London, the government of the United States has printed much and ought to print much more! Our government may even, when it wakes up to its duty toward history, consider those between our secretary of state and the British minister here, or between our minister in London and foreign secretary, to fall within its province, but I should not expect it to take such a view of the communications between the British minister here and the foreign secretary in London. Nor should I think it likely that in the *Calendars of State Papers, Foreign,* which I believe have now reached 1583, or in any other series, the British government would embark on any extensive publication of this material. Your foreign relations have been so extensive that the earlier U. S.-G. B. relations subtend but a small arc in the circle.

Yet, looking forward to increased interest in diplomatic history, and wishing also to be serviceable to the promotion of good relations between the two countries, I cannot help thinking that a full publication of dispatches showing how the earlier relations appeared to British eyes will be helpful toward mutual understanding.

No doubt the earlier confidential communications, whether American or British, contain passages that will not be gratifying, to readers in one nation or the other; Francis James Jackson evidently thought as ill of us as we did of him. [238] But it is ancient history now. I expect we shall find a good many cases like that of Stratford Canning [239] and John Quincy Adams, each of whom confides, the one to his cousin, the other to his diary, his opinion that he has to do with an obstinate, ill-tempered and domineering person but withal an honest one that he cannot help respecting. Full knowledge will help toward mutual regard, I should feel sure.

Now, do you think the Foreign Office will have any objection to the project? Mr. William Phillips assures me that the Department of State would cordially welcome it. I should be glad of your advice as to the method of approach to Mr. Balfour, whether I should proceed through our ambassador [240]—doubtless a formally correct channel, but I doubt if he cares anything about such matters—or in some other way. I suppose we should have to confine ourselves to the dispatches, excluding the enclosures, though using them for purposes of annotation. I have yet to hear, though

---

[235] The letter to Prothero, written Feb. 28, 1919, found him at the peace conference as a member of the British delegation. He reported that he, Hume Brown, probably Firth, and possibly Bury, had been selected by the Russians as the British committee to plan for the next historical congress. He believed, however, that it was of little use to "contemplate another Historical Congress at present. Things are in so chaotic a state now, and the future is so uncertain that to do so would be 'tempting Providence!'" The suggestion of an international committee to plan cooperative projects he welcomed but felt that even that should not be considered for 1919 (Prothero to Jameson, Mar. 23, 1919).

[236] See *ante,* Mar. 19, 1919.

[237] The remainder of this long letter deals with projects for international cooperation which had already been outlined in letters to Lappo-Danilevskii or Firth.

[238] Francis James Jackson (1770-1814), minister plenipotentiary to the United States, 1809-1811. Some indications of Jackson's feelings are to be found in Adams, Henry, *History of the United States: the first administration of James Madison* I: 154-156, N. Y., Scribner's, 1890.

[239] Stratford Canning (1786-1880), envoy extraordinary and minister plenipotentiary to the United States, 1819-1823.

[240] John W. Davis, who had been a member of the Congress from 1911 to 1913 and solicitor-general from 1913 to 1918, served as American ambassador to Great Britain from 1918 to 1921.

a calculation is being made, how big an amount, from period to period, this series would make. I should however wish also, by all means, to include as much as I could find, or could be allowed to use, of the private and unofficial letters which ministers wrote home to the foreign secretaries and others, and which often tell a better story than the official public dispatches; and I am planning to come to England next May (after a little time in Spain and at some intervening cities) to pursue game of this sort. This is especially a field in which I should be glad of suggestions from you, at any future time when it may be convenient. For instance, Monsignor Barnes told me here last autumn that he was a great-grandson of George Hammond the first minister,[241] and that two cousins of his in London had two chests of papers of George and Edmond (Lord) Hammond, I fear mostly the latter; F. J. Jackson's papers are at the Public Record Office; a large mass of papers of Sir Charles Bagot [242] is in the Public Archives of Canada at Ottawa; Sir Charles Vaughan's papers are at All Souls.[243] Preparing the way by correspondence where practicable, I had planned to spend two or three months in England following up whatever clues I may get as to such papers.

The main resources will after all be papers of the foreign secretaries, and especially of Grenville, Canning, Castlereagh, and Palmerston. Mr. Ashley let Mr. Adams see what he wished among the papers of Palmerston. Do you think I could obtain the same privilege for the earlier period? The Grenville papers at Dropmore are already largely in print.[244] I suppose that those of Canning are in the hands of the present Earl of Cork and Orrery, and those of Castlereagh in the hands of Lord Londonderry. Do you suppose I could obtain access to these? My function will be in the main confined to the collecting of copies and to a general supervision. I shall put the work of editing in some competent hands. The whole thing would be the work of some years. Because the period from 1792 to 1815 is already better known than later periods, though it ought not to be neglected, and also perhaps because it contains more of the less amiable material than the years after the treaty of Ghent, and because Bagot's papers are certainly available, I have a notion of bringing out first the volume beginning at that later date, or perhaps the volumes for Bagot and Canning, then running back to pick up volume I. and its immediate successors. I expect to go up to Ottawa in October to go over the Bagot material. Possibly, if I can find the time to do it, and it would be acceptable, I might prepare a paper on Bagot's ministry for the British Academy or the Royal Historical Society, sessions of both of which I should enjoy attending. What with the beginning of 105 years of peace, and the Bagot-Rush convention and the disarmament on the lakes, that might be an agreeable subject on which to read a paper,[245] and the reading of which might bring grist to my mill from unexpected quarters. But this is merely a suggestion, made because you are so kind as to suggest some communication to the Academy and I do not easily think of anything I could do that would interest them.[246]

All that I have written is tentative and preliminary, but I wish to let you know what I have in mind, because I feel sure you will be interested—you made the office of minister here an instrument of mutual harmony that no one else could ever have made it, even with the aid of a century of peace.

Please to give my very kind regards to Lady Bryce. One of the chief pleasures of coming to England next spring will be that of seeing you and her again. I hope that you both are in good health.

To HENRY B. GARDNER

Bowdoin College Library
Brunswick, Maine.
July 10, 1919.

Dear Gardner:

Interesting news respecting Walter.[247] If he finally decides for political economy he has under the same roof, as I hope he is aware, the wisest advisor in these here United States. In the matter of history, there are many who know more than I do of the opportunities

---

[241] The Rt. Rev. Msgr. Arthur S. Barnes, first ordained in the Church of England, was received into the Roman Catholic Church in 1895, and later served as Catholic chaplain in the universities of Cambridge and Oxford. He visited the United States in 1917-1919. Jameson met him when he was in Washington to attend the golden jubilee of the episcopacy of Cardinal Gibbons.

George Hammond (1763-1853) came to Philadelphia as minister plenipotentiary to the United States in 1791, and remained until 1795, after which he became under-secretary at the Foreign Office.

[242] Sir Charles Bagot (1781-1843), minister to the United States, 1815-1820.

[243] Sir Charles Richard Vaughan (1774-1849), envoy extraordinary and minister plenipotentiary to the United States, 1825-1835.

[244] The papers of William Wyndham Grenville, contained in the *13th Report of the Historical Manuscripts Commission,* appendix, part 3, and the *14th Report,* appendix, part 5, the *Manuscripts of J. B. Fortescue preserved at Dropmore House.*

Grenville (1759-1834) was Foreign Secretary from 1791 to 1801; George Canning from 1807 to 1809 and again in 1822; Castlereagh (1769-1822) was head of the Foreign Office from 1812 to 1822; and Palmerston (1784-1865) for many of the years between 1830 and 1851.

[245] The Bagot-Rush convention of 1817, completed by mutual agreement on the part of the United States and Great Britain, limited the vessels to be maintained by the two nations on the Great Lakes, and began an era of unbroken peace between the two countries. Richard Rush (1780-1859) was at this time acting Secretary of State.

[246] With this letter should be read the letter to Lord Bryce, *post,* Jan. 4, 1922.

[247] Professor Gardner's letter of July 3, 1919, announced his son Walter's inclination to take up history or a combination of history and economics as a life work.

for its pursuit in England and France. Incidentally, it does seem as if economic history must before long come into its rights in this country. It is really a worrying thing, that it is so much less pursued among us than what it should be. I fear that some of the fault lies upon our habit of organizing universities and colleges in "departments," which has the effect of discouraging the pursuit of studies that are common to two of these air-tight "departments." Under present circumstances, the best young student of economic history might feel that he imperilled his chances of getting a job by pursuing economic history rather than "pure" history. But I should hope that this state of things would amend itself some time before long. I think that at least the larger universities feel their need of instruction in economic history by persons who have specially trained themselves along that line.

The pecuniary attractions of the Rhodes Scholarship are considerable, but it does not seem to present the ideal method of spending three years on the part of an American student. No doubt, the new regulations in England about the Ph.D. degree afford a system better suited to a young American; but even so, Oxford is ceasing to be typically England. McLaughlin returned from his tour of the British universities with a conviction that the real sap was running rather in the provincial universities. From what I hear from Firth, who is of course the best history man at Oxford, I should never think of advising a young American student of history to spend more than one year there. A year at Oxford under Firth's guidance, might be extremely profitable; also I presume, though about this I know less, a year in London. But I should think that Paris would afford advantages intrinsically just as great as either, and greater when one considers how much greater the difference is between the typical French point of view respecting modern European history and the American, than between the American and the British. If I were starting in for a period of two or three years of European study of modern history, I should spend one year in England and one in Paris. But I should also wish to have some contact, such as a third year might afford, with the teaching in universities in other countries, e.g., those of Italy, of Switzerland (Borgeaud of Geneva), Guilland, or Stern at Zurich, if Stern is still teaching [248]—you see I really do not know much about these men—or even those of Germany; and for another instance, I should not think a student of economic history could anywhere find a more stimulating teacher than Pirenne of Ghent, a wonderful and brilliant man.

Such a combination would, I feel sure, be better for the young man than three years spent as a Rhodes scholar. The education of the latter has, I should think, great defects as a preparation for American life. Indeed, I should not at all think of any curriculum of three years in Europe as dispensing the young man from the need of some portion of time spent in an American university—at least one year, and that preferably his first year, of graduate work. From what I know of the matter, I think that the faculties of history in American universities expend more pains on the first stages of the instruction of graduate students than the European, certainly than the English. Moreover, a point of practical importance, an American university where one has spent one's first graduate year feels always thereafter an interest in helping the student to find a place, whereas the young man who has spent all his years of study in Europe is (or would be, for hardly anybody has tried it) somewhat at a disadvantage in this respect.

Such a course as I have proposed makes it a little more difficult to get a degree than staying in one place, but that can probably sometime be arranged, and is not of the first consequence. I suppose many colleges are afraid to appoint a man who has not a doctor's degree; but the important universities would probably not feel that way, at any rate in engaging a specialist, e.g., specialist in economic history. . . .

If you happen to go to Cambridge before August 8, it would pay you to see Haskins, who is fresh from Paris, and always is full of knowledge about whatever is going on in the higher education.

To FERDINAND SCHEVILL

Bowdoin College Library
Brunswick, Maine.
July 18, 1919.

My dear Schevill: [249]

Let us not worry. The matter of Hazen's book is a very slight one, and indeed on looking at it again— I did not have the book with me when I wrote—I find that it is taken rather from his "Modern European History" than from his "Europe since 1815." [250]

As to this question of, What is History, give me a chance some time later to see more fully what conclusions you have come to. I do not myself incline toward heresy, but I like to hear about it, and would never burn anyone at the stake for it. Indeed, I usually do not understand it, having no mind for theoretical considerations or for philosophy. I hold that this terrible war, the greatest calamity that has ever befallen the human race, is mainly due to the fact that the

[248] Antoine Guilland of Zurich was the author of, German historical publications, 1914-1920, Amer. Hist. Rev. 25: 640-657, July, 1920. Alfred Stern was still in the University of Zurich.

[249] Ferdinand Schevill, connected with the department of history of the University of Chicago from 1892 until his retirement in 1937.

[250] In 1917, Charles Downer Hazen (1868-1941), at that time professor of history in Columbia after twenty years in Smith College, published Modern European history, N. Y., Henry Holt. Two years later he brought out Fifty years of Europe, Holt, 1919, which contained sections of the earlier volume with a chapter added on the First World War.

Germans have a capacity for taking philosophy seriously, which the English and Americans do not share. I assured my good old friend Mr. Henry Adams, apropos of his "Letter to American Teachers of History," that I was precisely like old Scottish Janet, in my father's story: "Dominie, that was a grand sermon ye gave us the Sawbath." "And did ye understond it, Janet?" "Wad I hae the presoomption?!" Like the man in Langlois and Seignobos, when one asks me what history is, I reply that it is (among other things) what I am doing. Mr. Adams maintained that all historical work was at present meaningless. As I earn my living by it, I told him that I was forced to be like Louis XVIII. when he said it was his *metier d'être royaliste*.[251]

Nevertheless I want to hear all about it some time. Get up on Mars Hill, and imagine me the Athenian audience. Any properly constituted editor of an historical journal, however ignorant he may be, wishes to keep his mind open to New Truth; like Christie's Boston lady, "I just dote on advanced thought."

To ELIZABETH DONNAN

North Edgecomb, Maine.
July 24, 1919.

My dear Miss Donnan:

When you are in Boston, I wish that you would privately examine a file of the *Boston Courier* for 1860, see if you can find and identify the letters which young Henry Adams wrote to it from Italy during that year of revolution, and see if they are very good, first consulting the passage relating to them in the *Education,* by which you will get your bearings.[252] I thought that if this youth of twenty-two wrote respecting what went on before his eyes in Italy with anything like the same intelligence with which he wrote that survey of the session of 1860-1861 at Washington, which his brother Charles found and published in the *Proceedings* of the Massachusetts Historical Society,[253] the letters might be very good stuff for the *Review;* but, if I remember rightly, you found none of them in such issues of the *Boston Courier* as were possessed by the Library of Congress. I forgot to look into the matter when I was last in Boston.[254] . . .

---

[251] Readers will recognize that Dr. Jameson had no objection to repeating a *bon mot* or a good story when it served his purpose.

[252] Chapter 6 of the *Education of Henry Adams* deals with his experiences in Rome at the time of Garibaldi's uprising: "Perhaps the most useful purpose he set himself to serve was that of his pen, for he wrote long letters, during the next three months, to his brother Charles, which his brother caused to be printed in the *Boston Courier;* and the exercise was good for him" (89).

[253] The great secession winter of 1860-1861, *Proc., Mass. Hist. Soc.* 43: 660-687, June, 1910.

[254] See *post,* Oct. 24, 1919, n. 273.

To GEORGE A. PLIMPTON

September 24, 1919.

My dear Mr. Plimpton:[255]

Your letter of September 9 was very interesting, and should have been answered before, but I have been travelling about, and got back to my office only a day or two ago.

I should not wish to suggest anything that would interfere with any definite plans of yours for the use of material which you have got together with so much interest and care, and I ought to be well content if your interesting material respecting the slave trade comes before the public in any form, and especially in the excellent form which you would know how to give it.

At the same time, trying to look at the matter from an impartial point of view, with only the interests of the public in mind, I really think there is something to be said in favor of associating your slave trade material —as distinguished from your material on the general history of slavery within the United States—with the large and comprehensive collection of material on the slave trade which this Department of the Carnegie Institution has for several years been accumulating. By this I do not mean that we have been purchasing, for that is never in our line, but finding and transcribing all available material of first rate importance, and so making up a body of documents and narratives that will illustrate in the fullest and most rounded manner the whole history of the African slave trade to the American colonies.

Perhaps I may do well to describe what we have been doing. What relation it bears to the general scheme of operations of this Department can be seen if you care to examine two or three of my recent Annual Reports which I am sending herewith.[256] It will suffice here to say that I started with the following convictions: that the history of the negro in America, the history of about a tenth of our population, is a very important topic in American history; that while the history of the agitation for the abolition of slavery has been very abundantly recounted, comparatively little has been done toward the history of slavery as an actual economic and social institution in America; that for its successful prosecution it needed a much larger body of documents made easily accessible to students; that neither Congress, nor the Southern state legislatures, nor the Southern historical societies, nor to any great extent the Southern universities, would ever be likely to take up the matter of such documentary publication;

---

[255] George A. Plimpton (1855-1936), A.B., Amherst, 1876, an Amherst trustee for many years and a collector in many fields. His letter of Sept. 9 briefly described those papers in his hands which related to the slave trade. Later he generously allowed the Department of Historical Research to make use of them in the edition of *Documents illustrative of the slave trade to America.* See 3: 266-267, n. 1.

[256] See *Year Book,* Carnegie Institution, 1916: 167; 1918: 143-144.

and that therefore there was a distinct call upon an endowed department like this to fill in this gap in the documentation of United States history. You will understand from my annual reports that this Department does not regard it as any part of its business to write histories or monographs. The function of an endowed institution, in matters of history, should on the whole lie further back than that, in the dealing with original documents.

As the project lies in my mind, it has several distinct divisions, each to be taken up in due time, as our means permit, and pushed along carefully and with thorough scholarship. One division that I planned, for ultimate execution, is a *corpus* of the laws of all the colonies and states respecting slavery. Another is a collection of statistical data from the unprinted schedules of the old censuses, which contain a good deal of "slag" which was not used at the time but from which much matter can be extracted that to-day would be valued by historians. Another is a collection of statistical material respecting prices, valuations, tax assessments, and other economic data, for various periods in the history of slavery. Another, a collection of material illustrating the law respecting slavery and showing how it operated in several hundreds of actual incidents, is a body of excerpts from the judicial reports of the Southern states. This last has been begun; the other projects have to wait their turn, but the two or three volumes of materials on the transatlantic slave trade, on which work was begun several years ago, are now far advanced.

I put this project in the hands of one of the most intelligent of my assistants, and the one having the largest knowledge of economics, Miss Elizabeth Donnan, a lady well trained in all historical matters and of excellent judgment, who has just left us to become assistant professor of economics in Mt. Holyoke College, but will be able to finish her book by working in vacations, being an exceptionally strong and energetic young woman.

The main object of her researches has been to illustrate the slave trade in respect to the sources and methods of supply, as well as to the transatlantic voyages, and I venture to say that she has a larger knowledge of the whole history of the trade on the West African coast than any one else in America possesses. She has been making up her volumes from the original material in old books, in whatever language (for most of these are accessible in very few American libraries), but also and especially from manuscript material, for the volumes will mostly consist of materials hitherto unprinted. Her selection of what is most important has been made with care and skill, and embraces material covering the whole period, not only the importations before the Revolution and down to the prohibition in 1807, but also the illicit importations between that date and the Civil War, for which the correspondence

and reports of the African squadron in the Navy Department and other archival materials here in Washington have been used.[257] Miss Donnan has also obtained whatever is to her purpose from the Manuscripts Division of the Library of Congress, from the archives of Virginia and South Carolina, and from the Laurens papers belonging to the South Carolina Historical Society at Charleston, where she spent five or six weeks last spring working in that very important body of material. Other materials have been obtained from the eighteenth century newspapers, from manuscript collections in the North, and to some extent from the British Museum and the Public Record Office in London. Miss Donnan expects to spend next summer in London, searching thoroughly those two repositories, from which a great deal more is yet to be obtained before we can consider that our collection is thoroughly completed; and I have promises of further opportunities in Great Britain, in such places as Bristol.

I enter thus into detail because such a description of the contents of our proposed work may lead you to think that, leaving at one side your documents respecting slavery *in* the United States, which have another sort of value, not distinctly related to that of any of our books, your diary of the man who went to Africa in 1789 and your report of the Newport-Congo-Cuba-Newport voyage might gain in effectiveness and usefulness if brought into conjunction with this comprehensive collection of materials on the slave trade which we have been accumulating—and which, by the way, contains a log of a slave voyage from Providence in 1795.[258]

I fear that this has proved to be a rather long-winded explanation. I submit it however for your consideration. There is no need for haste in considering what I have suggested, for Miss Donnan cannot go to England until next summer, and we shall be far from regarding the book as complete until after the researches she will there make. I think I shall be in New York in late October or early in November and perhaps we could then find an opportunity to talk further of the matter, if such should be your desire.

To EDMUND C. BURNETT

October 6, 1919.

My dear Burnett:

. . . The Department were invited to a reception yesterday afternoon on the yacht "Carnegie," which in a few days is to set forth on another voyage, this time of some 74,000 miles. It was a very interesting craft

---

[257] The material relating to the trade after 1807 has not been published.

[258] Mr. Plimpton later published The journal of an African slaver, 1789-1792, *Proc. Amer. Ant. Soc.*, n.s. **39** (2) : 379-465, Oct., 1929.

to inspect.[259] In their small library, I was delighted to perceive Bolton's *Guide* and Parker's *Calendar* and Allison's *Inventory,* with which I felt sure these voyagers would while away many weary hours—but then I perceived, on looking further, that they had in all a complete set of the publications of the Institution. My friend James Angell (who is in Washington now as chairman of the National Research Council) [260] said that they undoubtedly took them along for ballast. Of course it is a pity that they should sail without a copy of volume I. of the *Letters of Delegates to the Continental Congress,* but it can be forwarded to them at the Cape of Good Hope. . . .

As for the flume business,[261] I hope that your valor and success may be like that of Cassius and Caesar, when

> The torrent roared, and we did buffet it
> With lusty sinews, thrusting it aside
> And stemming it with hearts of controversy.

To EDWARD S. CORWIN

October 8, 1919.

My dear Mr. Corwin: [262]

In view of what you say about the attraction Marshall's personality has for you, you may be interested in the slight reminiscences of him which I had in Richmond in 1891 from old Dr. William P. Palmer, who sat next to me at the dinner table of a boarding house.[263]

He said that Marshall was enormously and immediately attractive to children. They instantly flocked to him. He himself had often sat on his knees (with some difficulty, the old gentleman having very thin legs). He and his brother used often to go out to a farm their father had, and the Chief Justice also had one in the same direction, and, riding in from it, used often to overtake them, and set up one boy on the saddle in front of him and the other behind him, and so ride into Richmond, with characteristic disregard of conventional appearances.

An old lady of Northern Virginia who in her childhood used to visit in Richmond, at a house opposite Marshall's, told me that she had often seen the Chief Justice, with a handkerchief over his head, sweeping for dear life, aiding the servants to get the job done quickly while Mrs. Marshall was absent, he having sent her out in a carriage and then—a piece of his tender regard for her—getting it done as quickly as possible, because she among the other peculiarities of her nervousness, could not bear to have it done while she was about.

Little touches, not very important, but they are among the things which help to explain how he could be, as I suppose he was, in his old age the most esteemed citizen of Richmond while holding political views that almost every one there abhorred. An old Mr. Ruffin, brother I think of Edmund [264] who fired the first shot at Fort Sumter, said to me "Chief Justice Marshall was my wife's great uncle (or something or other) and one of the greatest and most lovable of men, but he did this country more harm than any one else in all its history has ever done it."

Don't trouble to reply to these slight lines—unless you choose to reply by sending an article for the *Review.* I am quite lacking in good American-history material for the next number.

To ELIZABETH DONNAN

October 15, 1919.

My dear Miss Donnan:

. . . Thank you for calling my attention to the letters of Roosevelt and Trevelyan.[265] I must say I enjoyed Trevelyan's most, just as personally he has been more attractive than Roosevelt to me. There is a ripeness about his remarks that the other lacks, not having had twenty years of quiet reflection after the ending of an active political career. Indeed, quiet reflection can hardly be said to have been the Colonel's strong point, either during or after his public service. His remarks about books seem to me in general rather superficial, and yet it is of course perfectly wonderful how many

---

[259] The *Carnegie,* a non-magnetic ship, operated under the Department of Terrestrial Magnetism of the Carnegie Institution, made seven voyages before it was destroyed, Nov. 29, 1929, in the harbor of Apia, as the result of an explosion while refueling. Capt. J. P. Ault was killed and all equipment destroyed (*Carnegie News Service Bulletin,* Feb. 2, 1930).

[260] James Rowland Angell (1860-1949), who was connected with the University of Chicago from 1894 to 1919, was president of the Carnegie Corporation, 1920-1921, and of Yale University from 1921 to 1937.

The National Research Council, established in 1916 by the National Academy of Sciences at the request of President Wilson, as an aid in preparing for war, had been, in 1918, requested by the President to continue its activities in stimulating and organizing research and in gathering scientific and technical information, in cooperation with the government or with private agencies.

[261] Dr. Burnett frequently wrote of his troubles in connection with a survey across his Tennessee farm for a flume.

[262] Edward S. Corwin, McCormick professor of jurisprudence, Princeton University, author of *John Marshall and the Constitution: a chronicle of the Supreme Court,* New Haven, Yale Univ. Press, 1919, *Chronicles of America* ser. **16.**

[263] Of Corwin's volume on Marshall, Jameson wrote: "For myself, though I have enjoyed what I have read in it [Beveridge's *Marshall*] I think I have derived more real satisfaction from a little book on Marshall of about 50,000 words that young Corwin of Princeton wrote for Allen Johnson's series of Chronicles of America, a popular but excellent series of fifty volumes, 'sold only in sets,' so that you may not have a chance to see Corwin's little book. It is good reading, but the thought is far superior to Beveridge's" (Jameson to Lord Bryce, Apr. 5, 1920; Stock, L.F., ed., Some Bryce-Jameson correspondence, *Amer. Hist. Rev.* **50:** 291, Jan., 1945).

[264] Edmund Ruffin (1794-1865) is probably better known for his work on fertilization, crop rotation, and drainage of the exhausted soil of Virginia, and for his publications on agriculture than for this fateful shot.

[265] *Scribner's Magazine* **66:** 385-409, October, 1919.

of them he read and remembered—it would be wonderful even in a man who had nothing else to do.

As to the A. H. A., I certainly hope he was wrong, and rather think he was.[266] His declamations against those who considered that history ought to be dull, and that nothing is important except minute research, like those with which his friend Thayer has so often favored us, strike me as having little more than a rhetorical value.[267] Such persons are no doubt detestable, but do they exist? Could anybody name one person who thinks so? We all agree that there must be brick-makers and hod-carriers in our profession as well as in others and that geniuses will be few; only, say Roosevelt and Thayer, don't let these humble workers assume that they are superior to glorious architects, or preach that there is no need of such. No, by no means, don't let them propagate that view; but did they ever? Though I was brought up in the period of healthy reaction against superficial literary treatment of history, and doubtless have heard some mousers speak with scorn of those who did not mouse, I can't quite remember anybody who corresponds to the being that Roosevelt chastises. It is a man of straw, set up to be knocked down. We who toil at the underpinnings of history know our place. I at any rate can clear my skirts by pointing to different things I said, in the height of the movement toward more careful use of sources, namely in a book I wrote in 1886-7, being some Hopkins Hall lectures on the *History of American Historiography*, a youthful work, but, by the way, not so bad for a boy of twenty-six, so I thought on looking it over the other day.[268]

I haven't a doubt that the unbeatable Ford showed up those *Courier* letters to the Massachusetts Historical Society last Thursday afternoon and will print them in his *Proceedings*.[269] I asked my sister to send me the next day's *Transcript*, which ordinarily reports the society's doings, but I have not received it yet.

McGrane's Biddle is here.[270] I guess it is good. Thayer's Roosevelt [271] is very interesting, and very well done indeed, except that he of course thinks it necessary to pitch into President Wilson with extraordinary bitterness. On the other hand, not a word about Roosevelt's conduct in respect to the Progressive nomination in 1916, which was as black an exhibition of ingratitude and of indifference to programmes of social reform in comparison with personal advancement as I can remember any great man to have shown. But I suppose that to raise this objection is to align oneself with the pedants who wish all history to be drab and impersonal.

In deference to the sentiment of regard for the sources at which I have hinted, I will not tell the senators that Miss Woolley called them a parcel of old hens until I am sure that that was her exact language.[272] . . .

To ELIZABETH DONNAN

October 24, 1919.

My dear Miss Donnan:

. . . What Ford read at the meeting of the Massachusetts Historical Society was not from the Boston *Courier* of 1860. It was based on the Boston *Advertiser* of 1861, namely on letters which Henry Adams wrote from Washington, not from Italy. I may very likely use the Italian letters in the January number.[273] On the other hand I may use a portion of the material respecting early Virginia which the vivacious Miss Wright sent me from the Spanish archives including especially a description of Jamestown in 1612 by John Clark, who was afterward mate of the *Mayflower*. That ought to be interesting in 1920. I can put the Spanish in the *A. H. R.* and, maintaining the austere

---

[266] Roosevelt's remarks on the American Historical Association (387) begin: "In a very small way I have been waging war with their kind (pedants) on this side of the water for a number of years. We have a preposterous little historical organization which when I was just out of Harvard and very ignorant I joined." A column and a half follow which betray little knowledge of the character of many of the members of the Association or of the work which it was doing, although he had been its president in 1912.

[267] Thayer, who was president of the American Historical Association in 1919, had given some expression to these opinions in his presidential address, Fallacies in history, *Amer. Hist. Rev.* 25: 179-190, Jan., 1920: "For a while we were told with much stubborn assertion, that it makes no matter how a man writes, or how he presents his facts; if readers can discover all the facts in the historian's dump, his end was achieved. From this came the epigram: 'If a book of history is interesting, it is not history.' This doctrine of muddle, or slovenly writing, condemns itself, and though some still practice it, none praise it" (190).

[268] The "other day" may have been used loosely for a much longer period than the words imply. Jameson's attention had been called to this book by a statement from Max Farrand that he could obtain no copy. In reply, Jameson wrote: "It seems a shame that you should not have a copy of that little book if you want it, though apparently it has now come into the class of rare Americana. The edition was small, 500 I believe. Hunting at my house, I have found an additional copy, and I do not know where it can be better disposed of than to send it to you, so I send it herewith. The lectures, as you will see from the preface, were delivered in January and

February, 1887, I shall hope therefore that as you turn the pages again you will judge the book leniently, as the production of a youth of 27, exceptionally green in some matters; but I should think it might not unnaturally serve the purpose you have in mind, of showing what was the state of things in 1887" (Jameson to Farrand, Jan. 22, 1917).

[269] The *Proceedings* of the society for October (53: 8) contained no letter by Henry Adams, but reported that Ford read a paper entitled, Henry Adams, correspondent.

[270] Reginald C. McGrane, professor of history in the University of Cincinnati, was the editor of the *Correspondence of Nicholas Biddle*, Boston and N. Y., Houghton Mifflin, 1919.

[271] Thayer, William R., *Theodore Roosevelt: an intimate biography*, Boston and N. Y., Houghton Mifflin, 1919.

[272] This was written in the midst of the Senate debate over the League of Nations.

[273] Henry Adams and Garibaldi, 1860, *Amer. Hist. Rev.* 25: 241-255, Jan., 1920.

views generally maintained by that journal in the matter of translations, can send an English version to the *Proceedings* of the Massachusetts Historical Society, to which I owe something—zwei Fliegen mit einem Schlag.[274]

Do you remember my telling you in Wilmington of that ancient recluse, heir of all the Rodneys, who would not let anybody see their papers, or even come into the house, usually professing ignorance of such documents? He died last spring, and could not take them with him, and his executor has had three big sales in Philadelphia, from which we have got some additional *Letters of Delegates to the Continental Congress,* and even a diary kept during some of its later sessions by Thomas Rodney, which I hope the Library of Congress bought yesterday.[275] . . .

To MARTHA L. EDWARDS

November 19, 1919.

My dear Miss Edwards:[276]

Your pamphlets came a little after your letter, and I have had great pleasure in reading them. The article in the *Mississippi Valley Historical Review* I had already seen.[277] Your record concerning war work of the religious organizations in Ohio is very impressive.

Is it not striking, how much more such doings contribute to the unifying process of American Christendom than all the efforts the various denominations and ecclesiastics have made toward "Church unity." In the days of my first remembrance, when churches did little except hold Sunday services and one week day meeting, it was natural to think of unification as a process that was to be brought about only by organic union of disunited denominations. At the end of fifty years of such effort, the facades of the churches face each other across the village green or court house square with the same old isolation; but around at the back doors, where the parish houses or parish kitchens or other parish institutions are located, and where most of the real work is done, there is constant intercourse and cooperation in all sorts of good work common to all the churches, and unity of a real kind is coming about in that way.

Other passages in what you have written bring to my mind a very just remark made to me in Chicago by Professor Paul Miliukov, famous in recent years as a leader in Russia.[278] It had struck him as very surprising that the complete freedom Americans enjoyed in respect to religious organization had left them nevertheless gathered almost exclusively in church denominations of European origin. It is striking, when one thinks of it. Freedom of religious thought has in the main not caused Americans to think freely on religious

---

[274] Miss Wright's documents were printed in the April *Review;* contrary to the plan expressed here, a translation was printed with them (*Ibid.,* 448-479). See *ante,* Mar. 27, 1916, n. 68.

[275] The diary is among the Rodney Papers in the Library of Congress.

[276] Martha L. Edwards (d. 1926), of Lake Erie College. In 1920 she became assistant professor of history in the University of Wisconsin.

[277] Probably one pamphlet was Ohio's religious organizations and the War, first published in the *Ohio Archaeological and Historical Quarterly* **28**: 208-224, April, 1919. Her article, Religious forces in the United States, 1815-1830, appeared in the *Miss. Valley Hist. Rev.* **5**: 434-449, March, 1919.

[278] Among the Jameson Papers is a small group of letters written by Professor Paul Miliukov in 1904. At that time he was in Sofia and was planning to visit Bosnia, Herzogovina, Dalmatia and Montenegro before coming to Boston to deliver the Lowell lectures, and then go to Chicago, his second visit there, to lecture on the Slavs. He was evidently in this country again in 1907 or 1908, for on Feb. 4, 1908, Jameson wrote to Leland: "I want to keep the picture of Milyoukov which appears on page 150 of the *Review of Reviews.* . . . I saw him only a few minutes when he was here but it was a great pleasure for I am very fond of him. Knew him in Chicago." Before the Russian Revolution Miliukov was a leader of the Constitutional Democratic party. Of his situation during the Revolution Golder wrote to Jameson on Oct. 15, 1917: "Our friend Miliukov has suffered much and has aged a great deal during these six months. Before the revolution and during the first week of the excitement he was the great man, but pretty soon the socialist and anarchist started a campaign of distrust against him that it will take years to overcome. Even if the Conservatives should come into power Miliukov will have to be kept in the background, unless an abrupt change should take place regardless of public opinion. It is such a pity, for after all, he is the ablest of them all, although I am sorry to say, not very tactful. He and his party were not ready for the change that came, but you could hardly expect him to be for neither they nor any one else foresaw what was coming.

"I had a rather unusual opportunity to become well acquainted with him. Of course, I had met him before but I can not say that I knew him well until one very eventful night. I was travelling in Southern Russia with the American Railway Commission in a special train and one evening we came to a town where Miliukov was speaking. His friend persuaded the Russian officials in charge of the train to let him come aboard and go with us to Petrograd. They consented but after the train started, they regretted, fearing that since he was out of power and the socialists in power, complications might arise. These officials decided to put him off in the middle of the night in a lonely station. I protested and tried in vain to get our American railway engineers to back me. I could not allow the insult without some indication that I was with him and comfort the old gentleman. When they put him off I, too, left the train and from eleven o'clock to two in the morning we had plenty of time to talk over affairs. I was fully rewarded for my little effort for I learned a great deal of contemporary history and Miliukov and his friends are now my sworn friends. . . . Notwithstanding all that his enemies are doing Miliukov is still a strong power in Russia."

In the autumn of 1920 Golder wrote from London that he had met Miliukov, who was planning to come to America toward the end of the year (Golder to Jameson, Sept. 22, Oct. 26, 1920). On Sept. 2, 1920, the New York *Times* announced that Professor Miliukov was to be a member of General Wrangel's government in South Russia, but by November that general had been defeated and had left Russia. For some time in 1921 Miliukov was in Paris as a member of the Russian Constituent Assembly, which represented all the Russian elements opposed to the Bolsheviki. He and a companion sailed for New York in October, 1921, to present conditions in Russia to this country and to the Washington Conference. See New York *Times,* Oct. 30, sect. 7, p. 4, and Nov. 12, p. 10.

subjects. The nature of Billy Sunday's [279] appeals to the average man show that the average man, though as a rule he does not take his religion seriously, nevertheless when he does proceed to take it seriously has no other thoughts respecting the Bible or theology than those which were current in 1850. The theology of Bryan's *The Prince of Peace,* the most popular of all religious discourses in America, is, they tell me, precisely that of sixty years ago. Dowie,[280] whom I heard holding an audience of five or six thousand "spellbound," had no other thoughts on any of these subjects than those of the lower-middle-class British evangelist of the fifties. Though everybody reads the newspapers, and surely a little of modern biblical criticism filters into the newspapers every month or so, nearly all American mankind have been absolutely unaffected by all the scholarly work that has been done in that line for fifty years. One is entitled to say in the field of religion what in the field of politics Oxenstjerna said on his death bed to his son, "Nescis quantilla prudentia homines regantur."

I thank you for your kind thought of me, and shall look forward with pleasure to seeing some time your book on the missions to the Indians. There again (for another digression) is a strange evidence of human stupidity and narrow-mindedness. Hardly any among the thousands of good Protestants who devote themselves to the study of Christian missions pay the slightest attention to the wonderful achievements in that line of the Catholic church, or are willing to rate them as of any serious consequence. I have seen a History of Christian Missions which out of 400 pages had not two to give to the missions of the Catholics, although one may truly say that for nearly two hundred years after the birth of Protestantism it was, with insignificant exceptions, entirely devoid of the missionary spirit, nearly every bit of which, from 1530 to 1730, is to be found in the glowing annals of the Catholic church— not to say, an elementary statement with which one could shock nine hundred and ninety-nine Protestant Sunday-school teachers out of a thousand, that, in the subsequent two hundred years also, that church has been the world's chief organization for the promotion of Christianity. In my mother's town the Catholics are more numerous than all the rest put together—and her minister is not acquainted with any of the priests, though full of the spirit of unity so far as Protestant colleagues are concerned.

But anybody would think I was still a professor, and still lecturing. I congratulate you upon the good field you have, and the good work you are doing in it.

To James T. Shotwell

January 19, 1920.

My dear Shotwell:

Thank you for your interesting letter of December 31. I quite agree with the notion that much might be made of the archival problems of the present day as one of the means toward bringing about such an international historical congress as is possible under present circumstances or those of the immediate future. I am sure that you will have found Hubert Hall much interested in this.[281] An equally good incitement toward such an end might come from a feeling, which I suppose would exist in these days, that now is a good time for extensive publications of materials for diplomatic history especially of the nineteenth century—partly because there will surely be a quickened interest in the study of international relations between 1815 and 1914 and partly because governments now-a-days are, for one reason or another, giving access to their diplomatic papers down to a much more recent date than hitherto.

The first of the international congresses was an outgrowth of a previous congress for diplomatic history,[282] and it is still true that a good approach toward an international congress lies through that path. But I should hope that that, and the archival matter too, should be only two of various incentives toward such a gathering. I should think far more highly of a general gathering, expect more from it, than from one which should be limited to conference on one or two historical subjects.[283] . . .

The existence of the Union Académique makes such procedure quite possible now. The tenth article of its statutes seems to provide for such actions. I suppose the procedure would be that the Union might, if it chose, appoint an international committee of historical people to organize an international historical conference a few years later.

The constitution which Leland drew up for the American Council of Learned Societies, and which with slight amendment was adopted at the meeting of September 19, has now been accepted by more than the requisite number of societies, and the American Council, etc., may be supposed to exist.[284] It was thought

---

[279] The Rev. William Ashley Sunday (1863-1935), at one time a professional baseball player, whose unconventional methods as an evangelist drew large audiences.

[280] John Alexander Dowie (1847-1907), founder of the "Christian Catholic Apostolic Church in Zion" and of Zion City on the west shore of Lake Michigan.

[281] Shotwell had suggested that it might be well to present this point to Hubert Hall, hoping that it would be discussed at the meeting of the Royal Historical Society in January.

[282] The forerunner of the series of international congresses beginning with the Paris congress of 1900 was the Hague congress on diplomatic history, held in 1898.

[283] The omitted section, after referring to the death from starvation of Professor Lappo-Danilevskii in January, 1919, repeated the argument for an international committee, and suggested that it might now be possible for such a committee to meet and prepare projects to be considered whenever an international congress should be called.

[284] The American Council of Learned Societies was organized in 1919 with two delegates from each of the important national learned societies devoted to humanistic and social studies. Its aims are to advance the interests of the humanistic sciences in America by promoting research in those studies, and, through

that a meeting might be had in January, but apparently it will be held in New York, February 14. Haskins and I are to represent the American Historical Association, Turner and Bingham the American Antiquarian Society; others are G. M. Whicher and J. C. Rolfe. The American Institute of International Education (Duggan) [285] offers us the hospitality of its rooms, and indeed is very willing to provide a permanent place for the secretariat and many of the expenses thereof. I think this Council, though mainly called into existence in order to offer a means of American representation in the U. A. I., may ultimately have some useful functions within the United States, making cooperation of our humanistic societies easier and more effective; but on the whole I entertain only modest expectations for the Council in any respect, because all depends on money, and neither rich individuals nor the custodians of great funds in this country seem to have any such disposition to hand out money for humanistic enterprises as for undertakings in the physical sciences. Archaeology is in a way an exception, either because it works with a pick and shovel upon the material earth, or because it lends itself readily to pleasing photographs, which, as witness the *National Geographic Magazine,* are a sure means of captivating the prosperous mind in the U. S. A.[286] . . .

To Francis A. Christie

March 12, 1920.

Dear Christie:

. . . The world goes very badly but we are informed on all hands that the only way to make it better is to go to work—in the vernacular, to saw wood, and I must this minute proceed to do it, not even waiting to discover an ideal candidate for the presidency of Allegheny College—or Yale, or Cornell, or Cincin-

nati, or Minnesota, or the University of Pennsylvania, or the Carnegie Institution. Why not appoint Hoover to them all? He could do it. . . .

Mrs. Shorey was over here the other day from Baltimore; charming as ever. Shorey and I are to have a walk in early June (up the Susquehanna from Perryville perhaps) and on my return from Canada Sparks [287] and I have one in the mountains of southern Pennsylvania. I shall hope that you and I can have at least one day of walking while I am with you. If there is a day in the week in which you are free, you might put my lecture on the preceding evening.

I am sure that the American Catholic Historical Association welcomes Protestants. I told the secretary, as I went out of the meeting in Cleveland, that I wished to be a member, and he was so pleased that I perceived I should have said so, with much emphasis, at the end of my remarks. Roosevelt would not have failed to do this. . . .

To Francis A. Christie

April 20, 1920.

My dear Christie:

. . . I will lecture at the school at whatever hour is appointed on Friday afternoon and give the other one that evening. I should not expect to be tired by it at all.

> Though much is taken, much is left, and though
> We are not now that strength which in old days
> Moved earth and heaven, that which we are we
> are.[288] . . .

. . . As to spring flowers my attitude toward all vegetation is that of Peter Bell; in fact, I am not even sure that I know a primrose when I see one, as he seems to have done. The best spring flower that I shall see will be that hardy perennial Franciscus Christianus.

Thank you for the review of Moore. I will not struggle to convince you that it is excellent, but it is.[289] . . .

I suppose I leave here about Monday noon, to walk three days with Sparks, probably from Chambersburg to Bedford. I hope that you and I will be able to put in some kind of a walk on Saturday, May 1. We can take along a sledge hammer and cold-chisel to dig up the flowers, wherewith to crown you as queen of the May. . . .

---

its membership in the International Union of Academies, to serve as an agency for the conduct of relations between its constituent societies and other American organizations of scholars and analogous bodies in foreign countries. Jameson was interested in the project from the beginning and was a member of its committee on ways and means. Under its auspices he had great responsibility for bringing the *Dictionary of American Biography* into existence. For an account of the organization see, The American Council of Learned Societies, *Amer. Hist. Rev.* **25**: 440-447, April, 1920.

[285] Bingham was at this time professor of Latin American history in Yale University; G. M. Whicher (1860-1937), a Johns Hopkins graduate student in 1884-1885, was secretary of the Archaeological Institute, 1919-1921; J. C. Rolfe (1859-1943) taught Latin in the University of Pennsylvania from 1902 to 1932; Stephen Duggan (1870-1950) was director of the Institute for International Education from 1919 to 1946.

[286] On Nov. 13, 1920, Jameson wrote to Leland: we "are preparing a document intended to draw tears from the eyes and money from the chests of the custodians of big funds."

The paragraph here omitted deals with the Cleveland meeting of the American Historical Association and with the activities of various historians known to Shotwell.

[287] Edwin E. Sparks (1860-1924), president of Pennsylvania State College, 1908-1920. He was an associate professor of history in the University of Chicago during Dr. Jameson's service there.

[288] "Tho' much is taken, much abides." Tennyson's Ulysses.

[289] Moore, George F., *History of religions,* 2v., N. Y., Scribner's, 1913-1919; V. 2 was reviewed by Christie, *Amer. Hist. Rev.* **25**: 702-704, July, 1920.

To WILLIAM E. DODD

May 12, 1920.

My dear Dr. Dodd: [290]

. . . Yes indeed, I am very much distressed at the tone and turn of our national politics. It was natural that we should decline from the high level of national effort in 1918, but we need not have fallen so far. The blame can be pretty widely distributed. Almost none of the senators, on either side, have shown any largeness of view in respect to international relations. There has been little else than contemptible manoeuvring for position—what in the language of the ring is called "foot-work." And Heaven knows this poverty of imagination with respect to foreign affairs has not been balanced by any considerable amount of good thought and action by Congress on internal matters. For a party that was going to show us great things in the way of efficiency, the Republicans in Congress have made a pretty poor exhibit these last fourteen months.

I am more disposed than you are to blame the President. It seems as if, by showing (or pretending) only a little more respect for the senators, on both sides of the chamber, he could have got the few votes necessary in the early stages of the discussion to put his treaty across. It is a marvel to me that any man can possibly be so sure he is exactly right on all subjects, in a world which, as I see it, is so full of uncertainties. But I entirely agree with you that we are, so far as the presidency is concerned, destined to find ourselves in very commonplace hands, compared to the three great men we have just had. Wood seems to me to be dull, if not second rate, and none of the rest are more than that. As for Johnson, it passes my comprehension how anybody can think a man to be fit for the presidency who talks as he does, so unthinkingly, so violently, and so coarsely.[291] But what we shall have will be but a recurrence of the average president, for it was only by accident that we got Roosevelt, and only by his favor, a consequence of that accident, that we got Taft, and as for Wilson,

I never forget that the chances were that we should get Clark, whose mind is, I should think, a shade lower in the scale of primitive development than that of any other public men to whom we have given the speakership let alone the presidency. Democracies can't always be having good luck. Most commonly they must take what they deserve.

To GEORGE M. TREVELYAN

May 14, 1920.

My dear Mr. Trevelyan:

. . . I sat up late over your book, as I foresaw I should, and enjoyed it immensely.[292] You certainly have a wonderful gift in biography. The volume made me very envious, as indeed all first rate books of history do. I so much intended to be a historian, and should so much have liked to be; but, even assuming that I could have been, my "job" has lain elsewhere. I say with Sir Henry Wotton, though with much more exactitude, "I am but a gatherer and disposer of other men's stuff." [293] Well, I knew perfectly well that it would be so, when I came here and only hope it is useful; I suppose it must be.

To ELIZABETH OGDEN ADAMS

June 2, 1920.

My dear Miss Adams:

I do not think that Mr. Becker precisely throws your uncle's philosophy of history out of court, and certainly I do not think he has a philosophy of history between which and your uncle's as irreconcilable alternatives, one has to choose.[294] I think his difference has another form.

I can illustrate their difference of attitude toward history by recalling a letter I had from your uncle about twenty-four years ago. When the *American Historical Review* was founded, I naturally asked Mr. Adams for an article for the first number. He gave me one he happened to have at hand, a paper on

---

[290] Dodd had written: "Are you not a little distressed at the tone and turn of our politics? To me it seems that the dilemma we are in can hardly be straightened out either by Wood (very conservative) or Johnson (apparently without character)—and one of these is to be the Republican nominee. Hoover seems to have eliminated himself. The Democrats could not elect any but Hoover and he will not take their advances. Possibly Cox, but Cox is only an unimaginative Lowden. Unlike my friends I put most blame upon the people themselves, the rest upon the Senate. It may be blindness, but I do not see what the President could have done better than he did—except perhaps to conciliate some people a little" (W. E. Dodd to Jameson, Apr. 25, 1920).

[291] Major-General Leonard Wood (1860-1927), friend of Theodore Roosevelt, and Hiram Johnson (1866-1945), United States senator from California, 1917-1945, and former governor of California, were chief contenders for the Republican nomination which went to Warren G. Harding.

[292] George Macaulay Trevelyan, son of Sir George Otto Trevelyan. Jameson was probably reading *Lord Grey of the Reform Bill,* London, Longmans, 1920.

[293] Wotton, Sir Henry (1568-1639), *Preface to the elements of architecture.*

[294] Elizabeth Ogden Adams, who in her "Uncle Henry's" last years had supervised the running of his Washington home, was now at 1731 N Street, Washington. Dr. Jameson had sent to her a copy of Carl Becker's review of *The degradation of the democratic dogma,* three of her uncle's essays brought out by Brooks Adams after Henry's death. Miss Adams wrote: "My uncle as a result of a lifelong study of history evolved or attempted to formulate a philosophy of history which Mr. Becker throws out of court. Which is right?" (Elizabeth O. Adams to Jameson, May 30, 1920).

Count Edward de Crillon,[295] an interesting by-product of his History—a chip from his work-shop. When a few months later I asked him for another article, he wrote me that he had for the present at any rate abandoned the pursuit of history, believing that it was all futile, or, in his phrase, "like a Chinese play, with neither beginning, nor middle, nor ending," until we had discovered a true philosophy of history.[296] Now this decision was in accord with the nature of his subtle and penetrating mind, but it is not a doctrine to which all of us will feel that we need to come. When in more recent years he and I sometimes recurred to this thought, I used to say that, like the liberal-minded but practical king (Louis XVIII.) who said respecting liberal politics that after all it was his *métier d'être royaliste,* it was my *métier* to work at history, and as I got my living by it, I was obliged to assume that it was worth pursuing. More broadly, while theoretically it is a little absurd to shape one's course without a definite opinion as to the ultimate goal of mankind, still, since most of the elements of human life seem likely to go forward for a long time much as at present, and since plainly the study of what human beings have done in political and economic society is useful to the conduct of political and economic society, it seems to be a possible and defensible course to go on working at history as seen within measurable tracts of time, without prejudice one way or the other to theories of the sum total of human development, or to any one's philosophy of history. We can sail along from headland to headland, and make progress toward destinations that we know about, even when we do not know which way East lies on the great ocean. So I think that Mr. Becker may perhaps be estimated as one who neither accepts nor rejects Mr. Adams's philosophy, but concludes that, whether it is true or not true, his own personal task, and that of most other historians, remains much the same, and remains worth doing.[297]

For myself, it is a comfort to one who cannot understand a page of philosophy to think that such understanding is not essential to his salvation, but that a large and useful field is still open to one who has never framed a philosophy of history nor been capable of comprehending those framed by others.

I took a long walk on Monday to visit an old friend, convalescing in the Montgomery County Hospital, who was one of your uncle's companions in the Western excursion, Yellowstone, etc., which has so interesting a place in your uncle's autobiography.[298] My friend, who went as a young attendant geologist, speaks with the greatest pleasure of your uncle's kindness and of the extraordinary interest of his conversation. . . .

To Carl Becker

June 14, 1920.

My dear Becker:

Your letter has interested me very much.[299] Being asked by Willcox[300] to say what I thought about

---

figuration came about, leaving it to metaphysicians like Henry Adams to deal with the underlying agency, if it exists, and to determine, if they can, whether we are headed for the ash-heap or the millennium. The ash-heap, even on Henry Adams's calculation, is some millions of years distant; and there is good reason to think that the millennium, if that is to be our fate, is still sufficiently remote not to call for immediate preparation on our part. Whatever its ultimate end or its absolute value may be, and whether we know the ultimate end and the absolute value or whether we know them not, human life will remain essentially what it has been, and will have the same finite human values and meaning. It is the function of history, as I understand it, to deal with this meaning and these values as they are revealed in the thought and acts of men" (*Amer. Hist. Rev.* **25**: 482, April, 1920).

[298] Joseph Paxson Iddings (1857-1920), with the United States Geological Survey at the time Henry Adams visited the Yellowstone, was a professor of geology in the University of Chicago while Jameson taught there. He apparently never recovered from the illness indicated here for he died on Sept. 8, 1920. For a brief mention of his trip with Adams see, *The education of Henry Adams,* 350.

[299] On June 8, 1920, Becker had written: "Mr. Meiklejohn has been trying to tempt me away from Cornell, and to that end held up before me a lot of glittering lucre which was hard to resist in these days of H.C.L. However, I am not going. Every one is most kind in desiring me to remain here, and they have done what they could in the way of salary; all of which is due in no small part to letters written to the President on my behalf by some good friends, of whom I am told you are one. I mean I was told you wrote a letter; I did not need to be told you were a good friend, of which you have given too many evidences for me ever to be unaware of it. . . . I have a very good lot of graduate students, who seem to be under the illusion that I do a good deal to help them on their way. There is the library which is a joy forever, as well as a thing of beauty. Above all, there are such men as Burr and Hull, who are the finest of the wheat. I cannot see any reason at all for going to Amherst, except the money; and although I give up a good deal of that to remain here, I feel very comfortable about it."

[300] Walter F. Willcox, A.B., Amherst, 1884, professor of economics and statistics, Cornell University, 1891-1931.

---

[295] *Amer. Hist. Rev.* **1**: 51-69, October, 1895. In reply to Jameson's request for an article for the opening number of the *Review,* Adams wrote: "I would gladly aid you, but during the last years, since 1889, I have not written a line, and have forgotten what little history I ever knew. Being seldom here, and rarely staying longer than the occasion requires, I have accumulated no material, and have long ago burned whatever old manuscripts I had once on hand.

"To write an article is impossible. The best I could do would be to give you some unpublished material. Among the many blunders I have made in my history, are a few that might stand correction by document, and I might introduce the documents by a few lines of explanation. A few characters can be made a little clearer in this way. Of course I can use only scoundrels for the purpose, if your readers are to be amused, but in history the scoundrel is a simpler and easier study than elsewhere" (Adams to Jameson, June 10, 1895).

[296] See *ante,* Jan. 31, 1907, n. 45.

[297] Becker put it: "I am content . . . to regard the history of modern Europe as a series of 'changes in configuration,' and to attempt to understand, not in terms of physics, but in terms of human needs, purposes, and acts, how these changes of con-

your usefulness to Cornell, I said what I thought—no more, no less. Himself a good Amherst man, he did not tell me, nor did I know till now, that the tempter was Amherst. I suppose that that would not have made any difference, unless it had caused me to write a letter in similar terms, *mutatis mutandis,* to Meiklejohn,[301] but I do not much "butt in" affairs there. I am very glad for Cornell's sake that you concluded to stay where you are, and am not going to be discontented on Amherst's account, though I know better than they do what they are missing.

To OLIVER L. SPAULDING

North Edgecomb, Maine
August 14, 1920.

My dear Colonel Spaulding:[302]

The letter of Captain Phelan inclosed in your letter of August 11 is interesting, but I do not think that there is much that can be done in the United States along the lines of his suggestions.

The work and training of American librarians is very different from that of European librarians, the latter being mostly trained as custodians of learned deposits, in which medieval manuscripts have a considerable part, while the former are for the most part librarians of public libraries intended for popular use; and therefore the numerous library schools we already have give to prospective librarians a much more appropriate training, one more practical in view of what is actually before them, than what is supplied by the École des Chartes. I do not at the moment think of a library position in the United States for which the curriculum of that admirable institution would furnish the proper training.

Nearly the same is true of the profession of archivists. No doubt the number of archivists in the United States, now small, must be expected to increase, for interest in the proper care of our state and national archives is advancing, and it is also true that there is no special institution for the training of archivists. But for a good while the demand will be too small to justify the creation of an institution intended to supply it, and, what is much more important, the work of an American archivist is too different from that which the European archivist pursues to make the training given in the École des Chartes the appropriate preparation. The archiviste-paléo-

graphe is chiefly trained to deal with that portion of European archive deposits which is most difficult, and which, on the whole, has hitherto elicited the greatest amount of interest, namely, the medieval portion. I should estimate that more than three-quarters of the instruction offered at the École des Chartes is intended to enable the student to deal with documents of earlier date than any that the American archivist ever sees. Greek and Latin paleography, diplomatics, medieval French law and language, are of no use to the archivist of Iowa or Connecticut. In most states the requirements of an archivist are the requirements of a superior and talented filing clerk, who will deal with nineteenth-century and twentieth-century papers of a sort to which the École des Chartes pays no attention. Even in the oldest states, there are but few instances where the archivist needs anything more than this, except at times a knowledge of seventeenth-century handwriting or seventeenth-century French, Spanish, and Dutch, together with a knowledge of English law and colonial institutions, which the École des Chartes would not furnish. In short, to such extent as we need archivists, we shall have to train them ourselves, for purposes foreign to the work of the École des Chartes and by methods which it has not especially developed. One of their graduates, of the sort that Captain Phelan describes, would not find a useful career in the United States.

You will I am sure understand that the one who writes this rather discouraging letter is one of those most ardent for increase in numbers and improvement in method on the part of American archivists.

To WOODROW WILSON

December 3, 1920.

My dear Mr. President:

I hope I shall not seem to have neglected the letter you were so kind as to address to me on November 20. It reached me on the 26th, at my mother's house in Massachusetts, just as I was starting out on some journeys that made reply impossible until I should have reached Washington, where also I wished to make an inquiry or two before answering.[303]

On the day when you wrote to me, you were in my mind to an exceptional degree, for, in pursuance of your proclamation respecting the observance of November 21, I had been invited by President Faunce to come over from Boston to Providence and speak at Brown University on the Mayflower Compact and the Pilgrims,[304] and I was much reminded, and re-

---

[301] Alexander Meiklejohn, A.B., Brown, 1893, A.M., 1895, Ph.D., Cornell, 1897, was a teacher of philosophy in Brown from 1897 to 1912 and dean from 1901 to 1912. He served as president of Amherst from 1912 to 1924. At the time of his appointment Jameson had written a warmly cordial letter about his work as dean; but before the end of the Amherst term he felt some question as to the character of his administration.

[302] Lieut.-Col. Oliver L. Spaulding, U. S. A., chief of the historical branch of War Plans Division, General Staff. For an account of the organization of the historical branch under Spaulding, see *Amer. Hist. Rev.* **25:** 354, Jan., 1920.

[303] President Wilson had sent to Jameson a letter from R. C. Stuart, Jr., president of the Woodrow Wilson Club of Harvard University, and had asked that Jameson make suggestions as to the best way in which the club "could busy itself in the excellent work which it has set before it."

[304] *The arrival of the Pilgrims,* a lecture delivered at Brown University, Providence, R. I., Nov. 21, 1920, printed by the university.

minded the audience in a way that I thought they liked, of those old days at the Brown University Lecture Association, when you came over from Middletown and stayed with me and gave that brilliant series of lectures which many of my audiences remembered with pleasure.[305]

I am very glad that these young men of Harvard have established this Woodrow Wilson Club, and should be particularly gratified if I could make any valuable suggestions for their purposes.

1. It is possible that, beyond such collecting of material as anybody can do with money, in the open market, they might make a distinctive addition to the materials possessed by the Harvard College Library respecting the negotiations at Versailles, if there were any series of manifolded daily reports or summaries of the transactions of committees or other subdivisions of the Conference, that by your permission and at their expense could be copied for the Harvard College Library. If such materials are not yet open to public use, such a transcript might be deposited under restrictions operating up to a given date in the future.

2. While I have been led to suppose that files of French newspapers of the period of the Conference would not be a very valuable source for the knowledge of its history, I have been told that what was in the Paris edition of the *London Daily Mail* was exceptionally good. Perhaps, if this seems to you to have been the case, the club could procure for the Harvard College Library a file of that newspaper during the period.

3. At the expense of the Carnegie Institution, the National Board for Historical Service (a group of the best historical men) maintained for two years, ending in July, 1919, a service consisting in securing of files of eighteen or twenty of the most important German newspapers, sent from month to month, and in drawing off from them and translating such portions as supplied valuable intelligence toward the conduct of the war, which were constantly supplied here in Washington to the government departments to which one or another portion might be helpful. One complete set of all the translations has since been turned over to the Library of Congress, and constitutes the cream of the historical material contained in the German newspapers during those two years. The Library of Congress would furnish at a low rate photostat reproductions of all those parts relating to the negotiations at Versailles, if the club desired it. This material would, I should imagine, form a valuable means of getting the German view of the negotiations as they progressed.[306]

4. The club might reprint in a small pamphlet the Covenant of the League of Nations and place copies of it in the hands of all graduate students, law school students, and senior undergraduates at Harvard. But people in Cambridge would know, though I do not, whether this would or would not be a superfluous thing. It perhaps does not fall within the scope of operations proposed by the club, since Mr. Stuart's letter speaks primarily of fortifying the library.

5. They might have an annual dinner with a good speaker, who might bring home to the minds of the students the principles which your conduct at Versailles represents.

6. But after all, the best suggestions that I can make are, I feel sure, of quite secondary value to those which they could obtain in Cambridge by direct conference with Professor Haskins, who was at Versailles and knows far more than I do of what was done there and of the materials for its history, and who, as a warm supporter of your administration, would be glad to help the admirable work which the club has in mind. I return Mr. Stuart's letter.[307]

Though this letter is already too long, I do not wish to close it without a personal word. When you were first taken ill, I wished that such a message could go from me to you, but I felt sure that you ought not to be burdened by the task of even reading the multitude of such letters that would come, and that those about you would rightly see to it that you were not thus burdened. But let me now say what has been in my heart and mind. I have followed your administration, and especially your course in international affairs, with great admiration, with much pride in our early friendship and in the occasional evidences of friendly regards still continuing on your part, and with the earnest hope and belief that the high ideals which you have entertained respecting the position of America in the world will ultimately be realized in what is essential. I have followed your illness with the profoundest sympathy, have never passed in sight of the White House without deep feeling, and have rejoiced at all the evidences that have come to me of improvement in your health. I hope that the release from public cares, three months from now, may greatly speed this process of recuperation, and that you may be able to do still other great work for the country, and much of it. I wish you to know of my warm and abiding friendship and deep solicitude. Of my wish to be helpful in any matter, whenever I can I am glad to see that you are already fully aware.

Believe me to be, with old affection and with the highest regard.

---

[305] See *ante*, Aug. 22, 1888, n. 7, and Jan. 5, 1889.

[306] A further description of this work, which was done under the direction of Victor S. Clark, is to be found in the *Ann. Rept., Amer. Hist. Assn.*, 1919: 1: 181-183. Vassar College was the only eastern institution which purchased photostats of the collection.

[307] Professor Haskins *was* consulted, and on Apr. 16, 1921, Wilson's secretary, John Randolph Bolling, sent his reply to Jameson with a request from Wilson that he comment on it. This Jameson did on Apr. 19, 1921, for the most part emphasizing the value of the newspaper collection he had described in his first letter. On Apr. 21, Mr. Bolling wrote that Jameson's letter had been sent to Mr. Stuart.

To Edmond S. Meany

January 19, 1921.

My dear Meany:

Thank you for sending me Tyler's pamphlet.[308] I return it herewith. I should not think it need be taken very seriously. He is a very good fellow, hospitable and genial, but he never loses a chance to preach these same old doctrines of the primacy of Virginia and these same old defences of his father and of secession and these same old depreciations of Lincoln and most of his associates. It is perfectly true that many historical writers, especially those of the second and third rank of competence and importance, have unduly magnified Plymouth Rock [309] and forgotten Virginia because they did not happen to live there, and it is well for correctives to be applied in this, and in some of the other matters of which he speaks; but such exaggerations as Tyler's quite overshoot their mark. He writes with much more fervor than discrimination. To take just one thing, why should one assume that the estimate placed upon Lincoln by Charles Francis Adams the elder is the final and correct estimate of history? Adams was a great man, and of enormous value to the country, and very intelligent; but he never saw Lincoln but once, was unfavorably impressed then, and was by temperament and previous history certain to misunderstand and under-estimate him and to exalt Seward in comparison.[310]

---

[308] Tyler, Lyon Gardiner, *Barton and the lineage of Lincoln: claim that Lincoln was related to Lee refuted.*

[309] In Jameson's review of Campbell's *The Puritan in Holland, England, and America,* he wrote: "Indeed, one occasionally sees American history treated as if Plymouth Rock underlay the whole geological formation of the United States" (*Atlantic Monthly* **70**: 698, November, 1892).

[310] "Mr. Adams made at the time his own diary record of the single official interview he was ever destined to have with President Lincoln. His half-amused, half-mortified, altogether shocked description of it, given contemporaneously to members of his family was far more graphic." Adams had gone with Seward to the White House to discuss foreign policy. "Presently a door opened, and a tall, large-featured, shabbily dressed man, of uncouth appearance, slouched into the room. His much-kneed, ill-fitting trousers, coarse stockings, and worn slippers at once caught the eye. He seemed generally ill at ease,—in manner, constrained and shy. The secretary introduced the minister to the President, and the appointee of the last proceeded to make the usual conventional remarks, expressive of obligation, and his hope that the confidence implied in the appointment he had received might not prove to have been misplaced. They had all by this time taken chairs; and the tall man listened in silent abstraction. When Mr. Adams had finished,—and he did not take long,—the tall man remarked in an indifferent, careless way that the appointment in question had not been his, but was due to the secretary of state, and that it was to 'Governor Seward' rather than to himself that Mr. Adams should express any sense of obligation he might feel; then stretching out his legs before him, he said, with an air of great relief as he swung his long arms to his head:— 'Well, governor, I've this morning decided that Chicago post-office appointment.' Mr. Adams and the nation's foreign policy were dismissed together! . . . he never recovered from his

To Charles H. Firth

February 5, 1921.

My dear Firth:

I cannot thank you too warmly for your kindness in sending me a copy of your pamphlet on Modern History in Oxford and for the great interest I have had in reading it.[311] All such contributions to the knowledge of how things have been done in the field of historical work is always of interest to me but this contribution has been particularly so. Such knowledge of the Oxford system as I possess enables me to see partly the difficulties under which professors struggle forward, but what I have seen of American and other men trained in history at Oxford makes me think that you underestimate the good that you have been able to accomplish. . . .

I venture to comment on a passage on page 50. You say "They considered whether Oxford could offer American students the higher training which they had hitherto received in Germany." I comment on this because I have frequently seen the problem stated in that way by English academic authorities. The view appears to be that, before the war, American students habitually went to German universities. Forty years ago they did. When I was graduated from Amherst College, I fully expected, as the inevitable thing in pursuance of historical education, to go to Germany soon. Circumstances arose that defeated the plan in my case, and turned me to the Johns Hopkins University instead, but most of the men of my age who at that time were preparing themselves for the teaching of history did go to German universities. But for the last twenty years, however it may have been in medicine and some of the physical sciences, very few graduate students of history, have gone to Germany. If they have gone to Europe at all, they have been much more likely to go to Paris. Much the same has been true, I think, in subjects allied to history, though probably not to the same extent, for there is a special reason in the case of history which does not apply to the allied subjects, namely, that fully half of our graduate students devote themselves mainly to American history, and of course mainly to the periods since 1776, as being much the most important, and these feel little impulse to go to any European institution. Of course they are wrong about this, and give their work too narrow a basis; but there are many professorships of American history to be aspired to and most students cannot afford to go to Europe at all.

When I was teaching, I always tried to influence men to go and study or work in Europe, if I properly could, but usually told them—and that was from sixteen to

---

astonishment, nor did the impression then made ever wholly fade from his mind" (Adams, Charles Francis, Jr., *Charles Francis Adams,* 144-146, American Statesmen ser., Boston, Houghton Mifflin, 1900).

[311] *Modern history in Oxford, 1841-1918,* Oxford, Blackwell, 1920.

twenty years ago—to go to Paris chiefly. I see little mention in English writings respecting this topic, of the opportunities for work in France, where, among other things, the young American comes into profitable contact with ways of thinking more different from his own, more like those of Europe at large, than those he would find in England; and I also think it possible that English writers are not aware of the improvements which the last thirty years have brought into the teaching of history to graduate students in American universities. We are flexible and facile enough to introduce with a certain rapidity anything we think to be an improvement, though I am far from content with what we are doing, and am sadly aware that our universities do not now get graduate students of as good a grade as they did twenty years ago. But what I undertook to say is that, in respect to history at least, and a good number of other studies, the talk of diverting from German to English universities the stream of American graduate students rests upon error. Whatever the reasons, there has for many years been no such stream. If on any one place, our minds have been set rather on Paris. It was beginning to be so when Charles Haskins wrote his article on the study of History in Paris in the *American Historical Review* of April, 1898.

I am now able to look forward definitely, and with a great deal of pleasure, to the prospect of seeing you this summer. My sailing is engaged for June 24, Montreal to Liverpool, Canadian Pacific Steamship *Victorian*. I expect to spend July, August and September, in London and elsewhere in England, with various minor occupations in London, but have as my chief object the collecting of material for the series of volumes I propose of the Correspondence of the British ministers in Washington. Mr. Balfour, as perhaps I told you, gave his consent that I should make all needful use of the material—official instructions and dispatches—in the Public Record Office; but my main object and what will justify tarrying three months in England, will be the pursuit of such correspondence in private hands, such as those in the hands of the descendants of Foreign Secretaries or in those of the descendants of the ministers and their relatives and friends.

Please bear me in mind, if any clews come to your hands.

I shall also have in mind the matter of a general handbook of lists of diplomatic representatives, but do not now know with how much assurance I can pursue the matter. Under the present means possessed by the Carnegie Institution, or budgets of this department no larger than the present, I should not be able to carry out the project; but we are hoping that additional means may be secured by the Institution through our

new president.[312] At present the Institution, like everybody else that has a fixed income, is pinched by the increased cost of everything it is trying to do.

To Elizabeth Ogden Adams

March 21, 1921.

My dear Miss Adams:

I think you may be interested to see a review of *A Cycle of Adams Letters* that is more amiable than your uncle's, and, in my opinion, more judicious.[313] So, as you may not see the April number of this excellent journal which I edit, I ask leave to enclose proof-sheet of a review by Professor Fish. He was one of my Providence students years ago, but is now a professor in the University of Wisconsin.

I will also enclose, as a curiosity, a reproduction of the menu of the dinner given by George Peabody,[314] London, 1855, to ex-president Fillmore. If that is the way that ex-presidents were treated in former times, no wonder that they almost all died soon after becoming ex-presidents—with the exception of your great-grandfather and his father, who seem to have been composed of particularly durable materials, which I hope have come down to you.

I have meant to ask you if you knew Mrs. Oswald Ernst,[315] of Boston origin but living in Washington, and if so, if you would be so kind as to introduce me to her. I wish to ask her about a letter-book of an ancestor of hers, in the early eighteenth century, which I suppose she possesses, and which may contain some data that I should like to see, for the benefit of one of my publications. I should very much appreciate your mediation.

---

[312] The new president was John C. Merriam (1869-1945), president of the Carnegie Institution of Washington, 1921-1938.

[313] *Amer. Hist. Rev.* **26**: 546-548, Apr. 1921.

[314] George Peabody (1795-1869), after establishing the firm of George Peabody and Company in London, which specialized in foreign exchange and American securities, settled there in 1837. In 1854 he took into partnership Junius S. Morgan. The Peabody Institute of Baltimore, with its excellent library often frequented by Jameson during his years in Baltimore, was but one of many Peabody establishments in New England and the South. His biographer in the *Dictionary of American Biography* refers to his "large and elaborate Fourth-of-July dinners at which the English nobility met American visitors to London." This may have been the menu for one of such dinners.

[315] Since Mrs. Ernst before marriage was Elizabeth Amory Lee and a daughter was named Helen Amory, it is safe to assume that Dr. Jameson was in pursuit of the letter-books of the colonial merchant, Thomas Amory, whose mercantile dealings extended to the West Indies, the Azores, England, Ireland, and the continent of Europe. These letter-books came into the possession of the Division of Manuscripts of the Library of Congress while Jameson was chief of the division.

To Wilbur C. Abbott

April 12, 1921.

My dear Abbott: [316]

. . . I suppose that I do not know enough about the scope of your Lowell Institute lectures to advise as to printing, but I feel clear that there would be a considerable utility in a book on modern revolutions, indeed I have for some time been impressed with the thought that such a book is needed.[317] So many people, in so many different parts of the world, are talking of revolution as a natural expedient when things go wrong, that it seems as if many people needed to be informed more fully as to the natural history of revolution, based on a comparison of modern instances. I tried (in a hasty search) to find some good exposition of the subject but did not succeed,—though I found that a newspaperman of my acquaintance was delighted when, in response to his inquiries, I pointed him to the grave pages of Thucydides on the subject, out of which he told me that he had cribbed an article. I should think a pretty large public would be interested in knowing what kind of an expedient this frequently-suggested one is, and how it has worked in comparison with some of the alternative expedients for improving the world—for I understand that there are others though one hears less about them.[318]

To Paul Shorey

May 5, 1921.

My dear Shorey:

I thank you for sending me your remarks on Wells.[319] I meant to put the paper in my suitcase before going to New York, the day it arrived, but failed to do so. Since my return, I have read it, and read it with enjoyment. I still refuse to think as badly of his book as you do, but perhaps that is because I have not read it. Judging from what pages I have read, I feel more inclined toward the views expressed by our own review of it (editorial our) by Professor Becker, who devotes a brief article to it in the July number of this journal.[320] I mentioned this largely in order that you may buy

that number, or at any rate read some of it. "Come with us, and we will do thee good." When it comes out, I shall be on the bounding billow, so don't expect me to buy a copy and present it to you. Results in the way of conversion would be too uncertain.

Mrs. Shorey, whose much esteemed letter arrived this morning, tells me that you even scent propaganda in the *Best Short Stories of 1920*. In the same mail with her letter and its remarks on radicals came this week's issue of the Saturday Evening Post. While waiting for my furnace to do what it should, and thus unable to go to my office, I read the first piece in it, the first installment of a story by the gifted Nina Putnam Wilcox (or is it Nina Wilcox Putnam),[321] and was shocked to see in it the plain traces of bourgeois propaganda, attempting to undermine by unworthy ridicule the sacred cause of contemporary radicalism.

So we get it, going and coming. Happy are those who have no opinions which it seems worth while to propagate, such as

Yours very truly.

To Gaillard Hunt

May 16, 1921.

My dear Hunt: [322]

. . . I have so much appreciation of your intelligence and skill in matters of administration that I should not think of "butting in" upon any matters that lie within that sphere of State Department duty, even if I had any suggestions to make, but I hope it may not seem out of keeping for me to offer, at the very beginning of your term of service, when new plans are being considered, some modest suggestions in my own field of documentary historical publications, of things that are not regarded as among the necessary and inevitable functions of the Department of State, but might well be, things which corresponding departments in other countries take as a normal part of their functions, and which our own Department has from time to time undertaken in part, though without a continuous system, thought out on general lines.

First, however, I should like to urge upon you the necessity of a new edition of the historical *Register of the Department of State*. My copy is of 1874, and though I have heard there was an edition of 1876, I don't understand that anything of the sort has been issued since that date.[323] I should think that even for the constant routine duties of the Department it would be almost necessary, certainly of great con-

---

[316] Wilbur C. Abbott (1869-1947), after teaching history in the University of Michigan, Dartmouth, the University of Kansas, and Yale, had gone to Harvard in 1920; from 1938 to 1941, after retiring from Harvard, he was research associate in Yale.

[317] In a note to Jameson of Apr. 6, 1921, Abbott added a postscript: "I hardly think my Lowell Lectures on Modern Revolutionary Movements deserve a note in the *Review,* but I should be glad to know whether you think such a series is worth publishing in book form—as I am urged to write them."

[318] The volume embodying Professor Abbott's thoughts on the subject of revolutionary movements was *The new barbarians,* Boston, Little, Brown, 1925.

[319] Professor Shorey's severe review of the *Outline of history* by H. G. Wells appeared in *Art and Archaeology* 11: 223-224, May, 1921.

[320] Mr. Wells and the new history, *Amer. Hist. Rev.* 26: 641-656, July, 1921.

[321] Putnam, Nina Wilcox, West Broadway, which ran in the *Saturday Evening Post* from May 7 through June 25, 1921.

[322] Gaillard Hunt, who had returned to the Department of State in 1917 after service in the Library of Congress as chief of the Division of Manuscripts (1909-1917), was now chief of the Division of Publication and editor of the Department.

[323] Though the need for this was admitted and it was included in Mr. Hunt's plans for publication, no new volume of the *Register* has yet appeared.

venience, to have that manual brought down to date, together with the making of such corrections as the old book requires. I should think it would be useful, if not indispensable, in every embassy and legation, and helpful to foreign legations here in Washington, too. Of course your officials can pursue the facts down through a series of Annual *Registers* which I suppose exists, but this must be very inconvenient.

I am, however, much more impressed with the value of such a manual, properly completed to 1921, to American students of American diplomatic history, a growing body of intelligent men that need to be encouraged. For I certainly hope that the Division of Publications, under your management, is going to encourage better knowledge of the past doings of the Department, rather than to repress such desires on the old-fashioned theory that the doings of the Department of State are a sacred mystery, about which the less the public knows the better. If anything is certain in these days, it is that our citizens need a far better understanding of our foreign policy and its traditions than they now possess. The best management of the Department that ever was or ever will be cannot attain its full measure of success unless it is sustained by an intelligent public opinion, that approves what is being done because it sees why it is done and whither it tends, in the long course of our development as a nation among nations.

I do hope, therefore, that you will have in mind, as one of the great steps of progress that will signalize your administration as Chief of the new Division, the inauguration of an important series of documentary historical publications. It need not be grandiose, nor require an expenditure that will and ought to alarm Congress. Sometimes historical scholars have put forward the proposal that the government should continue and complete the old series of *American State Papers, Foreign Relations*. That was the doctrine of McLaughlin's *Report on the Diplomatic Archives of the Department of State, 1789-1840* (Publication No. 22 of the Carnegie Institution of Washington), and also of the *Report* of the committee on the documentary publications of the United States Government, submitted in 1909 to President Roosevelt by a committee of which I was secretary.[324] But as time has gone on, and Congress has shown no indication of a desire to do anything large or systematic in the way of historical publication, I have come to the conclusion that such proposals are too large and expensive. It is true that the A.S.P.F.R. contains only a fraction (perhaps about a quarter) of the useful material for our diplomatic history down to 1830 contained in the archives, but the whole is a great amount, and when you add to it the material for 1830-1861, it makes so big a project that there will be little use in asking Congress to undertake it.

My suggestion is that the Department of State should inaugurate a systematic publication of the *instructions* to ministers, from 1776 down, leaving out of course, those communications which, though called instructions, are of no significance. The instructions are the cream of the whole mass. A series of them would show the development of our foreign policy almost as well as the publishing of everything, and it has the merit of being practicable while the other is not. No doubt it would involve a good many volumes, but careful and sensible editing could keep the number down, and, since it takes time to prepare such volumes adequately, they would come out, one at a time, in a way that would not make excessive expense in any one year. Gradually they would illuminate to ourselves and the people of other nations the history of our international policy. Surely, nothing before 1850 needs to be concealed now, and by the time 1850 had been reached, 1870 would be as far in the past as 1850 is now. Anyhow, it is far better for all the world to know what we have been about, in international relations, than because of ignorance to suspect us of deep and dark designs that were never entertained.

I advocate this course of procedure largely because of the great success which has attended a similar procedure on the part of the French. Leaving out of account the volumes or the various-colored books that partially disclose current diplomatic doings, the different national governments have in their volumes of diplomatic history followed various courses. The British *Calendar of State Papers, Foreign,* started from the beginning, printing summaries of every document, and in sixty years have got only as far as 1582. The Dutch, beginning more recently, have published a splendid series that runs only from 1795 to 1840. Other nations have administered "first aid" to students of diplomatic history in a similarly fragmentary manner. But the French, with their characteristic sense of proportion, limited this to instructions, and in seventeen years (1884-1901) published seventeen volumes of their great *Recueil des Instructions données aux Ambassadeurs et Ministres de France depuis les Traités de Westphalie jusqu'a la Revolution* which has illuminated the diplomatic history of Europe from 1648 to 1789 more than any one single publication or series. The method was, one volume for instructions to the Ambassadors to Austria, edited by Albert Sorel, one to the Ambassadors to Prussia, by Albert Waddington,[325] etc.—each one prepared by competent specialists, who provided an elaborate and valuable introduction. Our method and order of arrangement would doubtless be different, but under any suitable

---

[324] See *ante,* Nov. 23, 1905, and Dec. 13, 1907.

[325] Albert Sorel (1842-1906), lecturer and writer on diplomatic history; Albert Waddington (1861-1926), author of works on Prussian history. The series of *Recueil* here mentioned consisted of twenty-five volumes, which appeared between 1884 and 1929.

method the series would not fail to be of great value, not only to historical students and the public, but to our diplomats themselves, who at present often have little other aid toward tracing the earlier history of our diplomacy than the extracts which Moore has picked out and printed in his *Digest*.[326]

Well, this is much more of a screed than I meant to inflict, but please do think this over carefully and give me an opportunity to talk further with you about the matter. Meantime, as I have said, my hearty congratulations, and, as always, my most sincere regards.

To Cornelia M. Pierce

24, Woburn Square,
London, W.C.1,
July 21, 1921.

My dear Miss Pierce,

. . . This Anglo-American Conference proved to be much more of an affair than I had counted on. Indeed, it was a little overwhelming in the multitude of things to do and places to go to and hospitable entertainments to enjoy. I shall send herewith a separate copy of the programme, which you can show or send to others, and which, from the very look of it, will sufficiently explain why I have not written, and will even, I hope, serve as an excuse to President Merriam as to why I have hardly got to work until yesterday and to-day—in case he enquires. Nothing could surpass the kindness and hospitality with which we have been treated, and it will be very difficult under our circumstances, with our capital divided between New York and Washington, to requite it in any degree when the time comes for a corresponding Conference on our side.[327]

Leland will be interested to know that the affair went more smoothly and systematically than that of 1913, but indeed, it was obviously much simpler, and confined to practical discussions. Many of these were very good, and some of them were useful to me. The Americans present were of course a somewhat casual lot, for probably nobody came over solely or even mainly for this occasion, but it was a good set. I will try to remember to cross off from the programme sent the names of those who did not actually come. The D. of H.R. in the C. I. of W. was adequately represented, as you see. Miss Davenport and Miss Donnan persuaded themselves, or I persuaded them, to absent themselves from their toil sufficiently to attend most of the occasions named on the pro-

gramme. I rather felt obliged to go to about everything, else I should not have seemed to be playing the game, and being the oldest person present of the Americans, was more put forward than my native modesty, which I hope has been often observed in the office, would naturally have suggested. Thus, I made sort of a speech on the first day, as the programme indicates, (did not know I was to do so till a little after I reached London, but they rightly assumed that I would be willing), had to preside at one Session and then at an adjourned Session of that same section, was called on for a little "remark" here and there, and dined at Lady Astor's, whose dinner and reception were really brilliant.

The whole thing wound up on this last Monday afternoon (this is Thursday) with a visit of 30 or 40 to Windsor, where the King's librarian, John Fortescue, showed us all over the Castle as well as the library, including many apartments not ordinarily seen, and wonderful treasures of portraits and other paintings and of books and manuscripts. He certainly showed unwearied kindness, keeping all this up for nearly three hours in a temperature of about 90, and if you have ever read the remarks about Americans in any of his Preface, you will think all this to have been extremely creditable to his politeness and amiability.[328] . . .

To Katrina Jameson

July 24, 1921.[329]

Dearest K.:

. . . I go over [to Belgium] to attend a meeting of the Royal Academy of Sciences (corresp. member), and see several Belgian and Dutch friends, and see a manuscript at Ghent and some archive material at Middelburg.

. . . Tomorrow morning I go early to Oxford, for two days, so must write briefly and then go home and

---

[326] *A digest of international law as embodied in diplomatic discussions, treaties and other international agreements, international awards, the decisions of municipal courts and the writings of jurists,* 8v., Washington, Government Printing Office, 1906.

[327] Some return for the hospitality enjoyed by Americans in 1921 was attempted by the invitation to British guests to attend the meeting of the American Historical Association in 1924. See *post,* July 19, 1923.

[328] Sir John Fortescue (1859-1933), librarian of Windsor Castle, 1905-1926, editor of the *Calendars of State Papers, colonial,* beginning with the volume for 1677-1680. A single quotation will explain Jameson's remark: "the various settlements show themselves in the present volume to have been for the most part unfit to manage their own affairs. The ceaseless wrangles of the New England Colonies, their harsh treatment of the Indians, which had been the origin of the Virginian rebellion, the high-handed dealing of the dominant cliques, whether political as in Virginia, or religious as in Massachusetts, and the general bitterness of their sectarian animosity, made the lives of many of the settlers a burden to them. . . . In all the other colonies [except Maryland] the Board of Trade and Plantations was compelled to interfere, and in every case it found itself confronted by dishonesty, shiftiness, and prevarication" (*Cal. St. Papers, Col., 1677-1680,* 1v).

[329] On July 22 Jameson wrote to Miss Pierce: "The date reminds me that 25 years ago today I saw Queen Victoria, as she came in from Windsor to attend the wedding of her granddaughter Maud to Prince Charles of Denmark. They are now King Haakon VII. and Queen Maud of Norway, and the papers say are celebrating their silver wedding."

pack. Dine in Oriel College tomorrow night, with several friends. Today took Miss Donnan out to St. Albans, went to church in the old Norman cathedral, formerly the church of the great abbey where Matthew Paris and other of the great chroniclers wrote their annals, the best of the English chroniclers, and where King Henry III. often visited him and told him what had happened. Then walked out to St. Michael's Ch. to see Lord Bacon's monument, showing him seated in his customary attitude ("sic sedebat," says the inscription), and parts of the Roman wall of Verulamium. Then across to Hatfield, to see Hatfield House, Marquess of Salisbury's place (met his famous brother Lord Robert Cecil the other day), and in the church of St. Etheldreda the tombs of the Cecils.

A good birthday to you. You are a dear girl, and I love you. Please read Milton's sonnet on attaining his 23rd Year. . . .

To WALDO G. LELAND

Middelburg, August 7, 1921.

Dear Leland:

Talk about archive-buildings! You ought to see this. Here is an ancient Premonstratensian abbey, so old that some of it is Romanesque, and so big that I think Lafayette Square would not equal its area. This old hotel, which only Dutch frequent, is one part of it. Another part is a fifteenth, or fourteenth century church about the size of St. Patrick's Cathedral in N. Y., only much taller, and with a tower 200 ft. high, and then another church about the size of the Shoreham, and all sorts of buildings inhabited by the govt. of Zeeland, and in the oldest part, in room after room, the Zeeland archives, admirably arranged in most picturesque installation. I look across at the old arches as I write, and on a bench in the linden-shaded courtyard that fills the minor space of the abbey sits a young woman in the typical Zeeland costume you see in the pictures—full black skirt, short sleeves, white cap with gold headdress under it. Call no place picturesque till you have seen Middelburg. Yesterday afternoon, in the Sat. P.M., market and in the merry-go-rounds and fair I saw scores of these costumes. I am going to walk over to Veere this afternoon, which I suppose is still more antique.

I wish I could tell you all about this excursion, which ends tomorrow with return to London, but my hand and the hotel pen forbid. Ghent, Brussels, Louvain, Hague, Utrecht, Leyden, Middelburg. Father Delehaye inquired kindly of you. Didn't see Cuvelier [330] or Muller of Utrecht. Must stop and go to church. Abbey chimes going at a lively pace.

To FRANCIS A. CHRISTIE

September 2, 1921.

My dear Christie:

This is not a very prompt reply to your good letter of August 2nd, but I have been expecting from day to day to see an old Marburg friend of yours, Theodor Sippell. I heard of his existence from Cheyney, who had apparently come across him at Penn Club, the Quaker meeting place where he resides, and as Cheyney mentioned to him that I was an intimate friend of yours, he wished to see me.

I resolved to call upon him, but was rather slow about it, and did not find him there. Last evening he called on me. He wished to hear all about you, said that you wrote to him a year or two ago, and that he had replied; recalled with great pleasure your stay in Marburg. He is not pleased at the thought that he must now drop his studies in the religious history of the 17th century, which he has been pursuing for eleven years but he has come to that conclusion—finds that the Quakers are not sufficiently interested in that history to sustain it, and is going back to Germany in a fortnight, to do something quite different. He paints the situation for Gelehrten in Germany in dark colours. Still he seemed naturally a cheerful spirit, and I think a rather fine one, who had been pursuing interesting researches. The centre of his studies in England seems to have been the Grindletonians, or men of Grindleton, somewhere in the north, precursors of pietism with whom George Fox, Anna Hutchinson and the Baptists and Independents of the Commonwealth had connections which he has traced. Their minister and leader, Roger Brerely, he described as holding and developing Luther's doctrine of justification without knowledge of Melanchthon or others of Luther's followers. All this may be familiar to you, for I suppose he has imparted some of it to Braithwaite and Rufus Jones,[331] and it may be in their books without my having seen it, though your eagle eye would have fastened upon it. However I do not believe that his small book or pam-

---

[330] Father Hippolyte Delehaye, superior of the Bollandists, in whose work, the *Acta Sanctorum* and the *Analecta Bollandiana*, Jameson was much interested. In 1920 when the society was in financial difficulties he circularized 140 persons and institu-

tions to raise money for it. Father Delehaye's *L'Œuvre des Bollandistes, 1615-1915* was dedicated to him.

J. Cuvelier, archivist, author of two pamphlets of interest to archivists: *La Construction des Dépôt d'Archives* (1910), and *Congrès de Bruxelles, 1910* (1912).

[331] William C. Braithwaite (1862-1922), president of the Woodbrooke Settlement near Birmingham, makes brief reference to Roger Brereley and to studies by Sippell in his *Beginnings of Quakerism*, 24, 25, n., London, Macmillan, 1912. Rufus M. Jones (1863-1948), in his preface to *Spiritual reformers in the 16th and 17th centuries*, London, Macmillan, 1914, says of Sippell: "I am under much obligation to my friend, Theodor Sippell of Schweinsberg, Germany. I am glad to announce that he is preparing a critical historical study of John Everard and the Ranters, which will throw important light on the religious ideas of the English Commonwealth. He has read my proofs, and has, throughout my period of research, given me the benefit of his extensive knowledge of this historical field."

phlet, *Zur Vorgeschichte des Quäkertums* is known to our students and I got him to give me a copy of it, that it might be noticed in the A.H.R. (if that periodical still lives) and am sending it to you herewith, hoping that you will give us a brief review of it, unless you are quite distinctly sure that there is some other man, unknown to me, who is in a better position to talk about it. If I get it when I get back to 1140, about November 15, it will be in season for the January number (if there is one).[332]

I expect to stay here until a certain meeting occurs on October 7., then go to Paris for a week, or less, and then to Spain for three weeks or less, and then sail for home. I have not been very happy here in London, partly because of remoteness from my family, and partly because I have not been succeeding very well in getting hold of the things I have wished to secure. Either one of the two could be borne with more or less equanimity, but the combination is bad. The things I saw do not exist in the quantities I supposed, or when they do it has been slow and difficult work to get at them. . . .

To EDMUND C. BURNETT

24 Woburn Square, W.C.1.
September 15, 1921.

My dear Burnett:

Returning to London and to my mail, I find that your volume I is out.[333] Hurrah! and also Vivat! The day should have been celebrated. If you were over here, I would take you out and give you a drink. It occurs to me that I might go and get one for myself, by way of celebration, but everything alcoholic is distinctly bad for me, so that in that respect the opportunity to go to Europe is wasted on this particular American.[334]

Well, it is a great and signal achievement and one of which you ought to be more proud than your modesty ever allows you to be. You have erected a *Monumentum aere perennius,* that is to say more enduring than the brassy products of less modest workers. I feel that "on behalf of the Management" as they say in the small theatres, I ought to express much gratitude for all the faithful labour, learning and highly intelligent scholarship that has gone into the making of this volume and its successors. . . .

To EDWARD P. CHEYNEY

24, Woburn Square, W. C. 1.
September 23, 1921.

My dear Cheyney:

I do not know that you are suffering for a report from me or indeed that you miss me at all, though I have greatly missed you and Miss Cheyney.[335] The situations are different. You are either at the Schoolhouse, eager in researches as to the condition of the cabbages, or the Ranunculus Boadicea, or the Benedicta Quindecimus; or else you are at the University, seeing how the hopeful plants there are going on, and in either case your mind is fully occupied with familiar surroundings, while I still languish in exile.

I have to report however that I feel much more cheerful about Great Britain and the course of the world in general since I have given up the vain endeavour to find papers that do not exist and have turned to the solid and entirely practicable task of exploiting the great mass which actually does exist at the Public Records Office, and also since I have found a very bright and clever American girl, well versed in American history, to help me there—a coloured girl, by the way, of quite unusual abilities, a graduate of Oberlin and student in the London School of Economics.[336]

But nevertheless there is a certain shadow over my proceedings, cast before by one coming event, namely my departure. There is a terrible amount to do, and yet tomorrow I must go to Cambridge and then on to Edinburgh, and cut out three or four days from work here. However, I shall get through somehow, and leave here October 8 for Paris and Spain, and, as now appears a glimpse of Portugal, because there are now no steamers from Gibraltar or Cadiz to New York except Spanish ships full of fleas and with food full of grease, so that I must go and take a French steamer at Lisbon. It is a pleasant prospect, but its date is such as to reduce my stay in Spain. I asked Bernard Moses what chief word of wise counsel he would give to one who proposed to make a brief visit to Spain for such purposes as mine. He said, "Never let them think you are in a hurry." How can I conceal the fact? . . .

To GERALD H. RENDALL

24 Woburn Square, W.C.1.
October 5, 1921.

My dear Sir: [337]

I think I promised you some further account of

---

[332] There *was* a January number and it contained an unsigned review of the pamphlet, probably the work of Christie (*Amer. Hist. Rev.* **27**: 344).

[333] Burnett, Edmund C., *Letters of members of the Continental Congress* **1**, Carnegie Institution, publication no. 299. The second volume appeared in 1923, and the eighth and final volume of the series in 1936.

[334] This was during the prohibition era.

[335] Professor Cheyney and his daughter, Alice, had been spending the summer in England but had returned to America at the beginning of the academic year. The "school house" was their home.

[336] Miss Ruth Anna Fisher, later in charge of the making of London transcripts for the Library of Congress.

[337] Jameson had appealed to the Reverend Gerald H. Rendall

Anthony Merry. First and last, from one source or another, I have accumulated a good many details respecting him, but I will not bore you with them all. It may suffice to say that he was the only son of a Spanish merchant of the same name dwelling in London, and apparently a grandson of another Anthony Merry Spanish merchant. Our Anthony was for a time associated in business with the British consul at Malaga, in 1787 was appointed consul at Madrid, and presently consul-general and filled that office well for several years. In 1801-1802 he was secretary to the embassy and Lord Cornwallis at Amiens which made peace with France. On January 21, 1803 he married the widow of John Leathes of Herringfleet Hall in Suffolk and about a year later went out to America as envoy extraordinary and minister plenipotentiary, was there from 1804-1806, then went to Sweden in a similar capacity and retired from the diplomatic service in 1809. Then he lived at Herringfleet till his wife died in 1824, and the rest you know.[338]

With the same American "cheek" which led me to write to you, I wrote to that person of the name of Merry in the London Directory, who seemed to be the most "respectable," a professional man, and by chance made a good shot, for he was a collateral descendant and had a good portrait which will be useful in my

book.[339] No other portrait is known. This Dr. Merry also had a seal bearing the same arms which you describe as engraved on the monument.[340] . . .

To Condé B. Pallen

November 26, 1921.

My dear Sir:

I am not in a position to reply to your inquiry of November 22 in any way that I can regard as satisfactory, because I have read only a small part of Wells's "Outline of History," and therefore I should not be willing to be quoted. I have no objection, however, to adding one voice to your collection of opinion, provided it is understood that what I say is based more on what others have said in print or in conversation than on any reading of the book.[341]

1. I have little right to an opinion as to the accuracy of Wells's statements of fact. Pains enough have probably been taken with them in all the earlier parts of the book, where he seems to have felt that it was wise to defer to the opinions of others. Reading however some parts of his account of the nineteenth century, where he seemed not to feel in any such need of guidance, knowing for himself what judgments ought to be expressed, I thought his deductions, though often acute, to be frequently marred by an unjustified contempt for the

---

of Dedham, Essex, for information about Merry, as Dedham was the village in which Merry died.

[338] In an unpublished lecture delivered to the trustees of the Carnegie Institution on Nov. 20, 1923, Dr. Jameson added further details concerning Merry, pieced out "from a most amusing variety of minute bits of evidence." Of his American service Jameson said: "he served here in pompous unhappiness from November 1803 to November 1806. Apart from his relations with Burr's conspiracy, he is chiefly remembered for the flaming indignation with which he resented the slights which he conceived that President Jefferson put upon him and his formidable wife in matters of etiquette. . . . I found that he was the son—the most exemplary and devoted son—of a bankrupt but respectable London merchant dealing in Spanish wine; that he had spent 23 years in Spain, latterly as consul-general and chargé des affaires, which might readily account for his over-estimate of etiquette and punctilio; and that his wife, who when he married her was the widow of a Suffolk squire, had originally been a farmer's daughter on the squire's estate, with the nowise aristocratic name of Elizabeth Death. Taken in connection with their lofty attitude about their position at President Jefferson's table, it all reminded me of the saying which Thomas Carlyle quotes from his Scottish mother, that 'when sole leathers get to be uppers they're awful stiff.' " From letters of Merry in Paris to Francis James Jackson, Jameson quoted Merry's cool consideration of his future wife: "I have done nothing the whole Day, but think whether I shall not make up to a Widow (though perhaps of 35) who is here, and who has a good Fortune, which though as a Jointure will only last her Life, will last the Time for which I shall want such an Assistance to my own Income, for as she never had any Children before, at least I have some Reason to suspect so, it is not likely that she would leave me with a great, or, in fact, any Burden at all of that Kind, and what spurs me still more on the Business is the Consideration that whenever I am called from hence I shall be hurried off to

America, and of course have no time to look about me in England."

For an account of the difficulties at Jefferson's dinner table to which Jameson refers, see Adams, Henry, *History of the United States of America during the first administration of Thomas Jefferson* 2: 367-376, N. Y., Scribner's, 1903.

[339] Correspondence of British ministers, see *ante*, June 12, 1919.

[340] Merry served as secretary in the negotiation of the treaty of Amiens and confided to a friend that it was he rather than the plenipotentiary, Lord Cornwallis, who had been doing the work. He reports that he is worn out with the "Fatigue of this Business, proceeding entirely from the total Incapacity of the old woman to whom I am unfortunately attached, and who sometimes in our Conferences betrays it so evidently that Joseph [Bonaparte] looks at me and smiles." Jameson added, "But if Joseph smiled, Anthony Merry, it is said, never did. The gravity of his deportment was such, we are told, that both Napoleon and George Canning delighted to call him, with a punning reference to his name, 'Monsieur Toujours Gai' (Lecture by Jameson, Nov. 20, 1923).

[341] Condé B. Pallen (1858-1929), from 1904 to 1920 editor of the *Catholic Encyclopedia* and a member of the executive council of the National Civic Federation, was "chairman of department on study of revolutionary movements." After stating that there was a well-defined movement on foot to substitute Wells's *Outline of history* for other historical texts, he asked Dr. Jameson's opinion of the accuracy of Wells's facts and deductions, of his qualifications as an historian, whether his social and moral philosophy qualified him to be a leader and teacher of youth, and whether the "gripping qualities," as described by an unnamed college president, were so important as to render accuracy and philosophy of little moment (Pallen to Jameson, Nov. 22, 1921).

intelligence of eminent statesmen, and by too great confidence that he himself could easily see much better methods of procedure than they had followed.

2. Mr. Wells doubtless has not all the acquirements needed for the prodigious task he undertook, but neither has anyone else, and, while some historical students deprecate the invasion of their field by an outsider, my own doctrine has been that, if we who are professional students of history cannot write it in such a manner that thousands and thousands of people will for the first time read with avidity an outline of history, we should welcome it when it is done by one outside our trade, and not take the attitude of the Pharisees, toward "this people that knoweth not our law"; for Mr. Wells certainly has wonderful penetration and insight, as well as an engaging style.

3. I do not sufficiently know Wells's social and moral philosophy to answer this question. From what I hear, I suppose that the book tends toward socialism, and what little I have read of other books of Wells has not led me to think that he has all the principles in which I was brought up or all the instincts of a gentleman. I do not think that all this disqualifies him wholly to be a leader and teacher of youth (in your phrase), for youth must obtain instruction from many persons having grave imperfections; but if I were teaching in a college I should not wish his book to be the sole or main guide of the young men's instruction in history. It is better adapted to be one of several books that a young man should use, than his constituted textbook. I somewhat discount your college president's judgment, partly because of what he says about "the profound interests to which our students vibrate, their currents of passionate thought," whereas, as one who taught 23 years in universities cannot help knowing, they have no currents of passionate thought, and the profound interests to which they vibrate are merely those of inter-collegiate contests in baseball and football. If Wells's book will interest them so intensely as your writer thinks, much use ought by all means to be made of it. But the teacher should have the sense to show them, by his own words or by the use of other books, whatever is amiss, either in respect to inaccuracies in Wells's book, which is quite an unimportant matter, or in respect to larger items of wrongheadedness or conceit or misjudgment as to the present and the future.

4. I cannot answer this question, but my notion as to how an answer might be arrived at is perhaps sufficiently indicated under 3.

If you have seen Professor Carl Becker's review of the book in the July number of the "American Historical Review," I will say that, so far as I can judge, I approach somewhat nearer to Professor Becker's views expressed in that article than might seem from some of my answers above. Some things in Wells displease me a little, some things a good deal; but after all, it is a great thing to cause people to read a mostly good account of human progress.

To Mrs. George M. Bolling

December 16, 1921.

My dear Mrs. Bolling:[342]

. . . I have never read Owen Wister's book of which you speak,[343] but I have dipped into it enough to get its general drift. On the general subject, I find myself occupying the middle ground, but varying somewhat from time to time in the degree of my severity or leniency of view. I do not think the British public policy has been much more or much less disinterested, in dealing with other countries, than that of other national governments. In the long history of their dealings with us, they have often shown themselves aggressive, and sometimes selfish, but there has been a distinct improvement, and in recent years this has been very marked. They exaggerate their own unselfishness, and Frenchmen and others often think them to be hypocritical, but I do not think they are; it is all an unconscious impression of their own disinterestedness, not much different from that which we entertain respecting ours. Their rule over races not white has been, it seems to me, though not always amiable or tactful, more just than has been usual among conquering races, and in recent years quite exceptionally liberal and considerate. Many of the faults of their rule, and also of their course with respect to the United States, have been due to the rule of a class which now no longer rules. England this summer, for instance, seems to me distinctly more democratic in sentiment than I ever found it before; and that increase of democracy produces a better attitude toward the United States. They seem to me to be mostly good people, a little deceived about themselves, a little inclined to narrow views, but just and right-minded in the main. I like our people better, but I agree with those who think that good relations between us and the English are of very great importance, more important than in the case of any other nation, and, by the way, I am preparing to do my part, in one small particular to improve those relations. The very object for which I spent the three summer months in England was the preparation of a series of volumes of the Correspondence of the British Ministers in Washington with Foreign Secretaries in London and other British authorities, doing this because I believe that a full disclosure of the instructions given and information sent, and of all the private consultations exhibiting British policy toward us, good or

---

[342] The former Miss Irene Johnson of Baltimore, who, in 1898, married George M. Bolling, then professor of Greek and Comparative Philology in the Catholic University of America, Washington, D. C., and after 1914 in Ohio State University.

[343] The book referred to was the second of a trilogy by Owen Wister (1860-1938): *Pentecost of calamity, A straight deal,* and *Neighbors henceforth,* N. Y., Macmillan, 1915, 1920, 1922. The burden of the second volume was that it was high time Americans forgot their ancient grudge against Great Britain and realized how often their government had been in the wrong when dealing with the British government. Mrs. Bolling was probably troubled by the emphasis on American shortcomings and Britain's benevolent failure to take advantage of them.

bad, is better than the prevalence of surmise and suspicion as to deep and dark designs of Downing Street against our liberties and prosperity. I had unrestricted access to whatever I desired to see in the Foreign Office Papers, and found these people acting in about the way in which one would expect educated human beings in their position to act. . . .

To Lord Bryce

January 4, 1922.

My dear Lord Bryce:

To me it is quite marvelous that, with a thousand political matters on your mind, and a thousand Americans troubling you with this and that, you should on getting back to London remember the historical quest on which you saw me starting more than three months before. I appreciate very warmly your kind inquiry and am glad to report that I came away from London (October 8) with a feeling of having measurably succeeded in the main branch of what I was trying to do, though not very successful in the minor branch which constituted my strongest reason for going over personally.

By the major branch of the work I mean the collecting of the material preserved in the Public Record Office. I knew that that would contribute much the greatest part of the material, but I thought of the getting it as a relatively easy matter, which I might have entrusted to someone else. When, however, after doing what I could in other lines, I settled down to the work at the Public Record Office, I found that my personal care over a good many details was worth while, and would bring me results that I might not so securely have obtained by correspondence at the distance of 3,000 miles. My work there was very interesting to me, and very well rewarded, and I found a very intelligent American young woman, with a good knowledge of American history and extraordinary quickness and sureness of mind, to carry on the work after I came away, and supervise the copying, on instructions which after my own experience there I was able to draw up much better than I could have done from here.

So I came away from London not at all discontented, though it must be confessed that I was far from obtaining any such store of letters in private hands as I had expected. If letters do not exist, however, one cannot find them, and no one can blame you if you do not use them. I remember that thirty-nine years ago, about the time I first had the pleasure of seeing you, I was one day calling on Mr. Henry Adams in Washington, and asked him if there was anything I could do for him in Baltimore. He said that he would be obliged if I could find the papers of Robert and Samuel Smith in Baltimore. I asked the grandson of one of them about the matter. He said, "I must say that is rather good, in view of the manner in which Mr. Henry Adams has

always spoken of my grandfather and great-uncle,[344] but in fact the papers were long since burned up by my aunt." I told Mr. Adams of their fate, when I next saw him in Washington, and he said, "That's good, that's good! Now I don't have to read them, and nobody can blame me."

Well, in the first place, the voluminous papers of two ministers, Francis James Jackson and Stratford Canning, have been presented to the Public Record Office, and so they were at my disposal; also, what remains of those of George Hammond, though they proved to contain almost nothing for my purposes. But in respect to papers that might be supposed to be still at large, I had all the different varieties of ill luck that could be imagined. In the case of the papers of ministers and of those Foreign Secretaries who had brief terms, most collections seem to have disappeared. In one case, a lawsuit tied up everything from observation at present. In another, the owner resides in East Africa, and his old papers are in the vaults of a bank. In another, where I know there is a whole volume of one minister's letters, some of them probably from Philadelphia, no answer ever came from the owner, who was perhaps in Fiji or the Himalayas. In another, the owner, who cordially invited me to come and see all he had, fell ill before the appointed time and has since died. In another, the owner had gone away, leaving instructions that no mail should be forwarded.

Of the major Secretaries, Mr. J. B. Fortescue kindly sent in from Dropmore three port-folios of Grenville's papers, which were supposed to include all the material that I might desire, but I doubt if they did, and from those three got nothing not already printed by the Historical Manuscripts Commission. Lord Lascelles was absent in Balmoral and elsewhere, upon errands which we now understand to have been important,[345] but finally gave me an opportunity to go over the relevant portions of George Canning's papers.[346] That

---

[344] Robert Smith (1757-1842), Secretary of the Navy under Jefferson; Secretary of State under Madison. Samuel Smith (1752-1839), a member of the Senate from Maryland. Adams's general verdict was that the two men aspired to careers calling for more ability than they possessed, that they were born intriguers, and that Samuel was the leader of trouble-makers in the Senate, where he was able to make use of Cabinet secrets confided to him by his brother.

[345] Lord Lascelles, sixth Earl of Harewood, in 1922 married H.R.H. the Princess Mary, sufficient reason for his presence at Balmoral Castle.

[346] George Canning, whose papers had been in the possession of Lord Clanricarde, Hubert George de Burgh-Canning (1832-1917). On Apr. 1, 1921, Jameson asked Temperley who had inherited the papers of George Canning on the death of Lord Clanricarde. Temperley replied, on Apr. 13, that he did not know but would try to find out. "It was supposed that they belonged to the late Marquess of Clanricard but he, as you know, was practically a lunatic and it was never any use approaching him in the matter." In a second letter, May 5, Temperley reported: "The real *clou* of the collection is now with the Earl of Harewood. . . . Harewood himself inherited them for his son (the legatee). He has not been very con-

was an opportunity I much appreciated, for though Lord Fitzmaurice told me that old Lord Clanricarde let him see Charles Canning's papers,[347] when he was writing his life of Granville, I judge that no one had ever used George Canning's papers since Stapleton's time, about 1830;[348] but it is a very uneven collection, a great deal of interesting matter on some portions of Canning's career, and almost nothing on others, such as relations to the United States, and I got only four letters. Finally, though Lord Grey very kindly wrote to Lord Londonderry[349] for me, and the latter expressed himself most amiably in the matter, Ulster politics seemed to prevent him from ever seeing me, which was what he naturally desired as a preliminary. However, in some of these directions better success may be had later.

I should have said that my opportunity to approach Lord Lascelles on the matter came through Lord George Hamilton,[350] whom I saw at Deal Castle, and that came about through the introduction which you kindly sent me by the Mersey pilot. I must also thank you, very cordially, for your introduction to Lord Fitzmaurice, with whom I had a delightful Sunday luncheon at Bradford-on-Avon, on my way to Bristol for the inspection of some slave-trade papers, along another line of the work of my Department here.

Though there was some ill luck, nobody was otherwise than amiable and obliging in respect to the whole matter, and I had a good deal of enjoyment out of my summer in London, with comfortable quarters, and with the privileges of the Athenaeum Club (through the kindness of Sir Sidney Lee),[351] which enabled me

to often continue work in their library after the Public Record Office and the British Museum had closed.[352]

From London I went down into Spain, to get a little better familiarity with Spanish archives and their circumstances, and enjoyed those two weeks very much, though I found I had to omit, for want of time, the walk in the Pyrenees, on which I had counted and for which you were so kind as to give an outline of a route.[353] I had some walking in Portugal however, while waiting at Lisbon for the steamer from Marseilles. The Portuguese had had their revolution a few days before I arrived, but it was interesting to see the "grandiosa manifestacão," consisting of a procession of 6,000 or 7,000 men, by which President Almeida was to be persuaded not to resign his somewhat unattractive job merely because he had been unable to prevent revolution and the assassination of several of his ministers.[354] They looked respectable, but they did not keep step nor form spontaneously into columns of fours, as any similar American procession would have done; wherefore I concluded that the Portuguese are

ciliatory but will, I think, ultimately yield to the blandishments of Hubert Hall and allow transcripts to be made for the Historical Society."

[347] Charles Canning (1812-1862), Earl Canning, third son of George Canning, under-secretary of State for Foreign Affairs, 1841-1846. His correspondence also was in the possession of Lord Clanricarde and his biographer in the *Dictionary of National Biography* states that he was not allowed to see it.

Lord Edmond George Fitzmaurice (1846-1935), second son of the fourth Marquis of Lansdowne, was under-secretary for Foreign Affairs, 1882-1885, and again from 1905 to 1908. As a member of the Royal Manuscripts Commission and author of the lives of William, Earl of Shelburne, and Earl Granville, he was able to be of much use to Jameson.

[348] Augustus Granville Stapleton (1800-1880) was the author of *The political life of the Right Honourable George Canning from 1822 to . . . August, 1827,* 1831, and *George Canning and his times,* 1859.

[349] Edward Grey (1862-1933), Secretary of State for Foreign Affairs, 1905-1916; ambassador to the United States for a brief period in 1919.

Lord Londonderry, Sir Charles Henry Vane Tempest Stewart (1878-1949), minister of Education for Northern Ireland, 1921-1926.

[350] Lord George Hamilton (1845-1927), Secretary of State for India, 1895-1908, author of *Parliamentary reminiscences and reflections,* London, Murray, 1922.

[351] Sir Sidney Lee (1859-1926), editor of the *Dictionary of National Biography* from 1891 to 1917; professor of English language and literature and dean of the Faculty of Arts, University of London, 1913-1924.

[352] For editing this work the leisure and the opportunity never came. A small part of Jameson's material appeared as *Instructions to the British ministers to the United States, 1791-1812,* edited by Bernard Mayo, *Ann. Rept., Amer. Hist. Assn.,* 1936: v. 3. This is dedicated "To the Memory of J. Franklin Jameson," of whom the editor wrote: "Dr. Jameson will long be honored by historians for his labors upon the raw materials of American history, for discovering and quarrying the original documents which the historian must use, and reprinting the most important of them with such interpretative comment as they required. During his long and fruitful life he conceived many important editorial projects, and brought most of them to completion. The present volume is a by-product of his constant efforts to meet the needs of historians and to give effective aid to the progress of history."

Evidence of Jameson's interest in Dr. Mayo's volume is to be found in a letter of May 28, 1937, to one of the editors of this volume, written while he was confined to his home by the accident which ultimately caused his death: "I am however making progress for I sit up some two hours each day. This afternoon, e. g., I hold here a meeting of a small committee of the American Historical Association of which I am chairman to comment on the makeup of the *Annual Report* for 1936, in which one volume will contain the instructions sent by Grenville and his successors to their envoys in Washington, 1791-1812. A piece of work my interest in which carries me back to my later days at the Department of Historical Research of the Carnegie Institution of Washington, not to say to the time when you were editing the papers of James A. Bayard."

[353] From Madrid Jameson wrote: I too enjoyed my glimpse of village life in Spain, but shouldn't like to live there long. The wretched village [Simancas] is 7 m. out from Valladolid, with no means of access but walking (and the hours at the archive are 8 to 2) and a ramshackle motor-bus that leaves V. at 6 A.M. It was however a very interesting place in which to spend two days, fine old castle with whose appearance you are familiar from the walls of the D. of H. R." (Jameson to Cornelia M. Pierce, Oct. 19, 1921).

[354] Dr. Antonio José de Almeida was elected president of the republic of Portugal on Aug. 6, 1919. The unrest and disorder which plagued his term culminated in October, 1921, in the murder of Antonio Granjo, the prime minister, Admiral Machado dos Santos, and other prominent persons. The appearance in the harbor of foreign battle ships checked the violence.

"lesser breeds without the law," and unfit for self-government.

I do not think I am able to tell you one fact about the Washington conference [355] except that I have had a great deal of pleasure in the presence here of my Amherst classmate Baron Kanda,[356] whom I used to sit beside in old days, who is here as one of the delegates. He is the father of the very intelligent young man whom I mentioned to you as professor-designate of American history and institutions in the University of Tokyo, Mr. Yasaka Takagi.[357]

From Baron Korff [358] and others I hear great praises for all that you did for the success of the Institute of Politics at Williamstown. The whole thing seems to be regarded as having been immensely successful, and great preparations are being made for its continuance. Now that I am likely for the next several summers to stay on this side of the Atlantic, I certainly hope that

you will be coming to Williamstown every summer.[359] Please give my very cordial regards to Lady Bryce, and believe me, with many thanks for your kind aid and interest in my work respecting your predecessors.

To Mary Hayden

January 26, 1922.

My dear Miss Hayden:

I had the privilege of sitting next to you at the dinner which Lord and Lady Astor gave last July on the occasion of the Anglo-American Conference of Professors of History. I did not know who "Miss Hayden" was, which I hope is pardonable in one who had been so little in Great Britain and hardly at all in Ireland, and all of that eight years ago at the most recent. Afterward, when I saw by the printed list that I had had the opportunity of sitting next to the professor of modern Irish history in the National University of Ireland, I was full of regret that I had not known this earlier, for there would have been many interesting things to enquire about.

Now comes to the office of the American Historical Review, *A Short History of the Irish People* which you and Mr. Moonan have prepared, and I have emboldened myself to write and tell you of the pleasure I have been having in reading large parts of it before it goes out to the reviewer. It happened that, two or three weeks ago, I had an inquiry from an unknown correspondent who wished to know of a good short history of Ireland, and I was at a loss to know how to answer, for though my acquaintance with books of Irish history is superficial, it seemed to me that all of the smaller sort were spoiled for his purposes by partisanship on one side or the other, usually so warmly evinced that one felt sure that there was exaggeration and wondered where the real truth lay. Your book however, impresses me greatly by its calmness and moderation of statement, its evident spirit of fairness, and I shall know hereafter what to say to such inquiries. Please accept my cordial congratulations, and allow me to say again, that I heartily wish I had known, that evening of the dinner, that you were Irish. It would have been a great pleasure and benefit to one whose knowledge of Ireland thus far has considered of two rather disagreeable days in Ulster (Coleraine, where my original Jameson came from), and three very happy days at Trinity College as the guest of Dr. Mahaffy. I remember asking him, after he had told me of his very interesting success with the Georgian Society, why he did not set on foot an Irish historical society, on the pattern of the Scottish Historical Society, which has done so much admirable work. I thought the work of such a society might pave the way to greater national

---

[355] The Washington Conference, assembled in November, 1921, considered limitation of the navies of the convening countries, the use of submarines and of poison gas in warfare, as well as problems of the Pacific. The conference is best known for the treaty on limitation of naval armament which was concluded on Feb. 6, 1922.

[356] Baron Kanda (1857-1923), who came to this country in 1875, had prepared for college in the Amherst high school, and was graduated from Amherst College in 1879. On his return to Japan he was for a time professor of English and Latin in the University of Tokyo, and was prominent in various educational movements. From 1902 to 1911 he was dean of the Peers' School. On the death of his father he became Baron Kanda and a member of the House of Peers. The Class Letter of Dec. 20, 1909, prepared by Jameson as class secretary, reported of him: "Kanda, accompanied by Baroness Kanda, a lady of much beauty and charm, came to the United States in August in company with the Japanese commercial commissioners who made the tour of the country in the late summer and autumn. He was the second in rank in the party, and its chief maker of speeches in English. With one exception, some ten years ago, he had not visited America since graduation. Learning his itinerary, I tried to bring him into connection with as many as possible of the boys, and I think he saw a dozen or more. To me he seemed the same friendly, solid, level-headed fellow as in the old days, although, like the rest of us, soberer and more deliberate by reason of thirty more years." He attended the commencement of 1921, accompanied by his second son, Yasaka Takagi (who also was educated in this country), and at this time the college bestowed upon him the degree of LL.D. He was hardly back in Japan when he was returned to America as special assistant to the Washington Conference on the Limitation of Armament. He died about two years after the close of the conference (*History of the class of 1879 in Amherst College, from 1919 to 1924*, 23-24, compiled by J. F. Jameson).

[357] Yasaka Takagi, mentioned in n. 356, finished a period of American study in March, 1923, attended the International Congress of Historical Sciences in Brussels in April, visited brothers in London and Berlin, then returned to Japan, to become professor of American history and institutions in the University of Tokyo.

[358] Sergius Alexander Korff (1876-1924) was at this time attached to the Foreign Service School of Georgetown University; the next year he added to his Georgetown duties work in Columbia as professor of Eastern European history.

[359] Viscount Bryce was one of the lecturers at the first session of the Institute of Politics, inaugurated by Williams College in the summer of 1921, by means of the generosity of Bernard Baruch.

unity, as the historical work of the 40's and 50's did in Italy, but he thought the divergencies to be too great. That was in 1913, and they have been greater since that; but now we all hope that they will diminish rapidly, and I feel sure that, whether through the method of which I spoke or some other, there will result a striking increase of interest and production in Irish history. Many examples of the past show such results from such increases of independence. I hope you will make many more contributions to so good a cause.

To MARY SCRUGHAM

February 11, 1922.

My dear Miss Scrugham:

I should be flattered if any one could justly think that my opinions on a monograph respecting the election and other events of 1860 and of 1861 were highly valuable, but I know what the fact is. I never had great knowledge of the period, and that knowledge has diminished with the years. The truth is that one who occupies the position which I hold is obliged thereby to spread himself out so thin that, while there are few periods of history of which he has not read or heard something, there are none in respect to which he can pose as an authoritative specialist. Therefore I should not feel able to express a definite judgment about your book, but it seems to me very good.[360] Sometimes I think you are carried a little beyond what is just by your natural aptitude for telling phrases, and sometimes I think that, when great and laudable results have flowed from actions that seemed not to have been caused by the desire for such results, but by more human and short-sighted motives, it may be safer for us to suspect that the major ends which such conduct might secure were in part present in the minds of the actors and, in connection with much else, formed in part the basis of their action. I am old enough to remember a good deal of the sentiment of New England Republicans in the '60's and '70's, and am inclined to think that their sentiments in 1860 must have partaken largely of the philosophical liberalism that was current all over the world at that time—more largely than one would think from your descriptions; and that those who represented them were moved less largely by political, and more largely by moral, motives than you perhaps think.

But very likely much of this is the reflection of a mind that is conscious of never having thoroughly understood that of the politician. At all events, with whatever small movements of dissent here and there, I have steadily admired your book—its fullness of research, its detachment, its cleverness of presenta-

tion; and it falls in with a tendency which I am sure will grow to regard the Civil War as having been avoidable, though I am not yet quite confident that it was.

As to what is euphemistically called the Adjusted Compensation Bill, I really think that I have as strong an impression of the President's weakness as you have, and I am certain that no one rates the cowardice of Congressmen higher than I do. At the same time, remembering as I do the whole history of the soldiers' vote after the Civil War, the constant iniquities of the pension legislation, and the progress of the G. A. R. toward unlimited rapacity, I will not conceal from you that I regard this Soldiers' Bonus Bill as pretty certain to prove (if it passes, as I judge it will) the most harmful piece of legislation that has ever been passed by Congress in my lifetime; and as the harmfulness is perfectly obvious to anyone who has been instructed in arithmetic (because the numerical results of constantly succumbing to the threats of the Grand Army men are a well-known matter of history), I should not hesitate to call it also the most iniquitous piece of legislation passed during my lifetime. Nevertheless, such is the cowardice upon the Hill that I suppose it will pass, accompanied by ostrich-like efforts to conceal the magnitude of the first hold-up—first of a long series.[361]

To MARY SCRUGHAM

February 20, 1922.

My dear Miss Scrugham:

I have just received your letter of February 15, and hasten to say that you have misunderstood me if I have seemed to you to think you have not succeeded in presenting properly your opinions or in forming them justly. I presume that on the whole they are sound, at any rate I should not presume to conclude that they were not; I merely thought that there was somewhat more to say in certain directions, or in the defense of certain sets of men.

You are quite right about the close relation between the Civil War pensions and the high tariff. In the early 80s the tariff was working in such a way that the government's receipts were exceeding its expenditure by a hundred million dollars. This was a blessed situation in one aspect, upon which we might look back from the present day with tearful eyes, and it enabled us to pay off the Civil War debt with astonishing rapidity, down to a certain point; but it was then seen by a high tariff people that this would

---

[360] Mary Scrugham, *The peaceable Americans of 1860-61: a study in public opinion*, Columbia Studies in History, Economics and Public Law **96**, N. Y., Columbia Univ. Press, 1921.

[361] The "adjusted compensation bill," better known as the soldiers' bonus bill, passed the House but failed in the Senate in 1921. In 1922 it passed both houses but was vetoed by President Harding on Sept. 19, 1922, one of his reasons being that the Congress had made no provision for the four billion dollars which he believed necessary under the terms of the measure. The House passed the bill over his veto but the Senate supported the President.

presently make so striking an impression of the needlessness of taking in such excessive revenues that the system would be in danger. This paved the way easily to that saturnalia of corrupt expenditure on pensions which brought it about that, thenceforth and for a good number of years the sum of expenditure on account of the debt plus the expenditure on account of pensions remained about constant, the latter rising and rising as the former diminished.

On the other hand, that acquisitive efforts of the American Legion are primarily an effort to cause war profiteers to disgorge their profits is a good doctrine for the enthusiastic atmosphere of a convention, but is not very convincing at a distance. We can convince people that we are actuated by altruism and public spirit if we insist that gains wrongfully obtained from the public shall be turned into the public treasury of a country which is staggering under a load of debt and can hardly make both ends meet, but we shall not thus convince people if we go beyond this to insist, with appropriate threats to congressmen, that when or if great millions in additional revenue have been obtained from these wicked profiteers (and incidentally also from all the rest of mankind) they should be handed over to us.

To ARTHUR B. CALL

April 12, 1922.

My dear Call:

Thank you very much for your pamphlet about the Federal Convention of 1787. It seems to be good throughout, well adapted to its purpose, and likely to help it. I do think however that both you and Dr. Scott, in his more elaborate treatments of the same theme,[362] exaggerate somewhat—I do not say in your text, but in the very idea of bringing forward this episode for the purpose you have in mind—the closeness of the analogy between the union then effected, between states which I do not persuade myself to call sovereign in the full sense and which were fairly harmonious in make-up, and the possible associations of diverse nations that are now so much contemplated. Nevertheless, the putting forward of the analogy no doubt helps toward its being realized.

I have sometimes thought, when thinking of Dr. Scott's books on this subject, that it might be quite as useful if somebody should produce a book or article showing forth the gradual growth of unity of sentiment among these American states. For that cause of unity and harmony and peace in the world

which we all desire, increasing unity of sentiment is more important than increasing the unity of organization, or at any rate is an indispensable prerequisite to the latter. Tying these states together into a federal union no doubt helped the creation of a national sentiment, but the growth of national feelings in the place of provincial feelings, a growth promoted by many other things than by federal union, was a prerequisite to the permanent success of that union. For instance, in the first years under the constitution the parties were state parties—Republicans and Constitutional parties in Pennsylvania, Schuyler and Clinton and Livingston, factions in New York,[363] etc.— and the realignment of all these international parties was, in the political field, a long step toward real union in the nation. As in the political field, so in many others, but the crystallization of the political parties is perhaps the easiest to trace.

What we mainly wish is this: As between Hungarians and Rumanians, for instance, we should be perfectly content if their feeling toward each other was no different from that of the Chicago man toward the St. Louis man, or vice versa, who instead of wishing to get out and cut each other's throats, content themselves with rivalry and chaffing and occasional indignation. Federal organization could not get the Athenian away from that desire to cut the Corinthian's throat; nothing could but the iron hand of Rome. Nevertheless federal organization does help very much. . . .

To WALDO G. LELAND

April 25, 1922.

Dear Leland:

I was absent all last week, and yesterday was more or less tied up by the arrival of a relative, so this is my one chance to send you my blessing before you sail. Enclosed with the blessing you will find three clippings. Clipping (a) will show you the University Center for Research, somewhat like yourself at the Bodleian, though it *is* not consulted and held in public regard, *could be*. Clipping (b) will show you how fine a provision the Carnegie Corporation has made for housing those excellent ones who are devoted to the physical (and biological) sciences. From the description, the place will be a palace of delights to the tourist, and perhaps incidentally, though that seems to be a secondary matter in the eyes of the scribe, it will have laboratories and other provisions for re-

---

[362] Arthur D. Call, *The Federal Convention of 1787: an international conference adequate to its purpose,* with an introductory note by James Brown Scott, Washington, American Peace Society, 1922. The reference to the work of Scott, secretary of the Carnegie Endowment for International Peace, is probably to his *James Madison's notes of debates in the Federal Convention of 1787 and their relation to a more perfect society of nations,* N. Y., Oxford Univ. Press, 1918.

[363] Philip J. Schuyler (1733-1804), father-in-law of Alexander Hamilton, advocate of a strong federal government; opposed by George Clinton (1739-1812), who delayed as long as he could the ratification of the Constitution by New York. Edward Livingston (1764-1836) first joined Schuyler in the movement for ratification, but, neglected by Washington, later went over to the Clintons. See *Dictionary of American Biography* for all three.

search.[364] Clipping (c) refers to a matter which you may have seen announced in the New York papers, as I did, and which I imagine must be the thing which Haskins reported A. A. Young [365] as mentioning to him, as a thing which the Carnegie Corporation had found it possible to support, though in his judgment of less merit than the ACLS [American Council of Learned Societies]. I hope that this new institute will prove to be of great value, but the list of trustees given in the New York paper seem to me to impose a heavy handicap. I do not remember the names, beyond those given in this clipping, except of course the inevitable Walcott, a professional trustee; but nearly all of them were of so capitalistic a class that I believe the data put forth by the institute would not be instantly accepted by all economists, or even by the A. F. of L. I shall be interested to see, however, who the hired men will be.[366]

As further signs of progress to cheer you on your voyage, I may mention that the old house of Senator Kean at Seventeenth and I, now bears an enormous sign, about 30 feet by 5 feet, designating it as the headquarters of the Victory Memorial Committee.[367] Also, I have had one interview with Mr. Raege down below, Eben Putnam [368] having telegraphed that he wanted you to see Raege at once, and you not being available; and Raege is confident that he can get an archive building right off the bat, from Langley's

committee or Madden's or anybody's.[369] His confidence is based on the success of his organization in getting rapidly, and recently, and quite outside of any consideration of the budget, an appropriation of $17,000,000 for additional hospitals for the soldiers of the late war, and not to speak of other successes less completely won. Some time before long, after I have had a chance to talk with Colonel Sherrill and perhaps with Smoot,[370] I will have a meeting of our committee on archives, to which he will summon Putnam, and we will try to make up our minds what is best to do, but I do not think the analogy with his $17,000,000 success is perfect. Seventeen hospitals in seventeen different congressional districts would be much more useful in the period preceding election than anything connected with a National Archive Building, and I apprehend that members of Congress may ask themselves whether the voters belonging to the American Legion will be as mad at not getting a National Archive Building as at not getting the bonus or the hospitals. However, we shall see.

To bring my little budget of news down to date, I will mention that while I have been dictating this letter Varela [371] has come in to show me the plans of the building which Brookings is beginning over on Jackson Place, for this Institute of Economics and other tenants, and into which Brookings would like to have this Department go. I should prefer to stay here, but it may be true that there are great advantages to the work in such association as would be contemplated. I understand that I am to have a talk with Brookings [372] about it before long—or rather, as I apprehend, he with me—but anyhow I do not regard the matter as lying wholly in my hands. Accordingly, you may have seen the last of room 1133, and also you may not.

Well, it seems a dreadful thing to have you remove to such a distance that I cannot talk all such things over with you, as they arise from day to day; but there we are. I shall be eager, but must not be impatient, to have you back. Please give my love to Mrs. Leland. I wish you both a good voyage and a happy legation.

---

[364] At a meeting of the National Academy of Sciences on Apr. 24, its president, Dr. C. D. Walcott, announced plans for the erection in Washington of a $1,300,000 building to be the home of the National Academy of Sciences and the National Research Council, and a center for all fields of science. The building, the gift of the Carnegie Corporation, was to contain a large auditorium and numerous exhibition rooms (New York *Times,* Apr. 25, 1922).

[365] Allyn A. Young (1876-1929), professor of economics, Harvard University, 1920-1929; visiting professor, London School of Economics at the time of his death.

[366] This is undoubtedly a reference to the Institute of Economics, which was to receive from the Carnegie Corporation $200,000 a year for five years, $150,000 annually for the next three years, and $100,000 a year for two years. In making the grant the Corporation stipulated that the collection and dissemination of facts, for which it was set up, was to be in the interest of no party, group, or faction. The government was to be in the hands of fifteen trustees, of whom Robert S. Brookings was president. Some of the other members of the board were Arthur T. Hadley, Paul M. Warburg, George Sutherland, and David F. Houston. Permanent quarters were to be in a new building on Jackson Place, Washington. The head of the new establishment was to be Harold G. Moulton (*Report of the acting president,* Carnegie Corporation of New York, 31-38, Sept. 30, 1922, New York *Times,* Apr. 21, 1922).

[367] John Kean (1852-1914), Senator from New Jersey, 1899-1911. In January, 1922, President Harding had endorsed the erection of a National Victory Memorial Building and a committee was set up to formulate plans for it.

[368] Eben Putnam (1868-1933), official historian of Massachusetts in World War I; editor of the *Genealogical Magazine,* 1890-1917; national historian of the American Legion. From this time until the archive building was assured Putnam and the Legion took an active part in the campaign for it.

[369] Martin B. Madden (1855-1928), member of the House of Representatives from Illinois, 1905-1927. He was chairman of the Appropriations Committee. John Wesley Langley, member of the House from Kentucky, 1907-1925, was chairman of the Committee on Public Buildings and Grounds.

[370] Col. Charles H. S. Sherrill (1867-1936), one-time American ambassador to Turkey; Reed Smoot (1862-1941), senator from Utah, 1903-1933, chairman of the Committee on Appropriations.

[371] Edmund A. Varela, with the Carnegie Institution from 1906, was bursar from 1933 until his retirement, Jan. 1, 1941.

[372] Robert S. Brookings was a trustee of the Carnegie Institution as well as chairman of the Brookings Institution. The Department of Historical Research did not move into the Brookings building.

To Lady Bryce

May 3, 1922.

Dear Lady Bryce:

I do not know what the London papers may have been saying about the announcement that the French government have designated a successor to Mr. Jusserand, but no doubt it has been mentioned, and I have thought that it might interest you to see two of the best pronouncements upon the subject in the American papers; therefore I enclose them herewith. One is an editorial from the New York Times,[373] the other is one of the statements which David Lawrence furnishes to the Washington Star [374] and a group of other papers, and which I should think he intentionally made a little less cordial than he might out of regard for French political susceptibilities of the moment—though that is merely my conjecture.

For my own part, I feel it deeply that there is a prospect of his going away, not only because I cannot see how any successor could do so well in the interests of both countries, but also on personal grounds. For, to me, he is the most interesting man in Washington. I have never felt warranted in consuming as much of his time as I should have liked, but I have seen something of him, and always with great pleasure and profit from his vivacious and stimulating talk. He is the last of four historical students older than myself (he only a little older) from whom I have had during my years in Washington a helpful and pleasant kind of association somewhat different from anything one gets from those younger—your husband and the two Adamses, and now Jusserand. I shall feel his departure very deeply, as I did that of all three who preceded.[375]

Mrs. Jameson and my daughter and I were at dinner at his house last evening, which was a party in honor of two members of the French Academy, and what Mr. Jusserand said—to another man who brought up the matter, rather than to me, but to us both—was, as you will expect, said with the composure and loyalty of an old public servant, who understands how to do his duty. I do however wish that the politicians might have left him to choose his own time.[376]

I venture to enclose also the page commemorative of Lord Bryce in the April number of the *American Historical Review,* thinking that you may like to possess all such things, however inadequate.[377]

Father Hippolyte Delehaye writes me from Brussels that an International Historical Congress of a sort is planned for next spring in that city. I have not yet received details, and when I was there at the beginning of August there was no definite talk of any such meeting as yet possible, but it may be that it would seem part of my duty to go to it, and in that case I shall hope to have the pleasure of seeing you again.

To Elizabeth Donnan

May 8, 1922.

My dear Miss Donnan:

. . . Getting at it slowly, from time to time, I have by now read about two-thirds of Sam Morison's *Maritime History of Massachusetts.*[378] It is a book of extraordinary interest to me, as you rightly divined it would be, and also it is an extraordinarily clever book and one, too, on which a great deal of labor was expended. I suppose you know that he is going to Oxford in October to occupy the Harmsworth professorship of American history for two years. Now here is a queer trick of memory—or rather of the want of it. I first learned of this appointment from Leland, soon after my return in November, and declared that it was the ideal appointment, so much so that I was very much chagrined that it had never

[373] "When the time actually comes to say good-bye to Ambassador Jusserand, he will surely know that he bears with him across the sea precious tokens of American approval and gratitude. His service has been in every way distinguished and acceptable. We shall part with him not only as a worthy representative of France but as a proved interpreter and a tested friend of the United States." New York *Times,* May 2, 1922: 18. The time to part with him did not come until 1925.

[374] The article by David Lawrence is headed, "War on Jusserand is now revealed, Opponents in France have made Ambassador's work here doubly difficult." The gist of the article is that in spite of the opposition at home, the sending of special agents to this country, and the inconsistency of French policy, M. Jusserand has maintained excellent relations with four administrations. "Jules Jusserand is dean of the diplomatic corps. He has served at Washington longer than the ambassador of any other country. His going will be regretted; though it is realized that he is anxious to be relieved of the burden and the strain" (Washington *Star,* May 1, 1922: 3).

[375] On Nov. 15 Jameson wrote to Leland: "I am sorry to hear that Jusserand is not likely to be with us more than a year longer, and wish I felt freer to go and use up his time and my own in listening to his talk. It would be a much pleasanter way of spending my time than 'this dry drudgery at desk's dead wood.' Of the four older persons in whose talk I have delighted during these years in Washington Bryce has gone, Charles Adams has gone, Henry Adams has gone, and Jusserand is going. Alas!" Jameson was not alone in enjoy-

ment of Jusserand's talk. At the time of his coming to Washington Henry White wrote to Theodore Roosevelt: "I am sure you will greatly enjoy talking with him on all sorts of literary and other questions—there are very few which he cannot discuss in an interesting way" (Nevins, *Henry White,* 223).

[376] Though Jusserand was not recalled immediately he spent some time in Paris during the summer of 1922. On Aug. 21 Leland wrote to Jameson: "I happened to see Monsieur Jusserand in the Bibliothèque Nationale this morning so I paid my respects to him. He was very pleasant as always and we chatted for a few minutes. He said that the new tariff will kill the Republican party. He said that he wrote to his government in 1910 that the then tariff would cause the Republicans to lose the next election and that Harmon or Woodrow Wilson would be elected president. But don't mention this in the hearing of reporters or *senators.*"

[377] *Amer. Hist. Rev.,* 27: 628-629, Apr., 1922.

[378] Samuel Eliot Morison, A.B., 1908, Ph.D., 1912, Harvard; M.A., Oxford, 1922; professor of history in Harvard since 1915. Harmsworth professor of American history at Oxford, 1922-1925. See *post,* May 23, 1922.

occurred to me when talking with Firth, who was consulting me, as to ways of filling that chair. Afterward, I found in my notebook, in very brief jottings of my conversation with Firth, the name of Morison. It must be that I made Morison my chief or sole recommendation, for no other name is mentioned, yet to this day I cannot remember having said a word about him, but have still the same distinct recollection that I found no satisfactory solution to Firth's inquiry. Still, if it were a political nomination, I should proceed to pose to Morison as "an original Morison man." How many people we have heard of who, during those midnight hours at Chicago, made Harding president—a great achievement. Well, anyhow, he has done better than I expected he would. It is even thought that he has backbone enough to veto this bonus bill, the most harmful piece of legislation, I think, all consequences considered, that has passed either house in my lifetime. . . .

As for the British ministers, I have the stuff for volume I., but can get no time to edit it. The other day, at the annual meeting of the American Philosophical Society in Philadelphia I discoursed twenty minutes on the ministers that served in Philadelphia and was rewarded by getting, not any letters, of which I had no serious hope, not wishing their letters to Americans, but long desired portraits of two men that I have looked for for my gallery, Phineas Bond, chargé d'affaires 1795-1796, and David Montagu Erskine, minister 1806-1807—both Stuarts, both in the possession of Mr. John Cadwalader,[379] who lets me have them photographed. . . .

To Claude H. Van Tyne

May 11, 1922.

Dear Van Tyne:

I wish I could say "Welcome to our city" but anyhow welcome to our country, which I hope you find more contented than India, if not at the moment so interesting. Why can we not always have our friends on tap? Few things would please me more than to sit here (or there) and listen to you by the hour respecting India's coral strands and tangled skeins. But it cannot be, as Lowry remarked the other day, "this business of earning one's living does break up the forenoons so." I am not even to have the pleasure of seeing you here at the approaching meeting of the Board of Editors, since the Council's Committee on Nominations in obedience to the "reform" principles of the Committee of Nine decreed that on the expiration of that term another should take your place as one of my five tyrants. Thus Amurath succeeds to Amurath, while the representative of the working classes (or fellahs) remains in statu quo.

Well, at any rate I shall hear from you by way of

the *Atlantic Monthly,* for I am sure I shall read your articles with eager interest.[380] . . .

To Woodrow Wilson

May 12, 1922.

My dear Wilson: [381]

I am delighted with the thought of being able to be in any way useful to you.[382] That is what I am for, to help real historians—an historical powder-monkey, to pass forward ammunition to historical gunners (or gunmen). But I shall be obliged, Yankee fashion, to reply to your question by asking another. When you speak of the effects wrought upon European politics by the establishment of our present national government, am I right in supposing that what you have in mind are the effects produced by the substitution in 1789 of an effective government for an ineffective one previously existing? That is to say, effects produced by the bringing into existence of an American power that must be reckoned with, rather than, in a more general sense, the effects produced by the creation, a few years earlier, of an independent American republic, *i.e.,* by the American Revolution and its consequences.

In either case it will not take me long to provide you with a certain number of references to the "literature" that has come out since you graduated from our professorial class—given the difficulty of proving such inferences as you are seeking and the consequent effect that most of the books one would mention be books from which conclusions could be gathered by inference rather than directly.[383]

---

[379] John Cadwalader (1862-1925), a Philadelphia lawyer.

[380] India in ferment, and The Indian ferment, *Atlantic* 130: 93-105, 401-413, July, Sept., 1922.

[381] President Wilson on leaving the White House moved to 2340 S Street, N. W., Washington. Here as he slowly regained strength he turned to some of his earlier associates. On Apr. 5, 1922, Mr. and Mrs. Jameson had tea at the S Street home. Of this call Jameson wrote to his sister Helen: "We went, and found him as cheerful and entertaining as of old, and Mrs. Wilson quite charming and hospitable, but physically it was sad to see an old friend so disabled. He may have gained a great deal, and of course has his ups and downs, but that [sic] he could not get up from his chair nor move his left arm, and his head seemed inclined to droop to one side, though his speech was not affected except that it is a little weak."

[382] On May 11 Wilson wrote to Jameson: "I am thinking of devoting a part of my (enforced and uncomfortable) leisure to a closer study than I have ever made before of the effects wrought upon European politics by the establishment of our present national government, and I would be greatly indebted to you if you would direct me to the books which are likely to be of the most service to me in carrying out that purpose."

[383] Wilson's answer was prompt: "What I want is as clear a picture as I can get of the effect on the minds and actions of European public men of the establishment of an independent government in America of a form likely to last and gather power to itself and more than that likely to have a very material effect upon the thinking and political sympathies of their own people who were already beginning to look critically at the forms of government under which they were living."

To SAMUEL E. MORISON

May 23, 1922.

My dear Dr. Morison:

. . . I think I told you at St. Louis that it [*Maritime History of Massachusetts*] had been given to me as a Christmas present, but I get so little time to read anything that I wish to read that I have only lately finished it, getting at it when I could, in evenings at home. Such a book was sure to appeal strongly to me, as one whose great grandfather was a Salem sea-captain who died of a sunstroke at Demerara, whose great uncle was another Salem sea-captain, poisoned at dinner by a rajah in Sumatra in the '40's, and who has enough salt water in his blood to be always interested in such books. But quite apart from that personal predilection, it seems to me one of the very best books of American history that has come under my eye in all the years I have edited the *American Historical Review*. . . .

Apropos of what you say on page 179 respecting traffic through the Sound, I wonder if you know of Madame Nina Bang's long continued labors on the records of ships passing through that strait, and of her *Tabeller over Skibsfart og Varetransport gennem öresund.*, of which volume I., 1497-1660, was published in 1906—and especially, if you know of any earthly source from which an American contribution toward the publication of that book could be obtained. The work was begun under the auspices of the Carlsberg Fond of Copenhagen, but before the war was sustained by contributions from various countries, Professor Dietrich Schäfer of Berlin being the chairman of the committee. In view of the share of the United States in abolishing the Sound dues,[384] and of the interesting material for American commercial history which lay in the later entries, I made some faint efforts to obtain an American contribution, but did not succeed; and it is much more needed now, when so many of the subscribers have fallen away. I have a series of the annual reports, which are printed in Danish and German, which would explain more fully, to any prospective donor, the nature and progress of the work.[385]

It seems incredible that your book should not come to another edition, so you may like to have a few corrections I have noted as possible. If I am right, the reading on page 99, line 7, should be "Edwin" instead of Edmund; on page 106, line 26, "per hundred tons" instead of per ton; on page 119, line 1, "to the uttermost gulf of rich India"; page 167, line 10, "strict construction" instead of "loose-construction". . . .

To WOODROW WILSON

May 26, 1922.

My dear Wilson:

When you asked me to mention what materials there might be that would show the effect exerted upon the minds of European public men by the institution of the new system of government in the United States in 1789, it appeared to me that not many such indications could be found, and after some search, I am obliged to continue in that opinion. It most certainly must be that public men whose position required them to deal with the government of the United States appreciated that now there was a government with which one could do business, more easily and more effectually, but I do not find that these men anywhere said so, and other men seem to have been little impressed by the significance of the change. If anywhere, one would expect to find such evidences of interest and appreciation in England, France, and Spain, but of course the French were intensely preoccupied with their own affairs in 1789 and 1790, and in the case of Spain, I do not remember to have seen any evidence of interest in the matter. Our first minister there was so extraordinarily inactive, hardly writing more than two or three letters a year, that one gets nothing through that channel;[386] and in Dr. W. R. Manning's elaborate monograph on the Nootka Sound affair of 1790,—in the course of which one would think that appreciation of the changed value of the United States would come out if it existed,—while it would seem that some of these powers would have been glad to draw the United States into certain of their endeavors, I do not see any evidence that they thought much more of that country and its government than they previously had. What light there is, at this point, can be got by reading chapter X of Manning's "Nootka Sound Controversy" in the *Annual Report* of the American Historical Association for 1904, pages 412 to 423.

In the preceding volume of that series, volume II. of the *Annual Report* for 1903, are the despatches of the French ministers in Philadelphia, edited by Turner, beginning with those of Ternant in the latter part of 1791. They do not show anything of such appreciation as we are seeking; perhaps they are too late for this, and those of Otto, the chargé d'affaires in the two preceding years, have, I think, never been published.[387]

As for Great Britain, I myself have transcripts of all Grenville's instructions and letters to George Hammond, first minister, 1791-1795, acquired during the past

---

[384] For centuries Denmark claimed control of the Sound—the waterway connecting the North Sea and the Baltic—and collected dues from countries using it. During the nineteenth century protests grew loud and in 1855 Denmark proposed a conference, in which the United States participated. Here the powers came to an agreement as to the terms of future use of this water. See *ante*, Aug. 3, 1917.

[385] Morison replied, on Aug. 28, 1922, that he had never heard of Madame Bang's book. He suggested five New England institutions that might well make contributions to it.

[386] William Carmichael (d. 1795), who between March, 1785, and April, 1791, received eighteen sets of instructions from America and sent from Spain two dispatches, Mar. 14 and Dec. 6, 1786. McLaughlin, A. C., *Report on the diplomatic archives of the Department of State, 1789-1840*, 12, Carnegie Institution, pub. no. 22, 1904.

[387] Jean Ternant was in Philadelphia from Aug. 10, 1791, to May 16, 1793; Louis-Guillaume Otto was in America from 1779 to 1792. See Correspondence of Ternant, *Ann. Rept., Amer. Hist. Assn.*, 1903: **2**: 43-200, esp. 94 n.

winter for the purposes of my proposed volumes of the *Correspondence of the British Ministers to the United States,*[388] and have not found in them any evidence of a heightening appreciation of the United States government under its new form, other than such as is to be found from the very fact that now for the first time, eight years after recognizing the independence of the United States, the British government sends over a minister. A curious trait is, by the way, that in all the correspondence of those four years there is hardly a mention of the president of the United States. It is, "you are to represent to the American Ministers," or "if you find the American Ministers averse to this," or "in my conversations with the American Ministers." All that sounds very much as if Grenville and Hammond underestimated the actual power of President Washington in the conduct of the government, but I do not lay too much stress upon this, for Hammond was a very intelligent young man, and Grenville was extraordinarily well-informed as a rule. However, in the three volumes of his correspondence for these years 1789-1795 ([Royal] Historical Manuscripts Commission, Report on the Manuscripts of Mr. J. B. Fortescue of Dropmore, I.-III.) I do not think that anyone can see any evidence of any concern about America until the troubles arise about neutrality in the war against France.

Really, I think I can point you to only three places where you will find discussion by European public men of the results of the establishment of the new government in America. These are:

1. Report of a Committee of the Privy Council on Trade and Commerce of the United States of America, January, 1791, pages 52-69 of the original edition (which, a rare book, and one not easy to find from the catalogue, is marked in the Library of Congress, HF 3025 G78). This report, which I imagine was prepared mostly by Hawkesbury (Charles Jenkinson),[389] was reprinted in a volume put forth in 1807 by the Society of Ship Owners, entitled *Collection of Interesting and Important Papers on Navigation,* HF 3025 S72, and the passage to which I have adverted may be found on pages 94-110, of that volume if the original happens to be out.

2. In the Windham Papers, edited by Lord Rosebery, volume I., pages 121 to 137, is an interesting anonymous memorandum on the United States, and especially its government, written in English, in 1793, by a Frenchman in Philadelphia, whom the editor does not identify, but who is clearly the Vicomte de Noailles.[390]

3. In the *Correspondance Diplomatique de Talleyrand: Mission de 1792,* ed. Pallain, on pages 421 to 444, there is a long letter of Talleyrand to Lansdowne, 1795,[391] in which he sets forth results of his observations on America, with such fullness as to make it a sort of *Vorschrift* to his Memoirs on America and the Colonial System which he read to the Institut National in 1797, and which are to be found in its *Memoires,* and also as pamphlets in English translation.

I ought to add that, since coming away from the Library yesterday afternoon, it has occurred to me that I ought to have looked also at the *Political Memoranda of Francis Fifth Duke of Leeds,* published by the Royal Historical Society in 1884, since Leeds preceded Grenville as foreign secretary, holding that office from 1783 to 1791; also that in an indirect manner something might be derived from the Diary and Letters of Gouverneur Morris.[392]

I am sorry to have been unable to do better with the inquiry, but the matter is somewhat elusive.[393]

P. S. I hope that "My dear Wilson" does not sound cheeky; for on the other hand "Mr. Wilson" seems more cool and distant than I like to be to one who is now a neighbor at about the same distance that he was on McCulloh street in 1883-1885.[394]

---

grated to America. Accepting command against the English in Santo Domingo, he was wounded and died in January, 1804. (*The Windham Papers, the life and correspondence of the Right Honorable William Windham, 1750-1810.,* London, Herbert Jenkins, 1913).

[391] William Petty, first Marquess of Lansdowne (1737-1805), better known as the Earl of Shelburne. His active years, during which he attempted to promote commercial intercourse between England and the United States, were over by the time this communication was sent to him.

[392] Gouverneur Morris (1752-1816) served as United States minister to France, 1792-1794, and was in England on a special mission in 1790-1791. "He went to France in 1788 to sell Virginia tobacco. He remained in Europe thereafter for twelve interesting years," wrote Samuel F. Bemis, whose account of those years gives good reason for turning to Morris for such material as Wilson desired (Bemis, *The American Secretaries of State and their diplomacy* 2: 21-23, N. Y., Knopf, 1927).

A second postscript to this letter, sent later, added: "*The political memoranda of Francis fifth Duke of Leeds* contains nothing relating to America.

"In the *Diary and letters of Gouverneur Morris,* the following passages are all that relate to the subject of Mr. Wilson's question, and they show the British official mind (Pitt, Leeds, et al.) hardly at all affected by anything occurring in the United States in 1788-1792—I. 311-312, 321-322, 345-348, 370. J. F. J. (May 30, 1922)."

[393] For this aid Wilson expressed warm gratitude (May 30) but it seems unlikely that he pursued the subject further. One additional evidence of his renewed interest in historical activities exists: his desire to meet the board of editors of the *American Historical Review.* See *post,* May 29, 1922, and n. 398.

[394] Wilson lived at no. 8, Jameson at 54, McCulloh Street. This neighborhood so teemed with graduate students that it was dubbed the Latin Quarter of Baltimore.

---

[388] See *ante,* Jan. 4, 1922, n. 347.

[389] Baron Hawkesbury, first Earl of Liverpool (1729-1808).

[390] The Vicomte de Noailles (1756-1804), served in America under Lafayette. In 1789 he was elected to the States-General but when the French Revolution grew more violent he emi-

To Paul Mijouef

May 27, 1922.

My dear Mr. Mijouef:[395]

. . . The Board of Editors of the *Review* meet here in a few days. I shall read your letter to them, and I feel sure that it will be as gratifying to them as it has been to me, to know that the journal, on which I really expend a good deal of pains, has been so highly valued by one living and working at so great a distance. They will also be appreciative of all that you have done to make American affairs better understood in Russia. I wish that our population had any such adequate knowledge of Russian affairs. Indeed, I wish that I had it myself, though I have been not inattentive to such knowledge, and have had some good Russian friends. Mr. Milyoukov I have known since 1904, when he lectured at the University of Chicago, where I then was a professor. I knew, and corresponded with, the late Professor Alexander Lappo-Danilevskii. Baron Korff, resident now in Washington, is my very good friend. I sat by him last night at a public dinner, and learned that he expects to revisit Finland this summer. Professor Rostovtseff I have known since 1913, and see him sometimes now, though it is far from here to the University of Wisconsin, where, by the way, he is succeeding admirably as a teacher of young Americans, so I hear.[396]

You speak of the absence from the *English Historical Review* of anything that would indicate that a war had been going on. That would seem natural to Dr. Poole,[397] for whom I have a very high regard. On the other hand, I thought that my very good friend M. Bémont of the *Revue Historique,* admitted to its pages during the war a good deal of matter that was highly colored with the passions of the hour, and perhaps if I had been a Frenchman, three thousand miles nearer to the enemy, I should have done the same. But for my part I thought I should prefer not to print anything of which I should be obliged to think, on looking it over ten or twenty years afterward, that it was not solid nor becoming to the pages of an historical journal, yet I believed it to be perfectly advisable, and a duty, to enlighten our public with respect to the issues of the war by printing articles dealing with analogous situations in the past, of one sort and another. Some such articles you will see in the numbers sent to you, and I think they did some good. . . .

To Waldo G. Leland

May 29, 1922.

Dear Leland:

. . . On Thursday the Board of Editors meets here. President Wilson asks us to drop in at three; I think Dodd is responsible for this, anyhow it will be pleasant.[398] The executive committee of the University Center for Research appoints a meeting for that forenoon, which I shall be unable to attend. I don't know what the business is. No earnest student of history has ever turned up except that Miss Reuter, our one ewe lamb, for whom we were able to do so little.

I have not done anything further about Brookings' building, which has now risen to its full height, and is being filled in. From what Mrs. Thomas W. Page said to me the other day, I judge that her husband, leaving the tariff board, will not go back to Charlottesville, but will stay here in charge of that new Institute of Economic Research.[399] It will be an agreeable position, in which one will not have to be grilled by Wood

---

[395] Professor Paul Mijouef, Petrograd, who between 1922 and 1925 wrote several times expressing his gratitude for American historical material sent to him by Jameson and his enthusiasm for all things American.

[396] Of Michael Ivanovich Rostovtzeff (the spelling used by Jameson), Haskins had written to Jameson on Mar. 12, 1918: "Robert P. Blake writes me from Petrograd that Rostovtsev, being a Constitutional Democrat, is anxious to spend a year or so in scholarly work outside of Russia, preferably in lecturing at universities in his field of ancient history and archaeology. As you know, he is the chief living authority on the economic history of antiquity, and with the exception of Eduard Meyer, probably has no superior in the general field of ancient history. You will doubtless recall meeting him at London; I have a distinct impression of vigor and energy gained from my meeting him there and in Berlin. He would like very much to come to America; the only thing upon which he insists is that he shall not be asked to lecture publicly on recent Russian history, though he will not conceal his opinions in private conversation. He wants to come, if at all, as a scholar rather than as a propagandist in any direction. . . . Rostovtsev can lecture readily in French and German, and guarantees to lecture in English at the end of six months." Professor Rostovtseff became professor of ancient history in the University of Wisconsin in 1920 and of ancient history and archaeology in Yale in 1925.

[397] Reginald Lane Poole (1857-1939), served the *English Historical Review* from the time it was established, 1885, until 1920, as assistant editor, joint editor with S. R. Gardiner, and editor. From 1886 to 1910 he was a lecturer in modern history in Oxford, and with Dr. William Hunt was joint editor of the *Political History of England*, 12v., London, Longmans, 1905-1910.

[398] William E. Dodd, at this time a member of the board of editors of the *Review,* was an ardent admirer of Wilson. The group which called, in addition to Dodd and Jameson, included Carl Becker and G. S. Ford. One of the number later reported that Wilson's conversation was characterized by a most "un-Wilsonlike lack of reserve." He spoke freely, often with a vehemence which approached violence, of the disappointments of the peace negotiations, of his lack of confidence in Poincaré, and of the fact that one could never predict from one day to the next what Lloyd George might do. Asked whether he meant to write his memoirs he responded with an emphatic negative. At the December meeting of the American Historical Association he was elected second vice-president in order that he might be president at the meeting of 1924 but he did not live to serve in that capacity. His life ended Feb. 3, 1924.

[399] Thomas W. Page (1866-1937), member of the United States Tariff Commission, 1918-1922, and again, 1930-1937. He was not made head of the Economic Institute but from 1922 to 1930 he was chief of the international policies division of its staff and prepared a study, published as *Making the tariff of the United States*, N. Y., McGraw-Hill, 1924.

of Indiana [400] and other representatives from the woods.

As to the archives, I had a talk with Colonel Sherrill the other day. It appears that Smoot and his public buildings commission mean to persuade Secretary Mellon to buy the designated square, as I imagine he has the authority to do, and so compel Congress to make the necessary appropriation.[401] Whether Mellon will agree to do it remains to be seen. Moore and I agree that to fly in the face of the House in that way would be a mistake, which would delay the whole thing by one year and make bad feeling for the whole project, and with which we had better have nothing to do. So, unless I get further light, I shall not fall in with Raege's plan of having the meeting of our committee and then jamming the appropriation through the House by the power of the American Legion.

The Carnegie Corporation had a meeting in New York last Wednesday. I sent a letter to Pritchett and Merriam,[402] additional to what Haskins sent to them before he sailed, attempting to point out some fresh aspects or merits of the A C L S, but they took no action, regretting their poverty. . . .

To JOHN SPENCER BASSETT

August 9, 1922.

Dear Bassett:

C. K. Webster, professor in the University of Liverpool,[403] sends me *A Journey to America in 1834,* by Robert Heywood of Bolton, an English Unitarian. It was privately printed by a descendant in 1919, and is rather interesting. On June 23, being in Washington, he was taken to see Jackson. His record of the interview does not illustrate high themes in political history, but you are entitled to see the record.[404] He says:

"At ten we were taken in a coach by Mr. White, M. P. for New York, to see the President; waited a short time in an ante-room with others, then were ushered into a large room furnished with books and papers. A tall, straight, old, thin-faced man with grey hair rose, and on my name being mentioned he bowed and shook hands. After a little conversation about losing his teeth by attempting artificial ones, which had dragged the remainder out until only his wise teeth remained, we left him, bowing and shaking hands again. Walked into parts of the house or palace; saw a very noble room where about 1500 attend five or six times a year. Rode in the same carriage to the Capitol; and were shown into the Hall of Representatives; a great many members present but not easily heard in consequence of the muttering in the House."

Perhaps you will say that the record of muttering in the House does contribute to knowledge of the events of that day; but without looking up the journal I do not know what they were muttering about, and I fear that during that reign it was chronic.[405]

To WALDO G. LELAND

August 31, 1922.

Dear Leland:

. . . I agree with anyone who says that the Republicans are going to lose the next House, though the Fordney-McCumber tariff is not the only sin which will be thus visited upon them.[406] In the matter of the bonus, for instance, I do not see how there can be anyone, either among those in favor of it or among those against it, who can fail to regard the course of Congress as plainly despicable. In this morning's *Post* the veracious George Rothwell Brown proclaims that they will have a majority of thirty in the House. If he does not venture to claim more than that at present, it confirms my estimate. The Bourbon Fordney having declined renomination and McCumber having failed to get it, Garrett of Tennessee [407] the other day labelled this conglomerate the "orphan tariff." A year from now, I think, no one will be anxious to figure in the *recherche à la paternité.* . . .

---

[400] William Robert Wood (1861-1933), member of the House of Representatives, 1915-1933.

[401] The House Committee on Appropriations had cut out the item from the appropriations bill and vigorous attempts by Simeon D. Fess and F. W. Dallinger had failed to restore it.
Andrew W. Mellon (1855-1937), secretary of the Treasury under Harding, Coolidge, and Hoover, 1921-1932.

[402] Henry S. Pritchett (1857-1937), was at this time president of the Carnegie Foundation for the Advancement of Teaching, as well as a trustee of the Carnegie Institution of Washington and the Carnegie Endowment for International Peace, and acting president of the Carnegie Corporation of New York.
John C. Merriam (1869-1945), president of the Carnegie Institution of Washington from the end of 1920 till 1938, was a trustee of the Carnegie Corporation.

[403] Charles K. Webster was professor of modern history in the University of Liverpool from 1914 to 1922, and Wilson professor of international politics in the University of Wales from 1922 to 1932.

[404] Bassett had begun his work on the *Correspondence of Andrew Jackson,* to be published by the Carnegie Institution.

[405] On June 23, 1834, the House was discussing resolutions from Rhode Island which called for the recharter of the bank and the restoration of deposits removed by Jackson. Mr. Pearce of Rhode Island maintained that these were not expressions of the people of the state but of the legislature, which did not represent the people because of the "rotten borough" system. He was convinced that the state was two to one against the bank; others felt that the resolutions were an expression of popular opinion. (*Debates in Congress* 10, (4): 4674-4703).

[406] Joseph W. Fordney (1853-1932), member of the House from Michigan, 1889-1923; Porter James McCumber (1858-1933), Senator from North Dakota, 1899-1923. Despite the fact that America's own best interests as well as the state of the world demanded lower tariffs the Fordney-McCumber tariff took no steps in that direction. Their majority was cut by the election of November, 1922, but the Republicans did not lose control of the Congress.

[407] Finis J. Garrett, member of the House from Tennessee, 1905-1929.

To LORD FITZMAURICE

October 12, 1922.

Dear Lord Fitzmaurice:

I am very greatly obliged by your kindness in copying, with your own hand, the letter of George Washington about which I wrote. It is not in his letter-books, here at the Library of Congress, and I am very glad to have it. I am also obliged by your kindness in consulting your nephew about Hammond letters.

I do not think that Kipling's remarks, or alleged remarks, of which you speak, have made any serious impression on American minds.[408] It was an incident of a day, soon forgotten. Those who like "England" (meaning the conduct of the British government) and the English, will continue to like them, and those who do not, will continue to feel otherwise, much as before. Perhaps you have seen the *Life and Letters of Walter H. Page* just published, mainly consisting of his letters. *There* is a book which seems to me extraordinarily interesting, and in which there are views of the English that *will* have a permanent influence upon many minds. . . .

To WALDO G. LELAND

November 6, 1922.

Dear Leland:

Pirenne and Madame Pirenne have come and gone. They were here only forty-eight hours, but gave us all a great deal of pleasure. We took them to drive soon after their arrival on Wednesday afternoon, and had a couple of friends in to dinner. On Thursday the Belgian minister took him to breakfast at Hoover's (though otherwise I think the Hoovers were a little shabby),[409] then I took them down to Mount Vernon, and Miss Putnam had luncheon for them.[410] Thursday afternoon they came in here to the works, saw all of the staff, and Pirenne gave them an interesting little

talk about the German post-war psychology and prospects. That evening we had a somewhat larger dinner party; Friday morning we did the Capitol and the Library of Congress, and Pirenne and a group of men lunched with me at the Cosmos Club, while some ladies lunched there with Madame Pirenne and Señora and Señorita Jameson. They charmed everybody, and went on to New York, Niagara, and other points west with assurances that we had not tired them.

I talked with him about the reviving of the *Jahresberichte,* in which W. W. Bishop,[411] president of the Bibliographical Society of America is also interested, and which perhaps may be discussed with that society if they meet at New Haven. I suggested a form of international organization whereby those chapters relating to specific countries might be done by inhabitants thereof, and printed in either English, French, German, or Italian. Pirenne approved, but thought such cooperation with the Germans as would be requisite would, for the next two or three years, be impossible to secure from the French, though not from the Belgians.

Secondly, Fish had suggested that we should have a session devoted especially to American history. This is well worth while. American history, between you and me, should be the chief pursuit of mankind henceforth. But I should not wish to have such a session if the audience would be entirely or almost entirely composed of Americans, who would feel it to be right to give moral support to their colleagues but would not need the edification. Pirenne thought there would be a good many others attending such a session, in spite of the competing attractions necessarily made simultaneous. As president he authorized me to assume that it might be done, but before writing to Ganshof,[412] I should like to know what you think about this matter of audience. I have no idea of the amount of interest in American history existing anywhere in Europe except in England, where I myself saw no signs of any, though others have assured me they exist. One consideration is that, if you will look over the enclosed list, you will see that most of these persons are addicted to European history, which is why they are in Europe. Messrs. Leland, Neeser, Westergaard, Johnson, and Golder, and Miss Wright [413] might

[408] Lord Fitzmaurice, on Sept. 19, 1922, had written: "I hope the 'Kipling' incident will not have too much importance attached to it on yr side of the Atlantic. Whatever he may have really said or meant—as to which there seems some doubt —he only represents a very small section of opinion, if any."
To a guest at tea—Clare Sheridan—Kipling had said that America had grown rich during the war, had played a very poor part in military operations, and had forced a premature peace. These remarks were published in the New York *World* as an interview with Kipling, who at once denied that he had given an interview or that he had had any idea that a guest would make public a private conversation. See *Nation* 115: 295, Sept. 27, 1922.
[409] The Belgian minister was the Baron de Cartier de Marchienne, appointed minister in 1918, ambassador in 1920, an office which he held until 1927. Hoover's wartime connection with Belgium doubtless explains the expectation that he would wish to see something of Professor and Madame Pirenne on this visit. He was at this time Secretary of Commerce.
[410] Ruth Putnam, sister of Herbert Putnam, the librarian of Congress. Much of her historical writing had dealt with the history of the Low Countries.

[411] William W. Bishop, librarian of the University of Michigan. Jameson here turned to problems connected with the International Congress to be held in Brussels in the spring to which he planned to propose a new international bibliography of current historical publications to take the place of the *Jahresberichte der Geschichtswissenschaft* of Berlin, which had ceased to appear after the war.
[412] François L. Ganshof of Brussels was secretary of the committee which was organizing the congress.
[413] Robert W. Neeser, manager for the Western Union Company in France and at work on a history of the ships in the American Navy.
Waldemar C. Westergaard, head of the department of his-

write interesting papers in Franco-American, Danish-American, Swedish-American, Russian-American, or Spanish-American history, but for merely U. S. A. history there would be only Alvord, if he goes, Fish, Morison, and Jameson, and Morison says he isn't going over because he was so bored by the London Congress of 1913.

You are perfectly right in thinking that H. B. L.[414] might make a ten-strike with a paper on the history of the relations between the President and the Senate, but until I find that I can make a good deal of impression by pushing the side of the Treasury building, I shall not try to divert him from the topic of the relations between Russia and America in the Civil War, on which he is fully engaged, as I am enabled daily to perceive.[415] He is getting out of it some very interesting things, that would be of much more interest to a meeting of the American Historical Association than the opinions of P. Lee Phillips's father on the Kansas-Nebraska act.[416] But there we are.

---

tory, Pomona College, 1916 to 1925, when he went to the University of California.

Amandus Johnson, assistant professor of history, University of Pennsylvania, 1915-1922.

Frank A. Golder and Irene A. Wright have already been identified. In the longer list of Americans actually attending the congress, given by Mr. Leland, of this group only Westergaard is named as present (The International Congress of Historical Sciences held at Brussels, *Amer. Hist. Rev.* **28**: 641, n. 3, July, 1923).

[414] Henry Barrett Learned (1868-1931), author of *The President's Cabinet,* New Haven, Yale Univ. Press, 1912. After periods of teaching in Sheffield Scientific School, Yale, and in Wesleyan and Stanford universities he was now located in Washington.

[415] Learned's long daily conversations with Jameson frequently consumed time which the latter could ill spare. Although he believed it futile to push, he had some influence in turning Learned's attention to the subject suggested by Mr. Leland: "Learned—for whom please understand that I have a warm and always increasing regard, in spite of occasional amusement at his attitude toward Time, that devours its offspring—has investigated very carefully the traditions respecting the purchase of Alaska, and has nearly convinced himself that after all Golder's explanation of the visit of the Russian fleet must stand against whatever of traditions and of old men's recollections. This being the case, his candor and justice of view will probably cause him to give up that subject, and, as I have given him a recent book on *The Control of Our Foreign Relations* to review, he may come around to the excellent topic which you have suggested" (Jameson to Leland, Nov. 27, 1922). The paper which Learned presented at the Congress, entitled, The temper of the United States Senate, 1918-1920, dealt with one aspect of the relations between President and Senate.

[416] At the meeting of the American Historical Association in 1920 Learned read a paper on the repeal of the Missouri Compromise, based on an investigation of contemporary newspapers and the private papers of Philip Phillips, father of P. Lee Phillips, cartographer of the Library of Congress. This was published as, The relation of Philip Phillips to the repeal of the Missouri Compromise, *Miss. Valley Hist. Rev.* **8**: 303-317, March, 1922.

To CHARLES O. PAULLIN

C. O. P.[417]

November 18, 1912-November 18, 1922.

Weak-winged is song, and cannot circle round
This ample sphere on which all lands are found;
Yet may the Muse in hasty flight survey
This little plot we call the U.S.A.,
May see, spread out beneath her as she flies,
Mountains and lakes and states of various size,
Discern in sundry quarters "rocks and rills,"
And elsewhere various "woods and templed hills,"
And mighty cities dotting all the plain,
From San Francisco to North Edgecomb, Maine.

Now who discovered this domain so fair?
Was it Columbus, as the books declare?
He sailed around the Caribbean Sea,
Landed on verdant islands, two or three,
Saw South America before Cabral,
But wholly missed the Panama Canal,
Bought Mild Havanas, very cheap I think,
But saw no archives and secured no drink.

Oh, what a glorious feather in his cap
Had he put U.S.A. upon the map!
But that was left for one of later time,
Whom here we celebrate with cake and rhyme;
For whom alone (such is the view *I've* gained)
Lee Phillips's division is maintained;
Who for ten years has studied every state,
Enlarged his knowledge and increased his weight,
Till all this copious learning, lightly worn,
Is like the world on Atlas' shoulders borne.
Long may he live his lurid maps to plot,
To draw the line and place the telling dot,
Till with the finished atlas we can go
And add the creature to our Barnum's show.[418]

To MABEL WEBBER

November 18, 1922.

Dear Miss Webber: [419]

I wish that, in response to your interesting letter of November 15, I could tell you where any manuscript letters of Thomas Pinckney,[420] that are not in

---

[417] Charles O. Paullin, who was at work upon the *Atlas of Historical Geography of the United States,* had completed ten years with the Institution.

[418] William Barnum came to the Carnegie Institution in November, 1903, as chief clerk of the Division of Publications; from July 1, 1909, until his resignation, June 30, 1925, he was editor of publications of the Institution.

[419] Miss Mabel Webber, secretary, treasurer, and librarian of the South Carolina Historical Society from 1906 until 1940, and editor of its magazine from 1909.

[420] Thomas Pinckney (1750-1828), son of Charles Pinckney, was minister to England, 1791-1795. His services to his country compared well with those of any New England patriot of his day.

the letter-books or elsewhere, can be found; but, at any rate, it does not appear that they are in the Library of Congress. What I found there, relative to the matter I was investigating, I found in the Washington and Jefferson Papers, and at the Department of State I found only the official correspondence that ought to be there.

I think that Washington's letter written jointly to C. C. Pinckney and Rutledge, which he himself seems to think unusual in form, is perhaps to be explained partly by the fact that, when he wrote it at Columbia, he had just been consorting with them, especially perhaps with C. C. Pinckney, at Charleston, and so knew of them as inseparables, neither of whom would have any feelings about the other one's being appointed to high office, except such as were dictated by public spirit. Still it remains a striking move.[421]

I know that the feeling of which you speak, respecting the underestimate of historical persons of the South, exists in certain quarters, and I am not surprised at it, but I really think that the underestimate does not spring from any intention to be unfair, nor even always from local conceit in the North, though there is plenty of the latter and all of us have partly provincial minds, admiring our own States in comparison with others, just as we so often admire the United States in comparison with other nations, though I suppose historians ought to free themselves from all such prepossessions. If, however, I should sum up what in forty years I have observed of the minds of northern, or let us say northeastern historical scholars, any underestimate on their part concerning the South or the West, or any southern or western State, comes not from an intention, or even a willingness to disparage, but from lack of an equal amount of knowledge respecting those, to what they have concerning their own part of the country. The amount of printed material available respecting the history of the northeastern part of the United States is enormous in comparison with what we have for the Southern States, and, partly, of the Western States. The western historical societies and writers have, however, in the last twenty years put forth so much material that we who were born in the northeast have little excuse for not appreciating duly their history or their public men. If we do not do so, it is mostly from a prejudice of those brought up in old and settled communities against those who dwell in regions newer and less seasoned by time—just such a prejudice as Englishmen have with respect to America. In the case of the South, however, there certainly is another element in the situation, namely, that far less historical material respecting them has been pub-

lished; especially is this true of those materials that exhibit the part played by Southern men in the building of the nation, for if one looks over the whole mass of the publications of the historical societies of the Southern States, one sees them to be mainly occupied with matter not likely to be of interest to persons outside the State, and not illustrating the action of its men in the national field so much as their action within the confines of the State itself. I appreciate the difficulties of such societies and the necessity they are under of keeping up the interest of persons who live in the State, to whom local matters make the chief appeal, yet I think they might sometimes do more to connect local and state history with the history of the United States, or with broader national interests.

What I mean to say is, that the historian writing in New England underestimates, for instance, South Carolina men because he has never had adequate means of knowing how excellent or how important they were. If, for example, he is of federalist inclination, as so often he is, he feels that General Charles Cotesworth Pinckney must have been a good deal of a man, in order to have been nominated on the presidential ticket alongside of John Adams, but he is somewhat at a loss how to prove it to himself, or to make real to his own mind the eminence of Pinckney. He has 10 octave volumes of John Adams's writings and scores of his letters and other publications; what has he of C. C. Pinckney? Your Professor Wallace's books on Laurens, and Professor Cook's Life of David R. Williams [422] are instances of the good done by bringing forward into fuller light the South Carolinians who have had national careers, but I wish there might be forty such, provided they were equally well made.

How interesting and important are these letters of Thomas Pinckney to Gouverneur Morris? Such groups of personal letters of diplomatists usually have more juice in them than could rightly be put into their public despatches. Might they not be good material for your magazine—or mine? [423] They certainly would be, if they have anything like the same degree of interest that Morris put into his letters; but there we are again—we have five big volumes of Morris, correspondence and diary taken together, and a dozen letters of T. Pinckney in his grandson's book.[424] . . .

---

[421] In 1791 Washington wrote a joint letter to Charles Cotesworth Pinckney (brother of Thomas) and Edward Rutledge, asking that one of them accept appointment as associate justice of the Supreme Court. See Ford, W. C., ed., *Writings of Washington* 12: 43-44, 14v., N. Y., Putnam's, 1889-1893.

[422] Wallace, D. D., *Life of Henry Laurens*, N. Y., Putnam's, 1915; Cook, H. T., *The life and legacy of David R. Williams*, N. Y., privately printed, 1916.

[423] The correspondence to which Jameson refers was not published in the *South Carolina Historical Quarterly*. Morris was in France part of the time that Pinckney was minister to England.

[424] Pinckney, C. C., *Life of Gen. Thomas Pinckney*, Boston, Houghton Mifflin, 1895.

To Hugh Chisholm

November 22, 1922.

Dear Mr. Chisholm: [425]

I can hardly think you will remember our meeting some years ago at the hospitable table of the late General Charles Francis Adams, but, having been asked to join in an appeal to you to disclose the author of the rather strange article about Secretary Baker in the new volumes of the Britannica, and not unnaturally declining to do so, because I do not care who wrote it, I have thought that I might write to you directly, to assure you that, however intemperate may be the various expressions on the subject which have been going to you, I think they are right in the central fact, that the article is very distinctly unfair and inadequate. In war-time there were many Republicans who thought and spoke of Secretary Baker's qualities and actions in such terms as those which your writer uses, but judicious persons, whether Republicans or Democrats, who were here in Washington through the war and saw him and his actions close at hand, held no such view. I feel sure that such contributors as my friends Professors Hart and Seymour, whose articles in your new volumes I have greatly admired, would join me in pronouncing the article to be both unjust and insufficient. [426]

When the American Historical Association met here in December 1920, our Committee engaged Secretary Baker to speak at our dinner, along with Mr. Jusserand and others. I was amused to hear, after the brilliant and extraordinary address he gave us, expressions of surprise from worthy members of our tribe from New England (where it was an article of faith that everything in the administration was unworthy and incompetent, and Mr. Wilson and all his works deserving only of contempt and reprobation), at the presence in the Secretary of War of an intelligence and a vigor of thought which they had no idea that he possessed. Our Washington members were not surprised, and, although as I have said I care not who wrote this little article, I am satisfied that it was no one in Washington, but someone who got his political history chiefly from partisan Republican newspapers. Those last two sentences of the article are really, to anyone who watched the proceedings of the War Department from near at hand, a most extraordinary travesty of what it did and of the skill with which it did it. [427]

I hope that these expressions, from one who is neither Republican nor Democrat, and has no official position, but is merely "a looker-on here in Vienna," may not seem obtrusive or in any way uncivil. I admire your three new volumes enormously; and congratulate you heartily upon them.

To Waldo G. Leland

November 27, 1922.

Dear Leland:

. . . As to politics, I don't know that, by reason of being nearer to the Capitol and the White House, I can interpret the recent election any better than it can be done in Paris. As a collection of individuals, I do not see that Congress has been improved by the election. There were some bad losses (I count Poindexter one), and some fair gains. But there are stirrings that seem to indicate that the Senate may be run somewhat differently. Both in Senate and in House there will be new leaders in the main, and though they may not be superior leaders personally, they will apparently represent more liberal tendencies. As to the meeting of the American Legion, our accounts here are to the same effect. [428] The truth is, that organization has rushed into the baser kind of politics more rapidly than the G. A. R. did, and, while the country will expect, and is likely, to be largely run for the next twenty years by the ex-soldiers, and it is perhaps well that it should be so, it will rapidly grow weary of the officers and leading spirits in this organization.

I don't quite share your view about Fortescue. [429] I thought very highly of his conduct as president of

[427] The closing sentences of the brief sketch of Newton D. Baker, characterized as an "American politician," read: "After America entered the war he recommended moderation towards conscientious objectors and forbade men in uniform to interfere with anti-conscription meetings. The charge of pacifism was often brought against him, and his career generally as Secretary was widely condemned throughout the United States as lacking in energy, foresight and ability, and especially for his failure to prepare adequately in the months immediately preceding the American declaration of war" (*Encyclopedia Britannica* 30: 366 [12th ed.]).

[428] Mr. Leland wrote on Nov. 14, 1922: "The reports reaching here of the recent convention of the American Legion are not very encouraging. Dr. Gros, who attended from here, and who is a respectable person, says that it was a case of mob rule, with great disorder, drunkenness, gaming and even rioting on a small scale."

[429] "I should judge that Weeks had pulled a pretty bad bone in cancelling Fortescue's invitation to make the address at West Point. I know that Fortescue has always shown deep prejudice, not to say animus, with regard to American matters, but after all I don't suppose that the Cadets at West Point are all likely to be turned into Benedict Arnolds if he should address them. Besides, I understand that he has changed his views. And anyhow, what sort of cheap sports are we? I hope that the Historical Association will find some way of making amends for Weeks' blurb" (Leland to Jameson, Nov. 14, 1922). John W. Weeks was Secretary of War, 1921-1925.

[425] Hugh Chisholm (1866-1924), one of the editors of the tenth edition and editor-in-chief of the eleventh and the three volumes which constituted the twelfth edition of the *Encyclopaedia Britannica*. From 1913 to 1920 he was financial editor of the London *Times*.

[426] Professor Hart made two contributions to the twelfth edition of the *Britannica,* one on Theodore Roosevelt, one on the United States. Jameson was probably writing of the first of these.

Charles Seymour, then professor of history in Yale, was the author of a carefully colorless article on Warren G. Harding.

the Royal Historical Society, and especially as the king's librarian at Windsor Castle, toward the Americans who attended the conference of July, 1921, but the many passages in his prefaces to his *Calendars of State Papers, Colonial,* and the passages which the Secretary of War quoted from his Oxford lectures, have always been very offensive to me, whenever I have read them.[430] A man may have his prejudices, but a responsible historian has no business to talk that way to an Oxford audience. It is having one's fling, in order to appear smart, at the expense of sobriety and clear thinking, and I think that Weeks was right and that Fortescue got what he deserved. At the same time, I have been so appreciative of his attentions to us at Windsor that I wished to do what I could to make his visit to Washington agreeable, and wrote him so both before and after his rebuke, but he finally decided not to come here at all. He sails for England in a few days now, but I don't think the A. H. A. would invite him after what has happened.[431] . . .

To Dwight W. Morrow

December 4, 1922.

Dear Mr. Morrow:

It has been a great pleasure to see, collected in one series, these thoughtful and exceedingly valuable papers written from time to time by our old friend

Morse.[432] I have read with much interest your excellent introduction, and have been glad that the duty of thus introducing the volume to the public has fallen into such competent and sympathetic hands. There are only two suggestions which it occurs to me to make. One is that, although the party can rightly be described historically and actually as the alternative to revolution, some mention might be made of the fact, though it seems to have been hardly noticed by writers, that another alternative was frequently tried during a considerable period. I refer to the "association," in the sense in which that word was used from Queen Elizabeth's time to that of George III. It was a much less flexible device than the party, much less capable of successful working, yet was a good deal in favor in a period when parties were looked upon as dangerous combinations, deserving to be reprobated. I said a little about this device in a paper read before the American Historical Association a few years ago, and venture to enclose herewith a copy of my little paper, which will explain more fully what I had in mind.[433] It may be only my predilection for a subject on which I worked a little, but I should think that this device of the "association" might deserve a sentence. If one has made a small contribution to a large subject, one is glad to have it taken up early into any surveys of the larger subject that are likely to receive a greater degree of thoughtful attention than is given to isolated small papers.

I should also venture to suggest that, in the last paragraph of your introduction but one, a little more might be made of our dear friend's extraordinary hold upon students. You speak of him in other aspects, but do not say much about his classroom dealings with the boys. If I am right in thinking that in the last days of his teaching he was the professor most esteemed by the students, it is rather remarkable and encouraging, for as a rule the "most popular professor" at any college attains that position by the conscious or unconscious use of arts similar to those whereby men acquire popularity among older men, children of a larger growth, but not less puerile in succumbing to these simple devices. For instance, the student's idol is apt to be one who manifests vociferous enthusiasm for intercollegiate athletics, though every sane man knows that

---

[430] "Now we know how the Americans—represented by their Government—have always dealt with us since they have been an independent state. They must always prevail, and never give way; they must always take and never concede; they enjoy the flouting of an older community as a proof of their superiority; and they esteem a good bargain, even if gained by dishonourable means, to mark the highest form of ability. The United States cannot engage in any form of competition with us, from athletics to diplomacy, without using foul play. They must win, if not by fair skill, then by pre-arranged trickery or violence; if not by open negotiations, then by garbled maps and forged documents. There is the fact. It may be unpleasant, but it cannot be denied" (Fortescue, J. W., *British Statesmen of the Great War, 1793-1814,* 25-26, Ford Lectures for 1911, Cambridge, England, Clarendon Press, 1911). For an illustrative quotation from the prefaces to the *Calendars,* see *ante,* July 21, 1921, n. 328.

[431] Since Fortescue's disagreeable remarks have been quoted, it is a pleasure to record what he wrote just before he sailed for England: "Never and nowhere have I met with such kindness and hospitality as in the United States, nor with greater courtesy and civility from all classes—elevator boys, taxi-drivers, every one. This is all that I shall remember of my visit; and I leave your wonderful country (of which I have seen about two inches only, relatively speaking) with the warmest feelings towards all within it" (Fortescue to Jameson, Nov. 28, 1922). The fact that the West Point lecture had been cancelled was announced on the first page of the New York *Times,* Nov. 11, 1922; the next day the *Times* carried an interview with Fortescue in which he said that America's conduct in the war and his growing friendship with many Americans had convinced him that he had been wrong and that he had intended to tell the West Point students this.

[432] Dwight W. Morrow, like Dr. Jameson a devoted student of Professor Morse of Amherst, was preparing for publication a collection of Morse's papers, to be one of the Amherst Books, published in connection with the centennial celebration of Amherst College: Morse, Anson Daniel, *Parties and party leaders,* with an introduction by Dwight W. Morrow, Boston, Marshall Jones Company, 1923. A sympathetic account of the influence of Morse on Morrow is to be found in Nicolson, Harold, *Dwight Morrow,* 37-38, 51, 56, N. Y., Harcourt, Brace, 1935.

[433] As published, Morrow's introduction contains material (xxiv-xxv, xxviii-xxix) on the Association and its part in the political action of the sixteenth and seventeenth centuries, with a reference to Jameson's article: The Association, *Ann. Rept., Amer. Hist. Assn.,* 1917: 305-312.

they are outrageously overdone; or he is a bright and showy talker, or one who pleases the youths by adopting at times their dialect of slang. That with none of these arts Morse could be, in a very real sense, the most popular of Amherst professors, merely because of wisdom and goodness, it is a striking thing, and worth remembering at times [*sic*] when one thinks one's worst of undergraduates.

I wish that I had time to read again, in the proof-sheets, all these essays of his, but this is a very busy time with me, and it would be no compliment to work like Morse's, to push through it hastily. What he wrote was food for thought, and just now I have no time to think; but the mere glancing through the proof-sheets (on which, by the way, I have out of habit noted a few corrections), has very pleasantly revived my remembrance of his sound doctrines and his careful exposition. I thank you for the pleasure, and add my gratitude to that of his other pupils for the service you have done to his memory.

To Worthington C. Ford

January 10, 1923.

My dear Ford:

. . . I am glad I did not know what was going on at the dinner to which you allude, for it might have spoiled my dinner. It certainly would have done so if I had heard that you were accepting, instead of temporarily declining.[434]

I remember that in Richmond in 1891 you thought I was occupied with a useless task.[435] It would not have been if I had ever written the book which I then thought of. Anyhow, it was not useless in one more immediate sense, for out of it I got the material for at least one article, and part of another. The former was a piece on Virginia Voting in the Colonial Period, which I sent to the *Nation,* and which it printed.[436] When it came to me in proof, Garrison had put it into the form of a letter, dating it April 13, 1893. I remonstrated to him, that 600 or 700 people had been notified that that was to be my wedding day, and I

thought that, as in Gilpin's case, "All the world would stare" at the sight of such evidence of calmness.[437] He changed the date to April 12, which was not much better, for several of my friends commented on such tranquillity before execution. Without taking up the question whether it was important to show how democratic Virginia was as compared with Massachusetts, the *Nation* undoubtedly paid me enough to cover Mrs. Jameson's and my car fare from Brooklyn to Washington, where we began our married life at the Shoreham hotel, diagonally opposite the building in which I now spend my days. That truly shows some value in the researches so lightly esteemed by you.

To Henry A. Forster

January 13, 1923.

Dear Sir:

This is in reply to your letter of January 12. From what you write, and from what I hear otherwise, I judge that Miss Rutherford[438] takes extreme positions —so extreme that she is certain to arouse opposition on the part of a large number of sensible and moderate people throughout the South. Their protests will have a hundred times the weight in their region that anything would have which should come from the North. I do not find myself sharing your belief that if her talk is not refuted, it may spread through all the schools, colleges, and universities in the South. It will be impossible to refute every extravagant thing she may say, and indeed it is the same old stuff, and has been sufficiently refuted time and time again. I know many of the professors of history in the southern colleges, perhaps all the important ones, and none of them would countenance such views of American history as those which Miss Rutherford is trying to propagate. Their opinions will in the end be far more potent than hers. Moderate and sensible views will anyhow always be more potent than extravagant ones. I am not in the least worried. There will for many years be a sentimental attachment to the Lost Cause, and a habit of investing the struggle of those who supported it with

---

[434] "It was especially thoughtful of you to give me your admirable tribute to Viscount Bryce. I could not help but recall, as I read it, the dinner which I gave at the Metropolitan Club to our Historical Commission, at which Mr. Bryce was present. I forget whether or not I ever told you that it was at that dinner that Mr. Adams told me of the desire of the Massachusetts Historical Society for an editor and intimated, in his usual distant and unrelated attitude, that it might appeal to me. I then declined, for I was too much interested in the Washington work" (Ford to Jameson, Jan. 4, 1923). Six weeks after the dinner, J. F. Rhodes reopened the question with Ford and he accepted the Massachusetts position.

[435] "Can you match for accidents, even from the day when I discovered you under the roof of the Westmoreland Club, I think it was, in Richmond, Virginia, digging out old election returns in colonial times?" (*Ibid.*).

[436] *Nation* **56**: 309-310, Apr. 27, 1893. Wendell Phillips Garrison (1840-1907) was the literary editor of the *Nation* at this time.

[437] "Said John, It is my wedding day,
    And all the world would stare,
    If wife should dine at Edmonton,
    And I should dine at Ware."
            Cowper, The diverting history of John Gilpin.

[438] Mildred Lewis Rutherford of Athens, Ga., was state historian of the Georgia division of the United Daughters of the Confederacy and from 1911 to 1916 historian general of that organization. She was also historian general of the Confederated Memorial Associations and the author of many booklets on southern history. At this time she had started *Miss Rutherford's Scrapbook,* which was to appear ten times a year. Of the first number Jameson's correspondent, a New York lawyer, wrote: "The first number is the hottest reading I have ever read in relation to the Confederacy. . . . If this is not refuted it might spread through all the schools, colleges and universities South of Mason and Dixon's line" (Forster to Jameson, Jan. 12, 1923).

the same sort of romantic glamor with which Scott and others of his time and later times invested the Jacobite cause; but it will have no more serious effect on the future of the country, or specifically on the stability of the government, than that had. The southern people cannot be expected to declare that their grandfathers were wicked traitors, but they no more think of being in the least disloyal to the United States government than the Scotsmen of 1830 thought of being disloyal to the government of Great Britain under the house of Hanover; and as for historical opinions in the whole matter, they will settle themselves as other historical opinions have been settled, by the general resultant of various divergent views, as more and more people read good historical writings that come from both sides rather than from their own party alone.

To WALDO G. LELAND

January 30, 1923.

Dear Leland:

Congress

. . . First, as to the Brussels Congress. I am not coming over.[439] I feel very deep regret at this conclusion, and I think I appreciate fully all the reasons you bring forward in favor of going, with one additional one, and one of those that appeal most, namely, that I should like to have some good long talks with you about a number of things. But if you were here in Washington, or if I could describe at full length the situation of a lot of the things that lie before me—in a physical sense or in respect to time and urgency—I believe you would see that it was impossible for me to conclude otherwise than that it was my duty to stay here and struggle with these things, rather than to cut out six or seven weeks during which I could give no

attention to any of them. I think I have taken such measures that my absence will not be misconstrued by Pirenne or anybody who expected me to come, and I have tried to do all that I could without going over. . . .

Of twenty-one American historical scholars whose views I have gathered by correspondence or conversation, eighteen take just my view respecting abstention, while of the other three, one is of German extraction, one born a British subject, and one a Quaker. We are perfectly justified in declaring our opinion to be the almost unanimous opinion of the Americans. On the other hand, of the two conspicuous Britons in Canada—Wrong and Basil Williams—one votes one way and one the other, just as you would expect of any two Englishmen—Wrong decidedly with us, Williams decidedly not. The latter wrote me a very nice letter, very well thought out, and subsequently asked me, if I had no objection, to send it to a friend for use in the London *Nation*.[440] I have sent it. While I had a fleeting wish that the American opinion might also be known in England, I do not suppose it would have any more effect than the opinion of the faculty of the University of Arkansas would have in Boston; and anyhow, I have sufficiently, and perhaps more than sufficiently, made my opinion known to various Englishmen. From most of them I shall probably be hearing soon, but—it just occurs to my mind—what they say is not likely to change my mind either. Well, anyhow, it is pleasant to know that everybody has the same desire as to the ultimate future and the next congress, though the present political situation in Europe makes one doubtful whether another one will ever be pulled off within another decade, or indeed whether this one may not be wrecked between now and April.[441]

"Among those present" you may expect to see Yasaka Takagi. He hopes, with his usual considerate politeness, that he will not on that occasion be in any

---

[439] Mr. Leland, seriously concerned for the International Congress to be held in April in Brussels, wrote on Dec. 18, 1922: "Notestein spent Thursday evening with me on his way south, and I am a good deal concerned about what he told me as to the attitude of the English. He says that the London group, under Pollard, but omitting Newton, have drawn up some sort of protest against not including the Germans, and that the Oxford people have done the same, though not joined by Oman. . . . He said that the Cambridge men were also holding off, and he thought the English attendance would be negligible. He says that they hold the view, or entertain the fear that the present committee on organization will as a matter of course name the place of the next Congress, and will put it in Paris, and that the French will continue to omit the Germans, and that then we shall be definitely divided. He hears that the Swedes are planning some sort of demonstration, such as a congress including the Germans."

On Jan. 16, 1923, Leland added: "You have an influence with the English that no [one] else has and the French all trust you implicitly, and if it should be necessary to arrange any sort of a compromise you will be in a better position to bring it about than anyone else. . . . It isn't as though you were just another American. The first thing people ask me is if you are coming. . . . If you are here the American branch of the profession is represented—if you are not—it makes a lot of difference."

[440] The letter was not published in the London *Nation*.

[441] Owing in large part to the American position, that it was not reasonable to expect the Belgian Committee to issue a formal invitation to Germany to take part in the Congress, although the committee would be glad to invite individual German scholars, and to the intention of the American delegation to propose the creation of a permanent international committee representative of all countries, which should have responsibility for the organization of future congresses. The English historians were well represented at Brussels. The decision as to the place of the next Congress, 1928, there being invitations from Warsaw and Oslo, was referred to the new permanent Committee which the Brussels Congress voted to establish. On Aug. 9, 1923, Jameson wrote: "Leland says that Pirenne told him that the Americans had saved the congress, and the King told him that they all highly appreciated the course which the Americans had taken in the matter. You may very likely know that the British note suggesting to the Belgian committee that the congress should be made truly international, though extensively signed was in the end not sent. Mr. Seton-Watson, who had it in charge, sent a circular around saying that in view of the American attitude toward the matter it was thought better not to send it" (Jameson to Harold Hazeltine, Aug. 9, 1923). See Leland's account of the Brussels Congress in *Amer. Hist. Rev.* **28**: 639-655, 1923.

way a burden to any of his friends or acquaintances. As to hearing things he must manage for himself; but please do what you can to make him acquainted. He is likely to go on the same steamer with Learned.

I shall try to send over some sort of proposal respecting an international substitute for the Jahresberichte,[442] but it is awfully hard to get anything finished, and anyhow, I suppose none but a quite provisional action, if any, can be expected to be taken at Brussels. I have three or four things here that are more urgent than that, every one of which ought to have my undivided attention for a month ahead. I do not understand Bishop's criticism about the index to the JBG. The index to the last one fills 130 pages in double columns. There is no contenting these bibliographers.

I am glad to know that Westergaard and Golder will be present. Of course many British abstentions will be due, whether the fact is known or not, to their natural unwillingness to flock together. I think not more than half of those of the conspicuous grade attended the London congress.

Archives

It is now the afternoon of January 30. I presume that by this hour the conferees have done their deadly work and my amendment is dead and buried and damned.[443] You will remember that last February our little patriots negatived the scheme on the ground that it would be a wicked shame for the government to buy any more land in the District of Columbia. Later in the session they bought seven squares in the region west of the Pan-American, paying a million and a half for the same. One of the seven, bounded by B and C and 20th and 21st, was big enough for the Archive Building, and otherwise suitable except that it was a little too far west. I placed in Poindexter's hands an amendment appropriating $500,000 for beginning the construction of a $2,500,000 building on that square, thinking that it might be substituted for Smoot's amendment appropriating $1,000,000 for steel stacks with

which to fill up the interior of the Pension Office Building. Poindexter rather skillfully got Smoot committed to saying that he would accept it after his was passed, and both ultimately passed the Senate. But after seeing all of the four House conferees on our act (the fifth being ill), I made up my mind that it would fail. It is maintained that it is attached to the wrong bill, but the real reason is the need of larger and better post-office accommodations in various parts of our loved country. Well, two things have been achieved: all the House members influential in the matter, and a number of others, have had it proved to them that the building is authorized; the president of the Senate overruled on that ground a point of order made there, and the speaker said he would do the same.[444] Secondly, I suppose that a vote in the Senate for an appropriation for actual construction is an advance over last year. We started with an almost fatal handicap in that the Director of the Budget turned the thing down. Perhaps he will not do so next year; but I fear that the thing will now have to take its chances with a raft of public buildings so large and loosely constructed that it will sink.

ACLS

Erskine never notified until October the persons appointed last January as a committee on a Dictionary of American Biography,[445] and when their acceptances

---

[442] See *Amer. Hist. Rev.* **28**: 653-654, July, 1923. The proposal sent to the Congress by Jameson was for the international publication of an annual bibliography of current historical works, which should be "a continuation in modified form" of the abandoned *Jahresberichte der Geschichtswissenschaft*. It was referred to the international committee authorized by this Congress, and out of the proposal grew the *International bibliography of historical sciences*.

[443] Jameson's amendment, introduced by Senator Poindexter, added to the Independent Office Appropriation bill provision for funds with which to begin an archive building at once. For its passage Jameson had been, as he wrote to W. H. Allison on Jan. 22, spending all his time at the Capitol but with little hope of success. The four House conferees were Wood of Indiana, Edward H. Wason of New Hampshire, L. J. Dickinson of Iowa, and J. W. Byrns of Tennessee. Jameson was right. The conferees did not retain the appropriation for an archive building and on their report to the House on Feb. 2, a lively debate ensued, Wood defending its omission, Fess of Ohio arguing for its retention (*Cong. Rec.* 67 Cong., 4 sess., 2899-2900).

[444] Calvin Coolidge was President of the Senate; Frederick H. Gillett of Massachusetts, Speaker of the House.

[445] At the first meeting of the American Council of Learned Societies, in February, 1920, Frederick J. Turner proposed that the Council undertake a dictionary of American biography, to be comparable to the *Dictionary of National Biography*. This proposal he repeated at the February meeting in 1921. A similar suggestion was made by the committee of policy of the American Historical Association in 1920, and in January, 1922, the Council appointed to consider the matter a committee consisting of Jameson, chairman, John Erskine, Thomas W. Page, Frederic L. Paxson, Frederick J. Turner, and Robert S. Woodward. This was the group whose meeting Jameson is here describing. They were ready with a report in January, 1924. See, Brief account of the enterprise, *Dictionary of American Biography* **20**: vii-xvi; *Ann. Rept., Amer. Hist. Assn.,* 1920: 72.

Already Jameson had written to Mr. Leland (Dec. 12, 1923): "Confidentially, I obtained through my old friend John Finley, some encouragement about the Dictionary of American Biography from Mr. Ochs of the New York Times, but there is nothing definite to be reported yet. All other sorts of efforts to find the needful angel have petered out." On May 5, 1924, to John S. Bassett, he reported: "I have found an 'angel,' indeed in my eyes an archangel, who is willing to supply $50,000 a year for ten years without visible anxiety as to how much of it he will ever get back." Bassett reported the news to the American Historical Association, with the added comment: "I cannot refrain from adding that to our own member, Dr. J. F. Jameson, this society [American Council of Learned Societies] and the Nation are indebted for this happy consummation." *Ann. Rept., Amer. Hist. Assn.,* 1924: 66.

Once the funds were assured, the direction of the work was placed in the hands of a committee of management of seven, four to be appointed by the Council, two by the New York Times Company, and the seventh, who was to be editor-in-chief, to be chosen by the six. They were J. F. Jameson,

were all in, and I felt that I could play them up in a circular, I started out to collect funds for two meetings. The first plan I tried failed, but last week—only two or three days before the meeting of the ACLS—I completed my ten 50's, namely, from Ayer, Beveridge, Bingham, Fairfax Harrison, Kellen, D. W. Morrow, Conyers Read, John D. Rockefeller, jr., Henry D. Sharpe, and one other not to be quoted just yet. On Friday I lunched with Colby, who is enthusiastic about raising the money for floating the DAB, and desired to be allowed to take a hand in that process. Well, you would have been amused to see, at the end of a somewhat gloomy morning session, what a pleasure it was to these worthies to hear, when it came to my report, that ten esteemed persons had given the concern $500 for any purpose whatever. It was pathetic, when one compares the eminence of the persons and the cause with the smallness of the sum. I felt that I was quite a little sunshine bringer. Now to prepare for the first meeting, within a month I hope, but it means a lot of work for little Pollyanna, if data are to be got into such shape that the meeting can be effective. By that time I think President Woodward will be well enough to attend, the meeting being held here, T. W. Page being here; the other three are Turner, Paxson, and Erskine, who is really interested in this matter. I saw quite a bit of Haskins, and was pained to find him in no better health, although very likely better than when you last saw him, and so unwontedly careful of himself. He walks a little lame, too. At the meeting, Erskine at last handed out Bulletin No. 2, marred by a good number of errors, and conveying last year's directory of presidents and secretaries of societies. I send you a copy, without attempting to correct these last. The final choice of delegates to the UAI [Union Académique Internationale] was left to the chairman—probably Shotwell and Beeson, Latin, Chicago.[446] Shotwell came in for a little time, with his arm in a sling. He will be in Washington this week, I suppose; and also Duggan will be here, whom I want to sound about combining an Anglo-American Conference of Professors of History (return match) with the Washington end of the Washington-Richmond meeting of the A. H. A. in December 1924. I think that might be made to go.[447]

Jahresberichte, etc.

As mentioned above, I am trying to get a tentative scheme of that sort into shape for the Brussels Congress, but have the usual article yet to write on the New Haven meeting, these preparations respecting the DAB, and a beautiful scheme that I want to put up to Charlie Hughes before he sets out for Santiago de Chile[448]—to say nothing of the more immediate tasks of the D. of H. R. of the C. I. of W., which we have always with us.

I perfectly agree with you that the project of a gigantic international library is profoundly silly. I should not give it a moment's consideration, and not many to this business of abstracts, which is all very well for the scientists, but is much less applicable in our field;[449] and anyhow, you and I have plenty to do without wandering off with these idealistic bibliographers into some scheme

> That with no middle flight intends to soar
> Above th'Aonian mount, while it pursues
> Things unattempted yet in prose or rhyme.

I think however that you took precisely the judicious course in regard to all these proposals, and certainly I am greatly interested to read about them, and greatly obliged to you for sending the documents. Millikan's[450] letter was good hard American commonsense, though perhaps a little bluntly put. I will send extracts from your letter to Haskins.

C. I. of W.

Merriam sets out for Yucatan next week. A long, friendly letter from McLaughlin mentions that Professor E. D. Burton has been chosen president there, which I think is surprising, as he will be 67 in a few days, and I supposed Edgar Goodspeed was booked for that job.[451] . . .

---

[448] This scheme, presented to Secretary Hughes orally and later more formally set forth in writing in the name of the committee on documentary historical publications of the United States government, was, briefly, that the Department of State should publish the Instructions sent by the secretaries of State to our foreign ministers. The Department of Historical Research stood ready to provide copy for the first volume for Great Britain, edited by a competent scholar (Jameson to the Secretary of State, Apr. 23, 1923, printed in *Ann. Rept., Amer. Hist. Assn.,* 1923, 89-90). As will be seen in later letters, Secretary Hughes gave his approval to the idea and for a time it looked as if the plan were to be carried out but it was eventually dropped. See *post,* Mar. 9, 1925.

[449] This is a reference to Leland's report, Jan. 5, 1923, of a meeting of a subcommittee of the International Committee on Intellectual Cooperation of the League of Nations, where the two proposals discussed were for an international library, to contain all books and periodicals published in the world after some fixed date, and a system of inclusive abstracts, to be universally distributed. The chief advocate of the second was Madame Curie.

[450] Robert A. Millikan, member of the department of physics of the University of Chicago, 1896-1921, and director of the Norman Bridge Laboratory of Physics, California Institute of Technology, 1921-1945, was the American member of the Committee on Intellectual Cooperation of the League of Nations in 1923, but was not present at the meeting which Mr. Leland had attended. He had, however, sent a letter (which was not read at the meeting) opposing the plan for an international library.

[451] E. J. Goodspeed had been secretary to the president of the University of Chicago since 1920; Ernest D. Burton (1856-1925) lived but two years after this appointment, and was succeeded by Max Mason.

---

chairman, F. L. Paxson, Carl Van Doren, Charles Warren, John H. Finley, and Mrs. Arthur H. Sulzberger, daughter of Mr. Ochs. The seventh was Professor Allen Johnson of Yale.

[446] Charles H. Beeson.

[447] See *post,* July 19, 1923.

About time to write *finis* and go home, carrying with me certain precious manuscripts, such as Burnett's preface to his volume II., which has taken him only seven weeks to write, Go and do thou not likewise. The market shows an active demand for French guides (edition of Paris, 1923).

To Alexander J. Wall

January 31, 1923.

My dear Mr. Wall:

. . . I appreciate what you say, and what Mr. Hammond says, of the difficulties under which the endowed societies of the eastern states now labor, but the difference between them and the other group lies not solely in the method of support.[452] It is true that state support, in spite of some drawbacks, has the great advantage, that you have to convince people who feel that they are acting in the interest of the public and anyhow are spending other people's money and not their own, so that an appeal to them on public grounds is more easily made than to private millionaires. I believe however that quite as large a part of the difference between the operations of the two groups arises from the fact that one is in the East and the other in the West, one in old communities or regions, the other in new. My experience is that the western societies, whether in their group of officers or in their rank and file, are distinctly more alive than those of the East, and more prone to take a large view of their tasks. In any effort to bring about co-operation of historical societies for any given object, it is easier to persuade a western historical society to take an interest in something lying outside the borders of its own state and, in proportion to its means, to support any such object, than in the case of the eastern societies. They turn out better to the annual Conference. You will notice that they respond more largely to the questionnaires sent out. We have to ask ourselves why this is, or why the one set is more successful than the other.

Fundamentally, it is for two reasons. One is that the influential members of the western historical societies, mainly because those states are younger, keep a closer connection with the actual present-day life of the state. That means that they have a more real sense as to what things in its past life have had importance in shaping its present life, and thereby a more real sense

of what will interest the men who are influential in its present life. The eastern historical societies are apt to be composed of, or drift into the hands of, men who have nothing to do, and a man of that class has too little sense of values in history or in the present. He reads in his library, or views the world from his club window, he interests himself in small antiquarian objects—liberty poles and regimental buttons, if you will pardon a local reference. Often he cares about nothing subsequent to the Revolution, which seventy or a hundred years ago, when some of these societies were founded, was an allowable *terminus ad quem*, but which is now seventy or a hundred years farther back in the past, with the most interesting and important portion of American history stretched between it and us, and clamoring for treatment. I sometimes think that the military history of the Revolution, and especially the local details of that military history, has been a most injurious obsession upon the minds of our eastern historical societies. So long as that should remain the *terminus ad quem* for any historical society, it has been prone to occupy itself with the history of small provincial or parochial concerns—those of a seventeenth-century or eighteenth-century province, or those of a village. All that is interesting to many people, but as a rule it is not interesting to important business men.

Might not the eastern historical societies help themselves if they would note down the reasons which make their states or their cities important at the present time, and then would ask themselves what things in the past have caused these various elements of greatness? That might give a different perspective. Why do we have a New York Historical Society except that New York City is the most important city in America, yet how many of the strands that go to make up its present greatness still remain untouched by the historian. But if they were touched and traced, this business man or that who sees and works that strand at its present end, might sit up and take notice.

Why is it that, taking the country over, those historical societies are most successful which keep in close relations with the neighboring professors of American history? Is it not because the man who has to teach American history, perhaps from its beginning to its end, sees the local history in its proper setting, in its relations to those larger matters in which men of affairs are more interested than in the problems and pursuits of antiquarianism. Here is a practical suggestion—that, to my mind, the chief event of 1923 in the life of the New York Historical Society might well be, if they saw it so, the removal of Professor Evarts B. Greene from the University of Illinois to Columbia next autumn. There is a man who, modest and quiet as can be, has been able to get what he will from the legislature of Illinois, partly because they have seen his perfect disinterestedness, partly because of his wisdom and wide look over the field of history, though the colonial period is his special field. Be sure that

---

[452] Alexander J. Wall (1884-1944), librarian and later director of the New-York Historical Society. This letter was called forth by one from Mr. Wall of Jan. 17, 1923, in which he expressed the feeling that the conferences of historical societies held at the annual meetings of the Historical Association tended to concentrate on problems which pertained to state-supported societies, for the most part in the west, and ignored the no less acute problems of the privately endowed eastern societies. Mr. Otis G. Hammond, head of the New Hampshire Historical Society, had, at the December meeting of the Historical Association, presented a gloomy picture of the future of his society (*Amer. Hist. Rev.* **28**: 424, Apr. 1923).

you get into touch with him as soon as he arrives and secure for him, if you can, that place of influence in your society which he ought to have.

As for the problems about which you wrote, perhaps Columbus will, for the reasons I mentioned at the beginning, be a less available place for their consideration than Richmond, where the Conference of December, 1924, will be held.[453] Meantime, I do not know what can be done, in societies whose lines of publication are for the present somewhat fixed by temporary tradition, unless to organize special exhibitions of a sort that will make their appeal to men of large affairs and not merely to antiquarians or bibliographers. I say this however without in the least knowing what kind of exhibitions you have been having lately, and so you may have been doing precisely this. If you have not, it occurs to me that an exhibition relative to the Scandinavians in New York, or to the Jews in New York, or to the port of New York, or to the Erie Canal, or to the development of the skyscraper, or to that of the park system, or squares and parks, or to that of the systems of local passenger transportation, might hit some minds that have not been hit before. But I presume that all these ideas have already occurred to you and your associates. . . .

To the Editor of the Washington *Post*

February 3, 1923.[454]

Sir:

I was much interested in the item in your issue of February 1, stating, on the authority of one who had been American Consul at Leghorn, Italy, that the archives of the consulate there contained interesting correspondence between Thomas Jefferson and the official who was consul there when Jefferson was Secretary of State. But I wish that your readers might know that this is by no means a unique instance, for in the archives of many of our legations and consulates abroad there is correspondence of great historic interest, large amounts of which are not represented, by duplicates or in any other way, in the archives of the Department of State here in Washington. Some of it is correspondence of famous Americans, like that which has been mentioned, some of it is correspondence with

European public men during the long period since 1789; some of it the evidence and record of American diplomatic action and observation in respect to the various interesting events in European history which have occurred before the eyes of our representatives.

I speak of all this because it has a bearing on the problem of the National Archive Building which has been so much under discussion during the last two or three weeks.[455] During that discussion much has been said (and not too much can ever be said) about the deplorable condition in which the papers of the government here in Washington are being kept, but no one seems to have said a word about the archives of the government outside of Washington, and yet these constitute a very important part of the records of the government's history and business. There is a government report on this subject, made in 1913, "Archives of Government Offices outside of the City of Washington" (62d Cong., 3d sess., House Doc. no. 1433), prepared by the Librarian of Congress in pursuance of an executive order by President Taft, requiring heads of executive departments to collect information on this matter. Leaving out of account the reports collected by other departments, respecting custom houses, post-offices, army posts, navy yards, and the like, the reports from our legations and consulates abroad show an enormous amount of archival material still retained there, some of it of great historic interest.

Now most of this matter is useless or unused where it now reposes. It is the uniform custom of other governments (all of which as a matter of course have National Archive Buildings) to draw all these materials back into the national repository at the home capital after a certain number of years. For instance, no one would find at any of the foreign embassies or legations in Washington letter-books or letters received, except for quite recent years. They have been sent back, and that is what ought to be done with ours—an important additional reason for having a National Archive Building.

For, and this is the unhappy part of the story, while a great deal that is of value remains in these remote consulates and legations, a far greater amount, especially from the earlier periods, is destroyed, as the direct result of their being kept abroad. The frequent changes of place, from one office to another, destruction by fire and flood, the inroads of insects and vermin, climates excessively hot or excessively moist, negligence of employees, have done an amount of damage beyond

---

[453] The reasons mentioned were that in Columbus, Ohio, where the Association meeting was to be held in 1923, the representation of state-supported historical societies was likely to be much larger than that of private societies, and the problem which Mr. Wall wished to have discussed—how to secure more generous support from private sources—would not make strong appeal to a conference so constituted. As Jameson surmised, Mr. Wall's subject received no attention at the conference of historical societies held in December, 1923.

[454] This letter appeared in the *Post*, Feb. 5, 1923, 6, headed Priceless Americana lost for lack of storage place. Historical papers in embassies, legations and consulates all over the world are unprotected. The letter was printed as written save for unimportant variations in capitalization and punctuation, and the insertion of sub-headings.

[455] The reference is of course to interest in the fate of the amendment referred to in Jameson's letter of Jan. 30. An added reason for an increase in public discussion may be found in a letter from Jameson to Leland of Jan. 9, 1923: "A reporter from the *Times-Herald* came in the other day to get ammunition for a campaign respecting the N. A. B. He said that the Hearst papers throughout this happy land, had orders direct from Mr. Hearst to go at the matter. Articles have appeared in three successive numbers now and it looks as if continuous bombardment were intended."

what would be believed if the report did not show it conclusively. Thus, although the mission to Great Britain began in 1785, there are no records at the embassy till 1828. At Copenhagen, there is no trace of the legation records of the period from 1812 to 1841. The legation at Portugal began in 1789, but the earliest archives are of 1824. All the consular archives at Valparaiso were burned in 1906; all at Guadeloupe, in the West Indies; and many of those at Yokohama in 1866, at Toronto in 1886, and at St. John's, Newfoundland, in 1892, while those at Tahiti were damaged by a tidal wave in 1906, and in many if not most consulates there are gaps and losses. In other words, here is a mass of government papers kept in even a worse manner and suffering even worse damage from it, than those here in Washington. If the history of American foreign relations and of American commerce is worth anything to the nation, here is another argument for the National Archive Building.

There is abundant evidence that thousands of people, all over the country, are genuinely concerned about this matter of the National Archive Building. Every government official, every senator, every member of the House, agrees that we ought to have one. To one who for fifteen years, as chairman of the appropriate committee of the American Historical Association, has been struggling to secure that result, it seems more than strange that in view of such unanimity it has not yet been possible to get an appropriation for beginning construction. If Canada and Denmark and Holland and Saxony, to say nothing of many of our own states, can afford such buildings, why must the richest of all nations keep its archives in the disgraceful manner now obtaining? Or, to put it another way, if this is the most businesslike of nations, and the United States government the largest business organization in the world, is it good business to pay out $110,000 a year in rent for warehouses not fireproof and other grossly unfit places for the deposit of records, instead of spending a million or two, once for all, to carry out plans that will give us the finest archive building in the world? The recent action of Congress holds us in our present evil plight.[456] Let us hope that the next session will come before the next conflagration.

To SAMUEL E. MORISON

February 26, 1923.

My dear Mr. Morison:

. . . I can match your tale of secretarial futility.[457]

An old friend and colleague of mine, now a professor in the University of Edinburgh, told me when I was last there, that the secretary of a charitable society of which he was president, insisted on keeping a record of every postage stamp, "Letter to Aeneas Mackay, 2 d., ditto to Jennie McTavish, 1 d., etc." However, I have to confess that, though I suppose I know twenty men in the State Department, a bureau chief whom I had not previously known, told me, on meeting him ten days ago, that certain materials which a year ago I had asked them to get from Budapest had arrived, but they had not known what was the address of the *American Historical Review,* so had not sent them to me, and that was ten days ago and they have not come yet. Efforts to transact business through the State Department often result that way, and I should not be surprised if you never got your *American State Papers, Folio.* However, you may.

As to what has become of the article on the "Odyssey of Thomas Muir," I wish I knew myself. I had amused myself for a long time with the effort to fill out the story, and after I had got everything I could get in the archives of London, Paris, and Seville, and what I could get *from* those of Mexico, and had completed the thing to my satisfaction, I sent it last August to the Australian lady to get her approval of the composite—in which by this time my part about equals hers—and I have never heard from her since. A month ago I wrote to her again. Her own copy of the original article went down with her in the Mediterranean in war time, when her steamer was torpedoed, and it did not come up, as she happily did. The article seems to be doomed to much the same unhappy Fates as Muir himself. Anyhow I had many pleasant hours with it.[458]

To WALDO G. LELAND

March 30, 1923.

Dear Leland:

. . . Yesterday was spent—very reluctantly and tediously, I must say—in an all-day conference with the National Research Council,[459] which however gave Haskins and me an opportunity to talk a few minutes with Crane of Michigan respecting C. E. Merriam's Social [Science] Research Council, in which Crane is

---

[456] On the defeat of the amendment the Washington *Post,* Feb. 1, commented: "The national archives building for Washington is dead in the home of its friends. The House has such a stronghold on the strong box now that the Senate can hardly squeeze a nickle into an appropriation bill."

[457] "The local secretary of the Historical Association here distributed no notices of the annual meeting of the Association at Exeter, because she 'didn't think anyone would care to go' —so no one here knew of it until it was all over" (Morison from Oxford, to Jameson, Feb. 6, 1923).

[458] Morison had asked in a letter of Feb. 2, 1923, where this article had been printed. The manuscript eventually reappeared and was published as, The Odyssey of Thomas Muir, by Marjorie Masson and J. F. Jameson, *Amer. Hist. Rev.* 29: 49-72, Oct. 1923.

[459] The National Research Council was established in 1916, to forward scientific research for purposes of defense. At the close of the war it was continued at the request of the President, and received financial support from the Rockefeller Foundation. Though its original purpose was technical and scientific research and it sprang from the National Academy of Sciences, it has cooperated with the Social Science Research Council, the Council of Learned Societies, and the Council on Education.

the other representative of the American Political Science Association.[460] The Sociologists have joined it; the Economic Association also joined it, perfunctorily, Page tells me. In these days, if anybody asks a person or society to join a new committee of co-ordination or council for doing something that one vaguely understands, it is customary to join if it does not cost anything. Niell [461] says it is a poor day on which a new council for considering the problems of transportation is not formed. Crane seemed to see all our points with respect to holding the humanistic studies together in an existing aggregation, and was rather persuaded that what the Social Research Council wants to do can be done under the aegis of the A. C. L. S., since its committees are by no means made up solely of its own membership. It remains to be seen whether Merriam will be equally open to conviction. I believe he plans to have a pow-wow within a month. I hope it will be less tiresome to me than yesterday's was, which was a conference of a special committee or subcommittee (don't ask me to tell you its name or relatives) of a Committee on the Problems of Human Migration. Haskins and I were invited at the last moment, to represent history, though so far as I am concerned I deem myself a misfit *dans cette galère*. The conference was presided over by Miss Mary Van Kleeck of the Sage Foundation,[462] whose object was to shape a programme of researches which one could certify were greatly needed by humanity, so greatly needed as to justify the NRC in supplying funds for it or in getting someone else to do so. Problems of human migration! —quite a job, eh, what? Why narrow it by restricting it to *human* migration, when there are so many other deserving species that wander here and there over the face of the globe without proper guidance, and, to all appearances, at any rate in the case of the insects, somewhat aimlessly and without scientific programme? I would fain have been back at my desk, giving my attention to one or two concrete problems of migration, such as, Where do we go next? Where do we eat? When does W. G. Leland return to America?, and the like. Taking up immediately this last topic (A. II. b. 3),

I find myself seeing eye to eye with you in the view that you may well write your volume with the notes now on hand, without trying to explore much more. It sounds plausible. I have long wondered whether it really is necessary to treat the materials for American history in the French archives with so much more minute care than has been applied in the much more important case of the English archives. At the beginning, it was held that this should be done because of the large scale on which certain parts of the field had been treated (or mistreated) by our Canadian brethren. That was rational, and yet a good deal of the edge has been taken off that argument (in the mind of a distant observer) by the fact that we have prepared an itemized calendar of 30,000 individual documents.

But I must go over and lunch with Haskins, and then confer with Dr. Carter G. Woodson [463] and read a lot of proof. The committee on the D. A. B. meets here next Friday. After great efforts, by letter and telegram, to get some word from Erskine as to dates, the rest having responded promptly, I have had to fix on that date regardless of him. From what Haskins reports of conversation with him in New York, I judge that he cannot be here on that day.

To HENRI REVERDIN

May 24, 1923.

Dear Sir:

I have the honor to make the following replies to your "Enquiry among specialists," C. L. 1 (a) 1923. XII.[464] The answers, which I give in the order of questions are in many cases necessarily vague. Full answers to questions so broad in their scope would require a volume, and in many cases there is much uncertainty as to the facts, opinions differing widely.

1. In the field of historical work in the United States, the last ten years have seen some increase of product, but not a large one. There has been some increase of interest in Latin-American history and in the social history of the United States, and a largely

[460] Robert Treat Crane, a teacher of political science in the University of Michigan from 1913 to 1933; Charles E. Merriam (1874-1953), teacher of the same subject in the University of Chicago from 1900. On Mar. 6, 1923, Jameson wrote to Mr. Leland: "Cheyney . . . dropped in to consult about C. E. Merriam's project of a council or combination of the four social sciences for purposes of research. Haskins holds out stoutly for maintaining the existing combination, the A. C. L. S., instead of starting a new one; but Merriam is averse. He has no money either but I think he hopes that the National Research Council will come across." Professor Merriam was president of the Social Science Research Council from 1924 to 1927.

[461] Charles P. Neill (1865-1942), Ph.D., Johns Hopkins, 1897, manager of the Bureau of Information of Southeastern Railways, from 1915 to 1939.

[462] Mary Van Kleeck was director of industrial studies for the Russell Sage Foundation from 1909 to 1948.

[463] Carter G. Woodson (1875-1950), director of the Association for the Study of Negro Life and History and editor of the *Journal of Negro History*. See *post*, Apr. 1, 1930.

[464] An answer to a questionnaire sent out by Professor Henri Reverdin of the League of Nations. To Mr. Leland, Jameson wrote on Apr. 21, 1923: "Oh, yes, indeed, I got from him a choice little questionnaire, and am going to write a book for him just as soon as I can. Most of the questions, plainly devised for application to the most unfortunate countries of Europe, have no value with respect to these fortunate United States, and are, indeed, when sent in this direction, of the most extreme futility, *e.g.,* 'Have any important changes taken place in the last ten years in the branch of intellectual work in which you are interested? What is required to ensure progress? To what extent does the public take an interest? Which of these societies are in a precarious condition? Has your work any influence abroad? Kindly mention to what extent, if any, the state of public morality exercises an influence on the kind of intellectual work in which you are interested, or is influenced by it?'"

increased interest in the political and diplomatic history of the Continent of Europe in the period since 1860. In what has been written there has been some improvement, going along with the general increase of knowledge in the country. Text-books of history used in schools and colleges have shown a considerable improvement in quality. The teachers of history in our schools, mostly young women, know more about history than they did ten years ago; on the other hand, school authorities, such as the superintendents of education in the individual states of the Union and cities, show an inclination to push sociology and economics into the schools, in simple forms, at the expense of history.

2. It does not appear to me that the interest of the public in history has increased. It does not have a larger place in schools. Public interest in education is of course peculiarly vivid in the United States, but in respect to history in the schools its main manifestation in the last few years has been an eager activity of the less educated and more prejudiced portions of the population in insisting upon a nationalistic, even chauvinistic, and anti-British attitude toward textbooks and teaching of American history. The enormous gifts by individuals in promotion of scientific research are seldom accompanied by such gifts in support of historical work. It does not appear that the commercial success of the best historical writing is as great, in proportion to our population, as it was fifty years ago. As to difficulty of production, there is little except such as arises from the high cost of printing, which has very seriously affected the work of historical societies and universities. On the other hand, because of the greatness of our school population, good text-books in history are often very profitable.

3. Specialists in history come from the graduate departments of our universities, where they are trained in large numbers. During the years of the war and immediately thereafter the number was much diminished, but it is now as great as ever, or greater. These young men and young women are training themselves for the career of teaching, however, and with nearly all of them historical research and production must be a secondary interest in their later lives. The pay of teachers of history in colleges and secondary schools is nominally greater than ten years ago, but actually not so great, having seldom kept pace with the rise in cost of living, which may be said to have been about seventy-five percent. Graduate students are therefore a less able body than they were ten years ago; the material rewards of the legal career, etc., tempting more strongly than those which may be expected by the teacher. On the whole, too, the mass of students in universities and colleges and high schools having much increased, teachers have to spend a larger part of their time in teaching than they did ten years ago. There is no difficulty in securing the degree of training which is required, education being cheap. Only a small number, however,

give themselves the broadening benefit of study in Europe.

4. The chief general historical society in the United States is the American Historical Association, which has a large membership, considerable resources, and much influence. All the individual states, and many special sections of states have historical societies, of which many have large resources and extensive libraries of local history. More than a score of them publish creditable journals of state or local history and volumes of documentary historical material. A dozen or twenty of the leading universities publish a greater or smaller number of historical monographs. There are also certain historical associations which are general to the whole United States, not local, but are confined to special subjects, such as the American Catholic Historical Association, the American Jewish Historical Society, etc. The leading historical journal, indeed the one important general historical journal is the *American Historical Review*. Most of the state historical societies west of the Alleghanies have subventions, sometimes large ones, from the state governments. The government of the United States does almost nothing for history.

5. Most of the historical work done in the United States relates to American history. In respect to this portion, the part played by foreign countries consists only in this, that, by reason of the colonial dependence of our earlier governments on Great Britain, France, Spain, and the Dutch republic, large masses of material for this earlier period of our history are to be found in the archives of those countries. These have been diligently exploited by American scholars and societies. As to whether American historical work has any influence abroad, it would be difficult for anyone here to pronounce. There seems to be little interest in Europe in American history, and, although the work of Americans in respect to European history has been extensive (as may be seen from Professor Haskins' address sent herewith),[465] my impression is that, as a rule, European historical scholars working in similar fields are most commonly not aware of its existence.

6. The best means for maintaining knowledge as to what goes on in the way of historical work in America are the *Annual Reports* of the American Historical Association and especially (for American history) the annual bibliography entitled *Writings on American History*, which has been maintained since the year 1906, and is now printed by the association named. The best single means of information regarding historical publications in other countries has been the successive volumes of the *Jahresberichte der Geschichtswissenschaft*, issued for the years 1878-1913, but then discontinued without hope of continuance. A proposal for

---

[465] Professor Haskins's presidential address, European history and American scholarship, delivered before the American Historical Association in December, 1922, and published in the *Amer. Hist. Rev.* 28: 215-227, Jan., 1923.

its revival in the form of an international survey of similar sort, in which the chapters relating to historical progress in the respective countries should be made by scholars of their own, was laid before the International Historical Congress lately held in Brussels, and was then referred to an International Historical Committee then created.

7. Many American historical workers correspond individually with European historical scholars. An international committee has been created, as mentioned under 6, and will be of some utility.

8. The tendency in America is somewhat more toward economic and social history. Also I think that, since the war, there has been an increasing tendency to work upon a subject whose importance has been demonstrated by the fact of large consequences in subsequent history, as contrasted with the habit of working upon conventional themes.

9. The Americans have quick and versatile minds, but superficial habits of thought. Most of them read only newspapers, and our newspapers, from the very fact that they are read by a larger number of people than in any other country, are adapted mainly to least developed minds. They help only very slowly toward the development of interest in work having any intellectual distinction. Also, the majority of the American public knows little of Europe and of European thought. Yet interest in the rest of the world has very greatly increased in the last few years, and that of course will largely work toward a greater interest in the history of other countries. The Americans are, apparently, somewhat exceptionally humane and sympathetic toward other populations, and have some natural tendency toward taking an interest in their history, though physical remoteness has hitherto kept their minds somewhat isolated from these connections. Their interest in their own history is very closely connected with *one* item of public morality, namely, with their patriotism, which is ardent but not critical—the kind of patriotism likely to be generated in a country whose population is 120,000,000, whose prosperity is great, and whose future seems unbounded.

To WALDO G. LELAND

June 4, 1923.

Dear Leland:

. . . I am very glad to get all the information that you sent respecting the proposed C. I. C. text-book,[466] but I do not think I will utilize it immediately for any spiel in the *Review*. I doubt if great numbers of persons have read about the proposal, or at any rate are

alarmed by it. If the manual is ever prepared, we will review it, and I have no doubt it would have its uses, though it will not be adopted in the schools of Boston or New York, and perhaps not in those of Nahant, or Peacham, Vermont. To speak of it at its present stage might create unfavorable impressions that later would seem to be unwarranted. Eben Putnam tells me that the American Legion is getting out a text-book of American history (by Lord Knowswho—not a British lord), and told me that I could learn all about it, for any preliminary announcement in the *Review*, from John W. Oliver [467]—which I have carefully neglected to do. The less said about it the better. I have a little piece in the July number respecting Wisconsin's pure history law.[468] Really we have more crazy people in the United States and more different kinds, than I had any idea of when I was a little boy. . . .

Go to London, and heaven go with you, but do not think of spending only three days upon it, just tiring yourself out. It is well that some American a little more central to matters than Notestein is should be present on that occasion. I dare say there will be others, but none will know so much about the A. H. A., or the general situation. However, I should not wish you to take this Anglo-American Conference too seriously. Pollard and Newton [469] of course make the best of it, but it is not much more than a University of London affair. I presume you have received the first Annual Report of the Institute of Historical Research. With all respect for the good work which it actually represents, it seems to me an excellent example of window-dressing, which could not be improved upon in this here bumptious America; it is somewhat like *The Americanization of Edward Bok,* who, as the book plainly shows, had no need of being Americanized. He was all that already.

---

[466] Millikan had proposed to the Committee on Intellectual Cooperation, the rewriting of text-books in order to present to students an international rather than a national point of view. The suggestion met with no approval in the committee (Leland to Jameson, May 21, 1923, with memorandum of the same date).

[467] John W. Oliver, who received his Ph.D. from the University of Wisconsin, served in the First World War as second lieutenant. He was a professor of history in the University of Pittsburgh.

[468] A pure history law, *Amer. Hist. Rev.* **28**: 699-701, July, 1923, quotes the law, the gist of which was that any text-book "which falsifies the facts regarding the war of independence, or the war of 1812 or which defames our nation's founders or misrepresents the ideals and causes for which they struggled and sacrificed, or which contains propaganda favorable to any foreign government," upon complaint of five citizens and after a hearing cannot be "adopted, sold, or exchanged" within the state. Dr. Jameson ended his comments on the significance of this measure by urging those who cared for historical truth to lift up their voices "in behalf of common sense, rational patriotism, and fair minded training of young Americans for citizenship." The New York *Evening Post* of Sept. 15, 1923, carried a pungent editorial on the same law.

[469] The Anglo-American Historical Conference was to convene, July 6-7. Wallace Notestein was at this time professor of English history at Cornell University. Albert F. Pollard and A. Percival Newton, both professors of history in the University of London, were, from the beginning the moving spirits in the Anglo-American historical conferences.

To Channing M. Ward

June 15, 1923.

My dear Mr. Ward: [470]

I have not forgotten your inquiry, but I have been so excessively busy that I could not answer it till now. I do not now answer it with any sense of security, because at many points in the list of fifteen, one could suggest something else for which quite as good a case could be made out. Moreover, and this is very important to your whole inquiry, there are many movements or changes in history which have come about so gradually that one could not put one's finger on any one date or event yet which may be of more importance than several of those which one readily dates.

However since you ask for a list, here is one:
1. The repulse of the Huns at Chalons in 451.
2. The preaching of Mohammed.
3. The repulse of the Saracens at Tours in 732.
4. The formation of the empire of Charlemagne.
5. The invention of gunpowder.
6. The invention of the mariner's compass.
7. The invention of printing.
8. The discovery of America.
9. The Protestant Reformation.
10. The invention of the steam-engine.
11. The Declaration of American Independence.
12. The French Revolution.
13. The rise of Napoleon to supreme power.
14. The beginning of the railroad system.
15. The invention of the telegraph, or perhaps of the internal combustion engine.

To Elihu Root

North Edgecomb, Maine
July 19, 1923.

Dear Mr. Root:

I ask your permission to consult you upon an Anglo-American matter respecting which a certain obligation rests on me and others of the historical profession.

In July 1921 the University of London, taking occasion of the opening of its new Institute of Historical Research, convened an Anglo-American Conference of Professors of History. Some eighty or a hundred British scholars were present, representing all the universities, and about forty Americans. Most of the latter were designated as representatives by their respective universities and colleges, but none were especially sent over for the purpose; those Americans attending were either persons then beginning a year's leave of absence or then finishing one, or persons who, like myself, were in London for a summer's work in the Public Record Office or the British Museum.

[470] Ward was a son of Mr. W. N. Ward of Washington and Virginia. He had asked Jameson to name what he regarded as the fifteen most important events in history.

The proceedings, arranged on a distinctly practical programme, were of real value and interest, and in all respects, especially those of hospitable entertainment, we were treated very handsomely, with a government dinner, a dinner and reception by Lord and Lady Astor, and luncheons and teas by various appropriate organizations or officials in London.

On both sides the hope was made plain that this occasion of concert should not be isolated, and indeed an Anglo-American Historical Committee was then formed, which has since functioned with some usefulness. It was certainly the hope of all the Americans present that we should have an opportunity before long to requite in some measure the kindness of our hosts by holding on this side of the water a second Anglo-American Conference of Professors of History. We should not wish to attempt it in the American summer, and we should not wish that it should be the affair of any one American university. It has seemed, to those of us who have considered it, that the happiest arrangement would be to associate it with one of the annual meetings of the American Historical Association, and especially to make it a feature of the annual meeting to be held in the last days of December, 1924, when the Association will meet in Washington and Richmond, with an excursion to Williamsburg and Jamestown. That would mean for the British representatives absence from their work during much of the winter term, but we think we see how that could be arranged.

I should not wish to leave the impression that the main reason for desiring any such thing lies in the fact that we were ourselves so handsomely entertained. We feel certain that more frequent and more intimate association between American and British professors is in itself a good thing; that this is particularly true of those whose office it is to teach history, most commonly to teach their own national history; that British professors of history, of the more open-minded variety, might gain a great deal from the opportunity to visit American universities and talk with American colleagues, and that most of that type would welcome the opportunity; and that, conversely, what some of these men might say at a meeting of the American Historical Association would be of much interest and value to our members and would add greatly to the distinction of one of our annual meetings. The benefits would be much heightened by the fact that, if the conference were thus arranged for the days just after Christmas, there would be opportunity and temptation for our universities to engage some of these men for lectures, and especially and most profitably for classroom courses, in history, during either the autumn or the winter quarter. Dr. Stephen Duggan, director of the Institute of International Education, with whom I have talked at length of the whole project, would find it easy to arrange for such courses, as he often has done, with great profit to some of our universities and colleges, on previous occasions.

It is however certain, and so Dr. Duggan assures me with emphasis, that the only way by which such a conference can be brought about is for us to pay the expenses of the British representatives. British universities clearly cannot afford to do it. Incidentally, such subvention would have the advantage, that we could invite those whom we thought it most expedient to invite, on the ground of their exceptional ability to contribute something to our edification, or on that of their being the persons who would gain most from the opportunity and would do most to make their experience beneficial to British students; whereas invitations to British universities to send delegates will often bring persons of great distinction who are dull talkers or past the age when new experiences will bring to their minds fresh impulses that can be utilized in education. A "handpicked" delegation of about ten or twelve would be the expedient thing. We think we know the British professors thoroughly enough to select, first, men who would be profitable and would profit and cause their students to profit; secondly, men who have not already had the experience of a visit to America; and, thirdly, men who would like to come on such an occasion—and indeed none who had not this third qualification would have the first. If ten acceptances were received, the cost might be about $10,000, for we should wish that the delegates, besides coming to America comfortably and seeing New York and Washington and Richmond and Jamestown, should have some margin for a little additional travel, in such directions as each might prefer.

My problem is therefore to find the $10,000. Without some assurance regarding this, I have not formally broached the matter to my colleagues in the Executive Council of the American Historical Association, and should not do so, though I have talked with some of them respecting the matter, especially with our president, Professor Edward Cheyney of the University of Pennsylvania, who was one of those present at the conference in July 1921.

When I talked of the matter with Dr. Duggan in Washington last spring, it was in both our minds that the most natural source from which to seek the necessary subvention was the Carnegie Endowment for International Peace. Since that time, however, I have learned that the Endowment has felt obliged to discontinue its support of Dr. Duggan's very useful establishment, the Institute of International Education, and that its support has been taken over for the present by the Carnegie Corporation. The object of this letter is to ask your advice as to the quarter in which it would be best to seek encouragement as to such a subvention. There seem to be three resources—the Endowment, the Carnegie Corporation, and the new International Education Board, recently

established. Though the last-named is an affair of the Rockefeller group, I have understood that you have been much consulted by them, and therefore I suppose that the situation of all three of these organizations is well known to you. In case you approve of the general design of what I have set forth, I should be very greatly obliged if you would advise me in which quarter I might have most prospect of success as to obtaining the desired means. I sincerely hope that you do thus approve, for to me, with the view I entertain of the influence of men's views of history upon their public conduct, it seems as if such conferences must almost certainly produce much good in international relations.

Please pardon me for inflicting upon you in summertime so long a letter, but I have wished to explain all aspects of the matter fully.[471]

To Edwin F. Gay

August 6, 1923.

My dear Gay:[472]

I reached my office this morning, after a week's devious journeys from Maine, and find here your letter of August 1.[473] I judge that my secretary looked up Freeman's birth, and, finding it to be August 2, concluded that nothing could be done, but I judge that you are planning to combine him with

---

[471] On August 9, 1923, Jameson sent this same letter to Henry S. Pritchett of the Carnegie Corporation, adding a final paragraph in which he explained that he wrote at the suggestion of Mr. Root, who had ended his reply to Jameson: "To sum up, you will perceive that I think highly of your project, but I have no authority to say anything definite about money for it, but that I may be relied upon to do the best I can towards helping to find the money" (Root to Jameson, July 30, 1923).

The source of the funds for which Jameson was searching proved to be the Carnegie Endowment for International Peace, which generously made it possible for the Association to invite a group of distinguished British historians to the meeting of 1924. They were: from Oxford, Alexander J. Carlyle, chaplain and lecturer at University College; from Cambridge, John H. Clapham, fellow and tutor of King's College, James R. M. Butler, fellow of Trinity, Major Harold Temperley, fellow of Peterhouse; from Edinburgh, Sir Richard Lodge; from London, Hubert Hall of the Public Record Office, and Albert F. Pollard and Robert W. Seton-Watson, University College, University of London; Mary T. Hayden, University College, Dublin; Frederick W. Powicke, University of Manchester; C. K. Webster, University of Wales; C. Grant Robertson, University of Birmingham, William L. Grant, Upper Canada College (*Amer. Hist. Rev.* 30: 454-455 n.). Of these, Professor Pollard was already teaching in Columbia, Harold Temperley came at his own expense, as W. L. Grant of Canada may also have done. This accounts for the fact that the number of the guests varies in different statements.

[472] Edwin F. Gay (1867-1946) interrupted a long career of teaching in Harvard University to become editor of the New York *Evening Post* from 1920 to 1923.

[473] Gay had written: "Freeman's birthday, I believe, came early in August, and Parkman's is the beginning of September, both 1823. I understand that you were at Johns Hopkins when Freeman was teaching there, and I hoped you might write us an article of reminiscence and appreciation."

Parkman, whose birthday was September 16. So I send the enclosed, rather hastily prepared, which you can use or not, according to your plans. I did not see enough of Freeman when he was in Baltimore, about 1883, to enable me to supply a large amount of valuable copy, and cannot today get up to the Library of Congress to inspect W. R. W. Stephens's Life and Letters of him, in order to verify or date my recollections.[474] I simply do what I can at the moment.

As I passed through New York in one direction on Friday, Dwight Morrow told me that he had written you something respecting Coolidge, I presume for the Saturday issue of the *Post*. Coming through New York in another direction on Sunday afternoon, on my way here, I sought Saturday's *Post* at five places, but could not get it. I wanted to see what he said, and should be much obliged if you would send me a copy.[475]

[Enclosure] August 6, 1923.

(On Edward Augustus Freeman) [476]

Mr. Freeman paid a visit to the United States in the autumn of 1881, and lectured in several cities, returning to England in April, 1882. The writer was at that time a graduate student in the Department of History of the Johns Hopkins University, and retains a vivid recollection of the eminent historian and of his methods of lecturing, though naturally he had no significant conversations with him.[477] Mr. Free-man was a man of striking appearance and with distinctive ways of his own, not to say eccentricities and prejudices. He was a short, stout man, with a long and broad-spreading beard, and was clad in baggy garments—his whole appearance unmistakably British. After his first lecture, given in New York, one of the reporters irreverently said in his newspaper that he had "a horrible British accent." In a letter to his wife, written a day or two afterward, and printed in Dean Stephens's biography, he reports the phrase, with the remark that he did not know what the man meant. However the accent should be described,—and of course to Mr. Freeman's mind a truly English accent could not possibly be horrible,— he had it with him when he arrived in Baltimore. He lectured with vigor and clearness, on the lines of his favorite thesis of the unity of the English people in Sleswick, England, and the United States, emphasizing often by striking upon the platform the butt end of the pointer he used in connection with his maps, and indicating plainly the points at which we were to applaud by giving a crescendo intonation to the last words of his paragraph, and reaching vigorously for his glass of water, to give us time for whatever might be the American equivalent of "Hear, hear"!

Our teacher, Professor Herbert B. Adams, a genial and hospitable soul, cultivated Mr. Freeman's friendship with assiduity and great pleasure, and reported to us students afterwards many of Mr. Freeman's sayings and oddities.[478] All this was two years before he was appointed Regius professor of Modern History in the University of Oxford; and he seemed always to resent being called professor. Still more he resented the question where he did his scholarly work, whether in the British Museum, for instance, or the Public Record Office. "Where but in my own library, in my own house in Somersetshire" he would say in his gruff manner, although I suppose that in reality some portions of his great work on the Norman Conquest and on William Rufus would have been

---

[474] Freeman's letters from America are to be found in Stephens, W. R. W., *Life and Letters of Edward A. Freeman* 2: 233-257, London and N. Y., Macmillan, 1895.

[475] To this Gay replied on Aug. 27: "Dwight Morrow promised me that he would write on Coolidge, but he did not do so, so I am unable to my great regret to send you a copy of the paper containing anything of the sort." For references to Morrow's relations with Coolidge, see Nicolson, *Dwight Morrow*, 33-35, 229, 269-272.

[476] This was published in the *Post* of Sept. 17, 1923, p. 6, as Memories of a great historian.

[477] The entries in Jameson's Diary show a considerable change of opinion during the course of Freeman's lectures: "*Tu. Nov 15* [*1881*]. I didn't expect much, a mere popular lecture [Freeman's first lecture] but really it was a poorer affair than I had supposed. I suppose he has written them since he came to this country. Not only was there nothing new in it, but it was made inexpressibly tedious by the worst iteration I ever heard. But it was something to see one of the three great living English historians. He is a little, short, fat, duck legged man, much like Sylvester. . . . Took home [from the library] Freeman' Historical Geography of Europe. . . . Mean to read a little for his lectures on the Eastern Question, though they may contain as little, and assume as profound ignorance on our part, as this on the English People in their three Homes. I think it is an imposition to give such lectures in this country."

"*Wed. Nov. 16*. At four Freeman gave his first talk on the Hist. Geog. of S. E. Europe, coming down to the time of Heraclius; while the same things are to be found in the book, and his manner shows he isn't used to extempore speaking, it was far more interesting than last night, and quite bright and good natured."

"*Thurs. Nov. 17*. Then to Freeman's lecture at eight. It was a little better than the first, still there wasn't much to it, and I guess I'll skip the rest."

"*Fri. Nov. 18*. Freeman's lecture was good; this time on the Saracens and Slaves."

"*Sat. Nov. 19*. Freeman's talk which was good."

"*Mon. Nov. 21*. Heard Freeman's talk which he gave with more than his usual stammering."

"*Wed. Nov. 23*. Freeman's lecture excellent. . . . Came in door next behind Freeman, who [had] a small audience but good lecture." By going to Washington for a Thanksgiving holiday Jameson missed Freeman's final lecture and also that of James Bryce who was lecturing in Baltimore at the same time.

[478] A sketch of Freeman's character with some account of his oddities to be found in the review by Herbert Baxter Adams of Stephen, *Life and letters of Edward A. Freeman*, see *Amer. Hist. Rev.* 1: 149-153, Oct., 1895. A brief account of the historian's Baltimore visit is to be found in the *Johns Hopkins University Circular*, Dec., 1882, 30-31; see also, Vincent, J. M., Memorial address, *Ann. Rept., Amer. Hist. Assn.*, 1901: 1: 205-206.

better if he had used some of the documents in London instead of relying almost entirely on printed books which he could have at Somerleaze.

His manner was indeed very brusque, and often he gave offense by the aggressive vigor with which he maintained his numerous prejudices or expressed his very individual opinions. Nevertheless he was, and showed himself to be, a man of warm affections, of much gift for friendship, and of a tender heart, as his passionate reprobation of fox-hunting and vivisection showed. He responded to Adams' friendliness with much warmth, and wrote long letters to him after his departure from Virginia, where he went to visit his son, and from England.[479] Among the trivial recollections of which I fear this narrative consists, I treasure a passage in which he wrote to Adams in Virgilian phrase, after an election in which it appeared (for a time) that the Baltimore bosses had been overthrown by the "better element," "Procumbit humi bos." I cherish also a passage in which, after tramping about in the red mud of his son's Virginian farm, he wrote to Adams that he could say of himself, in the language of Domesday Book, "Potuit ire quo voluit cum ista terra,—for the soil of Virginia is sticky, and cleaveth to the boots."

Visits of distinguished European scholars to American universities were not so common forty years ago as they are now, and if I have dwelt upon Freeman's picturesque oddities more than I should, it is right also to say that his lectures and talks to the students, and his presence among us, were a very stimulating force, which did us all much good. Also, he performed a memorable service to the State of Maryland, of which few persons are now aware, and which certainly deserves grateful commemoration. Adams took him down to Annapolis. There in the State House he saw the invaluable archives of the province and state of Maryland kept in the disgraceful condition in which it was customary forty years ago for states to keep their archives—in open boxes under stairways, in odd places in the garret, and the like. All this made its proper impression on Freeman's mind, and Adams got him to express himself on the subject to a group of influential persons in Maryland, which Freeman did with his accustomed frankness and force. Coming from one so highly respected in the historical world his reproaches and exhortations had great effect, and soon after the act was passed by which all the older archives of the state were to be transferred to the custody in Baltimore of the Mary-

land Historical Society, as soon as it should complete a fire-proof annex to its building, and, once there, were to be not only properly arranged and made accessible to historical students but set in the way of publication under the competent editorship provided by that excellent society. Since then, forty-two quarto volumes of the *Maryland Archives* have been printed in such a manner as gives Maryland a foremost place among the states in respect to the printing of the materials for its earlier history preserved in the archives of the state.

To Henri Pirenne

August 28, 1923.

My dear Mr. Pirenne:

I am very much obliged by your kindness in sending me a copy of the address which you delivered at the opening of the International Congress of History.[480] I have read it with a great deal of interest and pleasure. What you say of the value and necessity of the comparative method especially appeals to me at present, while I am working upon a proposed publication of the correspondence of the earlier British ministers in the United States. Anyone who works even a little in the field of diplomatic history must surely be impressed with the evil effects which are caught from the habit of looking at such things from a purely national point of view. Even in what concerns the eighteenth century, if you are reading a French book, you find that the French diplomatists were merely contending for their proper national rights, while the opposing diplomatists were engaged in less creditable efforts to outwit them. If you are reading an English book, or a Prussian book, it is the other way around. As a test, did anyone ever see the word "intrigues" employed by a diplomatic historian to indicate the actions of the representatives of his own country? I never did, unless in some case where the negotiations were in the hands of a political party to which the writer was opposed. It is always the others who are intriguing. To the inhabitants of Mars it must all seem very amusing. . . .

To Herbert D. Foster

October 26, 1923.

My dear Foster: [481]

I do not know whether the following is the kind of thought that you want, or have at all in mind, but it has often occurred to me that, among the reasons for giving school children some history, one is, that it is the only study they are likely to have that would

---

[479] Bryce's comment after Freeman's American visit was: "Freeman is in good health and cheery—fiercer than ever against 'Francis Joseph.' He does not seem to me to have been quite so much influenced by America or brought back quite so many new ideas from it as I should have expected, but those he brought back are mostly just" (Bryce to H. B. Adams, June 18, 1882, in Holt, *op. cit.*, 53-54). For Freeman's opinion of the work being done by the Johns Hopkins, see *ante*, Nov. 5, 1882, n. 33.

[480] De la méthode comparative en histoire, in *Compte rendu du Ve Congrès International des Sciences Historiques, Bruxelles, 1923*, Brussels, 1923.

[481] Herbert Darling Foster (1863-1927), professor of history in Dartmouth College from 1893 until his death.

teach them anything about human nature and human actions on the part of individual human beings.[482] Sociology and political economy do indeed teach them something about mass action and mass psychology, but if these young people are to play their part as citizens, voting and going through the other motions of citizenship, they need a better understanding of individual character and conduct than most people have. It will help them to vote for suitable instead of unsuitable persons for given offices; it will help them to be fair-minded in judging political action. I used to say to myself at Brown that in all probability all the historical facts I tried to teach the young men would evaporate from the minds of most of them; but that, if the result of my teaching should be some increase of fairness of mind on their part, some redemption from the customary habit of blind adherence to party, that might really be a solid residual gain, sufficient to justify my existence and salary. Whether it did, however, I do not know.

To HENRY K. ROWE

December 18, 1923.

My dear Rowe: [483]

I have read your two chapters with interest and pleasure and admiration. I am proud to number among my former students one who can write so well. The chapters seem to be models of what exposition should be, and I am confident that the book will do the good which you are planning that it shall do. If I make any suggestions, they are made simply because you have asked me to do something of that sort, and they are advanced with hesitation.[484]

While you have taken everywhere a broad view, it is natural for you to have the Baptist and Congregationalist denominations a little more in mind than some of the others, yet I do not think that I have noticed this in respect to any of the Protestant denominations, unless at possibly one of two points with the Episcopalians; but I do think that, especially in chapter V., you have not sufficiently had in mind the missionary efforts of the Catholics. This is a very

usual omission among Protestant writers on the history of religious work in America. I have seen books on the history of missions from which one would never gather that Christianity in the West, either among Indians or white men, owed anything serious to Catholic labours. Now the fact is that, for nearly two hundred years after the Reformation, nearly all the missionary activity displayed in the Christian body was that of the Catholic Church, the other churches being too exclusively national organizations to think much of such things; and in this country, the efforts of John Eliot and the Mayhews, which is about all that American Puritanism has to show, is hardly a drop in the bucket compared to what the Catholics were doing at that time.[485] I dare say you are familiar with such books as those about Father De Smet, or the Reports of the Leopoldine Association, or Father Dilhet's *Etat,* ed. Browne, and the various other books that are mentioned in the first six (American) volumes of the *Catholic Historical Review,* but such knowledge does not show out adequately in your narrative. If you have to read up on the subject, I imagine that the article "Missions" in the *Catholic Cyclopedia* provides at the end a short-cut to the literature.[486]

It is possible that, though nearly every statement you make is justified for the time of which you are speaking, you may not have always made it clear to non-historical readers just what time you are talking about at each point, but I quite understand that you did not wish to give a chronological diction to the matter.

In the chapter of your Consequences of Freedom, it might be worth while to draw attention to what I think is a rather striking fact, that, in spite of the entire freedom under which American religion has

---

[482] Foster had written: "P.S. Have finally accepted a summons from Lingelbach and Benton to spout at a Columbus luncheon of joint social sciences on function and contribution of history in schools. I aim to sparkle upon the theme that history should aid even school pupils to collect and weigh evidence in homeopathic doses and begin to try to discriminate between those things that are, and those 'that aint.'... Have you ideas on this subject, Professor, and if you haven't, will you offer prayer?" (Foster to Jameson, Oct. 23, 1923).

[483] Henry K. Rowe (1869-1941), A.B., 1892, A.M., 1895, Brown, professor of history and later of church history, Andover-Newton Theological School.

[484] Jameson had been reading the manuscript of chapters four and five—The consequences of freedom and religion on the frontier—of Rowe's *The history of religion in the United States,* N. Y., Macmillan, 1924, which is dedicated "To John Franklin Jameson, who taught me to study and teach history."

[485] A brief paragraph on pages 83-84 of the published volume may be the result of these suggestions.

[486] Pierre-Jean De Smet (1801-1873), a Belgian, began his missionary work among the Indians in 1838. In 1840 he was sent to the Indians of the northwest, and from headquarters in St. Louis (where he died) he went on many expeditions among them. On several occasions the United States government found him useful in making peace with troublesome tribes. See *Catholic Encyclopedia* 4: 752-753.

In 1828 Father Reze (Reese) visited Vienna to gain aid for American missions. The Archbishop of Vienna, Leopold Maximilian, Graf von Firmian, enlisted the favor of the royal family, and with the sanction of Leo XII the Leopoldine Society was formed in memory of Leopoldina, favorite daughter of Francis I and wife of Pedro I of Brazil. From its establishment in 1830 until about 1910 the society had sent to America more than half a million dollars. The chief centers of its work were Cincinnati, Detroit and St. Louis (*Catholic Encyclopedia* 16: 52). The first volume of the *Catholic Historical Review,* 51-63, Apr., 1913, begins the publication of the Annals of the Leopoldine Association.

Dilhet, Father Jean (1753-1811), *État de l'Église Catholique en diocèse des États-Unis de l'Amérique Septentrionale,* translated by the Rev. Patrick William Browne, Catholic University of America Studies in Church History, 1, Washington, the Salve Begina Press, 1922.

been allowed to develop, after all it has stuck pretty closely to the denominational organizations brought over from Europe; the Disciples and the Mormons have been almost our only innovations.[487]

Now let me descend to a few details. In chapter IV., toward the end of page 3, I do not understand the implication that the foreign-speaking churches have been gathered "among converts to Protestantism." Don't you mean adherents? . . . You would not lose sight of the fact that, in 1776 say, or in 1789, while New England was prevailingly Congregational and the Middle States prevailingly Presbyterian, the Southern states were prevailingly Episcopalian. You probably have read President Stiles's election sermon in 1783, in which he takes it for granted, most mistakenly, that the future of the country belonged to those three.[488]

Page 14, I should not say that the people of the interior were mainly Scotch-Irish in origin. Our Scotch-Irish societies would loudly acclaim that, but I believe that the proportions of Celtic and Presbyterian Irish, or of Irish among the other inhabitants of the frontier region, are not yet known with any certainty. They would be very hard to determine. The same comment on page 4 of your fifth chapter.

Page 6 of that chapter, at the end, Jackson is often thought of as a typical backwoodsman. He was a typical backswood gentleman. He had nearly all the qualities of the typical backwoodsman, but he had good manners, and a finer character and a better mind than I supposed until we, or Professor Bassett for us, set about to prepare an edition of his correspondence, q.v. (not yet out).[489]

Page 8, in the middle, is it not better to avoid the adjective evangelical? I am not sure in what sense you use the word. I think it is commonly used in New England in a sense to exclude Catholics, Episcopalians, Unitarians, and Universalists, but there is something of an assumption in that use of the adjective, and an assumption that may well give offense. . . .

If you have anything to say of Catholic missions, your point about the necessary deflection of the missionary activities from frontier regions to cities has great emphasis in that denomination. Down till after the Civil War, the Catholic missionary (to whites) found his chief occupation in gathering together, or reaching and confirming in their faith, wandering sheep of the flock who had more or less isolated themselves on farms and elsewhere. The enormous Catholic immigration of the last thirty years, Italian and Slavonic, has gone to the cities or engaged in our industrial rather than our agricultural life, so that there is a difference of the local direction of home missionary work, besides that difference of race and language which strikes the eye when one sees a Polish inscription on a fine new Catholic Church in Northampton, Massachusetts, or a multitude of Slavic names in a list of clergy in the provinces of St. Paul, Milwaukee, and Chicago.

I return your chapters. Thank you very much for the opportunity to read them.

To Hiram Bingham

January 9, 1924.

Dear Colonel Bingham: [490]

. . . As to the best of the American universities for graduate work on the part of a student of American constitutional and political history, I am glad to give my impressions. Having your son especially in mind, I omit Yale from consideration, in spite of its being one of the best in these respects, because I should suppose it to be expedient that he should go elsewhere for his graduate work, even if, as I can readily suppose, he has not yet got from Andrews and Farrand and Johnson all that they would be capable of giving him. Another reason for what I say is that two years from now things may be different, perhaps especially at Columbia, where the large effort lately made to repair the historical department, by the appointment of Greene, Baron Korff, and Westermann, is probably not yet completed, but may be carried forward by the addition of some one of equal value in the field of American constitutional and political history since where Greene leaves off—though Fox is good.[491]

On the whole, I should put Wisconsin first, for the purposes which you have in mind. Fish and Paxson are both extraordinary men, work together admirably, and have had remarkable success in the training of graduate students in the fields you have in mind. Perhaps I should put it first in the case of any student, but certainly one who, as I suppose, has thus far studied these subjects only in New England, ought

---

[487] This suggestion was not carried out by Professor Rowe, nor did he make the indicated modifications on pages 3, 4, and 14. See pages 54, 64, and 75 of the published volume.

[488] Ezra Stiles (1727-1795), president of Yale, 1778-1795. The election sermon of 1783, preached at Hartford on May 8, was entitled, The United States elevated to glory and honor.

[489] Bassett, John S., Correspondence of Andrew Jackson, 7v., Carnegie Institution, pub. no. 371, 1926-1935.

[490] Hiram Bingham, a pioneer in Latin American history, who had been professor in that field in Yale University, and who had discovered Machu Picchu, was now U. S. Senator from Connecticut, after serving as lieutenant governor and governor of that state. His eldest son, Woodbridge, then a senior at Yale, is now professor of Far Eastern history in the University of California and director of the Institute of East Asiatic Studies.

[491] William L. Westermann, professor of ancient history in Cornell University for three years, had been appointed to the faculty of Columbia in 1923. In the same year Evarts B. Greene was brought to Columbia to teach American history, and Baron Korff, the history of Eastern Europe. No further professorial appointment was made until that of Allan Nevins in 1929.

Dixon Ryan Fox (1887-1945) taught history in Columbia from 1912 to 1934, when he became president of Union College.

by all means to go out of that region for awhile, either to the West or to Washington—if only Washington had adequate means for his teaching. It has not at present, yet I mention it because there are signs that within two years, it may have, and if so, a period of contact with political life in Washington should be of great value to such a student.

The library facilities at Madison are of course remarkable, and one meets there a very fine body of graduate students, from a number of different states. Chicago also has that advantage, though the library facilities are, I suppose, still inferior to those at Madison. Perhaps I ought to bracket Chicago with Wisconsin. McLaughlin is certainly a very superior teacher of that particular subject, but gives about half his work to the older sort of undergraduates. Dodd is full of stimulating ideas, but is sometimes absent from Chicago. Jernegan [492] has a great deal of knowledge, and often teaches in that field, but he has not the fertility of mind that marks Fish and Paxson and Dodd.

Harvard in 1926 seems in these respects to be an uncertain quantity, for both Turner stops at the end of this year, and Channing, I suppose, before long; and I should also think that your son would get at Cambridge too much of the New England point of view which, ich erlaube mich zu ermelden (brought up in Boston though I was) is in respect to American history an eccentric (in the literal sense) and somewhat perverted point of view. In short, I adhere in this case to Greeley's aphorism "Go West young man, go West"—even though, after two years in Paris there will be a certain shock.

To HIRAM BINGHAM

January 11, 1924.

Dear Colonel Bingham:

. . . Further as to your son's problem. I believe that, for a young man intending to spend his life in American history, a year in Paris is of more advantage than a year in England. Some of the British universities, especially the University of London, have been making much effort to persuade us to send our young men to them, or, as they put it, "to divert from Germany to England the stream of American graduate students." As a matter of fact, there is no such stream. For some years before the war, very few American students of history were going to Germany, mainly because American universities have been learning to do the trick of educating graduate

students in history exceptionally well. They do it rather better than the English, perhaps, for though English instruction in history is probably on the whole more competent that American instruction in history, in the specific matter of the professional training of graduate students the English have not been ardently interested for so long a time as we, and they have been slow to adopt the specific methods appropriate to that work.

Nevertheless, I think this ability to get at home what they want has had a somewhat unfortunate effect on us (and the case of the Japanese universities is quite parallel) in diminishing the amount of the broadening influence our fellows used to get from European study. Perhaps two years of study in Europe to two in America, may be about the right proportions for your son, or possibly one and a half in Europe to two and a half in America might be better. He would not be farther along in his profession in five years, perhaps, but in ten years the broader training he had had would have begun to tell. Most of our graduate students in these days seem to me to be trying to make themselves professors of American history by reading nothing else but American history, and I bless Heaven that when I was in college, though I made up my mind in my freshman year to occupy my life with history, there was so little of it to be had in college, I was forced to acquire a good general education. I should suggest that your son, in his year in Paris and his half-year or year in England should pay little attention to any matters of American history. He will have years enough for that afterward, and most American history men suffer greatly from not having as their background a sufficient knowledge of European history and its methods.

I am not able to advise as to which place in England should be chosen for a year or a half-year, because I do not know how far it is a matter of one's choice with whom one should study at Oxford or Cambridge, or how far the system dictates the young man's gravitating to some tutor or other teacher whom I do not know, though I know most of the professors. Fish would be the best adviser as to this, from his experience of a year or two as Director of the British Branch of the American University Union. Perhaps C. A. Duniway,[493] the present director, may a year from now be the wisest adviser, though he is now new to the job, and is anyhow less sagacious than Fish. Perhaps, for half a year, the University of London might be the best. The ordinary fate of young people who go there is to be gathered in by Pollard and Newton, able persons but ambitious and grasping. If a man could keep from being absorbed by them, he would get his great good from the Uni-

---

[492] Marcus W. Jernegan (1872-1949), A.B., 1896, A.M., 1898, Brown; Ph.D., University of Chicago, 1906. From 1908 until 1937 he was a member of the department of history of the University of Chicago. Among his publications were: *The American colonies, 1492-1750*, N. Y., Longmans, 1929; *Laboring and dependent classes in Colonial America, 1607-1783*, Chicago, Univ. of Chicago Press, 1931; *Growth of the American people*, N. Y., Longmans, 1938.

---

[493] Clyde A. Duniway (1866-1944), who had taught history in Stanford and had been president of the University of Montana and of Colorado College, was director of the British division of the American University Union in 1923-1924.

versity of London out of the advantages coming from contact with those teachers less central to the usual business of history, but brilliant specialists, such as Ernest Barker or Seton-Watson or Gardner or Petrie or Pares or Toynbee,[494] or perhaps the people at the London School of Economics, though I know little about them. With the British Museum and all, London is a great place for the young man.

Of course it is the latter portion of the four years that should be spent in America, and on the whole two years in one place. This last is important toward getting a job, a mundane consideration, but not to be neglected.

I do not advise in such matters with any such security as if I were still occupied with teaching, but it is a pleasure to tell anything I think I know.

To RICHARD A. ROBERTS

January 29, 1924.

My dear Mr. Roberts:[495]

I thank you for your very interesting address on the birth of Georgia. I have read it with much interest, heightened rather than diminished by the fact that I had seen the Egmont volumes,[496] for I looked at them so hastily that I never got the essentials of the story you have told.

Your sending of it brings back the very pleasant remembrance, which indeed has often before been in my mind, of your kindly entertainment of me at tea in Hare Court. Perhaps I may ask you to be so kind as to present my compliments to Mrs. Roberts and your young people.

Since I shall have the address in the volumes of the Royal Historical Society,[497] I am going to send this pamphlet to a small, choice library, the Wymberley Jones DeRenne Library, where the effort is made to preserve everything that is valuable relating to the early history of Georgia. The former owner, a curious character, was a third son of a rich man who cut him off with a small allowance because he married a person, excellent in every way, whom the father did not wish him to marry. The young people went and lived in England till, the father and both the elder sons having

died, Wymberley Jones DeRenne came back to the possession of a large estate, a few miles outside of Savannah, which had been in the family since the foundation of the colony. He told me that at first he did not know what to do with himself; began driving a coach from Savannah to his house (those were the days of the coaching fad), but found that, in this busy land, nobody wanted to ride with him but people that he did not want, whereupon, so he told me, his life was saved by a friend who suggested to him the collecting of books on Georgia. He did it with great energy and lavish expenditure, so that, if for instance a Munich bookseller lighted upon one of those immensely rare, sometimes unique, Salzburger pamphlets, he knew that his plain course was to offer it first to Wymberley Jones DeRenne. The latter built a marble library near his house, in a beautiful grove of live oaks, and there kept his priceless treasures as long as he lived, and made such provision for it that it has now a regular librarian —the nephew of the man who first suggested that he should collect. So your pamphlet ought to go there.

To MAX FARRAND

February 4, 1924.

Dear Farrand:

Far be it from me to pretend to know more about Greek than the estimable Doctors Liddell and Scott. They declare that ἰστορία is from ἴστωρ, and that it originally means the search for knowledge. No doubt it is from the same root as οἶδα and Eng. "with," and not from that of any verb signifying being.[498]

However, I should think that your friend is entirely on the wrong track if he thinks that the significance of a word can be learned by following its derivation back to the simplest or oldest root from which it comes, or by observing what its original signification was. That is surely not a right method. By such means, one might conclude that, for instance, students are mainly characterized by zeal, because *studeo* means to be zealous. A word means what it means, in the mouths of the most intelligent people who use it, not what a word from which it descended meant three thousand years ago.

To EDWARD P. CHEYNEY

February 12, 1924.

My dear Cheyney:

It did me more good than you can easily imagine, to

[494] Ernest Barker, principal of Kings College, London; Robert W. Seton-Watson, Masaryk professor of European history, Ernest A. Gardner, professor of archaeology, Sir Flinders Petrie, professor of Egyptology, Sir Bernard Pares, professor of Russian language and history, Arnold J. Toynbee, professor of international history, all of the University of London.

[495] Richard A. Roberts, secretary of the Royal Commission on Historical Manuscripts, 1903-1912, had retired in 1916 from the Public Record Office, where he had been senior assistant keeper. He was at this time vice-president of the Royal Historical Society.

[496] *Hist. MSS. Comm. report on the manuscripts of the Earl of Egmont*, 1905-1909.

[497] The birth of an American state: Georgia, with the subtitle, An effort of philanthropy and Protestant propaganda, *Trans. Royal Hist. Soc.*, 4th ser. 6: 22-49.

[498] Farrand had passed on to Jameson a request which had come to him, for the derivation of the word history: "I had thought it was derived through the Sanskrit root of the verb 'esse' and the significance of the term was merely the thing that is, or the study of what has occurred. I have found, however, that some of the authorities traced the etymology of the word to the root 'id' in 'oida' (See Standard Dictionary). Perhaps this is one and the same thing" (Farrand to Jameson, Feb. 1, 1924).

receive a letter written with your own hand.[499] I am very grateful to Miss Alice, as I hope she knows, for the many letters of report which she has kindly sent, but to get one from yourself is something quite different again already yet.   It affects me like the patch of green grass I saw this morning.   The world is going forward, in other words, and you with it, though for a time you have seemed to lag a little in the procession.   Before long, I hope, you will be looking at your own green grass and other green things at Springfield school-house.

That we are progressing here in Washington, along with the rest of the world, is not so certain. Many things look pretty black, as you will have learned from such reading of the newspapers as your guardians permit.   However, I suppose the stirrings up of the mess, and the disclosures, tend to ultimate good—if only the stirring could be done with ladles less political in their composition.[500]   At all times nine words out of ten that are spoken in the halls of Congress seem to be spoken for the purpose of advancing the fortunes of the party or the individual, but I hope the tenth is for the good of the country. . . .

To Waldo G. Leland

March 24, 1924.

Dear Leland:

Thank you for your report.   I am not at all of your opinion that the Carnegie Institution ought to be compensated for every hour you spent upon your lectures and upon the work of the Commission on Intellectual Co-operation.[501] Some of that time may very appropriately be considered to have been so spent as to benefit the Carnegie Institution of Washington.   As for the interruptions and distractions which come upon you, you have my full sympathy, but it certainly is hard to see how any large part of them can be avoided.   Nevertheless I hope that you will try to dodge as many of these things as you decently can.   Concerning a goodly number of them, it must be legitimate to say to one's self, What would these fellows do if I were not here?

They would get along somehow.   I remember that when George Burr and I were in London, he found so much compulsion upon him to do something for every Cornell man or woman, or man or woman from up-state New York, that came into London, that he had to retire to an obscure inn in the midst of Epping Forest in order to write something that he had promised to write—probably also something that he could have dodged if a little more hard-hearted.   I hope that you will not be forced to seek an alibi by such inconvenient means in order to finish volume one of the Guide. . . .

I think it will remain true in the future, as it has in the past, that most of the solid and fruitful work in history can be and will be done by means within the power of the separate nations, if not of the separate individuals.   I know that I have not much imagination, but I have never been able to see a large future for international co-operation in matters of history—partly because history is from its nature more nationalized than any subject in the physical sciences, and many humanistic studies.   I have, as you know, been strongly in favor of devoting increased attention to subjects or aspects of history that transcend national boundaries, but most of these can be very well attended to without international organization, and, whatever may be the future of political organization, the fact that for the last four hundred years mankind has been chiefly organized in great states will impose upon history a necessity of continuing to be largely national.   I see only a restricted scope for international endeavor in history, and I do not believe that enough can be done along the lines in your agenda (and where nos. 2, 4, and 6 are the things which may possibly bring substantial results to history) or any similar list of projects, to justify any elaborate or extensive organization.   If one should be created, its secretary would doubtless exert his mind to the full to devise things for it to do, but most of them would remain paper schemes.[502]

Accordingly I say, if you ask my advice, do the best you can to get it properly started, but entertain moderate expectations of its results, and take no measures that are not likely to be justified by those moderate prospects.   Somebody can be found, somewhere in

---

[499] Professor Cheyney, at the close of the Association meeting at Columbus, where he had delivered his presidential address, was seriously ill and remained for many weeks in a Columbus hospital.

[500] The disclosures of the corruption of Harding's administration were filling the pages of the daily papers throughout 1924. In addition to the Teapot Dome scandal, which eventually sent a member of the Cabinet to prison, the Department of Justice, the Veterans' Bureau, and the Bureau of Internal Revenue, were all found to be in the hands of corrupt officials, who were, on a large scale, acquiring wealth at the expense of the public.

[501] Mr. Leland had served as James Hazen Hyde lecturer in the French universities in 1923-1924, lecturing on the history of the French regime in North America, and, at the request of Dr. Inazo Nitobé, under-secretary of the League of Nations, and of Professor Robert A. Millikan, U. S. Member of the International Commission on Intellectual Cooperation, had substituted for the latter in the sessions of that Commission in late 1924.

[502] Mr. Leland was a member of the continuing committee set up by the Fourth International Congress of Historical Sciences (Brussels) with instructions to proceed to the creation of a permanent international committee of historical sciences, which was finally done in 1926. He frequently wrote to Jameson with respect to historical projects which might be undertaken by means of international cooperation.   Among these was the proposal by Jameson, himself, laid before the Brussels Congress and referred to the Continuing Committee, for an international bibliography of historical sciences.   In the agenda which he had sent to Jameson, no. 2 is listed as International historical bibliography; no. 4, Byzantine history; report of provisional committee on an international review of Byzantine studies; no. 6, Economic history: report of provisional committee on international review of economic history (Leland to Jameson, Mar. 4, 1924).

Europe, to be a reasonably good secretary for it, if not ideal. After all, the whole future of the thing is limited within the extent to which the will to cooperate exists among the European scholars. As I see it, that will to co-operate exists in only a moderate measure. It deserves to be encouraged but, if I may use an illustration, if I were in Brussels in May I would not tear my shirt over the effort to get fellows like Tout [503] or Pollard or other persons who, though well disposed, yet have British temperaments, to co-operate in anything with people of other nations, or, in fact, to do anything but what they damn pleased. Do not think me to have become a disciple to Hiram Johnson,[504] willing to let Europe go to the ash can, but I am very anxious to keep my feet on the ground. . . .

To WALDO G. LELAND

March 24, 1924.

Dear Leland:

You will wish to know more about the three deaths which have made this month of March so much a time of grief to me, and which will have been sad news to you too, if you have heard it all.[505]

The clipping which I send respecting Baron Korff will tell you about all that I know, for I have not yet seen the Baroness, though I meant to do so as soon as I got back to Washington. His stroke at his Georgetown lecture must have come just about the hour that I was leaving Washington on the 7th. While I suppose that a stroke of apoplexy, in the case of a man of his figure, is pretty nearly unaccountable, I think it must be true that he had been overworking rather badly this year. He taught at Columbia from Monday to Thursday, but commuted to Washington at the week ends because for one year more, while Sergius was finishing at the Western High School, the Baroness and the children remained here with her father and mother, who are old. Korff came down by night train Thursday night, lectured at the Johns Hopkins Friday morning and at Georgetown on Friday evening, and sometimes, I think, at Princeton and George Washington. On Saturdays he was always tired enough to do very little, and I almost always saw him on that day, either here at the office or at the club. He was so bright and happy a spirit, so entertaining, and with such a quick and eager mind, that it is real suffering to think that I shall not see him again.

Hunt's death was also entirely unexpected. In January they fortunately moved into town, and were boarding not far from us, in Georgetown. Toward the end of that month he was taken ill, with an affection of the heart which was said not to be at all dangerous, but only to require complete rest—some straining of the muscles of the heart, I believe. For two or three weeks he was not allowed to see anyone, but after that I saw him at least on Sundays, and he was always cheerful and happy, and seemed to be distinctly on the mend. While I was absent they moved to the Hotel Everett, where he would not have to go up and down stairs. Each day last week from Monday to Thursday he went down to the State Department for a couple of hours in the forenoon. Thursday Henry came home from the Woodbury Forest School, for his spring vacation, and had a happy afternoon with his father. That evening Representative Walton Moore,[506] of Virginia, came in from the Powhatan, next door, to spend the evening with him, and Hunt suggested to Mrs. Hunt that she should take Henry out to the movies. He told Moore that he felt fine. In the midst of their talk, the little girls being in the next room, Hunt collapsed and died before the nephew, Commander Hewett, or the doctor arrived, though that was but a few minutes —competent little Eleanor having telephoned to them instantly. It is painful beyond words that so much brightness and affection and endearing goodness should be removed from us. There was a requiem mass at St. Matthews Church on Saturday (he died Thursday evening), and Guilday [507] read after it a really beautiful address or tribute. The Secretary and Under-Secretary were there,[508] representatives of the Sons of the Revolution, and many many friends. The service was solemn and beautiful. Mrs. Hunt showed me yesterday a very fine and appreciative letter from Mr. Hughes, a thing to be proud of, coming from a man not given to emotion, but whose words are all known to be deliberate and sincere. She seemed to me exceedingly brave. I do not know how women ever bear such things. Gaillard has gone back to the Tech; Henry has a week more here; the family will go back to the very pleasant house where they were in Georgetown—1620 Twenty-ninth—where they were the only occupants aside from the owners of the house, who were friends, and they boarded not far away.

I went up to Woburn to spend a week with my mother while it was still possible, for it seemed that some sudden attack of the heart was likely to carry her away before I could come up if then summoned. During the first three days that I was there we had many happy hours together, and even the last days were full

---

[503] Thomas Frederick Tout (1855-1929), professor of history, Manchester University, 1890-1925; Messenger lecturer in Cornell University, 1927-1928; president of the Royal Historical Society, 1929. His presidential address, History and historians in America, related chiefly to the mediaeval collections in the Huntington Library, where he had spent some weeks.

[504] Hiram W. Johnson (1866-1945), Senator from California, 1917-1945, who, it will be remembered, was a determined isolationist throughout his service in the Senate.

[505] The three deaths were those of Baron Korff on Mar. 7, of Gaillard Hunt, on Mar. 20, and of Jameson's mother, on Mar. 12.

[506] R. Walton Moore, (1859-1941), member of the House, 1919-1931, assistant secretary of State, 1933.

[507] The Right Reverend Monsignor Peter Guilday (1884-1947), professor of American church history, Catholic University of America.

[508] Charles Evans Hughes was Secretary of State, Joseph C. Grew, under-secretary.

of the remembrances of her gentle goodness and unselfishness. She died on March 12. Both my sisters were there and Mrs. Jameson and my brother came in a day or two. My younger sister has now gone back to the children at Plainfield [509] and the older one, after a few days with her, will come here for a month. My mother was 86 years old, and, as you know, strong and well until less than two years ago. It is a great and very unusual privilege to have had such a mother for so many years.

To Elizabeth Donnan

April 28, 1924.

Dear Miss Donnan:

. . . I think I somewhere saw the recommendation of my "Privateering and Piracy" as literature for the dentist's office, but do not remember whether it was expected to add to the pain or diminish it. . . .

I had two good days' hike with Francis last week in southern Maryland; not a very interesting country, but it was beautiful weather, and he is good company.

This morning I attended the dedication of the new building for the National Academy of Sciences, because my president was to give one of the speeches. This was preceded by one by the President of the United States, a very good one. I was "tickled to death" with his pronunciation of the words "truth" and "view," to which he gave the real New England twang, which I have almost never found anyone able to effect who was not born in rural New England. I remember how in one of Freeman's letters from Boston, he says, "Bryce has just come in, delighted with having heard a man say Európean." These are simple pleasures, but if I share them with Bryce they cannot be discreditable. Mrs. Ramage [510] writes from southern France of a young Oxford man at the *pension* who let her know plainly, doubtless for her good, he having visited America, that he liked Americans, but wished they would not eat with their knives. To the best of my recollection I have not seen a person do that since one day in the Adirondacks, in August, 1892; but to see it again would be a pleasure like those I have mentioned above, bringing back the old American days of simplicity and informal joy.

To the Belgian Ambassador

June 7, 1924.

Your Excellency: [511]

I am very greatly obliged by your kindness in sending me a copy of your remarks at the New York

celebration of May 20. I have read it with great interest, not only because, in earlier days, I interested myself a good deal in special studies on the beginnings of New Netherland, [512] but also because of Mrs. Jameson's connection with the matter. One of the passengers on the *Nieu Nederlandt* was Catelina Trico, born in Paris or Valenciennes, wife of Joris Rapalje (originally, I presume, Rapallié), from whom Mrs. Jameson is descended, her maternal grandmother having been a Rapalje, while her maternal grandfather was a Duryea (which was, I presume, originally du Rieu, Walloon). This Catelina Trico was mother of the first girl born in New Netherland, Sara Rapalje, from whom my wife's name of Sara comes down. Catelina Trico lived to a great old age, and two depositions made by her in 1685-1688 respecting that first voyage, give interesting details respecting the distribution of those first immigrants to various places in the province. She herself, with the majority, went up to Albany, but at the end of three years came down to the mouth of the river, where she and her husband had a farm of, I believe, four hundred acres centred where the Brooklyn Navy Yard is now. I wish the family still possessed it.

Thanking you most cordially for the interest I have had in your discourse.

To Ruth Anna Fisher

September 8, 1924.

My dear Miss Fisher:

On June 14, 1830, Jeremy Bentham of London wrote to Andrew Jackson that he was sending him his "Anti-Senatica Papers," but we have been unable to locate these papers anywhere on this side. It occurs to me however that it may be possible to trace them through a report made by T. Whittaker, in 1892, on Bentham's unpublished manuscripts in University College. I should therefore be much obliged if you would examine this report and let me know what, if anything, you are able to find out respecting these papers. It is possible that they have been published, but the fact cannot be established here. I will ask you to interrupt any other work that you may be doing for us in order to let us have the information at as early a date as possible. [513]

---

[509] The children of Jameson's brother Arthur, with whom his sister, Esther, had lived since the death of their mother.

[510] Mrs. Burr Ramage, widow of a Johns Hopkins friend of Jameson.

[511] Baron de Cartier de Marchienne spoke at the unveiling of a monument at Battery Park, erected to honor Belgian pioneers.

[512] See *Magazine of American History* 8: 315-330, 598-611, May, Sept., 1882, and *ante*, Jan. 30, 1881, n. 16.

[513] Miss Fisher reported that the papers had not been published, but were to be found in the library of University College. They discuss the Constitution of the United States, with special attention to the problem of a second chamber. In a letter from Bentham to President Jackson, June 14, 1830, Bentham says that he is sending to Jackson the "Anti-Senatica Papers" and asks that their receipt be acknowledged. They have not been located in this country but have now been printed in *Smith College Studies in History* 11 (4). See Bassett, *Correspondence of Andrew Jackson* 4: 146-147, 150, Carnegie Institution, pub. no. 371, 1933.

To GEORGE M. TREVELYAN

September 22, 1924.

My dear Trevelyan:

I have just been reading, with very great pleasure, your article on History and Literature in the *Yale Review* for October. It will do good among us, along a line in which we greatly need to be "done good to." There has however been, in the last few years, some searching of heart among the historical professors as to the inability of most of our historical scholars to write anything that people would want to read. The Council of the American Historical Association, two or three years ago, appointed an excellent committee of four to prepare a report on the writing of history, addressed to the purpose of getting it better written— if reports of committees can do anything toward that end.[514] The committee is composed of Jusserand, chairman, Bassett of Smith College, secretary of the Association, who has the matter much at heart, C. W. Colby, formerly of McGill University at Montreal, but now a financial magnate beginning to have some leisure, and W. C. Abbott of Harvard. I think they will hatch out something useful.

With such subjects in mind, it occurs to me that I never sent you a copy of an address I gave a year and a quarter ago at Ann Arbor, on occasion of the presentation of the William L. Clements Library to the University of Michigan. Some copies of the thing, in a reprinted form, have come in lately, and I venture to send you one.[515] The occasion at any rate was of interest, if the address wasn't, for the building is a beautiful one and the collection very remarkable. This Mr. Clements, a manufacturer, well educated and of cultivated taste, has spent, I suppose, thirty years and a million and a half of dollars in making this collection, and then gave it, with an appropriate building, to his university. Feeling a little shy about belauding him in his presence, I think I drew it mild in proportion to my real admiration of his action. You may find especial interest in the engraving opposite page 122 of the magazine, because of the portrait of Shelburne over the fireplace. The magazine ought not to call that room "Rare Book Room," for all the rooms are that; but this room contains, in the cases at right and left of the fireplace the mass of Shelburne Papers which Mr. Clements bought from Lord Lansdowne, papers mainly relating to American affairs. Lord Lansdowne told him that there was this portrait, secondary to the one he had at Bowwood [Bowood], and not in the best condition, which he would give him if he cared to have it done up. It is really a fine portrait.

To CHARLES H. HASKINS

September 26, 1924.

Dear Haskins:

Few things could have done more to make my birthday pleasant than to receive on it the *Review's* copy of your immensely learned and valuable book, and to read the very pleasant words with which it is dedicated to me and Hendrickson and Turner.[516] I took it home that evening to show that dedication to Mrs. Jameson and Katrina, who chanced to be at home from the Havana Embassy on vacation (went back yesterday, alas!). I was myself very much affected by those words, and am very proud to be associated in any way with so much learning. I should like to have written learned books myself, but since fate—or my inability to do as you have done, write them in addition to a full measure of administrative work—has prevented that, it is at least a consolation if anyone who does make such achievements can think enough of my early teachings to mention them in such connection. To me those early teachings, whenever I remember them, seem crude enough, but I "meant well." I certainly did *desire* to uphold good standards of scholarship—which however you would have upheld and exemplified without a word from me.

I thank you very warmly for all this; and now I have to thank you still further, for sending me this handsome and erudite book in a copy of my own. I read much of it, from the *Review* copy, that evening I have mentioned, but I had to bring it back presently, and I shall now be able to read more, at leisure. While doing so, I know I shall marvel further at the possibility of anyone's carrying on such elaborate investigations while teaching and deaning at Harvard and settling the world's affairs at Versailles.[517]

To WILBUR C. ABBOTT

October 6, 1924.

My dear Dr. Abbott:

Herewith I send back your manuscript intended for the report of the committee on the writing of history.[518] I have read it with great interest, and am sure that it will awaken interest in our profession and do real good to the younger members of it and to their teachers. I do not know enough about the manner in which the

---

[514] See *post,* Oct. 6, 1924.
[515] The American historian's raw materials, an address delivered at the dedication of the William L. Clements Library of Americana, June 15, 1923, Ann Arbor, University of Michigan, 1923.

[516] *Studies in the history of mediaeval science,* Cambridge, Harvard Univ. Press, 1924, was dedicated to "J. F. J., G. L. H. and F. J. T." The closing sentence of the preface read: "The book is dedicated to three friends who in my early years, one as teacher, two as fellow-students and colleagues, contributed most to the formation of my ideals of scholarship." George L. Hendrickson, long professor of Latin in the University of Chicago, received his A.B. from the Johns Hopkins in 1887, as did Haskins; F. J. Turner was a graduate student in the university in 1888-1889. He and Haskins taught together in the University of Wisconsin twelve or more years.
[517] See *ante,* Apr. 17, 1919, n. 232.
[518] This report, compiled by J. S. Bassett, was printed as *The writing of history,* N. Y., Scribner's, 1926. Its four essays

subject has been divided among the members of the committee to warrant me in any suggestions of additions, but can see there is a possibility of further development along the lines you have pencilled at the foot of the last page. For instance, I observe that the awards of the Pulitzer prize for the best work of history published during the year, though I presume competently and rightly made, are seldom given to a book by a professor. That looks as though the professor himself did not escape, any more than his students, the deadly influence of doctoral dissertations —the dyer's hand subdued to what it works in. I say competently and rightly given, not merely because the awards have seemed to me about right (though I have never taken the trouble to review the whole year's product in order to check upon the committee) but because the committee seemed to be composed of men who would look at their question from the point of view of the general public, or from Pulitzer's point of view, while keeping a due regard to excellence in respect to scholarship. Last summer's discussions as to the award of the dramatic prize may leave one uncertain whether the historical award is not after all made by the Columbia School of Journalism,[519] but even if so, they too would regard the question of popular appeal, perhaps even more than the committee.[520]. . .

In general, I am greatly pleased to have strong emphasis laid on the thought that graduate students should be led to read more extensively the best historians. I suppose I was the first in this country to conduct a class of graduate students in the history of modern historiography. That was in 1887-1888, at the Johns Hopkins. I was young, and did it very badly, but I spent most of my waking hours on it, for a year, and never have regretted what I thereby learned concerning the course of development of our art, though fate has prevented me from ever writing a history, and confined me to the simple role of a powder-monkey, passing forward ammunition for others to fire off. A dry summary of what I learned is to be found in an

article on the development of modern European historiography in the *Atlantic Monthly* of about 1890 [521] —one of those articles by which, according to the saying of the uncharitable Bostonians, Horace Scudder surpassed Moses, by drying up the Atlantic.

To IRENE A. WRIGHT

October 27, 1924.

My dear Miss Wright:

. . . I am incapable of remorse on account of not having taken Jamaica material which the English did take.[522] The readers of the *American Historical Review* (in whose interest alone, with becoming rigidity, it is edited) are far more interested in early Virginia than early Jamaica. The English, on the other hand, are far more interested in the history of colonies which they retain, even smaller ones than Jamaica, than they appear to be in the history of the empire they lost. It is astonishing how indifferent they are to the history of the major branch of the English speaking race; their attitude toward it reminds me sometimes of that of the elder brother toward the prodigal son. But that is aside from the main point. I did not know that you especially desired to publish an article in the *American Historical Review,* but I appreciate the compliment. If you have several subjects on which you think of thus writing, please let me know what they are, and I will give my opinion as to the respective degrees of their suitability to our readers. Please understand that I don't like to decline articles, though I do it every week or so, since after all we can hardly print more than a dozen a year. On the other hand, though I value your constant friendliness, no one can say that in these thirty years I have ever printed an article in order to please a friend. The old *North American Review* used to have on its cover the excellent motto "Tres Tyriusve mihi nullo discrimine agetur," and them are my sentiments. I am shocked at your thought that editors of historical reviews are like all other editors. I hope not; and if you were reading our newspaper editorials during this presidential campaign, I think you would have to hedge a little on that.

were: The historian's work, by Jean Jules Jusserand, The influence of graduate instruction on historical writing, by Wilbur C. Abbott, The craftsmanship of the historian, by Charles W. Colby, and The present state of history writing, by J. S. Bassett. In the final article there is a letter from Jameson dealing with the subject as an editor under whose eye many manuscripts passed (127-135).

[519] The award, made in May, 1924, for the "original American play performed in New York, which shall best represent the educational value and power of the stage in raising the standard of good morals, good taste and good manners," was given to "Hell-bent for Heaven," by Hatcher Hughes of Columbia University. The critics of the award proposed instead "The Show-off."

[520] The material omitted deals with minor criticisms of phrasing.

[521] See *ante,* Nov. 19, 1889, n. 65.

[522] Miss Irene A. Wright, by years of enthusiastic and unremitting labor, had become the outstanding authority on the contents of the Spanish archives. The article refused by Dr. Jameson was The early history of Jamaica, published in the *English Historical Review* 36: 70-95, Jan., 1921. She had already supplied to the *American Historical Review* two sets of documents from the archives of Seville and Simancas: The commencement of the cane sugar industry in America, 1519-1538, and Spanish policy toward Virginia, 1606-1612; Jamestown, Ecija, and John Clark of the Mayflower, *Amer. Hist. Rev.* 21: 755-780, July, 1915; 25: 448-479, Apr., 1920.

THE DEPARTMENT OF HISTORICAL RESEARCH OF THE CARNEGIE INSTITUTION OF WASHINGTON: LAST YEARS, 1925-1928

To ANDREW C. McLAUGHLIN

January 31, 1925.

Dear McLaughlin:

I enjoyed getting your letter, and Mrs. Jameson was especially gratified by your urgent words as to vacations, rest, and the like. I am with you (and her) on all theoretical grounds, but have a difficulty in seeing just who would do my work while I amused myself, by means which at the moment do not occur to me. According to Hosea Biglow; [1]

> The mass ought to labor, and we lay on sofies,
>   That's the reason I want to spread freedom's aree;
> It puts all the cunninest on us in office,
>   And realizes our Maker's original idee,
> Says John C. Calhoun, says he.

To descend to prose, my carbuncle is nearly well now. I have had no pain from it for two weeks. The end of last week I went up to New York, incidentally saw the eclipse from Columbia University, (which was not put into darkness at all, could not be, I suppose), attended a meeting of the Committee of Management of the DAB from ten to five on Friday, one of the ACLS from ten to four on Saturday, and one of the Endowment Committee of the A. H. A. from five to nine, and none the worse for it all. On Sunday I had four hours with Francis at Haverford, where, with some amusement, I watched him skating for almost the first time.

Oh come now, do stop in Washington in March. I did not have a fair chance at you at all.

To HUBERT HALL

February 5, 1925.

My dear Hall:

I was just about to write to Mrs. Hall, to thank her for *Sard Harker*,[2] when your letter from the *George Washington* arrived. I waited to write to her till I had read the book. Please tell her that I have read it with a great deal of interest and pleasure, and am grateful to her for the opportunity to read it. I fear that the reading will deter me from any expedition

to the tropical or equatorial portions of America, as I detest mud, thick vegetation, snakes, pistols, daggers, and prisons, but there was never very much likelihood of that anyhow.

You do not say what kind of a voyage you had, but I hope it was not too rough. In what you say of our libraries, I don't understand the dark allusion to Fisher, but I am glad you liked them.[3] The freedom of access to books on the part of students of course causes some losses; while this is regrettable, it is worth while to spend or lose some money, for the sake of increased contact with books, and those of much pecuniary value are kept in a special place or room, *muy reservada*.

Well, your visit was a great pleasure, and I hope you are none the worse for it, and I may perhaps be permitted to assure you that the British invasion of Washington in 1924, while just as successful as that of 1814, was undoubtedly a source of greater pleasure to the inhabitants.[4]

To IRENE A. WRIGHT

February 7, 1925.

My dear Miss Wright:

. . . Now about your question as to a subject on which you might, in fragments of leisure (if you ever get any), write an article for the *Review*, out of the abundant material still unconsumed in the Archive de Indias. But I am afraid I have not a sufficiently broad knowledge of Spanish American history—to say nothing of a knowledge of the archives—to enable me to suggest subjects that it would be both profit-

---

[1] Apposite quotations from Hosea Biglow, Jameson had always at hand, both in conversation and when writing. He made good use of his knowledge of the Biglow Papers in Lowell and public affairs, *Review of Reviews* 4: 287-291, Oct., 1891.

[2] John Masefield's tale of harrowing adventure.

[3] "Nothing has impressed me so much on your side as the advantages enjoyed by your students through the greater enterprize of those who make libraries (worthy of the name) for them and also through the efficiency shown in getting the books used. Besides the teachers also benefit and through them and the students, who will be teachers in their turn, the nation benefits. So much for Fisher, though naturally it is of mutual benefit to send Rhodes scholars to Oxford and Camb. Anyhow Fisher (as more or less of an historian) ought to have seen that the equipment of your History students is well ahead of ours if for no other reason than that you and those who back you have made of the A. H. A. and its off-shoots a great professional force equipped and inspired as no other national body of historical workers is found to be elsewhere. So more strength to your arm" (Hall to Jameson, Jan. 17, 1925, on board the S. S. *George Washington*, returning to England from his visit to the American Historical Association meeting in Richmond).

[4] See *post*, Feb. 18, 1925

able and easy to work up. It is not difficult to find an episode for which you can accumulate all the materials in a few legajos and make out of them an entertaining narrative, and I have no doubt that the history of the southern portions of the United States will ultimately be greatly filled out by the elaboration of a mulitude of such episodes. After all, however, most of these episodes are more or less local, and limited in scope, and treatments of them belong rather in state historical journals or the transactions of historical societies than in the *A. H. R.,* which, on the whole, ought to be devoted to articles dealing with larger themes. I wish I could talk the matter over with you, because much of what I might suggest would be speedily put out of court by objections arising from your superior knowledge. Let me however ask what you think of the following suggestion, arising partly from your question as to why Spain did not succeed better. It is this: We have now a pretty fair supply of studies of the Spanish *system,* of the institutions of Spain's colonial empire, and we have many studies of individual episodes and of the history of administration or events in particular countries or provinces. All these, and what has been printed about the financial history of the empire, help to explain the want of ultimate success to which you allude. But is there not one element in the problem about which we know a great deal less, namely, the character of the mass of human beings that came over? Maybe much more has been printed about them than I am aware of, but when I remember how much stress we have laid, in pursuing the history of the English colonies, upon old Stoughton's doctrine that God "sifted a whole nation to get choice grain" with which to people this continent, and on the effort to find out how far this doctrine is true,[5] I feel as if there was a line of investigation that had not in the Spanish case been followed out with equal assiduity. I doubt if the Spanish American mind is sufficiently self-critical to grapple with it, and Native Sons of the Golden West and other North American students do not stay long enough in Spain to permit of the examination of such a theme, for it can not be found in any small number of legajos nor interpreted by one who does not know well the different parts of Spain. As I see it, one would have to salt down the little bits of information as one came upon them, during a considerable period of time, before he would be able to answer such questions as, How large a part of those Spaniards who settled in Mexico, in

Colombia, in Venezuela, in the regions of La Plata came from Asturias or from Galicia or from Andalusia, how large a part of them was clerical, secular or regular, friars or nuns, how large a part of them were gentlemen, and what did that mean? What was the actual character and mental furnishings of this or that element in the great migration?

Quite apart from the question whether anything can be discovered in this way as to the reasons for Spanish colonial success or the opposite, one of the greatest, and on the whole the most peculiar, of the fundamental facts of American history is that it springs from and represents the most extensive human migration in the world's history, and it would be well that we should know more of the nature of that migration. I wish, in short, that I knew as much about the conquistadores and those who came with them as I do about the Pilgrim Fathers, or the other choice grain, and some not so choice, that came to New England in the seventeenth century. (By the way, we have lately made for our proposed Atlas of the Historical Geography of the United States two little maps of England, on which we have noted, by dots representing every Englishman whose place of origin we can trace, the countries from which the seventeenth century settlers of New England came, and those from which emigrants came to Virginia after 1700. For the other colonies, it can not be done, but the differences between these two have quite a little interest).

What do you think of all this? Is it anything of the sort that you like to do, or are you better pleased with histories in which the actions of individuals are more especially traceable?[6] It is merely a suggestion from yours very truly, q. b. l. m.[7]

To ABRAHAM FLEXNER

February 13, 1925.

My dear Dr. Flexner:

Thank you very much for your kindness in sending me a copy of your valuable, and to my mind wonderful, volume on *Medical Education.* I find in it a great deal to interest me, and certainly am highly appreciative of the effort on your part which such a book has demanded, and of the beneficial results which are sure to follow from its publication. I think it is

---

[5] William Stoughton's (1631-1701) much-quoted remark: "God sifted a whole Nation that He might send Choice Grain over into this wilderness," was uttered in an election sermon in 1668 (*New England's true interest—a sermon,* 1670, 19; see *Dictionary American Biography*). Charles Francis Adams made good use of this phrase in an address delivered at the dedication of the building of the State Historical Society of Wisconsin, on Oct. 19, 1900, later printed: The sifted grain and grain sifters, *Amer. Hist. Rev.* 5: 197-234, Jan., 1901.

[6] Though Miss Wright published a number of works gathered from the rich stores of the Spanish archives, so far as the editors know she never acted on this suggestion or offered to the *Review* any further articles. The English conquest of Jamaica, 1655-1656, and Spanish narratives of the English attack on Santo Domingo, 1650, appeared in the *Camden Miscellany* of the Royal Historical Society, 13, 1924; 14, 1926. She later edited two valuable volumes for the Hakluyt Society; *Spanish documents concerning English voyages to the Caribbean, 1527-1568,* selected from the archives of the Indies at Seville, 2d ser., no. 62, 1929; and *Documents concerning English voyages to the Spanish Main, 1569-1580,* 2d ser., no. 71, 1932.

[7] Que besa los manos; who kisses your hands.

legitimate for me to take pride in having once had its author as a student in one of my classes, little as I was then able to teach anyone, and far removed as the field of the book is from that of my teaching or knowledge.[8]

To RUTH PUTNAM

February 18, 1925.

My dear Miss Putnam:[9]

. . . The meeting of the American Historical Association, concerning which you inquire, passed off very successfully indeed. After President Wilson's death[10] the thought of having part of the meeting in Washington was abandoned, and the sessions were held in Richmond on the Saturday after Christmas and the Monday and Tuesday following. The Sunday between was very useful by way of promoting sociability and of giving a chance for excursions to the battlefields or to Westover or about town. From the point of social pleasure, Richmond can not be beaten as a place of meeting; those people do know how to welcome and entertain strangers. A great deal was done for us there, and on the day following there was an excursion to Jamestown and Williamsburg, where the College of William and Mary was very hospitable. The attendance was large, and the programme good. There was plenty of business for the Council, in which, by the way, Miss Williams[11] does very well, and at any rate never makes the least trouble about anything. I enclose a slip which will show what was done in the way of elections, but for a fuller account of the meeting I must refer you to the usual article in the April number. I have not finished it yet, and perhaps ought to be working upon it this morning, for it is already late. I think it is the twentieth of these chronicles that I have ground out, and it goes slowly.[12]

Our nine British delegates made a very acceptable and interesting addition to the affair. They all behaved most amiably, gave much pleasure, and seemed to receive much, and their contributions were of course much above the average, they being a handpicked delegation. Most of them stayed through a part of January, and lectured here and there. Dr. Alexander J. Carlyle of Oxford, indeed, came over in October, gave lectures at the Lowell Institute and elsewhere, and stayed until after Christmas; and on the other hand C. K. Webster, of the University of Wales, came just before Christmas and stays till May, teaching at various places, just now at the University of Minnesota. On their way up from Richmond the Washington members of the Association, with any others who chose to come as they went home, gave a dinner to them at Rauscher's, which went off very well indeed. Dr. David J. Hill presided, and the British ambassador[13] and Sir Richard Lodge and A. F. Pollard spoke, and then Charles Moore gave, in an admirable fashion, one of his illustrated talks on Washington and its past and future development. . . .

I wish I could tell you a large amount about politics, but I know little of what is going on that is not in the newspapers, and I think you probably see some American newspapers in the library of the League. Lately, the Senate has been behaving a little worse than usual. It has lost quite a little ground in the public's estimation with respect to its conduct in the nomination of Attorney General Stone[14] to the Supreme Court, for the long wrangling over that had the appearance of being based, on the part of a number of Senators, on the ground that if the Attorney General followed up a prosecution against a Senator (Wheeler)[15] on whatever evidence, he should not be allowed to attain the supreme bench. Apart from passing the appropriations, it looks as if Congress would pass little significant legislation before March 4. The President may have a more successful time with the next Congress, but perhaps not much better if he does not exert more courageously the power which he might have.

However, this is not a lecture. It is a letter, mainly written in order to send to you and Miss Edith my very kind regards and my best wishes for all the year.

---

[8] This brought in reply: "It is a long time since I was a student of yours, but it is no exaggeration when I say that you and one or two other men in Baltimore taught me in my brief two years there everything I know about scholarship. You were the first person I ever saw who really knew anything thoroughly and I may add I have met no one since, for whose learning I have had more respect than I had and still have for yours" (Abraham Flexner to Jameson, Feb. 18, 1925).

[9] Ruth Putnam, sister of the librarian Herbert Putnam and an historian of the Netherlands, after the First World War, with her sister, Edith, left this country to make her home in Switzerland and Italy until her death in 1931. At the time of this letter she must have been completing her edition of the *Life and letters of Mary Putnam Jacobi*, N. Y., Putnam's, 1925.

[10] Wilson died on Feb. 3, 1924.

[11] Mary W. Williams, professor of history in Goucher College, was a member of the executive council of the American Historical Association from 1923 to 1927.

[12] Meeting of the American Historical Association at Richmond, *Amer. Hist. Rev.* 30: 451-473, Apr., 1925.

[13] Sir Esme Howard, ambassador to the United States, 1924-1930.

[14] Harlan Fiske Stone (1872-1946), Attorney General, 1924, was at length confirmed by the Senate and served as Associate Justice from Mar. 2, 1925, until June, 1941, and as Chief Justice from 1941 until 1946.

[15] Burton K. Wheeler, Senator from Montana, 1923-1947. Evidence collected by the Department of Justice caused the grand jury in the District of Columbia to bring indictment against Senator Wheeler on the charge of conspiring illegally to obtain use of government oil and gas lands in Montana. The indictment was later quashed.

To Nathan G. Goodman

February 27, 1925.

Dear Sir: [16]

As a rule, it is not worth while to pay much attention to what is said in newspaper editorials, and today I have not the time to comment at any great length on that which is mentioned in your letter of February 27. [17]

By "academic mind" is meant, we may assume, the mind of the whole body of teachers in universities and colleges. That would embrace, in the United States alone, at least 20,000 people. Some of them are dull and some of them are not. In every profession, the brilliant members are a minority, presumably a small minority. If by saying that the academic mind is usually deadly dull the *World* means that academics have duller minds than the average person, and it is to be presumed that that is what is meant, it would seem very unlikely that that should be true, that the people of the United States, or their officials or trustees, should select persons of less active minds than the majority to teach the rest, or the younger portion of them. Probably what the editor has really in mind is that the academics seem to him duller than the newspaper writers, the class with whose minds he is most familiar.

Well, we can't have everything in any one man or set of men. Each profession has its superiorities in some qualities and its deficiencies in others. Newspaper men are, on the average, brighter minded than college teachers, but they make up for it by their extraordinary superficiality and unscrupulousness of statement. Their profession abounds in "bright, breezy, brainy" fellows, who would say anything provided it sounds smart, on the one hand talking confidently about things of which they have not taken the pains to acquire any thorough knowledge, and on the other hand careless against all conscience in saying what is favorable to the party or cause to which they adhere. Most commonly, when you read in a newspaper an account of some transaction or matter that you yourself know all about, you find its account to be incorrect in many particulars. It is not so difficult to write brightly if you do not much care what you say.

On the other hand, the academic, whose duty it is to know things thoroughly and to state them correctly, is thereby inhibited from much of that brightness of style and free use of popular rhetoric which makes the newspapers bright. The patience required in order to obtain thorough knowledge and the gravity requisite for correctness of statement will often leave him dull. Moreover, academic pay is not good enough to attract many brilliant young men into the profession of academic teaching. The fault of that lies with the public, which cares more for brightness of writing in the newspapers, which constitutes almost its sole reading, and are bought for two cents and thrown away, than it cares for engaging the most valuable kind of mind in teaching its young people.

As I say, you can't have everything. The world needs bright minds to keep it alive and stirred up, and it needs solid minds to instruct it, but we can not expect to find all good qualities in every profession.

P. S.—Most scientific men are dull, too, and they write even worse than most history men, but the newspapers forgive them because from time to time they produce striking "discoveries" which make the writers and readers of newspapers sit up and take notice.

To Charles K. Webster

March 9, 1925.

My dear Mr. Webster:

I wish to thank you most cordially for your kindness in causing a copy of your book on *The Foreign Policy of Castlereagh* to be sent to me. It came some three weeks ago. If I have been slow to acknowledge it, it is because I did not wish to write about it until I had had an opportunity to read at least the greater part of it. Allow me to express now, besides my thanks, my great admiration for this admirable book. I do not know that I have ever seen a book of diplomatic history that was the fruit of so much labor among state papers; but, what is much more important and impresses me much more, I have seldom, if ever, seen one that was marked by the evidence of so much thought and deliberate consideration of everything involved, throughout its whole field. You have taken the needful time, have saturated yourself with the subject, and have not been content to bring out your book till all the deductions and interpretations and reflections in it were well matured. I am very grateful for the opportunity of reading so much good history, and am sure that the production of the book will redound greatly to your credit.

I am asking the publishers to send a copy for notice in the *American Historical Review,* but I shall not wait upon that chance, for my copy will be immediately at the service of the reviewer if he accepts my invitation. You will think it strange that I should entertain any

[16] Nathan G. Goodman was both journalist and historian, having taught history in the University of Pennsylvania, 1922-1924, and being a frequent contributor to newspapers and magazines.

[17] An editorial in the New York *World* of Feb. 21 had said: "After all the 'academic mind' is . . . usually deadly dull. That is the reason that history written mostly by men with the 'academic mind' is so little read." Jameson might well have adverted to his address, The influence of universities upon historical writing, delivered at the fortieth convocation of the University of Chicago, Sept. 17, 1901, in which he considered the merits and defects of history written under the influence of university training, that is, by those whom the newspaper would have called men with academic minds (*University Record* 6: 294-300, Jan., 1902).

doubt about getting the book, but, as a matter of fact, my requests to English publishers for books to review in that journal are almost invariably refused. Longmans and Macmillan and the Oxford and Cambridge University Presses have establishments in New York, and from those four branches I can get books, but when I send one of our requests to any publishing house in London, "the answer is in the negative," or else I am told that the book is published in this country by such and such a house, and if I then write to that house I am informed that they have too few copies for review purposes to admit of their sending one to me. As a rule, they have already wasted them on our daily papers.

All this is, however, not very important or very interesting to you. I have however one thing to say, that from my point of view at any rate, is of real importance. Namely, unless you have definite plans on which you have come to a fixed conclusion, respecting what you should do next, I wish you would consider whether it may not be a duty to occupy yourself with some part or aspect of the diplomatic relations between Great Britain and the United States. Have they not been, on the whole, at least when the future is considered, the most important relations that the government of Great Britain has had with any other power? The British public and our public ought alike to be instructed upon their history. Our public is in a fair way to be ultimately instructed, for a good number of Americans have worked and will work in that field. But, as in every other case in diplomatic history, we can not expect the best results unless the matter is treated from both sides. Yet if any Briton is occupying himself with the subject, I do not know who it is. When the editors of the *Cambridge History of British Foreign Policy* wished to have the relations between Great Britain and the United States treated, they had to ask Newton to get it up after a fashion; and he, in the training of his young people, finds it better to have them work up Lagos and Goree and Dominica, or the like dots on the earth's surface than anything in the history of the largest of nations and the one most closely connected with Great Britain and Canada. With the one admirable exception of Egerton, who in Great Britain bothers himself with the history of the United States?

Now, while nearly all of your book lies outside the bounds of my knowledge, I know a little about Bagot and Stratford Canning, and your chapter on relations with the United States is so wise and just and discriminating that, taking also into consideration the time you have spent in America and the time you could in future spend in Washington, I do believe you might well consider yourself specially marked out for this work, if it attracts you at all. Please do me the favor to consider it carefully, and perhaps you will give me a chance to talk with you more fully when you are in Washington, where I hope you are planning to come

soon and stay long.[18] Meantime, you will perhaps be interested to know that my plan for an American *Recueil des Instructions* to ministers abroad, which found great favor with Secretary Hughes, has been provided by him with State Department means for going forward.[19] The volumes for Great Britain will be the first to be prepared, instead of, as in the French case, the last—Jusserand having had the other things to do during the last twenty-three years; but he told me he was going to return to that job. . . .

To DIXON RYAN FOX

March 16, 1925.

My dear Mr. Fox:

No, I am afraid I can make only one suggestion respecting papers on the organization and conduct of stage-coach companies, and that is, naturally, a Massachusetts suggestion. If your young man can get hold of the papers of Ginery Twitchell, he will find much of what he wants of that state. Ginery Twitchell's extraordinary name first attracted my attention about 1869, when I saw it on one of the locomotives of the Boston and Albany Railroad. Years afterward I learned from my father who he was. He was the great *entrepreneur* of the stage-coach business in Massachusetts about 1840. As a specimen of his abilities, my father told me that on the morning after the election of 1840, when no railroad in Massachusetts ran west of Worcester, the Boston *Atlas* had returns from every town in the state except two, and that this was because Ginery Twitchell organized a special service for the purpose by means of his coaches and otherwise. I don't know whether Twitchell's papers survive, but Worthington Ford or Julius Tuttle or Clarence Brigham may know.[20]

To SIMEON D. FESS

March 17, 1925.

Dear Senator Fess:[21]

. . . You asked me to make what suggestions I could

---

[18] Before Webster left this country he confided to E. D. Adams that on his return to England he meant to work on Anglo-American diplomatic relations (Adams to Jameson, July 21, Jameson to Adams, July 29, 1925). Though he subsequently published work in the field of diplomatic history, it dealt but incidentally with those relations.

[19] In spite of the favor with which Secretary Hughes looked upon this project, it has never been carried out.

[20] Julius H. Tuttle (1857-1945), assistant librarian and librarian of the Massachusetts Historical Society, 1878-1934; Clarence S. Brigham, librarian of the American Antiquarian Society, 1908-1930, and after that time director of the society. For his first work for it see *ante,* Oct. 18, 1906, n. 23. The Ginery Twitchell Papers are now in the American Antiquarian Society.

[21] Simeon D. Fess (1861-1936), president of Antioch College, 1907-1917, representative from Ohio, 1915-1923, Senator, 1923-1935, was a graduate student in history in the University of Chicago, 1905-1907.

respecting suitable commemoration of the two hundredth anniversary of the birth of George Washington. I suppose that all you would expect at present would be outlines of suggestions, of a preliminary nature, which could be elaborated in much better form, in times of more leisure, before the meeting of the commission in December. I quite understand that, both on the present occasion and at that time, my part in the matter would be confined to those specific lines of suggestion that lie within my particular field, and that there are many other forms of commemoration, about which I could make no useful suggestions, but which will be abundantly treated by others.

My line of work causes me to think of commemorations having the form of printed volumes of historical material. Though this is only one variety of commemoration, and not the most popular one, I am persuaded nevertheless that is very important. We should wish that the commemoration of Washington's life, his services to the nation, and his incomparable character, should not expire with the speeches and the fireworks, but that some things having the nature of permanent commemoration should remain, and not merely monuments or structures which a few can look at, but printed memorials that can circulate everywhere throughout the country and can cause young people and old to think—to understand Washington and his greatness, to follow him through the successive events of his life with real and exact appreciation. Three things of this sort occur to me at present:

1. It is a surprising fact that, with all the print that has been lavished upon every little engagement of the Revolutionary War, the General Orders of the Commander-in-Chief, which may fairly be called the central documents of the war, the skeleton of its military history, have never been printed as a series, and a large number of them, I think the majority, have never been printed at all. Writers respecting individual events have printed some of them here and there, and a number of them appear in various regimental books and the like; but they should undoubtedly be printed as a series. They are the authoritative source for all such matters as orders of battle of the army, its orders of march, the organization of brigades and divisions, appointment of boards of officers for various purposes, instructions for the general officers of the day and of field officers of the day, directions for the care of arms and equipment, directions as to the formation of troops, directions for the march, changes in organization, courts martial, and the like. It is probable that a complete series can still be made up. In the Manuscript Division of the Library of Congress there are seven volumes of manuscript which are copies of the original Orders, but do not give them as a complete series. In the Old Record Office of the Adjutant General's department (in the Munitions Building) are fifty-four orderly books of divisions, brigades, and regiments,

some of them decaying and fading, among which there may be some of the original orderly books kept in Washington's headquarters by the adjutant general. With these and other materials, to be found elsewhere, a complete series can probably be made up. Ought not this to be done well before 1932? Ought it not to be undertaken soon, especially as we are entering upon the period of sesquicentennial commemoration of the events of the Revolutionary War? [22]

2. I should very greatly like to see a volume prepared that would make the man Washintgon real to all readers, young and old. I mean, a volume in which should be gathered together, in order of time from his youth to his death, all those interesting descriptions of the man, or records of interviews with him, or visits to him at Mt. Vernon, which were written by the many persons who actually saw and visited him. There are a great many of these, scattered through a great many different volumes. The cumulative effect of such a book would be a lifelike presentation of one who, I still think, ought to be our chief hero. Possibly another kind of portraiture might be attempted in a book which, made artistically and yet at small expense, might be distributed to schools, containing reproductions of all those portraits of Washington which have any claim to an authentic value. But the book of "Washington as seen by Contemporaries," of which I have spoken, would do a good deal more to make the man lifelike to modern readers than any series of pictures.

3. Jared Sparks's edition of the *Writings of Washington* (12 vols., 1837) is of course long since out of print; but Worthington Ford's edition (14 vols., 1889-1893) is equally so, and both are now hard to procure. Now that situation ought not to be allowed to continue past 1932. His youthful letters, his letters as general, those he wrote during the critical period from 1783 to 1789, and perhaps most of all the letters he wrote while President, ought to be reasonably accessible to all citizens. Ford prints a good many letters that Sparks did not print, and vice-versa. A collection that should contain all the letters that are in both collections, and some others of importance, yet without being swollen to an inordinate number of volumes, might well be produced at government expense. I do not mean in order to be given away, for I believe that time honored congressional procedure involves a shocking amount of waste, but I mean sold at cost or a little less. To my mind Washington's letters are admirable, and I do not see what better monument or memorial of him could be made than such a collection as I have indicated.[23]

---

[22] The General Orders were printed in the *Writings of Washington* described in the next note.

[23] One of Jameson's suggestions was acted upon and resulted in the appearance of *The writings of George Washington from the original manuscript sources, 1745-1799;* prepared under the direction of the United States George Washington Bicentennial

Perhaps other suggestions will occur to me later, but I strongly believe that these three are worthy of some consideration on the part of your commission. At all events, I have taken pleasure in sketching them for submission to you. . . .

To CONYERS READ

April 17, 1925.

Dear Dr. Read: [24]

In a precise sense, the original Mayflower Compact is not in existence. The nearest thing to an original, and the source from which we know the text, is a passage in Bradford's *Plymouth Plantation,* the original manuscript of which is in the Massachusetts State Library. I published a facsimile of page 54 of that manuscript, on which that document is written, in an edition of Bradford, which I published in the series called "Original Narratives of Early American History," of which I was the general editor— and also partly the editor of this volume. You will find this facsimile at page 107 of that book. If a satisfactory reproduction can not be obtained from it, the Clarendon Press can no doubt rather easily get a photograph from the Massachusetts State Library, or, more conveniently, they can probably obtain a satisfactory reproduction from the photographic facsimile of the Bradford manuscript which was printed in London in 1896, with an introduction by the late John A. Doyle. [25]

To FREDERICK J. TURNER

May 5, 1925.

Dear Turner:

Thank you very much for sending me a "separate" of your article on "The Significance of the Section in American History." It has been a source of great pleasure to me, as well as of great interest. The only fault I can find with it is that it is a "separate" from the *Wisconsin Magazine of History* instead of from the *American Historical Review;* but I shall continue to

hope that you have not forgotten this journal, to whose launching you contributed, in the very first number, so vigorous a push, and for which for years you did so much. [26]

How fortunate we have been, with our sectional rivalries confined by forces and arrangements that keep us from the unhappy fate of Europe. South America, I often think, is almost as well off; at any rate it represents a middle stage. The elements are less unified than ours, but after all, with their community of language and religion and modes of thought, they are much better unified than poor old Europe. We think of them as addicted to fighting (and an Irish lady the other day amused me greatly by exclaiming over their quarrelsomeness), but really in those countries they almost never fight each other, and here in Washington, especially since our patron St. Andrew gave them a building, [27] a local habitation as well as a name, they behave most fraternally.

Washington is at its best just now. I wish you were here, and would go to lunch tomorrow with me and C. K. Webster and a few others. I understand there is going to be a vacancy in the representation of Wisconsin in the Senate after March 4, 1927. [28] I wish you would get yourself elected. If this is to be brought about, it is not too soon to begin now.

To WILLIAM K. BOYD

North Edgecomb, Maine
July 10, 1925.

My dear Dr. Boyd: [29]

Dr. James A. Robertson tells me that there is a possibility that Duke University may be willing to sustain the revival of the "Hispanic-American Historical Review." [30] I hope that it will. I do not think of a way in which the amount of money which this would require could be better spent. It was always an excellent journal, which maintained a very

Commission and published by authority of Congress, John C. Fitzpatrick, ed., 39v., 1931-1944. The Congress also authorized sixteen pamphlets on Washington, of which Fitzpatrick wrote no. 5, *Washington as a religious man.* He was also the editor of *The diaries of George Washington, 1748-1799,* sponsored by the Mount Vernon Ladies' Association, Boston, Houghton Mifflin, 1925.

[24] Conyers Read, connected with the department of history of the University of Chicago from 1910 to 1920, was at this time in business in Philadelphia. He returned to academic life as professor of English history in the University of Pennsylvania in 1934. From 1933 to 1941 he served as executive secretary of the American Historical Association and in 1949 was its president.

[25] An edition of Bradford's *Plymouth Plantation* was printed "by Order of the General Court," two years after the facsimile edition. The latter appeared in the United States under the imprint of Houghton Mifflin.

[26] The article in question appeared in the March number of the *Wisconsin Magazine of History* and was later reprinted in *The significance of sections in American history,* 22-51, N. Y., Holt, 1932, arranged and published after Turner's death. The opening number of the *Review* 1: 70-87, Oct., 1895, contained the first of two articles by Turner on Western state making in the revolutionary era.

[27] The Pan-American Union, Constitution Ave., Washington, D. C.

[28] The term of Senator Irving L. Lenroot was to expire in 1927. Actually there was an earlier vacancy, caused by the death of Robert M. LaFollette, on June 18, 1925. To this seat Robert M. LaFollette, Jr., was appointed.

[29] William K. Boyd (1879-1938), professor of history, Trinity College (later Duke University), 1906-1938.

[30] With the fifth volume of the *Hispanic-American Historical Review,* 1922, the financial support, which had come chiefly from Mr. Juan C. Cebrian of San Francisco, ceased and the publication of the journal was suspended. Volume 6, 1926, and subsequent volumes appeared under the auspices of Duke University, James A. Robertson managing editor, as he had been from the beginning.

high quality, got good contributions, and certainly helped to stimulate work among those interested in Hispanic-American history and to keep them together in interest and effort. I do not think that there is any field of history in which American work has gone forward more rapidly in the last fifteen or twenty years than in this, and Robertson has and deserves the good-will of all those occupied with it, so that he can elicit what is best. Another consideration I will allude to, though it is undoubtedly in your mind, namely, that the cultivation of this field has, more than any other, a public importance in the field of political relations, for the maintenance of a good journal of this sort will be of real help in bringing Latin American and North American minds into contact and harmony, so that it may fairly be called a patriotic service. . . .

To JOHN H. FINLEY

September 18, 1925.

My dear Finley: [31]

I wish to enlist the aid of the *Times* in a good cause here in Washington.

The annual volumes of *Foreign Relations,* put forth by the Department of State, and from which writers and the public derive their most authoritative knowledge of what the government does in respect to foreign affairs, have got sadly into arrears. The last volume published was that for 1915.[32] Secretary Hughes, who fully appreciated the importance of such means of keeping the public informed, and indeed was alive to the importance of familiarizing the public with the whole course of our diplomatic history as well as of its recent years, took up with vigor the problem of bringing this series up to date, and, chiefly with that object in view, brought into the Department, as Editor of Publications, one who is both an excellent historical scholar and a man of vigor and energy, Dr. Tyler Dennett,[33] whose book on *Roosevelt and the Russo-Japanese War* you may have seen. Secretary Kellogg[34] is less interested in the past of the Department, even its recent past, than in the tasks of the moment, and many exigencies of the Department combine to press upon the editor of publications, as taking absolute precedence, confidential day-to-day publications and, when Congress is in session, the printing of the laws. Therefore, though Secretary Hughes planned to secure appropriations which provide the needful clerical assistance for going forward with the volumes of *Foreign Relations,* if there is any cut in the appropriations for this branch of the Department its effect is likely to be the pushing aside of this series. As things now are, though Congress is not in session, the editorial division has not been able to do a stroke of work on *Foreign Relations* since July 1.

Now, in the preparations now making for the next budget, various members of the Department, cordially agreeing as to the importance of this work, have with some difficulty persuaded the Secretary to retain in the estimates the item providing for it. It is probable, however, that the Director of the Budget will cut it out, and if he does, it is doubtful whether the Secretary will make an ardent fight for it before the Committee on Appropriations.

I tell you these things confidentially and from conversations, but if you need fuller or more exact information your representative here could be sent to Dr. Dennett to get it. I wish that you would take the matter up in your editorial council, and see if something vigorous can not be said in your columns as to the value of this work and the necessity of maintaining it. I do not think the Secretary is aware, as Mr. Hughes certainly was, of the enormous heightening of public interest in foreign affairs which has occurred since 1914. To me it seems as plain as day. The very existence of such a journal as *Foreign Affairs* may be taken as a proof of it, for certainly such a journal as that could not have been floated in this country fifteen years ago. Still better, as an indication of a more popular interest, is the circulation of the *Living Age;* a journal composed as that is would not have had a chance of success in 1910, whereas now, I dare say, it has a circulation of 50,000 or so. Or again, is there a woman's club in the United States that does not have at least one lecture or address on our foreign relations during its season? Right out in the Secretary's own state, this last winter, an English professor of international politics (C. K. Webster of the University of Wales, who taught in the University of Minnesota through January and February) said to friends of mine that if anybody supposed the Minnesota farmers and shop-keepers were not deeply interested in foreign relations and did not ask intelligent and searching questions about European affairs, he was very much mistaken. Stalled in his train by snow at one small town, he found the Chamber of Commerce immediately gathering all its members together and commandeering him, while they had him, to discourse to them of such things. I can't see how anybody can doubt the value of the State Department volumes or question the absolute necessity of bringing them up from their present discreditable arrears. Do see if you can do something

---

[31] John H. Finley was associate editor of the New York *Times* from 1921 to 1937, editor-in-chief, 1937-1938.

[32] *Papers relating to the foreign relations of the United States.* The volume for 1915 bears the imprint 1924, but it was probably not in circulation until 1925. The series continued to appear but the gap between the date of subject-matter and of the appearance of the volumes was not lessened.

[33] Tyler Dennett (1883-1949), chief of the Division of Publications of the Department of State and editor of the division, 1924-1929.

[34] Frank B. Kellogg (1856-1937), secretary of State, 1925-1929.

about it. The Secretary is plainly quite sensitive to public opinion and newspaper criticism.[35]

To J. HOLLAND ROSE

September 19, 1925.

Dear Dr. Rose:

I think you were notified of my absence from Washington at the time when your letter of August 27 was received, so I hope you will excuse the tardiness of this reply. I am indeed glad to know that the proposed *Cambridge History of the British Empire* is making so good a start.[36]

You ask for suggestions respecting men, for the American portion of the enterprise, and respecting new information now available. With regard to the second particular, I do not know of anything of so large a scope that it would deserve emphatic notice, and in that case could hardly answer the question without entering into some hundreds of items, which I presume is not what you want. With regard to men, I should say as follows:

The chief authority upon our colonial period, it would be universally agreed, is Professor Charles M. Andrews of Yale University, president this year of the American Historical Association. His knowledge is most extensive and minute, and he writes well. Of him, and indeed of most of the others I might

mention, I am unable to say how closely he is tied up by literary undertakings in which he is already engaged. Next to him in general command of the period, and knowledge and wisdom respecting it, I should place Professor Evarts B. Greene of Columbia University. Dr. Clarence W. Alvord, and his range and capabilities, must by this time be well enough known in England to permit me merely to mention him. Winfred T. Root till lately professor of colonial history in the University of Wisconsin, but now head of the department of history in the State University of Iowa, is a sound scholar with a large knowledge of colonial history; his one book is on *Pennsylvania and her Relations to the British Empire*. T. J. Wertenbaker of Princeton is an able man, who has produced good books in Virginia history, but has a much wider range than that.

For the period of the Revolution our most prominent writer is Claude H. Van Tyne of the University of Michigan, whose volume on the "Causes of the Revolution" is to be the first of a series of volumes on that period. A. M. Schlesinger of Harvard, a younger man of much ability, whose book on *The Colonial Merchants and the American Revolution* you may have seen, has much knowledge and good judgment. Carl Becker of Cornell is a man of very acute mind and an excellent writer, whose book on *The Eve of the Revolution* is quite a gem in its way. Among younger men A. H. Basye of Dartmouth has studied tentatively some of the institutional relations of the British government with the colonies, and R. G. Albion, of Princeton, knows much about the naval history of the War for Independence.

Later parts of the history of the British Empire are well known by A. L. P. Dennis of Clark University; he and his abilities are, I think, well known to you. Another who has worked in a later field is R. L. Schuyler of Columbia; another is Cecil F. Lavell, whose *Imperial England* (1918), could be looked at, and who I think is still professor in Grinnell College, Grinnell, Iowa—an Englishman, I believe.

For Canadian history you will naturally rely upon Canadians, and the only man in the United States whom I ought to mention seems to be C. D. Allin of the University of Minnesota. He is a Canadian by origin, and probably your Canadian informants would not forget him. His special line is the economic and tariff history of Canada.

In the West Indian field, I should mention Professor Clarence H. Haring of Harvard for the seventeenth century, and Frank W. Pitman, now professor in Pomona College, Claremont, California, for the eighteenth century. His book is the *Development of the British West Indies, 1700-1763* (1917).

I merely mention these men's books because no doubt they are all in the library of the British Museum and could be examined there, if you wish to use them in estimating the men. Perhaps I could

---

[35] Jameson also sent to the Director of the Budget, Brigadier-General Herbert M. Lord, a plea for volumes supplementary to the regular series, illustrating World War I, and an edition of the *Historical Register*.

At the suggestion of its committee on historical publications of the United States government, the Association at its December meeting passed resolutions urging the State Department to bring the volumes on *Foreign Relations* nearer to date. *Amer. Hist. Rev.* 21: 437, Apr., 1926.

On Feb. 12, 1926, Jameson returned to the subject in a letter to Rollo Ogden, editor of the New York *Times,* explaining that the State Department was having difficulty in getting the necessary appropriation: "The programme of economy is being carried out by the Bureau of the Budget with such rigidity that any government activities that make for civilization have hard work to maintain themselves, unless, as in the case of certain of the physical sciences, it is obvious that they put money into the national pocket." With this letter he enclosed a copy of one which he had sent to Representative Shreve, of the House Committee on Appropriations. In response to this plea, the *Times* on Feb. 16 published a long and cogent editorial, using the facts which Jameson had supplied and arguing that though there was much wasteful printing too little money was being devoted to the publication of *Foreign Relations*. The Department of State had asked for $50,000 to provide five volumes a year until the serial was brought to date. This the Director of the Budget cut out. The editorial concluded with the statement that economy was excellent but should be discriminating.

[36] Professor J. Holland Rose, of Cambridge University, had written for advice on "(1) any 'authorities' in the U. S. Universities on different topics connected with Canada, the W. Indies, or other more general topics connected with the Brit. Empire, and its disruption in 1776-1783. (2) Any new information now available on such topics or more recent ones." As a postscript, "I had a great time in U. S. and recd the $\Phi\beta\kappa$ key from the Iowa Chapter."

give more useful advice at a later stage, if at any time you are considering any of these men with respect to specific chapters of your first three volumes. I should be glad to be helpful in any way, if I can.

With best wishes for the whole great undertaking, and with great expectations from it.[37]

To BERTRAM Z. HAYS

September 21, 1925.

Dear Sir:

I owe you an apology. Your letter of November 5, 1924, addressed to the American Historical Association, was handed to me for reply, and I put it in the wrong place, and have just come across it. Please pardon the tardiness of this reply.

You ask whether it is true that certain additional verses, of which you furnish a copy, were originally a part of the hymn commonly called "America." [38] There is absolutely no foundation for any such statement. The author of that hymn was the Rev. Samuel F. Smith. He was living in my youth, and I have or had letters from him, and know an old gentleman who had heard the hymn sung the first time it was made public. It was prepared for a definite and known occasion, a children's celebration of July 4, 1832, in the Park Street Church, Boston, the church to which I used to go in the late sixties. Mr. Smith was very often requested to write out autograph copies of his famous hymn, and a number of such are in existence. You can challenge anyone to show you one of these autograph copies containing the verses (of very poor poetry) of which you have sent me a copy.

To ABRAHAM FLEXNER

October 28, 1925.

My dear Dr. Flexner:

Thank you very much for your kindness in sending me a copy of your *Atlantic* article on "A Modern University." [39] I am reading it with the greatest interest and pleasure. I know so much less of the matter than you do that I venture no comment, except to express a doubt whether you are right in thinking that the main motive of the Johns Hopkins for offering undergraduate instruction was to ensure a stream of graduate students. My remembrance may be at fault, but I think it was otherwise. Baltimore had no college, and I think it was felt at the outset that it

would be hardly considerate of local interests to omit all provision for young local students of the undergraduate stage.[40] Then, when it became plain that, by reason of the decline of income from shares of the B. and O., Mr. Hopkins's bequest would be insufficient and that the university must look to the Baltimore community for additional means, there was, in the middle 80's, a distinct effort to fortify the undergraduate department and to bring it into increasing favor with the well-to-do classes in Baltimore. I do not know all the details about the recent move toward getting rid of undergraduate work at the Hopkins, but I find myself wondering whether a city of nearly 800,000 inhabitants is not entitled to a strong organization of undergraduate instruction, and where Baltimore will get it if the Johns Hopkins ceases to offer it. However, perhaps the Lord will provide.

To HERBERT D. FOSTER

November 30, 1925.

Dear Foster:

Thank you for the clipping of Mead's remarks on Lodge and Wilson. Good stuff, I thought, though perhaps a little too sure and emphatic.[41] I knew Mead well when I lived in New England, and valued him as a choice spirit, but I had an impression that he had died or had become incapable of work, though I see from time to time outpourings of his wife's somewhat hysterical pacificism in the newspapers.[42]

I am incapable of forming any judgment about the conduct of the Senate with respect to the Versailles treaty, but Lodge's Parthian shot from the grave has not raised or altered my opinion of him.[43] For many years he had the position of the "Scholar in politics."

---

[37] To the first volume of the *Cambridge History of the British Empire,* Cambridge, Univ. Press, 1929, Charles M. Andrews contributed chapters IX and XIV: The acts of trade and The government of the Empire, 1660-1763. The chapter on the American Revolution was to have been written by Clarence W. Alvord but he died before the work was done and his place was taken by Cecil Headlam.

[38] This question came from Iroquois, South Dakota.

[39] Flexner, Abraham, A modern university, *Atlantic* 136: 530-541, Oct., 1925.

[40] French, in his *History of the university,* 64-65, calls attention to the fact, often forgotten, that the university accepted undergraduates from its foundation, and offers for this policy two reasons: the one here suggested by Jameson, and the one presented by Dr. Flexner. In support of the first, French quotes from President Gilman's report of 1880: "We have thought from the outset that the youth of Baltimore and the adjacent region had peculiar claims upon this university, for our founder was a Baltimore merchant who gave his fortune to build up in this place the institutions of charity and of education. His gifts were too generous to be restricted by any geographical consideration and they are administered in a most liberal spirit; at the same time it would not be reasonable that the boys of Baltimore should be obliged to go away from the city of their residence in order to secure the requisite preparation for university work." The second reason was presented in a later report of the president.

[41] Edwin D. Mead (1849-1937), editor of the *New England Magazine,* 1889-1901, and of *Old South Leaflets,* director of the World Peace Foundation. The clipping has not been found.

[42] Lucia True Ames Mead (1856-1936), a lecturer on international affairs, had been especially active in the interests of the League. Some of her comments on Senator Lodge's position may be found in the New York *Times,* Mar. 9, 1919, sect. III, p. 2, and Aug. 25, 1919, p. 10.

[43] Lodge, H. C., *The Senate and the League of Nations,* N. Y., Scribner's 1925. Lodge died on Nov. 9, 1924.

He was a scholar, with very great breadth of reading and, I am told, a wonderful memory of what he read. But he was not a scrupulous writer of history. He would say with solemn and resounding emphasis things that had no other foundation than partizan prejudice, wrote things in the oracular style of Senators that had cost them no serious labor of investigation, and his edition of "Hamilton" was an easy and shabby performance. I rather think that he was in many ways a valuable statesman, but he was cold and mean, and his book shows it.

To HARRY N. GARDINER

December 10, 1925.

Dear John: [44]

It so happens that I have not seen the last issue of the *Amherst Graduates Quarterly,* but partly share your indignation about the name of the inn.[45] If that sounds hesitant it is because I am not sure of the spelling of General Amherst's first name. I always regard the *Dictionary of National Biography* as more authoritative than anything else in such matters, even than the *Britannica,* and the Dictionary of National Biography spells the first name "Jeffrey." In Winsor's *Narrative and Critical History of America,* V. 527, you will see a facsimile of his signature, which is what we ordinarily look to as the most authoritative source of information respecting a man's name, but unfortunately he writes it simply "Jeff," and I rather think that that is the way in which he always signs his name. I have an assistant who used to be in the Canadian archives, and has handled quantities of his letters, but he is absent this morning.[46] I will try to find out, for I really think the name should be spelled rightly.

However, the objection which you say I expressed to you in vigorous terms was, I think, not with regard to the first name, but with regard to the whole business of calling the man Lord Jeffrey Amherst, which of course he never was. He never could have had such a designation, but by being the younger son of a duke or marquis, which of course he was not.

He was plain Jeffrey Amherst, or Colonel or General Amherst, till he became Sir Jeffrey Amherst in 1761, and Lord Amherst (that is to say, Baron Amherst) in 1776. But I imagine that one could din these truths into the ears of Amherst graduates till one was black in the face without producing any other effect than that of being thought to be fussy. These subtle distinctions of dukes and lords and sirs are matters of indifference to these highly educated persons. Probably I went on to express still further objections to the whole silly business of playing up Lord Amherst so much as has recently been the custom at the college. Perhaps they got the idea from Dartmouth, which in its earliest days had a real connection with the Earl of Dartmouth at that time, whereas, Amherst College, of course has not the slightest connection with Lord Amherst beyond the mere fact that the town was named for him, in 1758, I believe, and that when a college was founded there sixty-three years afterward, it was naturally called Amherst College. Lord Dartmouth gave Dartmouth College some money, but I don't believe Amherst College could get a cent out of Lord Amherst, even if he had not been dead twenty-four years when the college was founded. I suppose the song has fastened him upon the college, and they tell me that personally speaking it is an excellent song, though the words seem to me to be quite unworthy of a college.

If I can find out how the old gentleman did spell his name, I will let you know in a few days.

To SAMUEL E. MORISON

January 5, 1926.

Dear Mr. Morison:

. . . Upon the other, and very interesting matter spoken of in your letter of December 21, I am not able to give a reply that I think will be very satisfactory or helpful.[47] It is a fine project, one that deserves success, and one that I should be happy to see succeed.[48] There is, in a sense, a real need for it, because there is a real need for further cultivation of New England history along new lines—lines in which the present generation is or should be interested, not a little different from those which were of primary interest in the times of Justin Winsor or Charles Deane.

I am not equally certain that so good a project will be well sustained. It is plain, for instance, that the Massachusetts Historical Society has a much

[44] Harry Norman Gardiner (1855-1927), A.B., 1878, A.M., 1885, Amherst, known to his college friends as John because of his English birth, after two years' study in Germany had become instructor and then professor of philosophy in Smith College, where he taught from 1884 to 1924. On Jan. 10, 1928, Professor Bassett wrote to Jameson of the death of this college friend, who had been struck by an automobile on the streets of Northampton. In this letter Bassett referred to his own coming visit to Washington on Jan. 27. On that visit he was killed on the street.

[45] Professor Gardiner had complained of the way General Amherst's first name was spelled in, The Lord Jeffery Inn (*Amherst Graduates' Quarterly* 15: 3-8, Nov., 1925). A letter of Dec. 31, from Gardiner indicates that Jameson had found and sent to him some confirmation of the spelling, Jeffery, which he so deplored.

[46] David W. Parker.

[47] The first request in Professor Morison's letter was that Jameson bear in mind at the meeting of the Association in Ann Arbor his desire for an assistant during the second semester of 1924-1925.

[48] The project under consideration by Professor Kenneth Murdock and Morison was that of a periodical devoted to New England. The result of their planning was the *New England Quarterly,* which the Colonial Society helped to support.

smaller amount of working force than it had fifty years ago. I am sure that it tries to recruit its members from among people who will do something, but it seems to have difficulty in doing that, and to fill the gap with cultivated Bostonians, usually of the right families, who take an interest in New England history, but will not write anything about it, and in many cases have no ideas about it. It looks as if Ford had hard work to fill up his monthly programme and as if without him the volumes of Proceedings would contain few things of importance.

The same seems to me quite as true of the Colonial Society. I say this with hesitation, for it could not seem very polite for one who was long ago honored with corresponding membership to speak thus of the society's volumes, if what he said should be communicated to other members; but I am writing to you with freedom, because you asked me for my thoughts. Frankly, the volumes of Transactions seem to me a little thin, the substance often not strong enough to carry the heavy weight of embroidery which the most meticulous of editors heaps upon it by way of annotation. Now it would seem as if members of these two societies ought to be your best reliance for contributions. Can you get a lot more of good material, better on the average than what the Proceedings of the one society and the Transactions of the other contain? I do not feel sure. There is a younger element to draw upon, but they would mostly produce pieces of doctoral dissertations, not all captivating. I suppose you would also include Maine, New Hampshire, Vermont, Rhode Island, and Connecticut, and some of these might bring good help, though their historical societies seem mostly to be becalmed at present, even a prey to ship worms—meaning genealogists, who turn their old timbers into sawdust. Still, there is a good deal of writing talent still left in old New England, and among the descendants of New England elsewhere, and a live editor may be able to draw out enough to keep a journal going; but I would not start with it too large.

As to circulation, I could not estimate. Publishing people in Boston could do that much better. I have never had to work up a circulation, and should not know how. Members of the A. H. A. have to take my journal, whether they like it or not.

As to the amount of trouble involved in editing such a journal, do not underestimate it. The "American Historical Review," though I have good assistance, costs me a good deal of time. I do not suppose that the editing of a volume of the journal would take as much time as is taken by the editing of one of your biennial volumes of Transactions. But somewhat depends on how much you try to have besides "body-articles," for the latter make less trouble than reviews and notes of news; but I judge, from what I am told, that most readers of the A. H. R. turn first

to that last section and get more interest, if not more profit, from that portion than from what precedes.

Nothing better than the above occurs to me at the moment, but I shall be much interested in any further progress of the plan, glad to help if it is pursued, and am always ready to answer any questions that are at all in my line of experience.

To DANA C. MUNRO

January 25, 1926

Dear Munro:

If I understand the matter rightly, you want from me a series of suggestions as to what the A.H.A. might do with a budget of $7,000 for five years, especially intended for purposes of research and publication. What follows are therefore suggestions; if it were a question of a program a committee would take into account many such suggestions, coming from different men. The following are merely submitted for what they are worth, merely as illustrative specimens of the kind of things that might be done.

First of all, I should recommend the finishing of several tasks on which the association has already embarked, but which for want of means it has not brought to a conclusion. After that should follow any new enterprises.

1. My foremost suggestion would be that the association should enlarge greatly its contribution to the fund for making the annual bibliography entitled "Writings on American History." Miss Griffin is now paid only $100 a month, which is very much less than what ought to be paid for such superior and expert service, but the fund which I collect each year with some difficulty from various societies and individuals does not permit of a higher rate of payment. The association now contributes $200. I wish it could contribute $600 more. This piece of work is fundamental to the progress of American historical work, if anything is.

2. The Historical Manuscripts Commission used to have an appropriation of $500 per annum. This was for editorial expenses, in the bringing together, copying, and preparing for publication of historical materials that were found in private hands, and the like. For some years we have made them no appropriation, and while the Austin papers have been on our hands the Commission can get along; but henceforward it ought to have $600 per annum, chiefly for the preservation in print of historical materials that otherwise are in danger of destruction. Their printing is, as you know, provided for at the Government Printing Office.

3. We ought to finish that Bibliography of Travel in the United States. If constructed as planned, it would be a volume of so widespread interest that its printing and publication could be taken care of commercially, but the editorial work yet to be done would call for a

thousand dollars per annum during the first two years of the five.

4. We owe it to the keepers of records of states and counties and cities to finish that Primer of Archive Work which has been so long on the stocks, a small book partly done, for which $800 in one year ought to finish the editorial work and $1200 in the next year to provide the printing.[49]

5. We ought to finish that Bibliography of Modern English History of which our committee undertook the 16th Century, while the British committee undertook the 17th. The members of the committee have spent a great deal of time and labor on this, but, as busy professors, they cannot be expected to find the time to do all the labor and detail which is necessary in order to bring down to date the manuscript which they had nearly ready in 1914 and make the book completely ready for publication. A thousand dollars would do this task, for which they are now anxiously trying to find small sums of money; provisions, and indeed contracts, for the publication of this book have already been made.

6. Turning now to new tasks, I should advocate some expenditure of money in the exploitation of European sources for American History. Of all such enterprises, I should put foremost a piece of work in the Archives of the Indies at Seville, which would be interesting and helpful to the many students who are working on the history of those parts of the United States that were once under Spain. We have much less knowledge of those materials, and much less ease in getting at them, than in the case of the materials in England and France. I have done what I could, in the making of Hill's "Descriptive Catalogue of the Papeles de Cuba," but have no present prospect of further appropriation for this line of work. If I could go further in this field, I should take up that section of the Archives of the Indies which is next most abundant in material for United States History, namely, the "Audiencia," specifically, the sections devoted to the audiencias of Mexico, Guadalajara and Santo Domingo. A calendar of United States papers in this section could be made by Miss Wright in Seville for $2,000, which could be spread over two years, and the book could be printed for $3,000 in the third year.

7. The rest of the money I should devote to the preparing for print of collections of historical source-material, and its printing and publication, in accordance with the scheme which I have laid out in the tabular view which is annexed. This would mean the preparation and publishing of materials which we could not, as in the case of the Historical Manuscripts Commission, insert in our Annual reports that are printed by the Government Printing Office—unless indeed we should so grow in favor with Congress that they would en-

large our appropriation for the printing of the Annual Report; but I am not banking on that. As to what materials should be edited and printed, opinions of course would differ. I should advocate documentary material and not monographs, lest we be turned into a machine for publishing doctoral dissertations, for which university means exist or ought to exist. I should advocate the making of volumes each composed of documents illustrative of a particular subject in our history. For instance: (1) A body of documents illustrating the transition from the land-holding system that prevailed in 1775 to that which prevailed in 1800, a transition which, as I explained in the Vanuxem Lectures,[50] seems to me fundamental to our history, as promoting that economic democracy which in an agricultural nation led the way to political democracy; (2) A very important thing would be a collection of documents—convention proceedings, platforms, correspondence, etc.—illustrative of the growth of the system of party organization in the states, preliminary to the first national nominating conventions; (3) Something in the revolutionary period, which is now coming again into special prominence in the public mind, and for which I should especially suggest some body of documents from the Admiralty Papers in the British Public Record Office, since we know much less of the maritime history of the Revolution than of the struggles on the land; (4) The papers of Presidents Johnson and Grant, now in the Library of Congress, which lie as far back from the present day as the papers of Washington and Jefferson did when Sparks and Congress brought them forth.

In the tabular view which follows, I have computed that each one hundred pages of print would require about $60 for assistance in the process of search, about $60 for copying, about $50 for miscellaneous assistance in the process of editing, about $600 for printing and binding, and $30 for indexing, making about $800 in all.

If all this is useful, merely as a suggestion of possibilities, I shall be glad.[51]

---

[49] This has never been completed.

[50] These were the lectures on the American Revolution delivered at Princeton University and printed as *The American Revolution considered as a social movement*.

[51] The tabular view, here omitted, so arranges the work that the annual cost would be $7,000, and summarizes the five years as follows: "What the Association would have to show for the subvention at the end of the five years would be:

A. Published from the Government Printing Office.
  5 volumes annual bibliography Writings on American History
  5 vols. of Hist. MSS. Comm., Historical correspondence or papers.
B. Published by means heretofore provided.
  Bibliography of Modern English History (Tudor)
C. Published otherwise.
  Bibliography of Travel in U.S.
  Primer of Archive Science
  Calendar of 'Audencia' section, Archives of Indies 2400 pp. (5 vols.) of historical materials."

To JOHN S. BASSETT

February 8, 1926.

My dear Bassett:

I have thought from time to time of your question about topics in the history of the transition of civilization from Europe to America. If I remember rightly, your desire was to hit upon a topic within that field, on which you could write effectively during a period of some months in England. I do not know that I have hit upon a topic that will suit your desires, and that which has occurred to me as most eligible, while it is within the history of civilization, broadly considered, might not be reckoned by everyone to lie within that field. However, it is a topic of great importance to the history of life in America, and especially of that business life or economic life with which you have been at times a good deal concerned. Also, according to any recollection I have it has hardly been worked at all, and it could hardly be worked upon effectively on this side of the water.

What I suggest is, a study of the means and methods used in England, and perhaps also in Germany, Switzerland, and Holland, by persons having large grants of land in America, to persuade men to come over and settle upon it—the *modus operandi* of the business of "selling America" in the seventeenth and eighteenth centuries. Of course some of the printed matter by which this was done can be found in this country in libraries of Americana, but on the whole the pamphlets and broadsides and newspaper advertisements and correspondence by which this was done are preserved in English and German and Swiss and Dutch archives and libraries, rather than here. Is it not an important subject, when one considers how completely this was an agricultural nation and how largely its future depended upon population? But it may be important, and yet not at all what you want.[52]

[52] In reply Bassett wrote: "What I have in mind is a study into the intellectual background of American colonization from Great Britain, *i.e.*, before the Revolution. If we could have a clear statement of the religious, intellectual, musical, moral and other similar thinking of the plain people of England in the period mentioned, we should get near to the basis of Americanism" (Bassett to Jameson, Feb. 12, 1926).

To this Jameson replied: "I should wish, if it were my case, to study pretty fully the extent to which portions of the field have been covered by monographs written in America. . . . But I should especially wish, if it were practicable, to wait for the publication of Jernegan's book on the history of American education in the colonial period. Twenty-one or twenty-two years ago I started him upon that line, suggesting the making of his doctoral dissertation on the education or mental furnishings of that generation that made the American Revolution. He however has gone back from that over the whole field, and first of all he spent more than a year in England studying, not the well-cultivated field of the English universities and other matters of higher education, but the systems of elementary education in England in the seventeenth, and I presume, the eighteenth centuries. When I went over some of his work in that field after he first came back, it seemed to me that he had studied English elementary education of the Stuart period with much more thoroughness than any Englishman had ever done,

To ROSCOE R. HILL

February 9, 1926.

My dear Hill:

I have just had occasion to write to a man in San Salvador, who had sent me something historical, and that naturally brings up to my mind the duty and pleasure of writing to a good friend in the adjoining country.[53] I was very greatly interested in your December letter, and appreciative of your good wishes. I can not imagine that I have anything so interesting to write in response, for there are no revolutions here, except the daily revolutions of the earth, which are accomplished very quietly, and nobody shoots anybody in the streets for political reasons, although, as you may have heard, when it comes to ordinary murders, the United States holds a position of undisputed primacy among the great nations of the earth. On the other hand, with the departure of Dana Munro[54] to Panama, I no longer have anyone to tell me what goes on in Central America, so with respect to Nicaraguan news since December 8, and how President Solorazano finally came out,[55] I am much in the position of the Yale graduate who had a course in Shakespeare with Lounsbury,[56] in which they read Macbeth, studying carefully the first four acts, but not going farther when the end of the term came; meeting the professor years

and with most excellent results." Jameson also expressed his belief that many monographs must be written before Bassett's idea could be adequately developed. Jameson to Bassett, Feb. 23, 1926.

In Professor Jernegan's *Laboring and dependent classes in Colonial America, 1607-1783,* Chicago, Univ. of Chicago Press, 1931, the author devotes part II to Free education for poor children and apprentices in New England, and part III to Free education for poor children and apprentices in the South but these sections contain little information on English education.

[53] Since 1912 Nicaragua had been a virtual protectorate of the United States with the Marines at hand to keep order. R. R. Hill was from 1920 to 1928 a member of the Nicaraguan High Commission and financial advisor to the government.

[54] Dana G. Munro, son of Jameson's friend Dana C. Munro, after dealing with Central American affairs in the Department of State, was sent to Panama by that department in 1925.

[55] The Nicaraguan election of 1924 had made Solorazano president and Juan B. Sacasa vice-president. In the autumn of 1925 Gen. Emiliano Chamorro, a defeated candidate, led a coup d'état which drove out Sacasa and Solorazano, and allowed Chamorro to become president, though a president unrecognized by the United States and European countries. Sacasa came to Washington for aid but he also was refused recognition, on the ground that he had left the country and was completely without power to establish a government. Failing in Washington, he turned to Mexico and gained from President Calles arms and men. At that point the United States landed marines in Nicaragua to restore order. Chamorro fled and the Nicaraguan senate elected Adolfo Diaz. The cry was at once raised that Diaz held his place only by means of the force of the United States. A personal visit by Col. Henry L. Stimson brought an armistice between the hostile factions and a surrender of arms. On Nov. 24, 1928, by an election supervised by American forces, Gen. José M. Moncada was elected president and order was restored.

[56] Thomas R. Lounsbury (1838-1915), a professor in Sheffield Scientific School, Yale, from 1870 until 1906.

afterward the student said that he had always wished he knew how the story came out at the end.

Relatively quiet though our politics are, we have Congress with us, so there is interest if not excitement in the Washington atmosphere. The President does not seem to get his own way much more completely than Solorazano does, and yet, rather marvellously, in spite of that his prestige and favor with the people seem to continue unimpaired, though I do not suppose they would survive a period of financial pressure, which may come within two years. The Senate has agreed to our entrance into the World Court, provided forty-eight or forty-nine other states will accept all our reservations, one of which is of a nature to make the whole thing, as I see it, an action of not much value.[57] They are now struggling with the problems of taxation, in which their effort of course is to do what will seem popular, like reducing taxation on as many as possible of those who have votes, making gestures of economy, and seeming to soak the rich while also favoring the prosperity of business. The movement for a National Archive Building, which is the piece of legislation I am most interested in, is likely to be carried along by the general eagerness of Congress for an omnibus public buildings bill. The President two years ago urged upon them the necessity of providing $50,000,000 in ten years for public buildings in Washington; but, as I felt sure would be the case, it has proved that the only way to get this was to let them add appropriations of $115,000,00 more for all public buildings in the districts. That does not seem much like economy; enlargements of many post-offices are justifiable, but nearly all the new ones added will be merely so much pie.

But why should I poison your young mind with reflections upon the rulers of the people. Turn we to happier themes, of more domestic interest. . . .

To ANDREW C. McLAUGHLIN

February 15, 1926.

Dear McLaughlin:

. . . What you say about John Taylor of Caroline and Spencer Roane wakes long-forgotten memories. In Virginia in 1891 I picked up nearly all of John Taylor's publications, and read as much of them as I could bear to read, not being able long to pursue with equanimity the fine-spun threads of Virginian arguments of the old

school.[58] My mind was pedestrian then, and I guess is more so now, and John Taylor of Caroline and his friends seemed to me like Milton's angels that

> "sat on a hill retired,
> In thoughts more elevate, and reasoned high
> Of Providence, foreknowledge, will, and fate;
> Fixed fate, free will, foreknowledge absolute,
> And found no end, in wandering mazes lost."

Myself certainly finding no end, I interested myself more in such questions as, How the committee system came into existence, and what was the history of the previous question. By the way, that last, pursued in both the House of Commons and the House of Representatives, is not a bad subject for a doctoral dissertation. I hope your Constitutional History[59] is going to deal with that rather neglected area, the history of portions of our form of government that are not mentioned in the Constitution, but would make the Fathers sit up and take notice. As I see it, nearly all Americans, including especially those hundred-percenters that think it of vital importance to "have the Constitution taught," take a very distorted and erroneous view of their own form of government by paying very little attention to those parts of it that are not mentioned in the fundamental document but consist of law and custom, just as the whole of the English Constitution does. I hope that your Constitutional History, to whose issue I look forward as of a classical publication, is going to take due account of the history of these accretions, as well as of all that concerns the good old document itself.

With apologies to Baker for just using him as a springboard, I come down to earth, thanking you however for your graceful metaphors from the marine element.[60]

---

[57] In accepting membership in the World Court the Senate stipulated that: (1) the United States was to share in electing its judges; (2) the Congress was to decide the share of the expense to be borne by the United States; (3) the constitution of the Court was not to be changed without the consent of the United States; (4) it was to be understood that the Court had no legal relation to the League, and that the United States was assuming no obligations under the Versailles Treaty; (5) the Court was to render no decision affecting the United States without the consent of the United States. This fifth reservation other nations of course refused to accept.

[58] McLaughlin had written: "I have spent some days recently going over more systematically than ever before Spencer Roane and John Taylor. What sail those fellows carried! No wonder Marshall had to put up his staysail and flying jib and spinnaker and baloon topsails. No not his spinnaker which I am told is used only for running before the wind. Marshall was running into a heavy head sea, I guess—or was he? He had time and tide with him for the long stretch, but he must have thought he was beating to winward. What would have happened to Taylor and Roane, had they gone over to Jamie Madison's farm and borrowed his *Notes?*" (McLaughlin to Jameson, Feb. 12, 1926).

To the *Cambridge history of American literature* **2** (2): 70-92, N. Y., Putnam's, 1918, McLaughlin contributed a chapter on Publicists and orators, 1800-1850, in which he gave brief attention to these two. John Taylor of Caroline (1753-1824), three times a member of the United States Senate and the author of many political pamphlets, foreshadowed Calhoun's position on state sovereignty; Judge Spencer Roane (1762-1822) argued against the right of federal review in cases involving state legislation.

[59] McLaughlin, A. C., *Foundations of American constitutionalism*, N. Y., New York Univ. Press, 1932; *A constitutional history of the United States*, N. Y., Appleton-Century, 1935.

[60] This letter began with a brief reference to Newton D. Baker's *Progress and the Constitution*, N. Y., Scribner's, 1925,

To Charles M. Andrews

March 16, 1926.

Dear Andrews:

To receive such a letter from such a friend helps the day very much, and will help its successors, "Daughters of Time, the hypocritic days," for though I enjoy having you think that I carry my burdens here with ease, the truth is that they are heavy, and I often feel not only their weight but a sense of insufficiency to cope with so various a job.[61] However, if you and others will not expect me to keep up with it with perfect promptitude—will forgive the publication of the next number of the *American Historical Review* about April 8 instead of April 1, a distressing fact, bringing sorrow to many households—I will struggle on, and endeavor to do so cheerfully. You do not in your letter make any allowance for the help which good fellows like you have for twenty years rendered to the work of this Department on every occasion. The best wish I can give you in return is to desire that your own job may soon be simplified as much as you wish. The world is too much with us, and is too full of a number of things, and I do not agree with the poet that this last sort of abundance should make us all as happy as kings. Quite the contrary, in my case, "however" as Queen Elizabeth said to Mrs. Matthew Parker on a celebrated occasion, "I thank you for your good cheer.[62]

of which McLaughlin wrote: "It's scholarly and able, but slight and frail, though not feeble. Unfortunately a good deal of it is presented in pretty bad style, confusing and not effective. Must have been dictated or, more likely, taken down by a stenographer during delivery. If it were clear, direct and arresting it would be of some popular value" (McLaughlin to Jameson, Feb. 12, 1926).

[61] Andrews had written on Mar. 14: "I want to send you a word of congratulation on your last report, which you were good enough to send me. It contains a notable record of a year's plans and activities. You win my admiration constantly for your vigor and the scope of your interests. You seem to have no difficulty in keeping a dozen things going at once, apparently giving to each a maximum amount of attention. I do not wonder that you expressed surprise at my thought of retiring at an early date, when you are yourself so much on the job and so remote from such a contingency. May your flag be at the top of the mast until you have matched the record of Mr. Justice Holmes and are headed for that of Dr. Eliot and Mr. Depew. If I can get rid of the 'daily dozen' departmental activities I too shall nail my flag to the mast and head the same way, trailing along in your rear.

"I am eager to get down to real work; the last four years have been almost completely absorbed with *chores* and I don't call 'them things' work of a real man, of the two gun variety."

[62] The story is quoted in the article on Matthew Parker, archbishop of Canterbury, in the *Dictionary of National Biography* 15: 261-262, "In the exercise of hospitality he was materially aided by his wife, whose tact and genial disposition signally fitted her for such duties; and Elizabeth herself, touched by the grace and courtesy of her reception when on a visit to Lambeth Palace, but unable altogether to suppress her dislike of clerical matrimony, took leave of her hostess with the oft-quoted words: 'Madam I may not call you; mistress I am ashamed to call you; but yet I thank you.'"

To Max Farrand

June 4, 1926.

Dear Farrand:

There is a legend at North Edgecomb such as you describe.[63] The house still stands in the village, right opposite the post-office and the house which this Department used to have for an office; therefore you must have seen it,—a square, white, hip-roofed house, four rooms to a floor, such as retired sea captains in New England were in the habit of building. It was originally erected on the island opposite, probably somewhere about 1793, but eighty or ninety years ago was rolled down the hill, pushed on to scows, brought across to North Edgecomb, and then pushed up the slope to its present position. The legend is that a certain man or certain men of Maine built it as a residence for Marie Antoinette, intending to sail over and rescue her from prison. A small local book was written to this effect a few years ago, but I have always taken it for granted that it was pure delusion, though doubtless many of the chivalrous sons of Maine felt an impulse to go and rescue the lady for whom "ten thousand swords must have leaped from their scabbards to avenge even a look that threatened her with insult."[64]

As to Franklin's autobiography, I do not remember whether the late Albert H. Smyth gave a better edition of it than Bigelow's.[65] Of persons now living, Dr. William S. Mason, of Evanston, has the largest collection of Franklin material in the country, and I believe is a good scholar, though not a professional one. At a meeting of the American Antiquarian Society, a year or so ago, George S. Eddy read a paper on some of Franklin's printed works which, as I remember it, showed him to be a very close student of them, at least from a bibliographical point of view.[66] I do not know

[63] "Again and again in Maine I have run across the story that a house in Edgecomb was built and furnished for Marie Antoinette. Some time when you have a few minutes leisure —or shall I say—some time will you make the opportunity to dictate to a stenographer a brief statement of what the real historical basis for that story is" (Farrand to Jameson, June 3, 1926).

[64] From Burke's *Reflections on the Revolution in France* 3: 331, 1790.

[65] John Bigelow (1817-1911) published the *Autobiography,* Philadelphia, Lippincott, 1868; a *Life of Benjamin Franklin,* Lippincott, 1874; and the *Complete works,* 12v., N. Y., Putnam's, 1887-1888. Albert H. Smyth (1863-1907) edited the *Writings and correspondence,* 10v., N. Y., Macmillan, 1905-1907. Carl Becker, the author of the life of Franklin in the *Dictionary of American Biography,* pronounced Bigelow's to be the best edition of the *Autobiography.* For an account of early collections of Franklin's writings, see Philbrick, Francis S., Notes on early editions and editors of Franklin, *Proc. Amer. Philos. Soc.* 97: 525-564, Oct. 30, 1953.

[66] The paper was, Dr. Benjamin Franklin's library, *Proc. Amer. Ant. Soc., n. s.* 34 (2): 206-226, 1925. Mr. Eddy also published that same year, A suit of Benjamin Franklin's clothes, *N. Y. Hist. Soc. Bull.* 9: 88-92, Oct., 1925. The collection of Frankliniana of the American Philosophical Society was probably then, as it is now, the largest single collection of such material.

that there are now any other higher authorities on Franklin than these two.[67]

To Austin P. Evans

August 10, 1926.

Dear Dr. Evans:

. . . I did not get, or at any rate did not take, an opportunity to consult Professor Burr at serious length upon the problems of the book, though I talked with him a little about it, and he seemed quite to approve the general idea.[68] If I were you, or Church, I do not think that I should hesitate to ask him to suggest pieces that ought to be included, because, with his enormous range of knowledge, he might think of excellent things that nobody else would think of. Phrases could be used that would guard him from spending too much time upon the matter. Within such limits, I do not hesitate to ask him questions once in a while. I have always longed—all of us have always longed—that he should produce either or both of two great books, one on the history of witchcraft and one on the history of toleration, but I am pretty convinced that he never will. He will always devote himself to doing the work of others, or work which others impose upon him. I rather resent his occupation with these matters of Henry C. Lea and President White,[69] but if he were not doing them, he would be doing what the Tompkins County Historical Society or the Literary Club of McGrawville asked him to do, and if that is the case, he might as well be answering worth while questions for deserving historical scholars like you and me. The world does not contain a more unselfish man, but it is perhaps a pity for the world that the unselfishness and

the wonderful learning have not been entrusted to two separate individuals.

To Charles A. Beard

August 10, 1926.

My dear Mr. Beard:

I send you my thanks for the very pleasant review of my little book which I have just been reading in the *New Republic*.[70] With one exception, this is the only serious review of it that I have happened to see, though perhaps the publishers have encountered others. Anyhow, it is very gratifying to be so much commended by so high an authority.

I do not suppose I shall be warranted in inferring from your phrases that my little book has given you the impression that I am a late convert to the economic interpretation of history; but there is some probability that you may think so, and therefore I will tell you confidentially that the four lectures only convey the substance of six that I gave to a small audience at Columbia University in *1895*. I say confidentially, not because my sponsors at Princeton are not well aware of the fact; I did not deceive them, but there is no need to make the fact extensively known. I rewrote, with care as to additional facts or illustrations, but nearly everything that is a matter of doctrine was already in the text read in 1895. I say this because I think there is some tendency to classify historical scholars particularly rigidly, as of old and new schools, as if one must be distinctly of one school or the other, and as if there had been a sharp transition, whereas I should think there had been a gradual one, and the new history does not seem so altogether new to me as many represent. I am rather inept in all matters of philosophy and theory, and nothing that I said in this little book is said because I am committed to an economic interpretation of history, but many things that look that way are said merely because it appeared to me that the facts tended to support the remark I was making. A special reason for thanking you is that I really would like to have some of the younger students study the American Revolution (or anything else in our history) from the point of view which I assumed in these lectures. When I came, after so many years, to rewrite them for Princeton use, and set out to add or modify whatever it seemed needful to add or modify by reason of researches along the same lines published in monographs or dissertations during the interval, I

[67] Farrand published in the *Huntington Library Bull.* 10, Oct., 1936, Franklin's *Memoirs*, reissued by the Harvard University Press, 1936. In 1949 the University of California in cooperation with the Huntington Library published parallel text editions of Franklin's *Memoirs* and *Autobiography*, prepared by Farrand, who for the first used two French translations, the version of William Temple Franklin, and Franklin's manuscript; and for the second, two French translations, W. T. Franklin's version of 1818, and Bigelow's version of 1868.

[68] Austin P. Evans, once a student of Professor Burr, and after 1915 a teacher of history in Columbia University, had in 1925 been made editor of the *Records of civilization: sources and studies,* under the auspices of the Department of History of Columbia. In 1926 Jameson wrote to Professor Carlton J. Hayes, suggesting for the series a volume illustrative of the transition from manuscript to printed book and mentioning Frederic C. Church, also a former student of Burr and at that time a professor of history in the University of Idaho, as a possible editor. Some correspondence ensued but nothing came of the project. Information supplied by Professor Evans.

[69] When Henry C. Lea of Philadelphia died, in 1909, he left undone a projected work on the history of witchcraft. His notes and papers were given to Burr to prepare for publication. Burr was also given the charge of Andrew D. White's papers after Dr. White's death. Burr died leaving both the collections unpublished. Since his death the diaries of Andrew D. White have been found and Cornell University is planning an extensive publication program for the White papers.

[70] *The American Revolution considered as a social movement* was reviewed in the *New Republic* 47: 344, Aug. 11, 1926, under the caption, A challenge to windbags. Of it Beard wrote: "A truly notable book, this is, carefully organized, cut with a diamond point to a finish, studded with novel illustrative materials, gleaming with new illumination, serenely engaging in style, and sparingly garnished with genial humor." There is at one point in the review the implication that there is here new doctrine to be coming from the older generation of historians but no such statement is specifically made.

was surprised and disappointed to see how little had been done to illuminate the history of that period from the social and economic point of view—how little needed to be changed in my statements. I wish the studies along those lines might be so heartily encouraged that in a few years my small book may seem a primer of commonplaces. Therefore, again, I thank you.[71]

To WILLIAM BEER

October 5, 1926.

Dear Mr. Beer:[72]

Thank you for the newspaper article respecting Laffite.[73] I wonder if there is any scoundrel or ruffian in American history that has not been whitewashed. I expect that I should live long enough to see a movement for the canonization of Benedict Arnold, were it not for the fact that the Irish would not have it.

To CAROLINE HAZARD

October 8, 1926.

My dear Miss Hazard:[74]

Thank you for your letter of October 6. While we are speaking of ways in which a moderate amount of money could do something for the cause of Rhode Island history, I will mention one that occurs to me.

The history of our Revolution, as of most other revolutions, has naturally and most easily been treated by writing up the picturesque events that occurred in the main theatres of action—in this case, in such places as Boston, Philadelphia, or Charleston. But would it not be interesting and valuable if we could learn how the Revolutionary movement advanced in rural townships and other places more remote from the great scenes—for after all, one of the main questions is, What did the somewhat inarticulate mass of mankind think about the matter?

Studies in the history of the French Revolution have very greatly profited by turning attention to the task of studying the movement locally, province by province, parish by parish. Many years ago I proposed to the Rhode Island Historical Society that a smallish volume should be made up by collecting from the records of the town meetings the votes showing township action toward the Revolution and independence. It never has been done, but I think we can hardly understand the real nature of the Revolution in Rhode Island until somebody goes through the records of town meetings in the various towns (if I remember rightly there were only sixteen) and draws off from them all votes that are relevant to this particular study. If this quest should at all appeal to you in these days of fresh commemoration of the Revolution, it would be possible without great expense to engage some young man or woman who is sufficiently trained for such work, to make the necessary excerpts, out of which I should think there might emerge a rather interesting book. This is however merely a suggestion.

To ELIZABETH DONNAN

October 25, 1926.

Dear Miss Donnan:

Being in Baltimore on Saturday, I went through the papers of Henry Callister, but found nothing relating to the slave-trade. The papers are a series of letter-books extending from 1744 to 1752 and from 1759 to 1765. Callister was an interesting man, well educated, and writing intelligently, with a good many interests beside business. He came from Douglas in the Isle of Man to Oxford, Maryland, as assistant factor for Foster Cunliffe and Company[75] in 1741, having at first a salary of £40 per annum, some freedom of trade, and the privilege of sending home four hogsheads of tobacco, freight free, each year. In a letter of 1749 he uses the phrase, "After 8 years service in the most considerable house concern'd in the Maryland Trade, and under the immediate Direction of the most accomplish'd Factor (without Exception) of all Maryland the famous Robert Morris." That was the merchant, by the way, of whom the really famous Robert Morris was an illegitimate son.

---

[71] To Jameson, who persistently denied any understanding of philosophy or of the philosophy of history, Beard's comment on his *American Revolution* in answering this letter—"The most noteworthy contribution to the philosophy of American history, I think, that has yet been made, with the possible exception of the Education of Henry Adams"—must have brought surprise and some amusement. Beard continued: "Your letter gave me one decided regret. I wish that some wise rich man or wise college president (if such there be) had, in 1895 when you first drafted these lectures, emancipated you from all routine work, freed your powers, and given you unlimited mechanical service, and permitted you to devote your talents to the theme of your book. If that had been done we should now have at least one great historical work in America lifted above 'was uns alle bändigt, das Gemeine.' Grateful as I am for all the good work you have done in many fields I shall not cease to deplore the diversion of your energies from the grand topic of the American revolution" (Beard to Jameson, Aug. 14, 1926).

[72] William Beer (1849-1927), librarian of the Howard Memorial Library, New Orleans, since 1891.

[73] The Lafittes, Pierre and Jean, were notorious Louisiana pirates. Jean, the younger, was pardoned by Madison because of his aid to Jackson in New Orleans but turned pirate again and for a time had headquarters near Galveston. Eventually he left this country for South America.

[74] Caroline Hazard, whose home was Peace Dale, R. I., where Jameson visited when he taught in Brown, served for ten years as president of Wellesley College, but was probably better known as the author of many essays, poems, and biographical works. The suggestion here made she never acted upon.

[75] Foster, Ellis, and Robert Cunliffe, a Liverpool firm, shipped slaves to Virginia and South Carolina and it was therefore thought that the papers of their agent in Maryland might illuminate the Maryland trade in slaves. See *Documents illustrative of the history of the slave trade to America* 4: 303, n. 1.

But absolutely all the trade shown in the letters is export of tobacco from Maryland, and import and sale of all sorts of manufactured goods from Liverpool. It seems that in one letter, which I did not find (some of the letter-books being fragmentary) he must have suggested to them the importation of slaves, for in a letter of October 2, 1750, he mentions the arrival of the *Cunliffe* without one slave, "If we had the slaves as I told you in my last we should have managed better." It may be that there was slave trading in the years 1752-1759, for which there is a gap. From 1759 on he was settled at another place, Townside on the Chester River in Queen Anne County, but his connection with the Liverpool firm ended about then, and from that time on his affairs became increasingly involved, and his letters are wails of despair. I judge that he was even reduced in his old age to the dreadful business of teaching, for there are lists of pupils in Queen Anne County from 1784 to 1789, apparently in his handwriting, but just falling short of the year when my Queen Anne County great grandmother ought to have begun going to school, preparatory to her migration to Woburn.

"An inventory of sundry merchandize the property of Foster Cunliffe and Sons Esq. in Store at Oxford taken 12th October 1756" shows an enormous variety of articles, as many as there are in the general store at Head Tide, Maine, and valued in the total at about £3000.

I went over to attend the semi-centennial of the Johns Hopkins University, in my capacity as a "spared monument," who went there in 1880, and was the first to get the doctor's degree in history. There was a reunion of former members of each department. I did not find that of history as interesting as I had expected, but greatly enjoyed seeing quite a little of Woodburn.[76] There was a departmental dinner at the house of Professor Latané, to which I was invited by the three professors, but I was unfortunately unable to go to that house.

Off to Ithaca Wednesday. The Cornell people are trying an experiment this year of having certain ones come and talk for two or three days to the students of American history and with the teachers. I shall of course enjoy going there, and staying with Burr at the Telluride House.

To CHESTER P. HIGBY

December 13, 1926.

My dear Mr. Higby:[77]

If a journal of Modern European History should be founded in America, under good auspices (as would be likely to be the case if it were founded at all), you may be sure that I should gladly help it in whatever ways I could. To the question, however, whether it is best now to attempt to establish one, I should think it difficult to reply with any security. That is to say, that I find it difficult to judge how successful it could be made to be. If I were to judge of the supply of articles by what comes to me in this office, I should not feel able to make a very encouraging estimate. It is true that, taking all fields together, I receive in the course of a year three or four times as many articles as I can use, and I should suppose that in the special field of modern European history the proportion would be about the same; and it is true that I can print in this journal only about fifteen or sixteen articles a year. Seldom however do I find myself obliged on that ground to decline an article that I really wish to print. Sometimes an article is declined because it is too special or technical for a general historical review, and in some such cases it might be an excellent article for a journal specializing in the field of modern European history; but as a rule the articles that are declined seem to me second-rate, or occupied with subjects in which few persons are or ought to be interested or are not at all interesting, or are ill written. In other words, no excess of supply of good articles, which it is a pity not to print, is made manifest in the experience of this office.

I am aware that this does not tell the whole story—that a good many articles might be produced which would not be offered here and might be offered to a new journal of more restricted scope, but I am unable to judge how many there would be. The historical profession in the United States does not seem to me highly productive in the field of modern European history, except in the case of the doctoral dissertation, which is produced in great quantities but under compulsion, a hot-house product intended to meet the early spring market. The interest of older as well as of younger students seems to be confined almost entirely to the Reformation, the French Revolution, and the World War, with the diplomatic preliminaries of the latter. When I have occasion to find a reviewer for an English or French or German book in any other field of modern European history than these three, there are exceedingly few persons upon whom I can call as having paid any attention whatever to the subject. When I first began editing this journal, in 1895, I was surprised to see how many fields there were which no American had made especially his own; in 1926 the surprise is hardly less.

In short, there might be a sufficient supply of excellent material to maintain a good journal now, but I should be inclined to think that it might be better to wait some years more.

I think that I ought to add a warning that the labor of editing such a journal, at any rate if it is edited in so troublesome a manner as the *American Historical*

[76] James A. Woodburn (1856-1943), professor of American history, Indiana University, 1890-1924, when he became professor emeritus; president of the Indiana Historical Society, 1923-1931.

[77] Chester P. Higby from 1923 to 1927 was a member of the department of history of the University of North Carolina; after 1927 he taught in the University of Wisconsin.

Review, is very very great. I have good assistance, but sometimes the weight and amount of editorial work seems more than I can bear. I know of course that many journals are edited lightly and easily—but often they look to me as if they were.

I am afraid I can not cast much light on the general question. How well such a journal would prosper is a matter of prophecy which, we are often told, is not the province of the historical worker.[78]

To MARCUS W. JERNEGAN

December 22, 1926.

Dear Jernegan:

For reasons given in another letter, I have not been able to prepare any full answer to your inquiries, and what I briefly write now may not reach you in season to be of any possible use. I will however say one or two things that come uppermost in my mind.

In the first place, I should hope that any report made will not give the impression that the main business of the young men under consideration is to produce historical print.[79] Nearly all of them hold teaching positions, and the main business of a teacher is to teach. It is true that most teachers of history can not keep themselves thoroughly alive if they do nothing else than to teach their classes and make the necessary preparations. But many excellent scholars and cultivated persons keep themselves thoroughly alive by reading—the reading of things that they don't positively have to read in order to confront their classes—without proceeding to print results of reading. That may answer all purposes, *provided* the man has learned how to conduct a prolonged investigation and write a book, and could do it well if he chose.

As to why Ph.D.'s do not produce more historical matter subsequent to the doctoral dissertation, many reasons will have been given to you, and the reasons which young men allege in their own cases will be much more to your purpose than the reasons which old men imagine may have been the prevalent ones. However, I will say that there is one on which I myself should think that a good deal of stress should be laid, and which may not have been mentioned by everyone else. Namely, I am convinced that most universities make too formidable a job of the doctoral dissertation, and that therefore a good many young men, wearied by the magnitude of the effort and disheartened by its expense, have little courage to tackle anything more. Is it not true that the dissertation usually takes a year

of a young man's time? I think that that is too much —too much in proportion to the value of the dissertation-work to the young man's preparation for his career. He can learn those arts of continuous research and methodical construction and composition, which it is of course necessary for him to learn, quite as well by producing a monograph of a hundred pages as by producing one of six or seven hundred. Often the subjects which result in these enormous tomes are really too big for a beginner, require more maturity.

(I have just gone over, and sent to the printer, this year's List of Doctoral Dissertations. I always feel like expressing disapproval of many of them as ill-adapted to their purpose, but I never do). It seems possible if a young man began with a small publication, treating a very limited subject, that he would feel more encouraged to go on later to produce something larger in that field or in some other field.

Forty years ago, as I can well remember, doctoral dissertations were not so formidable. They were of about the size current in German universities. Now, we have advanced to the size of the French or Russian theses, but we have not done so because we have removed the doctorate to a higher grade of advancement, some ten years after the baccalaureate, as in the French or Russian case, but, I fear, because the unhallowed competitive ambitions of universities have drawn them into a desire to produce bigger dissertations than their competitors—"the world's biggest theses." However, this is merely one suggestion, and may be the fruit of imagination, where the returns you get from the young men themselves will give you the facts.

To ALBERT BUSHNELL HART

January 14, 1927.

Dear Hart:

I am glad to know, from your note, that the historical interests centering around the proposed celebration of 1932 have been put in your hands; none could be better. I shall be glad to co-operate with you in any way that occurs to you. At any rate, when next you come to Washington, consider yourself engaged to me for luncheon at the least, and for as much more of your time as you can give.

The list in the *Evening Star* of the seventeen or eighteen proposals submitted to your Commission was not impressive;[80] most of those who sent them in were

---

[78] The *Journal of Modern History* was established in 1927. From 1935 to 1938 it was edited by Mr. Higby.

[79] See Marcus W. Jernegan, Productivity of doctors of philosophy in history, *Amer. Hist. Rev.* **33**: 1-22, Oct., 1927; for a summary of the report see *ibid.* **32**: 433-435, Apr., 1927. Jernegan was chairman of a committee to draw up a program for research and publication, the other members of which were D. C. Munro, C. J. H. Hayes, A. M. Schlesinger, and W. K. Boyd.

[80] The proposals made to the Commission for the Celebration of the 200th anniversary of the birth of George Washington included suggestions for buildings, for memorial highways or parkways, for expositions, and for a history of the city of Washington. Hart, the historian of the commission, submitted a group of proposals, all intended to illuminate the life and character of Washington, and in a meeting of the commission advocated the publication of Washington's letters, as offering the best revelation of the man. Jameson's suggestions are to be found in his letter to Senator Fess, Mar. 17, 1925. For the list of suggestions, see Washington *Star*, Jan. 13, 1927, pp. 1-2.

obviously thinking less about any real commemoration of Washington than about ways of getting government money to spend for desirable objects—desirable to themselves or to the automobile industry. I have never been able to see any close connection between the "Lincoln Highway" and Abraham Lincoln, but am quite clear about its relation to the industry named. I had the vanity to think that hardly any proposals except Charles Moore's and mine would do anything toward commemorating, in a literal sense, our "Leading Man"; anyhow, all that *I* am interested in are things that will bring back to people's minds the actual character, personality, and career of that wonderful man. When I was a boy, the obvious chief American hero was George Washington, or if there were two, Washington and Lincoln. To the boys (and most older persons) of the present day it is all Lincoln. The dignified eighteenth-century gentleman is a character that makes much less appeal to their minds than the prairie democrat. That rather afflicts me. I wish every member of your Commission could be made to read the splendid passages about him in Lowell's "Under the Old Elm." When we think of Mirabeau, Gambetta, Bolivar, Lenin, what an incomparable benefit it has been to this republic to have such a figure at its origins! And then it is proposed, as the best way of commemorating him, to erect in Washington forty-eight state buildings, every one made by a different architect, chosen by the respective governors! But I am beginning to preach, and had better stop. Extract from the situation the best you can.

It was good to have a talk with you.

To Max Farrand

February 23, 1927.

Dear Farrand:

This is magnificent news, which you give in your letter of February 21. I do not think that there is anyone in the country who could be more gratified by it than I am, for it is one among several signs, but is the largest and most potent of all, that the United States is somewhat waking up to the importance of research in the humanities.[81] Moreover, it opens the way along just the lines that I have long believed to be most hopeful. In the great mass of comment and discussion excited this autumn and at the Rochester meeting by Jernegan's questionnaire and report on the reasons why Ph.D.'s do not go forward into further research, it was universally assumed that a great deal of historical research ought to be carried on in America, but it was almost universally assumed that universities and colleges were the natural place in which it should go forward and university and college teachers the natural persons to carry it on. I remember one of the innumerable discourses of President Butler in which it

was argued that universities furnished the ideal soil for research to grow in. My belief is quite different. Let university professors conduct all the research they can, and let universities encourage research, lest otherwise it be not done, but their main business is to teach, and often the only way in which they can carry on this habit of giving professors years of absence for research is by withdrawing the best minds from that contact of teacher with student for which alone universities and colleges were founded. I think that, at any rate in the field of history, institutions of research, which can reflect deliberately as to what is most needed for the progress of history, and can get it carried out by the best human instruments for each task, have a much better chance of securing results that are worth while than the relegating of research to the occasional leisures and casual choices of professors, who choose a line of research merely because it interests them individually, and are not likely either individually or collectively to proceed *programmartig* [*programmässig?*] the only way in which, in most lines of endeavor, highly fruitful advances are made.

Therefore I very greatly rejoice in the creation of an institution for research in history and other human subjects which will have, I hope, much larger resources than this Department of mine has, and will not be, as this has—though it has been very well treated—a lone human department in a group of departments otherwise devoted to the physical sciences, so that it is always in danger of being treated *stiefmütterlich* in the future.

Well, Heaven be with you, and if there is any way in which I can help, I shall always be glad to do so. Whatever there is of the journalist in the editor of the *American Historical Review* would enjoy proclaiming the glad tidings, but I suppose that an old-fashioned three-decker quarterly like this has no business with journalistic scoops, and I shall be content if you will send me, when the time arrives for publicity, whatever statement you can then make. The Ides of March will be about the last date for the April number, those of June about the last for the July number; meanwhile I shall hold your letter strictly confidential. . . .

To Roscoe R. Hill

March 1, 1927.

My dear Hill:

I hope that the automatic card thanking you for your review of that book on the viceroys was duly sent and duly reached you.[82] I was also grateful for your informing letter about the situation in Nicaragua.[83] The

---

[81] The news was that of Farrand's appointment to the Huntington Library.

[82] Hill's review of *Viceregal administration in the Spanish-American colonies*, by Lillian Estelle Fisher, appeared in the *Amer. Hist. Rev.* 32: 673-674, Apr., 1927.

[83] On Jan. 14, 1927, Mr. Hill wrote that General Chamorro had left the country and that American marines were guarding the legation in Managua but that two governments were still claiming control, one at Managua and one on the east coast. See *ante*, Feb. 9, 1926, n. 55.

members of the staff here were much interested in it. I told them of course that they should not quote you. It is not of much use for me to say much in reply on that topic, for the situation may have changed rapidly before this reaches you. One event which will occur in the meantime will certainly be an improvement, namely, the adjournment of Congress. Of the two semi-hostile camps in this town, the executive and the legislative, I almost always side with the former. The Department of State may often not manage rightly— it is hard for an outsider to judge—but I am well convinced that most of the Senators have no such knowledge of foreign countries as would invest their opinions with any great weight. Senator Borah's astonishing proposal that he and his committee should go down to Mexico and Guatemala in the recess and see for themselves what the facts are has very rightly been pushed aside.[84] No Senator ever comes back from a foreign country having seen anything that changed his mind. He knows it all before he goes, and sees only confirmation of the wisdom he has already expressed, can not afford as a Senator to take back anything he has ever said, and is merely more dogmatic and conceited than ever. Borah's next move, of direct correspondence with Calles,[85] is really a violation of the Logan Act,[86] but I do not expect to see him "punished by a fine of not more than $5000, and by imprisonment during a term not less than six months or more than three years," for while he has of course carried on this correspondence "with an intent to influence the measures or conduct of a foreign government in relation to disputes or controversies with the United States" he would of course deny that he had any other intention than to

find out the truth. But the Senate is a strange institution. A system of procedure that gave us William J. Stone,[87] of Missouri, for chairman of the Senate Committee on Foreign Relations at the time when we entered into the war with Germany, or which gives us Borah now in that position, is one of the strangest governmental devices in history. I wish Mr. Kellogg had John Hay's sharp tongue, or Elihu Root's adroitness in putting those fellows in their places.[88]

I hasten to say that I do not profess to know whether the administration is doing rightly or wrongly in the matter of either Nicaragua or Mexico. I only mean to say that it is always far more probable that the Senate is making blunders than that the Department of State is. . . .

To JOSEPH SCHAFER

June 23, 1927.

My dear Schafer:

I did indeed prepare the bibliography which accompanies President Gilman's *James Monroe*, but did almost nothing else.[89] Not a sentence of the text, I think, was written by me. When President Gilman had finished it, he wanted some young person to check it in respect to names and dates and such details, also mentioning any suggestions that might occur to him. I did that, and only that. Though he paid me for the service, he was so good as to mention in the preface the aid that I had given, saying that it sometimes was not done in such cases, but that he thought it was right to do it. In fact it seldom was or is done, and it was very decent of him to do it, and his reward has been that, as I have often had occasion to see, many persons have supposed that I did a large part, or most of the work, but that he after the manner of men, minimized the obligation.

To HERBERT PUTNAM

North Edgecomb, Maine,
July 26, 1927.

My dear Dr. Putnam:

. . . Schlesinger is a man of great ability, a man of thought, one fertile in suggestions, and of excellent judgment. I do not know him so intimately that I could declare him ideally fitted for the work in every particular, but I should think he would conduct it in general exceedingly well.[90] He would be persona grata

---

[84] William E. Borah (1865-1940), Senator from Idaho, 1907-1940.

[85] Plutarco Elías Calles, President of Mexico, 1924-1928. Seldom has there been greater friction between this country and Mexico than in the years 1925-1927, American investors feeling that their interests were threatened by the petroleum and the alien lands acts passed in December, 1925, to go into effect on Jan. 1, 1927. Under the first of these, Mexico declared sub-soil deposits inalienable; under the second, no foreigner might own land within one hundred kilometers of the border and no foreign corporation might own a majority of the stock of any Mexican corporation. The promise of President Calles that the laws would be so administered as to work no injury to the United States was discounted by those concerned.

A second cause of friction was the fact that Mexico was supporting the revolutionaries of Nicaragua under Sacasa, while the United States recognized Diaz as legitimate head of the government. A group of Senators joined with Borah in active opposition to the policy of the Department of State toward Mexico and Nicaragua. In the autumn of 1927 Dwight Morrow was sent as ambassador to Mexico and the friction subsided both between the United States and Mexico and between the Executive and the Senate.

[86] When, in 1798 the Philadelphia Quaker, Dr. George Logan, convinced that he could settle all matters of dispute between the United States and France, visited Paris, the Congress passed an act (Jan. 30, 1799) providing fine and imprisonment for any person who should in future attempt such unofficial negotiations.

[87] William J. Stone (1848-1918), member of the House, 1885-1891, Senator, 1903-1918, a mid-western isolationist.

[88] Frank B. Kellogg (1856-1937), Secretary of State, 1925-1929; John Hay (1838-1905), served in that position from 1898 to 1905; Elihu Root, from 1905 to January, 1909.

[89] See *ante*, Nov. 5, 1882, n. 34.

[90] Jameson was writing of Professor Schlesinger as a possible chief of the Division of Manuscripts of the Library of Congress, a position which he himself had previously declined but which he was to accept a few months later.

with the profession. In the work of collecting, especially in the rich field of the South, a Southern gentleman like U. B. Phillips [91] would have certain advantages, might be more pleasing to dowagers and maiden aunts, for instance, but his range of thought is perhaps not so wide, his judgment not so secure. Ford, whose niece he married, would tell candidly all about him. He is very clever and likeable, and writes very well. Had you thought at all of R. D. W. Connor of N. C. Univ.? Of men now in the South (a freer field for your collecting than any other) I should think him much the best. He has had much and successful experience in work like that of your Manuscripts Division, has had excellent connections (at any rate a wise and influential father),[92] is I believe very much liked, knows the professorial business too (for I suppose he has been nearly ten years in the University, after I suppose some ten years as secretary of the N. C. Historical Commission), and has also some of that facility in public speaking which Hunt had—if that would be an asset. Leland knows him better than I do. He could be more easily detached from his university than a Harvard professor, I imagine. You ask as to how that would be with Schlesinger. I don't know at all. I should think most likely he would not consent; but he would be worth trying for. . . .

To YASAKA TAKAGI

October 1, 1927.

My dear Takagi:

I have just been writing to Professor Fukuda about the volumes of the *Memorials of Naibu Kanda* which he was kind enough to send to me, and about the presentation of two of them to President Coolidge.[93] When I first received the volumes, the President had just come back to Washington from a vacation in the Far West, but I received an opportunity for an interview with him a few days ago, and presented the two volumes in person. He received them with much pleasure and interest, looked them over with some care, asked questions about some of the pictures, and subsequently sent me a letter of thanks, which I am transmitting to Professor Fukuda. You will be interested to know that one of the questions he asked was, as he looked at the picture of the Class of 1879 taken at the time of our graduation, "Who is the man in the front row, with a beard"? I was particularly pleased to tell him that that was George Sherman, a classmate whom you perhaps will not remember, but who was Mr. Coolidge's teacher for three years in Ludlow Academy, near his birthplace in Vermont, a modest man, who has led a very inconspicuous life, but an excellent teacher and a man of the highest character, of whom I have understood that he had a good deal of influence upon the President when he was from fifteen to seventeen, and for whom the President entertains a high regard. Immediately after that, my classmate Hardy,[94] whom you will remember as living at Amherst, was a teacher of the future President for one year.

But let me say a little more about the book, which I have been reading with extreme pleasure. Besides being in itself a good book, it is of particular interest to one who for four years, fifty years ago, shared almost every day of your father's life. It has also done me a great deal of good to read the narratives of the subsequent years, to see how much your father did for the benefit of his country, how noble a character he always manifested, and how strongly his high example of faithfulness and public spirit influenced those around him. It is a fine record, of which I am sure that you and your mother and your brothers and sisters (to all of them please commend me most heartily) have reason to be very proud. Alas, that such spirits can not dwell among us always, but you and your associates have made sure that your father's life will continue to be remembered and to be an influence on the subsequent generations. . . .

To WALTER M. GILBERT

October 6, 1927.

Dear Mr. Gilbert: [95]

Referring to your letter of September 30, and to that of Mr. Clyde Furst [96] dated September 29, I should not think it desirable for the Carnegie Institution to publish the proposed Franklin volume, or to take any part in doing so. Books composed in that manner will, I should think, always have a sufficient market without being subsidized.

I also do not think that the publication of such a volume would be creditable to the Carnegie Institution. The table of contents is made up on the assumption that one will get authoritative accounts of each of Franklin's many aspects by confiding the treatment of each to some man who, in the public eye, will seem to represent that speciality, *e.g.*, "America's First Great

---

[91] Ulrich B. Phillips (1877-1934), at this time professor of history in the University of Michigan, which he was soon to leave for Yale.

[92] R. D. W. Connor's father was Henry Groves Connor (1852-1924), appointed by President Taft as a federal district judge. For an account of his personality and of his work see the *Dictionary of American Biography*. The son became the first archivist of the United States on recommendation of a committee of historians headed by Dr. Jameson.

[93] In response to a request from Baron Kanda's family, transmitted to President Coolidge by Jameson, the President, as a graduate of Amherst, had written the preface to this volume.

[94] Audubon L. Hardy, who as a teacher in St. Johnsbury Academy signed Mr. Coolidge's certificate for admission to Amherst College.

[95] Walter M. Gilbert, administrative secretary of the Carnegie Institution of Washington.

[96] Clyde B. Furst, lecturer in Columbia University and author of works on education. His plan for a book on Franklin was not carried out.

Humorist," to be written by the president of the American Press Humorists, "America's First Cartoonist," by some one representing the Cartoonists of America, "Our First Great Athlete," by the president of the Amateur Athletic Union, "Father of Daylight Saving," by the president of the National Daylight Saving Association, and the like. Any such assumption is however fallacious. The public may think that good contributions would be got in this way, and therefore, as I have indicated, such a table of contents will sell the book, as it is intended to do, but while some of the contributions will be excellent, most will be worthless. I feel confident that the Carnegie Institution ought to have nothing to do with the project. I return the enclosures of your letter.

To ROBERT B. MOWAT

October 18, 1927.

My dear Mr. Mowat:

What is proposed in your letter of October 3 is certainly a matter of great interest.[97] I wish that I could cast more effective and useful light on your question than I fear would be possible on the part of one who is not in any sense a specialist in modern European history. I will however tell you now what I think. In two days I am going up to New England, by way of Philadelphia, Princeton, and New York, and may find opportunities to consult persons much more expert, and more occupied with the work of teaching.

My immediate thought is that you exaggerate the competence of the American historical scholars in the wide field of modern European history. Especially do I think this is true of the period between 1550 and the French Revolution. We have a few excellent students of the period of the Reformation, but very few of our scholars have made any deep study of all the period from 1550 to 1789. I do not think that they have a great deal that is valuable to add to what is in the vols. III.-VI. of the *Cambridge Modern History,* if indeed to vols. I. and II.

I believe that the Americans, if they were minded to combine for the purpose, could make a very respectable, large treatment of the period of European history beginning in 1789, but I do not think it would be so good as the chapters treating the same period in the Cambridge series, except in two particulars; the first, that it could be brought more nearly up to date, both in scope and in use of additional materials, and secondly, that the Americans might be expected to treat

of the recent portions of European history with a degree of detachment and impartiality less easily achieved by the members of the large European nations. After all there would, however, be a sufficient number of American chapters to bring out from readers the inquiry, Why America? Why not bring to bear upon these various subjects the thoughts and acquirements of historians in England, France, Germany, and perhaps especially the minor countries, whose historians, other things equal, have some distinct advantages of detached position?

I do not know how largely it would be found possible to secure co-operation on the part of the best men, many of whom have their own dishes cooking or simmering on the stove; but in any case I should believe in a more restricted scope for any such enterprise, both as to period and as to the number of volumes. I will not fail however to consult other members of the American Historical Association. It would not be of much good in bringing it before the American Historical Association as a body, but perhaps there will be some possibility that it may be canvassed among those who have come especially to take part in the session devoted to Modern European History.[98]

To THE COUNCIL OF THE AMERICAN HISTORICAL ASSOCIATION AND BOARD OF EDITORS OF THE *American Historical Review*

November 9, 1927.

Dear Mr. Taylor:[99]

In view of the meeting of the Executive Council of the American Historical Association on November 18, and as much in advance as I possibly could, I am sending this circular letter to the members of the Council and of the Board of Editors of the "American Historical Review," to mention that I have this day resigned my position as Director of this Department of the Carnegie Institution of Washington. I should wish that the communication should be regarded as confidential until November 20.

A few weeks ago it became known to me that, whereas I had supposed I could continue my present work as long as I was fit for it, it was the intention of President Merriam that I should be retired at the age of seventy (September, 1929). It is evidently also his intention that no successor shall be appointed; that the present workers in the Department shall be allowed to finish their present tasks, some general supervision being nominally exercised by Dr. A. V. Kidder, who was appointed last spring "Associate in Early American

---

[97] Robert B. Mowat of Corpus Christi College, Oxford, had written of a plan which he had been considering since 1925-1926, when he taught in the University of Wisconsin. This was for an *American Modern History* comparable to the *Cambridge Modern History* which he argued was sadly out of date. The appropriate agent for achieving such a cooperative project was, he believed, the American Historical Association, and he wished Jameson to bring the idea to the Association for discussion.

[98] Jameson collected opinions from Henry E. Bourne, Sidney B. Fay, Carlton Hayes, William E. Lingelbach and Bernadotte E. Schmitt. Of these only Hayes and Schmitt evinced enthusiasm for the enterprise.

[99] Henry O. Taylor was president of the American Historical Association, in 1927 and therefore the presiding officer of the council for the year.

History," meaning archaeology of the Southwest, Mexico, and Central America; but that no further work in United States history shall be undertaken.

While I was meditating upon these provisions for dissolving the Department to which I have given twenty-two years of labor, Dr. Herbert Putnam, a few days ago, offered me the chair of history at the Library of Congress for which funds have been given to the new Library of Congress Trust Fund.[100] This means that I should be able, until I was seventy-four, to continue work of somewhat the same sort as I have been doing, to continue close relations with the members of the historical profession, who have so heartily supported my past endeavors, and perhaps to do some useful things not yet attempted, Dr. Putnam offering all needful latitude for developing the new office.

In view of these prospects, and of the limited duration of any prospects in the present direction, I have thought that I had no alternative but to accept Dr. Putnam's very gratifying offer, and I have done so. I have proposed that my resignation from the service of the Carnegie Institution, and my assumption of the new duties, should take place at some time between April 1 and July 1 next.

In coming to this decision I have kept in mind, as intently as I could, the interests of the American Historical Association, but whatever results will come to them would anyhow have come in less than two years from now. The one portion of my professional estate at 1140 Woodward Building on which the Association will necessarily have to administer is the "American Historical Review." My tenure of the office of Managing Editor must end when I leave the service of the Institution. By this letter I offer my resignation of that office, either to the Council, or to the board of Editors that chose me in 1895 and in 1905, whichever may now be considered the proper legal form. It is certain that the Carnegie Institution, which has hitherto aided the Review by permitting myself and others to do its editing, will not continue to do so after 1928. I am sorry to precipitate upon the Council the problem of the Review's future, but I see no help for this, for apparently it ought to be considered at the approaching meeting.

In conclusion, I give my hearty thanks to the members of the Council and of the Board of Editors, as representatives of the whole historical profession, for the cordial support they have always given to my various efforts to serve that profession.

To FREDERICK J. TURNER
                                            November 25, 1927.
Dear Turner:

I thank you very cordially for your warm and friendly letter. I have needed all that I have received

of such letters, for the situation has been very afflicting. However, the president and his executive committee (apparently the other trustees have known nothing of these plans) have the power to do as they see fit, and I can do nothing but to thank Fortune and Putnam for giving me further opportunities to go on with work not wholly dissimilar.

Much as I am oppressed by reflections and apprehensions as to the fate of this Department and of these good friends who will remain in it, I try to think from time to time about my future work. After a little, I shall be able to think of it with more spirit. You, with your fertile mind, ought to be able to make good suggestions. Please do. I realize the truth of what you intimate, respecting the desirability of turning more toward the field of social and economic history and doing things that will help the new generation toward such studies. Yet at present whatever thinking I do toward that direction is hampered, apart from my own insufficient equipment in economics, by two considerations. First, one's activities will have to retain a close relation with the materials actually possessed by the Division of Manuscripts (as I suppose Farrand's will with the actual present collections at San Gabriel),[101] and those materials are far more largely appropriate to political than to social or economic history.

In the second place, I have always thought it much more difficult to document, with any sense of security, the social and economic history of the United States than the political or constitutional. You do not have definitely limited bodies of materials, handed down by authority, like statutes or other manageable series, but a vast lot of miscellaneous material from which the historian picks out what he wants, and so the effort to document must often be by a process of selection, and if selection, always open to the suspicion of being a biassed selection, or one made to sustain a set of views. Take for instance Phillips's two volumes in *A Documentary History of American Industrial Society*. If that selection of documents respecting the plantation and slavery was made by a Massachusetts man named Jameson it might be thought to have been selected with one set of prepossessions in mind, if by a Georgian named Phillips it might be thought to have been selected with another set. I please myself with the notion that my plan for Mrs. Catterall's volumes of *Judicial Cases concerning Slavery and the Negro* is inevitably immune from accusation of this sort, because it includes all cases that could be found, but I do not believe this can often be true of schemes for documenting aspects of social history.

I should be glad if, with these two difficulties in mind, and the *Handbook* of the L. of C. in hand, you would make to me any suggestions that occur. Do not however give yourself too much trouble about it, for one of the drawbacks to the future office is that helpfulness

---

[100] William Evarts Benjamin (1859-1940) was the benefactor who provided for a chair of American history.

[101] A reference to Farrand's recent appointment to the Huntington Library.

to the historical profession largely calls for print, and the Lord only knows what amount or varieties of print Congress will sustain. Also, one does not know how much elasticity of mind a man of sixty-eight, belonging to the older generation, can manifest; not very much, I suspect. Not enough to cut him loose from old habits and preoccupations.

Once more I thank you for your cheering words. I am glad to think of you as finding so much pleasure in your present occupation.[102]

AN EDITOR'S FAREWELL

[Feb. 24, 1928.] [103]

'Tis sweet to wield the azure pencil
    O'er manuscripts that come and go;
To seize the good, with hand prehensile,
    And doom the rest to flames below;
    To see that A shall strike no blow
Below the belt, reviewing B,
    Nor Y shall vex the soul of X
By caustic words unduly free.

'Tis sweet, in moods of exaltation,
    To read the proof of archive-guides;
To mend defects of punctuation
    A supersensual joy provides—
    To seize the comma where it hides
And see its force aright displayed,
    And swift invoke, with happy stroke,
The modest semi-colon's aid.

'Tis sweet to see historic learning
    Progress among the hoi polloi;
With Rupert Hughes a penny turning
    And Thompson guarding Everyboy
    From Britain's wiles with vocal joy,[104]
It rushes forward with a dash,
    While bold committees, in twenty cities,
Relieve the faithful of their cash.[105]

But sweeter far the friendly kindness
    That lies behind your presence here,
That views my faults with genial blindness,
    And sends me forward full of cheer.
    O golden friends, forever dear,
May all your days and years be bright,
    And younger fry your pulse send high,
As you have quickened mine tonight.

---

[102] Turner was research associate at the Huntington Library from 1927 to 1930.

[103] Read by Dr. Jameson at a dinner given in his honor, in New York, on Feb. 24, 1928.

[104] Rupert Hughes had recently published his biography of Washington; William Hale Thompson, Mayor of Chicago, was fulminating against Great Britain.

[105] A reference to the efforts of the Association to increase its endowment.

To ARTHUR I. ANDREWS

March 5, 1928.

Dear Arthur:

. . . As to members wearing their hats in the Vermont House of Representatives, except while addressing the chair, they must have taken their practice from that of the British House of Commons, either directly or by imitation of some other legislature. If your library contains a copy of the first volume of W. W. Hening's *Statutes at Large of Virginia,* you will find in it under date of about 1658, the rules of order of the Virginian House of Burgesses, in which it is prescribed that members addressing the chair shall rise and take off their hats, upon which Hening says in a foot-note that according to this it must then have been the practice, in the House of Burgesses, for members to sit with their hats on, as was done in the British House of Representatives and now (1809) in the federal House of Representatives in Washington, though the practice has long since been abandoned in the Virginian House of Delegates. I may add that my father told me that when he first visited as a youth the gallery of the Massachusetts House of Representatives the form in which the speaker put the question was, as well as I can remember it, "They that be in the affirmative will rise and stand uncovered until their number is counted," a form implying that once they had worn their hats, though in the time of which he spoke they certainly did not do so, though they preserved the old form of words.

To ELIZABETH DONNAN

March 6, 1928.

Dear Miss Donnan:

. . . I greatly appreciated your coming so far to my obsequies—or perhaps more properly my wake.[106] I was lauded enough to last the rest of my lifetime, but I could not help feeling, as I sat there endeavoring to blush, that all this was hardly fair to the rest of you, to whom no similar turn of fortune may give opportunity to hear their own eulogies pronounced while still alive and able to enjoy them. However, I certainly enjoyed mine. . . .

To WORTHINGTON C. FORD

March 19, 1928.

Dear Ford:

Your list of French edicts, etc., is apparently going to save us many pages of print in Leland's long-awaited Guide to the Materials for American History in Paris Archives.[107] With that in view, could you send me a copy of the last April serial? I seem to have mislaid mine.

---

[106] A reference to the dinner of Feb. 24, 1928.

[107] French edicts on America, *Proc. Mass. Hist. Soc.* 60: 250-304, Apr., 1927.

I regard the compilation as a prize exhibit of your incredible industry. Your mode of employing a bit of leisure reminds me of the opening passage of Walter Bagehot's essay on Lord Brougham, which he begins by quoting the beginning of Tennyson's "Lady Godiva":

"I waited for the train at Coventry
I lounged with grooms and porters on the bridge
And shaped the city's ancient legend thus."

Whereupon Bagehot goes on to say how differently Brougham, with his energy, would have employed an interval between trains at Coventry.[108]

To JOHN B. STETSON, JR.

March 28, 1928

Memorandum concerning Transcripts from Spanish Archives. [109]

1. Inasmuch as the territory of a dozen of our forty-eight states, and more than a fourth of the area of the continental United States, to say nothing of Porto Rico and the Philippines, were once under the dominion of Spain, naturally the Spanish archives are of enormous importance to United States history. Partly because the population of those areas was in the Spanish period not proportionately great, partly because the original Thirteen States were of English origin, the tendency of American historians was for a long time to concentrate attention on materials relating to the history of those states, that were found within their borders or in English archives. Of recent years, however, there has been a great awakening of interest in the history of those parts of the United States that once were under Spanish rule. I do not know of any branch of American history that has made more rapid progress in public attention during the last twenty years. Thereupon it is found that the historical materials preserved within those areas are quite insufficient, and often are fragmentary, and that any

satisfactory treatment of the early history of those regions, from Florida across to California, must be based on materials in Spanish archives. I should think it no exaggeration to say that, as regards their Spanish period, something like nine-tenths of the necessary material is, so far as originals are concerned, in Spain, to one-tenth within the United States,—excepting in so far as transcripts from Spain have already improved the situation.

2. Naturally therefore copies of many documents in the Spanish archives have been sought by those American institutions which try to meet the needs of historical students, but it has been done piecemeal and somewhat haphazard, various institutions seeking various documents, but without that degree of system which would enable the history of the whole period and area to be rightly understood.

3. Yet a right understanding of the history of the Spanish period in Florida, Louisiana, New Mexico, California, and other states is of very great importance, not only to those who live in those states, but to all Americans who wish intelligent knowledge of the remarkable composite called the "American Nation." Many matters of law in those regions can not be rightly understood without fuller knowledge of Spanish organization and administration in earlier years. Many matters concerning land, or the Indians, or mining interests, or trade relations call for better information respecting Spanish procedents. And there is in these masses of documents material for literary productions that will cause better knowledge and appreciation to be spread among our people concerning those elements of Spanish-American character that have entered into the general life of the United States.

4. Moreover, just as it is impossible to understand the history of the Old Thirteen colonies without studying the whole eighteenth-century British Empire, West Indian as well as Continental, so the study of those portions of the present United States that were once under Spain can not be severed from the study of the Spanish empire in America at large. If this is rightly pursued, the thorough study of the history of our formerly Spanish states will inevitably lead to that better appreciation of the development of Spanish-American life and institutions which all of us would desire to foster who wish that relations of cordial good-will should subsist between this nation and the republics to the southward. All that makes for better knowledge of their history makes for better appreciation of their qualities and for happier mutual relations. For example, can anyone name an historian, past or present, who has occupied himself with prolonged study of the history of another nation than his own and has not always been noted thereafter as a cordial friend of the nation whose story he has exploited? I dwell somewhat upon this because I think there is an argument here that may well appeal to Spanish authorities. That cordial appreciation of Spanish life and character should

---

[108] Ford begins his introduction thus: "While awaiting in the *Archives*, Paris, a reply to my request for permission to examine records that could be seen only by special grace of the Ministry from which they came, I called for certain boxes of printed material which required no privilege beyond admission to the Archives, already granted without delay on my application."

[109] This memorandum, called forth by the objections of officials in the Spanish archives to the photographing of documents, was written for the use of John B. Stetson, Jr., son of the founder of Stetson University, Deland, Florida, who expected soon to visit the archives. Stetson was the founder of the Florida State Historical Society, established in 1921 for the purpose of publishing material on Florida history. Jameson, a member of the council of the society, was much interested in its work and was in correspondence with Mrs. Jeannette T. Connor, whose edition of *Colonial records of Spanish Florida*, New Haven, Yale Univ. Press, 1925, was one of the publications of the society, and with Miss Irene Wright, who did much copying in Spain for Mr. Stetson and Mrs. Connor.

prevail among us is of great value to us, first of all, but it is not without its advantage to Spain also, as would be true in any similar case of two countries. Therefore I feel that the liberality and courtesy with which Spain has made her archives accessible to foreign students for a generation past deserves warm appreciation and gratitude, and has done good on both sides of the water; and I hope that such liberality, and the attendant good results, may always continue.

5. Not only is it highly important, for the above reasons, that there should be in one or more American libraries a copious supply of copies of Spanish documents relating to the formerly Spanish portions of the United States, but it is impossible to get the very best supply of such copies otherwise than by some of the photographic processes. I say this on the basis of twenty-three years' experience in the directing of this Department of the Carnegie Institution, during which time a considerable portion of my work has consisted in the making of guides to materials for American history in foreign archives. In those editorial processes I have had to work much with copies—handwritten, typewritten, and photographic—of documents from a wide variety of national and local archives in Europe. There is no comparison between the satisfaction I have had from photographic copies and that which can be got from those made by hand. The best of copyists make mistakes, and the average copyist makes a good many. That is always true, but in the case of materials relating to American history, a European copyist is sure to misread a multitude of proper names, from want of familiarity with American geography and biography, and especially a multitude of those Indian and other early names now disused which can not therefore be found in any books of reference that a Spanish copiest [sic] is likely to have at hand. With handwritten or typewritten transcripts, I have had again and again to write back to Europe to learn whether the word was not perhaps so-and-so, instead of what the copyist made of it, whereas the testimony of the photograph is irrefragable. Moreover, a photograph shows clearly the position of additions, interpolations, postscripts, addresses, subscriptions and the like, and, what is still more important, shows the handwriting, and so may lead to conclusions as to authorship that can not be got otherwise.

6. In some of the recent Spanish discussions, distinction seems to have been attempted between the copying of individual documents and the copying of whole series, but it is difficult to see how such a distinction can be defended and maintained in practice. Some historical facts can indeed be determined by data in a single letter, but others, of a more important order, such as those relating to the whole course of a given policy, can not be determined but by having before the investigator a whole series of despatches, or the like complete body of evidence.

7. I may add that, so far as the experience of this

office is concerned, I have in other European countries had no difficulty, except in one instance, in obtaining photographic or other copies of any series of papers that I have desired. If the Spanish government concludes to deal with the matter of transcripts in a manner different from that pursued by other governments, I shall hope that at least it will be a manner not less liberal.[110]

To Alice Louise McDuffee

April 13, 1928.

My dear Madam:[111]

. . . You ask as to methods by which the Daughters of the American Revolution might further the interests of historical knowledge. There is certainly one method which I should like to see them undertake. I spoke of it years ago to one who was then President-General, but the time was not then ripe. My thought rested upon the principle that, however interesting and stimulating, and valuable often, the essays and monographs and addresses may be which are produced by members of historical and other societies, they are of much more temporary and uncertain value than what are called source-materials for history, the original documents on which histories and monographs must be based; and that, useful as are the scattered individual documents which are often brought out in magazines, the work of the historian is much more furthered by unified collections of related documents, carefully edited, by first-rate scholars. You probably know the series of volumes of *Letters of Members of the Continental Congress,* which under my general supervision have been prepared by my associate Dr. Edmund C. Burnett, and know how those volumes, models of editing, have illuminated the history of that body and thereby of the Revolution. Why should not the Daughters of the American Revolution produce documentary volumes of that sort? The National Society of the Colonial Dames of America, whose Committee on Publication for fifteen or twenty years used me as their historical adviser, did just that, with five different documentary collections, of a volume or two each, and have won for themselves great credit among historical scholars. It would be easy to name half a dozen collections of documentary historical material relating to the Revolutionary War which are

---

[110] On Mar. 22, 1910, Jameson had written a comparable statement on the value of the material in Spain for American history. This time the argument was addressed not to the Spanish government but to those in this country who might foster exploitation of the archives: "I feel able to say with confidence that the greatest mass of unused (I may almost say unexplored) material of genuine importance for American history is in the Spanish archives" (Jameson to John W. Perrin, librarian of the Case Library, Cleveland, Mar. 22, 1910). Much work had been done since 1910 but in Jameson's opinion much still remained to be done.

[111] Miss Alice Louise McDuffee was Historian General of the National Society of the Daughters of the American Revolution from 1926 to 1929.

suffering to be brought out, the publication of which would do more good to the advancement of history than any one volume of essays, however brilliant.[112]

But if you think at all seriously of this, don't let it be started upon without careful deliberation and the application of the best scholarship available. In forty years' occupation with this sort of thing, I have seen many enterprises spoiled by the lack of those two lines of precaution. . . .

To the Earl of Dunmore

28th June, 1928.

My Lord,

It is perhaps known to you that the little "city" (village, in size) of Williamsburg, Virginia, is, on the plans provided by a Virginian organization, to be restored as nearly as possible to the condition in which it stood in the latter part of the eighteenth century. One who has principal charge of the rather grandiose antiquarian plans for this purpose told me lately in Washington that there was much anxiety in their Committee to procure closer and more minute information regarding certain of the public buildings of that time, and asked me to see whether any further details of that nature could be obtained in London.[113] The period which this Committee has in mind for making Williamsburg into a sort of outdoor museum is so nearly that in which your ancestor the fourth Earl was Governor of Virginia,[114] residing at Williamsburg, then the capital, that this has led me to suppose that it might be possible that among his papers, if any such are still preserved, there might be drawings or statements respecting the building called the Governor's Palace, and perhaps respecting those of the College of William and Mary and the House of Burgesses. I therefore venture to address to you this letter, by way of enquiry as to whether such papers survive, and as to whether, by your kindness, I might be permitted to examine them.

At present I am in London only until Saturday morning, when I have to go to Belgium for a week, but by next Friday I shall again be in London for a week, at 4 Montague Street, Russell Square.

I hope that my enquiry may not be a troublesome one.

---

[112] During the years since 1905 Jameson had been frequently called on for advice by the Daughters of the American Revolution but so far as the editors know they had never acted on his suggestions about publishing projects, though when approached by Jameson they had contributed to the support of *Writings on American History* and the *Acts of the Privy Council, Colonial,* and had responded to his request for letters to members of the Congress on the subject of an archive building.

[113] On Mar. 20, 1928, the Rev. W. A. R. Goodwin wrote to Jameson, asking whether he could guide those in charge of the Williamsburg restoration to any plans or descriptions of its colonial buildings. Jameson replied that he knew of nothing not already known in Williamsburg and referred to the drawings which he had discovered in 1912, which had been published in the *Virginia Magazine of History* (see *ante,* to L. G. Tyler, Nov. 1, 1912). This letter, written three months later, seems to indicate that Jameson had again been asked for aid.

[114] James Murray, Earl of Dunmore (1732-1809), appointed Governor of Virginia in 1771. After five stormy years he returned to England in 1776. Jameson's correspondence indicates that ten years before the date of this letter, when the then Earl of Dunmore was visiting in this country Jameson had asked for an interview in order to enquire about his ancestor's papers. It would seem that the interview never took place or Jameson would have known whether any of the papers of the colonial governor had been preserved. No answer to the request of this letter has been discovered.

To Clarence E. Carter

Library of Congress [1]
Division of Manuscripts
September 20, 1928

My dear Dr. Carter: [2]

On arriving in New York I did not immediately come to Washington. I began work here at the Library yesterday, and I did not until then see your letter of August 28. Some uncertainty about its concluding phrase led me to telegraph and inquire as to your arrival.

Your letter raises two questions, one as to the possible future of General Gage's papers, the other as to the copies for your use of what you want from Lord Gage's Collection. [3]

As to the first, the Library of Congress would not wish to compete with Mr. Clements, if he wishes to acquire that collection. His collections of manuscripts relating to the period of the Revolution are of such a character that one could hardly contest the appropriateness of his having also the papers of General Gage, and it might even be maintained that they were more appropriately associated with the papers of Clinton and Germain than with what we have here. Dr. Putnam has, and wishes to maintain, the most cordial relations of co-operation with Mr. Clements. Moreover, we could not compete with him successfully if we desired to do so. It might, however, be useful to learn positively, if we can, whether Mr. Clements does in fact have designs upon this collection. Would you be willing to sound him as to this? In some respects it would be better to have this done by you than from here. If he has no intention of trying to acquire the collection, it is possible that the Library might make an attempt, although, I suppose, not immediately. If you should be willing to do this, I suggest that you should not go beyond something like this:

"For some years I have been preparing an edition of the correspondence of General Thomas Gage. Being now assured of means for its publication when completed, I spent the past summer in London, where, by the kindness of Lord Gage, I had the opportunity to examine all those papers of his ancestor which are in his possession, and am to be allowed to take copies of such documents as I need and have not otherwise obtained. In London, however, it was reported to me that although Lord Gage had no present intention of disposing of these manuscripts, such an event was thought not impossible, and you had shown some inclination toward attempting negotiation for them. If this should be true, and if the manuscripts should come to Ann Arbor, it would obviously be of advantage to my enterprise, if I might be permitted to have further access to them. Would it be indiscreet for me to ask if you have any plans in this direction? If you have not, I suppose it is possible that the Library might be persuaded to make an effort, though I do not think they would wish to do so if you have any desire to add them to the collection at Ann Arbor." [4]

As to copies for your use, the Librarian authorizes me to say that probably an arrangement that would meet your views could be effected, similar to that made in the case of the Haldimand Collection. [5] Something would depend on the relation of what you want to the larger masses which you do not want but which other investigators might wish us to have here; and of course, everything depends on the consent of Lord Gage to the substitution of that process of photographic reproduction for whatever he has consented to in your individual case. I should be glad to have any suggestions from you as to the nature of your permissions and what should be done in the case of the Library; but I suppose

---

[1] From the files of Dr. Clarence E. Carter. As the letter indicates, Dr. Jameson had but recently returned from Europe, where he had acted both for the Department of Historical Research of the Carnegie Institution and for the Division of Manuscripts of the Library of Congress.

[2] Clarence E. Carter, Ph.D., University of Illinois, 1908, was teaching history in Miami University. He had spent a part of the summer of 1928 in England, examining the papers of General Gage.

[3] Dr. Carter's correspondence with Jameson over the Gage letters began in 1906 and continued intermittently for more than twenty years. During these years Jameson aided in locating letters and in obtaining access to collections and procuring copies of material. He also made various suggestions as to means of publication. On Aug. 9, 1928, he had written to Dr. Carter that he had it in mind to see whether Lord Gage would dispose of his papers to the Library of Congress, but was waiting until he had particulars from Carter as to the nature and extent of the collection. He suggested: "You might go so far as to say you wished they were in America, where American students could profit by them, and see what he says" (Files of C. E. Carter).

As a result of his work Professor Carter published *The correspondence of General Thomas Gage with the Secretaries of State, 1763-1775*, 2v., Yale Historical Publications: Manuscripts and Edited Texts, New Haven, Yale Univ. Press, 1931-1933.

[4] The collection was purchased by Mr. Clements from the sixth Viscount Gage in 1930 and was shipped to America in the chests in which Gen. Thomas Gage had stored it. In 1937, with the settlement of the Clements estate, the papers were transferred from his home to the Clements Library in Ann Arbor. See *Guide to the manuscript collections in the William L. Clements Library,* compiled by Howard H. Peckham, 82-100, Ann Arbor, Univ. of Michigan Press, 1942.

[5] The Haldiman collection was one of the first photostated for the Library of Congress by means of the Rockefeller grant.

that any action in the matter will have to wait until you have finished your inventory and can make the Library definite proposals.

Meantime I thank you very much for your full and interesting statement respecting the whole matter. I am sorry that I was not able to remain in London in July until your arrival.

To John C. Merriam

[Oct. 2, 1928].

To the President of the
  Carnegie Institution of Washington: [6]

It seems to me appropriate that I should put on record some report of transactions for the Institution in Europe this past summer, since by date such doings fall outside the limits of my last annual report, for the year ending with June, 1928, and from their nature are not likely to be narrated in any subsequent report made on behalf of the Department by other hands.

I sailed from New York on June 9, and disembarked from the return voyage on September 10. The period spent in Europe was 73 days, from disembarkation at Plymouth on June 18 to embarkation at Copenhagen on August 30. It was understood that part of this time was to be spent in affairs of the Carnegie Institution, part in affairs of the Library of Congress (to whose service I passed, officially or technically, on July 1), part in the needful travel between places involved in these pieces of work, and partly in travel of other sorts, for purposes of my own (and of course at my own expense).

In London I made the necessary arrangements for the photographing, in the Public Record Office, of a number of treaties and parts of treaties concerning America that are needed for Dr. Paullin's continuation of Miss Davenport's work. This photographing has since been effected by Miss Fisher, and the photographs have arrived at the office of the Department.

At the British Museum I carried out a thorough search for manuscript reports of debates concerning America in the British and Irish parliaments, preserved in the manuscript section of the Museum. This was in continuance of a search made in 1912 for such materials coming from the seventeenth century, and will have as its result some valuable additions to the parliamentary materials for the period since 1702, in the perfecting and editing of which Dr. Stock is at present engaged.

In Paris I made arrangements with Mr. Doysié [7]

for the photographing of certain treaties, or parts of treaties, of which the ratified texts are best found in archives of the Ministry of Foreign Affairs. I also made what efforts I could, with the director of those archives and with the American ambassador, toward extending to a later date than the present terminus the permissions to examine and describe those papers of Franco-American diplomacy which are to figure in the second volume of Mr. Leland's *Guide*.

The most important work was that done in the Hague. My annual reports since 1919 have described (in part) the difficulties and delays which have impeded the production of a *Guide to the Materials for American History in Dutch Archives* for which Mr. van Laer took the necessary notes in that year. Those difficulties had by last spring been mostly surmounted, and, by various means and hands, something approaching a complete manuscript had been produced from those notes.[8] But it was to be expected that in nine years such archives would receive many accessions and undergo some changes of classification, and though the late Miss Griffin and I endeavored, by scrutiny of the successive issues of the *Nederlandsch Archievenblad* and the official *Verslagen*, to keep *au courant* of these changes, it seemed indispensable that a careful revision of at least certain sections of the book should be made on the spot, in consultation with the official experts.

At the Rijksarchief this was achieved, with the exception of one section, through the kindness of the director, Dr. R. Fruin, who placed at my disposal the expert aid of Mjfr. S. Drossaers. The exception is that of the section on ecclesiastical archives. For this the proper authority, Dr. L. W. A. M. Lasonder, archivist of the Dutch Reformed Church, was not accessible at the Hague when I sought him, but I encountered him afterward in Norway, and he promised to give the needful revision to this section. At the archives of the House of Orange the archivist, Dr. N. Japikse, personally revised the text relating to that very interesting repository.

I also went through, in the Rijksarchief, a long series of reports from the Dutch ambassadors in London during the earlier part of the eighteenth century, on information that reports of proceedings or debates in Parliament, useful to Dr. Stock's third volume, would be found in them; but this proved not to be the case.

A visit to the Danish Regsarkiv in Copenhagen brought some material for improving one part of our manuscript of a *Guide to the Materials for American History in Scandinavian Archives*, and arrangements were concerted with Professor Waldemar Westergaard for completing the one section still lacking to that manuscript.[9]

Of the International Congress of Historical Sciences at Oslo, August 14-18, at which I was one of the representatives of the Carnegie Institution, there is little

[6] Report of J. F. Jameson covering work for the Department in Europe, in the summer of 1928.

[7] Abel Doysié, principal assistant of Mr. Leland from 1908 in the Paris mission of the Carnegie Institution and joint author of the later volumes of the *Guide*, has had immediate charge, under Mr. Leland's direction, since 1913 of copying American materials for the Library of Congress. See, Report on transcripts of documents from French Archives, by Waldo G. Leland in Report of the Librarian of Congress, 1921, app. IV.

[8] See *ante*, Feb. 13, 1919, n. 208.

[9] See *ante*, Feb. 13, 1919, n. 200

for me to report from the point of view of that institution. I was made president of the American delegation, and as such attended various social functions, and at the final dinner in Bergen was asked to respond on behalf of the Americans and British and did so, but I read no paper. I occupied myself mostly with certain interests of the *American Historical Review,* and with the work of a sub-committee of which I am chairman, formed two years ago by the International Committee of Historical Sciences for the purpose described under C. 3 in my budget proposals of August 15, 1927.[10] Since however the Carnegie Institution did not take up that matter, I judge it to be foreign to the present report.

Of the Congress in its general aspects, interesting to American students of history, I am preparing an account to be printed in the January number of the *American Historical Review,*[11] to which I beg leave to refer, merely saying here that it was very interesting and successful, especially in bringing together once more, in harmonious scientific co-operation and social intercourse, the representatives of lately warring nations. I am grateful to the Institution for the opportunity to be present. . . .

To CHARLES EVANS HUGHES

October 25, 1928.

My dear Mr. Hughes:[12]

The Executive Secretary of the American Council of Learned Societies is asking you to come and speak at the dinner to be given on the evening of November 13 in connection with the publication of the first volume of *The Dictionary of American Biography,* which the Council originated and is sponsoring through a committee of management of which I am chairman. I write to supplement the invitation. I do most earnestly hope that you will find it possible and convenient and agreeable to come and speak on that occasion. Your good wishes and observations on the launching of this important series would do it a great deal of good, and I hope that the occasion will seem to you not unworthy of the effort, and the enterprise itself not undeserving of your commendation and support.

What our committee has aimed to do is to provide

this nation with a biographical dictionary (some twenty large volumes of it) of a quality superior to anything that we have had before—of the same grade as *The Dictionary of National Biography.* I had no difficulty in persuading Mr. Adolph Ochs[13] to subsidize the making of the manuscript to the extent of $500,000.00, that we might enlist the best biographical historical scholars, and get each of the 15,000 biographies prepared by fresh effort from the original sources by the right expert. In Dr. Allen Johnson, formerly professor of American history at Yale, we secured an editor who has proved himself consummate in resourcefulness, energy and good judgment, and I think our first volume will convince you that we have attained the mark at which we aimed. Mr. Ochs's gift to the nation is a magnificent one, and deserves the commemoration we are planning, mostly in his honor. I hope you can come and help us to make it a commemoration of the high quality that we desire. I am sure that if you do so the publishers (Messrs. Charles Scribner's Sons) will be glad to send you an advanced copy of the first volume, that you may see the undertaking in physical form.

To GILBERT CHINARD

November 15, 1928.[14]

My dear Mr. Chinard:[15]

I am trying to organize a series of informal lectures or talks to be given here in the rooms of the Division of Manuscripts on Friday afternoons this winter, at 4:30 p.m., of which the object would be to give to the sixty or seventy persons in Washington who are professionally occupied with history (teachers, graduate students, etc., and some officials) a fuller knowledge of the contents of some of the collections in this rich repository than they can get from a mere *Handbook of Manuscripts.*[16] I wish this limited class of people to know more fully what we have in order that they may use it more largely and more fruitfully.

For instance, after a preliminary lecture which I am to give on the general subject of collections of modern historical manuscripts in some European libraries, Dr. Burnett of the Carnegie Institution, who, I suppose, knows more about the papers of the Continental Congress than anybody else, will give a talk on that collection. Dr. Fitzpatrick has promised me to discourse on

[10] This was a proposal that the department be granted $1200 for work on a list of ambassadors, ministers, and other diplomatic representatives from all governments to all governments, a project discussed in Jameson's letter to Firth of Mar. 19, 1919.

[11] International Historical Congress at Oslo, *Amer. Hist. Rev.* 34: 265-273, Jan., 1929.

[12] Mr. Hughes, at this time member of the Permanent Court of Arbitration at The Hague, was with the law firm of Hughes, Schurman, and Dwight. He wrote in response to this invitation that another engagement prevented him from accepting it.

Jameson assumed his new duties on his return from Europe in the autumn of 1928. From this time on he writes as chief of the Division of Manuscripts of the Library of Congress.

[13] Adolph Ochs (1858-1935) had been publisher and controlling owner of the New York *Times* since 1896.

[14] Division of Manuscripts, Library of Congress.

[15] At this time a member of the Walter Hines Page School of International Relations, and professor of French and comparative literature in the Johns Hopkins University.

[16] A reference to the *Handbook* edited by John C. Fitzpatrick, published in 1918; it was and remains the only basic printed guide to the Library's manuscript collections. These special afternoon lectures were held only during the first winter (1928-1929) of Jameson's term as chief of the Division of Manuscripts.

the Washington collection. Prof. Sioussat agrees about the Polk and Donelson papers.[17]

I write to inquire whether you would be so good as to help in the work of interpretation by giving us a talk about the Jefferson papers, or, if you prefer not to talk about the whole collection, to speak of particular portions or aspects of it.[18] I should be exceedingly obliged. I have not, I regret to say, any way of offering compensation beyond the expenses of the journey from Baltimore over here and back, but, in common with the audience, should be very grateful.

If you are able and willing to do what I request, may I ask whether 4:30 p.m. on Friday, January 4, would be a convenient time for you. If not, some later Friday could be chosen.

To VISCOUNT ASTOR

December 18, 1928.[19]

My Lord: [20]

You will not remember me from so remote a date as 1921, when I had the pleasure of dining at your table on the occasion of the first Anglo-American Conference of Professors of History, but I hope that I am not taking a liberty in writing to you upon a matter which comes before me officially.

A correspondent in Oregon, deeply interested in the early history of that State, writes that he and many others would be much helped by the information which, it would seem, must be contained in the original journal of Astoria, 1811-1813, which is referred to by the late Lord Astor [21] in an article in the Pall Mall Magazine for June 1899. In that article, entitled "John Jacob Astor," the writer says (page 176): "The first incidents of the settlement of Astoria, as graphically set forth day by day in the manuscript journal of its existence *in my possession* were not fortunate."

Of course the great collection of manuscripts, of which I have lately come in charge, embracing the papers of three-fourths of the Presidents and numberless documents of high value for American history, would welcome with greatest warmth the possession of an historical document of so great importance as the original journal of Astoria, but I should scarcely muster the hardihood to ask for it. We are, however, engaged in a large enterprise of reproducing by photostat, at the charge of an ample fund given by the younger Mr. Rockefeller, documents in the public archives of various European countries having a bearing on the history of the United States. For this purpose, we have photostats installed at the Public Record Office and the British Museum and in operation at present, under the general supervision of Professor Samuel F. Bemis, of George Washington University, as director of such work for the Library in Europe. I am enclosing this letter to him and beg to inquire through him whether you would be willing to have the manuscript of which I have spoken carried to the Museum or Public Record Office for photographic reproduction.

An access of hardihood as I write emboldens me to say frankly that if you *could* be prevailed upon to transfer this journal from your archives to the Library of Congress, where all history scholars could profit by it, it would be extremely gratifying; but, of course, it may be an integral part of a record that you would not wish to disrupt.[22]

To CHARLES M. ANDREWS

December 22, 1928.[23]

Dear Andrews: [24]

Your letter of December 6 [25] has been sent up to me for fuller reply but that reply could not be made at once, or until some inquiries and searches had been made.

The present instructions to Stevens and Brown require them to finish certain series on which they are now engaged, after which their work for us ceases, in view of the substitution of the photostat processes to which the Librarian's letter of December 8th refers. It does not appear that any of the work done by Stevens and Brown, except a very little about Guade-

[17] Edmund C. Burnett was then editing *Letters of members of the Continental Congress,* 8v., Washington, D. C., Carnegie Institution, 1921-1936. John C. Fitzpatrick, assistant chief of the Division of Manuscripts, 1902-1928, had recently resigned to devote his full time to editing the bicentennial edition of the *Writings of George Washington,* 39v., Washington, D. C., GPO, 1931-1944. St. George L. Sioussat, Ph.D., Johns Hopkins University, 1899, was then professor of American history in the University of Pennsylvania; he succeeded Jameson as chief of the Division of Manuscripts.

[18] Chinard had already published *Jefferson et les idéologues,* Baltimore, Johns Hopkins Press, 1925, *The Literary Bible of Thomas Jefferson,* Baltimore, Johns Hopkins Press, 1928, *Thomas Jefferson, the apostle of Americanism,* Boston, Little Brown & Co., 1929, and had edited *The commonplace book of Thomas Jefferson,* Baltimore, Johns Hopkins Press, 1926. His edition of *The letters of Jefferson and Du Pont de Nemours* appeared in 1931.

[19] Division of Manuscripts, Library of Congress; enclosed in Jameson's letter of the same date to Samuel Flagg Bemis, director of the European mission of the Library of Congress.

[20] William Waldorf Astor, 2nd Viscount Astor (1879-1952).

[21] William Waldorf Astor, 1st Viscount Astor (1848-1919), became proprietor of the *Pall Mall Gazette* in 1893, and afterwards started the *Pall Mall Magazine.*

[22] The Library of Congress failed to acquire either the original manuscript or a photostat of the Astoria journal.

[23] Division of Manuscripts, Library of Congress.

[24] As early as 1905 Andrews and Herbert L. Osgood had defined the pattern for the Library's copying program in England. The chief direction of this work was in Andrews' hands, and was carried on in conjunction with his preparation of the Carnegie *Guides* until he resigned as Library advisor in 1915. Actual transcription was done by the London firm of B. F. Stevens & Brown. Andrews always remained available for consultation, and in 1923 provided the Library with a plan for further work in England (see p. 93, n. 8, and p. 114, n. 56).

[25] Andrews had inquired about the extent of copying of West Indian materials in the Public Record Office.

loupe, has gone in to the West Indian classes of C.O.,[26] which I suppose is what you refer to.   As to the series which is progressing under the present policy of photostat reproductions, that was all placed sixteen months ago in the hands of Professor Samuel F. Bemis,[27] of George Washington University, who has general charge of all the operations under the great fund for photostatting which has been presented to the Library.   It is left to Bemis' discretion which materials shall in each country be subjected to the photostat.   What has been received from him thus far does not embrace West Indian materials, although, of course, we are far from having received yet all that has thus far been done in London, for the transmitting takes time.

To answer your question, I should say that the document of 1923, to which you allude, has been and is being observed as general doctrine.   But this "Outline of Plan" is not sufficiently specific to have been sent to Stevens and Brown, or anybody, as adequate instructions for copy.[28]   Those instructions have had to be made specific, taking up one class or group after another.   The West Indian classes have apparently not been tackled yet.   I think they should be, agreeing with you that students of the history of the old British Empire need to have them.   However, they do not need to have everything that is in them.   A selection must be made, and on the whole a less ample selection than in the case of the Mainland Colonies.   If you have any suggestions as to what things in these West Indian classes of C.O. most certainly require to be copied, we should be glad to have them.

One of the assistants has made the enclosed memorandum of West Indian material in the recently acquired transcripts and facsimiles from England. I send it as possibly of use to you.

If you have before you a copy of the "Outline of Plan" made in 1923, I would like to ask you what is meant by Section IV.[29]   I do not find that such calendars have been made as are there referred to, and I should think that to make calendars of all the docu-

ments, or even of all significant documents, relating to the American Colonies in all the series that you name would be a work of many years by a number of experienced workers, and would cost several scores of thousands of dollars.   I should fear that the best we could do, with the means at our disposal, would be to let our supervisor of work in the Public Record Office pick out for the photostat operator what ought to be copied, and accompany the copy with index cards when they are transmitted to the Library.   This is the course which is now being followed.   Of late, work has lain mostly in F.O. 4, 5, and 115.[30]

Do not think that I have forgotten or neglected your very kind personal letter.   It did my heart good, but I have wished to send in reply some non-mechanical letter, not dictated, possibly A.L.S., but I am so burdened with work that I seem never to get a chance for anything of that sort.

To FRANCE V. SCHOLES

January 22, 1929.[31]

My dear Mr. Scholes: [32]

This is [a] much belated reply to your letter of December 14 about the proposed bibliography,[33] but various journeys have made it difficult to keep up with correspondence, especially in cases where one had to think things over, and certainly one should do that in the case of a plan of such large dimensions as that which you suggest.

I know little of the bibliography of New Mexican history; but, assuming the type of bibliography which you seem to have in mind, I should think that the schedule you set forth presented little to criticize, except the magnitude of the task.   That is, however, a very serious consideration.   It is ordinarily not wise for a young man to enter upon any plan that will take more than five years for its completion, because changes of circumstances arise, help that one hopes to get from others usually fails, in whole or in part, and then one is disappointed, achieving a fragment, which does not look impressive when one has put forth so much larger a total.

There is one reason why I might question, not the details of your scheme, but its general type.   One must ask the question, why is one making a bibliography. Is it to satisfy bibliographers, and their ideal of bibli-

---

[26] Colonial Office series, Public Record Office, London.

[27] Samuel Flagg Bemis, Ph.D., Harvard, 1916, then professor of history in George Washington University, now Sterling professor of diplomatic history in Yale, initiated and directed, 1927-1929, Project A of the Library of Congress, subventioned by John D. Rockefeller, Jr., for continuing and expanding the copying of American materials in European depositories.

[28] Andrews's "Outline of Plan for Making Transcripts from British Archives" was dated Feb. 7, 1923; a copy was enclosed in the letter of Charles Moore to Jameson, Feb. 24, 1923 (Division of Manuscripts, Library of Congress). This plan included the transcription of British West Indian materials in the Public Record Office through the year 1783.

[29] Section IV concerned colonial documents not listed in B. F. Stevens's Catalogue index of manuscripts in the archives of England, France, Holland, and Spain relating to America, 1763 to 1783, a set of 180 MS. volumes purchased by the Library of Congress in 1906. The Andrews plan called for the preparation of calendars of the materials not listed by Stevens, to serve both as guides for further copying and also as indexes to the documents when copied (see p. 94, n. 10).

[30] Foreign Office series 4, 5, 115, Public Record Office, relate to diplomatic relations between Great Britain and the United States.

[31] Division of Manuscripts, Library of Congress.

[32] At this time Scholes was at the University of New Mexico. A graduate of Harvard, he was in Mexico in 1927 on the Woodbury Lowery Fellowship, where he studied seventeenth-century materials relating to New Mexico. In June, 1929, Scholes became the agent for Project A in Mexico, and served there for a year.

[33] The proposed bibliography was not published.

ography, or is it to be helpful in the highest degree in the most direct way to workers in New Mexican history? The passion of bibliographers for doing everything in the manner that they call complete, leads usually to the inclusion, for the sake of completeness, of much that has little actual value to the worker in historical research. For example, in your Part I, under "Bibliographical Aids" you would probably include Channing, Hart and Turner's Manual; under "Periodical Literature," the *American Historical Review,* and, under "General Secondary Works on the History of the United States and Latin America," a variety of books that everybody knows of. A lot of things would be included for the sake of completeness that no one is likely anyhow to miss, one might almost say are "known by the light of nature." I have myself grown rather impatient of these omnium-gatherum bibliographies, and think that there is far more utility to the research students whom we wish to help, in properly classified lists of sources. Nearly all secondary writings that are of any real use can already be found by means of Miss Griffin's annuals, *Writings on American History,* and other such repertories.

Another consideration, of a practical order, is that such lists of sources, first of the 17th century, and then for the other periods, can probably get themselves printed in the New Mexican Historical *Review,* strung along from time to time as they are severally completed, while a big book of New Mexican bibliography, perhaps in several volumes, runs a risk of being too expensive to be printed. One asks himself how many copies of it would be sold. It would be intended for a small number of persons, most of whom could not afford to buy it but would use it in their University library.

These are notes of caution as to the whole scheme, which I think ought to be looked upon with a practical eye to the interests of the ultimate consumer. As to character, my own belief is that there is little utility in those bibliographies that are mere lists; that the user is really helped most by those bibliographies which, after each title, tell why that particular book or source is useful, or what it contains—bibliographies like that which Manning put at the end of his "Nootka Sound Controversy" in the *Annual Report* of the American Historical Association for 1904.[34] As to the proposed collection of unpublished sources, I should feel sure that that is useful too, but with a similar caution as to planning on too extensive a scale. If you print a volume of such material, you have visibly done a good stroke to help students. Is the benefit increased by your saying beforehand that you are going to print twenty similar volumes which you may never succeed in completing?

As I have said, I do not feel myself to be on very secure ground, not really knowing how large a need

there may be, how many workers are to be helped, but I believe what I have said deserves to be considered; anyhow, I very much applaud your desire to help forward the study of New Mexican history. The primary business of a teacher is to teach, but he certainly does it better for having an eye to the interests of research, both what he himself can engage in, and what he can induce others to undertake.

To Charles M. Andrews

February 2, 1929.[35]

Dear Andrews:

At the moment, I am not writing at the Library, and tomorrow I go to New York for a few days but I will give attention, as early as possible, to the request made by you in respect to the East Florida Claims papers,[36] which, of course, we should wish to supply. If transcripts or photostats of them are at the Library, they shall be sent; if to my regret they are not they shall be sent for at once.

Ragatz [37] is a young associate professor in the George Washington University, author of the book published in December by the American Historical Association Committee (of which I am a member) on Publications from the Revolving Fund given by the Carnegie Corporation. The book is a treatise on the decline of the planter class in the British West Indies, 1763-1833 (Century Company). It seems to me a performance of high grade. I think no one, unless it is Pitman,[38] has so large a knowledge of West Indian affairs during at least that period, or of the West Indian classes in C.O. It may be that to copy all the West Indian materials prior to 1815 in the Public Record Office is not beyond the resources of the Library of Congress, but my thought had been that such inclusion of everything would be out of scale, in view of the fact, or what I supposed to be the fact, that we had never copied, or undertaken to copy everything of the P.R.O. relating to the Old Thirteen. I had supposed that a selection had been made in that case, and if so, do not think it inappropriate that a selection would be made in the case of the West Indian material. If so, I feel sure that we shall get from Ragatz a very intelligent selection—or, to put it more exactly, an intelligent elimination of what

---

[34] Manning, William R., Nootka Sound controversy, *Ann. Rept., Amer. Hist. Assoc.,* 1904: 279.

[35] Division of Manuscripts, Library of Congress.

[36] East Florida Claims, Treasury Papers, Public Record Office (see, Andrews, *Guide* 2: 264-265).

[37] Lowell Joseph Ragatz, Ph.D., University of Wisconsin, 1925, author of *The old plantation system in the British Caribbean,* London, Bryan Edwards Press, 1925, and *The fall of the planter class in the British Caribbean,* N. Y., Century Co., 1928; compiler of A guide for the study of British Caribbean history 1763-1834, *Ann. Rept., Amer. Hist. Assoc.,* 1930: **3.**

[38] Frank Wesley Pitman, Ph.D., Yale, 1914, author of *Development of the British West Indies, 1700-1763,* New Haven, Yale Press, 1917, at this time professor of history in Pomona College.

is likely to be useless, for certainly he and I mean to include everything that is likely to be of value.

Considering the vast mass of stuff relating to the United States in European archives—e.g. more than a million papers, perhaps two or three million, in the A.G.I.[39] at Seville alone—it is impossible to think of reproducing everything. Therefore, all repositories attacked, and all sections of them, must be treated with some regard to scale, considering all the various interests of present and future historical scholars as well as we can see them.

The use of the photostat, or in many cases of another kind of photographic apparatus, was resolved upon a good while ago, before I had anything to do with the matter. I rather have had to regard it as fixed in policy; but anyhow I have had to be very greatly impressed with the imperfections of transcripts made by hand, in nearly all cases, and I believe that, on the whole and in nearly all cases, the photographs will be more satisfactory.

I must stop now without saying more than to raise the question, in view of the long list that is sent to you herewith, whether such sending of lists to you will hereafter be useful, to a degree balancing the great expenditure of time and labor involved in making them, and if photostats and the like are to come to us, as is apparent, at the rate of several thousand a month, the truth is that if we succeed in keeping up to date our own index cards it will be all that we can do. This makes the case different from what it was when the procedure of sending such lists started. At any time when you or any of your students want anything from the P.R.O., and will send an inquiry here, we will reply or lend at once, the probability henceforth being that we shall have it.

To Mrs. Woodrow Wilson

April 1, 1929.[40]

My dear Mrs. Wilson:

I had thought to write to you more promptly, but illness in my staff has produced some delay. Perhaps, however, the delay will have enabled me to express more deliberately and more carefully what I agreed to say in pursuance of our conversation. Papers of public men come to the Library and the Division of Manuscripts in two ways: on deposit, the property and control remaining in the depositor, and by way of gift. I see no advantage to either party in following the method of deposit, unless it is desired that there shall be power of withdrawal, and I can recall only one or two instances of papers having been withdrawn, and none in the case of any of the Presidential series. It is usually not difficult for the donor to segregate and

retain whatever it is desirable to retain, or for the Library to segregate and return any material that can be definitely described, and therefore definitely specified in any document attending the process of gift. Also, deposits are apt to produce awkward situations at later dates, as when, after the lifetime of the depositor it becomes uncertain, possibly disputable, who has by succession the right to withdraw or control. Gifts work much better—meaning gift with whatever conditions expressed and agreed upon, it being certain, not only during my tenure of the office but during that of anyone likely to be entrusted with such a position, that the conditions would be observed with rigid care. All such conditions and restrictions are codified in a book known and accessible to all members of the staff.

In all cases of papers of public men of so recent a date that among the papers may be found letters of persons still living, it is our custom to maintain what are called "Library restrictions." That means that, quite apart from any restrictions suggested by the donor or in the absence of such, we forbid all quoting from letters of living persons; we do our best to discourage sensational exploitation of the papers, or their use for purposes having no serious historical value. To that end, we scrutinize applications and applicants with some care, expecting applicants when not already known to us (as in most cases they are) to afford some evidence that they are persons having serious aims, and of some qualifications for doing historical work in a right manner. In cases where it seems needful, we require investigators to let us examine the notes they have taken and preclude the use of quotations which we think would be undesirable to publish.

These standard restrictions, applicable in all modern cases, I mention with a view to the future, because, though plainly it would be expedient to establish more drastic restrictions for a time in the case of Mr. Wilson's papers, I should wish you to know that, in any period after these have expired by limitation, proper care is still exercised in the interest of such sobriety as befits the use of the nation's chief collection of unprinted historical material. As to these further restrictions, the usual practice has been to make it a condition that access should be had to the papers only on written permission from the donor. That is the condition, rigidly maintained by us, in the case of Mrs. Roosevelt and Mrs. Benjamin Harrison, as to the papers of their respective husbands, and in the case of the Chief Justice as to his papers—all of which, I will frankly say, seem up to the present time to be deposits rather than gifts, though all the other Presidential papers are the property of the Library.[41] I think there is one infelicity, in an arrangement of precisely that form, that it leaves us somewhat at sea as to status after the lifetime of the donor or depositor. Legally,

---

[39] Archivo General de Indias, relating to the former dominions of Spain in America and to the Philippine Islands.
[40] Division of Manuscripts, Library of Congress.

[41] The papers of Theodore Roosevelt, Benjamin Harrison, and William H. Taft are now owned by the Library of Congress.

a discretionary power does not pass with the estate; so, if Mrs. Roosevelt should suddenly die, no one else, in the absence of testamentary provision (and no one else at all in case the papers had been made the property of the Library), would have any control over access. That question would then rest solely in our discretion. It seems that it would be better, to set a definite date and to provide that up to that date access should be had only on written permission (specifying what portion of the papers) from the donor or his executors. For instance one might set as the date January 1, 1936, substantially fifteen years from the end of Mr. Wilson's presidency.

I understood your desire that no one should have the use of the papers till Mr. Baker had finished his biography, but such a date as I have mentioned would lie well outside that period, and anyhow I do not suppose that any papers for which he still had use would be transferred to Washington until he had done with them.[42]

As I said when we talked, it would be a great pleasure to me if you could give me an opportunity to show you our collection, and the various methods of our treatment of papers; and, as I said to Mr. Bolling,[43] that could easily be accomplished without publicity, for, though the Division of Manuscripts closes at four-thirty, I am almost always here until six with no one else present in these rooms. I could therefore, on any day on which you might like to come a little after half-past four, show you our collections with a greater freedom than within the ordinary hours. I would take the greatest pleasure in doing so, and I feel sure that we have things here that you would be interested to see. I am quite at your disposal in regard to this, and could meet you at the automobile entrance of the Library at any minute.

I thank you again for the public-spirited and generous action which you have in mind. If it suits Mr. Baker's convenience to send here successive portions of the papers as he finishes with them respectively, the Library will be glad to take care of them serially; and I, as an old friend of Mr. Wilson, shall be proud to be their custodian.

[42] Ray Stanard Baker (1870-1946) with William E. Dodd, ed., *The public papers of Woodrow Wilson,* 6v., N. Y., Harper, 1925-1927. Baker was also the author of *Woodrow Wilson, life and letters,* 8v., Garden City, N. Y., Doubleday, Page & Co., 1927-1939. The papers of President Wilson, numbering about 196,000 pieces, were presented to the Library of Congress by Mrs. Wilson, and started coming to the Library in 1930, but it was not until 1939 that the main body of the collection was received. In July, 1940, they were opened for use under special restrictions.

[43] John Randolph Bolling, brother of Mrs. Wilson, and formerly secretary to Woodrow Wilson.

To L. C. SUTTORP

April 4, 1929.[44]

Dear Sir:[45]

I should be much obliged if, without interrupting too inconveniently your regular work, you would also supply the Library of Congress with photographic reproductions of such narrations respecting the arrival in Japan of the first American naval commander, Commodore M. C. Perry, and the first American diplomatic representative, Townsend Harris, which may be found in that section of the Rijksarchief which is concerned with correspondence from Japan. I refer to the *Verslagen over 's Rijks Oude Archieven* for 1910, pages 37 to 48, and specifically to numbers 11, 12, 28, 167, and 168.

Commodore Perry came to Japan in the summer of 1853. Townsend Harris came there in 1856 and remained about three years, negotiating a treaty at the beginning of 1859. It has seemed to me that in all probability somewhat full narrations respecting them were sent from Desima or Nagasaki to the Foreign Office in the Hague, and that this would be interesting material for American students of early relations with Japan; certainly it would be so to one, on whose behalf I am making the present request. Please search, as time permits, and send me what you find, to any amount that is really pertinent and instructive.[46]

To WORTHINGTON C. FORD

June 22, 1929.[47]

My dear Ford:

I am much pleased to know that the letter-book of Henry Hotze has been found, and I am greatly obliged to you for sending it here and also for sending the letters belonging to the Welles papers. This is to acknowledge, according to your request, the receipt of two volumes and two packages of letters. I suppose

[44] Division of Manuscripts, Library of Congress.

[45] Suttorp, of the Algemeen Rijksarchief, The Hague, was Bemis's Dutch agent for the European mission of the Library of Congress.

[46] The small island of Deshima in the harbor at Nagasaki had been a Dutch trading post since the seventeenth century. For two centuries it remained the only direct European contact with Japan. In 1853 Matthew C. Perry made his famous visit to Japan, but the American squadron was never at Nagasaki and carefully avoided any contact with the Dutch factors. The Dutch, however, knew of the plans for the expedition and began, in 1852, to make overtures to the Japanese which might have been prejudicial to the United States, but the negotiations failed to proceed. The effect of the American mission to the Orient is reflected in the Dutch concern for future operations at Deshima. Townsend Harris, the famous missionary, spent many years in Japan. The material which Jameson assumed would exist in the Dutch archives was, indeed, found and microfilmed for the Library of Congress (Suttorp to Bemis, May 17, 1929, Division of Manuscripts).

[47] Division of Manuscripts, Library of Congress.

that the library's formal acknowledgment will go to you in due time, though my own gratitude also goes out to good old Mr. Vignaud for their preservation, though he is beyond the reach or need of thanks.[48]

Dr. Putnam is expected to land in New York on July 1. I shall be here till July 26. Any need of your coming to Washington does not rest on our processes of keeping and caring for reproductions received from Europe. It is not very necessary for you to know the details of all that. In so far as they concern the dozen or so of workers under Project A in various European archives and libraries, they have been made known to those persons abundantly and with great particularity. You can learn from them anything that you need to know as to our instructions in those respects, to which we hold them rigorously, though I hope with due consideration of difficulties, and of differences of circumstance in different places.[49]

I should, however, consider it to be impossible for you to carry on the system now established without very full information as to the arrangements which Bemis has made in different places, and the processes in which his agents are embarked. I judge that you suppose that you can learn all this from him in conferences of no great length in Europe. If so, I think you are mistaken. He has made provision, with what I consider wonderful energy and resourcefulness, for a wide variety of matters in different places, by methods adapted to different circumstances. With all my confidence in your quickness of apprehension, I cannot help thinking that oral discussion of a day or two would never put you so thoroughly *au courant* as a reading of Bemis's letters in which more things are set forth in detail than anyone would be likely to remember to explain. The letters are numerous, as a rule several each week, Bemis reporting to me about everything and I giving such instructions as I can. If you don't want to come down here to read them I presume that I could legally send them up to you to read—though I speak, as I perpetually live, in terror of governmental red-tape restrictions.

To ALFRED E. STAMP

June 27, 1929.[50]

My dear Mr. Stamp: [51]

Williamsburg, Virginia, is, for the American, an old town and old in appearance—enough so to cause a Virginian organization to resolve upon restoring as many as possible of its buildings into the aspect which they wore in the eighteenth century. They have obtained from Mr. John D. Rockefeller a promise of the necessary money, and are going into the matter rather elaborately. The Rev. W. A. R. Goodwin[52] of Williamsburg, who, I believe, is the chief executive of the matter, is sailing for England on July 3 in order to pick up whatever information he can find in British archives as to the earlier buildings in that town. The town was brought into existence and made the capital of the province about 1690, and the range which he speaks of covering is that of the years from 1690 to 1729. Since the Calendars of State Papers Colonial stop short of the latter date, I venture to suggest to him that, in all probability, Mr. Headlam[53] has manuscripts of them prepared for some years beyond the point at which print ends, and that perhaps, though such manuscripts would have no index, it may be possible for him, through your kindness and that of Mr. Headlam to go a little further down in date by means of it than he might otherwise. I hope I have not gone too far in making such a suggestion, which may involve trouble to your office. I have, however, given him a letter of introduction to you, and therewith leave him at your mercy.

---

[48] See *post*, Jameson to Ira E. Bennett, Mar. 18, 1936, for further reference to the Hotze letter book and its connection with Henry Vignaud; see also, p. 109, n. 68, p. 120, n. 113, p. 121, n. 114 for additional references. The Welles papers were additions to those of Gideon Welles, Secretary of the Navy during the Civil War.

[49] At this time Ford was editor for the Massachusetts Historical Society. On Sept. 1, 1929, he succeeded Samuel Flagg Bemis as director of the European mission of the Library of Congress. By then operations were confined chiefly to England, France, and Spain. Ford directed the activity of Project A until 1935. Among the more outstanding achievements in connection with the work was his success in having the French diplomatic archives opened for copying up to the year 1830, an action in which Bemis shares part of the honor for having completed the complicated groundwork during his years as director.

[50] Division of Manuscripts, Library of Congress.

[51] Deputy Keeper of Public Records, Public Record Office, London.

[52] Rev. William Archer Rutherford Goodwin (1869-1939), rector of Bruton Parish Church in Williamsburg, who conceived the idea of restoring the colonial capital of Virginia. Since Rockefeller was also supplying the funds for Project A, the Library of Congress was anxious to aid Dr. Goodwin in his British explorations. Jameson's letter of June 27, 1929 to Miss Ruth Anna Fisher (Division of Manuscripts), the Library's research assistant in London, also discusses plans for this research. Dr. Goodwin's own letter of July 31, 1929, to the London *Times*, expresses at considerable length the proposed restoration at Williamsburg. The most important result of his mission to England was the discovery of the now famous copper plate in the Bodleian Library at Oxford. Using the Carnegie *Guide* prepared by Charles M. Andrews during his survey of the Bodleian in 1903, Miss Mary Goodwin, a niece of the rector, was able to identify the series of buildings depicted on the copper plate as the original palace, capitol, and school erected at Williamsburg. The palace and capitol had both vanished years before, but, on the basis of this striking evidence, they were reproduced with great accuracy. The plate was later presented to Mr. Rockefeller by the Bodleian trustees in recognition of his munificent gift to Oxford University (particularly the Bodleian Library Extension), and is now on display at Williamsburg.

[53] Cecil Headlam, editor of *Calendar of state papers, colonial* (v. 17-40) had only brought his work through the year 1715 (v. 28).

To Mrs. Robert Todd Lincoln

July 12, 1929.[54]

Dear Madam: [55]

According to the understanding entertained in the Library of Congress respecting the conditions attendant upon its custody of the papers of President Lincoln deposited here by the late Mr. Robert T. Lincoln, any permission to examine any portion of them must come from you. No such permission has, so far as I know, ever been sought by any of my predecessors as custodians of the manuscripts in the Library; certainly none has been sought during the ten months during which I have served as chief of the Division of Manuscripts. It is my understanding, and that of the Librarian, that such permissions should be sought only very rarely, and only on occasions invested with a special importance.[56]

I believe, however, and in this the Librarian agrees with me, that an occasion has now arisen which may justify our asking your permission to give certain privileges of examination to one applicant, Professor James G. Randall of the University of Illinois, of whose letter on the subject I enclose a photostat copy. Professor Randall is a scholar of real distinction, whose book entitled "Constitutional Problems of Lincoln" is very highly regarded, and who is well known to be a man of scrupulous integrity and keen sense of propriety. I vouch for all this, on the basis of a dozen years acquaintance.[57]

The occasion for his request arises, as you will see, from the invitation he has received from the editor of the *Dictionary of American Biography* to write a biography of Lincoln in that work. If you have not seen this Dictionary of which two volumes (out of twenty) have been published by Messrs. Charles Scribner's Sons, permit me to explain that the enterprise origi-

nates from the American Council of Learned Societies, of which I am a member, representing in the Council the American Historical Association. I am chairman of the Committee of Management, the editor is Mr. Allen Johnson, for many years professor of American history in Yale University. The *Dictionary* represents an effort to provide something far above the common run of biographical dictionaries, of the same high character as the British *Dictionary of National Biography*. The great expense of preparing so elaborate a series of biographies, worked out with so much scholarship as is required, is met by a fund of half a million dollars which I obtained from the generosity of Mr. Adolph S. Ochs of the New York Times.

I hope it will appear from the above that the occasion on which the present request is based is no ordinary one. It is far from my intention to trouble you often with such applications. I may never do it again. The *Dictionary,* however, is a work of national importance, with which I am proud to be associated, and for which I should wish to provide every possible advantage; and in the judgments of the editor, Professor Johnson, and myself there is no one in the country to whom we would rather confide the difficult task of preparing a biography of President Lincoln than Professor Randall. I hope you may think it possible to give him the opportunity to make the examinations he desires, within the definitely restricted limits which he suggests.[58]

Believe me to be, with the highest regard, and with apologies if this letter is the source of any trouble or inconvenience, . . .

To Hoke Donithen

November 12, 1929.[59]

Dear Sir: [60]

This is in reply to your letter of November 8, which I find here on returning from New York. Permit me first to explain that the facts in relation to those papers of the late President Harding which were left in the White House are somewhat different from what you supposed when writing your letter. These papers are not now in my custody, and indeed never were a part of the possessions of the Library of Congress though temporarily here at one time. I had corresponded somewhat with Mr. Frelinghuysen [61] about the possi-

---

[54] Division of Manuscripts, Library of Congress.

[55] Mrs. Lincoln (who died Mar. 31, 1937) held the right of access to the papers of President Lincoln, but was careful to keep her husband's wish inviolate.

[56] The papers of Abraham Lincoln were placed in the Library of Congress on May 7, 1919, for safe-keeping by Robert Todd Lincoln (1843-1926), the President's only surviving child; they became a formal deposit in 1923. Under the terms of his will, and by a special deed of gift, the papers became the property of the government of the United States, to be preserved at the Library. Additional protection afforded by the deed of gift (Jan. 23, 1923) provided that the papers be withheld from public inspection until twenty-one years after Robert Lincoln's death. The papers were opened to the public on July 26, 1947. For a full and able account see, Mearns, David C., The Lincoln papers, 2v., Garden City, N. Y., Doubleday & Co., 1: 1-136, 1948.

[57] James Garfield Randall, Ph.D., University of Chicago, 1911, professor of history in the University of Illinois, a leading Lincoln scholar, had recently published *Constitutional problems under Lincoln*, N. Y., D. Appleton & Co., 1926. His later work included *Lincoln the President*, 2v., N. Y., Dodd Mead & Co., 1945, and *Lincoln the liberal statesman*, N. Y., Dodd Mead & Co., 1947.

[58] Professor Randall (1881-1953), like other applicants, was denied access to the papers until they became generally available in 1947. Mrs. Lincoln felt bound to comply with the injunction of her husband and, having refused other applications, could make no exceptions (Mrs. Robert T. Lincoln to Jameson, July 22, 1929, Division of Manuscripts).

[59] Division of Manuscripts, Library of Congress.

[60] Donithen was secretary, trustee, and member of the executive committee of the Harding Memorial Association at Marion, Ohio.

[61] On May 7, 1929, Jameson had written to Joseph S. Frelinghuysen of New York, chairman of the board of trustees of the

bility of their being given to the Library of Congress, or placed here, on deposit (as manuscripts sometimes are when the owners do not wish to give them outright), when suddenly, one day last July, an official of the White House staff, superintendent of the building, I believe, telephoned to say that, by reason of some structural changes which were to be made in the basement, it would be necessary to send these papers out of the building, and would I take them here. I agreed because it was plainly better, that, if they must go out of the White House, they should go to a fire-proof building, and to that portion of it where we have the habit and daily duty of caring for manuscripts. I explained, however, to him and to Mr. Frelinghuysen that the transfer was effected solely in order to meet this exigency, and without prejudice to the question whether the papers were ultimately to come to the Library of Congress or not.

The papers remained here two months. In September Mr. Charles D. Schaffner, whom I understand to be executor of the wills of both President and Mrs. Harding, and with whom I therefore had some correspondence about the ultimate disposition of these papers, requested that they should all be sent to him. My understanding, derived from secretaries at the White House who had been there in President Harding's time, was that Mr. Schaffner had a right to give such an instruction. I therefore caused the papers, amounting, I believe, to thirty-nine steel filing cases, to be sent back to the White House. I understand that on September 23 the officials there sent them to Mr. Schaffner. There my knowledge of them and their whereabouts ends, for, since they were not here as a gift or regular deposit, I made no examination of them, and can give no description. Mr. Schaffner's purpose seemed to be identical with that which you had indicated in your letter—to see for himself what the papers are.

Harding Memorial Association, to learn what disposition had been made of the papers. He urged that every consideration be given to adding the Harding papers to the growing collection of presidential papers in the Library of Congress. Referring to another matter, he added: "I hope I may take this occasion to send a word of thanks for a bit of action in the Senate some years ago, which you have probably forgotten, but which gratified me very much. I was listening from the gallery to a debate about the National Archives Building, a matter in which for twenty years I have been agitating on behalf of the American Historical Association. There seemed to be real danger that a proposal to use the interior court-yard of the old Pension Building might be adopted, instead of erecting a suitable building—a makeshift device which would have been fatal to any real solution of the problem. You chanced to come into the Senate chamber at that moment, to listen for a few moments, and then absolutely killed the makeshift proposal by a few convincing words as to the character of the Pension Office Building from the point of view of an insurance expert. Now that we have fixed assurance of a suitable National Archives Building, as a part of Triangle Project, I feel like embracing the first opportunity to send you a word of thanks" (Jameson to Frelinghuysen, May 7, 1929, Division of Manuscripts).

May I not, however, take this opportunity to impress upon you the desirability—I think I may say the public duty—of sending these papers to the Library of Congress—and sending the whole mass, not merely a selection? I can see that there might be something attractive in the thought of keeping them in the Harding Memorial Building at Marion, but after all, experience proves that in such a situation they would be exceedingly little used in comparison with the use that would come to them if they were placed here, where the papers of nearly all the other presidents are collected. The enclosed list will show you, in what I think a very impressive way, how largely the papers of the presidents are here and in the case of the recent presidents how uniform has been the opinion of those who possessed the papers that they had best come to this place. For instance, more than a hundred historical scholars have in this present year come to work for longer or shorter periods in the manuscripts in this Division of the Library of Congress while, I venture to say, not more than two or three at the most have labored among the papers of President Hayes at Fremont.

Those who care for the memory of President Harding and wish that he should have his due place in history may well be reminded that that end is best secured by placing his papers where not merely the biographer interested solely in him is working, but where also all those historians or biographers who are working on any aspect of the period of his public life resort for printed and unprinted material; and that is surely the Library of Congress. If in the future all such persons have the opportunity to make use of the Harding papers, as they have of the papers of those other presidents, that alone insures to him proper place in a multitude of historical books. If a departed statesman's papers have value, it is for use, and not as a monument.

The reasons for such disposition are well set forth in the accompanying circular, made by one of my predecessors in this office, to which I ask leave to invite your attention.

Let me also emphasize the desirability of sending the papers here in their integrity, not a mere selection from them. Letters and papers that seem unimportant now will be valued in the future, and are part of the record. A day does not pass in this establishment in which some point of history in which some one is interested is not solved by means of papers which in their own time might easily have been regarded as not worth keeping.

I feel so strongly about the interest of historians in having the papers of President Harding brought here that I should gladly come out to Marion to discuss the matter with you if I thought that this would be useful or needed. I hope that you will conclude, without this, that any other course would be a mistake. I will, however, beg you, at any rate, not to make any adverse decision without giving me the opportunity to come out and see you or else to answer any objections that may occur to your mind.[62]

To Worthington C. Ford

February 10, 1930.[63]

Dear Ford:

Ten days ago, when I was in New York, Professor Bemis, on the basis of the appointment of the Duke of Alba to the Minister of Education, gave Dr. Putnam a memorandum which was transmitted to you, with almost all of which I should agree, but on the last paragraph of which I wish to make a comment.[64]

In England, France, and Spain, it seems an obvious duty, and a rational part of our program, to photograph, so far as we can, the correspondence that passed between the representatives of each of those countries and Washington (or, previously, Philadelphia or New York) with the minister of foreign affairs in their respective capitals. As to the materials respecting the history of the United States that are to be found in the correspondence of the Spanish ambassadors in France and Spain, while I am aware of their importance and interest, my own judgment would be that they can have only a secondary claim upon our attention, and that it would be of doubtful expediency to attack them before completing, and probably at the expense of not completing, those primary series of which I speak first. This is said with reference to Bemis's suggestion that the letter books of the Conde Aranda as Spanish ambassador to Paris from 1776 to 1784, be photographed for us, arrangements being first made for their transfer from Simancas to Madrid for that purpose.

Bemis knows of my conviction on this subject, though doubtless Dr. Putnam does not. The question came up with respect to the correspondence at the Affaires Etrangères [65] between the French government and the French ambassador in Madrid. I showed Bemis that this would mean the copying of 30 volumes, Espagne 592-621 about 17,000 pages to be photographed, of which it is obvious from the descriptions in the *Inventaire* [66] only a minor fraction concerns America. I of course did not deny that a body of reproduced material would have its uses, but I held that, if we would maintain any sense of proportion, we could not copy all this, within the limits of our total. Important as the diplomatic history of 1776-1783 is, and especially as Bemis is interested in its revision,[67] it is only one septennium in our diplomatic history, and if we should try to carry out the principle of such inclusions logically, and take in all the cross correspondence of the British foreign office with all its ambassadors abroad, for the sake of the minor fraction therein that concerns American history, from 1776 to 1878, we should land in the Bankruptcy Court.

However, all this is for your consideration for I am aware that in Spain progress can sometimes be made more easily in some lines than in others and it is possible that what Bemis suggests in the paragraph named may offer a better means of dealing with the difficult problem of Simancas than anything more *planmässig*.

To John D. Rockefeller, Jr.

April 1, 1930.

My dear Mr. Rockefeller:

Dr. Carter G. Woodson has told me somewhat concerning his project for the collection of manuscript materials held in possession of negro families and contributing to or illustrating the history of their race. As some of the fruits of the efforts he has already made have come to the Division of Manuscripts of the Library of Congress (of which I now have charge), he thinks that I am in a position to support his application for means for continuing his endeavor. I am very glad to write in such support, for I believe thoroughly in what he is trying to do, and have a very high opinion of his qualifications for such work and skill and tact in pursuing it.

The negro race comprises ten per cent of our population, yet how much less we know of the history of that element than of any equal portion of the rest. It was for that reason that when in charge of the Department of Historical Research in the Carnegie Institution of Washington, I devoted a quite considerable portion

---

[62] The Harding papers have remained in Ohio.

[63] Division of Manuscripts, Library of Congress.

[64] On Jan. 30, 1930, Bemis informed the Librarian of Congress that the time had come to ask for more liberal privileges for Project A in Spain. The recent change in government, by which the Duke of Alba, as Minister of Public Instruction, directed archival administration, led to a more liberal attitude toward the Library mission. The Duke of Alba, already president of the Royal Academy of History at Madrid, and himself a patron of learning, had befriended Bemis in the early and difficult stages of work in Spain, when a royal decree against copying in series threatened to prevent the acquisition of archival materials altogether. By June, 1930, the restrictive measures had been reduced to a point where copying could be resumed and carried as far as the year 1870; and it was no longer necessary to deposit duplicates of selected copies with the Spanish authorities. In his memorandum to Putnam, Bemis proposed that fullest attention be given to all diplomatic materials, particularly those of England and France, aside from the United States series (Bemis to Putnam, Jan. 30, 1930, Division of Manuscripts).

[65] Archives du Ministère des Affaires Etrangères, Quai d'Orsay, Paris.

[66] *Inventaire sommaire des archives du département des affaires étrangères, correspondance politique* **2** (2) *Espagne*, Paris, Imprimerie Nationale, 1919.

[67] Professor Bemis's work in this field includes several notable contributions: *Jay's treaty, a study in commerce and diplomacy*, N. Y., Macmillan, 1923; *Pinckney's treaty, a study of America's advantage from Europe's distress*, Baltimore, Johns Hopkins Press, 1926; and *The diplomacy of the American Revolution*, N. Y., D. Appleton-Century Co., 1935.

of its annual appropriations to the history of the American negro. There is, however, a great deal of illustrative material in negro hands which a competent and persuasive negro worker can attain for permanent preservation more easily than any white collector. Dr. Woodson, abundantly qualified for the task by education and experience, has had much success in effecting such persuasion. He has deposited a large amount of such material in this Division of the Library of Congress, partly because this fireproof building gives it exceptional security which cannot be attained elsewhere, and partly because he finds that negro possessors of such papers can more readily be persuaded to give up their papers for historical purposes if they are told that the papers are coming to the Library of Congress.

Dr. Woodson has turned in here several hundred papers, which for my part I find very interesting— miscellaneous, to be sure, but having a wide range, from a bill of sale of a slave of Thomas Jefferson to James Madison to the journal of a negro bishop and the autobiography of a negro leader in the period of reconstruction. If he can keep on, on a good scale, he will make here a very rich collection such as I do not know of as existing elsewhere.

I should add that I believe he administers funds with care and prudence. At one time he had for some years a considerable grant from the Carnegie Corporation with the proviso that I should each quarter, when payments were to be made, certify general approval of the expenditures.[68] Observing them as carefully as I was expected to observe them, it seemed to me that the money was judiciously and economically spent. I hope you will be able to do what he asks. I regard his enterprise as very distinctly deserving of support.

To JOHN M. VINCENT

June 18, 1930.[69]

Dear Vincent:[70]

I have received your letter of June 12, and hasten to assure you that there was no lack of deliberation in planning for the Union Catalogue of Manuscripts. If you will look at the description of the project on page 74 of the Report of the Library of Congress for 1929, you will see that the American Council of Learned Societies appointed an Advisory Committee of just such persons as you suggest should be consulted—R. P.

Blake of Harvard, chairman, Burr of Cornell, H. A. Sanders of Michigan, Karl Young of Yale, and J. T. Gerould of Princeton. We had a meeting of that committee at Cambridge in September and formed a plan. I do not know that Mr. Seymour de Ricci[71] has conformed to it in every particular, his sheets thus far completed not being here but in Paris; and when we employ an expert of his eminence, it is natural for us to allow some discretion with respect to variations from perfect uniformity. However, he is not an intractable man, and will, I am sure, pay due attention to the criticisms received because of the publication made in the *Bulletin* of the New York Public Library.[72] If you could take the trouble to make criticisms in detail, I am sure they would be valued.

It would be necessary to bear in mind, however, that the descriptions cannot be amplified much beyond the point shown in the *Bulletin*. We have just so much money to spend, and must cut our coat according to our cloth. Such elaboration as is shown in many catalogues of manuscripts is therefore impossible. Our committee made a conclusion as to about how much could be done, on the whole field, with the means we had. More of one sort can be included only at the expense of subtraction from another.

As to the order of arrangement, our committee was not of your mind, that listing the manuscripts by libraries would be a disaster. They thought there were strong reasons for pursuing that order, and I do not think would change it. They thought it not difficult to make a suitable and practical index. They saw great difficulties in an alphabetical arrangement, especially in the case of the many composite volumes and the many manuscripts and parts of manuscripts that have neither title nor author.

But by all means let us have your criticisms of the specimens.[73]

To HARRIET S. TAPLEY

March 5, 1931.[74]

My dear Miss Tapley:[75]

I am very glad that you sent me the documents which

---

[68] In 1921, through the efforts of Jameson, with the cooperation of James B. Angell, president of the Carnegie Corporation, the corporation granted to the Association for the Study of Negro Life and History, $25,000, to be paid in quarterly installments of $1,200 each, after $2,500 was turned over to the association to pay its debts (C. G. Woodson to J. E. Moorland, June 25, 1921; from the files of Howard University, Washington, D. C.).

[69] Division of Manuscripts, Library of Congress.

[70] John Martin Vincent, Ph.D., Johns Hopkins University, 1890, professor of European history, 1905-1925, and professor emeritus thereafter, in the Johns Hopkins University.

[71] Seymour de Ricci (1881-1942), eminent paleographer and bibliographer, who prepared (with the assistance of William Jerome Wilson) the *Census of medieval and renaissance manuscripts in the United States and Canada*, 3v., N. Y., H. W. Wilson Co., 1935-1940. The Census was planned by the American Council of Learned Societies, administered by the Library of Congress as its Project C, and supervised by Jameson.

[72] De Ricci, Medieval manuscripts in the New York Public Library, N. Y. Public Library *Bulletin* 34: 297-322.

[73] The material was published according to geographical arrangement of repositories.

[74] Division of Manuscripts, Library of Congress.

[75] Miss Tapley of the Essex Institute, Salem, Mass., later edited *Early coastwise and foreign shipping of Salem*, Salem, Mass., Essex Institute, 1934.

have accompanied your letter of March 2,[76] for now I can understand just what your agent is doing. I am rather surprised to find that you have apparently not been making use of the three large volumes which I caused to be published fifteen or sixteen years ago for guidance of all American searchers in the wilderness of the Public Record Office, and that your searcher apparently does not know of their existence, although copies which I caused to be presented to the literary search room of the Public Record Office are, or were when I was last there, on the shelves of that room. I earnestly beg you to procure for the library of the Essex Institute, if it so happens that you have not them already, the three volumes of which I speak, "Guide to the materials for American history to 1783 in the Public Record Office of Great Britain" by Charles M. Andrews, 2 volumes, and "Guide to the materials in London archives for the history of the United States since 1783" by C. O. Paullin and F. L. Paxson, all published by the Carnegie Institution of Washington in or about 1914. I should think you ought also to have Andrews and Davenport, "Guide to the materials for American history in the British Museum, and minor libraries and archives in London, Oxford, and Cambridge," published by the same institution a few years earlier. I spent the greater part of my time during ten years in bringing out such volumes as these, for the archives in various European countries, and fondly hoped that those I have named were the vade-mecum of everyone undertaking research in London archives for purposes of American history. My reason for thinking that your agent does not know of them is that at the foot of page 3 of his letter of November 4, he naïvely says, "at the same time we have been working on an idea which occurred to us, viz. that the proper place to find particulars of Massachusetts shipping at a time when Massachusetts was a colony would be among the records of the Colonial Office." Of course it is. Where else? If he had looked on page 171 of volume I of Andrews's *Guide* and other corresponding pages, he would have found mention of this volume, C.O. 5: 848, which he has "unearthed," and of 30 other similar volumes for the other colonies.

I speak of all this with some earnestness because of the proposals made by Mr. Bernau in his letter of November 29, 1929. He is proposing to you, in all innocence, I daresay, a general search for Massachusetts materials in the Public Record Office, quite as if there were no existing guidance to that material. If I may advise, you should not let him stray from C.O. 5: 848-851 and H. C. Adm., Prize 1728-1815 [77] (assuming that you are satisfied with his work in those sections) until you have made a careful study of the pages respecting Massachusetts history in the volumes I have named, especially in Andrews I. 167-171, II. 304-340, and Paullin and Paxson, 481-484. What he proposes would cost many thousands of dollars, would last for many years, would duplicate work which has already been done or is being done, and all this to be put in the hands of one who has not informed himself of the existence of the fundamental inventories! One is always likely to run into this sort of thing with English searchers, only a very few of whom are at all aware of the extent to which the Americans have exploited for themselves the materials in the P.R.O.

Perhaps all this is not at all what you want from me, but an answer to your original question. To that I should have to say that the Library of Congress cannot enter upon the plan of purchasing sets of typewritten sheets such as you are getting. In the first place, we have as far as possible abandoned all getting of other than photographic copies from foreign archives, partly because copyists there seldom copy with perfect accuracy and in most cases make a particularly large number of mistakes in the transcribing of proper names from ignorance of American history. But also, for the main matter, in our position as a national library we cannot well enter upon the photostatting of these Massachusetts bundles unless we are prepared to go through a whole series, for all the colonies, of 34 volumes or bundles in C.O. 5 or 1826 (actually about 800 in H. C. Adm.). This we could not undertake to do, because to my mind it would be out of scale. Our grant from Mr. Rockefeller runs less than two years more and at the Public Record Office where we have our own photostat we can not expect to make more than 15,000 or 20,000 photostat sheets per annum. For that, we must make choice of the things which seem here to be most important and useful to American historical scholars, and while I have listed for our supervisor in London (an accomplished American young woman, who knows the American material in the P.R.O. from *a* to *z*) a long list of Admiralty papers, I have not dared, with the material at our command, to enter upon the general scheme of exploitation of the High Court of Admiralty Papers. I think therefore that you shall have to count us out. If, however, in any other way any of our work can at any time be made useful to you, I should be glad to know of it.

---

[76] Miss Tapley wrote that the Essex Institute was obtaining records of prizes for the periods of the American Revolution and the War of 1812, and also early shipping records, entrances, and clearances for ports in Massachusetts (Harriet S. Tapley to Jameson, Mar. 2, 1931, Division of Manuscripts).

[77] Colonial Office Papers, and High Court of Admiralty Papers, Public Record Office, London.

To Marcus W. Jernegan

March 13, 1931.[78]

Dear Jernegan:[79]

The case respecting materials on German immigration in the United States is not so desperate as in your letter of March 11[80] you seem to think. When I wrote my report I supposed our work in Germany was very near its end, on account of advice tending in that direction which I had given to Ford. Since then, however, his Germans have persuaded him to continue, being naturally anxious that their work should not stop, and he in view of their excellent work has been disposed to defer to their desires. I do not know, not interfering with him very often, and not having minute reports from him, just what they are doing at present, but perhaps it is more immigration material.

Do not infer from my report that I am not alive to the desirability of accumulating materials for the economic and social history of the United States. Anyone managing this work, and doing so in Washington, will be apt to think that, on account of the presence here of the archives of the Department of State, there is a particularly strong obligation upon him to give a foremost place to materials for our diplomatic history. This is the one place where that is inevitable. For the rest of the materials for political and military history, it must be remembered that such enterprises of copying cannot possibly be managed successfully in any other way than by following existing lists, and lists that really tell you something about the nature and value of the material. The main lists are those provided by the Carnegie Institution *Guides*. Most of the materials for American history which they list are materials for political and military history. If one tries to obtain through them, or through any other useable lists, any considerable amount of material for social history, the only indications he finds are, as a rule, indications of material which, however great in bulk, is inevitably so described that one expects, as is so often the case in the materials for social and economic history, that there is a small amount of wheat to bushels of chaff. That is, as you know, a standing difficulty in documenting social history as compared with documenting constitutional, political, or military history; you have voluminous masses of low-grade ore, from which to get a little gold.

Take Learned's *Guide*,[81] for instance, I suppose it mentions a thousand, anyhow several hundred bundles or portfolios, with only the designation "Auswanderungswesen." Now what are you going to do with that? You don't know whether it is any good or not. You presume that it mostly consists of lists of names. The genealogists might clamor for these, but I am not much concerned to help genealogists.

However, you have made a valiant attempt to select entries in Learned that really have a more general quality than this, and though the amount you designate is enormous, I shall be willing to send to Ford a duplicate of your lists and suggest to him that he instruct his people in Germany to proceed to attack it, unless they are already occupied with things which he thinks must have a prior claim. I am not sufficiently informed as to what is going on there now, or how many people he has at work, to give any guess as to when we shall be receiving any of this material. Some months hence, I should imagine.

The terms of our grant have been held not to include the reproduction of printed matter, but I think I can make an exception of the printed pieces you have included, embedded as they are in archival matter, and quite as rare and inaccessible in America as if they were so much manuscript.

The matter listed on the page which I return is already here.

I do not guarantee that the Swiss material you list will be secured in this present year, since, so far as I know, Ford has not yet made any arrangements whatever for operations in Switzerland.

If there is any obstacle that prevents us from carrying all this out, and you have to make your own bargain with our men, I may mention that it is not necessary that the workers should be itinerant from archive to archive, for German archival regulations permit the transfer of specified bundles or portfolios from minor archives to such places as Hamburg, and Berlin where our work is being done.[82]

To Worthington C. Ford

April 16, 1931.[83]

Dear Ford:

I am indebted to you for three official letters of April 7, and one private note, to which I shall reply this afternoon from the Cosmos Club, for I have here (today) no abiding place but must go immediately after luncheon to a meeting, I rather hope the final meeting, of our interdepartmental committee on the

---

[78] Division of Manuscripts, Library of Congress.

[79] Marcus W. Jernegan, Ph.D., University of Chicago, 1906, student of Jameson at Brown and temporary member (1907-1908) of his staff in the Carnegie Institution. In 1920 he became professor of American history in the University of Chicago. For some account of his work in social and economic history see p. 296, n. 492, and p. 316, n. 52.

[80] Jernegan was fearful that materials for social and economic history were being neglected in the acquisitions program for Project A.

[81] Learned, Marion D., *Guide to the manuscript materials relating to American history in the German state archives*, Washington, D. C., Carnegie Institution, 1912.

[82] The excellent inter-archival loan system in Germany enabled the Library of Congress to copy many items in outlying repositories.

[83] Division of Manuscripts, Library of Congress.

new archive building (or Archives Building, as our legislators have very regrettably, after grave discussion and full presentation of correct doctrine, decreed that it shall be called).

The process of trying to combine the desiderata on which our committee were disposed to insist with the architectural requirements advanced by the architect and the Board of Architectural Consultants has worked out much more satisfactorily than any of us expected. We are certainly going to have a very handsome building, and I think that, in almost all particulars, though not quite in all, the internal arrangements will be very satisfactory. Along with the chairman, Louis Simon, chief draftsman in [the] Supervising Architect's Office,[84] the most useful member of the committee has been Tyler Dennett of the State Department. He is so very able an administrator, and so much in sympathy with the work of historical scholars, himself an excellent one, that I would to Heaven that he might be the first archivist of the United States, but there is no hope of that. He has resigned from the State Department, the resignation to take effect at the end of this month, and is going to a professorship at Princeton.[85]

I thank you for your very interesting accounts of your journey to Buda-Pest and elsewhere, and of the conference of archivists at Paris.

It is very gratifying that the remaining journals of the S. P. G.[86] will soon be coming this way. I am sorry to hear of Miss Fisher's cold and absence.[87] As you are going over to London soon, I send you a copy of a recent letter I sent to her. As to Oxford and Cambridge, all the American material there, that was there in 1907, is well listed, item by item, in the Andrews and Davenport *Guide*, which you have. The European *Guides* that you lack have just been sent to you by the Carnegie Institution.

As to Edinburgh, just as well leave it alone, I should say. I believe that all the Darien stuff of any serious importance has been put into print, and Francis Hart's list at the end of the first serial of the *Proceedings* of the Massachusetts Historical Society for last year, just issued, does not seem to show much Scottish material not already exploited, though plenty of new stuff in Spain, which, however, he has used in his book.[88]

As for anything else, I imagined in 1913 that, after covering the British archives, the Carnegie Institution of Washington ought to do something with respect to those of Scotland and Ireland, so went to Edinburgh and Dublin that spring after the London Congress, and made brief inspections.[89] The Irish archives later removed themselves from consideration, as you indicate.[90] I had various young women, one after another, make various assaults upon the materials in the General Register Office at Edinburgh, Miss Fisher making the final expedition in 1922. There seemed to me to be only two portions of the deposits there that contained enough material respecting the history of America to make it worth while to go into them. One was certain papers of the Parliament which were duly got and printed in Stock's volumes.[91] The other was the papers of the High Court of Admiralty. Notes were taken to form a calendar of all the American cases, from 1703 to 1783, and these I have lately had copied, and have edited them for publication in the next Annual Report of the American Historical Association.[92] The cases themselves being voluminous and individually unimportant, or important only to local historians, I think every need is satisfied by a calendar. Extended photostatting would not be worth while.

I am, however, delighted that you are just at this time going over to England, for this morning Colonel Stephen Bonsal has shown me a clipping from the London *Times* of March 17 describing the provisions of the will of Dr. Alfred Maudslay, who bequeathed to the Library of Congress all the diaries and letters and papers of Gouverneur Morris.[93] This was most de-

[84] Louis A. Simon, chief of the Architectural Division, Treasury Department, 1905-1933; supervising architect of the Public Buildings Commission, 1933-1941.

[85] Tyler Dennett was professor of international relations in Princeton University from 1931 to 1934, when he became president of Williams College. For additional data see p. 310, n. 33.

[86] Society for the Propagation of the Gospel in Foreign Parts, London, founded in 1701 as the missionary organ of the Church of England. The American colonies were its chief field of activity during the eighteenth century.

[87] Miss Ruth Anna Fisher, research assistant in London for the European mission of the Library of Congress.

[88] Hart, Francis Russell, ed., Spanish documents relating to the Scots' settlement of Darien, *Proc. Mass. Hist. Soc.* **63**: 154-168, 1930. Hart also edited Spanish documents relating to the siege of Havana, *Proc. Mass. Hist. Soc.* **64**: 432-439, 1932.

[89] International Congress of Historical Studies, London, April, 1913; see *ante,* Jameson to Sara Jameson, Apr. 2, 6, 13, 15, 30, 1913, for some account of his visit to England. His letter of Apr. 30, from Dublin, contains no reference to the Irish archives. Jameson made some arrangements for work at Edinburgh, where he engaged Miss Margaret Adam, a specialist in the field of Scottish immigration to America. The work was interrupted by the war but was resumed in 1921 by Miss Sibyl Norman formerly of the Paris mission staff. In 1920 he renewed inquiries in Dublin, and during 1921 had Herbert C. Bell (then at work in London upon the Carnegie guide to West Indian materials) make a survey of the Irish Record Office.

[90] The Irish archives were destroyed during the civil war in June, 1922, and Jameson abandoned his intention of publishing Bell's survey.

[91] Stock, Leo. F., ed., *Proceedings and debates of British parliaments respecting North America, 1542-1754,* 5v., Washington, D. C., Carnegie Institution, 1924-1941.

[92] Jameson, J. F., Notes from the archives of Scotland concerning America, *Ann. Rept., Amer. Hist. Assoc.,* 1930: 1: 97-122.

[93] The papers of Gouverneur Morris had descended to Anne Cary Morris, wife of Dr. Alfred Percival Maudslay, of Morney Cross, Fownhope, co. Hereford, England, noted anthropologist and ethnologist. Stephen Bonsal (1865-1951), newspaper correspondent and author, had also married a descendant of Morris, and was anxious that this historic collection be returned to America. Some years prior to Dr. Maudslay's death (which occurred Jan. 22, 1931), Bonsal attempted to persuade him to give the manuscripts to the Library of Congress. Under

lightful news, and a surprise to Bonsal, for he argued with the possessors to this effect a few years ago, but thought he did not succeed. I rather think we are, however, indebted to him for the result, but there is yet something to do in the matter, and you, quite in the nick of time, are just the person to make sure that we get everything that belongs to us, and that no letters of Washington, etc. escape. Among his papers is a list, he tells me, of all the papers that went to Sparks, with indications of some that did not come back.[94]

To RUTH ANNA FISHER

May 14, 1931.[95]

My dear Miss Fisher:[96]

In 1921 Miss Mary Thornton, daughter of Sir Edward Thornton, British minister here for some years about 1870, and granddaughter of an earlier Edward Thornton who was secretary of legation and chargé des affaires in Washington from 1800 to 1803, after some previous service as a secretary in Philadelphia and a vice consul in Baltimore, showed me a rather extensive manuscript account of that earlier Edward Thornton (afterwards Sir Edward) of the whole of his earlier life. It was a very interesting autobiography. Miss Thornton allowed me to have copies made of certain portions which I desired for a publication then in contemplation but never executed. It now occurs to me that it might well be possible, as it certainly would be advantageous, for the Library of Congress to obtain that manuscript. My remembrance is that Miss Thornton had a sister, but that there was no one in her branch of the family to continue the Thornton name and descent, her nephew having died as a young man in Central America. Therefore, if she is still living, I wish you would find her and see if she cannot be persuaded to transfer the document to the Library of Congress. She spent several years of her youth in Washington, she is a lady of much intelligence, and she may well appreciate that so valuable a record ought not to be subjected to any chances of future destruction or loss, and on the whole, being mainly of American interest, might best be preserved permanently in a place to which American historical scholars are accustomed to resort for manuscript materials. The enclosed circular may be helpful.

Please leave no stone unturned in the effort to find Miss Thornton. Since, however, she was already beginning to be old when I saw her, it is quite possible that she, and her sister, if I am right in thinking there was one, are no longer living. In that case, please use all endeavors to find the manuscript.

The question whether it should be a gift or a purchase is one of some delicacy, which I should have to leave to your own diplomacy. It seemed to me that their circumstances were by no means affluent, and certainly the Library of Congress would be glad to pay what is right for the possession of the manuscript, and I suppose that twenty or thirty pounds would be a fair price. I do not sufficiently remember the total extent, respecting matters subsequent to 1803, to say that we should go so far as forty pounds. But if I were myself to see her, or any present representative, I should not first of all bring up the question of purchase, which might seem to assume a need of money and willingness to sell ancestral possessions, nor distinctly put the question forward first as of a gift, speaking of transfer or some such term, and feeling my way, and allowing her to make the suggestion of sale if she thought fit. In other words, while we should be perfectly willing to pay, there would be susceptibilities to be regarded if Miss Thornton is still the owner—and perhaps there would be in the case of any successor. I leave all this with confidence to you, asking you to report as to possibilities, and to understand that my function also is in such matters only one of recommendation to the Librarian.

In 1921 Miss Thornton lived at 10 West Halkin St., S.W.[97]

To MAX FARRAND

June 1, 1931.[98]

Dear Farrand:[99]

Your letter of May 25 makes me anxious that you should fully understand the whole situation respecting the new edition, *The Writings of George Washington*. Please do not think of it as intended to be anything else than the completest and best that can be achieved. When the Bicentennial Commission was formed, with Senator Fess as practically chairman, I took advantage of his having once been a student of mine to press upon him the thought that, of all ways of commemorating Washington, the one indispensable one was the making of a new edition of his writings, the earlier

---

the terms of Dr. Maudslay's will these were bequeathed to the Library, with certain restrictions in favor of Miss Beatrix Cary Davenport, his wife's niece. The collection fills over fifty volumes, including Morris's diary (13v., 1789-1816), official and private letter books for the same period, and numerous account and bank books, as well as others relating to the settlement of his estate. The papers reached the Library in 1937, but remained in a restricted category until 1943. See *post,* Jameson to Bonsal, Feb. 17, 1937.

[94] Presumably in connection with Jared Spark's *Life and correspondence of Gouverneur Morris,* 3v., Boston, 1832.

[95] Division of Manuscripts, Library of Congress.

[96] Miss Fisher was at this time American representative of the Library of Congress in London.

[97] Before Miss Thornton was located Miss Fisher had "turned many stones" but she was finally successful both in finding Miss Thornton and in presenting the desire of the Library so persuasively that the owner presented the autobiography to the Division of Manuscripts with great pleasure.

[98] Division of Manuscripts, Library of Congress.

[99] Max Farrand (1869-1945) was at this time director of the Henry E. Huntington Library at San Marino, Calif.

editions being almost entirely out of print.[100] Other people no doubt made the same suggestion and it was one of the first things resolved upon by the Commission. Hart [101] having been officially appointed the "Historian" of the Commission, the enterprise was naturally put under his general supervision, and he has been useful to it in various ways. It was understood on all hands that Fitzpatrick [102] was on all accounts the right man to do the editing, and he began upon it as soon as the appropriations were available, indeed somewhat before that date (July 1, 1930). An Advisory Committee was appointed, of which I have been chairman, and which also includes Paltsits, Randolph Adams, Tyler Dennett, Charles Moore, and General John M. Palmer.[103]

As such chairman, and also in the interests of the Washington collection in this Division of the Library (where the work of editing is going on) I have for two years past been diligently gathering in photostats of all letters of Washington possessed elsewhere, that I could hear of. I have raked the country pretty well, getting, I suppose, six or seven hundred letters, from the Historical Society of Massachusetts, Pennsylvania, New York, etc., the New York Public Library, various state archives, and a multitude of private owners of from one to one hundred thirty letters. Everyone has been most amiable about it. All have understood the purpose, and, though of course in many cases we had in the Washington collection the drafts or letter-book copies, still it is of course better to found the texts on the letters actually sent.

Now I have to confess that, with respect to the photostats of Washington letters that came from the Huntington Library, it never crossed my mind that they perhaps stood on a different basis, and that I never had asked your permission to make use of them in this way. They came here two years before I did, namely in 1926, and I know that Fitzpatrick was using them for his texts, when needful (he is not printing *every* letter of Washington), but I never looked at them till I received your letter of May 25. I then found that your photostats did not bear the inscription you now put upon such, restraining from printing not authorized by specific permission, and Fitzpatrick has assumed that he was as free to use these as any other of our photostats. I do not find in the files of this Division any correspondence that says anything about permis-

sions to print—nothing in fact but some correspondence with Mr. Bliss [104] with lists of what you have, that we could obtain under the Wilbur Fund,[105] all this being before the time of the Rockefeller Grant on which Project A, which I administer, is founded. There may be correspondence downstairs, but I probably can't get at it today.

All these things considered, I ask you to overlook any remissness on the part of our Advisory Committee or of the Bicentennial Commission, or of the Chief of the Division of Manuscripts, in not making formal request, as should have been done, for permission to publish letters coming from your library, and to receive with favor my present request for such permission.

To EMMET L. RICHARDSON

November 16, 1931.[106]

My dear Mr. Richardson: [107]

I am delighted beyond measure by the receipt of your letter of November 12. I hope that you and Mrs. Richardson will not have thought, by reason of the restrained language of my last letter, that I did not have in mind, with adequate appreciation, what you and she had said to me when you were here respecting your intention or disposition to give to the Library of Congress the invaluable original manuscript of the Autobiography of Abraham Lincoln. I had that fully in mind, and have always entertained with much gratitude the hope that such would be the conclusion of the matter, and that it might happen during my time of service to the Library. When, however, you sent me the extract from Miss Fell's will, it seemed to me not proper to anticipate in my reply a benefaction which your letter did not expressly declare, and I confined myself to an acknowledgment of the letter, with thanks for your kindness in sending the extract.[108]

Now, however, that your intention in the matter is

---

[104] Leslie Edgar Bliss, librarian of the Henry E. Huntington Library.

[105] A Library of Congress trust fund provided by James B. Wilbur of Manchester, Vermont, in 1925, the income from which is used for the acquisition of foreign materials for American history.

[106] Division of Manuscripts, Library of Congress.

[107] Emmet L. Richardson of Milwaukee, Wis., married a granddaughter of Jesse W. Fell of Normal, Ill., close friend and political associate of Abraham Lincoln. In 1859, at Fell's request, Lincoln prepared a three-page autobiography. This he sent to Fell on December 20 of that year. This document was later owned by his daughter, Miss Fannie Fell (who died in 1931), who bequeathed it to her niece, Mrs. Richardson, and the latter's son, Robert D. Richardson, with the provision that they place the document in some public institution where it would be preserved and made available to the public, particularly to Lincoln scholars. In compliance with this, the Autobiography was presented to the Library of Congress in 1947 where it is now displayed in the main hall with other important Lincoln memorabilia.

[108] In connection with the Autobiography it should be noted that Jameson made an attempt to acquire the letter sent by

---

[100] The two best known editions were Sparks, Jared, *The life and writings of George Washington*, 12v., 1834-1837, and subsequent editions; and Ford, Worthington C., *Writings of Washington*, 14v., N. Y., Putnam's, 1890.

[101] Albert Bushnell Hart of Harvard.

[102] John C. Fitzpatrick, previously identified, pp. 308-309, n. 23.

[103] Victor H. Paltsits, keeper of manuscripts, New York Public Library; Randolph G. Adams, director of the William L. Clements Library of American History; Tyler Dennett, historical advisor, Department of State; Charles Moore, chairman of the National Commission of Fine Arts; and General John M. Palmer, U.S.A. (ret.), soldier and author.

fully declared, let me express to you in the warmest terms my gratitude and appreciation. The Autobiography will surely be regarded by the Library as one of its chiefest treasures, and will always enhance, in the minds of the multitudes who will see it, the regard for the Library of Congress, which, I am glad to see, is already very widely entertained.

I cannot think there is any ground for doubt as to the most appropriate place for such a memorial, if you and Mrs. Richardson have the generosity to place it out of your own possession anywhere. I have read attentively Mr. Raney's argument.[109] It has its points, but after all, Lincoln belongs to the nation more than he belongs to Illinois. By the generosity and public spirit of his son, Robert T. Lincoln, the papers which the President left behind are in the Library of Congress. A million people visit the Library of Congress every year, where thousands would see such a memento in any other place. Whatever Mr. Raney says or might say regarding the University of Chicago as a place of education, I should not be likely to dispute, having myself been for four years the head of its historical department, and appreciating the University as I do; but, what he says respecting study of Lincoln's life there by a multitude of young students is to my mind not relevant, since all such study could be adequately

based on its printed text, and no custodian would expect to have them, unless very rarely, turning the pages of the precious manuscript. I would also correct the notion that the document prepared for Scripps[110] would overshadow that which you possess. I will take Mr. Raney's word that it is here, but if so, it is among the papers bequeathed by Mr. Robert Lincoln.[111] As he gave them on condition that they should not be examined for twenty-five years (till 1947), I have myself carefully refrained (though this is perhaps construing the obligation too closely) from ever looking inside the boxes or knowing anything about their contents.

Since you ask me to suggest any variation from the text of your circular, I should have to express a doubt whether it is physically possible to group the Lincoln Autobiography, in the most complete sense, in one special exhibit with the Declaration of Independence and the Constitution of the United States. These have an architectural setting specially devised for them, to which it would be difficult, artistically or practically, to make an addition.[112] What I think the Librarian would more probably have in mind is the giving of a special treatment to the Lincoln Autobiography in a setting of the most important other memorials of President Lincoln that we have—the family Bible recording his marriage, the Bible on which he took the oath of office as President, Queen Victoria's splendid letter to Mrs. Lincoln,[113] etc.—doing this in the same upper hall in which the Declaration and the Constitution are, and in such a position as would mark our very high appreciation of its importance and value; but, not having yet had an opportunity to talk with him of the matter, I am not in a position to make definite promises as to details. We should probably wish to discuss them with you and Mrs. Richardson.

Lincoln to Fell on Dec. 20, 1859. During the last century it became separated from the Autobiography and passed into the hands of Osborn H. Oldroyd (1842-1930), an important Lincoln collector, who sold much of his collection to the federal government in 1926. This sale, however, did not include the letter. In 1931 Jameson made an unsuccessful attempt to acquire it for the Library of Congress. The letter was purchased from Oldroyd's heirs by the late Oliver R. Barrett, the noted collector, in whose hands it remained until 1950 when the Library finally purchased it at auction. It is now exhibited with the Autobiography. In his inquiry of Feb. 28, 1931, Jameson mentioned to Oldroyd's widow that Fell's descendants were considering the Library of Congress as a suitable repository for the Autobiography, and that Robert Todd Lincoln had already presented his father's papers to the government. He wrote: "They would, however, like to join with it [the Autobiography] the letter of Lincoln to Mr. Fell by which the autobiography was transmitted to the latter. It is remembered by one of the family that, years ago, both the autobiography and the letter were sent to Colonel Oldroyd, and that while the autobiography came back from him to the family, this seems not to have been the case with the transmitting letter. Allow me therefore to ask whether the letter is among the papers of Colonel Oldroyd, or, if you have not yet made so complete an examination of those papers that you can answer this question, to ask you to keep on the watch for it during the further examination of the papers in your hands, and to let me know if it is found, that correspondence may be undertaken with a view to its being joined to the autobiography. You will, I am sure, agree with me that it would be a pity for the transmitting letter to pass, through some dealer's hands, into the possession of some private collector, instead of being preserved in immediate relation to the autobiography to which it refers. . . ." (Jameson to Mrs. O. H. Oldroyd, Feb. 28, 1931, Division of Manuscripts.)

[109] McKendree Llewellyn Raney, Ph.D., Johns Hopkins University, 1904, director of the University of Chicago libraries, 1927-1942.

To CHARLES CHENEY HYDE

November 17, 1931.

My dear Mr. Hyde:[114]

The Washington *Star* mentions that Columbia Uni-

[110] John Locke Scripps (1818-1866), Chicago newspaperman, author of *The first published life of Abraham Lincoln written in the year MDCCCLX,* reprinted Detroit, Cranbrook Press, 1900. The account was originally published as a campaign document in the New York *Tribune* and in the Chicago *Press and Tribune,* in 1860.

[111] See *ante,* Jameson to Mrs. Robert Todd Lincoln, July 12, 1929, n. 56.

[112] At this time the Declaration of Independence and the Constitution were displayed in special cases on the upper floor of the main hall of the Library. They have since been removed to the National Archives where they are exhibited today.

[113] A reference to the Queen's letter of condolence to Mrs. Lincoln, dated Apr. 29, 1865, three days after word of the assassination reached England.

[114] Charles Cheney Hyde, professor of law in Northwestern University Law School, 1907-1925, Hamilton Fish Professor of International Law and Diplomacy, Columbia University, 1925-1945.

versity has bought the late Secretary Lansing's and Secretary Foster's house on Eighteenth Street.[115] I imagine that this purchase is connected with some purpose entertained with regard to the late Judge Edwin B. Parker's fund for a school or institution of international relations, and I know that you are, naturally, a member of the committee for making plans respecting the use of that fund.[116] Therefore I venture to break in with a suggestion. I do this without knowing anything of the plans of your committee, but merely presuming that an important school or institute of international relations will be likely to arrange for some Washington connections.

If so, let me mention the project which has been in the minds of several professors of American history at all times since 1901. In that year I first broached it to the American Historical Association, and they, through a committee of which I was a member, proposed it to the Carnegie Institution of Washington, then just come into existence, a plan whereby there should be brought into existence in Washington an establishment to which graduate students of American history, from whatever university, might come for periods of three months or more and get the advantages of Washington and its archives and the Library of Congress, and the competent guidance of a qualified professor, their time spent here of course counting as residence toward their degrees. It was a plan for doing for students of that subject what is done for classical students in the American schools of classical studies at Athens and Rome. The Carnegie Institution, however, resolved from the beginning not to engage in educational work, and so established a Department of Historical Research of a different type; but the idea has been constantly entertained, and from time to time revived in the constitution of committees and other short-lived machinery for carrying out the same purpose, in history and other fields, without adequate means for doing anything substantial and permanent.[117]

If you are planning that one result of Judge Parker's bequest shall be the creation of something like a branch establishment for the promotion of the studies which he had in mind, let me plead that there shall be a special and adequate provision for the pursuit of American diplomatic history. This is obviously the one place in the country for the most successful pursuit of that subject. Here are the archives of the Department of

State, and in this division of the Library of Congress the personal papers of most of the Secretaries of State (list enclosed). Moreover, under the operation of Mr. Rockefeller's great gift for photostating materials for American history in foreign archives ($100,000 a year), I have been gathering in here such a mass of photostats and other photographic reproductions of the correspondence of the British, French, Spanish, Dutch, German, Italian, Swedish, and Russian envoys to the United States with their respective foreign ministers, as provides here an additional resource, of the highest value and of great magnitude, towards the studying of diplomatic history from the point of view of the other chancelleries the importance of which procedure I do not need to emphasize.[118] . . .

To HERBERT E. BOLTON

November 4, 1932.[119]

My dear Mr. Bolton: [120]

I have been slower than I intended in responding to your inquiry of October 18,[121] but my recent long illness has left me in a shape that does not admit of full hours at the Library, and what time I spend there has in recent days been subjected to a great deal of interruption.

I am asking a man in the Catalogue Division, who especially keeps track of printed books on Hispanic-America, to furnish information about that, but unfortunately overlooked that sentence in your letter, so that the response must come a few days later.

Of original manuscript materials, in that field, much the most important thing we have is the Harkness collection, given by Mr. Edward S. Harkness some three years ago.[122] It consists of two parts, one relating to early Spanish times in Mexico, the other to the early period in Peru. The Peruvian section is briefly described in the preface to Miss Clemence's *Calendar*,[123] published last summer, which no doubt you have; or, is fully described by the *Calendar* itself. It embraces

---

[115] This was no. 1323 Eighteenth Street, N. W.

[116] Judge Edwin B. Parker (1868-1929), who had assisted in organizing the War Industries Board of the first World War, and had served as umpire on the Mixed Claims Commission after the war, left by will to Columbia University some two million dollars with which to establish a Graduate School of International Affairs. The present acting director of the school believes that the Washington purchase had no connection with the Parker School of Foreign and Comparative Law established by Columbia under Judge Parker's will.

[117] See *ante*, Oct. 15, 1901.

[118] The paragraph omitted deals with the qualifications of Professor Samuel F. Bemis, then of George Washington University, to guide the work of advanced students of American history.

[119] Division of Manuscripts, Library of Congress.

[120] Herbert E. Bolton (1870-1953) at this time chairman of the department of history and director of the Bancroft Library in the University of California, was a leading scholar in the field of Hispanic-American history.

[121] Bolton had asked for a brief account of what the Library of Congress had done during the past twenty years toward building up a collection of materials for the study of Hispanic-American history.

[122] Acquired in 1929 (see, Librarian of Congress, *Ann. Rept.*, 1928-1929: 45-46; *Ann. Rept.*, 1931-1932: 52).

[123] Clemence, Stella R., ed., *The Harkness collection in the Library of Congress: calendar of Spanish manuscripts concerning Peru 1531-1651*, Washington, D. C., Govt. Print. Off., 1932. Miss Clemence later edited *The Harkness collection in the Library of Congress: documents from early Peru, the Pizarros, and the Almagros 1531-1598*, Washington, D. C., Govt. Print. Off., 1936.

1030 pieces. The Mexican section is of about the same magnitude, but is more restricted in scope, most of the pieces relating to a series of legal proceedings concerning Martin Cortés, the son of the Conqueror.[124]

The other original manuscripts in the Library are but moderately numerous, and mostly concern the 19th century. For Mexico we have the collection of the papers of Augustin de Yturbide, some 21 portfolios; several volumes of papers of Louis Berlandier, chiefly illustrative of his scientific explorations of 1826-1834; and a few volumes, each, of papers of Col. John T. Pickett, Confederate agent in Mexico, 1860-1862, Edward L. Plumb, Secretary of Legation in Mexico, 1866-1877, and Andrew Talcott, concerned with the building of the Imperial Mexican Railway, 1865-1866. For matters further south there are the papers of Ephraim G. Squier, 10 volumes of correspondence and 7 portfolios of archaeological material; 2 letterbooks of Thomas H. Nelson, minister to Chile, 1861-1865; 2 portfolios of notes and memoranda of Joel R. Poinsett, 1810-1812, and a dozen or so volumes or portfolios of Jeremy Robinson, 1808-1842.

As regards reproductions of manuscript material preserved in other countries, what the Library has done in respect to Hispanic-American history is but a part of large general operations toward building up the Library in this side. From 1902 to 1928 the Library obtained each year a considerable number of transcripts from England, and later from France and Spain and Mexico, amounting in the whole to many thousands of pages, handwritten in the case of England and France, typewritten in the case of Spain and Mexico. The five years from September 1, 1927, to August 31, 1932, were marked by a special and more extensive endeavor to accelerate progress in this direction by a larger expenditure and fuller organization, possible by a grant of $450,000 made available for this purpose by Mr. John D. Rockefeller, Jr. These operations have been conducted under the general supervision of the Division of Manuscripts, but in Europe were managed during the first two years by Professor Samuel F. Bemis, and in the last three by Dr. Worthington C. Ford. Operations under Mr. Rockefeller's grant extended to all the European countries in which large materials for American history are preserved, and to Canada and Mexico. Since the expiration of the period during which that grant was to be available, namely since September 1 last, the work has gone on, upon a reduced and still considerable scale, in England, France, and Spain. The operations under this grant have been entirely photographic. They have resulted in the addition to the resources of the Library of nearly two million pages of photocopies.[125]

The portions of this material which can be counted as materials for Hispanic-American history have come from five places, Seville, Madrid, Simancas, Mexico City, and Vienna. The amount is about 180,000 pages from Seville, 160,000 from Madrid and Simancas, and 80,000 from the City of Mexico. What were obtained from Vienna were reproductions of that portion of the archives of the Emperor Maximilian which concerned his Mexican adventure. The material from Seville is mainly from the section called Papeles procedentes de la Isla de Cuba,[126] of which we now have reproductions of all the most important legajos—specifically, all those marked "Listed" in Dr. Hill's *Descriptive Catalogue*,[127] and some others; but also a considerable number of legajos have been obtained from the Audiencia Section—Audiencias de Guadalajara, Mexico, and Santo Domingo. The material from Madrid and Simancas is supposed to cover pretty well the essential papers of Spanish diplomacy with respect to the American colonies and the United States down to about 1880. The endeavors with respect to Mexico were directed chiefly to those materials in the archives of the Ministry of Foreign Relations, the Archivo General and the Biblioteca Nacional, which illustrate the relations between the republics of the United States and Mexico from the beginning of Mexican independence to a rather late period, in some cases 1882. Little attempt has been made to exploit the vast masses of material in the Archivo General and Library for the Colonial History of New Spain, because, it was felt that there should be one place in which material regarding the relations of the United States and Mexico should be fully represented in such copying, and that one place was obviously Washington, inevitably the mecca of students of diplomatic history, while the colonial history of Mexico might in the main be left to be the province of states and universities in California and the southwest. Aside from the diplomatic papers obtained from the Ministry of Foreign Affairs our collection of photocopies embraces such material from those sections of the Archivo General called Operaciones de Guerra, Viajes y Descubrimientos, Marine, and Tierras. Analogous material has been obtained from the National Library.

In addition to all the above, described as fruits of the operations of the last five years under the Rockefeller grant, it will not be forgotten that many thousands of papers in Spanish and Mexican archives were transcribed for the Library of Congress in earlier years, though it would be easily understood that these handwritten or typewritten transcripts do not give the same satisfaction to the researcher as he may obtain from the photographic facsimiles made in recent years and in the case of Spain, still being made.

---

[124] Miss Clemence has prepared a catalogue of the Mexican materials which is scheduled for publication within the next year.

[125] See *ante*, Jameson to Charles M. Andrews, Dec. 22, 1928, n. 27; and Jameson to Worthington C. Ford, June 22, 1929, n. 49.

[126] This huge series of documents was transferred from Havana to the Archives of the Indies at Seville in 1888-1889; it contains much relating to Florida and Louisiana.

[127] For Hill's catalogue see p. 134, n. 164.

It is proper also to mention the great mass of copies made for the late Mrs. Jeannette Thurber Connor,[128] respecting Florida, presented to the Library by her husband, but not yet available for general study; and 45 volumes of transcripts from the papers of the Inquisition in Mexico, presented more recently by G. R. G. Conway.[129]

As to technical processes, the Library's photographic work in foreign countries has consisted, in about equal measure, of the making of negative photostats, of the familiar type, and of the reproducing of pages of manuscript on photographic films of a type resembling those used in moving pictures and their subsequent enlargement to the size of the originals, in a form which gives positives, black on white. Our reproductions from Mexico are photostats; those from Spain are almost all films, not all of which have yet been enlarged.

I hope the above is about what you want.

To Arthur G. Doughty, C.M.G.

December 6, 1932.[130]

Dear Doughty: [131]

For a period of three years, which to my regret has now come to an end, the Library of Congress has been carrying on in your building a large enterprise of photocopying which, considerate as the workers have surely intended to be, must have been a source of some labor and difficulty on your part and that of your staff. You and I have hardly corresponded at all in that period, which of itself shows with how much patience and good will you have borne whatever infelicities may have attended such an invasion from without; but, now that it is ended, let me express to you my very cordial thanks for all the facilities and favors which have been shown to Miss MacSporran and to Mr. Hammond,[132] and my appreciation of the extraordinary amount of help given to our operations. We have been carrying on this sort of work in many archives and many countries, but nowhere, I think, have we been quite so generously treated as by you. I shall always remember it with gratitude.

The results are really notable. I set out to accomplish two things in the Public Archives of Canada, and they have been accomplished. We have here, in more than ten thousand pages, all the correspondence which the most careful and intelligent search could find in your archives that passed between the successive British ministers in Washington, down to recent times, and the governors general, provincial governors etc. in Canada and its provinces. Secondly, we have the essential series of your documents relating to the War of 1812. If means had held out, I should have liked to have obtained, thirdly, reproductions of a lot of your papers respecting the Indians, but that will have to wait for more prosperous times and the two collections named have been, I think the things that will be most useful to our writers and students.

Miss MacSporran has done a remarkably fine piece of work, thorough and untiring in research, most careful and intelligent in selection, and perfect in presentation. Mr. Hammond's photographic work has been of a very high order. I do not think that from any country or archive we have received better prints, and indeed hardly any have been quite so good. From what Miss MacSporran tells me he must be an exceptionally skillful and resourceful photographer.

If I were going to be able to attend the meeting of the American Historical Association at Toronto I should certainly make the expedition to Ottawa and to you in person, but I have felt obliged to give that up. I had an attack of the heart in March which laid me up in bed for five months. I came back to my work at the end of September, and find myself increasingly able to carry on, but it is thought not quite prudent for me to make the journey to Toronto at the end of the month. I am very sorry, not only because I have not missed a meeting before in nearly forty years, but especially because I know how happy a time you and your Canadian associates will be giving us.

However, here are my best greetings for Christmas and the new year, and my very hearty thanks for the unstinted generosity with which you have helped forward our work.

To Albert Bushnell Hart

March 27, 1933.

Dear Hart:

I am glad you are writing something of the sort which you describe. As to the Committee on the International [sic, National] Archive Building, however, you are a little off the track.[133]   Charles Francis Adams

[128] Mrs. Washington E. Connor (d. 1927) of New York. She and John B. Stetson, Jr., were the chief organizers of the Florida State Historical Society. In 1921, with James A. Robertson as adviser, they began a program of gathering all references in the Spanish archives relating to Florida. From this acquisition Mrs. Connor selected material for her publication on Spanish Florida (see p. 329, n. 109). Prior to her death she made additional selections with the intention of publishing, but deposited this group of materials in the Library of Congress, where it has since remained.

[129] For a useful account of George R. G. Conway of Mexico City (who died in 1951) see, Williams, Schafer, The G. R. G. Conway collection in the Library of Congress, a checklist, *Hisp. Amer. Hist. Rev.* **35**: 386-397, 1955.

[130] Division of Manuscripts, Library of Congress.

[131] See *ante,* Jameson to Doughty, Dec. 28, 1906.

[132] Miss Maysie S. MacSporran and Mr. Hammond, the photographer. Work continued in Canada until 1935.

[133] Hart had written: "Of late I have busied myself in getting together data upon my professional activities extending over the course of years. Can you give me the dates of the Committee or Commission on Public Archives of which Charles Francis Adams was chairman? The purpose was to put a pressure on Congress for a national archive building, which later was carried out to a very considerable degree through your efforts" (Hart to Jameson, Mar. 21, 1933).

was never chairman of it, and I don't think he was ever a member of it. I began a little agitation about it in 1907, before I ceased to be president, and in 1908 a committee was appointed, of which I was chairman from that time till Dec. 1928. It was at first a committee of the Council, and therefore its membership is not listed in the Proceedings of the Association as recorded in the *Annual Report* until 1919, when it begins to be listed as a committee of the Association.

To add a little to this, the agitation went very well in its first year, and by 1913 Senators and Representatives generally were aware that the thing should be done, and in the Omnibus Public Buildings Bill of March 3, 1913, it was provided for, but before it was actually authorized or any appropriations were made, came the War and a period of economy, so that the project made no further progress until the general provision was made for filling the triangle with public buildings. Then the archives project was taken up into that general scheme, and has since moved forward with the slow glacial movement of that program, till in this February the cornerstone was laid, and now the building is going up. I am hoping that it will be done by December 1934, when the AHA will hold here its annual meeting, celebrating its semi-centennial. That will be only twenty-seven years from the time when the agitation started, but one Francis Bacon, in 1593, [recommended] creation of a Public Record Office for Great Britain and they got it in 1859.[134]

To Lady Foster

                                        May 26, 1933.[135]

Dear Lady Foster:[136]

Your letter of May 5 was a source of great interest

and pleasure to me. If Sir Augustus's notes on the United States are of anything like the interest and high quality of the quotations printed from them in the Quarterly Review for June 1841 (and though a reviewer is prone to pick out plums, I think this can hardly fail to be the case), your find must be one of the greatest interest for readers of American history.[137]

I should greatly like to know more about these Notes. The Quarterly reviewer does not say, in the heading of his article, "Privately Printed," as perhaps in a former letter, writing from memory, I may have said, but "Unpublished," and I judge from your brief description that the five volumes of which you speak are manuscript. If they are as interesting as the reviewer's quotations, my thought would be that they ought to be printed if this is possible, in these bad times for the publishing business, or if not, that a manuscript of so much interest and historical value should somehow become available to students of the period of American history which is involved, if you and Sir Vere Foster could bring yourselves to part with it. Is it right that it should remain *perdu* in a country house in Ireland?

---

[134] In speaking to the American Library Association on May 26, 1914, Dr. Jameson used the dates 1616 and 1838 for this comparison. Here he doubtless refers to the petition presented to Queen Elizabeth by "great lawyers"; in the earlier speech, to the action under James I. The petitioners under James, after frequent conferences formed a plan and "jointly laid the same before his majesty, who having referred the same, together with the several former plans and reports, to the consideration of Sir Francis Bacon, then lord keeper of the great seal, and several of the king's council, they certified to his majesty, as their opinions, that the establishment of *an office of general remembrance of matters of record would be beneficial to the commonwealth,* and in no way prejudicial to any of the record officers in their several offices and places of employment. In consequence of this opinion the king by his letters patent, dated 9th October, in the fifteenth year of his reign, . . . *'granted, ordained, created, and appointed,* that there should be forever thereafter an office which should be called *the Office of general remembrance of matters of record,'"* Hall, Hubert, *Studies in English official historical documents,* 25, Cambridge Univ. Press, 1908; Ayloff, Sir Joseph, *Calendar of the ancient charters,* xxx-xxxi, Benjamin White, 1774. The variation in terminal dates results from the fact that in one instance Jameson used the date when the construction of the Public Record Office was authorized, in the other, the date when a section was ready for use.

[135] Division of Manuscripts, Library of Congress.

[136] Wife of Sir Augustus Vere Foster, 4th Bart. (1873-1947),

of Glyde Court, Ardee, co. Louth, Ireland, who was the grandson of Sir Augustus John Foster, Bart. Lady Foster died in 1938.

[137] Sir Augustus John Foster, Bart. (1780-1848), of Glyde Court, diplomat, was secretary of legation at Washington, 1804-1807; chargé d'affaires at Stockholm, 1808-1811; minister plenipotentiary at Washington, 1811-1812, at Copenhagen, 1814-1824, at Turin, 1824-1840. His "Notes on the United States of America" were compiled many years after his residency at Washington, and drawn from diaries and correspondence. Portions were published by John Gibson Lockhart in the *Quarterly Review* **68**: 20-57, with editorial comments. Two copies of the manuscript notes, each filling five notebooks, are extant: a copy in the Henry E. Huntington Library, acquired at a London auction in 1926, and the Library of Congress copy (believed to be a later version), purchased from Sir Vere Foster in 1933. The Library had already acquired from a London dealer, in 1929, eight bound volumes of correspondence and sixty-four volumes of journals and diaries of Sir Augustus John Foster. The Lockhart extracts had so excited Jameson's interest that he undertook to locate the original manuscript long before he became chief of the Division of Manuscripts. This led to his correspondence with the family at Glyde Court. In her letter of May 5, 1933 (to which reference is made in the text, above), Lady Foster wrote: "Today it struck me to look in an old bureau that had lately to be broken open in search of a Deed, and I have found the notes on the United States of America. . . ." (Division of Manuscripts).

In recent years the "Notes" have attracted the interest of scholars, and the following selections have been published: Tinkcom, Margaret B., Caviar along the Potomac: Sir Augustus John Foster's "Notes on the United States," 1804-1812, *Wm. & Mary Quart.,* 3rd ser., **8**: 88-107, 1951; Kinard, Margaret, Sir Augustus J. Foster and "The Wild Natives of the Woods," 1805-1807, *Wm. & Mary Quart.,* 3rd ser., **9**: 191-214 (with introduction by Dorothy Wollon), 1952; Tinkcom, Harry M., Sir Augustus in Pennsylvania, *Pa. Mag. of Hist. and Biog.* **75**: 369-399, 1951; Latimer, Margaret Kinard, Sir Augustus J. Foster in Maryland, *Md. Hist. Mag.* **47**: 283-296; and Davis, Richard Beale, ed., *Jeffersonian America: notes on the United States of America collected in the years 1805-6-7 and 11-12 by Sir Augustus John Foster, Bart.,* San Marino, Huntington Library, 1954.

I think certainly not, if I can judge from the long quotations in the Quarterly, which are marked by unusual gifts of observation and style, and by a fairness and mellowness of judgment that marks the advance from the intelligent youth of twenty-five or thirty who writes sprightly and satirical letters to his mother (in, *The Two Duchesses*),[138] to the experienced old diplomat of sixty.

I should greatly delight to have these volumes of manuscript here, associated with that section of Sir Augustus's papers that we bought at a London sale two or three years ago. Miss Thornton, granddaughter of that Sir Edward Thornton who was in charge of British interests here from 1800 to 1803, has presented us with the manuscript of an interesting though fragmentary body of memoirs which he similarly wrote in later years,[139] but that was a small manuscript, and I should not think it reasonable to ask you to give us Sir Augustus Foster's five volumes of notes. Could you bring yourselves to sell them to us? The Library has not money at present, but will have some after the new fiscal year begins, July 1, though indeed much less than in previous years, Congress having, properly enough, cut down our appropriations in view of the general situation. If you could entertain this thought, you would perhaps have a notion of price.[140]

Meantime, I should be greatly obliged if you would give me some statistical data as to such matters as the number and sizes of the pages of manuscript or proof sheets.

To PHILIPPE BUNAU-VARILLA

June 26, 1933.[141]

Dear Sir:[142]

The Division of Manuscripts in the Library of Congress has much the largest and most important collection of manuscript material for the history of the United States. It embraces the papers of nearly all our Presidents, most of our Secretaries of State, many Senators and Representatives, Generals and Admirals, and other public characters, and is constantly used by historians. The enclosed circular sets forth some of the reasons which have caused them or their descendants to give or bequeath papers concerning their public lives to this depository, for permanent preservation.

Few episodes in the history of the United States have been of more momentous importance than the development of those public relations with the Isthmus of Panama in which you had so distinguished a share. I take it for granted that a collection of papers in your possession illuminates the history of that episode as nothing else can do. It is very likely that many papers in such a collection are so confidential in nature that they should not be submitted to examination, even by serious historical writers, till a later date; but, on the other hand, would it not be a great pity that a body of materials so necessary to the true understanding of events so momentous in their future consequences should be exposed to any of those chances of destruction which await materials left permanently in private hands. I write therefore to inquire whether it would not seem to you possible that, under whatever conditions or restrictions may seem to you desirable, arrangements might be made whereby such records and correspondence as you have kept might ultimately be transferred to a permanent institution like this, the national library of the nation most concerned. I should hope that it might be so, and that the necessary conditions could be worked out without difficulty. We have much material that is temporarily reserved from examination—one large collection till 1947, another till 1951[143]—and all conditions agreed to are maintained with the utmost rigidity. I should like to feel that the record of your part in the Panama transactions would not be lost to the historians of the future.

If anything in these suggestions appeals to your mind, I should be glad of further correspondence.[144]

To SOL BLOOM

January 24, 1934.[145]

My dear Mr. Bloom:[146]

Now that the work of the Commission for Celebrating the Two Hundredth Anniversary of the Birth of George Washington is drawing to its close, I wish to

---

[138] Foster, Vere, *The Two Duchesses*, London, Blackie & Son, 1898, an edition of the correspondence of Georgiana, Duchess of Devonshire, and of Elizabeth, Duchess of Devonshire, containing biographical data on the latter's son, Sir Augustus John Foster. Lady Foster (née Hervey) married secondly the Fifth Duke of Devonshire. The editor of this correspondence, Sir Vere Henry Lewis Foster (1819-1900) was a younger son of Sir Augustus John Foster, and an uncle of the gentleman with whom the Library of Congress was negotiating.

[139] See *ante*, Jameson to Ruth Anna Fisher, May 14, 1931.

[140] The "Notes" were purchased by the Library late in 1933 (see, Librarian of Congress, *Ann. Rept.*, 1933-1934: 35).

[141] Division of Manuscripts, Library of Congress.

[142] Col. Philippe Bunau-Varilla (1859-1940), French soldier and diplomat, was chief engineer for the New Panama Canal Company, and later represented the newly established isthmian republic in its negotiations with the United States in 1903.

[143] These dates refer to the Lincoln papers (opened in 1947), and probably to portions of the papers of Secretary of State Robert Lansing, though the latter material was actually opened in 1949.

[144] In reply to Jameson's inquiry Colonel Bunau-Varilla signified that he had already specified in his will that the Library of Congress was to receive his papers (Bunau-Varilla to Jameson, Sept. 17, 1933, Division of Manuscripts). In 1938, two years prior to his death, the Library received the first group of material from him. In 1947 additional papers were received from his son, Etienne; these also related to the Panama Canal Zone (see, Librarian of Congress, *Ann. Rept.*, 1938-1939: 51, and *Ann. Rept.*, 1947: 42).

[145] Division of Manuscripts, Library of Congress.

[146] Sol Bloom (1870-1949), member of Congress from New York, 1923-1949, and director of the U. S. George Washington Bicentennial Commission.

take the occasion to say to you personally, what I have said to many other persons in recent months, that your activities in the work of the Commission have been of extraordinary value to the country. I had feared that the memory of Washington was becoming a little dim with the lapse of years and the change in the character of public sentiments, for it is no longer as easy as it once was for our people, especially our young people, to appreciate a dignified eighteenth-century gentleman, a Virginian squire and magnate. I ardently desired that the bicentennial celebrations should have the effect of freshening that image in the popular mind. It is you, more than anyone else, who has brought this about, by enterprise and enthusiasm and painstaking work; and I can hardly see how anyone, whose mind is open to any impressions at all, can have failed to have the figure of Washington made clearer and grander and more impressive by reason of the labors which you have carried through under the auspices of the Commission. The country is much to be congratulated.

To HERBERT PUTNAM.

1899   April 5   1934 [147]

In vain, as April Fifth draws near,
You yield yourself to modest fear
          Of laudatory talk;
In vain, betimes you speed away
And give it out that you shall stay
          Till Friday in New York.

For, after all, one seldom hears
Of terms of five-and-thirty years,
          To which to "point with pride";
And in this case, and on this date,
Man's cosmic urge to celebrate
          Is amply justified.

The Muses' fountain must not gush;
We must not make our chieftain blush
          By saying all we feel;
But admiration for his skill,
Affection deep, and right good will,
          Don't ask us to conceal!

Bear with us if, in this mild way,
We ask to celebrate the day;
          The verses soon will stop.
You do not have to make a speech,
And Lewis [148] has, within your reach,
          Your customary chop.

---

[147] Verses for the thirty-fifth anniversary of Herbert Putnam's appointment as Librarian of Congress, read at luncheon at the "Round Table," where Dr. Putnam, members of the library staff, and guests were accustomed to gather.

[148] Lewis Alexander, a familiar and beloved figure in the Library, who was the Librarian's messenger, and doubled as major domo of the "Round Table."

To SAMUEL FLAGG BEMIS

June 26, 1934.

Dear Bemis: [149]

. . . It is true that on the whole, in the conference, the Senate bill prevailed over the House bill, and a pity it is 'tis true, for the House bill was distinctly better, and some of the provisions of the Senate bill, left in the residuum, are distinctly unfortunate. Still, they are no wise fatal or disastrous, and on the whole the act is a pretty good one. It is of course a pity that there ever was a McKellar bill, but its most objectionable features had been removed from it before the matter came to conference.[150]

The exemption from the Civil Service laws will do no harm if the right kind of man is appointed archivist. The Classification Acts ought to have been applied, and Fess told me that he would see to it that they were, but he did not. The provision as to senatorial confirmation of one or two of the most highly paid assistants is regrettable, but even Fess thought that desirable, in the case of positions so important, and the representatives yielded.

I will see that you have a copy of the act, when I get some. As to appointment of an archivist, I judge that none will be made till after the President's return from Honolulu. The Executive Committee of the A. H. A. wishes to advocate the nomination of R. D. W. Connor of North Carolina, but his obligations to his university are making him hesitate about allowing his name to be used.[151] . . .

To HERMAN P. KOPPLEMANN

January 19, 1935.[152]

My dear Mr. Kopplemann: [153]

I am sorry that I have not been able until today to

---

[149] From the files of Professor Samuel F. Bemis.

[150] The bills under discussion were for the organization of the archives. The House bill was introduced by Representative Sol Bloom, that in the Senate by Senator McKellar. In a letter of June 19, Jameson wrote to Professor Bemis: "I am somewhat disappointed that the final result is not better, but the conferees labored with the matter in great haste, with their minds distracted by other things, on the morning of what was expected to be the last day of the session, and therefore their combination of the Senate bill with the House bill (which was distinctly better), proved to be a little clumsy in some respects. In spite of whatever efforts were made to inform them, and to steer them right, they had not the time to digest the whole matter perfectly. However, the act is good in the main, and workable. Anyhow, the main point is that an act was passed. There was a time when I feared that session would end without this."

[151] Professor Connor yielded and became the first archivist.

[152] Division of Manuscripts, Library of Congress.

[153] Member of Congress from Connecticut, 1933-1939, 1941-1943, 1945-1947.

make formal reply to your letter of January 16.[154] First let me say that I must pointedly disclaim any position of authority with respect to early Connecticut history. Any pronouncements that I might make in that field would be only of secondary importance. The high authorities on Connecticut history are in Connecticut. Everyone who has any real position in American history would immediately agree that the foremost authority in Colonial history that we now have, or ever have had, is Professor Charles M. Andrews of New Haven, who, I think, was the original chairman of the historical committee provided by Connecticut's Tercentenary Commission. The present chairman, Professor Dutcher[155] of Middletown (Wesleyan University) is also an excellent scholar. I say these things merely to indicate that if the Tercentenary Commission has decided on the year 1636, it is certain to have done so on the best grounds, and certainly there is no one in Washington who will be qualified to upset or contradict its conclusions.

You say the Post Office Department desires to know, first, the date of the first real settlement in Connecticut, and secondly, the name of the town in which such settlement was made. I think that this is to take up the matter in the wrong way, with notions resting on an insecure basis. It assumes that the first settlement of any state or colony is necessarily made by a large mass of people settling themselves on the same date within the area of one township. That is not always the case. It was not the case with Connecticut. The Dutch at Manhattan sent out in 1633 some small expedition that built a trading post or fort within the present limits of Hartford, and these men whose number and names no one knows, continued there for a time until they were engulfed or "frozen out" by the increasing multitude of English settlers and gave up their enterprise. In the same year a party of men from the Plymouth Colony did much the same thing at another point on the Connecticut River. No one, however, could properly regard these events as the foundation of Connecticut, for what were established were only posts for trading with the Indians. The "settlements," if one could call them so, were purely temporary, and nothing substantial came from the endeavors—certainly not the Connecticut that we know and whose foundation we wish to celebrate.

I believe that some exploring parties from the Massachusetts towns came into the present Connecticut area in 1634, but I think it is not known that they stayed through the winter of 1634-1635 or can be said to have founded a settlement. In 1634 a moderate number of

Massachusetts settlers planted themselves at Newtown, Dorchester, and Watertown, now called Hartford, Windsor, and Wethersfield, and before the winter set in another party, acting on authority from England, stationed themselves at the mouth of the River and began a fort at what is now called Saybrook. The main body of settlers, however, for the three towns up the River, came in 1636, and in April of that year they held the first meeting of their legislative body or court.

I presume that this is why the Tercentenary Commission has settled upon 1636. I should think their decision might well be thought conclusive.

I think the above statements are substantially correct, but, as I have said, I do not profess to have any authoritative knowledge.

To WALDO G. LELAND

March 26, 1935.

Dear Leland:

I quite agree with you that the John Carter Brown Library might be made of more use. It will always be used spontaneously by persons from elsewhere who come to consult its wonderful resources, but its use might also be extended into forms that would bring credit directly to the college, and, what is more important, that would bring results more systematic and tangible, and of more direct and visible benefit to the scholarship of the country.

More broadly, there are in Providence extraordinary resources for the pursuit of the earlier part of American history, embracing not only those of the John Carter Brown Library, but those of the University library, the Rhode Island Historical Society, the Athenaeum, and the Public Library; so I have always thought that Providence was a particularly favorable place for work in the history of the period before 1800. Things might well be so organized as to produce more systematic results from all this material. This will need primarily a qualified man, and as you indicate, the most eligible mode of providing him would be through some sort of chair in the University. I should hardly think, however, that the best means would be through a professor whose primary function was the teaching of Colonial history. That will never appeal to more than a few undergraduates, and I should agree with them in thinking that young Rhode Islanders had better be studying the later and more important periods of American history. The number of graduate students of American history, too, will never be large. I could conceive of a chair whose incumbent, while offering a course or two in Colonial history, or the history of the period before 1800, should have as his main function the organizing of fruitful activities in that field by his own agency and that of others. A series of publications in that field might be devised that would be of real credit to the University and of more importance than the mere bibliographical notes and monographs that the

---

[154] Kopplemann had appealed to the Post Office Department for a special stamp commemorating the three hundredth anniversary of the settlement of Connecticut, but found it was first necessary to ascertain the date and place of the first settlement (Kopplemann to Jameson, Jan. 16, 1935, Division of Manuscripts).

[155] George M. Dutcher, Ph.D., Cornell, 1903, professor of history in Wesleyan University.

librarians of such libraries are apt to generate. I know too little of the University's means to advocate positively such an establishment, but I should hope it might be possible. There are now a considerable number of research professorships in the country, but they are of course expensive. It might be possible to find some young Providence man of excellent scholarship, who has a strong interest in this direction, such as Brigham [156] had when he was in college, and who perhaps, having some means of his own, might be content with a moderate stipend for a congenial task not overexacting. I have seen and known of instances of this sort of chair. The nearest was perhaps that professorship of Maryland Colonial History which they had, and I suppose still have, at Georgetown University, and which was occupied very happily by Father Devitt during my early years in Washington.[157] His endowment was slight, but he was a priest.

These are only suggestions. I shall hope, however, that in some way or other the thought you have outlined to me may be able to take effect through some young man who, besides adequate scholarship, has some gift of planning and managing.

To WILLIAM EVARTS BENJAMIN

June 17, 1935.[158]

My dear Mr. Benjamin: [159]

In view of your generosity with respect to the foundation for our Chair of American History, I have never thought it proper to trouble you with suggestions of further benevolence to the Library, unless some very signal occasion should arise. Such an occasion has, however, now arisen. In brief, Mr. Franklin Bache, engineer, of Philadelphia, has resolved that he must sell his collection of papers of his great-great-grandfather, Benjamin Franklin. As neither the American Philosophical Society, the Historical Society of Pennsylvania, nor the University of Pennsylvania, feels able or disposed to undertake the purchase of the collection *en bloc* he is preparing to dispose of the collection by sale at auction.

It seems to me, and I think it will seem to you, a real calamity that this collection should be broken up and dispersed. It is one of very great value and interest, which has come down in the family with very little access or use on the part of historical investigators, and constitutes an important fraction of Franklin's papers—not so large as that possessed by the American Philosophical Society, perhaps not as large as that which is in the Library of Congress, but certainly larger than any other (unless Mr. Mason's,[160] the extent of which I do not accurately know).

Am I not fully warranted in saying that, if there is any possible way of keeping this collection intact, and adding it to one of the existing great collections of Franklin material, I ought to do everything I can to preserve it from such dispersion? And surely the Library of Congress is the best place for it.

These are papers of one who was (save perhaps Washington) not only the most famous American of his time, but the one who as diplomat and otherwise did more than anyone else to bring the United States into being as a national power. If any papers should be a national possession, surely these. Yet it would apparently be out of the question at present to try to get Congress to appropriate money for the purpose, and Mr. Bache, though he would very greatly prefer to have the papers kept together, does not entertain the thought of any such proposal. I believe it is only by the generosity of some individual who is able to appreciate the importance that the collection could be secured by the Library of Congress.

I write, as you see, to learn whether this opportunity appeals to you as a possibility. I cannot make the enquiry more definite by any indication as to price. I have never said more to Mr. Bache than that I knew one person who might possibly resolve to make such a gift to the Library, and he has not gone beyond saying that in such case, which he would very heartily welcome, he should propose a valuation by three qualified persons. He has a manuscript catalogue covering the whole collection.

So I write, merely in a tentative way. I cannot, however, conceal my ardent hope that the prospect of such a splendid gift to the nation may appeal to you.[161]

To MRS. GRATTAN DOYLE

December 9, 1935

My dear Mrs. Doyle: [162]

An Ithaca friend has sent me the enclosed clipping from the *Ithaca Journal* in which Professor Becker sets forth in full, his defense against the almost incredibly

---

[156] Clarence S. Brigham. Mr. Leland, who had been elected a member of the Board of Fellows of the Corporation of Brown University in 1933, was concerned that the John Carter Brown Library, one of the most important collections of Americana in the world, was not more resorted to for research, especially by graduate students.

[157] Rev. E. I. Devitt, S.J., professor of colonial history, Georgetown University, died on Jan. 26, 1920, and no one was appointed to the position after that time.

[158] Division of Manuscripts, Library of Congress.

[159] William Evarts Benjamin of New York (see p. 327, n. 100), financier, collector of historical documents and objets d'art, in 1927 had provided the Library of Congress with an endowment of $75,000, the income from which sustains the Chair of American History, a dignity since held by the chiefs of the Division of Manuscripts.

[160] William Smith Mason (1866) formerly of Evanston, Ill., who had accumulated a large collection of Franklin material which he later presented to Yale University.

[161] The Bache collection was acquired by the American Philosophical Society by private purchase.

[162] Mrs. Henry Grattan Doyle was president of the Board of Education, Washington, D. C.

silly attack which has been made upon him and his textbook of modern history.[163] It may be that you already have a copy of it, but even so, you might find use for a duplicate.

Thinking that the real point in the matter is not whether Professor Becker is a Communist (which, of course, he isn't) but what the book actually says, I have just been reading those pages of his textbook which deal with the Russian Revolution and its consequences during the subsequent years. If I were not already familiar with the kind of attacks which ignorant and unthinking people make on textbooks of history, I should think it incredible that anyone could find in those pages anything to which to object. They give a straightforward, true, and well-balanced account of these Russian movements, setting forth plainly the tyranny and horrors which have accompanied them, but also, as an honest man should, stating two or three notable successes of the movement,—and all in a very interesting manner.

The head and front of Mr. Becker's offending seems to be that he has declared the Russian Revolution and its consequences to have been perhaps the most interesting and most important movement of recent times. If a total change of the political and social system of a population of one hundred and forty millions is not enormously interesting and important, in heaven's name what is? I see that some zealots maintain that Communism should not even be mentioned in our schools. If a textbook in modern history is to omit all the recent history of Russia because we do not like Communism, all the recent history of Germany, Italy, Hungary and Poland, because we do not like Dictatorships, and all the recent history of England, Belgium, the Netherlands, Denmark, Sweden and Norway, because we do not like Monarchies, surely the ostrich has nothing on us.

There is an aspect of the matter which I have not seen mentioned, but which is of great importance. During the fifty-six years that I have been occupied with history, few things have been more gratifying than the improvement of textbooks of history. When I was a boy, they were dull and lifeless compendiums, made by second-rate minds, which the pupil was expected to memorize and hoped soon to forget. Of late, they have often been made by historians of the highest quality, such as Professor Becker, whom I think to be the most brilliant historical writer that we have in this country. If various "pressure groups," securing the aid of timid school boards and time-serving publishers, are to control our textbooks of history, we cannot expect that such men as he will be willing to prepare them. We shall slip back into the old system of machine-made books, prepared by persons who have no thought but to seem orthodox, and to get past all critics by abandoning all thought. I ardently hope that the School Board of Washington will, as on some previous occasions, refuse to succumb to the clamor of ignorant zealots.

To Allen French

March 5, 1936.[164]

My dear Mr. French: [165]

This is in reply to your letter of March 4.

I do not know of anyone who is preparing a book, or is engaged in any serious writing upon the Andros period in New England history. It is possible that Miss Viola F. Barnes of Mt. Holyoke College, whose work in that field you doubtless know, is further engaged in it.[166] At any rate, I think she would know if anyone else is so engaged. It seems likely also that Mr. Clifford K. Shipton would be likely to have heard of any such person, by reason of his work on the Harvard Graduates (Sibley) of that period.[167]

---

[163] Professor Becker's text-book, *Modern history,* N. Y., Silver, Burdett, 1931, had been attacked by the Federation of Citizens Association of the District of Columbia, and an investigation was being conducted by the Board of Education of the District. This attack Becker answered in the Ithaca *Journal,* Nov. 27, 1935. Here he emphasized the fact that to expound the ideas of Marx or Lenin did not mean agreement with them; to state that Russia was producing in 1930 as much as it had produced in 1913 did not mean that he preferred the Russian industrial system to our own; and to say that the Russian Revolution was one of the most important movements of our time was not to say that he approved of that movement. Obviously his critics also found it an important movement. Mr. Sullivan had called him a "well-known communist writer"; Mr. Hacker, in the *New Republic* deplored the fact that he was an "old-fashioned Liberal," whose "fine and independent mind" was not sufficiently fine and independent to subscribe to the Marxian doctrine of history. For his actual opinions, Becker refers to passages in *Every man his own historian,* 125, N. Y., Appleton-Century-Crofts, 1935. "I have no faith in force and oppression as the primary means of achieving the good life. I am not as yet a non-resistance pacifist. Any government is probably better than none, and all governments rest at least [last] on force. But I believe that the essential test of civilized society is the extent to which law and public authority rest on free discussion and voluntary consent. . . . I have no faith in the possibility of abolishing oppression by oppressing oppressors. . . . I believe therefore that all the great and permanently valuable achievements of civilization have been won by the free play of intelligence in opposition to, or in spite of, the pressure of mass emotion and the effort of organized authority to enforce conformity to [sic] in conduct and opinions. I do not believe that there has been, or that there will be, a high civilization in any country in which the mind of man is limited to the expression of ideas authorized by public authority." He adds: "If this makes me out a Communist then there is *no* meaning in words." For the attack on the textbook, see Washington *Herald,* Nov. 21, 1935.

[164] Division of Manuscripts, Library of Congress.

[165] Allen French (1870-1946) of Concord, Mass., who wrote on New England subjects, including *First year of the American Revolution,* N. Y., Houghton Mifflin Co., 1934.

[166] Viola F. Barnes, author of *Dominion of New England, a study in British colonial history,* New Haven, Yale Univ. Press, 1923.

[167] Sibley, John Langdon, *Biographical sketches of graduates of Harvard University* (continued by Clifford K. Shipton), 8v., Boston, Mass. Hist. Soc., 1873-1951.

In the matter of photographic copies of early New England documents, also, I am obliged to say that people in Boston are likely to be better informed than I. In the large work of photocopying from English archives in which this Division of Manuscripts has been engaged during the past eight years that I have been here, I have thus far given attention, in the case of the Public Record Office, somewhat more to the diplomatic materials (correspondence of the British Ministers here with the foreign office) than to the Colonial period, and in the Colonial period, while we have copies of most of the useful material relating to the Colonies from New York to Virginia, I have refrained from copying New England material at the one end, and that relating to the Carolinas and Georgia at the other end. People come to us more largely for materials relating to colonies relatively near to Washington. The southern-most colonies and those of New England have done so much copying and are likely to do so much more, and students of their history are so much more likely to work in local repositories than here, that I have up to the present time preserved this (confessed) inequality of treatment. I have to say, however, that as to anything now going forward in New England, respecting copying some British sources, I know only that some effort is being made by the Essex Institute,[168] through an organization in England calling itself by some such name as Historical Record Agency, or the like, but consisting, I rather fear, of two or three men in London of the antiquarian type, not especially wise as to what is important in American history.

For avoidance of going to England for historical researches, my best suggestion, for anything one can bear to have done through the eyes of another, is to put any searches in the hands of Miss Ruth A. Fisher, 29 Abercorn Place, St. John's Wood, London. N.W. 8. She is a very clever American woman, who knows the American materials in the Public Record Office better than anyone else does or ever has, except Charles Andrews, and who makes her living by just such services. She is and has been for eight years the researcher and agent employed by this Division of the Library of Congress in all its procuring of photocopies and in searches, and before that for several years I made use of her services for the Department of Historical Research in the Carnegie Institution of Washington. She is intelligent, learned, accurate, businesslike, and a good diplomatist.[169]

So far as the British Museum is concerned, you probably know that we have copies of all their materials relating to the United States. I could send you a list of the New England volumes from the PRO of which we have copies, if that would be useful to you. These and the BM materials can be sent out on loan to any reasonably fireproof libraries.

To Ira E. Bennett

March 18, 1936.[170]

My dear Mr. Bennett: [171]

You have asked me whether some of the manuscripts in the Library of Congress have no stories attached to them which would be of interest to the general public. I can think of several.

Certainly one of the most valuable and interesting manuscripts which we (or anyone else) have is our Codex of Christopher Columbus's book of privileges. In 1502, between his third and fourth voyages, Columbus, anxious to preserve with all certainty the records of his various grants and titles received from Ferdinand and Isabella, gathered scribes into his house in Seville and caused several copies of all these documents to be transcribed on parchment. Of the resulting books, two were sent to Genoa, and one of them is there now, while the other, carried to Paris by Napoleon, is still in Paris. Columbus's descendant, the Duke of Veragua, has another copy. The fourth, and apparently the only other complete copy, was bought by Edward Everett in Florence in 1818, for a quite moderate sum. For a long time after his death, it could not be found, but at the end of the century it was found by his son, Dr. William Everett, in the lower and disused part of a cupboard in the old house at Medford, Massachusetts. In 1902 he sold it to the Library of Congress for a sum much less than its value, if indeed, its value could be calculated. It is a beautifully written book of about 200 pages containing a text of about 40 documents, attested at the end by the public notary of Seville.

That cupboards, while they have their uses, have also their fatalities, is also illustrated by the story of a manuscript written by Sir Augustus Foster, a very intelligent British diplomat who was Minister to the United States in 1811 and up to the outbreak of the war in July, 1812. In 1841 there appeared in the *Quarterly Review* an article (anonymous, but written by Lockhart the editor, Sir Walter Scott's son-in-law and biographer) the heading of which indicates it as being based on "Notes on the United States of America by Sir Augustus Foster, unpublished." Lockhart gives long and interesting extracts from them, but the book itself could nowhere be found in our time, either as a privately printed volume or in manuscript. Search was made for it, among other places, in the country house in Ireland in which the present descendant of the writer, Sir Vere Foster, now resides. Then, suddenly,

<hr>

[168] See *ante,* Jameson to Harriet S. Tapley, Mar. 5, 1931.

[169] See *ante,* Jameson to Ruth Anna Fisher, Sept. 8, 1924, May 14, 1931.

[170] Division of Manuscripts, Library of Congress.

[171] Ira E. Bennett of Washington, D. C., journalist, who replied that he hoped to write upon the vicissitudes of manuscripts (Bennett to Jameson, Mar. 20, 1936, Division of Manuscripts).

it came to light in 1933, found in that very house, in a cupboard of which the key had been broken in the lock. Singularly, the provision regarding it in the will of Sir Augustus Foster prescribes that the "Notes" shall not be published until ninety years from the time of his death! The manuscript consists of five volumes, with a total of some 700 pages, and is replete with interest for the student of the times of Jefferson and Madison.[172]

There is also some romance in the story of the Harkness collection of manuscripts coming down from the early days of Spanish conquest and settlement in Peru and Mexico, documents of great interest and value, most generously presented to the Library some years ago by Mr. Edward S. Harkness.[173] The Spanish habit in those early days was for a notary to make copies of letters and documents, who then gave the attested copy to the applicant and retained the signed original. An English mining engineer ranging around through various parts of Peru, cultivated everywhere the families of old notaries, and amassed a collection of extraordinary interest, embracing such things as a number of documents subscribed by Pizarro with his mark (for the great conqueror could not write) or a tailor's bill for Hernando De Soto.

Papers of much later times also have their stories. Twenty-odd years ago, a scholar in this city was asked by the late Charles Francis Adams, then writing on the diplomatic history of the Civil War period, to see if there could be found in France the papers of John Slidell, whom the Confederate government had sent as envoy to Napoleon III. The friend to whom application was made wrote to the late Mr. Henri Vignaud,[174] for many years secretary of our Embassy in Paris, who, however, had first gone there as secretary to Slidell. Mr. Vignaud wrote that Slidell's daughters had burned all his papers, but he would send what little he himself had of papers of the Confederate period, and that, after Mr. Adams had done with them, the correspondent might put them where he thought best. Apart from some letters, the main item was a letterbook kept by Henry Hotze who served the Confederacy in London as a sort of Consul General. After Mr. Adams's death, these materials for some years could not be found, but finally turned up and came to the Library of Congress. Hotze's letters to Secretaries Hunter and Benjamin are already among the papers of the Confederate State Department in the Library, and so the letterbook might not have been of much interest in itself, but, in the end of the volume, Hotze had inserted accounts of all the secret-service expenditures of the Confederate Government that passed through his hands, a curious record.[175]

Another instance. A school master in New Jersey reported from one of his pupils that the latter's mother, very poor, lately removing to some rented house, had found under the eaves a little packet of papers of unknown origin, which the Library gladly bought, for one of them was a letter of blazing indignation, narrating the affair of the *Chesapeake* and the *Leopard,* written to his father by William H. Allen, at that time third lieutenant of the *Chesapeake,* who fired the one shot that was fired in its defense, and took the lead in the junior officers' denunciation of Barron's misconduct. Allen was one of the naval heroes of the War of 1812, who, in 1813, went in command of the *Argus,* after a spectacular destruction of commerce in the English Channel (23 British vessels in 19 days) and was mortally wounded in the fight of the *Pelican.*[176]

If these are of use to you, I shall be much gratified.

To Tracy W. McGregor

April 22, 1936

Dear Mr. McGregor: [177]

    . . . I now shall speak of another matter because of what you said of your tentative thoughts respecting Charlottesville. I hope you will sometime take into consideration the alternative possibility, as to the future of your remarkable library, of doing something like what my Amherst classmate, Henry Folger, did with his Shakespeare library. He had no connection with Washington, but, after considering everything very carefully, as was his wont, he decided to make his collection, not precisely a national property (for it has its own trustees, the trustees of Amherst College), but essentially a national possession and, for that purpose, to put it in juxtaposition with the Library of Congress. The effect is, that all who come to his library for purposes of research, in the special rooms behind the scenes, enjoy the great advantage of having at their disposal, with convenience, all the resources of America's largest library. There is a good deal in that, for almost daily I am impressed, by various happenings, with the advantage one has here with any enquiry, from the abundance of all sorts of learned material, beyond what can be had anywhere else.

---

[172] See *ante,* Jameson to Lady Foster, May 26, 1933.

[173] See *ante,* Jameson to Herbert E. Bolton, Nov. 4, 1932.

[174] See *ante,* Jameson to Henry Vignaud, Mar. 8, 1909.

[175] See *ante,* Jameson to Worthington C. Ford, June 22, 1929. Jameson later made use of the Hotze material in an article (see p. 121, n. 114).

[176] The letters of William Henry Allen, naval officer, include the letter to his father, General William Allen, of Providence, R. I., July 17, 1807, in which Barron is denounced. The papers were purchased by the Library in 1934.

[177] Tracy William McGregor (1869-1936), a Detroit business man, much interested in education and in civic services. A few years before this he had settled in Washington. Dr. Jameson had come to know him in connection with what was called the McGregor plan, a plan to encourage in college students a love of rare books. To selected colleges, $500 a year was granted if they would add an equal sum. The $1000 was used, chiefly, for the purchase of Americana, which the committee managing the plan, acquired and turned over to the college.

Two weeks from the date of this letter Mr. McGregor suddenly died. The headquarters for administering the plan were moved to Ann Arbor, where the work was carried on under the direction of a committee of the American Historical Association. The purchases were brought to an official close in 1943.

I shall naturally be thought to be speaking as an official of the Library of Congress, but I have been here only eight years, out of thirty-one spent in Washington at large, and I have always been very eager to see Washington made, much more largely than hitherto, the place of resort of scholars and men of learning and investigation. Anything that helps toward that end ought always to command a favorable word from me, even at the risk of seeming to "butt in." [178] . . .

To HENRY E. BOURNE, DUMAS MALONE, AND HARRIS E. STARR

June 11, 1936 [179]

'Tis sweet to wield the azure pencil
    O'er manuscripts that come and go,
To seize the good with hand prehensile,
    And doom the rest to flames below,
    To see that A shall strike no blow
Beneath the belt, reviewing B,
    Nor Y shall vex the soul of X
By caustic words unduly free. [180]

But also sweet to be returning
    To Cleveland's academic shades
To steady in the paths of learning
    The feet of her aspiring maids,
    And, ranging over past decades,
With children's children round one's chair,
    Once more relate the grisly fate
Of Danton and of Robespierre.

---

[178] Mr. McGregor replied to this letter on Apr. 24: "Such an idea has once or twice passed through my own mind in a vague sort of way, but without arousing any enthusiasm on my part. The chief reason against Washington seemed to be that, at the present time at least, my collection of books was not important enough nor of sufficient size to stand alone under such circumstances. Now that you have brought forward such an idea in more definite fashion than I had myself, I shall be pleased to think about it and to hear from you again or to talk with you at some convenient time." According to the terms of his will, made some time before this, his library was to go to a southern university and the trustees, after his death, decided upon the University of Virginia.

[179] "Sometime in June, probably early in the month, some of us are planning—Charles Warren and Leland and I—to have a dinner at the Mayflower in compliment to both Bourne and Dumas Malone, Bourne's service ending at the end of June and Malone's residence ending here in that same month, for he goes to be director of the Harvard University Press and will wind up the work of the *Dictionary* as well as he can in the summer with only occasional visits here for that purpose. I am sure that it would be a great pleasure to both of them, and to us all, if you could find the time to send some message that could be read at the dinner" (Jameson to Ambassador William E. Dodd, Berlin, Apr. 28, 1936).

Bourne was retiring as editor of the *American Historical Review,* to return to Cleveland; Harris E. Starr, associate editor of the *Dictionary* was to be in New Haven.

[180] Here Jameson stole a stanza from the lines which he read at the dinner of Feb. 24, 1928.

'Tis sweet to spend one's days assessing
    The merits of the mighty dead;
With streaks of cursing and of blessing
    All down the line from A to Zed,
    Till scoundrels on their dying bed
To paths of virtue quickly flee
    Because they fear, as death draws near,
The judgment of the D. A. B.

Yet sweet New Haven's spires to bless,
    And be once more its guiding Starr;
To turn the crank of Harvard's press
    And spread its products near and far;
    To give complacency a jar,
With golden breezes fill the sail,
    And so confound the grudging sound
Of those who cry, To Hell with Yale.

But what of us, who sit here grieving
    As you disperse to various parts?
Do you not know that you are leaving
    A void in forty friendly hearts?
    But none the less, as each departs,
To heavy toil or light repose,
    At Fate's command we press his hand,
And wish him joy where'er he goes. [181]

To THOMAS A. ČAPEK

September 28, 1936. [182]

My dear Mr. Čapek: [183]

On reporting to the Librarian, Dr. Putnam, respecting your very remarkable and interesting collection of Bohemica, I find he entirely agrees with me that it is of very great value for present and future students and that, if you should be so generous as to present it to the Library of Congress, it would be received with most cordial gratitude. Institutions can not make such collections by their own efforts; to do so requires the enthusiasm, patient labor, and special knowledge of one who, as you have done in this case, devotes years to the pursuit of the rarer objects, and devotes the needful pains to the completing of series less rare.

---

[181] On the appearance of the last volume of the *Dictionary,* Charles Warren (1868-1954) wrote to Jameson, Jan. 21, 1937: "As I thus refreshed my memory, I was the more and more amazed with the manner in which your original conception had been so completely realized. As I wrote to Dr. Malone, it seemed to me that it is very rare than any man's idea could be so fully and satisfactorily carried out, as has been your original conception. I wish now to again extend to you personally, my very warm congratulations on the successful completion of the great work whose success is entirely due to four men—Mr. Ochs, Dr. Allen Johnson, Dr. Malone, and yourself."

[182] Division of Manuscripts, Library of Congress.

[183] Thomas A. Čapek (1861-1950), born in Czechoslovakia, came to the United States in 1880, and became an eminent lawyer, journalist, and banker. Čapek collected much valuable material on the Czechs in America, and was the author of a number of works including *The Czechs (Bohemians) in America,* N. Y., Houghton Mifflin Co., 1920.

I have been looking over the books, more than a thousand in number, I should think, found on our shelves relating to the history of the various non-English elements that have entered into the composite of American population, and it has quite confirmed the opinion I expressed to you, that work upon the history of migration into the United States and of the varieties of immigrating population is centered in the United States rather than in the countries of origin. The chief publications on the history of the German element in the United States have been made in Philadelphia; the researches lying behind those publications have mostly been made by Americans, and in the United States, not in Germany. Work on the history of the Norwegians in America is centered in the Minnesota Historical Society; of the Swedes, in the Swedish Colonial Society or the northwestern libraries. The Irish-American Historical Society is an affair of Boston and New York, not of Dublin. The study of the Scotch-Irish element has been pursued by Americans, hardly at all by Ulstermen. The books on the French in America, the Italians in America, the Armenians, the Swiss, have been produced on this side of the water. I think that it will always be so, that there will be far more impulse to pursue such studies on the part of those who, by descent or otherwise, represent the immigrants who made their adventure into the new world than on the part of scholars in the country of origin, who will always be more interested in the history of their respective lands than in that of any offshoots, and are apt to feel deterred by the consciousness of not having a sufficient understanding of American conditions. Indeed, to appreciate all this, we have only to look at the case of the main ingredient in our population, the English. The number of books, pamphlets, and articles on American history produced each year in the United States is about three thousand; certainly the number produced in England is much less than three hundred.

I say all this because I understand your main question to be whether this wonderful collection of Bohemica, on the making of which you have lavished so much time and thought and effort, would be better placed in the Museum at Prague than in the Library of Congress. If, as I think we must always hold, the best place of deposit for any books is the place where they are most likely to be fruitfully used, I can not doubt that the most appropriate home for any such collection as yours is the National Library, to which more students come for researches in American history than to any other place.

In saying this, I include in my opinion the materials in Czech as well as those in English. It is of course true that there are more people who read Czech in any Bohemian city than in Washington; but persons who set out to pursue the history of the Czechs in America will be persons who already either read Czech or, having some other Slavic language, know that they must

acquire a reading knowledge of Czech in order to progress. The recent policy of restrictions on immigration—quotas and the like—has caused a definite increase of interest in the history of immigration. (And by the way, I am sending you, in a day or two, a copy of the report upon linguistic elements in the American population of 1790, which I caused to be prepared by the American Historical Association).[184] So, I should hope that your Czech material, both printed and manuscript, might come here, as well as the English Bohemica.

I hope that you and Mrs. Čapek can find the time to come down and inspect the Library of Congress and its provisions for special students, and I think you would be much impressed with what is done for them here. The Librarian joins me in this wish, and bids me say that, if at any time you and Mrs. Čapek can come here, he will be happy to have you take luncheon with him at his daily "Round Table."

You would, I think, be especially impressed by the provisions made for the preservation of the rarities in the newly constructed Rare Book Room, where conditions which we think ideal have been made for the security and permanence of such material. Also, remembering the fragile condition of some of your most precious pieces, I mention that the staff of our repair room is considered exceptionally skilful in all such work of preservation.

By all means come if you can, you and Mrs. Čapek. At all events accept my cordial thanks for the kindness with which you and she showed me your treasures. If they can ultimately come here, it will be a great gratification to one who, as you perceived, has long been especially interested in the history of immigration into the United States.[185]

P.S. I notice, by the way, that we have very few books on Czech immigration—two copies of your book, and a few others.[186]

To Stephen Bonsal

February 17, 1937.[187]

My dear Colonel Bonsal:[188]

You will be glad to know that the manuscripts of Senator Gouverneur Morris are in the possession of the Library of Congress, and on their way to this place.

---

[184] Howard F. Barker and Marcus L. Hansen, American Council of Learned Societies report of committee on linguistic and national stocks in the population of the United States, *Ann. Rept., Amer. Hist. Assoc.,* 1931: **1**: 103-441.

[185] The collection was presented to the Library of Congress in 1951 by Čapek's widow (see, *Amer. Hist. Rev.* **59**: 821).

[186] Probably his *Czechs in America,* mentioned above.

[187] Division of Manuscripts, Library of Congress.

[188] See *ante,* Jameson to Worthington C. Ford, Apr. 16, 1931, n. 93, for Colonel Bonsal's connection with Morris.

Letters received today from Miss Davenport,[189] and from our agent Miss Fisher, show that the transfer was effected on February 1, and that the whole mass has been turned over by the latter to the forwarding agents in London of whom the Library of Congress makes use. No doubt the consignment is on the water now, and will soon be here.

The list which Miss Fisher sends, a copy of her receipt to the solicitors of the executors, shows that she succeeded in obtaining, not only all the volumes which had been in the custody of Miss Davenport, but also, apparently, all the material that came to the executors and was rightly included in Mr. Maudslay's bequest.

I consider that, for this most gratifying achievement and accession, we are primarily indebted to you, and I hope it will give you much pleasure that the good seed you cast on an ambiguous ground so many years ago has borne fruit to so great advantage to the Library of Congress, and through it to future students of American history.

TO HENRY ADAMS

March 17, 1937.[190]

My dear Mr. Adams: [191]

Dr. Worthington Ford tells me that he has sent to you, after answering it to me, a letter I wrote him not long ago respecting the volumes he edited of the *Correspondence of John Quincy Adams*.[192] This was a little premature, for though I expected to write to you upon the matter some time, I had expected to delay this until I had acquired certain pieces of information and made various reflections. However, I suppose no harm is done, for though I suggested to Dr. Ford that my letter should be regarded as confidential, this was because the whole matter is in a tentative stage, not because there was anything in the letter that called for secrecy. I shall hope to write again later. Meanwhile

however I shall be glad if you will at times consider at least the possibility that the papers of John Adams, John Quincy Adams, and of your grandfather might follow the course which has been followed by the papers of nearly all the other Presidents—indeed, all but four of those not now living, and those four are regrettable exceptions, which, in three of the cases at least, operate to prevent those Presidents from having their meed of proper attention from historians. The careers of your great-great-grandfather, your great-grandfather, and your grandfather are so large a part of the history of the United States that all the historians that I ever see are agreed in lamenting that it is not definitely assured that their papers shall, when the proper time comes, take their rightful place here along with those of Washington, Jefferson, Madison, Monroe, and so many others.[193]

But of all this later, if I may. I write now chiefly to assure you that it was no part of my intention that my preliminary thoughts, concerning primarily the correspondence of John Quincy Adams, should go from Dr. Ford to you.

TO CARL HAYDEN

April 16, 1937.

Senator: [194]

I hear the legislation looking toward further appropriation for the series of volumes entitled "Territorial Papers of the United States" will soon be introduced in the Senate. I sincerely hope that such legislation will be secured. When measures toward that end were first brought forward, in 1925, by the late Senator Ralston,[195] it fell to me, as chairman of one of the committees of the American Historical Association, to exert myself to the utmost to promote the enterprise at its inception, and I have constantly taken great interest in its progress.[196] More than twenty years ago, being then director of the department of historical research in the Carnegie Institution of Washington, I had been greatly struck by the multitude of inquiries that came to me from western states concerning documents of their territorial periods, which were to be found in great numbers in the various archives of Washington, but were greatly scattered. I then caused the preparation, and publication by the Carnegie Institution, of a stout volume entitled *Calendar of Papers in*

---

[189] Beatrix Cary Davenport had been allowed special use of the Morris papers under the terms of Dr. Maudslay's will, before the material became available at the Library of Congress. She edited *A diary of the French Revolution by Gouverneur Morris, 1752-1816*, 2v., Boston, Houghton Mifflin Co., 1939. In a letter to Miss Davenport Jameson wrote: "I can well appreciate that parting with the papers of Senator Morris has cost you a pang, but I truly believe that in the interest of his future fame it is more desirable that they should be in a permanent national repository than that they should remain permanently in private hands, however devoted and solicitous. I appreciate the considerable care with which you have managed the transfer. In view of the lamentable accidents that have befallen the papers of American statesmen (as I could testify from fifty years of observation) we have occasion to be very gratified to those descendants who have so thoroughly preserved Senator Morris's papers. . . ." (Jameson to Beatrix C. Davenport, Feb. 17, 1937, Division of Manuscripts).
[190] Division of Manuscripts, Library of Congress.
[191] The late Henry Adams, 2nd, of Boston, nephew of Henry Adams (1838-1918), the historian.
[192] Ford, Worthington C., ed., *Writings of John Quincy Adams*, 7v., N. Y., Macmillan Co., 1913-1917.

[193] In a brief, blunt note Adams replied that Jameson's suggestion did not appeal to him (Henry Adams to Jameson, Mar. 22, 1937, Division of Manuscripts). The papers are included in the Adams Manuscript Trust, and have remained at the Massachusetts Historical Society, where they are now being edited for publication.
[194] Carl Hayden, Senator from Arizona since 1927; member of the Senate Committee on Appropriations.
[195] Samuel M. Ralston (1857-1925), Senator from Indiana, 1923-1925.
[196] The committee was that on documentary historical publications of the government.

Washington Archives Relating to the Territories of the United States (to 1873). This volume, prepared by David W. Parker, and listing some 10,000 such documents was made by Senator Ralston the foundation of the act of March 3, 1925, which goes by his name, and has been the basis of the work done under that act. Any brief examination of that volume will show that, scattered through the various Government depositories in Washington, there is a great wealth of material for the early history of more than thirty of the states, and the volumes already published in the series show them to be of great importance toward the illustration of that history.

I am sure that, with a little time, very abundant testimony could be obtained from these states as to the value which their historical scholars and writers attach to the contents of this collection.

The case is parallel to that of the efforts made by all thirteen of the original states to secure from London, Paris, and elsewhere, and put in print for the use of historical scholars materials for the earlier history of those states, of the period when they were colonies of Great Britain and other European powers. The archives of Washington stand, to the history of all the newer states, in the position which the archives of London, etc., stand to that of the Old Thirteen. In view however of the changes in territorial and state boundaries, such an enterprise of exploitation cannot be rightly carried out except as a Federal undertaking, which will illustrate the history of the old Northwest, the Louisiana region, Florida, and the whole area west of the Mississippi.

When so large a part of the enterprise has already been carried out, and carried out in so scholarly and excellent a manner, it would be distinctly discreditable to the nation if the whole project should not be carried to completion. No historical publication by the United States Government has illuminated so many different portions of our history, and the workmanship has commended itself in the highest degree, as I can securely testify, to the members of the historical profession.[197]

---

[197] For collecting and copying the papers at the beginning of the enterprise, Jameson recommended Newton D. Mereness. For editing them, Dr. Clarence E. Carter was chosen. He had received the Justin Winsor Prize of the American Historical Association for *Great Britain and the Illinois Country, 1763-1774*, and had been associated with Professor Alvord in preparing many volumes of the Illinois Historical Collections. On the appearances of Dr. Carter's first volumes Jameson wrote: "My congratulations upon a very distinguished achievement. Edited so carefully and presented in such fine shape, they fulfill the designs of those who instigated the publication, to a degree which, I am sure, far surpasses what those persons could have expected. The series reflects, and will reflect, great credit upon you" (From the files of Dr. Carter). The series was

To THEODORE FRANCIS GREEN

April 28, 1937.

Dear Senator Green:[198]

Thank you for your kindness in sending me a copy of your address at the dinner of the Law Society of Massachusetts.[199] A man lying in bed with a broken leg is in no position to debate effectively with a Senator. Your argument is a good one, and if I am not convinced by it, you are at liberty to lay it to the fact that I am over seventy, and no longer (if ever) easily convinced. On the specific question, not whether a piece of legislation is desirable, but whether it is really in accord with the Constitution, I should not be content to take the judgment of the people, or of the Congress, as of equal validity with that of the Supreme Court. After living in Washington thirty-five years and seeing multitudes of acts passed—perhaps in ten minutes, certainly without having been read by more than a few members —I do not consider that the passage of an act indicates that Congress, in any real sense, has deliberately concluded that it is constitutional—still less that the nation has so concluded. The average Congressman, whether a lawyer or not, contents himself with thinking "I guess that will get by the Supreme Court." Such judgments, or popular judgments, do not seem to me capable of being regarded as superior in convincing power, as to the specific question of constitutionality, to the deliberate judgment of nine lawyers of the calibre usually represented in the Supreme Court, who have deliberated over that specific question during adequate periods of time. I set out with refusing to debate. I am in danger of proceeding to do so. But I am an old Federalist—not of the Hamiltonian, but of the Adams-Bayard-Marshall variety—not much enamoured of popular opinion. Dismiss all the above, if you like, as vagaries of the sickroom, but I thank you for the opportunity to read your excellent argument.

---

continued, being in 1950 transferred from the Department of State to the National Archives. In 1953, the nineteenth volume, edited by Dr. Carter, appeared.

[198] Theodore Francis Green, A.B., 1887, A.M., 1890, Brown, instructor in Roman law, Brown, 1894-1897, Governor of Rhode Island, 1933-1937, had just entered the Senate from that state.

[199] The address sent to Jameson was on Proposed Supreme Court changes, delivered before the Law Society on Apr. 14, 1937. In this he argued that the existing court had actually been passing not on the constitutionality but on the wisdom of legislation, which was not their function; that age hardened the mind and those members of the court over seventy had not kept up with the country; that to enlarge the court a constitutional amendment was not necessary; and that the plan of President Roosevelt to increase its size could not lead to dictatorship and was imperative, in order to restore respect for the court and confidence in it. *Journal*, Mass. Law Society, May, 1937: 806-814.

LIST OF CORRESPONDENTS